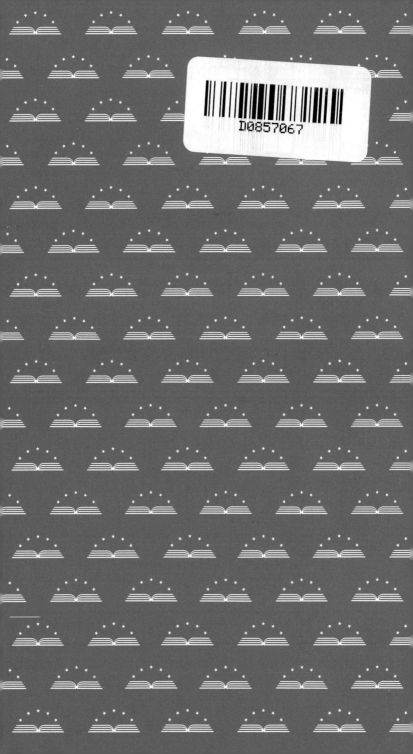

ALEXANDER HAMILTON

ALEXANDER HAMILTON

WRITINGS

THE LIBRARY OF AMERICA

Texts copyright © 1961, 1962, 1963, 1964, 1965, 1966, 1967,
1969, 1972, 1973, 1974, 1975, 1976, 1977, 1979 by Columbia
University Press. Reprinted by permission. See Note on the
Texts, page 1052, for further acknowledgments.

The paper used in this publication meets the
minimum requirements of the American National Standard for
Information Sciences—Permanence of Paper for Printed
Library Materials, ANSI Z39.48—1984.

Distributed to the trade
in the United States by Penguin Putnam, Inc.
and in Canada by Penguin Books Canada Ltd.

Library of Congress Catalog Number: 2001023043
For cataloging information, see end of Index.
ISBN 1–931082–04–9

First Printing
The Library of America—129

JOANNE B. FREEMAN
SELECTED THE CONTENTS AND WROTE THE NOTES
FOR THIS VOLUME

This volume has been published with support from The John M. Olin Foundation.

Contents

xi

FEDERALIST LEADER AND ATTORNEY, 1795–1804

THE WEST INDIES,
THE REVOLUTION,
AND THE CONFEDERATION
1769–1786

To Edward Stevens

Dear Edward   St Croix Novemr. 11th 1769
   This just serves to acknowledge receipt of yours per Cap Lowndes which was delivered me Yesterday. The truth of Cap Lightbourn & Lowndes information is now verifyd by the Presence of your Father and Sister for whose safe arrival I Pray, and that they may convey that Satisfaction to your Soul that must naturally flow from the sight of Absent Friends in health, and shall for news this way refer you to them. As to what you say respecting your having soon the happiness of seeing us all, I wish, for an accomplishment of your hopes provided they are Concomitant with your welfare, otherwise not, tho doubt whether I shall be Present or not for to confess my weakness, Ned, my Ambition is prevalent that I contemn the grov'ling and condition of a Clerk or the like, to which my Fortune &c. condemns me and would willingly risk my life tho' not my Character to exalt my Station. Im confident, Ned that my Youth excludes me from any hopes of immediate Preferment nor do I desire it, but I mean to prepare the way for futurity. Im no Philosopher you see and may be jusly said to Build Castles in the Air. My Folly makes me ashamd and beg youll Conceal it, yet Neddy we have seen such Schemes successfull when the Projector is Constant I shall Conclude saying I wish there was a War.
   I am   Dr Edward   Yours   Alex Hamilton

PS   I this moment receivd yours by William Smith and am pleasd to see you Give such Close Application to Study.

COUNTING-HOUSE BUSINESS

To Nicholas Cruger

Dr. Sir   St Croix February 24 1772

Herewith you have duplicate of my two last Letters of the 27 November & 10th Ulto. and I now congratulate myself upon the pleasure of addressing you again, but am sorry I shall be obligd to communicate some dissatisfactory occurrencies.

Your Sloop Thunderbolt arrivd here the 29th of the preceding Month with 41 More Skeletons. A worse parcel of Mules never was seen; she took in at first 48 & lost 7 on the passage. I sent all that were able to walk to pasture, in Number 33. The other 8 could hardly stand for 2 Minutes together & in spite of the greatest care 4 of them are now in Limbo. The Surviving 4 I think are out of Danger, and shall likewise be shortly sent to pasture. I refusd two great offers made me upon their first landing to Wit 70 ps. a head for the Choice of 20, and 15 ps. a Head for the abovementioned Invalids, which may give you a proper idea of the condition they were in. Taking this along with it—that if they had been such as we had reason to hope they would be—I could with pleasure have had £40 round, so unfortunate has the Voyage been. However by sending them to pasture I expect to get £100 round for those now alive. 17 are already gone at that price and as they recruit fast the rest I hope will soon go at the same. I pay 2 ps. a Head Montly for pasturage. The Sloop was 27 days on her passage from the Main—not for want of swiftness, for tis now known she Sails well, but from continual Calms & the little wind she had was quite against her. Capt Newton seemd to be much concernd at his Ill luck tho I believe he had done all in his power to make the voyage Successful. But no Man can command the Winds. The Mules were pretty well chosen & had been once a good parcel. I receivd only a few lines from your Brother: no Sales nor anything else; he excusd himself being Sick. I desird him as directed to furnish the Sloop with a few Guns but she went intirely defenceless to the Main; notwithstanding several Vessells had been obligd to put back to get out of the way of the

Launches with which the Coast swarms. When Capt Newton urgd him to hire a few Guns for the Sloop He replied to this effect—that I only had mentiond the matter to him but that you had never said a word about it. This last time I mentiond it again & begd the Captain to hire 4 Guns himself if your Brother did not which he has promisd to do. The Expence will not be above 15. or 20 ps., and one escape may not be followd by a second, neither do I see any reason to run the risque of it. I sent down on your account 10 Hhds Codfish, 8 Hhds Rum, 40 Philad. barrels & 8 Teirces Bread. The Rum Cost 2/7½ & is worth 5 bits a Gallon at Curacoa. I believe those Articles will answer pretty well.

Upon application to Mr Heyns I found I had been misinformd & that Mr Hunter has no Attorney here; whereupon I wrote him a Letter to St Thomas & have sent him three Copys of the Same without receiving any answer. Mr. Ringger is here and is going over in a day or two. I intend to give him a Letter & beg he'll ask for an answer and send it over. I am a good deal surprisd at Capt Hunters Silence.

Brig Nancys Accounts are inclosd. The Tea is arrivd; it Cost 20¼ Sti, but there is a discount of 4 ⅌ Ct. for prompt payment. I shall send Copy of the Invoice &c. to Mess Walton & Cruger. The Lumber you contracted for is arrivd & I am a good deal puzzled to fulfil your engagements; it is rather early you know to receivd & Cash is scarce. Mr Beekman would Ship on freight which would ease the matter but he can receive none yet. However I must manage some how or other. It would be a pity to pay dead freight.

As to introducing Wine, it depends upon Circumstances. There is none here at present and if yours could be brought while the scarcity continues, it would not be difficult to obtain permission to land it. Other-wise it will be impracticable, unless our General who is momently expected should bring any new indulgence concerning that article. But the whole is a chance.

Many changes of Officers are talkd of; in particular tis said Judge Sevel will be superceded by Jeger the informer—& the Collector by the present Comptroler, which is all that occurs to me now. Therefore Ill conclude wishing you safe passage out.

I am   Sir   Your Obdt Serv   AH

ACCOUNT OF A HURRICANE

To The Royal Danish American Gazette

Honoured Sir,   St. Croix, Sept. 6, 1772

I take up my pen just to give you an imperfect account of one of the most dreadful Hurricanes that memory or any records whatever can trace, which happened here on the 31st ultimo at night.

It began about dusk, at North, and raged very violently till ten o'clock. Then ensued a sudden and unexpected interval, which lasted about an hour. Meanwhile the wind was shifting round to the South West point, from whence it returned with redoubled fury and continued so 'till near three o'clock in the morning. Good God! what horror and destruction. Its impossible for me to describe or you to form any idea of it. It seemed as if a total dissolution of nature was taking place. The roaring of the sea and wind, fiery meteors flying about it in the air, the prodigious glare of almost perpetual lightning, the crash of the falling houses, and the ear-piercing shrieks of the distressed, were sufficient to strike astonishment into Angels. A great part of the buildings throughout the Island are levelled to the ground, almost all the rest very much shattered; several persons killed and numbers utterly ruined; whole families running about the streets, unknowing where to find a place of shelter; the sick exposed to the keeness of water and air without a bed to lie upon, or a dry covering to their bodies; and our harbours entirely bare. In a word, misery, in all its most hideous shapes, spread over the whole face of the country. A strong smell of gunpowder added somewhat to the terrors of the night; and it was observed that the rain was surprizingly salt. Indeed the water is so brackish and full of sulphur that there is hardly any drinking it.

My reflections and feelings on this frightful and melancholy occasion, are set forth in the following self-discourse.

Where now, oh! vile worm, is all thy boasted fortitude and resolution? What is become of thine arrogance and self sufficiency? Why dost thou tremble and stand aghast? How humble, how helpless, how contemptible you now appear. And for why? The jarring of elements—the discord of clouds? Oh! impotent presumptuous fool! how durst thou offend that Omnipotence, whose nod alone were sufficient to quell the destruction that hovers over thee, or crush thee into atoms? See thy wretched helpless state, and learn to know thyself. Learn to know thy best support. Despise thyself, and adore thy God. How sweet, how unutterably sweet were now, the voice of an approving conscience; Then couldst thou say, hence ye idle alarms, why do I shrink? What have I to fear? A pleasing calm suspense! A short repose from calamity to end in eternal bliss? Let the Earth rend. Let the planets forsake their course. Let the Sun be extinguished and the Heavens burst asunder. Yet what have I to dread? My staff can never be broken—in Omnipotence I trusted.

He who gave the winds to blow, and the lightnings to rage—even him have I always loved and served. His precepts have I observed. His commandments have I obeyed—and his perfections have I adored. He will snatch me from ruin. He will exalt me to the fellowship of Angels and Seraphs, and to the fullness of never ending joys.

But alas! how different, how deplorable, how gloomy the prospect! Death comes rushing on in triumph veiled in a mantle of tenfold darkness. His unrelenting scythe, pointed, and ready for the stroke. On his right hand sits destruction, hurling the winds and belching forth flames: Calamity on his left threatening famine disease and distress of all kinds. And Oh! thou wretch, look still a little further; see the gulph of eternal misery open. There mayest thou shortly plunge—the just reward of thy vileness. Alas! whither canst thou fly? Where hide thyself? Thou canst not call upon thy God; thy life has been a continual warfare with him.

Hark—ruin and confusion on every side. 'Tis thy turn next; but one short moment, even now, Oh Lord help. Jesus be merciful!

Thus did I reflect, and thus at every gust of the wind, did I conclude, 'till it pleased the Almighty to allay it. Nor did my emotions proceed either from the suggestions of too much natural fear, or a conscience over-burthened with crimes of an uncommon cast. I thank God, this was not the case. The scenes of horror exhibited around us, naturally awakened such ideas in every thinking breast, and aggravated the deformity of every failing of our lives. It were a lamentable insensibility indeed, not to have had such feelings, and I think inconsistent with human nature.

Our distressed, helpless condition taught us humility and contempt of ourselves. The horrors of the night, the prospect of an immediate, cruel death—or, as one may say, of being crushed by the Almighty in his anger—filled us with terror. And every thing that had tended to weaken our interest with him, upbraided us in the strongest colours, with our baseness and folly. That which, in a calm unruffled temper, we call a natural cause, seemed then like the correction of the Deity. Our imagination represented him as an incensed master, executing vengeance on the crimes of his servants. The father and benefactor were forgot, and in that view, a consciousness of our guilt filled us with despair.

But see, the Lord relents. He hears our prayer. The Lightning ceases. The winds are appeased. The warring elements are reconciled and all things promise peace. The darkness is dispell'd and drooping nature revives at the approaching dawn. Look back Oh! my soul, look back and tremble. Rejoice at thy deliverance, and humble thyself in the presence of thy deliverer.

Yet hold, Oh vain mortal! Check thy ill timed joy. Art thou so selfish to exult because thy lot is happy in a season of universal woe? Hast thou no feelings for the miseries of thy fellow-creatures? And art thou incapable of the soft pangs of sympathetic sorrow? Look around thee and shudder at the view. See desolation and ruin where'er thou turnest thine eye! See thy fellow-creatures pale and lifeless; their bodies mangled, their souls snatched into eternity, unexpecting. Alas! perhaps unprepared! Hark the bitter groans of distress. See sickness and infirmities exposed to the inclemencies of wind and water! See tender infancy pinched with hunger and hanging on the mothers knee for food! See the unhappy mothers anxiety. Her poverty denies relief, her breast heaves with pangs of maternal pity, her heart is bursting, the tears gush down her cheeks. Oh sights of woe! Oh distress unspeakable! My heart bleeds, but I have no power to solace! O ye, who revel in affluence, see the afflictions of humanity and bestow your superfluity to ease them. Say not, we have suffered also, and thence withold your compassion. What are your sufferings compared to those? Ye have still more than enough left. Act wisely. Succour the miserable and lay up a treasure in Heaven.

I am afraid, Sir, you will think this description more the effort of imagination than a true picture of realities. But I can affirm with the greatest truth, that there is not a single circumstance touched upon, which I have not absolutely been an eye witness to.

Our General has issued several very salutary and humane regulations, and both in his publick and private measures, has shewn himself *the Man*.

A Full Vindication of the
Measures of the Congress,

from the Calumnies of their Enemies;
In Answer to A Letter, Under the Signature of A. W. Farmer.
Whereby His Sophistry is exposed, his Cavils confuted, his
Artifices detected, and his Wit ridiculed; in a General Address
To the Inhabitants of America, And A Particular Address
To the Farmers of the Province of New-York.
Veritas magna est & prævalebit.
Truth is powerful, and will prevail.

FRIENDS AND COUNTRYMEN,   New-York 1774

It was hardly to be expected that any man could be so presumptuous, as openly to controvert the equity, wisdom, and
authority of the measures, adopted by the congress: an
assembly truly respectable on every account! Whether we
consider the characters of the men, who composed it; the
number, and dignity of their constituents, or the important
ends for which they were appointed. But, however improbable such a degree of presumption might have seemed, we find
there are some, in whom it exists. Attempts are daily making
to diminish the influence of their decisions, and prevent the
salutary effects, intended by them. The impotence of such insidious efforts is evident from the general indignation they are
treated with; so that no material ill-consequences can be
dreaded from them. But lest they should have a tendency to
mislead, and prejudice the minds of a few; it cannot be
deemed altogether useless to bestow some notice upon them.

And first, let me ask these restless spirits, whence arises that
violent antipathy they seem to entertain, not only to the natural rights of mankind; but to common sense and common
modesty. That they are enemies to the natural rights of
mankind is manifest, because they wish to see one part of
their species enslaved by another. That they have an invincible
aversion to common sense is apparent in many respects: They
endeavour to persuade us, that the absolute sovereignty of
parliament does not imply our absolute slavery; that it is a

Christian duty to submit to be plundered of all we have, merely because some of our fellow-subjects are wicked enough to require it of us, that slavery, so far from being a great evil, is a great blessing; and even, that our contest with Britain is founded entirely upon the petty duty of 3 pence per pound on East India tea; whereas the whole world knows, it is built upon this interesting question, whether the inhabitants of Great-Britain have a right to dispose of the lives and properties of the inhabitants of America, or not? And lastly, that these men have discarded all pretension to common modesty, is clear from hence, first, because they, in the plainest terms, call an august body of men, famed for their patriotism and abilities, fools or knaves, and of course the people whom they represented cannot be exempt from the same opprobrious appellations; and secondly, because they set themselves up as standards of wisdom and probity, by contradicting and censuring the public voice in favour of those men.

A little consideration will convince us, that the congress instead of having "ignorantly misunderstood, carelessly neglected, or basely betrayed the interests of the colonies," have, on the contrary, devised and recommended the only effectual means to secure the freedom, and establish the future prosperity of America upon a solid basis. If we are not free and happy hereafter, it must proceed from the want of integrity and resolution, in executing what they have concerted; not from the temerity or impolicy of their determinations.

Before I proceed to confirm this assertion by the most obvious arguments, I will premise a few brief remarks. The only distinction between freedom and slavery consists in this: In the former state, a man is governed by the laws to which he has given his consent, either in person, or by his representative: In the latter, he is governed by the will of another. In the one case his life and property are his own, in the other, they depend upon the pleasure of a master. It is easy to discern which of these two states is preferable. No man in his senses can hesitate in choosing to be free, rather than a slave.

That Americans are intitled to freedom, is incontestible upon every rational principle. All men have one common original: they participate in one common nature, and consequently have one common right. No reason can be assigned why one man should exercise any power, or pre-eminence over his fellow creatures more than another; unless they have voluntarily vested him with it. Since then, Americans have not by any act of their's impowered the British Parliament to make laws for them, it follows they can have no just authority to do it.

Besides the clear voice of natural justice in this respect, the fundamental principles of the English constitution are in our favour. It has been repeatedly demonstrated, that the idea of legislation, or taxation, when the subject is not represented, is inconsistent with *that*. Nor is this all, our charters, the express conditions on which our progenitors relinquished their native countries, and came to settle in this, preclude every claim of ruling and taxing us without our assent.

Every subterfuge that sophistry has been able to invent, to evade or obscure this truth, has been refuted by the most conclusive reasonings; so that we may pronounce it a matter of undeniable certainty, that the pretensions of Parliament are contradictory to the law of nature, subversive of the British constitution, and destructive of the faith of the most solemn compacts.

What then is the subject of our controversy with the mother country? It is this, whether we shall preserve that se-curity to our lives and properties, which the law of nature, the genius of the British constitution, and our charters afford us; or whether we shall resign them into the hands of the British House of Commons, which is no more privileged to dispose of them than the Grand Mogul? What can actuate those men, who labour to delude any of us into an opinion, that the object of contention between the parent state and the colonies is only three pence duty upon tea? or that the commotions in America originate in a plan, formed by some turbulent men to erect it into a republican government? The parliament claims a right to tax us in all cases whatsoever: Its late acts are in virtue of that claim. How ridiculous then is it to affirm, that we are quarrelling for the trifling sum of three pence a pound on tea; when it is evidently the principle against which we contend.

The design of electing members to represent us in general congress, was, that the wisdom of America might be collected in devising the most proper and expedient means to repel this atrocious invasion of our rights. It has been accordingly done. Their decrees are binding upon all, and demand a religious observance.

We did not, especially in this province, circumscribe them by any fixed boundary, and therefore as they cannot be said to have exceeded the limits of their authority, their act must be esteemed the act of their constituents. If it should be objected, that they have not answered the end of their election; but have fallen upon an improper and ruinous mode of proceeding: I reply, by asking, Who shall be the judge? Shall any individual oppose his private sentiment to the united counsels of men, in whom America has reposed so high a confidence? The attempt must argue no small degree of arrogance and self-sufficiency.

Yet this attempt has been made, and it is become in some measure necessary to vindicate the conduct of this venerable assembly from the aspersions of men, who are their adversaries, only because they are foes to America.

When the political salvation of any community is depending, it is incumbent upon those who are set up as its guardians, to embrace such measures, as have justice, vigour, and a probability of success to recommend them: If instead of this, they take those methods which are in themselves feeble, and little likely to succeed; and may, through a defect in vigour, involve the community in still greater danger; they may be justly considered as its betrayers. It is not enough in times of eminent peril to use only possible means of preservation: Justice and sound policy dictate the use of probable means.

The only scheme of opposition, suggested by those, who have been, and are averse from a non-importation and non-exportation agreement, is, by REMONSTRANCE and PETITION. The authors and abettors of this scheme, have never been able to *invent* a single argument to prove the likelihood of its succeeding. On the other hand, there are many standing facts, and valid considerations against it.

In the infancy of the present dispute, we had recourse to this method only. We addressed the throne in the most loyal and respectful manner, in a legislative capacity; but what was the consequence? Our address was treated with contempt and neglect. The first American congress did the same, and met with similar treatment. The total repeal of the stamp act, and the partial repeal of the revenue acts took place, not because the complaints of America were deemed just and reasonable; but because these acts were found to militate against the commercial interests of Great Britain: This was the declared motive of the repeal.

These instances are sufficient for our purpose; but they derive greater validity and force from the following:

The legal assembly of Massachusetts Bay, presented, not long since, a most humble, dutiful, and earnest petition to his Majesty, requesting the dismission of a governor, highly odious to the people, and whose misrepresentations they regarded as one chief source of all their calamities. Did they succeed in their request? No, it was treated with the greatest indignity, and stigmatized as "a seditious, vexatious, and scandalous libel."

I know the men I have to deal with will acquiesce in this stigma. Will they also dare to calumniate the noble and spirited petition that came from the Mayor and Aldermen of the city of London? Will they venture to justify that unparalelled stride of power, by which popery and arbitrary dominion were established in Canada? The citizens of London remonstrated against it; they signified its repugnancy to the principles of the revolution; but like ours, their complaints were unattended to. From thence we may learn how little dependence ought to be placed on this method of obtaining the redress of grievances.

There is less reason now than ever to expect deliverance, in this way, from the hand of oppression. The system of slavery, fabricated against America, cannot at this time be considered as the effect of inconsideration and rashness. It is the offspring of mature deliberation. It has been fostered by time, and strengthened by every artifice human subtilty is capable of. After the claims of parliament had lain dormant for awhile, they are again resumed and prosecuted with more than common ardour. The Premier has advanced too far to recede with safety: He is deeply interested to execute his purpose, if possible: we know he has declared, that he will never desist, till he has brought America to his feet; and we may conclude, nothing but necessity will induce him to abandon his aims. In common life, to retract an error even in the beginning, is no easy task. Perseverance confirms us in it, and rivets the difficulty; but in a public station, to have been in an error, and to have persisted in it, when it is detected, ruins both reputation and fortune. To this we may add, that disappointment and opposition inflame the minds of men, and attach them, still more, to their mistakes.

What can we represent which has not already been represented? what petitions can we offer, that have not already been offered? The rights of America, and the injustice of parliamentary pretensions have been clearly and repeatedly stated, both in and out of parliament. No new arguments can be framed to operate in our favour. Should we even resolve the errors of the ministry and parliament into the fallibility of human understanding, if they have not yet been convinced, we have no prospect of being able to do it by any thing further we can say. But if we impute their conduct to a wicked thirst of domination and disregard to justice, we have no hope of prevailing with them to alter it, by expatiating on our rights, and suing to their compassion for relief; especially since we have found, by various experiments, the inefficacy of such methods.

Upon the whole, it is morally certain, this mode of opposition would be fruitless and defective. The exigency of the times requires vigorous and probable remedies; not weak and improbable. It would therefore be the extreme of folly to place any confidence in, much less, confine ourselves wholly to it.

This being the case, we can have no resource but in a restriction of our trade, or in a resistance *vi & armis*. It is impossible to conceive any other alternative. Our congress, therefore, have imposed what restraint they thought necessary. Those, who condemn or clamour against it, do nothing more, nor less, than advise us to be slaves.

I shall now examine the principal measures of the congress, and vindicate them fully from the charge of injustice or impolicy.

Were I to argue in a philosophical manner, I might say, the obligation to a mutual intercourse in the way of trade with the inhabitants of Great-Britain, Ireland and the West-Indies is of the *imperfect* kind. There is no law, either of nature, or of the civil society in which we live, that obliges us to purchase, and make use of the products and manufactures of a different land, or people. It is indeed a dictate of humanity to contribute to the support and happiness of our fellow creatures and more especially those who are allied to us by the ties of blood, interest, and mutual protection; but humanity does not require us to sacrifice our own security and welfare to the convenience, or advantage of others. Self preservation is the first principle of our nature. When our lives and properties are at stake, it would be foolish and unnatural to refrain from such measures as might preserve them, because they would be detrimental to others.

But we are justified upon another principle besides this. Though the manufacturers of Great Britain and Ireland, and the Inhabitants of the West Indies are not chargeable with any actual crime towards America, they may, in a political view, be esteemed criminal. In a civil society, it is the duty of each particular branch to promote, not only the good of the whole community, but the good of every other particular branch: If one part endeavours to violate the rights of another, the rest ought to assist in preventing the injury: When they do not, but remain neutral, they are deficient in their duty, and may be regarded, in some measure, as accomplices.

The reason of this is obvious, from the design of civil society, which is, that the united strength of the several members might give stability and security to the whole body, and each respective member; so that one part cannot encroach upon another, without becoming a common enemy, and eventually endangering the safety and happiness of all the other parts.

Since then the persons who will be distressed by the methods we are using for our own protection, have by their neutrality first committed a breach of an obligation, similar to that which bound us to consult their emolument, it is plain, the obligation upon us is annulled, and we are blameless in what we are about to do.

With respect to the manufacturers of Great Britain, they are criminal in a more particular sense. Our oppression arises from that member of the great body politic, of which they compose a considerable part. So far as their influence has been wanting to counteract the iniquity of their rulers, so far they acquiesced in it, and are to be deemed confederates in their guilt. It is impossible to exculpate a people, that suffers its rulers to abuse and tyrannize over others.

It may not be amiss to add, that we are ready to receive with open arms, any who may be sufferers by the operation of our measures, and recompense them with every blessing our country affords to honest industry. We will receive them as brethren, and make them sharers with us in all the advantages we are struggling for.

From these plain and indisputable principles, the mode of opposition we have chosen is reconcileable to the strictest maxims of Justice. It remains now to be examined, whether it has also the sanction of good policy.

To render it agreeable to good policy, three things are requisite. First, that the necessity of the times require it: Secondly, that it be not the probable source of greater evils, than those it pretends to remedy: And lastly, that it have a probability of success.

That the necessity of the times demands it needs but little elucidation. We are threatened with absolute slavery; it has been proved, that resistance by means of REMONSTRANCE and PETITION, would not be efficacious, and of course, that a restriction on our trade, is the only peaceable method, in our power, to avoid the impending mischief: It follows therefore, that such a restriction is necessary.

That it is not the probable source of greater evils than those it pretends to remedy, may easily be determined. The most abject slavery, which comprehends almost every species of human misery, is what it is designed to prevent.

The consequences of the means are a temporary stagnation of commerce, and thereby a deprivation of the luxuries and some of the conveniencies of life. The necessaries, and many of the conveniencies, our own fertile and propitious soil affords us.

No person, that has enjoyed the sweets of liberty, can be insensible of its infinite value, or can reflect on its reverse, without horror and detestation. No person, that is not lost to every generous feeling of humanity, or that is not stupidly blind to his own interest, could bear to offer himself and posterity as victims at the shrine of despotism, in preference to enduring the short lived inconveniencies that may result from an abridgment, or even entire suspension of commerce.

Were not the disadvantages of slavery too obvious to stand in need of it, I might enumerate and describe the hideous train of calamities, inseparable from it. I might shew that it is fatal to religion and morality; that it tends to debase the mind, and corrupt its noblest springs of action. I might shew, that it relaxes the sinews of industry, clips the wings of commerce, and introduces misery and indigence in every shape.

Under the auspices of tyranny, the life of the subject is often sported with; and the fruits of his daily toil are consumed in oppressive taxes, that serve to gratify the ambition, avarice and lusts of his superiors. Every court minion riots in the spoils of the honest labourer, and despises the hand by which he is fed. The page of history is replete with instances that loudly warn us to beware of slavery.

Rome was the nurse of freedom. She was celebrated for her justice and lenity; but in what manner did she govern her dependent provinces? They were made the continual scene of rapine and cruelty. From thence let us learn, how little confidence is due to the wisdom and equity of the most exemplary nations.

Should Americans submit to become the vassals of their fellow-subjects in Great Britain, their yoke will be peculiarly grievous and intolerable. A vast majority of mankind is intirely biassed by motives of self-interest. Most men are glad to remove any burthens off themselves, and place them upon the necks of their neighbours. We cannot therefore doubt, but that the British Parliament, with a view to the ease and advantage of itself, and its constituents, would oppress and grind the Americans as much as possible. Jealousy would concur with selfishness; and for fear of the future independence of America, if it should be permitted to rise to too great a height of splendor and opulence, every method would be taken to drain it of its wealth and restrain its prosperity. We are already suspected of aiming at independence, and that is one principal cause of the severity we experience. The same cause will always operate against us, and produce an uniform severity of treatment.

The evils which may flow from the execution of our measures, if we consider them with respect to their extent and duration, are comparatively nothing. In all human probability they will scarcely be felt. Reason and experience teach us, that the consequences would be too fatal to Great Britain to admit of delay. There is an immense trade between her and the colonies. The revenues arising from thence are prodigious. The consumption of her manufactures in these colonies supplies the means of subsistence to a vast number of her most useful inhabitants. The experiment we have made heretofore, shews us of how much importance our commercial connexion is to her; and gives us the highest assurance of obtaining immediate redress by suspending it.

From these considerations it is evident, she must do something decisive. She must either listen to our complaints, and restore us to a peaceful enjoyment of our violated rights; or she must exert herself to enforce her despotic claims by fire and sword. To imagine she would prefer the latter, implies a charge of the grossest infatuation of madness itself. Our numbers are very considerable; the courage of Americans has been tried and proved. Contests for liberty have ever been found the most bloody, implacable and obstinate. The disciplined troops Great Britain could send against us, would be but few, Our superiority in number would over balance our inferiority in discipline. It would be a hard, if not an impracticable task to subjugate us by force.

Besides, while Great Britain was engaged in carrying on an unnatural war against us, her commerce would be in a state of decay. Her revenues would be decreasing. An armament, sufficient to enslave America, would put her to an insupportable expence.

She would be laid open to the attacks of foreign enemies. Ruin, like a deluge, would pour in from every quarter. After lavishing her blood and treasure to reduce us to a state of vassalage, she would herself become a prey to some triumphant neighbour.

These are not imaginary mischiefs. The colonies contain above three millions of people. Commerce flourishes with the most rapid progress throughout them. This commerce Great-Britain has hitherto regulated to her own advantage. Can we think the annihilation of so exuberant a source of wealth, a matter of trifling import. On the contrary, must it not be productive of the most disastrous effects? It is evident it must. It is equally evident, that the conquest of so numerous a people, armed in the animating cause of liberty could not be accomplished without an inconceivable expence of blood and treasure.

We cannot therefore suspect Great-Britain to be capable of such frantic extravagance as to hazard these dreadful consequences; without which she must necessarily desist from her unjust pretensions, and leave us in the undisturbed possession of our privileges.

Those, who affect to ridicule the resistance America might make to the military force of Great-Britain, and represent its humiliation as a matter the most easily to be achieved, betray, either a mind clouded by the most irrational prejudices, or a total ignorance of human nature. However, it must be the wish of every honest man never to see a trial.

But should we admit a possibility of a third course, as our pamphleteer supposes, that is, the endeavouring to bring us to a compliance by putting a stop to our whole trade: Even this would not be so terrible as he pretends. We can live without trade of any kind. Food and clothing we have within ourselves. Our climate produces cotton, wool, flax and hemp, which, with proper cultivation would furnish us with summer apparel in abundance. The article of cotton indeed would do more, it would contribute to defend us from the inclemency of winter. We have sheep, which, with due care in improving and increasing them, would soon yield a sufficiency of wool. The large quantity of skins, we have among us, would never let us want a warm and comfortable suit. It would be no unbecoming employment for our daughters to provide silks of their own country. The silk-worm answers as well here as in any part of the world. Those hands, which may be deprived of business by the cessation of commerce, may be occupied in various kinds of manufactures and other internal improvements. If by the necessity of the thing, manufactures should once be established and take root among us, they will pave the way, still more, to the future grandeur and glory of America, and by lessening its need of external commerce, will render it still securer against the encroachments of tyranny.

It is however, chimerical to imagine that the circumstances of Great-Britain will admit of such a tardy method of subjecting us, for reasons, which have been already given, and which shall be corroborated by others equally forcible.

I come now to consider the last and principal ingredient that constitutes the policy of a measure, which is a probability of success. I have been obliged to anticipate this part of my subject, in considering the second requisite, and indeed what I have already said seems to me to leave no room for doubting, that the means we have used will be successful, but I shall here examine the matter more thoroughly, and endeavour to evince it more fully.

The design of the Congress in their proceedings, it cannot, and need not be denied, was either, by a prospect of the evil consequences, to influence the ministry to give up their enterprize; or should they prove inflexible, to affect the inhabitants of Great-Britain, Ireland and the West-Indies in such a manner, as to rouse them from their state of neutrality, and engage them to unite with us in opposing the lawless hand of tyranny, which is extended to ravish our liberty from us, and might soon be extended for the same purpose against them.

The FARMER mentions, as one probable consequence of our measures, "clamours, discord, confusion, mobs, riots, insurrections, rebellions in Great-Britain, Ireland and the West-Indies;" though at the same time that he thinks *it is*, he also thinks *it is not* a probable consequence. For my part, without hazarding any such seeming contradictions, I shall, in a plain way, assert, that I verily believe a non-importation and non-exportation will effect all the purposes they are intended for.

It is no easy matter to make any tolerably exact estimate of the advantages that acrue to Great-Britain, Ireland and the West-Indies from their commercial intercourse with the colonies, nor indeed is it necessary. Every man, the least acquainted with the state and extent of our trade, must be convinced, it is the source of immense revenues to the parent state, and gives employment and bread to a vast number of his Majesty's subjects. It is impossible but that a suspension of it for any time, must introduce beggary and wretchedness in an eminent degree, both in England and Ireland; and as to the West-India plantations, they could not possibly subsist without us. I am the more confident of this, because I have a pretty general acquaintance with their circumstances and dependencies.

We are told, "that it is highly improbable, we shall succeed in distressing the people of Great-Britain, Ireland and the West-Indies, so far as to oblige them to join with us in getting the acts of Parliament, which we complain of, repealed: The first distress (it is said) will fall on ourselves; it will be more severely felt by us, than any part of all his Majesty's dominions, and will affect us the longest. The fleets of Great-Britain command respect throughout the globe. Her influence extends to every part of the earth. Her manufactures are equal to any: Superior to most in the world. Her wealth is great. Her people enterprizing and persevering in their attempts to extend, and enlarge, and protect her trade. The total loss of our trade will be felt only for a time. Her merchants would turn their attention another way: New sources of trade and wealth would be opened: New schemes pursued. She would soon find a vent for all her manufactures in spite of all we could do. Our malice would hurt only ourselves. Should our schemes distress some branches of her trade, it would be only for a time; and there is ability and humanity enough in the nation to relieve those, that are distressed by us, and put them in some other way of getting their living."

The omnipotence and all sufficiency of Great-Britain may be pretty good topics for her passionate admirers to exercise their declamatory powers upon, for amusement and trial of skill; but they ought not to be proposed to the world as matters of truth and reality. In the calm, unprejudiced eye of reason, they are altogether visionary. As to her wealth, it is notorious that she is oppressed with a heavy national debt, which it requires the utmost policy and œconomy ever to discharge. Luxury has arrived to a great pitch; and it is an universal maxim that luxury indicates the declension of a state. Her subjects are loaded with the most enormous taxes: All circumstances agree in declaring their distress. The continual emigrations, from Great-Britain and Ireland, to the continent, are a glaring symptom, that those kingdoms are a good deal impoverished.

The attention of Great-Britain has hitherto been constantly awake to expand her commerce. She has been vigilant to explore every region, with which it might be her interest to trade. One of the principal branches of her commerce is with the colonies. These colonies, as they are now settled and peopled, have been the work of near two centuries: They are blessed with every advantage of soil, climate and situation. They have advanced with an almost incredible rapidity. It is therefore an egregious piece of absurdity to affirm, that the loss of our trade would be felt for a time (which must signify a short time.) No new schemes could be pursued that would not require, at least, as much time to repair the loss of our trade, as was spent in bringing it to its present degree of perfection, which is near two centuries. Nor can it be reasonably imagined, that the total and sudden loss of so extensive and lucrative a branch, would not produce the most violent effects to a nation that subsists entirely upon its commerce.

It is said, "there is ability and humanity enough in the nation to relieve those that are distressed by us; and to put them into some other way of getting their living." I wish the gentleman had obliged his readers so much, as to have pointed out this other way; I must confess, I have racked my brains to no purpose to discover it, and am fully of opinion it is purely ideal. Besides the common mechanic arts, which are subservient to the ordinary uses of life, and which are the instruments of commerce; I know no other ways in time of peace, in which men can be employed, except in agriculture and the liberal arts. Persons employed in the mechanic arts, are those, whom the abridgment of commerce would immediately affect, and as to such branches as might be less affected, they are already sufficiently stocked with workmen, and could give bread to no more; not only so, but I can't see by what legerdemain, a weaver, or clothier could be at once converted into a carpenter or black-smith. With respect to agriculture, the lands of Great Britain and Ireland have been long ago distributed and taken up; nor do they require any additional labourers to till them; so that there could be no employment in this way. The liberal arts cannot maintain those who are already devoted to them; not to say, it is more than probable, the generality of mechanics, would make but indifferent philosophers, poets, painters and musicians.

What poor shifts is sophistry obliged to have recourse to! we are threatened with the resentment of those against whom our measures will operate. It is said, that "instead of conciliating, we shall alienate the affections of the people of Great-Britain, of friends, we shall make them our enemies;" and further, that "we shall excite the resentment of the government at home against us, which will do us no good, but, on the contrary, much harm."

Soon after, we are told that "we shall probably raise the resentment of the Irish and West-Indians: The passions of human nature" it is said, "are much the same in all countries. If they find us disposed wantonly to distress them, to serve our own purposes, they will look out for some method to do without us: will they not look elsewhere for a supply of those articles, they used to take from us? They would deserve to be despised for their meanness did they not."

To these objections I reply, first with respect to the inhabitants of Great-Britain, that if they are our friends, as is supposed, and as we have reason to believe; they cannot, without being destitute of rationality, be incensed against us for using the only peaceable and probable means, in our power, to preserve our invaded rights: They know by their own experience how fruitless remonstrances and petitions are: They know, we have tried them over and over to no purpose: They know also, how dangerous to their liberties, the loss of ours must be. What then could exite their resentment if they have the least regard to common justice? The calamities, that threaten them, proceed from the weakness, or wickedness of their own rulers; which compels us to take the measures we do. The insinuation, that we *wantonly* distress them to serve our own purposes, is futile and unsupported by a single argument. I have shewn, we could have no other resource; nor can they think our conduct such, without a degree of infatuation, that it would be impossible to provide against, and therefore useless to consult. It is most reasonable to believe, they will revenge the evils they may feel on the true authors of them, on an aspiring and ill-judging ministry; not on us, who act out of a melancholy necessity, and are the innocent causes in self-defence.

With respect to the ministry, it is certain, that any thing, which has a tendency to frustrate their designs, will not fail to excite their displeasure; but since we have nothing to expect from their justice and lenity, it can be no objection to a measure, that it tends to stir up their resentment. But their resentment (it is often said) may ruin us. The impossibility of doing that, without at the same time, ruining Great-Britain, is a sufficient security.

The same may be said with regard to the Irish and the West-Indians, which has been said concerning the people of Great-Britain. The Irish, in particular, by their own circumstances will be taught to sympathise with us, and commend our conduct. Justice will direct their resentment to its proper objects.

It is true self-love will prompt both the Irish and the West-Indians to take every method in their power, to escape the miseries they are in danger of; but what methods can they take? "The Irish (it is said) may be supplied with flax-seed from Holland, the Baltic, and the river St. Lawrence: Canada produces no inconsiderable quantity already." And as to the West-Indies, "they produce now many of the necessaries of life. The quantity may be easily increased. Canada will furnish them with many articles they now take from us; flour, lumber, horses, &c. Georgia, the Floridas, and the Mississippi abound in lumber: Nova Scotia in fish."

The Dutch are rivals to the English in their commerce. They make large quantities of fine linens, gause, laces, &c. which require the flax to be picked before it comes to seed; for which reason, it is not in their power to raise much more seed than they want for their own use. Ireland has always had the surplus from them. They could, if they were ever so willing, enlarge their usual supplies but very little. It is indeed probable they may withold them. They may choose to improve the occasion for the advancement of their own trade: They may take advantage of the scarcity of materials in Ireland, to increase and put off their own manufactures.

The Baltic has ever supplied Ireland with its flax, and she has been able to consume that, with all she could derive from other quarters.

As to Canada, I am well informed it could at present afford, but a very inconsiderable quantity. It has had little encouragement, hitherto, to raise that article, and of course has not much attended to it. The instances mentioned, of seed being "bought up there at a low price, brought to New-York, and sold to the Irish factors at a great advance," does not prove there is any quantity raised there. Its cheapness proceeds from there being no demand for it; and where there was no demand, there was no inducement to cultivate it.

Upon the whole, it appears, that the supplies of flax-seed, which Ireland might draw elsewhere, would be trifling in comparison with those received from us, and not at all equivalent to her wants. But if this were not the case, if she might procure a sufficiency without our help, yet could she not do without us. She would want purchasers for her linens after they were manufactured; and where could she find any so numerous and wealthy as we are? I must refer it to the profound sagacity of Mr. A. W. Farmer, to explore them, it is too arduous a task for me.

Much less could the West-Indies subsist independent of us. Notwithstanding the continual imports from hence, there is seldom or ever, in any of the islands, a sufficient stock of provisions to last six months, which may give us an idea, how great the consumption is. The necessaries they produce within themselves, when compared with the consumption, are scarcely worth mentioning. Very small portions of the lands are appropriated to the productions of such necessaries, indeed it is too valuable to admit of it. Nor could the quantity be increased to any material degree, without applying the whole of the land to it. It is alledged, that Canada will furnish them with "flour, lumber, horses, &c. and that Georgia, the Floridas and Mississipi abound in lumber; Nova Scotia in fish." These countries have been all-along carrying on a trade to the West-Indies, as well as we; and can it be imagined that alone, they will be able to supply them tolerably? The Canadians have been indolent, and have not improved their country as they ought to have done. The wheat they raise at present, over and above what they have occasion for themselves, would be found to go but little way among the islands. Those, who think the contrary, must have mistaken notions of them. They must be unapprized of the number of souls they contain: Almost every 150 or 200 acres of land, exclusive of populous towns, comprehend a hundred people. It is not a small quantity of food that will suffice for so many. Ten or fifteen years diligence, I grant, might enable Canada to perform what is now expected from her; but, in the mean time, the West-Indians might have the satisfaction of starving.

To suppose the best, which is, that by applying their canelands to the purpose of procuring sustenance, they may preserve themselves from starving: still the consequences must be very serious or pernicious. The wealthy planters would but ill relish the loss of their crops, and such of them as were considerably in debt would be ruined. At any rate, the revenues of Great-Britain would suffer a vast diminution.

The FARMER, I am inclined to hope, builds too much upon the present disunion of Canada, Georgia, the Floridas, the Mississippi, and Nova Scotia from other colonies. A little time, I trust, will awaken them from their slumber, and bring them to a proper sense of their indiscretion. I please myself with the flattering prospect, that they will, ere long, unite in one indissoluble chain with the rest of the colonies. I cannot believe they will persist in such a conduct as must exclude them from the secure enjoyment of those heaven-descended immunities we are contending for.

There is one argument I have frequently heard urged, which it may be of some use to invalidate. It is this, that if the mother country should be inclined to an accommodation of our disputes, we have by our rash procedure thrown an insurmountable obstacle in her way; we have made it disgraceful to her to comply with our requisitions, because they are proposed in a hostile manner.

Our present measures, I have proved, are the only peaceable ones we could place the least confidence in. They are the least exceptionable, upon the score of irritating Great-Britain, of any our circumstances would permit. The congress have petitioned his Majesty for the redress of grievances. They have, no doubt, addressed him in the most humble, respectful and affectionate terms; assured him, of their own loyalty, and fidelity and of the loyalty and fidelity of his American subjects in general; endeavoured to convince him, that we have been misrepresented and abused; and expressed an earnest desire to see an amicable termination of the unhappy differences now existing. Can a pretext be wanting, in this case, to preserve the dignity of this parent state, and yet remove the complaints of the colonies? How easy would it be to overlook our particular agreements, and grant us redress in consequence of our petitions? It is easy to perceive there would be no difficulty in this respect.

I have omitted many considerations, which might be adduced to shew the impolicy of Great-Britains, delaying to accommodate matters, and attempting to enforce submission by cutting off all external sources of trade. To say all the subject allows, would spin out this piece to an immoderate length; I shall, therefore, content myself with mentioning only three things more. First, it would be extremely hurtful to the commerce of Great-Britain to drive us to the necessity of laying a regular foundation for manufactories of our own; which, if once established, could not easily, if at all, be undermined, or abolished. Secondly, it would be very expensive to the nation to maintain a fleet for the purpose of blocking up our ports, and destroying our trade: nor could she interrupt our intercourse with foreign climes without, at the same time, retrenching her own revenues; for she must then lose the duties and customs upon the articles we are wont to export to, and import from them. Added to this, it would not be prudent to risk the displeasure of those nations, to whom our trade is useful and beneficial. And lastly, a perseverance in ill-treatment would naturally beget such deep-rooted animosities in America, as might never be eradicated; and which might operate to the prejudice of the empire to the latest period.

Thus have I clearly proved, that the plan of opposition concerted by our congress is perfectly consonant with justice and sound policy; and will, in all human probability, secure our freedom against the assaults of our enemies.

But, after all, it may be demanded why they have adopted a non-exportation; seeing many arguments tend to shew that a non-importation alone would accomplish the end desired?

I answer, that the continuance of our exports is the only thing which could lessen, or retard the efficacy of a non-importation. It is not indeed probable it should do that to any great degree; but it was adviseable to provide against every possible obstruction. Besides this, the prospect of its taking place, and of the evils attendant upon it, will be a prevailing motive with the ministry to abandon their malignant schemes. It will also serve to convince them, that we are not afraid of putting ourselves to any inconveniencies, sooner than be the victims of their lawless ambition.

The execution of this measure has been wisely deferred to a future time, because we have the greatest reason to think affairs will be settled without it, and because its consequences would be too fatal to be justified by any thing but absolute necessity. This necessity there will be, should not our disputes terminate before the time allotted for its commencement.

Before I conclude this part of my address, I will answer two very singular interrogatories proposed by the FARMER, "Can we think (says he) to threaten, and bully, and frighten the supreme government of the nation into a compliance with our demands? Can we expect to force submission to our peevish and petulant humours, by exciting clamours and riots in England?" No, gentle Sir. We neither desire, nor endeavour to threaten, bully, or frighten any persons into a compliance with our demands. We have no peevish and petulant humours to be submitted to. All we aim at, is to convince your high and mighty masters, the ministry, that we are not such asses as to let them ride us as they please. We are determined to shew them, that we know the value of freedom; nor shall their rapacity extort, that inestimable jewel from us, without a manly and virtuous struggle. But for your part, sweet Sir! tho' we cannot much applaud your wisdom, yet we are compelled to admire your valour, which leads you to hope you may be able to *swear*, threaten, bully and frighten all America into a compliance with your sinister designs. When properly accoutered and armed with your formidable hiccory cudgel, what may not the ministry expect from such a champion? alas! for the poor committee gentlemen, how I tremble when I reflect on the many wounds and scars they must receive from your tremendous arm! Alas! for their supporters and abettors; a very large part indeed of the continent; but what of that? they must all be soundly drubbed with that confounded hiccory cudgel; for surely you would not undertake to drub one of them, without knowing yourself able to treat all their friends and adherents in the same manner; since 'tis plain you would bring them all upon your back.

I am now to address myself in particular to the Farmers of New-York.

MY GOOD COUNTRYMEN,

The reason I address myself to you, in particular, is, not because I am one of your number, or connected with you in interest more than with any other branch of the community. I love to speak the truth, and would scorn to prejudice you in favour of what I have to say, by taking upon me a fictitious character as other people have done. I can venture to assure you, the true writer of the piece signed A. W. FARMER, is not in reality a Farmer. He is some ministerial emissary, that has assumed the name to deceive you, and make you swallow the intoxicating potion he has prepared for you. But I have a better opinion of you than to think he will be able to succeed. I am persuaded you love yourselves and children better than to let any designing men cheat you out of your liberty and property, to serve their own purposes. You would be a disgrace to your ancestors, and the bitterest enemies to yourselves and to your posterity, if you did not act like men, in protecting and defending those rights you have hitherto enjoyed.

I say, my friends, I do not address you in particular, because I have any greater connexion with you, than with other people. I despise all false pretentions, and mean arts. Let those have recourse to dissimulation and falshood, who can't defend their cause without it. 'Tis my maxim to let the plain naked truth speak for itself; and if men won't listen to it, 'tis their own fault: they must be contented to suffer for it. I am neither merchant, nor farmer. I address you, because I wish well to my country, and of course to you, who are one chief support of it; and because an attempt has been made to lead you astray in particular. You are the men too who would lose most should you be foolish enough to counteract the prudent measures our worthy congress has taken for the preservation of our liberties. Those, who advise you to do it, are not your friends, but your greatest foes. They would have you made slaves, that they may pamper themselves with the fruits of your honest labour. 'Tis the Farmer who is most oppressed in all countries where slavery prevails.

You have seen how clearly I have proved, that a non-importation and non-exportation are the only peaceable means in our power to save ourselves from the most dreadful state of slavery. I have shewn there is not the least hope, to be placed in any thing else. I have confuted all the principal cavils raised by the pretended Farmer, and I hope, before I finish, to satisfy you, that he has attempted to frighten you with the prospect of evils, which will never happen. This indeed I have, in a great measure, done already, by making appear the great probability, I may almost say certainty, that our measures will procure us the most speedy redress.

Are you willing then to be slaves without a single struggle? Will you give up your freedom, or, which is the same thing, will you resign all security for your life and property, rather than endure some small present inconveniencies? Will you not take a little trouble to transmit the advantages you now possess to those, who are to come after you? I cannot doubt it. I would not suspect you of so much baseness and stupidity, as to suppose the contrary.

Pray who can tell me why a farmer in America, is not as honest and good a man, as a farmer in England? or why has not the one as good a right to what he has earned by his labour, as the other? I can't, for my life, see any distinction between them. And yet it seems the English farmers are to be governed and taxed by their own Assembly, or Parliament; and the American farmers are not. The former are to choose their own Representatives from among themselves, whose interest is connected with theirs, and over whom they have proper controul. The latter are to be loaded with taxes by men three thousand miles off; by men, who have no interest, or connexions among them; but whose interest it will be to burden them as much as possible; and over whom they cannot have the least restraint. How do you like this doctrine my friends? Are you ready to own the English farmers for your masters? Are you willing to acknowledge their right to take your property from you, how and when they please? I know you scorn the thought. You had rather die, than submit to it.

But some people try to make you believe, we are disputing about the foolish trifle of three pence duty upon tea. They may as well tell you, that black is white. Surely you can judge for yourselves. Is a dispute, whether the Parliament of Great-Britain shall make what laws, and impose what taxes they please upon us, or not; I say, is this a dispute about three pence duty upon tea? The man that affirms it, deserves to be laughed at.

It is true, we are denying to pay the duty upon tea; but it is not for the value of the thing itself. It is because we cannot submit to that, without acknowledging the principle upon which it is founded, and that principle is *a right to tax us in all cases whatsoever.*

You have, heretofore experienced the benefit of being taxed by your own Assemblies only. Your burdens are so light, that you scarcely feel them. You'd soon find the difference if you were once to let the Parliament have the management of these matters.

How would you like to pay four shillings a year,* out of every pound your farms are worth, to be squandered, (at least a great part of it) upon ministerial tools and court syco-phants? What would you think of giving a tenth part of the yearly products of your lands to the clergy? Would you not think it very hard to pay 10s. sterling per annum, for every wheel of your waggons and other carriages, a shilling or two for every pane of glass in your houses, and two or three shillings for every one of your hearths? I might mention taxes upon your mares, cows, and many other things; but those I have already mentioned are sufficient. Methinks I see you stare, and hear you ask how you could live, if you were to pay such heavy taxes? Indeed my friends I can't tell you. You are to look out for that, and take care you do not run yourselves in the way of danger, by following the advice of those, who want to betray you. This you may depend upon, if ever you let the Parliament carry its point, you will have these and more to pay. Perhaps before long, your tables, and chairs, and platters, and dishes, and knives and forks, and every thing else would be taxed. Nay, I don't know but they would find

---

*i. e. the full price of your farms every five years.

means to tax you for every child you got, and for every kiss your daughters received from their sweet-hearts, and God knows, that would soon ruin you. The people of England would pull down the Parliament House, if their present heavy burdens were not transferred from them to you. Indeed there is no reason to think the Parliament would have any inclination to spare you: The contrary is evident.

But being ruined by taxes is not the worst you have to fear. What security would you have for your lives? How can any of you be sure you would have the free enjoyment of your religion long? would you put your religion in the power of any set of men living? Remember civil and religious liberty always go together, if the foundation of the one be sapped, the other will fall of course.

Call to mind one of our sister colonies, Boston. Reflect upon the situation of Canada, and then tell me whether you are inclined to place any confidence in the justice and humanity of the parliament. The port of Boston is blocked up, and an army planted in the town. An act has been passed to alter its charter, to prohibit its assemblies, to license the murder of its inhabitants, and to convey them from their own country to Great Britain, to be tried for their lives. What was all this for? Just because a small number of people, provoked by an open and dangerous attack upon their liberties, destroyed a parcel of Tea belonging to the East India Company. It was not public but private property they destroyed. It was not the act of the whole province, but the act of a part of the citizens; instead of trying to discover the perpetrators, and commencing a legal prosecution against them; the parliament of Great-Britain interfered in an unprecedented manner, and inflicted a punishment upon a whole province, "untried, unheard, unconvicted of any crime." This may be justice, but it looks so much like cruelty, that a man of a humane heart would be more apt to call it by the latter, than the former name.

The affair of Canada, if possible, is still worse. The English laws have been superceded by the French laws. The Romish faith is made the established religion of the land, and his Majesty is placed at the head of it. The free exercise of the protestant faith depends upon the pleasure of the Governor and Council. The subject is divested of the right of trial by jury, and an innocent man may be imprisoned his whole life, without being able to obtain any trial at all. The parliament was not contented with introducing arbitrary power and popery in Canada, with its former limits, but they have annexed to it the vast tracts of land that surround all the colonies.

Does not your blood run cold, to think an English parliament should pass an act for the establishment of arbitrary power and popery in such an extensive country? If they had had any regard to the freedom and happiness of mankind, they would never have done it. If they had been friends to the protestant cause, they would never have provided such a nursery for its great enemy: They would not have given such encouragement to popery. The thought of their conduct, in this particular shocks me. It must shock you too my friends. Beware of trusting yourselves to men, who are capable of such an action! They may as well establish popery in New-York and the other colonies as they did in Canada. They had no more right to do it there than here.

Is it not better, I ask, to suffer a few present inconveniencies, than to put yourselves in the way of losing every thing that is precious. Your lives, your property, your religion are all at stake. I do my duty. I warn you of your danger. If you should still be so mad, as to bring destruction upon yourselves; if you should still neglect what you owe to God and man, you cannot plead ignorance in your excuse. Your consciences will reproach you for your folly, and your children's children will curse you.

You are told, the schemes of our Congress will ruin you. You are told, they have not considered your interest; but have neglected, or betrayed you. It is endeavoured to make you look upon some of the wisest and best men in the America, as rogues and rebels. What will not wicked men attempt! They will scruple nothing, that may serve their purposes. In truth, my friends, it is very unlikely any of us shall suffer much; but let the worst happen, the farmers will be better off, than other people.

Many of those that made up the Congress have large possessions in land, and may, therefore be looked upon as farmers themselves. Can it be supposed, they would be careless about the farmer's interest, when they could not injure that, without injuring themselves? You see the absurdity of such a supposition.

The merchants and a great part of the tradesmen get their living by commerce. These are the people that would be hurt most, by putting a stop to it. As to the farmers, "they furnish food for the merchant and mechanic; the raw materials for most manufactures are the produce of their industry." The merchants and mechanics are already dependent upon the farmers for their food, and if the non-importation should continue any time, they would be dependent upon them for their cloaths also.

It is a false assertion, that the merchants have imported more than usual this year. That report has been raised by your enemies to poison your minds with evil suspicions. If our disputes be not settled within eighteen months, the goods we have among us will be consumed; and then the materials for making cloaths must be had from you. Manufactures must be promoted with vigour, and a high price will be given for your wool, flax and hemp. It will be your interest to pay the greatest care and attention to your sheep. Increase and improve the breed as much as possible: *Kill them sparingly*, and such only as will not be of use towards the increase and improvement of them. In a few months we shall know what we have to trust to. If matters be not accommodated by spring, enlarge the quantity of your flax and hemp. You will experience the benefit of it. All those articles will be very much wanted: They will bring a great deal higher price than they used to do. And while you are supplying the wants of the community, you will be enriching yourselves.

Should we hereafter, find it necessary to stop our exports, you can apply more of your land to raising flax and hemp, and less of it to wheat, rye, &c. By which means, you will not have any of those latter articles to lie upon hand. There will be a consumption for as much of the former as you can raise, and the great demand they will be in, will make them very profitable to you.

Patience good Mr. Critic! *Kill them sparingly, I said,* what objection have you to the phrase? You'll tell me, it is not *classical*; but I affirm it is, and if you will condescend to look into

Mr. Johnson's dictionary, you will find I have his authority for it. Pray then, for the future, *spare* your wit, upon such occasions, otherwise the world will not be disposed to *spare* its ridicule. And though the man that *spares* nobody does not deserve to be *spared* himself, yet will I *spare* you, for the present, and proceed to things of more importance.

Pardon me, my friends, for taking up your time with this digression; but I could not forbear stepping out of the way a little, to shew the world, I am as able a critic, and as good a punster as Mr. Farmer. I now return to the main point with pleasure.

It is insinuated, "That the bustle about non-importation, &c. has its rise, not from patriotism, but selfishness;" and is only made by the merchants, that they may get a high price for their goods.

By this time, I flatter myself you are convinced, that we are not disputing about trifles. It has been clearly proved to you, that we are contending for every thing dear in life, and that the measures adopted by the congress, are the only ones which can save us from ruin. This is sufficient to confute that insinuation. But to confirm it, let me observe to you, that the merchants have not been the foremost to bring about a non-importation. All the members of the congress were unanimous in it; and *many* of them were not merchants. The warmest advocates for it, every where, are not concerned in trade, and, as I before remarked, the traders will be the principal sufferers, if it should continue any time.

But it is said it will not continue, because, "when the stores are like to become empty, they will have weight enough to break up the agreement." I don't think they would attempt it; but if they should, it is impossible a few mercenary men could have influence enough to make the whole body of people give up the only plan their circumstances admit of for the preservation of their rights, and, of course, to forfeit all they have been so long striving to secure. The making of a non-importation agreement did not depend upon the merchants; neither will the breaking of it depend upon them. The congress have provided against the breach of the non-importation, by the non-consumption agreement. They have resolved for themselves and us their constituents, "not to purchase, or use any East-India

Tea whatsoever; nor any goods, wares, or merchandize, from Great-Britain or Ireland, imported after the first of December, nor molasses, &c. from the West Indies, nor wine from Madeira, or the Western Islands, nor foreign Indigo." If we do not purchase or use these things, the merchant will have no inducement to import them.

Hence you may perceive the reason of a non-consumption agreement. It is to put it out of the power of dishonest men, to break the non importation. *Is this a slavish regulation?* Or is it a hardship upon us to submit to it? Surely not. Every sensible, every good man must approve of it. Whoever tries to disaffect you to it, ought to meet with your contempt.

Take notice, my friends, how these men are obliged to contradict themselves. In one place you are told, that all the bustle about non-importation, &c. has its rise, not from patriotism, but from selfishness, "or, in other words, that it is made by the merchants to get a higher price for their goods." In another place it is said, that all we are doing is instigated by some turbulent men, who want to establish a republican form of government among us.

The Congress is censured for appointing committees to carry their measures into execution, and directing them "to establish such further regulations, as they may think proper for that purpose." Pray, did we not appoint our Delegates to make regulations for us? What signified making them, if they did not provide some persons to see them executed? Must a few bad men be left to do what they please, contrary to the general sense of the people, without any persons to controul them, or to look into their behaviour and mark them out to the public? The man that desires to screen his knavery from the public eye, will answer yes; but the honest man, that is determined to do nothing hurtful to his country, and who is conscious his actions will bear the light, will heartily answer no.

The high prices of goods are held up to make you dissatisfied with the non-importation. If the arguments on this head were true, it would be much better to subject yourselves to that disadvantage, for a time, than to bring upon yourselves all the mischiefs I have pointed out to you. Should you submit to claims of the Parliament, you will not only be oppressed with the taxes upon your lands, &c. which I have already mentioned; but you will have to pay heavy taxes upon all the goods we import from Great-Britain. Large duties will be laid upon them at home; and the merchants, of course, will have a greater price for them, or it would not be worth their while to carry on trade. The duty laid upon paper, glass, painter's colours, &c. was a beginning of this kind. The present duty upon tea is preparatory to the imposition of duties upon all other articles. Do you think the Parliament would make such a serious matter of three pence a pound upon tea, if it intended to stop there? It is absurd to imagine it. You would soon find your mistake if you did. For fear of paying somewhat a higher price to the merchants for a year or two, you would have to pay an endless list of taxes, within and without, as long as you live, and your children after you.

But I trust, there is no danger that the prices of goods will rise much, if at all. The same congress that put a stop to the importation of them, has also forbid raising the prices of them. The same committee that is to regulate the one, is also to regulate the other. All care will be taken to give no cause of dissatisfaction. Confide in the men whom you, and the rest of the continent have chosen the guardians of our common liberties. They are men of sense and virtue. They will do nothing but what is really necessary for the security of your lives and properties.

A sad pother is made too about prohibiting the exportation of sheep, without excepting weathers. The poor Farmer is at a mighty loss to know how weathers can improve, or increase the breed. Truly I am not such a conjurer, as to be able to inform him; but if you please, my friends, I can give you two pretty good reasons, why the congress has not excepted weathers. One is, that for some time, we shall have occasion for all the wool we can raise; so that it would be imprudent to export sheep of any kind: and the other is, that, if you confine yourself chiefly to killing weathers, as you ought to do, you will have none to export. The gentleman who made the objection, must have known these things, as well as myself; but he loves to crack a jest, and could not pass by so fair an opportunity.

He takes notice of the first of these reasons himself; but in order to weaken its force, cries, "let me ask you, brother farmers, which of you would keep a flock of sheep, barely, for the sake of their wool?" To this he answers, "not one of you. If you cannot sell your sheep to advantage, at a certain age, you cannot keep them to any profit." He thinks, because he calls you brother farmers, that he can cajole you into believing what he pleases; but you are not the fools he takes you for. You know what is for your own interest better than he can tell you. And we all know, that in a little time, if our affairs be not settled, the demand for wool will be very great. You will be able to obtain such a price, as will make it worth your while to bestow the greatest attention upon your sheep.

In another place, this crafty writer tells you, that, "from the day our exports, from this province are stopped, the farmers may date the commencement of their ruin." He asks, "will the shop-keeper give you his goods? will the weaver, shoemaker, black-smith, carpenter work for you without pay?" I make no doubt, you are satisfied, from what I have said, that we shall never have occasion to stop our exports; but if things turn out contrary to our expectation, and it should become necessary to take that step, you will find no difficulty in getting what you want from the merchants and mechanics. They will not be able to do without you, and, consequently, they cannot refuse to supply you with what you stand in need of from them. Where will the merchants and mechanics get food and materials for clothing, if not from the farmer? And if they are dependent upon you, for those two grand supports of life, how can they withold what they have from you?

I repeat it (my friends) we shall know, how matters are like to be settled by the spring. If our disputes be not terminated to our satisfaction by that time, it will be your business to plant large parts of your lands with flax and hemp. Those articles will be wanted for manufactures, and they will yield you a greater profit than any thing else. In the interim, take good care of your sheep.

I heartily concur with the farmer, in condemning all illicit trade. Perjury is, no doubt, a most heinous and detestable crime; and for my part, I had rather suffer any thing, than have my wants relieved at the expence of truth and integrity.

I know, there are many pretended friends to liberty, who will take offence at this declaration; but I speak the sentiments of my heart without reserve. I do not write for a party. I should scorn to be of any. All I say, is from a disinterested regard to the public weal.

The congress, I am persuaded, were of the same opinion: They, like honest men, have, as much as was in their power, provided against this kind of trade, by agreeing to use no East-India tea whatever, after the first day of March next.

I shall now consider what has been said, with respect to the payment of debts, and stopping of the courts of justice. Let what will happen, it will be your own faults, if you are not able to pay your debts. I have told you, in what manner you may make as much out of your lands as ever: by bestowing more of your attention upon raising flax and hemp, and less upon other things. Those articles (as I have more than once observed) will be in the highest demand: There will be no doing without them; and, of course, you will be able to get a very profitable price for them. How can it be, that the farmers should be at a loss for money to pay their debts, at a time, when the whole community must buy, not only their food, but all the materials for their cloaths from them? You have no reason to be uneasy on that account.

As to the courts of justice, no violence can, or will be used to shut them up; but, if it should be found necessary, we may enter into solemn agreement to cease from all litigations at law, except in particular cases. We may regulate law suits, in such a manner, as to prevent any mischief that might arise from them. Restrictions may be laid on to hinder merciless creditors, from taking advantage of the times, to oppress and ruin their debtors but, at the same time, not to put it in the power of the debtors, *wantonly*, to withold their just dues from their creditors, when they are able to pay them. The law ruins many a good honest family. Disputes may be settled in a more friendly way; one or two virtuous neighbours may be chosen by each party to decide them. If the next congress should think any regulations concerning the courts of justice requisite, they will make them; and proper persons will be appointed to carry them into execution, and to see, that no individuals deviate from them. It will be your duty to elect persons, whose fidelity and zeal for your interest you can depend upon, to represent you in *that* congress; which is to meet at Philadelphia, in May ensuing.

The Farmer cries, "tell me not of delegates, congresses committees, mobs, riots, insurrections, associations; a plague on them all. Give me the steady, uniform, unbiassed influence of the courts of justice. I have been happy under their protection, and I trust in God, I shall be so again."

I say, tell me not of the British Commons, Lords, ministry, ministerial tools, placemen, pensioners, parasites. I scorn to let my life and property depend upon the pleasure of any of them. Give me the steady, uniform, unshaken security of constitutional freedom; give me the right to be tried by a jury of my own neighbours, and to be taxed by my own representatives only. What will become of the law and courts of justice without this? The shadow may remain, but the substance will be gone. I would die to preserve the law upon a solid foundation; but take away liberty, and the foundation is destroyed.

The last thing I shall take notice of, is the complaint of the Farmer, that the congress will not allow you "a dish of tea to please your wives with, nor a glass of Madeira to cheer your spirits, nor a spoonful of molasses, to sweeten your butter milk with." You would have a right to complain, if the use of these things had been forbidden to you alone; but it has been equally forbidden to all sorts of people. The members of the congress themselves are no more permitted to please their wives with a dish of tea, or to cheer their spirits with a glass of wine, or to sweeten their butter milk with a spoonful of molasses, than you are. They are upon a footing with you in this respect.

By him! but, with your leave, my friends, we'll try, if we can, to do without swearing. I say, it is enough to make a man mad, to hear such ridiculous quibbles offered instead of sound argument; but so it is, the piece I am writing against contains nothing else.

When a man grows warm, he has a confounded itch for swearing. I have been going, above twenty times, to rap out an oath, *by him that made me*, but I have checked myself, with this reflection, that it is rather *unmannerly*, to treat him that made us with so much freedom.

Thus have I examined and confuted, all the cavils and objections, of any consequence, stated by this Farmer. I have only passed over such things, as are of little weight, the fallacy of which will easily appear. I have shewn, that the congress have neither "ignorantly misunderstood, carelessly neglected, nor basely betrayed you;" but that they have devised and recommended the *only* effectual means to preserve your invaluable privileges. I have proved, that their measures cannot fail of success; but will procure the most speedy relief for us. I have also proved, that the farmers are the people who would suffer least, should we be obliged to carry all our measures into execution.

Will you then, my friends, allow yourselves, to be duped by this artful enemy? will you follow his advice, disregard the authority of your congress, and bring ruin on yourselves and posterity? will you act in such a manner as to deserve the hatred and resentment of all the rest of America? I am sure you will not. I should be sorry to think, any of my countrymen would be so mean, so blind to their own interest, so lost to every generous and manly feeling.

The sort of men I am opposing give you fair words, to persuade you to serve their own turns; but they think and speak of you in common in a very disrespectful manner. I have heard some of their party talk of you, as the most ignorant and mean-spirited set of people in the world. They say, that you have no sense of honour or generosity; that you don't care a farthing about your country, children or any body else, but yourselves; and that you are so ignorant, as not to be able to look beyond the present; so that if you can once be persuaded to believe the measures of your congress will involve you in some little present perplexities, you will be glad to do any thing to avoid them; without considering the much greater miseries that await you at a little distance off. This is the character they give of you. Bad men are apt to paint others like themselves. For my part, I will never entertain such an opinion of you, unless you should verify their words, by wilfully falling into the pit they have prepared for you. I flatter myself you will convince them of their error, by shewing the world, you are capable of judging what is right and best, and have resolution to pursue it.

All I ask is, that you will judge for yourselves. I don't desire you to take my opinion or any man's opinion, as the guide of your actions. I have stated a number of plain arguments; I have supported them with several well-known facts: It is your business to draw a conclusion and act accordingly.

I caution you, again and again, to beware of the men who advise you to forsake the plain path, marked out for you by the congress. They only mean to deceive and betray you. Our representatives in general assembly cannot take any wiser or better course to settle our differences, than our representatives in the continental congress have taken. If you join with the rest of America in the same common measure, you will be sure to preserve your liberties inviolate; but if you separate from them, and seek for redress alone, and unseconded, you will certainly fall a prey to your enemies, and repent your folly as long as you live.

May God give you wisdom to see what is your true interest, and inspire you with becoming zeal for the cause of virtue and mankind.

A Friend to America.

December 15, 1774

THE DANGER OF TRUSTING IN VIRTUE

To John Jay

Dear Sir   New York Novem 26. 1775

I take the liberty to trouble you with some remarks on a matter which to me appears of not a little importance; doubting not that you will use your influence in Congress to procure a remedy for the evil I shall mention, if you think the considerations I shall urge are of that weight they seem in my judgment to possess.

You will probably ere this reaches you have heard of the late incursion made into this city by a number of horsemen from New England under the command of Capt Sears, who took away Mr. Rivington's types, and a Couteau or two.

Though I am fully sensible how dangerous and pernicious Rivington's press has been, and how detestable the character of the man is in every respect, yet I cannot help disapproving and condemning this step.

In times of such commotion as the present, while the passions of men are worked up to an uncommon pitch there is great danger of fatal extremes. The same state of the passions which fits the multitude, who have not a sufficient stock of reason and knowlege to guide them, for opposition to tyranny and oppression, very naturally leads them to a contempt and disregard of all authority. The due medium is hardly to be found among the more intelligent, it is almost impossible among the unthinking populace. When the minds of these are loosened from their attachment to ancient establishments and courses, they seem to grow giddy and are apt more or less to run into anarchy. These principles, too true in themselves, and confirmed to me both by reading and my own experience, deserve extremely the attention of those, who have the direction of public affairs. In such tempestuous times, it requires the greatest skill in the political pilots to keep men steady and within proper bounds, on which account I am always more or less alarmed at every thing which is done of mere will and pleasure, without any proper authority. Irregularities I know are to be expected, but they are nevertheless dangerous and ought to be checked, by every prudent and moderate mean. From these general maxims, I disapprove of the irruption in question, as serving to cherish a spirit of disorder at a season when men are too prone to it of themselves.

Moreover, New England is very populous and powerful. It is not safe to trust to the virtue of any people. Such proceedings will serve to produce and encourage a spirit of encroachment and arrogance in them. I like not to see potent neighbours indulged in the practice of making inroads at pleasure into this or any other province.

You well know too, sir, that antipathies and prejudices have long subsisted between this province and New England. To this may be attributed a principal part of the disaffection now prevalent among us. Measures of the present nature, however they may serve to intimidate, will secretly revive and increase those ancient animosities, which though smothered for a while will break out when there is a favorable opportunity.

Besides this, men coming from a neighbouring province to chastise the notorious friends of the ministry here, will hold up an idea to our ennemies not very advantageous to our affairs. They will imagine that the New Yorkers are totally, or a majority of them, disaffected to the American cause, which makes the interposal of their neighbours necessary: or that such violences will breed differences and effect that which they have been so eagerly wishing, a division and qurrelling among ourselves. Every thing of such an aspect must encourage their hopes.

Upon the whole the measure is condemned, by all the cautious and prudent among the whigs, and will evidently be productive of secret jealousy and ill blood if a stop is not put to things of the kind for the future.

All the good purposes that could be expected from such a step will be answered; and many ill consequences will be prevented if your body gently interposes a check for the future. Rivington will be intimidated & the tories will be convinced that the other colonies will not tamely see the general cause betrayed by the Yorkers. A favourable idea will be impressed of your justice & impartiality in discouraging the encroachments of any one province on another; and the apprehensions of prudent men respecting the ill-effects of an ungoverned spirit in the people of New England will be quieted. Believe me sir it is a matter of consequence and deserves serious attention

The tories it is objected by some are growing insolent and clamorous: It is necessary to repress and overawe them. There is truth in this; but the present remedy is a bad one. Let your body station in different parts of the province most tainted, with the ministerial infection, a few regiments of troops, raised in Philadelphia the Jerseys or any other province except New England. These will suffice to strengthen and support the Whigs who are still I flatter myself a large majority and to suppress the efforts of the tories. The pretence for this would be plausible. There is no knowing how soon the Ministry may make an attempt upon New York. There is reason to believe they will not be long before they turn their attention to it. In this there will be some order & regularity, and no grounds of alarm to our friends.

I am sir with very great Esteem—   Your most hum servant
A. Hamilton

THE NEW YORK CONSTITUTION

To Gouverneur Morris

Head Quarters Morris Town
Dear Sir,   May 19th. 1777

I this moment received the favour of your letter of the 16th instant.

I partly agree and partly disagree with you respecting the deficiencies of your constitution. That there is a want of vigor in the executive, I believe will be found true. To determine the qualifications proper for the chief executive Magistrate requires the deliberate wisdom of a select assembly, and cannot be safely lodged with the people at large. That instability is inherent in the nature of popular governments, I think very disputable; unstable democracy, is an epithet frequently in the mouths of politicians; but I believe that from a strict examination of the matter, from the records of history, it will be found that the fluctuation of governments in which the popular principle has borne a considerable sway, has proceeded from its being compounded with other principles and from its being made to operate in an improper channel. Compound governments, though they may be harmonious in the beginning, will introduce distinct interests; and these interests will clash, throw the state into convulsions & produce a change or dissolution. When the deliberative or judicial powers are vested wholly or partly in the collective body of the people, you must expect error, confusion and instability. But a representative democracy, where the right of election is well secured and regulated & the exercise of the legislative, executive and judiciary authorities, is vested in select persons, chosen *really* and not *nominally* by the people, will in my opinion be most likely to be happy, regular and durable. That the complexity of your legislative will occasion delay and dilatoriness is evident and I fear may be attended with much greater, evil; as expedition is not very material *in making* laws, especially when the government is well digested and matured by time. The evil I mean is, that in time, your senate, from the very name and from the mere circumstance of its being a separate member of the legislature, will be liable to degenerate into a body purely aristocratical. And I think the danger of an abuse of power from a simple legislative would not be very great, in a government where the equality and fulness of popular representation is so wisely provided for as in yours. On the whole, though I think there are the defects intimated, I think your Government far the best that we have yet seen, and capable of giving long and substantial happiness to the people. Objections to it should be suggested with great caution and reserve.

Nothing particular in the military line— The enemy still in the Jersies, though they have been some time sending away their stores baggage &c. and are raising new works of defence. All this may be preparatory to an evacuation at all events, and they may be only intended to pave the way for a retreat, in case of an attack, or any accident. Advices from the West Indies, that have an appearance of authenticity, mention a french vessel bound for the Continent, being taken by the British frigate, Perseus, and carried into Dominique; and a remonstrance being made by the Governor of Martinique, threatening reprisals in case of a detention. Nay, some accounts say he has actually seized all the English vessels in the harbour of Martinique and imprisonned their seamen 'till restitution shall be made. If these accounts be true, they are important, and may be considered as an earnest of more general hostility.

Perhaps your next favour will find me at Bound brook. Head Quarters will soon be moved there. Our family seem desirous of cultivating a closer acquaintance with the enemy than we have had the pleasure of, for some time past.

With real regard, I am Sir,   Your most obedt servant
A Hamilton

*

Relying on your punctuality in favouring me with any important intelligence your way, I am likely to lose a beaver hat, which was staked against the truth of the report of the stores at St. John's being destroyed. If you forget me in future, I will certainly excommunicate you.

THE TROUBLE WITH CONGRESS

To George Clinton

Dear Sir,   Head Quarters Feb'y 13, 1778.

I did myself the honor of writing to you, immediately after my arrival at Head Quarters, in answer to two letters I found here, from you.

There is a matter, which often obtrudes itself upon my mind, and which requires the attention of every person of sense and influence, among us. I mean a degeneracy of representation in the great council of America. It is a melancholy truth Sir, and the effects of which we dayly see and feel, that there is not so much wisdom in a certain body, as there ought to be, and as the success of our affairs absolutely demands. Many members of it are no doubt men in every respect, fit for the trust, but this cannot be said of it as a body. Folly, caprice a want of foresight, comprehension and dignity, characterise the general tenor of their actions. Of this I dare say, you are sensible, though you have not perhaps so many opportunities of knowing it as I have. Their conduct with respect to the army especially is feeble indecisive and improvident—insomuch, that we are reduced to a more terrible situation than you can conceive. False and contracted views of economy have prevented them, though repeatedly urged to it, from making that provision for officers which was requisite to interest them in the service; which has produced such carelessness and indifference to the service, as is subversive of every officer-like quality. They have disgusted the army by repeated instances of the most whimsical favouritism in their promotions; and by an absurd prodigality of rank to foreigners and to the meanest staff of the army. They have not been able to summon resolution enough to withstand the impudent importunity and vain boasting of foreign pretenders; but have manifested such a ductility and inconstancy in their proceedings, as will warrant the charge of suffering themselves to be bullied, by every petty rascal, who comes armed with ostentatious pretensions of military merit and experience. Would you believe it Sir, it is become almost proverbial in the mouths of the French officers and other foreigners, that they have nothing more to do, to obtain whatever they please, than to assume a high tone and assert their own merit with confidence and perserverance? These things wound my feelings as a republican more than I can express; and in some degree make me contemptible in my own eyes.

By injudicious changes and arrangements in the Commissary's department, in the middle of a campaign, they have exposed the army frequently to temporary want, and to the danger of a dissolution, from absolute famine. At this very day there are complaints from the whole line, of having been three or four days without provisions; desertions have been immense, and strong features of mutiny begin to show themselves. It is indeed to be wondered at, that the soldiery have manifested so unparalleled a degree of patience, as they have. If effectual measures are not speedily adopted, I know not how we shall keep the army together or make another campaign.

I omit saying any thing of the want of Cloathing for the army. It may be disputed whether more could have been done than has been done.

If you look into their conduct in the civil line, you will equally discover a deficiency of energy dignity and extensiveness of views; but of this you can better judge than myself, and it is unnecessary to particularise.

America once had a representation, that would do honor to any age or nation. The present falling off is very alarming and dangerous. What is the cause? or how is it to be remedied? are questions that the welfare of these states requires should be well attended to. The great men who composed our first council; are they dead, have they deserted the cause, or what has become of them? Very few are dead and still fewer have deserted the cause;—they are all except the few who still remain in Congress either in the field, or in the civil offices of their respective states; far the greater part are engaged in the latter. The only remedy then is to take them out of these employments and return them to the place, where their presence is infinitely more important.

Each State in order to promote its own internal government and prosperity, has selected its best members to fill the offices within itself, and conduct its own affairs. Men have been fonder of the emoluments and conveniences, of being employed at home, and local attachment, falsely operating, has made them more provident for the particular interests of the states to which they belonged, than for the common interests of the confederacy. This is a most pernicious mistake, and must be corrected. However important it is to give form and efficiency to your interior constitutions and police; it is infinitely more important to have a wise general council; otherwise a failure of the measures of the union will overturn all your labours for the advancement of your particular good and ruin the common cause. You should not beggar the councils of the United States to enrich the administration of the several members. Realize to yourself the consequences of having a Congress despised at home and abroad. How can the common force be exerted, if the power of collecting it be put in weak foolish and unsteady hands? How can we hope for success in our European negociations, if the nations of Europe have no confidence in the wisdom and vigor, of the great Continental Government? This is the object on which their eyes are fixed, hence it is America will derive its importance or insignificance, in their estimation.

Arguments to you Sir, need not be multiplied to enforce the necessity of having a good general council, neither do I think we shall very widely differ as to the fact that the present is very far from being such.

The sentiments I have advanced are not fit for the vulgar ear; and circumstanced as I am, I should with caution utter them except to those in whom I may place an entire confidence. But it is time that men of weight and understanding should take the alarm, and excite each other to a proper remedy. For my part, my insignificance, allows me to do nothing more, than to hint my apprehensions to those of that description who are pleased to favour me with their confidence. In this view, I write to you.

As far, as I can judge, the remarks I have made do not apply to your state nearly so much as to the other twelve. You have a Duane a Morris and may I not add a Duer? But why do you not send your Jay and your R. R. Livingston? I wish General Schuyler was either explicitly in the army or in the Congress. For yourself Sir, though I mean no compliments you must not be spared from where you are.

But the design of this letter is not so much that you may use your influence, in improving or enlarging your own representation, as in, discreetly, giving the alarm to other states, through the medium of your confidential friends. Indeed Sir it is necessary there should be a change. America will shake to its center, if there is not.

You and I had some conversation when I had the pleasure of seeing you last with respect to the existence of a certain faction. Since I saw you, I have discovered such convincing traits of the monster, that I cannot doubt its reality in the most extensive sense. I dare say, you have seen and heard enough to settle the matter, in your own mind. I believe it unmasked its batteries too soon and begins to hide its head; but as I imagine it will only change the storm to a sap; all the true and sensible friends to their country, and of course to a certain great man, ought to be upon the watch, to counterplot the secret machinations of his enemies. Have you heard any thing of Conway's history? He is one of the vermin bred in the entrails of this chimera dire, and there does not exist a more villainous calumniator and incendiary. He is gone to Albany on a certain expedition.

I am with great regard & respect, Sir, Your most Obed. servant

Alex. Hamilton

THE BATTLE OF MONMOUTH

To Elias Boudinot

My dear Sir,

You will by this time imagine that I have forgotten my promise of writing to you, as I have been so long silent on an occasion, which most people will be fond of celebrating to their friends. The truth is, I have no passion for scribbling and I know you will be at no loss for the fullest information. But that you may not have a right to accuse me of negligence, I will impose upon myself the drugery of saying something about the transactions of the 28th, in which the American arms gained very signal advantages; and might have gained much more signal ones.

Indeed, I can hardly persuade myself to be in good humour with success so far inferior to what we, in all probability should have had, had not the finest opportunity America ever possessed been fooled away by a man, in whom she has placed a large share of the most ill judged confidence. You will have heard enough to know, that I mean General Lee. This man is either a driveler in the business of soldiership or something much worse. To let you fully into the silly and pitiful game he has been playing, I will take the tale up from the beginning; expecting you will consider what I say, as in the most perfect confidence.

When we came to Hopewell Township, The General un-luckily called a council of war, the result of which would have done honor to the most honorable society of midwives, and to them only. The purport was, that we should keep at a com-fortable distance from the enemy, and keep up a vain parade of annoying them by detachment. In persuance of this idea, a detachment of 1500 men was sent off under General Scot to join the other troops near the enemy's lines. General Lee was *primum mobile* of this sage plan; and was even opposed to sending so considerable a force. The General, on mature re-consideration of what had been resolved on, determined to persue a different line of conduct at all hazards. With this view, he marched the army the next morning towards King-ston and there made another detachment of 1000 men under General Wayne; and formed all the detached troops into an advanced corps under the command of the Marquis De la fayette. The project was, that this advanced corps should take the first opportunity to attack the enemy's rear on the march, to be supported or covered as circumstances should require by the whole army.

General Lee's conduct with respect to the command of this corps was truly childish. According to the incorrect notions of our army his seniority would have intitled him to the command of the advanced corps; but he in the first instance declined it, in favour of the Marquis. Some of his friends having blamed him for doing it, and Lord Stirling having shown a disposition to interpose his claim, General Lee very inconsistently reasserted his pretensions. The matter was a second time accommodated; General Lee and Lord Stirling agreed to let the Marquis command. General Lee a little time after, recanted again and became very importunate. The General, who had all along observed the greatest candor in the matter, grew tired of such fickle behaviour and ordered the Marquis to proceed.

The enemy in marching from Allen Town had changed their disposition and thrown all their best troops in the rear; this made it necessary, to strike a stroke with propriety, to reinforce the advanced corps. Two brigades were detached for this purpose, and the General, willing to accommodate General Lee, sent him with them to take the command of the whole advanced corps, which rendezvoused the forenoon of the 27th at English Town, consisting of at least 5000 rank & file, most of them select troops. General Lee's orders were, the moment he received intelligence of the enemy's march to persue them & to attack their rear.

This intelligence was received about five oClock the morning of the 28th. and General Lee put his troops in motion accordingly. The main body did the same. The advanced corps came up with the enemys rear a mile or two beyond the court House; I saw the enemy drawn up, and am persuaded there were not a thousand men; their front from different accounts was then ten miles off. However favourable this situation may seem for an attack it was not made; but after changing their position two or three times by retrograde movements our advanced corps got into a general confused retreat and even route would hardly be too strong an expression. Not a word of all this was officially communicated to the General; as we approached the supposed place of action we heard some flying rumours of what had happened in consequence of which the General rode forward and found the troops retiring in the greatest disorder and the enemy pressing upon their rear. I never saw the general to so much advantage. His coolness and firmness were admirable. He instantly took measures for checking the enemy's advance, and giving time for the army, which was very near, to form and make a proper disposition. He then rode back and had the troops formed on a very advantageous piece of ground; in which and in other transactions of the day General Greene & Lord Stirling rendered very essential service, and did themselves great honor. The sequel is, we beat the enemy and killed and wounded at least a thousand of their best troops. America owes a great deal to General Washington for this day's work; a general route dismay and disgrace would have attended the whole army in any other hands but his. By his own good sense and fortitude he turned the fate of the day. Other officers have great merit in performing their parts well; but he directed the whole with the skill of a Master workman. He did not hug himself at a distance and leave an Arnold to win laurels for him; but by his own presence, he brought order out of confusion, animated his troops and led them to success.

A great number of our officers distinguished themselves this day. General Wayne was always foremost in danger. Col Stewart & Lt Col Ramsay were with him among the first to oppose the enemy. Lt Col Olney at the Head of Varnum's Brigade made the next stand. I was with him, got my horse wounded and myself much hurt by a fall in consequence. Col Livingston behaved very handsomely. Our friend Barber was remarkably active; towards the close of the day, he received a ball through his side—which the doctors think will not be fatal. Col: Silly, & Lt Col: Parker were particularly useful on the left—Col Craig, with General Wayne, on the right. The Artillery acquitted themselves most charmingly. I was spectator to Lt Col: Oswalds behaviour, who kept up a gallant fire from some pieces commanded by him, uncovered and unsupported. In short one can hardly name particulars without doing injustice to the rest. The behaviour of the officers and men in general was such as could not easily be surpassed. Our troops, after the first impulse from mismanagement, behaved with more spirit & moved with greater order than the British troops. You know my way of thinking about our army, and that I am not apt to flatter it. I assure you I never was pleased with them before this day.

What part our family acted let others say. I hope you will not suspect me of vanity when I tell you that one of them Fitsgerald, had a slight contusion with a Musket ball, another, Laurens, had a slight contusion also—and his horse killed—a third, Hamilton, had his horse wounded in the first part of the action with a musket ball. If the rest escaped, it is only to be ascribed to better fortune, not more prudence in keeping out of the way. That Congress is not troubled with any messenger-aids to give swords and other pretty toys to, let them ascribe to the good sense of the Commander in Chief, and to a certain turn of thinking in those about him which put them above such shifts.

What think you now of General Lee? You will be ready to join me in condemning him: And yet, I fear a Court Martial will not do it. A certain preconceived and preposterous opinion of his being a very great man will operate much in his favour. Some people are very industrious in making interest for him. Whatever a court Martial may decide, I shall continue to believe and say—his conduct was monstrous and unpardonable.

I am Dr Sir   Yrs. Affecty   Alex Hamilton

Brunswick
July 5th. 78

One wing of the army marched this morning towards the North River, another goes tomorrow. The enemy by our last accounts were embarking their baggage. They lie three miles below Middletown. French importunity cannot be resisted. I have given two frenchmen letters to you. I am very serious about Mr. Toussard, and as far as a Majority in some Corps Armands, Pulaskis or such like, would wish you to interest yourself for him. The Marquis De Vienne, I am so far in earnest concerning, that if his pretensions are moderate and he can be gratified I should be glad of it, but I fear they will be pretty high.

ENLISTING SLAVES AS SOLDIERS

To John Jay

Dear Sir,

Col Laurens, who will have the honor of delivering you this letter, is on his way to South Carolina, on a project, which I think, in the present situation of affairs there, is a very good one and deserves every kind of support and encouragement. This is to raise two three or four batalions of negroes; with the assistance of the government of that state, by contributions from the owners in proportion to the number they possess. If you should think proper to enter upon the subject with him, he will give you a detail of his plan. He wishes to have it recommended by Congress to the state; and, as an inducement, that they would engage to take those batalions into Continental pay.

It appears to me, that an expedient of this kind, in the present state of Southern affairs, is the most rational, that can be adopted, and promises very important advantages. Indeed, I hardly see how a sufficient force can be collected in that quarter without it; and the enemy's operations there are growing infinitely serious and formidable. I have not the least doubt, that the negroes will make very excellent soldiers, with proper management; and I will venture to pronounce, that they cannot be put in better hands than those of Mr. Laurens. He has all the zeal, intelligence, enterprise, and every other qualification requisite to succeed in such an undertaking. It is a maxim with some great military judges, that with sensible officers soldiers can hardly be too stupid; and on this principle it is thought that the Russians would make the best troops in the world, if they were under other officers than their own. The King of Prussia is among the number who maintain this doctrine and has a very emphatical saying on the occasion, which I do not exactly recollect. I mention this, because I frequently hear it objected to the scheme of embodying negroes that they are too stupid to make soldiers. This is so far from appearing to me a valid objection that I think their want of cultivation (for their natural faculties are probably as good as ours) joined to that habit of subordination which they acquire from a life of servitude, will make them sooner became soldiers than our White inhabitants. Let officers be men of sense and sentiment, and the nearer the soldiers approach to machines perhaps the better.

I foresee that this project will have to combat much opposition from prejudice and self-interest. The contempt we have been taught to entertain for the blacks, makes us fancy many things that are founded neither in reason nor experience; and an unwillingness to part with property of so valuable a kind will furnish a thousand arguments to show the impracticability or pernicious tendency of a scheme which requires such a sacrifice. But it should be considered, that if we do not make use of them in this way, the enemy probably will; and that the best way to counteract the temptations they will hold out will be to offer them ourselves. An essential part of the plan is to give them their freedom with their muskets. This will secure their fidelity, animate their courage, and I believe will have a good influence upon those who remain, by opening a door to their emancipation. This circumstance, I confess, has no small weight in inducing me to wish the success of the project; for the dictates of humanity and true policy equally interest me in favour of this unfortunate class of men.

When I am on the subject of Southern affairs, you will excuse the liberty I take, in saying, that I do not think measures sufficiently vigorous are persuing for our defence in that quarter. Except the few regular troops of South Carolina, we seem to be relying wholly on the militia of that and the two neighbouring states. These will soon grow impatient of service and leave our affairs in a very miserable situation. No considerable force can be uniformly kept up by militia—to say nothing of many obvious and well known inconveniences, that attend this kind of troops. I would beg leave to suggest, Sir, that no time ought to be lost in making a draft of militia to serve a twelve month from the States of North and South Carolina and Virginia. But South Carolina being very weak in her population of whites may be excused from the draft on condition of furnishing the black batalions. The two others may furnish about 3,500 men and be exempted on that account from sending any succours to this army. The states to the Northward of Virginia will be fully able to give competent supplies to the army here; and it will require all the force and exertions of the three states I have mentioned to withstand the storm which has arisen and is increasing in the South.

The troops drafted must be thrown into batalions and officered in the best manner we can. The supernumerary officers may be made use of as far as they will go.

If arms are wanted for these troops and no better way of supplying them is to be found, we should endeavour to levy a contribution of arms upon the militia at large. Extraordinary exigencies demand extraordinary means. I fear this Southern business will become a very *grave* one.

With the truest respect & esteem   I am Sir   Your most Obed servant   Alex Hamilton

Want of time to copy it, will apologise for sending this letter in its present state.

Head Quarters   March 14th. 79

HOPE FOR A WIFE

To John Laurens

Cold in my professions, warm in my friendships, I wish, my Dear Laurens, it might be in my power, by action rather than words, to convince you that I love you. I shall only tell you that 'till you bade us Adieu, I hardly knew the value you had taught my heart to set upon you. Indeed, my friend, it was not well done. You know the opinion I entertain of mankind, and how much it is my desire to preserve myself free from particular attachments, and to keep my happiness independent on the caprice of others. You should not have taken advantage of my sensibility to steal into my affections without my consent. But as you have done it and as we are generally indulgent to those we love, I shall not scruple to pardon the fraud you have committed, on condition that for my sake, if not for your own, you will always continue to merit the partiality, which you have so artfully instilled into me.

I have received your two letters one from Philadelphia the other from Chester. I am pleased with your success, so far, and I hope the favourable omens, that precede your application to the Assembly may have as favourable an issue, provided the situation of affairs should require it which I fear will be the case. But both for your country's sake and for my own I wish the enemy may be gone from Georgia before you arrive and that you may be obliged to return and share the fortunes of your old friends. In respect to the Commission, which you received from Congress, all the world must think your conduct perfectly right. Indeed your ideas upon this occasion seem not to have their wonted accuracy; and you have had scruples, in a great measure, without foundation. By your appointment as Aide De Camp to the Commander in Chief, you had as much the rank of Lieutenant Colonel, as any officer in the line—your receiving a commission as Lieutenant Colonel from the date of that appointment, does not in the least injure or interfere with one of them; unless by virtue of it you are introduced into a particular regiment in violation of the right of succession; which is not the case at present neither is it a necessary consequence. As you were going to command a batalion, it was proper you should have a commission; and if this commission had been dated posterior to your appointment as Aide De Camp, I should have considered it as derogatory to your former rank, to mine, and to that of the whole corps. The only thing I see wrong in the affair is this—Congress by their conduct, both on the former and present occasion, appear to have intended to confer a privilege, an honor, a mark of distinction, a something upon you; which they withold from other Gentlemen in the family. This carries with it an air of preference, which, though we can all truly say, we love your character, and admire your military merit, cannot fail to give some of us uneasy sensations. But in this, my Dear J I wish you to understand me well. The blame, if there is any, falls wholly upon Congress. I repeat it, your conduct has been perfectly right and even laudable; you rejected the offer when you ought to have rejected it; and you accepted it when you ought to have accepted it; and let me add with a degree of overscrupulous delicacy. It was necessary to your project; your project was the public good; and *I* should have done the same. In hesitating, you have refined upon the refinements of generosity.

There is a total stagnation of news here, political and military. Gates has refused the Indian command. Sullivan is come to take it. The former has lately given a fresh proof of his impudence, his folly and his rascality. *'Tis no great matter;* but a peculiarity in the case prevents my saying *what.*

I anticipate by sympathy the pleasure you must feel from the sweet converse of your dearer self in the inclosed letters. I hope they may be recent. They were brought out of New York by General Thompson delivered to him there by a Mrs. Moore not long from England, *soi-disante parente de Madame votre épouse.* She speaks of a daughter of yours, well when she left England, perhaps [   ].

And Now my Dear as we are upon the subject of wife, I empower and command you to get me one in Carolina. Such a wife as I want will, I know, be difficult to be found, but if you succeed, it will be the stronger proof of your zeal and dexterity. Take her description— She must be young, handsome (I lay most stress upon a good shape) sensible (a little learning will do), well bred (but she must have an aversion to the word *ton*) chaste and tender (I am an enthusiast in my notions of fidelity and fondness) of some good nature, a great deal of generosity (she must neither love money nor scolding, for I dislike equally a termagent and an œconomist). In politics, I am indifferent what side she may be of; I think I have arguments that will easily convert her to mine. As to religion a moderate stock will satisfy me. She must believe in god and hate a saint. But as to fortune, the larger stock of that the better. You know my temper and circumstances and will therefore pay special attention to this article in the treaty. Though I run no risk of going to Purgatory for my avarice; yet as money is an essential ingredient to happiness in this world— as I have not much of my own and as I am very little calculated to get more either by my address or industry; it must needs be, that my wife, if I get one, bring at least a sufficiency to administer to her own extravagancies. NB You will be pleased to recollect in your negotiations that I have no invincible antipathy to the *maidenly beauties* & that I am willing to take the *trouble* of them upon myself.

If you should not readily meet with a lady that you think answers my description you can only advertise in the public papers and doubtless you will hear of many competitors for most of the qualifications required, who will be glad to become candidates for such a prize as I am. To excite their emulation, it will be necessary for you to give an account of the lover—his *size*, make, quality of mind and *body*, achievements, expectations, fortune, &c. In drawing my picture, you will no doubt be civil to your friend; mind you do justice to the length of my nose and don't forget, that I [   ].

After reviewing what I have written, I am ready to ask myself what could have put it into my head to hazard this Jeu *de follie*. Do I want a wife? No—I have plagues enough without desiring to add to the number that *greatest of all*; and if I were silly enough to do it, I should take care how I employ a proxy. Did I mean to show my wit? If I did, I am sure I have missed my aim. Did I only intend to frisk? In this I have succeeded, but I have done more. I have gratified my feelings, by lengthening out the only kind of intercourse now in my power with my friend. Adieu

Yours.   A Hamilton

P.S—Fleury shall be taken care of. All the family send their love. In this join the General & Mrs. Washington & what is best, tis not in the stile of ceremony but sincerity.

c. April 1779

AN INSULT TO HONOR

To William Gordon

Sir

I have received your letter of the 25th of August, which you will probably not be surprised to hear, is by no means satisfactory. Instead of giving up the author of the accusation, you charitably suppose me guilty & amuse yourself in a strain of conjecture (which whatever *ingenuity* it may have, was certainly unnecessary) about the manner in which the affair happen'd, & the motives that produced it. Your entering a volunteer to apologise for me is, no doubt, a mark of your condescension & of your benevolence, & would make it ungrateful, as well as indecent, to suspect, that the conditions, with which you fetter a compliance with my request, proceed from any other cause than a laudable, though, perhaps, in this instance, an officious zeal for the interests of religion & for the good of society. It shall never be said, that you had a recourse to a pitiful evasion, & attempted to cover the dishonor of a refusal under a specious pretence of terms, which you knew, as a gentleman, I should be obliged to reject. I venture however, with every allowance for the sanctity of your intentions, & with all possible deference for your judgment, to express my doubts of the propriety of the concessions, you require, on my part, as preliminaries to a discovery, which I still think you are bound to make, as an act of justice—This is a principle from which I can never depart; & I am convinced, I shall have the common sense & feelings of mankind on my side. An opinion of my *inexperience* seems to have betrayed you into mistakes: Whatever you may imagine, Sir, I have read the *world* sufficiently to know that, though it may often be *convenient* to the propagator of a calumny to conceal the inventor, he will stand in need of no small address, to escape the suspicions & even the indignation of the honest & of the disinterested. Nor can I but persist in believing, that, notwithstanding the confidence, which, from a very natural partiality, you place in your own character, the delicacy of your sentiments will be alarmed at the possibility of incurring this danger, & will prevent your exposing yourself to it, by refusing or delaying any longer, to comply with so reasonable a demand.

It often happens, that our zeal is at variance with our understanding. Had it not been for this, you might have recollected, that we do not now live in the days of chivalry; & you would have judged your precautions, on the subject of duelling, at least, useless. The good sense of the present times has happily found out, that to prove your own innocence, or the malice of an accuser, the worst method, you can take, is to run him through the body, or shoot him through the head. And permit me to add, that while you felt an aversion to du-elling, on the principles of religion, you ought, in charity, to have supposed others possessed of the same scruples,—of whose impiety you had no proofs. But whatever may be my final determination, on this point, ought to be a matter of in-difference. 'Tis a good old maxim, to which we may safely ad-here in most cases, that we ought to do our duty, & leave the rest to the care of heaven. The crime alleged to me is of such enormity, that, if I am guilty, it ought not to go unpunished; &, if I am innocent I should have an opportunity of indicat-ing my innocence. The truth in either case should appear; & it is incumbent upon you, Sir, to afford the means, either by accusing me to my civil, or military superiors, or by disclosing the author of the information.

Your anxiety to engage me "to admit of the matter's being thoroughly examined into by Congress, or individuals of the first character" was equally superfluous. I am, at all times, amenable to the authority of the state & of the laws, & when-ever it should be the pleasure of Congress, the means of bringing me to justice, for any crime, I may have committed, are obvious & easy, without the assistance of informal stipulation on my side. I shall not expose myself to the ridicule of self-importance by applying to Congress for an inquiry; nor shall I invite the charge of impertinence, by promising to do what I have no power to refuse. I shall only declare, for my own satisfaction, that so far as concerns myself, nothing would give me greater pleasure than to undergo the strictest scrutiny, in any legal mode, into the rectitude of my conduct on this & on every other occasion, as a soldier or as a citizen. With respect to an examination by individuals of character, whenever I have it in my power to confront my accuser, I shall take care to do it in presence of witnesses of the first respectability, who will be able, from what they see & hear, to tell the world, that I am innocent & injured, & that he is a contemptable defamer. It is no doubt unfortunate for me, that you have prejudged the case & are of a different opinion. You profess to give credit to the story, because you say, "your informer is a man of veracity

& *could not be mistaken*." From this description, he is probably not a soldier, or you would have been more inclined to
suppose him *fallible*. But whoever he may be, you have certainly shown a facility in believing, that does honor to your
credulity at the expence of your candour. I protest, Sir, this is
the first time I have heard my own veracity called in question.
Had you not given a sanction to the contrary by your example, I should have indulgently flattered myself that I had as
much right to be believed as another, & that my denial was
a counterballance to the assertion of your informant, & left
the affair in suspence to be decided by the future circumstances. You persue a different line, & in the overflowings of
your pious hatred to political heresy, have determined, that I
must be guilty at all events. You ascribe the denial to a defect
of memory, & pretend to think it more likely, that I should
have lost all recollection of the fact, than that you should
have been misinformed. Far from accepting, I absolutely reject the apology, you make for me, & continue to believe it
impossible, I could have made a declaration similar to the one
reported: For I abhor the sentiment it contains, & am confident, it never could have had a momentary place in my mind,
consequently could never have dishonoured my lips. The supposition is absurd, that I could have used the expressions,
when I cannot recognise the remotest trace of an idea, at any
period, that could possibly have led to them. In this consciousness, I again appeal to you, & demand, by all the ties
of truth, justice & honor, that you immediately give up your
author. I stake my life & reputation upon the issue, & defy
all the craft of malevolence, or of cabal to support the charge.
If you decline a discovery, I shall then not have it in my
choice to make any other, than *one conclusion*.

You have blended several matters foreign to the purpose,
which might as well have been omitted. I shall only answer in
general, that I religiously believe, the officers of the army are
among the best citizens in America, & inviolably attached to
the liberties of the community,—infinitely more so, than any
of those splenetic patriots out of it, who endeavour, for sinister
purposes to instil jealousies & alarms, which they themselves,
know to be as groundless, as they are impolitic & ridiculous.

But if any individuals have been imprudent, or unprincipled, let them answer for themselves. I am responsible, only for my own conduct. Your fears for the injury, which the indiscretions of such persons might do to the General, were kind, but I hope unnecessary. The decided confidence of Congress & the hearts of the people of America are the witnesses to his integrity. The blame of the unmeaning petulance of a few impatient spirits will never rest upon him; for whoever knows his character will be satisfied, that an officer would be ashamed to utter in his hearing, any sentiments, that would disgrace a citizen.

I am Sir   Your most obedient servant   Alex Hamilton

West Point   Sept 5. 1779

"I AM NOT FIT FOR THIS TERRESTREAL COUNTRY"

To John Laurens

Jany 8t.
I had written the enclosed and was called off. Some ruffian hand has treated it in the manner you see. I have no time to copy it. I shall take up the story where I left it.

Another reason for believing the destination is your way, is that Governor Martin and divers others refugees of Georgia South and North Carolina are said to have gone in the fleet. You will have a busy time; acquit yourselves well. We hope however that some late violent winds will drown them all on their way. There is no other military news.

Believe me my Dr Laurens I am not insensible of the first mark of your affection in recommending me to your friends for a certain commission. However your partiality may have led you to overrate my qualifications that very partiality must endear you to me; and all the world will allow that your struggles and scruples upon the occasion deserve the envy of men of vertue. I am happy you placed the matter upon the footing you did, because I hope it will ultimately engage you to accept the appointment. Had it fallen to my lot, I should have been flattered by such a distinction but I should have felt all your embarrassments.

Of this however I need have no apprehension. Not one of the four in nomination but would stand a better chance than myself; and yet my vanity tells me they do not all merit a preference. But I am a stranger in this country. I have no property here, no connexions. If I have talents and integrity, (as you say I have) these are justly deemed very spurious titles in these enlightened days, when unsupported by others more solid; and were it not for your example, I should be inclined in considering the composition of a certain body, to suppose that three fourths of them are mortal enemies to the first and three fourths of the other fourth have a laudable contempt for the last.

Adieu God preserve and prosper you   A Hamilton

I have strongly sollicited leave to go to the Southward. It could not be refused; but arguments have been used to dissuade me from it, which however little weight they may have had in my judgment gave law to my feelings. I am chagrined and unhappy but I submit. In short Laurens I am disgusted with every thing in this world but yourself and *very* few more honest fellows and I have no other wish than as soon as possible to make a brilliant exit. 'Tis a weakness; but I feel I am not fit for this terrestreal Country.

All the Lads embrace you. The General sends his love. Write to him as often as you can.

January 8, 1780

"EXAMINE WELL YOUR HEART"

To Elizabeth Schuyler

Impatiently My Dearest have I been expecting the return of your father to bring me a letter from my charmer with the answers you have been good enough to promise me to the little questions asked in mine by him. I long to see the workings of my Betseys heart, and I promise my self I shall have ample gratification to my fondness in the sweet familiarity of her pen. She will there I hope paint me her feelings without re-serve—even in those tender moments of pillowed retirement, when her soul abstracted from every other object, delivers it-self up to Love and to me—yet with all that delicacy which suits the purity of her mind and which is so conspicuous in whatever she does.

It is now a week my Betsey since I have heard from you. In that time I have written you twice. I think it will be adviseable in future to number our letters, for I have reason to suspect they do not all meet with fair play. This is number one.

Meade just comes in and interrupts me by sending his love to you. He tells you he has written a long letter to his widow asking her opinion of the propriety of quitting the service; and that if she does not disapprove it, he will certainly take his final leave after the campaign. You see what a fine opportunity she has to be enrolled in the catalogue of heroines, and I dare say she will set you an example of fortitude and patriotism. I know too you have so much of the Portia in you, that you will not be out done in this line by any of your sex, and that if you saw me inclined to quit the service of your country, you would dissuade me from it. I have promised you, you recol-lect, to conform to your wishes, and I persist in this intention. It remains with you to show whether you are a *Roman* or an *American wife.*

Though I am not sanguine in expecting it, I am not with-out hopes this Winter will produce a peace and then you must submit to the mortification of enjoying more domestic happi-ness and less fame. This I know you will not like, but we can-not always have things as we wish.

The affairs of England are in so bad a plight that if no for-tunate events attend her this campaign, it would seem im-possible for her to proceed in the war. But she is an obstinate old dame, and seems determined to ruin her whole family, rather than to let Miss America go on flirting it with her new lovers, with whom, as giddy young girls often do, she eloped in contempt of her mothers authority. I know you will be ready to justify her conduct and to tell me the ill treatment she received was enough to make any girl of spirit act in the same manner. But I will one day cure you of these refractory notions about the right of resistance, (of which I foresee you will be apt to make a very dangerous application), and teach you the great advantage and absolute necessity of implicit obedience.

But now we are talking of times to come, tell me my pretty damsel have you made up your mind upon the subject of housekeeping? Do you soberly relish the pleasure of being a poor mans wife? Have you learned to think a home spun preferable to a brocade and the rumbling of a waggon wheel to the musical rattling of a coach and six? Will you be able to see with perfect composure your old acquaintances flaunting it in gay life, tripping it along in elegance and splendor, while you hold an humble station and have no other enjoyments than the sober comforts of a good wife? Can you in short be an Aquileia and chearfully plant turnips with me, if fortune should so order it? If you cannot my Dear we are playing a comedy of all in the wrong, and you should correct the mistake before we begin to act the tragedy of the unhappy couple.

I propose you a set of new questions my lovely girl; but though they are asked with an air of levity, they merit a very serious consideration, for on their being resolved in the affirmative stripped of all the colorings of a fond imagination our happiness may absolutely depend. I have not concealed my circumstances from my Betsey; they are far from splendid; they may possibly even be worse than I expect, for every day brings me fresh proof of the knavery of those to whom my little affairs are entrusted. They have already filed down what was in their hands more than one half, and I am told they go on diminishing it, 'till I *fear* they will reduce it below my *former fears*. An indifference to property enters into my character too much, and what affects me now as my Betsey is concerned in it, I should have laughed at or not thought of at all a year ago. But I have thoroughly examined my own heart. Beloved by you, I can be happy in any situation, and can struggle with every embarrassment of fortune with patience and firmness. I cannot however forbear entreating you to realize our union on the dark side and satisfy, without deceiving yourself, how far your affection for me can make you happy in a privation of those elegancies to which you have been accustomed. If fortune should smile upon us, it will do us no harm to have been prepared for adversity; if she frowns upon us, by being prepared, we shall encounter it without the chagrin of disappointment. Your future rank in life is a perfect lottery; you may move in an exalted you may move in a very humble sphere; the last is most probable; examine well your heart. And in doing it, don't figure to yourself a cottage in romance, with the spontaneous bounties of nature courting you to enjoyment. Don't imagine yourself a shepherdess, your hair embroidered with flowers a crook in your hand tending your flock under a shady tree, by the side of a cool fountain, your faithful shepherd sitting near and entertaining you with gentle tales of love. These are pretty dreams and very apt to enter into the heads of lovers when they think of a connection without the advantages of fortune. But they must not be indulged. You must apply your situation to real life, and think how you should feel in scenes of which you may find examples every day. So far My Dear Betsey as the tenderest affection can compensate for other inconveniences in making your estimate, you cannot give too large a credit for this article. My heart overflows with every thing for you, that admiration, esteem and love can inspire. *I would this moment give the world to be near you only to kiss your sweet hand.* Believe what I say to be truth and imagine what are my feelings when I say it. Let it awake your sympathy and let our hearts melt in a prayer to be soon united, never more to be separated.

Adieu loveliest of your sex AH

Instead of inclosing your letter to your father I inclose his to you because I do not know whether he may not be on his way here. If he is at home he will tell you the military news. If he has set out for camp, you may open and read my letters to him. The one from Mr. Mathews you will return by the first opportunity.

August 1780

To James Duane

Dr. Sir

Agreeably to your request and my promise I sit down to give you my ideas of the defects of our present system, and the changes necessary to save us from ruin. They may perhaps be the reveries of a projector rather than the sober views of a politician. You will judge of them, and make what use you please of them.

The fundamental defect is a want of power in Congress. It is hardly worth while to show in what this consists, as it seems to be universally acknowleged, or to point out how it has happened, as the only question is how to remedy it. It may however be said that it has originated from three causes—an excess of the spirit of liberty which has made the particular states show a jealousy of all power not in their own hands; and this jealousy has led them to exercise a right of judging in the last resort of the measures recommended by Congress, and of acting according to their own opinions of their propriety or necessity, a diffidence in Congress of their own powers, by which they have been timid and indecisive in their resolutions, constantly making concessions to the states, till they have scarcely left themselves the shadow of power; a want of sufficient means at their disposal to answer the public exigencies and of vigor to draw forth those means; which have occasioned them to depend on the states individually to fulfil their engagements with the army, and the consequence of which has been to ruin their influence and credit with the army, to establish its dependence on each state separately rather than *on them*, that is rather than on the whole collectively.

It may be pleaded, that Congress had never any definitive powers granted them and of course could exercise none—could do nothing more than recommend. The manner in which Congress was appointed would warrant, and the public good required, that they should have considered themselves as vested with full power *to preserve the republic from harm.*

They have done many of the highest acts of sovereignty, which were always chearfully submitted to—the declaration of independence, the declaration of war, the levying an army, creating a navy, emitting money, making alliances with foreign powers, appointing a dictator &c. &c.—all these implications of a complete sovereignty were never disputed, and ought to have been a standard for the whole conduct of Administration. Undefined powers are discretionary powers, limited only by the object for which they were given—in the present case, the independence and freedom of America. The confederation made no difference; for as it has not been generally adopted, it had no operation. But from what I recollect of it, Congress have even descended from the authority which the spirit of that act gives them, while the particular states have no further attended to it than as it suited their pretensions and convenience. It would take too much time to enter into particular instances, each of which separately might appear inconsiderable; but united are of serious import. I only mean to remark, not to censure.

But the confederation itself is defective and requires to be altered; it is neither fit for war, nor peace. The idea of an uncontrolable sovereignty in each state, over its internal police, will defeat the other powers given to Congress, and make our union feeble and precarious. There are instances without number, where acts necessary for the general good, and which rise out of the powers given to Congress must interfere with the internal police of the states, and there are as many instances in which the particular states by arrangements of internal police can effectually though indirectly counteract the arrangements of Congress. You have already had examples of this for which I refer you to your own memory.

The confederation gives the states individually too much influence in the affairs of the army; they should have nothing to do with it. The entire formation and disposal of our military forces ought to belong to Congress. It is an essential cement of the union; and it ought to be the policy of Congress to destroy all ideas of state attachments in the army and make it look up wholly to them. For this purpose all appointments promotions and provisions whatsoever ought to be made by them. It may be apprehended that this may be dangerous to liberty. But nothing appears more evident to me, than that we run much greater risk of having a weak and disunited federal government, than one which will be able to usurp upon the rights of the people. Already some of the lines of the army would obey their states in opposition to Congress notwithstanding the pains we have taken to preserve the unity of the army—if any thing would hinder this it would be the personal influence of the General, a melancholy and mortifying consideration.

The forms of our state constitutions must always give them great weight in our affairs and will make it too difficult to bend them to the persuit of a common interest, too easy to oppose whatever they do not like and to form partial combinations subversive of the general one. There is a wide difference between our situation and that of an empire under one simple form of government, distributed into counties provinces or districts, which have no legislatures but merely magistratical bodies to execute the laws of a common sovereign. Here the danger is that the sovereign will have too much power to oppress the parts of which it is composed. In our case, that of an empire composed of confederated states each with a government completely organised within itself, having all the means to draw its subjects to a close dependence on itself—the danger is directly the reverse. It is that the common sovereign will not have power sufficient to unite the different members together, and direct the common forces to the interest and happiness of the whole.

The leagues among the old Grecian republics are a proof of this. They were continually at war with each other, and for want of union fell a prey to their neighbours. They frequently held general councils, but their resolutions were no further observed than as they suited the interests and inclinations of all the parties and at length, they sunk intirely into contempt.

The Swiss-cantons are another proof of the doctrine. They have had wars with each other which would have been fatal to them, had not the different powers in their neighbourhood been too jealous of one-another and too equally matched to suffer either to take advantage of their quarrels. That they have remained so long united at all is to be attributed to their weakness, to their poverty, and to the cause just mentioned.

These ties will not exist in America; a little time hence, some of the states will be powerful empires, and we are so remote from other nations that we shall have all the leisure and opportunity we can wish to cut each others throats.

The Germanic corps might also be cited as an example in favour of the position.

The United provinces may be thought to be one against it. But the family of the stadtholders whose authority is interwoven with the whole government has been a strong link of union between them. Their physical necessities and the habits founded upon them have contributed to it. Each province is too inconsiderable by itself to undertake any thing. An analysis of their present constitutions would show that they have many ties which would not exist in ours; and that they are by no means a proper mode for us.

Our own experience should satisfy us. We have felt the difficulty of drawing out the resources of the country and inducing the states to combine in equal exertions for the common cause. The ill success of our last attempt is striking. Some have done a great deal, others little or scarcely any thing. The disputes about boundaries &c. testify how flattering a prospect we have of future tranquillity, if we do not frame in time a confederacy capable of deciding the differences and compelling the obedience of the respective members.

The confederation too gives the power of the purse too intirely to the state legislatures. It should provide perpetual funds in the disposal of Congress—by a land tax, poll tax, or the like. All imposts upon commerce ought to be laid by Congress and appropriated to their use, for without certain revenues, a government can have no power; that power, which holds the purse strings absolutely, must rule. This seems to be a medium, which without making Congress altogether independent will tend to give reality to its authority.

Another defect in our system is want of method and energy in the administration. This has partly resulted from the other defect, but in a great degree from prejudice and the want of a proper executive. Congress have kept the power too much into their own hands and have meddled too much with details of every sort. Congress is properly a deliberative corps and it forgets itself when it attempts to play the executive. It is impossible such a body, numerous as it is, constantly fluctuating, can ever act with sufficient decision, or with system. Two thirds of the members, one half the time, cannot know what has gone before them or what connection the subject in hand has to what has been transacted on former occasions. The members, who have been more permanent, will only give information, that promotes the side they espouse, in the present case, and will as often mislead as enlighten. The variety of business must distract, and the proneness of every assembly to debate must at all times delay.

Lately Congress, convinced of these inconveniences, have gone into the measure of appointing boards. But this is in my opinion a bad plan. A single man, in each department of the administration, would be greatly preferable. It would give us a chance of more knowlege, more activity, more responsibility and of course more zeal and attention. Boards partake of a part of the inconveniencies of larger assemblies. Their decisions are slower their energy less their responsibility more diffused. They will not have the same abilities and knowlege as an administration by single men. Men of the first pretensions will not so readily engage in them, because they will be less conspicuous, of less importance, have less opportunity of distinguishing themselves. The members of boards will take less pains to inform themselves and arrive to eminence, because they have fewer motives to do it. All these reasons conspire to give a preference to the plan of vesting the great executive departments of the state in the hands of individuals. As these men will be of course at all times under the direction of Congress, we shall blend the advantages of a monarchy and republic in our constitution.

A question has been made, whether single men could be found to undertake these offices. I think they could, because there would be then every thing to excite the ambition of candidates. But in order to this Congress by their manner of appointing them and the line of duty marked out must show that they are in earnest in making these offices, offices of real trust and importance.

I fear a little vanity has stood in the way of these arrangements, as though they would lessen the importance of Con-

gress and leave them nothing to do. But they would have precisely the same rights and powers as heretofore, happily dis-
encumbered of the detail. They would have to inspect the
conduct of their ministers, deliberate upon their plans, originate others for the public good—only observing this rule that
they ought to consult their ministers, and get all the information and advice they could from them, before they entered
into any new measures or made changes in the old.

A third defect is the fluctuating constitution of our army.
This has been a pregnant source of evil; all our military misfortunes, three fourths of our civil embarrassments are to be
ascribed to it. The General has so fully enumerated the mischief of it in a late letter of the   to Congress that I
could only repeat what he has said, and will therefore refer
you to that letter.

The imperfect and unequal provision made for the army is
a fourth defect which you will find delineated in the same letter. Without a speedy change the army must dissolve; it is
now a mob, rather than an army, without cloathing, without
pay, without provision, without morals, without discipline.
We begin to hate the country for its neglect of us; the country begins to hate us for our oppressions of them. Congress
have long been jealous of us; we have now lost all confidence in them, and give the worst construction to all they
do. Held together by the slenderest ties we are ripening for a
dissolution.

The present mode of supplying the army—by state purchases—is not one of the least considerable defects of our system. It is too precarious a dependence, because the states will
never be sufficiently impressed with our necessities. Each will
make its own ease a primary object, the supply of the army a
secondary one. The variety of channels through which the
business is transacted will multiply the number of persons employed and the opportunities of embezzling public money.
From the popular spirit on which most of the governments
turn, the state agents, will be men of less character and ability, nor will there be so rigid a responsibility among them as
there might easily be among those in the employ of the continent, of course not so much diligence care or economy. Very
little of the money raised in the several states will go into the

Continental treasury, on pretence, that it is all exhausted in providing the quotas of supplies, and the public will be without funds for the other demands of governments. The expence will be ultimately much greater and the advantages much smaller. We actually feel the insufficiency of this plan and have reason to dread under it a ruinous extremity of want.

These are the principal defects in the present system that now occur to me. There are many inferior ones in the organization of particular departments and many errors of administration which might be pointed out; but the task would be troublesome and tedious, and if we had once remedied those I have mentioned the others would not be attended with much difficulty.

I shall now propose the remedies, which appear to me applicable to our circumstances, and necessary to extricate our affairs from their present deplorable situation.

The first step must be to give Congress powers competent to the public exigencies. This may happen in two ways, one by resuming and exercising the discretionary powers I suppose to have been originally vested in them for the safety of the states and resting their conduct on the candor of their country men and the necessity of the conjuncture: the other by calling immediately a convention of all the states with full authority to conclude finally upon a general confederation, stating to them beforehand explicit the evils arising from a want of power in Congress, and the impossibility of supporting the contest on its present footing, that the delegates may come possessed of proper sentiments as well as proper authority to give to the meeting. Their commission should include a right of vesting Congress with the whole or a proportion of the unoccupied lands, to be employed for the purpose of raising a revenue, reserving the jurisdiction to the states by whom they are granted.

The first plan, I expect will be thought too bold an expedient by the generality of Congress; and indeed their practice hitherto has so rivetted the opinion of their want of power, that the success of this experiment may very well be doubted.

I see no objection to the other mode, that has any weight in competition with the reasons for it. The Convention should assemble the 1st of November next, the sooner, the better; our disorders are too violent to admit of a common or lingering remedy. The reasons for which I require them to be vested with plenipotentiary authority are that the business may suffer no delay in the execution, and may in reality come to effect. A convention may agree upon a confederation; the states individually hardly ever will. We must have one at all events, and a vigorous one if we mean to succeed in the contest and be happy hereafter. As I said before, to engage the states to comply with this mode, Congress ought to confess to them plainly and unanimously the impracticability of supporting our affairs on the present footing and without a solid coercive union. I ask that the Convention should have a power of vesting the whole or a part of the unoccupied land in Congress, because it is necessary that body should have some property as a fund for the arrangements of finance; and I know of no other kind that can be given them.

The confederation in my opinion should give Congress complete sovereignty; except as to that part of internal police, which relates to the rights of property and life among individuals and to raising money by internal taxes. It is necessary, that every thing, belonging to this, should be regulated by the state legislatures. Congress should have complete sovereignty in all that relates to war, peace, trade, finance, and to the management of foreign affairs, the right of declaring war of raising armies, officering, paying them, directing their motions in every respect, of equipping fleets and doing the same with them, of building fortifications arsenals magazines &c. &c., of making peace on such conditions as they think proper, of regulating trade, determining with what countries it shall be carried on, granting indulgencies laying prohibitions on all the articles of export or import, imposing duties granting bounties & premiums for raising exporting importing and applying to their own use the product of these duties, only giving credit to the states on whom they are raised in the general account of revenues and expences, instituting Admiralty courts &c., of coining money, establishing banks on such terms, and with such privileges as they think proper, appropriating funds and doing whatever else relates to the operations of finance, transacting every thing with foreign nations, making alliances offensive and defensive, treaties of commerce, &c. &c.

The confederation should provide certain perpetual revenues, productive and easy of collection, a land tax, poll tax or the like, which together with the duties on trade and the unlocated lands would give Congress a substantial existence, and a stable foundation for their schemes of finance. What more supplies were necessary should be occasionally demanded of the states, in the present mode of quotas.

The second step I would recommend is that Congress should instantly appoint the following great officers of state—A secretary for foreign affairs—a President of war—A President of Marine—A Financier—A President of trade; instead of this last a board of Trade may be preferable as the regulations of trade are slow and gradual and require prudence and experience (more than other qualities), for which boards are very well adapted.

Congress should choose for these offices, men of the first abilities, property and character in the continent—and such as have had the best opportunities of being acquainted with the several branches. General Schuyler (whom you mentioned) would make an excellent President of War, General McDougall a very good President of Marine. Mr. Robert Morris would have many things in his favour for the department of finance. He could by his own personal influence give great weight to the measures he should adopt. I dare say men equally capable may be found for the other departments.

I know not, if it would not be a good plan to let the Financier be President of the Board of trade; but he should only have a casting voice in determining questions there. There is a connection between trade and finance, which ought to make the director of one acquainted with the other; but the Financier should not direct the affairs of trade, because for the sake of acquiring reputation by increasing the revenues, he might adopt measures that would depress trade. In what relates to finance he should be alone.

These offices should have nearly the same powers and functions as those in France analogous to them, and each should be chief in his department, with subordinate boards composed of assistant clerks &c. to execute his orders.

In my opinion a plan of this kind would be of inconceivable utility to our affairs; its benefits would be very speedily felt. It would give new life and energy to the operations of government. Business would be conducted with dispatch method and system. A million of abuses now existing would be corrected, and judicious plans would be formed and executed for the public good.

Another step of immediate necessity is to recruit the army for the war, or at least for three years. This must be done by a mode similar to that which is practiced in Sweeden. There the inhabitants are thrown into classes of sixteen, and when the sovereign wants men each of these classes must furnish one. They raise a fixed sum of money, and if one of the class is willing to become a soldier, he receives the money and offers himself a volunteer; if none is found to do this, a draft is made and he on whom the lot falls receives the money and is obliged to serve. The minds of the people are prepared for a thing of this kind; the heavy bounties they have been obliged to pay for men to serve a few months must have disgusted them with this mode, and made them desirous of another, that will once for all answer the public purposes, and obviate a repetition of the demand. It ought by all means to be attempted, and Congress should frame a general plan and press the execution upon the states. When the confederation comes to be framed, it ought to provide for this by a fundamental law, and hereafter there would be no doubt of the success. But we cannot now wait for this; we want to replace the men whose times of service will expire the 1st of January, for then, without this, we shall have no army remaining and the enemy may do what they please. The General in his letter already quoted has assigned the most substantial reasons for paying immediate attention to this point.

Congress should endeavour, both upon their credit in Europe, and by every possible exertion in this country, to provide cloathing for their officers, and should abolish the whole system of state supplies. The making good the depreciation of the currency and all other compensations to the army should be immediately taken up by Congress, and not left to the states; if they would have the accounts of depreciation liquidated, and governmental certificates given for what is due in specie or an equivalent to specie, it would give satisfaction; appointing periodical settlements for future depreciation.

The placing the officers upon half pay during life would be a great stroke of policy, and would give Congress a stronger tie upon them, than any thing else they can do. No man, that reflects a moment, but will prefer a permanent provision of this kind to any temporary compensation, nor is it opposed to economy; the difference between this and between what has been already done will be insignificant. The benefit of it to the widows should be confined to those whose husbands die during the war. As to the survivors, not more than one half on the usual calculation of mens lives will exceed the seven years for which the half pay is already established. Besides this whatever may be the visionary speculations of some men at this time, we shall find it indispensable after the war to keep on foot a considerable body of troops; and all the officers retained for this purpose must be deducted out of the half pay list. If any one will take the pains to calculate the expence on these principles, I am persuaded he will find the addition of expence from the establishment proposed, by no means a national object.

The advantages of securing the attachment of the army to Congress, and binding them to the service by substantial ties are immense. We should then have discipline, an army in reality, as well as in name. Congress would then have a solid basis of authority and consequence, for to me it is an axiom that in our constitution an army is essential to the American union.

The providing of supplies is the pivot of every thing else (though a well constituted army would not in a small degree conduce to this, by giving consistency and weight to government). There are four ways all which must be united—a foreign loan, heavy pecuniary taxes, a tax in kind, a bank founded on public and private credit.

As to a foreign loan I dare say, Congress are doing every thing in their power to obtain it. The most effectual way will be to tell France that without it, we must make terms with great Britain. This must be done with plainness and firmness, but with respect and without petulance, not as a menace, but as a candid declaration of our circumstances. We need not fear to be deserted by France. Her interest and honor are too deeply involved in our fate; and she can make no possible compromise. She can assist us, if she is convinced it is absolutely necessary, either by lending us herself or by becoming our surety or by influencing Spain. It has been to me astonishing how any man could have doubted at any period of our affairs of the necessity of a foreign loan. It was self evident, that we had not a fund of wealth in this country, capable of affording revenues equal to the expences. We must then create artificial revenues, or borrow; the first was done, but it ought to have been foreseen, that the expedient could not last; and we should have provided in time for its failure.

Here was an error of Congress. I have good reason to believe, that measures were not taken in earnest early enough, to procure a loan abroad. I give you my honor that from our first outset, I thought as I do now and wished for a foreign loan not only because I foresaw it would be essential but because I considered it as a tie upon the nation from which it was derived and as a mean to prop our cause in Europe.

Concerning the necessity of heavy pecuniary taxes I need say nothing, as it is a point in which everybody is agreed; nor is there any danger, that the product of any taxes raised in this way will over burthen the people, or exceed the wants of the public. Indeed if all the paper in circulation were drawn annually into the treasury, it would neither do one, nor the other.

As to a tax in kind, the necessity of it results from this principle—that the money in circulation is not a sufficient representative of the productions of the country, and consequently no revenues raised from it as a medium can be a competent representative of that part of the products of the country, which it is bound to contribute to the support of the public. The public therefore to obtain its due or satisfy its just demands and its wants must call for a part of those products themselves. This is done in all those countries which are not commercial, in Russia, Prussia, Denmark Sweden &c. and is peculiarly necessary in our case.

Congress in calling for specific supplies seem to have had this in view; but their intention has not been answered. The states in general have undertaken to furnish the supplies by purchase, a mode as I have observed, attended with every inconvenience and subverting the principle on which the supplies were demanded—the insufficiency of our circulating medium as a representative for the labour and commodities of the Country. It is therefore necessary that Congress should be more explicit, should form the outlines of a plan for a tax in kind, and recommend it to the states, as a measure of absolute necessity.

The general idea I have of a plan, is that a respectable man should be appointed by the state in each county to collect the taxes and form magazines, that Congress should have in each state an officer to superintend the whole and that the state collectors should be subordinate and responsible to them. This Continental superintendent might be subject to the general direction of the Quarter Master General, or not, as might be deemed best; but if not subject to him, he should be obliged to make monthly returns to the President at War, who should instruct him what proportion to deliver to the Quarter Master General. It may be necessary that the superintendents should sometimes have power to dispose of the articles in their possession on public account; for it would happen that the contributions in places remote from the army could not be transported to the theatre of operations without too great expence, in which case it would be eligible to dispose of them and purchase with the money so raised in the countries near the immediate scene of war.

I know the objections which may be raised to this plan—its tendency to discourage industry and the like; but necessity calls for it; we cannot proceed without, and less evils must give place to greater. It is besides practiced with success in other countries, and why not in this? It may be said, the examples cited are from nations under despotic governments and that the same would not be practicable with us; but I contend where the public good is evidently the object more may be effected in governments like ours than in any other. It has been a constant remark that free countries have ever paid the heaviest taxes. The obedience of a free people to general laws however hard they bear is ever more perfect than that of slaves to the arbitrary will of a prince. To this it may be added that Sweden was always a free government, and is so now in a great degree, notwithstanding the late revolution.

How far it may be practicable to erect a bank on the joint credit of the public and of individuals can only be certainly determined by the experiment; but it is of so much importance that the experiment ought to be fully tried. When I saw the subscriptions going on to the bank established for supplying the army, I was in hopes it was only the embryo of a more permanent and extensive establishment. But I have reason to believe I shall be disappointed. It does not seem to be at all conducted on the true principles of a bank. The directors of it are purchasing with their stock instead of bank notes as I expected; in consequence of which it must turn out to be a mere subscription of a particular sum of money for a particular purpose.

Paper credit never was long supported in any country, on a national scale, where it was not founded on the joint basis of public and private credit. An attempt to establish it on public credit alone in France under the auspices of Mr. Law had nearly ruined the kingdom; we have seen the effects of it in America, and every successive experiment proves the futility of the attempt. Our new money is depreciating almost as fast as the old, though it has in some states as real funds as paper money ever had. The reason is, that the monied men have not an immediate interest to uphold its credit. They may even in many ways find it their interest to undermine it. The only certain manner to obtain a permanent paper credit is to engage the monied interest immediately in it by making them contribute the whole or part of the stock and giving them the whole or part of the profits.

The invention of banks on the modern principle originated in Venice. There the public and a company of monied men are mutually concerned. The Bank of England unites public authority and faith with private credit; and hence we see what a vast fabric of paper credit is raised on a visionary basis. Had it not been for this, England would never have found sufficient funds to carry on her wars; but with the help of this she has done, and is doing wonders. The bank of Amsterdam is on a similar foundation.

And why can we not have an American bank? Are our monied men less enlightened to their own interest or less enterprising in the persuit? I believe the fault is in our government which does not exert itself to engage them in such a scheme. It is true, the individuals in America are not very rich, but this would not prevent their instituting a bank; it would only prevent its being done with such ample funds as in other countries. Have they not sufficient confidence in the government and in the issue of the cause? Let the Government endeavour to inspire that confidence, by adopting the measures I have recommended or others equivalent to them. Let it exert itself to procure a solid confederation, to establish a good plan of executive administration, to form a permanent military force, to obtain at all events a foreign loan. If these things were in a train of vigorous execution, it would give a new spring to our affairs; government would recover its respectability and individuals would renounce their diffidence.

The object I should propose to myself in the first instance from a bank would be an auxiliary mode of supplies; for which purpose contracts should be made between Government and the bank on terms liberal and advantageous to the latter. Every thing should be done in the first instance to encourage the bank; after it gets well established it will take care of itself and government may make the best terms it can for itself.

The first step to establishing the bank will be to engage a number of monied men of influence to relish the project and make it a business. The subscribers to that lately established are the fittest persons that can be found; and their plan may be interwoven.

The outlines of my plan would be to open subscriptions in all the states for the stock, which we will suppose to be one million of pounds. Real property of every kind, as well as specie should be deemed good stock, but at least a fourth part of the subscription should be in specie or plate. There should be one great company in three divisions in Virginia, Philadelphia, and at Boston or two at Philadelphia and Boston. The bank should have a right to issue bank notes bearing two per Cent interest for the whole of their stock; but not to exceed it. These notes may be payable every three months or oftener, and the faith of government must be pledged for the support of the bank. It must therefore have a right from time to time to inspect its operations, and must appoint inspectors for the purpose.

The advantages of the bank may consist in this, in the profits of the contracts made with government, which should bear interest to be annually paid in specie, in the loan of money at interest say six per Cent, in purchasing lives by annuities as practiced in England &c. The benefit resulting to the company is evident from the consideration, that they may employ in circulation a great deal more money than they have specie in stock, on the credit of the real property which they will have in other use; this money will be employed either in fulfilling their contracts with the public by which also they will gain a profit, or in loans at an advantageous interest or in annuities.

The bank may be allowed to purchase plate and bullion and coin money allowing government a part of the profit. I make the bank notes bear interest to obtain a readie currency and to induce the holders to prefer them to specie to prevent too great a run upon the bank at any time beyond its ability to pay.

If Government can obtain a foreign loan it should lend to the bank on easy terms to extend its influence and facilitate a compliance with its engagements. If government could engage the states to raise a sum of money in specie to be deposited in bank in the same manner, it would be of the greatest consequence. If government could prevail on the enthusiasm of the people to make a contribution in plate for the same purpose it would be a master stroke. Things of this kind sometimes succeed in popular contests; and if undertaken with address; I should not despair of its success; but I should not be sanguine.

The bank may be instituted for a term of years by way of trial and the particular privilege of coining money be for a term still shorter. A temporary transfer of it to a particular company can have no inconvenience as the government are in no condition to improve this resource nor could it in our circumstances be an object to them, though with the industry of a knot of individuals it might be.

A bank of this kind even in its commencement would answer the most valuable purposes to government and to the proprietors; in its progress the advantages will exceed calculation. It will promote commerce by furnishing a more extensive medium which we greatly want in our circumstances. I mean a more extensive valuable medium. We have an enormous nominal one at this time; but it is only a name.

In the present unsettled state of things in this country, we can hardly draw inferences from what has happened in others, otherwise I should be certain of the success of this scheme; but I think it has enough in its favour to be worthy of trial.

I have only skimmed the surface of the different subjects I have introduced. Should the plans recommended come into contemplation in earnest and you desire my further thoughts, I will endeavour to give them more form and particularity. I am persuaded a solid confederation a permanent army a reasonable prospect of subsisting it would give us treble consideration in Europe and produce a peace this winter.

If a Convention is called the minds of all the states and the people ought to be prepared to receive its determinations by sensible and popular writings, which should conform to the views of Congress. There are epochs in human affairs, when *novelty* even is useful. If a general opinion prevails that the old way is bad, whether true or false, and this obstructs or relaxes the operation of the public service, a change is necessary if it be but for the sake of change. This is exactly the case now. 'Tis an universal sentiment that our present system is a bad one, and that things do not go right on this account. The measure of a Convention would revive the hopes of the people and give a new direction to their passions, which may be improved in carrying points of substantial utility. The Eastern states have already pointed out this mode to Congress; they ought to take the hint and anticipate the others.

And, in future, My Dear Sir, two things let me recommend, as fundamental rules for the conduct of Congress—to attach the army to them by every motive, to maintain an air of authority (not domineering) in all their measures with the states. The manner in which a thing is done has more influence than is commonly imagined. Men are governed by opinion; this opinion is as much influenced by appearances as by realities; if a Government appears to be confident of its own powers, it is the surest way to inspire the same confidence in others; if it is diffident, it may be certain, there will be a still greater diffidence in others, and that its authority will not only be distrusted, controverted, but contemned.

I wish too Congress would always consider that a kindness consists as much in the manner as in the thing: the best things done hesitatingly and with an ill grace lose their effect, and produce disgust rather than satisfaction or gratitude. In what Congress have at any time done for the army, they have commonly been too late: They have seemed to yield to importunity rather than to sentiments of justice or to a regard to the accommodation of their troops. An attention to this idea is of more importance than it may be thought. I who have seen all the workings and progress of the present discontents, am convinced, that a want of this has not been among the most inconsiderable causes.

You will perceive My Dear Sir this letter is hastily written and with a confidential freedom, not as to a member of Congress, whose feelings may be sore at the prevailing clamours; but as to a friend who is in a situation to remedy public disorders, who wishes for nothing so much as truth, and who is desirous of information, even from those less capable of judging than himself. I have not even time to correct and copy and only enough to add that I am very truly and affectionately D Sir   Your most Obed ser   A. Hamilton

Liberty Pole
Sept. 3d 1780

OPINIONS REGARDING THE SEXES

To Elizabeth Schuyler

I wrote you last night the inclosed hasty note in expectation that your papa would take his leave of us this morning early; a violent storm in which our house is tumbling about our ears prevents him. He and Meade are propping the house (I mean the Marquis), and I sit down to indulge the pleasure I always feel in writing to you.

The little song you sent me I have read over and over. It is very pretty and contains precisely those sentiments I would wish my betsey to feel, and she tells me it is an exact copy of her heart. You seem by sympathy to have anticipated the inquiries I made in one of mine lately, and to have answered them all by this little song; a pretty method indeed when I am asking a set of sober questions, of the greatest importance, to answer me with a song. I confess however that they scarcely deserved a better and that if you should in reality refer me to your song, I shall be very well served. For after all the proofs I have of your tenderness and readiness to share every kind of fortune with me it is a presumptuous diffidence of your heart to propose the examination I did. But be assured My angel it is not a diffidence of my betsey's heart, but of a *female* heart, that dictated the questions. I am ready to believe everything in favour of yours; but am restrained by the experience I have had of human nature, and of the softer part of it. Some of your sex possess every requisite to please delight, and inspire esteem friendship and affection; but there are too few of this description. We are full of vices. They are full of weaknesses; though I will not agree with the poet that they are, "Matter too soft, a lasting mark to bear. And best distinguished by black brown or fair." Nor will I join in the exclamation of Adam against the Creators having formed woman, "*a fair defect of nature.*" Yet I have reason to think that these portraits are applicable to too many of the sex; and though I am satisfied, whenever I trust my senses and my judgment that you are one of the exceptions, I cannot forbear having moments when I feel a disposition to make a more perfect discovery of your temper, and character. In one of those moments I wrote the letter in question.

Do not however I entreat you suppose that I entertain an ill opinion of all your sex. I have a much worse of my own. I have seen more of yours that merited esteem and love, but the truth is, My Dear girl, there are very few of either that are not very worthless. You know my sentiments on this head. I think I have found a precious jewel. I pray you do not think your sex injured and undertake to be their champion; for it will be taking an unfair advantage of your influence over me.

We have been fortunate of late in Quarters. I gave you a description of a fair one in those we had at Tappan. We have found another here; a pretty little dutch girl of fifteen. Every body makes love to her, and she receives every body kindly. She grants every thing that is asked and has too much simplicity to refuse any thing; but she has so much innocence to shield her, that the most determined rake would not dare to take advantage of her simplicity. This you will say is a very favourable character; but I have summed up all her excellencies—beauty, innocence, youth, simplicity. If all her sex were like her, I would become a disciple of Mahomet. I am persuaded she has no soul; and as I am squeamish enough to require a soul in a woman, I run no great risk of becoming one of her captives.

You see I give you an account of all the pretty females I meet with; you tell me nothing of the pretty fellows you see. I suppose you will pretend there is none of them engages the least of your attention, but you know I have been told you were something of a coquette, and I shall take care what degree of credit, I give to this pretence. When your sister returns home, I shall try to get her in my interest and make her tell me of all your flirtations. Have you heard any thing more of what I hinted to you about Fleury? When she returns, give my love to her and tell her, I expected, she would have outstripped you in the Hymenial line.

Adieu My love   A Hamilton

Sep. 3d

THE PLIGHT OF MRS. ARNOLD

To Elizabeth Schuyler

Sepr 25

In the midst of my letter, I was interrupted by a scene that shocked me more than any thing I have met with—the discovery of a treason of the deepest dye. The object was to sacrifice West Point. General Arnold had sold himself to André for this purpose. The latter came but in disguise and in returning to New York was detected. Arnold hearing of it immediately fled to the enemy. I went in pursuit of him but was much too late, and I could hardly regret the disappointment, when on my return, I saw an amiable woman frantic with distress for the loss of a husband she tenderly loved—a traitor to his country and to his fame, a disgrace to his connections. It was the most affecting scene I ever was witness to. She for a considerable time intirely lost her senses. The General went up to see her and she upbraided him with being in a plot to murder her child; one moment she raved; another she melted into tears; sometimes she pressed her infant to her bosom and lamented its fate occasioned by the imprudence of its father in a manner that would have pierced insensibility itself. All the sweetness of beauty, all the loveliness of innocence, all the tenderness of a wife and all the fondness of a mother showed themselves in her appearance and conduct. We have every reason to believe she was intirely unacquainted with the plan, and that her first knowlege of it was when Arnold went to tell her he must banish himself from his Country and from her forever. She instantly fell into a convulsion and he left her in that situation.

This morning she is more composed. I paid her a visit and endeavoured to sooth her by every method in my power, though you may imagine she is not easily to be consoled. Added to her other distresses, She is very apprehensive the resentment of her country will fall upon her (who is only unfortunate) for the guilt of her husband. I have tried to persuade her, her apprehensions are ill founded; but she has too many proofs of the illiberality of the state to which she belongs to be convinced. She received us in bed, with every circumstance that could interest our sympathy. Her sufferings were so eloquent that I wished myself her brother, to have a right to become her defender. As it is, I have entreated her to enable me to give her proofs of my friendship.

Could I forgive Arnold for sacrificing his honor reputation and duty I could not forgive him for acting a part that must have forfieted the esteem of so fine a woman. At present she almost forgets his crime in his misfortune, and her horror at the guilt of the traitor is lost in her love of the man. But a virtuous mind cannot long esteem a base one, and time will make her despise, if it cannot make her hate.

Indeed my angelic Betsey, I would not for the world do any thing that would hazard your esteem. 'Tis to me a jewel of inestimable price & I think you may rely I shall never make you blush.

I thank you for all the goodness of which your letters are expressive, and I entreat you my lovely girl to believe that my tenderness for you every day increases and that no time or circumstances can abate it. I quarrel with the hours that they do not fly more rapidly and give us to each other.

THE FATE OF MAJOR ANDRÉ

To Elizabeth Schuyler

Since my last to you, I have received your letters No. 3 & 4; the others are yet on the way. Though it is too late to have the advantage of novelty, to comply with my promise, I send you my account of Arnold's affair; and to justify myself to your sentiments, I must inform you that I urged a compliance with Andre's request to be shot and I do not think it would have had an ill effect; but some people are only sensible to motives of policy, and sometimes from a narrow disposition mistake it. When André's tale comes to be told, and present resentment is over, the refusing him the privilege of choosing the manner of death will be branded with too much obduracy.

It was proposed to me to suggest to him the idea of an exchange for Arnold; but I knew I should have forfieted his esteem by doing it, and therefore declined it. As a man of honor he could not but reject it and I would not for the world have proposed to him a thing, which must have placed me in the unamiable light of supposing him capable of a meanness, or of not feeling myself the impropriety of the measure. I confess to you I had the weakness to value the esteem of a *dying* man; because I reverenced his merit.

I fear you will admire the picture so much as to forget the painter. I wished myself possessed of André's accomplishments for your sake; for I would wish to charm you in every sense. You cannot conceive my avidity for every thing that would endear me more to you. I shall never be satisfied with giving you pleasure, and I am mortified that I do not unite in myself every valuable and agreeable qualification. I do not my love affect modesty. I am conscious of the advantages I possess. I know I have talents and a good heart; but why am I not handsome? Why have I not every acquirement that can embellish human nature? Why have I not fortune, that I might hereafter have more leisure than I shall have to cultivate those improvements for which I am not entirely unfit?

Tis not the vanity of excelling others, but the desire of pleasing my Betsey that dictates these wishes. In her eyes I should wish to be the first the most amiable the most accomplished of my sex; but I will make up all I want in love.

Two days since, the bundle directed to your papa was delivered to me. I beg you to present my affectionate compliments with it to your mama.

I am in very good health and shall be in very good spirits when I meet my Betsey.

Adieu   A Hamilton

How is your little sister? Is she as sprightly as ever? Does she set so much value upon a certain kiss as she seemed to do when we entered the carriage at Hartford? I forgot to tell you that she fell in love there with an old man of fifty.

October 2, 1780

ADVICE ABOUT MARRIAGE

To Margarita Schuyler

Because your sister has the talent of growing more amiable every day, or because I am a fanatic in love, or both—or if you prefer another interpretation, because I have address enough to be a good dissembler, she fancies herself the happiest woman in the world, and would need persuade all her friends to embark with her in the matrimonial voyage. But I pray you do not let her advice have so much influence as to make you matrimony-mad. 'Tis a very good thing when their stars unite two people who are fit for each other, who have souls capable of relishing the sweets of friendship, and sensibilities. The conclusion of the sentence I trust to your fancy. But its a dog of life when two dissonant tempers meet, and 'tis ten to one but this is the case. When therefore I join her in advising you to marry, I add be cautious in the choice. Get a man of sense, not ugly enough to be pointed at—with some good-nature—a few grains of feeling—a little taste—a little imagination—and above all a good deal of decision to keep you in order; for that I foresee will be no easy task. If you can find one with all these qualities, willing to marry you, marry him as soon as you please.

I must tell you in confidence that I think I have been very fortunate.

January 21, 1781

To Philip Schuyler

Head Quarters New
My Dear Sir.   Windsor Feby 18, 81
Since I had the pleasure of writing you last an unexpected change has taken place in my situation. I am no longer a member of the General's family. This information will surprise you and the manner of the change will surprise you more.— Two day ago The General and I passed each other on the stairs. He told me he wanted to speak to me. I answered that I would wait upon him immediately. I went below and delivered Mr. Tilghman a letter to be sent to The Commissary containing an order of a pressing and interesting nature. Returning to The General I was stopped in the way by the

Marquis De la Fayette, and we conversed together about a minute on a matter of business. He can testify how impatient I was to get back, and that I left him in a manner which but for our intimacy would have been more than abrupt. Instead of finding the General as usual in his room, I met him at the head of the stairs, where accosting me in a very angry tone, "Col Hamilton (said he), you have kept me waiting at the head of the stairs these ten minutes. I must tell you Sir you treat me with disrespect." I replied without petulancy, but with decision "I am not conscious of it Sir, but since you have thought it necessary to tell me so we part" "Very well Sir (said he) if it be your choice" or something to this effect and we separated.

I sincerely believe my absence which gave so much umbrage did not last two minutes.

In less than an hour after, Tilghman came to me in the Generals name assuring me of his great confidence in my abilities, integrity usefulness &c and of his desire in a candid conversation to heal a difference which could not have happened but in a moment of passion. I requested Mr. Tilghman to tell him, [1] that I had taken my resolution in a manner not to be revoked: [2] that as a conversation could serve no other purpose than to produce explanations mutually disagreeable, though I certainly would not refuse an interview if he desired it yet I should be happy he would permit me to decline it [4] that however I did not wish to distress him or the public business, by quitting him before he could derive other assistance by the return of some of the Gentlemen who were absent: [3] that though determined to leave the family the same principles which had kept me so long in it would continue to direct my conduct towards him when out of it. [5] And that in the mean time it depended on him to let our behaviour to each other be the same as if nothing had happened.

He consented to decline the conversation and thanked me for my offer of continuing my aid, in the manner I had mentioned.

Thus we stand. I wait Mr. Humphrey's return from the Eastward and may perhaps be induced to wait the return of Mr. Harrison from Virginia.

I have given you so particular a detail of our difference from the desire I have to justify myself in your opinion.

Perhaps you may think I was precipitate in rejecting the overture made by the general to an accommodation. I assure you My Dr Sir it was not the effect of resentment it was the deliberate result of maxims I had long formed for the government of my own conduct.

I always disliked the office of an Aide de Camp as having in it a kind of personal dependance. I refused to serve in this capacity with two Major General's at an early period of the war. Infected however with the enthusiasm of the times, an idea of the Generals character which experience soon taught me to be unfounded, overcame my scruples and induced me to *accept his invitation* to enter into his family. I believe you know the place I held in The Generals confidence and councils of which will make it the more extraordinary to you to learn that for three years past I have felt no friendship for him and have professed none. The truth is our own dispositions are the opposites of each other & the pride of my temper would not suffer me to profess what I did not feel. Indeed when advances of this kind have been made to me on his part, they were received in a manner that showed at least I had no inclination to court them, and that I wished to stand rather upon a footing of military confidence than of private attachment. You are too good a judge of human nature not to be sensible how this conduct in me must have operated on a man to whom all the world is offering incense. With this key you will easily unlock the present mystery. At the end of the war I may say many things to you concerning which I shall impose upon myself 'till then an inviolable silence.

The General is a very honest man. His competitors have slender abilities and less integrity. His popularity has often been essential to the safety of America, and is still of great importance to it. These considerations have influenced my past conduct respecting him, and will influence my future. I think it is necessary he should be supported.

His estimation in your mind, whatever may be its amounts, I am persuaded has been formed on principles which a circumstance like this cannot materially affect; but if I thought it could diminish your friendship for him, I should almost forego the motives that urge me to justify myself to you. I wish what I have said to make no other impression than to satisfy you I have not been in the wrong. It is also said in confidence, for as a public knowlege of the breach would in many ways have an ill effect. it will probably be the policy of both sides to conceal it and cover the separation with some plausible pretext. I am importuned by such friends as are privy to the affair, to listen to a reconciliation: but my resolution is unalterable.

As I cannot think of quitting the army during the war, I have a project of re-entering into the artillery, by taking Lieutenant-Colonel Forrest's place, who is desirous of retiring on half pay. I have not however made up my mind upon this head, as I should be obliged to come in the youngest Lt Col instead of the eldest, which I ought to have been by natural succession had I remained in the corps; and at the same time to resume studies relative to the profession which, to avoid inferiority, must be laborious.

If a handsome command for the campaign in the light infantry should offer itself, I shall ballance between this and the artillery. My situation in the latter would be more solid and permanent; but as I hope the war will not last long enough to make it progressive, this consideration has the less force. A command for the campaign would leave me the winter to prosecute studies relative to my future career in life. With respect to the former, I have been materially the worse for going into his family.

I have written to you on this subject with all the freedom and confidence to which you have a right and with an assurance of the interest you take in all that concerns me.

Very sincerely & Affectionately I am Dr Sir Yr. most Obed

A Hamilton

WASHINGTON WILL REPENT HIS ILL-HUMOUR

To James McHenry

I have, Dear Mac, several of your letters. I shall soon have time enough to write my friends as often as they please.

The Great man and I have come to an open rupture. Proposals of accomodation have been made on his part but rejected. I pledge my honor to you that he will find me inflexible. He shall for once at least repent his ill-humour. Without a shadow of reason and on the slightest ground, he charged me in the most affrontive manner with treating him with disrespect. I answered very decisively—"Sir I am not conscious of it but since you have thought it necessary to tell me so, we part." I wait till more help arrives. At present there is besides myself only Tilghman, who is just recovering from a fit of illness the consequence of too close application to business.

We have often spoken freely our sentiments to each other. Except to a very few friends our difference will be a secret; therefore be silent. I shall continue to support a popularity that has been essential, is still useful.

Adieu my friend. May the time come when characters may be known in their true light.   AH

Madame sends her friendship to you.

February 18, 1781

The Continentalist No. I

MR. LOUDON.

I send you the first number of a series of papers which I intend to publish on matters of the greatest importance to these States; I hope they will be read with as much candour and attention as the object of them deserve, and that no conclusions will be drawn till these are fully developed.

I am, Sir, Your most obedient humble servant, A.B.

THE CONTINENTALIST. NO. I

It would be the extreme of vanity in us not to be sensible, that we began this revolution with very vague and confined notions of the practical business of government. To the greater part of us it was a novelty: Of those, who under the former constitution had had opportunities of acquiring experience, a large proportion adhered to the opposite side, and the remainder can only be supposed to have possessed ideas adapted to the narrow colonial sphere, in which they had been accustomed to move, not of that enlarged kind suited to the government of an INDEPENDENT NATION.

There were no doubt exceptions to these observations— men in all respects qualified for conducting the public affairs, with skill and advantage; but their number was small; they were not always brought forward in our councils; and when they were, their influence was too commonly borne down by the prevailing torrent of ignorance and prejudice.

On a retrospect however, of our transactions, under the disadvantages with which we commenced, it is perhaps more to be wondered at, that we have done so well, than that we have not done better. There are indeed some traits in our conduct, as conspicuous for sound policy, as others for magnanimity. But, on the other hand, it must also be confessed, there have been many false steps, many chimerical projects and utopian speculations, in the management of our civil as well as of our military affairs. A part of these were the natural effects of the spirit of the times dictated by our situation. An

extreme jealousy of power is the attendant on all popular revolutions, and has seldom been without its evils. It is to this
source we are to trace many of the fatal mistakes, which have
so deeply endangered the common cause; particularly that defect, which will be the object of these remarks, A WANT OF
POWER IN CONGRESS.

The present Congress, respectable for abilities and integrity,
by experience convinced of the necessity of a change, are
preparing several important articles to be submitted to the respective states, for augmenting the powers of the Confederation. But though there is hardly at this time a man of
information in America, who will not acknowledge, as a general proposition, that in its present form, it is unequal, either
to a vigorous prosecution of the war, or to the preservation of
the union in peace; yet when the principle comes to be applied to practice, there seems not to be the same agreement
in the modes of remedying the defect; and it is to be feared,
from a disposition which appeared in some of the states on a
late occasion, that the salutary intentions of Congress may
meet with more delay and opposition, than the critical posture of the states will justify.

It will be attempted to shew in a course of papers what
ought to be done, and the mischiefs of a contrary policy.

In the first stages of the controversy it was excuseable to
err. Good intentions, rather than great skill, were to have
been expected from us. But we have now had suffecent time
for reflection and experience, as ample as unfortunate, to rectify our errors. To persist in them, becomes disgraceful and
even criminal, and belies that character of good sense and a
quick discernment of our interests, which, in spite of our mistakes, we have been hitherto allowed. It will prove, that our
sagacity is limited to interests of interior moment; and that we
are incapable of those enlightened and liberal views, necessary
to make us a great and a flourishing people.

History is full of examples, where in contests for liberty, a
jealousy of power has either defeated the attempts to recover
or preserve it in the first instance, or has afterwards subverted
it by clogging government with too great precautions for its
security, or by leaving too wide a door for sedition and
popular licenciousness. In a government framed for durable

liberty, not less regard must be paid to giving the magistrate a proper degree of authority, to make and execute the laws with vigour, than to guarding against encroachments upon the rights of the community. As too much power leads to despotism, too little leads to anarchy, and both eventually to the ruin of the people. These are maxims well known, but never sufficiently attended to, in adjusting the frames of governments. Some momentary interest or passion is sure to give a wrong biass, and pervert the most favourable opportunities.

No friend to order or to rational liberty, can read without pain and disgust the history of the commonwealths of Greece. Generally speaking, they were a constant scene of the alternate tyranny of one part of the people over the other, or of a few usurping demagogues over the whole. Most of them had been originally governed by kings, whose despotism (the natural disease of monarchy) had obliged their subjects to murder, expel, depose, or reduce them to a nominal existence, and institute popular governments. In these governments, that of Sparta excepted, the jealousy of power hindered the people from trusting out of their own hands a competent authority, to maintain the repose and stability of the commonwealth; whence originated the frequent revolutions and civil broils with which they were distracted. This, and the want of a solid fœderal union to restrain the ambition and rivalship of the different cities, after a rapid succession of bloody wars, ended in their total loss of liberty and subjugation to foreign powers.

In a comparison of our governments with those of the ancient republics, we must, without hesitation, give the preference to our own; because, every power with us is exercised by representation, not in tumultuary assemblies of the collective body of the people, where the art or impudence of the ORATOR or TRIBUNE, rather than the utility or justice of the measure could seldom fail to govern. Yet whatever may be the advantage on our side, in such a comparison, men who estimate the value of institutions, not from prejudices of the moment, but from experience and reason, must be persuaded, that the same JEALOUSY of POWER has prevented our reaping all the advantages, from the examples of other nations, which we ought to have done, and has rendered our particular constitutions in many respects feeble and imperfect.

Perhaps the evil is not very great in respect to our constitutions; for notwithstanding their imperfections, they may, for some time, be made to operate in such a manner, as to answer the purposes of the common defence and the maintenance of order; and they seem to have, in themselves, and in the progress of society among us, the seeds of improvement.

But this is not the case with respect to the FOEDERAL GOVERNMENT; if it is too weak at first, it will continually grow weaker. The ambition and local interests of the respective members, will be constantly undermining and usurping upon its prerogatives, till it comes to a dissolution; if a partial combination of some of the more powerful ones does not bring it to a more SPEEDY and VIOLENT END.

The New-York Packet, and
the American Advertiser, July 12, 1781

The Continentalist No. III

The situation of these states is very unlike that of the United Provinces. Remote as we are from Europe, in a little time, we should fancy ourselves out of the reach of attempts from abroad, and in full liberty, at our leisure and convenience, to try our strength at home. This might not happen at once; but if the FOEDERAL GOVERNMENT SHOULD LOSE ITS AUTHORITY, it would CERTAINLY FOLLOW. Political societies, in close neighbourhood, must either be strongly united under one government, or there will infallibly exist emulations and quarrels. This is in human nature; and we have no reason to think ourselves wiser, or better, than other men. Some of the larger states, a small number of years hence, will be in themselves populous, rich and powerful, in all those circumstances calculated to inspire ambition and nourish ideas of separation and independence. Though it will ever be their true interest to preserve the union, their vanity and self importance, will be very likely to overpower that motive, and make them seek to place themselves at the head of particular confederacies independent of the general one. A

schism once introduced, competitions of boundary and rivalships of commerce will easily afford pretexts for war. European powers may have inducements for fomenting these
divisions and playing us off against each other. But without
such a disposition in them, if separations once take place, we
shall, of course, embrace different interests and connections.
The particular confederacies, leaguing themselves with rival
nations, will naturally be involved in their disputes; into which
they will be the more readily tempted by the hope of making
acquisitions upon each other, and upon the colonies of the
powers with whom they are respectively at enmity.

WE ALREADY SEE SYMPTOMS OF THE EVILS TO
BE APPREHENDED. In the midst of a war for our existence
as a nation; in the midst of dangers too serious to be trifled
with, some of the states have evaded, or refused, compliance
with the demands of Congress in points of the greatest moment to the common safety. If they act such a part at this perilous juncture, what are we to expect in a time of peace and
security? Is it not to be feared, that the resolutions of Congress would soon become like the decisions of the Greek am-
phyctions, or like the edicts of a German diet?

But as these evils are at a little distance, we may perhaps be
insensible and short sighted enough to disregard them. There
are others that threaten our immediate safety. Our whole system is in disorder; our currency depreciated, till in many
places it will hardly obtain a circulation at all, public credit at
its lowest ebb, our army deficient in numbers, and unpro-
vided with every thing, the government, in its present condition, unable to command the means to pay, clothe, or feed
their troops, the enemy making an alarming progress in the
southern states, lately in complete possession of two of them,
though now in part rescued by the genius and exertions of a
General without an army, a force under Cornwallis still formidable to Virginia.

We ought to blush to acknowledge, that this is a true picture of our situation, when we reflect, that the enemy's
whole force in the United States, including their American
levies and the late reinforcement, is little more than fourteen
thousand effective men; that our population, by recent examination, has been found to be greater, than at the com-

mencement of the war; that the quantity of our specie has also increased, that the country abounds with all the necessaries of life, and has a sufficiency of foreign commodities, with a considerable and progressive commerce; that we have beyond comparison a better stock of warlike materials, than when we began the contest, and an ally as willing as able to supply our further wants: And that we have, on the spot, five thousand auxiliary troops, paid and subsisted by that ally, to assist in our defence.

Nothing but a GENERAL DISAFFECTION of the PEOPLE, or MISMANAGEMENT in their RULERS, can account for the figure we make, and for the distresses and perplexities we experience, contending against so small a force.

Our enemies themselves must now be persuaded, that the first is not the cause; and WE KNOW it is not. The most decided attachment of the people could alone have made them endure, without a convulsion, the successive shocks in our currency, added to the unavoidable inconveniences of war. There is perhaps not another nation in the world, that would have shown equal patience and perseverance in similar circumstances. The enemy have now tried the temper of almost every part of America; and they can hardly produce in their ranks a thousand men, who without their arts and seductions have voluntarily joined their standard. The miseries of a rigorous captivity, may perhaps have added half as many more to the number of the American levies, at this time in their armies. This small accession of force is the more extraordinary, as they have at some periods, been apparently in the full tide of success, while every thing wore an aspect tending to infuse despondency into the people of this country. This has been remarkably the case in the southern states. They for a time had almost undisturbed possession of two of them; and Cornwallis, after overruning a great part of a third; after two victorious battles, only brought with him into Virginia, about two hundred tories. In the state where he thought himself so well established, that he presumptuously ventured to assure the minister, there was not a rebel left, a small body of Continental troops, have been so effectually seconded by the militia of that vanquished country, as to have been able to capture a number of his troops more than equal to their own, and to repossess the principal part of the state.

As in the explanation of our embarrassments nothing can be alledged to the disaffection of the people, we must have recourse to the other cause of IMPOLICY and MISMAN-AGEMENT in their RULERS.

Where the blame of this may lie is not so much the question as what are the proper remedies; yet it may not be amiss to remark, that too large a share has fallen upon Congress. That body is no doubt chargeable with mistakes; but perhaps its greatest has been too much readiness to make concessions of the powers implied in its original trust. This is partly to be attributed to an excessive complaisance to the spirit, which has evidently actuated a majority of the states, a desire of monopolizing all power in themselves. Congress have been responsible for the administration of affairs, without the means of fulfilling that responsibility.

It would be too severe a reflection upon us to suppose, that a disposition to make the most of the friendship of others, and to exempt ourselves from a full share of the burthens of the war has had any part in the backwardness, which has appeared in many of the states, to confer powers and adopt measures adequate to the exigency. Such a sentiment would neither be wise, just, generous, nor honorable; nor do I believe the accusation would be well founded, yet our conduct makes us liable to a suspicion of this sort. It is certain, however, that too sanguine expectations from Europe have unintentionally relaxed our efforts, by diverting a sense of danger, and begetting an opinion, that the inequality of the contest would make every campaign the last.

We did not consider how difficult it must be to exhaust the resources of a nation circumstanced like that of Great Britain; whose government has always been distinguished for energy, and its people for enthusiasm. Nor did we, in estimating the superiority of our friends make sufficient allowance for that want of concert, which will ever characterise the operations of allies, or for the immense advantage to the enemy, of having their forces, though inferior, under a single direction. Finding the rest of Europe either friendly, or pacific, we never calculated the contingencies, which might alter that disposition;

nor reflected that the death* of a single prince, the change or caprice of a single minister, was capable of giving a new face to the whole system.

We are at this time more sanguine than ever. The war with the Dutch, we believe, will give such an addition of force to our side, as will make the superiority irresistible. No person can dispute this, if things remain in their present state; but the extreme disparity of the contest is the very reason, why this cannot be the case. The neutral powers will either effect a particular, or a general accommodation, or they will take their sides. There are three suppositions to be made: one, that there will be a compromise *between the united* provinces and England; for which we are certain the mediation of Austria and Russia have been offered; another, a pacification between all the belligerent powers, for which we have reason to believe the same mediation has been offered; the third, a rejection of the terms of mediation and a more general war.

Either of these suppositions is a motive for exertion. The first will place things in the same, probably in a worse situation, than before the declaration of the war against Holland. The composing of present differences may be accompanied with a revival of ancient connections; and at least would be productive of greater caution and restraint in a future intercourse with us.

The second, it is much to be dreaded, would hazard a dismemberment[†] of a part of these states; and we are bound in honor, in duty and in interest, to employ every effort to dispossess the enemy of what they hold. A natural basis of the negociation, with respect to this continent, will be, that each party shall retain what it possesses at the conclusion of the

---

* The death of the Empress Queen has actually produced a change: Her politics, if not friendly to our connections, were at least pacific: and while she lived no hostile interference of the House of Austria was to be expected. The Emperor, her son, by her death, left more at liberty to pursue his inclinations, averse to the aggrandisement of France, of course afraid of the abasement of England, has given several indications of an unfriendly disposition. It should be a weighty consideration with us, that among the potentates which we look upon as amicable, three of the principal ones are at a very advanced stage of life. The King of Spain, the King of Prussia, and the Empress of Russia. We know not what may be the politics of successors.

[†] Perhaps not expressly and directly, but virtually, under the plausible form of a new arrangement of limits.

treaty, qualified perhaps by a cession of particular points for an equivalent elsewhere. It is too delicate to dwell on the motives to this apprehension; but if such a compromise sometimes terminates the disputes of nations originally independent, it will be less extraordinary where one party was originally under the dominion of the other.

If we are determined, as we ought to be with the concurrence of our allies, not to accept such a condition, then we ought to prepare for the third event, a more general and more obstinate war.

Should this take place, a variety of new interests will be involved, and the affairs of America MAY CEASE TO BE OF PRIMARY IMPORTANCE. In proportion as the objects and operations of the war become complicated and extensive, the final success must become uncertain; and in proportion as the interests of others in our concerns may be weakened, or supplanted by more immediate interests of their own, ought our attention to ourselves, and exertions in our own behalf to be awakened and augmented.

We ought therefore, not only to strain every nerve for complying with the requisitions, to render the present campaign as decisive as possible; but we ought without delay, to ENLARGE THE POWERS OF CONGRESS. Every plan of which, this is not the foundation, will be illusory. The separate exertions of the states will never suffice. Nothing but a well-proportioned exertion of the resources of the whole, under the direction of a Common Council, with power sufficient to give efficacy to their resolutions, can preserve us from being a CONQUERED PEOPLE now, or can make us a HAPPY PEOPLE hereafter.

The New-York Packet, and
the American Advertiser, August 9, 1781

The Continentalist No. IV

The preceding numbers are chiefly intended to confirm an opinion, already pretty generally received, that it is necessary to augment the powers of the confederation. The principal difficulty yet remains, to fix the public judgment, definitively, on the points, which ought to compose that augmentation.

It may be pronounced with confidence, that nothing short of the following articles can suffice.

1st, THE POWER OF REGULATING TRADE, comprehending a right of granting bounties and premiums by way of encouragement, of imposing duties of every kind, as well for revenue as regulation, of appointing all officers of the customs, and of laying embargoes, in extraordinary emergencies.

2d, A moderate land-tax* throughout the United States, at a specific rate per pound, or per acre, granted to the FOEDERAL GOVERNMENT in perpetuity, and, if Congress think proper, to be levied by their own collectors.

3d, A moderate capitation tax[†] on every male inhabitant above fifteen years of age; exclusive of common soldiers, common seamen, day-labourers, cottagers and paupers; to be also vested in perpetuity, and with the same condition of collection.

4th, The disposal of all unlocated land, for the benefit of the United States (so far as respects the profits of the first sale and the quit-rents) the jurisdiction remaining to the respective States in whose limits they are contained.

5th, A certain proportion of the product of all mines, discovered, or to be discovered, for the same duration and with the same right of collection, as in the second and third articles.

6th, The appointment of all land (as well as naval) officers of every rank.

The three first articles are of IMMEDIATE NECESSITY; the three last would be of great present but of much greater future utility; the whole combined would give solidity and permanency to the union.

The great defect of the confederation is, that it gives the United States no property, or in other words, no revenue, nor

---

* Two-pence an acre on cultivated and a half penny on uncultivated land, would answer the purpose, and would be so moderate as not to be felt. A small tax on uncultivated land would have the good effect of obliging the proprietor either to cultivate it himself, or to dispose of it to some person, that would do it.

[†] Suppose a dollar or even a half a dollar per head.

the means of acquiring it, inherent in themselves, and independent on the temporary pleasure of the different members; and power without revenue in political society is a name. While Congress continue altogether dependent on the occasional grants of the several States, for the means of defraying the expences of the FOEDERAL GOVERNMENT, it can neither have dignity vigour nor *credit*. CREDIT supposes specific and permanent funds for the punctual payment of interest, with a moral certainty of a final redemption of the principal. In our situation it will probably require more, on account of the general diffidence, which has been excited by the past disorder in our finances. It will perhaps be necessary, in the first instance, to appropriate funds for the redemption of the principal* in a determinate period, as well as for the payment of interest.

It is essential, that the property in such funds should be in the contractor himself, and the appropriation dependent on his own will; if instead of this the possession, or disposal of them, is to float on the voluntary and occasional concurrence of a number of different wills, not under his absolute controul, both the one and the other will be too precarious to be trusted.

The most wealthy and best established nations are obliged to pledge their funds to obtain credit; and it would be the height of absurdity in us, in the midst of a revolution, to expect to have it on better terms. This credit being to be procured through Congress, the funds ought to be provided, declared, and vested in them. It is a fact, that besides the want of specific funds, a circumstance which operates powerfully against our obtaining credit abroad, is, not a distrust of our becoming independent, but of our continuing united; and with our present confederation the distrust is natural. Both foreigners and the thinking men among ourselves, would have much more confidence in the duration of the union, if they were to see it supported on the foundation here proposed.

* It might indeed be a good restraint upon the spirit of running in debt with which governments are too apt to be infected, to make it a condition of the grants to Congress, that they shall be obliged in all their loans to appropriate funds for the payment of principal as well as interest; and such a restriction might be serviceable to public credit.

There are some among us ignorant enough to imagine, that the war may be carried on without credit; defraying the expences of the year with what may be raised within the year. But this is for want of a knowledge of our real resources and expenses. It may be demonstrated, that the whole amount of the revenue, which these States are capable of affording, will be deficient annually five or six millions of dollars, for the support of civil government and of the war. This is not a conjecture hazarded at random, but the result of experiment and calculation; nor can it appear surprising, when it is considered, that the revenues of the United Provinces equal to these States in population, beyond comparison superior in industry, commerce and riches, do not exceed twenty five millions of guilders, or about nine millions and an half of dollars. In times of war, they have raised a more considerable sum; but has been chiefly by gratuitous contributions of rich individuals; a resource we cannot employ, because there are few men of large fortunes in this country, and these for the most part in land. Taxes in the United Provinces are carried to an extreme, which would be impracticable here; not only the living are made to pay for every necessary of life; but even the dead are tributary to the public for the liberty of interment at particular hours. These considerations make it evident, that we could not raise an equal amount of revenue in these States; yet in seventy-six, when the currency was not depreciated, Congress emitted for the expences of the year fourteen millions of dollars. It cannot be denied, that there was a want of order and œconomy, in the expenditure of public money, nor that we had a greater military force to maintain at that time, than we now have; but, on the other hand, allowing for the necessary increase in our different civil lists, and for the advanced prices of many articles, it can hardly be supposed possible to reduce our annual expence very much below that sum. This simple idea of the subject, without entering into details, may satisfy us, that the deficiency which has been stated is not to be suspected of exaggeration.

Indeed nations the most powerful and opulent are obliged to have recourse to loans, in time of war; and hence it is, that most of the States of Europe are deeply immersed in debt. France is among the number, notwithstanding her immense population, wealth and resources. England owes the enormous sum of two hundred millions sterling. The United Provinces, with all their prudence and parsimony, owe a debt of the generality of fifty millions sterling, besides the particular debts of each province. Almost all the other powers are more or less in the same circumstances.

While this teaches us how contracted and uninformed are the views of those who expect to carry on the war, without running in debt; it ought to console us, with respect to the amount of that which we now owe, or may have occasion to incur, in the remainder of the war. The whole, without burthening the people, may be paid off in twenty years after the conclusion of peace.

The principal part of the deficient five or six millions must be procured by loans from private persons, at home and abroad.

Every thing may be hoped, from the generosity of France, which her means will permit; but she has full employment for her revenues and credit, in the prosecution of the war on her own part. If we judge of the future by the past, the pecuniary succours from her must continue to be far short of our wants: And the contingency of a war on the continent of Europe makes it possible, they may diminish rather than increase.

We have in a less degree experienced the friendship of Spain in this article.

The government of the United Provinces, if disposed to do it, can give us no assistance. The revenues of the Republic are chiefly mortgaged for former debts. Happily it has extensive credit, but it will have occasion for the whole to supply its own exigencies.

Private men, either foreigners, or natives, will not lend to a large amount, but on the usual security of funds properly established. This security Congress cannot give, till the several States vest them with revenue, or the means of revenue for that purpose.

Congress have wisely appointed a Superintendant of their Finances; a man of acknowledged abilities and integrity, as well as of great personal credit and pecuniary influence. It was impossible, that the business of finance could be ably conducted by a body of men, however well composed or well intentioned. Order in the future management of our monied concerns, a strict regard to the performance of public engagements, and of course, the restoration of public credit may be reasonably and confidently expected from Mr. Morris's administration, if he is furnished with materials upon which to operate—that is, if the fœderal government can acquire funds as the basis of his arrangements. He has very judiciously proposed a national bank, which, by uniting the influence and interest of the monied men with the resources of government, can alone give it that durable and extensive credit of which it stands in need. This is the best expedient he could have devised for relieving the public embarrassments, but to give success to the plan, it is essential, that Congress should have it in their power to support him with unexceptionable funds.

Had we begun the practice of funding four years ago, we should have avoided that depreciation of the currency, which has been as pernicious to the morals as to the credit of the nation: And there is no other method than this to prevent a continuance and multiplication of the evils flowing from that prolific source.

The New-York Packet, and
the American Advertiser, August 30, 1781

The Continentalist No. VI

Let us see what will be the consequences of not authorising the Fœderal Government to regulate the trade of these states.

Besides the want of revenue and of power, besides the immediate risk to our independence, the danger of all the future evils of a precarious union, besides the deficiency of a wholesome concert and provident superintendence to advance the general prosperity of trade, the direct consequence will be, that the landed interest and the labouring poor will in the first place fall a sacrifice to the trading interest, and the whole eventually to a bad system of policy, made necessary by the want of such regulating power.

Each state will be afraid to impose duties on its commerce,

lest the other states, not doing the same, should enjoy greater advantages than itself; by being able to afford native commodities cheaper abroad, and foreign commodities cheaper at home.

A part of the evils resulting from this would be: A loss to the revenue of those moderate duties, which, without being injurious to commerce, are allowed to be the most agreeable species of taxes to the people.

Articles of foreign luxury while they would contribute nothing to the income of the state, being less dear by an exemption from duties, would have a more extensive consumption.

Many branches of trade hurtful to the common interest would be continued for want of proper checks and discouragements.

As revenues must be found to satisfy the public exigencies in peace and in war, too great a proportion of taxes will fall directly upon land and upon the necessaries of life, the produce of that land.

The influence of these evils will be, to render landed property fluctuating and less valuable, to oppress the poor by raising the prices of necessaries, to injure commerce by encouraging the consumption of foreign luxuries, by encreasing the value of labor, by lessening the quantity of home productions, enhancing their prices at foreign markets, of course, obstructing their sale and enabling other nations to supplant us.

Particular caution ought at present to be observed in this country, not to burthen the soil itself and its productions, with heavy impositions; because the quantity of unimproved land will invite the husbandmen to abandon old settlements for new, and the disproportion of our population for some time to come, will necessarily make labor dear, to reduce which, and not to increase it, ought to be a capital object of our policy.

Easy duties therefore on commerce, especially on imports, ought to lighten the burthens, which will unavoidably fall upon land. Though it may be said, that on the principle of a reciprocal influence of prices, whereon the taxes are laid in the first instance, they will in the end be borne by all classes; yet it is of the greatest importance that no one should sink under the immediate pressure. The great art is to distribute the public burthens well and not suffer them, either first, or last, to fall too heavily upon parts of the community; else distress and disorder must ensue. A shock given to any part of the political machine vibrates through the whole.

As a sufficient revenue could not be raised from trade to answer the public purposes, other articles have been proposed.

A moderate land and poll tax, being of easy and unexpensive collection, and leaving nothing to discretion, are the simplest and best, that could be devised.

It is to be feared, the avarice of many of the landholders will be opposed to a perpetual tax upon land, however moderate. They will ignorantly hope to shift the burthens of the national expence from themselves to others; a disposition as iniquitous as it is fruitless. The public necessities must be satisfied; this can only be done by the contributions of the whole society. Particular classes are neither able nor will be willing to pay for the protection and security of the others; and where so selfish a spirit discovers itself in any member, the rest of the community will unite to compel it to do its duty.

Indeed many theorists in political œconomy have held, that all taxes, wherever they originate fall ultimately upon land; and have therefore been of opinion, that it would be best to draw the whole revenue of the state immediately from that source, to avoid the expence of a more diversified collection, and the accumulations which will be heaped in their several stages upon the primitive sums advanced in those taxes, which are imposed on our trade.* But though it has been demonstrated, that this theory has been carried to an extreme, impracticable in fact, yet it is evident, in tracing the matter, that a large part of all taxes, however remotely laid, will by an insensible circulation, come at last to settle upon land; the source of most of the materials employed of commerce.

It appears from calculation made by the ablest masters of political arithmetic, about sixty years ago, that the yearly product of all the lands in England amounted to £42,000,000 sterling, and the whole annual consumption, at that period,

---

* The merchant it is said will have an advance on the duty he pays, the shop keeper a further advance &c.

of foreign as well as domestic commodities, did not exceed
£49,000,000, and the surplus of the exportation above the
importation £2,000,000; on which sums, must arise all the
revenues in whatever shape which go into the treasury. It is
easy to infer from this, how large a part of them must directly,
or indirectly be derived from land.

Nothing can be more mistaken, than the collision and rivalship, which almost always subsist between the landed and
trading interests, for the truth is they are so inseparably interwoven, that one cannot be injured, without injury, nor benefitted, without benefit to the other. Oppress trade, lands sink
in value, make it flourish, their value rises, incumber husbandry, trade declines, encourage agriculture, commerce revives. The progress of this mutual reaction might easily be
delineated, but it is too obvious to every man, who turns his
thoughts, however superficially, upon the subject, to require
it. It is only to be regretted that it is too often lost sight of,
when the seductions of some immediate advantage or exemption tempt us to sacrifice the future to the present.

But perhaps the class is more numerous than those, who
not unwilling to bear their share of public burthens, are yet
averse to the idea of perpetuity, as if there ever would arrive a
period, when the state would cease to want revenues and
taxes become unnecessary. It is of importance to unmask this
delusion and open the eyes of the people to the truth. It is
paying too great a tribute to the idol of popularity to flatter
so injurious and so visionary an expectation. The error is too
gross to be tolerated any where, but in the cottage of the
peasant; should we meet with it in the senate house, we must
lament the ignorance or despise the hypocrisy, on which it is
ingrafted. Expence is in the present state of things entailed
upon all governments. Though if we continue united, we
shall be hereafter less exposed to wars by land, than most
other countries; yet while we have powerful neighbours on either extremity, and our frontier is embraced by savages, whose
alliance they may without difficulty command, we cannot, in
prudence, dispense with the usual precautions for our interior
security. As a commercial people, maritime power must be a
primary object of our attention, and a navy cannot be created
or maintained without ample revenues. The nature of our

popular constitutions requires a numerous magistracy, for whom competent provision must be made; or we may be certain our affairs will always be committed to improper hands; and experience will teach us, that no government costs so much as a bad one.

We may preach till we are tired of the theme, the necessity of disinterestedness in republics, without making a single proselyte. The virtuous declaimer will neither persuade himself nor any other person to be content with a double mess of porridge,* instead of a reasonable stipend for his services. We might as soon reconcile ourselves to the Spartan community of goods and wives, to their iron coin, their long beards, or their black broth. There is a total dissimulation in the circumstances, as well as the manners, of society among us; and it is as ridiculous to seek for models in the simple ages of Greece and Rome, as it would be to go in quest of them among the Hottentots and Laplanders.

The public, for the different purposes, that have been mentioned, must always have large demands upon its constituents, and the only question is whether these shall be satisfied by annual grants perpetually renewed—by a perpetual grant once for all or by a compound of permanent and occasional supplies. The last is the wisest course. The Fœderal Government should neither be independent nor too much dependent. It should neither be raised above responsibility or controul, nor should it want the means of maintaining its own weight, authority, dignity and credit. To this end permanent funds are indispensable, but they ought to be of such a nature and so moderate in their amount, as never to be inconvenient. Extraordinary supplies can be the objects of extraordinary grants; and in this salutary medium will consist our true wisdom.

It would seem as if no mode of taxation could be relished but that worst of all modes which now prevails, by assessment. Every proposal for a specific tax is sure to meet with opposition. It has been objected to a poll tax, at a fixed rate, that it will be unequal, as the rich will pay no more than the poor. In the form under which it has been offered in these

---

* It was a custom with the Lacedaemonians when any new Senator was elected, to present him at their public tables with a double allowance as a mark of distinction.

papers, the poor properly speaking are not comprehended, though it is true that beyond the exclusion of the indigent the tax has no reference to the proportion of property; but it should be remembered that it is impossible to devise any specific tax, that will operate equally on the whole community. It must be the province of the legislature to hold the scales with a judicious hand and ballance one by another. The rich must be made to pay for their luxuries; which is the only proper way of taxing their superior wealth.

Do we imagine that our assessments opperate equally? Nothing can be more contrary to the fact. Wherever a discretionary power is lodged in any set of men over the property of their neighbours, they will abuse it. Their passions, prejudices, partialities, dislikes, will have the principal lead in measuring the abilities of those over whom their power extends; and assessors will ever be a set of petty tyrants, too unskilful, if honest, to be possessed of so delicate a trust, and too seldom honest to give them the excuse of want of skill. The genius of liberty reprobates every thing arbitrary or discretionary in taxation. It exacts that every man by a definite and general rule should know what proportion of his property the state demands. Whatever liberty we may boast in theory, it cannot exist in fact, while assessments continue. The admission of them among us is a new proof, how often human conduct reconciles the most glaring opposites; in the present case the most vicious practice of despotic governments, with the freest constitutions and the greatest love of liberty.

The establishment of permanent funds would not only answer the public purposes infinitely better than temporary supplies; but it would be the most effectual way of easing the people. With this basis for procuring credit, the amount of present taxes might be greatly diminished. Large sums of money might be borrowed abroad at a low interest, and introduced into the country to defray the current expences and pay the public debts; which would not only lessen the demand for immediate supplies, but would throw more money into circulation, and furnish the people with greater means of paying the taxes. Though it be a just rule, that we ought not to run in debt to avoid present expence, so far as our faculties extend; yet the propriety of doing it cannot be disputed when

it is apparent, that these are incompetent to the public necessities. Efforts beyond our abilities can only tend to individual
distress and national disappointment.

The product of the three forgoing articles will be as little as
can be required to enable Congress to pay their debts, and restore order into their finances. In addition to these—

The disposal of the unlocated lands will hereafter be a valuable source of revenue, and an immediate one of credit. As it
may be liable to the same condition with the duties on trade,
that is the product of the sales within each state, to be credit-
ted to that state, and as the rights of jurisdiction are not infringed, it seems to be susceptible of no reasonable objection.

Mines in every country constitute a branch of the revenue.
In this where nature has so richly impregnated the bowels of
the earth, they may in time become a valuable one; and as
they require the care and attention of government to bring
them to perfection, this care and a share in the profits of it,
will very properly devolve upon Congress. All the precious
metals should absolutely be the property of the Fœderal Government, and with respect to the others, it should have a discretionary power of reserving in the nature of a tax, such part
as it may judge not inconsistent with the encouragement due
to so important an object. This is rather a future than a present resource.

The reason of allowing Congress to appoint its own officers
of the customs, collectors of taxes, and military officers of
every rank, is to create in the interior of each state a mass of
influence in favour of the Fœderal Government. The great
danger has been shown to be, that it will not have power
enough to defend itself and preserve the union, not that it
will ever become formidable to the general liberty. A mere regard to the interests of the confederacy will never be a principle sufficiently active to curb the ambition and intrigues of
different members. Force cannot effect it: A contest of arms
will seldom be between the common sovereign and a single
refractory member; but between distinct combinations of the
several parts against each other. A sympathy of situations will
be apt to produce associates to the disobedient. The application of force is always disagreeable, the issue uncertain. It will
be wise to obviate the necessity of it, by interesting such a

number of individuals in each state in support of the Fœderal Government, as will be counterpoised to the ambition of others; and will make it difficult for them to unite the people in opposition to the just and necessary measures of the union.

There is something noble and magnificent in the perspective of a great Fœderal Republic, closely linked in the pursuit of a common interest, tranquil and prosperous at home, respectable abroad; but there is something proportionably diminutive and contemptible in the prospect of a number of petty states, with the appearance only of union, jarring, jealous and perverse, without any determined direction, fluctuating and unhappy at home, weak and insignificant by their dissentions, in the eyes of other nations. Happy America! if those, to whom thou hast intrusted the guardianship of thy infancy, know how to provide for thy future repose; but miserable and undone, if their negligence or ignorance permits the spirit of discord to erect her banners on the ruins of thy tranquillity!

*The New-York Packet, and
the American Advertiser, July 4, 1782*

THE BIRTH OF A SON

To Richard Kidder Meade

Albany Augt 27th. 1782

I thank you my dear Meade for your letter of the first of this month which you will perceive has travelled much faster than has been usual with our letters. Our correspondence hitherto has been unfortunate, nor in fact can either of us compliment himself on his punctuality but you were right in concluding that however indolence or accident may interrupt our intercourse, nothing will interrupt our friendship. Mine for you is built on the solid basis of a full conviction that you deserve it and that it is reciprocal and it is the more firmly fixed because you have few competitors. Experience is a continued comment on the worthlessness of the human race and the few exceptions we find have the greater right to be valued in proportion as they are rare. I know few men estimable, fewer amiable & when I meet with one of the last description it is not in my power to withhold my affection.

You reproach me with not having said enough about our little stranger. When I wrote last I was not sufficiently acquainted with him to give you his character. I may now assure you that your daughter when she sees him will not consult you about the choice or will only do it in respect to the rules of decorum. He is truly a very fine young gentleman, the most agreable in his conversation and manners of any I ever knew— nor less remarkable for his intelligence and sweetness of temper. You are not to imagine by my beginning with his mental qualifications that he is defective in personal. It is agreed on all hands, that he is handsome, his features are good, his eye is not only sprightly and expressive but it is full of benignity. His attitude in sitting is by connoisseurs esteemed graceful and he has a method of waving his hand that announces the future orator. He stands however rather awkwardly and his legs have not all the delicate slimness of his fathers. It is feared He may never excel as much in dancing which is probably the only accomplishment in which he will not be a model. If he has any fault in manners, he laughs too much. He has now passed his Seventh Month.

I am glad to find your prospect of being settled approaches. I am sure you will realize all the happiness you promise yourself with your amiable partner. I wish Fortune had not cast our lots at such a distance, Mrs. Meade you, Betsy & myself would make a most affectionate & most happy *partie* quarré.

As to myself I shall sit down in New York when it opens & the period we are told approaches. No man looks forward to a Peace with more pleasure than I do, though no man would sacrifice less to it than myself, If I were not convinced the people sigh for peace. I have been studying the Law for some months and have lately been licenced as an attorney. I wish to prepare myself by October for Examination as a Counsellor but some public avocations may possibly prevent me.

I had almost forgotten to tell you, that I have been pretty unanimously elected by the legislature of this state, a member of Congress to begin to serve in November. I do not hope to reform the State although I shall endeavour to do all the good I can.

Suffer Betsey & me to present our love to Mrs. Meade; she has a sisterly affection for you. My respects if you please to Mr. & Mrs. Fitzhugh.

God Bless you   A Hamilton

Remarks in Congress on Raising Funds

Mr. Hamilton went extensively into the subject; the sum of it was as follows: he observed that funds considered as permanent sources of revenue were of two kinds: 1st. Such as wd. extend generally & uniformly throughout the U.S., & wd. be collected under the authority of Congs. 2dly., such as might be established separately within each State, & might consist of any objects which were chosen by the States, and which might be collected either under the authority of the States or of Congs. Funds of the 1st. kind he contended were preferable; as being 1st., more simple, the difficulties attending the mode of fixing the quotas laid down in the Confederation rendering it extremely complicated & in a manner insuperable; 2d, as being more certain; since the States according to the secd. plan wd. probably retain the collection of the revenue and a vicious system of collection prevailed generally throughout the U.S. a system by which the collectors were chosen by the people & made their offices more subservient to their popularity than to the public revenue; 3d. & as being more œconomical since the collection would be effected with fewer officers under the management of Congress, than under that of the States.

January 27, 1783

Remarks in Congress on Collecting Funds

Mr. Hamilton, in reply to Mr. Elseworth dwelt long on the inefficacy of State funds. He supposed too that greater obstacles would arise to the execution of the plan than to that of a general revenue. As an additional reason for the latter to be collected by officers under the appointment of Congress, he signified that as the energy of the fœderal Govt. was evidently short of the degree necessary for pervading & uniting the States it was expedient to introduce the influence of officers deriving their emoluments from & consequently interested in supporting the power of Congress.

January 28, 1783

THE PROSPECT OF A MUTINY

To George Washington

Sir

Flattering myself that your knowlege of me will induce you to receive the observations I make as dictated by a regard to the public good, I take the liberty to suggest to you my ideas on some matters of delicacy and importance. I view the present juncture as a very interesting one. I need not observe how far the temper and situation of the army make it so. The state of our finances was perhaps never more critical. I am under injunctions which will not permit me to disclose some facts that would at once demonstrate this position, but I think it probable you will be possessed of them through another channel. It is however certain that there has scarcely been a period of the revolution which called more for wisdom and decision in Congress. Unfortunately for us we are a body not governed by reason or foresight but by circumstances. It is probable we shall not take the proper measures, and if we do not a few months may open an embarrassing scene. This will be the case whether we have peace or a continuance of the war.

If the war continues it would seem that the army must in June subsist itself *to defend the* country; if peace should take place it *will* subsist itself to *procure justice to itself.* It appears to be a prevailing opinion in the army that the disposition to recompence their services will cease with the necessity for them, and that if they once lay down their arms, they will part with the means of obtaining justice. It is to be lamented that appearances afford too much ground for their distrust.

It becomes a serious inquiry what will be the true line of policy. The claims of the army urged with moderation, but with firmness, may operate on those weak minds which are influenced by their apprehensions more than their judgments; so as to produce a concurrence in the measures which the exigencies of affairs demand. They may add weight to the applications of Congress to the several states. So far an useful turn may be given to them. But the difficulty will be to keep a *complaining* and *suffering army* within the bounds of moderation.

This Your Excellency's influence must effect. In order to it, it will be adviseable not to discountenance their endeavours to procure redress, but rather by the intervention of confidential and prudent persons, *to take the direction of them.* This however must not appear: it is of moment to the public tranquillity that Your Excellency should preserve the confidence of the army without losing that of the people. This will enable you in case of extremity to guide the torrent, and bring order perhaps even good, out of confusion. 'Tis a part that requires address; but 'tis one which your own situation as well as the welfare of the community points out.

I will not conceal from Your Excellency a truth which it is necessary you should know. An idea is propagated in the army that delicacy carried to an extreme prevents your espousing its interests with sufficient warmth. The falsehood of this opinion no one can be better acquainted with than myself; but it is not the less mischievous for being false. Its tendency is to impair that influence, which you may exert with advantage, should any commotions unhappily ensue, to moderate the pretensions of the army and make their conduct correspond with their duty.

The great *desideratum* at present is the establishment of general funds, which alone can do justice to the Creditors of

the United States (of whom the army forms the most meritorious class), restore public credit and supply the future wants
of government. This is the object of all men of sense; in this
the influence of the army, properly directed, may cooperate.

The intimations I have thrown out will suffice to give Your
Excellency a proper conception of my sentiments. You will
judge of their reasonableness or fallacy; but I persuade myself
you will do justice to my motives.

I have the honor to be With great respect   Your Excel-
lencys Most Obedt servt.   Alex Hamilton

General Knox has the confidence of the army & is a man of
sense. I think he may be safely made use of. Situated as I am
Your Excellency will feel the confidential nature of these observations.

Philadelphia
Feby. 13th, 1783

"CONTENDING FOR A SHADOW"

To George Washington

Sir   Philadelphia, March 17. 1783
   I am duely honored with Your Excellency's letter of the
4th. and 12th. instant. It is much to be regretted though not
to be wondered at, that steps of so inflammatory a tendency
have been taken in the army. Your Excellency has in my opinion acted wisely. The best way is ever not to attempt to stem
a torrent but to divert it.

I am happy to find You coincide in opinion with me on the
conduct proper to be observed by yourself. I am persuaded
more and more it is that which is most consistent with your
own reputation and the public safety.

Our affairs wear a most serious aspect as well foreign as domestic. Before this gets to hand Your Excellency will probably
have seen the provisional articles between Great Britain and
these states. It might at first appearance be concluded that

these will be the prelude to a general peace; but there are strong reasons to doubt the truth of such a conclusion. Obstacles may arise from different quarters, from the demands of Spain & Holland, from the hope in France of greater acquisitions in the East, and perhaps still more probably from the insincerity and duplicity of Lord Shelburne, whose politics founded in the peculiarity of his situation, as well as in the character of the man may well be suspected of insidiousness. I am really apprehensive if peace does not take place, that the negotiations will tend to sow distrusts among the allies and weaken the force of the common league. We have I fear men among us and men in trust who have a hankering after British connection. We have others whose confidence in France savours of credulity. The intrigues of the former and the incautiousness of the latter may be both, though in different degrees, injurious to the American interests; and make it difficult for prudent men to steer a proper course. There are delicate circumstances with respect to the late foreign transactions which I am not at liberty to reveal; but which joined to our internal weaknesses, disorders, follies & prejudices make this country stand upon precarious ground.

Some use perhaps may be made of these ideas to induce moderation in the army. An opinion that their country does not stand upon a secure footing will operate upon the patriotism of the officers against hazarding any domestic commotions.

When I make these observations I cannot forbear adding that if no excesses take place I shall not be sorry that ill-humours have appeared. I shall not regret importunity, if temperate, from the army.

There are good intentions in the Majority of Congress; but there is not sufficient wisdom or decision. There are dangerous prejudices in the particular states opposed to those measures which alone can give stability & prosperity to the Union. There is a fatal opposition to Continental views. Necessity alone can work a reform. But how apply it and how keep it within salutary bounds?

I fear we have been contending for a shadow.

The affair of accounts I considered as having been put on a satisfactory footing. The particular states have been required to settle 'till the first of August 80 and the Superintendant of Finance has been directed to take measures for settling since that period. I shall immediately see him on the subject.

We have had Eight states and a half in favour of a commutation of the half pay for an average of ten years purchase, that is five years full pay instead of half pay for life, which on a calculation of annuities is nearly an equivalent. I hope this will now shortly take place.

We have made considerable progress in a plan to be recommended to the several states for funding all the public debts including those of the army; which is certainly the only way to restore public credit and enable us to continue the war, by borrowing abroad, if it should be necessary to continue it.

I omitted mentioning to Your Excellency that from European intelligence, there is great reason to believe at all events, peace or War, New York will be evacuated in the Spring. It will be a pity if any domestic disturbances should change the plans of the British Court.

I have the honor to be With the greatest respect   Yr Excellency's Most Obed servant

P.S Your Excellency mentions that it has been surmised the plan in agitation was formed in Philadelphia; that combinations have been talked of between the public creditors and the army; and that members of Congress had incouraged the idea. This is partly true. I have myself urged in Congress the propriety of uniting the influence of the public creditors, & the army as a part of them, to prevail upon the states to enter into their views. I have expressed the same sentiments out of doors. Several other members of Congress have done the same. The meaning however of all this was simply that Congress should adopt such a plan as would embrace the relief of all the public creditors including the army; in order that the personal influence of some, the connections of others, and a sense of justice to the army as well as the apprehension of ill consequences might form a mass of influence in each state in favour of the measures of Congress. In this view, as I mentioned to Your Excellency in a former letter, I thought the discontents of the army might be turned to a good account.

I am still of opinion that their earnest, but respectful applications for redress will have a good effect.

As to any combination of *Force* it would only be productive of the horrors of a civil war, might end in the ruin of the Country & would certainly end in the ruin of the army.

A Letter from Phocion
to the Considerate Citizens of New-York
on the Politics of the Day

WHILE not only every personal artifice is employed by a few heated and inconsiderate spirits, to practise upon the passions of the people, but the public papers are made the channel of the most inflammatory and pernicious doctrines, tending to the subversion of all private security and genuine liberty; it would be culpable in those who understand and value the true interests of the community to be silent spectators. It is, however, a common observation, that men, bent upon mischief, are more active in the pursuit of their object, than those who aim at doing good. Hence it is in the present moment, we see the most industrious efforts to violate, the constitution of this state, to trample upon the rights of the subject, and to chicane or infringe the most solemn obligations of treaty; while dispassionate and upright men almost totally neglect the means of counteracting these dangerous attempts. A sense of duty alone calls forth the observations which will be submitted to the good sense of the people in this paper, from one who has more inclination than leisure to serve them; and who has had too deep a share in the common exertions in this revolution, to be willing to see its fruits blasted by the violence of rash or unprincipled men, without at least protesting against their designs.

The persons alluded to, pretend to appeal to the spirit of Whiggism, while they endeavour to put in motion all the furious and dark passions of the human mind. The spirit of Whiggism, is generous, humane, beneficent and just. These men inculcate revenge, cruelty, persecution, and perfidy. The spirit of Whiggism cherishes legal liberty, holds the rights of every individual sacred, condemns or punishes no man without regular trial and conviction of some crime declared by antecedent laws, reprobates equally the punishment of the citizen by arbitrary acts of legislature, as by the lawless combinations of unauthorised individuals: While these men are advocates for expelling a large number of their fellow-citizens unheard, untried; or if they cannot effect this, are for disfranchising them, in the face of the constitution, without the judgment of their peers, and contrary to the law of the land.

The 13th article of the constitution declares, "that no member of this state shall be *disfranchised* or *defrauded of any of the rights or privileges* sacred to the subjects of this state by the constitution, unless *by the law of the land or the judgment of his peers.*" If we enquire what is meant by the law of the land, the best commentators will tell us, that it means *due process of law, that is, by indictment or presentment of good and lawful men*,* and trial and conviction in consequence.

It is true, that *in England,* on extraordinary occasions, attainders for high treason, by act of parliament have been practiced, but many of the ablest advocates for civil liberty have condemned this practice, and it has commonly been exercised with great caution upon individuals only by name, never against *general descriptions* of men. The sense of our constitution on this practice, we may gather from the 41st article, where all attainders, other than for crimes committed during the late war, are forbidden.

If there had been no treaty in the way, the legislature might, by *name,* have attainted particular persons of high treason for crimes committed during the war, but independent of the treaty it could not, and cannot, without tyranny, disfranchise or punish whole classes of citizens by general descriptions, without trial and conviction of offences known by laws previously established declaring the offence and prescribing the penalty.

This is a dictate of natural justice, and a fundamental principle of law and liberty.

Nothing is more common than for a free people, in times of heat and violence, to gratify momentary passions, by letting into the government, principles and precedents which afterwards prove fatal to themselves. Of this kind is the doctrine of disqualification, disfranchisement and banishment by acts of legislature. The dangerous consequences of this power are manifest. If the legislature can disfranchise any number of citizens at pleasure by general descriptions, it may soon con-

---

* Coke upon Magna Charta, Chap. 29, Page 50.

fine all the votes to a small number of partizans, and establish an aristocracy or an oligarchy; if it may banish at discretion all those whom particular circumstances render obnoxious, without hearing or trial, no man can be safe, nor know when he may be the innocent victim of a prevailing faction. The name of liberty applied to such a government would be a mockery of common sense.

The English Whigs, after the revolution, from an overweening dread of popery and the Pretender, from triennial, voted the parliament septennial. They have been trying ever since to undo this false step in vain, and are repenting the effects of their folly in the overgrown power of the new family. Some imprudent Whigs among us, from resentment to those who have taken the opposite side, (and many of them from worse motives) would corrupt the principles of our government, and furnish precedents for future usurpations on the rights of the community.

Let the people beware of such Counsellors. However, a few designing men may rise in consequence, and advance their private interests by such expedients, the people, at large, are sure to be the losers in the event whenever they suffer a departure from the rules of general and equal justice, or from the true principles of universal liberty.

These men, not only overleap the barriers of the constitution without remorse, but they advise us to become the scorn of nations, by violating the solemn engagements of the United States. They endeavour to mould the Treaty with Great-Britain, into such form as pleases them, and to make it mean any thing or nothing as suits their views. They tell us, that all the stipulations, with respect to the Tories, are merely that Congress will recommend, and the States may comply or not as they please.

But let any man of sense and candour read the Treaty, and it will speak for itself. The fifth article is indeed recommendatory; but the sixth is as positive as words can make it. "*There shall be* no future confiscations made, nor prosecutions commenced against any person or persons, for, or by reason of the part which he or they may have taken in the present war, and no person shall, on that account, suffer any future loss or damage, either in his person, liberty, or property."

As to the restoration of confiscated property which is the subject of the fifth article, the states may restore or not as they think proper, because Congress engage only to recommend; but there is not a word about recommendation in the 6th article.

Quotations are made from the debates in Parliament to prove that the whole is understood as recommendatory; but the expressions in those quotations, turn altogether upon those persons who have been actually proscribed and their property confiscated; they have no relation to those who come under the sixth article, or who might be the objects of future prosecution or punishment. And to this it may be added, that it is absurd and inadmissible in fair reasoning, to combat the plain and authentic language of solemn treaty by loose recitals of debates in newspapers.

The sound and ingenuous construction of the two articles taken collectively, is this—that where the property of any persons, other than those who have been in arms against the United States, had been actually confiscated and themselves proscribed, there Congress are to recommend a restoration of estates, rights and properties; and with respect to those who had been in arms, they are to recommend permission for them to remain a twelvemonth in the country to solicit a like restoration: But with respect to all those who were not in this situation, and who had not already been the objects of confiscation and banishment, they were to be absolutely secured from all future injury to person, liberty or property.

To say that this exemption from positive injury, does not imply a right to live among us as citizens, is a pitiful sophistry; it is to say that the banishment of a person from his country, connexions and resources (one of the greatest punishments that can befal a man) is no punishment at all.

The meaning of the word *liberty* has been contested. Its true sense must be the enjoyment of the common privileges of subjects under the same government. There is no middle line of just construction between this sense and a mere exemption from personal imprisonment! If the last were adopted, the stipulation would become nugatory; and by depriving those who are the subjects of it, of the protection of government, it would amount to a virtual confiscation and banishment; for they could not have the benefit of the laws against those who should be aggressors.

Should it be said that they may receive protection without being admitted to a full enjoyment of the privileges of citizens, this must be either matter of right under the treaty, or matter of grace in the government. If the latter, the government may refuse it, and then the objection presents itself, that the treaty would by this construction be virtually defeated; if matter of right, then it follows that more is intended by the word liberty, than a mere exemption from imprisonment, and where shall the line be drawn—not a capricious and arbitrary line, but one warranted by rational and legal construction?

To say that by espousing the cause of Great-Britain they became aliens, and that it will satisfy the treaty to allow them the same protection to which aliens are entitled is to admit that subjects may at pleasure renounce their allegiance to the state of which they are members, and devote themselves to a foreign jurisdiction; a principle contrary to law and subversive of government. But even this will not satisfy the treaty; for aliens cannot hold real property under our government; and if they are aliens, all their real estates belong to the public. This will be to all intents and purposes, a confiscation of property. But this is not all, how does it appear that the persons who are thus to be stripped of their citizenship, have been guilty of such an adherence to the enemy, as in legal contemplation amounts to a crime. Their merely remaining in their possessions under the power of the conqueror does not imply this; but is executed by the laws and customs of all civilized nations. To adjudge them culpable, they must be first tried and convicted; and this the treaty forbids. These are the difficulties involved, by recurring to subtle and evasive instead of simple and candid construction, which will teach us that the stipulations in the treaty, amount to an amnesty and act of oblivion.

There is a very simple and conclusive point of view in which this subject may be placed. No citizen can be deprived of any right which the citizens in general are entitled to, unless forfeited by some offence. It has been seen that the regular and constitutional mode of ascertaining whether this forfeiture has been incurred, is by legal process, trial and conviction. This *ex vi termini*, supposes prosecution. Now consistent with the treaty there can be no future prosecution for any thing done on account of the war. Can we then do by act of legislature, what the treaty disables us from doing by due course of law? This would be to imitate the Roman General, who having promised Antiochus to restore half his vessels, caused them to be sawed in two before their delivery; or the Platææ, who having promised the Thebans to restore their prisoners, had them first put to death and returned them dead.

Such fraudulent subterfuges are justly considered more odious than an open and avowed violation of treaty.

When these posture-masters in logic are driven from this first ground of the meaning of the treaty; they are forced to that of attacking the right of Congress to make such a stipulation, and arraigning the impudence of Great-Britain in attempting to make terms for our own subjects. But here as every where else, they are only successful in betraying their narrowness and ignorance.

Does not the act of confederation place the exclusive right of war and peace in the United States in Congress? Have they not the sole power of making treaties with foreign nations? Are not these among the first rights of sovereignty, and does not the delegation of them to the general confederacy, so far abridge the sovereignty of each particular state? Would not a different doctrine involve the contradiction of *imperium in imperio*? What reasonable limits can be assigned to these prerogatives of the union, other than the general safety and the *fundamentals* of the constitution? Can it be said that a treaty for arresting the future operation of positive acts of legislature, and which has indeed no other effect than that of a pardon for past offences committed against these acts, is an attack upon the fundamentals of the state constitutions? Can it be denied that the peace which was made, taken collectively, was manifestly for the general good; that it was even favourable to the solid interests of this country, beyond the expectation of the most sanguine? If this cannot be denied; and none can deny it who know either the value of the objects gained by the treaty, or the necessity these states were under at the time of making peace?—It follows that Congress and their Ministers acted wisely in making the treaty which has been made; and it follows from this, that these states are bound by it, and ought religiously to observe it.

The *uti possiedetis, each party to hold what it possesses*, is the point from which nations set out in framing a treaty of peace; if one side gives up a part of its acquisitions, the other side renders an equivalent in some other way. What is the equivalent given to Great-Britain for all the important concessions she has made. She has rendered the capital of this state and its large dependencies. She is to surrender our immensely valuable posts on the frontier, and to yield to us a vast tract of western territory, with one half of the Lakes, by which we shall command almost the whole furr trade; she renounces to us her claim to the navigation of the Mississippi, and admits us a share in the fisheries, even on better terms than we formerly enjoyed it. As she was in possession by right of war of all these objects, whatever may have been our original pretensions to them, they are by the laws of nations to be considered as so much given up on her part; and what do we give in return? We stipulate that there shall be no future injury to her adherents among us. How insignificant the equivalent in comparison with the acquisition! A man of sense would be ashamed to compare them: A man of honesty, not intoxicated with passion, would blush to lisp a question of the obligation to observe the stipulation on our part.

If it be said that Great-Britain has only restored to us what she had unjustly taken from us, and that therefore we are not bound to make compensation—This admits of several answers. First, That the fact is not true, for she had ceded to us a large tract of country to which we had even no plausible claim: Secondly, That however the principle of the objection might have been proper to prevent our promising an equivalent, it comes too late after the promise has been made: Thirdly, That as to the external effects of war, the voluntary law of nations knows no distinction between the justice or injustice of the quarrel; but in the treaty of peace puts the contracting parties upon an equal footing; which is a necessary consequence of the independence of nations; for as they acknowledge no common judge, if in concluding peace both parties were not to stand upon the same ground of right, there never could be an adjustment of differences or an end of war. This is a settled principle.

Let us examine the pretext upon which it is disputed. Congress, say our political jugglers, have no right to meddle with our internal police. They would be puzzled to tell what they mean by the expression. The truth is, it has no definite meaning; for it is impossible for Congress to do a single act which will not directly or indirectly affect the internal police of every state. When in order to procure privileges of commerce to the citizens of these states in foreign countries, they stipulate a reciprocity of privileges here, does not such an admission of the subjects of foreign countries to certain rights within these states operate, immediately upon their internal police? And were this not done, would not the power of making commercial treaties vested in Congress, become a mere nullity? In short if nothing was to be done by Congress that would affect our internal police, in the large sense in which it has been taken, would not all the powers of the confederation be annihilated and the union dissolved?

But say they again, such a thing was never heard of as an indemnity for traiterous subjects stipulated in a treaty of peace. History will inform them that it is a stipulation often made. Two examples shall be cited: The treaty of Munster which put an end to the differences between Spain and the United Provinces, after the revolution of those provinces: The treaty concluded in 1738, between the Empire, France, Spain, Poland, and several other powers, called the Christian peace. The war which preceded this treaty was one of the most complicated in which Europe had been engaged; the succession to the Spanish Monarchy, and the right to the throne of Poland had been included in it, Stanislaus having been obliged to abdicate the crown. Different parts of the nations concerned had taken opposite sides. Many of the German Princes had been in arms against the Empire to which they owed obedience: This treaty not only mutually stipulates indemnity to the subjects of the respective powers, but even restitution of *property* and *offices*. The Emperor, who contracted in behalf of the Empire, has much less extensive powers as head of the Empire, than Congress as representative of the United States.

But let it be admitted that Congress had no right to enter into this article. Do not equity and prudence strongly urge the several states to comply with it? We have in part enjoyed the benefit of the treaty; in consequence of which, we of this state are now in possession of our capital; and this implies an obligation in conscience, to perform what is to be performed on our part. But there is a consideration which will perhaps have more force with men, who seem to be superior to conscientious obligations; it is that the British are still in possession of our frontier posts, which they may keep in spite of us; and that they may essentially exclude us from the fisheries if they are so disposed. Breach of treaty on our part will be a just ground for breaking it on theirs. The treaty must stand or fall together. The wilful breach of a single article annuls the whole.* Congress are appointed by the constitution to manage our foreign concerns. The nations with whom they contract are to suppose they understand their own powers and will not exceed them. If they do it in any instance, and we think it proper to disavow the act, it will be no apology to those with whom they contract that they had exceeded their authority. One side cannot be bound unless the obligation is reciprocal.

Suppose then Great-Britain should be induced to refuse a further compliance with the treaty, in consequence of a breach of it on our part, what situation should we be in? Can we renew the war to compel a compliance? We know, and all the world knows, it is out of our power. Will those who have heretofore assisted us take our part? Their affairs require peace as well as ours, and they will not think themselves bound to undertake an unjust war to regain to us rights which we have forfeited by a childish levity and a wanton contempt of public faith.

We should then have sacrificed important interests to the little vindictive selfish mean passions of a few. To say nothing of the loss of territory, of the disadvantage to the whole commerce of the union, by obstructions in the fisheries; this state would loose an annual profit of more than £.50,000 *Sterling*, from the furr trade.

---

* Vatel, Book 4, Ch. 4, § 47. Grotius, Book 3, Ch. 19, § 14.

But not to insist on possible inconveniences, there is a certain evil which attends our intemperance, a loss of character in Europe. Our Ministers write that our conduct, hitherto, in this respect, has done us infinite injury, and has exhibited us in the light of a people, destitute of government, on whose engagements of course no dependence can be placed.

The men who are at the head of the party which contends for disqualification and expulsion, endeavoured to inlist a number of people on their side by holding out motives of private advantage to them. To the trader they say, you will be overborne by the large capitals of the Tory merchants; to the Mechanic, your business will be less profitable, your wages less considerable by the interference of Tory workmen. A man, the least acquainted with trade, will indeed laugh at such suggestion. He will know, that every merchant or trader has an interest in the aggregate mass of capital or stock in trade; that what he himself wants in capital, he must make up in credit; that unless there are others who possess large capitals, this credit cannot be had, and that in the diminution of the general capital of the State, commerce will decline, and his own prospects of profit will diminish.

These arguments, if they were understood, would be conclusive with the Mechanic: "There is already employment enough for all the workmen in the city, and wages are sufficiently high. If you could raise them by expelling those who have remained in the city, and whom you consider as rivals, the extravagant price of wages would have two effects; it would draw persons to settle here, not only from other parts of this State, but from the neighbouring States: Those classes of the community who are to employ you, will make a great many shifts rather than pay the exorbitant prices you demand; a man will wear his old cloaths so much longer before he gets a new suit; he will buy imported shoes cheap rather than those made here at so dear a rate: The owner of a house will defer the repairs as long as possible; he will only have those which are absolutely necessary made; he will not attend to elegant improvement, and the like will happen in other branches. These circumstances will give you less employment, and in a very little time bring back your wages to what they now are, and even sink them lower. But this is not all: You are not required merely to expel your rival mechanics, but you must drive away the rich merchants and others who are called Tories, to please your leaders, who will persuade you they are dangerous to your liberty (though in fact they only mean their own consequence.) By this conduct you will drive away the principal part of those who have the means of becoming large undertakers. The Carpenters and Masons in particular, must be content with patching up the houses already built and building little huts upon the vacant lots, instead of having profitable and durable employment in erecting large and elegant edifices."

There is a certain proportion or level in all the departments of industry. It is folly to think to raise any of them, and keep them long above their natural height. By attempting to do it the œconomy of the political machine is disturbed, and till things return to their proper state, the society at large suffers. The only object of concern with an industrious artisan, as such, ought to be, that there may be plenty of money in the community, and a brisk commerce to give it circulation and activity. All attempts at profit, through the medium of monopoly or violence, will be as fallacious as they are culpable.

But say some, to suffer these wealthy disaffected men to remain among us, will be dangerous to our liberties; enemies to our government, they will be always endeavouring to undermine it and bring us back to the subjection of Great-Britain. The safest reliance of every government is on mens interests. This is a principle of human nature, on which all political speculation to be just, must be founded. Make it the interest of those citizens, who, during the revolution, were opposed to us to be friends to the new government, by affording them not only protection, but a participation in its privileges, and they will undoubtedly become its friends. The apprehension of returning under the dominion of Great Britain is chimerical; if there is any way to bring it about, the measures of those men, against whose conduct these remarks are aimed, lead directly to it. A disorderly or a violent government may disgust the best citizens, and make the body of the people tired of their Independence.

The embarrassed and exhausted state of Great-Britain, and the political system of Europe, render it impossible for her ever to reacquire the dominion of this country. Her former partizans must be convinced of this, and abandon her cause as desperate. They will never be mad enough to risk their fortunes a second time in the hopeless attempt of restoring her authority; nor will they have any inclination to do it, if they are allowed to be happy under the government of the society in which they live. To make it practicable, if they should be so disposed, they must not only get the government of this state, but of the United States into their hands. To suppose this possible, is to suppose that a majority of the numbers, property and abilities of the United States has been and is in opposition to the revolution. Its success is a clear proof that this has not been the case; and every man of information among us, knows the contrary. The supposition itself would show the absurdity, of expelling a small number from the city, which would constitute so insignificant a proportion of the whole, as without diminishing their influence, would only increase their disposition to do mischief. The policy in this case would be evident, of appealing to their interests rather than to their fears.

Nothing can be more ridiculous than the idea of expelling a few from this city and neighbourhood, while there are numbers in different parts of this and other states, who must necessarily partake in our governments, and who can never expect to be the objects of animadversion or exclusion. It is confirming *many* in their enmity and prejudices against the state, to indulge our enmity and prejudices against a few.

The idea of suffering the Tories to live among us under disqualifications, is equally mischievous and absurd. It is necessitating a large body of citizens in the state to continue enemies to the government, ready, at all times, in a moment of commotion, to throw their weight into that scale which meditates a change whether favourable or unfavourable to public liberty.

Viewing the subject in every possible light, there is not a single interest of the community but dictates moderation rather than violence. That honesty is still the best policy; that justice and moderation are the surest supports of every government, are maxims, which however they may be called trite, at all times true, though too seldom regarded, but rarely neglected with impunity. Were the people of America, with one voice, to ask, What shall we do to perpetuate our liberties and secure our happiness? The answer would be, "govern well" and you have nothing to fear either from internal disaffection or external hostility. Abuse not the power you possess, and you need never apprehend its diminution or loss. But if you make a wanton use of it, if you furnish another example, that despotism may debase the government of the many as well as the few, you like all others that have acted the same part, will experience that licentiousness is the forerunner to slavery.

How wise was that policy of Augustus, who after conquering his enemies, when the papers of Brutus were brought to him, which would have disclosed all his secret associates, immediately ordered them to be burnt. He would not even know his enemies, that they might cease to hate when they had nothing to fear.

How laudable was the example of Elizabeth, who when she was transfered from the prison to the throne, fell upon her knees and thanking Heaven, for the deliverance it had granted her, from her bloody persecutors; dismissed her resentment. "This act of pious gratitude says the historian, seems to have been the last circumstance in which she remembered any past injuries and hardships. With a prudence and magnanimity truly laudable, she buried all offences in oblivion, and received with affability even those, who had acted with the greatest virulence against her." She did more—she retained many of the opposite party in her councils.

The reigns of these two sovereigns, are among the most illustrious in history. Their moderation gave a stability to their government, which nothing else could have affected. This was the secret of uniting all parties.

These sentiments are delivered to you in the frankness of conscious integrity, by one who *feels* that solicitude for the good of the community which the zealots, whose opinions he encounters profess, by one who pursues not as they do, the honour or emoluments of his country, by one who, though he has had, in the course of the Revolution, a very *confidential* share in the public councils, civil and military, and has as often, at least, met danger in the common cause as any of those who now assume to be the guardians of the public liberty, asks no other reward of his countrymen, than to be heard without prejudice for their own interest.   PHOCION.

P.S. While the writer hopes the sentiments of this letter will meet the approbation of discreet and honest men, he thinks it necessary to apologize for the hasty and incorrect manner. Perhaps too, expressions of too much asperity have been employed against those who take the lead in the principles which are here opposed; and feelings of indignation against the pernicious tendency of their measures, have not admitted sufficient allowances for what is, in some instances, an honest, though mistaken, zeal. Though the writer entertains the worst opinion of the motives of many of them, he believes there are some who act from principle.

January 1784

"I FEEL ALL THE SENTIMENT OF A BROTHER"

To James Hamilton

My Dear Brother: New York, June 22, 1785.
I have received your letter of the 31st of May last, which, and one other, are the only letters I have received from you in many years. I am a little surprised you did not receive one which I wrote to you about six months ago. The situation you describe yourself to be in gives me much pain, and nothing will make me happier than, as far as may be in my power, to contribute to your relief. I will cheerfully pay your draft upon me for fifty pounds sterling, whenever it shall appear. I wish it was in my power to desire you to enlarge the sum; but though my future prospects are of the most flattering kind my present engagements would render it inconvenient to me to advance you a larger sum. My affection for you, however, will not permit me to be inattentive to your welfare, and I hope time will prove to you that I feel all the sentiment of a brother. Let me only request of you to exert your industry for a year or two more where you are, and at the end of that time

I promise myself to be able to invite you to a more comfortable settlement in this Country. Allow me only to give you one caution, which is to avoid if possible getting in debt. Are you *married* or *single*? If the *latter*, it is my wish for many reasons it may be agreeable to you to continue in that state.

But what has become of our dear father? It is an age since I have heared from him or of him, though I have written him several letters. Perhaps, alas! he is no more, and I shall not have the pleasing opportunity of contributing to render the close of his life more happy than the progress of it. My heart bleeds at the recollection of his misfortunes and embarrassments. Sometimes I flatter myself his brothers have extended their support to him, and that he now enjoys tranquillity and ease. At other times I fear he is suffering in indigence. I entreat you, if you can, to relieve me from my doubts, and let me know how or where he is, if alive, if dead, how and where he died. Should he be alive inform him of my inquiries, beg him to write to me, and tell him how ready I shall be to devote myself and all I have to his accommodation and happiness.

I do not advise your coming to this country at present, for the war has also put things out of order here, and people in your business find a subsistence difficult enough. My object will be, by-and-by, to get you settled on a farm.

Believe me always your affectionate friend and brother,

Alex. Hamilton.

Address of the Annapolis Convention

To the Honorable the Legislatures of Virginia, Delaware Pennsylvania, New Jersey, and New York.

The Commissioners from the said states, respectively assembled at Annapolis, humbly beg leave to report.

That, pursuant to their several appointments, they met, at Annapolis in the State of Maryland, on the eleventh day of September Instant, and having proceeded to a Communication of their powers; they found, that the States of New York, Pennsylvania and Virginia had, in substance, and nearly in the same terms, authorised their respective Commissioners "to meet such commissioners as were, or might be, appointed by the other States in the Union, at such time and place, as should be agreed upon by the said Commissioners to take into consideration the trade and Commerce of the United States, to consider how far an uniform system in their commercial intercourse and regulations might be necessary to their common interest and permanent harmony, and to report to the several States, such an Act, relative to this great object, as when unanimously ratified by them would enable the United States in Congress assembled effectually to provide for the same."

That the State of Delaware, had given similar powers to their Commissioners, with this difference only that the Act to be framed in virtue of those powers, is required to be reported "to the United States in Congress Assembled, to be agreed to by them, and confirmed by the Legislatures of every State."

That the State of New Jersey had enlarged the object of their Appointment, empowering their Commissioners, "to consider how far an uniform system in their commercial regulations and *other important matters*, might be necessary to the common interest and permanent harmony of the several States," and to report such an Act on the subject, as when ratified by them "would enable the United States in Congress Assembled, effectually to provide for the exigencies of the Union."

That appointments of Commissioners have also been made

by the States of New Hampshire, Massachusetts, Rhode Island, and North Carolina, none of whom however have attended; but that no information has been received by your Commissioners of any appointments having been made by the States of Connecticut, Maryland, South Carolina, or Georgia.

That the express terms of the powers to your Commissioners supposing a deputation from all the States, and having for object the Trade and Commerce of the United States, Your Commissioners did not conceive it advisable to proceed on the business of their mission, under the Circumstance of so partial and defective a representation.

Deeply impressed however with the magnitude and importance of the object confided to them on this occasion, your Commissioners cannot forbear to indulge an expression of their earnest and unanimous wish, that speedy measures may be taken, to effect a general meeting, of the States, in a future Convention, for the same and such other purposes, as the situation of public affairs, may be found to require.

If in expressing this wish, or in intimating any other sentiment, your Commissioners should seem to exceed the strict bounds of their appointment, they entertain a full confidence, that a conduct, dictated by an anxiety for the welfare, of the United States, will not fail to receive an indulgent construction.

In this persuasion your Commissioners submit an opinion, that the Idea of extending the powers of their Deputies, to other objects, than those of Commerce, which has been adopted by the State of New Jersey, was an improvement on the original plan, and will deserve to be incorporated into that of a future Convention; they are the more naturally led to this conclusion, as in the course of their reflections on the subject, they have been induced to think, that the power of regulating trade is of such comprehensive extent, and will enter so far into the general System of the fœderal government, that to give it efficacy, and to obviate questions and doubts concerning its precise nature and limits, may require a correspondent adjustment of other parts of the Fœderal System.

That there are important defects in the system of the Fœderal Government is acknowledged by the Acts of all those States, which have concurred in the present Meeting; That the defects, upon a closer examination, may be found greater and more numerous, than even these acts imply, is at least so far probable, from the embarrassments which characterise the present State of our national affairs—foreign and domestic, as may reasonably be supposed to merit a deliberate and candid discussion, in some mode, which will unite the Sentiments and Councils of all the States. In the choice of the mode your Commissioners are of opinion, that a Convention of Deputies from the different States, for the special and sole purpose of entering into this investigation, and digesting a plan for supplying such defects as may be discovered to exist, will be entitled to a preference from consideration, which will occur, without being particularised.

Your Commissioners decline an enumeration of those national circumstances on which their opinion respecting the propriety of a future Convention with more enlarged powers, is founded; as it would be an useless intrusion of facts and observations, most of which have been frequently the subject of public discussion, and none of which can have escaped the penetration of those to whom they would in this instance be addressed. They are however of a nature so serious, as, in the view of your Commissioners to render the Situation of the United States delicate and critical, calling for an exertion of the united virtue and wisdom of all the members of the Confederacy.

Under this impression, Your Commissioners, with the most respectful deference, beg leave to suggest their unanimous conviction, that it may essentially tend to advance the interests of the union, if the States, by whom they have been respectively delegated, would themselves concur, and use their endeavours to procure the concurrence of the other States, in the appointment of Commissioners, to meet at Philadelphia on the second Monday in May next, to take into consideration the situation of the United States, to devise such further provisions as shall appear to them necessary to render the constitution of the Fœderal Government adequate to the exigencies of the Union; and to report such an Act for that purpose to the United States in Congress Assembled, as when agreed to, by them, and afterwards confirmed by the Legislatures of every State will effectually provide for the same.

Though your Commissioners could not with propriety address these observations and sentiments to any but the States they have the honor to Represent, they have nevertheless concluded from motives of respect, to transmit Copies of this report to the United States in Congress assembled, and to the executives of the other States.

By order of the Commissioners

Dated at Annapolis ⎫
September 14th. 1786 ⎭

Resolved that the Chairman sign the aforegoing Report in behalf of the Commissioners

Then adjourned without day.

Egbt: Benson Alexander Hamilton	New York
Abra: Clark Wm Chls Houston Js. Schureman	New Jersey
Tench Coxe	Pennsylvania
Geo: Read John Dickinson Richard Bassett	Delaware
Edmund Randolph Js. Madison Jr. St. George Tucker	Virginia

FRAMING AND RATIFYING
THE CONSTITUTION
1787–1789

Plan of Government

I   The Supreme Legislative Power of the United States of America to be vested in two distinct bodies of men—the one to be called the *Assembly* the other the *senate*; who together shall form the Legislature of the United States, with power to pass all *laws whatsoever*, subject to the *negative* hereafter mentioned.

II   The Assembly to consist of persons elected *by the People* to serve for three years.

III   The Senate to consist of persons elected to serve during *good behaviour*. Their election to be made by *Electors* chosen for that purpose by the People. In order to this The States to be divided into election districts. On the death removal or resignation of any senator his place to be filled out of the district from which he came.

IV   The Supreme Executive authority of the United States to be vested in a *governor* to be elected to serve *during good behaviour*. His election to be made by *Electors* chosen by *electors* chosen by the people in the election districts aforesaid or by electors chosen for that purpose by the respective legislatures—provided that if an election be not made within a limited time the President of the Senate shall be the Governor. The Governor to have *a negative* upon all laws about to be passed and to have the execution of all laws passed—to be the Commander in Chief of the land and naval forces and of the Militia of the United States—to have the direction of war, when authorised or began—to have with the *advice* and *approbation* of the Senate the power of making all treaties—to have the appointment of the *heads or chief* officers of the departments of finance war and foreign affairs—to have the *nomination* of all other officers (ambassadors to foreign nations included) subject to the approbation or rejection of the Senate—to have the power of pardoning all offences but *treason*, which he shall not pardon without the approbation of the Senate.

V   On the death resignation or removal of the Governor his authorities to be exercised by the President of the Senate.

K   VI   The Senate to have the sole power of *declaring war*—the power of advising and approving all treaties—the power of approving or rejecting all appointments of officers except the heads or chiefs of the departments of finance war and foreign affairs.

VII   The Supreme Judicial authority of the United States to be vested in twelve Judges, to hold their offices during good behaviour with adequate and permanent salaries. This Court to have original jurisdiction in all causes of capture and an appellative jurisdiction (from the Courts of the several states) in all causes in which the revenues of the general government or the citizens of foreign nations are concerned.

L   VIII   The Legislature of the United States to have power to institute Courts in each state for the determination of all causes of capture and of all matters relating to their revenues, or in which the citizens of foreign nations are concerned.

IX   The Governor Senators and all Officers of the United States to be liable to impeachment for mal and corrupt conduct, and upon conviction to be removed from office and disqualified for holding any place of trust or profit. All impeachments to be tried by a Court to consist of the judges of the Supreme Court chief or Senior Judge of the superior Court of law of each state—provided that such judge hold his place during good behaviour and have a permanent salary.

X   All laws of the particular states contrary to the constitution or laws of the United States to be utterly void. And the better to prevent such laws being passed the Governor or President of each state shall *be appointed by the general gov-*

M   *ernment* and shall have a *negative* upon the laws about to be passed in the state of which he is governor or President.

XI   No state to have any forces land or naval—and the *Mili-*

N   *tia* of all the states to be under the sole and *exclusive direction* of the United States *the officers* of which to be appointed and commissioned by them.

c. June 18, 1787

Speech in the Constitutional Convention
on a Plan of Government

Version recorded by James Madison

Mr. Hamilton, had been hitherto silent on the business before the Convention, partly from respect to others whose superior abilities age & experience rendered him unwilling to bring forward ideas dissimilar to theirs, and partly from his delicate situation with respect to his own State, to whose sentiments as expressed by his Colleagues, he could by no means accede. The crisis however which now marked our affairs, was too serious to permit any scruples whatever to prevail over the duty imposed on every man to contribute his efforts for the public safety & happiness. He was obliged therefore to declare himself unfriendly to both plans. He was particularly opposed to that from N. Jersey, being fully convinced, that no amendment of the Confederation, leaving the States in possession of their Sovereignty could possibly answer the purpose. On the other hand he confessed he was much discouraged by the amazing extent of Country in expecting the desired blessings from any general sovereignty that could be substituted. As to the powers of the Convention, he thought the doubts started on that subject had arisen from distinctions & reasonings too subtle. A *federal* Govt. he conceived to mean an association of independent Communities into one. Different Confederacies have different powers, and exercise them in different ways. In some instances the powers are exercised over collective bodies; in others over individuals, as in the German Diet—& among ourselves in cases of piracy. Great latitude therefore must be given to the signification of the term. The plan last proposed departs itself from the *federal* idea, as understood by some, since it is to operate eventually on individuals. He agreed moreover with the Honble gentleman from Va. (Mr. R.) that we owed it to our Country, to do on this emergency whatever we should deem essential to its happiness. The States sent us here to provide for the exigences of the Union. To rely on & propose any plan not adequate to these exigences, merely because it was not clearly within our powers, would be to sacrifice the means to the end. It may be said that the *States* can not *ratify* a plan not within the purview of the article of Confederation providing for alterations & amendments. But may not the States themselves in which no constitutional authority equal to this purpose exists in the Legislatures, have had in view a reference to the people at large. In the Senate of N. York, a proviso was moved, that no act of the Convention should be binding untill it should be referred to the people & ratified; and the motion was lost by a single voice only, the reason assigned agst. it being, that it might possibly be found an inconvenient shackle.

The great question is what provision shall we make for the happiness of our Country? He would first make a comparative examination of the two plans—prove that there were essential defects in both—and point out such changes as might render a *national one*, efficacious. The great & essential principles necessary for the support of Government are 1. an active & constant interest in supporting it. This principle does not exist in the States in favor of the federal Govt. They have evidently in a high degree, the esprit de corps. They constantly pursue internal interests adverse to those of the whole. They have their particular debts—their particular plans of finance &c. All these when opposed to, invariably prevail over the requisitions & plans of Congress. 2. The love of power. Men love power. The same remarks are applicable to this principle. The States have constantly shewn a disposition rather to regain the powers delegated by them than to part with more, or to give effect to what they had parted with. The ambition of their demagogues is known to hate the controul of the Genl. Government. It may be remarked too that the Citizens have not that anxiety to prevent a dissolution of the Genl. Govt. as of the particular Govts. A dissolution of the latter would be fatal; of the former would still leave the purposes of Govt. attainable to a considerable degree. Consider what such a State as Virga. will be in a few years, a few compared with the life of nations. How strongly will it feel its importance & self-sufficiency? 3. An habitual attachment of the people. The whole force of this tie is on the side of the State Govt. Its sovereignty is immediately before the eyes of the people: its protection is immediately enjoyed by them. From its hand distributive justice, and all those acts which familiarize & endear Govt. to a people, are dispensed to them. 4. *Force* by which may be understood a *coertion of laws* or *coertion of arms.* Congs. have not the former except in few cases. In particular States, this coercion is nearly sufficient; tho' he held it in most cases, not entirely so. A certain portion of military force is absolutely necessary in large communities. Masss. is now feeling this necessity & making provision for it. But how can this force be exerted on the States collectively. It is impossible. It amounts to a war between the parties. Foreign powers also will not be idle spectators. They will interpose, the confusion will increase, and a dissolution of the Union will ensue. 5. *influence.* he did not mean corruption, but a dispensation of those regular honors & emoluments, which produce an attachment to the Govt. Almost all the weight of these is on the side of the States; and must continue so as long as the States continue to exist. All the passions then we see, of avarice, ambition, interest, which govern most individuals, and all public bodies, fall into the current of the States, and do not flow in the stream of the Genl. Govt. The former therefore will generally be an overmatch for the Genl. Govt. and render any confederacy, in its very nature precarious. Theory is in this case fully confirmed by experience. The Amphyctionic Council had it would seem ample powers for general purposes. It had in particular the power of fining and using force agst. delinquent members. What was the consequence. Their decrees were mere signals of war. The Phocian war is a striking example of it. Philip at length taking advantage of their disunion, and insinuating himself into their Councils, made himself master of their fortunes. The German Confederacy affords another lesson. The authority of Charlemagne seemed to be as great as could be necessary. The great feudal chiefs however, exercising their local sovereignties, soon felt the spirit & found the means of, encroachments, which reduced the imperial authority to a nominal sovereignty. The Diet has succeeded, which tho' aided by a Prince at its head, of great authority independently of his imperial attributes, is a striking illustration of the weakness of Confederated Governments.

Other examples instruct us in the same truth. The Swiss cantons have scarce any Union at all, and have been more than once at war with one another. How then are all these evils to be avoided? only by such a compleat sovereignty in the general Governmt. as will turn all the strong principles & passions above mentioned on its side. Does the scheme of N. Jersey produce this effect? does it afford any substantial remedy whatever? On the contrary it labors under great defects, and the defect of some of its provisions will destroy the efficacy of others. It gives a direct revenue to Congs. but this will not be sufficient. The balance can only be supplied by requisitions: which experience proves can not be relied on. If States are to deliberate on the mode, they will also deliberate on the object of the supplies, and will grant or not grant as they approve or disapprove of it. The delinquency of one will invite and countenance it in others. Quotas too must in the nature of things be so unequal as to produce the same evil. To what standard will you resort? Land is a fallacious one. Compare Holland with Russia: France or Engd. with other countries of Europe. Pena. with N. Carola. will the relative pecuniary abilities in those instances, correspond with the relative value of land. Take numbers of inhabitants for the rule and make like comparison of different countries, and you will find it to be equally unjust. The different degrees of industry and improvement in different Countries render the first object a precarious measure of wealth. Much depends too on *situation*. Cont. N. Jersey & N. Carolina, not being commercial States & contributing to the wealth of the commercial ones, can never bear quotas assessed by the ordinary rules of proportion. They will & must fail in their duty, their example will be followed, and the Union itself be dissolved. Whence then is the national revenue to be drawn? from Commerce? even from exports which notwithstanding the common opinion are fit objects of moderate taxation, from excise, &c &c. These tho' not equal, are less unequal than quotas. Another destructive ingredient in the plan, is that equality of suffrage which is so much desired by the small States. It is not in human nature that Va. & the large States should consent to it, or if they did that they shd. long abide by it. It shocks too much the ideas of Justice, and every human feeling. Bad principles in a Govt. tho slow are sure in their operation, and will gradually destroy it. A doubt has been raised whether Congs. at present have a right to keep Ships or troops in time of peace. He leans to the negative. Mr. Ps. plan provides no remedy. If the powers proposed were adequate, the organization of Congs. is such that they could never be properly & effectually exercised. The members of Congs. being chosen by the States & subject to recall, represent all the local prejudices. Should the powers be found effectual, they will from time to time be heaped on them, till a tyrannic sway shall be established. The general power whatever be its form if it preserves itself, must swallow up the State powers. Otherwise it will be swallowed up by them. It is agst. all the principles of a good Government to vest the requisite powers in such a body as Congs. Two Sovereignties can not co-exist within the same limits. Giving powers to Congs. must eventuate in a bad Govt. or in no Govt. The plan of N. Jersey therefore will not do. What then is to be done? Here he was embarrassed. The extent of the Country to be governed, discouraged him. The expence of a general Govt. was also formidable; unless there were such a diminution of expence on the side of the State Govts. as the case would admit. If they were extinguished, he was persuaded that great œconomy might be obtained by substituting a general Govt. He did not mean however to shock the public opinion by proposing such a measure. On the other hand he saw no *other* necessity for declining it. They are not necessary for any of the great purposes of commerce, revenue, or agriculture. Subordinate authorities he was aware would be necessary. There must be district tribunals: corporations for local purposes. But cui bono, the vast & expensive apparatus now appertaining to the States. The only difficulty of a serious nature which occurred to him, was that of drawing representatives from the extremes to the center of the Community. What inducements can be offered that will suffice? The moderate wages for the 1st. branch would only be a bait to little demagogues. Three dollars or thereabouts he supposed would be the utmost. The Senate he feared from a similar cause, would be filled by certain undertakers who wish for particular offices under the Govt. This view of the subject almost led him to despair that a Republican Govt. could be established over so great an extent. He was sensible at the same time that it would be unwise to propose one of any other form. In his private opinion he had no scruple in declaring, supported as he was by the opinions of so many of the wise & good, that the British Govt. was the best in the world: and that he doubted much whether any thing short of it would do in America. He hoped Gentlemen of different opinions would bear with him in this, and begged them to recollect the change of opinion on this subject which had taken place and was still going on. It was once thought that the power of Congs. was amply sufficient to secure the end of their institution. The error was now seen by every one. The members most tenacious of republicanism, he observed, were as loud as any in declaiming agst. the vices of democracy. This progress of the public mind led him to anticipate the time, when others as well as himself would join in the praise bestowed by Mr. Neckar on the British Constitution, namely, that it is the only Govt. in the world "which unites public strength with individual security." In every community where industry is encouraged, there will be a division of it into the few & the many. Hence separate interests will arise. There will be debtors & creditors &c. Give all power to the many, they will oppress the few. Give all power to the few, they will oppress the many. Both therefore ought to have power, that each may defend itself agst. the other. To the want of this check we owe our paper money, instalment laws &c. To the proper adjustment of it the British owe the excellence of their Constitution. Their house of Lords is a most noble institution. Having nothing to hope for by a change, and a sufficient interest by means of their property, in being faithful to the national interest, they form a permanent barrier agst. every pernicious innovation, whether attempted on the part of the Crown or of the Commons. No temporary Senate will have the firmness eno' to answer the purpose. The Senate (of Maryland) which seems to be so much appealed to, has not yet been sufficiently tried. Had the people been unanimous & eager, in the late appeal to them on the subject of a paper emission they would have yielded to the torrent. Their acquiescing in such an appeal is a proof of it. Gentlemen differ in their opinions concerning the necessary checks, from the different estimates they form of the human passions. They suppose seven years a sufficient period to give the senate an adequate firmness, from not duly considering the amazing violence & turbulence of the democratic spirit. When a great object of Govt. is pursued, which seizes the popular passions, they spread like wild fire, and become irresistable. He appealed to the gentlemen from the N. England States whether experience had not there verified the remark. As to the Executive, it seemed to be admitted that no good one could be established on Republican principles. Was not this giving up the merits of the question: for can there be a good Govt. without a good Executive. The English model was the only good one on this subject. The Hereditary interest of the King was so interwoven with that of the Nation, and his personal emoluments so great, that he was placed above the danger of being corrupted from abroad—and at the same time was both sufficiently independent and sufficiently controuled, to answer the purpose of the institution at home. one of the weak sides of Republics was their being liable to foreign influence & corruption. Men of little character, acquiring great power become easily the tools of intermedling Neibours. Sweeden was a striking instance. The French & English had each their parties during the late Revolution which was effected by the predominant influence of the former. What is the inference from all these observations? That we ought to go as far in order to attain stability and permanency, as republican principles will admit. Let one branch of the Legislature hold their places for life or at least during good behaviour. Let the Executive also be for life. He appealed to the feelings of the members present whether a term of seven years, would induce the sacrifices of private affairs which an acceptance of public trust would require, so so as to ensure the services of the best Citizens. On this plan we should have in the Senate a permanent will, a weighty interest, which would answer essential purposes. But is this a Republican Govt., it will be asked? Yes if all the Magistrates are appointed, and vacancies are filled, by the people, or a process of election originating with the people. He was sensible that an Executive constituted as he proposed would have in fact but little of the power and independence that might be necessary. On the other plan of appointing him for 7 years, he thought the Executive ought to have but little power. He would be ambitious, with the means of making creatures; and as the object of his ambition wd. be to *prolong* his power, it is probable that in case of a war, he would avail himself of the emergence, to evade or refuse a degradation from his place. An Executive for life has not this motive for forgetting his fidelity, and will therefore be a safer depository of power. It will be objected probably, that such an Executive will be an *elective Monarch*, and will give birth to the tumults which characterize that form of Govt. He wd. reply that *Monarch* is an indefinite term. It marks not either the degree or duration of power. If this Executive Magistrate wd. be a monarch for life—the other propd. by the Report from the Comtte of the whole, wd. be a monarch for seven years. The circumstance of being elective was also applicable to both. It had been observed by judicious writers that elective monarchies wd. be the best if they could be guarded agst. the *tumults* excited by the ambition and intrigues of competitors. He was not sure that tumults were an inseparable evil. He rather thought this character of Elective Monarchies had been taken rather from particular cases than from general principles. The election of Roman Emperors was made by the *Army*. In *Poland* the election is made by great rival *princes* with independent power, and ample means, of raising commotions. In the German Empire, the appointment is made by the Electors & Princes, who have equal motives & means, for exciting cabals & parties. Might not such a mode of election be devised among ourselves as will defend the community agst. these effects in any dangerous degree? Having made these observations he would read to the Committee a sketch of a plan which he shd. prefer to either of those under consideration. He was aware that it went beyond the ideas of most members. But will such a plan be adopted out of doors? In return he would ask will the people adopt the other plan? At present they will adopt neither. But he sees the Union dissolving or already dissolved—he sees evils operating in the States which must soon cure the people of their fondness for democracies—he sees that a great progress has been already made & is still going on in the public mind. He thinks therefore that the people will in time be unshackled from their prejudices; and whenever that happens, they will themselves not be satisfied at stopping where the plan of Mr. R. wd. place them, but be ready to go as far at least as he proposes. He did not mean to offer the paper he had sketched as a proposition to the Committee. It was meant only to give a more correct view of his ideas, and to suggest the amendments which he should probably propose to the plan of Mr. R. in the proper stages of its future discussion. He read his sketch in the words following: towit. . . ."

On these several articles he entered into explanatory observations corresponding with the principles of his introductory reasoning.

Version recorded by Robert Yates

Mr. Hamilton. To deliver my sentiments on so important a subject, when the first characters in the union have gone before me, inspires me with the greatest diffidence, especially when my own ideas are so materially dissimilar to the plans now before the committee. My situation is disagreeable, but it would be criminal not to come forward on a question of such magnitude. I have well considered the subject, and am convinced that no amendment of the confederation can answer the purpose of a good government, so long as state sovereignties do, in any shape, exist; and I have great doubts whether a national government on the Virginia plan can be made effectual. What is federal? An association of several independent states into one. How or in what manner this association is formed, is not so clearly distinguishable. We find the diet of Germany has in some instances the power of legislation on individuals. We find the United States of America have it in an extensive degree in the cases of piracies.

Let us now review the powers with which we are invested. We are appointed for the *sole* and *express* purpose of revising the confederation, and to *alter* or *amend* it, so as to render it effectual for the purposes of a good government. Those who suppose it must be federal, lay great stress on the terms *sole* and *express*, as if these words intended a confinement to a federal government; when the manifest import is no more than that the institution of a good government must be the *sole* and *express* object of your deliberations. Nor can we suppose an annihilation of our powers by forming a national government, as many of the states have made in their constitutions no provision for any alteration; and thus much I can say for the state I have the honor to represent, that when our credentials were under consideration in the senate, some members were for inserting a restriction in the powers, to prevent an encroachment on the constitution: it was answered by others, and thereupon the resolve carried on the credentials, that it might abridge some of the constitutional powers of the state, and that possibly in the formation of a new union it would be found necessary. This appears reasonable, and therefore leaves us at liberty to form such a national government as we think best adapted for the good of the whole. I have therefore no difficulty as to the extent of our powers, nor do I feel myself restrained in the exercise of my judgment under them. We can only propose and recommend—the power of ratifying or rejecting is still in the states. But on this great question I am still greatly embarrassed. I have before observed my apprehension of the inefficacy of either plan, and I have great doubts whether a more energetic government can pervade this wide and extensive country. I shall now show, that both plans are materially defective.

1. A good government ought to be constant, and ought to contain an active principle.

2. Utility and necessity.

3. An habitual sense of obligation.

4. Force.

5. Influence.

I hold it, that different societies have all different views and interests to pursue, and always prefer local to general concerns. For example: New-York legislature made an external compliance lately to a requisition of congress; but do they not at the same time counteract their compliance by gratifying the local objects of the state so as to defeat their concession? And this will ever be the case. Men always love power, and states will prefer their particular concerns to the general welfare; and as the states become large and important, will they not be less attentive to the general government? What, in process of time will Virginia be? She contains now half a million inhabitants—in twenty-five years she will double the number. Feeling her own weight and importance, must she not become indifferent to the concerns of the union? And where, in such a situation, will be found national attachment to the general government?

By *force*, I mean the *coercion* of law and the coercion of arms. Will this remark apply to the power intended to be vested in the government to be instituted by theire plan? A delinquent must be compelled to obedience by force of arms. How is this to be done? If you are unsuccessful, a dissolution of your government must be the consequence; and in that case the individual legislatures will reassume their powers; nay, will not the interest of the states be thrown into the state governments?

By *influence*, I mean the regular weight and support it will receive from those who will find it their interest to support a government intended to preserve the peace and happiness of the community of the whole. The state governments, by either plan, will exert the means to counteract it. They have their state judges and militia all combined to support their state interests; and these will be influenced to oppose a national government. Either plan is therefore precarious. The national government cannot long exist when opposed by such a weighty rival. The experience of ancient and modern confederacies evince this point, and throw considerable light on the subject. The amphyctionic council of Greece had a right to require of its members troops, money and the force of the country. Were they obeyed in the exercise of those powers? Could they preserve the peace of the greater states and republics? or where were they obeyed? History shows that their decrees were disregarded, and that the stronger states, regardless of their power, gave law to the lesser.

Let us examine the federal institution of Germany. It was instituted upon the laudable principle of securing the independency of the several states of which it was composed, and to protect them against foreign invasion. Has it answered these good intentions? Do we not see that their councils are weak and distracted, and that it cannot prevent the wars and confusions which the respective electors carry on against each other? The Swiss cantons, or the Helvetic union, are equally inefficient.

Such are the lessons which the experience of others affords us, and from whence results the evident conclusion that all federal governments are weak and distracted. To avoid the evils deducible from these observations, we must establish a general and national government, completely sovereign, and annihilate the state distinctions and state operations; and unless we do this, no good purpose can be answered. What does the Jersey plan propose? It surely has not this for its object. By this we grant the regulation of trade and a more effectual collection of the revenue, and some partial duties. These, at five or ten per cent, would only perhaps amount to a fund to discharge the debt of the corporation.

Let us take a review of the variety of important objects, which must necessarily engage the attention of a national government. You have to protect your rights against Canada on the north, Spain on the south, and your western frontier against the savages. You have to adopt necessary plans for the settlement of your frontiers, and to institute the mode in which settlements and good government are to be made.

How is the expense of supporting and regulating these important matters to be defrayed? By requisition on the states, according to the Jersey plan? Will this do it? We have already found it ineffectual. Let one state prove delinquent, and it will encourage others to follow the example; and thus the whole will fail. And what is the standard to quota among the states their respective proportions? Can lands be the standard? How would that apply between Russia and Holland? Compare Pennsylvania with North-Carolina, or Connecticut with New-York. Does not commerce or industry in the one or other make a great disparity between these different countries, and may not the comparative value of the states from these circumstances, make an unequal disproportion when the data is numbers? I therefore conclude that either system would ultimately destroy the confederation, or any other government which is established on such fallacious principles. Perhaps imposts, taxes on specific articles, would produce a more equal system of drawing a revenue.

Another objection against the Jersey plan is, the unequal representation. Can the great States consent to this? If they did it would eventually work its own destruction. How are forces to be raised by the Jersey plan? By quotas? Will the states comply with the requisition? As much as they will with the taxes.

Examine the present confederation, and it is evident they can raise no troops nor equip vessels before war is actually declared. They cannot therefore take any preparatory measure before an enemy is at your door. How unwise and inadequate their powers! and this must ever be the case when you attempt to define powers. Something will always be wanting. Congress, by being annually elected, and subject to recall, will ever come with the prejudices of their states rather than the good of the union. Add therefore additional powers to a body thus organized, and you establish a *sovereignty* of the worst kind, consisting of a single body. Where are the checks? None. They must either prevail over the state governments, or the prevalence of the state governments must end in their dissolution. This is a conclusive objection to the Jersey plan.

Such are the insuperable objections to both plans: and what is to be done on this occasion? I confess I am at a loss. I foresee the difficulty on a consolidated plan of drawing a representation from so extensive a continent to one place. What can be the inducements for gentlemen to come 600 miles to a national legislature? The expense would at least amount to £100,000. This however can be no conclusive objection if it eventuates in an extinction of state governments. The burthen of the latter would be saved, and the expense then would not be great. State distinctions would be found unnecessary, and yet I confess, to carry government to the extremities, the state governments reduced to corporations, and with very limited powers, might be necessary, and the expense of the national government become less burthensome.

Yet, I confess, I see great difficulty of drawing forth a good representation. What, for example, will be the inducements for gentlemen of fortune and abilities to leave their houses and business to attend annually and long? It cannot be the wages; for these, I presume, must be small. Will not the power, therefore, be thrown into the hands of the demagogue or middling politician, who, for the sake of a small stipend and the hopes of advancement, will offer himself as a candidate, and the real men of weight and influence, by remaining at home, add strength to the state governments? I am at a loss to know what must be done; I despair that a republican form of government can remove the difficulties. Whatever may be my opinion, I would hold it however unwise to change that form of government. I believe the British government forms the best model the world ever produced, and such has been its progress in the minds of the many, that this truth gradually gains ground. This government has for its object *public strength* and *individual security*. It is said with us to be unattainable. If it was once formed it would maintain itself. All communities divide themselves into the few and the many. The first are the rich and well born, the other the mass of the people. The voice of the people has been said to be the voice of God; and however generally this maxim has been quoted and believed, it is not true in fact. The people are turbulent and changing; they seldom judge or determine right. Give therefore to the first class a distinct, permanent share in the government. They will check the unsteadiness of the second, and as they cannot receive any advantage by a change, they therefore will ever maintain good government. Can a democratic assembly, who annually revolve in the mass of the people, be supposed steadily to pursue the public good? Nothing but a permanent body can check the imprudence of democracy. Their turbulent and uncontrouling disposition requires checks. The senate of New-York, although chosen for four years, we have found to be inefficient. Will, on the Virginia plan, a continuance of seven years do it? It is admitted, that you cannot have a good executive upon a democratic plan. See the excellency of the British executive. He is placed above temptation. He can have no distinct interests from the public welfare. Nothing short of such an executive can be efficient. The weak side of a republican government is the danger of foreign influence. This is unavoidable, unless it is so constructed as to bring forward its first characters in its support. I am therefore for a general government, yet would wish to go the full length of republican principles.

Let one body of the legislature be constituted during good behaviour or life.

Let one executive be appointed who dares execute his powers.

It may be asked is this a republican system? It is strictly so, as long as they remain elective.

And let me observe, that an executive is less dangerous to the liberties of the people when in office during life, than for seven years.

It may be said, this constitutes an elective monarchy? Pray, what is a monarchy? May not the governors of the respective states be considered in that light? But by making the executive subject to impeachment, the term monarchy cannot apply. These elective monarchs have produced tumults in Rome, and are equally dangerous to peace in Poland; but this cannot apply to the mode in which I would propose the election. Let electors be appointed in each of the states to elect the executive—(*Here Mr. H. produced his plan, a copy whereof is hereunto annexed,*) to consist of two branches—and I would give them the unlimited power of passing *all laws* without exception. The assembly to be elected for three years by the people in districts—the senate to be elected by the electors to be chosen for that purpose by the people, and to remain in office during life. The executive to have the power of negativing all laws—to make war or peace, with the advice of the senate—to make treaties with their advice, but to have the sole direction of all military operations, and to send ambassadors and appoint all military officers, and to pardon all offenders, treason excepted, unless by advice of the senate. On his death or removal, the president of the senate to officiate, with the same powers, until another is elected. Supreme judicial officers to be appointed by the executive and the senate. The legislature to appoint courts in each state, so as to make the state governments unnecessary to it.

All state laws to be absolutely void which contravene the general laws. An officer to be appointed in each state to have a negative on all state laws. All the militia and the appointment of officers to be under the national government.

I confess that this plan and that from Virginia are very remote from the idea of the people. Perhaps the Jersey plan is

nearest their expectation. But the people are gradually ripening in their opinions of government—they begin to be tired
of an excess of democracy—and what even is the Virginia
plan, but *pork still, with a little change of the sauce.*

June 18, 1787

To George Washington

Dr. Sir.

In my passage through the Jerseys and since my arrival here
I have taken particular pains to discover the public sentiment
and I am more and more convinced that this is the critical opportunity for establishing the prosperity of this country on a
solid foundation. I have conversed with men of information
not only of this City but from different parts of the state; and
they agree that there has been an astonishing revolution for
the better in the minds of the people. The prevailing apprehension among thinking men is that the Convention, from a
fear of shocking the popular opinion, will not go far enough.
They seem to be convinced that a strong well mounted
government will better suit the popular palate than one of a
different complexion. Men in office are indeed taking all
possible pains to give an unfavourable impression of the Convention; but the current seems to be running strongly the
other way.

A plain but sensible man, in a conversation I had with him
yesterday, expressed himself nearly in this manner. The people
begin to be convinced that their "excellent form of government" as they have been used to call it, will not answer their
purpose; and that they must substitute something not very remote from that which they have lately quitted.

These appearances though they will not warrant a conclusion that the people are yet ripe for such a plan as I advocate,
yet serve to prove that there is no reason to despair of their
adopting one equally energetic, if the Convention should

think proper to propose it. They serve to prove that we ought not to allow too much weight to objections drawn from the supposed repugnancy of the people to an efficient constitution. I confess I am more and more inclined to believe that former habits of thinking are regaining their influence with more rapidity than is generally imagined.

Not having compared ideas with you, Sir, I cannot judge how far our sentiments agree; but as I persuade myself the genuineness of my representations will receive credit with you, my anxiety for the event of the deliberations of the Convention induces me to make this communication of what appears to be the tendency of the public mind. I own to you Sir that I am seriously and deeply distressed at the aspect of the Councils which prevailed when I left Philadelphia. I fear that we shall let slip the golden opportunity of rescuing the American empire from disunion anarchy and misery. No motley or feeble measure can answer the end or will finally receive the public support. Decision is true wisdom and will be not less reputable to the Convention than salutary to the community.

I shall of necessity remain here ten or twelve days; if I have reason to believe that my attendance at Philadelphia will not be mere waste of time, I shall after that period rejoin the Convention.

I remain with sincere esteem Dr Sir   Yr. Obed serv

A Hamilton

July 3d. 87

Conjectures About the New Constitution

The new constitution has in favour of its success these circumstances—a very great weight of influence of the persons who framed it, particularly in the universal popularity of General Washington—the good will of the commercial interest throughout the states which will give all its efforts to the establishment of a government capable of regulating protecting and extending the commerce of the Union—the good will of most men of property in the several states who wish a government of the union able to protect them against domestic violence and the depredations which the democratic spirit is apt to make on property; and who are besides anxious for the respectability of the nation—the hopes of the Creditors of the United States that a general government possessing the means of doing it will pay the debt of the Union—a strong belief in the people at large of the insufficiency of the present confederation to preserve the existence of the Union and of the necessity of the union to their safety and prosperity; of course a strong desire of a change and a predisposition to receive well the propositions of the Convention.

Against its success is to be put the dissent of two or three important men in the Convention; who will think their characters pledged to defeat the plan—the influence of many *inconsiderable* men in possession of considerable offices under the state governments who will fear a diminution of their consequence, power and emolument by the establishment of the general government and who can hope for nothing there—the influence of some *considerable* men in office possessed of talents and popularity who partly from the same motives and partly from a desire of *playing a part* in a convulsion for their own aggrandisement will oppose the quiet adoption of the new government—(some considerable men out of office, from motives of ambition may be disposed to act the same part)—add to these causes the disinclination of the people to taxes, and of course to a strong government—the opposition of all men much in debt who will not wish to see a government established one object of which is to restrain the means of cheating Creditors—the democratical jealousy of the people which may be alarmed at the appearance of institutions that may seem calculated to place the power of the community in few hands and to raise a few individuals to stations of great preeminence—and the influence of some foreign powers who from different motives will not wish to see an energetic government established throughout the states.

In this view of the subject it is difficult to form any judgment whether the plan will be adopted or rejected. It must be essentially a matter of conjecture. The present appearances and all other circumstances considered the probability seems to be on the side of its adoption.

But the causes operating against its adoption are powerful and there will be nothing astonishing in the Contrary.

If it do not finally obtain, it is probable the discussion of the question will beget such struggles animosities and heats in the community that this circumstance conspiring with the *real necessity* of an essential change in our present situation will produce civil war. Should this happen, whatever parties prevail it is probable governments very different from the present in their principles will be established. A dismemberment of the Union and monarchies in different portions of it may be expected. It may however happen that no civil war will take place; but several republican confederacies be established between different combinations of the particular states.

A reunion with Great Britain, from universal disgust at a state of commotion, is not impossible, though not much to be feared. The most plausible shape of such a business would be the establishment of a son of the present monarch in the supreme government of this country with a family compact.

If the government be adopted, it is probable general Washington will be the President of the United States. This will insure a wise choice of men to administer the government and a good administration. A good administration will conciliate the confidence and affection of the people and perhaps enable the government to acquire more consistency than the proposed constitution seems to promise for so great a Country. It may then triumph altogether over the state governments and reduce them to an intire subordination, dividing the larger states into smaller districts. The *organs* of the general government may also acquire additional strength.

If this should not be the case, in the course of a few years, it is probable that the contests about the boundaries of power between the particular governments and the general government and the *momentum* of the larger states in such contests will produce a dissolution of the Union. This after all seems to be the most likely result.

But it is almost arrogance in so complicated a subject, depending so intirely on the incalculable fluctuations of the human passions, to attempt even a conjecture about the event.

It will be Eight or Nine months before any certain judgment can be formed respecting the adoption of the Plan.

c. late September 1787

The Federalist No. 1

To the People of the State of New York.

After an unequivocal experience of the inefficacy of the subsisting Fœderal Government, you are called upon to deliberate on a new Constitution for the United States of America. The subject speaks its own importance; comprehending in its consequences, nothing less than the existence of the UNION, the safety and welfare of the parts of which it is composed, the fate of an empire, in many respects, the most interesting the world. It has been frequently remarked, that it seems to have been reserved to the people of this country, by their conduct and example, to decide the important question, whether societies of men are really capable or not, of establishing good government from reflection and choice, or whether they are forever destined to depend, for their political constitutions, on accident and force. If there be any truth in the remark, the crisis, at which we are arrived, may with propriety be regarded as the æra in which that decision is to be made; and a wrong election of the part we shall act, may, in this view, deserve to be considered as the general misfortune of mankind.

This idea will add the inducements of philanthropy to those of patriotism to heighten the sollicitude, which all considerate and good men must feel for the event. Happy will it be if our choice should be directed by a judicious estimate of our true interests, unperplexed and unbiassed by considerations not connected with the public good. But this is a thing more ardently to be wished, than seriously to be expected. The plan offered to our deliberations, affects too many particular interests, innovates upon too many local institutions, not to involve in its discussion a variety of objects foreign to its merits, and of views, passions and prejudices little favourable to the discovery of truth.

Among the most formidable of the obstacles which the new Constitution will have to encounter, may readily be distinguished the obvious interest of a certain class of men in every State to resist all changes which may hazard a diminution of the power, emolument and consequence of the offices they hold under the State-establishments—and the perverted ambition of another class of men, who will either hope to aggrandise themselves by the confusions of their country, or will flatter themselves with fairer prospects of elevation from the subdivision of the empire into several partial confederacies, than from its union under one government.

It is not, however, my design to dwell upon observations of this nature. I am well aware that it would be disingenuous to resolve indiscriminately the opposition of any set of men (merely because their situations might subject them to suspicion) into interested or ambitious views: Candour will oblige us to admit, that even such men may be actuated by upright intentions; and it cannot be doubted, that much of the opposition which has made its appearance, or may hereafter make its appearance, will spring from sources, blameless at least, if not respectable, the honest errors of minds led astray by preconceived jealousies and fears. So numerous indeed and so powerful are the causes, which serve to give a false bias to the judgment, that we upon many occasions, see wise and good men on the wrong as well as on the right side of questions, of the first magnitude to society. This circumstance, if duly attended to, would furnish a lesson of moderation of those, who are ever so much persuaded of their being in the right, in any controversy. And a further reason for caution, in this respect, might be drawn from the reflection, that we are not always sure, that those who advocate the truth are influenced by purer principles than their antagonists. Ambition, avarice, personal animosity, party opposition, and many other motives, not more laudable than these, are apt to operate as well upon those who support as upon those who oppose the right side of a question. Were there not even these inducements to moderation, nothing could be more illjudged than that intolerant spirit, which has, at all times, characterised political parties. For, in politics as in religion, it is equally absurd to aim at making proselytes by fire and sword. Heresies in either can rarely be cured by persecution.

And yet however just these sentiments will be allowed to be, we have already sufficient indications, that it will happen in this as in all former cases of great national discussion. A torrent of angry and malignant passions will be let loose. To judge from the conduct of the opposite parties, we shall be led to conclude, that they will mutually hope to evince the justness of their opinions, and to increase the number of their converts by the loudness of their declamations, and by the bitterness of their invectives. An enlightened zeal for the energy and efficiency of government will be stigmatised, as the off-spring of a temper fond of despotic power and hostile to the principles of liberty. An overscrupulous jealousy of danger to the rights of the people, which is more commonly the fault of the head than of the heart, will be represented as mere pretence and artifice; the bait for popularity at the expence of public good. It will be forgotten, on the one hand, that jealousy is the usual concomitant of violent love, and that the noble enthusiasm of liberty is too apt to be infected with a spirit of narrow and illiberal distrust. On the other hand, it will be equally forgotten, that the vigour of government is essential to the security of liberty; that, in the contemplation of a sound and well informed judgment, their interest can never be separated; and that a dangerous ambition more often lurks behind the specious mask of zeal for the rights of the people, than under the forbidding appearance of zeal for the firmness and efficiency of government. History will teach us, that the former has been found a much more certain road to the introduction of despotism, than the latter, and that of those men who have overturned the liberties of republics the greatest number have begun their carreer, by paying an obsequious court to the people, commencing Demagogues and ending Tyrants.

In the course of the preceeding observations I have had an eye, my Fellow Citizens, to putting you upon your guard against all attempts, from whatever quarter, to influence your decision in a matter of the utmost moment to your welfare by any impressions other than those which may result from the evidence of truth. You will, no doubt, at the same time, have collected from the general scope of them that they proceed from a source not unfriendly to the new Constitution. Yes, my Countrymen, I own to you, that, after having given it an attentive consideration, I am clearly of opinion, it is your interest to adopt it. I am convinced, that this is the safest course for your liberty, your dignity, and your happiness. I effect not reserves, which I do not feel. I will not amuse you with an appearance of deliberation, when I have decided. I frankly acknowledge to you my convictions, and I will freely lay before you the reasons on which they are founded. The consciousness of good intentions disdains ambiguity. I shall not however multiply professions on this head. My motives must remain in the depository of my own breast: My arguments will be open to all, and may be judged of by all. They shall at least be offered in a spirit, which will not disgrace the cause of truth.

I propose in a series of papers to discuss the following interesting particulars—*The utility of the UNION to your political prosperity—The insufficiency of the present Confederation to preserve that Union—The necessity of a government at least equally energetic with the one proposed to the attainment of this object—The conformity of the proposed constitution to the true principles of republican government—Its analogy to your own state constitution*—and lastly, *The additional security, which its adoption will afford to the preservation of that species of government, to liberty and to property.*

In the progress of this discussion I shall endeavour to give a satisfactory answer to all the objections which shall have made their appearance that may seem to have any claim to your attention.

It may perhaps be thought superfluous to offer arguments to prove the utility of the UNION, a point, no doubt, deeply engraved on the hearts of the great body of the people in every state, and one, which it may be imagined has no adversaries. But the fact is, that we already hear it whispered in the private circles of those who oppose the new constitution, that the Thirteen States are of too great extent for any general system, and that we must of necessity resort to separate confederacies of distinct portions of the whole.* This doctrine will, in all probability, be gradually propagated, till it has votaries enough to countenance an open avowal of it. For nothing can be more evident, to those who are able to take an enlarged

---

* The same idea, tracing the arguments to their consequences, is held out in several of the late publications against the New Constitution.

view of the subject than the alternative of an adoption of the new Constitution, or a dismemberment of the Union. It will therefore be of use to begin by examining the advantages of that Union, the certain evils and the probable dangers, to which every State will be exposed from its dissolution. This shall accordingly constitute the subject of my next address.

PUBLIUS.

The Independent Journal, October 27, 1787

The Federalist No. 6

To the People of the State of New-York.

The three last numbers of this Paper have been dedicated to an enumeration of the dangers to which we should be exposed, in a state of disunion, from the arms and arts of foreign nations. I shall now proceed to delineate dangers of a different, and, perhaps, still more alarming kind, those which will in all probability flow from dissentions between the States themselves, and from domestic factions and convulsions. These have been already in some instances slightly anticipated, but they deserve a more particular and more full investigation.

A man must be far gone in Utopian speculations who can seriously doubt, that if these States should either be wholly disunited, or only united in partial confederacies, the subdivisions into which they might be thrown would have frequent and violent contests with each other. To presume a want of motives for such contests, as an argument against their existence, would be to forget that men are ambitious, vindictive and rapacious. To look for a continuation of harmony between a number of independent unconnected sovereignties, situated in the same neighbourhood, would be to disregard the uniform course of human events, and to set at defiance the accumulated experience of ages.

The causes of hostility among nations are innumerable. There are some which have a general and almost constant operation upon the collective bodies of society: Of this description are the love of power or the desire of preeminence and dominion—the jealousy of power, or the desire of equality and safety. There are others which have a more circumscribed, though an equally operative influence, within their spheres: Such are the rivalships and competitions of commerce between commercial nations. And there are others, not less numerous than either of the former, which take their origin intirely in private passions; in the attachments, enmities, interests, hopes and fears of leading individuals in the communities of which they are members. Men of this class, whether the favourites of a king or of a people, have in too many instances abused the confidence they possessed; and assuming the pretext of some public motive, have not scrupled to sacrifice the national tranquility to personal advantage, or personal gratification.

The celebrated Pericles, in compliance with the resentments of a prostitute, (A) at the expence of much of the blood and treasure of his countrymen, attacked, vanquished and destroyed, the city of the *Samnians*. The same man, stimulated by private pique against the *Megarensians*, (B) another nation of Greece, or to avoid a prosecution with which he was threatened as an accomplice in a supposed theft of the statuary *Phidias*, (C) or to get rid of the accusations prepared to be brought against him for dissipating the funds of the State in the purchase of popularity, (D) or from a combination of all these causes, was the primitive author of that famous and fatal war, distinguished in the Grecian annals by the name of the *Pelopponesian* war; which, after various vicissitudes, intermissions and renewals, terminated in the ruin of the Athenian commonwealth.

The ambitious Cardinal, who was Prime Minister to Henry VIIIth. permitting his vanity to aspire to the Tripple-Crown, (E) entertained hopes of succeeding in the acquisition of that splendid prize by the influence of the Emperor Charles Vth. To secure the favour and interest of this enterprising and powerful Monarch, he precipitated England into a war with France, contrary to the plainest dictates of Policy, and at the hazard of the safety and independence, as well of the Kingdom over which he presided by his councils, as of Europe in general—For if there ever was a Sovereign who bid fair to realise the project of universal monarchy it was the Emperor Charles Vth, of whose intrigues Wolsey was at once the instrument and the dupe.

(A) *ASPASIA*, vide *PLUTARCH'S* life of Pericles.
(B) ------ Idem.
(C) --- Idem. Phidias was supposed to have stolen some public gold with the connivance of Pericles for the embelishment of the statue of Minerva.
(D) Idem.
(E) Worn by the Popes.

The influence which the bigottry of one female, (F) the petulancies of another, (G) and the cabals of a third, (H) had in the cotemporary policy, ferments and pacifications of a considerable part of Europe are topics that have been too often descanted upon not to be generally known.

To multiply examples of the agency of personal considerations in the production of great national events, either foreign or domestic, according to their direction would be an unnecessary waste of time. Those who have but a superficial acquaintance with the sources from which they are to be drawn will themselves recollect a variety of instances; and those who have a tolerable knowledge of human nature will not stand in need of such lights, to form their opinion either of the reality or extent of that agency. Perhaps however a reference, tending to illustrate the general principle, may with propriety be made to a case which has lately happened among ourselves. If SHAYS had not been a *desperate debtor* it is much to be doubted whether Massachusetts would have been plunged into a civil war.

But notwithstanding the concurring testimony of experience, in this particular, there are still to be found visionary, or designing men, who stand ready to advocate the paradox of perpetual peace between the States, though dismembered and alienated from each other. The genius of republics (say they) is pacific; the spirit of commerce has a tendency to soften the manners of men and to extinguish those inflammable humours which have so often kindled into wars. Commercial republics, like ours, will never be disposed to waste themselves in ruinous contentions with each other. They will be governed by mutual interest, and will cultivate a spirit of mutual amity and concord.

Is it not (we may ask these projectors in politics) the true interest of all nations to cultivate the same benevolent and philosophic spirit? If this be their true interest, have they in fact pursued it? Has it not, on the contrary, invariably been found, that momentary passions and immediate interests have a more active and imperious controul over human conduct

(F) Madame De Maintenon
(G) Dutchess of Marlborough.
(H) Madame De Pompadoure.

than general or remote considerations of policy, utility or justice? Have republics in practice been less addicted to war than monarchies? Are not the former administered by *men* as well as the latter? Are there not aversions, predilections, rivalships and desires of unjust acquisition that affect nations as well as kings? Are not popular assemblies frequently subject to the impulses of rage, resentment, jealousy, avarice, and of other irregular and violent propensities? Is it not well known that their determinations are often governed by a few individuals, in whom they place confidence, and are of course liable to be tinctured by the passions and views of those individuals? Has commerce hitherto done any thing more than change the objects of war? Is not the love of wealth as domineering and enterprising a passion as that of power or glory? Have there not been as many wars founded upon commercial motives, since that has become the prevailing system of nations, as were before occasioned by the cupidity of territory or dominion? Has not the spirit of commerce in many instances administered new incentives to the appetite both for the one and for the other? —Let experience the least fallible guide of human opinions be appealed to for an answer to these inquiries.

Sparta, Athens, Rome and Carthage were all Republics; two of them, Athens and Carthage, of the commercial kind. Yet were they as often engaged in wars, offensive and defensive, as the neighbouring Monarchies of the same times. Sparta was little better than a well regulated camp; and Rome was never sated of carnage and conquest.

Carthage, though a commercial Republic, was the aggressor in the very war that ended in her destruction. Hannibal had carried her arms into the heart of Italy and to the gates of Rome, before Scipio, in turn, gave him an overthrow in the territories of Carthage and made a conquest of the Commonwealth.

Venice in latter times figured more than once in wars of ambition; 'till becoming an object of terror to the other Italian States, Pope Julius the Second found means to accomplish that formidable league, (I) which gave a deadly blow to the power and pride of this haughty Republic.

(I) The LEAGUE OF CAMBRAY, comprehending the Emperor, the King of France, the King of Arragon, and most of the Italian Princes and States.

The Provinces of Holland, 'till they were overwhelmed in debts and taxes, took a leading and conspicuous part in the wars of Europe. They had furious contests with England for the dominion of the sea; and were among the most persevering and most implacable of the opponents of Lewis XIV.

In the government of Britain the representatives of the people compose one branch of the national legislature. Commerce has been for ages the predominant pursuit of that country. Few nations, nevertheless, have been more frequently engaged in war; and the wars, in which that kingdom has been engaged, have in numerous instances proceeded from the people.

There have been, if I may so express it, almost as many popular as royal wars. The cries of the nation and the importunities of their representatives have, upon various occasions, dragged their monarchs into war, or continued them in it contrary to their inclinations, and, sometimes, contrary to the real interests of the State. In that memorable struggle for superiority, between the rival Houses of *Austria* and *Bourbon* which so long kept Europe in a flame, it is well known that the antipathies of the English against the French, seconding the ambition, or rather the avarice of a favourite leader, (K), protracted the war beyond the limits marked out by sound policy and for a considerable time in opposition to the views of the Court.

The wars of these two last mentioned nations have in a great measure grown out of commercial considerations—The desire of supplanting and the fear of being supplanted either in particular branches of traffic or in the general advantages of trade and navigation and sometimes even the more culpable desire of sharing in the commerce of other nations, without their consent.

The last war but two between Britain and Spain sprang from the attempts of the English merchants, to prosecute an illicit trade with the Spanish main. These unjustifiable practices on their part produced severities on the part of the Spaniards, towards the subjects of Great Britain, which were not more justifiable; because they exceeded the bounds of a

(K) The Duke of Marlborough.

just retaliation, and were chargeable with inhumanity and cruelty. Many of the English who were taken on the Spanish coasts were sent to dig in the mines of Potosi; and by the usual progress of a spirit of resentment, the innocent were after a while confounded with the guilty in indiscriminate punishment. The complaints of the merchants kindled a violent flame throughout the nation, which soon after broke out in the house of commons, and was communicated from that body to the ministry. Letters of reprisal were granted and a war ended, which in its consequences overthrew all the alliances that but twenty years before had been formed, with sanguine expectations of the most beneficial fruits.

From this summary of what has taken place in other countries, whose situations have borne the nearest resemblance to our own, what reason can we have to confide in those reveries, which would seduce us into an expectation of peace and cordiality between the members of the present confederacy, in a state of separation? Have we not already seen enough of the fallacy and extravagance of those idle theories which have amused us with promises of an exemption from the imperfections, weaknesses and evils incident to society in every shape? Is it not time to awake from the deceitful dream of a golden age, and to adopt as a practical maxim for the direction of our political conduct, that we, as well as the other inhabitants of the globe, are yet remote from the happy empire of perfect wisdom and perfect virtue?

Let the point of extreme depression to which our national dignity and credit have sunk—let the inconveniences felt every where from a lax and ill administration of government—let the revolt of a part of the State of North-Carolina—the late menacing disturbances in Pennsylvania and the actual insurrections and rebellions in Massachusetts declare—!

So far is the general sense of mankind from corresponding with the tenets of those, who endeavour to lull asleep our apprehensions of discord and hostility between the States, in the event of disunion, that it has from long observation of the progress of society become a sort of axiom in politics, that vicinity, or nearness of situation, constitutes nations natural enemies. An intelligent writer expresses himself on this subject to this effect—"NEIGHBOURING NATIONS (says he) are naturally ENEMIES of each other, unless their common weakness forces them to league in a CONFEDERATE RE-PUBLIC, and their constitution prevents the differences that neighbourhood occasions, extinguishing that secret jealousy, which disposes all States to aggrandise themselves at the ex-pence of their neighbours." (L) This passage, at the same time points out the EVIL and suggests the REMEDY.

PUBLIUS.

(L) Vide Principes des Negotiations par L'Abbe de Mably.

The Independent Journal, November 14, 1787

The Federalist No. 7

To the People of the State of New-York.

It is sometimes asked, with an air of seeming triumph, what inducements could the States have, if disunited, to make war upon each other? It would be a full answer to this question to say—precisely the same inducements, which have, at different times, deluged in blood all the nations in the world. But unfortunately for us, the question admits of a more particular answer. There are causes of difference within our immediate contemplation, of the tendency of which, even under the restraints of a Fœderal Constitution, we have had sufficient experience, to enable us to form a judgment of what might be expected, if those restraints were removed.

Territorial disputes have at all times been found one of the most fertile sources of hostility among nations. Perhaps the greatest proportion of the wars that have desolated the earth have sprung from this origin. This cause would exist, among us, in full force. We have a vast tract of unsettled territory within the boundaries of the United States. There still are discordant and undecided claims between several of them; and the dissolution of the Union would lay a foundation for similar claims between them all. It is well known, that they have heretofore had serious and animated discussions concerning the right to the lands which were ungranted at the time of the revolution, and which usually went under the name of crown-lands. The States within the limits of whose colonial governments they were comprised have claimed them as their property; the others have contended that the rights of the crown in this article devolved upon the Union; especially as to all that part of the Western territory which either by actual possession or through the submission of the Indian proprietors was subjected to the jurisdiction of the King of Great Britain, till it was relinquished in the treaty of peace. This, it has been said, was at all events an acquisition to the confederacy by compact with a foreign power. It has been the prudent policy of Congress to appease this controversy, by prevailing upon the States to make cessions to the United

States for the benefit of the whole. This has been so far accomplished, as under a continuation of the Union, to afford a decided prospect of an amicable termination of the dispute. A dismemberment of the confederacy however would revive this dispute, and would create others on the same subject. At present, a large part of the vacant Western territory is by cession at least, if not by any anterior right, the common property of the Union. If that were at an end, the States which made the cession on a principle of Fœderal compromise, would be apt, when the motive of the grant had ceased, to reclaim the lands as a reversion. The other States would no doubt insist on a proportion, by right of representation. Their argument would be that a grant, once made, could not be revoked, and that the justice of their participating in territory acquired, or secured by the joint efforts of the confederacy remained undiminished—If contrary to probability it should be admitted by all the States, that each had a right to a share of this common stock, there would still be a difficulty to be surmounted, as to a proper rule of apportionment. Different principles would be set up by different States for this purpose; and as they would affect the opposite interests of the parties, they might not easily be susceptible of a pacific adjustment.

In the wide field of Western territory, therefore, we perceive an ample theatre for hostile pretensions, without any umpire or common judge to interpose between the contending parties. To reason from the past to the future we shall have good ground to apprehend, that the sword would sometimes be appealed to as the arbiter of their differences. The circumstances of the dispute between Connecticut and Pennsylvania, respecting the land at Wyoming admonish us, not to be sanguine in expecting an easy accommodation of such differences. The articles of confederation obliged the parties to submit the matter to the decision of a Fœderal Court. The submission was made, and the Court decided in favour of Pennsylvania. But Connecticut gave strong indications of dissatisfaction with that determination; nor did she appear to be intirely resigned to it, till by negotiation and management something like an equivalent was found for the loss she supposed herself to have sustained. Nothing here said is intended to convey the slightest censure on the conduct of that State. She no doubt sincerely believed herself to have been injured by the decision; and States like individuals acquiesce with great reluctance in determinations to their disadvantage.

Those, who had an opportunity of seeing the inside of the transactions, which attended the progress of the controversy between this State and the district of Vermont, can vouch the opposition we experienced, as well from States not interested as from those which were interested in the claim; and can attest the danger, to which the peace of the Confederacy might have been exposed, had this State attempted to assert its rights by force. Two motives preponderated in that opposition—one a jealousy entertained of our future power—and the other, the interest of certain individuals of influence in the neighbouring States, who had obtained grants of lands under the actual government of that district. Even the States which brought forward claims, in contradiction to ours, seemed more solicitous to dismember this State, than to establish their own pretentions. These were New-Hampshire, Massachussets and Connecticut. New-Jersey and Rhode-Island upon all occasions discovered a warm zeal for the independence of Vermont; and Maryland, 'till alarmed by the appearance of a connection between Canada and that place, entered deeply into the same views. These being small States, saw with an unfriendly eye the perspective of our growing greatness. In a review of these transactions we may trace some of the causes, which would be likely to embroil the States with each other, if it should be their unpropitious destiny to become disunited.

The competitions of commerce would be another fruitful source of contention. The States less favourably circumstanced would be desirous of escaping from the disadvantages of local situation, and of sharing in the advantages of their more fortunate neighbours. Each State, or separate confederacy, would pursue a system of commercial polity peculiar to itself. This would occasion distinctions, preferences and exclusions, which would beget discontent. The habits of intercourse, on the basis of equal privileges, to which we have been accustomed from the earliest settlement of the country, would give a keener edge to those causes of discontent, than they would naturally have, independent of this circumstance. *We should be ready to denominate injuries those things which were in reality the justifiable acts of independent sovereignties consulting a distinct interest.* The spirit of enterprise, which characterises the commercial part of America, has left no occasion of displaying itself unimproved. It is not at all probable that this unbridled spirit would pay much respect to those regulations of trade, by which particular States might endeavour to secure exclusive benefits to their own citizens. The infractions of these regulations on one side, the efforts to prevent and repel them on the other, would naturally lead to outrages, and these to reprisals and wars.

The opportunities, which some States would have of rendering others tributary to them, by commercial regulations, would be impatiently submitted to by the tributary States. The relative situation of New-York, Connecticut and New Jersey, would afford an example of this kind. New-York, from the necessities of revenue, must lay duties on her importations. A great part of these duties must be paid by the inhabitants of the two other States in the capacity of consumers of what we import. New York would neither be willing nor able to forego this advantage. Her citizens would not consent that a duty paid by them should be remitted in favour of the citizens of her neighbours; nor would it be practicable, if there were not this impediment in the way, to distinguish the customers in our own markets. Would Connecticut and New-Jersey long submit to be taxed by New-York for her exclusive benefit? Should we be long permitted to remain in the quiet and undisturbed enjoyment of a metropolis, from the possession of which we derived an advantage so odious to our neighbours, and, in their opinion, so oppressive? Should we be able to preserve it against the incumbent weight of Connecticut on the one side, and the co-operating pressure of New-Jersey on the other? These are questions that temerity alone will answer in the affirmative.

The public debt of the Union would be a further cause of collision between the separate States or confederacies. The apportionment, in the first instance, and the progressive extinguishment, afterwards, would be alike productive of ill humour and animosity. How would it be possible to agree upon a rule of apportionment satisfactory to all? There is scarcely any, that can be proposed, which is entirely free from real objections. These, as usual, would be exaggerated by the adverse interests of the parties. There are even dissimilar views among the States, as to the general principle of discharging the public debt. Some of them, either less impressed with the importance of national credit, or because their citizens have little, if any, immediate interest in the question, feel an indifference, if not a repugnance to the payment of the domestic debt, at any rate. These would be inclined to magnify the difficulties of a distribution. Others of them, a numerous body of whose citizens are creditors to the public, beyond the proportion of the State in the total amount of the national debt, would be strenuous for some equitable and effectual provision. The procrastinations of the former would excite the resentments of the latter. The settlement of a rule would in the mean time be postponed, by real differences of opinion and affected delays. The citizens of the States interested, would clamour, foreign powers would urge, for the satisfaction of their just demands; and the peace of the States would be hazarded to the double contingency of external invasion and internal contention.

Suppose the difficulties of agreeing upon a rule surmounted, and the apportionment made. Still there is great room to suppose, that the rule agreed upon would, upon experiment, be found to bear harder upon some States than upon others. Those which were sufferers by it would naturally seek for a mitigation of the burthen. The others would as naturally be disinclined to a revision, which was likely to end in an increase of their own incumbrances. Their refusal would be too plausible a pretext to the complaining States to withhold their contributions, not to be embraced with avidity; and the non compliance of these States with their engagements would be a ground of bitter dissention and altercation. If even the rule adopted should in practice justify the equality of its principle, still delinquencies in payment, on the part of some of the States, would result from a diversity of other causes—the real deficiency of resources—the mismanagement of their finances, accidental disorders in the administration of the government—and in addition to the rest the reluctance with which men commonly part with money for purposes, that have outlived the exigencies which produced them, and interfere with the supply of immediate wants. Delinquencies from whatever causes would be productive of complaints, recriminations and quarrels. There is perhaps nothing more likely to disturb the tranquillity of nations, than their being bound to mutual contributions for any common object, which does not yield an equal and coincident benefit. For it is an observation as true, as it is trite, that there is nothing men differ so readily about as the payment of money.

Laws in violation of private contracts as they amount to aggressions on the rights of those States, whose citizens are injured by them, may be considered as another probable source of hostility. We are not authorised to expect, that a more liberal or more equitable spirit would preside over the legislations of the individual States hereafter, if unrestrained by any additional checks, than we have heretofore seen, in too many instances, disgracing their several codes. We have observed the disposition to retaliation excited in Connecticut, in consequence of the enormities perpetrated by the legislature of Rhode-Island; and we may reasonably infer, that in similar cases, under other circumstances, a war not of *parchment* but of the sword would chastise such atrocious breaches of moral obligation and social justice.

The probability of incompatible alliances between the different States, or confederacies, and different foreign nations, and the effects of this situation upon the peace of the whole, have been sufficiently unfolded in some preceding papers. From the view they have exhibited, of this part of the subject, this conclusion is to be drawn, that America, if not connected at all, or only by the feeble tie of a simple league offensive and defensive, would by the operation of such opposite and jarring alliances be gradually entangled in all the pernicious labyrinths of European politics and wars; and by the destructive contentions of the parts, into which she was divided, would be likely to become a prey to the artifices and machinations of powers equally the enemies of them all. *Divide et impera** must be the motto of every nation, that either hates, or fears us.

PUBLIUS

* Divide and command.

The Independent Journal, November 17, 1787

The Federalist No. 8

Assuming it therefore as an established truth that the several States, in case of disunion, or such combinations of them as might happen to be formed out of the wreck of the general confederacy, would be subject to those vicissitudes of peace and war, of friendship and enmity with each other, which have fallen to the lot of all neighbouring nations not united under one government, let us enter into a concise detail of some of the consequences, that would attend such a situation.

War between the States, in the first periods of their separate existence, would be accompanied with much greater distresses than it commonly is in those countries, where regular military establishments have long obtained. The disciplined armies always kept on foot on the continent of Europe, though they bear a malignant aspect to liberty and œconomy, have notwithstanding been productive of the signal advantage, of rendering sudden conquests impracticable, and of preventing that rapid desolation, which used to mark the progress of war, prior to their introduction. The art of fortification has contributed to the same ends. The nations of Europe are incircled with chains of fortified places, which mutually obstruct invasion. Campaigns are wasted in reducing two or three frontier garrisons, to gain admittance into an enemy's country. Similar impediments occur at every step, to exhaust the strength and delay the progress of an invader. Formerly an invading army would penetrate into the heart of a neighbouring country, almost as soon as intelligence of its approach could be received; but now a comparatively small force of disciplined troops, acting on the defensive with the aid of posts, is able to impede and finally to frustrate the enterprises of one much more considerable. The history of war, in that quarter of the globe, is no longer a history of nations subdued and empires overturned, but of towns taken and retaken, of battles that decide nothing, of retreats more beneficial than victories, of much effort and little acquisition.

In this country the scene would be altogether reversed. The jealousy of military establishments, would postpone them as long as possible. The want of fortifications leaving the frontiers of one State open to another, would facilitate inroads. The populous States would with little difficulty overrun their less populous neighbours. Conquests would be as easy to be made, as difficult to be retained. War therefore would be desultory and predatory. PLUNDER and devastations ever march in the train of irregulars. The calamities of individuals would make the principal figure in the events, which would characterise our military exploits.

This picture is not too highly wrought, though I confess, it would not long remain a just one. Safety from external danger is the most powerful director of national conduct. Even the ardent love of liberty will, after a time, give way to its dictates. The violent destruction of life and property incident to war—the continual effort and alarm attendant on a state of continual danger, will compel nations the most attached to liberty, to resort for repose and security, to institutions, which have a tendency to destroy their civil and political rights. To be more safe they, at length, become willing to run the risk of being less free.

The institutions alluded to are STANDING ARMIES, and the correspondent appendages of military establishments. Standing armies it is said are not provided against in the new constitution; and it is therefore inferred, that they may exist under it.* Their existence however from the very terms of the proposition, is, at most, problematical & uncertain. But standing armies, it may be replied, must inevitably result from a dissolution of the confederacy. Frequent war and constant apprehension, which require a state of as constant preparation, will infallibly produce them. The weaker States or confederacies, would first have recourse to them, to put themselves upon an equality with their more potent neighbours. They would endeavour to supply the inferiority of population and

---

* This objection will be fully examined in its proper place, and it will be shown that the only rational precaution which could have been taken on this subject has been taken; and a much better one than is to be found in any constitution that has been heretofore framed in America, most of which contain no guard at all on this subject.

resources, by a more regular and effective system of defence, by disciplined troops and by fortifications. They would, at the same time, be necessitated to strengthen the executive arm of government; in doing which, their constitutions would acquire a progressive direction towards monarchy. It is of the nature of war to increase the executive at the expence of the legislative authority.

The expedients which have been mentioned, would soon give the States or confederacies that made use of them, a superiority over their neighbours. Small States, or States of less natural strength, under vigorous governments, and with the assistance of disciplined armies, have often triumphed over larger States, or States of greater natural strength, which have been destitute of these advantages. Neither the pride, nor the safety of the more important States, or confederacies, would permit them long to submit to this mortifying and adventitious inferiority. They would quickly resort to means similar to those by which it had been effected, to reinstate themselves in their lost pre-eminence. Thus we should in a little time see established in every part of this country, the same engines of despotism, which have been the scourge of the old world. This at least would be the natural course of things, and our reasonings will be the more likely to be just, in proportion as they are accommodated to this standard.

These are not vague inferrences drawn from supposed or speculative defects in a constitution, the whole power of which is lodged in the hands of the people, or their representatives and delegates, but they are solid conclusions drawn from the natural and necessary progress of human affairs.

It may perhaps be asked, by way of objection to this, why did not standing armies spring up out of the contentions which so often distracted the ancient republics of Greece? Different answers equally satisfactory may be given to this question. The industrous habits of the people of the present day, absorbed in the pursuits of gain, and devoted to the improvements of agriculture and commerce are incompatible with the condition of a nation of soldiers, which was the true condition of the people of those republics. The means of revenue, which have been so greatly multiplied by the encrease of gold and silver, and of the arts of industry, and the science of finance, which is the offspring of modern times, concurring with the habits of nations, have produced an intire revolution in the system of war, and have rendered disciplined armies, distinct from the body of the citizens, the inseparable companion of frequent hostility.

There is a wide difference also, between military establishments in a country, seldom exposed by its situation to internal invasions, and in one which is often subject to them, and always apprehensive of them. The rulers of the former can have no good pretext, if they are even so inclined, to keep on foot armies so numerous as must of necessity be maintained in the latter. These armies being, in the first case, rarely, if at all, called into activity for interior defence, the people are in no danger of being broken to military subordination. The laws are not accustomed to relaxations, in favor of military exigencies—the civil state remains in full vigor, neither corrupted nor confounded with the principles or propensities of the other state. The smallness of the army renders the natural strength of the community an overmatch for it; and the citizens, not habituated to look up to the military power for protection, or to submit to its oppressions, neither love nor fear the soldiery: They view them with a spirit of jealous acquiescence in a necessary evil, and stand ready to resist a power which they suppose may be exerted to the prejudice of their rights. The army under such circumstances, may usefully aid the magistrate to suppress a small faction, or an occasional mob, or insurrection; but it will be unable to enforce encroachments against the united efforts of the great body of the people.

In a country, in the predicament last described, the contrary of all this happens. The perpetual menacings of danger oblige the government to be always prepared to repel it—its armies must be numerous enough for instant defence. The continual necessity for their services enhances the importance of the soldier, and proportionably degrades the condition of the citizen. The military state becomes elevated above the civil. The inhabitants of territories, often the theatre of war, are unavoidably subjected to frequent infringements on their rights, which serve to weaken their sense of those rights; and by degrees, the people are brought to consider the soldiery not only as their protectors, but as their superiors. The transition from this disposition to that of considering them as masters, is neither remote, nor difficult: But it is very difficult to prevail upon a people under such impressions, to make a bold, or effectual resistance, to usurpations, supported by the military power.

The kingdom of Great Britain falls within the first description. An insular situation, and a powerful marine, guarding it in a great measure against the possibility of foreign invasion, supercede the necessity of a numerous army within the kingdom. A sufficient force to make head against a sudden descent, till the militia could have time to rally and embody, is all that has been deemed requisite. No motive of national policy has demanded, nor would public opinion have tolerated a larger numbers of troops upon its domestic establishment. There has been, for a long time past, little room for the operation of the other causes, which have been enumerated as the consequences of internal war. This peculiar felicity of situation has, in a great degree, contributed to preserve the liberty, which that country to this day enjoys, in spite of the prevalent venality and corruption. If, on the contrary, Britain had been situated on the continent, and had been compelled, as she would have been, by that situation, to make her military establishments at home co-extensive with those of the other great powers of Europe, she, like them, would in all probability, be at this day a victim to the absolute power of a single man. 'Tis possible, though not easy, that the people of that island may be enslaved from other causes, but it cannot be by the powers of an army so inconsiderable as that which has been usually kept up in that kingdom.

If we are wise enough to preserve the Union, we may for ages enjoy an advantage similar to that of an insulated situation. Europe is at a great distance from us. Her colonies in our vicinity, will be likely to continue too much disproportioned in strength, to be able to give us any dangerous annoyance. Extensive military establishments cannot, in this position, be necessary to our security. But if we should be disunited, and the integral parts should either remain separated, or which is most probable, should be thrown together into two or three confederacies, we should be in a short course of time, in the predicament of the continental powers of Europe—our liberties would be a prey to the means of defending ourselves against the ambition and jealousy of each other.

This is an idea not superficial nor futile, but solid and weighty. It deserves the most serious and mature consideration of every prudent and honest man of whatever party. If such men will make a firm and solemn pause, and meditate dispassionately on the importance of this interesting idea, if they will contemplate it, in all its attitudes, and trace it to all its consequences, they will not hesitate to part with trivial objections to a constitution, the rejection of which would in all probability put a final period to the Union. The airy phantoms that flit before the distempered imaginations of some of its adversaries, would quickly give place to the more substantial forms of dangers real, certain, and formidable.

PUBLIUS.

The New-York Packet, November 20, 1787

The Federalist No. 9

To the People of the State of New-York.

A Firm Union will be of the utmost moment to the peace and liberty of the States as a barrier against domestic faction and insurrection. It is impossible to read the history of the petty Republics of Greece and Italy, without feeling sensations of horror and disgust at the distractions with which they were continually agitated, and at the rapid succession of revolutions, by which they were kept in a state of perpetual vibration, between the extremes of tyranny and anarchy. If they exhibit occasional calms, these only serve as short-lived contrasts to the furious storms that are to succeed. If now and then intervals of felicity open themselves to view, we behold them with a mixture of regret arising from the reflection that the pleasing scenes before us are soon to be overwhelmed by the tempestuous waves of sedition and party-rage. If momentary rays of glory break forth from the gloom, while they dazzle us with a transient and fleeting brilliancy, they at the same time admonish us to lament that the vices of government should pervert the direction and tarnish the lustre of those bright talents and exalted indowments, for which the favoured soils, that produced them, have been so justly celebrated.

From the disorders that disfigure the annals of those republics, the advocates of despotism have drawn arguments, not only against the forms of republican government, but against the very principles of civil liberty. They have decried all free government, as inconsistent with the order of society, and have indulged themselves in malicious exultation over its friends and partizans. Happily for mankind, stupendous fabrics reared on the basis of liberty, which have flourished for ages, have in a few glorious instances refuted their gloomy sophisms. And, I trust, America will be the broad and solid foundation of other edifices not less magnificent, which will be equally permanent monuments of their errors.

But it is not to be denied that the portraits, they have

sketched of republican government, were too just copies of the originals from which they were taken. If it had been found impracticable, to have devised models of a more perfect structure, the enlightened friends to liberty would have been obliged to abandon the cause of that species of government as indefensible. The science of politics, however, like most other sciences has received great improvement. The efficacy of various principles is now well understood, which were either not known at all, or imperfectly known to the ancients. The regular distribution of power into distinct departments—the introduction of legislative ballances and checks—the institution of courts composed of judges, holding their offices during good behaviour—the representation of the people in the legislature by deputies of their own election—these are either wholly new discoveries or have made their principal progress towards perfection in modern times. They are means, and powerful means, by which the excellencies of republican government may be retained and its imperfections lessened or avoided. To this catalogue of circumstances, that tend to the amelioration of popular systems of civil government, I shall venture, however novel it may appear to some, to add one more on a principle, which has been made the foundation of an objection to the New Constitution, I mean the ENLARGEMENT of the ORBIT within which such systems are to revolve either in respect to the dimensions of a single State, or to the consolidation of several smaller States into one great confederacy. The latter is that which immediately concerns the object under consideration. It will however be of use to examine the principle in its application to a single State which shall be attended to in another place.

The utility of a confederacy, as well to suppress faction and to guard the internal tranquillity of States, as to increase their external force and security, is in reality not a new idea. It has been practiced upon in different countries and ages, and has received the sanction of the most applauded writers, on the subjects of politics. The opponents of the PLAN proposed have with great assiduity cited and circulated the observations of Montesquieu on the necessity of a contracted territory for a republican government. But they seem not to have been apprised of the sentiments of that great man expressed in another part of his work, nor to have adverted to the consequences of the principle to which they subscribe, with such ready acquiescence.

When Montesquieu recommends a small extent for republics, the standards he had in view were of dimensions, far short of the limits of almost every one of these States. Neither Virginia, Massachusetts, Pennsylvania, New-York, North-Carolina, nor Georgia, can by any means be compared with the models, from which he reasoned and to which the terms of his description apply. If we therefore take his ideas on this point, as the criterion of truth, we shall be driven to the alternative, either of taking refuge at once in the arms of monarchy, or of splitting ourselves into an infinity of little jealous, clashing, tumultuous commonwealths, the wretched nurseries of unceasing discord and the miserable objects of universal pity or contempt. Some of the writers, who have come forward on the other side of the question, seem to have been aware of the dilemma; and have even been bold enough to hint at the division of the larger States, as a desirable thing. Such an infatuated policy, such a desperate expedient, might, by the multiplication of petty offices, answer the views of men, who possess not qualifications to extend their influence beyond the narrow circles of personal intrigue, but it could never promote the greatness or happiness of the people of America.

Referring the examination of the principle itself to another place, as has been already mentioned, it will be sufficient to remark here, that in the sense of the author who has been most emphatically quoted upon the occasion, it would only dictate a reduction of the SIZE of the more considerable MEMBERS of the Union; but would not militate against their being all comprehended in one Confederate Government. And this is the true question, in the discussion of which we are at present interested.

So far are the suggestions of Montesquieu from standing in opposition to a general Union of the States, that he explicitly treats of a CONFEDERATE REPUBLIC as the expedient for extending the sphere of popular government and reconciling the advantages of monarchy with those of republicanism.

"It is very probable (says he)* that mankind would have been obliged, at length, to live constantly under the government of a SINGLE PERSON, had they not contrived a kind of constitution, that has all the internal advantages of a republican, together with the external force of a monarchical government. I mean a CONFEDERATE REPUBLIC.

"This form of Government is a Convention, by which several smaller *States* agree to become members of a larger *one*, which they intend to form. It is a kind of assemblage of societies, that constitute a new one, capable of encreasing by means of new associations, till they arrive to such a degree of power as to be able to provide for the security of the united body.

"A republic of this kind, able to withstand an external force, may support itself without any internal corruption. The form of this society prevents all manner of inconveniencies.

"If a single member should attempt to usurp the supreme authority, he could not be supposed to have an equal authority and credit, in all the confederate states. Were he to have too great influence over one, this would alarm the rest. Were he to subdue a part, that which would still remain free might oppose him with forces, independent of those which he had usurped, and overpower him before he could be settled in his usurpation.

"Should a popular insurrection happen, in one of the confederate States, the others are able to quell it. Should abuses creep into one part, they are reformed by those that remain sound. The State may be destroyed on one side, and not on the other; the confederacy may be dissolved, and the confederates preserve their sovereignty.

"As this government is composed of small republics it enjoys the internal happiness of each, and with respect to its external situation it is possessed, by means of the association of all the advantages of large monarchies."

I have thought it proper to quote at length these interesting passages, because they contain a luminous abrigement of the principal arguments in favour of the Union, and must effectually remove the false impressions, which a misapplication of other parts of the work was calculated to produce.

* Spirit of Laws, Vol. I. Book IX. Chap. I.

They have at the same time an intimate connection with the more immediate design of this Paper; which is to illustrate the tendency of the Union to repress domestic faction and insurrection.

A distinction, more subtle than accurate has been raised between *a confederacy* and a *consolidation* of the States. The essential characteristic of the first is said to be, the restriction of its authority to the members in their collective capacities, without reaching to the individuals of whom they are composed. It is contended that the national council ought to have no concern with any object of internal administration. An exact equality of suffrage between the members has also been insisted upon as a leading feature of a Confederate Government. These positions are in the main arbitrary; they are supported neither by principle nor precedent. It has indeed happened that governments of this kind have generally operated in the manner, which the distinction, taken notice of, supposes to be inherent in their nature—but there have been in most of them extensive exceptions to the practice, which serve to prove as far as example will go, that there is no absolute rule on the subject. And it will be clearly shewn, in the course of this investigation, that as far as the principle contended for has prevailed, it has been the cause of incurable disorder and imbecility in the government.

The definition of a *Confederate Republic* seems simply to be, an "assemblage of societies" or an association of two or more States into one State. The extent, modifications and objects of the Fœderal authority are mere matters of discretion. So long as the separate organisation of the members be not abolished, so long as it exists by a constitutional necessity for local purposes, though it should be in perfect subordination to the general authority of the Union, it would still be, in fact and in theory, an association of States, or a confederacy. The proposed Constitution, so far from implying an abolition of the State Governments, makes them constituent parts of the national sovereignty by allowing them a direct representation in the Senate, and leaves in their possession certain exclusive and very important portions of sovereign power. This fully corresponds, in every rational import of the terms, with the idea of a Fœderal Government.

In the Lycian confederacy, which consisted of twenty three CITIES, or republics, the largest were intitled to *three* votes in the COMMON COUNCIL, those of the middle class to *two* and the smallest to *one*. The COMMON COUNCIL had the appointment of all the judges and magistrates of the respective CITIES. This was certainly the most delicate species of interference in their internal administration; for if there be any thing, that seems exclusively appropriated to the local jurisdictions, it is the appointment of their own officers. Yet Montesquieu, speaking of this association, says "Were I to give a model of an excellent confederate republic, it would be that of Lycia." Thus we perceive that the distinctions insisted upon were not within the contemplation of this enlightened civilian, and we shall be led to conclude that they are the novel refinements of an erroneous theory.

PUBLIUS.

The Independent Journal, November 21, 1787

The Federalist No. 11

To the People of the State of New-York.

The importance of the Union, in a commercial light, is one of those points, about which there is least room to entertain a difference of opinion, and which has in fact commanded the most general assent of men, who have any acquaintance with the subject. This applies as well to our intercourse with foreign countries, as with each other.

There are appearances to authorise a supposition, that the adventurous spirit, which distinguishes the commercial character of America, has already excited uneasy sensations in several of the maritime powers of Europe. They seem to be apprehensive of our too great interference in that carrying trade, which is the support of their navigation and the foundation of their naval strength. Those of them, which have colonies in America, look forward, to what this country is capable of becoming, with painful solicitude. They foresee the dangers, that may threaten their American dominions from the neighbourhood of States, which have all the dispositions, and would possess all the means, requisite to the creation of a powerful marine. Impressions of this kind will naturally indicate the policy of fostering divisions among us, and of depriving us as far as possible of an ACTIVE COMMERCE in our own bottoms. This would answer the threefold purpose of preventing our interference in their navigation, of monopolising the profits of our trade, and of clipping the wings, by which we might soar to a dangerous greatness. Did not prudence forbid the detail, it would not be difficult to trace by facts the workings of this policy to the cabinets of Ministers.

If we continue united, we may counteract a policy so unfriendly to our prosperity in a variety of ways. By prohibitory regulations, extending at the same time throughout the States, we may oblige foreign countries to bid against each other, for the privileges of our markets. This assertion will not appear chimerical to those who are able to appreciate the importance of the markets of three millions of people—increasing in rapid progression, for the most part exclusively addicted to agriculture, and likely from local circumstances to remain so—to any manufacturing nation; and the immense difference there would be to the trade and navigation of such a nation, between a direct communication in its own ships, and an indirect conveyance of its products and returns, to and from America, in the ships of another country. Suppose, for instance, we had a government in America, capable of excluding Great-Britain (with whom we have at present no treaty of commerce) from all our ports, what would be the probable operation of this step upon her politics? Would it not enable us to negotiate with the fairest prospect of success for commercial privileges of the most valuable and extensive kind in the dominions of that kingdom? When these questions have been asked, upon other occasions, they have received a plausible but not a solid or satisfactory answer. It has been said, that prohibitions on our part would produce no change in the system of Britain; because she could prosecute her trade with us, through the medium of the Dutch, who would be her immediate customers and paymasters for those articles which were wanted for the supply of our markets. But would not her navigation be materially injured, by the loss of the important advantage of being her own carrier in that trade? Would not the principal part of its profits be intercepted by the Dutch, as a compensation for their agency and risk? Would not the mere circumstance of freight occasion a considerable deduction? Would not so circuitous an intercourse facilitate the competitions of other nations, by enhancing the price of British commodities in our markets, and by transferring to other hands the management of this interesting branch of the British commerce?

A mature consideration of the objects, suggested by these questions, will justify a belief, that the real disadvantages to Britain, from such a state of things, conspiring with the prepossessions of a great part of the nation in favour of the American trade, and with the importunities of the West-India islands, would produce a relaxation in her present system, and would let us into the enjoyment of privileges in the markets of those islands and elsewhere, from which our trade would derive the most substantial benefits. Such a point gained from the British government, and which could not be expected without an equivalent in exemptions and immunities in our markets, would be likely to have a correspondent effect on the conduct of other nations, who would not be inclined to see themselves, altogether supplanted in our trade.

A further resource for influencing the conduct of European nations towards us, in this respect would arise from the establishment of a fœderal navy. There can be no doubt, that the continuance of the Union, under an efficient government, would put it in our power, at a period not very distant, to create a navy, which, if it could not vie with those of the great maritime powers, would at least be of respectable weight, if thrown into the scale of either of two contending parties. This would be more particularly the case in relation to operations in the West-Indies. A few ships of the line sent opportunely to the reinforcement of either side, would often be sufficient to decide the fate of a campaign, on the event of which interests of the greatest magnitude were suspended. Our position is in this respect a very commanding one. And if to this consideration we add that of the usefulness of supplies from this country, in the prosecution of military operations in the West-Indies, it will readily be perceived, that a situation so favourable would enable us to bargain with great advantage for commercial privileges. A price would be set not only upon our friendship, but upon our neutrality. By a steady adherance to the Union we may hope ere long to become the Arbiter of Europe in America; and to be able to incline the ballance of European competitions in this part of the world as our interest may dictate.

But in the reverse of this elegible situation we shall discover, that the rivalships of the parts would make them checks upon each other, and would frustrate all the tempting advantages, which nature has kindly placed within our reach. In a state so insignificant, our commerce would be a prey to the wanton intermeddlings of all nations at war with each other; who, having nothing to fear from us, would with little scruple or remorse supply their wants by depredations on our property, as often as it fell in their way. The rights of neutrality will only be respected, when they are defended by an adequate power. A nation, despicable by its weakness, forfeits even the privilege of being neutral.

Under a vigorous national government, the natural strength

and resources of the country, directed to a common interest, would baffle all the combinations of European jealousy to restrain our growth. This situation would even take away the motive to such combinations, by inducing an impracticability of success. An active commerce, an extensive navigation, and a flourishing marine would then be the inevitable offspring of moral and physical necessity. We might defy the little arts of little politicians to controul, or vary, the irresistible and unchangeable course of nature.

But in a state of disunion these combinations might exist, and might operate with success. It would be in the power of the maritime nations, availing themselves of our universal impotence, to prescribe the conditions of our political existence; and as they have a common interest in being our carriers, and still more in preventing our being theirs, they would in all probability combine to embarrass our navigation in such a manner, as would in effect destroy it, and confine us to a PASSIVE COMMERCE. We should thus be compelled to content ourselves with the first price of our commodities, and to see the profits of our trade snatched from us to enrich our enemies and persecutors. That unequalled spirit of enterprise, which signalises the genius of the American Merchants and Navigators, and which is in itself an inexhaustible mine of national wealth, would be stifled and lost; and poverty and disgrace would overspread a country, which with wisdom might make herself the admiration and envy of the world.

There are rights of great moment to the trade of America, which are rights of the Union. I allude to the fisheries, to the navigation of the Western lakes and to that of the Mississippi. The dissolution of the confederacy would give room for delicate questions, concerning the future existence of these rights; which the interest of more powerful partners would hardly fail to solve to our disadvantage. The disposition of Spain with regard to the Mississippi needs no comment. France and Britain are concerned with us in the fisheries; and view them as of the utmost moment to their navigation. They, of course, would hardly remain long indifferent to that decided mastery of which experience has shewn us to be possessed in this valuable branch of traffic; and by which we are able to undersell those nations in their own markets. What more natural, than that they should be disposed to exclude, from the lists, such dangerous competitors?

This branch of trade ought not to be considered as a partial benefit. All the navigating States may in different degrees advantageously participate in it and under circumstances of a greater extension of mercantile capital would not be unlikely to do it. As a nursery of seamen it now is, or when time shall have more nearly assimilated the principles of navigation in the several States, will become an universal resource. To the establishment of a navy it must be indispensible.

To this great national object of a NAVY, Union will contribute in various ways. Every institution will grow and flourish in proportion to the quantity and extent of the means concentered towards its formation and support. A navy of the United States, as it would embrace the resources of all, is an object far less remote than a navy of any single State, or partial confederacy, which would only embrace the resources of a part. It happens indeed that different portions of confederated America possess each some peculiar advantage for this essential establishment. The more Southern States furnish in greater abundance certain kinds of naval stores—tar, pitch and turpentine. Their wood for the construction of ships is also of a more solid and lasting texture. The difference in the duration of the ships of which the navy might be composed, if chiefly constructed of Southern wood would be of signal importance either in the view of naval strength or of national œconomy. Some of the Southern and of the middle States yield a greater plenty of iron and of better quality. Seamen must chiefly be drawn from the Northern hive. The necessity of naval protection to external or maritime commerce, does not require a particular elucidation, no more than the conduciveness of that species of commerce to the prosperity of a navy. They, by a kind of reaction, mutually beneficial, promote each other.

An unrestrained intercourse between the States themselves will advance the trade of each, by an interchange of their respective productions, not only for the supply of reciprocal wants at home, but for exportation to foreign markets. The veins of commerce in every part will be replenished, and will acquire additional motion and vigour from a free circulation of the commodities of every part. Commercial enterprise will have much greater scope, from the diversity in the productions of different States. When the staple of one fails, from a bad harvest or unproductive crop, it can call to its aid the staple of another. The variety not less than the value of products for exportation, contributes to the activity of foreign commerce. It can be conducted upon much better terms, with a large number of materials of a given value, than with a small number of materials of the same value; arising from the competitions of trade and from the fluctuations of markets. Particular articles may be in great demand, at certain periods, and unsaleable at others; but if there be a variety of articles it can scarcely happen that they should all be at one time in the latter predicament; and on this account the operations of the merchant would be less liable to any considerable obstruction, or stagnation. The speculative trader will at once perceive the force of these observations; and will acknowledge that the aggregate ballance of the commerce of the United States would bid fair to be much more favorable, than that of the thirteen States, without union, or with partial unions.

It may perhaps be replied to this, that whether the States are united, or disunited, there would still be an intimate intercourse between them which would answer the same ends: But this intercourse would be fettered, interrupted and narrowed by a multiplicity of causes; which in the course of these Papers have been amply detailed. An unity of commercial, as well as political interests, can only result from an unity of government.

There are other points of view, in which this subject might be placed, of a striking and animating kind. But they would lead us too far into the regions of futurity, and would involve topics not proper for a Newspaper discussion. I shall briefly observe, that our situation invites, and our interests prompt us, to aim at an ascendant in the system of American affairs. The world may politically, as well as geographically, be divided into four parts, each having a distinct set of interests. Unhappily for the other three, Europe by her arms and by her negociations, by force and by fraud, has, in different degrees, extended her dominion over them all. Africa, Asia, and

America have successively felt her domination. The superiority, she has long maintained, has tempted her to plume herself as the Mistress of the World, and to consider the rest of mankind as created for her benefit. Men admired as profound philosophers have, in direct terms, attributed to her inhabitants a physical superiority; and have gravely asserted that all animals, and with them the human species, degenerate in America—that even dogs cease to bark after having breathed a while in our atmosphere.* Facts have too long supported these arrogant pretensions of the European: It belongs to us to vindicate the honor of the human race, and to teach that assuming brother moderation. Union will enable us to do it. Disunion will add another victim to his triumphs. Let Americans disdain to be the instruments of European greatness! Let the thirteen States, bound together in a strict and indissoluble union, concur in erecting one great American system, superior to the controul of all trans-atlantic force or influence, and able to dictate the terms of the connection between the old and the new world!

PUBLIUS.

* Recherches philosophiques sur les Americains.

The Independent Journal, November 24, 1787

The Federalist No. 12

To the People of the State of New-York.

The effects of union upon the commercial prosperity of the States have been sufficiently delineated. Its tendency to promote the interests of revenue will be the subject of our present enquiry.

The prosperity of commerce is now perceived and acknowledged, by all enlightened statesmen, to be the most useful as well as the most productive source of national wealth; and has accordingly become a primary object of their political cares. By multiplying the means of gratification, by promoting the introduction and circulation of the precious metals, those darling objects of human avarice and enterprise, it serves to vivify and invigorate the channels of industry, and to make them flow with greater activity and copiousness. The assiduous merchant, the laborious husbandman, the active mechanic, and the industrious manufacturer, all orders of men look forward with eager expectation and growing alacrity to this pleasing reward of their toils. The often-agitated question, between agriculture and commerce, has from indubitable experience received a decision, which has silenced the rivalships, that once subsisted between them, and has proved to the satisfaction of their friends, that their interests are intimately blended and interwoven. It has been found, in various countries, that in proportion as commerce has flourished, land has risen in value. And how could it have happened otherwise? Could that which procures a free vent for the products of the earth—which furnishes new incitements to the cultivators of land—which is the most powerful instrument in encreasing the quantity of money in a state—could that, in fine, which is the faithful handmaid of labor and industry in every shape, fail to augment the value of that article, which is the prolific parent of far the greatest part of the objects upon which they are exerted? It is astonishing, that so simple a truth should ever have had an adversary; and it is one among a multitude of proofs, how apt a spirit of ill-informed jealousy, or of too great abstraction and refinement is to lead men astray from the plainest paths of reason and conviction.

The ability of a country to pay taxes must always be proportioned, in a great degree, to the quantity of money in circulation, and to the celerity with which it circulates. Commerce, contributing to both these objects, must of necessity render the payment of taxes easier, and facilitate the requisite supplies to the treasury. The hereditary dominions of the Emperor of Germany, contain a great extent of fertile, cultivated and populous territory, a large proportion of which is situated in mild and luxuriant climates. In some parts of this territory are to be found the best gold and silver mines in Europe. And yet, from the want of the fostering influence of commerce, that monarch can boast but slender revenues. He has several times been compelled to owe obligations to the pecuniary succours of other nations, for the preservation of his essential interests; and is unable, upon the strength of his own resources, to sustain a long or continued war.

But it is not in this aspect of the subject alone, that union will be seen to conduce to the purposes of revenue. There are other points of view, in which its influence will appear more immediate and decisive. It is evident from the state of the country, from the habits of the people, from the experience we have had on the point itself, that it is impracticable to raise any very considerable sums by direct taxation. Tax laws have in vain been multiplied—new methods to enforce the collection have in vain been tried—the public expectation has been uniformly disappointed, and the treasuries of the States have remained empty. The popular system of administration, inherent in the nature of popular government, coinciding with the real scarcity of money, incident to a languid and mutilated state of trade, has hitherto defeated every experiment for extensive collections, and has at length taught the different Legislatures the folly of attempting them.

No person, acquainted with what happens in other countries, will be surprised at this circumstance. In so opulent a nation as that of Britain, where direct taxes from superior wealth, must be much more tolerable, and from the vigor of the government, much more practicable, than in America, far the greatest part of the national revenue is derived from taxes of the indirect kind; from imposts and from excises. Duties on imported articles form a large branch of this latter description.

In America it is evident, that we must a long time depend, for the means of revenue, chiefly on such duties. In most parts of it, excises must be confined within a narrow compass. The genius of the people will ill brook the inquisitive and peremptory spirit of excise laws. The pockets of the farmers, on the other hand, will reluctantly yield but scanty supplies in the unwelcome shape of impositions on their houses and lands. And personal property is too precarious and invisible a fund to be laid hold of in any other way, than by the imperceptible agency of taxes on consumption.

If these remarks have any foundation, that state of things, which will best enable us to improve and extend so valuable a resource, must be best adapted to our political welfare. And it cannot admit of a serious doubt, that this state of things must rest on the basis of a general union. As far as this would be conducive to the interests of commerce, so far it must tend to the extention of the revenue to be drawn from that source. As far as it would contribute to rendering regulations for the collection of the duties more simple and efficacious, so far it must serve to answer the purposes of making the same rate of duties more productive, and of putting it in the power of the government to increase the rate, without prejudice to trade.

The relative situation of these States, the number of rivers, with which they are intersected, and of bays that wash their shores, the facility of communication in every direction, the affinity of language, and manners, the familiar habits of intercourse; all these are circumstances, that would conspire to render an illicit trade between them, a matter of little difficulty, and would insure frequent evasions of the commercial regulations of each other. The seperate States, or confederacies would be necessitated by mutual jealousy to avoid the temptations to that kind of trade, by the lowness of their duties. The temper of our governments, for a long time to come, would not permit those rigorous precautions, by which the European nations guard the avenues into their respective countries, as well by land as by water; and which even there are found insufficient obstacles to the adventurous stratagems of avarice.

In France there is an army of patrols (as they are called) constantly employed to secure her fiscal regulations against the inroads of the dealers in contraband trade. Mr. *Neckar* computes the number of these patrols at upwards of twenty thousand. This shews the immense difficulty in preventing that species of traffic, where there is an inland communication, and places in a strong light the disadvantages with which the collection of duties in this country would be incumbered, if by disunion the States should be placed in a situation, with respect to each other, resembling that of France with respect to her neighbours. The arbitrary and vexatious powers with which the patrols are necessarily armed would be intolerable in a free country.

If on the contrary, there be but one government pervading all the States, there will be as to the principal part of our commerce but ONE SIDE to guard, the ATLANTIC COAST. Vessels arriving directly from foreign countries, laden with valuable cargoes, would rarely choose to hazard themselves to the complicated and critical perils, which would attend attempts to unlade prior to their coming into port. They would have to dread both the dangers of the coast, and of detection as well after as before their arrival at the places of their final destination. An ordinary degree of vigilance would be competent to the prevention of any material infractions upon the rights of the revenue. A few armed vessels, judiciously stationed at the entrances of our ports, might at a small expence be made useful centinels of the laws. And the government having the same interests to provide against violations every where, the co-operation of its measures in each State would have a powerful tendency to render them effectual. Here also we should preserve by union an advantage which nature holds out to us, and which would be relinquished by seperation. The United States lie at a great distance from Europe, and at a considerable distance from all other places with which they would have extensive connections of foreign trade. The passage from them to us, in a few hours, or in a single night, as between the coasts of France and Britain, and of other neighbouring nations, would be impracticable. This is a prodigious security against a direct contraband with foreign countries; but a circuitous contraband to one State, through the medium of another, would be both easy and safe. The difference between a direct importation from abroad and an indirect importation, through the channel of a neighbouring State, in small parcels, according to time and opportunity, with the additional facilities of inland communication, must be palpable to every man of discernment.

It is therefore, evident, that one national government would be able, at much less expence, to extend the duties on imports, beyond comparison further, than would be practicable to the States separately, or to any partial confederacies: Hitherto I believe it may safely be asserted, that these duties have not upon an average exceeded in any States three per cent. In France they are estimated to be about fifteen per cent and in Britain they exceed this proportion.* There seems to be nothing to hinder their being increased in this country, to at least treble their present amount. The single article of ardent spirits, under Fœderal regulation, might be made to furnish a considerable revenue. Upon a ratio to the importation into this State, the whole quantity imported into the United States may be estimated at four millions of Gallons; which at a shilling per gallon would produce two hundred thousand pounds. That article would well bear this rate of duty: and if it should tend to diminish the consumption of it, such an effect would be equally favorable to the agriculture, to the œconomy, to the morals and to the health of the society. There is perhaps nothing so much a subject of national extravagance, as these spirits.

What will be the consequence, if we are not able to avail ourselves of the resource in question in its full extent? A nation cannot long exist without revenue. Destitute of this essential support, it must resign its independence and sink into the degraded condition of a province. This is an extremity to which no government will of choice accede. Revenue therefore must be had at all events. In this country, if the principal part be not drawn from commerce, it must fall with oppressive weight upon land. It has been already intimated, that excises in their true signification are too little in unison with the feelings of the people, to admit of great use being made of

* If my memory be right they amount to 20 per cent.

that mode of taxation, nor indeed, in the States where almost the sole employment is agriculture, are the objects, proper for excise sufficiently numerous to permit very ample collections in that way. Personal estate, (as has been before remarked) from the difficulty of tracing it cannot be subjected to large contributions, by any other means, than by taxes on consumption. In populous cities, it may be enough the subject of conjecture, to occasion the oppression of individuals, without much aggregate benefit to the State; but beyond these circles it must in a great measure escape the eye and the hand of the tax-gatherer. As the necessities of the State, nevertheless, must be satisfied, in some mode or other, the defect of other resources must throw the principal weight of the public burthens on the possessors of land. And as, on the other hand, the wants of the government can never obtain an adequate supply, unless all the sources of revenue are open to its demands, the finances of the community under such embarrassments, cannot be put into a situation consistent with its respectability, or its security. Thus we shall not even have the consolations of a full treasury to atone for the oppression of that valuable class of the citizens, who are employed in the cultivation of the soil. But public and private distress will keep pace with each other in gloomy concert; and unite in deploring the infatuation of those councils, which led to disunion.

PUBLIUS.

The New-York Packet, November 27, 1787

The Federalist No. 13

To the People of the State of New-York.

As connected with the subject of revenue, we may with propriety consider that of œconomy. The money saved from one object may be usefully applied to another; and there will be so much the less to be drawn from the pockets of the people. If the States are united under one government, there will be but one national civil list to support; if they are divided into several confederacies, there will be as many different national civil lists to be provided for; and each of them, as to the principal departments coextensive with that which would be necessary for a government of the whole. The entire separation of the States into thirteen unconnected sovereignties is a project too extravagant and too replete with danger to have many advocates. The ideas of men who speculate upon the dismemberment of the empire, seem generally turned towards three confederacies; one consisting of the four northern, another of the four middle, and a third of the five southern States. There is little probability that there would be a greater number. According to this distribution each confederacy would comprise an extent of territory larger than that of the kingdom of Great-Britain. No well informed man will suppose that the affairs of such a confederacy can be properly regulated by a government, less comprehensive in its organs or institutions, than that, which has been proposed by the Convention. When the dimensions of a State attain to a certain magnitude, it requires the same energy of government and the same terms of administration; which are requisite in one of much greater extent. This idea admits not of precise demonstration, because there is no rule by which we can measure the momentum of civil power, necessary to the government of any given number of individuals; but when we consider that the island of Britain, nearly commensurate with each of the supposed confederacies, contains about eight millions of people, and when we reflect upon the degree of authority required to direct the passions of so large a society to the public good, we shall see no reason to doubt that the like portion of power would be sufficient to perform the same task in a society far more numerous. Civil power properly organised and exerted is capable of diffusing its force to a very great extent; and can in a manner reproduce itself in every part of a great empire by a judicious arrangement of subordinate institutions.

The supposition, that each confederacy into which the States would be likely to be divided, would require a government not less comprehensive, than the one proposed, will be strengthened by another supposition, more probable than that which presents us with three confederacies as the alternative to a general union. If we attend carefully to geographical and commercial considerations, in conjunction with the habits and prejudices of the different States, we shall be led to conclude, that in case of disunion they will most naturally league themselves under two governments. The four eastern States, from all the causes that form the links of national sympathy and connection, may with certainty be expected to unite. New-York, situated as she is, would never be unwise enough to oppose a feeble and unsupported flank to the weight of that confederacy. There are obvious reasons, that would facilitate her accession to it. New-Jersey is too small a State to think of being a frontier, in opposition to this still more powerful combination; nor do there appear to be any obstacles to her admission into it. Even Pennsylvania would have strong inducements to join the northern league. An active foreign commerce on the basis of her own navigation is her true policy, and coincides with the opinions and dispositions of her citizens. The more southern States, from various circumstances, may not think themselves much interested in the encouragement of navigation. They may prefer a system, which would give unlimited scope to all nations, to be the carriers as well as the purchasers of their commodities. Pennsylvania may not choose to confound her interests in a connection so adverse to her policy. As she must at all events be a frontier, she may deem it most consistent with her safety to have her exposed side turned towards the weaker power of the southern, rather than towards the stronger power of the northern confederacy. This would give her the fairest chance to avoid being the FLANDERS of America. Whatever may be the determination of Pennsylvania, if the northern confederacy includes New-Jersey, there is no likelihood of more than one confederacy to the south of that State.

Nothing can be more evident than that the thirteen States will be able to support a national government, better than one half, or one third, or any number less than the whole. This reflection must have great weight in obviating that objection to the proposed plan, which is founded on the principle of expence; an objection however, which, when we come to take a nearer view of it, will appear in every light to stand on mistaken ground.

If in addition to the consideration of a plurality of civil lists, we take into view the number of persons who must necessarily be employed to guard the inland communication, between the different confederacies, against illicit trade, and who in time will infallibly spring up out of the necessities of revenue; and if we also take into view the military establishments, which it has been shewn would unavoidably result from the jealousies and conflicts of the several nations, into which the States would be divided, we shall clearly discover, that a separation would be not less injurious to the œconomy than to the tranquillity, commerce, revenue and liberty of every part.

PUBLIUS.

The Independent Journal, November 28, 1787

The Federalist No. 15

To the People of the State of New-York.

In the course of the preceding papers, I have endeavoured, my Fellow Citizens, to place before you in a clear and convincing light, the importance of Union to your political safety and happiness. I have unfolded to you a complication of dangers to which you would be exposed should you permit that sacred knot which binds the people of America together to be severed or dissolved by ambition or by avarice, by jealousy or by misrepresentation. In the sequel of the inquiry, through which I propose to accompany you, the truths intended to be inculcated will receive further confirmation from facts and arguments hitherto unnoticed. If the road, over which you will still have to pass, should in some places appear to you tedious or irksome, you will recollect, that you are in quest of information on a subject the most momentous which can engage the attention of a free people: that the field through which you have to travel is in itself spacious, and that the difficulties of the journey have been unnecessarily increased by the mazes with which sophistry has beset the way. It will be my aim to remove the obstacles to your progress in as compendious a manner, as it can be done, without sacrificing utility to dispatch.

In pursuance of the plan, which I have laid down for the discussion of the subject, the point next in order to be examined is the "insufficiency of the present confederation to the preservation of the Union." It may perhaps be asked, what need is there of reasoning or proof to illustrate a position, which is not either controverted or doubted; to which the understandings and feelings of all classes of men assent; and which in substance is admitted by the opponents as well as by the friends of the New Constitution? It must in truth be acknowledged that however these may differ in other respects, they in general appear to harmonise in this sentiment at least, that there are material imperfections in our national system, and that something is necessary to be done to rescue us from impending anarchy. The facts that support this opinion are no longer objects of speculation. They have forced themselves upon the sensibility of the people at large, and have at length extorted from those, whose mistaken policy has had the principal share in precipitating the extremity, at which we are arrived, a reluctant confession of the reality of those defects in the scheme of our Fœderal Government, which have been long pointed out and regretted by the intelligent friends of the Union.

We may indeed with propriety be said to have reached almost the last stage of national humiliation. There is scarcely any thing that can wound the pride, or degrade the character of an independent nation, which we do not experience. Are there engagements to the performance of which we are held by every tie respectable among men? These are the subjects of constant and unblushing violation. Do we owe debts to foreigners and to our own citizens contracted in a time of imminent peril, for the preservation of our political existence? These remain without any proper or satisfactory provision for their discharge. Have we valuable territories and important posts in the possession of a foreign power, which by express stipulations ought long since to have been surrendered? These are still retained, to the prejudice of our interests not less than of our rights. Are we in a condition to resent, or to repel the aggression? We have neither troops nor treasury nor government.* Are we even in a condition to remonstrate with dignity? The just imputations on our own faith, in respect to the same treaty, ought first to be removed. Are we entitled by nature and compact to a free participation in the navigation of the Mississippi? Spain excludes us from it. Is public credit an indispensable resource in time of public danger? We seem to have abandoned its cause as desperate and irretrievable. Is commerce of importance to national wealth? Ours is at the lowest point of declension. Is respectability in the eyes of foreign powers a safe guard against foreign encroachments? The imbecility of our Government even forbids them to treat with us: Our ambassadors abroad are the mere pageants of mimic sovereignty. Is a violent and unnatural decrease in the value of land a symptom of national distress? The price of improved

* I mean for the Union.

land in most parts of the country is much lower than can be accounted for by the quantity of waste land at market, and can only be fully explained by that want of private and public confidence, which are so alarmingly prevalent among all ranks and which have a direct tendency to depreciate property of every kind. Is private credit the friend and patron of industry? That most useful kind which relates to borrowing and lending is reduced within the narrowest limits, and this still more from an opinion of insecurity than from the scarcity of money. To shorten an enumeration of particulars which can afford neither pleasure nor instruction it may in general be demanded, what indication is there of national disorder, poverty and insignificance that could befal a community so peculiarly blessed with natural advantages as we are, which does not form a part of the dark catalogue of our public misfortunes?

This is the melancholy situation, to which we have been brought by those very maxims and councils, which would now deter us from adopting the proposed constitution; and which not content with having conducted us to the brink of a precipice, seem resolved to plunge us into the abyss, that awaits us below. Here, my Countrymen, impelled by every motive that ought to influence an enlightened people, let us make a firm stand for our safety, our tranquillity, our dignity, our reputation. Let us at last break the fatal charm which has too long seduced us from the paths of felicity and prosperity.

It is true, as has been before observed, that facts too stubborn to be resisted have produced a species of general assent to the abstract proposition that there exist material defects in our national system; but the usefulness of the concession, on the part of the old adversaries of fœderal measures, is destroyed by a strenuous opposition to a remedy, upon the only principles, that can give it a chance of success. While they admit that the Government of the United States is destitute of energy; they contend against conferring upon it those powers which are requisite to supply that energy: They seem still to aim at things repugnant and irreconcilable—at an augmentation of Fœderal authority without a diminution of State authority—at sovereignty in the Union and complete independence in the members. They still in fine seem to cherish with blind devotion the political monster of an *imperium in imperio.* This renders a full display of the principal defects of the confederation necessary, in order to shew, that the evils we experience do not proceed from minute or partial imperfections, but from fundamental errors in the structure of the building which cannot be amended otherwise than by an alteration in the first principles and main pillars of the fabric.

The great and radical vice in the construction of the existing Confederation is in the principle of LEGISLATION for STATES or GOVERNMENTS, in their CORPORATE or COLLECTIVE CAPACITIES and as contradistinguished from the INDIVIDUALS of whom they consist. Though this principle does not run through all the powers delegated to the Union; yet it pervades and governs those, on which the efficacy of the rest depends. Except as to the rule of apportionment, the United States have an indefinite discretion to make requisitions for men and money; but they have no authority to raise either by regulations extending to the individual citizens of America. The consequence of this is, that though in theory their resolutions concerning those objects are laws, constitutionally binding on the members of the Union, yet in practice they are mere recommendations, which the States observe or disregard at their option.

It is a singular instance of the capriciousness of the human mind, that after all the admonitions we have had from experience on this head, there should still be found men, who object to the New Constitution for deviating from a principle which has been found the bane of the old; and which is in itself evidently incompatible with the idea of GOVERNMENT; a principle in short which if it is to be executed at all must substitute the violent and sanguinary agency of the sword to the mild influence of the Magistracy.

There is nothing absurd or impracticable in the idea of a league or alliance between independent nations, for certain defined purposes precisely stated in a treaty; regulating all the details of time, place, circumstance and quantity; leaving nothing to future discretion; and depending for its execution on the good faith of the parties. Compacts of this kind exist among all civilized nations subject to the usual vicissitudes of peace and war, of observance and non observance, as the interests or passions of the contracting powers dictate. In the early part of the present century, there was an epidemical rage in Europe for this species of compacts; from which the politicians of the times fondly hoped for benefits which were never realised. With a view to establishing the equilibrium of power and the peace of that part of the world, all the resources of negotiation were exhausted, and triple and quadruple alliances were formed; but they were scarcely formed before they were broken, giving an instructive but afflicting lesson to mankind how little dependence is to be placed on treaties which have no other sanction than the obligations of good faith; and which oppose general considerations of peace and justice to the impulse of any immediate interest and passion.

If the particular States in this country are disposed to stand in a similar relation to each other, and to drop the project of a general DISCRETIONARY SUPERINTENDENCE, the scheme would indeed be pernicious, and would entail upon us all the mischiefs that have been enumerated under the first head; but it would have the merit of being at least consistent and practicable. Abandoning all views towards a confederate Government, this would bring us to a simple alliance offensive and defensive; and would place us in a situation to be alternately friends and enemies of each other as our mutual jealousies and rivalships nourished by the intrigues of foreign nations should prescribe to us.

But if we are unwilling to be placed in this perilous situation; if we will still adhere to the design of a national government, or which is the same thing of a superintending power under the direction of a common Council, we must resolve to incorporate into our plan those ingredients which may be considered as forming the characteristic difference between a league and a government; we must extend the authority of the union to the persons of the citizens,—the only proper objects of government.

Government implies the power of making laws. It is essential to the idea of a law, that it be attended with a sanction; or, in other words, a penalty or punishment for disobedience. If there be no penalty annexed to disobedience, the resolutions or commands which pretend to be laws will in fact amount to nothing more than advice or recommendation.

This penalty, whatever it may be, can only be inflicted in two ways; by the agency of the Courts and Ministers of Justice, or by military force; by the COERTION of the magistracy, or by the COERTION of arms. The first kind can evidently apply only to men—the last kind must of necessity be employed against bodies politic, or communities or States. It is evident, that there is no process of a court by which their observance of the laws can in the last resort be enforced. Sentences may be denounced against them for violations of their duty; but these sentences can only be carried into execution by the sword. In an association where the general authority is confined to the collective bodies of the communities that compose it, every breach of the laws must involve a state of war, and military execution must become the only instrument of civil obedience. Such a state of things can certainly not deserve the name of government, nor would any prudent man choose to commit his happiness to it.

There was a time when we were told that breaches, by the States, of the regulations of the fœderal authority were not to be expected—that a sense of common interest would preside over the conduct of the respective members, and would beget a full compliance with all the constitutional requisitions of the Union. This language at the present day would appear as wild as a great part of what we now hear from the same quarter will be thought, when we shall have received further lessons from that best oracle of wisdom, experience. It at all times betrayed an ignorance of the true springs by which human conduct is actuated, and belied the original inducements to the establishment of civil power. Why has government been instituted at all? Because the passions of men will not conform to the dictates of reason and justice, without constraint. Has it been found that bodies of men act with more rectitude or greater disinterestedness than individuals? The contrary of this has been inferred by all accurate observers of the conduct of mankind; and the inference is founded upon obvious reasons. Regard to reputation has a less active influence, when the infamy of a bad action is to be divided among a number, than when it is to fall singly upon one. A spirit of faction which is apt to mingle its poison in the deliberations of all bodies of men, will often hurry the persons of whom they are composed into improprieties and excesses, for which they would blush in a private capacity.

In addition to all this, there is in the nature of sovereign power an impatience of controul, that disposes those who are invested with the exercise of it, to look with an evil eye upon all external attempts to restrain or direct its operations. From this spirit it happens that in every political association which is formed upon the principle of uniting in a common interest a number of lesser sovereignties, there will be found a kind of excentric tendency in the subordinate or inferior orbs, by the operation of which there will be a perpetual effort in each to fly off from the common center. This tendency is not difficult to be accounted for. It has its origin in the love of power. Power controuled or abridged is almost always the rival and enemy of that power by which it is controuled or abriged. This simple proposition will teach us how little reason there is to expect, that the persons, entrusted with the administration of the affairs of the particular members of a confederacy, will at all times be ready, with perfect good humour, and an un-biassed regard to the public weal, to execute the resolutions or decrees of the general authority. The reverse of this results from the constitution of human nature.

If therefore the measures of the confederacy cannot be ex-ecuted, without the intervention of the particular administra-tions, there will be little prospect of their being executed at all. The rulers of the respective members, whether they have a constitutional right to do it or not, will undertake to judge of the propriety of the measures themselves. They will con-sider the conformity of the thing proposed or required to their immediate interests or aims, the momentary conve-niences or inconveniences that would attend its adoption. All this will be done, and in a spirit of interested and suspicious scrutiny, without that knowledge of national circumstances and reasons of state, which is essential to a right judgment, and with that strong predilection in favour of local objects, which can hardly fail to mislead the decision. The same process must be repeated in every member of which the body is constituted; and the execution of the plans, framed by the councils of the whole, will always fluctuate on the discretion of the ill-informed and prejudiced opinion of every part.

Those who have been conversant in the proceedings of popular assemblies; who have seen how difficult it often is, when there is no exterior pressure of circumstances, to bring them to harmonious resolutions on important points, will readily conceive how impossible it must be to induce a number of such assemblies, deliberating at a distance from each other, at different times, and under different impressions, long to cooperate in the same views and pursuits.

In our case, the concurrence of thirteen distinct sovereign wills is requisite under the confederation to the complete execution of every important measure, that proceeds from the Union. It has happened as was to have been foreseen. The measures of the Union have not been executed; and the delinquencies of the States have step by step matured themselves to an extreme; which has at length arrested all the wheels of the national government, and brought them to an awful stand. Congress at this time scarcely possess the means of keeping up the forms of administration; 'till the States can have time to agree upon a more substantial substitute for the present shadow of a fœderal government. Things did not come to this desperate extremity at once. The causes which have been specified produced at first only unequal and disproportionate degrees of compliance with the requisitions of the Union. The greater deficiencies of some States furnished the pretext of example and the temptation of interest to the complying, or to the least delinquent States. Why should we do more in proportion than those who are embarked with us in the same political voyage? Why should we consent to bear more than our proper share of the common burthen? These were suggestions which human selfishness could not withstand, and which even speculative men, who looked forward to remote consequences, could not, without hesitation, combat. Each State yielding to the persuasive voice of immediate interest and convenience has successively withdrawn its support, 'till the frail and tottering edifice seems ready to fall upon our heads and to crush us beneath its ruins.

PUBLIUS

The Independent Journal, December 1, 1787

The Federalist No. 16

To the People of the State of New-York.

The tendency of the principle of legislation for States, or communities, in their political capacities, as it has been exemplified by the experiment we have made of it, is equally attested by the events which have befallen all other governments of the confederate kind, of which we have any account, in exact proportion to its prevalence in those systems. The confirmations of this fact will be worthy of a distinct and particular examination. I shall content myself with barely observing here, that of all the confederacies of antiquity, which history has handed down to us, the Lycian and Achæan leagues, as far as there remain vestiges of them, appear to have been most free from the fetters of that mistaken principle, and were accordingly those which have best deserved, and have most liberally received the applauding suffrages of political writers.

This exceptionable principle may as truly as emphatically be stiled the parent of anarchy: It has been seen that delinquencies in the members of the Union are its natural and necessary offspring; and that whenever they happen, the only constitutional remedy is force, and the immediate effect of the use of it, civil war.

It remains to enquire how far so odious an engine of government, in its application to us, would even be capable of answering its end. If there should not be a large army, constantly at the disposal of the national government, it would either not be able to employ force at all, or when this could be done, it would amount to a war between different parts of the confederacy, concerning the infractions of a league; in which the strongest combination would be most likely to prevail, whether it consisted of those who supported, or of those who resisted the general authority. It would rarely happen that the delinquency to be redressed would be confined to a single member, and if there were more than one, who had neglected their duty, similarity of situation would induce them to unite for common defence. Independent of this motive of sympathy, if a large and influential State should happen to be the aggressing member, it would commonly have weight enough with its neighbours, to win over some of them as associates to its cause. Specious arguments of danger to the common liberty could easily be contrived; plausible excuses for the deficiencies of the party, could, without difficulty be invented, to alarm the apprehensions, inflame the passions, and conciliate the good will even of those States which were not chargeable with any violation, or omission of duty. This would be the more likely to take place, as the delinquencies of the larger members might be expected sometimes to proceed from an ambitious premeditation in their rulers, with a view to getting rid of all external controul upon their designs of personal aggrandizement; the better to effect which, it is presumable they would tamper beforehand with leading individuals in the adjacent States. If associates could not be found at home, recourse would be had to the aid of foreign powers, who would seldom be disinclined to encouraging the dissentions of a confederacy, from the firm Union of which they had so much to fear. When the sword is once drawn, the passions of men observe no bounds of moderation. The suggestions of wounded pride, the instigations of irritated resentment, would be apt to carry the States, against which the arms of the Union were exerted to any extremes necessary to revenge the affront, or to avoid the disgrace of submission. The first war of this kind would probably terminate in a dissolution of the Union.

This may be considered as the violent death of the confederacy. Its more natural death is what we now seem to be on the point of experiencing, if the fœderal system be not speedily renovated in a more substantial form. It is not probable, considering the genius of this country, that the complying States would often be inclined to support the authority of the Union by engaging in a war against the non-complying States. They would always be more ready to pursue the milder course of putting themselves upon an equal footing with the delinquent members, by an imitation of their example. And the guilt of all would thus become the security of all. Our past experience has exhibited the operation of this spirit in its full light. There would in fact be an insuperable difficulty in ascertaining when force could with propriety be employed. In the article of pecuniary contribution, which would be the most usual source of delinquency, it would often be impossible to decide whether it has proceeded from disinclination, or inability. The pretence of the latter would always be at hand. And the case must be very flagrant in which its fallacy could be detected with sufficient certainty to justify the harsh expedient of compulsion. It is easy to see that this problem alone, as often as it should occur, would open a wide field for the exercise of factious views, of partiality and of oppression, in the majority that happened to prevail in the national council.

It seems to require no pains to prove that the States ought not to prefer a national constitution, which could only be kept in motion by the instrumentality of a large army, continually on foot to execute the ordinary requisitions or decrees of the government. And yet this is the plain alternative involved by those who wish to deny it the power of extending its operations to individuals. Such a scheme, if practicable at all, would instantly degenerate into a military despotism; but it will be found in every light impracticable. The resources of the Union would not be equal to the maintenance of an army considerable enough to confine the larger States within the limits of their duty; nor would the means ever be furnished of forming such an army in the first instance. Whoever considers the populousness and strength of several of these States singly at the present juncture, and looks forward to what they will become, even at the distance of half a century, will at once dismiss as idle and visionary any scheme, which aims at regulating their movements by laws, to operate upon them in their collective capacities, and to be executed by a coertion applicable to them in the same capacities. A project of this kind is little less romantic than that monster-taming spirit, which is attributed to the fabulous heroes and demi-gods of antiquity.

Even in those confederacies, which have been composed of members smaller than many of our counties, the principle of legislation for sovereign States, supported by military coertion, has never been found effectual. It has rarely been attempted to be employed, but against the weaker members. And in most instances attempts to coerce the refractory and disobedient, have been the signals of bloody wars; in which one half of the confederacy has displayed its banners against the other half.

The result of these observations to an intelligent mind must be clearly this, that if it be possible at any rate to construct a Fœderal Government capable of regulating the common concerns and preserving the general tranquility, it must be founded, as to the objects committed to its care, upon the reverse of the principle contended for by the opponents of the proposed constitution. It must carry its agency to the persons of the citizens. It must stand in need of no intermediate legislations; but must itself be empowered to employ the arm of the ordinary magistrate to execute its own resolutions. The majesty of the national authority must be manifested through the medium of the Courts of Justice. The government of the Union, like that of each State, must be able to address itself immediately to the hopes and fears of individuals; and to attract to its support, those passions, which have the strongest influence upon the human heart. It must in short, possess all the means and have a right to resort to all the methods of executing the powers, with which it is entrusted, that are possessed and exercised by the governments of the particular States.

To this reasoning it may perhaps be objected, that if any State should be disaffected to the authority of the Union, it could at any time obstruct the execution of its laws, and bring the matter to the same issue of force, with the necessity of which the opposite scheme is reproached.

The plausibility of this objection will vanish the moment we advert to the essential difference between a mere NON COMPLIANCE and a DIRECT and ACTIVE RESISTANCE. If the interposition of the State-Legislatures be necessary to give effect to a measure of the Union, they have only NOT TO ACT or TO ACT EVASIVELY, and the measure is defeated. This neglect of duty may be disguised under affected but unsubstantial provisions, so as not to appear, and of course not to excite any alarm in the people for the safety of the constitution. The State leaders may even make a merit of their surreptitious invasions of it, on the ground of some temporary convenience, exemption, or advantage.

But if the execution of the laws of the national government, should not require the intervention of the State Legislatures; if they were to pass into immediate operation upon the citizens themselves, the particular governments could not interrupt their progress without an open and violent exertion of an unconstitutional power. No omissions, nor evasions would answer the end. They would be obliged to act, and in such a manner, as would leave no doubt that they had encroached on the national rights. An experiment of this nature would always be hazardous—in the face of a constitution in any degree competent to its own defence, and of a people enlightened enough to distinguish between a legal exercise and an illegal usurpation of authority. The success of it would require not merely a factious majority in the Legislature, but the concurrence of the courts of justice, and of the body of the people. If the Judges were not embarked in a conspiracy with the Legislature they would pronounce the resolutions of such a majority to be contrary to the supreme law of the land, unconstitutional and void. If the people were not tainted with the spirit of their State representatives, they, as the natural guardians of the constitution, would throw their weight into the national scale, and give it a decided preponderancy in the contest. Attempts of this kind would not often be made with levity or rashness; because they could seldom be made without danger to the authors; unless in cases of a tyrannical exercise of the Fœderal authority.

If opposition to the national government should arise from the disorderly conduct of refractory, or seditious individuals, it could be overcome by the same means which are daily employed against the same evil, under the State governments. The Magistracy, being equally the Ministers of the law of the land, from whatever source it might emanate, would doubtless be as ready to guard the national as the local regulations from the inroads of private licentiousness. As to those partial commotions and insurrections which sometimes disquiet society, from the intrigues of an inconsiderable faction, or from sudden or occasional ill humours that do not infect the great body of the community, the general government could command more extensive resources for the suppression of disturbances of that kind, than would be in the power of any single member. And as to those mortal feuds, which in certain con-junctures spread a conflagration through a whole nation, or through a very large proportion of it, proceeding either from weighty causes of discontent given by the government, or from the contagion of some violent popular paroxism, they do not fall within any ordinary rules of calculation. When they happen, they commonly amount to revolutions and dis-memberments of empire. No form of government can always either avoid or controul them. It is in vain to hope to guard against events too mighty for human foresight or precaution, and it would be idle to object to a government because it could not perform impossibilities.

PUBLIUS.

The New-York Packet, December 4, 1787

The Federalist No. 17

To the People of the State of New-York.

An objection of a nature different from that which has been stated and answered, in my last address, may perhaps be likewise urged against the principle of legislation for the individual citizens of America. It may be said, that it would tend to render the government of the Union too powerful, and to enable it to absorb in itself those residuary authorities, which it might be judged proper to leave with the States for local purposes. Allowing the utmost latitude to the love of power, which any reasonable man can require, I confess I am at a loss to discover what temptation the persons entrusted with the administration of the general government could ever feel to divest the States of the authorities of that description. The regulation of the mere domestic police of a State appears to me to hold out slender allurements to ambition. Commerce, finance, negociation and war seem to comprehend all the objects, which have charms for minds governed by that passion; and all the powers necessary to these objects ought in the first instance to be lodged in the national depository. The administration of private justice between the citizens of the same State, the supervision of agriculture and of other concerns of a similar nature, all those things in short which are proper to be provided for by local legislation, can never be desirable cares of a general jurisdiction. It is therefore improbable that there should exist a disposition in the Fœderal councils to usurp the powers with which they are connected; because the attempt to exercise those powers would be as troublesome as it would be nugatory; and the possession of them, for that reason, would contribute nothing to the dignity, to the importance, or to the splendour of the national government.

But let it be admitted for argument sake, that mere wantonness and lust of domination would be sufficient to beget that disposition, still it may be safely affirmed, that the sense of the constituent body of the national representatives, or in other words of the people of the several States would controul the indulgence of so extravagant an appetite. It will always be far more easy for the State governments to encroach upon the national authorities, than for the national government to encroach upon the State authorities. The proof of this proposition turns upon the greater degree of influence, which the State governments, if they administer their affairs with uprightness and prudence, will generally possess over the people; a circumstance which at the same time teaches us, that there is an inherent and intrinsic weakness in all Fœderal Constitutions; and that too much pains cannot be taken in their organization, to give them all the force which is compatible with the principles of liberty.

The superiority of influence in favour of the particular governments would result partly from the diffusive construction of the national government; but chiefly from the nature of the objects to which the attention of the State administrations would be directed.

It is a known fact in human nature that its affections are commonly weak in proportion to the distance or diffusiveness of the object. Upon the same principle that a man is more attached to his family than to his neighbourhood, to his neighbourhood than to the community at large, the people of each State would be apt to feel a stronger byass towards their local governments than towards the government of the Union; unless the force of that principle should be destroyed by a much better administration of the latter.

This strong propensity of the human heart would find powerful auxiliaries in the objects of State regulation.

The variety of more minute interests, which will necessarily fall under the superintendence of the local administrations, and which will form so many rivulets of influence running through every part of the society, cannot be particularised without involving a detail too tedious and uninteresting to compensate for the instruction it might afford.

There is one transcendent advantage belonging to the province of the State governments which alone suffices to place the matter in a clear and satisfactory light—I mean the ordinary administration of criminal and civil justice. This of all others is the most powerful, most universal and most attractive source of popular obedience and attachment. It is that, which—being the immediate and visible guardian of life and property—having its benefits and its terrors in constant activity before the public eye—regulating all those personal interests and familiar concerns to which the sensibility of individuals is more immediately awake—contributes more than any other circumstance to impressing upon the minds of the people affection, esteem and reverence towards the government. This great cement of society which will diffuse itself almost wholly through the channels of the particular governments, independent of all other causes of influence, would ensure them so decided an empire over their respective citizens, as to render them at all times a complete counterpoise and not unfrequently dangerous rivals to the power of the Union.

The operations of the national government on the other hand falling less immediately under the observation of the mass of the citizens the benefits derived from it will chiefly be perceived and attended to by speculative men. Relating to more general interests, they will be less apt to come home to the feelings of the people; and, in proportion, less likely to inspire a habitual sense of obligation and an active sentiment of attachment.

The reasoning on this head has been abundantly exemplified by the experience of all Fœderal constitutions, with which we are acquainted, and of all others, which have borne the least analogy to them.

Though the ancient feudal systems were not strictly speaking confederacies, yet they partook of the nature of that species of association. There was a common head, chieftain, or sovereign, whose authority extended over the whole nation; and a number of subordinate vassals; or feudatories, who had large portions of land allotted to them and numerous trains of *inferior* vassals or retainers, who occupied and cultivated that land upon the tenure of fealty or obedience to the persons of whom they held it. Each principal vassal was a kind of sovereign within his particular demesnes. The consequences of this situation were a continual opposition to the authority of the sovereign, and frequent wars between the great barons, or chief feudatories themselves. The power of the head of the nation was commonly too weak either to preserve the public peace or to protect the people against the oppressions of their immediate lords. This period of European affairs is emphatically stiled by historians the times of feudal anarchy.

When the sovereign happened to be a man of vigorous and warlike temper and of superior abilities, he would acquire a personal weight and influence, which answered for the time the purposes of a more regular authority. But in general the power of the barons triumphed over that of the prince; and in many instances his dominion was entirely thrown off, and the great fiefs were erected into independent principalities or states. In those instances in which the monarch finally prevailed over his vassals, his success was chiefly owing to the tyranny of those vassals over their dependents. The barons, or nobles equally the enemies of the sovereign and the oppressors of the common people were dreaded and detested by both; till mutual danger and mutual interest effected an union between them fatal to the power of the aristocracy. Had the nobles, by a conduct of clemency and justice, preserved the fidelity and devotion of their retainers and followers, the contests between them and the prince must almost always have ended in their favour and in the abrigement or subversion of the royal authority.

This is not an assertion founded merely in speculation or conjecture. Among other illustrations of its truth which might be cited Scotland will furnish a cogent example. The spirit of clanship which was at an early day introduced into that kingdom, uniting the nobles and their dependents by ties equivalent to those of kindred, rendered the aristocracy a constant overmatch for the power of the monarch; till the incorporation with England subdued its fierce and ungovernable spirit, and reduced it within those rules of subordination, which a more rational and a more energetic system of civil polity had previously established in the latter kingdom.

The separate governments in a confederacy may aptly be compared with the feudal baronies; with this advantage in their favour, that from the reasons already explained, they will generally possess the confidence and good will of the people; and with so important a support will be able effectually to oppose all incroachments of the national government. It will be well if they are not able to conteract its legitimate and necessary authority. The points of similitude consist in the rivalship

of power, applicable to both, and in the CONCENTRA-
TION of large portions of the strength of the community
into particular depositories, in one case at the disposal of individuals, in the other case at the disposal of political bodies.

A concise review of the events that have attended confederate governments will further illustrate this important doctrine;
an inattention to which has been the great source of our
political mistakes, and has given our jealousy a direction to
the wrong side. This review shall form the subject of some
ensuing papers.

PUBLIUS.

The Independent Journal, December 5, 1787

The Federalist No. 21

Having in the three last numbers taken a summary review of the principal circumstances and events, which have depicted the genius and fate of other confederate governments; I shall now proceed in the enumeration of the most important of those defects, which have hitherto disappointed our hopes from the system established among ourselves. To form a safe and satisfactory judgment of the proper remedy, it is absolutely necessary that we should be well acquainted with the extent and malignity of the disease.

The next most palpable defect of the subsisting confederation is the total want of a SANCTION to its laws. The United States as now composed, have no power to exact obedience, or punish disobedience to their resolutions, either by pecuniary mulcts by a suspension or divestiture of privileges, or in any other constitutional mode. There is no express delegation of authority to them to use force against delinquent members; and if such a right should be ascribed to the fœderal head, as resulting from the nature of the social compact between the States, it must be by inference and construction, in the face of that part of the second article, by which it is declared, "each State shall retain every power, jurisdiction and right, not *expressly* delegated to the United States in Congress assembled." There is doubtless, a striking absurdity in supposing that a right of this kind does not exist, but we are reduced to the dilemma either of embracing that supposition, preposterous as it may seem, or of contravening or explaining away a provision, which has been of late a repeated theme of the eulogies of those, who oppose the new constitution; and the want of which in that plan, has been the subject of much plausible animadversion and severe criticism. If we are unwilling to impair the force of this applauded provision, we shall be obliged to conclude, that the United States afford the extraordinary spectacle of a government, destitute even of the shadow of a constitutional power to enforce the execution of its own laws. It will appear from the specimens which have been cited, that the American confederacy in this particular, stands discriminated from every other institution of a similar kind, and exhibits a new and unexampled phenomenon in the political world.

The want of a mutual guarantee of the State governments is another capital imperfection in the fœderal plan. There is nothing of this kind declared in the articles that compose it; and to imply a tacit guarantee from considerations of utility, would be a still more flagrant departure from the clause which has been mentioned, than to imply a tacit power of coertion, from the like considerations. The want of a guarantee, though it might in its consequences endanger the Union, does not so immediately attack its existence as the want of a constitutional sanction to its laws.

Without a guarantee, the assistance to be derived from the Union in repelling those domestic dangers, which may sometimes threaten the existence of the State constitutions, must be renounced. Usurpation may rear its crest in each State, and trample upon the liberties of the people; while the national government could legally do nothing more than behold its encroachments with indignation and regret. A successful faction may erect a tyranny on the ruins of order and law, while no succour could constitutionally be afforded by the Union to the friends and supporters of the government. The tempestuous situation, from which Massachusetts has scarcely emerged, evinces that dangers of this kind are not merely speculative. Who can determine what might have been the issue of her late convulsions, if the mal-contents had been headed by a Caesar or by a Cromwell? Who can predict what effect a despostism established in Massachusetts, would have upon the liberties of New-Hampshire or Rhode-Island; of Connecticut or New-York?

The inordinate pride of State importance has suggested to some minds an objection to the principle of a guarantee in the fœderal Government; as involving an officious interference in the domestic concerns of the members. A scruple of this kind would deprive us of one of the principal advantages to be expected from Union; and can only flow from a misapprehension of the nature of the provision itself. It could be no impediment to reforms of the State Constitutions by a majority of the people in a legal and peaceable mode. This right would remain undiminished. The guarantee could only operate against changes to be effected by violence. Towards the prevention of calamities of this kind too many checks cannot be provided. The peace of society, and the stability of government, depend absolutely on the efficacy of the precautions adopted on this head. Where the whole power of the government is in the hands of the people, there is the less pretence for the use of violent remedies, in partial or occasional distempers of the State. The natural cure for an ill administration, in a popular or representative constitution, is a change of men. A guarantee by the national authority would be as much levelled against the usurpations of rulers, as against the ferments and outrages of faction and sedition in the community.

The principle of regulating the contributions of the States to the common treasury by QUOTAS is another fundamental error in the confederation. Its repugnancy to an adequate supply of the national exigencies has been already pointed out, and has sufficiently appeared from the trial which has been made of it. I speak of it now solely with a view to equality among the States. Those who have been accustomed to contemplate the circumstances, which produce and constitute natural wealth, must be satisfied that there is no common standard, or barometer, by which the degrees of it can be ascertained. Neither the value of lands nor the numbers of the people, which have been successively proposed as the rule of State contributions, has any pretension to being a just representative. If we compare the wealth of the United Netherlands with that of Russia or Germany or even of France; and if we at that same time compare the total value of the lands, and the aggregate population of that constricted district, with the total value of the lands, and the aggregate population of the immense regions of either of the three last mentioned countries, we shall at once discover that there is no comparison between the proportion of either of these two objects and that of the relative wealth of those nations. If the like parallel were to be run between several of the American States; it would furnish a like result. Let Virginia be contrasted with North-Carolina, Pennsylvania with Connecticut, or Maryland with New-Jersey, and we shall be convinced that the respective abilities of those States, in relation to revenue, bear little or no analogy to their comparative stock in lands or to their comparative population. The position may be equally illustrated by a similar process between the counties of the same State. No man who is acquainted with the State of New-York will doubt, that the active wealth of Kings County bears a much greater proportion to that of Montgomery, than it would appear to do, if we should take either the total value of the lands or the total numbers of the people as a criterion!

The wealth of nations depends upon an infinite variety of causes. Situation, soil, climate, the nature of the productions, the nature of the government, the genius of the citizens—the degree of information they possess—the state of commerce, of arts, of industry—these circumstances and many much too complex, minute, or adventitious, to admit of a particular specification, occasion differences hardly conceivable in the relative opulence and riches of different countries. The consequence clearly is, that there can be no common measure of national wealth; and of course, no general or stationary rule, by which the ability of a State to pay taxes can be determined. The attempt therefore to regulate the contributions of the members of a confederacy, by any such rule, cannot fail to be productive of glaring inequality and extreme oppression.

This inequality would of itself be sufficient in America to work the eventual destruction of the Union, if any mode of inforcing a compliance with its requisitions could be devised. The suffering States would not long consent to remain associated upon a principle which distributed the public burthens with so unequal a hand; and which was calculated to impoverish and oppress the citizens of some States, while those of others would scarcely be conscious of the small proportion of the weight they were required to sustain. This however is an evil inseparable from the principle of quotas and requisitions.

There is no method of steering clear of this inconvenience but by authorising the national government to raise its own revenues in its own way. Imposts, excises and in general all duties upon articles of consumption may be compared to a fluid, which will in time find its level with the means of paying them. The amount to be contributed by each citizen will in a degree be at his own option, and can be regulated by an attention to his resources. The rich may be extravagant, the poor can be frugal. And private oppression may always be avoided by a judicious selection of objects proper for such impositions. If inequalities should arise in some States from duties on particular objects, these will in all probability be counterballanced by proportional inequalities in other States from the duties on other objects. In the course of time and things, an equilibrium, as far as it is attainable, in so complicated a subject, will be established every where. Or if inequalities should still exist they would neither be so great in their degree, so uniform in their operation, nor so odious in their appearance, as those which would necessarily spring from quotas upon any scale, that can possibly be devised.

It is a signal advantage of taxes on articles of consumption, that they contain in their own nature a security against excess. They prescribe their own limit; which cannot be exceeded without defeating the end proposed—that is an extension of the revenue. When applied to this object, the saying is as just as it is witty, that "in political arithmetic, two and two do not always make four." If duties are too high they lessen the consumption—the collection is eluded; and the product to the treasury is not so great as when they are confined within proper and moderate bounds. This forms a complete barrier against any material oppression of the citizens, by taxes of this class, and is itself a natural limitation of the power of imposing them.

Impositions of this kind usually fall under the denomination of indirect taxes, and must always constitute the chief part of the revenue raised in this country. Those of the direct kind, which principally relate to lands and buildings, may admit of a rule of apportionment. Either the value of land, or the number of the people may serve as a standard. The state of agriculture, and the populousness of a country, have been considered as nearly connected with each other. And as a rule for the purpose intended, numbers in the view of simplicity and certainty, are entitled to a preference. In every country it is an Herculean task to obtain a valuation of the land; in a country imperfectly settled and progressive in improvement, the difficulties are increased almost to impracticability. The expence of an accurate valuation is in all situations a formidable objection. In a branch of taxation where no limits to the discretion of the government are to be found in the nature of things, the establishment of a fixed rule, not incompatible with the end, may be attended with fewer inconveniencies than to leave that discretion altogether at large.

PUBLIUS.

The Independent Journal, December 12, 1787

The Federalist No. 22

To the People of the State of New-York.

In addition to the defects already enumerated in the existing Fœderal system, there are others of not less importance, which concur in rendering it altogether unfit for the administration of the affairs of the Union.

The want of a power to regulate commerce is by all parties allowed to be of the number. The utility of such a power has been anticipated under the first head of our inquiries; and for this reason as well as from the universal conviction entertained upon the subject, little need be added in this place. It is indeed evident, on the most superficial view, that there is no object, either as it respects the interests of trade or finance that more strongly demands a Fœderal superintendence. The want of it has already operated as a bar to the formation of beneficial treaties with foreign powers; and has given occasions of dissatisfaction between the States. No nation acquainted with the nature of our political association would be unwise enough to enter into stipulations with the United States, by which they conceded privileges of any importance to them, while they were apprised that the engagements on the part of the Union, might at any moment be violated by its members; and while they found from experience that they might enjoy every advantage they desired in our markets, without granting us any return, but such as their momentary convenience might suggest. It is not therefore to be wondered at, that Mr. Jenkinson in ushering into the House of Commons a bill for regulating the temporary intercourse between the two countries, should preface its introduction by a declaration that similar provisions in former bills had been found to answer every purpose to the commerce of Great Britain, & that it would be prudent to persist in the plan until it should appear whether the American government was likely or not to acquire greater consistency.*

---

* This as nearly as I can recollect was the sense of his speech in introducing the last bill.

Several States have endeavoured by separate prohibitions, restrictions and exclusions, to influence the conduct of that kingdom in this particular; but the want of concert, arising from the want of a general authority, and from clashing, and dissimilar views in the States, has hitherto frustrated every experiment of the kind; and will continue to do so as long as the same obstacles to an uniformity of measures continue to exist.

The interfering and unneighbourly regulations of some States, contrary to the true spirit of the Union, have in different instances given just cause of umbrage and complaint to others; and it is to be feared that examples of this nature, if not restrained by a national controul, would be multiplied and extended till they became not less serious sources of animosity and discord, than injurious impediments to the intercourse between the different parts of the confederacy. "The commerce of the German empire,* is in continual trammels from the multiplicity of the duties which the several Princes and States exact upon the merchandizes passing through their territories; by means of which the fine streams and navigable rivers with which Germany is so happily watered, are rendered almost useless." Though the genius of the people of this country might never permit this description to be strictly applicable to us, yet we may reasonably expect, from the gradual conflicts of State regulations, that the citizens of each, would at length come to be considered and treated by the others in no better light than that of foreigners and aliens.

The power of raising armies, by the most obvious construction of the articles of the confederation, is merely a power of making requisitions upon the States for quotas of men. This practice, in the course of the late war, was found replete with obstructions to a vigorous and to an œconomical system of defence. It gave birth to a competition between the States, which created a kind of auction for men. In order to furnish the quotas required of them, they outbid each other, till bounties grew to an enormous and insupportable size. The hope of a still further increase afforded an inducement to those who were disposed to serve to procrastinate their inlist-

* Encyclopedie *article* empire.

ment; and disinclined them to engaging for any considerable periods. Hence slow and scanty levies of men in the most critical emergencies of our affairs—short inlistments at an unparalleled expence—continual fluctuations in the troops, ruinous to their discipline, and subjecting the public safety frequently to the perilous crisis of a disbanded army. Hence also those oppressive expedients for raising men which were upon several occasions practised, and which nothing but the enthusiasm of liberty would have induced the people to endure.

This method of raising troops is not more unfriendly to œconomy and vigor, than it is to an equal distribution of the burthen. The States near the seat of war, influenced by motives of self preservation, made efforts to furnish their quotas, which even exceeded their abilities, while those at a distance from danger were for the most part as remiss as the others were diligent in their exertions. The immediate pressure of this inequality was not in this case, as in that of the contributions of money, alleviated by the hope of a final liquidation. The States which did not pay their proportions of money, might at least be charged with their deficiencies; but no account could be formed of the deficiencies in the supplies of men. We shall not, however, see much reason to regret the want of this, when we consider how little prospect there is, that the most delinquent States will ever be able to make compensation for their pecuniary failures. The system of quotas and requisitions, whether it be applied to men or money, is in every view a system of imbecility in the union, and of inequality and injustice among the members.

The right of equal suffrage among the States is another exceptionable part of the confederation. Every idea of proportion, and every rule of fair representation conspire to condemn a principle, which gives to Rhode-Island an equal weight in the scale of power with Massachusetts, or Connecticut, or New-York; and to Delaware, an equal voice in the national deliberations with Pennsylvania or Virginia, or North-Carolina. Its operation contradicts that fundamental maxim of republican government, which requires that the sense of the majority should prevail. Sophistry may reply, that sovereigns are equal, and that a majority of the votes of the States will be a majority of confederated America. But this kind of logical legerdemain, will never counteract the plain suggestions of justice and common sense. It may happen that this majority of States is a small minority of the people of America;* and two thirds of the people of America, could not long be persuaded, upon the credit of artificial distinctions and syllogistic subtleties, to submit their interests to the management and disposal of one third. The larger States would after a while revolt from the idea of receiving the law from the smaller. To acquiesce in such a privation of their due importance in the political scale, would be not merely to be insensible to the love of power, but even to sacrifice the desire of equality. It is neither rational to expect the first, nor just to require the last—the smaller States considering how peculiarly their safety and welfare depend on union, ought readily to renounce a pretension; which, if not relinquished would prove fatal to its duration.

It may be objected to this, that not seven but nine States, or two thirds of the whole number must consent to the most important resolutions; and it may be thence inferred, that nine States would always comprehend a majority of the inhabitants of the Union. But this does not obviate the impropriety of an equal vote between States of the most unequal dimensions and populousness; nor is the inference accurate in point of fact; for we can enumerate nine States which contain less than a majority of the people;† and it is constitutionally possible, that these nine may give the vote. Besides there are matters of considerable moment determinable by a bare majority; and there are others, concerning which doubts have been entertained, which if interpreted in favor of the sufficiency of a vote of seven States, would extend its operation to interests of the first magnitude. In addition to this, it is to be observed, that there is a probability of an increase in the number of States, and no provision for a proportional augmentation of the ratio of votes.

But this is not all; what at first sight may seem a remedy, is

---

* New-Hampshire, Rhode-Island, New-Jersey, Delaware, Georgia, South-Carolina and Maryland, are a majority of the whole number of the States, but they do not contain one third of the people.

† Add New-York and Connecticut, to the foregoing seven, and they will still be less than a majority.

in reality a poison. To give a minority a negative upon the majority (which is always the case where more than a majority is requisite to a decision) is in its tendency to subject the sense of the greater number to that of the lesser number. Congress from the non-attendance of a few States have been frequently in the situation of a Polish Diet, where a single veto has been sufficient to put a stop to all their movements. A sixtieth part of the Union, which is about the proportion of Delaware and Rhode-Island, has several times been able to oppose an intire bar to its operations. This is one of those refinements which in practice has an effect, the reverse of what is expected from it in theory. The necessity of unanimity in public bodies, or of something approaching towards it, has been founded upon a supposition that it would contribute to security. But its real operation is to embarrass the administration, to destroy the energy of government, and to substitute the pleasure, caprice or artifices of an insignificant, turbulent or corrupt junto, to the regular deliberations and decisions of a respectable majority. In those emergencies of a nation, in which the goodness or badness, the weakness or strength of its government, is of the greatest importance, there is commonly a necessity for action. The public business must in some way or other go forward. If a pertinacious minority can controul the opinion of a majority respecting the best mode of conducting it; the majority in order that something may be done, must conform to the views of the minority; and thus the sense of the smaller number will over-rule that of the greater, and give a tone to the national proceedings. Hence tedious delays—continual negotiation and intrigue—contemptible compromises of the public good. And yet in such a system, it is even happy when such compromises can take place: For upon some occasions things will not admit of accommodation; and then the measures of government must be injuriously suspended or fatally defeated. It is often, by the impracticability of obtaining the concurrence of the necessary number of votes, kept in a state of inaction. Its situation must always savour of weakness—sometimes border upon anarchy.

It is not difficult to discover that a principle of this kind gives greater scope to foreign corruption as well as to domestic faction, than that which permits the sense of the majority to decide; though the contrary of this has been presumed. The mistake has proceeded from not attending with due care to the mischiefs that may be occasioned by obstructing the progress of government at certain critical seasons. When the concurrence of a large number is required by the constitution to the doing of any national act, we are apt to rest satisfied that all is safe, because nothing improper will be likely *to be done*; but we forget how much good may be prevented, and how much ill may be produced, by the power of hindering the doing what may be necessary, and of keeping affairs in the same unfavorable posture in which they may happen to stand at particular periods.

Suppose for instance we were engaged in a war, in conjunction with one foreign nation against another. Suppose the necessity of our situation demanded peace, and the interest or ambition of our ally led him to seek the prosecution of the war, with views that might justify us in making separate terms. In such a state of things, this ally of ours would evidently find it much easier by his bribes and intrigues to tie up the hands of government from making peace, where two thirds of all the votes were requisite to that object, than where a simple majority would suffice. In the first case he would have to corrupt a smaller number; in the last a greater number. Upon the same principle it would be much easier for a foreign power with which we were at war, to perplex our councils and embarrass our exertions. And in a commercial view we may be subjected to similar inconveniences. A nation, with which we might have a treaty of commerce, could with much greater facility prevent our forming a connection with her competitor in trade; tho' such a connection should be ever so beneficial to ourselves.

Evils of this description ought not to be regarded as imaginary. One of the weak sides of republics, among their numerous advantages, is that they afford too easy an inlet to foreign corruption. An hereditary monarch, though often disposed to sacrifice his subjects to his ambition, has so great a personal interest in the government, and in the external glory of the nation, that it is not easy for a foreign power to give him an equivalent for what he would sacrifice by treachery to the State. The world has accordingly been witness to few examples of this species of royal prostitution, though there have been abundant specimens of every other kind.

In republics, persons elevated from the mass of the community, by the suffrages of their fellow-citizens, to stations of great pre-eminence and power, may find compensations for betraying their trust, which to any but minds animated and guided by superior virtue, may appear to exceed the proportion of interest they have in the common stock, and to overbalance the obligations of duty. Hence it is that history furnishes us with so many mortifying examples of the prevalency of foreign corruption in republican governments. How much this contributed to the ruin of the ancient commonwealths has been already delineated. It is well known that the deputies of the United Provinces have, in various instances been purchased by the emissaries of the neighbouring kingdoms. The Earl of Chesterfield (if my memory serves me right) in a letter to his court, intimates that his success in an important negotiation, must depend on his obtaining a Major's commission for one of those deputies. And in Sweden, the parties were alternately bought by France and England, in so barefaced and notorious a manner that it excited universal disgust in the nation; and was a principal cause that the most limited monarch in Europe, in a single day, without tumult, violence, or opposition, became one of the most absolute and uncontrouled.

A circumstance, which crowns the defects of the confederation, remains yet to be mentioned—the want of a judiciary power. Laws are a dead letter without courts to expound and define their true meaning and operation. The treaties of the United States to have any force at all, must be considered as part of the law of the land. Their true import as far as respects individuals, must, like all other laws, be ascertained by judicial determinations. To produce uniformity in these determinations, they ought to be submitted in the last resort, to one SUPREME TRIBUNAL. And this tribunal ought to be instituted under the same authority which forms the treaties themselves. These ingredients are both indispensable. If there is in each State, a court of final jurisdiction, there may be as many different final determinations on the same point, as there are courts. There are endless diversities in the opinions of men. We often see not only different courts, but the Judges of the same court differing from each other. To avoid the confusion which would unavoidably result from the contradictory decisions of a number of independent judicatories, all nations have found it necessary to establish one court paramount to the rest—possessing a general superintendance, and authorised to settle and declare in the last resort, an uniform rule of civil justice.

This is the more necessary where the frame of the government is so compounded, that the laws of the whole are in danger of being contravened by the laws of the parts. In this case if the particular tribunals are invested with a right of ultimate jurisdiction, besides the contradictions to be expected from difference of opinion, there will be much to fear from the bias of local views and prejudices, and from the interference of local regulations. As often as such an interference was to happen, there would be reason to apprehend, that the provisions of the particular laws might be preferred to those of the general laws; for nothing is more natural to men in office, than to look with peculiar deference towards that authority to which they owe their official existence.

The treaties of the United States, under the present constitution, are liable to the infractions of thirteen different Legislatures, and as many different courts of final jurisdiction, acting under the authority of those Legislatures. The faith, the reputation, the peace of the whole union, are thus continually at the mercy of the prejudices, the passions, and the interests of every member of which it is composed. Is it possible that foreign nations can either respect or confide in such a government? Is it possible that the People of America will longer consent to trust their honor, their happiness, their safety, on so precarious a foundation?

In this review of the Confederation, I have confined myself to the exhibition of its most material defects; passing over those imperfections in its details, by which even a great part of the power intended to be conferred upon it has been in a great measure rendered abortive. It must be by this time evident to all men of reflection, who can divest themselves of the prepossessions of preconceived opinions, that it is a system so radically vicious and unsound, as to admit not of amendment but by an entire change in its leading features and characters.

The organization of Congress, is itself utterly improper for the exercise of those powers which are necessary to be deposited in the Union. A single Assembly may be a proper receptacle of those slender, or rather fettered authorities, which have been heretofore delegated to the fœderal head; but it would be inconsistent with all the principles of good government, to intrust it with those additional powers which even the moderate and more rational adversaries of the proposed constitution admit ought to reside in the United States. If that plan should not be adopted; and if the necessity of union should be able to withstand the ambitious aims of those men, who may indulge magnificent schemes of personal aggrandizement from its dissolution; the probability would be, that we should run into the project of conferring supplementary powers upon Congress as they are now constituted; and either the machine, from the intrinsic feebleness of its structure, will moulder into pieces in spite of our ill-judged efforts to prop it; or by successive augmentations of its force and energy, as necessity might prompt, we shall finally accumulate in a single body, all the most important prerogatives of sovereignty; and thus entail upon our posterity, one of the most execrable forms of government that human infatuation ever contrived. Thus we should create in reality that very tyranny, which the adversaries of the new constitution either are, or affect to be solicitous to avert.

It has not a little contributed to the infirmities of the existing fœderal system, that it never had a ratification by the PEOPLE. Resting on no better foundation than the consent of the several Legislatures; it has been exposed to frequent and intricate questions concerning the validity of its powers; and has in some instances given birth to the enormous doctrine of a right of legislative repeal. Owing its ratification to the law of a State, it has been contended, that the same authority might repeal the law by which it was ratified. However gross a heresy it may be, to maintain that *a party* to *a compact* has a right to revoke that *compact*, the doctrine itself has had respectable advocates. The possibility of a question of this nature, proves the necessity of laying the founda-

tions of our national government deeper than in the mere sanction of delegated authority. The fabric of American Empire
ought to rest on the solid basis of THE CONSENT OF THE
PEOPLE. The streams of national power ought to flow
immediately from that pure original fountain of all legitimate
authority.

PUBLIUS.

The New-York Packet, December 14, 1787

The Federalist No. 23

To the People of the State of New-York.

The necessity of a Constitution, at least equally energetic with the one proposed, to the preservation of the Union, is the point, at the examination of which we are now arrived.

This enquiry will naturally divide itself into three branches —the objects to be provided for by a Fœderal Government—the quantity of power necessary to the accomplishment of those objects—the persons upon whom that power ought to operate. Its distribution and organization will more properly claim our attention under the succeeding head.

The principal purposes to be answered by Union are these— The common defence of the members—the preservation of the public peace as well against internal convulsions as external attacks—the regulation of commerce with other nations and between the States—the superintendence of our intercourse, political and commercial, with foreign countries.

The authorities essential to the care of the common defence are these—to raise armies—to build and equip fleets—to prescribe rules for the government of both—to direct their operations—to provide for their support. These powers ought to exist without limitation: *Because it is impossible to foresee or define the extent and variety of national exigencies, or the correspondent extent & variety of the means which may be necessary to satisfy them.* The circumstances that endanger the safety of nations are infinite; and for this reason no constitutional shackles can wisely be imposed on the power to which the care of it is committed. This power ought to be co-extensive with all the possible combinations of such circumstances; and ought to be under the direction of the same councils, which are appointed to preside over the common defence.

This is one of those truths, which to a correct and unprejudiced mind, carries its own evidence along with it; and may be obscured, but cannot be made plainer by argument or reasoning. It rests upon axioms as simple as they are universal. The *means* ought to be proportioned to the *end*; the persons, from whose agency the attainment of any *end* is expected, ought to possess the *means* by which it is to be attained.

Whether there ought to be a Fœderal Government intrusted with the care of the common defence, is a question in the first instance open to discussion; but the moment it is decided in the affirmative, it will follow, that that government ought to be cloathed with all the powers requisite to the complete execution of its trust. And unless it can be shewn, that the circumstances which may affect the public safety are reducible within certain determinate limits; unless the contrary of this position can be fairly and rationally disputed, it must be admitted, as a necessary consequence, that there can be no limitation of that authority, which is to provide for the defence and protection of the community, in any matter essential to its efficiency; that is, in any matter essential to the *formation, direction* or *support* of the NATIONAL FORCES.

Defective as the present Confederation has been proved to be, this principle appears to have been fully recognized by the framers of it; though they have not made proper or adequate provision for its exercise. Congress have an unlimited discretion to make requisitions of men and money—to govern the army and navy—to direct their operations. As their requisitions were made constitutionally binding upon the States, who are in fact under the most solemn obligations to furnish the supplies required of them, the intention evidently was, that the United States should command whatever resources were by them judged requisite to "the common defence and general welfare." It was presumed that a sense of their true interests, and a regard to the dictates of good faith, would be found sufficient pledges for the punctual performance of the duty of the members to the Fœderal Head.

The experiment has, however demonstrated, that this expectation was ill founded and illustory; and the observations made under the last head, will, I imagine, have sufficed to convince the impartial and discerning, that there is an absolute necessity for an entire change in the first principles of the system: That if we are in earnest about giving the Union energy and duration, we must abandon the vain project of legislating upon the States in their collective capacities: We must extend the laws of the Fœderal Government to the individual citizens of America: We must discard the fallacious scheme of quotas and requisitions, as equally impracticable and unjust. The result from all this is, that the Union ought to be invested with full power to levy troops; to build and equip fleets, and to raise the revenues, which will be required for the formation and support of an army and navy, in the customary and ordinary modes practiced in other governments.

If the circumstances of our country are such, as to demand a compound instead of a simple, a confederate instead of a sole government, the essential point which will remain to be adjusted, will be to discriminate the OBJECTS, as far as it can be done, which shall appertain to the different provinces or departments of power; allowing to each the most ample authority for fulfilling the objects committed to its charge. Shall the Union be constituted the guardian of the common safety? Are fleets and armies and revenues necessary to this purpose? The government of the Union must be empowered to pass all laws, and to make all regulations which have relation to them. The same must be the case, in respect to commerce, and to every other matter to which its jurisdiction is permitted to extend. Is the administration of justice between the citizens of the same State, the proper department of the local governments? These must possess all the authorities which are connected with this object, and with every other that may be allotted to their particular cognizance and direction. Not to confer in each case a degree of power, commensurate to the end, would be to violate the most obvious rules of prudence and propriety, and improvidently to trust the great interests of the nation to hands, which are disabled from managing them with vigour and success.

Who so likely to make suitable provisions for the public defence, as that body to which the guardianship of the public safety is confided—which, as the center of information, will best understand the extent and urgency of the dangers that threaten—as the representative of the WHOLE will feel itself most deeply interested in the preservation of every part—which, from the responsibility implied in the duty assigned to it, will be most sensibly impressed with the necessity of proper exertions—and which, by the extension of its authority throughout the States, can alone establish uniformity and concert in the plans and measures, by which the common safety is to be secured? Is there not a manifest inconsistency in devolving upon the Fœderal Government the care of the general defence, and leaving in the State governments the *effective* powers, by which it is to be provided for? Is not a want of co-operation the infallible consequence of such a system? And will not weakness, disorder, an undue distribution of the burthens and calamities of war, an unnecessary and intolerable increase of expence, be its natural and inevitable concomitants? Have we not had unequivocal experience of its effects in the course of the revolution, which we have just accomplished?

Every view we may take of the subject, as candid enquirers after truth, will serve to convince us, that it is both unwise and dangerous to deny the Fœderal Government an unconfined authority, as to all those objects which are intrusted to its management. It will indeed deserve the most vigilant and careful attention of the people, to see that it be modelled in such a manner, as to admit of its being safely vested with the requisite powers. If any plan which has been, or may be offered to our consideration, should not, upon a dispassionate inspection, be found to answer this description, it ought to be rejected. A government, the Constitution of which renders it unfit to be trusted with all the powers, which a free people *ought to delegate to any government*, would be an unsafe and improper depository of the NATIONAL INTERESTS, wherever THESE can with propriety be confided, the co-incident powers may safely accompany them. This is the true result of all just reasoning upon the subject. And the adversaries of the plan, promulgated by the Convention, ought to have confined themselves to showing that the internal structure of the proposed government, was such as to render it unworthy of the confidence of the people. They ought not to have wandered into inflammatory declamations, and unmeaning cavils about the extent of the powers. The POWERS are not too extensive for the OBJECTS of Fœderal administration, or in other words, for the management of our NATIONAL INTERESTS; nor can any satisfactory argument be framed to shew that they are chargeable with such an excess. If it be true, as has been insinuated by some of the writers on the other side, that the difficulty arises from the nature of the thing, and that the extent of the country will not permit us to form a government, in which such ample powers can safely be reposed, it would prove that we ought to contract our views, and resort to the expedient of separate Confederacies, which will move within more practicable spheres. For the absurdity must continually stare us in the face of confiding to a government, the direction of the most essential national interests, without daring to trust it with the authorities which are indispensable to their proper and efficient management. Let us not attempt to reconcile contradictions, but firmly embrace a rational alternative.

I trust, however, that the impracticability of one general system cannot be shewn. I am greatly mistaken, if any thing of weight, has yet been advanced of this tendency; and I flatter myself, that the observations which have been made in the course of these papers, have sufficed to place the reverse of that position in as clear a light as any matter still in the womb of time and experience can be susceptible of. This at all events must be evident, that the very difficulty itself drawn from the extent of the country, is the strongest argument in favor of an energetic government; for any other can certainly never preserve the Union of so large an empire. If we embrace the tenets of those, who oppose the adoption of the proposed Constitution, as the standard of our political creed, we cannot fail to verify the gloomy doctrines, which predict the impracticability of a national system, pervading the entire limits of the present Confederacy.

PUBLIUS.

The New-York Packet, December 18, 1787

The Federalist No. 24

To the People of the State of New-York.

To the powers proposed to be conferred upon the Federal Government, in respect to the creation and direction of the national forces, I have met with but one specific objection, which, if I understand it rightly is this—that proper provision has not been made against the existence of standing armies in time of peace; an objection which I shall now endeavor to shew, rests on weak and unsubstantial foundations.

It has indeed been brought forward in the most vague and general form, supported only by bold assertions—without the appearance of argument—without even the sanction of theoretical opinions, in contradiction to the practice of other free nations, and to the general sense of America, as expressed in most of the existing Constitutions. The propriety of this remark will appear the moment it is recollected, that the objection under consideration turns upon a supposed necessity of restraining the LEGISLATIVE authority of the nation, in the article of military establishments; a principle unheard of except in one or two of our State Constitutions, and rejected in all the rest.

A stranger to our politics, who was to read our news-papers, at the present juncture, without having previously inspected the plan reported by the Convention, would be naturally led to one of two conclusions: either that it contained a positive injunction that standing armies should be kept up in time of peace; or that it vested in the EXECUTIVE the whole power of levying troops, without subjecting his discretion in any shape, to the controul of the Legislature.

If he came afterwards to peruse the plan itself, he would be surprised to discover, that neither the one nor the other was the case; that the whole power of raising armies was lodged in the *Legislature*, not in the *Executive*; that this Legislature was to be a popular body, consisting of the representatives of the people, periodically elected; and that, instead of the provision he had supposed in favor of standing armies, there was to be found, in respect to this object, an important qualification even of the Legislative discretion, in that clause which forbids the appropriation of money for the support of an army for any longer period than two years: a precaution, which, upon a nearer view of it, will appear to be a great and real security against the keeping up of troops, without evident necessity.

Disappointed in his first surmise, the person I have supposed would be apt to pursue his conjectures a little further. He would naturally say to himself, it is impossible that all this vehement and pathetic declamation can be without some colorable pretext. It must needs be, that this people so jealous of their liberties, have in all the preceding models of the Constitutions, which they have established, inserted the most precise and rigid precautions on this point, the omission of which in the new plan has given birth to all this apprehension and clamour.

If under this impression he proceeded to pass in review the several State Constitutions, how great would be his disappointment to find that *two only* of them* contained an interdiction of standing armies in time of peace; that the other eleven had either observed a profound silence on the subject, or had in express terms admitted the right of the legislature to authorise their existence.

Still however he would be persuaded that there must be some plausible foundation for the cry raised on this head. He would never be able to imagine, while any source of information remained unexplored, that it was nothing more than an experiment upon the public credulity, dictated either by a

---

* This statement of the matter is taken from the printed collections of state constitutions—Pennsylvania and North-Carolina are the two which contain the interdiction in these words—"as standing armies in time of peace are dangerous to liberty, *they ought not* to be kept up." This is in truth rather a *caution* than a *prohibition*. New-Hampshire, Massachusetts, Delaware, and Maryland, have in each of their bills of rights a clause to this effect—"standing armies are dangerous to liberty, and ought not to be raised or kept up *without the consent of the legislature*;" which is a formal admission of the authority of the legislature. New-York has no bill of her rights and her Constitution says not a word about the matter. No bills of rights appear annexed to the constitutions of the other States, except the foregoing and their constitutions are equally silent— I am told, however, that one or two states have bills of rights which do not appear in this collection, but that those also recognize the right of the legislative authority in this respect.

deliberate intention to deceive or by the overflowings of a zeal too intemperate to be ingenuous. It would probably occur to him that he would be likely to find the precautions he was in search of in the primitive compact between the States. Here, at length, he would expect to meet with a solution of the enigma. No doubt he would observe to himself the existing confederation must contain the most explicit provisions against military establishments in time of peace; and a departure from this model in a favourite point has occasioned the discontent which appears to influence these political champions.

If he should now apply himself to a careful and critical survey of the articles of Confederation, his astonishment would not only be encreased but would acquire a mixture of indignation at the unexpected discovery that these articles instead of containing the prohibition he looked for, and tho' they had with a jealous circumspection restricted the authority of the State Legislatures in this particular, had not imposed a single restraint on that of the United States. If he happened to be a man of quick sensibility or ardent temper, he could now no longer refrain from regarding these clamours as the dishonest artifices of a sinister and unprincipled opposition to a plan which ought at least to receive a fair and candid examination from all sincere lovers of their country. How else (he would say) could the authors of them have been tempted to vent such loud censures upon that plan, about a point, in which it seems to have conformed itself to the general sense of America, as declared in its different forms of Government; and in which it has even superadded a new and powerful guard unknown to any of them? If on the contrary he happened to be a man of calm and dispassionate feelings—he would indulge a sigh for the frailty of human nature; and would lament that in a matter so interesting to the happiness of millions the true merits of the question should be discolored and perplexed by expedients so unfriendly to an impartial and right determination. Even such a man could hardly forbear remarking that a conduct of this kind has too much the appearance of an intention to mislead the people by alarming their passions rather than to convince them by arguments addressed to their understandings.

But however little this objection may be countenanced even by precedents among ourselves, it may be satisfactory to take a nearer view of its intrinsic merits. From a close examination it will appear that restraints upon the discretion of the Legislature in respect to military establishments in time of peace would be improper to be imposed; and, if imposed, from the necessities of society, would be unlikely to be observed.

Though a wide ocean separates the United States from Europe; yet there are various considerations that warn us against an excess of confidence or security. On one side of us and stretching far into our rear are growing settlements subject to the dominion of Britain. On the other side and extending to meet the British settlements are colonies and establishments subject to the dominion of Spain. This situation and the vicinity of the West-India Islands belonging to these two powers create between them, in respect to their American possessions, and in relation to us, a common interest. The Savage tribes, on our western frontier, ought to be regarded as our natural enemies, their natural allies; because they have most to fear from us and most to hope from them. The improvements in the art of navigation have, as to the facility of communication, rendered distant nations in a great measure neighbours. Britain and Spain are among the principal maritime powers of Europe. A future concert of views between these nations ought not to be regarded as impracticable. The increasing remoteness of consanguinity is every day diminishing the force of the family-compact between France and Spain. And politicians have ever with great reason estimated the ties of blood as feeble and precarious links of political connection. These circumstances combined admonish us not to be sanguine in considering ourselves as intirely out of the reach of danger.

Previous to the revolution, and even since the peace, there has been a constant necessity for keeping small garrisons on our western frontier. No person can doubt that these will continue to be indispensible, if it should only be against the ravages and depredations of the Indians. These garrisons must either be furnished by occasional detachments from the militia, or by permanent corps in the pay of the government. The first is impracticable; and if practicable, would be pernicious. The militia would not long, if at all, submit to be dragged from their occupations and families to perform that most disagreeable duty in times of profound peace. And if they could be prevailed upon, or compelled to do it, the increased expence of a frequent rotation of service and the loss of labor and disconcertion of the industrious pursuits of individuals, would form conclusive objections to the scheme. It would be as burthensome and injurious to the public, as ruinous to private citizens. The latter resource of permanent corps in the pay of Government amounts to a standing army in time of peace; a small one indeed, but not the less real for being small. Here is a simple view of the subject that shows us at once the impropriety of a constitutional interdiction of such establishments, and the necessity of leaving the matter to the discretion and prudence of the Legislature.

In proportion to our increase in strength, it is probable, nay it may be said certain, that Britain and Spain would augment their military establishments in our neighbourhood. If we should but be willing to be exposed in a naked and defenceless condition to their insults or encroachments, we should find it expedient to encrease our frontier garrisons in some ratio to the force by which our western settlements might be annoyed. There are and will be particular posts the possession of which will include the command of large districts of territory and facilitate future invasions of the remainder. It may be added that some of those posts will be keys to the trade with the Indian nations. Can any men think it would be wise to leave such posts in a situation to be at any instant seized by one or the other of two neighbouring and formidable powers? To act this part would be to desert all the usual maxims of prudence and policy.

If we mean to be a commercial people or even to be secure on our Atlantic side, we must endeavour as soon as possible to have a navy. To this purpose there must be dock-yards and arsenals; and, for the defence of these, fortifications and probably garrisons. When a nation has become so powerful by sea, that it can protect its dock-yards by its fleets, this supersedes the necessity of garrisons for that purpose; but where naval establishments are in their infancy, moderate garrisons will, in all likelihood, be found an indispensible precaution against descents for the destruction of the arsenals and dock-yards, and sometimes of the fleet itself.

PUBLIUS.

The Daily Advertiser, December 19, 1787

The Federalist No. 25

To the People of the State of New-York.

It may perhaps be urged, that the objects enumerated in the preceding number ought to be provided for by the State Governments, under the direction of the Union. But this would be in reality an inversion of the primary principle of our political association; as it would in practice transfer the care of the common defence from the fœderal head to the individual members: A project oppressive to some States, dangerous to all, and baneful to the confederacy.

The territories of Britain, Spain and of the Indian nations in our neighbourhood, do not border on particular States; but incircle the Union from MAINE to GEORGIA. The danger, though in different degrees, is therefore common. And the means of guarding against it ought in like manner to be the objects of common councils and of a common treasury. It happens that some States, from local situation, are more directly exposed. NEW-YORK is of this class. Upon the plan of separate provisions, New-York would have to sustain the whole weight of the establishments requisite to her immediate safety, and to the mediate or ultimate protection of her neighbours. This would neither be equitable as it respected New-York, nor safe as it respected the other States. Various inconveniences would attend such a system. The States, to whose lot it might fall to support the necessary establishments, would be as little able as willing, for a considerable time to come, to bear the burthen of competent provisions. The security of all would thus be subjected to the parsimony, improvidence or inability of a part. If the resources of such part becoming more abundant and extensive, its provisions should be proportionably enlarged, the other States would quickly take the alarm at seeing the whole military force of the Union in the hands of two or three of its members; and those probably amongst the most powerful. They would each choose to have some counterpoise; and pretences could easily be contrived. In this situation, military establishments, nourished by mutual jealousy, would be apt to swell beyond their natural or proper size; and being at the separate disposal of the members, they would be engines for the abridgment, or demolition of the national authority.

Reasons have been already given to induce a supposition, that the State Governments will too naturally be prone to a rivalship with that of the Union, the foundation of which will be the love of power; and that in any contest between the fœderal head and one of its members, the people will be most apt to unite with their local government: If in addition to this immense advantage, the ambition of the members should be stimulated by the separate and independent possession of military forces, it would afford too strong a temptation, and too great facility to them to make enterprises upon, and finally to subvert the constitutional authority of the Union. On the other hand, the liberty of the people would be less safe in this state of things, than in that which left the national forces in the hands of the national government. As far as an army may be considered as a dangerous weapon of power, it had better be in those hands, of which the people are most likely to be jealous, than in those of which they are least likely to be jealous. For it is a truth which the experience of all ages has attested, that the people are always most in danger, when the means of injuring their rights are in the possession of those of whom they entertain the least suspicion.

The framers of the existing confederation, fully aware of the danger to the Union from the separate possession of military forces by the States, have in express terms, prohibited them from having either ships or troops, unless with the consent of Congress. The truth is, that the existence of a Fœderal Government and military establishments, under State authority, are not less at variance with each other, than a due supply of the fœderal treasury and the system of quotas and requisitions.

There are other lights besides those already taken notice of, in which the impropriety of restraints on the discretion of the national Legislature will be equally manifest. The design of the objection, which has been mentioned, is to preclude standing armies in time of peace; though we have never been informed how far it is desired the prohibition should extend; whether to raising armies as well as to *keeping them up* in a season of tranquility or not. If it be confined to the latter, it will have no precise signification, and it will be ineffectual for the purpose intended. When armies are once raised, what shall be denominated "keeping them up," contrary to the sense of the constitution? What time shall be requisite to ascertain the violation? Shall it be a week, a month, or a year? Or shall we say, they may be continued as long as the danger which occasioned their being raised continues? This would be to admit that they might be kept up *in time of peace* against threatening, or impending danger; which would be at once to deviate from the literal meaning of the prohibition, and to introduce an extensive latitude of construction. Who shall judge of the continuance of the danger? This must undoubtedly be submitted to the national government—and the matter would then be brought to this issue, that the national government, to provide against apprehended danger, might, in the first instance, raise troops, and might afterwards keep them on foot, as long as they supposed the peace or safety of the community was in any degree of jeopardy. It is easy to perceive, that a discretion so latitudinary as this, would afford ample room for eluding the force of the provision.

The supposed utility of a provision of this kind, must be founded upon a supposed probability, or at least possibility, of a combination between the executive and the legislative in some scheme of usurpation. Should this at any time happen, how easy would it be to fabricate pretences of approaching danger? Indian hostilities instigated by Spain or Britain, would always be at hand. Provocations to produce the desired appearances, might even be given to some foreign power, and appeased again by timely concessions. If we can reasonably presume such a combination to have been formed, and that the enterprize is warranted by a sufficient prospect of success; the army when once raised, from whatever cause, or on whatever pretext, may be applied to the execution of the project.

If to obviate this consequence, it should be resolved to extend the prohibition to the *raising* of armies in time of peace, the United States would then exhibit the most extraordinary spectacle, which the world has yet seen—that of a nation incapacitated by its constitution to prepare for defence, before it was actually invaded. As the ceremony of a formal denunciation of war has of late fallen into disuse, the presence of an enemy within our territories must be waited for as the legal warrant to the government to begin its levies of men for the protection of the State. We must receive the blow before we could even prepare to return it. All that kind of policy by which nations anticipate distant danger, and meet the gathering storm, must be abstained from, as contrary to the genuine maxims of a free government. We must expose our property and liberty to the mercy of foreign invaders, and invite them, by our weakness, to seize the naked and defenceless prey, because we are afraid that rulers, created by our choice—dependent on our will—might endanger that liberty, by an abuse of the means necessary to its preservation.

Here I expect we shall be told, that the Militia of the country is its natural bulwark, and would be at all times equal to the national defence. This doctrine in substance had like to have lost us our independence. It cost millions to the United States, that might have been saved. The facts, which from our own experience forbid a reliance of this kind, are too recent to permit us to be the dupes of such a suggestion. The steady operations of war against a regular and disciplined army, can only be successfully conducted by a force of the same kind. Considerations of œconomy, not less than of stability and vigor, confirm this position. The American Militia, in the course of the late war, have by their valour on numerous occasions, erected eternal monuments to their fame; but the bravest of them feel and know, that the liberty of their country could not have been established by their efforts alone, however great and valuable they were. War, like most other things, is a science to be acquired and perfected by diligence, by perseverance, by time, and by practice.

All violent policy, contrary to the natural and experienced course of human affairs, defeats itself. Pennsylvania at this instant affords an example of the truth of this remark. The bill of rights of that State declares, that standing armies are dangerous to liberty, and ought not to be kept up in time of peace. Pennsylvania, nevertheless, in a time of profound peace, from the existence of partial disorders in one or two of her counties, has resolved to raise a body of troops; and in all probability, will keep them up as long as there is an appearance of danger to the public peace. The conduct of Massachusetts affords a lesson on the same subject, though on different ground. That State (without waiting for the sanction of Congress as the articles of the confederation require) was compelled to raise troops to quell a domestic insurrection, and still keeps a corps in pay to prevent a revival of the spirit of revolt. The particular constitution of Massachusets opposed no obstacle to the measure; but the instance is still of use to instruct us, that cases are likely to occur under our governments, as well as under those of other nations, which will sometimes render a military force in time of peace essential to the security of the society; and that it is therefore improper, in this respect, to controul the legislative discretion. It also teaches us, in its application to the United States, how little the rights of a feeble government are likely to be respected, even by its own constituents. And it teaches us, in addition to the rest, how unequal parchment provisions are to a struggle with public necessity.

It was a fundamental maxim of the Lacedemonian commonwealth, that the post of Admiral should not be conferred twice on the same person. The Pelopponesian confederates, having suffered a severe defeat at sea from the Athenians, demanded LYSANDER, who had before served with success in that capacity, to command the combined fleets. The Lacedemonians, to gratify their allies, and yet preserve the semblance of an adherence to their ancient institutions, had recourse to the flimsy subterfuge of investing LYSANDER with the real power of Admiral, under the nominal title of Vice-Admiral. This instance is selected from among a multitude that might be cited to confirm the truth already advanced and illustrated by domestic examples; which is, that nations pay little regard to rules and maxims calculated in their very nature to run counter to the necessities of society. Wise politicians will be cautious about fettering the government with restrictions, that cannot be observed; because they know that every breach of the fundamental laws, though dictated by necessity, impairs that sacred reverence, which ought to be maintained in the breasts of rulers towards the constitution of a country, and forms a precedent for other breaches, where the same plea of necessity does not exist at all, or is less urgent and palpable.

PUBLIUS.

The New-York Packet, December 21, 1787

The Federalist No. 26

To the People of the State of New-York.

It was a thing hardly to be expected, that in a popular revolution the minds of men should stop at that happy mean, which marks the salutary boundary between POWER and PRIVILEGE, and combines the energy of government with the security of private rights. A failure in this delicate and important point is the great source of the inconveniences we experience; and if we are not cautious to avoid a repetition of the error, in our future attempts to rectify and ameliorate our system, we may travel from one chimerical project to another; we may try change after change; but we shall never be likely to make any material change for the better.

The idea of restraining the Legislative authority, in the means of providing for the national defence, is one of those refinements, which owe their origin to a zeal for liberty more ardent than enlightened. We have seen however that it has not had thus far an extensive prevalency: That even in this country, where it has made its first appearance, Pennsylvania and North-Carolina are the only two States by which it has been in any degree patronised: And that all the others have refused to give it the least countenance; wisely judging that confidence must be placed some where; that the necessity of doing it is implied in the very act of delegating power; and that it is better to hazard the abuse of that confidence, than to embarrass the government and endanger the public safety, by impolitic restrictions on the Legislative authority. The opponents of the proposed Constitution combat in this respect the general decision of America; and instead of being taught by experience the propriety of correcting any extremes, into which we may have heretofore run, they appear disposed to conduct us into others still more dangerous and more extravagant. As if the tone of government had been found too high, or too rigid, the doctrines they teach are calculated to induce us to depress, or to relax it, by expedients which upon other occasions have been condemned or forborn. It may be affirmed without the imputation of invective, that if the principles they inculcate on various points could so far obtain as to become the popular creed, they would utterly unfit the people of this country for any species of government whatever. But a danger of this kind is not to be apprehended. The citizens of America have too much discernment to be argued into anarchy: And I am much mistaken if experience has not wrought a deep and solemn conviction in the public mind, that greater energy of government is essential to the welfare and prosperity of the community.

It may not be amiss in this place concisely to remark the origin and progress of the idea which aims at the exclusion of military establishments in time of peace. Though in speculative minds it may arise from a contemplation of the nature and tendency of such institutions fortified by the events that have happened in other ages and countries; yet as a national sentiment it must be traced to those habits of thinking, which we derive from the nation from whom the inhabitants of these States have in general sprung.

In England for a long time after the Norman conquest the authority of the monarch was almost unlimited. Inroads were gradually made upon the prerogative, in favour of liberty, first by the Barons and afterwards by the people, 'till the greatest part of its most formidable pretensions became extinct. But it was not 'till the revolution in 1688, which elevated the Prince of Orange to the throne of Great Britain, that English liberty was completely triumphant. As incident to the undefined power of making war, an acknowleged prerogative of the crown, Charles IId. had by his own authority kept on foot in time of peace a body of 5,000 regular troops. And this number James IId. increased to 30,000; which were paid out of his civil list. At the revolution, to abolish the exercise of so dangerous an authority, it became an article of the bill of rights then framed, that "the raising or keeping a standing army within the kingdom in time of peace, *unless with the consent of Parliament*, was against law."

In that kingdom, when the pulse of liberty was at its highest pitch, no security against the danger of standing armies was thought requisite, beyond a prohibition of their being raised or kept up by the mere authority of the executive magistrate. The patriots, who effected that memorable revolution, were too temperate and too well informed, to think of any restraint in the legislative discretion. They were aware that a certain number of troops for guards and garrisons were indispensable, that no precise bounds could be set to the national exigencies; that a power equal to every possible contingency must exist somewhere in the government; and that when they referred the exercise of that power to the judgement of the legislature, they had arrived at the ultimate point of precaution, which was reconciliable with the safety of the community.

From the same source, the people of America may be said to have derived a hereditary impression of danger to liberty from standing armies in time of peace. The circumstances of a revolution quickened the public sensibility on every point connected with the security of popular rights; and in some instances raised the warmth of our zeal beyond the degree which consisted with the due temperature of the body politic. The attempts of two of the states to restrict the authority of the legislature in the article of military establishments are of the number of these instances. The principles, which had taught us to be jealous of the power of an hereditary monarch, were by an injudicious excess extended to the representatives of the people in their popular assemblies. Even in some of the States, where this error was not adopted, we find unnecessary declarations, that standing armies ought not to be kept up, in time of peace WITHOUT THE CONSENT OF THE LEGISLATURE—I call them unnecessary, because the reason, which had introduced a similar provision into the English bill of rights, is not applicable to any of the state constitutions. The power of raising armies at all, under those constitutions, can by no construction be deemed to reside any where else, than in the legislatures themselves; and it was superfluous, if not absurd, to declare that a matter should not be done without the consent of a body, which alone had the power of doing it. Accordingly in some of those constitutions, and among others in that of this State of New-York; which has been justly celebrated both in Europe and in America as one of the best of the forms of government established in this country, there is a total silence upon the subject.

It is remarkable, that even in the two States, which seem to have meditated an interdiction of military establishments in time of peace, the mode of expression made use of is rather cautionary than prohibitory. It is not said, that standing armies *shall not be* kept up, but that they *ought not* to be kept up in time of peace. This ambiguity of terms appears to have been the result of a conflict between jealousy and conviction, between the desire of excluding such establishments at all events, and the persuasion that an absolute exclusion would be unwise and unsafe.

Can it be doubted that such a provision, whenever the situation of public affairs was understood to require a departure from it, would be interpreted by the Legislature into a mere admonition and would be made to yield to the necessities or supposed necessities of the State? Let the fact already mentioned with respect to Pennsylvania decide. What then (it may be asked) is the use of such a provision, if it cease to operate, the moment there is an inclination to disregard it?

Let us examine whether there be any comparison, in point of efficacy, between the provision alluded to and that which is contained in the New Constitution, for restraining the appropriations of money for military purposes to the period of two years. The former by aiming at too much is calculated to effect nothing; the latter, by steering clear of an imprudent extreme, and by being perfectly compatible with a proper provision for the exigencies of the nation, will have a salutary and powerful operation.

The Legislature of the United States will be *obliged* by this provision, once at least in every two years, to deliberate upon the propriety of keeping a military force on foot; to come to a new resolution on the point; and to declare their sense of the matter, by a formal vote in the face of their constituents. They are not *at liberty* to vest in the executive department permanent funds for the support of an army; if they were even incautious enough to be willing to repose in it so improper a confidence. As the spirit of party, in different degrees, must be expected to infect all political bodies, there will be no doubt persons in the national Legislature willing enough to arraign the measures and criminate the views of the majority. The provision for the support of a military force will always be a favourable topic for declamation. As often as the question comes forward, the public attention will be roused and attracted to the subject, by the party in opposition: And if the majority should be really disposed to exceed the proper limits the community will be warned of the danger and will have an opportunity of taking measures to guard against it. Independent of parties in the national Legislature itself, as often as the period of discussion arrived, the state Legislatures, who will always be not only vigilant but suspicious and jealous guardians of the rights of the citizens, against incroachments from the Fœderal government, will constantly have their attention awake to the conduct of the national rulers and will be ready enough, if any thing improper appears, to sound the alarm to the people and not only to be the VOICE but if necessary the ARM of their discontent.

Schemes to subvert the liberties of a great community *require time to* mature them for execution. An army so large as seriously to menace those liberties could only be formed by progressive augmentations; which would suppose, not merely a temporary combination between the legislature and executive, but a continued conspiracy for a series of time. Is it probable that such a combination would exist at all? Is it probable that it would be persevered in and transmitted along, through all the successive variations in the representative body, which biennial elections would naturally produce in both houses? Is it presumable, that every man, the instant he took his seat in the national senate, or house of representatives, would commence a traitor to his constituents and to his country? Can it be supposed, that there would not be found one man, discerning enough to detect so atrocious a conspiracy, or bold or honest enough to apprise his constituents of their danger? If such presumptions can fairly be made, there ought to be at once an end of all delegated authority. The people should resolve to recall all the powers they have heretofore parted with out of their own hands; and to divide themselves into as many states as there are counties, in order that they may be able to manage their own concerns in person.

If such suppositions could even be reasonably made, still the concealment of the design, for any duration, would be impracticable. It would be announced by the very circumstance of augmenting the army to so great an extent in time of profound peace. What colorable reason could be assigned in a country so situated, for such vast augmentations of the military force? It is impossible that the people could be long deceived; and the destruction of the project and of the projectors would quickly follow the discovery.

It has been said that the provision, which limits the appropriation of money for the support of an army to the period of two years would be unavailing; because the executive, when once possessed of a force large enough to awe the people into submission, would find resources in that very force sufficient to enable him to dispense with supplies from the acts of the legislature. But the question again recurs: Upon what pretence could he be put into possession of a force of that magnitude in time of peace? If we suppose it to have been erected, in consequence of some domestic insurrection, or foreign war, then it becomes a case not within the principle of the objection; for this is levelled against the power of keeping up troops in time of peace. Few persons will be so visionary, as seriously to contend, that military forces ought not to be raised to quell a rebellion, or resist an invasion; and if the defence of the community, under such circumstances, should make it necessary to have an army, so numerous as to hazard its liberty, this is one of those calamities for which there is neither preventative nor cure. It cannot be provided against by any possible form of government: It might even result from a simple league offensive and defensive; if it should ever be necessary for the confederates or allies to form an army for common defence.

But it is an evil infinitely less likely to attend us in an united than in a disunited state; nay it may be safely asserted that it is an evil altogether unlikely to attend us in the better situation. It is not easy to conceive a possibility, that dangers so formidable can assail the whole Union, as to demand a force considerable enough to place our liberties in the least jeopardy; especially if we take into our view the aid to be derived from the militia, which ought always to be counted upon, as a valuable and powerful auxiliary. But in a state of disunion (as has been fully shewn in another place) the contrary of this supposition would become not only probable but almost unavoidable.

PUBLIUS.

The Independent Journal, December 22, 1787

The Federalist No. 27

To the People of the State of New-York.

It has been urged in different shapes that a constitution of the kind proposed by the Convention, cannot operate without the aid of a military force to execute its laws. This however, like most other things that have been alledged on that side, rests on mere general assertion; unsupported by any precise or intelligible designation of the reasons upon which it is founded. As far as I have been able to divine the latent meaning of the objectors, it seems to originate in a pre-supposition that the people will be disinclined to the exercise of fœderal authority in any matter of an internal nature. Waving any exception that might be taken to the inaccuracy or inexplicitness of the distinction between internal and external, let us enquire what ground there is to pre-suppose that disinclination in the people? Unless we presume, at the same time, that the powers of the General Government will be worse administered than those of the State governments, there seems to be no room for the presumption of ill-will, disaffection or opposition in the people. I believe it may be laid down as a general rule, that their confidence in and obedience to a government, will commonly be proportioned to the goodness or badness of its administration. It must be admitted that there are exceptions to this rule; but these exceptions depend so entirely on accidental causes, that they cannot be considered as having any relation to the intrinsic merits or demerits of a constitution. These can only be judged of by general principles and maxims.

Various reasons have been suggested in the course of these papers, to induce a probability that the General Government will be better administered than the particular governments: The principal of which reasons are that the extension of the spheres of election will present a greater option, or latitude of choice to the people, that through the medium of the State Legislatures, which are select bodies of men, and who are to appoint the members of the national Senate,—there is reason to expect that this branch will generally be composed with peculiar care and judgment: That these circumstances promise greater knowledge and more extensive information in the national councils: And that they will be less apt to be tainted by the spirit of faction, and more out of the reach of those occasional ill humors or temporary prejudices and propensities, which in smaller societies frequently contaminate the public councils, beget injustice and oppression of a part of the community, and engender schemes, which though they gratify a momentary inclination or desire, terminate in general distress, dissatisfaction and disgust. Several additional reasons of considerable force, to fortify that probability, will occur when we come to survey with a more critic eye, the interior structure of the edifice, which we are invited to erect. It will be sufficient here to remark, that until satisfactory reasons can be assigned to justify an opinion, that the fœderal government is likely to be administered in such a manner as to render it odious or contemptible to the people, there can be no reasonable foundation for the supposition, that the laws of the Union will meet with any greater obstruction from them, or will stand in need of any other methods to enforce their execution, than the laws of the particular members.

The hope of impunity is a strong incitement to sedition—the dread of punishment—a proportionately strong discouragement to it—will not the government of the Union, which, if possessed of a due degree of power, can call to its aid the collective resources of the whole confederacy, be more likely to repress the *former* sentiment, and to inspire the *latter*, than that of a single State, which can only command the resources within itself? A turbulent faction in a State may easily suppose itself able to contend with the friends to the government in that State; but it can hardly be so infatuated as to imagine itself a match for the combined efforts of the Union. If this reflection be just, there is less danger of resistance from irregular combinations of individuals, to the authority of the confederacy, than to that of a single member.

I will in this place hazard an observation which will not be the less just, because to some it may appear new; which is, that the more the operations of the national authority are intermingled in the ordinary exercise of government, the more the citizens are accustomed to meet with it in the common occurrences of their political life; the more it is familiarised to their sight and to their feelings; the further it enters into those objects which touch the most sensible cords, and put in motion the most active springs of the human heart; the greater will be the probability that it will conciliate the respect and attachment of the community. Man is very much a creature of habit. A thing that rarely strikes his senses will generally have but little influence upon his mind. A government continually at a distance and out of sight, can hardly be expected to interest the sensations of the people. The inference is, that the authority of the Union, and the affections of the citizens towards it, will be strengthened rather than weakened by its extension to what are called matters of internal concern; and will have less occasion to recur to force in proportion to the familiarity and comprehensiveness of its agency. The more it circulates through those channels and currents, in which the passions of mankind naturally flow, the less will it require the aid of the violent and perilous expedients of compulsion.

One thing at all events, must be evident, that a government like the one proposed, would bid much fairer to avoid the necessity of using force, than that species of league contended for by most of its opponents; the authority of which should only operate upon the States in their political or collective capacities. It has been shewn, that in such a confederacy, there can be no sanction for the laws but force; that frequent delinquencies in the members, are the natural offspring of the very frame of the government; and that as often as these happen they can only be redressed, if at all, by war and violence.

The plan reported by the Convention, by extending the authority of the fœderal head to the individual citizens of the several States, will enable the government to employ the ordinary magistracy of each in the execution of its laws. It is easy to perceive that this will tend to destroy, in the common apprehension, all distinction between the sources from which they might proceed; and will give the Fœderal Government the same advantage for securing a due obedience to its authority, which is enjoyed by the government of each State; in addition to the influence on public opinion, which will result from the important consideration of its having power to call to its assistance and support the resources of the whole

Union. It merits particular attention in this place, that the laws of the confederacy, as to the *enumerated* and *legitimate* objects of its jurisdiction, will become the SUPREME LAW of the land; to the observance of which, all officers legislative, executive and judicial in each State, will be bound by the sanctity of an oath. Thus the Legislatures, Courts and Magistrates of the respective members will be incorporated into the operations of the national government, *as far as its just and constitutional authority extends*; and will be rendered auxiliary to the enforcement of its laws.* Any man, who will pursue by his own reflections the consequences of this situation, will perceive that there is good ground to calculate upon a regular and peaceable execution of the laws of the Union; if its powers are administered with a common share of prudence. If we will arbitrarily suppose the contrary, we may deduce any inferences we please from the supposition; for it is certainly possible, by an injudicious exercise of the authorities of the best government, that ever was or ever can be instituted, to provoke and precipitate the people into the wildest excesses. But though the adversaries of the proposed constitution should presume that the national rulers would be insensible to the motives of public good, or to the obligations of duty; I would still ask them, how the interests of ambition, or the views of encroachment, can be promoted by such a conduct?

PUBLIUS.

* The sophistry which has been employed to show that this will tend to the distruction of the State Governments will, in its proper place, be fully detected.

The New-York Packet, December 25, 1787

The Federalist No. 28

To the People of the State of New-York.

That there may happen cases, in which the national government may be necessitated to resort to force, cannot be denied. Our own experience has corroborated the lessons taught by the examples of other nations; that emergencies of this sort will sometimes arise in all societies, however constituted; that seditions and insurrections are unhappily maladies as inseparable from the body politic, as tumours and eruptions from the natural body; that the idea of governing at all times by the simple force of law (which we have been told is the only admissible principle of republican government) has no place but in the reveries of those political doctors, whose sagacity disdains the admonitions of experimental instruction.

Should such emergencies at any time happen under the national government, there could be no remedy but force. The means to be employed must be proportioned to the extent of the mischief. If it should be a slight commotion in a small part of a State, the militia of the residue would be adequate to its suppression: and the natural presumption is, that they would be ready to do their duty. An insurrection, whatever may be its immediate cause, eventually endangers all government: Regard to the public peace, if not to the rights of the Union, would engage the citizens, to whom the contagion had not communicated itself, to oppose the insurgents: And if the general government should be found in practice conducive to the prosperity and felicity of the people, it were irrational to believe that they would be disinclined to its support.

If on the contrary the insurrection should pervade a whole State, or a principal part of it, the employment of a different kind of force might become unavoidable. It appears that Massachusetts found it necessary to raise troops for repressing the disorders within that State; that Pennsylvania, from the mere apprehension of commotions among a part of her citizens, has thought proper to have recourse to the same measure. Suppose the State of New-York had been inclined to re-establish her lost jurisdiction over the inhabitants of Vermont; could she have hoped for success in such an enterprise from the efforts of the militia alone? Would she not have been compelled to raise and to maintain a more regular force for the execution of her design? If it must then be admitted that the necessity of recurring to a force different from the militia in cases of this extraordinary nature, is applicable to the State governments themselves, why should the possibility that the national government might be under a like necessity in similar extremities, be made an objection to its existence? Is it not surprising that men, who declare an attachment to the union in the abstract, should urge, as an objection to the proposed constitution, what applies with tenfold weight to the plan for which they contend; and what as far as it has any foundation in truth is an inevitable consequence of civil society upon an enlarged scale? Who would not prefer that possibility to the unceasing agitations and frequent revolutions which are the continual scourges of petty republics?

Let us pursue this examination in another light. Suppose, in lieu of one general system, two or three or even four confederacies were to be formed, would not the same difficulty oppose itself to the operations of either of these confederacies? Would not each of them be exposed to the same casualties; and, when these happened, be obliged to have recourse to the same expedients for upholding its authority, which are objected to a government for all the States? Would the militia in this supposition be more ready or more able to support the federal authority than in the case of a general union? All candid and intelligent men must upon due consideration acknowledge that the principle of the objection is equally applicable to either of the two cases; and that whether we have one government for all the States, or different governments for different parcels of them, or even if there should be an intire separation of the States, there might sometimes be a necessity to make use of a force constituted differently from the militia to preserve the peace of the community, and to maintain the just authority of the laws against those violent invasions of them which amount to insurrections and rebellions.

Independent of all other reasonings upon the subject, it is a full answer to those who require a more peremptory provision against military establishments in time of peace, that the whole power of the proposed government is to be in the hands of the representatives of the people. This is the essential, and after all the only efficacious security for the rights and privileges of the people which is attainable in civil society.*

If the representatives of the people betray their constituents, there is then no resource left but in the exertion of that original right of self-defence, which is paramount to all positive forms of government; and which, against the usurpations of the national rulers, may be exerted with infinitely better prospect of success, than against those of the rulers of an individual State. In a single State, if the persons entrusted with supreme power became usurpers, the different parcels, subdivisions or districts, of which it consists, having no distinct government in each, can take no regular measures for defence. The citizens must rush tumultuously to arms, without concert, without system, without resource; except in their courage and despair. The usurpers, cloathed with the forms of legal authority, can too often crush the opposition in embryo. The smaller the extent of territory, the more difficult will it be for the people to form a regular or systematic plan of opposition; and the more easy will it be to defeat their early efforts. Intelligence can be more speedily obtained of their preparations and movements; and the military force in the possession of the usurpers, can be more rapidly directed against the part where the opposition has begun. In this situation, there must be a peculiar coincidence of circumstances to ensure success to the popular resistance.

The obstacles to usurpation and the facilities of resistance increase with the increased extent of the state; provided the citizens understand their rights and are disposed to defend them. The natural strength of the people in a large community, in proportion to the artificial strength of the government, is greater than in a small; and of course more competent to a struggle with the attempts of the government to establish a tyranny. But in a confederacy the people, without exaggeration, may be said to be entirely the masters of their own fate. Power being almost always the rival of

* Its full efficacy will be examined hereafter.

power; the General Government will at all times stand ready to check the usurpations of the state governments; and these will have the same disposition towards the General Government. The people, by throwing themselves into either scale, will infallibly make it preponderate. If their rights are invaded by either, they can make use of the other, as the instrument of redress. How wise will it be in them by cherishing the Union to preserve to themselves an advantage which can never be too highly prised!

It may safely be received as an axiom in our political system, that the state governments will in all possible contingencies afford complete security against invasions of the public liberty by the national authority. Projects of usurpation cannot be masked under pretences so likely to escape the penetration of select bodies of men as of the people at large. The Legislatures will have better means of information. They can discover the danger at a distance; and possessing all the organs of civil power and the confidence of the people, they can at once adopt a regular plan of opposition, in which they can combine all the resources of the community. They can readily communicate with each other in the different states; and unite their common forces for the protection of their common liberty.

The great extent of the country is a further security. We have already experienced its utility against the attacks of a foreign power. And it would have precisely the same effect against the enterprises of ambitious rulers in the national councils. If the fœderal army should be able to quell the resistance of one state, the distant states would be able to make head with fresh forces. The advantages obtained in one place must be abandoned to subdue the opposition in others; and the moment the part which had been reduced to submission was left to itself its efforts would be renewed and its resistance revive.

We should recollect that the extent of the military force must at all events be regulated by the resources of the country. For a long time to come, it will not be possible to maintain a large army: and as the means of doing this increase, the population and natural strength of the community will proportionably increase. When will the time arrive, that the fœderal Government can raise and maintain an army capable of erecting a despotism over the great body of the people of an immense empire; who are in a situation, through the medium of their state governments, to take measures for their own defence with all the celerity, regularity and system of independent nations? The apprehension may be considered as a disease, for which there can be found no cure in the resources of argument and reasoning.

PUBLIUS.

The Independent Journal, December 26, 1787

The Federalist No. 29

To the People of the State of New-York.

The power of regulating the militia and of commanding its services in times of insurrection and invasion are natural incidents to the duties of superintending the common defence, and of watching over the internal peace of the confederacy.

It requires no skill in the science of war to discern that uniformity in the organization and discipline of the militia would be attended with the most beneficial effects, whenever they were called into service for the public defence. It would enable them to discharge the duties of the camp and of the field with mutual intelligence and concert; an advantage of peculiar moment in the operations of an army; And it would fit them much sooner to acquire the degree of proficiency in military functions, which would be essential to their usefulness. This desirable uniformity can only be accomplished by confiding the regulation of the militia to the direction of the national authority. It is therefore with the most evident propriety that the plan of the Convention proposes to empower the union "to provide for organizing, arming and disciplining the militia, and for governing such part of them as may be employed in the service of the United States, *reserving to the states respectively the appointment of the officers and the authority of training the militia according to the discipline prescribed by Congress.*"

Of the different grounds which have been taken in opposition to the plan of the Convention, there is none that was so little to have been expected, or is so untenable in itself, as the one from which this particular provision has been attacked. If a well regulated militia be the most natural defence of a free country, it ought certainly to be under the regulation and at the disposal of that body which is constituted the guardian of the national security. If standing armies are dangerous to liberty, an efficacious power over the militia, in the body to whose care the protection of the State is committed, ought as far as possible to take away the inducement and the pretext to such unfriendly institutions. If the fœderal government can command the aid of the militia in those emergencies which call for the military arm in support of the civil magistrate, it can the better dispense with the employment of a different kind of force. If it cannot avail itself of the former, it will be obliged to recur to the latter. To render an army unnecessary will be a more certain method of preventing its existence than a thousand prohibitions upon paper.

In order to cast an odium upon the power of calling forth the militia to execute the Laws of the Union, it has been remarked that there is no where any provision in the proposed Constitution for calling out the POSSE COMITATUS to assist the magistrate in the execution of his duty; whence it has been inferred that military force was intended to be his only auxiliary. There is a striking incoherence in the objections which have appeared, and sometimes even from the same quarter, not much calculated to inspire a very favourable opinion of the sincerity or fair dealing of their authors. The same persons who tell us in one breath that the powers of the federal government will be despotic and unlimited, inform us in the next that it has not authority sufficient even to call out the POSSE COMITATUS. The latter fortunately is as much short of the truth as the former exceeds it. It would be as absurd to doubt that a right to pass all laws *necessary* and *proper* to execute its declared powers would include that of requiring the assistance of the citizens to the officers who may be entrusted with the execution of those laws; as it would be to believe that a right to enact laws necessary and proper for the imposition and collection of taxes would involve that of varying the rules of descent and alienation of landed property or of abolishing the trial by jury in cases relating to it. It being therefore evident that the supposition of a want of power to require the aid of the POSSE COMITATUS is entirely destitute of colour, it will follow that the conclusion which has been drawn from it, in its application to the authority of the federal government over the militia is as uncandid as it is illogical. What reason could there be to infer that force was intended to be the sole instrument of authority merely because there is a power to make use of it when necessary? What shall we think of the motives which could induce men of sense to reason in this manner? How shall we prevent a conflict between charity and judgment?

By a curious refinement upon the spirit of republican jealousy, we are even taught to apprehend danger from the militia itself in the hands of the federal government. It is observed that select corps may be formed, composed of the young and ardent, who may be rendered subservient to the views of arbitrary power. What plan for the regulation of the militia may be pursued by the national government is impossible to be foreseen. But so far from viewing the matter in the same light with those who object to select corps as dangerous, were the Constitution ratified, and were I to deliver my sentiments to a member of the federal legislature from this State on the subject of a militia establishment, I should hold to him in substance the following discourse:

"The project of disciplining all the militia of the United States is as futile as it would be injurious, if it were capable of being carried into execution. A tolerable expertness in military movements is a business that requires time and practice. It is not a day or even a week that will suffice for the attainment of it. To oblige the great body of the yeomanry and of the other classes of the citizens to be under arms for the purpose of going through military exercises and evolutions as often as might be necessary, to acquire the degree of perfection which would intitle them to the character of a well regulated militia, would be a real grievance to the people, and a serious public inconvenience and loss. It would form an annual deduction from the productive labour of the country to an amount which, calculating upon the present numbers of the people, would not fall far short of the whole expence of the civil establishments of all the States. To attempt a thing which would abridge the mass of labour and industry to so considerable an extent would be unwise; and the experiment, if made, could not succeed, because it would not long be endured. Little more can reasonably be aimed at with respect to the people at large than to have them properly armed and equipped; and in order to see that this be not neglected, it will be necessary to assemble them once or twice in the course of a year.

"But though the scheme of disciplining the whole nation must be abandoned as mischievous or impracticable; yet it is a matter of the utmost importance that a well digested plan should as soon as possible be adopted for the proper establishment of the militia. The attention of the government ought particularly to be directed to the formation of a select corps of moderate size upon such principles as will really fit it for service in case of need. By thus circumscribing the plan it will be possible to have an excellent body of well trained militia ready to take the field whenever the defence of the State shall require it. This will not only lessen the call for military establishments; but if circumstances should at any time oblige the government to form an army of any magnitude, that army can never be formidable to the liberties of the people, while there is a large body of citizens little if at all inferior to them in discipline and the use of arms, who stand ready to defend their own rights and those of their fellow citizens. This appears to me the only substitute that can be devised for a standing army; the best possible security against it, if it should exist."

Thus differently from the adversaries of the proposed constitution should I reason on the same subject; deducing arguments of safety from the very sources which they represent as fraught with danger and perdition. But how the national Legislature may reason on the point is a thing which neither they nor I can foresee.

There is something so far fetched and so extravagant in the idea of danger to liberty from the militia, that one is at a loss whether to treat it with gravity or with raillery; whether to consider it as a mere trial of skill, like the paradoxes of rhetoricians, as a disingenuous artifice to instill prejudices at any price or as the serious offspring of political fanaticism. Where in the name of common sense are our fears to end if we may not trust our sons, our brothers, our neighbours, our fellow-citizens? What shadow of danger can there be from men who are daily mingling with the rest of their countrymen; and who participate with them in the same feelings, sentiments, habits and interests? What reasonable cause of apprehension can be inferred from a power in the Union to prescribe regulations for the militia and to command its services when necessary; while the particular States are to have the *sole and exclusive appointment of the officers*? If it were possible seriously to indulge a jealousy of the militia upon any conceivable establishment under the Fœderal Government, the circumstance of the officers being in the appointment of the States ought at once to extinguish it. There can be no doubt that this circumstance will always secure to them a preponderating influence over the militia.

In reading many of the publications against the Constitution, a man is apt to imagine that he is perusing some ill written tale or romance; which instead of natural and agreeable images exhibits to the mind nothing but frightful and distorted shapes—Gorgons Hydras and Chimeras dire—discoloring and disfiguring whatever it represents and transforming every thing it touches into a monster.

A sample of this is to be observed in the exaggerated and improbable suggestions which have taken place respecting the power of calling for the services of the militia. That of New-Hampshire is to be marched to Georgia, of Georgia to New Hampshire, of New-York to Kentuke and of Kentuke to Lake Champlain. Nay the debts due to the French and Dutch are to be paid in Militia-men instead of Louis d'ors and ducats. At one moment there is to be a large army to lay prostrate the liberties of the people; at another moment the militia of Virginia are to be dragged from their homes five or six hundred miles to tame the republican contumacy of Massachusetts; and that of Massachusetts is to be transported an equal distance to subdue the refractory haughtiness of the aristocratic Virginians. Do the persons, who rave at this rate, imagine, that their art or their eloquence can impose any conceits or absurdities upon the people of America for infallible truths?

If there should be an army to be made use of as the engine of despotism what need of the militia? If there should be no army, whither would the militia, irritated by being called upon to undertake a distant and hopeless expedition for the purpose of rivetting the chains of slavery upon a part of their countrymen direct their course, but to the seat of the tyrants, who had meditated so foolish as well as so wicked a project; to crush them in their imagined intrenchments of power and to make them an example of the just vengeance of an abused and incensed people? Is this the way in which usurpers stride to dominion over a numerous and enlightened nation? Do they begin by exciting the detestation of the very instruments of their intended usurpations? Do they usually commence their career by wanton and disgustful acts of power calculated to answer no end, but to draw upon themselves universal hatred and execration? Are suppositions of this sort the sober admonitions of discerning patriots to a discerning people? Or are they the inflammatory ravings of chagrined incendiaries or distempered enthusiasts? If we were even to suppose the national rulers actuated by the most ungovernable ambition, it is impossible to believe that they would employ such preposterous means to accomplish their designs.

In times of insurrection or invasion it would be natural and proper that the militia of a neighbouring state should be marched into another to resist a common enemy or to guard the republic against the violences of faction or sedition. This was frequently the case in respect to the first object in the course of the late war; and this mutual succour is indeed a principal end of our political association. If the power of affording it be placed under the direction of the union, there will be no danger of a supine and listless inattention to the dangers of a neighbour, till its near approach had superadded the incitements of self preservation to the too feeble impulses of duty and sympathy.

PUBLIUS.

The Independent Journal, January 9, 1788

The Federalist No. 30

It has been already observed, that the Fœderal Government ought to possess the power of providing for the support of the national forces; in which proposition was intended to be included the expence of raising troops, of building and equiping fleets, and all other expences in any wise connected with military arrangements and operations. But these are not the only objects to which the jurisdiction of the Union, in respect to revenue, must necessarily be empowered to extend—It must embrace a provision for the support of the national civil list—for the payment of the national debts contracted, or that may be contracted—and in general for all those matters which will call for disbursements out of the national treasury. The conclusion is, that there must be interwoven in the frame of the government, a general power of taxation in one shape or another.

Money is with propriety considered as the vital principle of the body politic; as that which sustains its life and motion, and enables it to perform its most essential functions. A complete power therefore to procure a regular and adequate supply of it, as far as the resources of the community will permit, may be regarded as an indispensable ingredient in every constitution. From a deficiency in this particular, one of two evils must ensue; either the people must be subjected to continual plunder as a substitute for a more eligible mode of supplying the public wants, or the government must sink into a fatal atrophy, and in a short course of time perish.

In the Ottoman or Turkish empire, the sovereign, though in other respects absolute master of the lives and fortunes of his subjects, has no right to impose a new tax. The consequence is, that he permits the Bashaws or Governors of provinces to pillage the people without mercy; and in turn squeezes out of them the sums of which he stands in need to satisfy his own exigencies and those of the State. In America, from a like cause, the government of the Union has gradually dwindled into a state of decay, approaching nearly to annihilation. Who can doubt that the happiness of the people in both countries would be promoted by competent authorities in the proper hands, to provide the revenues which the necessities of the public might require?

The present confederation, feeble as it is, intended to repose in the United States, an unlimited power of providing for the pecuniary wants of the Union. But proceeding upon an erroneous principle, it has been done in such a manner as entirely to have frustrated the intention. Congress by the articles which compose that compact (as has been already stated) are authorised to ascertain and call for any sums of money necessary, in their judgment, to the service of the United States; and their requisitions, if conformable to the rule of apportionment, are in every constitutional sense obligatory upon the States. These have no right to question the propriety of the demand—no discretion beyond that of devising the ways and means of furnishing the sums demanded. But though this be strictly and truly the case; though the assumption of such a right be an infringement of the articles of Union; though it may seldom or never have been avowedly claimed; yet in practice it has been constantly exercised; and would continue to be so, as long as the revenues of the confederacy should remain dependent on the intermediate agency of its members. What the consequences of this system have been, is within the knowledge of every man, the least conversant in our public affairs, and has been amply unfolded in different parts of these inquiries. It is this which has chiefly contributed to reduce us to a situation which affords ample cause, both of mortification to ourselves, and of triumph to our enemies.

What remedy can there be for this situation but, in a change of the system, which has produced it? In a change of the fallacious and delusive system of quotas and requisitions? What substitute can there be imagined for this *ignis fatuus* in finance, but that of permitting the national government to raise its own revenues by the ordinary methods of taxation, authorised in every well ordered constitution of civil government? Ingenious men may declaim with plausibility on any subject; but no human ingenuity can point out any other expedient to rescue us from the inconveniences and embarrassments, naturally - resulting from defective supplies of the public treasury.

The more intelligent adversaries of the new constitution admit the force of this reasoning; but they qualify their admission by a distinction between what they call *internal* and *external* taxation. The former they would reserve to the State governments; the latter, which they explain into commercial imposts, or rather duties on imported articles, they declare themselves willing to concede to the Fœderal Head. This distinction, however, would violate that fundamental maxim of good sense and sound policy, which dictates that every POWER ought to be proportionate to its OBJECT; and would still leave the General Government in a kind of tutelage to the State governments, inconsistent with every idea of vigor or efficiency. Who can pretend that commercial imposts are or would be alone equal to the present and future exigencies of the Union? Taking into the account the existing debt, foreign and domestic, upon any plan of extinguishment, which a man moderately impressed with the importance of public justice and public credit could approve, in addition to the establishments, which all parties will acknowledge to be necessary, we could not reasonably flatter ourselves, that this resource alone, upon the most improved scale, would even suffice for its present necessities. Its future necessities admit not of calculation or limitation; and upon the principle, more than once adverted to, the power of making provision for them as they arise, ought to be equally unconfined. I believe it may be regarded as a position, warranted by the history of mankind, that *in the usual progress of things, the necessities of a nation in every stage of its existence will be found at least equal to its resources.*

To say that deficiencies may be provided for by requisitions upon the States, is on the one hand, to acknowledge that this system cannot be depended upon; and on the other hand, to depend upon it for every thing beyond a certain limit. Those who have carefully attended to its vices and deformities as they have been exhibited by experience, or delineated in the course of these papers, must feel an invincible repugnancy to trusting the national interests, in any degree, to its operation. Its inevitable tendency, whenever it is brought into activity, must be to enfeeble the Union and sow the seeds of discord and contention between the Fœderal Head and its members, and between the members themselves. Can it be expected that the deficiencies would be better supplied in this mode, than the total wants of the Union have heretofore been supplied, in the same mode? It ought to be recollected, that if less will be required from the States, they will have proportionably less means to answer the demand. If the opinions of those who contend for the distinction which has been mentioned, were to be received as evidence of truth, one would be led to conclude that there was some known point in the œconomy of national affairs, at which it would be safe to stop, and say, thus far the ends of public happiness will be promoted by supplying the wants of government, and all beyond this is unworthy of our care or anxiety. How is it possible that a government half supplied and always necessitous, can fulfil the purposes of its institution—can provide for the security of—advance the prosperity—or support the reputation of the commonwealth? How can it ever possess either energy or stability, dignity or credit, confidence at home or respectability abroad? How can its administration be any thing else than a succession of expedients temporising, impotent, disgraceful? How will it be able to avoid a frequent sacrifice of its engagements to immediate necessity? How can it undertake or execute any liberal or enlarged plans of public good?

Let us attend to what would be the effects of this situation in the very first war in which we should happen to be engaged. We will presume for argument sake, that the revenue arising from the impost-duties answer the purposes of a provision for the public debt, and of a peace establishment for the Union. Thus circumstanced, a war breaks out. What would be the probable conduct of the government in such an emergency? Taught by experience that proper dependence could not be placed on the success of requisitions: unable by its own authority to lay hold of fresh resources, and urged by considerations of national danger, would it not be driven to the expedient of diverting the funds already appropriated from their proper objects to the defence of the State? It is not easy to see how a step of this kind could be avoided; and if it should be taken, it is evident that it would prove the destruction of public credit at the very moment that it was become essential to the public safety. To imagine that at such a crisis credit might be dispensed with, would be the extreme of infatuation. In the modern system of war, nations the most wealthy are obliged to have recourse to large loans. A country so little opulent as ours, must feel this necessity in a much stronger degree. But who would lend to a government that prefaced its overtures for borrowing, by an act which demonstrated that no reliance could be placed on the steadiness of its measures for paying? The loans it might be able to procure, would be as limited in their extent as burthensome in their conditions. They would be made upon the same principles that usurers commonly lend to bankrupt and fraudulent debtors; with a sparing hand, and at enormous premiums.

It may perhaps be imagined, that from the scantiness of the resources of the country, the necessity of diverting the established funds in the case supposed, would exist; though the national government should possess an unrestrained power of taxation. But two considerations will serve to quiet all apprehension on this head; one is, that we are sure the resources of the community in their full extent, will be brought into activity for the benefit of the Union; the other is, that whatever deficiencies there may be, can without difficulty be supplied by loans.

The power of creating new funds upon new objects of taxation by its own authority, would enable the national government to borrow, as far as its necessities might require. Foreigners as well as the citizens of America, could then reasonably repose confidence in its engagements; but to depend upon a government, that must itself depend upon thirteen other governments for the means of fulfilling its contracts, when once its situation is clearly understood, would require a degree of credulity, not often to be met with in the pecuniary transactions of mankind, and little reconcileable with the usual sharp-sightedness of avarice.

Reflections of this kind, may have trifling weight with men, who hope to see realized in America, the halcyon scenes of the poetic or fabulous age; but to those who believe we are likely to experience a common portion of the vicissitudes and calamities, which have fallen to the lot of other nations, they must appear entitled to serious attention. Such men must behold the actual situation of their country with painful solicitude, and deprecate the evils which ambition or revenge might, with too much facility, inflict upon it.

PUBLIUS.

The New-York Packet, December 28, 1787

The Federalist No. 31

To the People of the State of New-York.

In disquisitions of every kind there are certain primary truths or first principles upon which all subsequent reasonings must depend. These contain an internal evidence, which antecedent to all reflection or combination commands the assent of the mind. Where it produces not this effect, it must proceed either from some defect or disorder in the organs of perception, or from the influence of some strong interest, or passion, or prejudice. Of this nature are the maxims in geometry, that "The whole is greater than its part; that things equal to the same are equal to one another; that two straight lines cannot inclose a space; and that all right angles are equal to each other." Of the same nature are these other maxims in ethics and politics, that there cannot be an effect without a cause; that the means ought to be proportioned to the end; that every power ought to be commensurate with its object; that there ought to be no limitation of a power destined to effect a purpose, which is itself incapable of limitation. And there are other truths in the two latter sciences, which if they cannot pretend to rank in the class of axioms, are yet such direct inferences from them, and so obvious in themselves, and so agreeable to the natural and unsophisticated dictates of common sense, that they challenge the assent of a sound and unbiassed mind, with a degree of force and conviction almost equally irresistable.

The objects of geometrical enquiry are so intirely abstracted from those pursuits which stir up and put in motion the unruly passions of the human heart, that mankind without difficulty adopt not only the more simple theorems of the science, but even those abstruse paradoxes, which however they may appear susceptible of demonstration, are at variance with the natural conceptions which the mind, without the aid of philosophy, would be led to entertain upon the subject. The INFINITE DIVISIBILITY of matter, or in other words, the INFINITE divisibility of a FINITE thing, extending even to the minutest atom, is a point agreed among geometricians;

though not less incomprehensible to common sense, than any of those mysteries in religion, against which the batteries of infidelity have been so industriously levelled.

But in the sciences of morals and politics men are found far less tractable. To a certain degree it is right and useful, that this should be the case. Caution and investigation are a necessary armour against error and imposition. But this untractableness may be carried too far, and may degenerate into obstinacy, perverseness or disingenuity. Though it cannot be pretended that the principles of moral and political knowledge have in general the same degree of certainty with those of the mathematics; yet they have much better claims in this respect, than to judge from the conduct of men in particular situations, we should be disposed to allow them. The obscurity is much oftener in the passions and prejudices of the reasoner than in the subject. Men upon too many occasions do not give their own understandings fair play; but yielding to some untoward bias they entangle themselves in words and confound themselves in subtleties.

How else could it happen (if we admit the objectors to be sincere in their opposition) that positions so clear as those which manifest the necessity of a general power of taxation in the government of the union, should have to encounter any adversaries among men of discernment? Though these positions have been elsewhere fully stated, they will perhaps not be improperly recapitulated in this place, as introductory to an examination of what may have been offered by way of objection to them. They are in substance as follow:

A government ought to contain in itself every power requisite to the full accomplishment of the objects committed to its care, and to the complete execution of the trusts for which it is responsible; free from every other control, but a regard to the public good and to the sense of the people.

As the duties of superintending the national defence and of securing the public peace against foreign or domestic violence, involve a provision for casualties and dangers, to which no possible limits can be assigned, the power of making that provision ought to know no other bounds than the exigencies of the nation and the resources of the community.

As revenue is the essential engine by which the means of answering the national exigencies must be procured, the power of procuring that article in its full extent, must necessarily be comprehended in that of providing for those exigencies.

As theory and practice conspire to prove that the power of procuring revenue is unavailing, when exercised over the States in their collective capacities, the Federal government must of necessity be invested with an unqualified power of taxation in the ordinary modes.

Did not experience evince the contrary, it would be natural to conclude that the propriety of a general power of taxation in the national government might safely be permitted to rest on the evidence of these propositions, unassisted by any additional arguments or illustrations. But we find in fact, that the antagonists of the proposed constitution, so far from acquiescing in their justness or truth, seem to make their principal and most zealous effort against this part of the plan. It may therefore be satisfactory to analize the arguments with which they combat it.

Those of them, which have been most labored with that view, seem in substance to amount to this: "It is not true, because the exigencies of the Union may not be susceptible of limitation, that its power of laying taxes ought to be unconfined. Revenue is as requisite to the purposes of the local administrations as to those of the Union; and the former are at least of equal importance with the latter to the happiness of the people. It is therefore as necessary, that the State Governments should be able to command the means of supplying their wants, as, that the National Government should possess the like faculty, in respect to the wants of the Union. But an indefinite power of taxation in the *latter* might, and probably would in time deprive the former of the means of providing for their own necessities; and would subject them entirely to the mercy of the national Legislature. As the laws of the Union are to become the supreme law of the land; as it is to have power to pass all laws that may be NECESSARY for carrying into execution, the authorities with which it is proposed to vest it; the national government might at any time abolish the taxes imposed for State objects, upon the pretence of an

interference with its own. It might alledge a necessity of doing this, in order to give efficacy to the national revenues:
And thus all the resources of taxation might by degrees, become the subjects of fœderal monopoly, to the intire exclusion and destruction of the State Governments."

This mode of reasoning appears some times to turn upon
the supposition of usurpation in the national government; at
other times it seems to be designed only as a deduction from
the constitutional operation of its intended powers. It is only
in the latter light, that it can be admitted to have any pretensions to fairness. The moment we launch into conjectures
about the usurpations of the fœderal Government, we get
into an unfathomable abyss, and fairly put ourselves out of the
reach of all reasoning. Imagination may range at pleasure till
it gets bewildered amidst the labyrinths of an enchanted
castle, and knows not on which side to turn to extricate itself
from the perplexities into which it has so rashly adventured.
Whatever may be the limits or modifications of the powers of
the Union, it is easy to imagine an endless train of possible
dangers; and by indulging an excess of jealousy and timidity,
we may bring ourselves to a state of absolute scepticism and
irresolution. I repeat here what I have observed in substance
in another place that all observations founded upon the danger of usurpation, ought to be referred to the composition
and structure of the government, not to the nature or extent
of its powers. The State governments, by their original constitutions, are invested with complete sovereignty. In what
does our security consist against usurpations from that quarter? Doubtless in the manner of their formation, and in a due
dependence of those who are to administer them upon the
people. If the proposed construction of the Fœderal Government, be found upon an impartial examination of it, to be
such as to afford, to a proper extent, the same species of security, all apprehensions on the score of usurpation ought to
be discarded.

It should not be forgotten, that a disposition in the State
governments to encroach upon the rights of the Union, is
quite as probable, as a disposition in the Union to encroach
upon the rights of the State Governments. What side would
be likely to prevail in such a conflict, must depend on the

means which the contending parties could employ towards ensuring success. As in republics, strength is always on the side of the people; and as there are weighty reasons to induce a belief, that the State governments will commonly possess most influence over them, the natural conclusion is, that such contests will be most apt to end to the disadvantage of the Union; and that there is greater probability of encroachments by the members upon the Fœderal Head, than by the Fœderal Head upon the members. But it is evident, that all conjectures of this kind, must be extremely vague and fallible, and that it is by far the safest course to lay them altogether aside; and to confine our attention wholly to the nature and extent of the powers as they are delineated in the constitution. Every thing beyond this, must be left to the prudence and firmness of the people; who, as they will hold the scales in their own hands, it is to be hoped, will always take care to preserve the constitutional equilibrium between the General and the State Governments. Upon this ground, which is evidently the true one, it will not be difficult to obviate the objections, which have been made to an indefinite power of taxation in the United States.

PUBLIUS.

The New-York Packet, January 1, 1788

The Federalist No. 32

Although I am of opinion that there would be no real danger of the consequences, which seem to be apprehended to the State Governments, from a power in the Union to controul them in the levies of money; because I am persuaded that the sense of the people, the extreme hazard of provoking the resentments of the State Governments, and a conviction of the utility and necessity of local administrations, for local purposes, would be a complete barrier against the oppressive use of such a power: Yet I am willing here to allow in its full extent the justness of the reasoning, which requires that the individual States should possess an independent and uncontrolable authority to raise their own revenues for the supply of their own wants. And making this concession I affirm that (with the sole exception of duties on imports and exports) they would under the plan of the Convention retain that authority in the most absolute and unqualified sense; and that an attempt on the part of the national Government to abrige them in the exercise of it would be a violent assumption of power unwarranted by any article or clause of its Constitution.

An intire consolidation of the States into one complete national sovereignty would imply an intire subordination of the parts; and whatever powers might remain in them would be altogether dependent on the general will. But as the plan of the Convention aims only at a partial Union or consolidation, the State Governments would clearly retain all the rights of sovereignty which they before had and which were not by that act *exclusively* delegated to the United States. This exclusive delegation or rather this alienation of State sovereignty would only exist in three cases; where the Constitution in express terms granted an exclusive authority to the Union; where it granted in one instance an authority to the Union; and in another prohibited the States from exercising the like authority; and where it granted an authority to the Union, to which a similar authority in the States would be absolutely and totally *contradictory* and *repugnant*. I use these terms to distinguish this last case from another which might appear to resemble it; but which would in fact be essentially different; I mean where the exercise of a concurrent jurisdiction might be productive of occasional interferences in the *policy* of any branch of administration, but would not imply any direct contradiction or repugnancy in point of constitutional authority. These three cases of exclusive jurisdiction in the Fœderal Government may be exemplified by the following instances: The last clause but one in the 8th section of the 1st. article provides expressly that Congress shall exercise "*exclusive legislation*" over the district to be appropriated as the seat of government. This answers to the first case. The first clause of the same section impowers Congress "*to lay and collect taxes, duties, imposts or excises*" and the 2d. clause of the 10th. section of the same article declares that "*no State shall* without the consent of Congress, *lay any imposts or duties on imports or exports* except for the purpose of executing its inspection laws." Hence would result an exclusive power in the Union to lay duties on imports and exports with the particular exception mentioned; but this power is abriged by another clause which declares that no tax or duty shall be laid on articles exported from any State; in consequence of which qualification it now only extends to the *duties on imports*. This answers to the second case. The third will be found in that clause, which declares that Congress shall have power "to establish an UNIFORM RULE of naturalization throughout the United States." This must necessarily be exclusive; because if each State had power to prescribe a DISTINCT RULE there could be no UNIFORM RULE.

A case which may perhaps be thought to resemble the latter, but which is in fact widely different, affects the question immediately under consideration. I mean the power of imposing taxes on all articles other than exports and imports. This, I contend, is manifestly a concurrent and coequal authority in the United States and in the individual States. There is plainly no expression in the granting clause which makes that power *exclusive* in the Union. There is no independent clause or sentence which prohibits the States from exercising it. So far is this from being the case, that a plain and conclusive argument to the contrary is to be deduced from the restraint laid upon the States in relation to duties on imports and exports. This restriction implies an admission, that if it were not inserted the States would possess the power it excludes, and it implies a further admission, that as to all other taxes the authority of the States remains undiminished. In any other view it would be both unnecessary and dangerous; it would be unnecessary because if the grant to the Union of the power of laying such duties implied the exclusion of the States, or even their subordination in this particular there could be no need of such a restriction; it would be dangerous because the introduction of it leads directly to the conclusion which has been mentioned and which if the reasoning of the objectors be just, could not have been intended; I mean that the States in all cases to which the restriction did not apply would have a concurrent power of taxation with the Union. The restriction in question amounts to what lawyers call a NEGATIVE PREGNANT; that is a *negation* of one thing and an *affirmance* of another; a negation of the authority of the States to impose taxes on imports and exports, and an affirmance of their authority to impose them on all other articles. It would be mere sophistry to argue that it was meant to exclude them *absolutely* from the imposition of taxes of the former kind, and to leave them at liberty to lay others *subject to the controul* of the national Legislature. The restraining or prohibitory clause only says, that they shall not *without the consent of Congress* lay such duties; and if we are to understand this in the sense last mentioned, the Constitution would then be made to introduce a formal provision for the sake of a very absurd conclusion; which is that the States *with the consent* of the national Legislature might tax imports and exports; and that they might tax every other article *unless controuled* by the same body. If this was the intention why not leave it in the first instance to what is alleged to be the natural operation of the original clause conferring a general power of taxation upon the Union? It is evident that this could not have been the intention and that it will not bear a construction of the kind.

As to a supposition of repugnancy between the power of taxation in the States and in the Union, it cannot be supported in that sense which would be requisite to work an exclusion of the States. It is indeed possible that a tax might be laid on a particular article by a State which might render it *inexpedient* and that thus a further tax should be laid on the same article by the Union; but it would not imply a constitutional inability to impose a further tax. The quantity of the imposition, the expediency or inexpediency of an increase on either side, would be mutually questions of prudence; but there would be involved no direct contradiction of power. The particular policy of the national and the State systems of finance might now and then not exactly coincide, and might require reciprocal forbearances. It is not however a mere possibility of inconvenience in the exercise of powers, but an immediate constitutional repugnancy, that can by implication alienate and extinguish a pre-existing right of sovereignty.

The necessity of a concurrent jurisdiction in certain cases results from the division of the sovereign power; and the rule that all authorities of which the States are not explicitly divested in favour of the Union remain with them in full vigour, is not only a theoretical consequence of that division, but is clearly admitted by the whole tenor of the instrument which contains the articles of the proposed constitution. We there find that notwithstanding the affirmative grants of general authorities, there has been the most pointed care in those cases where it was deemed improper that the like authorities should reside in the States, to insert negative clauses prohibiting the exercise of them by the States. The tenth section of the first article consists altogether of such provisions. This circumstance is a clear indication of the sense of the Convention, and furnishes a rule of interpretation out of the body of the act which justifies the position I have advanced, and refutes every hypothesis to the contrary.

PUBLIUS

The Independent Journal, January 2, 1788

The Federalist No. 33

To the People of the State of New-York.

The residue of the argument against the provisions in the constitution, in respect to taxation, is ingrafted upon the following clauses; the last clause of the eighth section of the first article of the plan under consideration, authorises the national legislature "to make all laws which shall be *necessary* and *proper*, for carrying into execution *the powers* by that Constitution vested in the government of the United States, or any department or officer thereof;" and the second clause of the sixth article declares, that "the Constitution and the Laws of the United States made *in pursuance thereof*, and the treaties made by their authority shall be the *supreme law* of the land; any thing in the constitution or laws of any State to the contrary notwithstanding."

These two clauses have been the sources of much virulent invective and petulant declamation against the proposed constitution, they have been held up to the people, in all the exaggerated colours of misrepresentation, as the pernicious engines by which their local governments were to be destroyed and their liberties exterminated—as the hideous monster whose devouring jaws would spare neither sex nor age, nor high nor low, nor sacred nor profane; and yet strange as it may appear, after all this clamour, to those who may not have happened to contemplate them in the same light, it may be affirmed with perfect confidence, that the constitutional operation of the intended government would be precisely the same, if these clauses were entirely obliterated, as if they were repeated in every article. They are only declaratory of a truth, which would have resulted by necessary and unavoidable implication from the very act of constituting a Fœderal Government, and vesting it with certain specified powers. This is so clear a proposition, that moderation itself can scarcely listen to the railings which have been so copiously vented against this part of the plan, without emotions that disturb its equanimity.

What is a power, but the ability or faculty of doing a thing? What is the ability to do a thing but the power of employing the *means* necessary to its execution? What is a LEGISLA-TIVE power but a power of making LAWS? What are the *means* to execute a LEGISLATIVE power but LAWS? What is the power of laying and collecting taxes but a *legislative power*, or a power of *making laws*, to lay and collect taxes? What are the proper means of executing such a power but *necessary* and *proper* laws?

This simple train of enquiry furnishes us at once with a test by which to judge of the true nature of the clause complained of. It conducts us to this palpable truth, that a power to lay and collect taxes must be a power to pass all laws *necessary* and *proper* for the execution of that power; and what does the unfortunate and calumniated provision in question do more than declare the same truth; to wit, that the national legisla-ture to whom the power of laying and collecting taxes had been previously given, might in the execution of that power pass all laws *necessary* and *proper* to carry it into effect? I have applied these observations thus particularly to the power of taxation, because it is the immediate subject under considera-tion, and because it is the most important of the authorities proposed to be conferred upon the Union. But the same process will lead to the same result in relation to all other powers declared in the constitution. And it is *expressly* to exe-cute these powers, that the sweeping clause, as it has been af-fectedly called, authorises the national legislature to pass all *necessary* and *proper* laws. If there is any thing exceptionable, it must be sought for in the specific powers, upon which this general declaration is predicated. The declaration itself, though it may be chargeable with tautology or redundancy, is at least perfectly harmless.

But SUSPICION may ask why then was it introduced? The answer is, that it could only have been done for greater cau-tion, and to guard against all cavilling refinements in those who might hereafter feel a disposition to curtail and evade the legitimate authorities of the Union. The Convention proba-bly foresaw what it has been a principal aim of these papers to inculcate that the danger which most threatens our political welfare, is, that the State Governments will finally sap the foundations of the Union; and might therefore think it necessary, in so cardinal a point, to leave nothing to construction. Whatever may have been the inducement to it, the wisdom of the precaution is evident from the cry which has been raised against it; as that very cry betrays a disposition to question the great and essential truth which it is manifestly the object of that provision to declare.

But it may be again asked, who is to judge of the *necessity* and *propriety* of the laws to be passed for executing the powers of the Union? I answer first that this question arises as well and as fully upon the simple grant of those powers, as upon the declaratory clause: And I answer in the second place, that the national government, like every other, must judge in the first instance of the proper exercise of its powers; and its constituents in the last. If the Fœderal Government should overpass the just bounds of its authority, and make a tyrannical use of its powers; the people whose creature it is must appeal to the standard they have formed, and take such measures to redress the injury done to the constitution, as the exigency may suggest and prudence justify. The propriety of a law in a constitutional light, must always be determined by the nature of the powers upon which it is founded. Suppose by some forced constructions of its authority (which indeed cannot easily be imagined) the Fœderal Legislature should attempt to vary the law of descent in any State; would it not be evident that in making such an attempt it had exceeded its jurisdiction and infringed upon that of the State? Suppose again that upon the pretence of an interference with its revenues, it should undertake to abrogate a land tax imposed by the authority of a State, would it not be equally evident that this was an invasion of that concurrent jurisdiction in respect to this species of tax which its constitution plainly supposes to exist in the State governments? If there ever should be a doubt on this head the credit of it will be intirely due to those reasoners, who, in the imprudent zeal of their animosity to the plan of the Convention, have laboured to invelope it in a cloud calculated to obscure the plainest and simplest truths.

But it is said, that the laws of the Union are to be the *supreme law* of the land. But what inference can be drawn from this or what would they amount to, if they were not to be supreme? It is evident they would amount to nothing. A LAW by the very meaning of the term includes supremacy. It is a rule which those to whom it is prescribed are bound to observe. This results from every political association. If individuals enter into a state of society the laws of that society must be the supreme regulator of their conduct. If a number of political societies enter into a larger political society, the laws which the latter may enact, pursuant to the powers entrusted to it by its constitution, must necessarily be supreme over those societies, and the individuals of whom they are composed. It would otherwise be a mere treaty, dependent on the good faith of the parties, and not a government; which is only another word for POLITICAL POWER AND SUPREMACY. But it will not follow from this doctrine that acts of the larger society which are *not pursuant* to its constitutional powers but which are invasions of the residuary authorities of the smaller societies will become the supreme law of the land. These will be merely acts of usurpation and will deserve to be treated as such. Hence we perceive that the clause which declares the supremacy of the laws of the Union, like the one we have just before considered, only declares a truth, which flows immediately and necessarily from the institution of a Fœderal Government. It will not, I presume, have escaped observation that it *expressly* confines this supremacy to laws made *pursuant to the Constitution*; which I mention merely as an instance of caution in the Convention; since that limitation would have been to be understood though it had not been expressed.

Though a law therefore for laying a tax for the use of the United States would be supreme in its nature, and could not legally be opposed or controuled; yet a law for abrogating or preventing the collection of a tax laid by the authority of a State (unless upon imports and exports) would not be the supreme law of the land, but an usurpation of power not granted by the constitution. As far as an improper accumulation of taxes on the same object might tend to render the collection difficult or precarious, this would be a mutual inconvenience not arising from a superiority or defect of power on either side, but from an injudicious exercise of power by one or the other, in a manner equally disadvantageous to both. It is to be hoped and presumed however that mutual interest would dictate a concert in this respect which would avoid any material inconvenience. The inference from the whole is—that the individual States would, under the proposed constitution, retain an independent and uncontroulable authority to raise revenue to any extent of which they may stand in need by every kind of taxation except duties on imports and exports. It will be shewn in the next paper that this CONCURRENT JURISDICTION in the article of taxation was the only admissible substitute for an intire subordination, in respect to this branch of power, of the State authority to that of the Union.

PUBLIUS.

The Independent Journal, January 2, 1788

The Federalist No. 34

I flatter myself it has been clearly shewn in my last number, that the particular States, under the proposed Constitution, would have CO-EQUAL authority with the Union in the article of revenue, except as to duties on imports. As this leaves open to the States far the greatest part of the resources of the community, there can be no color for the assertion, that they would not possess means, as abundant as could be desired, for the supply of their own wants, independent of all external control. That the field is sufficiently wide, will more fully appear, when we come to advert to the inconsiderable share of the public expences, for which, it will fall to the lot of the State Governments to provide.

To argue upon abstract principles, that this co-ordinate authority cannot exist, is to set up supposition and theory, against fact and reality. However proper such reasonings might be, to show that a thing *ought not to exist*, they are wholly to be rejected, when they are made use of to prove that it does not exist, contrary to the evidence of the fact itself. It is well known, that in the Roman Republic, the Legislative authority in the last resort, resided for ages in two different political bodies; not as branches of the same Legislature, but as distinct and independent Legislatures, in each of which an opposite interest prevailed; in one, the Patrician—in the other, the Plebeian. Many arguments might have been adduced to prove the unfitness of two such seemingly contradictory authorities, each having power to *annul* or *repeal* the acts of the other. But a man would have been regarded as frantic, who should have attempted at Rome, to disprove their existence. It will readily be understood, that I allude to the COMITIA CENTURIATA, and COMITIA TRIBUTA. The former, in which the people voted by Centuries, was so arranged as to give a superiority to the Patrician interest: in the latter, in which numbers prevailed, the Plebeian interest had an entire predominancy. And yet these two Legislatures co-existed for ages, and the Roman Republic attained to the utmost height of human greatness.

In the case particularly under consideration, there is no such contradiction as appears in the example cited, there is no power on either side to annul the acts of the other. And in practice, there is little reason to apprehend any inconvenience; because, in a short course of time, the wants of the States will naturally reduce themselves within *a very narrow compass*; and in the interim, the United States will, in all probability, find it convenient to abstain wholly from those objects, to which the particular States would be inclined to resort.

To form a more precise judgment of the true merits of this question, it will be well to advert to the proportion between the objects that will require a Federal provision in respect to revenue; and those which will require a State provision. We shall discover that the former are altogether unlimited; and, that the latter are circumscribed within very moderate bounds. In pursuing this enquiry, we must bear in mind, that we are not to confine our view to the present period, but to look forward to remote futurity. Constitutions of civil Government are not to be framed upon a calculation of existing exigencies; but upon a combination of these, with the probable exigencies of ages, according to the natural and tried course of human affairs. Nothing therefore can be more fallacious, than to infer the extent of any power, proper to be lodged in the National Government, from an estimate of its immediate necessities. There ought to be a CAPACITY to provide for future contingencies, as they may happen; and, as these are illimitable in their nature, it is impossible safely to limit that capacity. It is true, perhaps, that a computation might be made, with sufficient accuracy to answer the purpose of the quantity of revenue, requisite to discharge the subsisting engagements of the Union, and to maintain those establishments, which for some time to come, would suffice in time of peace. But would it be wise, or would it not rather be the extreme of folly, to stop at this point, and to leave the Government entrusted with the care of the National defence, in a state of absolute incapacity to provide for the protection of the community, against future invasions of the public peace, by foreign war, or domestic convulsions? If, on the contrary, we ought to exceed this point, where can we stop, short of an indefinite power of providing for emergencies as they might arise? Though it is easy to assert, in general terms, the possibility of forming a rational judgment of a due provision against probable dangers; yet we may safely challenge those who make the assertion, to bring forward their data, and may affirm, that they would be found as vague and uncertain, as any that could be produced to establish the probable duration of the world. Observations, confined to the mere prospects of internal attacks, can deserve no weight, though even these will admit of no satisfactory calculation: But if we mean to be a commercial people, it must form a part of our policy, to be able one day to defend that commerce. The support of a navy, and of naval wars must baffle all the efforts of political arithmetic admitting that we ought to try the novel and absurd experiment in politics, of tying up the hands of Government from offensive war, founded upon reasons of state: Yet, certainly we ought not to disable it from guarding the community against the ambition or enmity of other Nations. A cloud has been for some time hanging over the European world. If it should break forth into a storm, who can insure us, that in its progress, a part of its fury would not be spent upon us? No reasonable man would hastily pronounce that we are entirely out of its reach. Or if the combustible materials that now seem to be collecting, should be dissipated without coming to maturity; or, if a flame should be kindled, without extending to us, what security can we have, that our tranquility will long remain undisturbed from some other cause, or from some other quarter? Let us recollect, that peace or war, will not always be left to our option; that however moderate or unambitious we may be, we cannot count upon the moderation, or hope to extinguish the ambition of others. Who could have imagined, at the conclusion of the last war, that France and Britain, wearied and exhausted as they both were, would so soon have looked with so hostile an aspect upon each other? To judge from the history of mankind, we shall be compelled to conclude, that the fiery and destructive passions of war, reign in the human breast, with much more powerful sway, than the mild and beneficent sentiments of peace; and, that to model our political systems upon speculations of lasting tranquility, is to calculate on the weaker springs of the human character.

What are the chief sources of expence in every Government? What has occasioned that enormous accumulation of debts with which several of the European Nations are oppressed? The answer, plainly is, wars and rebellions—the support of those institutions which are necessary to guard the body politic, against these two most mortal diseases of society. The expences arising from those institutions, which are relative to the mere domestic police of a State—to the support of its Legislative, Executive and Judicial departments, with their different appendages, and to the internal encouragement of agriculture and manufactures, (which will comprehend almost all the objects of State expenditure) are insignificant, in comparison with those which relate to the National defence.

In the kingdom of Great-Britain, where all the ostentatious apparatus of Monarchy is to be provided for, not above a fifteenth part of the annual income of the nation is appropriated to the class of expences last mentioned; the other fourteen fifteenths are absorbed in the payment of the interest of debts, contracted for carrying on the wars in which that country has been engaged, and in the maintenance of fleets and armies. If on the one hand it should be observed, that the expences incurred in the prosecution of the ambitious enterprizes and vain-glorious pursuits of a Monarchy, are not a proper standard by which to judge of those which might be necessary in a republic; it ought on the other hand to be remarked, that there should be as great a disproportion, between the profusion and extravagance of a wealthy kingdom in its domestic administration, and the frugality and œconomy, which, in that particular, become the modest simplicity of republican Government. If we balance a proper deduction from one side against that which it is supposed ought to be made from the other, the proportion may still be considered as holding good.

But let us advert to the large debt which we have ourselves contracted in a single war, and let us only calculate on a common share of the events which disturb the peace of nations, and we shall instantly perceive without the aid of any elaborate illustration, that there must always be an immense disproportion between the objects of Federal and State expenditures. It is true that several of the States separately are incumbered with considerable debts, which are an excrescence of the late war. But when these are discharged, the only call for revenue of any consequence, which the State Governments will continue to experience, will be for the mere support of their respective civil lists; to which, if we add all contingencies, the total amount in every State, ought not to exceed two hundred thousand pounds.

In framing a Government for posterity as well as ourselves, we ought in those provisions which are designed to be permanent, to calculate not on temporary, but on permanent causes of expence. If this principle be a just one, our attention would be directed to a provision in favor of the State Governments for an annual sum of about 200,000 pounds; while the exigencies of the Union could be susceptible of no limits, even in imagination. In this view of the subject by what logic can it be maintained, that the local Governments ought to command in perpetuity, an EXCLUSIVE source of revenue for any sum beyond the extent of 200,000 pounds? To extend its power further, in *exclusion* of the authority of the Union, would be to take the resources of the community out of those hands which stood in need of them for the public welfare, in order to put them in other hands, which could have no just or proper occasion for them.

Suppose then the Convention had been inclined to proceed upon the principle of a repartition of the objects of revenue between the Union and its members, in *proportion* to their comparative necessities; what particular fund could have been selected for the use of the States, that would not either have been too much or too little; too little for their present, and too much for their future wants. As to the line of separation between external and internal taxes, this would leave to the States at a rough computation, the command of two thirds of the resources of the community, to defray from a tenth to a twentieth part of its expences, and to the Union, one third of the resources of the community, to defray from nine tenths to nineteen twentieths of its expences. If we desert this boundary, and content ourselves with leaving to the States an exclusive power of taxing houses and lands, there would still be a great disproportion between the *means* and the *end*; the possession of one third of the resources of the community, to supply at most one tenth of its wants. If any fund could have been selected and appropriated equal to and not greater than the object, it would have been inadequate to the discharge of the existing debts of the particular States, and would have left them dependent on the Union for a provision for this purpose.

The preceeding train of observations will justify the position which has been elsewhere laid down, that, "A CON-CURRENT JURISDICTION in the article of taxation, was the only admissible substitute for an entire subordination, in respect to this branch of power, of the State authority to that of the Union." Any separation of the objects of revenue, that could have been fallen upon, would have amounted to a sacrifice of the great INTERESTS of the Union to the POWER of the individual States. The Convention thought the concurrent jurisdiction preferable to that subordination; and it is evident that it has at least the merit of reconciling an indefinite constitutional power of taxation in the Federal Government, with an adequate and independent power in the States to provide for their own necessities. There remain a few other lights, in which this important subject of taxation will claim a further consideration.

PUBLIUS.

The Daily Advertiser, January 5, 1788

The Federalist No. 35

Before we proceed to examine any other objections to an indefinite power of taxation in the Union, I shall make one general remark; which is, that if the jurisdiction of the national government in the article of revenue should be restricted to particular objects, it would naturally occasion an undue proportion of the public burthens to fall upon those objects. Two evils would spring from this source, the oppression of particular branches of industry, and an unequal distribution of the taxes, as well among the several States as among the citizens of the same State.

Suppose, as has been contended for, the fœderal power of taxation were to be confined to duties on imports, it is evident that the government, for want of being able to command other resources, would frequently be tempted to extend these duties to an injurious excess. There are persons who imagine that this can never be carried to too great a length; since the higher they are, the more it is alleged they will tend to discourage an extravagant consumption, to produce a favourable balance of trade, and to promote domestic manufactures. But all extremes are pernicious in various ways. Exorbitant duties on imported articles would beget a general spirit of smuggling; which is always prejudicial to the fair trader, and eventually to the revenue itself: They tend to render other classes of the community tributary in an improper degree to the manufacturing classes to whom they give a premature monopoly of the markets: They sometimes force industry out of its more natural channels into others in which it flows with less advantage. And in the last place they oppress the merchant, who is often obliged to pay them himself without any retribution from the consumer. When the demand is equal to the quantity of goods at market, the consumer generally pays the duty; but when the markets happen to be overstocked, a great proportion falls upon the merchant, and sometimes not only exhausts his profits, but breaks in upon his capital. I am apt to think that a division of the duty between the seller and the buyer more often happens than is commonly imagined. It is not always possible to raise the price of a commodity, in exact proportion to every additional imposition laid upon it. The merchant especially, in a country of small commercial capital, is often under a necessity of keeping prices down, in order to a more expeditious sale.

The maxim that the consumer is the payer, is so much oftener true than the reverse of the proposition, that it is far more equitable the duties on imports should go into a common stock, than that they should redound to the exclusive benefit of the importing States. But it is not so generally true as to render it equitable that those duties should form the only national fund. When they are paid by the merchant, they operate as an additional tax upon the importing State; whose citizens pay their proportion of them in the character of consumers. In this view they are productive of inequality among the States; which inequality would be encreased with the encreased extent of the duties. The confinement of the national revenues to this species of imposts, would be attended with inequality, from a different cause between the manufacturing and the non-manufacturing States. The States which can go furthest towards the supply of their own wants, by their own manufactures, will not, according to their numbers of wealth, consume so great a proportion of imported articles, as those States which are not in the same favourable situation; they would not therefore in this mode alone contribute to the public treasury in a ratio to their abilities. To make them do this, it is necessary that recourse be had to excises; the proper objects of which are particular kinds of manufactures. New-York is more deeply interested in these considerations than such of her citizens as contend for limiting the power of the Union to external taxation can be aware of—New-York is an importing State, and is not likely speedily to be to any great extent a manufacturing State. She would of course suffer in a double light from restraining the jurisdiction of the Union to commercial imposts.

So far as these observations tend to inculcate a danger of the import duties being extended to an injurious extreme it may be observed, conformably to a remark made in another part of these papers, that the interest of the revenue itself would be a sufficient guard against such an extreme. I readily admit that this would be the case as long as other resources were open; but if the avenues to them were closed HOPE stimulated by necessity would beget experiments fortified by rigorous precautions and additional penalties; which for a time would have the intended effect, till there had been leisure to contrive expedients to elude these new precautions. The first success would be apt to inspire false opinions; which it might require a long course of subsequent experience to correct. Necessity, especially in politics, often occasions false hopes, false reasonings and a system of measures, correspondently erroneous. But even if this supposed excess should not be a consequence of the limitation of the fœderal power of taxation the inequalities spoken of would still ensue, though not in the same degree, from the other causes that have been noticed. Let us now return to the examination of objections—

One, which if we may judge from the frequency of its repetition seems most to be relied on, is that the house of representatives is not sufficiently numerous for the reception of all the different classes of citizens; in order to combine the interests and feelings of every part of the community, and to produce a due sympathy between the representative body and its constituents. This argument presents itself under a very specious and seducing form; and is well calculated to lay hold of the prejudices to those to whom it is addressed. But when we come to dissect it with attention it will appear to be made up of nothing but fair sounding words. The object it seems to aim at is in the first place impracticable, and in the sense in which it is contended for is unnecessary. I reserve for another place the discussion of the question which relates to the sufficiency of the representative body in respect to numbers; and shall content myself with examining here the particular use which has been made of a contrary supposition in reference to the immediate subject of our inquiries.

The idea of an actual representation of all classes of the people by persons of each class is altogether visionary. Unless it were expressly provided in the Constitution that each different occupation should send one or more members the thing would never take place in practice. Mechanics and manufacturers will always be inclined with few exceptions to give their votes to merchants in preference to persons of their own professions or trades. Those discerning citizens are well aware that the mechanic and manufacturing arts furnish the materials of mercantile enterprise and industry. Many of them indeed are immediately connected with the operations of commerce. They know that the merchant is their natural patron and friend; and they are aware that however great the confidence they may justly feel in their own good sense, their interests can be more effectually promoted by the merchant than by themselves. They are sensible that their habits in life have not been such as to give them those acquired endowments, without which in a deliberative assembly the greatest natural abilities are for the most part useless; and that the influence and weight and superior acquirements of the merchants render them more equal to a contest with any spirit which might happen to infuse itself into the public councils unfriendly to the manufacturing and trading interests. These considerations and many others that might be mentioned prove, and experience confirms it, that artisans and manufacturers will commonly be disposed to bestow their votes upon merchants and those whom they recommend. We must therefore consider merchants as the natural representatives of all these classes of the community.

With regard to the learned professions, little need be observed; they truly form no distinct interest in society; and according to their situation and talents will be indiscriminately the objects of the confidence and choice of each other and of other parts of the community.

Nothing remains but the landed interest; and this in a political view and particularly in relation to taxes I take to be perfectly united from the wealthiest landlord to the poorest tenant. No tax can be laid on land which will not affect the proprietor of millions of acres as well as the proprietor of a single acre. Every land-holder will therefore have a common interest to keep the taxes on land as low as possible; and common interest may always be reckoned upon as the surest bond of sympathy. But if we even could suppose a distinction of interest between the opulent land-holder and the middling farmer, what reason is there to conclude that the first would

stand a better chance of being deputed to the national legislature than the last? If we take fact as our guide and look into
our own senate and assembly we shall find that moderate proprietors of land prevail in both; nor is this less the case in the
senate which consists of a smaller number than in the Assembly, which is composed of a greater number. Where the qualifications of the electors are the same, whether they have to
choose a small or a large number their votes will fall upon
those in whom they have most confidence; whether these
happen to be men of large fortunes or of moderate property
or of no property at all.

It is said to be necessary that all classes of citizens should
have some of their own number in the representative body, in
order that their feelings and interests may be the better understood and attended to. But we have seen that this will
never happen under any arrangement that leaves the votes of
the people free. Where this is the case, the representative
body, with too few exceptions to have any influence on the
spirit of the government, will be composed of land-holders,
merchants, and men of the learned professions. But where is
the danger that the interests and feelings of the different
classes of citizens will not be understood or attended to by
these three descriptions of men? Will not the land-holder
know and feel whatever will promote or injure the interests of
landed property? and will he not from his own interest in that
species of property be sufficiently prone to resist every attempt to prejudice or incumber it? Will not the merchant understand and be disposed to cultivate as far as may be proper
the interests of the mechanic and manufacturing arts to which
his commerce is so nearly allied? Will not the man of the
learned profession, who will feel a neutrality to the rivalships
between the different branches of industry, be likely to prove
an impartial arbiter between them, ready to promote either,
so far as it shall appear to him conducive to the general interests of the society?

If we take into the account the momentary humors or dispositions which may happen to prevail in particular parts of
the society, and to which a wise administration will never be
inattentive, is the man whose situation leads to extensive
inquiry and information less likely to be a competent judge of

their nature, extent and foundation than one whose observation does not travel beyond the circle of his neighbours and acquaintances? Is it not natural that a man who is a candidate for the favour of the people and who is dependent on the suffrages of his fellow-citizens for the continuance of his public honors should take care to inform himself of their dispositions and inclinations and should be willing to allow them their proper degree of influence upon his conduct. This dependence, and the necessity of being bound himself and his posterity by the laws to which he gives his assent are the true, and they are the strong chords of sympathy between the representatives and the constituent.

There is no part of the administration of government that requires extensive information and a thorough knowledge of the principles of political economy so much as the business of taxation. The man who understands those principles best will be least likely to resort to oppressive expedients, or to sacrifice any particular class of citizens to the procurement of revenue. It might be demonstrated that the most productive system of finance will always be the least burthensome. There can be no doubt that in order to a judicious exercise of the power of taxation it is necessary that the person in whose hands it is should be acquainted with the general genius, habits and modes of thinking of the people at large and with the resources of the country. And this is all that can be reasonably meant by a knowledge of the interests and feelings of the people. In any other sense the proposition has either no meaning, or an absurd one. And in that sense let every considerate citizen judge for himself where the requisite qualification is most likely to be found.

PUBLIUS.

The Independent Journal, January 5, 1788

The Federalist No. 36

To the People of the State of New-York.

We have seen that the result of the observations, to which the foregoing number has been principally devoted, is that from the natural operation of the different interests and views of the various classes of the community, whether the representation of the people be more or less numerous, it will consist almost entirely of proprietors of land, of merchants and members of the learned professions, who will truly represent all those different interests and views. If it should be objected that we have seen other descriptions of men in the local Legislatures; I answer, that it is admitted there are exceptions to the rule, but not in sufficient number to influence the general complexion or character of the government. There are strong minds in every walk of life that will rise superior to the disadvantages of situation, and will command the tribute due to their merit, not only from the classes to which they particularly belong, but from the society in general. The door ought to be equally open to all; and I trust, for the credit of human nature, that we shall see examples of such vigorous plants flourishing in the soil of Fœderal, as well as of State Legislation; but occasional instances of this sort, will not render the reasoning founded upon the general course of things less conclusive.

The subject might be placed in several other lights that would lead all to the same result; and in particular it might be asked, what greater affinity or relation of interest can be conceived between the carpenter and blacksmith, and the linen manufacturer or stocking weaver, than between the merchant and either of them? It is notorious, that there are often as great rivalships between different branches of the mechanic or manufacturing arts, as there are between any of the departments of labor and industry; so that unless the representative body were to be far more numerous than would be consistent with any idea of regularity or wisdom in its deliberations, it is impossible that what seems to be the spirit of the objection we have been considering, should ever be realised in practice.

But I forbear to dwell any longer on a matter, which has hitherto worn too loose a garb to admit even of an accurate inspection of its real shape or tendency.

There is another objection of a somewhat more precise nature that claims our attention. It has been asserted that a power of internal taxation in the national Legislature could never be exercised with advantage, as well from the want of a sufficient knowledge of local circumstances as from an interference between the revenue laws of the Union and of the particular States. The supposition of a want of proper knowledge, seems to be entirely destitute of foundation. If any question is depending in a State Legislature respecting one of the counties which demands a knowledge of local details, how is it acquired? No doubt from the information of the members of the county. Cannot the like knowledge be obtained in the national Legislature from the representatives of each State? And is it not to be presumed that the men who will generally be sent there, will be possessed of the necessary degree of intelligence, to be able to communicate that information? Is the knowledge of local circumstances, as applied to taxation, a minute topographical acquaintance with all the mountains, rivers, streams, high-ways and bye-paths in each State, or is it a general acquaintance with its situation and resources—with the state of its agriculture, commerce, manufactures—with the nature of its products and consumptions—with the different degrees and kinds of its wealth, property and industry?

Nations in general, even under governments of the more popular kind, usually commit the administration of their finances to single men or to boards composed of a few individuals, who digest and prepare, in the first instance, the plans of taxation, which are afterwards passed into laws by the authority of the sovereign or Legislature.

Inquisitive and enlightened Statesmen are deemed every where best qualified to make a judicious selection of the objects proper for revenue; which is a clear indication, as far as the sense of mankind can have weight in the question, of the species of knowledge of local circumstances requisite to the purposes of taxation.

The taxes intended to be comprised under the general denomination of internal taxes, may be subdivided into those of the *direct* and those of the *indirect* kind. Though the objection be made to both, yet the reasoning upon it seems to be confined to the former branch. And indeed, as to the latter, by which must be understood duties and excises on articles of consumption, one is at a loss to conceive what can be the nature of the difficulties apprehended. The knowledge relating to them, must evidently be of a kind that will either be suggested by the nature of the article itself, or can easily be procured from any well informed man, especially of the mercantile class. The circumstances that may distinguish its situation in one State from its situation in another must be few, simple, and easy to be comprehended. The principal thing to be attended to would be to avoid those articles which had been previously appropriated to the use of a particular State; and there could be no difficulty in ascertaining the revenue system of each. This could always be known from the respective codes of laws, as well as from the information of the members of the several States.

The objection when applied to real property, or to houses and lands, appears to have, at first sight, more foundation; but even in this view, it will not bear a close examination. Land taxes are commonly laid in one or two modes, either by *actual* valuations permanent or periodical, or by occasional assessments, at the discretion or according to the best judgment of certain officers, whose duty it is to make them. In either case the EXECUTION of the business, which alone requires the knowledge of local details, must be devolved upon discreet persons in the character of commissioners or assessors, elected by the people or appointed by the government for the purpose. All that the law can do must be to name the persons or to prescribe the manner of their election or appointment, to fix their numbers and qualifications; and to draw the general outlines of their powers and duties. And what is there in all this, that cannot as well be performed by the national Legislature as by a State Legislature? The attention of either can only reach to general principles; local details, as already observed, must be referred to those who are to execute the plan.

But there is a simple point of view in which this matter may be placed, that must be altogether satisfactory. The national Legislature can make use of the *system of each State within that State*. The method of laying and collecting this species of taxes in each State, can, in all its parts, be adopted and employed by the Fœderal Government.

Let it be recollected, that the proportion of these taxes is not to be left to the discretion of the national Legislature: but is to be determined by the numbers of each State as described in the second section of the first article. An actual census or enumeration of the people must furnish the rule; a circumstance which effectually shuts the door to partiality or oppression. The abuse of this power of taxation seems to have been provided against with guarded circumspection. In addition to the precaution just mentioned, there is a provision that "all duties, imposts and excises, shall be UNIFORM throughout the United States."

It has been very properly observed by different speakers and writers on the side of the Constitution, that if the exercise of the power of internal taxation by the Union, should be discovered on experiment, to be really inconvenient, the Fœderal Government may then forbear the use of it and have recourse to requisitions in its stead. By way of answer to this, it has been triumphantly asked, why not in the first instance omit that ambiguous power and rely upon the latter resource? Two solid answers may be given; the first is, that the exercise of that power, if convenient, will be preferable, because it will be more effectual; and it is impossible to prove in theory or otherwise than by the experiment that it cannot be advantageously exercised. The contrary indeed appears most probable. The second answer is, that the existence of such a power in the Constitution, will have a strong influence in giving efficacy to requisitions. When the States know that the Union can supply itself without their agency, it will be a powerful motive for exertion on their part.

As to the interference of the revenue laws of the Union, and of its members; we have already seen that there can be no clashing or repugnancy of authority. The laws cannot therefore in a legal sense, interfere with each other; and it is far from impossible to avoid an interference even in the policy of their different systems. An effectual expedient for this purpose will be mutually to abstain from those objects, which either side may have first had recourse to. As neither can *controul* the other, each will have an obvious and sensible interest in this reciprocal forbearance. And where there is an *immediate* common interest, we may safely count upon its operation. When the particular debts of the States are done away, and their expences come to be limited within their natural compass, the possibility almost of interference will vanish. A small land tax will answer the purposes of the States, and will be their most simple and most fit resource.

Many spectres have been raised out of this power of internal taxation to excite the apprehensions of the people—double sets of revenue officers—a duplication of their burthens by double taxations, and the frightful forms of odious and oppressive poll taxes, have been played off with all the ingenious dexterity of political legerdemain.

As to the first point, there are two cases, in which there can be no room for double sets of officers; one where the right of imposing the tax is exclusively vested in the Union, which applies to the duties on imports; and the other, where the object has not fallen under any State regulation or provision, which may be applicable to a variety of objects. In other cases, the probability is, that the United States will either wholly abstain from the objects pre-occupied for local purposes, or will make use of the State officers and State regulations, for collecting the additional imposition. This will best answer the views of revenue, because it will save expence in the collection, and will best avoid any occasion of disgust to the State governments and to the people. At all events, here is a practicable expedient for avoiding such an inconvenience; and nothing more can be required than to show that evils predicted do not necessarily result from the plan.

As to any argument derived from a supposed system of influence, it is a sufficient answer to say, that it ought not to be presumed; but the supposition is susceptible of a more precise answer. If such a spirit should infest the councils of the Union, the most certain road to the accomplishment of its aim would be to employ the State officers as much as possible, and to attach them to the Union by an accumulation of their emoluments. This would serve to turn the tide of State influence into the channels of the national government, instead of making fœderal influence flow in an opposite and adverse current. But all suppositions of this kind are invidious, and ought to be banished from the consideration of the great question before the people. They can answer no other end than to cast a mist over the truth.

As to the suggestion of double taxation, the answer is plain. The wants of the Union are to be supplied in one way or another; if to be done by the authority of the Fœderal Government, it will not be to be done by that of the State governments. The quantity of taxes to be paid by the community, must be the same in either case; with this advantage, if the provision is to be made by the Union, that the capital resource of commercial imposts, which is the most convenient branch of revenue, can be prudently improved to a much greater extent under fœderal than under State regulation, and of course will render it less necessary to recur to more inconvenient methods; and with this further advantage, that as far as there may be any real difficulty in the exercise of the power of internal taxation, it will impose a disposition to greater care in the choice and arrangement of the means; and must naturally tend to make it a fixed point of policy in the national administration to go as far as may be practicable in making the luxury of the rich tributary to the public treasury, in order to diminish the necessity of those impositions, which might create dissatisfaction in the poorer and most numerous classes of the society. Happy it is when the interest which the government has in the preservation of its own power, coincides with a proper distribution of the public burthens, and tends to guard the least wealthy part of the community from oppression!

As to poll taxes, I, without scruple, confess my disapprobation of them; and though they have prevailed from an early period in those States* which have uniformly been the most tenacious of their rights, I should lament to see them introduced into practice under the national government. But does it follow because there is a power to lay them, that they will actually be laid? Every State in the Union has power to impose taxes of this kind; and yet in several of them they are unknown in practice. Are the State governments to be

* The New-England States.

stigmatised as tyrannies because they possess this power? If they are not, with what propriety can the like power justify such a charge against the national government, or even be urged as an obstacle to its adoption? As little friendly as I am to the species of imposition, I still feel a thorough conviction, that the power of having recourse to it ought to exist in the Fœderal Government. There are certain emergencies of nations, in which expedients that in the ordinary state of things ought to be foreborn, become essential to the public weal. And the government from the possibility of such emergencies ought ever to have the option of making use of them. The real scarcity of objects in this country; which may be considered as productive sources of revenue, is a reason peculiar to itself, for not abridging the discretion of the national councils in this respect. There may exist certain critical and tempestuous conjunctures of the State, in which a poll tax may become an inestimable resource. And as I know nothing to exempt this portion of the globe from the common calamities that have befallen other parts of it, I acknowledge my aversion to every project that is calculated to disarm the government of a single weapon, which in any possible contingency might be usefully employed for the general defence and security.

I have now gone through the examination of those powers proposed to be conferred upon the federal government; which relate more peculiarly to its energy, and to its efficiency for answering the great and primary objects of union. There are others, which though omitted here, will in order to render the view of the subject more complete, be taken notice of under the next head of our enquiries. I flatter myself the progress already made will have sufficed to satisfy the candid and judicious part of the community, that some of the objections which have been most strenuously urged against the constitution, and which were most formidable in their first appearance, are not only destitute of substance, but if they had operated in the formation of the plan, would have rendered it incompetent to the great ends of public happiness and national prosperity. I equally flatter myself that a further and more critical investigation of the system will serve to recommend it still more to every sincere and disinterested advocate for good government; and will leave no doubt with men of this character of the propriety and expediency of adopting it. Happy will it be for ourselves, and most honorable for human nature, if we have wisdom and virtue enough, to set so glorious an example to mankind!

PUBLIUS.

The New-York Packet, January 8, 1788

The Federalist No. 59

To the People of the State of New-York.

The natural order of the subject leads us to consider in this place, that provision of the Constitution which authorises the national Legislature to regulate in the last resort the election of its own members. It is in these words—"The *times, places* and *manner* of holding elections for Senators and Representatives, shall be prescribed in each State by the Legislature thereof; but the Congress may at any time by law, make or alter *such regulations* except as to *places* of choosing senators."* This provision has not only been declaimed against by those who condemn the Constitution in the gross; but it has been censured by those, who have objected with less latitude and greater moderation; and in one instance, it has been thought exceptionable by a gentleman who has declared himself the advocate of every other part of the system.

I am greatly mistaken, notwithstanding, if there be any article in the whole plan more completely defensible than this. Its propriety rests upon the evidence of this plain proposition, that *every government ought to contain in itself the means of its own preservation*. Every just reasoner will at first sight, approve an adherence to this rule, in the work of the Convention; and will disapprove every deviation from it, which may not appear to have been dictated by the necessity of incorporating into the work some particular ingredient, with which a rigid conformity to the rule was incompatible. Even in this case, though he may acquiesce in the necessity; yet he will not cease to regard a departure from so fundamental a principle, as a portion of imperfection in the system which may prove the seed of future weakness and perhaps anarchy.

It will not be alledged that an election law could have been framed and inserted into the Constitution, which would have been always applicable to every probable change in the situation of the country; and it will therefore not be denied that a discretionary power over elections ought to exist somewhere.

* I Clause, 4 Sect. of the Ist Art.

It will, I presume, be as readily conceded, that there were only three ways, in which this power could have been reasonably modified and disposed, that it must either have been lodged wholly in the National Legislature, or wholly in the State Legislatures, or primarily in the latter, and ultimately in the former. The last mode has with reason been preferred by the Convention. They have submitted the regulation of elections for the Fœderal Government in the first instance to the local administrations; which in ordinary cases, and when no improper views prevail, may be both more convenient and more satisfactory; but they have reserved to the national authority a right to interpose, whenever extraordinary circumstances might render that interposition necessary to its safety.

Nothing can be more evident, than that an exclusive power of regulating elections for the National Government, in the hands of the State Legislatures, would leave the existence of the Union entirely at their mercy. They could at any moment annihilate it, by neglecting to provide for the choice of persons to administer its affairs. It is to little purpose to say that a neglect or omission of this kind, would not be likely to take place. The constitutional possibility of the thing, without an equivalent for the risk, is an unanswerable objection. Nor has any satisfactory reason been yet assigned for incurring that risk. The extravagant surmises of a distempered jealousy can never be dignified with that character. If we are in a humour to presume abuses of power, it is as fair to presume them on the part of the State Governments, as on the part of the General Government. And as it is more consonant to the rules of a just theory to intrust the Union with the care of its own existence, than to transfer that care to any other hands; if abuses of power are to be hazarded, on the one side, or on the other, it is more rational to hazard them where the power would naturally be placed, than where it would unnaturally be placed.

Suppose an article had been introduced into the Constitution, empowering the United States to regulate the elections for the particular States, would any man have hesitated to condemn it, both as an unwarrantable transposition of power, and as a premeditated engine for the destruction of the State governments? The violation of principle in this case would have required no comment; and to an unbiassed observer, it will not be less apparent in the project of subjecting the existence of the National Government, in a similar respect to the pleasure of the State governments. An impartial view of the matter cannot fail to result in a conviction, that each, as far as possible, ought to depend on itself for its own preservation.

As an objection to this position, it may be remarked, that the Constitution of the national Senate, would involve in its full extent the danger which it is suggested might flow from an exclusive power in the State Legislatures to regulate the fœderal elections. It may be alledged, that by declining the appointment of Senators they might at any time give a fatal blow to the Union; and from this, it may be inferred, that as its existence would be thus rendered dependent upon them in so essential a point, there can be no objection to entrusting them with it, in the particular case under consideration. The interest of each State, it may be added, to maintain its representation in the national councils, would be a complete security against an abuse of the trust.

This argument though specious, will not upon examination be found solid. It is certainly true, that the State Legislatures, by forbearing the appointment of Senators, may destroy the National Government. But it will not follow, that because they have the power to do this in one instance, they ought to have it in every other. There are cases in which the pernicious tendency of such a power may be far more decisive, without any motive, equally cogent with that which must have regulated the conduct of the Convention, in respect to the construction of the Senate, to recommend their admission into the system. So far as that construction may expose the Union to the possibility of injury from the State Legislatures, it is an evil; but it is an evil, which could not have been avoided without excluding the States, in their political capacities, wholly from a place in the organization of the National Government. If this had been done, it would doubtless have been interpreted into an entire dereliction of the fœderal principle; and would certainly have deprived the State governments of that absolute safe-guard, which they will enjoy under this provision. But however wise it may have been, to have submitted in this instance to an inconvenience, for the attainment of a necessary advantage, or a greater good, no inference can be drawn from thence to favor an accumulation of the evil, where no necessity urges, nor any greater good invites.

It may easily be discerned also, that the National Government would run a much greater risk from a power in the State Legislatures over the elections of its House of Representatives, than from their power of appointing the members of its Senate. The Senators are to be chosen for the period of six years; there is to be a rotation, by which the seats of a third part of them are to be vacated, and replenished every two years; and no State is to be entitled to more than two Senators: A quorum of the body is to consist of sixteen members. The joint result of these circumstances would be, that a temporary combination of a few States, to intermit the appointment of Senators, could neither annul the existence nor impair the activity of the body: And it is not from a general or permanent combination of the States, that we can have any thing to fear. The first might proceed from sinister designs in the leading members of a few of the State Legislatures; the last would suppose a fixed and rooted disaffection in the great body of the people; which will either never exist at all, or will in all probability proceed from an experience of the inaptitude of the General Government to the advancement of their happiness; in which event no good citizen could desire its continuance.

But with regard to the Fœderal House of Representatives, there is intended to be a general election of members once in two years. If the State Legislatures were to be invested with an exclusive power of regulating these elections, every period of making them would be a delicate crisis in the national situation; which might issue in a dissolution of the Union, if the leaders of a few of the most important States should have entered into a previous conspiracy to prevent an election.

I shall not deny that there is a degree of weight in the observation, that the interest of each State to be represented in the fœderal councils will be a security against the abuse of a power over its elections in the hands of the State Legislatures. But the security will not be considered as complete, by those who attend to the force of an obvious distinction between the interest of the people in the public felicity, and the interest of their local rulers in the power and consequence of their offices. The people of America may be warmly attached to the government of the Union at times, when the particular rulers of particular States, stimulated by the natural rivalship of power and by the hopes of personal aggrandisement, and supported by a strong faction in each of those States, may be in a very opposite temper. This diversity of sentiment, between a majority of the people and the individuals who have the greatest credit in their councils, is exemplified in some of the States, at the present moment, on the present question. The scheme of separate confederacies, which will always multiply the chances of ambition, will be a never failing bait to all such influential characters in the State administrations as are capable of preferring their own emolument and advancement to the public weal; with so effectual a weapon in their hands as the exclusive power of regulating elections for the National Government a combination of a few such men, in a few of the most considerable States, where the temptation will always be the strongest, might accomplish the destruction of the Union, by seizing the opportunity of some casual dissatisfaction among the people (and which perhaps they may themselves have excited) to discontinue the choice of members for the Fœderal House of Representatives. It ought never to be forgotten, that a firm Union of this country, under an efficient government, will probably be an encreasing object of jealousy to more than one nation of Europe; and that enterprises to subvert it will sometimes originate in the intrigues of foreign powers, and will seldom fail to be patronised and abetted by some of them. Its preservation therefore ought in no case, that can be avoided, to be committed to the guardianship of any but those, whose situation will uniformly beget an immediate interest in the faithful and vigilant performance of the trust.

PUBLIUS.

The New-York Packet, February 22, 1788

The Federalist No. 60

To the People of the State of New-York.

We have seen that an incontroulable power over the elections for the federal government could not without hazard be committed to the state legislatures. Let us now see what would be the dangers on the other side; that is, from confiding the ultimate right of regulating its own elections to the union itself. It is not pretended, that this right would ever be used for the exclusion of any state from its share in the representation. The interest of all would in this respect at least be the security of all. But it is alledged that it might be employed in such a manner as to promote the election of some favourite class of men in exclusion of others; by confining the places of election to particular districts, and rendering it impracticable to the citizens at large to partake in the choice. Of all chimerical suppositions, this seems to be the most chimerical. On the one hand no rational calculation of probabilities would lead us to imagine, that the disposition, which a conduct so violent and extraordinary would imply, could ever find its way into the national councils; and on the other, it may be concluded with certainty, that if so improper a spirit should ever gain admittance into them, it would display itself in a form altogether different and far more decisive.

The improbability of the attempt may be satisfactorily inferred from this single reflection, that it could never be made without causing an immediate revolt of the great body of the people,—headed and directed by the state governments. It is not difficult to conceive that this characteristic right of freedom may, in certain turbulent and factious seasons, be violated in respect to a particular class of citizens by a victorious and overbearing majority; but that so fundamental a privilege, in a country so situated and so enlightened, should be invaded to the prejudice of the great mass of the people, by the deliberate policy of the government; without occasioning a popular revolution, is altogether inconceivable and incredible.

In addition to this general reflection, there are considerations of a more precise nature, which forbid all apprehension on the subject. The dissimilarity in the ingredients, which will compose the national government; and still more in the manner in which they will be brought into action in its various branches must form a powerful obstacle to a concert of views, in any partial scheme of elections. There is sufficient diversity in the state of property, in the genius, manners, and habits of the people of the different parts of the union to occasion a material diversity of disposition in their representatives towards the different ranks and conditions in society. And though an intimate intercourse under the same government will promote a gradual assimilation, in temper and sentiment, yet there are causes as well physical as moral, which may in a greater or less degree permanently nourish different propensities and inclinations in this particular. But the circumstance, which will be likely to have the greatest influence in the matter, will be the dissimilar modes of constituting the several component parts of the government. The house of representatives being to be elected immediately by the people; the senate by the state legislatures; the president by electors chosen for that purpose by the people; there would be little probability of a common interest to cement these different branches in a predilection for any particular class of electors.

As to the senate it is impossible that any regulation of "time and manner," which is all that is proposed to be submitted to the national government in respect to that body, can affect the spirit which will direct the choice of its members. The collective sense of the state legislatures can never be influenced by extraneous circumstances of that sort: A consideration, which alone ought to satisfy us that the discrimination apprehended would never be attempted. For what inducement could the senate have to concur in a preference, in which itself would not be included? Or to what purpose would it be established in reference to one branch of the legislature; if it could not be extended to the other? The composition of the one would in this case counteract that of the other. And we can never suppose that it would embrace the appointments to the senate, unless we can at the same time suppose the voluntary co-operation of the state legislatures. If we make the latter supposition, it then becomes immaterial where the power in question is placed; whether in their hands or in those of the union.

But what is to be the object of this capricious partiality in the national councils? Is it to be exercised in a discrimination between the different departments of industry, or between the different kinds of property, or between the different degrees of property? Will it lean in favor of the landed interest, or the monied interest, or the mercantile interest, or the manufacturing interest? Or to speak in the fashionable language of the adversaries of the Constitution; will it court the elevation of the "wealthy and the well born" to the exclusion and debasement of all the rest of the society?

If this partiality is to be exerted in favor of those who are concerned in any particular description of industry or property, I presume it will readily be admitted that the competition for it will lie between landed men and merchants. And I scruple not to affirm, that it is infinitely less likely, that either of them should gain an ascendant in the national councils, than that the one or the other of them should predominate in all the local councils. The inference will be, that a conduct tending to give an undue preference to either is much less to be dreaded from the former than from the latter.

The several states are in various degrees addicted to agriculture and commerce. In most, if not all of them, agriculture is predominant. In a few of them, however, commerce nearly divides its empire, and in most of them has a considerable share of influence. In proportion as either prevails, it will be conveyed into the national representation, and for the very reason that this will be an emanation from a greater variety of interests, and in much more various proportions, than are to be found in any single state, it will be much less apt to espouse either of them, with a decided partiality, than the representation of any single state.

In a country consisting chiefly of the cultivators of land where the rules of an equal representation obtain the landed interest must upon the whole preponderate in the government. As long as this interest prevails in most of the state legislatures, so long it must maintain a correspondent superiority in the national senate, which will generally be a faithful copy of the majorities of those assemblies. It cannot therefore be presumed that a sacrifice of the landed to the mercantile class will ever be a favorite object of this branch of the federal legislature. In applying thus particularly to the senate a general observation suggested by the situation of the country, I am governed by the consideration, that the credulous votaries of state power, cannot upon their own principles suspect that the state legislatures would be warped from their duty by any external influence. But as in reality the same situation must have the same effect in the primitive composition at least of the federal house of representatives; an improper byass towards the mercantile class is as little to be expected from this quarter or from the other.

In order perhaps to give countenance to the objection at any rate, it may be asked, is there not danger of an opposite byass in the national government, which may dispose it to endeavour to secure a monopoly of the federal administration to the landed class? As there is little likelihood that the supposition of such a byass will have any terrors for those who would be immediately injured by it, a laboured answer to this question will be dispensed with. It will be sufficient to remark, first, that for the reasons elsewhere assigned, it is less likely that any decided partiality should prevail in the councils of the union than in those of any of its members. Secondly that there would be no temptation to violate the constitution in favor of the landed class, because that class would in the natural course of things enjoy as great a preponderancy as itself could desire. And thirdly that men accustomed to investigate the sources of public prosperity, upon a large scale, must be too well convinced of the utility of commerce, to be inclined to inflict upon it so deep a wound as would result from the entire exclusion of those who would best understand its interest from a share in the management of them. The importance of commerce in the view of revenue alone must effectually guard it against the enmity of a body which would be continually importuned in its favour by the urgent calls of public necessity.

I the rather consult brevity in discussing the probability of a preference founded upon a discrimination between the different kinds of industry and property; because, as far as I understand the meaning of the objectors, they contemplate a discrimination of another kind. They appear to have in view, as the objects of the preference with which they endeavour to alarm us, those whom they designate by the description of the "wealthy and the well born." These, it seems, are to be exalted to an odious pre-eminence over the rest of their fellow citizens. At one time however their elevation is to be a necessary consequence of the smallness of the representative body; at another time it is to be effected by depriving the people at large of the opportunity of exercising their right of suffrage in the choice of that body.

But upon what principle is the discrimination of the places of election to be made in order to answer the purpose of the meditated preference? Are the wealthy and the well born, as they are called, confined to particular spots in the several states? Have they by some miraculous instinct or foresight set apart in each of them a common place of residence? Are they only to be met with in the towns or cities? Or are they, on the contrary, scattered over the face of the country as avarice or chance may have happened to cast their own lot, or that of their predecessors? If the latter is the case, (as every intelligent man knows it to be)* is it not evident that the policy of confining the places of elections to particular districts would be as subversive of its own aim as it would be exceptionable on every other account? The truth is that there is no method of securing to the rich the preference apprehended, but by prescribing qualifications of property either for those who may elect, or be elected. But this forms no part of the power to be conferred upon the national government. Its authority would be expressly restricted to the regulation of the *times*, the *places*, and the *manner* of elections. The qualifications of the persons who may choose or be chosen, as has been remarked upon another occasion, are defined and fixed in the constitution; and are unalterable by the legislature.

Let it however be admitted, for argument sake, that the expedient suggested might be successful; and let it at the same time be equally taken for granted that all the scruples which a sense of duty or an apprehension of the danger of the experiment might inspire, were overcome in the breasts of the na-

* Particularly in the Southern States and in this State.

tional rulers; still, I imagine, it will hardly be pretended, that they could ever hope to carry such an enterprise into execution, without the aid of a military force sufficient to subdue, the resistance of the great body of the people. The improbability of the existence of a force equal to that object, has been discussed and demonstrated in different parts of these papers; but that the futility of the objection under consideration may appear in the strongest light, it shall be conceded for a moment that such a force might exist; and the national government shall be supposed to be in the actual possession of it. What will be the conclusion? With a disposition to invade the essential rights of the community, and with the means of gratifying that disposition, is it presumable that the persons who were actuated by it would amuse themselves in the ridiculous task of fabricating election laws for securing a preference to a favourite class of men? Would they not be likely to prefer a conduct better adapted to their own immediate aggrandisement? Would they not rather boldly resolve to perpetuate themselves in office by one decisive act of usurpation, than to trust to precarious expedients, which in spite of all the precautions that might accompany them, might terminate in the dismission, disgrace and ruin of their authors? Would they not fear that citizens not less tenacious than conscious of their rights would flock from the remotest extremes of their respective states to the places of election, to overthrow their tyrants, and to substitute men who would be disposed to avenge the violated majesty of the people?

PUBLIUS.

The Independent Journal, February 23, 1788

The Federalist No. 61

To the People of the State of New-York.
The more candid opposers of the provision respecting elections contained in the plan of the Convention, when pressed in argument, will sometimes concede the propriety of that provision; with this qualification however that it ought to have been accompanied with a declaration that all elections should be had in the counties where the electors resided. This say they, was a necessary precaution against an abuse of the power. A declaration of this nature, would certainly have been harmless: So far as it would have had the effect of quieting apprehensions, it might not have been undesirable. But it would in fact have afforded little or no additional security against the danger apprehended; and the want of it will never be considered by an impartial and judicious examiner as a serious, still less, as an insuperable objection to the plan. The different views taken of the subject in the two preceding papers must be sufficient to satisfy all dispassionate and discerning men, that if the public liberty should ever be the victim of the ambition of the national rulers, the power under examination at least will be guiltless of the sacrifice.

If those who are inclined to consult their jealousy only would exercise it in a careful inspection of the several State Constitutions, they would find little less room for disquietude and alarm from the latitude which most of them allow in respect to elections, than from the latitude which is proposed to be allowed to the National Government in the same respect. A review of their situation, in this particular, would tend greatly to remove any ill impressions which may remain in regard to this matter. But as that review would lead into lengthy and tedious details, I shall content myself with the single example of the State in which I write. The Constitution of New-York makes no other provision for *locality* of elections, than that the members of the Assembly shall be elected in the *counties*, those of the Senate in the great districts into which the State is or may be divided; these at present are four in number, and comprehend each from two to six counties. It may readily be perceived that it would not be more difficult to the Legislature of New-York to defeat the suffrages of the citizens of New-York by confining elections to particular places, than to the Legislature of the United States to defeat the suffrages of the citizens of the Union, by the like expedient. Suppose for instance, the city of Albany was to be appointed the sole place of election for the county and district of which it is a part, would not the inhabitants of that city speedily become the only electors of the members both of the Senate and Assembly, for that county and district? Can we imagine that the electors who reside in the remote subdivisions of the county of Albany, Saratoga, Cambridge, &c. or in any part of the county of Montgomery, would take the trouble to come to the city of Albany to give their votes for members of the Assembly or Senate, sooner than they would repair to the city of New-York to participate in the choice of the members of the Fœderal House of Representatives? The alarming indifference discoverable in the exercise of so invaluable a privilege under the existing laws, which afford every facility to it, furnishes a ready answer to this question. And, abstracted from any experience on the subject, we can be at no loss to determine that when the place of election is at an *inconvenient distance* from the elector, the effect upon his conduct will be the same whether that distance be twenty miles or twenty thousand miles. Hence it must appear that objections to the particular modification of the fœderal power of regulating elections will in substance apply with equal force to the modification of the like power in the Constitution of this State; and for this reason it will be impossible to acquit the one and to condemn the other. A similar comparison would lead to the same conclusion in respect to the Constitutions of most of the other States.

If it should be said that defects in the State Constitutions furnish no apology for those which are to be found in the plan proposed; I answer, that as the former have never been thought chargeable with inattention to the security of liberty, where the imputations thrown on the latter can be shown to be applicable to them also, the presumption is that they are rather the cavilling refinements of a predetermined opposition, than the well founded inferences of a candid research after truth. To those who are disposed to consider, as innocent ommissions in the State Constitutions, what they regard as unpardonable blemishes in the plan of the Convention, nothing can be said; or at most they can only be asked to assign some substantial reason why the representatives of the people in a single State should be more impregnable to the lust of power or other sinister motives, than the representatives of the people of the United States? If they cannot do this, they ought at least to prove to us, that it is easier to subvert the liberties of three millions of people, with the advantage of local governments to head their opposition, than of two hundred thousand people, who are destitute of that advantage. And in relation to the point immediately under consideration, they ought to convince us that it is less probable a predominant faction in a single State, should, in order to maintain its superiority, incline to a preference of a particular class of electors, than that a similar spirit should take possession of the representatives of thirteen States spread over a vast region, and in several respects distinguishable from each other by a diversity of local circumstances, prejudices and interests.

Hitherto my observations have only aimed at a vindication of the provision in question, on the ground of theoretic propriety, on that of the danger of placing the power elsewhere, and on that of the safety of placing it in the manner proposed. But there remains to be mentioned a positive advantage which will result from this disposition, and which could not as well have been obtained from any other: I allude to the circumstance of uniformity in the time of elections for the Fœderal House of Representatives. It is more than possible, that this uniformity may be found by experience to be of great importance to the public welfare; both as a security against the perpetuation of the same spirit in the body; and as a cure for the diseases of faction. If each State may choose its own time of election, it is possible there may be at least as many different periods as there are months in the year. The times of election in the several States as they are now established for local purposes, vary between extremes as wide as March and November. The consequence of this diversity would be, that there could never happen a total dissolution or renovation of the body at one time. If an improper spirit of any kind should happen to prevail in it, that spirit would be apt to infuse itself into the new members as they come forward in succession. The mass would be likely to remain nearly the same; assimilating constantly to itself its gradual accretions. There is a contagion in example which few men have sufficient force of mind to resist. I am inclined to think that treble the duration in office, with the condition of a total dissolution of the body at the same time, might be less formidable to liberty, than one third of that duration, subject to gradual and successive alterations.

Uniformity in the time of elections seems not less requisite for executing the idea of a regular rotation in the Senate; and for conveniently assembling the Legislature at a stated period in each year.

It may be asked, why then could not a time have been fixed in the Constitution? As the most zealous adversaries of the plan of the Convention in this State, are in general not less zealous admirers of the Constitution of the State, the question may be retorted, and it may be asked, why was not a time for the like purpose fixed in the Constitution of this State? No better answer can be given, than that it was a matter which might safely be entrusted to legislative discretion, and that if a time had been appointed, it might upon experiment have been found less convenient than some other time. The same answer may be given to the question put on the other side. And it may be added, that the supposed danger of a gradual change being merely speculative, it would have been hardly adviseable upon that speculation to establish, as a fundamental point, what would deprive several States of the convenience of having the elections for their own governments, and for the National Government, at the same epoch.

PUBLIUS.

The New-York Packet, February 26, 1788

The Federalist No. 65

To the People of the State of New-York.

The remaining powers, which the plan of the Convention allots to the Senate, in a distinct capacity, are comprised in their participation with the Executive in the appointment to offices, and in their judicial character as a court for the trial of impeachments. As in the business of appointments the Executive will be the principal agent, the provisions relating to it will most properly be discussed in the examination of that department. We will therefore conclude this head with a view of the judicial character of the Senate.

A well constituted court for the trial of impeachments, is an object not more to be desired than difficult to be obtained in a government wholly elective. The subjects of its jurisdiction are those offenses which proceed from the misconduct of public men, or in other words from the abuse or violation of some public trust. They are of a nature which may with peculiar propriety be denominated POLITICAL, as they relate chiefly to injuries done immediately to the society itself. The prosecution of them, for this reason, will seldom fail to agitate the passions of the whole community, and to divide it into parties, more or less friendly or inimical, to the accused. In many cases, it will connect itself with the pre-existing factions, and will inlist all their animosities, partialities, influence and interest on one side, or on the other; and in such cases there will always be the greatest danger, that the decision will be regulated more by the comparitive strength of parties than by the real demonstrations of innocence or guilt.

The delicacy and magnitude of a trust, which so deeply concerns the political reputation and existence of every man engaged in the administration of public affairs, speak for themselves. The difficulty of placing it rightly in a government resting entirely on the basis of periodical elections will as readily be perceived, when it is considered that the most conspicuous characters in it will, from that circumstance, be too often the leaders, or the tools of the most cunning or the most numerous faction; and on this account can hardly be expected to possess the requisite neutrality towards those, whose conduct may be the subject of scrutiny.

The Convention, it appears, thought the Senate the most fit depositary of this important trust. Those who can best discern the intrinsic difficulty of the thing will be least hasty in condemning that opinion; and will be most inclined to allow due weight to the arguments which may be supposed to have produced it.

What it may be asked is the true spirit of the institution itself? Is it not designed as a method of NATIONAL INQUEST into the conduct of public men? If this be the design of it, who can so properly be the inquisitors for the nation, as the representatives of the nation themselves? It is not disputed that the power of originating the inquiry, or in other words of preferring the impeachment ought to be lodged in the hands of one branch of the legislative body; will not the reasons which indicate the propriety of this arrangement, strongly plead for an admission of the other branch of that body to a share in the inquiry? The model, from which the idea of this institution has been borrowed, pointed out that course to the Convention: In Great Britain, it is the province of the house of commons to prefer the impeachment; and of the house of lords to decide upon it. Several of the State constitutions have followed the example. As well the latter as the former seem to have regarded the practice of impeachments, as a bridle in the hands of the legislative body upon the executive servants of the government. Is not this the true light in which it ought to be regarded?

Where else, than in the Senate could have been found a tribunal sufficiently dignified, or sufficiently independent? What other body would be likely to feel *confidence enough in its own situation*, to preserve unawed and uninfluenced the necessary impartiality between an *individual* accused, and the *representatives of the people, his accusers?*

Could the Supreme Court have been relied upon as answering this description? It is much to be doubted whether the members of that tribunal would, at all times, be endowed with so eminent a portion of fortitude, as would be called for in the execution of so difficult a task; & it is still more to be doubted, whether they would possess the degree of credit and authority, which might, on certain occasions, be indispensable, towards reconciling the people to a decision, that should happen to clash with an accusation brought by their immediate representatives. A deficiency in the first would be fatal to the accused; in the last, dangerous to the public tranquillity. The hazard in both these respects could only be avoided, if at all, by rendering that tribunal more numerous than would consist with a reasonable attention to œconomy. The necessity of a numerous court for the trial of impeachments is equally dictated by the nature of the proceeding. This can never be tied down by such strict rules, either in the delineation of the offence by the prosecutors, or in the construction of it by the judges, as in common cases serve to limit the discretion of courts in favor of personal security. There will be no jury to stand between the Judges, who are to pronounce the sentence of the law and the party who is to receive or suffer it. The awful discretion, which a court of impeachments must necessarily have, to doom to honor or to infamy the most confidential and the most distinguished characters of the community, forbids the commitment of the trust to a small number of persons.

These considerations seem alone sufficient to authorise a conclusion, that the Supreme Court would have been an improper substitute for the Senate, as a court of impeachments. There remains a further consideration which will not a little strengthen this conclusion. It is this—The punishment, which may be the consequence of conviction upon impeachment, is not to terminate the chastisement of the offender. After having been sentenced to a perpetual ostracism from the esteem and confidence, and honors and emoluments of his country; he will still be liable to prosecution and punishment in the ordinary course of law. Would it be proper that the persons, who had disposed of his fame and his most valuable rights as a citizen in one trial, should in another trial, for the same offence, be also the disposers of his life and his fortune? Would there not be the greatest reason to apprehend, that error in the first sentence would be the parent of error in the second sentence? That the strong bias of one decision would be apt to overrule the influence of any new lights, which might be brought to vary the complexion of another decision? Those, who know any thing of human nature, will not hesitate to answer these questions in the affirmative; and will be at no loss to perceive, that by making the same persons Judges in both cases, those who might happen to be the objects of prosecution would in a great measure be deprived of the double security, intended them by a double trial. The loss of life and estate would often be virtually included in a sentence, which, in its terms, imported nothing more than dismission from a present, and disqualification for a future office. It may be said, that the intervention of a jury, in the second instance, would obviate the danger. But juries are frequently influenced by the opinions of Judges. They are sometimes induced to find special verdicts which refer the main question to the decision of the court. Who would be willing to stake his life and his estate upon the verdict of a jury, acting under the auspices of Judges, who had predetermined his guilt?

Would it have been an improvement of the plan, to have united the Supreme Court with the Senate, in the formation of the court of impeachments? This Union would certainly have been attended with several advantages; but would they not have been overballanced by the signal disadvantages, already stated, arising from the agency of the same Judges in the double prosecution to which the offender would be liable? To a certain extent, the benefits of that Union will be obtained from making the Chief Justice of the Supreme Court the President of the court of impeachments, as is proposed to be done in the plan of the Convention; while the inconveniencies of an intire incorporation of the former into the latter will be substantially avoided. This was perhaps the prudent mean. I forbear to remark upon the additional pretext for clamour, against the Judiciary, which so considerable an augmentation of its authority would have afforded.

Would it have been desirable to have composed the court for the trial of impeachments of persons wholly distinct from the other departments of the government? There are weighty arguments, as well against, as in favor of such a plan. To some minds, it will not appear a trivial objection, that it would tend to increase the complexity of the political machine; and to add a new spring to the government, the utility of which would at best be questionable. But an objection, which will not be thought by any unworthy of attention, is this—A court formed upon such a plan would either be attended with heavy expence, or might in practice be subject to a variety of casualties and inconveniencies. It must either consist of permanent officers stationary at the seat of government, and of course entitled to fixed and regular stipends, or of certain officers of the State governments, to be called upon whenever an impeachment was actually depending. It will not be easy to imagine any third mode materially different, which could rationally be proposed. As the court, for reasons already given, ought to be numerous; the first scheme will be reprobated by every man, who can compare the extent of the public wants, with the means of supplying them; the second will be espoused with caution by those, who will seriously consider the difficulty of collecting men dispersed over the whole union; the injury to the innocent, from the procrastinated determination of the charges which might be brought against them; the advantage to the guilty, from the opportunities which delay would afford to intrigue and corruption; and in some cases the detriment to the State, from the prolonged inaction of men, whose firm and faithful execution of their duty might have exposed them to the persecution of an intemperate or designing majority in the House of Representatives. Though this latter supposition may seem harsh, and might not be likely often to be verified; yet it ought not to be forgotten, that the demon of faction will at certain seasons extend his sceptre over all numerous bodies of men.

But though one or the other of the substitutes which have been examined, or some other that might be devised, should be thought preferable to the plan, in this respect, reported by the Convention, it will not follow, that the Constitution ought for this reason to be rejected. If mankind were to resolve to agree in no institution of government, until every part of it had been adjusted to the most exact standard of perfection, society would soon become a general scene of anarchy, and the world a desert. Where is the standard of perfection to be found? Who will undertake to unite the discordant opinions of a whole community, in the same judgment of it; and to prevail upon one conceited projector to renounce his *infallible* criterion, for the *fallible* criterion of his more *conceited neighbor*? To answer the purpose of the adversaries of the Constitution, they ought to prove, not merely, that particular provisions in it are not the best, which might have been imagined; but that the plan upon the whole is bad and pernicious.

PUBLIUS.

The New-York Packet, March 7, 1788

The Federalist No. 66

To the People of the State of New-York.

A review of the principal objections that have appeared against the proposed court for the trial of impeachments, will not improbably eradicate the remains of any unfavourable impressions, which may still exist, in regard to this matter.

The *first* of these objections is, that the provision in question confounds legislative and judiciary authorities in the same body; in violation of that important and well established maxim, which requires a separation between the different departments of power. The true meaning of this maxim has been discussed and ascertained in another place, and has been shewn to be entirely compatible with a partial intermixture of those departments for special purposes, preserving them in the main distinct and unconnected. This partial intermixture is even in some cases not only proper, but necessary to the mutual defence of the several members of the government, against each other. An absolute or qualified negative in the executive, upon the acts of the legislative body, is admitted by the ablest adepts in political science, to be an indefensible barrier against the encroachments of the latter upon the former. And it may perhaps with not less reason be contended that the powers relating to impeachments are as before intimated, an essential check in the hands of that body upon the encroachments of the executive. The division of them between the two branches of the legislature; assigning to one the right of accusing, to the other the right of judging; avoids the inconvenience of making the same persons both accusers and judges; and guards against the danger of persecution from the prevalency of a factious spirit in either of those branches. As the concurrence of two-thirds of the senate will be requisite to a condemnation, the security to innocence, from this additional circumstance, will be as complete as itself can desire.

It is curious to observe with what vehemence this part of the plan is assailed, on the principle here taken notice of, by men who profess to admire without exception the constitution of this state; while that constitution makes the senate, together with the chancellor and judges of the supreme court, not only a court of impeachments, but the highest judicatory in the state in all causes, civil and criminal. The proportion, in point of numbers, of the chancellor and judges to the senators, is so inconsiderable, that the judiciary authority of New-York in the last resort may, with truth, be said to reside in its senate. If the plan of the convention be in this respect chargeable with a departure from the celebrated maxim which has been so often mentioned, and seems to be so little understood, how much more culpable must be the constitution of New-York?*

A *second* objection to the senate, as a court of impeachments, is, that it contributes to an undue accumulation of power in that body, tending to give to the government a countenance too aristocratic. The senate, it is observed, is to have concurrent authority with the executive in the formation of treaties, and in the appointment to offices: If, say the objectors, to these prerogatives is added that of deciding in all cases of impeachment, it will give a decided predominancy to senatorial influence. To an objection so little precise in itself, it is not easy to find a very precise answer. Where is the measure or criterion to which we can appeal, for determining what will give the senate too much, too little, or barely the proper degree of influence? Will it not be more safe, as well as more simple, to dismiss such vague and uncertain calculations, to examine each power by itself, and to decide on general principles where it may be deposited with most advantage and least inconvenience?

If we take this course it will lead to a more intelligible, if not to a more certain result. The disposition of the power of making treaties, which has obtained in the plan of the convention, will then, if I mistake not, appear to be fully justified by the considerations stated in a former number, and by others which will occur under the next head of our enquiries. The expediency of the junction of the senate with the executive will, I trust, be placed in a light not less satisfactory, in

---

*In that of New-Jersey also the final judiciary authority is in a branch of the legislature. In New-Hampshire, Massachusetts, Pennsylvania, and South-Carolina, one branch of the legislature is the court for the trial of impeachments.

the disquisitions under the same head. And I flatter myself the observations in my last paper must have gone no inconsiderable way towards proving that it was not easy, if practicable, to find a more fit receptacle for the power of determining impeachments, than that which has been chosen. If this be truly the case, the hypothetical danger of the too great weight of the senate ought to be discarded from our reasonings.

But this hypothesis, such as it is has already been refuted in the remarks applied to the duration in office prescribed for the senators. It was by them shewn, as well on the credit of historical examples, as from the reason of the thing, that the most *popular* branch of every government, partaking of the republican genius, by being generally the favorite of the people, will be as generally a full match, if not an overmatch, for every other member of the government.

But independent of this most active and operative principle; to secure the equilibrium of the national house of representatives, the plan of the convention has provided in its favor, several important counterpoises to the additional authorities, to be conferred upon the senate. The exclusive privilege of originating money bills will belong to the house of representatives. The same house will possess the sole right of instituting impeachments: Is not this a complete counterballance to that of determining them? The same house will be the umpire in all elections of the president, which do not unite the suffrages of a majority of the whole number of electors; a case which it cannot be doubted will sometimes, if not frequently, happen. The constant possibility of the thing must be a fruitful source of influence to that body. The more it is contemplated, the more important will appear this ultimate, though contingent power of deciding the competitions of the most illustrious citizens of the union, for the first office in it. It would not perhaps be rash to predict, that as a mean of influence it will be found to outweigh all the peculiar attributes of the senate.

A third objection to the senate as a court of impeachments is drawn from the agency they are to have in the appointments to office. It is imagined that they would be too indulgent judges of the conduct of men, in whose official creation they had participated. The principle of this objection would condemn a practice, which is to be seen in all the state governments, if not in all the governments with which we are acquainted: I mean that of rendering those, who hold offices during pleasure, dependent on the pleasure of those, who appoint them. With equal plausibility might it be alledged in this case that the favoritism of the latter would always be an asylum for the misbehavior of the former. But that practice, in contradiction to this principle, proceeds upon the presumption, that the responsibility of those who appoint, for the fitness and competency of the persons, on whom they bestow their choice, and the interest they will have in the respectable and prosperous administration of affairs, will inspire a sufficient disposition, to dismiss from a share in it, all such, who, by their conduct, shall have proved themselves unworthy of the confidence reposed in them. Though facts may not always correspond with this presumption, yet if it be in the main just, it must destroy the supposition, that the senate, who will merely sanction the choice of the executive, should feel a byass towards the objects of that choice, strong enough to blind them to the evidences of guilt so extraordinary as to have induced the representatives of the nation to become its accusers.

If any further argument were necessary to evince the improbability of such a byass, it might be found in the nature of the agency of the senate, in the business of appointments. It will be the office of the president to *nominate*, and with the advice and consent of the senate to *appoint*. There will of course be no exertion of *choice* on the part of the senate. They may defeat one choice of the executive, and oblige him to make another; but they cannot themselves *choose*—they can only ratify or reject the choice, of the president. They might even entertain a preference to some other person, at the very moment they were assenting to the one proposed; because there might be no positive ground of opposition to him; and they could not be sure, if they withheld their assent, that the subsequent nomination would fall upon their own favorite, or upon any other person in their estimation more meritorious than the one rejected. Thus it could hardly happen that the majority of the senate would feel any other complacency towards the object of an appointment, than such, as the appearances of merit, might inspire, and the proofs of the want of it, destroy.

A fourth objection to the senate, in the capacity of a court of impeachments, is derived from their union with the executive in the power of making treaties. This, it has been said, would constitute the senators their own judges, in every case of a corrupt or perfidious execution of that trust. After having combined with the executive in betraying the interests of the nation in a ruinous treaty, what prospect, it is asked, would there be of their being made to suffer the punishment, they would deserve, when they were themselves to decide upon the accusation brought against them for the treachery of which they had been guilty?

This objection has been circulated with more earnestness and with greater show of reason, than any other which has appeared against this part of the plan; and yet I am deceived if it does not rest upon an erroneous foundation.

The security essentially intended by the constitution against corruption and treachery in the formation of treaties, is to be sought for in the numbers and characters of those who are to make them. The JOINT AGENCY of the chief magistrate of the union, and of two-thirds of the members of a body selected by the collective wisdom of the legislatures of the several states, is designed to be the pledge for the fidelity of the national councils in this particular. The convention might with propriety have meditated the punishment of the executive, for a deviation from the instructions of the senate, or a want of integrity in the conduct of the negociations committed to him: They might also have had in view the punishment of a few leading individuals in the senate, who should have prostituted their influence in that body, as the mercenary instruments of foreign corruption: But they could not with more or with equal propriety have contemplated the impeachment and punishment of two-thirds of the senate, consenting to an improper treaty, than of a majority of that or of the other branch of the national legislature, consenting to a pernicious or unconstitutional law: a principle which I believe has never been admitted into any government. How in fact could a majority of the house of representatives impeach themselves? Not better, it is evident, than two-thirds of the senate might try themselves. And yet what reason is there, that a majority of the house of representatives, sacrificing the interests of the society, by an unjust and tyrannical act of legislation, should escape with impunity more than two-thirds of the senate, sacrificing the same interests in an injurious treaty with a foreign power? The truth is, that in all such cases it is essential to the freedom and to the necessary independence of the deliberations of the body, that the members of it should be exempt from punishment for acts done in a collective capacity; and the security to the society must depend on the care which is taken to confide the trust to proper hands, to make it their interest to execute it with fidelity, and to make it as difficult as possible for them to combine in any interest opposite to that of the public good.

So far as might concern the misbehaviour of the executive in perverting the instructions, or contravening the views of the senate, we need not be apprehensive of the want of a disposition in that body to punish the abuse of their confidence, or to vindicate their own authority. We may thus far count upon their pride, if not upon their virtue. And so far even as might concern the corruption of leading members, by whose arts and influence the majority may have been inveigled into measures odious to the community; if the proofs of that corruption should be satisfactory, the usual propensity of human nature will warrant us in concluding, that there would be commonly no defect of inclination in the body, to divert the public resentment from themselves, by a ready sacrifice of the authors of their mismanagement and disgrace.

PUBLIUS.

The Independent Journal, March 8, 1788

The Federalist No. 67

To the People of the State of New-York.

The Constitution of the executive department of the proposed government claims next our attention.

There is hardly any part of the system which could have been attended with greater difficulty in the arrangement of it than this; and there is perhaps none, which has been inveighed against with less candor, or criticised with less judgment.

Here the writers against the Constitution seem to have taken pains to signalize their talent of misrepresentation, calculating upon the aversion of the people to monarchy, they have endeavoured to inlist all their jealousies and apprehensions in opposition to the intended President of the United States; not merely as the embryo but as the full grown progeny of that detested parent. To establish the pretended affinity they have not scrupled to draw resources even from the regions of fiction. The authorities of a magistrate, in few instances greater, and in some instances less, than those of a Governor of New-York, have been magnified into more than royal prerogatives. He has been decorated with attributes superior in dignity and splendor to those of a King of Great-Britain. He has been shown to us with the diadem sparkling on his brow, and the imperial purple flowing in his train. He has been seated on a throne surrounded with minions and mistresses; giving audience to the envoys of foreign potentates, in all the supercilious pomp of majesty. The images of Asiatic despotism and voluptuousness have scarcely been wanting to crown the exaggerated scene. We have been almost taught to tremble at the terrific visages of murdering janizaries; and to blush at the unveiled mysteries of a future seraglio.

Attempts so extravagant as these to disfigure, or it might rather be said, to metamorphose the object, render it necessary to take an accurate view of its real nature and form; in order as well to ascertain its true aspect and genuine appearance, as to unmask the disingenuity and expose the fallacy of the counterfeit resemblances which have been so insidiously as well as industriously propagated.

In the execution of this task there is no man, who would not find it an arduous effort, either to behold the moderation or to treat with seriousness the devices, not less weak than wicked, which have been contrived to pervert the public opinion in relation to the subject. They so far exceed the usual, though unjustifiable, licenses of party-artifice, that even in a disposition the most candid and tolerant they must force the sentiments which favor an indulgent construction of the conduct of political adversaries to give place to a voluntary and unreserved indignation. It is impossible not to bestow the imputation of deliberate imposture and deception upon the gross pretence of a similitude between a King of Great-Britain and a magistrate of the character marked out for that of the President of the United States. It is still more impossible to withhold that imputation from the rash and barefaced expedients which have been employed to give success to the attempted imposition.

In one instance, which I cite as a sample of the general spirit, the temerity has proceeded so far as to ascribe to the President of the United States a power, which by the instrument reported is *expressly* allotted to the executives of the individual States. I mean the power of filling casual vacancies in the Senate.

This bold experiment upon the discernment of his countrymen, has been hazarded by a writer who (whatever may be his real merit) has had no inconsiderable share in the applauses of his party;* and who upon this false and unfounded suggestion, has built a series of observations equally false and unfounded. Let him now be confronted with the evidence of the fact; and let him, if he be able, justify or extenuate the shameful outrage he has offered to the dictates of truth and to the rules of fair dealing.

The second clause of the second section of the second article empowers the President of the United States "to nominate, and by and with the advice and consent of the Senate to appoint ambassadors, other public ministers and consuls, judges of the Supreme Court, and all other *officers* of the United States, whose appointments are *not* in the Constitution

* See Cato No. 5.

otherwise provided for, and *which shall be established by law.*" Immediately after this clause follows another in these words— "The President shall have power to fill up all *vacancies* that may happen *during the recess of the Senate*, by granting commissions which shall *expire at the end of their next session.*" It is from this last provision that the pretended power of the President to fill vacancies in the Senate has been deduced. A slight attention to the connection of the clauses and to the obvious meaning of the terms will satisfy us that the deduction is not even colorable.

The first of these two clauses it is clear only provides a mode for appointing such officers, "whose appointments are *not otherwise provided for* in the Constitution, and which *shall be established by law*;" of course it cannot extend to the appointment of senators; whose appointments are *otherwise provided for* in the Constitution,* and who are *established by the Constitution*, and will not require a future establishment by law. This position will hardly be contested.

The last of these two clauses, it is equally clear, cannot be understood to comprehend the power of filling vacancies in the Senate, for the following reasons—*First.* The relation in which that clause stands to the other, which declares the general mode of appointing officers of the United States, denotes it to be nothing more than a supplement to the other; for the purpose of establishing an auxiliary method of appointment in cases, to which the general method was inadequate. The ordinary power of appointment is confided to the President and Senate *jointly*, and can therefore only be exercised during the session of the Senate; but as it would have been improper to oblige this body to be continually in session for the appointment of officers; and as vacancies might happen *in their recess*, which it might be necessary for the public service to fill without delay, the succeeding clause is evidently intended to authorise the President *singly* to make temporary appointments "during the recess of the Senate, by granting commissions which should expire at the end of their next session." *Secondly.* If this clause is to be considered as supplementary to the one which precedes, the *vacancies* of which it speaks must

* Article I. § 3. Clause I.

be construed to relate to the "officers" described in the preceding one; and this we have seen excludes from its description the members of the Senate. *Thirdly.* The time within which the power is to operate "during the recess of the Senate" and the duration of the appointments "to the end of the next session" of that body, conspire to elucidate the sense of the provision; which if it had been intended to comprehend Senators would naturally have referred the temporary power of filling vacancies to the recess of the State Legislatures, who are to make the permanent appointments, and not to the recess of the national Senate, who are to have no concern in those appointments; and would have extended the duration in office of the temporary Senators to the next session of the Legislature of the State, in whose representation the vacancies had happened, instead of making it to expire at the end of the ensuing session of the national Senate. The circumstances of the body authorised to make the permanent appointments, would of course have governed the modification of a power which related to the temporary appointments; and as the national Senate is the body whose situation is alone contemplated in the clause upon which the suggestion under examination has been founded, the vacancies to which it alludes can only be deemed to respect those officers, in whose appointment that body has a concurrent agency with the President. But, *lastly,* the first and second clauses of the third section of the first article, not only obviate the possibility of doubt, but destroy the pretext of misconception. The former provides that "the Senate of the United States shall be composed of two Senators from each State, chosen *by the Legislature thereof* for six years," and the latter directs that "if vacancies in that body should happen by resignation or otherwise *during the recess of the Legislature of* ANY STATE, the Executive THEREOF may make temporary appointments until the *next meeting of the Legislature,* which shall then fill such vacancies." Here is an express power given, in clear and unambiguous terms, to the State executives to fill the casual vacancies in the Senate by temporary appointments; which not only invalidates the supposition, that the clause before considered could have been intended to confer that power upon the President of the United States; but proves that this supposition, destitute as it is even of the merit of plausibility, must have originated in an intention to deceive the people, too palpable to be obscured by sophistry, and too atrocious to be palliated by hypocrisy.

I have taken the pains to select this instance of misrepresentation, and to place it in a clear and strong light, as an unequivocal proof of the unwarrantable arts which are practised to prevent a fair and impartial judgment of the real merits of the constitution submitted to the consideration of the people. Nor have I scrupled in so flagrant a case to allow myself in a severity of animadversion little congenial with the general spirit of these papers. I hesitate not to submit it to the decision of any candid and honest adversary of the proposed government, whether language can furnish epithets of too much asperity for so shameless and so prostitute an attempt to impose on the citizens of America.

PUBLIUS.

The New-York Packet, March 11, 1788

The Federalist No. 68

To the People of the State of New-York.

The mode of appointment of the chief magistrate of the United States is almost the only part of the system, of any consequence, which has escaped without severe censure, or which has received the slightest mark of approbation from its opponents. The most plausible of these, who has appeared in print, has even deigned to admit, that the election of the president is pretty well guarded.* I venture somewhat further; and hesitate not to affirm, that if the manner of it be not perfect, it is at least excellent. It unites in an eminent degree all the advantages; the union of which was to be desired.

It was desireable, that the sense of the people should operate in the choice of the person to whom so important a trust was to be confided. This end will be answered by committing the right of making it, not to any pre-established body, but to men, chosen by the people for the special purpose, and at the particular conjuncture.

It was equally desirable, that the immediate election should be made by men most capable of analizing the qualities adapted to the station, and acting under circumstances favourable to deliberation and to a judicious combination of all the reasons and inducements, which were proper to govern their choice. A small number of persons, selected by their fellow citizens from the general mass, will be most likely to possess the information and discernment requisite to so complicated an investigation.

It was also peculiarly desirable, to afford as little opportunity as possible to tumult and disorder. This evil was not least to be dreaded in the election of a magistrate, who was to have so important an agency in the administration of the government, as the president of the United States. But the precautions which have been so happily concerted in the system under consideration, promise an effectual security against this mischief. The choice of *several* to form an intermediate body

* Vide Federal Farmer.

of electors, will be much less apt to convulse the community, with any extraordinary or violent movements, than the choice of *one* who was himself to be the final object of the public wishes. And as the electors, chosen in each state, are to assemble and vote in the state, in which they are chosen, this detached and divided situation will expose them much less to heats and ferments, which might be communicated from them to the people, than if they were all to be convened at one time, in one place.

Nothing was more to be desired, than that every practicable obstacle should be opposed to cabal, intrigue and corruption. These most deadly adversaries of republican government might naturally have been expected to make their aproaches from more than one quarter, but chiefly from the desire in foreign powers to gain an improper ascendant in our councils. How could they better gratify this, than by raising a creature of their own to the chief magistracy of the union? But the convention have guarded against all danger of this sort with the most provident and judicious attention. They have not made the appointment of the president to depend on any pre-existing bodies of men who might be tampered with before hand to prostitute their votes; but they have referred it in the first instance to an immediate act of the people of America, to be exerted in the choice of persons for the temporary and sole purpose of making the appointment. And they have excluded from eligibility to this trust, all those who from situation might be suspected of too great devotion to the president in office. No senator, representative, or other person holding a place of trust or profit under the United States, can be of the number of the electors. Thus, without corrupting the body of the people, the immediate agents in the election will at least enter upon the task, free from any sinister byass. Their transient existence, and their detached situation, already taken notice of, afford a satisfactory prospect of their continuing so, to the conclusion of it. The business of corruption, when it is to embrace so considerable a number of men, requires time, as well as means. Nor would it be found easy suddenly to embark them, dispersed as they would be over thirteen states, in any combinations, founded upon motives, which though they could not properly be denominated corrupt, might yet be of a nature to mislead them from their duty.

Another and no less important desideratum was, that the executive should be independent for his continuance in office on all, but the people themselves. He might otherwise be tempted to sacrifice his duty to his complaisance for those whose favor was necessary to the duration of his official consequence. This advantage will also be secured, by making his re-election to depend on a special body of representatives, deputed by the society for the single purpose of making the important choice.

All these advantages will be happily combined in the plan devised by the convention; which is, that the people of each state shall choose a number of persons as electors, equal to the number of senators and representatives of such state in the national government, who shall assemble within the state and vote for some fit person as president. Their votes, thus given, are to be transmitted to the seat of the national government, and the person who may happen to have a majority of the whole number of votes will be the president. But as a majority of the votes might not always happen to centre on one man and as it might be unsafe to permit less than a majority to be conclusive, it is provided, that in such a contingency, the house of representatives shall select out of the candidates, who shall have the five highest numbers of votes, the man who in their opinion may be best qualified for the office.

This process of election affords a moral certainty, that the office of president, will seldom fall to the lot of any man, who is not in an eminent degree endowed with the requisite qualifications. Talents for low intrigue and the little arts of popularity may alone suffice to elevate a man to the first honors in a single state; but it will require other talents and a different kind of merit to establish him in the esteem and confidence of the whole union, or of so considerable a portion of it as would be necessary to make him a successful candidate for the distinguished office of president of the United States. It will not be too strong to say, that there will be a constant probability of seeing the station filled by characters pre-eminent for ability and virtue. And this will be thought no inconsiderable recommendation of the constitution, by those, who are able to estimate the share, which the executive in every government must necessarily have in its good or ill administration. Though we cannot acquiesce in the political heresy of the poet who says—

"For forms of government let fools contest—
"That which is best administered is best."

—yet we may safely pronounce, that the true test of a good government is its aptitude and tendency to produce a good administration.

The vice-president is to be chosen in the same manner with the president; with this difference, that the senate is to do, in respect to the former, what is to be done by the house of representatives, in respect to the latter.

The appointment of an extraordinary person, as vice president, has been objected to as superfluous, if not mischievous. It has been alledged, that it would have been preferable to have authorised the senate to elect out of their own body an officer, answering that description. But two considerations seem to justify the ideas of the convention in this respect. One is, that to secure at all times the possibility of a definitive resolution of the body, it is necessary that the president should have only a casting vote. And to take the senator of any state from his seat as senator, to place him in that of president of the senate, would be to exchange, in regard to the state from which he came, a constant for a contingent vote. The other consideration is, that as the vice-president may occasionally become a substitute for the president, in the supreme executive magistracy, all the reasons, which recommend the mode of election prescribed for the one, apply with great, if not with equal, force to the manner of appointing the other. It is remarkable, that in this as in most other instances, the objection, which is made, would be against the constitution of this state. We have a Lieutenant Governor chosen by the people at large, who presides in the senate, and is the constitutional substitute for the Governor in casualties similar to those, which would authorise the vice-president to exercise the authorities and discharge the duties of the president.

PUBLIUS.

The Independent Journal, March 12, 1788

The Federalist No. 69

To the People of the State of New-York.

I proceed now to trace the real characters of the proposed executive as they are marked out in the plan of the Convention. This will serve to place in a strong light the unfairness of the representations which have been made in regard to it.

The first thing which strikes our attention is that the executive authority, with few exceptions, is to be vested in a single magistrate. This will scarcely however be considered as a point upon which any comparison can be grounded; for if in this particular there be a resemblance to the King of Great-Britain, there is not less a resemblance to the Grand Signior, to the Khan of Tartary, to the man of the seven mountains, or to the Governor of New-York.

That magistrate is to be elected for *four* years; and is to be re-eligible as often as the People of the United States shall think him worthy of their confidence. In these circumstances, there is a total dissimilitude between *him* and a King of Great-Britain; who is an *hereditary* monarch, possessing the crown as a patrimony descendible to his heirs forever; but there is a close analogy between *him* and a Governor of New-York, who is elected for *three* years, and is re-eligible without limitation or intermission. If we consider how much less time would be requisite for establishing a dangerous influence in a single State, than for establishing a like influence throughout the United States, we must conclude that a duration of *four* years for the Chief Magistrate of the Union, is a degree of permanency far less to be dreaded in that office, than a duration of *three* years for a correspondent office in a single State.

The President of the United States would be liable to be impeached, tried, and upon conviction of treason, bribery, or other high crime or misdemeanors, removed from office; and would afterwards be liable to prosecution and punishment in the ordinary course of law. The person of the King of Great-Britain is sacred and inviolable: There is no constitutional tribunal to which he is amenable; no punishment to which he can be subjected without involving the crisis of a national revolution. In this delicate and important circumstance or personal responsibility, the President of confederated America would stand upon no better ground than a Governor of New-York and upon worse ground than the Governors of Virginia and Delaware.

The President of the United States is to have power to return a bill, which shall have passed the two branches of the Legislature, for re-consideration; but the bill so returned is to become a law, if upon that re-consideration it be approved by two thirds of both houses. The King of Great Britain, on his part, has an absolute negative upon the acts of the two houses of Parliament. The disuse of that power for a considerable time past, does not affect the reality of its existence; and is to be ascribed wholly to the crown's having found the means of substituting influence to authority, or the art of gaining a majority in one or the other of the two houses, to the necessity of exerting a prerogative which could seldom be exerted without hazarding some degree of national agitation. The qualified negative of the President differs widely from this absolute negative of the British sovereign; and tallies exactly with the revisionary authority of the Council of revision of this State, of which the Governor is a constituent part. In this respect, the power of the President would exceed that of the Governor of New-York; because the former would possess singly what the latter shares with the Chancellor and Judges: But it would be precisely the same with that of the Governor of Massachusetts, whose constitution, as to this article, seems to have been the original from which the Convention have copied.

The President is to be the "Commander in Chief of the army and navy of the United States, and of the militia of the several States, when called to the actual service of the United States. He is to have power to grant reprieves and pardons for offences against the United States, *except in cases of impeachment*; to recommend to the consideration of Congress such measures as he shall judge necessary and expedient; to convene on extraordinary occasions both houses of the Legislature, or either of them, and in case of disagreement between them *with respect to the time of adjournment*, to adjourn them to such time as he shall think proper; to take care that the laws be faithfully executed; and to commission all officers of the United States." In most of these particulars the power of the President will resemble equally that of the King of Great-Britain and of the Governor of New-York. The most material points of difference are these—First; the President will have only the occasional command of such part of the militia of the nation, as by legislative provision may be called into the actual service of the Union. The King of Great Britain and the Governor of New-York have at all times the entire command of all the militia within their several jurisdictions. In this article therefore the power of the President would be inferior to that of either the Monarch or the Governor. Secondly; the President is to be Commander in Chief of the army and navy of the United States. In this respect his authority would be nominally the same with that of the King of Great-Britain, but in substance much inferior to it. It would amount to nothing more than the supreme command and direction of the military and naval forces, as first General and Admiral of the confederacy; while that of the British King extends to the *declaring* of war and to the *raising* and *regulating* of fleets and armies; all which by the Constitution under consideration would appertain to the Legislature.* The Governor of New-York on the other hand, is by the Constitution of the State vested only with the command of its militia and navy. But the Constitutions of several of the States, expressly declare their Governors to be the Commanders in Chief as well of the army as navy; and it may well be a question whether those of New-Hampshire and Massachusetts, in particular, do not in this instance confer larger powers upon their respective gov-

---

* A writer in a Pennsylvania paper, under the signature of *Tamony* has asserted that the King of Great-Britain owes his prerogatives as Commander in Chief to an annual mutiny bill. The truth is on the contrary that his prerogative in this respect is immemorial, and was only disputed "contrary to all reason and precedent," as Blackstone, vol. I, p. 262, expresses it, by the long parliament of Charles the first, but by the statute the 13, of Charles second, ch. 6, it was declared to be in the King alone, for that the sole supreme government and command of the militia within his Majesty's realms and dominions, and of all forces by sea and land, and of all forts and places of strength, *ever was and is* the undoubted right of his Majesty and his royal predecessors Kings and Queens of England, and that both or either House of Parliament cannot nor ought to pretend to the same.

ernors, than could be claimed by a President of the United States. Thirdly; the power of the President in respect to pardons would extend to all cases, *except those of impeachment.* The Governor of New-York may pardon in all cases, even in those of impeachment, except for treason and murder. Is not the power of the Governor in this article, on a calculation of political consequences, greater than that of the President? All conspiracies and plots against the government, which have not been matured into actual treason, may be screened from punishment of every kind, by the interposition of the prerogative of pardoning. If a Governor of New-York therefore should be at the head of any such conspiracy, until the design had been ripened into actual hostility, he could ensure his accomplices and adherents an entire impunity. A President of the Union on the other hand, though he may even pardon treason, when prosecuted in the ordinary course of law, could shelter no offender in any degree from the effects of impeachment & conviction. Would not the prospect of a total indemnity for all the preliminary steps be a greater temptation to undertake and persevere in an enterprise against the public liberty than the mere prospect of an exemption from death and confiscation, if the final execution of the design, upon an actual appeal to arms, should miscarry? Would this last expectation have any influence at all, when the probability was computed that the person who was to afford that exemption might himself be involved in the consequences of the measure; and might be incapacitated by his agency in it, from affording the desired impunity? The better to judge of this matter, it will be necessary to recollect that by the proposed Constitution the offence of treason is limited "to levying war upon the United States, and adhering to their enemies, giving them aid and comfort," and that by the laws of New-York it is confined within similar bounds. Fourthly; the President can only adjourn the national Legislature in the single case of disagreement about the time of adjournment. The British monarch may prorogue or even dissolve the Parliament. The Governor of New-York may also prorogue the Legislature of this State for a limited time; a power which in certain situations may be employed to very important purposes.

The President is to have power with the advice and consent

of the Senate to make treaties; provided two thirds of the Senators present concur. The King of Great-Britain is the sole and absolute representative of the nation in all foreign transactions. He can of his own accord make treaties of peace, commerce, alliance, and of every other description. It has been insinuated, that his authority in this respect is not conclusive, and that his conventions with foreign powers are subject to the revision, and stand in need of the ratification of Parliament. But I believe this doctrine was never heard of 'till it was broached upon the present occasion. Every jurist* of that kingdom, and every other man acquainted with its constitution knows, as an established fact, that the prerogative of making treaties exists in the crown in its utmost plenitude; and that the compacts entered into by the royal authority have the most complete legal validity and perfection, independent of any other sanction. The Parliament, it is true, is sometimes seen employing itself in altering the existing laws to conform them to the stipulations in a new treaty; and this may have possibly given birth to the imagination that its co-operation was necessary to the obligatory efficacy of the treaty. But this parliamentary interposition proceeds from a different cause; from the necessity of adjusting a most artificial and intricate system of revenue and commercial laws to the changes made in them by the operation of the treaty; and of adapting new provisions and precautions to the new state of things, to keep the machine from running into disorder. In this respect therefore, there is no comparison between the intended power of the President, and the actual power of the British sovereign. The one can perform alone, what the other can only do with the concurrence of a branch of the Legislature. It must be admitted that in this instance the power of the fœderal executive would exceed that of any State executive. But this arises naturally from the exclusive possession by the Union of that part of the sovereign power, which relates to treaties. If the confederacy were to be dissolved, it would become a question, whether the executives of the several States were not solely invested with that delicate and important prerogative.

The President is also to be authorised to receive Ambassadors

* Vide Blackstone's Commentaries, vol. I, page 257.

and other public Ministers. This, though it has been a rich theme of declamation, is more a matter of dignity than of authority. It is a circumstance, which will be without consequence in the administration of the government; and it was far more convenient that it should be arranged in this manner, than that there should be a necessity of convening the Legislature, or one of its branches, upon every arrival of a foreign minister; though it were merely to take the place of a departed predecessor.

The President is to nominate and *with the advice and consent of the Senate* to appoint Ambassadors and other public Ministers, Judges of the Supreme Court, and in general all officers of the United States established by law and whose appointments are not otherwise provided for by the Constitution. The King of Great-Britain is emphatically and truly stiled the fountain of honor. He not only appoints to all offices, but can create offices. He can confer titles of nobility at pleasure; and has the disposal of an immense number of church preferments. There is evidently a great inferiority, in the power of the President in this particular, to that of the British King; nor is it equal to that of the Governor of New-York, if we are to interpret the meaning of the constitution of the State by the practice which has obtained under it. The power of appointment is with us lodged in a Council composed of the Governor and four members of the Senate chosen by the Assembly. The Governor *claims* and has frequently *exercised* the right of nomination, and is *entitled* to a casting vote in the appointment. If he really has the right of nominating, his authority is in this respect equal to that of the President, and exceeds it in the article of the casting vote. In the national government, if the Senate should be divided, no appointment could be made: In the government of New-York, if the Council should be divided the Governor can turn the scale and confirm his own nomination.* If we compare

* Candor however demands an acknowledgement; that I do not think the claim of the Governor to a right of nomination well founded. Yet it is always justifiable to reason from the practice of a government till its propriety has been constitutionally questioned. And independent of this claim, when we take into view the other considerations and pursue them through all their consequences, we shall be inclined to draw much the same conclusion.

the publicity which must necessarily attend the mode of appointment by the President and an entire branch of the national Legislature, with the privacy in the mode of appointment by the Governor of New-York, closeted in a secret apartment with at most four, and frequently with only two persons; and if we at the same time consider how much more easy it must be to influence the small number of which a Council of Appointment consists than the considerable number of which the national Senate would consist, we cannot hesitate to pronounce, that the power of the Chief Magistrate of this State in the disposition of offices must in practice be greatly superior to that of the Chief Magistrate of the Union.

Hence it appears, that except as to the concurrent authority of the President in the article of treaties, it would be difficult to determine whether that Magistrate would in the aggregate, possess more or less power than the Governor of New-York. And it appears yet more unequivocally that there is no pretence for the parallel which has been attempted between him and the King of Great-Britain. But to render the contrast, in this respect, still more striking, it may be of use to throw the principal circumstances of dissimilitude into a closer groupe.

The President of the United States would be an officer elected by the people for *four* years. The King of Great-Britain is a perpetual and *hereditary* prince. The one would be amenable to personal punishment and disgrace: The person of the other is sacred and inviolable. The one would have a qualified negative upon the acts of the legislative body: The other has an *absolute* negative. The one would have a right to command the military and naval forces of the nation: The other in addition to this right, possesses that of *declaring* war, and of *raising* and *regulating* fleets and armies by his own authority. The one would have a concurrent power with a branch of the Legislature in the formation of treaties: The other is the *sole possessor* of the power of making treaties. The one would have a like concurrent authority in appointing to offices: The other is the sole author of all appointments. The one can infer no privileges whatever: The other can make denizens of aliens, noblemen of commoners, can erect corporations with all the rights incident to corporate bodies. The one can prescribe no rules concerning the commerce or currency of the nation: The other is in several respects the arbiter of commerce, and in this capacity can establish markets and fairs, can regulate weights and measures, can lay embargoes for a limited time, can coin money, can authorise or prohibit the circulation of foreign coin. The one has no particle of spiritual jurisdiction: The other is the supreme head and Governor of the national church! What answer shall we give to those who would persuade us that things so unlike resemble each other? The same that ought to be given to those who tell us, that a government, the whole power of which would be in the hands of the elective and periodical servants of the people, is an aristocracy, a monarchy, and a despotism.

PUBLIUS.

The New-York Packet, March 14, 1788

The Federalist No. 70

To the People of the State of New-York.

There is an idea, which is not without its advocates, that a vigorous executive is inconsistent with the genius of republican government. The enlightened well wishers to this species of government must at least hope that the supposition is destitute of foundation; since they can never admit its truth, without at the same time admitting the condemnation of their own principles. Energy in the executive is a leading character in the definition of good government. It is essential to the protection of the community against foreign attacks: It is not less essential to the steady administration of the laws, to the protection of property against those irregular and high handed combinations, which sometimes interrupt the ordinary course of justice to the security of liberty against the enterprises and assaults of ambition, of faction and of anarchy. Every man the least conversant in Roman story knows how often that republic was obliged to take refuge in the absolute power of a single man, under the formidable title of dictator, as well against the intrigues of ambitious individuals, who aspired to the tyranny, and the seditions of whole classes of the community, whose conduct threatened the existence of all government, as against the invasions of external enemies, who menaced the conquest and destruction of Rome.

There can be no need however to multiply arguments or examples on this head. A feeble executive implies a feeble execution of the government. A feeble execution is but another phrase for a bad execution: And a government ill executed, whatever it may be in theory, must be in practice a bad government.

Taking it for granted, therefore, that all men of sense will agree in the necessity of an energetic executive; it will only remain to inquire, what are the ingredients which constitute this energy—how far can they be combined with those other ingredients which constitute safety in the republican sense? And how far does this combination characterise the plan, which has been reported by the convention?

The ingredients, which constitute energy in the executive, are first unity, secondly duration, thirdly an adequate provision for its support, fourthly competent powers.

The circumstances which constitute safety in the republican sense are, 1st. a due dependence on the people, secondly a due responsibility.

Those politicians and statesmen, who have been the most celebrated for the soundness of their principles, and for the justness of their views, have declared in favor of a single executive and a numerous legislature. They have with great propriety considered energy as the most necessary qualification of the former, and have regarded this as most applicable to power in a single hand; while they have with equal propriety considered the latter as best adapted to deliberation and wisdom, and best calculated to conciliate the confidence of the people and to secure their privileges and interests.

That unity is conducive to energy will not be disputed. Decision, activity, secrecy, and dispatch will generally characterise the proceedings of one man, in a much more eminent degree, than the proceedings of any greater number; and in proportion as the number is increased, these qualities will be diminished.

This unity may be destroyed in two ways; either by vesting the power in two or more magistrates of equal dignity and authority; or by vesting it ostensibly in one man, subject in whole or in part to the controul and co-operation of others, in the capacity of counsellors to him. Of the first the two consuls of Rome may serve as an example; of the last we shall find examples in the constitutions of several of the states. New-York and New-Jersey, if I recollect right, are the only states, which have entrusted the executive authority wholly to single men.* Both these methods of destroying the unity of the executive have their partisans; but the votaries of an executive council are the most numerous. They are both liable, if not to equal, to similar objections; and may in most lights be examined in conjunction.

* New-York has no council except for the single purpose of appointing to offices; New-Jersey has a council, whom the governor may consult. But I think from the terms of the constitution their resolutions do not bind him.

The experience of other nations will afford little instruction on this head. As far however as it teaches any thing, it teaches us not to be inamoured of plurality in the executive. We have seen that the Achæans on an experiment of two Prætors, were induced to abolish one. The Roman history records many instances of mischiefs to the republic from the dissentions between the consuls, and between the military tribunes, who were at times substituted to the consuls. But it gives us no specimens of any peculiar advantages derived to the state, from the circumstance of the plurality of those magistrates. That the dissentions between them were not more frequent, or more fatal, is matter of astonishment; until we advert to the singular position in which the republic was almost continually placed and to the prudent policy pointed out by the circumstances of the state, and pursued by the consuls, of making a division of the government between them. The Patricians engaged in a perpetual struggle with the Plebeians for the preservation of their antient authorities and dignities; the consuls, who were generally chosen out of the former body, were commonly united by the personal interest they had in the defence of the privileges of their order. In addition to this motive of union, after the arms of the republic had considerably expanded the bounds of its empire, it became an established custom with the consuls to divide the administration between themselves by lot; one of them remaining at Rome to govern the city and its environs; the other taking the command in the more distant provinces. This expedient must no doubt have had great influence in preventing those collisions and rivalships, which might otherwise have embroiled the peace of the republic.

But quitting the dim light of historical research, and attaching ourselves purely to the dictates of reason and good sense, we shall discover much greater cause to reject than to approve the idea of plurality in the executive, under any modification whatever.

Wherever two or more persons are engaged in any common enterprize or pursuit, there is always danger of difference of opinion. If it be a public trust or office in which they are cloathed with equal dignity and authority, there is peculiar danger of personal emulation and even animosity. From either and especially from all these causes, the most bitter dissentions are apt to spring. Whenever these happen, they lessen the respectability, weaken the authority, and distract the plans and operations of those whom they divide. If they should unfortunately assail the supreme executive magistracy of a country, consisting of a plurality of persons, they might impede or frustrate the most important measures of the government, in the most critical emergencies of the state. And what is still worse, they might split the community into the most violent and irreconcilable factions, adhering differently to the different individuals who composed the magistracy.

Men often oppose a thing merely because they have had no agency in planning it, or because it may have been planned by those whom they dislike. But if they have been consulted and have happened to disapprove, opposition then becomes in their estimation an indispensable duty of self love. They seem to think themselves bound in honor, and by all the motives of personal infallibility to defeat the success of what has been resolved upon, contrary to their sentiments. Men of upright, benevolent tempers have too many opportunities of remarking with horror, to what desperate lengths this disposition is sometimes carried, and how often the great interests of society are sacrificed to the vanity, to the conceit and to the obstinacy of individuals, who have credit enough to make their passions and their caprices interesting to mankind. Perhaps the question now before the public may in its consequences afford melancholy proofs of the effects of this despicable frailty, or rather detestable vice in the human character.

Upon the principles of a free government, inconveniencies from the source just mentioned must necessarily be submitted to in the formation of the legislature; but it is unnecessary and therefore unwise to introduce them into the constitution of the executive. It is here too that they may be most pernicious. In the legislature, promptitude of decision is oftener an evil than a benefit. The differences of opinion, and the jarrings of parties in that department of the government, though they may sometimes obstruct salutary plans, yet often promote deliberations and circumspection; and serve to check excesses in the majority. When a resolution too is once taken, the opposition must be at an end. That resolution is a law,

and resistance to it punishable. But no favourable circumstances palliate or atone for the disadvantages of dissention in
the executive department. Here they are pure and unmixed.
There is no point at which they cease to operate. They serve
to embarrass and weaken the execution of the plan or measure, to which they relate, from the first step to the final conclusion of it. They constantly counteract those qualities in the
executive, which are the most necessary ingredients in its
composition, vigour and expedition, and this without any
counterballancing good. In the conduct of war, in which the
energy of the executive is the bulwark of the national security,
every thing would be to be apprehended from its plurality.

It must be confessed that these observations apply with
principal weight to the first case supposed, that is to a plurality of magistrates of equal dignity and authority; a scheme the
advocates for which are not likely to form a numerous sect:
But they apply, though not with equal, yet with considerable
weight, to the project of a council, whose concurrence is
made constitutionally necessary to the operations of the ostensible executive. An artful cabal in that council would be
able to distract and to enervate the whole system of administration. If no such cabal should exist, the mere diversity of
views and opinions would alone be sufficient to tincture the
exercise of the executive authority with a spirit of habitual feebleness and delatoriness.

But one of the weightiest objections to a plurality in the executive, and which lies as much against the last as the first
plan, is that it tends to conceal faults, and destroy responsibility. Responsibility is of two kinds, to censure and to punishment. The first is the most important of the two; especially
in an elective office. Man, in public trust, will much oftener
act in such a manner as to render him unworthy of being any
longer trusted, than in such a manner as to make him obnoxious to legal punishment. But the multiplication of the executive adds to the difficulty of detection in either case. It often
becomes impossible, amidst mutual accusations, to determine
on whom the blame or the punishment of a pernicious measure, or series of pernicious measures ought really to fall. It is
shifted from one to another with so much dexterity, and under such plausible appearances, that the public opinion is left

in suspense about the real author. The circumstances which may have led to any national miscarriage or misfortune are sometimes so complicated, that where there are a number of actors who may have had different degrees and kinds of agency, though we may clearly see upon the whole that there has been mismanagement, yet it may be impracticable to pronounce to whose account the evil which may have been incurred is truly chargeable.

"I was overruled by my council. The council were so divided in their opinions, that it was impossible to obtain any better resolution on the point." These and similar pretexts are constantly at hand, whether true or false. And who is there that will either take the trouble or incur the odium of a strict scrutiny into the secret springs of the transaction? Should there be found a citizen zealous enough to undertake the unpromising task, if there happen to be a collusion between the parties concerned, how easy is it to cloath the circumstances with so much ambiguity, as to render it uncertain what was the precise conduct of any of those parties?

In the single instance in which the governor of this state is coupled with a council, that is in the appointment to offices, we have seen the mischiefs of it in the view now under consideration. Scandalous appointments to important offices have been made. Some cases indeed have been so flagrant, that ALL PARTIES have agreed in the impropriety of the thing. When enquiry has been made, the blame has been laid by the governor on the members of the council; who on their part have charged it upon his nomination: While the people remain altogether at a loss to determine by whose influence their interests have been committed to hands so unqualified, and so manifestly improper. In tenderness to individuals, I forbear to descend to particulars.

It is evident from these considerations, that the plurality of the executive tends to deprive the people of the two greatest securities they can have for the faithful exercise of any delegated power; first, the restraints of public opinion, which lose their efficacy as well on account of the division of the censure attendant on bad measures among a number, as on account of the uncertainty on whom it ought to fall; and secondly, the opportunity of discovering with facility and clearness the misconduct of the persons they trust, in order either to their removal from office, or to their actual punishment, in cases which admit of it.

In England the king is a perpetual magistrate; and it is a maxim, which has obtained for the sake of the public peace, that he is unaccountable for his administration, and his person sacred. Nothing therefore can be wiser in that kingdom than to annex to the king a constitutional council, who may be responsible to the nation for the advice they give. Without this there would be no responsibility whatever in the executive department; an idea inadmissible in a free government. But even there the king is not bound by the resolutions of his council, though they are answerable for the advice they give. He is the absolute master of his own conduct, in the exercise of his office; and may observe or disregard the council given to him at his sole discretion.

But in a republic, where every magistrate ought to be personally responsible for his behaviour in office, the reason which in the British constitution dictates the propriety of a council not only ceases to apply, but turns against the institution. In the monarchy of Great-Britain, it furnishes a substitute for the prohibited responsibility of the chief magistrate; which serves in some degree as a hostage to the national justice for his good behaviour. In the American republic it would serve to destroy, or would greatly diminish the intended and necessary responsibility of the chief magistrate himself.

The idea of a council to the executive, which has so generally obtained in the state constitutions, has been derived from that maxim of republican jealousy, which considers power as safer in the hands of a number of men than of a single man. If the maxim should be admitted to be applicable to the case, I should contend that the advantage on that side would not counterballance the numerous disadvantages on the opposite side. But I do not think the rule at all applicable to the executive power. I clearly concur in opinion in this particular with a writer whom the celebrated Junius pronounces to be "deep, solid and ingenious," that, "the executive power is more easily confined when it is one:"* That it is far more safe there

* De Lome.

should be a single object for the jealousy and watchfulness of the people; and in a word that all multiplication of the executive is rather dangerous than friendly to liberty.

A little consideration will satisfy us, that the species of security sought for in the multiplication of the executive is unattainable. Numbers must be so great as to render combination difficult; or they are rather a source of danger than of security. The united credit and influence of several individuals must be more formidable to liberty than the credit and influence of either of them separately. When power therefore is placed in the hands of so small a number of men, as to admit of their interests and views being easily combined in a common enterprise, by an artful leader, it becomes more liable to abuse and more dangerous when abused, than if it be lodged in the hands of one man; who from the very circumstance of his being alone will be more narrowly watched and more readily suspected, and who cannot unite so great a mass of influence as when he is associated with others. The Decemvirs of Rome, whose name denotes their number,* were more to be dreaded in their usurpation than any ONE of them would have been. No person would think of proposing an executive much more numerous than that body, from six to a dozen have been suggested for the number of the council. The extreme of these numbers is not too great for an easy combination; and from such a combination America would have more to fear, than from the ambition of any single individual. A council to a magistrate, who is himself responsible for what he does, are generally nothing better than a clog upon his good intentions, are often the instruments and accomplices of his bad, and are almost always a cloak to his faults.

I forbear to dwell upon the subject of expence; though it be evident that if the council should be numerous enough to answer the principal end, aimed at by the institution, the salaries of the members, who must be drawn from their homes to reside at the seat of government, would form an item in the catalogue of public expenditures, too serious to be incurred for an object of equivocal utility.

* Ten.

I will only add, that prior to the appearance of the constitution, I rarely met with an intelligent man from any of the
states, who did not admit as the result of experience, that the
UNITY of the Executive of this state was one of the best of
the distinguishing features of our constitution.

PUBLIUS.

The Independent Journal, March 15, 1788

The Federalist No. 71

Duration in office has been mentioned as the second requisite to the energy of the executive authority. This has relation to two objects: To the personal firmness of the Executive Magistrate in the employment of his constitutional powers; and to the stability of the system of administration which may have been adopted under his auspices. With regard to the first, it must be evident, that the longer the duration in office, the greater will be the probability of obtaining so important an advantage. It is a general principle of human nature, that a man will be interested in whatever he possesses, in proportion to the firmness or precariousness of the tenure, by which he holds it; will be less attached to what he holds by a momentary or uncertain title, than to what he enjoys by a durable or certain title; and of course will be willing to risk more for the sake of the one, than for the sake of the other. This remark is not less applicable to a political privilege, or honor, or trust, than to any article of ordinary property. The inference from it is, that a man acting in the capacity of Chief Magistrate, under a consciousness, that in a very short time he *must* lay down his office, will be apt to feel himself too little interested in it, to hazard any material censure or perplexity, from the independent exertion of his powers, or from encountering the ill-humors, however transient, which may happen to prevail either in a considerable part of the society itself, or even in a predominant faction in the legislative body. If the case should only be, that he *might* lay it down, unless continued by a new choice; and if he should be desirous of being continued, his wishes conspiring with his fears would tend still more powerfully to corrupt his integrity, or debase his fortitude. In either case feebleness and irresolution must be the characteristics of the station.

There are some, who would be inclined to regard the servile pliancy of the executive to a prevailing current, either in the community, or in the Legislature, as its best recommendation. But such men entertain very crude notions, as well of the purposes for which government was instituted, as of the true means by which the public happiness may be promoted. The republican principle demands, that the deliberate sense of the community should govern the conduct of those to whom they entrust the management of their affairs; but it does not require an unqualified complaisance to every sudden breese of passion, or to every transient impulse which the people may receive from the arts of men, who flatter their prejudices to betray their interests. It is a just observation, that the people commonly *intend* the PUBLIC GOOD. This often applies to their very errors. But their good sense would despise the adulator, who should pretend that they always *reason right* about the *means* of promoting it. They know from experience, that they sometimes err; and the wonder is, that they so seldom err as they do; beset as they continually are by the wiles of parasites and sycophants, by the snares of the ambitious, the avaricious, the desperate; by the artifices of men, who possess their confidence more than they deserve it, and of those who seek to possess, rather than to deserve it. When occasions present themselves in which the interests of the people are at variance with their inclinations, it is the duty of the persons whom they have appointed to be the guardians of those interests, to withstand the temporary delusion, in order to give them time and opportunity for more cool and sedate reflection. Instances might be cited, in which a conduct of this kind has saved the people from very fatal consequences of their own mistakes, and has procured lasting monuments of their gratitude to the men, who had courage and magnanimity enough to serve them at the peril of their displeasure.

But however inclined we might be to insist upon an unbounded complaisance in the executive to the inclinations of the people, we can with no propriety contend for a like complaisance to the humors of the Legislature. The latter may sometimes stand in opposition to the former; and at other times the people may be entirely neutral. In either supposition, it is certainly desirable that the executive should be in a situation to dare to act his own opinion with vigor and decision.

The same rule, which teaches the propriety of a partition between the various branches of power, teaches us likewise that this partition ought to be so contrived as to render the one independent of the other. To what purpose separate the executive, or the judiciary, from the legislative, if both the executive and the judiciary are so constituted as to be at the absolute devotion of the legislative? Such a separation must be merely nominal and incapable of producing the ends for which it was established. It is one thing to be subordinate to the laws, and another to be dependent on the legislative body. The first comports with, the last violates, the fundamental principles of good government; and whatever may be the forms of the Constitution, unites all power in the same hands. The tendency of the legislative authority to absorb every other, has been fully displayed and illustrated by examples, in some preceding numbers. In governments purely republican, this tendency is almost irresistable. The representatives of the people, in a popular assembly, seem sometimes to fancy that they are the people themselves; and betray strong symptoms of impatience and disgust at the least sign of opposition from any other quarter; as if the exercise of its rights by either the executive or judiciary, were a breach of their privilege and an outrage to their dignity. They often appear disposed to exert an imperious controul over the other departments; and as they commonly have the people on their side, they always act with such momentum as to make it very difficult for the other members of the government to maintain the balance of the Constitution.

It may perhaps be asked how the shortness of the duration in office can affect the independence of the executive on the legislature, unless the one were possessed of the power of appointing or displacing the other? One answer to this enquiry may be drawn from the principle already remarked, that is from the slender interest a man is apt to take in a short lived advantage, and the little inducement it affords him to expose himself on account of it to any considerable inconvenience or hazard. Another answer, perhaps more obvious, though not more conclusive, will result from the consideration of the influence of the legislative body over the people, which might be employed to prevent the re-election of a man, who by an upright resistance to any sinister project of that body, should have made himself obnoxious to its resentment.

It may be asked also whether a duration of four years would answer the end proposed, and if it would not, whether a less period which would at least be recommended by greater security against ambitious designs, would not for that reason be preferable to a longer period, which was at the same time too short for the purpose of inspiring the desired firmness and independence of the magistrate?

It cannot be affirmed, that a duration of four years or any other limited duration would completely answer the end proposed; but it would contribute towards it in a degree which would have a material influence upon the spirit and character of the government. Between the commencement and termination of such a period there would always be a considerable interval, in which the prospect of annihilation would be sufficiently remote not to have an improper effect upon the conduct of a man endued with a tolerable portion of fortitude; and in which he might reasonably promise himself, that there would be time enough, before it arrived, to make the community sensible of the propriety of the measures he might incline to pursue. Though it be probable, that as he approached the moment when the public were by a new election to signify their sense of his conduct, his confidence and with it, his firmness would decline; yet both the one and the other would derive support from the opportunities, which his previous continuance in the station had afforded him of establishing himself in the esteem and good will of his constituents. He might then hazard with safety, in proportion to the proofs he had given of his wisdom and integrity, and to the title he had acquired to the respect and attachment of his fellow citizens. As on the one hand, a duration of four years will contribute to the firmness of the executive in a sufficient degree to render it a very valuable ingredient in the composition; so on the other, it is not long enough to justify any alarm for the public liberty. If a British House of Commons, from the most feeble beginnings, *from the mere power of assenting or disagreeing to the imposition of a new tax*, have by rapid strides, reduced the prerogatives of the crown and the privileges of the nobility within the limits they conceived to be compatible with the principles of a free government; while they raised themselves to the rank and consequence of a coequal branch of the Legislature; if they have been able in one instance to abolish both the royalty and the aristocracy, and to overturn all the ancient establishments as well in the church as State; if they have been able on a recent occasion to make the monarch tremble at the prospect of an innovation* attempted by them; what would be to be feared from an elective magistrate of four years duration, with the confined authorities of a President of the United States? What but that he might be unequal to the task which the Constitution assigns him? I shall only add that if his duration be such as to leave a doubt of his firmness, that doubt is inconsistent with a jealousy of his encroachments.

PUBLIUS.

* This was the case with respect to Mr. Fox's India bill which was carried in the House of Commons, and rejected in the House of Lords, to the entire satisfaction, as it is said, of the people.

The New-York Packet, March 18, 1788

The Federalist No. 72

The administration of government, in its largest sense, comprehends all the operations of the body politic, whether legislative, executive or judiciary, but in its most usual and perhaps in its most precise signification, it is limited to executive details, and falls peculiarly within the province of the executive department. The actual conduct of foreign negotiations, the preparatory plans of finance, the application and disbursement of the public monies, in conformity to the general appropriations of the legislature, the arrangement of the army and navy, the direction of the operations of war; these and other matters of a like nature constitute what seems to be most properly understood by the administration of government. The persons therefore, to whose immediate management these different matters are committed, ought to be considered as the assistants or deputies of the chief magistrate; and, on this account, they ought to derive their offices from his appointment, at least from his nomination, and ought to be subject to his superintendence. This view of the subject will at once suggest to us the intimate connection between the duration of the executive magistrate in office, and the stability of the system of administration. To reverse and undo what has been done by a predecessor is very often considered by a successor, as the best proof he can give of his own capacity and desert; and, in addition to this propensity, where the alteration has been the result of public choice, the person substituted is warranted in supposing, that the dismission of his predecessor has proceeded from a dislike to his measures, and that the less he resembles him the more he will recommend himself to the favor of his constituents. These considerations, and the influence of personal confidences and attachments, would be likely to induce every new president to promote a change of men to fill the subordinate stations; and these causes together could not fail to occasion a disgraceful and ruinous mutability in the administration of the government.

With a positive duration of considerable extent, I connect the circumstance of re-eligibility. The first is necessary to give to the officer himself the inclination and the resolution to act his part well, and to the community time and leisure to observe the tendency of his measures, and thence to form an experimental estimate of their merits. The last is necessary to enable the people, when they see reason to approve of his conduct, to continue him in the station, in order to prolong the utility of his talents and virtues, and to secure to the government, the advantage of permanency in a wise system of administration.

Nothing appears more plausible at first sight, nor more ill founded upon close inspection, than a scheme, which in relation to the present point has had some respectable advocates—I mean that of continuing the chief magistrate in office for a certain time, and then excluding him from it, either for a limited period, or for ever after. This exclusion whether temporary or perpetual would have nearly the same effects; and these effects would be for the most part rather pernicious than salutary.

One ill effect of the exclusion would be a diminution of the inducements to good behaviour. There are few men who would not feel much less zeal in the discharge of a duty, when they were conscious that the advantages of the station, with which it was connected, must be relinquished at a determinate period, than when they were permitted to entertain a hope of *obtaining* by *meriting* a continuance of them. This position will not be disputed, so long as it is admitted that the desire of reward is one of the strongest incentives of human conduct, or that the best security for the fidelity of mankind is to make their interest coincide with their duty. Even the love of fame, the ruling passion of the noblest minds, which would prompt a man to plan and undertake extensive and arduous enterprises for the public benefit, requiring considerable time to mature and perfect them, if he could flatter himself with the prospect of being allowed to finish what he had begun, would on the contrary deter him from the undertaking, when he foresaw that he must quit the scene, before he could accomplish the work, and must commit that, together with his own reputation, to hands which might be unequal or unfriendly to the task. The most to be expected from the generality of men, in such a situation, is the negative merit of not doing harm instead of the positive merit of doing good.

Another ill effect of the exclusion would be the temptation to sordid views, to peculation, and in some instances, the usurpation. An avaricious man, who might happen to fill the offices, looking forward to a time when he must at all events yield up the emoluments he enjoyed, would feel a propensity, not easy to be resisted by such a man, to make the best use of the opportunity he enjoyed, while it lasted; and might not scruple to have recourse to the most corrupt expedients to make the harvest as abundant as it was transitory; though the same man probably, with a different prospect before him, might content himself with the regular perquisites of his station, and might even be unwilling to risk the consequences of an abuse of his opportunities. His avarice might be a guard upon his avarice. Add to this, that the same man might be vain or ambitious as well as avaricious. And if he could expect to prolong his honors, by his good conduct, he might hesitate to sacrifice his appetite for them to his appetite for gain. But with the prospect before him of approaching and inevitable annihilation, his avarice would be likely to get the victory over his caution, his vanity or his ambition.

An ambitious man too, when he found himself seated on the summit of his country's honors, when he looked forward to the time at which he must descend from the exalted eminence forever; and reflected that no exertion of merit on his part could save him from the unwelcome reverse: Such a man, in such a situation, would be much more violently tempted to embrace a favorable conjuncture for attempting the prolongation of his power, at every personal hazard, than if he had the probability of answering the same end by doing his duty.

Would it promote the peace of the community, or the stability of the government, to have half a dozen men who had had credit enough to be raised to the seat of the supreme magistracy, wandering among the people like discontented ghosts, and sighing for a place which they were destined never more to possess?

A third ill effect of the exclusion would be the depriving the community of the advantage of the experience gained by the chief magistrate in the exercise of his office. That experience is the parent of wisdom is an adage, the truth of which is recognized by the wisest as well as the simplest of mankind. What more desirable or more essential than this quality in the governors of nations? Where more desirable or more essential than in the first magistrate of a nation? Can it be wise to put this desirable and essential quality under the ban of the constitution; and to declare that the moment it is acquired, its possessor shall be compelled to abandon the station in which it was acquired, and to which it is adapted? This nevertheless is the precise import of all those regulations, which exclude men from serving their country, by the choice of their fellow citizens, after they have, by a course of service fitted themselves for doing it with a greater degree of utility.

A fourth ill effect of the exclusion would be the banishing men from stations, in which in certain emergencies of the state their presence might be of the greatest moment to the public interest or safety. There is no nation which has not at one period or another experienced an absolute necessity of the services of particular men, in particular situations, perhaps it would not be too strong to say, to the preservation of its political existence. How unwise therefore must be every such self-denying ordinance, as serves to prohibit a nation from making use of its own citizens, in the manner best suited to its exigences and circumstances! Without supposing the personal essentiality of the man, it is evident that a change of the chief magistrate, at the breaking out of a war, or at any similar crisis, for another even of equal merit, would at all times be detrimental to the community; inasmuch as it would substitute inexperience to experience, and would tend to unhinge and set afloat the already settled train of the administration.

A fifth ill effect of the exclusion would be, that it would operate as a constitutional interdiction of stability in the administration. *By necessitating* a change of men, in the first office in the nation, it would necessitate a mutability of measures. It is not generally to be expected, that men will vary; and measures remain uniform. The contrary is the usual course of things. And we need not be apprehensive there will be too much stability, while there is even the option of changing; nor need we desire to prohibit the people from continuing their confidence, where they think it may be safely placed, and where by constancy on their part, they may obviate the fatal inconveniences of fluctuating councils and a variable policy.

These are some of the disadvantages, which would flow from the principle of exclusion. They apply most forcibly to the scheme of a perpetual exclusion; but when we consider that even a partial exclusion would always render the re-admission of the person a remote and precarious object, the observations which have been made will apply nearly as fully to one case as to the other.

What are the advantages promised to counterballance these disadvantages? They are represented to be 1st. Greater independence in the magistrate: 2dly. Greater security to the people. Unless the exclusion be perpetual there will be no pretence to infer the first advantage. But even in that case, may he have no object beyond his present station to which he may sacrifice his independence? May he have no connections, no friends, for whom he may sacrifice it? May he not be less willing, by a firm conduct, to make personal enemies, when he acts under the impression, that a time is fast approaching, on the arrival of which he not only MAY, but MUST be exposed to their resentments, upon an equal, perhaps upon an inferior footing? It is not an easy point to determine whether his independence would be most promoted or impaired by such an arrangement.

As to the second supposed advantage, there is still greater reason to entertain doubts concerning it. If the exclusion were to be perpetual, a man of irregular ambition, of whom alone there could be reason in any case to entertain apprehensions, would with infinite reluctance yield to the necessity of taking his leave forever of a post, in which his passion for power and pre-eminence had acquired the force of habit. And if he had been fortunate or adroit enough to conciliate the good will of people he might induce them to consider as a very odious and unjustifiable restraint upon themselves, a provision which was calculated to debar them of the right of giving a fresh proof of their attachment to a favorite. There may be conceived circumstances, in which this disgust of the people, seconding the thwarted ambition of such a favour-ite, might occasion greater danger to liberty, than could ever reasonably be dreaded from the possibility of a perpetuation in office, by the voluntary suffrages of the community, exercising a constitutional privilege.

There is an excess of refinement in the idea of disabling the people to continue in office men, who had entitled themselves, in their opinion, to approbation and confidence; the advantages of which are at best speculative and equivocal; and are over-balanced by disadvantages far more certain and decisive.

PUBLIUS.

The Independent Journal, March 19, 1788

The Federalist No. 73

To the People of the State of New-York.

The third ingredient towards constituting the vigor of the executive authority is an adequate provision for its support. It is evident that without proper attention to this article, the separation of the executive from the legislative department would be merely nominal and nugatory. The Legislature, with a discretionary power over the salary and emoluments of the Chief Magistrate, could render him as obsequious to their will, as they might think proper to make him. They might in most cases either reduce him by famine, or tempt him by largesses, to surrender at discretion his judgment to their inclinations. These expressions taken in all the latitude of the terms would no doubt convey more than is intended. There are men who could neither be distressed nor won into a sacrifice of their duty; but this stern virtue is the growth of few soils: And in the main it will be found, that a power over a man's support is a power over his will. If it were necessary to confirm so plain a truth by facts, examples would not be wanting, even in this country, of the intimidation or seduction of the executive by the terrors, or allurements, of the pecuniary arrangements of the legislative body.

It is not easy therefore to commend too highly the judicious attention which has been paid to this subject in the proposed Constitution. It is there provided that "The President of the United States shall, at stated times, receive for his services a compensation, *which shall neither be increased nor diminished, during the period for which he shall have been elected,* and he shall *not receive within that period any other emolument* from the United States or any of them." It is impossible to imagine any provision which would have been more eligible than this. The Legislature on the appointment of a President is once for all to declare what shall be the compensation for his services during the time for which he shall have been elected. This done, they will have no power to alter it either by increase or diminution, till a new period of service by a new election commences.

They can neither weaken his fortitude by operating upon his necessities; nor corrupt his integrity, by appealing to his avarice. Neither the Union nor any of its members will be at liberty to give, nor will he be at liberty to receive any other emolument, than that which may have been determined by the first act. He can of course have no pecuniary inducement to renounce or desert the independence intended for him by the Constitution.

The last of the requisites to energy which have been enumerated are competent powers. Let us proceed to consider those which are proposed to be vested in the President of the United States.

The first thing that offers itself to our observation, is the qualified negative of the President upon the acts or resolutions of the two Houses of the Legislature; or in other words his power of returning all bills with objections; to have the effect of preventing their becoming laws, unless they should afterwards be ratified by two thirds of each of the component members of the legislative body.

The propensity of the legislative department to intrude upon the rights and to absorb the powers of the other departments, has been already suggested and repeated; the insufficiency of a mere parchment delineation of the boundaries of each, has also been remarked upon; and the necessity of furnishing each with constitutional arms for its own defence, has been inferred and proved. From these clear and indubitable principles results the propriety of a negative, either absolute or qualified, in the executive, upon the acts of the legislative branches. Without the one or the other the former would be absolutely unable to defend himself against the depredations of the latter. He might gradually be stripped of his authorities by successive resolutions, or annihilated by a single vote. And in the one mode or the other, the legislative and executive powers might speedily come to be blended in the same hands. If even no propensity had ever discovered itself in the legislative body, to invade the rights of the executive, the rules of just reasoning and theoretic propriety would of themselves teach us, that the one ought not to be left at the mercy of the other, but ought to possess a constitutional and effectual power of self defence.

But the power in question has a further use. It not only serves as a shield to the executive, but it furnishes an additional security against the enaction of improper laws. It establishes a salutary check upon the legislative body calculated to guard the community against the effects of faction, precipitancy, or of any impulse unfriendly to the public good, which may happen to influence a majority of that body.

The propriety of a negative, has upon some occasions been combated by an observation, that it was not to be presumed a single man would possess more virtue or wisdom, than a number of men; and that unless this presumption should be entertained, it would be improper to give the executive magistrate any species of controul over the legislative body.

But this observation when examined will appear rather specious than solid. The propriety of the thing does not turn upon the supposition of superior wisdom or virtue in the executive: But upon the supposition that the legislative will not be infallible: That the love of power may sometimes betray it into a disposition to encroach upon the rights of the other members of the government; that a spirit of faction may sometimes pervert its deliberations; that impressions of the moment may sometimes hurry it into measures which itself on maturer reflection would condemn. The primary inducement to conferring the power in question upon the executive, is to enable him to defend himself; the secondary one is to encrease the chances in favor of the community, against the passing of bad laws, through haste, inadvertence, or design. The oftener a measure is brought under examination, the greater the diversity in the situations of those who are to examine it, the less must be the danger of those errors which flow from want of due deliberation, or of those misteps which proceed from the contagion of some common passion or interest. It is far less probable, that culpable views of any kind should infect all the parts of the government, at the same moment and in relation to the same object, than that they should by turns govern and mislead every one of them.

It may perhaps be said, that the power of preventing bad laws includes that of preventing good ones; and may be used to the one purpose as well as to the other. But this objection will have little weight with those who can properly estimate the mischiefs of that inconstancy and mutability in the laws, which form the greatest blemish in the character and genius of our governments. They will consider every institution calculated to restrain the excess of law-making, and to keep things in the same state, in which they may happen to be at any given period, as much more likely to do good than harm; because it is favorable to greater stability in the system of legislation. The injury which may possibly be done by defeating a few good laws will be amply compensated by the advantage of preventing a number of bad ones.

Nor is this all. The superior weight and influence of the legislative body in a free government, and the hazard to the executive in a trial of strength with that body, afford a satisfactory security, that the negative would generally be employed with great caution, and that there would oftener be room for a charge of timidity than of rashness, in the exercise of it. A King of Great-Britain, with all his train of sovereign attributes, and with all the influence he draws from a thousand sources, would at this day hesitate to put a negative upon the joint resolutions of the two houses of Parliament. He would not fail to exert the utmost resources of that influence to strangle a measure disagreeable to him, in its progress to the throne, to avoid being reduced to the dilemma of permitting it to take effect, or of risking the displeasure of the nation, by an opposition to the sense of the legislative body. Nor is it probable that he would ultimately venture to exert his prerogative, but in a case of manifest propriety, or extreme necessity. All well informed men in that kingdom will accede to the justness of this remark. A very considerable period has elapsed since the negative of the crown has been exercised.

If a magistrate, so powerful and so well fortified as a British monarch, would have scruples about the exercise of the power under consideration, how much greater caution may be reasonably expected in a President of the United States, cloathed for the short period of four years with the executive authority of a government wholly and purely republican?

It is evident that there would be greater danger of his not using his power when necessary, than of his using it too often, or too much. An argument indeed against its expediency has been drawn from this very source. It has been represented on

this account as a power odious in appearance; useless in practice. But it will not follow, that because it might be rarely exercised, it would never be exercised. In the case for which it is
chiefly designed, that of an immediate attack upon the constitutional rights of the executive, or in a case in which the
public good was evidently and palpably sacrificed, a man of
tolerable firmness would avail himself of his constitutional
means of defence, and would listen to the admonitions of duty
and responsibility. In the former supposition, his fortitude
would be stimulated by his immediate interest in the power of
his office; in the latter by the probability of the sanction of his
constituents; who though they would naturally incline to the
legislative body in a doubtful case, would hardly suffer their
partiality to delude them in a very plain case. I speak now with
an eye to a magistrate possessing only a common share of firmness. There are men, who under any circumstances will have
the courage to do their duty at every hazard.

But the Convention have pursued a mean in this business;
which will both facilitate the exercise of the power vested in
this respect in the executive magistrate, and make its efficacy to
depend on the sense of a considerable part of the legislative
body. Instead of an absolute negative, it is proposed to give the
executive the qualified negative already described. This is a
power, which would be much more readily exercised than the
other. A man who might be afraid to defeat a law by his single
VETO, might not scruple to return it for re-consideration;
subject to being finally rejected only in the event of more than
one third of each house concurring in the sufficiency of his objections. He would be encouraged by the reflection, that if his
opposition should prevail, it would embark in it a very respectable proportion of the legislative body, whose influence
would be united with his in supporting the propriety of his
conduct, in the public opinion. A direct and categorical negative has something in the appearance of it more harsh, and
more apt to irritate, than the mere suggestion of argumenta-
tive objections to be approved or disapproved, by those to
whom they are addressed. In proportion as it would be less apt
to offend, it would be more apt to be exercised; and for this
very reason it may in practice be found more effectual. It is to
be hoped that it will not often happen, that improper views will

govern so large a proportion as two-thirds of both branches of the Legislature at the same time; and this too in defiance of the counterpoising weight of the executive. It is at any rate far less probable, that this should be the case, than that such views should taint the resolutions and conduct of a bare majority. A power of this nature, in the executive, will often have a silent and unperceived though forcible operation. When men engaged in unjustifiable pursuits are aware, that obstructions may come from a quarter which they cannot controul, they will often be restrained, by the bare apprehension of opposition, from doing what they would with eagerness rush into, if no such external impediments were to be feared.

This qualified negative, as has been elsewhere remarked, is in this State vested in a council, consisting of the Governor, with the Chancellor and Judges of the Supreme Court, or any two of them. It has been freely employed upon a variety of occasions, and frequently with success. And its utility has become so apparent, that persons who in compiling the Constitution were violent opposers of it, have from experience become its declared admirers.*

I have in another place remarked, that the Convention in the formation of this part of their plan, had departed from the model of the Constitution of this State, in favor of that of Massachusetts—two strong reasons may be imagined for this preference. One is that the Judges, who are to be the interpreters of the law, might receive an improper bias from having given a previous opinion in their revisionary capacities. The other is that by being often associated with the executive they might be induced to embark too far in the political views of that magistrate, and thus a dangerous combination might by degrees be cemented between the executive and judiciary departments. It is impossible to keep the Judges too distinct from every other avocation than that of expounding the laws. It is peculiarly dangerous to place them in a situation to be either corrupted or influenced by the executive.

PUBLIUS.

* Mr. Abraham Yates, a warm opponent of the plan of the Convention, is of this number.

The New-York Packet, March 21, 1788

The Federalist No. 74

To the People of the State of New-York.

The President of the United States is to be "Commander in Chief of the army and navy of the United States, and of the militia of the several States *when called into the actual service* of the United States." The propriety of this provision is so evident in itself; and it is at the same time so consonant to the precedents of the State constitutions in general, that little need be said to explain or enforce it. Even those of them, which have in other respects coupled the Chief Magistrate with a Council, have for the most part concentrated the military authority in him alone. Of all the cares or concerns of government, the direction of war most peculiarly demands those qualities which distinguish the exercise of power by a single hand. The direction of war implies the direction of the common strength; and the power of directing and employing the common strength, forms an usual and essential part in the definition of the executive authority.

"The President may require the opinion in writing of the principal officer in each of the executive departments upon any subject relating to the duties of their respective offices." This I consider as a mere redundancy in the plan; as the right for which it provides would result of itself from the office.

He is also to be authorised "to grant reprieves and pardons for offences against the United States *except in cases of impeachment.*" Humanity and good policy conspire to dictate, that the benign prerogative for pardoning should be as little as possible fettered or embarrassed. The criminal code of every country partakes so much of necessary severity, that without an easy access to exceptions in favor of unfortunate guilt, justice would wear a countenance too sanguinary and cruel. As the sense of responsibility is always strongest in proportion as it is undivided, it may be inferred that a single man would be most ready to attend to the force of those motives, which might plead for a mitigation of the rigor of the law, and least apt to yield to considerations, which were calculated to shelter a fit object of its vengeance. The reflection, that the fate of a fellow creature depended on his *sole fiat*, would naturally inspire scrupulousness and caution: The dread of being accused of weakness or connivance would beget equal circumspection, though of a different kind. On the other hand, as men generally derive confidence from their numbers, they might often encourage each other in an act of obduracy, and might be less sensible to the apprehension of suspicion or censure for an injudicious or affected clemency. On these accounts, one man appears to be a more eligible dispenser of the mercy of the government than a body of men.

The expediency of vesting the power of pardoning in the President has, if I mistake not, been only contested in relation to the crime of treason. This, it has been urged, ought to have depended upon the assent of one or both of the branches of the legislative body. I shall not deny that there are strong reasons to be assigned for requiring in this particular the concurrence of that body or of a part of it. As treason is a crime levelled at the immediate being of the society, when the laws have once ascertained the guilt of the offender, there seems a fitness in refering the expediency of an act of mercy towards him to the judgment of the Legislature. And this ought the rather to be the case, as the supposition of the connivance of the Chief Magistrate ought not to be entirely excluded. But there are also strong objections to such a plan. It is not to be doubted that a single man of prudence and good sense, is better fitted, in delicate conjunctures, to balance the motives, which may plead for and against the remission of the punishment, than any numerous body whatever. It deserves particular attention, that treason will often be connected with seditions, which embrace a large proportion of the community; as lately happened in Massachusetts. In every such case, we might expect to see the representation of the people tainted with the same spirit, which had given birth to the offense. And when parties were pretty equally matched, the secret sympathy of the friends and favorers of the condemned person, availing itself of the good nature and weakness of others, might frequently bestow impunity where the terror of an example was necessary. On the other hand, when the sedition had proceeded from causes which had inflamed the resentments of the major party, they might often be found obstinate

and inexorable, when policy demanded a conduct of forbearance and clemency. But the principal argument for reposing
the power of pardoning in this case in the Chief Magistrate is
this—In seasons of insurrection or rebellion, there are often
critical moments, when a well timed offer of pardon to the insurgents or rebels may restore the tranquility of the commonwealth; and which, if suffered to pass unimproved, it may
never be possible afterwards to recall. The dilatory process of
convening the Legislature, or one of its branches, for the purpose of obtaining its sanction to the measure, would frequently be the occasion of letting slip the golden opportunity.
The loss of a week, a day, an hour, may sometimes be fatal. If
it should be observed that a discretionary power with a view
to such contingencies might be occasionally conferred upon
the President; it may be answered in the first place, that it is
questionable whether, in a limited constitution, that power
could be delegated by law; and in the second place, that it
would generally be impolitic before-hand to take any step
which might hold out the prospect of impunity. A proceeding
of this kind, out of the usual course, would be likely to be
construed into an argument of timidity or of weakness, and
would have a tendency to embolden guilt.

PUBLIUS.

The New-York Packet, March 25, 1788

The Federalist No. 75

The president is to have power "by and with the advice and consent of the senate, to make treaties, provided two-thirds of the senators present concur." Though this provision has been assailed on different grounds, with no small degree of vehemence, I scruple not to declare my firm persuasion, that it is one of the best digested and most unexceptionable parts of the plan. One ground of objection is, the trite topic of the intermixture of powers; some contending that the president ought alone to possess the power of making treaties; and others, that it ought to have been exclusively deposited in the senate. Another source of objection is derived from the small number of persons by whom a treaty may be made: Of those who espouse this objection, a part are of opinion that the house of representatives ought to have been associated in the business, while another part seem to think that nothing more was necessary than to have substituted two-thirds of *all* the members of the senate to two-thirds of the members *present.* As I flatter myself the observations made in a preceding number, upon this part of the plan, must have sufficed to place it to a discerning eye in a very favourable light, I shall here content myself with offering only some supplementary remarks, principally with a view to the objections which have been just stated.

With regard to the intermixture of powers, I shall rely upon the explanations already given, in other places of the true sense of the rule, upon which that objection is founded; and shall take it for granted, as an inference from them, that the union of the executive with the senate, in the article of treaties, is no infringement of that rule. I venture to add that the particular nature of the power of making treaties indicates a peculiar propriety in that union. Though several writers on the subject of government place that power in the class of executive authorities, yet this is evidently an arbitrary disposition: For if we attend carefully to its operation, it will be found to partake more of the legislative than of the executive character, though it does not seem strictly to fall within the definition of either of them. The essence of the legislative authority is to enact laws, or in other words to prescribe rules for the regulation of the society, while the execution of the laws and the employment of the common strength, either for this purpose or for the common defence, seem to comprise all the functions of the executive magistrate. The power of making treaties is plainly neither the one nor the other. It relates neither to the execution of the subsisting laws, nor to the enaction of new ones, and still less to an exertion of the common strength. Its objects are CONTRACTS with foreign nations, which have the force of law, but derive it from the obligations of good faith. They are not rules prescribed by the sovereign to the subject, but agreements between sovereign and sovereign. The power in question seems therefore to form a distinct department, and to belong properly neither to the legislative nor to the executive. The qualities elsewhere detailed, as indispensable in the management of foreign negotiations, point out the executive as the most fit agent in those transactions; while the vast importance of the trust, and the operation of treaties as laws, plead strongly for the participation of the whole or a part of the legislative body in the office of making them.

However proper or safe it may in governments where the executive magistrate is an hereditary monarch, to commit to him the entire power of making treaties, it would be utterly unsafe and improper to entrust that power to an elective magistrate for four years duration. It has been remarked upon another occasion, and the remark is unquestionably just, that an hereditary monarch, though often the oppressor of his people, has personally too much at stake in the government to be in any material danger of being corrupted by foreign powers. But a man raised from the station of a private citizen to the rank of chief magistrate, possessed of but a moderate or slender fortune, and looking forward to a period not very remote, when he may probably be obliged to return to the station from which he was taken, might sometimes be under temptations to sacrifice his duty to his interest, which it would require superlative virtue to withstand. An avaricious man might be tempted to betray the interests of the state to the acquisition of wealth. An ambitious man might make his own aggrandizement, by the aid of a foreign power, the price of his treachery to his constituents. The history of human conduct does not warrant that exalted opinion of human virtue which would make it wise in a nation to commit interests of so delicate and momentous a kind as those which concern its intercourse with the rest of the world to the sole disposal of a magistrate, created and circumstanced, as would be a president of the United States.

To have entrusted the power of making treaties to the senate alone, would have been to relinquish the benefits of the constitutional agency of the president, in the conduct of foreign negotiations. It is true, that the senate would in that case have the option of employing him in this capacity; but they would also have the option of letting it alone; and pique or cabal might induce the latter rather than the former. Besides this, the ministerial servant of the senate could not be expected to enjoy the confidence and respect of foreign powers in the same degree with the constitutional representative of the nation; and of course would not be able to act with an equal degree of weight or efficacy. While the union would from this cause lose a considerable advantage in the management of its external concerns, the people would lose the additional security, which would result from the co-operation of the executive. Though it would be imprudent to confide in him solely so important a trust; yet it cannot be doubted, that his participation in it would materially add to the safety of the society. It must indeed be clear to a demonstration, that the joint possession of the power in question by the president and senate would afford a greater prospect of security, than the separate possession of it by either of them. And whoever has maturely weighed the circumstances, which must concur in the appointment of a president will be satisfied, that the office will always bid fair to be filled by men of such characters as to render their concurrence in the formation of treaties peculiarly desirable, as well on the score of wisdom as on that of integrity.

The remarks made in a former number, which has been alluded to in an other part of this paper, will apply with conclusive force against the admission of the house of representatives to a share in the formation of treaties. The fluctuating and taking its future increase into the account, the multitudinous composition of that body, forbid us to expect in it those qualities which are essential to the proper execution of such a trust. Accurate and comprehensive knowledge of foreign politics; a steady and systematic adherence to the same views; a nice and uniform sensibility to national character, decision, *secrecy* and dispatch; are incompatible with the genius of a body so variable and so numerous. The very complication of the business by introducing a necessity of the concurrence of so many different bodies, would of itself afford a solid objection. The greater frequency of the calls upon the house of representatives, and the greater length of time which it would often be necessary to keep them together when convened, to obtain their sanction in the progressive stages of a treaty, would be source of so great inconvenience and expence, as alone ought to condemn the project.

The only objection which remains to be canvassed is that which would substitute the proportion of two thirds of all the members composing the senatorial body to that of two thirds of the members *present*. It has been shewn under the second head of our inquiries that all provisions which require more than the majority of any body to its resolutions have a direct tendency to embarrass the operations of the government and an indirect one to subject the sense of the majority to that of the minority. This consideration seems sufficient to determine our opinion, that the convention have gone as far in the endeavour to secure the advantage of numbers in the formation of treaties as could have been reconciled either with the activity of the public councils or with a reasonable regard to the major sense of the community. If two thirds of the whole number of members had been required, it would in many cases from the non attendance of a part amount in practice to a necessity of unanimity. And the history of every political establishment in which this principle has prevailed is a history of impotence, perplexity and disorder. Proofs of this position might be adduced from the examples of the Roman tribuneship, the Polish diet and the states general of the Netherlands; did not an example at home render foreign precedents unnecessary.

To require a fixed proportion of the whole body would not in all probability contribute to the advantages of a numerous agency, better than merely to require a proportion of the attending members. The former by making a determinate number at all times requisite to a resolution diminishes the motives to punctual attendance. The latter by making the capacity of the body to depend on a *proportion* which may be varied by the absence or presence of a single member, has the contrary effect. And as, by promoting punctuality, it tends to keep the body complete, there is great likelihood that its resolutions would generally be dictated by as great a number in this case as in the other; while there would be much fewer occasions of delay. It ought not to be forgotten that under the existing confederation two members *may* and usually *do* represent a state; whence it happens that Congress, who now are solely invested with *all the powers* of the union, rarely consists of a greater number of persons than would compose the intended senate. If we add to this, that as the members vote by states, and that where there is only a single member present from a state, his vote is lost, it will justify a supposition that the active voices in the senate, where the members are to vote individually, would rarely fall short in number of the active voices in the existing Congress. When in addition to these considerations we take into view the co-operation of the president, we shall not hesitate to infer that the people of America would have greater security against an improper use of the power of making treaties, under the new constitution, than they now enjoy under the confederation. And when we proceed still one step further, and look forward to the probable augmentation of the senate, by the erection of new states, we shall not only perceive ample ground of confidence in the sufficiency of the numbers, to whose agency that power will be entrusted; but we shall probably be led to conclude that a body more numerous than the senate would be likely to become, would be very little fit for the proper discharge of the trust.

PUBLIUS.

The Independent Journal, March 26, 1788

The Federalist No. 76

To the People of the State of New-York.

The President is "to *nominate* and by and with the advice and consent of the Senate to appoint Ambassadors, other public Ministers and Consuls, Judges of the Supreme Court, and all other officers of the United States, whose appointments are not otherwise provided for in the Constitution. But the Congress may by law vest the appointment of such inferior officers as they think proper in the President alone, or in the Courts of law, or in the heads of departments. The President shall have power to fill up *all vacancies* which may happen *during the recess of the Senate*, by granting commissions which shall *expire* at the end of their next session."

It has been observed in a former paper, "that the true test of a good government is its aptitude and tendency to produce a good administration." If the justness of this observation be admitted, the mode of appointing the officers of the United States contained in the foregoing clauses, must when examined be allowed to be entitled to particular commendation. It is not easy to conceive a plan better calculated than this, to produce a judicious choice of men for filling the offices of the Union; and it will not need proof, that on this point must essentially depend the character of its administration.

It will be agreed on all hands, that the power of appointment in ordinary cases ought to be modified in one of three ways. It ought either to be vested in a single man—or in a *select* assembly of a moderate number—or in a single man with the concurrence of such an assembly. The exercise of it by the people at large, will be readily admitted to be impracticable; as, waving every other consideration it would leave them little time to do any thing else. When therefore mention is made in the subsequent reasonings of an assembly or body of men, what is said must be understood to relate to a select body or assembly of the description already given. The people collectively from their number and from their dispersed situation cannot be regulated in their movements by that systematic spirit of cabal and intrigue, which will be urged as the chief objections to reposing the power in question in a body of men.

Those who have themselves reflected upon the subject, or who have attended to the observations made in other parts of these papers, in relation to the appointment of the President, will I presume agree to the position that there would always be great probability of having the place supplied by a man of abilities, at least respectable. Premising this, I proceed to lay it down as a rule, that one man of discernment is better fitted to analise and estimate the peculiar qualities adapted to particular offices, than a body of men of equal, or perhaps even of superior discernment.

The sole and undivided responsibility of one man will naturally beget a livelier sense of duty and a more exact regard to reputation. He will on this account feel himself under stronger obligations, and more interested to investigate with care the qualities requisite to the stations to be filled, and to prefer with impartiality the persons who may have the fairest pretentions to them. He will have *fewer* personal attachments to gratify than a body of men, who may each be supposed to have an equal number, and will be so much the less liable to be misled by the sentiments of friendship and of affection. A single well directed man by a single understanding, cannot be distracted and warped by that diversity of views, feelings and interests, which frequently distract and warp the resolutions of a collective body. There is nothing so apt to agitate the passions of mankind as personal considerations, whether they relate to ourselves or to others, who are to be the objects of our choice or preference. Hence, in every exercise of the power of appointing to offices by an assembly of men, we must expect to see a full display of all the private and party likings and dislikes, partialities and antipathies, attachments and animosities, which are felt by those who compose the assembly. The choice which may at any time happen to be made under such circumstances will of course be the result either of a victory gained by one party over the other, or of a compromise between the parties. In either case, the intrinsic merit of the candidate will be too often out of sight. In the first, the qualifications best adapted to uniting the suffrages of the party will be more considered than those which fit the person for the station. In the last the coalition will commonly turn upon some interested equivalent—"Give us the man we wish for this office, and you shall have the one you wish for that." This will be the usual condition of the bargain. And it will rarely happen that the advancement of the public service will be the primary object either of party victories or of party negociations.

The truth of the principles here advanced seems to have been felt by the most intelligent of those who have found fault with the provision made in this respect by the Convention. They contend that the President ought solely to have been authorized to make the appointments under the Fœderal Government. But it is easy to shew that every advantage to be expected from such an arrangement would in substance be derived from the power of *nomination*, which is proposed to be conferred upon him; while several disadvantages which might attend the absolute power of appointment in the hands of that officer, would be avoided. In the act of nomination his judgment alone would be exercised; and as it would be his sole duty to point out the man, who with the approbation of the Senate should fill an office, his responsibility would be as complete as if he were to make the final appointment. There can in this view be no difference between nominating and appointing. The same motives which would influence a proper discharge of his duty in one case would exist in the other. And as no man could be appointed, but upon his previous nomination, every man who might be appointed would be in fact his choice.

But might not his nomination be overruled? I grant it might, yet this could only be to make place for another nomination by himself. The person ultimately appointed must be the object of his preference, though perhaps not in the first degree. It is also not very probable that his nomination would often be overruled. The Senate could not be tempted by the preference they might feel to another to reject the one proposed; because they could not assure themselves that the person they might wish would be brought forward by a second or by any subsequent nomination. They could not even be certain that a future nomination would present a candidate in any degree more acceptable to them: And as their dissent might cast a kind of stigma upon the individual rejected; and might have the appearance of a reflection upon the judgment of the chief magistrate; it is not likely that their sanction would often be refused, where there were not special and strong reasons for the refusal.

To what purpose then require the co-operation of the Senate? I answer that the necessity of their concurrence would have a powerful, though in general a silent operation. It would be an excellent check upon a spirit of favoritism in the President, and would tend greatly to preventing the appointment of unfit characters from State prejudice, from family connection, from personal attachment, or from a view to popularity. And, in addition to this, it would be an efficacious source of stability in the administration.

It will readily be comprehended, that a man, who had himself the sole disposition of offices, would be governed much more by his private inclinations and interests, than when he was bound to submit the propriety of his choice to the discussion and determination of a different and independent body; and that body an entire branch of the Legislature. The possibility of rejection would be a strong motive to care in proposing. The danger to his own reputation, and, in the case of an elective magistrate, to his political existence, from betraying a spirit of favoritism, or an unbecoming pursuit of popularity, to the observation of a body, whose opinion would have great weight in forming that of the public, could not fail to operate as a barrier to the one and to the other. He would be both ashamed and afraid to bring forward for the most distinguished or lucrative stations, candidates who had no other merit, than that of coming from the same State to which he particularly belonged, or of being in some way or other personally allied to him, or of possessing the necessary insignificance and pliancy to render them the obsequious instruments of his pleasure.

To this reasoning, it has been objected, that the President by the influence of the power of nomination may secure the compliance of the Senate to his views. The supposition of universal venality in human nature is little less an error in political reasoning than the supposition of universal rectitude. The institution of delegated power implies that there is a portion of virtue and honor among mankind, which may be a reasonable foundation of confidence. And experience justifies the theory: It has been found to exist in the most corrupt periods of the most corrupt governments. The venality of the British House of Commons has been long a topic of accusation against that body, in the country to which they belong, as well as in this; and it cannot be doubted that the charge is to a considerable extent well founded. But it is as little to be doubted that there is always a large proportion of the body, which consists of independent and public spirited men, who have an influential weight in the councils of the nation. Hence it is (the present reign not excepted) that the sense of that body is often seen to controul the inclinations of the monarch, both with regard to men and to measures. Though it might therefore be allowable to suppose, that the executive might occasionally influence some individuals in the Senate; yet the supposition that he could in general purchase the integrity of the whole body would be forced and improbable. A man disposed to view human nature as it is, without either flattering its virtues or exaggerating its vices, will see sufficient ground of confidence in the probity of the Senate, to rest satisfied not only that it will be impracticable to the Executive to corrupt or seduce a majority of its members; but that the necessity of its co-operation in the business of appointments will be a considerable and salutary restraint upon the conduct of that magistrate. Nor is the integrity of the Senate the only reliance. The constitution has provided some important guards against the danger of executive influence upon the legislative body: It declares that "No Senator, or representative shall, during the time *for which he was elected*, be appointed to any civil office under the United States, which shall have been created, or the emoluments whereof shall have been encreased during such time; and no person holding any office under the United States shall be a member of either house during his continuance in office."

PUBLIUS.

The New-York Packet, April 1, 1788

The Federalist No. 77

It has been mentioned as one of the advantages to be expected from the co-operation of the senate, in the business of appointments, that it would contribute to the stability of the administration. The consent of that body would be necessary to displace as well as to appoint. A change of the chief magistrate therefore would not occasion so violent or so general a revolution in the officers of the government, as might be expected if he were the sole disposer of offices. Where a man in any station had given satisfactory evidence of his fitness for it, a new president would be restrained from attempting a change, in favour of a person more agreeable to him, by the apprehension that the discountenance of the senate might frustrate the attempt, and bring some degree of discredit upon himself. Those who can best estimate the value of a steady administration will be most disposed to prize a provision, which connects the official existence of public men with the approbation or disapprobation of that body, which from the greater permanency of its own composition, will in all probability be less subject to inconstancy, than any other member of the government.

To this union of the senate with the president, in the article of appointments, it has in some cases been objected, that it would serve to give the president an undue influence over the senate; and in others, that it would have an opposite tendency; a strong proof that neither suggestion is true.

To state the first in its proper form is to refute it. It amounts to this—The president would have an improper *influence over* the senate; because the senate would have the power of *restraining* him. This is an absurdity in terms. It cannot admit of a doubt that the intire power of appointment would enable him much more effectually to establish a dangerous empire over that body, than a mere power of nomination subject to their controul.

Let us take a view of the converse of the proposition— "The senate would influence the executive." As I have had

occasion to remark in several other instances, the indistinct-
ness of the objection forbids a precise answer. In what manner is this influence to be exerted? In relation to what objects?
The power of influencing a person, in the sense in which it is
here used, must imply a power of conferring a benefit upon
him. How could the senate confer a benefit upon the president by the manner of employing their right of negative upon
his nominations? If it be said they might sometimes gratify
him by an acquiesence in a favorite choice, when public motives might dictate a different conduct; I answer that the instances in which the president could be personally interested
in the result, would be too few to admit of his being materially affected by the compliances of the senate. The POWER
which can *originate* the disposition of honors and emoluments, is more likely to attract than to be attracted by the
POWER which can merely obstruct their course. If by influencing the president be meant *restraining* him, this is precisely what must have been intended. And it has been shewn
that the restraint would be salutary, at the same time that it
would not be such as to destroy a single advantage to be
looked for from the uncontrouled agency of that magistrate.
The right of nomination would produce all the good of that
of appointment, and would in a great measure avoid its ills.

Upon a comparison of the plan for the appointment of the
officers of the proposed government with that which is established by the constitution of this state a decided preference
must be given to the former. In that plan the power of nomination is unequivocally vested in the executive. And as there
would be a necessity for submitting each nomination to the
judgment of an entire branch of the legislature, the circumstances attending an appointment, from the mode of conducting it, would naturally become matters of notoriety; and
the public would be at no loss to determine what part had
been performed by the different actors. The blame of a bad
nomination would fall upon the president singly and absolutely. The censure of rejecting a good one would lie entirely
at the door of the senate; aggravated by the consideration
of their having counteracted the good intentions of the
executive. If an ill appointment should be made the
executive for nominating and the senate for approving would

participate though in different degrees in the opprobrium and disgrace.

The reverse of all this characterises the manner of appointment in this state. The council of appointment consists of from three to five persons, of whom the governor is always one. This small body, shut up in a private apartment, impenetrable to the public eye, proceed to the execution of the trust committed to them. It is known that the governor claims the right of nomination, upon the strength of some ambiguous expressions in the constitution; but it is not known to what extent, or in what manner he exercises it; nor upon what occasions he is contradicted or opposed. The censure of a bad appointment, on account of the uncertainty of its author, and for want of a determinate object, has neither poignancy nor duration. And while an unbounded field for cabal and intrigue lies open, all idea of responsibility is lost. The most that the public can know is, that the governor claims the right of nomination: That *two* out of the considerable number of *four* men can too often be managed without much difficulty: That if some of the members of a particular council should happen to be of an uncomplying character, it is frequently not impossible to get rid of their opposition, by regulating the times of meeting in such a manner as to render their attendance inconvenient: And that, from whatever cause it may proceed, a great number of very improper appointments are from time to time made. Whether a governor of this state avails himself of the ascendant he must necessarily have, in this delicate and important part of the administration, to prefer to offices men who are best qualified for them: Or whether he prostitutes that advantage to the advancement of persons, whose chief merit is their implicit devotion to his will, and to the support of a despicable and dangerous system of personal influence, are questions which unfortunately for the community can only be the subjects of speculation and conjecture.

Every mere council of appointment, however constituted, will be a conclave, in which cabal and intrigue will have their full scope. Their number, without an unwarrantable increase of expence, cannot be large enough to preclude a facility of combination. And as each member will have his friends and connections to provide for, the desire of mutual gratification will beget a scandalous bartering of votes and bargaining for places. The private attachments of one man might easily be satisfied; but to satisfy the private attachments of a dozen, or of twenty men, would occasion a monopoly of all the principal employments of the government, in a few families, and would lead more directly to an aristocracy or an oligarchy, than any measure that could be contrived. If to avoid an accumulation of offices, there was to be a frequent change in the persons, who were to compose the council, this would involve the mischiefs of a mutable administration in their full extent. Such a council would also be more liable to executive influence than the senate, because they would be fewer in number, and would act less immediately under the public inspection. Such a council in fine as a substitute for the plan of the convention, would be productive of an increase of expence, a multiplication of the evils which spring from favouritism and intrigue in the distribution of the public honors, a decrease of stability in the administration of the government, and a diminution of the security against an undue influence of the executive. And yet such a council has been warmly contended for as an essential amendment in the proposed constitution.

I could not with propriety conclude my observations on the subject of appointments, without taking notice of a scheme, for which there has appeared some, though but a few advocates; I mean that of uniting the house of representatives in the power of making them. I shall however do little more than mention it, as I cannot imagine that it is likely to gain the countenance of any considerable part of the community. A body so fluctuating, and at the same time so numerous, can never be deemed proper for the exercise of that power. Its unfitness will appear manifest to all, when it is recollected that in half a century it may consist of three or four hundred persons. All the advantages of the stability, both of the executive and of the senate, would be defeated by this union; and infinite delays and embarrassments would be occasioned. The example of most of the states in their local constitutions, encourages us to reprobate the idea.

The only remaining powers of the executive, are comprehended in giving information to congress of the state of the union; in recommending to their consideration such measures as he shall judge expedient; in convening them, or either branch, upon extraordinary occasions; in adjourning them when they cannot themselves agree upon the time of adjournment; in receiving ambassadors and other public ministers; in faithfully executing the laws; and in commissioning all the officers of the United States.

Except some cavils about the power of convening *either* house of the legislature and that of receiving ambassadors, no objection has been made to this class of authorities; nor could they possibly admit of any. It required indeed an insatiable avidity for censure to invent exceptions to the parts which have been excepted to. In regard to the power of convening either house of the legislature, I shall barely remark, that in respect to the senate at least, we can readily discover a good reason for it. As this body has a concurrent power with the executive in the article of treaties, it might often be necessary to call it together with a view to this object, when it would be unnecessary and improper to convene the house of representatives. As to the reception of ambassadors, what I have said in a former paper will furnish a sufficient answer.

We have now compleated a survey of the structure and powers of the executive department, which, I have endeavoured to show, combines, as far as republican principles would admit, all the requisites to energy. The remaining enquiry is; does it also combine the requisites to safety in the republican sense—a due dependence on the people—a due responsibility? The answer to this question has been anticipated in the investigation of its other characteristics, and is satisfactorily deducible from these circumstances, from the election of the president once in four years by persons immediately chosen by the people for that purpose; and from his being at all times liable to impeachment, trial, dismission from office, incapacity to serve in any other; and to the forfeiture of life and estate by subsequent prosecution in the common course of law. But these precautions, great as they are, are not the only ones, which the plan of the convention has provided in favor of the public security. In the only instances in which the abuse of the executive authority was materially to be feared, the chief magistrate of the United States would by that plan be subjected to the controul of a branch of the legislative body. What more could be desired by an enlightened and reasonable people?

PUBLIUS.

The Independent Journal, April 2, 1788

COORDINATING A CAMPAIGN

To James Madison

Some days since I wrote to you, My Dear Sir, inclosing a letter from a Mr. V Der Kemp &c.

I then mentioned to you that the question of a majority for or against the constitution would depend upon the County of Albany. By the latter accounts from that quarter I fear much that the issue there has been against us.

As Clinton is truly the leader of his party, and is inflexibly obstinate I count little on overcoming opposition by reason. Our only chances will be the previous ratification by nine states, which may shake the firmness of his followers; and a change in the sentiments of the people which have been for some time travelling towards the constitution, though the first impressions made by every species of influence and artifice were too strong to be eradicated in time to give a decisive turn to the elections. We shall leave nothing undone to cultivate a favourable disposition in the citizens at large.

The language of the Antifœderalists is that if all the other states adopt, New York ought still to hold out. I have the most direct intelligence, but in a manner, which forbids a public use being made of it, that Clinton has in several conversations declared his opinion of the *inutility* of the UNION. Tis an unhappy reflection, that the friends to it should by quarrelling for straws among themselves promote the designs of its adversaries.

We think here that the situation of your state is critical. Let me know what you now think of it. I believe you meet nearly at the time we do. It will be of vast importance that an exact communication should be kept up between us at that period; and the moment *any decisive* question is taken, if favourable, I request you to dispatch an express to me with pointed orders to make all possible diligence, by changing horses &c. All expences shall be thankfully and liberally paid.

I executed your commands respecting the first vol of the Fœderalist. I sent 40 of the common copies & twelve of the finer ones addressed to the care of Governor Randolph. The Printer announces the second vol in a day or two, when an equal number of the two kinds shall also be forwarded. He informs that the Judicial department trial by jury bill of rights &c. is discussed in some additional papers which have not yet appeared in the Gazettes.

I remain with great sincerity & attachment

New York May 19. 1788

The Federalist No. 78

We proceed now to an examination of the judiciary department of the proposed government.

In unfolding the defects of the existing confederation, the utility and necessity of a federal judicature have been clearly pointed out. It is the less necessary to recapitulate the considerations there urged; as the propriety of the institution in the abstract is not disputed: The only questions which have been raised being relative to the manner of constituting it, and to its extent. To these points therefore our observations shall be confined.

The manner of constituting it seems to embrace these several objects— 1st. The mode of appointing the judges— 2d. The tenure by which they are to hold their places— 3d. The partition of the judiciary authority between different courts, and their relations to each other.

First. As to the mode of appointing the judges: This is the same with that of appointing the officers of the union in general, and has been so fully discussed in the two last numbers, that nothing can be said here which would not be useless repetition.

Second. As to the tenure by which the judges are to hold their places: This chiefly concerns their duration in office; the provisions for their support; and the precautions for their responsibility.

According to the plan of the convention, all the judges who may be appointed by the United States are to hold their offices *during good behaviour*, which is conformable to the most approved of the state constitutions; and among the rest, to that of this state. Its propriety having been drawn into question by the adversaries of that plan, is no light symptom of the rage for objection which disorders their imaginations and judgments. The standard of good behaviour for the continuance in office of the judicial magistracy is certainly one of the most valuable of the modern improvements in the practice of government. In a monarchy it is an excellent barrier to the despotism of the prince: In a republic it is a no less excellent barrier to the encroachments and oppressions of the representative body. And it is the best expedient which can be devised in any government, to secure a steady, upright and impartial administration of the laws.

Whoever attentively considers the different departments of power must perceive, that in a government in which they are separated from each other, the judiciary, from the nature of its functions, will always be the least dangerous to the political rights of the constitution; because it will be least in a capacity to annoy or injure them. The executive not only dispenses the honors, but holds the sword of the community. The legislature not only commands the purse, but prescribes the rules by which the duties and rights of every citizen are to be regulated. The judiciary on the contrary has no influence over either the sword or the purse, no direction either of the strength or of the wealth of the society, and can take no active resolution whatever. It may truly be said to have neither FORCE nor WILL, but merely judgment; and must ultimately depend upon the aid of the executive arm even for the efficacy of its judgments.

This simple view of the matter suggests several important consequences. It proves incontestibly that the judiciary is beyond comparison the weakest of the three departments of power;* that it can never attack with success either of the other two; and that all possible care is requisite to enable it to defend itself against their attacks. It equally proves, that though individual oppression may now and then proceed from the courts of justice, the general liberty of the people can never be endangered from that quarter; I mean, so long as the judiciary remains truly distinct from both the legislative and executive. For I agree that "there is no liberty, if the power of judging be not separated from the legislative and executive powers."† And it proves, in the last place, that as liberty can have nothing to fear from the judiciary alone, but would have every thing to fear from its union with either of

---

* The celebrated Montesquieu speaking of them says, "of the three powers above mentioned, the JUDICIARY is next to nothing." Spirit of Laws, vol. I, page 186.

† Idem. page 181.

the other departments; that as all the effects of such an union must ensue from a dependence of the former on the latter, notwithstanding a nominal and apparent separation; that as from the natural feebleness of the judiciary, it is in continual jeopardy of being overpowered, awed or influenced by its co-ordinate branches; and that as nothing can contribute so much to its firmness and independence, as permanency in office, this quality may therefore be justly regarded as an indispensable ingredient in its constitution; and in a great measure as the citadel of the public justice and the public security.

The complete independence of the courts of justice is peculiarly essential in a limited constitution. By a limited constitution I understand one which contains certain specified exceptions to the legislative authority; such for instance as that it shall pass no bills of attainder, no *ex post facto* laws, and the like. Limitations of this kind can be preserved in practice no other way than through the medium of the courts of justice; whose duty it must be to declare all acts contrary to the manifest tenor of the constitution void. Without this, all the reservations of particular rights or privileges would amount to nothing.

Some perplexity respecting the right of the courts to pronounce legislative acts void, because contrary to the constitution, has arisen from an imagination that the doctrine would imply a superiority of the judiciary to the legislative power. It is urged that the authority which can declare the acts of another void, must necessarily be superior to the one whose acts may be declared void. As this doctrine is of great importance in all the American constitutions, a brief discussion of the grounds on which it rests cannot be unacceptable.

There is no position which depends on clearer principles, than that every act of a delegated authority, contrary to the tenor of the commission under which it is exercised, is void. No legislative act therefore contrary to the constitution can be valid. To deny this would be to affirm that the deputy is greater than his principal; that the servant is above his master; that the representatives of the people are superior to the people themselves; that men acting by virtue of powers may do not only what their powers do not authorise, but what they forbid.

If it be said that the legislative body are themselves the constitutional judges of their own powers, and that the construction they put upon them is conclusive upon the other departments, it may be answered, that this cannot be the natural presumption, where it is not to be collected from any particular provision in the constitution. It is not otherwise to be supposed that the constitution could intend to enable the representatives of the people to substitute their *will* to that of their constituents. It is far more rational to suppose that the courts were designed to be an intermediate body between the people and the legislature, in order, among other things, to keep the latter within the limits assigned to their authority. The interpretation of the laws is the proper and peculiar province of the courts. A constitution is in fact, and must be, regarded by the judges as a fundamental law. It therefore belongs to them to ascertain its meaning as well as the meaning of any particular act proceeding from the legislative body. If there should happen to be an irreconcileable variance between the two, that which has the superior obligation and validity ought of course to be preferred; or in other words, the constitution ought to be preferred to the statute, the intention of the people to the intention of their agents.

Nor does this conclusion by any means suppose a superiority of the judicial to the legislative power. It only supposes that the power of the people is superior to both; and that where the will of the legislature declared in its statutes, stands in opposition to that of the people declared in the constitution, the judges ought to be governed by the latter, rather than the former. They ought to regulate their decisions by the fundamental laws, rather than by those which are not fundamental.

This exercise of judicial discretion in determining between two contradictory laws, is exemplified in a familiar instance. It not uncommonly happens, that there are two statutes existing at one time, clashing in whole or in part with each other, and neither of them containing any repealing clause or expression. In such a case, it is the province of the courts to liquidate and fix their meaning and operation: So far as they can by any fair construction be reconciled to each other; reason and law conspire to dictate that this should be done: Where this is impracticable, it becomes a matter of necessity to give effect to one, in exclusion of the other. The rule which has obtained in the courts for determining their relative validity is that the last in order of time shall be preferred to the first. But this is mere rule of construction, not derived from any positive law, but from the nature and reason of the thing. It is a rule not enjoined upon the courts by legislative provision, but adopted by themselves, as consonant to truth and propriety, for the direction of their conduct as interpreters of the law. They thought it reasonable, that between the interfering acts of an *equal* authority, that which was the last indication of its will, should have the preference.

But in regard to the interfering acts of a superior and subordinate authority, of an original and derivative power, the nature and reason of the thing indicate the converse of that rule as proper to be followed. They teach us that the prior act of a superior ought to be prefered to the subsequent act of an inferior and subordinate authority; and that, accordingly, whenever a particular statute contravenes the constitution, it will be the duty of the judicial tribunals to adhere to the latter, and disregard the former.

It can be of no weight to say, that the courts on the pretence of a repugnancy, may substitute their own pleasure to the constitutional intentions of the legislature. This might as well happen in the case of two contradictory statutes; or it might as well happen in every adjudication upon any single statute. The courts must declare the sense of the law; and if they should be disposed to exercise *will* instead of *judgment*, the consequence would equally be the substitution of their pleasure to that of the legislative body. The observation, if it proved any thing, would prove that there ought to be no judges distinct from that body.

If then the courts of justice are to be considered as the bulwarks of a limited constitution against legislative encroachments, this consideration will afford a strong argument for the permanent tenure of judicial offices, since nothing will contribute so much as this to that independent spirit in the judges, which must be essential to the faithful performance of so arduous a duty.

This independence of the judges is equally requisite to guard the constitution and the rights of individuals from the effects of those ill humours which the arts of designing men, or the influence of particular conjunctures, sometimes disseminate among the people themselves, and which, though they speedily give place to better information and more deliberate reflection, have a tendency in the mean time to occasion dangerous innovations in the government, and serious oppressions of the minor party in the community. Though I trust the friends of the proposed constitution will never concur with its enemies* in questioning that fundamental principle of republican government, which admits the right of the people to alter or abolish the established constitution whenever they find it inconsistent with their happiness; yet it is not to be inferred from this principle, that the representatives of the people, whenever a momentary inclination happens to lay hold of a majority of their constituents incompatible with the provisions in the existing constitution, would on that account be justifiable in a violation of those provisions; or that the courts would be under a greater obligation to connive at infractions in this shape, than when they had proceeded wholly from the cabals of the representative body. Until the people have by some solemn and authoritative act annulled or changed the established form, it is binding upon themselves collectively, as well as individually; and no presumption, or even knowledge of their sentiments, can warrant their representatives in a departure from it, prior to such an act. But it is easy to see that it would require an uncommon portion of fortitude in the judges to do their duty as faithful guardians of the constitution, where legislative invasions of it had been instigated by the major voice of the community.

But it is not with a view to infractions of the constitution only that the independence of the judges may be an essential safeguard against the effects of occasional ill humours in the society. These sometimes extend no farther than to the injury of the private rights of particular classes of citizens, by unjust and partial laws. Here also the firmness of the judicial magistracy is of vast importance in mitigating the severity, and confining the operation of such laws. It not only serves to

* Vide Protest of the minority of the convention of Pennsylvania, Martin's speech, &c.

moderate the immediate mischiefs of those which may have been passed, but it operates as a check upon the legislative body in passing them; who, perceiving that obstacles to the success of an iniquitous intention are to be expected from the scruples of the courts, are in a manner compelled by the very motives of the injustice they meditate, to qualify their attempts. This is a circumstance calculated to have more influence upon the character of our governments, than but few may be aware of. The benefits of the integrity and moderation of the judiciary have already been felt in more states than one; and though they may have displeased those whose sinister expectations they may have disappointed, they must have commanded the esteem and applause of all the virtuous and disinterested. Considerate men of every description ought to prize whatever will tend to beget or fortify that temper in the courts; as no man can be sure that he may not be to-morrow the victim of a spirit of injustice, by which he may be a gainer to-day. And every man must now feel that the inevitable tendency of such a spirit is to sap the foundations of public and private confidence, and to introduce in its stead, universal distrust and distress.

That inflexible and uniform adherence to the rights of the constitution and of individuals, which we perceive to be indispensable in the courts of justice, can certainly not be expected from judges who hold their offices by a temporary commission. Periodical appointments, however regulated, or by whomsoever made, would in some way or other be fatal to their necessary independence. If the power of making them was committed either to the executive or legislature, there would be danger of an improper complaisance to the branch which possessed it; if to both, there would be an unwillingness to hazard the displeasure of either; if to the people, or to persons chosen by them for the special purpose, there would be too great a disposition to consult popularity, to justify a reliance that nothing would be consulted but the constitution and the laws.

There is yet a further and a weighty reason for the permanency of the judicial offices; which is deducible from the nature of the qualifications they require. It has been frequently remarked with great propriety, that a voluminous code of laws is one of the inconveniences necessarily connected with the advantages of a free government. To avoid an arbitrary discretion in the courts, it is indispensable that they should be bound down by strict rules and precedents, which serve to define and point out their duty in every particular case that comes before them; and it will readily be conceived from the variety of controversies which grow out of the folly and wickedness of mankind, that the records of those precedents must unavoidably swell to a very considerable bulk, and must demand long and laborious study to acquire a competent knowledge of them. Hence it is that there can be but few men in the society, who will have sufficient skill in the laws to qualify them for the stations of judges. And making the proper deductions for the ordinary depravity of human nature, the number must be still smaller of those who unite the requisite integrity with the requisite knowledge. These considerations apprise us, that the government can have no great option between fit characters; and that a temporary duration in office, which would naturally discourage such characters from quitting a lucrative line of practice to accept a seat on the bench, would have a tendency to throw the administration of justice into hands less able, and less well qualified to conduct it with utility and dignity. In the present circumstances of this country, and in those in which it is likely to be for a long time to come, the disadvantages on this score would be greater than they may at first sight appear; but it must be confessed that they are far inferior to those which present themselves under the other aspects of the subject.

Upon the whole there can be no room to doubt that the convention acted wisely in copying from the models of those constitutions which have established *good behaviour* as the tenure of their judicial offices in point of duration; and that so far from being blameable on this account, their plan would have been inexcuseably defective if it had wanted this important feature of good government. The experience of Great Britain affords an illustrious comment on the excellence of the institution.

PUBLIUS.

The Federalist, May 28, 1788

The Federalist No. 79

To the People of the State of New-York.

Next to permanency in office, nothing can contribute more to the independence of the judges than a fixed provision for their support. The remark made in relation to the president, is equally applicable here. In the general course of human nature, *a power over a man's subsistence amounts to a power over his will.* And we can never hope to see realised in practice the complete separation of the judicial from the legislative power, in any system, which leaves the former dependent for pecuniary resources on the occasional grants of the latter. The enlightened friends to good government, in every state, have seen cause to lament the want of precise and explicit precautions in the state constitutions on this head. Some of these indeed have declared that *permanent** salaries should be established for the judges; but the experiment has in some instances shewn that such expressions are not sufficiently definite to preclude legislative evasions. Something still more positive and unequivocal has been evinced to be requisite. The plan of the convention accordingly has provided, that the judges of the United States "shall at *stated times* receive for their services a compensation, which shall not be *diminished* during their continuance in office."

This, all circumstances considered, is the most eligible provision that could have been devised. It will readily be understood, that the fluctuations in the value of money, and in the state of society, rendered a fixed rate of compensation in the constitution inadmissible. What might be extravagant to day, might in half a century become penurious and inadequate. It was therefore necessary to leave it to the discretion of the legislature to vary its provisions in conformity to the variations in circumstances; yet under such restrictions as to put it out of the power of that body to change the condition of the individual for the worse. A man may then be sure of the ground upon which he stands, and can never be deterred from his

* Vide Constitution of Massachusetts, Chap. 2, Sect. 1. Art. 13.

duty by the apprehension of being placed in a less eligible situation. The clause which has been quoted combines both advantages. The salaries of judicial offices may from time to time be altered, as occasion shall require, yet so as never to lessen the allowance with which any particular judge comes into office, in respect to him. It will be observed that a difference has been made by the convention between the compensation of the president and of the judges. That of the former can neither be increased nor diminished. That of the latter can only not be diminished. This probably arose from the difference in the duration of the respective offices. As the president is to be elected for no more than four years, it can rarely happen that an adequate salary, fixed at the commencement of that period, will not continue to be such to the end of it. But with regard to the judges, who, if they behave properly, will be secured in their places for life, it may well happen, especially in the early stages of the government, that a stipend, which would be very sufficient at their first appointment, would become too small in the progress of their service.

This provision for the support of the judges bears every mark of prudence and efficacy; and it may be safely affirmed that, together with the permanent tenure of their offices, it affords a better prospect of their independence than is discoverable in the constitutions of any of the states, in regard to their own judges.

The precautions for their responsibility are comprised in the article respecting impeachments. They are liable to be impeached for mal-conduct by the house of representatives, and tried by the senate, and if convicted, may be dismissed from office and disqualified for holding any other. This is the only provision on the point, which is consistent with the necessary independence of the judicial character, and is the only one which we find in our own constitution in respect to our own judges.

The want of a provision for removing the judges on account of inability, has been a subject of complaint. But all considerate men will be sensible that such a provision would either not be practiced upon, or would be more liable to abuse than calculated to answer any good purpose. The mensuration of the faculties of the mind has, I believe, no place in the catalogue of known arts. An attempt to fix the boundary between the regions of ability and inability, would much oftener give scope to personal and party attachments and enmities, than advance the interests of justice, or the public good. The result, except in the case of insanity, must for the most part be arbitrary; and insanity without any formal or express provision, may be safely pronounced to be a virtual disqualification.

The constitution of New-York, to avoid investigations that must forever be vague and dangerous, has taken a particular age as the criterion of inability. No man can be a judge beyond sixty. I believe there are few at present, who do not disapprove of this provision. There is no station in relation to which it is less proper than to that of a judge. The deliberating and comparing faculties generally preserve their strength much beyond that period, in men who survive it; and when in addition to this circumstance, we consider how few there are who outlive the season of intellectual vigour, and how improbable it is that any considerable proportion of the bench, whether more or less numerous, should be in such a situation at the same time, we shall be ready to conclude that limitations of this sort have little to recommend them. In a republic, where fortunes are not affluent, and pensions not expedient, the dismission of men from stations in which they have served their country long and usefully, on which they depend for subsistence, and from which it will be too late to resort to any other occupation for a livelihood, ought to have some better apology to humanity, than is to be found in the imaginary danger of a superannuated bench.

PUBLIUS.

The Federalist, May 28, 1788

The Federalist No. 80

To the People of the State of New-York.

To judge with accuracy of the proper extent of the federal judicature, it will be necessary to consider in the first place what are its proper objects.

It seems scarcely to admit of controversy that the judiciary authority of the union ought to extend to these several descriptions of causes. 1st. To all those which arise out of the laws of the United States, passed in pursuance of their just and constitutional powers of legislation; 2d. to all those which concern the execution of the provisions expressly contained in the articles of union; 3d. to all those in which the United States are a party; 4th to all those which involve the PEACE of the CONFEDERACY, whether they relate to the intercourse between the United States and foreign nations, or to that between the States themselves; 5th. to all those which originate on the high seas, and are of admiralty or maritime jurisdiction; and lastly, to all those in which the state tribunals cannot be supposed to be impartial and unbiassed.

The first point depends upon this obvious consideration that there ought always to be a constitutional method of giving efficacy to constitutional provisions. What for instance would avail restrictions on the authority of the state legislatures, without some constitutional mode of enforcing the observance of them? The states, by the plan of the convention are prohibited from doing a variety of things; some of which are incompatible with the interests of the union, and others with the principles of good government. The imposition of duties on imported articles, and the emission of paper money, are specimens of each kind. No man of sense will believe that such prohibitions would be scrupulously regarded, without some effectual power in the government to restrain or correct the infractions of them. This power must either be a direct negative on the state laws, or an authority in the federal courts, to over-rule such as might be in manifest contravention of the articles of union. There is no third course that I can imagine. The latter appears to have been thought by the convention preferable to the former, and I presume will be most agreeable to the states.

As to the second point, it is impossible by any argument or comment to make it clearer than it is in itself. If there are such things as political axioms, the propriety of the judicial power of a government being co-extensive with its legislative, may be ranked among the number. The mere necessity of uniformity in the interpretation of the national laws, decides the question. Thirteen independent courts of final jurisdiction over the same causes, arising upon the same laws, is a hydra in government, from which nothing but contradiction and confusion can proceed.

Still less need be said in regard to the third point. Controversies between the nation and its members or citizens, can only be properly referred to the national tribunals. Any other plan would be contrary to reason, to precedent, and to decorum.

The fourth point rests on this plain proposition, that the peace of the WHOLE ought not to be left at the disposal of a PART. The union will undoubtedly be answerable to foreign powers for the conduct of its members. And the responsibility for an injury ought ever to be accompanied with the faculty of preventing it. As the denial or perversion of justice by the sentences of courts, as well as in any other manner, is with reason classed among the just causes of war, it will follow that the federal judiciary ought to have cognizance of all causes in which the citizens of other countries are concerned. This is not less essential to the preservation of the public faith, than to the security of the public tranquility. A distinction may perhaps be imagined between cases arising upon treaties and the laws of nations, and those which may stand merely on the footing of the municipal law. The former kind may be supposed proper for the federal jurisdiction, the latter for that of the states. But it is at least problematical whether an unjust sentence against a foreigner, where the subject of controversy was wholly relative to the *lex loci*, would not, if unredressed, be an aggression upon his sovereign, as well as one which violated the stipulations in a treaty or the general laws of nations. And a still greater objection to the distinction would result from the immense difficulty, if not impossibility, of a practical discrimination between the cases of one complection and those of the other. So great a proportion of the cases in which foreigners are parties involve national questions, that it is by far most safe and most expedient to refer all those in which they are concerned to the national tribunals.

The power of determining causes between two states, between one state and the citizens of another, and between the citizens of different states, is perhaps not less essential to the peace of the union than that which has been just examined. History gives us a horrid picture of the dissentions and private wars which distracted and desolated Germany prior to the institution of the IMPERIAL CHAMBER by Maximilian, towards the close of the fifteenth century; and informs us at the same time of the vast influence of that institution in appeasing the disorders and establishing the tranquility of the empire. This was a court invested with authority to decide finally all differences between the members of the Germanic body.

A method of terminating territorial disputes between the states, under the authority of the federal head, was not unattended to, even in the imperfect system by which they have been hitherto held together. But there are many other sources, besides interfering claims of boundary, from which bickerings and animosities may spring up among the members of the union. To some of these we have been witnesses in the course of our past experience. It will readily be conjectured that I allude to the fradulent laws which have been passed in too many of the states. And though the proposed constitution establishes particular guards against the repetition of those instances which have heretofore made their appearance, yet it is warrantable to apprehend that the spirit which produced them will assume new shapes that could not be foreseen, nor specifically provided against. Whatever practices may have a tendency to disturb the harmony between the states, are proper objects of federal superintendence and control.

It may be esteemed the basis of the union, that "the citizens of each state shall be entitled to all the privileges and immunities of citizens of the several states." And if it be a just principle that every government *ought to possess the means of executing its own provisions by its own authority*, it will follow, that in order to the inviolable maintenance of that equality of privileges and immunities to which the citizens of the union will be entitled, the national judiciary ought to preside in all cases in which one state or its citizens are opposed to another state or its citizens. To secure the full effect of so fundamental a provision against all evasion and subterfuge, it is necessary that its construction should be committed to that tribunal, which, having no local attachments, will be likely to be impartial between the different states and their citizens, and which, owing its official existence to the union, will never be likely to feel any bias inauspicious to the principles on which it is founded.

The fifth point will demand little animadversion. The most bigotted idolizers of state authority have not thus far shewn a disposition to deny the national judiciary the cognizance of maritime causes. These so generally depend on the laws of nations, and so commonly affect the rights of foreigners, that they fall within the considerations which are relative to the public peace. The most important part of them are by the present confederation submitted to federal jurisdiction.

The reasonableness of the agency of the national courts in cases in which the state tribunals cannot be supposed to be impartial, speaks for itself. No man ought certainly to be a judge in his own cause, or in any cause in respect to which he has the least interest or bias. This principle has no inconsiderable weight in designating the federal courts as the proper tribunals for the determination of controversies between different states and their citizens. And it ought to have the same operation in regard to some cases between the citizens of the same state. Claims to land under grants of different states, founded upon adverse pretensions of boundary, are of this description. The courts of neither of the granting states could be expected to be unbiassed. The laws may have even prejudged the question, and tied the courts down to decisions in favour of the grants of the state to which they belonged. And even where this had not been done, it would be natural that the judges, as men, should feel a strong predilection to the claims of their own government.

Having thus laid down and discussed the principles which ought to regulate the constitution of the federal judiciary, we will proceed to test, by these principles, the particular powers of which, according to the plan of the convention, it is to be composed. It is to comprehend, "all cases in law and equity arising under the constitution, the laws of the United States, and treaties made, or which shall be made under their authority; to all cases affecting ambassadors, other public ministers and consuls; to all cases of admiralty and maritime jurisdiction; to controversies to which the United States shall be a party; to controversies between two or more states, between a state and citizens of another state, between citizens of different states, between citizens of the same state claiming lands under grants of different states, and between a state or the citizens thereof, and foreign states, citizens and subjects." This constitutes the entire mass of the judicial authority of the union. Let us now review it in detail. It is then to extend,

First. To all cases in law and equity *arising under the constitution* and *the laws of the United States.* This corresponds to the two first classes of causes which have been enumerated as proper for the jurisdiction of the United States. It has been asked what is meant by "cases arising under the constitution," in contradistinction from those "arising under the laws of the United States." The difference has been already explained. All the restrictions upon the authority of the state legislatures, furnish examples of it. They are not, for instance, to emit paper money; but the interdiction results from the constitution, and will have no connection with any law of the United States. Should paper money, notwithstanding, be emitted, the controversies concerning it would be cases arising upon the constitution, and not upon the laws of the United States, in the ordinary signification of the terms. This may serve as a sample of the whole.

It has also been asked, what need of the word "equity"? What equitable causes can grow out of the constitution and laws of the United States? There is hardly a subject of litigation between individuals, which may not involve those ingredients of *fraud, accident, trust* or *hardship,* which would render the matter an object of equitable, rather than of legal jurisdiction, as the distinction is known and established in several of the states. It is the peculiar province, for instance, of a court of equity to relieve against what are called hard bargains: These are contracts, in which, though there may have been no direct fraud or deceit, sufficient to invalidate them in a court of law; yet there may have been some undue and unconscionable advantage taken of the necessities or misfortunes of one of the parties, which a court of equity would not tolerate. In such cases, where foreigners were concerned on either side, it would be impossible for the federal judicatories to do justice without an equitable, as well as a legal jurisdiction. Agreements to convey lands claimed under the grants of different states, may afford another example of the necessity of an equitable jurisdiction in the federal courts. This reasoning may not be so palpable in those states where the formal and technical distinction between LAW and EQUITY is not maintained as in this state, where it is exemplified by every day's practice.

The judiciary authority of the union is to extend—

Second. To treaties made, or which shall be made under the authority of the United States, and to all cases affecting ambassadors, other public ministers and consuls. These belong to the fourth class of the enumerated cases, as they have an evident connection with the preservation of the national peace.

Third. To cases of admiralty and maritime jurisdiction. These form altogether the fifth of the enumerated classes of causes proper for the cognizance of the national courts.

Fourth. To controversies to which the United States shall be a party. These constitute the third of those classes.

Fifth. To controversies between two or more states, between a state and citizens of another state, between citizens of different states. These belong to the fourth of those classes, and partake in some measure of the nature of the last.

Sixth. To cases between the citizens of the same state, *claiming lands under grants of different states.* These fall within the last class, and *are the only instance in which the proposed constitution directly contemplates the cognizance of disputes between the citizens of the same state.*

Seventh. To cases between a state and the citizens thereof, and foreign states, citizens, or subjects. These have been already explained to belong to the fourth of the enumerated classes, and have been shewn to be in a peculiar manner the proper subjects of the national judicature.

From this review of the particular powers of the federal judiciary, as marked out in the constitution, it appears, that they are all conformable to the principles which ought to have governed the structure of that department, and which were necessary to the perfection of the system. If some partial inconveniencies should appear to be connected with the incorporation of any of them into the plan, it ought to be recollected that the national legislature will have ample authority to make such *exceptions* and to prescribe such regulations as will be calculated to obviate or remove these inconveniencies. The possibility of particular mischiefs can never be viewed by a well-informed mind as a solid objection to a general principle, which is calculated to avoid general mischiefs, and to obtain general advantages.

PUBLIUS.

The Federalist, May 28, 1788

The Federalist No. 81

To the People of the State of New-York.

Let us now return to the partition of the judiciary authority between different courts, and their relations to each other.

"The judicial power of the United States is (by the plan of the convention) to be vested in one supreme court, and in such inferior courts as the congress may from time to time ordain and establish."*

That there ought to be one court of supreme and final jurisdiction is a proposition which has not been, and is not likely to be contested. The reasons for it have been assigned in another place, and are too obvious to need repetition. The only question that seems to have been raised concerning it, is whether it ought to be a distinct body, or a branch of the legislature. The same contradiction is observable in regard to this matter, which has been remarked in several other cases. The very men who object to the senate as a court of impeachments, on the ground of an improper intermixture of powers, advocate, by implication at least, the propriety of vesting the ultimate decision of all causes in the whole, or in a part of the legislative body.

The arguments or rather suggestions, upon which this charge is founded, are to this effect: "The authority of the proposed supreme court of the United States, which is to be a separate and independent body, will be superior to that of the legislature. The power of construing the laws, according to the *spirit* of the constitution, will enable that court to mould them into whatever shape it may think proper; especially as its decisions will not be in any manner subject to the revision or correction of the legislative body. This is as unprecedented as it is dangerous. In Britain, the judicial power in the last resort, resides in the house of lords, which is a branch of the legislature; and this part of the British government has been imitated in the state constitutions in general. The parliament of Great-Britain, and the legislatures of the

---

* Article 3. Sec. 1.

several states, can at any time rectify by law, the exceptionable decisions of their respective courts. But the errors and usurpations of the supreme court of the United States will be uncontrolable and remediless." This, upon examination, will be found to be altogether made of false reasoning upon misconceived fact.

In the first place, there is not a syllable in the plan under consideration, which *directly* empowers the national courts to construe the laws according to the spirit of the constitution, or which gives them any greater latitude in this respect, than may be claimed by the courts of every state. I admit however, that the constitution ought to be the standard of construction for the laws, and that wherever there is an evident opposition, the laws ought to give place to the constitution. But this doctrine is not deducible from any circumstance peculiar to the plan of the convention; but from the general theory of a limited constitution; and as far as it is true, is equally applicable to most, if not to all the state governments. There can be no objection therefore, on this account, to the federal judicature, which will not lie against the local judicatures in general, and which will not serve to condemn every constitution that attempts to set bounds to the legislative discretion.

But perhaps the force of the objection may be thought to consist in the particular organization of the proposed supreme court; in its being composed of a distinct body of magistrates, instead of being one of the branches of the legislature, as in the government of Great-Britain and in that of this state. To insist upon this point, the authors of the objection must renounce the meaning they have laboured to annex to the celebrated maxim requiring a separation of the departments of power. It shall nevertheless be conceded to them, agreeably to the interpretation given to that maxim in the course of these papers, that it is not violated by vesting the ultimate power of judging in a *part* of the legislative body. But though this be not an absolute violation of that excellent rule; yet it verges so nearly upon it, as on this account alone to be less eligible than the mode preferred by the convention. From a body which had had even a partial agency in passing bad laws, we could rarely expect a disposition to temper and moderate them in the application. The same spirit, which had operated in making them would be too apt to operate in interpreting them: Still less could it be expected, that men who had infringed the constitution, in the character of legislators, would be disposed to repair the breach, in the character of judges. Nor is this all: Every reason, which recommends the tenure of good behaviour for judicial offices, militates against placing the judiciary power in the last resort in a body composed of men chosen for a limited period. There is an absurdity in referring the determination of causes in the first instance to judges of permanent standing, and in the last to those of a temporary and mutable constitution. And there is a still greater absurdity in subjecting the decisions of men selected for their knowledge of the laws, acquired by long and laborious study, to the revision and control of men, who for want of the same advantage cannot but be deficient in that knowledge. The members of the legislature will rarely be chosen with a view to those qualifications which fit men for the stations of judges; and as on this account there will be great reason to apprehend all the ill consequences of defective information; so on account of the natural propensity of such bodies to party divisions, there will be no less reason to fear, that the pestilential breath of faction may poison the fountains of justice. The habit of being continually marshalled on opposite sides, will be too apt to stifle the voice both of law and of equity.

These considerations teach us to applaud the wisdom of those states, who have committed the judicial power in the last resort, not to a part of the legislature, but to distinct and independent bodies of men. Contrary to the supposition of those, who have represented the plan of the convention in this respect as novel and unprecedented, it is but a copy of the constitutions of New-Hampshire, Massachusetts, Pennsylvania, Delaware, Maryland, Virginia, North-Carolina, South-Carolina and Georgia; and the preference which has been given to these models is highly to be commended.

It is not true, in the second place, that the parliament of Great Britain, or the legislatures of the particular states, can rectify the exceptionable decisions of their respective courts, in any other sense than might be done by a future legislature of the United States. The theory neither of the British, nor the state constitutions, authorises the revisal of a judicial sentence, by a legislative act. Nor is there anything in the proposed constitution more than in either of them, by which it is forbidden. In the former as well as in the latter, the impropriety of the thing, on the general principles of law and reason, is the sole obstacle. A legislature without exceeding its province cannot reverse a determination once made, in a particular case; though it may prescribe a new rule for future cases. This is the principle, and it applies in all its consequences, exactly in the same manner and extent, to the state governments, as to the national government, now under consideration. Not the least difference can be pointed out in any view of the subject.

It may in the last place be observed that the supposed danger of judiciary encroachments on the legislative authority, which has been upon many occasions reiterated, is in reality a phantom. Particular misconstructions and contraventions of the will of the legislature may now and then happen; but they can never be so extensive as to amount to an inconvenience, or in any sensible degree to affect the order of the political system. This may be inferred with certainty from the general nature of the judicial power; from the objects to which it relates; from the manner in which it is exercised; from its comparative weakness, and from its total incapacity to support its usurpations by force. And the inference is greatly fortified by the consideration of the important constitutional check, which the power of instituting impeachments, in one part of the legislative body, and of determining upon them in the other, would give to that body upon the members of the judicial department. This is alone a complete security. There never can be danger that the judges, by a series of deliberate usurpations on the authority of the legislature, would hazard the united resentment of the body entrusted with it, while this body was possessed of the means of punishing their presumption by degrading them from their stations. While this ought to remove all apprehensions on the subject, it affords at the same time a cogent argument for constituting the senate a court for the trial of impeachments.

Having now examined, and I trust removed the objections to the distinct and independent organization of the supreme court, I proceed to consider the propriety of the power of constituting inferior courts,* and the relations which will subsist between these and the former.

The power of constituting inferior courts is evidently calculated to obviate the necessity of having recourse to the supreme court, in every case of federal cognizance. It is intended to enable the national government to institute or *authorise* in each state or district of the United States, a tribunal competent to the determination of matters of national jurisdiction within its limits.

But why, it is asked, might not the same purpose have been accomplished by the instrumentality of the state courts? This admits of different answers. Though the fitness and competency of those courts should be allowed in the utmost latitude; yet the substance of the power in question, may still be regarded as a necessary part of the plan, if it were only to empower the national legislature to commit to them the cognizance of causes arising out of the national constitution. To confer the power of determining such causes upon the existing courts of the several states, would perhaps be as much "to constitute tribunals," as to create new courts with the like power. But ought not a more direct and explicit provision to have been made in favour of the state courts? There are, in my opinion, substantial reasons against such a provision: The most discerning cannot foresee how far the prevalency of a local spirit may be found to disqualify the local tribunals for the jurisdiction of national causes; whilst every man may discover that courts constituted like those of some of the states, would be improper channels of the judicial authority of the union. State judges, holding their offices during pleasure, or from year to year, will be too little independent to be relied upon for an inflexible execution of the national laws. And if there was a necessity for confiding the original cognizance of causes

---

* This power has been absurdly represented as intended to abolish all the county courts in the several states, which are commonly called inferior courts. But the expressions of the constitution are to constitute "tribunals INFERIOR TO THE SUPREME COURT," and the evident design of the provision is to enable the institution of local courts subordinate to the supreme, either in states or larger districts. It is ridiculous to imagine that county courts were in contemplation.

arising under those laws to them, there would be a correspondent necessity for leaving the door of appeal as wide as
possible. In proportion to the grounds of confidence in, or
diffidence of the subordinate tribunals, ought to be the facility or difficulty of appeals. And well satisfied as I am of the
propriety of the appellate jurisdiction in the several classes of
causes to which it is extended by the plan of the convention,
I should consider every thing calculated to give in practice, an
unrestrained course to appeals as a source of public and private
inconvenience.

I am not sure but that it will be found highly expedient and
useful to divide the United States into four or five, or half a
dozen districts; and to institute a federal court in each district,
in lieu of one in every state. The judges of these courts, with
the aid of the state judges, may hold circuits for the trial of
causes in the several parts of the respective districts. Justice
through them may be administered with ease and dispatch;
and appeals may be safely circumscribed within a very narrow
compass. This plan appears to me at present the most eligible
of any that could be adopted, and in order to it, it is necessary that the power of constituting inferior courts should exist in the full extent in which it is to be found in the proposed
constitution.

These reasons seem sufficient to satisfy a candid mind, that
the want of such a power would have been a great defect in
the plan. Let us now examine in what manner the judicial authority is to be distributed between the supreme and the inferior courts of the union.

The supreme court is to be invested with original jurisdiction, only "in cases affecting ambassadors, other public ministers and consuls, and those in which A STATE shall be a
party." Public ministers of every class, are the immediate representatives of their sovereigns. All questions in which they
are concerned, are so directly connected with the public
peace, that as well for the preservation of this, as out of respect to the sovereignties they represent, it is both expedient
and proper, that such questions should be submitted in the
first instance to the highest judicatory of the nation. Though
consuls have not in strictness a diplomatic character, yet as
they are the public agents of the nations to which they

belong, the same observation is in a great measure applicable to them. In cases in which a state might happen to be a party, it would ill suit its dignity to be turned over to an inferior tribunal. Though it may rather be a digression from the immediate subject of this paper, I shall take occasion to mention here, a supposition which has excited some alarm upon very mistaken grounds: It has been suggested that an assignment of the public securities of one state to the citizens of another, would enable them to prosecute that state in the federal courts for the amount of those securities. A suggestion which the following considerations prove to be without foundation.

It is inherent in the nature of sovereignty, not to be amenable to the suit of an individual *without its consent*. This is the general sense and the general practice of mankind; and the exemption, as one of the attributes of sovereignty, is now enjoyed by the government of every state in the union. Unless therefore, there is a surrender of this immunity in the plan of the convention, it will remain with the states, and the danger intimated must be merely ideal. The circumstances which are necessary to produce an alienation of state sovereignty, were discussed in considering the article of taxation, and need not be repeated here. A recurrence to the principles there established will satisfy us, that there is no colour to pretend that the state governments, would by the adoption of that plan, be divested of the privilege of paying their own debts in their own way, free from every constraint but that which flows from the obligations of good faith. The contracts between a nation and individuals are only binding on the conscience of the sovereign, and have no pretensions to a compulsive force. They confer no right of action independent of the sovereign will. To what purpose would it be to authorise suits against states, for the debts they owe? How could recoveries be enforced? It is evident that it could not be done without waging war against the contracting state; and to ascribe to the federal courts, by mere implication, and in destruction of a pre-existing right of the state governments, a power which would involve such a consequence, would be altogether forced and unwarrantable.

Let us resume the train of our observations; we have seen that the original jurisdiction of the supreme court would be

THE FEDERALIST NO. 81 445

confined to two classes of causes, and those of a nature rarely to occur. In all other causes of federal cognizance, the original jurisdiction would appertain to the inferior tribunals, and the supreme court would have nothing more than an appellate jurisdiction, "with such *exceptions*, and under such *regulations* as the congress shall make."

The propriety of this appellate jurisdiction has been scarcely called in question in regard to matters of law; but the clamours have been loud against it as applied to matters of fact. Some well intentioned men in this state, deriving their notions from the language and forms which obtain in our courts, have been induced to consider it as an implied supersedure of the trial by jury, in favour of the civil law mode of trial, which prevails in our courts of admiralty, probates and chancery. A technical sense has been affixed to the term "appellate", which in our law parlance is commonly used in reference to appeals in the course of the civil law. But if I am not misinformed, the same meaning would not be given to it in any part of New-England. There an appeal from one jury to another is familiar both in language and practice, and is even a matter of course, until there have been two verdicts on one side. The word "appellate" therefore will not be understood in the same sense in New-England as in New-York, which shews the impropriety of a technical interpretation derived from the jurisprudence of any particular state. The expression taken in the abstract, denotes nothing more than the power of one tribunal to review the proceedings of another, either as to the law or fact, or both. The mode of doing it may depend on ancient custom or legislative provision, (in a new government it must depend on the latter) and may be with or without the aid of a jury, as may be judged adviseable. If therefore the re-examination of a fact once determined by a jury, should in any case be admitted under the proposed constitution, it may be so regulated as to be done by a second jury, either by remanding the cause to the court below for a second trial of the fact, or by directing an issue immediately out of the supreme court.

But it does not follow that the re-examination of a fact once ascertained by a jury, will be permitted in the supreme court. Why may it not be said, with the strictest propriety, when a writ of error is brought from an inferior to a superior court of law in this state, that the latter has jurisdiction of the fact, as well as the law? It is true it cannot institute a new enquiry concerning the fact, but it takes cognizance of it as it appears upon the record, and pronounces the law arising upon it.* This is jurisdiction of both fact and law, nor is it even possible to separate them. Though the common law courts of this state ascertain disputed facts by a jury, yet they unquestionably have jurisdiction of both fact and law; and accordingly, when the former is agreed in the pleadings, they have no recourse to a jury, but proceed at once to judgment. I contend therefore on this ground, that the expressions, "appellate jurisdiction, both as to law and fact," do not necessarily imply a re-examination in the supreme court of facts decided by juries in the inferior courts.

The following train of ideas may well be imagined to have influenced the convention in relation to this particular provision. The appellate jurisdiction of the supreme court (may it have been argued) will extend to causes determinable in different modes, some in the course of the COMMON LAW, and others in the course of the CIVIL LAW. In the former, the revision of the law only, will be, generally speaking, the proper province of the supreme court; in the latter, the re-examination of the fact is agreeable to usage, and in some cases, of which prize causes are an example, might be essential to the preservation of the public peace. It is therefore necessary, that the appellate jurisdiction should, in certain cases, extend in the broadest sense to matters of fact. It will not answer to make an express exception of cases, which shall have been originally tried by a jury, because in the courts of some of the states, *all causes* are tried in this mode;† and such an exception would preclude the revision of matters of fact, as well where it might be proper, as where it might be improper. To avoid all inconveniencies, it will be safest to declare generally, that the supreme court shall possess appellate jurisdic-

* This word is a compound of JUS and DICTIO, juris, dictio, or a speaking or pronouncing of the law.
† I hold that the states will have concurrent jurisdiction with the subordinate federal judicatories, in many cases of federal cognizance, as will be explained in my next paper.

tion, both as to law and *fact*, and that this jurisdiction shall be subject to such *exceptions* and regulations as the national legislature may prescribe. This will enable the government to modify it in such a manner as will best answer the ends of public justice and security.

This view of the matter, at any rate puts it out of all doubt that the supposed *abolition* of the trial by jury, by the operation of this provision, is fallacious and untrue. The legislature of the United States would certainly have full power to provide that in appeals to the supreme court there should be no re-examination of facts where they had been tried in the original causes by juries. This would certainly be an authorised exception; but if for the reason already intimated it should be thought too extensive, it might be qualified with a limitation to such causes only as are determinable at common law in that mode of trial.

The amount of the observations hitherto made on the authority of the judicial department is this—that it has been carefully restricted to those causes which are manifestly proper for the cognizance of the national judicature, that in the partition of this authority a very small portion of original jurisdiction has been reserved to the supreme court, and the rest consigned to the subordinate tribunals—that the supreme court will possess an appellate jurisdiction both as to law and fact in all the cases referred to them, but subject to any *exceptions* and *regulations* which may be thought adviseable; that this appellate jurisdiction does in no case *abolish* the trial by jury, and that an ordinary degree of prudence and integrity in the national councils will insure us solid advantages from the establishment of the proposed judiciary, without exposing us to any of the inconveniencies which have been predicted from that source.

PUBLIUS.

The Federalist, May 28, 1788

The Federalist No. 82

To the People of the State of New-York.

The erection of a new government, whatever care or wisdom may distinguish the work, cannot fail to originate questions of intricacy and nicety; and these may in a particular manner be expected to flow from the establishment of a constitution founded upon the total or partial incorporation of a number of distinct sovereignties. 'Tis time only that can mature and perfect so compound a system, can liquidate the meaning of all the parts, and can adjust them to each other in a harmonious and consistent WHOLE.

Such questions accordingly have arisen upon the plan proposed by the convention, and particularly concerning the judiciary department. The principal of these respect the situation of the state courts in regard to those causes, which are to be submitted to federal jurisdiction. Is this to be exclusive, or are those courts to possess a concurrent jurisdiction? If the latter, in what relation will they stand to the national tribunals? These are inquiries which we meet with in the mouths of men of sense, and which are certainly intitled to attention.

The principles established in a former paper* teach us, that the states will retain all *pre-existing* authorities, which may not be exclusively delegated to the federal head; and that this exclusive delegation can only exist in one of three cases; where an exclusive authority is in express terms granted to the union; or where a particular authority is granted to the union, and the exercise of a like authority is prohibited to the states, or where an authority is granted to the union with which a similar authority in the states would be utterly incompatible. Though these principles may not apply with the same force to the judiciary as to the legislative power; yet I am inclined to think that they are in the main just with respect to the former as well as the latter. And under this impression I shall lay it down as a rule that the state courts will *retain* the jurisdiction they now have, unless it appears to be taken away in one of the enumerated modes.

* Vol. I, No. XXXII.

The only thing in the proposed constitution, which wears the appearance of confining the causes of federal cognizance to the federal courts is contained in this passage—"The JUDICIAL POWER of the United States *shall be vested* in one supreme court, and in *such* inferior courts as the congress shall from time to time ordain and establish." This might either be construed to signify, that the supreme and subordinate courts of the union should alone have the power of deciding those causes, to which their authority is to extend; or simply to denote that the organs of the national judiciary should be one supreme court and as many subordinate courts as congress should think proper to appoint, or in other words, that the United States should exercise the judicial power with which they are to be invested through one supreme tribunal and a certain number of inferior ones to be instituted by them. The first excludes, the last admits the concurrent jurisdiction of the state tribunals: And as the first would amount to an alienation of state power by implication, the last appears to me the most natural and the most defensible construction.

But this doctrine of concurrent jurisdiction is only clearly applicable to those descriptions of causes of which the state courts have previous cognizance. It is not equally evident in relation to cases which may grow out of, and be *peculiar* to the constitution to be established: For not to allow the state courts a right of jurisdiction in such cases can hardly be considered as the abridgement of a pre-existing authority. I mean not therefore to contend that the United States in the course of legislation upon the objects entrusted to their direction may not commit the decision of causes arising upon a particular regulation to the federal courts solely, if such a measure should be deemed expedient; but I hold that the state courts will be divested of no part of their primitive jurisdiction, further than may relate to an appeal; and I am even of opinion, that in every case in which they were not expressly excluded by the future acts of the national legislature, they will of course take cognizance of the causes to which those acts may give birth. This I infer from the nature of judiciary power, and from the general genius of the system. The judiciary power of every government looks beyond its own local or municipal laws, and in civil cases lays hold of all subjects of litigation between parties within its jurisdiction though the causes of dispute are relative to the laws of the most distant part of the globe. Those of Japan not less than of New-York may furnish the objects of legal discussion to our courts. When in addition to this, we consider the state governments and the national governments as they truly are, in the light of kindred systems and as parts of ONE WHOLE, the inference seems to be conclusive that the state courts would have a concurrent jurisdiction in all cases arising under the laws of the union, where it was not expressly prohibited.

Here another question occurs—what relation would subsist between the national and state courts in these instances of concurrent jurisdiction? I answer that an appeal would certainly lie from the latter to the supreme court of the United States. The constitution in direct terms, gives an appellate jurisdiction to the supreme court in all the enumerated cases of federal cognizance, in which it is not to have an original one; without a single expression to confine its operation to the inferior federal courts. The objects of appeal, not the tribunals from which it is to be made, are alone contemplated. From this circumstance and from the reason of the thing it ought to be construed to extend to the state tribunals. Either this must be the case, or the local courts must be excluded from a concurrent jurisdiction in matters of national concern, else the judiciary authority of the union may be eluded at the pleasure of every plantiff or prosecutor. Neither of these consequences ought without evident necessity to be involved; the latter would be intirely inadmissible, as it would defeat some of the most important and avowed purposes of the proposed government, and would essentially embarrass its measures. Nor do I perceive any foundation for such a supposition. Agreeably to the remark already made, the national and state systems are to be regarded as ONE WHOLE. The courts of the latter will of course be natural auxiliaries to the execution of the laws of the union, and an appearl from them will as naturally lie to that tribunal, which is destined to unite and assimilate the principles of national justice and the rules of national decisions. The evident aim of the plan of the convention is that all the causes of the specified classes, shall for weighty public reasons receive their original or final determination in the courts of the union. To confine therefore the general expressions giving appellate jurisdiction to the supreme court to appeals from the subordinate federal courts, instead of allowing their extension to the state courts, would be to abridge the latitude of the terms, in subversion of the intent, contrary to every sound rule of interpretation.

But could an appeal be made to lie from the state courts to the subordinate federal judicatories? This is another of the questions which have been raised, and of greater difficulty than the former. The following considerations countenance the affirmative. The plan of the convention in the first place authorises the national legislature "to constitute tribunals inferior to the supreme court"*. It declares in the next place that, "the JUDICIAL POWER of the United States *shall be vested* in one supreme court and in such inferior courts as congress shall ordain and establish;" and it then proceeds to enumerate the cases to which this judicial power shall extend. It afterwards divides the jurisdiction of the supreme court into original and appelate, but gives no definition of that of the subordinate courts. The only outlines described for them are that they shall be "inferior to the supreme court" and that they shall not exceed the specified limits of the federal judiciary. Whether their authority shall be original or appellate or both is not declared. All this seems to be left to the discretion of the legislature. And this being the case, I perceive at present no impediment to the establishment of an appeal from the state courts to the subordinate national tribunals; and many advantages attending the power of doing it may be imagined. It would diminish the motives to the multiplication of federal courts, and would admit of arrangements calculated to contract the appellate jurisdiction of the supreme court. The state tribunals may then be left with a more entire charge of federal causes; and appeals in most cases in which they may be deemed proper instead of being carried to the supreme court, may be made to lie from the state courts to district courts of the union.

PUBLIUS

* Section 8th, Article 1st.

The Federalist, May 28, 1788

The Federalist No. 83

To the People of the State of New-York.

The objection to the plan of the convention, which has met with most success in this state, and perhaps in several of the other states, is *that* relative to *the want of a constitutional provision* for the trial by jury in civil cases. The disingenuous form in which this objection is usually stated, has been repeatedly adverted to and exposed; but continues to be pursued in all the conversations and writings of the opponents of the plan. The mere silence of the constitution in regard to *civil causes*, is represented as an abolition of the trial by jury; and the declamations to which it has afforded a pretext, are artfully calculated to induce a persuasion that this pretended abolition is complete and universal; extending not only to every species of civil, but even to *criminal causes*. To argue with respect to the latter, would, however, be as vain and fruitless, as to attempt the serious proof of the *existence* of *matter*, or to demonstrate any of those propositions which by their own internal evidence force conviction, when expressed in language adapted to convey their meaning.

With regard to civil causes, subtleties almost too contemptible for refutation, have been adopted to countenance the surmise that a thing, which is only *not provided for*, is entirely *abolished*. Every man of discernment must at once perceive the wide difference between *silence* and *abolition*. But as the inventors of this fallacy have attempted to support it by certain *legal maxims* of interpretation, which they have perverted from their true meaning, it may not be wholly useless to explore the ground they have taken.

The maxims on which they rely are of this nature, "a specification of particulars is an exclusion of generals;" or, "the expression of one thing is the exclusion of another." Hence, say they, as the constitution has established the trial by jury in criminal cases, and is silent in respect to civil, this silence is an implied prohibition of trial by jury in regard to the latter.

The rules of legal interpretation are rules of *common sense*, adopted by the courts in the construction of the laws. The true test therefore, of a just application of them, is its conformity to the source from which they are derived. This being the case, let me ask if it is consistent with reason or common sense to suppose, that a provision obliging the legislative power to commit the trial of criminal causes to juries, is a privation of its right to authorise or permit that mode of trial in other cases? Is it natural to suppose, that a command to do one thing, is a prohibition to the doing of another, which there was a previous power to do, and which is not incompatible with the thing commanded to be done? If such a supposition would be unnatural and unreasonable, it cannot be rational to maintain that an injunction of the trial by jury in certain cases is an interdiction of it in others.

A power to constitute courts, is a power to prescribe the mode of trial; and consequently, if nothing was said in the constitution on the subject of juries, the legislature would be at liberty either to adopt that institution, or to let it alone. This discretion in regard to criminal causes is abridged by the express injunction of trial by jury in all such cases; but it is of course left at large in relation to civil causes, there being a total silence on this head. The specification of an obligation to try all criminal causes in a particular mode, excludes indeed the obligation or necessity of employing the same mode in civil causes, but does not abridge *the power* of the legislature to exercise that mode if it should be thought proper. The pretence therefore, that the national legislature would not be at full liberty to submit all the civil causes of federal cognizance to the determination of juries, is a pretence destitute of all just foundation.

From these observations, this conclusion results, that the trial by jury in civil cases would not be abolished, and that the use attempted to be made of the maxims which have been quoted, is contrary to reason and common sense, and therefore not admissible. Even if these maxims had a precise technical sense, corresponding with the ideas of those who employ them upon the present occasion, which, however, is not the case, they would still be inapplicable to a constitution of government. In relation to such a subject, the natural and obvious sense of its provisions, apart from any technical rules, is the true criterion of construction.

Having now seen that the maxims relied upon will not bear the use made of them, let us endeavour to ascertain their proper use and true meaning. This will be best done by examples. The plan of the convention declares that the power of congress or in other words of the *national legislature*, shall extend to certain enumerated cases. This specification of particulars evidently excludes all pretension to a general legislative authority; because an affirmative grant of special powers would be absurd as well as useless, if a general authority was intended.

In like manner, the judicial authority of the federal judicatures, is declared by the constitution to comprehend certain cases particularly specified. The expression of those cases marks the precise limits beyond which the federal courts cannot extend their jurisdiction; because the objects of their cognizance being enumerated, the specification would be nugatory if it did not exclude all ideas of more extensive authority.

These examples might be sufficient to elucidate the maxims which have been mentioned, and designate the manner in which they should be used. But that there may be no possibility of misapprehension upon this subject I shall add one case more, to demonstrate the proper use of these maxims, and the abuse which has been made of them.

Let us suppose that by the laws of this state, a married woman was incapable of conveying her estate, and that the legislature, considering this as an evil, should enact that she might dispose of her property by deed executed in the presence of a magistrate. In such a case there can be no doubt but the specification would amount to an exclusion of any other mode of conveyance; because the woman having no previous power to alienate her property, the specification determines the particular mode which she is, for that purpose, to avail herself of. But let us further suppose that in a subsequent part of the same act it should be declared that no woman should dispose of any estate of a determinate value without the consent of three of her nearest relations, signified by their signing the deed; could it be inferred from this regulation that a married woman might not procure the approbation of her relations to a deed for conveying property of inferior value? The position is too absurd to merit a refutation, and yet this is precisely the position which those must establish who contend that the trial by juries, in civil cases, is abolished, because it is expressly provided for in cases of a criminal nature.

From these observations it must appear unquestionably true that trial by jury is in no case abolished by the proposed constitution, and it is equally true that in those controversies between individuals in which the great body of the people are likely to be interested, that institution will remain precisely in the same situation in which it is placed by the state constitutions, and will be in no degree altered or influenced by the adoption of the plan under consideration. The foundation of this assertion is that the national judiciary will have no cognizance of them, and of course they will remain determinable as heretofore by the state courts only, and in the manner which the state constitutions and laws prescribe. All land causes, except where claims under the grants of different states come into question, and all other controversies between the citizens of the same state, unless where they depend upon positive violations of the articles of union by acts of the state legislatures, will belong exclusively to the jurisdiction of the state tribunals. Add to this that admiralty causes, and almost all those which are of equity jurisdiction are determinable under our own government without the intervention of a jury, and the inference from the whole will be that this institution, as it exists with us at present, cannot possibly be affected to any great extent by the proposed alteration in our system of government.

The friends and adversaries of the plan of the convention, if they agree in nothing else, concur at least in the value they set upon the trial by jury: Or if there is any difference between them, it consists in this; the former regard it as a valuable safeguard to liberty, the latter represent it as the very palladium of free government. For my own part, the more the operation of the institution has fallen under my observation, the more reason I have discovered for holding it in high estimation; and it would be altogether superfluous to examine to what extent it deserves to be esteemed useful or essential in a representative republic, or how much more merit it may be entitled to as a defence against the oppressions of an hereditary monarch, than as a barrier to the tyranny of popular magistrates in a popular government. Discussions of this kind would be more curious than beneficial, as all are satisfied of the utility of the institution, and of its friendly aspect to liberty. But I must acknowledge that I cannot readily discern the inseparable connection between the existence of liberty and the trial by jury in civil cases. Arbitrary impeachments, arbitrary methods of prosecuting pretended offences, and arbitrary punishments upon arbitrary convictions have ever appeared to me to be the great engines of judicial despotism; and these have all relation to criminal proceedings. The trial by jury in criminal cases, aided by the *habeas corpus* act, seems therefore to be alone concerned in the question. And both of these are provided for in the most ample manner in the plan of the convention.

It has been observed, that trial by jury is a safeguard against an oppressive exercise of the power of taxation. This observation deserves to be canvassed.

It is evident that it can have no influence upon the legislature, in regard to the *amount* of the taxes to be laid, to the *objects* upon which they are to be imposed, or to the *rule* by which they are to be apportioned. If it can have any influence therefore, it must be upon the mode of collection, and the conduct of the officers entrusted with the execution of the revenue laws.

As to the mode of collection in this state, under our own constitution, the trial by jury is in most cases out of use. The taxes are usually levied by the more summary proceeding of distress and sale, as in cases of rent. And it is acknowledged on all hands, that this is essential to the efficacy of the revenue laws. The dilatory course of a trial at law to recover the taxes imposed on individuals, would neither suit the exigencies of the public, nor promote the convenience of the citizens. It would often occasion an accumulation of costs, more burthensome than the original sum of the tax to be levied.

And as to the conduct of the officers of the revenue, the provision in favor of trial by jury in criminal cases, will afford the security aimed at. Wilful abuses of a public authority, to the oppression of the subject, and every species of official extortion, are offences against the government; for which, the persons who commit them, may be indicted and punished according to the circumstances of the case.

The excellence of the trial by jury in civil cases, appears to depend on circumstances foreign to the preservation of liberty. The strongest argument in its favour is, that it is a security against corruption. As there is always more time and better opportunity to tamper with a standing body of magistrates than with a jury summoned for the occasion, there is room to suppose, that a corrupt influence would more easily find its way to the former than to the latter. The force of this consideration, is however, diminished by others. The sheriff who is the summoner of ordinary juries, and the clerks of courts who have the nomination of special juries, are themselves standing officers, and acting individually, may be supposed more accessible to the touch of corruption than the judges, who are a collective body. It is not difficult to see that it would be in the power of those officers to select jurors who would serve the purpose of the party as well as a corrupted bench. In the next place, it may fairly be supposed that there would be less difficulty in gaining some of the jurors promiscuously taken from the public mass, than in gaining men who had been chosen by the government for their probity and good character. But making every deduction for these considerations the trial by jury must still be a valuable check upon corruption. It greatly multiplies the impediments to its success. As matters now stand, it would be necessary to corrupt both court and jury; for where the jury have gone evidently wrong, the court will generally grant a new trial, and it would be in most cases of little use to practice upon the jury, unless the court could be likewise gained. Here then is a doubt security; and it will readily be perceived that this complicated agency tends to preserve the purity of both institutions. By increasing the obstacles to success it discourages attempts to seduce the integrity of either. The temptations to prostitution, which the judges might have to surmount, must certainly be much fewer while the co-operation of a jury is necessary, than they might be if they had themselves the exclusive determination of all causes.

Notwithstanding therefore the doubts I have expressed as to the essentiality of trial by jury, in civil cases, to liberty, I admit that it is in most cases, under proper regulations, an excellent method of determining questions of property; and that on this account alone it would be entitled to a constitutional provision in its favour, if it were possible to fix the limits within which it ought to be comprehended. There is however, in all cases, great difficulty in this; and men not blinded by enthusiasm, must be sensible that in a federal government which is a composition of societies whose ideas and institutions in relation to the matter materially vary from each other, that difficulty must be not a little augmented. For my own part, at every new view I take of the subject, I become more convinced of the reality of the obstacles, which we are authoritatively informed, prevented the insertion of a provision on this head in the plan of the convention.

The great difference between the limits of the jury trial in different states is not generally understood. And as it must have considerable influence on the sentence we ought to pass upon the omission complained of, in regard to this point, an explanation of it is necessary. In this state our judicial establishments resemble more nearly, than in any other, those of Great-Britain. We have courts of common law, courts of probates (analogous in certain matters to the spiritual courts in England) a court of admiralty, and a court of chancery. In the courts of common law only the trial by jury prevails, and this with some exceptions. In all the others a single judge presides and proceeds in general either according to the course of the cannon or civil law, without the aid of a jury.* In New-Jersey there is a court of chancery which proceeds like ours, but neither courts of admiralty, nor of probates, in the sense in which these last are established with us. In that state the courts of common law have the cognizance of those causes, which with us are determinable in the courts of admiralty and of probates, and of course the jury trial is more extensive in New-Jersey than in New-York. In Pennsylvania this is perhaps still more the case, for there is no court of chancery in that state, and its common law courts have equity jurisdiction. It has a

---

* It has been erroneously insinuated, with regard to the court of chancery, that this court generally tries disputed facts by a jury. The truth is, that references to a jury in that court rarely happen, and are in no case necessary, but where the validity of a devise of land comes into question.

court of admiralty, but none of probates, at least on the plan of ours. Delaware has in these respects imitated Pennsylvania. Maryland approaches more nearly to New-York, as does also Virginia, except that the latter has a plurality of chancellors. North-Carolina bears most affinity to Pennsylvania; South-Carolina to Virginia. I believe however that in some of those states which have distinct courts of admiralty, the causes depending in them are triable by juries. In Georgia there are none but common law courts, and an appeal of course lies from the verdict of one jury to another, which is called a special jury, and for which a particular mode of appointment is marked out. In Connecticut they have no distinct courts, either of chancery or of admiralty, and their courts of probates have no jurisdiction of causes. Their common law courts have admiralty, and to a certain extent, equity jurisdiction. In cases of importance their general assembly is the only court of chancery. In Connecticut therefore the trial by jury extends in *practice* further than in any other state yet mentioned. Rhode Island is I believe in this particular pretty much in the situation of Connecticut. Massachusetts and New-Hampshire, in regard to the blending of law, equity and admiralty, jurisdictions are in a similiar predicament. In the four eastern states the trial by jury not only stands upon a broader foundation than in the other states, but it is attended with a peculiarity unknown in its full extent to any of them. There is an appeal *of course* from one jury to another till there have been two verdicts out of three on one side.

From this sketch it appears, that there is a material diversity as well in the modification as in the extent of the institution of trial by jury in civil cases in the several states; and from this fact, these obvious reflections flow. First, that no general rule could have been fixed upon by the convention which would have corresponded with the circumstances of all the states; and secondly, that more, or at least as much might have been hazarded, by taking the system of any one state for a standard, as by omitting a provision altogether, and leaving the matter as it has been left, to legislative regulation.

The propositions which have been made for supplying the omission, have rather served to illustrate than to obviate the difficulty of the thing. The minority of Pennsylvania have proposed this mode of expression for the purpose—"trial by jury shall be as heretofore"—and this I maintain would be absolutely senseless and nugatory. The United States, in their united or collective capacity, are the OBJECT to which all general provisions in the constitution must necessarily be construed to refer. Now it is evident, that though trial by jury with various limitations is known in each state individually, yet in the United States *as such*, it is at this time altogether unknown, because the present federal government has no judiciary power whatever; and consequently there is no proper antecedent or previous establishment to which the term *heretofore* could relate. It would therefore be destitute of a precise meaning, and inoperative from its uncertainty.

As on the one hand, the form of the provision would not fulfil the intent of its proposers; so on the other, if I apprehend that intent rightly, it would be in itself inexpedient. I presume it to be, that causes in the federal courts should be tried by jury, if in the state where the courts sat, that mode of trial would obtain in a similiar case in the state courts—that is to say admiralty causes should be tried in Connecticut by a jury, and in New-York without one. The capricious operation of so dissimilar a method of trial in the same cases, under the same government, is of itself sufficient to indispose every well regulated judgment towards it. Whether the cause should be tried with or without a jury, would depend in a great number of cases, on the accidental situation of the court and parties.

But this is not in my estimation the greatest objection. I feel a deep and deliberate conviction, that there are many cases in which the trial by jury is an ineligible one. I think it so particularly in cases which concern the public peace with foreign nations; that is in most cases where the question turns wholly on the laws of nations. Of this nature among others are all prize causes. Juries cannot be supposed competent to investigations, that require a thorough knowledge of the laws and usages of nations, and they will sometimes be under the influence of impressions which will not suffer them to pay sufficient regard to those considerations of public policy which ought to guide their enquiries. There would of course be always danger that the rights of other nations might be infringed by their decisions, so as to afford occasions of reprisal and war. Though the proper province of juries be to determine matters of fact, yet in most cases legal consequences are complicated with fact in such a manner as to render a separation impracticable.

It will add great weight to this remark in relation to prize causes to mention that the method of determining them has been thought worthy of particular regulation in various treaties between different powers of Europe, and that pursuant to such treaties they are determinable in Great-Britain in the last resort before the king himself in his privy council, where the fact as well as the law undergoes a re-examination. This alone demonstrates the impolicy of inserting a fundamental provision in the constitution which would make the state systems a standard for the national government in the article under consideration, and the danger of incumbering the government with any constitutional provisions, the propriety of which is not indisputable.

My convictions are equally strong that great advantages result from the separation of the equity from the law jurisdiction; and that the causes which belong to the former would be improperly committed to juries. The great and primary use of a court of equity is to give relief *in extraordinary cases*, which are *exceptions** to general rules. To unite the jurisdiction of such cases with the ordinary jurisdiction must have a tendency to unsettle the general rules and to subject every case that arises to a *special* determination. While the separation of the one from the other has the contrary effect of rendering one a sentinel over the other, and of keeping each within the expedient limits. Besides this the circumstances that constitute cases proper for courts of equity, are in many instances so nice and intricate, that they are incompatible with the genius of trials by jury. They require often such long, deliberate and critical investigation as would be impracticable to men called from their occupations and obliged to decide before they were permitted to return to them. The simplicity and expedition which form the distinguishing characters of this mode of trial require that the matter to be decided should be

---

* It is true that the principles by which that relief is governed are now reduced to a regular system, but it is not the less true that they are in the main, applicable to SPECIAL circumstances which form exceptions to general rules.

reduced to some single and obvious point; while the litigations usual in chancery frequently comprehend a long train of minute and independent particulars.

It is true that the separation of the equity from the legal jurisdiction is peculiar to the English system of jurisprudence; which is the model that has been followed in several of the states. But it is equally true, that the trial by jury has been unknown in every case in which they have been united. And the separation is essential to the preservation of that institution in its pristine purity. The nature of a court of equity will readily permit the extension of its jurisdiction to matters of law, but it is not a little to be suspected, that the attempt to extend the jurisdiction of the courts of law to matters of equity will not only be unproductive of the advantages which may be derived from courts of chancery, on the plan upon which they are established in this state, but will tend gradually to change the nature of the courts of law, and to undermine the trial by jury, by introducing questions too complicated for a decision in that mode.

These appear to be conclusive reasons against incorporating the systems of all the states in the formation of the national judiciary; according to what may be conjectured to have been the intent of the Pennsylvania minority. Let us now examine how far the proposition of Massachusetts is calculated to remedy the supposed defect.

It is in this form—"In civil actions between citizens of different states, every issue of fact, arising in *actions at common law*, may be tried by a jury, if the parties, or either of them, request it."

This at best is a proposition confined to one description of causes; and the inference is fair either that the Massachusetts convention considered that as the only class of federal causes, in which the trial by jury would be proper; or that if desirous of a more extensive provision, they found it impracticable to devise one which would properly answer the end. If the first, the omission of a regulation respecting so partial an object, can never be considered as a material imperfection in the system. If the last, it affords a strong corroboration of the extreme difficulty of the thing.

But this is not all: If we advert to the observations already made respecting the courts that subsist in the several states of the union, and the different powers exercised by them, it will appear, that there are no expressions more vague and indeterminate than those which have been employed to characterise *that* species of causes which it is intended shall be entitled to a trial by jury. In this state the boundaries between actions at common law and actions of equitable jurisdiction are ascertained in conformity to the rules which prevail in England upon that subject. In many of the other states, the boundaries are less precise. In some of them, every cause is to be tried in a court of common law, and upon that foundation every action may be considered as an action at common law to be determined by a jury, if the parties or either of them chuse it. Hence the same irregularity and confusion would be introduced by a compliance with this proposition, that I have already noticed as resulting from the regulation proposed by the Pennsylvania minority. In one state a cause would receive its determination from a jury, if the parties or either of them requested it; but in another state a cause exactly similar to the other must be decided without the intervention of a jury, because the state judicatories varied as to common law jurisdiction.

It is obvious therefore that the Massachusetts proposition, upon this subject, cannot operate as a general regulation until some uniform plan, with respect to the limits of common law and equitable jurisdictions shall be adopted by the different states. To devise a plan of that kind is a task arduous in itself, and which it would require much time and reflection to mature. It would be extremely difficult, if not impossible, to suggest any general regulation that would be acceptable to all the states in the union, or that would perfectly quadrate with the several state institutions.

It may be asked, why could not a reference have been made to the constitution of this state, taking that, which is allowed by me to be a good one, as a standard for the United States? I answer that it is not very probable the other states should entertain the same opinion of our institutions which we do ourselves. It is natural to suppose that they are hitherto more attached to their own, and that each would struggle for the preference. If the plan of taking one state as a model for the whole had been thought of in the convention, it is to be presumed that the adoption of it in that body, would have been rendered difficult by the predilection of each representation in favour of its own government; and it must be uncertain which of the states would have been taken as the model. It has been shewn that many of them would be improper ones. And I leave it to conjecture whether, under all circumstances, it is most likely that New-York or some other state would have been preferred. But admit that a judicious selection could have been effected in the convention, still there would have been great danger of jealousy and disgust in the other states, at the partiality which had been shewn to the institutions of one. The enemies of the plan would have been furnished with a fine pretext for raising a host of local prejudices against it, which perhaps might have hazarded in no inconsiderable degree, its final establishment.

To avoid the embarrassments of a definition of the cases which the trial by jury ought to embrace, it is some times suggested by men of enthusiastic tempers, that a provision might have been inserted for establishing it in all cases whatsoever. For this I believe no precedent is to be found in any member of the union; and the considerations which have been stated in discussing the proposition of the minority of Pennsylvania, must satisfy every sober mind that the establishment of the trial by jury in *all* cases, would have been an unpardonable error in the plan.

In short, the more it is considered, the more arduous will appear the task of fashioning a provision in such a form, as not to express too little to answer the purpose, or too much to be adviseable; or which might not have opened other sources of opposition to the great and essential object of introducing a firm national government.

I cannot but persuade myself on the other hand, that the different lights in which the subject has been placed in the course of these observations, will go far towards removing in candid minds, the apprehensions they may have entertained on the point. They have tended to shew that the security of liberty is materially concerned only in the trial by jury in criminal cases, which is provided for in the most ample manner in the plan of the convention; that even in far the greatest proportion of civil cases, and those in which the great body of the community is interested, that mode of trial will remain in its full force, as established in the state constitutions, untouched and unaffected by the plan of the convention: That it is in no case abolished* by that plan; and that there are great if not insurmountable difficulties in the way of making any precise and proper provision for it in a constitution for the United States.

The best judges of the matter will be the least anxious for a constitutional establishment of the trial by jury in civil cases, and will be the most ready to admit that the changes which are continually happening in the affairs of society, may render a different mode of determining questions of property, preferable in many cases, in which that mode of trial now prevails. For my own part, I acknowledge myself to be convinced that even in this state, it might be advantageously extended to some cases to which it does not at present apply, and might as advantageously be abridged in others. It is conceded by all reasonable men, that it ought not to obtain in all cases. The examples of innovations which contract its ancient limits, as well in these states as in Great-Britain, afford a strong presumption that its former extent has been found inconvenient; and give room to suppose that future experience may discover the propriety and utility of other exceptions. I suspect it to be impossible in the nature of the thing, to fix the salutary point at which the operation of the institution ought to stop; and this is with me a strong argument for leaving the matter to the discretion of the legislature.

This is now clearly understood to be the case in Great-Britain, and it is equally so in the state of Connecticut; and yet it may be safely affirmed, that more numerous encroachments have been made upon the trial by jury in this state since the revolution, though provided for by a positive article of our constitution, than has happened in the same time either in Connecticut or Great-Britain. It may be added that

---

* Vide No. LXXXI, in which the supposition of its being abolished by the appellate jurisdiction in matters of fact being vested in the supreme court is examined and refuted.

these encroachments have generally originated with the men who endeavour to persuade the people they are the warmest defenders of popular liberty, but who have rarely suffered constitutional obstacles to arrest them in a favourite career. The truth is that the general GENIUS of a government is all that can be substantially relied upon for permanent effects. Particular provisions, though not altogether useless, have far less virtue and efficacy than are commonly ascribed to them; and the want of them will never be with men of sound discernment a decisive objection to any plan which exhibits the leading characters of a good government.

It certainly sounds not a little harsh and extraordinary to affirm that there is no security for liberty in a constitution which expressly establishes the trial by jury in criminal cases, because it does not do it in civil also; while it is a notorious fact that Connecticut, which has been always regarded as the most popular state in the union, can boast of no constitutional provision for either.

PUBLIUS.

The Federalist, May 28, 1788

The Federalist No. 84

To the People of the State of New-York.

In the course of the foregoing review of the constitution I have taken notice of, and endeavoured to answer, most of the objections which have appeared against it. There however remain a few which either did not fall naturally under any particular head, or were forgotten in their proper places. These shall now be discussed; but as the subject has been drawn into great length, I shall so far consult brevity as to comprise all my observations on these miscellaneous points in a single paper.

The most considerable of these remaining objections is, that the plan of the convention contains no bill of rights. Among other answers given to this, it has been upon different occasions remarked, that the constitutions of several of the states are in a similar predicament. I add, that New-York is of this number. And yet the opposers of the new system in this state, who profess an unlimited admiration for its constitution, are among the most intemperate partizans of a bill of rights. To justify their zeal in this matter, they alledge two things; one is, that though the constitution of New-York has no bill of rights prefixed to it, yet it contains in the body of it various provisions in favour of particular privileges and rights, which in substance amount to the same thing; the other is, that the constitution adopts in their full extent the common and statute law of Great-Britain, by which many other rights not expressed in it are equally secured.

To the first I answer, that the constitution proposed by the convention contains, as well as the constitution of this state, a number of such provisions.

Independent of those, which relate to the structure of the government, we find the following: Article I. section 3. clause 7. "Judgment in cases of impeachment shall not extend further than to removal from office, and disqualification to hold and enjoy any office of honour, trust or profit under the United States; but the party convicted shall nevertheless be liable and subject to indictment, trial, judgment and punishment, according to law." Section 9. of the same article, clause 2. "The privilege of the writ of *habeas corpus* shall not be suspended, unless when in cases of rebellion or invasion the public safety may require it." Clause 3. "No bill of attainder or *ex post facto* law shall be passed." Clause 7. "No title of nobility shall be granted by the United States: And no person holding any office of profit or trust under them, shall, without the consent of congress, accept of any present, emolument, office or title, of any kind whatever, from any king, prince or foreign state." Article III. section 2. clause 3. "The trial of all crimes, except in cases of impeachment, shall be by jury; and such trial shall be held in the state where the said crimes shall have been committed; but when not committed within any state, the trial shall be at such place or places as the congress may by law have directed." Section 3, of the same article, "Treason against the United States shall consist only in levying war against them, or in adhering to their enemies, giving them aid and comfort. No person shall be convicted of treason unless on the testimony of two witness to the same overt act, or on confession in open court." And clause 3, of the same section. "The congress shall have power to declare the punishment of treason, but no attainder of treason shall work corruption of blood, or forfeiture, except during the life of the person attainted."

It may well be a question whether these are not upon the whole, of equal importance with any which are to be found in the constitution of this state. The establishment of the writ of *habeas corpus*, the prohibition of *ex post facto* laws, and of TITLES OF NOBILITY, *to which we have no corresponding provisions in our constitution*, are perhaps greater securities to liberty and republicanism than any it contains. The creation of crimes after the commission of the fact, or in other words, the subjecting of men to punishment for things which, when they were done, were breaches of no law, and the practice of arbitrary imprisonments have been in all ages the favourite and most formidable instruments of tyranny. The observations of the judicious Blackstone* in reference to the latter, are well worthy of recital. "To bereave a man of life (says he)

---

* Vide Blackstone's Commentaries, vol. I, page 136.

or by violence to confiscate his estate, without accusation or trial, would be so gross and notorious an act of despotism, as must at once convey the alarm of tyranny throughout the whole nation; but confinement of the person by secretly hurrying to goal, where his sufferings are unknown or forgotten, is a less public, a less striking, and therefore *a more dangerous engine* of arbitrary government." And as a remedy for this fatal evil, he is every where peculiarly emphatical in his encomiums on the *habeas corpus* act, which in one place he calls "the BULWARK of the British constitution."*

Nothing need be said to illustrate the importance of the prohibition of titles of nobility. This may truly be denominated the corner stone of republican government; for so long as they are excluded, there can never be serious danger that the government will be any other than that of the people.

To the second, that is, to the pretended establishment of the common and statute law by the constitution, I answer, that they are expressly made subject "to such alterations and provisions as the legislature shall from time to time make concerning the same." They are therefore at any moment liable to repeal by the ordinary legislative power, and of course have no constitutional sanction. The only use of the declaration was to recognize the ancient law, and to remove doubts which might have been occasioned by the revolution. This consequently can be considered as no part of a declaration of rights, which under our constitutions must be intended as limitations of the power of the government itself.

It has been several times truly remarked, that bills of rights are in their origin, stipulations between kings and their subjects, abridgments of prerogative in favor of privilege, reservations of rights not surrendered to the prince. Such was MAGNA CHARTA, obtained by the Barons, sword in hand, from king John. Such were the subsequent confirmations of that charter by subsequent princes. Such was the *petition of right* assented to by Charles the First, in the beginning of his reign. Such also was the declaration of right presented by the lords and commons to the prince of Orange in 1688, and afterwards thrown into the form of an act of parliament,

* Idem, vol. 4, page 438.

called the bill of rights. It is evident, therefore, that according to their primitive signification, they have no application to constitutions professedly founded upon the power of the people, and executed by their immediate representatives and servants. Here, in strictness, the people surrender nothing, and as they retain every thing, they have no need of particular reservations. "WE THE PEOPLE of the United States, to secure the blessings of liberty to ourselves and our posterity, do *ordain* and *establish* this constitution for the United States of America." Here is a better recognition of popular rights than volumes of those aphorisms which make the principal figure in several of our state bills of rights, and which would sound much better in a treatise of ethics than in a constitution of government.

But a minute detail of particular rights is certainly far less applicable to a constitution like that under consideration, which is merely intended to regulate the general political interests of the nation, than to a constitution which has the regulation of every species of personal and private concerns. If therefore the loud clamours against the plan of the convention on this score, are well founded, no epithets of reprobation will be too strong for the constitution of this state. But the truth is, that both of them contain all, which in relation to their objects, is reasonably to be desired.

I go further, and affirm that bills of rights, in the sense and in the extent in which they are contended for, are not only unnecessary in the proposed constitution, but would even be dangerous. They would contain various exceptions to powers which are not granted; and on this very account, would afford a colourable pretext to claim more than were granted. For why declare that things shall not be done which there is no power to do? Why for instance, should it be said, that the liberty of the press shall not be restrained, when no power is given by which restrictions may be imposed? I will not contend that such a provision would confer a regulating power; but it is evident that it would furnish, to men disposed to usurp, a plausible pretence for claiming that power. They might urge with a semblance of reason, that the constitution ought not to be charged with the absurdity of providing against the abuse of an authority, which was not given, and that the provision against restraining the liberty of the press afforded a clear implication, that a power to prescribe proper regulations concerning it, was intended to be vested in the national government. This may serve as a specimen of the numerous handles which would be given to the doctrine of constructive powers, by the indulgence of an injudicious zeal for bills of rights.

On the subject of the liberty of the press, as much has been said, I cannot forbear adding a remark or two: In the first place, I observe that there is not a syllable concerning it in the constitution of this state, and in the next, I contend that whatever has been said about it in that of any other state, amounts to nothing. What signifies a declaration that "the liberty of the press shall be inviolably preserved?" What is the liberty of the press? Who can give it any definition which would not leave the utmost latitude for evasion? I hold it to be impracticable; and from this, I infer, that its security, whatever fine declarations may be inserted in any constitution respecting it, must altogether depend on public opinion, and on the general spirit of the people and of the government.* And here, after all, as intimated upon another occasion, must we seek for the only solid basis of all our rights.

There remains but one other view of this matter to conclude the point. The truth is, after all the declamation we

---

* To show that there is a power in the constitution by which the liberty of the press may be affected, recourse has been had to the power of taxation. It is said that duties may be laid upon publications so high as to amount to a prohibition. I know not by what logic it could be maintained that the declarations in the state constitutions, in favour of the freedom of the press, would be a constitutional impediment to the imposition of duties upon publications by the state legislatures. It cannot certainly be pretended that any degree of duties, however low, would be an abridgement of the liberty of the press. We know that newspapers are taxed in Great-Britain, and yet it is notorious that the press no where enjoys greater liberty than in that country. And if duties of any kind may be laid without a violation of that liberty, it is evident that the extent must depend on legislative discretion, regulated by public opinion; so that after all, general declarations respecting the liberty of the press will give it no greater security than it will have without them. The same invasions of it may be effected under the state constitutions which contain those declarations through the means of taxation, as under the proposed constitution which has nothing of the kind. It would be quite as significant to declare that government ought to be free, that taxes ought not to be excessive, &c., as that the liberty of the press ought not to be restrained.

have heard, that the constitution is itself in every rational sense, and to every useful purpose, A BILL OF RIGHTS. The several bills of rights, in Great-Britain, form its constitution, and conversely the constitution of each state is its bill of rights. And the proposed constitution, if adopted, will be the bill of rights of the union. Is it one object of a bill of rights to declare and specify the political privileges of the citizens in the structure and administration of the government? This is done in the most ample and precise manner in the plan of the convention, comprehending various precautions for the public security, which are not to be found in any of the state constitutions. Is another object of a bill of rights to define certain immunities and modes of proceeding, which are relative to personal and private concerns? This we have seen has also been attended to, in a variety of cases, in the same plan. Adverting therefore to the substantial meaning of a bill of rights, it as absurd to allege that it is not to be found in the work of the convention. It may be said that it does not go far enough, though it will not be easy to make this appear; but it can with no propriety be contended that there is no such thing. It certainly must be immaterial what mode is observed as to the order of declaring the rights of the citizens, if they are to be found in any part of the instrument which establishes the government. And hence it must be apparent that much of what has been said on this subject rests merely on verbal and nominal distinctions, which are entirely foreign from the substance of the thing.

Another objection, which has been made, and which from the frequency of its repetition it is to be presumed is relied on, is of this nature: It is improper (say the objectors) to confer such large powers, as are proposed, upon the national government; because the seat of that government must of necessity be too remote from many of the states to admit of a proper knowledge on the part of the constituent, of the conduct of the representative body. This argument, if it proves any thing, proves that there ought to be no general government whatever. For the powers which it seems to be agreed on all hands, ought to be vested in the union, cannot be safely intrusted to a body which is not under every requisite controul. But there are satisfactory reasons to shew that the objection is in reality not well founded. There is in most of the arguments which relate to distance a palpable illusion of the imagination. What are the sources of information by which the people in Montgomery county must regulate their judgment of the conduct of their representatives in the state legislature? Of personal observation they can have no benefit. This is confined to the citizens on the spot. They must therefore depend on the information of intelligent men, in whom they confide—and how must these men obtain their information? Evidently from the complection of public measures, from the public prints, from correspondences with their representatives, and with other persons who reside at the place of their deliberation. This does not apply to Montgomery county only, but to all the counties, at any considerable distance from the seat of government.

It is equally evident that the same sources of information would be open to the people, in relation to the conduct of their representatives in the general government; and the impediments to a prompt communication which distance may be supposed to create, will be overballanced by the effects of the vigilance of the state governments. The executive and legislative bodies of each state will be so many centinels over the persons employed in every department of the national administration; and as it will be in their power to adopt and pursue a regular and effectual system of intelligence, they can never be at a loss to know the behaviour of those who represent their constituents in the national councils, and can readily communicate the same knowledge to the people. Their disposition to apprise the community of whatever may prejudice its interests from another quarter, may be relied upon, if it were only from the rivalship of power. And we may conclude with the fullest assurance, that the people, through that channel, will be better informed of the conduct of their national representatives, than they can be by any means they now possess of that of their state representatives.

It ought also to be remembered, that the citizens who inhabit the country at and near the seat of government, will in all questions that affect the general liberty and prosperity, have the same interest with those who are at a distance; and that they will stand ready to sound the alarm when necessary, and to point out the actors in any pernicious project. The public papers will be expeditious messengers of intelligence to the most remote inhabitants of the union.

Among the many extraordinary objections which have appeared against the proposed constitution, the most extraordinary and the least colourable one, is derived from the want of some provision respecting the debts due *to* the United States. This has been represented as a tacit relinquishment of those debts, and as a wicked contrivance to screen public defaulters. The newspapers have teemed with the most inflammatory railings on this head; and yet there is nothing clearer than that the suggestion is entirely void of foundation, and is the offspring of extreme ignorance or extreme dishonesty. In addition to the remarks I have made upon the subject in another place, I shall only observe, that as it is a plain dictate of common sense, so it is also an established doctrine of political law, that *"States neither lose any of their rights, nor are discharged from any of their obligations by a change in the form of their civil government."**

The last objection of any consequence which I at present recollect, turns upon the article of expence. If it were even true that the adoption of the proposed government would occasion a considerable increase of expence, it would be an objection that ought to have no weight against the plan. The great bulk of the citizens of America, are with reason convinced that union is the basis of their political happiness. Men of sense of all parties now, with few exceptions, agree that it cannot be preserved under the present system, nor without radical alterations; that new and extensive powers ought to be granted to the national head, and that these require a different organization of the federal government, a single body being an unsafe depository of such ample authorities. In conceding all this, the question of expence must be given up, for it is impossible, with any degree of safety, to narrow the foundation upon which the system is to stand. The two branches of the legislature are in the first instance, to consist of only sixty-five persons, which is the same number of which

---

* Vide Rutherford's Institutes, vol. 2. book II. chap. x. sec. xiv, and xv.— Vide also Grotius, book II, chap. ix, sect. viii, and ix.

congress, under the existing confederation, may be composed. It is true that this number is intended to be increased; but this is to keep pace with the increase of the population and resources of the country. It is evident, that a less number would, even in the first instance, have been unsafe; and that a continuance of the present number would, in a more advanced stage of population, be a very inadequate representation of the people.

Whence is the dreaded augmentation of expence to spring? One source pointed out, is the multiplication of offices under the new government. Let us examine this a little.

It is evident that the principal departments of the administration under the present government, are the same which will be required under the new. There are now a secretary at war, a secretary for foreign affairs, a secretary for domestic affairs, a board of treasury consisting of three persons, a treasurer, assistants, clerks, &c. These offices are indispensable under any system, and will suffice under the new as well as under the old. As to ambassadors and other ministers and agents in foreign countries, the proposed constitution can make no other difference, than to render their characters, where they reside, more respectable, and their services more useful. As to persons to be employed in the collection of the revenues, it is unquestionably true that these will form a very considerable addition to the number of federal officers; but it will not follow, that this will occasion an increase of public expence. It will be in most cases nothing more than an exchange of state officers for national officers. In the collection of all duties, for instance, the persons employed will be wholly of the latter description. The states individually will stand in no need of any for this purpose. What difference can it make in point of expence, to pay officers of the customs appointed by the state, or those appointed by the United States? There is no good reason to suppose, that either the number or the salaries of the latter, will be greater than those of the former.

Where then are we to seek for those additional articles of expence which are to swell the account to the enormous size that has been represented to us? The chief item which occurs to me, respects the support of the judges of the United States. I do not add the president, because there is now a president of congress, whose expences may not be far, if any thing, short of those which will be incurred on account of the president of the United States. The support of the judges will clearly be an extra expence, but to what extent will depend on the particular plan which may be adopted in practice in regard to this matter. But it can upon no reasonable plan amount to a sum which will be an object of material consequence.

Let us now see what there is to counterballance any extra expences that may attend the establishment of the proposed government. The first thing that presents itself is, that a great part of the business, which now keeps congress sitting through the year, will be transacted by the president. Even the management of foreign negociations will naturally devolve upon him according to general principles concerted with the senate, and subject to their final concurrence. Hence it is evident, that a portion of the year will suffice for the session of both the senate and the house of representatives: We may suppose about a fourth for the latter, and a third or perhaps a half for the former. The extra business of treaties and appointments may give this extra occupation to the senate. From this circumstance we may infer, that until the house of representatives shall be increased greatly beyond its present number, there will be a considerable saving of expence from the difference between the constant session of the present, and the temporary session of the future congress.

But there is another circumstance, of great importance in the view of the economy. The business of the United States has hitherto occupied the state legislatures as well as congress. The latter has made requisitions which the former have had to provide for. Hence it has happened that the sessions of the state legislatures have been protracted greatly beyond what was necessary for the execution of the mere local business of the states. More than half their time has been frequently employed in matters which related to the United States. Now the members who compose the legislatures of the several states amount to two thousand and upwards; which number has hitherto performed what under the new system will be done in the first instance by sixty-five persons, and probably at no future period by above a fourth or a fifth of that number. The congress under the proposed government will do all the business of the United States themselves, without the intervention of the state legislatures, who thenceforth will have only to attend to the affairs of their particular states, and will not have to sit in any proportion as long as they have heretofore done. This difference, in the time of the sessions of the state legislatures, will be all clear gain, and will alone form an article of saving, which may be regarded as an equivalent for any additional objects of expence that may be occasioned by the adoption of the new system.

The result from these observations is, that the sources of additional expence from the establishment of the proposed constitution are much fewer than may have been imagined, that they are counterbalanced by considerable objects of saving, and that while it is questionable on which side the scale will preponderate, it is certain that a government less expensive would be incompetent to the purposes of the union.

PUBLIUS.

The Federalist, May 28, 1788

The Federalist No. 85

According to the formal division of the subject of these papers, announced in my first number, there would appear still to remain for discussion, two points, "the analogy of the proposed government to your own state constitution," and "the additional security, which its adoption will afford to republican government, to liberty and to property." But these heads have been so fully anticipated and exhausted in the progress of the work, that it would now scarcely be possible to do any thing more than repeat, in a more dilated form, what has been heretofore said; which the advanced stage of the question, and the time already spent upon it conspire to forbid.

It is remarkable, that the resemblance of the plan of the convention to the act which organizes the government of this state holds, not less with regard to many of the supposed defects, than to the real excellencies of the former. Among the pretended defects, are the re-eligibility of the executive, the want of a council, the omission of a formal bill of rights, the omission of a provision respecting the liberty of the press: These and several others, which have been noted in the course of our inquiries, are as much chargeable on the existing constitution of this state, as on the one proposed for the Union. And a man must have slender pretensions to consistency, who can rail at the latter for imperfections which he finds no difficulty in excusing in the former. Nor indeed can there be a better proof of the insincerity and affectation of some of the zealous adversaries of the plan of the convention among us, who profess to be the devoted admirers of the government under which they live, than the fury with which they have attacked that plan, for matters in regard to which our own constitution is equally, or perhaps more vulnerable.

The additional securities to republican government, to liberty and to property, to be derived from the adoption of the plan under consideration, consist chiefly in the restraints which the preservation of the union will impose on local factions and insurrections, and on the ambition of powerful individuals in single states, who might acquire credit and influence enough, from leaders and favorites, to become the despots of the people; in the diminution of the opportunities to foreign intrigue, which the dissolution of the confederacy would invite and facilitate; in the prevention of extensive military establishments, which could not fail to grow out of wars between the states in a disunited situation; in the express guarantee of a republican form of government to each; in the absolute and universal exclusion of titles of nobility; and in the precautions against the repetition of those practices on the part of the state governments, which have undermined the foundations of property and credit, have planted mutual distrust in the breasts of all classes of citizens, and have occasioned an almost universal prostration of morals.

Thus have I, my fellow citizens, executed the task I had assigned to myself; with what success, your conduct must determine. I trust at least you will admit, that I have not failed in the assurance I gave you respecting the spirit with which my endeavours should be conducted. I have addressed myself purely to your judgments, and have studiously avoided those asperities which are too apt to disgrace political disputants of all parties, and which have been not a little provoked by the language and conduct of the opponents of the constitution. The charge of a conspiracy against the liberties of the people, which has been indiscriminately brought against the advocates of the plan, has something in it too wanton and too malignant not to excite the indignation of every man who feels in his own bosom a refutation of the calumny. The perpetual changes which have been rung upon the wealthy, the well-born and the great, have been such as to inspire the disgust of all sensible men. And the unwarrantable concealments and misrepresentations which have been in various ways practiced to keep the truth from the public eye, have been of a nature to demand the reprobation of all honest men. It is not impossible that these circumstance may have occasionally betrayed me into intemperances of expression which I did not intend: It is certain that I have frequently felt a struggle between sensibility and moderation, and if the former has in some instances prevailed, it must be my excuse that it has been neither often nor much.

Let us now pause and ask ourselves whether, in the course of these papers, the proposed constitution has not been satisfactorily vindicated from the aspersions thrown upon it, and whether it has not been shewn to be worthy of the public approbation, and necessary to the public safety and prosperity. Every man is bound to answer these questions to himself, according to the best of his conscience and understanding, and to act agreeably to the genuine and sober dictates of his judgment. This is a duty, from which nothing can give him a dispensation. 'Tis one that he is called upon, nay, constrained by all the obligations that form the bands of society, to discharge sincerely and honestly. No partial motive, no particular interest, no pride of opinion, no temporary passion or prejudice, will justify to himself, to his country or to his posterity, an improper election of the part he is to act. Let him beware of an obstinate adherence to party. Let him reflect that the object upon which he is to decide is not a particular interest of the community, but the very existence of the nation. And let him remember that a majority of America has already given its sanction to the plan, which he is to approve or reject.

I shall not dissemble, that I feel an intire confidence in the arguments, which recommend the proposed system to your adoption; and that I am unable to discern any real force in those by which it has been opposed. I am persuaded, that it is the best which our political situation, habits and opinions will admit, and superior to any the revolution has produced.

Concessions on the part of the friends of the plan, that it has not a claim to absolute perfection, have afforded matter of no small triumph to its enemies. Why, say they, should we adopt an imperfect thing? Why not amend it, and make it perfect before it is irrevocably established? This may be plausible enough, but it is only plausible. In the first place I remark, that the extent of these concessions has been greatly exaggerated. They have been stated as amounting to an admission, that the plan is radically defective; and that, without material alterations, the rights and the interests of the community cannot be safely confided to it. This, as far as I have understood the meaning of those who make the concessions, is an intire perversion of their sense. No advocate of the measure can be found who will not declare as his sentiment, that the system, though it may not be perfect in every part, is upon the whole a good one, is the best that the present views and circumstances of the country will permit, and is such an one as promises every species of security which a reasonable people can desire.

I answer in the next place, that I should esteem it the extreme of imprudence to prolong the precarious state of our national affairs, and to expose the union to the jeopardy of successive experiments, in the chimerical pursuit of a perfect plan. I never expect to see a perfect work from imperfect man. The result of the deliberations of all collective bodies must necessarily be a compound as well of the errors and prejudices, as of the good sense and wisdom of the individuals of whom they are composed. The compacts which are to embrace thirteen distinct states, in a common bond of amity and union, must as necessarily be a compromise of as many dissimilar interests and inclinations. How can perfection spring from such materials?

The reasons assigned in an excellent little pamphlet lately published in this city* are unanswerable to shew the utter improbability of assembling a new convention, under circumstances in any degree so favourable to a happy issue, as those in which the late convention met, deliberated and concluded. I will not repeat the arguments there used, as I presume the production itself has had an extensive circulation. It is certainly well worthy the perusal of every friend to his country. There is however one point of light in which the subject of amendments still remains to be considered; and in which it has not yet been exhibited to public view. I cannot resolve to conclude, without first taking a survey of it in this aspect.

It appears to me susceptible of absolute demonstration, that it will be far more easy to obtain subsequent than previous amendments to the constitution. The moment an alteration is made in the present plan, it becomes, to the purpose of adoption, a new one, and must undergo a new decision of each state. To its complete establishment throughout the union, it will therefore require the concurrence of thirteen states. If, on the contrary, the constitution proposed should

---

* Intitled "An Address to the people of the state of New-York."

once be ratified by all the states as it stands, alterations in it may at any time be affected by nine states. Here then the chances are as thirteen to nine* in favour of subsequent amendments, rather than of the original adoption of an intire system.

This is not all. Every constitution for the United States must inevitably consist of a great variety of particulars, in which thirteen independent states are to be accommodated in their interests or opinions of interest. We may of course expect to see, in any body of men charged with its original formation, very different combinations of the parts upon different points. Many of those who form the majority on one question may become the minority on a second, and an association dissimilar to either may constitute the majority on a third. Hence the necessity of moulding and arranging all the particulars which are to compose the whole in such a manner as to satisfy all the parties to the compact; and hence also an immense multiplication of difficulties and casualties in obtaining the collective assent to a final act. The degree of that multiplication must evidently be in a ratio to the number of particulars and the number of parties.

But every amendment to the constitution, if once established, would be a single proposition, and might be brought forward singly. There would then be no necessity for management or compromise, in relation to any other point, no giving nor taking. The will of the requisite number would at once bring the matter to a decisive issue. And consequently whenever nine† or rather ten states, were united in the desire of a particular amendment, that amendment must infallibly take place. There can therefore be no comparison between the facility of effecting an amendment, and that of establishing in the first instance a complete constitution.

In opposition to the probability of subsequent amendments it has been urged, that the persons delegated to the administration of the national government, will always be disinclined to yield up any portion of the authority of which they were once possessed. For my own part I acknowledge a thorough

---

*† It may rather be said TEN for though two-thirds may set on foot the measure, three-fourths must ratify.

conviction that any amendments which may, upon mature consideration, be thought useful, will be applicable to the organization of the government, not to the mass of its powers; and on this account alone, I think there is no weight in the observation just stated. I also think there is little weight in it on another account. The intrinsic difficulty of governing THIRTEEN STATES at any rate, independent of calculations upon an ordinary degree of public spirit and integrity, will, in my opinion, constantly *impose* on the national rulers the *necessity* of a spirit of accommodation to the reasonable expectations of their constituents. But there is yet a further consideration, which proves beyond the possibility of doubt, that the observation is futile. It is this, that the national rulers, whenever nine states concur, will have no option upon the subject. By the fifth article of the plan the congress will be *obliged*, "on the application of the legislatures of two-thirds of the states, (which at present amounts to nine) to call a convention for proposing amendments, which *shall be valid* to all intents and purposes, as part of the constitution, when ratified by the legislatures of three-fourths of the states, or by conventions in three-fourths thereof." The words of this article are peremptory. The Congress "*shall* call a convention." Nothing in this particular is left to the discretion of that body. And of consequence all the declamation about their disinclination to a change, vanishes in air. Nor however difficult it may be supposed to unite two-thirds or three-fourths of the state legislatures, in amendments which may affect local interest, can there be any room to apprehend any such difficulty in a union on points which are merely relative to the general liberty or security of the people. We may safely rely on the disposition of the state legislatures to erect barriers against the encroachments of the national authority.

If the foregoing argument is a fallacy, certain it is that I am myself deceived by it; for it is, in my conception, one of those rare instances in which a political truth can be brought to the test of mathematical demonstration. Those who see the matter in the same light with me, however zealous they may be for amendments, must agree in the propriety of a previous adoption, as the most direct road to their own object.

The zeal for attempts to amend, prior to the establishment of the constitution, must abate in every man, who, is ready to accede to the truth of the following observations of a writer, equally solid and ingenious: "To balance a large state or society (says he) whether monarchical or republican, on general laws, is a work of so great difficulty, that no human genius, however comprehensive, is able by the mere dint of reason and reflection, to effect it. The judgments of many must unite in the work: EXPERIENCE must guide their labour: Time must bring it to perfection: And the FEELING of inconveniences must correct the mistakes which they inevitably fall into, in their first trials and experiments."* These judicious reflections contain a lesson of moderation to all the sincere lovers of the union, and ought to put them upon their guard against hazarding anarchy, civil war, a perpetual alienation of the states from each other, and perhaps the military despotism of a victorious demagogue, in the pursuit of what they are not likely to obtain, but from TIME and EXPERIENCE. It may be in me a defect of political fortitude, but I acknowledge, that I cannot entertain an equal tranquillity with those who affect to treat the dangers of a longer continuance in our present situation as imaginary. A NATION without a NATIONAL GOVERNMENT is, in my view, an awful spectacle. The establishment of a constitution, in time of profound peace, by the voluntary consent of a whole people, is a PRODIGY, to the completion of which I look forward with trembling anxiety. I can reconcile it to no rules of prudence to let go the hold we now have, in so arduous an enterprise, upon seven out of the thirteen states; and after having passed over so considerable a part of the ground to recommence the course. I dread the more the consequences of new attempts, because I KNOW that POWERFUL INDIVIDUALS, in this and in other states, are enemies to a general national government, in every possible shape.

PUBLIUS.

* Hume's Essays, vol. I, page 128.—The rise of arts and sciences.

The Federalist, May 28, 1788

FEARS OF CIVIL WAR

To James Madison

My Dear Sir

In my last I think I informed you that the elections had turned out, beyond expectation, favourable to the Anti-fœderal party. They have a majority of two thirds in the Convention and according to the best estimate I can form of about four sevenths in the community. The views of the leaders in this City are pretty well ascertained to be turned towards a *long* adjournment say till next spring or Summer. Their incautious ones observe that this will give an opportunity to the state to *see how the government works and to act according to circumstances.*

My reasonings on the fact are to this effect. The leaders of the party hostile to the constitution are equally hostile to the Union. They are however afraid to reject the constitution at once because that step would bring matters to a crisis between this state and the states which had adopted the Constitution and between the parties in the state. A separation of the Southern district from the other part of the state it is perceived would become the object of the Fœderalists and of the two neighbouring states. They therefore resolve upon a long adjournment as the safest and most artful course to effect their final purpose. They suppose that when the Government gets into operation it will be obliged to take some steps in respect to revenue &c. which will furnish topics of declamation to its enemies in the several states and will strengthen the minorities. If any considerable discontent should show itself they will stand ready to head the opposition. If on the contrary the thing should go on smoothly and the sentiments of our own people should change they can then elect to come into the Union. They at all events take the chances of time and the chapter of accidents.

How far their friends in the Country will go with them I am not able to say, but as they have always been found very obsequious we have little reason to calculate upon an uncompliant temper in the present instance.

For my own part the more I can penetrate the views of the Antifœderal party in this state, the more I dread the consequences of the non adoption of the Constitution by any of the other states, the more I fear an eventual disunion and civil war. God grant that Virginia may accede. Her example will have a vast influence on our politics. New Hampshire, all accounts give us to expect, will be an assenting state.

The number of the volumes of the Fœderalist which you desired have been forwarded as well the second as first, to the care of Governor Randolph. It was impossible to correct a certain error.

In a former letter I requested you to communicate to me by express the event of any decisive question in favour of the constitution authorising changes of horses &c with an assurance to the person sent that he will be liberally paid for his diligence.

June 8, 1788

Speech in the New York Ratifying Convention on Representation

Mr. *Hamilton* then reassumed his argument. When, said he, I had the honor to address the committee yesterday, I gave a history of the circumstances which attended the Convention, when forming the Plan before you. I endeavored to point out to you the principles of accommodation, on which this arrangement was made; and to shew that the contending interests of the States led them to establish the representation as it now stands. In the second place I attempted to prove, that, in point of number, the representation would be perfectly secure.

Sir, no man agrees more perfectly than myself to the main principle for which the gentlemen contend. I agree that there should be a broad democratic branch in the national legislature. But this matter, Sir, depends on circumstances; It is impossible, in the first instance to be precise and exact with regard to the number; and it is equally impossible to determine to what point it may be proper in future to increase it. On this ground I am disposed to acquiesce. In my reasonings on the subject of government, I rely more on the interests and the opinions of men, than on any speculative parchment provisions whatever. I have found, that Constitutions are more or less excellent, as they are more or less agreeable to the natural operation of things: I am therefore disposed not to dwell long on curious speculations, or pay much attention to modes and forms; but to adopt a system, whose principles have been sanctioned by experience; adapt it to the real state of our country; and depend on probable reasonings for its operation and result. I contend that sixty-five and twenty-six in two bodies afford perfect security, in the present state of things; and that the regular progressive enlargement, which was in the contemplation of the General Convention, will leave not an apprehension of danger in the most timid and suspicious mind. It will be the interest of the large states to increase the representation: This will be the standing instruction to their delegates. But, say the gentlemen, the Members of Congress will be interested not to increase the number, as it will diminish their relative influence. In all their reasoning upon the subject, there seems to be this fallacy: They suppose that the representative will have no motive of action, on the one side, but a sense of duty; or on the other, but corruption: They do not reflect, that he is to return to the community; that he is dependent on the will of the people, and that it cannot be his interest to oppose their wishes. Sir, the general sense of the people will regulate the conduct of their representatives. I admit that there are exceptions to this rule: There are certain conjunctures, when it may be necessary and proper to disregard the opinions which the majority of the people have formed: But in the general course of things, the popular views and even prejudices will direct the actions of the rulers.

All governments, even the most despotic, depend, in a great degree, on opinion. In free republics, it is most peculiarly the case: In these, the will of the people makes the essential principle of the government; and the laws which control the community, receive their tone and spirit from the public wishes. It is the fortunate situation of our country, that the minds of the people are exceedingly enlightened and refined: Here then we may expect the laws to be proportionably agreeable to the standard of perfect policy; and the wisdom of public measures to consist with the most intimate conformity between the views of the representative and his constituent. If the general voice of the people be for an increase, it undoubtedly must take place: They have it in their power to instruct their representatives; and the State Legislatures, which appoint the Senators, may enjoin it also upon them. Sir, if I believed that the number would remain at sixty-five, I confess I should give my vote for an amendment; though in a different form from the one proposed.

The amendment proposes a ratio of one for twenty thousand: I would ask, by what rule or reasoning it is determined, that one man is a better representative for twenty than thirty thousand? At present we have three millions of people; in twenty-five years, we shall have six millions; and in forty years, nine millions: And this is a short period, as it relates to the existence of States. Here then, according to the ratio of one for thirty thousand, we shall have, in forty years, three hundred representatives. If this be true, and if this be a safe representation, why be dissatisfied? why embarrass the Constitution with amendments, that are merely speculative and useless. I agree with the gentleman, that a very small number might give some colour for suspicion: I acknowledge, that ten would be unsafe; on the other hand, a thousand would be too numerous. But I ask him, why will not ninety-one be an adequate and safe representation? This at present appears to be the proper medium. Besides, the President of the United States will be himself the representative of the people. From the competition that ever subsists between the branches of government, the President will be induced to protect their rights, whenever they are invaded by either branch. On whatever side we view this subject, we discover various and powerful checks to the encroachments of Congress. The true and permanent interests of the members are opposed to corruption: Their number is vastly too large for easy combination: The rivalship between the houses will forever prove an insuperable obstacle: The people have an obvious and powerful protection in their own State governments: Should any thing dangerous be attempted, these bodies of perpetual observation, will be capable of forming and conducting plans of regular opposition. Can we suppose the people's love of liberty will not, under the incitement of their legislative leaders, be roused into resistance, and the madness of tyranny be extinguished at a blow? Sir, the danger is too distant; it is beyond all rational calculations.

It has been observed by an honorable gentleman, that a pure democracy, if it were practicable, would be the most perfect government. Experience has proved, that no position in politics is more false than this. The ancient democracies, in which the people themselves deliberated, never possessed one feature of good government. Their very character was tyranny; their figure deformity: When they assembled, the field of debate presented an ungovernable mob, not only incapable of deliberation, but prepared for every enormity. In these assemblies, the enemies of the people brought forward their plans of ambition systematically. They were opposed by their enemies of another party; and it became a matter of contingency, whether the people subjected themselves to be led blindly by one tyrant or by another.

It was remarked yesterday, that a numerous representation was necessary to obtain the confidence of the people. This is not generally true. The confidence of the people will easily be gained by a good administration. This is the true touchstone. I could illustrate the position, by a variety of historical examples, both ancient and modern. In Sparta, the Ephori were a body of magistrates, instituted as a check upon the senate, and representing the people. They consisted of only five men: But they were able to protect their rights, and therefore enjoyed their confidence and attachment. In Rome, the people were represented by three Tribunes, who were afterwards increased to ten. Every one acquainted with the history of that republic, will recollect how powerful a check to the senatorial encroachments, this small body proved; how unlimited a confidence was placed in them by the people whose guardians they were; and to what a conspicuous station in the government, their influence at length elevated the Plebians. Massachusetts has three hundred representatives; New York has sixty-five. Have the people in this state less confidence in their representation, than the people of that? Delaware has twenty-one: Do the inhabitants of New-York feel a higher confidence than those of Delaware? I have stated these examples, to prove that the gentleman's principle is not just. The popular confidence depends on circumstances very distinct from considerations of number. Probably the public attachment is more strongly secured by a train of prosperous events, which are the result of wise deliberation and vigorous execution, and to which large bodies are much less competent than small ones. If the representative conducts with propriety, he will necessarily enjoy the good will of the constituent. It appears then, if my reasoning be just, that the clause is perfectly proper, upon the principles of the gentleman who contends for the amendment: as there is in it the greatest degree of present security, and a moral certainty of an increase equal to our utmost wishes.

It has been farther, by the gentlemen in opposition, observed, that a large representation is necessary to understand the interests of the people. This principle is by no means true in the extent to which the gentleman seems to carry it. I would ask, why may not a man understand the interests of thirty as well as of twenty? The position appears to be made upon the unfounded presumption, that all the interests of all parts of the community must be represented. No idea is more erroneous than this. Only such interests are proper to be represented, as are involved in the powers of the General Government. These interests come compleatly under the observation of one, or a few men; and the requisite information is by no means augmented in proportion to the increase of number. What are the objects of the Government? Commerce, taxation, &c. In order to comprehend the interests of commerce, is it necessary to know how wheat is raised, and in what proportion it is produced in one district and in another? By no means. Neither is this species of knowledge necessary in general calculations upon the subject of taxation. The information necessary for these purposes, is that which is open to every intelligent enquirer; and of which, five men may be as perfectly possessed as fifty. In royal governments, there are usually particular men to whom the business of taxation is committed. These men have the forming of systems of finance; and the regulation of the revenue. I do not mean to commend this practice. It proves however, this point; that a few individuals may be competent to these objects; and that large numbers are not necessary to perfection in the science of taxation. But granting, for a moment, that this minute and local knowledge the gentlemen contend for, is necessary, let us see, if under the New Constitution, it will not probably be found in the representation. The natural and proper mode of holding elections, will be to divide the state into districts, in proportion to the number to be elected. This state will consequently be divided at first into six. One man from each district will probably possess all the knowledge the gentlemen can desire. Are the senators of this state more ignorant of the interests of the people, than the assembly? Have they not ever enjoyed their confidence as much? Yet, instead of six districts, they are elected in four; and the chance of their being collected from the smaller divisions of the state consequently diminished. Their number is but twenty-four; and their powers are co-extensive with those of the assembly, and reach objects, which are most dear to the people—life, liberty and property.

Sir, we hear constantly a great deal, which is rather calculated to awake our passions, and create prejudices, than to conduct us to truth, and teach us our real interests. I do not suppose this to be the design of the gentlemen. Why then are we told so often of an aristocracy? For my part, I hardly know the meaning of this word as it is applied. If all we hear be true, this government is really a very bad one. But who are the aristocracy among us? Where do we find men elevated to a perpetual rank above their fellow citizens; and possessing powers entirely independent of them? The arguments of the gentlemen only go to prove that there are men who are rich, men who are poor, some who are wise, and others who are not— That indeed every distinguished man is an aristocrat. This reminds me of a description of the aristocrats, I have seen in a late publication, styled the Federal Farmer. The author reckons in the aristocracy, all governors of states, members of Congress, chief magistrates, and all officers of the militia. This description, I presume to say, is ridiculous. The image is a phantom. Does the new governmen render a rich man more eligible than a poor one? No. It requires no such qualification. It is bottomed on the broad and equal principle of your state constitution.

Sir, if the people have it in their option, to elect their most meritorious men; is this to be considered as an objection? Shall the constitution oppose their wishes, and abridge their most invaluable privilege? While property contines to be pretty equally divided, and a considerable share of information pervades the community; the tendency of the people's suffrages, will be to elevate merit even from obscurity. As riches increase and accumulate in few hands; as luxury prevails in society; virtue will be in a greater degree considered as only a graceful appendage of wealth, and the tendency of things will be to depart from the republican standard. This is the real disposition of human nature: It is what, neither the honorable member nor myself can correct. It is a common misfortune, that awaits our state constitution, as well as all others.

There is an advantage incident to large districts of election, which perhaps the gentlemen, amidst all their apprehensions of influence and bribery, have not adverted to. In large districts, the corruption of the electors is much more difficult:

Combinations for the purposes of intrigue are less easily formed: Factions and cabals are little known. In a small district, wealth will have a more complete influence; because the people in the vicinity of a great man, are more immediately his dependants, and because this influence has fewer objects to act upon. It has been remarked, that it would be disagreeable to the middle class of men to go to the seat of the new government. If this be so, the difficulty will be enhanced by the gentleman's proposal. If his argument be true, it proves, that the larger the representation is, the less will be your choice of having it filled. But, it appears to me frivolous to bring forward such arguments as these. It has answered no other purpose, than to induce me, by way of reply, to enter into discussions, which I consider as useless, and not applicable to our subject.

It is a harsh doctrine, that men grow wicked in proportion as they improve and enlighten their minds. Experience has by no means justified us in the supposition, that there is more virtue in one class of men than in another. Look through the rich and the poor of the community; the learned and the ignorant. Where does virtue predominate? The difference indeed consists, not in the quantity but kind of vices, which are incident to the various classes; and here the advantage of character belongs to the wealthy. Their vices are probably more favorable to the prosperity of the state, than those of the indigent; and partake less of moral depravity.

After all, Sir, we must submit to this idea, that the true principle of a republic is, that the people should choose whom they please to govern them. Representation is imperfect, in proportion as the current of popular favour is checked. This great source of free government, popular election, should be perfectly pure, and the most unbounded liberty allowed. Where this principle is adhered to; where, in the organization of the government, the legislative, executive and judicial branches are rendered distinct; where again the legislative is divided into separate houses, and the operations of each are controuled by various checks and balances, and above all, by the vigilance and weight of the state governments; to talk of tyranny, and the subversion of our liberties, is to speak the language of enthusiasm. This balance between the national and state governments ought to be dwelt on with peculiar attention, as it is of the utmost importance. It forms a double security to the people. If one encroaches on their rights, they will find a powerful protection in the other. Indeed they will both be prevented from overpassing their constitutional limits, by a certain rivalship, which will ever subsist between them. I am persuaded, that a firm union is as necessary to perpetuate our liberties, as it is to make us respectable; and experience will probably prove, that the national government will be as natural a guardian of our freedom, as the state legislatures themselves.

Suggestions, Sir, of an extraordinary nature, have been frequently thrown out in the course of the present political controversy. It gives me pain to dwell on topics of this kind; and I wish they might be dismissed. We have been told, that the old Confederation has proved inefficacious, only because intriguing and powerful men, aiming at a revolution, have been forever instigating the people, and rendering them disaffected with it. This, Sir, is a false insinuation. The thing is impossible. I will venture to assert, that no combination of designing men under Heaven, will be capable of making a government unpopular, which is in its principles a wise and good one; and vigorous in its operations.

The Confederation was framed amidst the agitation and tumult of society. It was composed of unfound materials put together in haste. Men of intelligence discovered the feebleness of the structure, in the first stages of its existence; but the great body of the people, too much engrossed with their distresses, to contemplate any but the immediate causes of them, were ignorant of the defects of their Constitution. But, when the dangers of war were removed, they saw clearly what they had suffered, and what they had yet to suffer from a feeble form of government. There was no need of discerning men to convince the people of their unhappy situation—the complaint was co-extensive with the evil, and both were common to all classes of the community. We have been told, that the spirit of patriotism and love of liberty are almost extinguished among the people; and that it has become a prevailing doctrine, that republican principles ought to be hooted out of the world. Sir, I am confident that such remarks as these are rather occasioned by the heat of argument, than by a cool conviction of their truth and justice. As far as my experience has extended, I have heard no such doctrine, nor have I discovered any diminution of regard for those rights and liberties, in defence of which, the people have fought and suffered. There have been, undoubtedly, some men who have had speculative doubts on the subject of government; but the principles of republicanism are founded on too firm a basis to be shaken by a few speculative and sceptical reasoners. Our error has been of a very different kind. We have erred through excess of caution, and a zeal false and impracticable. Our counsels have been destitute of consistency and stability. I am flattered with a hope, Sir, that we have now found a cure for the evils under which we have so long labored. I trust, that the proposed Constitution affords a genuine specimen of representative and republican government—and that it will answer, in an eminent degree, all the beneficial purposes of society.

June 21, 1788

Speech in the New York Ratifying Convention on Interests and Corruption

The Hon. Mr. *Hamilton.* Mr. Chairman I rise to take notice of the observations of the hon. member from Ulster. I imagine the objections he has stated, are susceptible of a complete and satisfactory refutation. But before I proceed to this, I shall attend to the arguments advanced by the gentlemen from Albany and Dutchess. These arguments have been frequently urged, and much confidence has been placed in their strength: The danger of corruption has been dwelt upon with peculiar emphasis, and presented to our view in the most heightened and unnatural colouring: Events, merely possible have been magnified by distempered imagination into inevitable realities; and the most distant and doubtful conjectures have been formed into a serious and infallible prediction. In the same spirit, the most fallacious calculations have been made: The lowest possible quorum has been contemplated as the number to transact important business; and a majority of these to decide in all cases on questions of infinite moment. Allowing, for the present, the propriety and truth of these apprehensions, it would be easy, in comparing the two constitutions, to prove that the chances of corruption under the new, are much fewer that those to which the old one is exposed. Under the old confederation, the important powers of declaring war, making peace, &c. can be exercised by nine states. On the presumption that the smallest constitutional number will deliberate and decide, those interesting powers will be committed to fewer men, under the ancient than under the new government. In the former, eighteen members, in the latter, not less than twenty-four may determine all great questions. Thus on the principles of the gentlemen, the fairer prospect of safety is clearly visible in the new government. That we may have the fullest conviction of the truth of this position, it ought to be suggested, as a decisive argument, that it will ever be the interest of the several states to maintain, under the new government, an ample representation: For, as every member has a vote, the relative influence and authority of each state will be in proportion to the number of representatives she has in Congress. There is not therefore a shadow of probability, that the number of acting members in the general legislature, will be ever reduced to a bare quorum; especially as the expence of their support is to be defrayed from a federal treasury: But under the existing confederation, as each state has but one vote, it will be a matter of indifference, on the score of influence, whether she delegates two or six representatives: And the maintenance of them forming a striking article in the state expenditures, will forever prove a capital inducement to retain or withdraw from the federal legislature, those delegates which her selfishness may too often consider as superfluous.

There is another source of corruption, in the old government, which the proposed plan is happily calculated to remedy. The concurrence of nine states, as has been observed, is necessary to pass resolves the most important, and on which, the safety of the republic may depend. If these nine states are at any time assembled, a foreign enemy, by dividing a state and gaining over and silencing a single member, may frustrate the most indispensible plan of national policy, and totally prevent a measure, essential to the welfare or existence of the empire. Here, then, we find a radical, dangerous defect, which will forever embarrass and obstruct the machine of government; and suspend our fate on the uncertain virtue of an individual. What a difference between the old and new constitution strikes our view! In the one, corruption must embrace a majority; in the other, her poison administered to a single man, may render the efforts of a majority totally vain. This mode of corruption is still more dangerous, as its operations are more secret and imperceptible: The exertions of active villainy are commonly accompanied with circumstances, which tend to its own exposure: But this negative kind of guilt has so many plausible apologies as almost to elude suspicion.

In all reasonings on the subject of corruption, much use has been made of the examples furnished by the British house of commons. Many mistakes have arisen from fallacious comparisons between our government and theirs. It is time, that the real state of this matter should be explained. By far the

greatest part of the house of commons is composed of representatives of towns or boroughs: These towns had antiently
no voice in parliament; but on the extension of commercial
wealth and influence, they were admitted to a seat. Many of
them are in the possession and gift of the king; and from their
dependence on him, and the destruction of the right of free
election, they are stigmatized with the appellation of rotten
boroughs. This is the true source of the corruption, which
has so long excited the severe animadversion of zealous politicians and patriots. But the knights of the shire, who form another branch of the house of commons, and who are chosen
from the body of the counties they represent, have been generally esteemed a virtuous and incorruptible set of men. I appeal, Sir, to the history of that house: This will shew us, that
the rights of the people have been ever very safely trusted to
their protection; that they have been the ablest bulwarks of
the British commons; and that in the conflict of parties, by
throwing their weight into one scale or the other, they have
uniformly supported and strengthened the constitutional
claims of the people. Notwithstanding the cry of corruption that has been perpetually raised against the house of
commons, it has been found, that that house, sitting at first
without any constitutional authority, became, at length, an
essential member of the legislature, and have since, by regular
gradations, acquired new and important accessions of privilege: That they have, on numerous occasions, impaired the
overgrown prerogative, and limited the incroachments of
monarchy.

An honorable member from Dutchess, (*Mr. Smith*) has observed, that the delegates from New-York, (for example) can
have very little information of the local circumstances of
Georgia or South-Carolina, except from the representatives of
those states; and on this ground, insists upon the expediency
of an enlargment of the representation; since, otherwise, the
majority must rely too much on the information of a few. In
order to determine whether there is any weight in this reasoning, let us consider the powers of the national government, and compare them with the objects of state legislation.
The powers of the new government are general, and calculated to embrace the aggregate interest of the Union, and the

general interest of each state, so far as it stands in relation to the whole. The object of the state governments is to provide for their internal interests, as unconnected with the United States, and as composed of minute parts or districts. A particular knowledge, therefore, of the local circumstances of any state, as they may vary in different districts, is unnecessary for the federal representative. As he is not to represent the interests or local wants of the county of Dutchess or Montgomery; neither is it necessary that he should be acquainted with their particular resources: But in the state governments, as the laws regard the interests of the people, in all their various minute divisions; it is necessary, that the smallest interests should be represented. Taking these distinctions into view, I think it must appear evident, that one discerning and intelligent man will be as capable of understanding and representing the general interests of a state, as twenty; because, one man can be as fully acquainted with the general state of the commerce, manufactures, population, production and common resources of a state, which are the proper objects of federal legislation. It is to be presumed, that few men originally possess a complete knowledge of the circumstances of other states; They must rely, therefore, on the information, to be collected from the representatives of those states: And if the above reasoning be just, it appears evident, I imagine, that this reliance will be as secure as can be desired.

Sir, in my experience of public affairs, I have constantly remarked, in the conduct of members of Congress, a strong and uniform attachment to the interests of their own state: These interests have, on many occasions, been adhered to, with an undue and illiberal pertinacity; and have too often been preferred to the welfare of the Union. This attachment has given birth to an unaccommodating spirit of party, which has frequently embarrassed the best measures: It is by no means, however, an object of surprize. The early connections we have formed; the habits and prejudices in which we have been bred, fix our affection so strongly, that no future objects of association can easily eradicate them: This, together with the entire and immediate dependence the representative feels on his constituent, will generally incline him to prefer the particular before the public good.

The subject, on which this argument of a small representation has been most plausibly used, is taxation. As to internal taxation, in which the difficulty principally rests, it is not probable, that any general regulation will originate in the national legislature. If Congress in times of great danger and distress, should be driven to this resource, they will undoubtedly adopt such measures, as are most conformable to the laws and customs of each state: They will take up your own codes and consult your own systems: This is a source of information which cannot mislead, and which will be equally accessible to every member. It will teach them the most certain, safe and expeditious mode of laying and collecting taxes in each state. They will appoint the officers of revenue agreeably to the spirit of your particular establishments; or they will make use of your own.

Sir, the most powerful obstacle to the members of Congress betraying the interests of their constituents, is the state legislatures themselves; who will be standing bodies of observation, possessing the confidence of the people, jealous of federal encroachments, and armed with every power to check the first essays of treachery. They will institute regular modes of enquiry: The complicated domestic attachments, which subsist between the state legislators and their electors, will ever make them vigilant guardians of the people's rights: Possessed of the means, and the disposition of resistance, the spirit of opposition will be easily communicated to the people; and under the conduct of an organized body of leaders, will act with weight and system. Thus it appears, that the very structure of the confederacy affords the surest preventives from error, and the most powerful checks to misconduct.

Sir, there is something in an argument, that has been urged, which, if it proves any thing, concludes against all union and all government; it goes to prove, that no powers should be entrusted to any body of men, because they may be abused. This is an argument of possibility and chance; one that would render useless all reasonings upon the probable operation of things, and defeat the established principles of natural and moral causes. It is a species of reasoning, sometimes used to excite popular jealousies, but is generally discarded by wise and discerning men. I do not suppose that the

honorable member who advanced the idea, had any such design: He, undoubtedly, would not wish to extend his argument to the destruction of union or government; but this, Sir,
is its real tendency. It has been asserted, that the interests,
habits and manners of the Thirteen States are different; and
hence it is inferred, that no general free government can suit
them. This diversity of habits, &c. has been a favorite theme
with those who are disposed for a division of our empire; and
like many other popular objections, seems to be founded on
fallacy. I acknowledge, that the local interests of the states are
in some degree various; and that there is some difference in
their habits and manners: But this I will presume to affirm;
that, from New-Hampshire to Georgia, the people of America are as uniform in their interests and manners, as those of
any established in Europe. This diversity, to the eye of a spec-
ulatist, may afford some marks of characteristic discrimination, but cannot form an impediment to the regular operation
of those general powers, which the Constitution gives to the
united government. Were the laws of the union to new-model
the internal police of any state; were they to alter, or abrogate
at a blow, the whole of its civil and criminal institutions; were
they to penetrate the recesses of domestic life, and controul,
in all respects, the private conduct of individuals, there might
be more force in the objection: And the same constitution,
which was happily calculated for one state, might sacrifice the
wellfare of another. Though the difference of interests may
create some difficulty and apparent partiality, in the first operations of government, yet the same spirit of accommodation,
which produced the plan under discussion, would be exercised in lessening the weight of unequal burthens. Add to this
that, under the regular and gentle influence of general laws,
these varying interests will be constantly assimilating, till they
embrace each other, and assume the same complexion.

June 21, 1788

Speech in the New York Ratifying Convention on the Distribution of Powers

The hon. Mr. *Hamilton*. This is one of those subjects, Mr. Chairman, on which objections very naturally arise, and assume the most plausible shape. Its address is to the passions, and its first impressions create a prejudice, before cool examination has an opportunity for exertion. It is more easy for the human mind to calculate the evils, than the advantages of a measure; and vastly more natural to apprehend the danger, than to see the necessity, of giving powers to our rulers. Hence I may justly expect, that those who hear me, will place less confidence in those arguments which oppose, than in those which favour, their prepossessions.

After all our doubts, our suspicions and speculations, on the subject of government, we must return at last to this important truth—that when we have formed a constitution upon free principles, when we have given a proper balance to the different branches of administration, and fixed representation upon pure and equal principles, we may with safety furnish it with all the powers, necessary to answer, in the most ample manner, the purposes of government. The great desiderata are a free representation, and mutual checks: When these are obtained, all our apprehension of the extent of powers are unjust and imaginary. What then is the structure of this constitution? One branch of the legislature is to be elected by the people—by the same people, who choose your state representatives: Its members are to hold their office two years, and then return to their constituents. Here, sir, the people govern: Here they act by their immediate representatives. You have also a senate, constituted by your state legislatures—by men, in whom you place the highest confidence; and forming another representative branch. Then again you have an executive magistrate, created by a form of election, which merits universal admiration. In the form of this government, and in the mode of legislation, you find all the checks which the greatest politicians and the best writers have ever conceived. What more can reasonable men desire? Is

there any one branch, in which the whole legislative and executive powers are lodged? No. The legislative authority is
lodged in three distinct branches properly balanced: The executive authority is divided between two branches; and the judicial is still reserved for an independent body, who hold their
office during good behaviour. This organization is so complex,
so skillfully contrived, that it is next to impossible that an impolitic or wicked measure should pass the great scrutiny with
success. Now what do gentlemen mean by coming forward
and declaiming against this government? Why do they say we
ought to limit its powers, to disable it, and to destroy its capacity of blessing the people? Has philosophy suggested—has
experience taught, that such a government ought not to be
trusted with every thing necessary for the good of society? Sir,
when you have divided and nicely balanced the departments of
government; When you have strongly connected the virtue of
your rulers with their interest; when, in short, you have rendered your system as perfect as human forms can be; you must
place confidence; you must give power.

We have heard a great deal of the sword and the purse: It
is said, our liberties are in danger, if both are possessed by
Congress. Let us see what is the true meaning of this maxim,
which has been so much used, and so little understood. It is,
that you shall not place these powers in either the legislative
or executive singly: Neither one nor the other shall have both;
Because this would destroy that division of powers, on which
political liberty is founded; and would furnish one body with
all the means of tyranny. But where the purse is lodged in one
branch, and the sword in another, there can be no danger. All
governments have possessed these powers. They would be
monsters without them, and incapable of exertion. What is
your state government? Does not your legislature command
what money it pleases? Does not your executive execute the
laws without restraint? These distinctions between the purse
and the sword have no application to the system, but only to
its separate branches. Sir, when we reason about the great interests of a great people, it is high time that we dismiss our
prejudices and banish declamation.

In order to induce us to consider the powers given by this
constitution as dangerous; In order to render plausible an

attempt to take away the life and spirit of the most important power in government; the gentleman complains that we shall not have a true and safe representation. I have asked him, what a safe representation is; and he has given no satisfactory answer. The assembly of New-York has been mentioned as a proper standard: But if we apply this standard to the general government, our Congress will become a mere mob, exposed to every irregular impulse, and subject to every breeze of faction. Can such a system afford security? Can you have confidence in such a body? The idea of taking the ratio of representation, in a small society, for the ratio of a great one, is a fallacy which ought to be exposed. It is impossible to ascertain to what point our representation will increase: It may vary from one, to two, three or four hundred. It depends upon the progress of population. Suppose it to rest at two hundred. Is not this number sufficient to secure it against corruption? Human nature must be a much more weak and despicable thing, than I apprehend it to be, if two hundred of our fellow citizens can be corrupted in two years. But suppose they are corrupted; can they in two years accomplish their designs? Can they form a combination, and even lay a foundation for a system of tyranny, in so short a period? It is far from my intention to wound the feelings of any gentleman; but I must, in this most interesting discussion, speak of things as they are; and hold up opinions in the light in which they ought to appear: and I maintain, that all that has been said of corruption, of the purse and the sword, and of the danger of giving powers, is not supported by principle or fact—That it is mere verbage, and idle declamation. The true principle of government is this—Make the system compleat in its structure; give a perfect proportion and balance to its parts; and the powers you give it will never affect your security. The question then, of the division of powers between the general and state governments, is a question of convenience: It becomes a prudential enquiry, what powers are proper to be reversed to the latter; and this immediately involves another enquiry into the proper objects of the two governments. This is the criterion, by which we shall determine the just distribution of powers.

The great leading objects of the federal government, in which revenue is concerned, are to maintain domestic peace, and provide for the common defence. In these are compre-hended the regulation of commerce; that is, the whole system of foreign intercourse; the support of armies and navies, and of the civil administration. It is useless to go into detail. Every one knows that the objects of the general government are nu-merous, extensive and important. Every one must acknowl-edge the necessity of giving powers, in all respects and in every degree, equal to these objects. This principle assented to, let us enquire what are the objects of the state govern-ments. Have they to provide against foreign invasion? Have they to maintain fleets and armies? Have they any concern in the regulation of commerce, the procuring alliances, or form-ing treaties of peace? No: Their objects are merely civil and domestic; to support the legislative establishment, and to pro-vide for the administration of the laws. Let any one compare the expence of supporting the civil list in a state, with the ex-pence of providing for the defence of the union. The differ-ence is almost beyond calculation. The experience of Great-Britain will throw some light on this subject. In that kingdom, the ordinary expences of peace to those of war, are as one to fourteen: But there they have a monarch, with his splendid court, and an enormous civil establishment, with which we have nothing in this country to compare. If, in Great-Britain, the expences of war and peace are so dispro-portioned; how wide will be their disparity in the United States; How infinitely wider between the general government and each individual state! Now, Sir, where ought the great resources to be lodged? Every rational man will give an im-mediate answer. To what extent shall these resources be pos-sessed? Reason says as far as possible exigencies can require; that is, without limitation. A constitution cannot set bounds to a nation's wants; it ought not therefore to set bounds to its resources. Unexpected invasions—long and ruinous wars, may demand all the possible abilities of the coun-try: Shall not your government have power to call these abilities into action? The contingencies of society are not re-ducible to calculations: They cannot be fixed or bounded, even in imagination. Will you limit the means of your de-fence, when you cannot ascertain the force or extent of the invasion? Even in ordinary wars, a government is frequently obliged to call for supplies, to the temporary oppression of the people.

Sir, if we adopt the idea of exclusive revenues, we shall be obliged to fix some distinguishing line, which neither government shall overpass. The inconveniencies of this measure must appear evident, on the slightest examination. The resources appropriated to one, may diminish or fail; while those of the other may increase, beyond the wants of government: One may be destitute of revenues, while the other shall possess an unnecessary abundance: and the constitution will be an eternal barrier to a mutual intercourse and relief. In this case, will the individual states stand on so good a ground, as if the objects of taxation were left free and open to the embrace of both the governments? Possibly, in the advancement of commerce, the imposts may increase to such a degree, as to render direct taxes unnecessary; These resources then, as the constitution stands, may be occasionally relinquished to the states: But on the gentleman's idea of prescribing exclusive limits, and precluding all reciprocal communication, this would be entirely improper. The laws of the states must not touch the appropriated resources of the United States, whatever may be their wants. Would it not be of more advantage to the states, to have a concurrent jurisdiction extending to all the sources of revenue, than to be confined to such a small resource, as, on calculation of the objects of the two governments, should appear to be their due proportion? Certainly you cannot hesitate on this question. The gentleman's plan would have a further ill effect; It would tend to dissolve the connexion and correspondence of the two governments, to estrange them from each other, and to destroy that mutual dependence, which forms the essence of union.

Sir, a number of arguments have been advanced by an honorable member from New-York, which to every unclouded mind must carry conviction. He has stated, that in sudden emergencies, it may be necessary to borrow; and that it is impossible to borrow, unless you have funds to pledge for the payment of your debts. Limiting the powers of government to certain resources, is rendering the fund precarious; and obliging the government to ask, instead of empowering them to command, is to destroy all confidence and credit. If the power of taxing is restricted, the consequence is, that on the breaking out of a war, you must divert the funds, appropriated to the payment of debts, to answer immediate exigencies. Thus you violate your engagements, at the very time you increase the burthen of them. Besides, sound policy condemns the practice of accumulating debts. A government, to act with energy, should have the possession of all its revenues to answer present purposes. The principle, for which I contend, is recognized in all its extent by our old constitution. Congress is authorized to raise troops, to call for supplies without limitation, and to borrow money to any amount. It is true, they must use the form of recommendations and requisitions: but the states are bound by the solemn ties of honor, of justice, of religion, to comply without reserve.

Mr. Chairman, it has been advanced as a principle, that no government but a despotism can exist in a very extensive country. This is a melancholy consideration indeed. If it were founded on truth, we ought to dismiss the idea of a republican government, even for the state of New-York. This idea has been taken from a celebrated writer, who, by being misunderstood, has been the occasion of frequent fallacies in our reasoning on political subjects. But the position has been misapprehended; and its application is entirely false and unwarrantable: It relates only to democracies, where the whole body of the people meet to transact business; and where representation is unknown. Such were a number of antient, and some modern independent cities. Men who read without attention, have taken these maxims respecting the extent of country; and, contrary to their proper meaning, have applied them to republics in general. This application is wrong, in respect to all representative governments; but especially in relation to a confederacy of states, in which the supreme legislature has only general powers, and the civil and domestic concerns of the people are regulated by the laws of the several states. This distinction being kept in view, all the difficulty will vanish, and we may easily conceive, that the people of a large country may be represented as truly, as those of a small one. An assembly constituted for general purposes, may be fully competent to every federal regulation, without being too numerous for deliberate conduct. If the state governments were to be abolished, the question would wear a different face: but this idea is inadmissible. They are absolutely necessary to the system. Their existence must form a leading principle in the most perfect constitution we could form. I insist, that it never can be the interest or desire of the national legislature, to destroy the state governments. It can derive no advantage from such an event; But, on the contrary, would lose an indispensable support, a necessary aid in executing the laws, and conveying the influence of government to the doors of the people. The union is dependent on the will of the state governments for its chief magistrate, and for its senate. The blow aimed at the members, must give a fatal wound to the head; and the destruction of the states must be at once a political suicide. Can the national government be guilty of this madness? what inducements, what temptations can they have? Will they attach new honors to their station; will they increase the national strength; will they multiply the national resources; will they make themselves more respectable, in the view of foreign nations, or of their fellow citizens, by robbing the states of their constitutional privileges? But imagine, for a moment, that a political frenzy should seize the government. Suppose they should make the attempt. Certainly, Sir, it would be forever impracticable. This has been sufficiently demonstrated by reason and experience. It has been proved, that the members of republics have been, and ever will be, stronger than the head. Let us attend to one general historical example. In the antient feudal governments of Europe, there were, in the first place a monarch; subordinate to him, a body of nobles; and subject to these, the vassals or the whole body of the people. The authority of the kings was limited, and that of the barons considerably independent. A great part of the early wars in Europe were contests between the king and his nobility. In these contests, the latter possessed many advantages derived from their influence, and the immediate command they had over the people; and they generally prevailed. The history of the feudal wars exhibits little more than a series of successful encroachments on the prerogatives of monarchy. Here, Sir, is one great proof of the superiority, which the members in limited governments possess over their head. As long as the barons enjoyed the confidence and attachment of the people, they had the strength of the country on their side, and were irresistable. I may be told, that in some instances the barons were overcome: But how did this happen? Sir, they took advantage of the depression of the royal authority, and the establishment of their own power, to oppress and tyrannise over their vassals. As commerce enlarged, and as wealth and civilization encreased, the people began to feel their own weight and consequence: They grew tired of their oppressions; united their strength with that of the prince; and threw off the yoke of artistocracy. These very instances prove what I contend for: They prove, that in whatever direction the popular weight leans, the current of power will flow: Wherever the popular attachments lie, there will rest the political superiority. Sir, can it be supposed that the state governments will become the oppressors of the people? Will they forfeit their affections? Will they combine to destroy the liberties and happiness of their fellow citizens, for the sole purpose of involving themselves in ruin? God forbid! The idea, Sir, is shocking! It outrages every feeling of humanity, and every dictate of common sense!

There are certain social principles in human nature, from which we may draw the most solid conclusions with respect to the conduct of individuals, and of communities. We love our families, more than our neighbours: We love our neighbours, more than our countrymen in general. The human affections, like the solar heat, lose their intensity, as they depart from the center; and become languid, in proportion to the expansion of the circle, on which they act. On these principles, the attachment of the individual will be first and forever secured by the states governments: They will be a mutual protection and support. Another source of influence, which has already been pointed out, is the various official connections in the states. Gentlemen endeavour to evade the force of this, by saying that these offices will be insignificant. This is by no means true. The state officers will ever be important, because they are necessary and useful. Their powers are such, as are extremely interesting to the people; such as affect their property, their liberty and life. What is more important, than the administration of justice, and the execution of the civil and criminal laws? Can the state governments become insignificant, while they have the power of raising money independently and without controul? If they are really useful; If they are calculated to promote the essential interests of the people; they must have their confidence and support. The states can never lose their powers, till the whole people of America are robbed of their liberties. These must go together, they must support each other, or meet one common fate. On the gentleman's principle, we may safely trust the state governments, tho' we have no means of resisting them: but we cannot confide in the national government, tho' we have an effectual, constitutional guard against every encroachment. This is the essence of their argument, and it is false and fallacious beyond conception.

With regard to the jurisdiction of the two governments, I shall certainly admit that the constitution ought to be so formed, as not to prevent the states from providing for their own existence; and I maintain that it is so formed; and that their power of providing for themselves is sufficiently established. This is conceded by one gentleman, and in the next breath, the concession is retracted. He says, Congress have but one exclusive right in taxation; that of duties on imports: Certainly then, their other powers are only concurrent. But to take off the force of this obvious conclusion, he immediately says that the laws of the United States are supreme; and that where there is one supreme, there cannot be a concurrent authority: and further, that where the laws of the union are supreme, those of the states must be subordinate; because, there cannot be two supremes. This is curious sophistry. That two supreme powers cannot act together, is false. They are inconsistent only when they are aimed at each other, or at one indivisible object. The laws of the United States are supreme, as to all their proper, constitutional objects: The laws of the states are supreme in the same way. These supreme laws may act on different objects, without clashing; or they may operate on different parts of the same common object, with perfect harmony. Suppose both governments should lay a tax of a penny on a certain article: Has not each an independent and uncontrolable power to collect its own tax? The meaning of the maxim—that there can not be two supremes—is simply this:—Two powers cannot be supreme over each other. This meaning is entirely perverted by the gentlemen. But, it is said, disputes between collectors are to be referred to the federal courts. This is again wandering in the field of conjecture. But suppose the fact certain: Is it not to be presumed, that they will express the true meaning of the constitution and the laws? Will they not be bound to consider the concurrent jurisdiction; to declare that both the taxes shall have equal operation; that both the powers, in that respect, are sovereign and co-extensive? If they transgress their duty, we are to hope that they will be punished. Sir, we can reason from probabilities alone. When we leave common sense, and give ourselves up to conjecture, there can be no certainty, no security in our reasonings.

I imagine I have stated to the committee abundant reasons to prove the entire safety of the state governments and of the people. I would go into a more minute consideration of the nature of the concurrent jurisdiction, and the operation of the laws, in relation to revenue; but at present I feel too much indisposed to proceed. I shall, with the leave of the committee, improve another opportunity of expressing to them more fully my ideas on this point. I wish the committee to remember, that the constitution under examination is framed upon truly republican principles; and that, as it is expressly designed to provide for the common protection and the general welfare of the United States, it must be utterly repugnant to this constitution, to subvert the state governments, or oppress the people.

June 27, 1788

CONVINCING WASHINGTON TO SERVE

To George Washington

Dear Sir   New York September 1788
    Your Excellency's friendly and obliging letter of the 28th Ulto. came safely to hand. I thank you for your assurance of seconding my application to General Morgan. The truth of that affair is, that he purchased the watch for a trifle of a

British soldier, who plundered Major Cochran at the moment of his fall at York Town.

I should be deeply pained my Dear Sir if your scruples in regard to a certain station should be matured into a resolution to decline it; though I am neither surprised at their existence nor can I but agree in opinion that the caution you observe in deferring an ultimate determination is prudent. I have however reflected maturely on the subject and have come to a conclusion, (in which I feel no hesitation) that every public and personal consideration will demand from you an acquiescence in what will *certainly* be the unanimous wish of your country. The absolute retreat which you meditated at the close of the late war was natural and proper. Had the government produced by the revolution gone on in a *tolerable* train, it would have been most adviseable to have persisted in that retreat. But I am clearly of opinion that the crisis which brought you again into public view left you no alterative but to comply—and I am equally clear in the opinion that you are by that act *pledged* to take a part in the execution of the government. I am not less convinced that the impression of this necessity of your filling the station in question is so universal that you run no risk of any uncandid imputation, by submitting to it. But even if this were not the case, a regard to your own reputation as well as to the public good, calls upon you in the strongest manner to run that risk.

It cannot be considered as a compliment to say that on your acceptance of the office of President the success of the new government in its commencement may materially depend. Your agency and influence will be not less important in preserving it from the future attacks of its enemies than they have been in recommending it in the first instance to the adoption of the people. Independent of all considerations drawn from this source the point of light in which you stand at home and abroad will make an infinite difference in the respectability with which the government will begin its operations in the alternative of your being or not being at the head of it. I forbear to urge considerations which might have a more personal application. What I have said will suffice for the inferences I mean to draw.

First— In a matter so essential to the well being of society as the prosperity of a newly instituted government a citizen of so much consequence as yourself to its success has no option but to lend his services if called for. Permit me to say it would be inglorious in such a situation not to hazard the glory however great, which he might have previously acquired.

Secondly. Your signature to the proposed system pledges your judgment for its being such an one as upon the whole was worthy of the public approbation. If it should miscarry (as men commonly decide from success or the want of it) the blame will in all probability be laid on the system itself. And the framers of it will have to encounter the disrepute of having brought about a revolution in government, without substituting any thing that was worthy of the effort. They pulled down one Utopia, it will be said, to build up another. This view of the subject, if I mistake not my dear Sir will suggest to your mind greater hazard to that fame, which must be and ought to be dear to you, in refusing your future aid to the system than in affording it. I will only add that in my estimate of the matter that aid is indispensable.

I have taken the liberty to express these sentiments to lay before you my view of the subject. I doubt not the considerations mentioned have fully occurred to you, and I trust they will finally produce in your mind the same result, which exists in mine. I flatter myself the frankness with which I have delivered myself will not be displeasing to you. It has been prompted by motives which you would not disapprove.

I remain My Dear Sir With the sincerest respect and regard Your Obd & hum serv   A Hamilton

The letter inclosed in yours was immediately forwarded.

WITHHOLDING VOTES FROM ADAMS

To James Wilson

My Dear Sir,
    A degree of anxiety about a matter of primary importance to the new government induces me to trouble you with this

letter. I mean the election of the President. We all feel of how much moment it is that Washington should be the man; and I own I cannot think there is material room to doubt that this will be the unanimous sense. But as a failure in this object would be attended with the worst consequences I cannot help concluding that even possibilities should be guarded against.

Every body is aware of that defect in the constitution which renders it possible that the man intended for Vice President may in fact turn up President. Every body sees that unanimity in Adams as Vice President and a few votes insidiously witheld from Washington might substitute the former to the latter. And every body must perceive that there is something to fear from machinations of Antifœderal malignity. What in this situation is wise?

By my accounts from the North I have every reason to believe that Adams will run there universally. I learn that he is equally espoused in Jersey Pensylvania & Delaware & that Maryland is not disinclined to him. I hear of no persons thought of to the South, but Rutlege in South Carolina and Clinton in Virginia. As the accounts of the appointments of electors will satisfy the partisans of those Gentlemen in each of those States that they will have no coadjustors elsewhere, it seems not improbable that they will relinquish the attempt in favour of their intended candidates. Here then is a *chance* of unanimity in Adams. Nothing so apt to beget it as the opinion that the current sets irresistibly towards him. Men are fond of going with the stream. Suppose personal caprice or hostility to the new system should occasion half a dozen votes only to be witheld from Washington—what may not happen? Grant there is little danger. If any, ought it to be run?

The votes from New Hampshire to Delaware inclusively & exclusive of New York are 41 South of Delaware 32. Here supposing equal unanimity on each side in a different candidate the chance is that there will be Eight votes to spare from Adams leaving him still a majority. Take the probability of unanimity in the North in Adams & of division in the South between different candidates and the chances are almost infinite in his favour. Hence I conclude it will be prudent to throw away a few votes say 7 or 8; giving these to persons not otherwise thought of. Under this impression I have proposed to friends in Connecticut to throw away two to others in Jersey to throw away an equal number & I submit it to you whether it will not be well to lose three or four in Pensylvania. Your advices from the South will serve you as the best guide; but for God's sake let not our zeal for a secondary object defeat or endanger a first. I admit that in several important views and particularly to avoid disgust to a man who would be a formidable head to Antifœderalists—it is much to be desired that Adams may have the plurality of suffrages for Vice President; but if risk is to be run on one side or on the other can we hesitate where it ought to be preferred?

If there appears to you to be any danger, will it not be well for you to write to Maryland to *qualify* matters there?

Yrs sincerely & affecly   A. Hamilton

New York Jany 25. 1789.

PRESIDENTIAL ETIQUETTE

To George Washington

Dr. Sir

In conformity to the intimation you were pleased to honor me with on   evening last I have reflected on the etiquette proper to be observed by the President and now submit the ideas which have occurred to me on the subject.

The public good requires as a primary object that the dignity of the office should be supported. Whatever is essential to this ought to be pursued though at the risk of partial or momentary dissatisfaction. But care will be necessary to avoid extensive disgust or discontent. Men's minds are prepared for a pretty high tone in the demeanour of the Executive; but I doubt whether for so high a tone as in the abstract might be desireable. The notions of equality are yet in my opinion too general and too strong to admit of such a distance being placed between the President and other branches of the government as might even be consistent with a due proportion.

The following plan will I think steer clear of extremes and involve no very material inconveniences.

I   The President to have a levee day once a week for receiving visits. An hour to be fixed at which it shall be understood that he will appear and consequently that the visitors are previously to be assembled. The President to remain half an hour, in which time he may converse cursorily on indifferent subjects with such persons as shall strike his attention, and at the end of that half hour disappear. Some regulation will be hereafter necessary to designate those who may visit. A mode of introduction through particular officers will be indispensable. No visits to be returned.

II   The President to accept no invitations: and to give formal entertainments only twice or four times a year on the anniversaries of important events in the revolution. If twice, the day of the declaration of Independence, and that of the inauguration of the President, which completed the organization of the Constitution, to be preferred; if four times, the day of the treaty of alliance with france & that of the definitive treaty with Britain to be added. The members of the two houses of the legislature Principal officers of the Government Foreign ministers and other distinguished strangers only to be invited. The numbers form in my mind an objection—But there may be separate tables in separate rooms. This is practiced in some European Courts. I see no other method in which foreign Ministers can with propriety be included in any attentions of the table which the President may think fit to pay.

III   The President on the levée days either by himself or some Gentleman of his household to give informal invitations to family dinners on the days of invitation. Not more than six or eight to be invited at a time & the matter to be confined essentially to members of the legislature and other official characters. The President never to remain long at table.

I think it probable that the last article will not correspond with the ideas of most of those with whom Your Excellency may converse but on pretty mature reflection I believe it will be necessary to remove the idea of too immense an inequality, which I fear would excite dissatisfaction and cabal. The thing may be so managed as neither to occasion much waste of time, nor to infringe on dignity.

It is an important point to consider what persons may have access to Your Excellency on business. The heads of departments will of course have this privilege. Foreign Ministers of some descriptions will also be intitled to it. In Europe I am informed ambassadors only have direct access to the Chief Magistrate. Something very *near* what prevails there would in my opinion be right. The distinction of rank between diplomatic characters requires attention and the door of access ought not to be too wide to that class of persons. I have thought that the members of the Senate should also have a right of *individual* access on matters relative to the *public administration*. In England & France Peers of the realm have this right. We have none such in this Country, but I believe that it will be satisfactory to the people to know that there is some body of men in the state who have a right of continual communication with the President. It will be considered as a safeguard against secret combinations to deceive him.

I have asked myself—will not the representatives expect the same privilege and be offended if they are not allowed to participate with the Senate? There is sufficient danger of this, to merit consideration. But there is a reason for the distinction in the constitution. The Senate are coupled with the President in certain executive functions; treaties and appointments. This makes them in a degree his constitutional counsellors and gives them a *peculiar* claim to the right of access. On the whole, I think the discrimination will be proper & may be hazarded.

I have chosen this method of communication, because I understood Your Excellency, that it would be most convenient to you. The unstudied and unceremonious manner of it will I hope not render it the less acceptable. And if in the execution of your commands at any time I consult frankness and simplicity more than ceremony or profession, I flatter myself you will not on that account distrust the sincerity of the assurance I now give of my cordial wishes for your personal happiness and the success of your administration. I have the honor to be with the highest respect

Your Excellency's   Most Obedient & humble servant

May 5, 1789

SECRETARY OF THE TREASURY
1789–1795

To Lafayette

My Dear Marquis   New York October 6th. 1789

I have seen with a mixture of Pleasure and apprehension the Progress of the events which have lately taken Place in your Country. As a friend to mankind and to liberty I rejoice in the efforts which you are making to establish it while I fear much for the final success of the attempts, for the fate of those I esteem who are engaged in it, and for the danger in case of success of innovations greater than will consist with the real felicity of your Nation. If your affairs still go well, when this reaches you, you will ask why this foreboding of ill, when all the appearences have been so much in your favor. I will tell you; I dread disagreements among those who are now united (which will be likely to be improved by the adverse party) about the nature of your constitution; I dread the vehement character of your people, whom I fear you may find it more easy to bring on, than to keep within Proper bounds, after you have put them in motion; I dread the interested refractoriness of your nobles, who cannot all be gratified and who may be unwilling to submit to the requisite sacrifices. And I dread the reveries of your Philosophic politicians who appear in the moment to have great influence and who being mere speculatists may aim at more refinement than suits either with human nature or the composition of your Nation.

These my dear Marquis are my apprehensions. My wishes for your personal success and that of the cause of liberty are incessant. Be virtuous amidst the Seductions of ambition, and you can hardly in any event be unhappy. You are combined with a great and good man; you will anticipate the name of Neckar. I trust you and he will never cease to harmonize.

You will, I presume, have heard before this gets to hand, that I have been appointed to the head of the Finances of this Country: this event I am sure will give you Pleasure. In undertaking the task, I hazard much, but I thought it an occasion that called upon me to hazard. I have no doubt that the reasonable expectation of the public may be satisfied, if I am properly supported by the Legislature, and in this respect, I stand at present on the most encouraging footing.

The debt due to France will be among the first objects of my attention. Hitherto it has been from necessity neglected. The Session of Congress is now over. It has been exhausted in the organization of the Government, and in a few laws of immediate urgency respecting navigation and commercial Imposts. The subject of the debt foreign and domestic has been referred to the next session which will commence the first Monday in January with an instruction to me to prepare and report a Plan comprehending an adequate Provision for the support of the Public Credit. There were many good reasons for a temporary adjournment.

From this sketch you will perceive that I am not in a situation to address any thing officially to your administration; but I venture to say to you, as my friend, that if the installments of the Principal of the debt could be suspended for a few years, it would be a valuable accommodation to the United States. In this suggestion I contemplate a speedy payment of the *arrears* of *interest* now due, and effectual Provision for the punctual payment of future interest as it arises. Could an arrangement of this sort meet the approbation of your Government, it would be best on every account that the offer should come unsolicited as a fresh mark of good will.

I wrote you last by Mr. De Warville. I presume you received my letter. As it touched some delicate issues I should be glad to know its fate.

Your with unalterable   esteem and affection

Alexander Hamilton

P. S. The latest accounts from France have abated some of my apprehensions. The abdications of priviledges patronised by your Nobility in the States General are truly noble, and bespeak a Patriotic and magnanimous policy, which promises good both to them and their Country.

Memorandum by George Beckwith on a Conversation with Hamilton

Seventh.   I have requested to see you on this occasion from a Wish to Explain Certain points, relative to our situation, and from a desire to suggest a measure, which I conceive to be both for the interest of Great Britain, and of this Country to adopt. We have lately Established a Government upon principles, that in my opinion render it safe for any Nation to Enter into Treaties with us, Either Commercial or Political, which has not hitherto been the Case; I have always preferred a Connexion with you, to that of any other Country, *We think in English*, and have a similarity of prejudices, and of predilections; I have been in the habits of considering this subject, We are a young and a growing Empire, with much Enterprize and vigour, but undoubtedly are, and must be for years, rather an Agricultural, than a manufacturing people; yet our policy has had a tendency to suggest the Necessity of introducing manufactures, which Accordingly have made some progress in Connecticut, where Cloth has been manufactured to some Extent, leaving already a clear profit of between six and seven per cent to the proprietors, and Pensylvania has gone further in her Exertions in different branches. These and similar Efforts are to no Comparative Extent, but doubtless their Encrease will be proportioned to your Conduct.

I am free to say, that Although France has been indulgent to us, in certain points, yet, what she can furnish, is by no means so Essential or so suited to us as Your productions, nor do our raw Materials suit her so well as they do you.

The Government of a Country Cannot altogether change Either the taste or the disposition of a people, but its influence may check or cherish it.

We wish to form a Commercial treaty with you to Every Extent, to which you may think it for Your interest to go. Lord Lansdowne at the close of his Administration had a plan of this nature upon a very broad scale indeed, and one which I do not think now Attainable, Considering the Spirit of your late Navigation and regulating Acts, As Well as from various publications by persons of Considerable weight in England; but when I view the rapid Encrease of this country, its Extent, taste and disposition, I do think a Treaty of Commerce might be formed upon terms advantageous to both Countries; for unless this can be done, I Know very well nothing of this nature Can be Effected, And Kingdoms so circumstanced, can have little friendly intercourse. I do think we are, and shall be, great Consumers, and I am of opinion, that it will be better for Great Britain to grant us admission into her Islands under certain limitations of size of vessels, so as merely to Enable us to Carry our produce there, and to bring from thence the productions of those Islands to our own ports, under such restrictions as to prevent the possibility of our interfering with Your Carrying trade in Europe, than by a rigid adherence to Your present plan to produce a system of warfare in Commercial matters, which however Encouraged by France in this Country, during the late Sessions here, with a view to promote coldness and animosity between the two Countries, I have Ever viewed with much regret, as being directly opposed to that system, which upon Mature reflexion, I have thought it most Eligible for us to pursue.

The present Moment I view as particularly favourable for a plan of this Nature. We are now so Circumstanced as to be free to Enter into a discussion of this sort, from our Condition with regard to the other Maritime powers; this may not be the case hereafter.

We have a matter of great Importance to settle with Spain, I mean the navigation of the Mississippi; this is of the first moment to our territories to the Westward, they *must have that outlet, without it they will be lost to us.* As to your provinces to the Northward, on that score there is no Cause for jealousy; it never Can be our interest to Extend our possessions in that quarter, Even if we had the power; our Country is Already sufficiently large, more so perhaps than prudence might wish, as its Extent tends to Encrease our difficulties in Certain points, and to weaken our Government. It is also a consideration not unworthy of your Attention, that as we may become considerable in half a Century or in less, if we are under the necessity of connecting ourselves with the House of Bourbon, such a connexion, in that Event, may become important to Your West India possessions. On the other hand, connected with you, by strong ties of Commercial, perhaps of political, friendships, our naval Exertions, in future wars, may in your scale be greatly important; And decisive. These are my opinions, they are the sentiments, which I have long Entertained, on which I have acted, and I think them suited to the future welfare of both Countries. I am not sufficiently Authorized to say so, it is not in my department, but I am inclined to think a *person will soon be sent to England to sound the disposition of Your Court upon* it.

Sir, I have mentioned to (see second) what would have been the Effect of Your Revenue Bill, had it passed in the form in which it appeared from Your Prints, with those discriminating clauses, which undoubtedly were levelled at us. . . . He requested My permission to communicate this to You, and I believe I may Conclude that this Conversation Arises from that source.

It does.

I thought it consistent with the spirit of that communication, not to with hold it, notwithstanding the modification, which afterwards took place, although I Can give no opinion whatever, as to the Effects, which it may produce, under its present form, nor to the light in which we may view it at home, I speak very freely to You, but you will of course readily comprehend, that now, this is merely private conversation.

Certainly, and in Your situation, mine cannot be Esteemed any thing more although I can assure you, that the ideas I have thrown out, may be depended upon, as the sentiments of the most Enlightened men in this Country, they are those of General Washington, I can Confidently assure You, as well as of a great majority in the Senate.

If I understand the Revenue and Tonnage Acts, You have placed us precisely upon the footing of every other foreign nation; during the discussion of this bill You doubtless took it into Your consideration, the condition of Your shipping in our Ports in Europe, and You would naturally compare it with that of other Foreign Shipping; you would then judge, whether we have been hostile to you, or not; now I beg leave to put a case, if, in consequence of Your late regulations, we should place you Exactly upon the footing of other foreigners in our ports, would it appear an unfair procedure?

Surely not, Every Nation has a clear right, as You remarked, to regulate its own Commerce.

An other thing strikes me. As the real views of communities, as well as of individuals, are rather to be gathered from their conduct than from their professions, it is not unnatural to suppose, that, prior to the Entering upon the discussion of a future Treaty we may think it reasonable to settle any matters, that may be supposed to respect the Treaty of Peace, still unadjusted.

Certainly, this is proper to both sides. There are two points only, that occur to me as being Complained of. The one, the Tender laws, and their Effects, I consider to be done away by the present Government, which has paid the most particular attention to this, in the formation and Establishment of its Judiciary branch; the District Courts will be in immediate operation, the supreme Court very shortly. The other regards the Confiscation Acts. I have seen the original Document, it was wholly recommendatory, and the Confiscations, that have taken place since the peace, have Arisen rather from mistakes, than intention, their Amount is comparatively nothing.

There has been I acknowledge a spirit of animosity, and rancour, in many instances, which I greatly condemn, but this, however uncreditable, I do not believe will amount to an infringement.

On our side there are Also two points still unadjusted, the *Western Forts, And the Negroes*, although, as to the latter I always decidedly approved Lord Dorchester's conduct on that occasion, he could not do otherwise. To have given up these men to their Masters, after the assurances of protection held out to them, was impossible, and the Reply of Your Cabinet to our application on this subject was to me perfectly satisfactory.

You have mentioned its being your intention to send a person to learn our disposition upon Certain points; You are indubitably the proper judges of the qualifications and disposition of the gentleman to be Employed in the business. I beg leave however to suggest, how much such a measure may be promoted, or impeded, by the predilections, possibly by the prejudices, of an individual so circumstanced. If his mind should have any bias towards any other foreign power such bias might Althogether frustrate the objects of his mission.

Undoubtedy, we have not in some former instances been Exempt from this sort of inconvenience, to which the manner of naming to public appointments under our old government not a little contributed. The Case is now altered, these nominations originate with General Washington, who is a good judge of men, and the gentleman, to be Employed in this business, is perfectly master of the subject, and if he leans in his bias towards any foreign Country, it is decidely to You.

As you have done me the honour of mentioning to me the turn of party, during Your late Sessions, I cannot avoid saying that I was much surprized to find amongst the gentlemen, who were so decidely hostile to us in their public conduct, the name of a Man, from whose Character for good sense, and other qualifications, I should have been led to Expect a very different conduct.

You mean Mr. Maddison from Virginia. I confess I was likewise rather surprized at it, as well as that the only opposition to General Washington was from thence. The truth is, that although this gentleman is a clever man, he is very little Acquainted with the world. That he is Uncorrupted And incorruptible I have not a doubt; he has the same End in view that I have, And so have those gentlemen, who Act with him, but their mode of attaining it is very different. You have I take it for granted seen our Debates?

I have them, but have not read them, Your observation of the manner of attaining the object, You profess to have in view, leads me to remark, that I cannot think Commercial Hostility with us, the mode to obtain Commercial Friendship. From what I have heard You say with respect to Mr. Pitt, & to our Cabinet, You will not wonder when I tell you, that their plan has been Evidently to hold the Nation high, in the opinion of the world, and they have accomplished it. You Cannot suppose, that those who follow up such a system will be influenced by compulsory measures. Upon such minds their tendency must be diametrically opposite. The purposes of National glory are best Attained by a close adherence to National honour, alike prepared to meet foreign friendship, and to repel foreign hostility.

Beyond all doubt, these are sentiments, that do honour to any nation, and I make no scruple to say, that both before I came into office and since, I have acted under that impression.

Whilst the Revenue and Tonnage Bills were under discussion, I was decidedly opposed to those discriminating Clauses, that were so warmly advocated by some gentlemen. I was at pains to obtain information from our mercantile body here upon this subject, who with a few Exceptions were against Every species of distinction, upon the principle that it would be productive of a War of Commerce. And in as far as I could judge by their Communications, there are Certain indulgencies, which our shipping Enjoy, in Your ports in Europe. If the Effect of our regulations determines you to place us precisely on the footing of all other foreign powers, we have not from that measure the smallest ground for Complaint, nor, as it appears to me would the Alteration be very momentous to us. I Cannot recollect that there is Any thing in the Impost Act, which marks a preference to Any other Foreign Power, when put into Competition with You, possibly some very trifling difference between French brandies and your West India spirits.

I think I clearly comprehend the scope of the Communication, that you have been pleased to make to me. Pray what use do you wish me to make of it? Is it with the view of my mentioning it to Lord Dorchester?

Yes, And by Lord Dorchester to Your Ministry, in whatever Manner His Lordship shall judge proper; but I should not chuse to have this go any further in America.

I am desirous to Know Your intentions Accurately upon this particular point, as you are the Judge of the Extent of Your Confidence.

This is very delicate in You, And I have been Anxious to hold this conversation with you from the opinion that I have always had of your Character, and from my conviction, that Lord Dorchester would not honour any man with his good opinion, and friendship, in whose integrity Every Confidence might not be placed.

If the present favourable occasion shall pass away, and a system of Commercial Warfare shall take place, it may lead to the adoption of an other idea, in the Contemplation of gentlemen, who are advocates for discrimination, and which did not respect a Tonnage, or Impost duties, but had in view a *much stronger measure.*

N. B. He did not say what it was, but I understood it to mean the idea of shutting their ports to our shipping, that might wish to clear out Either for our possessions in North America, or the West Indies, with lumber, provisions &ca.

I have understood that there has been some difficulty lately with respect to our Packet.

I hope it is settled?

The matter has been somewhat misrepresented. The fact was, the Collector of the Customs at this port had applied to me to Know in what light he was to Consider Your Packets, the Act passed by our Legislature during the summer having left that point unsettled. The law of nations Exempted Men of War from such duties undoubtedly, but it became requisite to know officially whether your Packet was a King's ship, or not, and the result of the Inquiry has been that she was so, in every respect, that the Captain held a Commission under Your Admiralty Board, and was debarred from Commerce.

The Matter therefore is settled.

N.B. The French Government have reestablished packets to New York but they are Merchant Vessels, come out occasionally with goods and with certain allowances or carrying the letters or Government dispatches. These are therefore obliged to clear at the Custom house, and consequently subject to the Effects, both of the Impost and Tonnage Acts. They are small Vessels.

October 1789

"SUSPICION IS EVER EAGLE EYED"

To Henry Lee

My Dear Friend

I have just received your letter of the 16th instant.

I am sure you are sincere when you say, you would not subject me to an impropriety. Nor do I know that there would be any in my answering your queries. But you remember the saying with regard to Caesar's Wife. I think the spirit of it applicable to every man concerned in the administration of the finances of a Country. With respect to the Conduct of such men—*Suspicion* is ever eagle eyed, And the most innocent things are apt to be misinterpreted.

Be assured of the affection & friendship of Yr.

A Hamilton

New York December 1st 1789

Report on Public Credit

Treasury Department, January 9, 1790.
The Secretary of the Treasury, in obedience to the resolution of the House of Representatives, of the twenty-first day of September last, has, during the recess of Congress, applied himself to the consideration of a proper plan for the support of the Public Credit, with all the attention which was due to the authority of the House, and to the magnitude of the object.

In the discharge of this duty, he has felt, in no small degree, the anxieties which naturally flow from a just estimate of the difficulty of the task, from a well-founded diffidence of his own qualifications for executing it with success, and from a deep and solemn conviction of the momentous nature of the truth contained in the resolution under which his investigations have been conducted, "That an *adequate* provision for the support of the Public Credit, is a matter of high importance to the honor and prosperity of the United States."

With an ardent desire that his well-meant endeavors may be conducive to the real advantage of the nation, and with the utmost deference to the superior judgment of the House, he now respectfully submits the result of his enquiries and reflections, to their indulgent construction.

In the opinion of the Secretary, the wisdom of the House, in giving their explicit sanction to the proposition which has been stated, cannot but be applauded by all, who will seriously consider, and trace through their obvious consequences, these plain and undeniable truths.

That exigencies are to be expected to occur, in the affairs of nations, in which there will be a necessity for borrowing.

That loans in times of public danger, especially from foreign war, are found an indispensable resource, even to the wealthiest of them.

And that in a country, which, like this, is possessed of little active wealth, or in other words, little monied capital, the necessity for that resource, must, in such emergencies, be proportionably urgent.

And as on the one hand, the necessity for borrowing in particular emergencies cannot be doubted, so on the other, it is equally evident, that to be able to borrow upon *good terms*, it is essential that the credit of a nation should be well established.

For when the credit of a country is in any degree questionable, it never fails to give an extravagant premium, in one shape or another, upon all the loans it has occasion to make. Nor does the evil end here; the same disadvantage must be sustained upon whatever is to be bought on terms of future payment.

From this constant necessity of *borrowing* and *buying dear*, it is easy to conceive how immensely the expences of a nation, in a course of time, will be augmented by an unsound state of the public credit.

To attempt to enumerate the complicated variety of mischiefs in the whole system of the social œconomy, which proceed from a neglect of the maxims that uphold public credit, and justify the solicitude manifested by the House on this point, would be an improper intrusion on their time and patience.

In so strong a light nevertheless do they appear to the Secretary, that on their due observance at the present critical juncture, materially depends, in his judgment, the individual and aggregate prosperity of the citizens of the United States; their relief from the embarrassments they now experience; their character as a People; the cause of good government.

If the maintenance of public credit, then, be truly so important, the next enquiry which suggests itself is, by what means it is to be effected? The ready answer to which question is, by good faith, by a punctual performance of contracts. States, like individuals, who observe their engagements, are respected and trusted: while the reverse is the fate of those, who pursue an opposite conduct.

Every breach of the public engagements, whether from choice or necessity, is in different degrees hurtful to public credit. When such a necessity does truly exist, the evils of it are only to be palliated by a scrupulous attention, on the part of the government, to carry the violation no farther than the necessity absolutely requires, and to manifest, if the nature of the case admits of it, a sincere disposition to make reparation, whenever circumstances shall permit. But with every possible mitigation, credit must suffer, and numerous mischiefs ensue. It is therefore highly important, when an appearance of necessity seems to press upon the public councils, that they should examine well its reality, and be perfectly assured, that there is no method of escaping from it, before they yield to its suggestions. For though it cannot safely be affirmed, that occasions have never existed, or may not exist, in which violations of the public faith, in this respect, are inevitable; yet there is great reason to believe, that they exist far less frequently than precedents indicate; and are oftenest either pretended through levity, or want of firmness, or supposed through want of knowledge. Expedients might often have been devised to effect, consistently with good faith, what has been done in contravention of it. Those who are most commonly creditors of a nation, are, generally speaking, enlightened men; and there are signal examples to warrant a conclusion, that when a candid and fair appeal is made to them, they will understand their true interest too well to refuse their concurrence in such modifications of their claims, as any real necessity may demand.

While the observance of that good faith, which is the basis of public credit, is recommended by the strongest inducements of political expediency, it is enforced by considerations of still greater authority. There are arguments for it, which rest on the immutable principles of moral obligation. And in proportion as the mind is disposed to contemplate, in the order of Providence, an intimate connection between public virtue and public happiness, will be its repugnancy to a violation of those principles.

This reflection derives additional strength from the nature of the debt of the United States. It was the price of liberty. The faith of America has been repeatedly pledged for it, and with solemnities, that give peculiar force to the obligation. There is indeed reason to regret that it has not hitherto been kept; that the necessities of the war, conspiring with inexperience in the subjects of finance, produced direct infractions; and that the subsequent period has been a continued scene of negative violation, or non-compliance. But a diminution of this regret arises from the reflection, that the last seven years have exhibited an earnest and uniform effort, on the part of the government of the union, to retrieve the national credit, by doing justice to the creditors of the nation; and that the embarrassments of a defective constitution, which defeated this laudable effort, have ceased.

From this evidence of a favorable disposition, given by the former government, the institution of a new one, cloathed with powers competent to calling forth the resources of the community, has excited correspondent expectations. A general belief, accordingly, prevails, that the credit of the United States will quickly be established on the firm foundation of an effectual provision for the existing debt. The influence, which this has had at home, is witnessed by the rapid increase, that has taken place in the market value of the public securities. From January to November, they rose thirty-three and a third per cent, and from that period to this time, they have risen fifty per cent more. And the intelligence from abroad announces effects proportionably favourable to our national credit and consequence.

It cannot but merit particular attention, that among ourselves the most enlightened friends of good government are those, whose expectations are the highest.

To justify and preserve their confidence; to promote the encreasing respectability of the American name; to answer the calls of justice; to restore landed property to its due value; to furnish new resources both to agriculture and commerce; to cement more closely the union of the states; to add to their security against foreign attack; to establish public order on the basis of an upright and liberal policy. These are the great and invaluable ends to be secured, by a proper and adequate provision, at the present period, for the support of public credit.

To this provision we are invited, not only by the general considerations, which have been noticed, but by others of a more particular nature. It will procure to every class of the community some important advantages, and remove some no less important disadvantages.

The advantage to the public creditors from the increased value of that part of their property which constitutes the public debt, needs no explanation.

But there is a consequence of this, less obvious, though not less true, in which every other citizen is interested. It is a well known fact, that in countries in which the national debt is properly funded, and an object of established confidence, it answers most of the purposes of money. Transfers of stock or public debt are there equivalent to payments in specie; or in other words, stock, in the principal transactions of business, passes current as specie. The same thing would, in all probability happen here, under the like circumstances.

The benefits of this are various and obvious.

First. Trade is extended by it; because there is a larger capital to carry it on, and the merchant can at the same time, afford to trade for smaller profits; as his stock, which, when unemployed, brings him in an interest from the government, serves him also as money, when he has a call for it in his commercial operations.

Secondly. Agriculture and manufactures are also promoted by it: For the like reason, that more capital can be commanded to be employed in both; and because the merchant, whose enterprize in foreign trade, gives to them activity and extension, has greater means for enterprize.

Thirdly. The interest of money will be lowered by it; for this is always in a ratio, to the quantity of money, and to the quickness of circulation. This circumstance will enable both the public and individuals to borrow on easier and cheaper terms.

And from the combination of these effects, additional aids will be furnished to labour, to industry, and to arts of every kind.

But these good effects of a public debt are only to be looked for, when, by being well funded, it has acquired an *adequate* and *stable* value. Till then, it has rather a contrary tendency. The fluctuation and insecurity incident to it in an unfunded state, render it a mere commodity, and a precarious one. As such, being only an object of occasional and particular speculation, all the money applied to it is so much diverted from the more useful channels of circulation, for which the thing itself affords no substitute: So that, in fact, one serious inconvenience of an unfunded debt is, that it contributes to the scarcity of money.

This distinction which has been little if at all attended to, is of the greatest moment. It involves a question immediately interesting to every part of the community; which is no other than this—Whether the public debt, by a provision for it on true principles, shall be rendered a *substitute* for money; or whether, by being left as it is, or by being provided for in such a manner as will wound those principles, and destroy confidence, it shall be suffered to continue, as it is, a pernicious drain of our cash from the channels of productive industry.

The effect, which the funding of the public debt, on right principles, would have upon landed property, is one of the circumstances attending such an arrangement, which has been least adverted to, though it deserves the most particular attention. The present depreciated state of that species of property is a serious calamity. The value of cultivated lands, in most of the states, has fallen since the revolution from 25 to 50 per cent. In those farthest south, the decrease is still more considerable. Indeed, if the representations, continually received from that quarter, may be credited, lands there will command no price, which may not be deemed an almost total sacrifice.

This decrease, in the value of lands, ought, in a great measure, to be attributed to the scarcity of money. Consequently whatever produces an augmentation of the monied capital of the country, must have a proportional effect in raising that value. The beneficial tendency of a funded debt, in this respect, has been manifested by the most decisive experience in Great-Britain.

The proprietors of lands would not only feel the benefit of this increase in the value of their property, and of a more prompt and better sale, when they had occasion to sell; but the necessity of selling would be, itself, greatly diminished. As the same cause would contribute to the facility of loans, there is reason to believe, that such of them as are indebted, would be able through that resource, to satisfy their more urgent creditors.

It ought not however to be expected, that the advantages, described as likely to result from funding the public debt, would be instantaneous. It might require some time to bring the value of stock to its natural level, and to attach to it that fixed confidence, which is necessary to its quality as money. Yet the late rapid rise of the public securities encourages an expectation, that the progress of stock to the desireable point, will be much more expeditious than could have been foreseen. And as in the mean time it will be increasing in value, there is room to conclude, that it will, from the outset, answer many of the purposes in contemplation. Particularly it seems to be probable, that from creditors, who are not themselves necessitous, it will early meet with a ready reception in payment of debts, at its current price.

Having now taken a concise view of the inducements to a proper provision for the public debt, the next enquiry which presents itself is, what ought to be the nature of such a provision? This requires some preliminary discussions.

It is agreed on all hands, that that part of the debt which has been contracted abroad, and is denominated the foreign debt, ought to be provided for, according to the precise terms of the contracts relating to it. The discussions, which can arise, therefore, will have reference essentially to the domestic part of it, or to that which has been contracted at home. It is to be regretted, that there is not the same unanimity of sentiment on this part, as on the other.

The Secretary has too much deference for the opinions of every part of the community, not to have observed one, which has, more than once, made its appearance in the public prints, and which is occasionally to be met with in conversation. It involves this question, whether a discrimination ought not to be made between original holders of the public securities, and present possessors, by purchase. Those who advocate a discrimination are for making a full provision for the securities of the former, at their nominal value; but contend, that the latter ought to receive no more than the cost to them, and the interest: And the idea is sometimes suggested of making good the difference to the primitive possessor.

In favor of this scheme, it is alledged, that it would be unreasonable to pay twenty shillings in the pound, to one who had not given more for it than three or four. And it is added, that it would be hard to aggravate the misfortune of the first owner, who, probably through necessity, parted with his property at so great a loss, by obliging him to contribute to the profit of the person, who had speculated on his distresses.

The Secretary, after the most mature reflection on the force of this argument, is induced to reject the doctrine it contains, as equally unjust and impolitic, as highly injurious, even to the original holders of public securities; as ruinous to public credit.

It is inconsistent with justice, because in the first place, it is a breach of contract; in violation of the rights of a fair purchaser.

The nature of the contract in its origin, is, that the public will pay the sum expressed in the security, to the first holder, or his *assignee*. The *intent*, in making the security assignable, is, that the proprietor may be able to make use of his property, by selling it for as much as it *may be worth in the market*, and that the buyer may be *safe* in the purchase.

Every buyer therefore stands exactly in the place of the seller, has the same right with him to the identical sum expressed in the security, and having acquired that right, by fair purchase, and in conformity to the original *agreement* and *intention* of the government, his claim cannot be disputed, without manifest injustice.

That he is to be considered as a fair purchaser, results from this: Whatever necessity the seller may have been under, was occasioned by the government, in not making a proper provision for its debts. The buyer had no agency in it, and therefore ought not to suffer. He is not even chargeable with having taken an undue advantage. He paid what the commodity was worth in the market, and took the risks of reimbursement upon himself. He of course gave a fair equivalent, and ought to reap the benefit of his hazard; a hazard which was far from inconsiderable, and which, perhaps, turned on little less than a revolution in government.

That the case of those, who parted with their securities from necessity, is a hard one, cannot be denied. But whatever complaint of injury, or claim of redress, they may have, respects the government solely. They have not only nothing to object to the persons who relieved their necessities, by giving them the current price of their property, but they are even under an implied condition to contribute to the reimbursement of those persons. They knew, that by the terms of the contract with themselves, the public were bound to pay to those, to whom they should convey their title, the sums stipulated to be paid to them; and, that as citizens of the United States, they were to bear their proportion of the contribution for that purpose. This, by the act of assignment, they tacitly engage to do; and if they had an option, they could not, with integrity or good faith, refuse to do it, without the consent of those to whom they sold.

But though many of the original holders sold from necessity, it does not follow, that this was the case with all of them. It may well be supposed, that some of them did it either through want of confidence in an eventual provision, or from the allurements of some profitable speculation. How shall these different classes be discriminated from each other? How shall it be ascertained, in any case, that the money, which the original holder obtained for his security, was not more beneficial to him, than if he had held it to the pressent time, to avail himself of the provision which shall be made? How shall it be known, whether if the purchaser had employed his money in some other way, he would not be in a better situation, than by having applied it in the purchase of securities, though he should now receive their full amount? And if neither of these things can be known, how shall it be determined whether a discrimination, independent of the breach of contract, would not do a real injury to purchasers; and if it included a compensation to the primitive proprietors, would not give them an advantage, to which they had no equitable pretension.

It may well be imagined, also, that there are not wanting instances, in which individuals, urged by a present necessity, parted with the securities received by them from the public, and shortly after replaced them with others, as an indemnity for their first loss. Shall they be deprived of the indemnity which they have endeavoured to secure by so provident an arrangement?

Questions of this sort, on a close inspection, multiply themselves without end, and demonstrate the injustice of a discrimination, even on the most subtile calculations of equity, abstracted from the obligation of contract.

The difficulties too of regulating the details of a plan for that purpose, which would have even the semblance of equity, would be found immense. It may well be doubted whether they would not be insurmountable, and replete with such absurd, as well as inequitable consequences, as to disgust even the proposers of the measure.

As a specimen of its capricious operation, it will be sufficient to notice the effect it would have upon two persons, who may be supposed two years ago to have purchased, each, securities at three shillings in the pound, and one of them to retain those bought by him, till the discrimination should take place; the other to have parted with those bought by him, within a month past, at nine shillings. The former, who had had most confidence in the government, would in this case only receive at the rate of three shillings and the interest; while the latter, who had had less confidence would receive *for what cost him the same money* at the rate of nine shillings, and his representative, *standing in his place*, would be entitled to a like rate.

The impolicy of a discrimination results from two considerations; one, that it proceeds upon a principle destructive of that *quality* of the public debt, or the stock of the nation, which is essential to its capacity for answering the purposes of money—that is the *security* of *transfer*; the other, that as well on this account, as because it includes a breach of faith, it renders property in the funds less valuable; consequently induces lenders to demand a higher premium for what they lend, and produces every other inconvenience of a bad state of public credit.

It will be perceived at first sight, that the transferable quality of stock is essential to its operation as money, and that this depends on the idea of complete security to the transferree, and a firm persuasion, that no distinction can in any circumstances be made between him and the original proprietor.

The precedent of an invasion of this fundamental principle, would of course tend to deprive the community of an advantage, with which no temporary saving could bear the least comparison.

And it will as readily be perceived, that the same cause would operate a diminution of the value of stock in the hands of the first, as well as of every other holder. The price, which any man, who should incline to purchase, would be willing to give for it, would be in a compound ratio to the immediate profit it afforded, and to the chance of the continuance of his profit. If there was supposed to be any hazard of the latter, the risk would be taken into the calculation, and either there would be no purchase at all, or it would be at a proportionably less price.

For this diminution of the value of stock, every person, who should be about to lend to the government, would demand a compensation; and would add to the actual difference, between the nominal and the market value, and equivalent for the chance of greater decrease; which, in a precarious state of public credit, is always to be taken into the account.

Every compensation of this sort, it is evident, would be an absolute loss to the government.

In the preceding discussion of the impolicy of a discrimination, the injurious tendency of it to those, who continue to be the holders of the securities, they received from the government, has been explained. Nothing need be added, on this head, except that this is an additional and interesting light, in which the injustice of the measure may be seen. It would not only divest present proprietors by purchase, of the rights they had acquired under the sanction of public faith, but it would depreciate the property of the remaining original holders.

It is equally unnecessary to add any thing to what has been already said to demonstrate the fatal influence, which the principle of discrimination would have on the public credit.

But there is still a point in view in which it will appear perhaps even more exceptionable, than in either of the former. It would be repugnant to an express provision of the Constitution of the United States. This provision is, that "all debts contracted and engagements entered into before the adoption of that Constitution shall be as valid against the United States under it, as under the confederation," which amounts to a constitutional ratification of the contracts respecting the debt, in the state in which they existed under the confederation. And resorting to that standard, there can be no doubt, that the rights of assignees and original holders, must be considered as equal.

In exploding thus fully the principle of discrimination, the Secretary is happy in reflecting, that he is the only advocate of what has been already sanctioned by the formal and express authority of the government of the Union, in these emphatic terms—"The remaining class of creditors (say Congress in their circular address to the states, of the 26th of April 1783) is composed, partly of such of our fellow-citizens as originally lent to the public the use of their funds, or have since manifested *most confidence* in their country, by receiving transfers from the lenders; and partly of those, whose property has been either advanced or assumed for the public service. To *discriminate* the merits of these several descriptions of creditors, would be a task equally unnecessary and invidious. If the voice of humanity plead more loudly in favor of some than of others, the voice of policy, no less than of justice, pleads in favor of all. A WISE NATION will never permit those who relieve the wants of their country, or who *rely most* on its *faith*, its *firmness*, and its *resources*, when either of them is distrusted, to suffer by the event."

The Secretary concluding, that a discrimination, between the different classes of creditors of the United States, cannot with propriety be *made*, proceeds to examine whether a difference ought to be permitted to *remain* between them, and another description of public creditors—Those of the states individually.

The Secretary, after mature reflection on this point, entertains a full conviction, that an assumption of the debts of the particular states by the union, and a like provision for them, as for those of the union, will be a measure of sound policy and substantial justice.

It would, in the opinion of the Secretary, contribute, in an eminent degree, to an orderly, stable and satisfactory arrangement of the national finances.

Admitting, as ought to be the case, that a provision must be made in some way or other, for the entire debt; it will follow, that no greater revenues will be required, whether that provision be made wholly by the United States, or partly by them, and partly by the states separately.

The principal question then must be, whether such a provision cannot be more conveniently and effectually made, by one general plan issuing from one authority, than by different plans originating in different authorities.

In the first case there can be no competition for resources; in the last, there must be such a competition. The consequences of this, without the greatest caution on both sides, might be interfering regulations, and thence collision and confusion. Particular branches of industry might also be oppressed by it. The most productive objects of revenue are not numerous. Either these must be wholly engrossed by one side, which might lessen the efficacy of the provisions by the other; or both must have recourse to the same objects in different modes, which might occasion an accumulation upon them, beyond what they could properly bear. If this should not happen, the caution requisite to avoiding it, would prevent the revenue's deriving the full benefit of each object. The danger of interference and of excess would be apt to impose restraints very unfriendly to the complete command of those resources, which are the most convenient; and to compel the having recourse to others, less eligible in themselves, and less agreeable to the community.

The difficulty of an effectual command of the public resources, in case of separate provisions for the debt, may be seen in another, and perhaps more striking light. It would naturally happen that different states, from local considerations, would in some instances have recourse to different objects, in others, to the same objects, in different degrees, for procuring the funds of which they stood in need. It is easy to conceive how this diversity would affect the aggregate revenue of the country. By the supposition, articles which yielded a full supply in some states, would yield nothing, or an insufficient product, in others. And hence the public revenue would not derive the full benefit of those articles, from state regulations. Neither could the deficiencies be made good by those of the union. It is a provision of the national constitution, that "all duties, imposts and excises, shall be uniform throughout the United States." And as the general government would be under a necessity from motives of policy, of paying regard to the duty, which may have been previously imposed upon any article, though but in a single state, it would be constrained, either to refrain wholly from any further imposition, upon such article, where it had been already rated as high as was proper, or to confine itself to the difference between the existing rate, and what the article would reasonably bear. Thus the pre-occupancy of an article by a single state, would tend to arrest or abridge the impositions of the union on that article. And as it is supposeable, that a great variety of articles might be placed in this situation, by dissimilar arrangements of the particular states, it is evident, that the aggregate revenue of the country would be likely to be very materially contracted by the plan of separate provisions.

If all the public creditors receive their dues from one source, distributed with an equal hand, their interest will be the same. And having the same interests, they will unite in the support of the fiscal arrangements of the government: As these, too, can be made with more convenience, where there is no competition: These circumstances combined will insure to the revenue laws a more ready and more satisfactory execution.

If on the contrary there are distinct provisions, there will be distinct interests, drawing different ways. That union and concert of views, among the creditors, which in every government is of great importance to their security, and to that of public credit, will not only not exist, but will be likely to give place to mutual jealousy and opposition. And from this cause, the operation of the systems which may be adopted, both by the particular states, and by the union, with relation to their respective debts, will be in danger of being counteracted.

There are several reasons, which render it probable, that the situation of the state creditors would be worse, than that of the creditors of the union, if there be not a national assumption of the state debts. Of these it will be sufficient to mention two; one, that a principal branch of revenue is exclusively vested in the union; the other, that a state must always be checked in the imposition of taxes on articles of consumption, from the want of power to extend the same regulation to the other states, and from the tendency of partial duties to injure its industry and commerce. Should the state creditors stand upon a less eligible footing than the others, it is unnatural to expect they would see with pleasure a provision for them. The influence which their dissatisfaction might have, could not but operate injuriously, both for the creditors, and the credit, of the United States.

Hence it is even the interest of the creditors of the union, that those of the individual states should be comprehended in a general provision. Any attempt to secure to the former either exclusive or peculiar advantages, would materially hazard their interests.

Neither would it be just, that one class of the public creditors should be more favoured than the other. The objects for which both descriptions of the debt were contracted, are in the main the same. Indeed a great part of the particular debts of the States has arisen from assumptions by them on account of the union. And it is most equitable, that there should be the same measure of retribution for all.

There is an objection, however, to an assumption of the state debts, which deserves particular notice. It may be supposed, that it would increase the difficulty of an equitable settlement between them and the United States.

The principles of that settlement, whenever they shall be discussed, will require all the moderation and wisdom of the government. In the opinion of the Secretary, that discussion, till further lights are obtained, would be premature.

All therefore which he would now think adviseable on the point in question, would be, that the amount of the debts assumed and provided for, should be charged to the respective states, to abide an eventual arrangement. This, the United States, as assignees to the creditors, would have an indisputable right to do.

But as it might be a satisfaction to the House to have before them some plan for the liquidation of accounts between the union and its members, which, including the assumption of the state debts, would consist with equity: The Secretary will submit in this place such thoughts on the subject, as have occurred to his own mind, or been suggested to him, most compatible, in his judgment, with the end proposed.

Let each state be charged with all the money advanced to it out of the treasury of the United States, liquidated according to the specie value, at the time of each advance, with interest at six per cent.

Let it also be charged with the amount, in specie value, of all its securities which shall be assumed, with the interest upon them to the time, when interest shall become payable by the United States.

Let it be credited for all monies paid and articles furnished to the United States, and for all other expenditures during the war, either towards general or particular defence, whether authorized or unauthorized by the United States; the whole liquidated to specie value, and bearing an interest of six per cent. from the several times at which the several payments, advances and expenditures accrued.

And let all sums of continental money now in the treasuries of the respective states, which shall be paid into the treasury of the United States, be credited at specie value.

Upon a statement of the accounts according to these principles, there can be little doubt, that balances would appear in favor of all the states, against the United States.

To equalize the contributions of the states, let each be then charged with its proportion of the aggregate of those balances, according to some equitable ratio, to be devised for that purpose.

If the contributions should be found disproportionate, the result of this adjustment would be, that some states would be creditors, some debtors to the union.

Should this be the case, as it will be attended with less inconvenience for the United States, to have to pay balances to, than to receive them from the particular states, it may perhaps, be practicable to effect the former by a second process, in the nature of a transfer of the amount of the debts of debtor states, to the credit of creditor states, observing the ratio by which the first apportionment shall have been made. This, whilst it would destroy the balances due from the former, would increase those due to the latter. These to be provided for by the United States, at a reasonable interest, but not to be transferable.

The expediency of this second process must depend on a knowledge of the result of the first. If the inequalities should be too great, the arrangement may be impracticable, without unduly increasing the debt of the United States. But it is not likely, that this would be the case. It is also to be remarked, that though this second process might not, upon the principle of apportionment, bring the thing to the point aimed at, yet it may approach so nearly to it, as to avoid essentially the embarrassment, of having considerable balances to collect from any of the states.

The whole of this arrangment to be under the superintendence of commissioners, vested with equitable discretion, and final authority.

The operation of the plan is exemplified in the schedule A.

The general principle of it seems to be equitable, for it appears difficult to conceive a good reason, why the expences for the particular defence of a part in a common war, should not be a common charge, as well as those incurred professedly for the general defence. The defence of each part is that of the whole; and unless all the expenditures are brought into a common mass, the tendency must be, to add, to the calamities suffered, by being the most exposed to the ravages of war, an increase of burthens.

This plan seems to be susceptible of no objection, which does not belong to every other, that proceeds on the idea of a final adjustment of accounts. The difficulty of settling a ratio, is common to all. This must, probably, either be sought for in the proportions of the requisitions, during the war, or in the decision of commissioners appointed with plenary power. The rule prescribed in the Constitution, with regard to representation and direct taxes, would evidently not be applicable to the situation of parties, during the period in question.

The existing debt of the United States is excluded from the computation, as it ought to be, because it will be provided for out of a general fund.

The only discussion of a preliminary kind, which remains, relates to the distinctions of the debt into principal and interest. It is well known, that the arrears of the latter bear a large proportion to the amount of the former. The immediate payment of these arrears is evidently impracticable, and a question arises, what ought to be done with them?

There is good reason to conclude, that the impressions of many are more favorable to the claim of the principal than to that of the interest; at least so far, as to produce an opinion, that an inferior provision might suffice for the latter.

But to the Secretary, this opinion does not appear to be

well founded. His investigations of the subject, have led him to a conclusion, that the arrears of interest have pretensions, at least equal to the principal.

The liquidated debt, traced to its origin, falls under two principal discriminations. One, relating to loans; the other to services performed and articles supplied.

The part arising from loans, was at first made payable at fixed periods, which have long since elapsed, with an early option to lenders, either to receive back their money at the expiration of those periods, or to continue it at interest, 'till the whole amount of continental bills circulating should not exceed the sum in circulation at the time of each loan. This contingency, in the sense of the contract, never happened; and the presumption is, that the creditors preferred continuing their money indefinitely at interest, to receiving it in a depreciated and depreciating state.

The other parts of it were chiefly for objects, which ought to have been paid for at the time, that is, when the services were performed or the supplies furnished; and were not accompanied with any contract for interest.

But by different acts of government and administration, concurred in by the creditors, these parts of the debt have been converted into a capital, bearing an interest of six per cent. per annum, but without any definite period of redemption. A portion of the loan-office debt has been exchanged for new securities of that import. And the whole of it seems to have acquired that character, after the expiration of the periods prefixed for re-payment.

If this view of the subject be a just one, the capital of the debt of the United States, may be considered in the light of an annuity at the rate of six per cent. per annum, redeemable at the pleasure of the government, by payment of the principal. For it seems to be a clear position, that when a public contracts a debt payable with interest, without any precise time being stipulated or understood for payment of the capital, that time is a matter of pure discretion with the government, which is at liberty to consult its own convenience respecting it, taking care to pay the interest with punctuality.

Wherefore, as long as the United States should pay the interest of their debt, as it accrued, their creditors would have no right to demand the principal.

But with regard to the arrears of interest, the case is different. These are now due, and those to whom they are due, have a right to claim immediate payment. To say, that it would be impracticable to comply, would not vary the nature of the right. Nor can this idea of impracticability be honorably carried further, than to justify the proposition of a new contract upon the basis of a commutation of that right for an equivalent. This equivalent too ought to be a real and fair one. And what other fair equivalent can be imagined for the detention of money, but a reasonable interest? Or what can be the standard of that interest, but the market rate, or the rate which the government pays in ordinary cases?

From this view of the matter, which appears to be the accurate and true one, it will follow, that the arrears of interest are entitled to an equal provision with the principal of the debt.

The result of the foregoing discussions is this—That there ought to be no discrimination between the original holders of the debt, and present possessors by purchase—That it is expedient, there should be an assumption of the state debts by the Union, and that the arrears of interest should be provided for on an equal footing with the principal.

The next enquiry, in order, towards determining the nature of a proper provision, respects the quantum of the debt, and the present rates of interest.

The debt of the union is distinguishable into foreign and domestic.

	Dollars.	Cents.
The foreign debt as stated in the schedule B, amounts to principal . . . . bearing an interest of four, and partly an interest of five per cent.	10,070,307	
Arrears of interest to the last of December, 1789, ...	1,640,071	62
Making together, dollars	11,710,378	62

The domestic debt may be subdivided into liquidated and unliquidated; principal and interest.

The principal of the liquidated part,
as stated in schedule C, amounts to. . .   27,383,917   74
bearing an interest of six per cent.

The arrears of interest as stated in
the schedule D. to the end of 1790,
amount to   13,030,168   20

Making together, dollars   40,414,085   94

This includes all that has been paid in indents (except what has come into the treasury of the United States) which, in the opinion of the Secretary, can be considered in no other light, than as interest due.

The unliquidated part of the domestic debt, which consists chiefly of the continental bills of credit, is not ascertained, but may be estimated at 2,000,000 dollars.

These several sums constitute the whole of the debt of the United States, amounting together to 54,124,464 dollars, and 56 cents.

That of the individual states is not equally well ascertained. The schedule E. shews the extent to which it has been ascertained by returns pursuant to the order of the House of the 21st September last; but this not comprehending all the states, the residue must be estimated from less authentic information. The Secretary, however, presumes, that the total amount may be safely stated at 25 millions of dollars, principal and interest. The present rate of interest of the state debts is in general, the same with that of the domestic debt of the union.

On the supposition, that the arrears of interest ought to be provided for, on the same terms with the principal, the annual amount of the interest, which, at the existing rates, would be payable on the entire mass of the public debt, would be,

Dollars. Cents.

On the foreign debt, computing
the interest on the principal, as it
stands, and allowing four per cent
on the arrears of interest, ...   542,599   66

On the domestic debt, including
that of the states   4,044,845   15

Making together, dollars   4,587,444   81

The interesting problem now occurs. Is it in the power of the United States, consistently with those prudential considerations, which ought not to be overlooked, to make a provision equal to the purpose of funding the whole debt, at the rates of interest which it now bears, in addition to the sum which will be necessary for the current service of the government?

The Secretary will not say that such provision would exceed the abilities of the country; but he is clearly of opinion, that to make it, would require the extension of taxation to a degree, and to objects, which the true interest of the public creditors forbids. It is therefore to be hoped, and even to be expected, that they will chearfully concur in such modifications of their claims, on fair and equitable principles, as will facilitate to the government an arrangement substantial, durable and satisfactory to the community. The importance of the last characteristic will strike every discerning mind. No plan, however flattering in appearance, to which it did not belong, could be truly entitled to confidence.

It will not be forgotten, that exigencies may, ere long, arise, which would call for resources greatly beyond what is now deemed sufficient for the current service; and that, should the faculties of the country be exhausted or even *strained* to provide for the public debt, there could be less reliance on the sacredness of the provision.

But while the Secretary yields to the force of these considerations, he does not lose sight of those fundamental principles of good faith, which dictate, that every practicable exertion ought to be made, scrupulously to fulfil the engagements of the government; that no change in the rights of its creditors ought to be attempted without their voluntary consent; and that this consent ought to be voluntary in fact, as well as in name. Consequently, that every proposal of a change ought to be in the shape of an appeal to their reason and to their interest; not to their necessities. To this end it is requisite, that a fair equivalent should be offered for what may be asked to be given up, and unquestionable security for the remainder. Without this, an alteration, consistently with the credit and honor of the nation, would be impracticable.

It remains to see, what can be proposed in conformity to these views.

It has been remarked, that the capital of the debt of the union is to be viewed in the light of an annuity at the rate of six per cent. per annum, redeemable at the pleasure of the government, by payment of the principal. And it will not be required, that the arrears of interest should be considered in a more favourable light. The same character, in general, may be applied to the debts of the individual states.

This view of the subject admits, that the United States would have it in their power to avail themselves of any fall in the market rate of interest, for reducing that of the debt.

This property of the debt is favourable to the public; unfavourable to the creditor. And may facilitate an arrangement for the reduction of interest, upon the basis of a fair equivalent.

Probabilities are always a rational ground of contract. The Secretary conceives, that there is good reason to believe, if effectual measures are taken to establish public credit, that the government rate of interest in the United States, will, in a very short time, fall at least as low as five per cent. and that in a period not exceeding twenty years, it will sink still lower, probably to four.

There are two principal causes which will be likely to produce this effect; one, the low rate of interest in Europe; the other, the increase of the monied capital of the nation, by the funding of the public debt.

From three to four per cent. is deemed good interest in several parts of Europe. Even less is deemed so, in some places. And it is on the decline; the increasing plenty of money continually tending to lower it. It is presumable, that no country will be able to borrow of foreigners upon better terms, than the United States, because none can, perhaps, afford so good security. Our situation exposes us less, than that of any other nation, to those casualties, which are the chief causes of expence; our incumbrances, in proportion to our real means, are less, though these cannot immediately be brought so readily into action, and our progress in resources from the early state of the country, and the immense tracts of unsettled territory, must necessarily exceed that of any other. The advantages of this situation have already engaged the attention of the European moneylenders, particularly among the Dutch. And as they become better understood, they will have the greater influence. Hence as large a proportion of the cash of Europe as may be wanted, will be, in a certain sense, in our market, for the use of government. And this will naturally have the effect of a reduction of the rate of interest, not indeed to the level of the places, which send their money to market, but to something much nearer to it, than our present rate.

The influence which the funding of the debt is calculated to have, in lowering interest, has been already remarked and explained. It is hardly possible, that it should not be materially affected by such an increase of the monied capital of the nation, as would result from the proper funding of seventy millions of dollars. But the probability of a decrease in the rate of interest, acquires confirmation from facts, which existed prior to the revolution. It is well known, that in some of the states, money might with facility be borrowed, on good security, at five per cent. and, not unfrequently, even at less.

The most enlightened of the public creditors will be most sensible of the justness of this view of the subject, and of the propriety of the use which will be made of it.

The Secretary, in pursuance of it, will assume, as a probability, sufficiently great to be a ground of calculation, both on the part of the government and of its creditors—That the interest of money in the United States will, in five years, fall to five per cent. and, in twenty, to four. The probability, in the mind of the Secretary, is rather that the fall may be more rapid and more considerable; but he prefers a mean, as most likely to engage the assent of the creditors, and more equitable in itself; because it is predicated on probabilities, which may err on one side, as well as on the other.

Premising these things, the Secretary submits to the House, the expediency of proposing a loan to the full amount of the debt, as well of the particular states, as of the union, upon the following terms.

First—That for every hundred dollars subscribed, payable in the debt (as well interest as principal) the subscribed be entitled, at his option, either

To have two thirds funded at an annuity, or yearly interest

of six per cent, redeemable at the pleasure of the government, by payment of the principal; and to receive the other third in lands in the Western Territory, at the rate of twenty cents per acre. Or,

To have the whole sum funded at an annuity or yearly interest of four per cent. irredeemable by any payment exceeding five dollars per annum on account both of principal and interest; and to receive, as a compensation for the reduction of interest, fifteen dollars and eighty cents, payable in lands, as in the preceding case. Or

To have sixty-six dollars and two thirds of a dollar funded immediately at an annuity or yearly interest of six per cent. irredeemable by any payment exceeding four dollars and two thirds of a dollar per annum, on account both of principal and interest; and to have, at the end of ten years, twenty-six dollars and eighty-eight cents, funded at the like interest and rate of redemption. Or

To have an annuity for the remainder of life, upon the contingency of living to a given age, not less distant than ten years, computing interest at four per cent. Or

To have an annuity for the remainder of life, upon the contingency of the survivorship of the youngest of two persons, computing interest, in this case also, at four per cent.

In addition to the foregoing loan, payable wholly in the debt, the Secretary would propose, that one should be opened for ten millions of dollars, on the following plan.

That for every hundred dollars subscribed, payable one half in specie, and the other half in debt (as well principal as interest) the subscriber be entitled to an annuity or yearly interest of five per cent. irredeemable by any payment exceeding six dollars per annum, on account both of principal and interest.

The principles and operation of these different plans may now require explanation.

The first is simply a proposition for paying one third of the debt in land, and funding the other two thirds, at the existing rate of interest, and upon the same terms of redemption, to which it is at present subject.

Here is no conjecture, no calculation of probabilities. The creditor is offered the advantage of making his interest principal, and he is asked to facilitate to the government an effectual provision for his demands, by accepting a third part of them in land, at a fair valuation.

The general price, at which the western lands have been, heretofore, sold, has been a dollar per acre in public securities; but at the time the principal purchases were made, these securities were worth, in the market, less than three shillings in the pound. The nominal price, therefore, would not be the proper standard, under present circumstances, nor would the precise specie value then given, be a just rule. Because, as the payments were to be made by instalments, and the securities were, at the times of the purchases, extremely low, the probability of a moderate rise must be presumed to have been taken into the account. Twenty cents, therefore, seem to bear an equitable proportion to the two considerations of value at the time, and likelihood of increase.

It will be understood, that upon this plan, the public retains the advantage of availing itself of any fall in the market rate of interest, for reducing that upon the debt, which is perfectly just, as no present sacrifice, either in the quantum of the principal, or in the rate of interest, is required from the creditor.

The inductment to the measure is, the payment of one third of the debt in land.

The second plan is grounded upon the supposition, that interest, in five years, will fall to five per cent. in fifteen more, to four. As the capital remains entire, but bearing an interest of four per cent. only, compensation is to be made to the creditor, for the interest of two per cent. per annum for five years, and of one per cent, per annum, for fifteen years, to commence at the distance of five years. The present value of these two sums or annuities, computed according to the terms of the supposition, is, by strict calculation, fifteen dollars and seven hundred and ninety-two thousandth parts of a dollar; a fraction less than the sum proposed.

The inducement to the measure here is, the reduction of interest to a rate, more within the compass of a convenient provision; and the payment of the compensation in lands.

The inducements to the individual are—the accommodation afforded to the public, the high probability of a complete equivalent—the chance even of gain, should the rate of interest fall, either more speedily or in a greater degree, than the calculation supposes. Should it fall to five per cent. sooner than five years; should it fall lower than five before the additional fifteen were expired; or should it fall below four, previous to the payment of the debt, there would be, in each case, an absolute profit to the creditor. As his capital will remain entire, the value of it will increase, with every decrease of the rate of interest.

The third plan proceeds upon the like supposition of a successive fall in the rate of interest. And upon that supposition offers an equivalent to the creditor. One hundred dollars, bearing an interest of six per cent. for five years; of five per cent. for fifteen years, and thenceforth of four per cent. (these being the successive rates of interest in the market) is

equal to a capital of . . . . 122 dollars, 510725 parts, bearing an interest of four per cent. which, converted into a capital, bearing a fixed rate of interest

of six per cent, is equal to . . . . . .81 dollars, 6738166 parts.

The difference between sixty-six dollars and two thirds of a dollar (the sum to be funded immediately) and this last sum is. . . . . .15 dollars, 0172 parts, which at six per cent per annum, amounts at the end of ten years, to . . . . 26 dollars, 8755 parts, the sum to be funded at the expiration of that period.

It ought, however, to be acknowledged, that this calculation does not make allowance for the principle of redemption, which the plan itself includes; upon which principle the equivalent in a capital of six per cent. would be by strict calculation, ... 87 dollars, 50766 parts.

But there are two considerations which induce the Secretary to think, that the one proposed would operate more equitably than this: One is, that it may not be very early in the power of the United States to avail themselves of the right of redemption reserved in the plan: The other is, that with regard to the part to be funded at the end of ten years, the principal of redemption is suspended during that time, and the full interest at six per cent. goes on improving at the same rate; which for the last five years will exceed the market rate of interest, according to the supposition.

The equivalent is regulated in this plan, by the circumstance of fixing the rate of interest higher, than it is supposed it will continue to be in the market; permitting only a gradual discharge of the debt, in an established proportion, and consequently preventing advantage being taken of any decrease of interest below the stipulated rate.

Thus the true value of eighty-one dollars and sixty-seven cents, the capital proposed, considered as a perpetuity, and bearing six per cent. interest, when the market rate of interest was five per cent. would be a small fraction more than ninety-eight dollars, when it was four per cent. would be one hundred and twenty-two dollars and fifty-one cents. But the proposed capital being subject to gradual redemption, it is evident, that its value, in each case, would be somewhat less. Yet from this may be perceived, the manner in which a less capital at a fixed rate of interest, becomes an equivalent for a greater capital, at a rate liable to variation and diminution.

It is presumable, that those creditors, who do not entertain a favorable opinion of property in western lands, will give a preference to this last mode of modelling the debt. The Secretary is sincere in affirming, that, in his opinion, it will be likely to prove, *to the full* as beneficial to the creditors, as a provision for his debt upon its present terms.

It is not intended, in either case to oblige the government to redeem, in the proportion specified, but to secure to it, the right of doing so, to avoid the inconvenience of a perpetuity.

The fourth and fifth plans abandon the supposition which is the basis of the two preceding ones, and offer only four per cent. throughout.

The reason of this is, that the payment being deferred, there will be an accumulation of compound interest, in the intermediate period against the public, which, without a very provident administration, would turn to its detriment. And the suspension of the burthen would be too apt to beget a relaxation of efforts in the mean time. The measure therefore, its object being temporary accommodation, could only be adviseable upon a moderate rate of interest.

With regard to individuals, the inducement will be sufficient at four per cent. There is no disposition of money, in private loans, making allowance for the usual delays and casualties, which would be equally beneficial as a future provision.

A hundred dollars advanced upon the life of a person of eleven years old, would produce an annuity*

	Dollars.	Parts.
If commencing at twenty-one, of	10	346
If commencing at thirty-one, of	18	803
If commencing at forty-one, of	37	286
If commencing at fifty-one, of	78	580

The same sum advanced upon the chance of the survivorship of the youngest of two lives, one of the persons being twenty-five, the other, thirty years old, would produce, if the youngest of the two, should survive, an annuity† for the remainder of life of   23 dollars, 556 parts.

From these instances may readily be discerned, the advantages, which these deferred annuities afford, for securing a comfortable provision for the evening of life, or for wives, who survive their husbands.

The sixth plan also relinquishes the supposition, which is the foundation of the second, and third, and offers a higher rate of interest upon similar terms of redemption, for the consideration of the payment of one half of the loan in specie. This is a plan highly advantageous to the creditors, who may be able to make that payment; while the specie itself could be applied in purchases of the debt, upon terms, which would fully indemnify the public for the increased interest.

It is not improbable, that foreign holders of the domestic debt, may embrace this as a desireable arrangement.

As an auxiliary expedient, and by way of experiment, the Secretary would propose a loan upon the principles of a tontine.‡

To consist of six classes, composed respectively of persons of the following ages:

First class, of those 20 years and under.

Second class, of those above 20, and not exceeding 30.

Third class, of those above 30, and not exceeding 40.

---

* See Schedule F
† Table Schedule G.
‡ See Table Schedule H.

Fourth class, of those above 40 and not exceeding 50.

Fifth class, of those above 50, and not exceeding 60.

Sixth class, of those above 60.

Each share to be two hundred dollars. The number of shares in each class, to be indefinite. Persons to be at liberty to subscribe on their own lives, or on those of others, nominated by them.

	Dollars.	Cents.
The annuity upon a share in the first class to be	8.	40
upon a share in the second	8.	65
upon a share in the third	9.	0
upon a share in the fourth	9.	65
upon a share in the fifth	10.	70
upon a share in the sixth	12.	80

The annuities of those who die, to be equally divided among the survivors, until four-fifths shall be dead, when the principle of survivorship shall cease, and each annuitant thenceforth enjoy his dividend as a several annuity during the life, upon which it shall depend.

These annuities are calculated upon the best life in each class, and at a rate of interest of four per cent. with some deductions in favor of the public. To the advantages which these circumstances present, the cessation of the right of survivorship on the death of four-fifths of the annuitants, will be no inconsiderable addition.

The inducements to individuals are, a competent interest for their money from the outset, secured for life, and the prospect of continual encrease, and even of large profit to those, whose fortune it is, to survive their associates.

It will have appeared, that in all the proposed loans, the Secretary has contemplated the putting the interest upon the same footing with the principal: *That* on the debt of the United States, he would have computed to the last of the present year: *That* on the debt of the particular states, to the last of the year 1791; the reason for which distinction will be seen hereafter.

In order to keep up a due circulation of money, it will be expedient, that the interest of the debt should be paid quarter-yearly. This regulation will, at the same time, conduce to the advantage of the public creditors, giving them, in fact, by the anticipation of payment, a higher rate of interest; which may, with propriety, be taken into the estimate of the compensation to be made to them. Six per cent. per annum, paid in this mode, will truly be worth six dollars, and one hundred and thirty-five thousandth parts of a dollar, computing the market interest at the same rate.

The Secretary thinks it advisable, to hold out various propositions, all of them compatible with the public interest, because it is, in his opinion, of the greatest consequence, that the debt should, with the consent of the creditors, be remoulded into such a shape, as will bring the expenditure of the nation to a level with its income. 'Till this shall be accomplished, the finances of the United States will never wear a proper countenance. Arrears of interest, continually accruing, will be as continual a monument, either of inability, or of ill faith; and will not cease to have an evil influence on public credit. In nothing are appearances of greater moment, than in whatever regards credit. Opinion is the soul of it, and this is affected by appearances, as well as realities. By offering an option to the creditors, between a number of plans, the change meditated will be more likely to be accomplished. Different tempers will be governed by different views of the subject.

But while the Secretary would endeavour to effect a change in the form of the debt, by new loans, in order to render it more susceptible of an adequate provision; he would not think it proper to aim at procuring the concurrence of the creditors by operating upon their necessities.

Hence whatever surplus of revenue might remain, after satisfying the interest of the new loans, and the demand for the current service, ought to be divided among those creditors, if any, who may not think fit to subscribe to them. But for this purpose, under the circumstance of depending propositions, a temporary appropriation will be most adviseable, and the sum must be limited to four per cent. as the revenues will only be calculated to produce, in that proportion, to the entire debt.

The Secretary confides for the success of the propositions, to be made, on the goodness of the reasons upon which they rest; on the fairness of the equivalent to be offered in each case; on the discernment of the creditors of their true interest; and on their disposition to facilitate the arrangements of the government, and to render them satisfactory to the community.

The remaining part of the task to be performed is, to take a view of the means of providing for the debt, according to the modification of it, which is proposed.

On this point the Secretary premises, that, in his opinion, the funds to be established, ought, for the present, to be confined to the existing debt of the United States; as well, because a progressive augmentation of the revenue will be most convenient, as because the consent of the state creditors is necessary, to the assumption contemplated; and though the obtaining of that consent may be inferred with great assurance, from their obvious interest to give it; yet 'till it shall be obtained, an actual provision for the debt, would be premature. Taxes could not, with propriety, be laid for an object, which depended on such a contingency.

All that ought now to be done, respecting it, is, to put the matter in an effectual train for a future provision. For which purpose, the Secretary will, in the course of this report, submit such propositions, as appear to him adviseable.

The Secretary now proceeds to a consideration of the necessary funds.

It has been stated that the debt of the United States consists of

	Dollars.	Cents.
The foreign debt, amounting, with arrears of interest, to	11,710,378	62
And the domestic debt amounting, with like arrears, computed to the end of the year 1790, to	42,414,085	94
Making together, Dollars	54,124,464	56

The interest on the domestic debt is computed to the end of this year, because the details of carrying any plan into execution, will exhaust the year.

	Dollars.	Cents.
The annual interest of the foreign debt has been stated at	542,599	66
And the interest on the domestic debt at four percent. would amount to	1,696,563	43
Making together, dollars	2,239,163	09

Thus to pay the interest of the foreign debt, and to pay four per cent on the whole of the domestic debt, principal and interest, forming a new capital,

    will require a yearly income of . . 2,239,163 dollars, 9 cents.

The sum which, in the opinion of the Secretary, ought now to be provided in addition to what the current service will require.

For, though the rate of interest, proposed by the third plan, exceeds four per cent. on the whole debt, and the annuities on the tontine will also exceed four per cent. on the sums which may be subscribed; yet, as the actual provision for a part is, in the former case, suspended; as measures for reducing the debt, by purchases, may be advantageously pursued, and as the payment of the deferred annuities will of course be postponed, four per cent. on the whole, will be a sufficient provision.

With regard to the instalments of the foreign debt, these, in the opinion of the Secretary, ought to be paid by new loans abroad. Could funds be conveniently spared, from other exigencies, for paying them, the United States could ill bear the drain of cash, at the present juncture, which the measure would be likely to occasion.

But to the sum which has been stated for payment of the interest, must be added a provision for the current service. This the Secretary estimates at six hundred thousand dollars;* making, with the amount of the interest, two millions, eight hundred and thirty-nine thousand, one hundred and sixty-three dollars, and nine cents.

This sum may, in the opinion of the Secretary, be obtained from the present duties on imports and tonnage, with the additions, which, without any possible disadvantage either to trade, or agriculture, may be made on wines, spirits, including those distilled within the United States, teas and coffee.

The Secretary conceives, that it will be sound policy, to carry the duties upon articles of this kind, as high as will be consistent with the practicability of a safe collection. This will lessen the necessity, both of having recourse to direct taxation, and of accumulating duties where they would be more

---

* See Schedule I.

inconvenient to trade, and upon objects, which are more to be regarded as necessaries of life.

That the articles which have been enumerated, will, better than most others, bear high duties, can hardly be a question. They are all of them, in reality—luxuries—the greatest part of them foreign luxuries; some of them, in the excess in which they are used, pernicious luxuries. And there is, perhaps, none of them, which is not consumed in so great abundance, as may, justly, denominate it, a source of national extravagance and impoverishment. The consumption of ardent spirits particularly, no doubt very much on account of their cheapness, is carried to an extreme, which is truly to be regretted, as well in regard to the health and the morals, as to the œconomy of the community.

Should the increase of duties tend to a decrease of the consumption of those articles, the effect would be, in every respect desirable. The saving which it would occasion, would leave individuals more at their ease, and promote a more favourable balance of trade. As far as this decrease might be applicable to distilled spirits, it would encourage the substitution of cyder and malt liquors, benefit agriculture, and open a new and productive source of revenue.

It is not however, probable, that this decrease would be in a degree, which would frustrate the expected benefit to the revenue from raising the duties. Experience has shewn, that luxuries of every kind, lay the strongest hold on the attachments of mankind, which, especially when confirmed by habit, are not easily alienated from them.

The same fact affords a security to the merchant, that he is not likely to be prejudiced by considerable duties on such articles. They will usually command a proportional price. The chief things in this view to be attended to, are, that the terms of payment be so regulated, as not to require inconvenient advances, and that the mode of collection be secure.

To other reasons, which plead for carrying the duties upon the articles which have been mentioned, to as great an extent as they will bear, may be added these; that they are of a nature, from their extensive consumption, to be very productive, and are amongst the most difficult objects of illicit introduction.

Invited by so many motives to make the best use of the resource, which these articles afford, the essential enquiry is—
in what mode can the duties upon them be most effectually
collected?

With regard to such of them, as will be brought from
abroad, a duty on importation recommends itself by two leading considerations; one is, that meeting the object at its first
entrance into the country, the collection is drawn to a point,
and so far simplified; the other is, that it avoids the possibility
of interference between the regulations of the United States,
and those of the particular states.

But a duty, the precautions for the collection of which
should terminate with the landing of the goods, as is essentially the case in the existing system, could not, with safety, be
carried to the extent, which is contemplated.

In that system, the evasion of the duties, depends as it
were, on a single risk. To land the goods in defiance of the
vigilance of the officers of the customs, is almost, the sole difficulty. No future pursuit, is materially, to be apprehended.
And where the inducement is equivalent to the risk, there will
be found too many, who are willing to run it. Consequently
there will be extensive frauds of the revenue, against which
the utmost rigor of the penal laws, has proved, as often as it
has been tried, an ineffectual guard.

The only expedient which has been discovered, for conciliating high duties with a safe collection, is, the establishment
of a *second*, or interior scrutiny.

By pursuing the article, from its importation, into the
hands of the dealers in it, the risk of detection is so greatly in-
hanced, that few, in comparison, will venture to incur it. Indeed every dealer, who is not himself the fraudulent importer,
then becomes, in some sort, a centinel upon him.

The introduction of a system, founded on this principle, in
some shape or other, is, in the opinion of the Secretary, essential to the efficacy of every attempt, to render the revenues
of the United States equal to their exigencies, their safety,
their prosperity, their honor.

Nor is it less essential to the interest of the honest and fair
trader. It might even be added, that every individual citizen,
besides his share in the general weal, has a particular interest

in it. The practice of smuggling never fails to have one of two effects, and sometimes unites them both. Either the smuggler undersells the fair trader, as, by saving the *duty*, he can afford to do, and makes *it* a charge upon him; or he sells at the increased price occasioned by the duty, and defrauds every man, who buys of him, of his share of what the public ought to receive. For it is evident, that the loss falls ultimately upon the citizens, who must be charged with other taxes to make good the deficiency, and supply the wants of the state.

The Secretary will not presume, that the plan, which he shall submit to the consideration of the house, is the best that could be devised. But it is the one, which has appeared to him freest from objections of any, that has occurred of equal efficacy. He acknowledges too, that it is susceptible of improvement, by other precautions in favor of the revenue, which he did not think it expedient to add. The chief outlines of the plan are not original, but it is no ill recommendation of it, that it has been tried with success.

The Secretary accordingly proposes,

That the duties heretofore laid upon wines, distilled spirits, teas and coffee, should, after the last day of May next, cease, and that instead of them, the following duties be laid.

Upon every gallon of Madeira Wine, of the quality of London particular, thirty-five cents.

Upon every gallon of other Madeira Wine, thirty cents.

Upon every gallon of Sherry, twenty-five cents.

Upon every gallon of other Wine, twenty cents.

Upon every gallon of distilled Spirits, more than ten per cent. below proof, according to Dicas's hydrometer, twenty cents.

Upon every gallon of those Spirits under five, and not more than ten per cent. below proof, according to the same hydrometer, twenty-one cents.

Upon every gallon of those Spirits of proof, and not more than five per cent. below proof, according to the same hydrometer, twenty-two cents.

Upon every gallon of those Spirits above proof, but not exceeding twenty per cent. according to the same hydrometer, twenty-five cents.

Upon every gallon of those spirits more than twenty, and

not more than forty per cent. above proof, according to the same hydrometer, thirty cents.

Upon every gallon of those spirits more than forty per cent. above proof, according to the same hydrometer, forty cents.

Upon every pound of Hyson Tea, forty cents.

Upon every pound of other Green Tea, twenty-four cents.

Upon every pound of Souchong and other black Teas, except Bohea, twenty cents.

Upon every pound of Bohea Tea, twelve cents.

Upon every pound of Coffee, five cents.

That upon Spirits distilled within the United States, from Molasses, Sugar, or other foreign materials, there be paid—

Upon every gallon of those Spirits, more than ten per cent below proof, according to Dicas's hydrometer, eleven cents.

Upon every gallon of those spirits under five, and not more than ten per cent. below proof, according to the same hydrometer, twelve cents.

Upon every gallon of those Spirits of proof, and not more than five per cent. below proof, according to the same hydrometer, thirteen cents.

Upon every gallon of those Spirits, above proof, but not exceeding twenty per cent. according to the same hydrometer, fifteen cents.

Upon every gallon of those Spirits, more than twenty, and not more than forty per cent. above proof, according to the same hydrometer, twenty cents.

Upon every gallon of those Spirits more than forty per cent. above proof, according to the same hydrometer, thirty cents.

That upon Spirits distilled within the United States, in any city, town or village, from materials of the growth or production of the United States, there be paid—

Upon every gallon of those Spirits more than ten per cent. below proof, according to Dicas's hydrometer, nine cents.

Upon every gallon of those Spirits under five, and not more than ten per cent. below proof, according to the same hydrometer, ten cents.

Upon every gallon of those Spirits of proof, and not more than five per cent. below proof, according to the same hydrometer, eleven cents.

Upon every gallon of those Spirits above proof, but not exceeding twenty per cent. according to the same hydrometer, thirteen cents.

Upon every gallon of those Spirits more than twenty, and not more than forty per cent. above proof, according to the same hydrometer, seventeen cents.

Upon every gallon of those Spirits, more than forty per cent. above proof, according to the same hydrometer, twenty-five cents.

That upon all Stills employed in distilling Spirits from materials of the growth or production of the United States, in any other place, than a city, town or village, there be paid the yearly sum of sixty cents, for every gallon, English wine measure, of the capacity of each Still, including its head.

The Secretary does not distribute the duties on Teas into different classes, as has been done in the impost act of the last session; because this distribution depends on considerations of commercial policy, not of revenue. It is sufficient, therefore, for him to remark, that the rates, above specified, are proposed with reference to the lowest class.

The Secretary conceiving, that he could not convey an accurate idea of the plan contemplated by him, for the collection of these duties, in any mode so effectual as by the draft of a bill for the purpose, begs leave respectfully to refer the House to that, which will be found annexed to this report, relatively to the article of distilled spirits; and which, for the better explanation of some of its parts, is accompanied with marginal remarks.

It would be the intention of the Secretary, that the duty on wines should be collected upon precisely the same plan with that on imported spirits.

But with regard to teas and coffee, the Secretary is inclined to think, that it will be expedient, till experience shall evince the propriety of going further, to exclude the *ordinary* right of the officers to visit and inspect the places in which those articles may be kept. The other precautions, without this, will afford, though not complete, considerable security.

It will not escape the observation of the House, that the Secretary, in the plan submitted, has taken the most scrupulous care, that those citizens upon whom it is immediately to

operate, be secured from every species of injury by the misconduct of the officers to be employed. There are not only
strong guards against their being guilty of abuses of authority; they are not only punishable, criminally, for any they may
commit, and made answerable in damages, to individuals, for
whatever prejudice these may sustain by their acts or neglects:
But even where seizures are made with probable cause, if
there be an acquittal of the article seized, a compensation
to the proprietors for the injury their property may suffer,
and even for its detention, is to be made out of the public
treasury.

So solicitous indeed has the Secretary been, to obviate
every appearance of hardship, that he has even included a
compensation to the dealers, for their agency in aid of the
revenue.

With all these precautions to manifest a spirit of moderation and justice on the part of government: And when it is
considered, that the object of the proposed system is the firm
establishment of public credit; that on this depends the character, security and prosperity of the nation; that advantages in
every light important, may be expected to result from it; that
the immediate operation of it will be upon an enlightened
class of citizens, zealously devoted to good government, and
to a liberal and enlarged policy, and that it is peculiarly the interest of the virtuous part of them to co-operate in whatever
will restrain the spirit of illicit traffic; there will be perceived
to exist, the justest ground of confidence, that the plan, if eligible in itself, will experience the chearful and prompt acquiescence of the community.

The Secretary computes the nett product of the duties proposed in this report at about one million seven hundred and
three thousand four hundred dollars, according to the estimate in schedule K, which if near the truth, will, together
with the probable product of the duties on imports and tonnage, complete the sum required. But it will readily occur,
that in so unexplored a field there must be a considerable degree of uncertainty in the data. And that, on this account, it
will be prudent to have an auxiliary resource for the first year,
in which the interest will become payable, that there may be
no possibility of disappointment to the public creditors, ere

there may be an opportunity of providing for any deficiency, which the experiment may discover. This will accordingly be attended to.

The proper appropriation of the funds provided, and to be provided, seems next to offer itself to consideration.

On this head, the Secretary would propose, that the duties on distilled spirits, should be applied in the first instance, to the payment of the interest of the foreign debt.

That reserving out of the residue of those duties an annual sum of six hundred thousand dollars, for the current service of the United States; the surplus, together with the product of the other duties, be applied to the payment of the interest on the new loan, by an appropriation, co-extensive with the duration of the debt.

And that if any part of the debt should remain unsubscribed, the excess of the revenue be divided among the creditors of the unsubscribed part, by a temporary disposition; with a limitation, however, to four per cent.

It will hardly have been unnoticed, that the Secretary had been thus far silent on the subject of the post-office. The reason is, that he has had in view the application of the revenue arising from that source, to the purposes of a sinking fund. The post-master-general gives it as his opinion, that the immediate product of it, upon a proper arrangement, would probably be, not less than one hundred thousand dollars. And from its nature, with good management, it must be a growing, and will be likely to become a considerable fund. The post-master-general is now engaged in preparing a plan,* which will be the foundation of a proposition for a new arrangement of the establishment. This, and some other points relative to the subject referred to the Secretary, he begs leave to reserve for a future report.

Persuaded as the Secretary is, that the proper funding of the present debt, will render it a national blessing: Yet he is so far from acceding to the position, in the latitude in which it is sometimes laid down, that "public debts are public benefits," a position inviting to prodigality, and liable to dangerous

---

* This plan, since the framing of this report, has been received, and will be, shortly, submitted.

abuse,—that he ardently wishes to see it incorporated, as a fundamental maxim, in the system of public credit of the United States, that the creation of debt should always be accompanied with the means of extinguishment. This he regards as the true secret for rendering public credit immortal. And he presumes, that it is difficult to conceive a situation, in which there may not be an adherence to the maxim. At least he feels an unfeigned solicitude, that this may be attempted by the United States, and that they may commence their measures for the establishment of credit, with the observance of it.

Under this impression, the Secretary proposes, that the nett product of the post-office, to a sum not exceeding one million of dollars, be vested in commissioners, to consist of the Vice-President of the United States or President of the Senate, the Speaker of the House of Representatives, the Chief Justice, Secretary of the Treasury and Attorney-General of the United States, for the time being, in trust, to be applied, by them, or any three of them, to the discharge of the existing public debt, either by purchases of stock in the market, or by payments on account of the principal, as shall appear to them most adviseable, in conformity to the public engagements; to continue so vested, until the whole of the debt shall be discharged.

As an additional expedient for effecting a reduction of the debt, and for other purposes which will be mentioned, the Secretary would further propose that the same commissioners be authorised, with the approbation of the President of the United States, to borrow, on their credit, a sum, not exceeding twelve millions of dollars, to be applied,

First. To the payment of the interest and instalments of the foreign debt, to the end of the present year, which will require 3,491,923 dollars, and 46 cents.

Secondly. To the payment of any deficiency which may happen in the product of the funds provided for paying the interest of the domestic debt.

Thirdly. To the effecting a change in the form of such part of the foreign debt, as bears an interest of five per cent. It is conceived, that, for this purpose, a new loan, at a lower interest, may be combined with other expedients. The remainder of this part of the debt, after paying the instalments, which will accrue in the course of 1790, will be 3,888,888 dollars, and 81 cents.

Fourthly. To the purchase of the public debt at the price it shall bear in the market, while it continues below its true value. This measure, which would be, in the opinion of the Secretary, highly dishonorable to the government, if it were to precede a provision for funding the debt, would become altogether unexceptionable, after that had been made. Its effect would be in favor of the public creditors, as it would tend to raise the value of stock. And all the difference, between its true value, and the actual price, would be so much clear gain to the public. The payment of foreign interest on the capital to be borrowed for this purpose, should that be a necessary consequence, would not, in the judgment of the Secretary, be a good objection to the measure. The saving by the operation would be itself, a sufficient indemnity; and the employment of that capital, in a country situated like this, would much more than compensate for it. Besides, if the government does not undertake this operation, the same inconvenience, which the objection in question supposes, would happen in another way, with a circumstance of aggravation. As long, at least, as the debt shall continue below its proper value, it will be an object of speculation to foreigners, who will not only receive the interest, upon what they purchase, and remit it abroad, as in the case of the loan, but will reap the additional profit of the difference in value. By the government's entering into competition with them, it will not only reap a part of this profit itself, but will contract the extent, and lessen the extra profit of foreign purchases. That competition will accelerate the rise of stock; and whatever greater rate this obliges foreigners to pay, for what they purchase, is so much clear saving to the nation. In the opinion of the Secretary, and contrary to an idea which is not without patrons, it ought to be the policy of the government, to raise the value of stock to its true standard as fast as possible. When it arrives to that point, foreign speculations (which, till then, must be deemed pernicious, further than as they serve to bring it to that point) will become beneficial. Their money laid out in this country, upon our agriculture, commerce and manufactures, will produce much more to us, than the income they will receive from it.

The Secretary contemplates the application of this money, through the medium of a national bank, for which, with the permission of the House, he will submit a plan in the course of the session.

The Secretary now proceeds, in the last place, to offer to the consideration of the House, his ideas, of the steps, which ought at the present session, to be taken, towards the assumption of the state debts.

These are briefly, that concurrent resolutions of the two Houses, with the approbation of the President, be entered into, declaring in substance,

That the United States do assume, and will at the first session in the year 1791, provide, on the same terms with the present debt of the United States, for all such part of the debts of the respective states, or any of them, as shall, prior to the first day of January in the said year 1791, be subscribed towards a loan to the United States, upon the principles of either of the plans, which shall have been adopted by them, for obtaining a re-loan of their present debt.

Provided that the provision to be made as aforesaid, shall be suspended, with respect to the debt, of any state, which may have exchanged the securities of the United States for others issued by itself, until the whole of the said securities shall, either be re-exchanged, or surrendered to the United States.

And provided also, that the interest upon the debt assumed, be computed to the end of the year 1791; and that the interest to be paid by the United States, commence on the first day of January, 1792.

That the amount of the debt of each state so assumed and provided for, be charged to such state in account with the United States, upon the same principles, upon which it shall be lent to the United States.

That subscriptions be opened for receiving loans of the said debts at the same times and places, and under the like regulations, as shall have been prescribed in relation to the debt of the United States.

The Secretary has now completed the objects, which he proposed to himself, to comprise in the present report. He has, for the most part, omitted details, as well to avoid fatiguing the attention of the House, as because more time would have been desirable even to digest the general principles of the plan. If these should be found right, the particular modifications will readily suggest themselves in the progress of the work.

The Secretary, in the views which have directed his pursuit of the subject, has been influenced, in the first place, by the consideration, that his duty from the very terms of the resolution of the House, obliged him to propose what appeared to him an adequate provision for the support of the public credit, adapted at the same time to the real circumstances of the United States; and in the next, by the reflection, that measures which will not bear the test of future unbiassed examination, can neither be productive of individual reputation, nor (which is of much greater consequence) public honor, or advantage.

Deeply impressed, as the Secretary is, with a full and deliberate conviction, that the establishment of public credit, upon the basis of a satisfactory provision, for the public debt, is, under the present circumstances of this country, the true desideratum towards relief from individual and national embarrassments; that without it, these embarrassments will be likely to press still more severely upon the community—He cannot but indulge an anxious wish, that an effectual plan for that purpose may, during the present session, be the result of the united wisdom of the legislature.

He is fully convinced, that it is of the greatest importance, that no further delay should attend the making of the requisite provision; not only, because it will give a better impression of the good faith of the country, and will bring earlier relief to the creditors; both which circumstances are of great moment to public credit: but, because the advantages to the community, from raising stock, as speedily as possible, to its natural value, will be incomparably greater, than any that can result from its continuance below that standard. No profit, which could be derived from purchases in the market, on account of the government, to any practicable extent, would be an equivalent for the loss, which would be sustained by the purchases of foreigners, at a low value. Not to repeat, that governmental purchases, to be honorable, ought to be preceded by a provision. Delay, by disseminating doubt, would sink the price of stock; and as the temptation to foreign speculations, from the lowness of the price, would be too great to be neglected, millions would probably be lost to the United States.

All which is humbly submitted.

Alexander Hamilton, *Secretary of the Treasury.*

Report on a National Bank

Treasury Department
December 13th, 1790

In obedience to the order of the House of Representatives of
the ninth day of August last, requiring the Secretary of
the Treasury to prepare and report on this day such further provision as may, in his opinion, be necessary for establishing the public Credit

The said Secretary further respectfully reports

That from a conviction (as suggested in his report No. 1
herewith presented) That a National Bank is an Institution of
primary importance to the prosperous administration of the
Finances, and would be of the greatest utility in the operations connected with the support of the Public Credit, his attention has been drawn to devising the plan of such an
institution, upon a scale, which will intitle it to the confidence, and be likely to render it equal to the exigencies of the
Public.

Previously to entering upon the detail of this plan, he en-
treats the indulgence of the House, towards some preliminary
reflections naturally arising out of the subject, which he hopes
will be deemed, neither useless, nor out of place. Public opinion being the ultimate arbiter of every measure of Government, it can scarcely appear improper, in deference to that, to
accompany the origination of any new proposition with explanations, which the superior information of those, to whom
it is immediately addressed, would render superfluous.

It is a fact well understood, that public Banks have found
admission and patronage among the principal and most enlightened commercial nations. They have successively obtained in Italy, Germany, Holland, England and France, as
well as in the United States. And it is a circumstance, which
cannot but have considerable weight, in a candid estimate of
their tendency, that after an experience of centuries, there exists not a question about their utility in the countries in which
they have been so long established. Theorists and men of
business unite in the acknowlegment of it.

Trade and industry, wherever they have been tried, have been indebted to them for important aid. And Government has been repeatedly under the greatest obligations to them, in dangerous and distressing emergencies. That of the United States, as well in some of the most critical conjunctures of the late war, as since the peace, has received assistance from those established among us, with which it could not have dispensed.

With this two fold evidence before us, it might be expected, that there would be a perfect union of opinions in their favour. Yet doubts have been entertained; jealousies and prejudices have circulated: and though the experiment is every day dissipating them, within the spheres in which effects are best known; yet there are still persons by whom they have not been intirely renounced. To give a full and accurate view of the subject would be to make a Treatise of a report; but there are certain aspects in which it may be cursorily exhibited, which may perhaps conduce to a just impression of its merits. These will involve a comparison of the advantages, with the disadvantages, real or supposed, of such institutions.

The following are among the principal advantages of a Bank.

First. The augmentation of the active or productive capital of a country. Gold and Silver, when they are employed merely as the instruments of exchange and alienation, have been not improperly denominated dead Stock; but when deposited in Banks, to become the basis of a paper circulation, which takes their character and place, as the signs or representatives of value, they then acquire life, or, in other words, an active and productive quality. This idea, which appears rather subtil and abstract, in a general form, may be made obvious and palpable, by entering into a few particulars. It is evident, for instance, that the money, which a merchant keeps in his chest, waiting for a favourable opportunity to employ it, produces nothing 'till that opportunity arrives. But if instead of locking it up in this manner, he either deposits it in a Bank, or invests it in the Stock of a Bank, it yields a profit, during the interval; in which he partakes, or not, according to the choice he may have made of being a depositor or a proprietor; and when any advantageous speculation offers, in order to be able to embrace it, he has only to withdraw his money, if a depositor, or if a proprietor to obtain a loan from the Bank, or to dispose of his Stock; an alternative seldom or never attended with difficulty, when the affairs of the institution are in a prosperous train. His money thus deposited or invested, is a fund, upon which himself and others can borrow to a much larger amount. It is a well established fact, that Banks in good credit can circulate a far greater sum than the actual quantum of their capital in Gold & Silver. The extent of the possible excess seems indeterminate; though it has been conjecturally stated at the proportions of two and three to one. This faculty is produced in various ways. First. A great proportion of the notes, which are issued and pass current as Cash, are indefinitely suspended in circulation, from the confidence which each holder has, that he can at any moment turn them into gold and silver. Secondly, Every loan, which a Bank makes is, in its first shape, a credit given to the borrower on its books, the amount of which it stands ready to pay, either in its own notes, or in gold or silver, at his option. But, in a great number of cases, no actual payment is made in either. The Borrower frequently, by a check or order, transfers his credit to some other person, to whom he has a payment to make; who, in his turn, is as often content with a similar credit, because he is satisfied, that he can, whenever he pleases, either convert it into cash, or pass it to some other hand, as an equivalent for it. And in this manner the credit keeps circulating, performing in every stage the office of money, till it is extinguished by a discount with some person, who has a payment to make to the Bank, to an equal or greater amount. Thus large sums are lent and paid, frequently through a variety of hands, without the intervention of a single piece of coin. Thirdly, There is always a large quantity of gold and silver in the repositories of the Bank, besides its own Stock, which is placed there, with a view partly to its safe keeping and partly to the accommodation of an institution, which is itself a source of general accommodation. These deposits are of immense consequence in the operations of a Bank. Though liable to be redrawn at any moment, experience proves, that the money so much oftener changes proprietors than place, and that what is drawn out is generally so speedily replaced, as to authorise the counting upon the sums deposited, as an *effective fund*; which, concurring with the Stock of the Bank, enables it to extend its loans, and to answer all the demands for coin, whether in consequence of those loans, or arising from the occasional return of its notes.

These different circumstances explain the manner, in which the ability of a bank to circulate a greater sum, than its actual capital in coin, is acquired. This however must be gradual; and must be preceded by a firm establishment of confidence; a confidence which may be bestowed on the most rational grounds; since the excess in question will always be bottomed on good security of one kind or another. This, every well conducted Bank carefully requires, before it will consent to advance either its money or its credit; and where there is an auxiliary capital (as will be the case in the plan hereafter submitted) which, together with the capital in coin, define the boundary, that shall not be exceeded by the engagements of the Bank, the security may, consistently with all the maxims of a reasonable circumspection be regarded as complete.

The same circumstances illustrate the truth of the position, that it is one of the properties of Banks to increase the active capital of a country. This, in other words is the sum of them. The money of one individual, while he is waiting for an opportunity to employ it, by being either deposited in the Bank for safe keeping, or invested in its Stock, is in a condition to administer to the wants of others, without being put out of his own reach, when occasion presents. This yields an extra profit, arising from what is paid for the use of his money by others, when he could not himself make use of it; and keeps the money itself in a state of incessant activity. In the almost infinite vicissitudes and competitions of mercantile enterprise, there never can be danger of an intermission of demand, or that the money will remain for a moment idle in the vaults of the Bank. This additional employment given to money, and the faculty of a bank to lend and circulate a greater sum than the amount of its stock in coin are to all the purposes of trade and industry an absolute increase of capital. Purchases and undertakings, in general, can be carried on by any given sum of bank paper or credit, as effectually as by an equal sum of gold and silver. And thus by contributing to enlarge the mass of industrious and commercial enterprise, banks become nurseries of national wealth: a consequence, as satisfactorily verified by experience, as it is clearly deducible in theory.

Secondly. Greater facility to the Government in obtaining pecuniary aids, especially in sudden emergencies. This is another and an undisputed advantage of public banks: one, which as already remarked, has been realised in signal instances, among ourselves. The reason is obvious: The capitals of a great number of individuals are, by this operation, collected to a point, and placed under one direction. The mass, formed by this union, is in a certain sense magnified by the credit attached to it: And while this mass is always ready, and can at once be put in motion, in aid of the Government, the interest of the bank to afford that aid, independent of regard to the public safety and welfare, is a sure pledge for its disposition to go as far in its compliances, as can in prudence be desired. There is in the nature of things, as will be more particularly noticed in another place, an intimate connection of interest between the government and the Bank of a Nation.

Thirdly. The facilitating of the payment of taxes. This advantage is produced in two ways. Those who are in a situation to have access to the Bank can have the assistance of loans to answer with punctuality the public calls upon them. This accommodation has been sensibly felt in the payment of the duties heretofore laid, by those who reside where establishments of this nature exist. This however, though an extensive, is not an universal benefit. The other way, in which the effect here contemplated is produced, and in which the benefit is general, is the encreasing of the quantity of circulating medium and the quickening of circulation. The manner in which the first happens has already been traced. The last may require some illustration. When payments are to be made between different places, having an intercourse of business with each other, if there happen to be no private bills, at market, and there are no Bank notes, which have a currency in both, the consequence is, that coin must be remitted. This is attended with trouble, delay, expence and risk. If on the contrary, there are bank notes current in both places, the transmission of these by the post, or any other speedy, or convenient conveyance answers the purpose; and these again, in the alternations of demand, are frequently returned, very soon after, to the place from whence they were first sent: Whence the transportation and retransportation of the metals are obviated; and a more convenient and more expeditious medium of payment is substituted. Nor is this all. The metals, instead of being suspended from their usual functions, during this process of vibration from place to place, continue in activity, and administer still to the ordinary circulation; which of course is prevented from suffering either diminution or stagnation. These circumstances are additional causes of what, in a practical sense, or to the purposes of business, may be called greater plenty of money. And it is evident, that whatever enhances the quantity of circulating money adds to the ease, with which every industrious member of the community may acquire that portion of it, of which he stands in need; and enables him the better to pay his taxes, as well as to supply his other wants. Even where the circulation of the bank paper is not general, it must still have the same effect, though in a less degree. For whatever furnishes additional supplies to the channels of circulation, in one quarter, naturally contributes to keep the streams fuller elsewhere. This last view of the subject serves both to illustrate the position, that Banks tend to facilitate the payment of taxes; and to exemplify their utility to business of every kind, in which money is an agent.

It would be to intrude too much on the patience of the house, to prolong the details of the advantages of Banks; especially as all those, which might still be particularized are readily to be inferred as consequences from those, which have been enumerated. Their disadvantages, real or supposed, are now to be reviewed. The most serious of the charges which have been brought against them are—

That they serve to increase usury:

That they tend to prevent other kinds of lending:

That they furnish temptations to overtrading:

That they afford aid to ignorant adventurers who disturb the natural and beneficial course of trade:

That they give to bankrupt and fraudulent traders a fictitious credit, which enables them to maintain false appearances and to extend their impositions: And lastly

That they have a tendency to banish gold and silver from the country.

There is great reason to believe, that on a close and candid survey, it will be discovered, that these charges are either destitute of foundation; or that, as far as the evils, they suggest, have been found to exist, they have proceeded from other, or partial, or temporary causes, are not inherent in the nature and permanent tendency of such institutions; or are more than counterbalanced by opposite advantages. This survey shall be had, in the order in which the charges have been stated.

The first of them is, that Banks serve to increase usury.

It is a truth, which ought not to be denied, that the method of conducting business, which is essential to bank operations, has among us, in particular instances, given occasion to usurious transactions. The punctuality, in payments, which they necessarily exact has sometimes obliged those, who have adventured beyond both their capital and their *credit* to procure money, at any price, and consequently to resort to usurers for aid.

But experience and practice gradually bring a cure to this evil. A general habit of punctuality among traders is the natural consequence of the necessity of observing it with the Bank; a circumstance which itself more than compensates for any occasional ill, which may have sprung from that necessity, in the particular, under consideration. As far therefore as Traders depend on each other for pecuniary supplies, they can calculate their expectations with greater certainty; and are in proportionably less danger of disappointments, which might compel them to have recourse to so pernicious an expedient, as that of borrowing at usury; the mischiefs of which, after a few examples, naturally inspire great care, in all but men of desperate circumstances, to avoid the possibility of being subjected to them. One, and not the least of the evils incident to the use of that expedient, if the fact be known or even strongly suspected, is loss of credit with the bank itself.

The Directors of a bank too, though in order to extend its business and its popularity, in the infancy of an institution, they may be tempted to go further in accommodations, than the strict rules of prudence will warrant, grow more circumspect of course, as its affairs become better established, and as the evils of too great facility are experimentally demonstrated.

They become more attentive to the situation and conduct of those, with whom they deal; they observe more narrowly their operations and pursuits; they œconomise the credit, they give to those of suspicious solidity; they refuse it to those whose career is more manifestly hazardous. In a word, in the course of practice, from the very nature of things, the *interest* will make it the *policy* of a Bank, to succour the wary and industrious; to discredit the rash and unthrifty; to discountenance both usurious lenders and usurious borrowers.

There is a leading view, in which the tendency of banks will be seen to be, to abrige rather than to promote usury. This relates to their property of increasing the quantity and quickening the circulation of money. If it be evident, that usury will prevail or diminish, according to the proportion which the demand for borrowing bears to the quantity of money at market to be lent; whatever has the property just mentioned, whether it be in the shape of paper or of coin, by contributing to render the supply more equal to the demand, must tend to counteract the progress of usury.

But bank-lending, it is pretended, is an impediment to other kinds of lending; which, by confining the resource of borrowing to a particular class, leaves the rest of the community more destitute, and therefore more exposed to the extortions of usurers. As the profits of bank stock exceed the legal rate of interest, the possessors of money, it is argued, prefer investing it in that article to lending it at this rate; to which there are the additional motives of a more prompt command of the capital, and of more frequent and exact returns, without trouble or perplexity in the collection. This constitutes the second charge, which has been enumerated.

The fact on which this charge rests is not to be admitted without several qualifications; particularly in reference to the state of things in this country. First. The great bulk of the Stock of a bank will consist of the funds of men in trade, among ourselves, and monied foreigners; the former of whom could not spare their capitals out of their reach, to be invested in loans, for long periods, on mortgages, or personal security; and the latter of whom would not be willing to be subjected to the casualties, delays and embarassments of such a disposition of their money in a distant country. Secondly. There will always be a considerable proportion of those, who are properly the money lenders of a Country, who from that spirit of caution, which usually characterises this description of men will incline rather to vest their funds in mortgages on real estate, than in the Stock of a Bank, which they are apt to consider as a more precarious security.

These considerations serve in a material degree to narrow the foundation of the objection, as to the point of fact. But there is a more satisfactory answer to it. The effect supposed, as far as it has existence, is temporary. The reverse of it takes place, in the general and permanent operation of the thing.

The capital of every public bank will of course be restricted within a certain defined limit. It is the province of legislative prudence so to adjust this limit, that while it will not be too contracted for the demand, which the course of business may create, and for the security, which the public ought to have for the solidity of the paper, which may be issued by the bank, it will still be within the compass of the pecuniary resources of the community; so that there may be an easy practicability of completing the subscriptions to it. When this is once done, the supposed effect of necessity ceases. There is then no longer room for the investment of any additional capital. Stock may indeed change hands by one person selling and another buying; but the money, which the buyer takes out of the common mass to purchase the stock, the seller receives, and restores to it. Hence the future surplusses, which may accumulate, must take their natural course, and lending at interest must go on, as if there were no such institution.

It must indeed flow in a more copious stream. The Bank furnishes an extraordinary supply for borrowers, within its immediate sphere. A larger supply consequently remains for borrowers elsewhere. In proportion, as the circulation of the Bank is extended, there is an augmentation of the aggregate mass of money, for answering the aggregate mass of demand. Hence a greater facility in obtaining it for every purpose.

It ought not to escape without a remark, that as far as the citizens of other countries become adventurers in the Bank, there is a positive increase of the gold and silver of the Country. It is true, that from this a half yearly rent is drawn back, accruing from the dividends upon the Stock. But as this rent arises from the employment of the capital, by our own citizens, it is probable, that it is more than replaced by the profits of that employment. It is also likely, that a part of it is, in the course of trade, converted into the products of our Country: And it may even prove an incentive, in some cases, to emigration to a country, in which the character of citizen is as easy to be acquired, as it is estimable and important. This view of the subject furnishes an answer to an objection, which has been deduced from the circumstance here taken notice of, namely the income resulting to foreigners from the part of the Stock, owned by them, which has been represented as tending to drain the country of its specie. In this objection, the original investment of the capital, and the constant use of it afterwards seem both to have been overlooked.

That Banks furnish temptations to overtrading is the third of the enumerated objections. This must mean, that by affording additional aids to mercantile enterprise, they induce the merchant sometimes to adventure beyond the prudent or salutary point. But the very statement of the thing shews, that the subject of the charge is an occasional ill, incident to a general good. Credit of every kind (as a species of which only can bank lending have the effect supposed) must be in different degrees, chargeable with the same inconvenience. It is even applicable to gold and silver, when they abound in circulation. But would it be wise on this account to decry the precious metals, to root out credit; or to proscribe the means of that enterprise, which is the main spring of trade and a principal source of national wealth, because it now and then runs into excesses, of which overtrading is one?

If the abuses of a beneficial thing are to determine its condemnation, there is scarcely a source of public prosperity, which will not speedily be closed. In every case, the evil is to be compared with the good; and in the present case such a comparison will issue in this, that the new and increased energies derived to commercial enterprise, from the aid of banks, are a source of general profit and advantage; which greatly outweigh the partial ills of the overtrading of a few individuals, at particular times, or of numbers in particular conjunctures.

The fourth and fifth charges may be considered together. These relate to the aid, which is sometimes afforded by banks to unskilful adventurers and fraudulent traders. These charges also have some degree of foundation; though far less than has been pretended, and they add to the instances of partial ills, connected with more extensive and overbalancing benefits.

The practice of giving fictitious credit to improper persons is one of those evils, which experience guided by interest speedily corrects. The bank itself is in so much jeopardy of being a sufferer by it, that it has the strongest of all inducements to be on its guard. It may not only be injured immediately by the delinquencies of the persons, to whom such credit is given; but eventually, by the incapacities of others, whom their impositions, or failures may have ruined.

Nor is there much danger of a bank's being betrayed into this error, from want of information. The Directors, themselves, being, for the most part, selected from the class of Traders are to be expected to possess individually an accurate knowlege of the characters and situations of those, who come within that description. And they have, in addition to this, the course of dealing of the persons themselves with the bank to assist their judgment, which is in most cases a good index of the state, in which those persons are. The artifices and shifts, which those in desperate or declining circumstances are obliged to employ, to keep up the countenance, which the rules of the Bank require, and the train of their connections, are so many prognostics, not difficult to be interpreted, of the fate which awaits them. Hence it not unfrequently happens, that Banks are the first to discover the unsoundness of such characters, and, by withholding credit, to announce to the public, that they are not intitled to it.

If banks, in spite of every precaution, are sometimes betrayed into giving a false credit to the persons described; they more frequently enable honest and industrious men, of small or perhaps of no capital to undertake and prosecute business, with advantage to themselves and to the community; and assist merchants of both capital and credit, who meet with fortuitous and unforeseen shocks, which might without such helps prove fatal to them and to others; to make head against their misfortunes, and finally to retrieve their affairs: Circumstances, which form no inconsiderable encomium on the utility of Banks.

But the last and heaviest charge is still to be examined. This is, that Banks tend to banish the gold and silver of the Country.

The force of this objection rests upon their being an engine of paper credit, which by furnishing a substitute for the metals, is supposed to promote their exportation. It is an objection, which if it has any foundation, lies not against Banks, peculiarly, but against every species of paper credit.

The most common answer given to it is, that the thing supposed is of little, or no consequence; that it is immaterial what serves the purpose of money, whether paper or gold and silver; that the effect of both upon industry is the same; and that the intrinsic wealth of a nation is to be measured, not by the abundance of the precious metals, contained in it, but by the quantity of the productions of its labor and industry.

This answer is not destitute of solidity, though not intirely satisfactory. It is certain, that the vivification of industry, by a full circulation, with the aid of a proper and well regulated paper credit, may more than compensate for the loss of a part of the gold and silver of a Nation; if the consequence of avoiding that loss should be a scanty or defective circulation.

But the positive and permanent increase or decrease of the precious metals, in a Country, can hardly ever be a matter of indifference. As the commodity taken in lieu of every other, it is a species of the most effective wealth; and as the money of the world, it is of great concern to the state, that it possess a sufficiency of it to face any demands, which the protection of its external interests may create.

The objection seems to admit of another and a more conclusive answer, which controverts the fact itself. A nation, that has no mines of its own, must derive the precious metals from others; generally speaking, in exchange for the products of its labor and industry. The quantity, it will possess, will therefore, in the ordinary course of things, be regulated by the favourable, or unfavourable balance of its trade; that is, by the proportion between its abilities to supply foreigners, and its wants of them; between the amount of its exportations and that of its importations. Hence the state of its agriculture and manufactures, the quantity and quality of its labor and industry must, in the main, influence and determine the increase or decrease of its gold and silver.

If this be true, the inference seems to be, that well constituted Banks favour the increase of the precious metals. It has
been shewn, that they augment in different ways, the active
capital of the country. This, it is, which generates employment; which animates and expands labor and industry. Every
addition, which is made to it, by contributing to put in motion a greater quantity of both, tends to create a greater quantity of the products of both: And, by furnishing more
materials for exportation, conduces to a favourable balance of
trade and consequently to the introduction and increase of
gold and silver.

This conclusion appears to be drawn from solid premises.
There are however objections to be made to it.

It may be said, that as Bank paper affords a substitute for
specie, it serves to counteract that rigorous necessity for the
metals, as a medium of circulation, which in the case of a
wrong balance, might restrain in some degree their exportation; and it may be added, that from the same cause, in the
same case, it would retard those œconomical and parsimonious reforms, in the manner of living, which the scarcity of
money is calculated to produce, and which might be necessary to rectify such wrong balance.

There is perhaps some truth in both these observations;
but they appear to be of a nature rather to form exceptions
to the generality of the conclusion, than to overthrow it.
The state of things, in which the *absolute exigencies* of circulation can be supposed to resist with any effect the urgent
demands for specie, which a wrong balance of trade may occasion, presents an *extreme case*. And a situation in which a
too expensive manner of living of a community, compared
with its means, can stand in need of a corrective, from distress or necessity, is one, which perhaps rarely results, but
from extraordinary and adventitious causes: such for example, as a national revolution, which unsettles all the established habits of a people, and inflames the appetite for
extravagance, by the illusions of an ideal wealth, engendered
by the continual multiplication of a depreciating currency or
some similar cause. There is good reason to believe, that
where the laws are wise and well executed, and the inviola-
bility of property and contracts maintained, the œconomy of

a people will, in the general course of things, correspond with its means.

The support of industry is probably in every case, of more consequence towards correcting a wrong balance of trade, than any practicable retrenchments, in the expences of families, or individuals: And the stagnation of it would be likely to have more effect, in prolonging, than any such savings in shortening its continuance. That stagnation is a natural consequence of an inadequate medium, which, without the aid of Bank circulation, would in the cases supposed, be severely felt.

It also deserves notice, that as the circulation is always in a compound ratio to the fund, upon which it depends, and to the demand for it, and as that fund is itself affected by the exportation of the metals, there is no danger of its being overstocked, as in the case of paper issued at the pleasure of the Government; or of its preventing the consequences of any unfavourable balance from being sufficiently felt, to produce the reforms alluded to, as far as circumstances may require and admit.

Nothing can be more fallible, than the comparisons, which have been made between different countries, to illustrate the truth of the position under consideration. The comparative quantity of gold and silver, in different countries, depends upon an infinite variety of facts and combinations, all of which ought to be known, in order to judge, whether the existence or non existence of paper currencies has any share in the relative proportions they contain. The *mass* and *value* of the productions of the labor and industry of each, compared with its wants; the nature of its establishments abroad; the kind of wars in which it is usually engaged; the relations it bears to the countries, which are the original possessors of those metals; the privileges it enjoys in their trade; these and a number of other circumstances are all to be taken into the account, and render the investigation too complex to justify any reliance on the vague and general surmises, which have been hitherto hazarded on the point.

In the foregoing discussion, the objection has been considered as applying to the permanent expulsion and diminution of the metals. Their temporary exportation, for particular purposes, has not been contemplated. This, it must be confessed is facilitated by Banks, from the faculty they possess of supplying their place. But their utility is in nothing more conspicuous, than in these very cases. They enable the Government to pay its foreign debts, and to answer any exigencies, which the external concerns of the community may have produced. They enable the Merchant to support his credit, (on which the prosperity of trade depends) when special circumstances prevent remittances in other modes. They enable him also to prosecute enterprises, which ultimately tend to an augmentation of the species of wealth in question. It is evident, that gold and silver may often be employed in procuring commodities abroad; which, in a circuitous commerce, replace the original fund, with considerable addition. But it is not to be inferred from this facility given to temporary exportation, that Banks, which are so friendly to trade and industry, are in their general tendency, inimical to the increase of the precious metals.

These several views of the subject appear sufficient to impress a full conviction, of the utility of Banks, and to demonstrate that they are of great importance, not only in relation to the administration of the finances, but in the general system of the political œconomy.

The judgment of many concerning them has no doubt been perplexed, by the misinterpreation of appearances, which were to be ascribed to other causes. The general devastation of personal property, occasioned by the late war, naturally produced, on the one hand, a great demand for money, and on the other a great deficiency of it to answer the demand. Some injudicious laws, which grew out of the public distresses, by impairing confidence and causing a part of the inadequate sum in the country to be locked up, aggravated the evil: The dissipated habits, contracted by many individuals, during the war, which after the peace plunged them into expences beyond their incomes: The number of adventurers without capital and in many instances, without information, who at that epoch rushed into trade, and were obliged to make any sacrifices to support a transient credit; the employment of considerable sums in speculations upon the public debt, which from its unsettled state was incapable of becoming itself a substitute: All these circumstances concurring necessarily led to usurious borrowing, produced most of the inconveniencies, and were the true causes of most of the appearances; which, where the Banks were established, have been by some erroneously placed to their account: a mistake, which they might easily have avoided, by turning their eyes towards places, where there were none, and where, nevertheless, the same evils would have been perceived to exist, even in a greater degree, than where those institutions had obtained.

These evils have either ceased, or been greatly mitigated. Their more complete extinction may be looked for, from that additional security to property, which the constitution of the United States happily gives (a circumstance of prodigious moment in the scale both of public and private prosperity) from the attraction of foreign capital, under the auspices of that security, to be employed upon objects & in enterprises, for which the state of this country opens a wide and inviting field, from the consistency and stability, which the public debt is fast acquiring, as well in the public opinion, at home and abroad, as in fact; from the augmentation of capital, which that circumstance and the quarter yearly payment of interest will afford; and from the more copious circulation, which will be likely to be created by a well constituted National Bank.

The establishment of Banks in this country seems to be recommended by reasons of a peculiar nature. Previously to the revolution circulation was in a great measure carried on by paper emitted by the several local governments. In Pennsylvania alone the quantity of it was near a million and a half of dollars. This auxiliary may be said to be now at an end. And it is generally supposed, that there has been for some time past, a deficiency of circulating medium. How far that deficiency is to be considered as real or imaginary is not susceptible of demonstration, but there are circumstances and appearances, which, in relation to the country at large, countenance the supposition of its reality.

The circumstances are, besides the fact just mentioned respecting paper emissions the vast tracts of waste land, and the little advanced state of manufactures. The progressive settlement of the former, while it promises ample retribution, in the generation of future resources, diminishes or obstructs, in the mean time, the *active* wealth of the country. It not only draws off a part of the circulating money, and places it in a more passive state, but it diverts into its own channels a portion of that species of labor and industry, which would otherwise be employed, in furnishing materials for foreign trade, and which by contributing to a favourable balance, would assist the introduction of specie. In the early periods of new settlements, the settlers not only furnish no surplus for exportation, but they consume a part of that which is produced by the labour of others. The same thing is a cause, that manufactures do not advance or advance slowly. And notwithstanding some hypotheses to the contrary, there are many things to induce a suspicion, that the precious metals will not abound, in any country, which has not mines or variety of manufactures. They have been sometimes acquired by the sword, but the modern system of war has expelled this resource, and it is one upon which it is to be hoped the United States will never be inclined to rely.

The appearances, alluded to, are, greater prevalency of direct barter, in the more interior districts of the country, which however has been for some time past gradually lessening; and greater difficulty, generally, in the advantageous alienation of improved real estate; which, also, has, of late, diminished, but is still seriously felt in different parts of the Union. The difficulty of getting money, which has been a general complaint, is not added to the number; because it is the complaint of all times, and one, in which imagination must ever have too great scope, to permit an appeal to it.

If the supposition of such a deficiency be in any degree founded, and some aid to circulation be desireable, it remains to inquire what ought to be the nature of that aid.

The emitting of paper money by the authority of Government is wisely prohibited to the individual States, by the National Constitution. And the spirit of that prohibition ought not to be disregarded, by the Government of the United States. Though paper emissions, under a general authority, might have some advantages, not applicable, and be free from some disadvantages, which are applicable, to the like emissions by the States separately; yet they are of a nature so liable to abuse, and it may even be affirmed so certain of being abused, that the wisdom of the Government will be shewn in never trusting itself with the use of so seducing and dangerous an expedient. In times of tranquillity, it might have no ill consequence, it might even perhaps be managed in a way to be productive of good; but in great and trying emergencies, there is almost a moral certainty of its becoming mischievous. The stamping of paper is an operation so much easier than the laying of taxes, that a government, in the practice of paper emissions, would rarely fail in any such emergency to indulge itself too far, in the employment of that resource, to avoid as much as possible one less auspicious to present popularity. If it should not even be carried so far as to be rendered an absolute bubble, it would at least be likely to be extended to a degree, which would occasion an inflated and artificial state of things incompatible with the regular and prosperous course of the political œconomy.

Among other material differences between a paper currency, issued by the mere authority of Government, and one issued by a Bank, payable in coin, is this—That in the first case, there is no standard to which an appeal can be made, as to the quantity which will only satisfy, or which will surcharge the circulation; in the last, that standard results from the demand. If more should be issued, than is necessary, it will return upon the bank. Its emissions, as elsewhere intimated, must always be in a compound ratio to the fund and to the demand: Whence it is evident, that there is a limitation in the nature of the thing: While the discretion of the government is the only measure of the extent of the emissions, by its own authority.

This consideration further illustrates the danger of emissions of that sort, and the preference, which is due to Bank paper.

The payment of the interest of the public debt, at thirteen different places, is a weighty reason, peculiar to our immediate situation, for desiring a Bank circulation. Without a paper, in general currency, equivalent to gold and silver, a considerable proportion of the specie of the country must always be suspended from circulation and left to accumulate, preparatorily to each day of payment; and as often as one approaches, there must in several cases be an actual transportation of the metals at both expence and risk, from their natural and proper reservoirs to distant places. This necessity will be felt very injuriously to the trade of some of the States; and will embarrass not a little the operations of the Treasury in those States. It will also obstruct those negociations, between different parts of the Union, by the instrumentality of Treasury bills, which have already afforded valuable accommodations to Trade in general.

Assuming it then as a consequence, from what has been said, that a national bank is a desireable institution; two inquiries emerge. Is there no such institution, already in being, which has a claim to that character, and which supersedes the propriety, or necessity of another? If there be none, what are the principles upon which one ought to be established?

There are at present three banks in the United States. That of North America, established in the city of Philadelphia; that of New York, established in the city of New York; that of Massachusetts, established in the city of Boston. Of these three, the first is the only one, which has at any time had a direct relation to the Government of the United States.

The Bank of North America originated in a resolution of Congress of the 26th of May 1781, founded upon a proposition of the Superintendant of finance, which was afterwards carried into execution, by an ordinance of the 31st of december following, entitled, "An Ordinance to incorporate the Subscribers to the Bank of North America."

The aid afforded to the United States, by this institution, during the remaining period of the war, was of essential consequence, and its conduct towards them since the peace, has not weakened its title to their patronage and favour. So far its pretensions to the character in question are respectable; but there are circumstances, which militate against them; and considerations, which indicate the propriety of an establishment on different principles.

The Directors of this Bank, on behalf of their constituents, have since *accepted* and *acted* under a new charter from the State of Pennsylvania, materially variant from their original one; and which so narrows the foundation of the institution, as to render it an incompetent basis for the extensive purposes of a National Bank.

The limit assigned by the ordinance of Congress to the Stock of the Bank is ten millions of Dollars. The last charter of Pennsylvania confines it to two millions. Questions naturally arise, whether there be not a direct repugnancy between two charters so differently circumstanced; and whether the acceptance of the one is not to be deemed a virtual surrender of the other. But perhaps it is neither adviseable nor necessary to attempt a solution of them.

There is nothing in the Acts of Congress, which imply an exclusive right in the institution, to which they relate, except during the term of the war. There is therefore nothing, if the public good require it, which prevents the establishment of another. It may however be incidentally remarked, that in the general opinion of the citizens of the United States, the Bank of North America has taken the station of a bank of Pennsylvania only. This is a strong argument for a new institution, or for a renovation of the old, to restore it to the situation in which it originally stood, in the view of the United States.

But though the ordinance of Congress contains no grant of exclusive privileges, there may be room to allege, that the Government of the United States ought not, in point of candour and equity, to establish any rival or interfering institution, in prejudice of the one already established; especially as this has, from services rendered, well founded claims to protection and regard.

The justice of such an observation ought within proper bounds to be admitted. A new establishment of the sort ought not to be made, without cogent and sincere reasons of public good. And in the manner of doing it every facility should be given to a consolidation of the old with the new, upon terms not injurious to the parties concerned. But there is no ground to maintain, that in a case, in which the Government has made no condition restricting its authority, it ought voluntarily to restrict it, through regard to the interests of a particular institution, when those of the state dictate a different course; especially too after such circumstances have intervened, as characterise the actual situation of the Bank of North America.

The inducements, to a new disposition of the thing are now to be considered. The first of them which occurs is, the, at least ambiguous, situation, in which the Bank of North America has placed itself, by the acceptance of its last charter. If this has rendered it the mere Bank of a particular State, liable to dissolution at the expiration of fourteen years, to which term the act of that state has restricted its duration, it would be neither fit nor expedient to accept it, as an equivalent for a Bank of the United States.

The restriction of its capital also, which according to the same supposition, cannot be extended beyond two millions of dollars, is a conclusive reason for a different establishment. So small a capital promises neither the requisite aid to government, nor the requisite security to the community. It may answer very well the purposes of local accommodation, but is an inadequate foundation for a circulation coextensive with the United States, embracing the whole of their revenues, and affecting every individual, into whose hands the paper may come.

And inadequate as such a capital would be to the essential ends of a National Bank, it is liable to being rendered still more so, by that principle of the constitution of the Bank of North America, contained equally in its old and in its new charter, which leaves the increase of the *actual* capital at any time (now far short of the allowed extent) to the discretion of the Directors, or Stockholders. It is naturally to be expected, that the allurements of an advanced price of Stock and of large dividends may disincline those, who are interested, to an extension of capital; from which they will be apt to fear a diminution of profits. And from this circumstance, the interest and accommodation of the public (as well individually as collectively) are made more subordinate to the interest, real or imagined, of the Stockholders, than they ought to be. It is true, that unless the latter be consulted, there can be no bank (in the sense at least in which institutions of this kind, worthy of confidence, can be established in this Country) but it does not follow, that this is alone to be consulted, or that it even ought to be paramount. Public utility is more truly the object of public Banks, than private profit. And it is the business of Government, to constitute them on such principles, that while the latter will result, in a sufficient degree, to afford competent motives to engage in them, the former be not made subservient to it. To effect this, a principal object of attention ought to be to give free scope to the creation of an ample capital; and with this view, fixing the bounds, which are deemed safe and convenient, to leave no discretion either to stop short of them or to overpass them. The want of this precaution, in the establishment of the Bank of North America, is a further and an important reason for desiring one differently constituted.

There may be room, at first sight, for a supposition, that as the profits of a Bank will bear a proportion to the extent of its operations, and as, for this reason, the interest of the Stockholders will not be disadvantageously affected, by any necessary augmentations of capital, there is no cause to apprehend, that they will be indisposed to such augmentations. But most men in matters of this nature, prefer the certainties, they enjoy, to probabilities depending on untried experiments; especially when these promise rather, that they will not be injured, than that they will be benefited.

From the influence of this principle, and a desire of enhancing its profits, the Directors of a Bank will be more apt to overstrain its faculties, in the attempt to face the additional demands, which the course of business may create, than to set on foot new subscriptions, which may hazard a diminution of the profits, and even a temporary reduction of the price of Stock.

Banks are among the best expedients for lowering the rate of interest, in a country; but to have this effect, their capitals must be completely equal to all the demands of business, and such as will tend to remove the idea, that the accommodations they afford, are in any degree favours; an idea very apt to accompany the parsimonious dispensation of contracted funds. In this, as in every other case, the plenty of the commodity ought to beget a moderation of the price.

The want of a principle of rotation, in the constitution of the Bank of North America, is another argument for a variation of the establishment. Scarcely one of the reasons, which militate against this principle in the constitution of a country, is applicable to that of a Bank; while there are strong reasons in favour of it, in relation to the one, which do not apply to the other. The knowlege, to be derived from experience, is the only circumstance common to both, which pleads against rotation in the directing officers of a Bank.

But the objects of the Government of a nation, and those of the government of a bank are so widely different, as greatly to weaken the force of that consideration, in reference to the latter. Almost every important case of legislation requires, towards a right decision, a general and an accurate acquaintance with the affairs of the state; and habits of thinking seldom acquired, but from a familiarity with public concerns. The administration of a bank, on the contrary, is regulated, by a few simple fixed maxims, the application of which is not difficult to any man of judgment, especially if instructed in the principles of trade. It is in general a constant succession of the same details.

But though this be the case, the idea of the advantages of experience is not to be slighted. Room ought to be left for the regular transmission of official information: And for this purpose the head of the direction ought to be excepted from the principle of rotation. With this exception, and with the aid of the information of the subordinate officers, there can be no danger of any ill effects from want of experience, or knowlege; especially as the periodical exclusion ought not to reach the whole of the Directors at one time.

The argument in favour of the principle of rotation is this, that by lessening the danger of combinations among the Directors, to make the institution subservient to party views, or to the accommodation, preferably, of any particular set of men, it will render the public confidence more firm, stable and unqualified.

When it is considered, that the Directors of a Bank are not elected by the great body of the community, in which a diversity of views will naturally prevail, at different conjunctures, but by a small and select class of men, among whom it is far more easy to cultivate a steady adherence to the same persons and objects; and that those Directors have it in their power so immediately to conciliate, by obliging the most influential of this class, it is easy to perceive, that without the principle of rotation, changes in that body can rarely happen, but as a concession which they may themselves think it expedient to make to public opinion.

The continual administration of an institution of this kind, by the same persons, will never fail, with, or without, cause, from their conduct, to excite distrust and discontent. The necessary secrecy of their transactions gives unlimited scope to imagination to infer that something is, or may be wrong. And this *inevitable* mystery is a solid reason, for inserting in the constitution of a Bank the necessity of a change of men. As neither the mass of the parties interested nor the public in general can be permitted to be witnesses of the interior management of the Directors, it is reasonable, that both should have that check upon their conduct, and that security against the prevalency of a partial or pernicious system, which will be produced by the certainty of periodical changes. Such too is the delicacy of the credit of a Bank, that every thing, which can fortify confidence and repel suspicion, without injuring its operations, ought carefully to be sought after in its formation.

A further consideration in favour of a change, is the improper rule, by which the right of voting for Directors is regulated in the plan, upon which the Bank of North America was originally constituted, namely a vote for each share, and the want of a rule in the last charter; unless the silence of it, on that point, may signify that every Stockholder is to have an equal and a single vote, which would be a rule in a different extreme not less erroneous. It is of importance that a rule should be established, on this head, as it is one of those things, which ought not to be left to discretion; and it is consequently, of equal importance, that the rule should be a proper one.

A vote for each share renders a combination, between a few principal Stockholders, to monopolise the power and benefits of the Bank too easy. An equal vote to each Stockholder, however great or small his interest in the institution, allows not that degree of weight to large stockholders, which it is reasonable they should have, and which perhaps their security and that of the bank require. A prudent mean is to be preferred. A conviction of this has produced a bye-law of the corporation of the bank of North America, which evidently aims at such a mean. But a reflexion arises here, that a like majority with that which enacted this law, may at any moment repeal it.

The last inducement, which shall be mentioned, is the want of precautions to guard against a foreign influence insinuating itself into the Direction of the Bank. It seems scarcely reconcileable with a due caution to permit, that any but citizens should be eligible as Directors of a National Bank, or that non-resident foreigners should be able to influence the appointment of Directors by the votes of their proxies. In the event however of an incorporation of the Bank of North America in the plan, it may be necessary to qualify this principle, so as to leave the right of foreigners, who now hold shares of its stock unimpaired; but without the power of transmitting the privilege in question to foreign alienees.

It is to be considered, that such a Bank is not a mere matter of private property, but a political machine of the greatest importance to the State.

There are other variations from the Constitution of the Bank of North America, not of inconsiderable moment, which appear desireable, but which are not of magnitude enough to claim a prliminary discussion. These will be seen in the plan, which will be submitted in the sequel.

If the objections, which have been stated to the constitution of the Bank of North America, are admitted to be well founded, they will nevertheless not derogate from the merit of the main design, or of the services which that bank has rendered, or of the benefits which it has produced. The creation of such an institution, at the time it took place, was a measure dictated by wisdom. Its utility has been amply evinced by its fruits. American Independence owes much to it. And it is very conceivable, that reasons of the moment may have rendered those features in it inexpedient which a revision, with a permanent view, suggests as desireable.

The order of the subject leads next to an inquiry into the principles, upon which a national Bank, ought to be organised.

The situation of the United States naturally inspires a wish, that the form of the institution could admit of a plurality of branches. But various considerations discourage from pursuing this idea. The complexity of such a plan would be apt to inspire doubts, which might deter from adventuring in it. And the practicability of a safe and orderly administration, though not to be abandoned as desparate cannot be made so manifest in perspective, as to promise the removal of those doubts, or to justify the Government in adopting the idea as an original experiment. The most that would seem adviseable, on this point, is to insert a provision, which may lead to it hereafter; if experience shall more clearly demonstrate its utility, and satisfy those, who may have the Direction, that it may be adopted with safety. It is certain, that it would have some advantages both peculiar and important. Besides more general accommodation, it would lessen the danger of a run upon the bank.

The argument, against it, is, that each branch must be under a distinct, though subordinate direction; to which a considerable latitude of discretion must of necessity be entrusted. And as the property of the whole institution would be liable for the engagements of each part, that and its credit would be at stake, upon the prudence of the Directors of every part. The mismanagement of either branch, miight hazard serious disorder in the whole.

Another wish, dictated by the particular situation of the country, is, that the Bank could be so constituted as to be made an immediate instrument of loans to the proprietors of land; but this wish also yields to the difficulty of accomplishing it. Land is alone an unfit fund for a bank circulation. If the notes issued upon it were not to be payable in coin, on demand, or at a short date; this would amount to nothing more than a repetition of the paper emissions, which are now exploded by the general voice. If the notes are to be payable in coin, the land must first be converted into it by sale, or mortgage. The difficulty of effecting the latter is the very thing, which begets the desire of finding another resource, and the former would not be practicable on a sudden emergency, but with sacrifices which would make the cure worse than the disease. Neither is the idea of constituting the fund partly of coin and partly of land free from impediments. These two species of property do not for the most part unite in the same hands. Will the monied man consent to enter into a partnership with the landholder by which *the latter* will share in the profits *which will be* made *by the money of the former*? The money it is evident will be the agent or efficient cause of the profits. The land can only be regarded as an additional security. It is not difficult to foresee, that an union, on such terms, will not readily be formed. If the landholders are to procure the money by sale or mortgage of a part of their lands, this they can as well do, when the Stock consists wholly of money, as if it were to be compounded of money and land.

To procure for the landholders the assistance of loans is the great desideratum. Supposing other difficulties surmounted, and a fund created, composed partly of coin and partly of land, yet the benefit contemplated could only then be obtained, by the banks advancing them its notes for the whole or part of the value of the lands, they had subscribed to the Stock. If this advance was small, the relief aimed at would not be given; if it was large, the quantity of notes issued would be a cause of *distrust*, and, if received at all, they would be likely to return speedily upon the Bank for payment; which, after exhausting its coin, might be under a necessity of turning its lands into money, at any price, that could be obtained for them, to the irreparable prejudice of the proprietors.

Considerations of public advantage suggest a further wish, which is, that the Bank could be established upon principles, that would cause the profits of it to redound to the immediate benefit of the State. This is contemplated by many, who speak of a National Bank, but the idea seems liable to insuperable objections. To attach full confidence to an institution of this nature, it appears to be an essential ingredient in its structure, that it shall be under a *private* not a *public* Direction, under the guidance of *individual interest*, not of *public policy*; which would be supposed to be, and in certain emergencies, under a feeble or too sanguine administration would, really, be, liable to being too much influenced by *public necessity*. The suspicion of this would most probably be a canker, that would continually corrode the vitals of the credit of the Bank, and would be most likely to prove fatal in those situations, in which the public good would require, that they should be most sound and vigorous. It would indeed be little less, than a miracle, should the credit of the Bank be at the disposal of the Government, if in a long series of time, there was not experienced a calamitous abuse of it. It is true, that it would be the real interest of the Government not to abuse it: its genuine policy to husband and cherish it with the most guarded circumspection as an inestimable treasure. But what Government ever uniformly consulted its true interest, in opposition to the temptations of momentary exigencies? What nation was ever blessed with a constant succession of upright and wise Administrators?

The keen, steady, and, as it were, magnetic sense, of their own interest, as proprietors, in the Directors of a Bank, pointing invariably to its true pole, the prosperity of the institution, is the only security, that can always be relied upon, for a careful and prudent administration. It is therefore the only basis on which an enlightened, unqualified and permanent confidence can be expected to be erected and maintained.

The precedents of the Banks established in several cities of Europe, Amsterdam, Hamburgh and others, may seem to militate against this position. Without a precise knowlege of all the peculiarities of their respective constitutions, it is difficult to pronounce how far this may be the case. That of Amsterdam, however, which we best know, is rather under a municipal than a governmental direction. Particular magistrates of the city, not officers of the republic, have the management of it. It is also a Bank of deposit, not of loan, or circulation; consequently less liable to abuse, as well as less useful. Its general business consists in receiving money for safekeeping; which if not called for within a certain time becomes a part of its Stock and irreclaimable: But a Credit is given for it on the books of the Bank, which being transferable, answers all the purposes of money.

The Directors being Magistrates of the city, and the Stockholders in general, its most influential citizens, it is evident, that the principle of private interest must be prevalent in the management of the Bank. And it is equally evident, that from the nature of its operations, that principle is less essential to it, than to an Institution, constituted with a view to the accommodation of the Public and Individuals by direct loans and a paper circulation.

As far as may concern the aid of the Bank, within the proper limits, a good government has nothing more to wish for, than it will always possess; though the management be in the hands of private individuals. As the institution, if rightly constituted, must depend for its renovation from time to time on the pleasure of the Government, it will not be likely to feel a disposition to render itself, by its conduct, unworthy of public patronage. The Government too in the administration of its finances, has it in its power to reciprocate benefits to the Bank, of not less importance, than those which the bank affords to the Government, and which besides are never un-attended with an immediate and adequate compensation. In-dependent of these more particular considerations, the natural weight and influence of a good Government will always go far towards procuring a compliance with its desires; and as the Directors will usually be composed of some of the most dis-creet, respectable and well informed citizens, it can hardly ever be difficult to make them sensible of the force of the in-ducements, which ought to stimulate their exertions.

It will not follow, from what has been said, that the State may not be the holder of a part of the Stock of a Bank, and consequently a sharer in the profits of it. It will only follow, that it ought not to desire any participation in the Direction of it, and therefore ought not to own the whole or a princi-pal part of the Stock; for if the mass of the property should belong to the public, and if the direction of it should be in private hands, this would be to commit the interests of the State to persons, not interested, or not enough interested in their proper management.

There is one thing, however, which the Government owes to itself and to the community; at least to all that part of it, who are not Stockholders; which is to reserve to itself a right of ascertaining, as often as may be necessary, the state of the Bank, excluding however all pretension to controul. This right forms an article in the primitive constitution of the Bank of North America. And its propriety stands upon the clearest reasons. If the paper of a Bank is to be permitted to insinuate itself into all the revenues and receipts of a country; if it is even to be tolerated as the substitute for gold and silver, in all the transactions of business, it becomes in either view a na-tional concern of the first magnitude. As such the ordinary rules of prudence require, that the Government should pos-sess the means of ascertaining, whenever it thinks fit, that so delicate a trust is executed with fidelity and care. A right of this nature is not only desireable, as it respects the Government; but it ought to be equally so to all those, concerned in the institution; as an additional title to public and private confidence; and as a thing which can only be formidable to practices, that imply mismanagement. The presumption must always be, that the characters who would be entrusted with the exercise of this right, on behalf of the Government, will not be deficient in the discretion, which it may require; at least the admitting of this presumption cannot be deemed too great a return of confidence for that very large portion of it, which the Government is required to place in the Bank.

Abandoning, therefore, ideas, which however agreeable or desireable, are neither practicable nor safe, the following plan for the constitution of a National Bank is respectfully submitted to the consideration of the House.

I. The capital Stock of the Bank shall not exceed ten Millions of Dollars, divided into Twenty five thousand shares, each share being four hundred Dollars; to raise which sum, subscriptions shall be opened on the first monday of april next, and shall continue open, until the whole shall be subscribed. Bodies politic as well as individuals may subscribe.

II. The amount of each share shall be payable, one fourth in gold and silver coin, and three fourths in that part of the public debt, which according to the loan proposed by the Act making provision for the debt of the United States, shall bear an accruing interest at the time of payment of six per centum per annum.

III. The respective sums subscribed shall be payable in four equal parts, as well specie as debt, in succession, and at the distance of six calendar months from each other; the first payment to be made at the time of subscription. If there shall be a failure in any subsequent payment, the party failing shall lose the benefit of any dividend which may have accrued, prior to the time for making such payment, and during the delay of the same.

IV. The Subscribers to the Bank and their successors shall be incorporated, and shall so continue until the final redemption of that part of its stock, which shall consist of the public debt.

V. The capacity of the corporation to hold real and personal estate shall be limited to fifteen millions of Dollars, including the amount of its capital, or original stock. The lands and tenements, which it shall be permitted to hold, shall be only such as shall be requisite for the immediate accommodation of the institution; and such as shall have been bona fide mortgaged to it by way of security, or conveyed to it in satisfaction of debts previously contracted, in the usual course of its dealings, or purchased at sales upon judgments which shall have been obtained for such debts.

VI. The totality of the debts of the company, whether by bond, bill, note, or other contract, (credits for deposits excepted) shall never exceed the amount of its capital stock. In case of excess, the Directors, under whose administration it shall happen, shall be liable for it in their private or separate capacities. Those who may have dissented may excuse themselves from this responsibility by immediately giving notice of the fact and their dissent to the President of the United States, and to the Stockholders, at a general meeting to be called by the President of the Bank at their request.

VII. The Company may sell or demise its lands and tenements, or may sell the whole, or any part of the public Debt, whereof its Stock shall consist; but shall *trade* in nothing, except bills of exchange, gold and silver bullion, or in the sale of goods pledged for money lent: nor shall take more than at the rate of six per centum, per annum, upon its loans or discounts.

VIII. No loan shall be made by the bank, for the use or on account of the Government of the United States, or of either of them to an amount exceeding fifty thousand Dollars, or of any foreign prince or State; unless previously authorised by a law of the United States.

IX. The Stock of the Bank shall be transferable according to such rules as shall be instituted by the Company in that behalf.

X. The affairs of the Bank shall be under the management of Twenty five Directors, one of whom shall be the President. And there shall be on the first monday of January, in each year, a choice of Directors, by plurality of suffrages of the Stockholders, to serve for a year. The Directors at their first meeting, after each election, shall choose one of their number as President.

XI. The number of votes, to which each Stockholder shall be entitled, shall be according to the number of shares he shall hold in the proportions following, that is to say, for one share and not more than two shares one vote; for every two shares, above two and not exceeding ten, one vote; for every four shares above ten and not exceeding thirty, one vote; for every six shares above thirty and not exceeding sixty, one vote; for every eight shares above sixty and not exceeding one hundred, one vote; and for every ten shares above one hundred, one vote; but no person, copartnership, or body politic, shall be entitled to a greater number than thirty votes. And after the first election, no share or shares shall confer a right of suffrage, which shall not have been holden three calendar months previous to the day of election. Stockholders actually resident within the United States and none other may vote in elections by proxy.

XII. Not more than three fourths of the Directors in office, exclusive of the President, shall be eligible for the next succeeding year. But the Director who shall be President at the time of an election may always be reelected.

XIII. None but a Stockholder being a citizen of the United States, shall be eligible as a Director.

XIV. Any number of Stockholders not less than sixty, who together shall be proprietors of two hundred shares, or upwards, shall have power at any time to call a general meeting of the Stockholders, for purposes relative to the Institution; giving at least six weeks notice in two public gazettes of the place where the Bank is kept, and specifying in such notice the object of the meeting.

XV. In case of the death, resignation, absence from the United States, or removal of a Director by the Stockholders, his place may be filled by a new choice for the remainder of the year.

XVI. No Director shall be entitled to any emolument, unless the same shall have been allowed by the Stockholders at a General meeting. The Stockholders shall make such compensation to the President, for his extraordinary attendance at the Bank, as shall appear to them reasonable.

XVII. Not less than seven Directors shall constitute a Board for the transaction of business.

XVIII. Every Cashier, or Treasurer, before he enters on the duties of his office shall be required to give bond, with two or more sureties, to the satisfaction of the Directors, in a sum not less than twenty thousand Dollars, with condition for his good behaviour.

XIX. Half yearly dividends shall be made of so much of the profits of the Bank as shall appear to the Directors adviseable: And once in every three years the Directors shall lay before the Stockholders, at a General Meeting, for their information, an exact and particular statement of the debts, which shall have remained unpaid, after the expiration of the original credit, for a period of treble the term of that credit; and of the surplus of profit, if any, after deducting losses and dividends.

XX. The bills and notes of the Bank originally made payable, or which shall have become payable on demand, in gold and silver coin, shall be receivable in all payments to the United States.

XXI. The Officer at the head of the Treasury Department of the United States, shall be furnished from time to time, as often as he may require, not exceeding once a week, with statements of the amount of the capital Stock of the Bank and of the debts due to the same; of the monies deposited therein; of the notes in circulation, and of the Cash in hand; and shall have a right to inspect such general account in the books of the bank as shall relate to the said statements; provided, that this shall not be construed to imply a right of inspecting this account of any private individual or individuals with the Bank.

XXII. No similar institution shall be established by any future act of the United States, during the continuance of the one hereby proposed to be established.

XXIII. It shall be lawful for the Directors of the Bank to establish offices, wheresoever they shall think fit, within the United States, for the purposes of discount and deposit only, and upon the same terms, and in the same manner, as shall be practiced at the Bank; and to commit the management of the said offices, and the making of the said discounts, either to Agents specially appointed by them, or to such persons as may be chosen by the Stockholders residing at the place where any such office shall be, under such agreements and subject to such regulations as they shall deem proper; not being contrary to law or to the Constitution of the Bank.

XXIV. And lastly. The President of the United States shall be authorised to cause a subscription to be made to the Stock of the said Company, on behalf of the United States, to an amount not exceeding two Millions of Dollars, to be paid out of the monies which shall be borrowed by virtue of either of the Acts, the one entitled "an Act making provision for the debt of the United States," and the other entitled "An Act making provision for the reduction of the Public Debt"; borrowing of the bank an equal sum, to be applied to the purposes for which the said monies shall have been procured, reimbursable in ten years by equal annual instalments; or at any time sooner, or in any greater proportions, that the Government may think fit.

The reasons for the several provisions contained in the foregoing plan, have been so far anticipated, and will, for the most part, be so readily suggested, by the nature of those provisions, that any comments, which need further be made, will be both few and concise.

The combination of a portion of the public Debt in the formation of the Capital, is the principal thing, of which an explanation is requisite. The chief object of this is, to enable the creation of a capital sufficiently large to be the basis of an extensive circulation, and an adequate security for it. As has been elsewhere remarked, the original plan of the Bank of North America contemplated a capital of ten millions of Dollars, which is certainly not too broad a foundation for the extensive operations, to which a National Bank is destined. But to collect such a sum in this country, in gold and silver, into one depository, may, without hesitation, be pronounced impracticable. Hence the necessity of an auxiliary which the public debt at once presents.

This part of the fund will be always ready to come in aid of the specie. It will more and more command a ready sale; and can therefore expeditiously be turned into coin if an exigency of the Bank should at any time require it. This quality of prompt convertibility into coin, renders it an equivalent for that necessary agent of Bank circulation; and distinguishes it from a fund in land of which the sale would generally be far less compendious and at great disadvantage. The quarter yearly receipts of interest will also be an actual addition to the specie fund during the intervals between them and the half yearly dividends of profits. The objection to combining land with specie, resulting from their not being generally in possession of the same persons, does not apply to the debt, which will always be found in considerable quantity among the monied and trading people.

The debt composing part of the capital, besides its collateral effect in enabling the Bank to extend its operations, and consequently to enlarge its profits, will produce a direct annual revenue of six per centum from the Government, which will enter into the half yearly dividends received by the Stockholders.

When the present price of the public debt is considered, and the effect which its conversion into Bank Stock, incorporated with a specie fund, would in all probability have to accelerate its rise to the proper point, it will easily be discovered, that the operation presents in its outset a very considerable advantage to those who may become subscribers; and from the influence, which that rise would have on the general mass of the Debt, a proportional benefit to all the public creditors, and, in a sense, which has been more than once adverted to, to the community at large.

There is an important fact, which exemplifies the fitness of the public Debt, for a bank fund, and which may serve to remove doubts in some minds on this point. It is this, that the Bank of England in its first erection rested wholly on that foundation. The subscribers to a Loan to Government of one million two hundred thousand pounds sterling were incorporated as a Bank; of which the Debt created by the Loan, and the interest upon it, were the sole fund. The subsequent augmentations of its capital, which now amounts to between eleven and twelve millions of pounds sterling, have been of the same nature.

The confining of the right of the Bank to contract debts to the amount of its capital is an important precaution, which is not to be found in the constitution of the Bank of North America, and which, while the fund consists wholly of coin, would be a restriction attended with inconveniencies, but would be free from any if the composition of it should be such as is now proposed. The restriction exists in the establishment of the Bank of England, and as a source of security is worthy of imitation. The consequence of exceeding the limit there is, that each Stockholder is liable to the excess, in proportion to his interest in the Bank. When it is considered, that the Directors owe their appointments to the choice of the Stockholders, a responsibility of this kind, on the part of the latter, does not appear unreasonable. But, on the other hand, it may be deemed a hardship upon those, who may have dissented from the choice. And there are many among us, whom it might perhaps discourage from becoming concerned in the institution. These reasons have induced the placing of the responsibility upon the Directors, by whom the limit prescribed should be transgressed.

The interdiction of loans on account of the United States, or of any particular State, beyond the moderate sum specified, or of any foreign power, will serve as a barrier to executive incroachments; and to combinations inauspicious to the safety or contrary to the policy of the Union.

The limitation of the rate of interest is dictated by the consideration, that different rates prevail in different parts of the Union; and as the operations of the Bank may extend through the whole, some rule seems to be necessary. There is room for a question, whether the limitation ought not rather to be to five than to six per cent, as proposed. It may with safety be taken for granted, that the former rate would yield an ample dividend; perhaps as much as the latter, by the extension which it would give to business. The natural effect of low interest is to increase trade and industry; because undertakings of every kind can be prosecuted with greater advantage. This is a truth generally admitted; but it is requisite to have analised the subject, in all its relations, to be able to form a just conception of the extent of that effect. Such an analysis cannot but satisfy an intelligent mind, that the difference of one per cent, in the rate at which money may be had, is often capable of making an essential change for the better in the situation of any country or place.

Every thing, therefore, which tends to lower the rate of interest is peculiarly worthy of the cares of Legislators. And though laws which violently sink the legal rate of interest greatly below the market level are not to be commended, because they are not calculated to answer their aim, yet whatever has a tendency to effect a reduction, without violence to the natural course of things, ought to be attended to and pursued. Banks are among the means most proper to accomplish this end; and the moderation of the rate at which their discounts are made, is a material ingredient towards it; with which their own interest, viewed on an enlarged and permanent scale, does not appear to clash.

But as the most obvious ideas are apt to have greater force, than those which depend on complex and remote combinations, there would be danger, that the persons whose funds must constitute the Stock of the Bank would be diffident of the sufficiency of the profits to be expected, if the rate of loans and discounts were to be placed below the point to which they have been accustomed; and might on this account be indisposed to embarking in the plan. There is, it is true, one reflection, which in regard to men actively engaged in trade ought to be a security against this danger; it is this, that the accommodations which they might derive in the way of their business, at a low rate, would more than indemnify them for any difference in the dividend, supposing even that some diminution of it were to be the consequence. But upon the whole, the hazard of contrary reasoning among the mass of monied men is a powerful argument against the experiment. The institutions of the kind already existing add to the difficulty of making it. Maturer reflection and a large capital may of themselves lead to the desired end.

The last thing, which will require any explanatory remark, is the authority proposed to be given to the President to subscribe to the amount of two millions of Dollars on account of the public. The main design of this is to enlarge the specie fund of the Bank, and to enable it to give a more early extension to its operations. Though it is proposed to borrow with one hand what is lent with the other, yet the disbursement of what is borrowed will be progressive, and Bank notes may be thrown into circulation, instead of the gold and silver. Besides, there is to be an annual reimbursement of a part of the sum borrowed, which will finally operate as an actual investment of so much specie. In addition to the inducements to this measure, which results from the general interest of the Government, to enlarge the sphere of the utility of the Bank, there is this more particular consideration, to wit, that as far as the dividend on the Stock shall exceed the interest paid on the loan, there is a positive profit.

The Secretary begs leave to conclude, with this general observation, that if the Bank of North America shall come forward with any propositions, which have for object the ingrafting upon that institution the characteristics, which shall appear to the Legislature necessary to the due extent and safety of a National Bank, there are, in his judgment, weighty inducements to giving every reasonable facility to the measure. Not only the pretensions of that institution, from its original relation to the Government of the United States, and from the services it has rendered, are such as to claim a disposition favourable to it, if those who are interested in it are willing on their part to place it on a footing satisfactory to the Government, and equal to the purposes of a Bank of the United States; but its cooperation would materially accelerate the accomplishment of the great object, and the collision, which might otherwise arise, might, in a variety of ways, prove equally disagreeable and injurious. The incorporation or union here contemplated, may be effected in different modes, under the auspices of an Act of the United States, if it shall be desired by the Bank of North America, upon terms, which shall appear expedient to the Government.

All which is humbly submitted

Alexander Hamilton,
Secy of the Treasury

Opinion on the Constitutionality of a National Bank

THE Secretary of the Treasury having perused with attention the papers containing the opinions of the Secretary of State and Attorney General concerning the constitutionality of the bill for establishing a National Bank proceeds according to the order of the President to submit the reasons which have induced him to entertain a different opinion.

It will naturally have been anticipated that, in performing this task he would feel uncommon solicitude. Personal considerations alone arising from the reflection that the measure originated with him would be sufficient to produce it: The sense which he has manifested of the great importance of such an institution to the successful administration of the department under his particular care; and an expectation of serious ill consequences to result from a failure of the measure, do not permit him to be without anxiety on public accounts. But the chief solicitude arises from a firm persuasion, that principles of construction like those espoused by the Secretary of State and the Attorney General would be fatal to the just & indispensible authority of the United States.

In entering upon the argument it ought to be premised, that the objections of the Secretary of State and Attorney General are founded on a general denial of the authority of the United States to erect corporations. The latter indeed expressly admits, that if there be any thing in the bill which is not warranted by the constitution, it is the clause of incorporation.

Now it appears to the Secretary of the Treasury, that this *general principle* is *inherent* in the very *definition* of *Government* and *essential* to every step of the progress to be made by that of the United States; namely—that every power vested in a Government is in its nature *sovereign*, and includes by *force* of the *term*, a right to employ all the *means* requisite, and fairly *applicable* to the attainment of the *ends* of such power; and which are not precluded by restrictions & exceptions specified in the constitution; or not immoral, or not contrary to the essential ends of political society.

This principle in its application to Government in general would be admitted as an axiom. And it will be incumbent upon those, who may incline to deny it, to *prove* a distinction; and to shew that a rule which in the general system of things is essential to the preservation of the social order is inapplicable to the United States.

The circumstances that the powers of sovereignty are in this country divided between the National and State Governments, does not afford the distinction required. It does not follow from this, that each of the *portions* of powers delegated to the one or to the other is not sovereign *with regard to its proper objects*. It will only *follow* from it, that each has sovereign power as to *certain things*, and not as to *other things*. To deny that the Government of the United States has sovereign power as to its declared purposes & trusts, because its power does not extend to all cases, would be equally to deny, that the State Governments have sovereign power in any case; because their power does not extend to every case. The tenth section of the first article of the constitution exhibits a long list of very important things which they may not do. And thus the United States would furnish the singular spectacle of a *political society* without *sovereignty*, or of a people *governed* without *government*.

If it would be necessary to bring proof to a proposition so clear as that which affirms that the powers of the fœderal government, *as to its objects*, are sovereign, there is a clause of its constitution which would be decisive. It is that which declares, that the constitution and the laws of the United States made in pursuance of it, and all treaties made or which shall be made under their authority shall be the supreme law of the land. The power which can create the *Supreme law* of the land, in any case, is doubtless sovereign *as to such case*.

This general & indisputable principle puts at once an end to the *abstract* question—Whether the United States have power to *erect a corporation?* that is to say, to give a *legal* or *artificial capacity* to one or more persons, distinct from the natural. For it is unquestionably incident to *sovereign power* to erect corporations, and consequently to *that* of the United States, in *relation to the objects* intrusted to the management of the government. The difference is this—where the authority of the government is general, it can create corporations in *all cases*, where it is confined to certain branches of legislation, it can create corporations only in those cases.

Here then as far as concerns the reasonings of the Secretary of State & the Attorney General, the affirmative of the constitutionality of the bill might be permitted to rest. It will occur to the President that the principle here advanced has been untouched by either of them.

For a more complete elucidation of the point nevertheless, the arguments which they have used against the power of the government to erect corporations, however foreign they are to the great & fundamental rule which has been stated, shall be particularly examined. And after shewing that they do not tend to impair its force, it shall also be shewn, that the power of incorporation incident to the government in certain cases, does fairly extend to the particular case which is the object of the bill.

The first of these arguments is, that the foundation of the constitution is laid on this ground "that all powers not delegated to the United States by the Constitution nor prohibited to it by the States are reserved to the States or to the people", whence it is meant to be inferred, that congress can in no case exercise any power not included in those enumerated in the constitution. And it is affirmed that the power of erecting a corporation is not included in any of the enumerated powers.

The main proposition here laid down, in its true signification is not to be questioned. It is nothing more than a consequence of this republican maxim, that all government is a delegation of power. But how much is delegated in each case, is a question of fact to be made out by fair reasoning & construction upon the particular provisions of the constitution— taking as guides the general principles & general ends of government.

It is not denied, that there are *implied*, as well as *express* powers, and that the former are as effectually delegated as the latter. And for the sake of accuracy it shall be mentioned, that there is another class of powers, which may be properly denominated *resulting* powers. It will not be doubted that if the United States should make a conquest of any of the territories of its neighbours, they would possess sovereign jurisdiction over the conquered territory. This would rather be a result from the whole mass of the powers of the government & from the nature of political society, than a consequence of either of the powers specially enumerated.

But be this as it may, it furnishes a striking illustration of the general doctrine contended for. It shews an extensive case, in which a power of erecting corporations is either implied in, or would result from some or all of the powers, vested in the National Government. The jurisdiction acquired over such conquered territory would certainly be competent to every species of legislation.

To return—It is conceded, that implied powers are to be considered as delegated equally with express ones.

Then it follows, that as a power of erecting a corporation may as well be *implied* as any other thing; it may as well be employed as an *instrument* or *mean* of carrying into execution any of the specified powers, as any other instrument or mean whatever. The only question must be, in this as in every other case, whether the mean to be employed, or in this instance the corporation to be erected, has a natural relation to any of the acknowledged objects or lawful ends of the government. Thus a corporation may not be erected by congress, for superintending the police of the city of Philadelphia because they are not authorised to *regulate* the *police* of that city; but one may be erected in relation to the collection of the taxes, or to the trade with foreign countries, or to the trade between the States, or with the Indian Tribes, because it is the province of the fœderal government to regulate those objects & because it is incident to a general *sovereign* or *legislative power* to *regulate* a thing, to employ all the means which relate to its regulation to the *best* & *greatest advantage*.

A strange fallacy seems to have crept into the manner of thinking & reasoning upon the subject. Imagination appears to have been unusually busy concerning it. An incorporation seems to have been regarded as some great, independent, substantive thing—as a political end of peculiar magnitude & moment; whereas it is truly to be considered as a *quality*, *capacity*, or *mean* to an end. Thus a mercantile company is formed with a certain capital for the purpose of carrying on a particular branch of business. Here the business to be prosecuted is the *end*; the association in order to form the requisite capital is the primary mean. Suppose that an incorporation were added to this; it would only be to add a new *quality* to that association; to give it an artificial capacity by which it would be enabled to prosecute the business with more safety & convenience.

That the importance of the power of incorporation has been exaggerated, leading to erroneous conclusions, will further appear from tracing it to its origin. The roman law is the source of it, according to which a *voluntary* association of individuals at *any time* or *for any purpose* was capable of producing it. In England, whence our notions of it are immediately borrowed, it forms a part of the executive authority, & the exercise of it has been often *delegated* by that authority. Whence therefore the ground of the supposition, that it lies beyond the reach of all those very important portions of sovereign power, legislative as well as executive, which belong to the government of the United States?

To this mode of reasoning respecting the right of employing all the means requisite to the execution of the specified powers of the Government, it is objected that none but *necessary* & proper means are to be employed, & the Secretary of State maintains, that no means are to be considered as *necessary*, but those without which the grant of the power would be *nugatory*. Nay so far does he go in his restrictive interpretation of the word, as even to make the case of *necessity* which shall warrant the constitutional exercise of the power to depend on *casual* & *temporary* circumstances, an idea which alone refutes the construction. The *expediency* of exercising a particular power, at a particular time, must indeed depend on *circumstances*; but the constitutional right of exercising it must be uniform & invariable—the same to day, as to morrow.

All the arguments therefore against the constitutionality of the bill derived from the accidental existence of certain State-banks: institutions which *happen* to exist to day, & for ought that concerns the government of the United States, may disappear to morrow, must not only be rejected as fallacious, but must be viewed as demonstrative, that there is a *radical* source of error in the reasoning.

It is essential to the being of the National government, that so erroneous a conception of the meaning of the word *necessary*, should be exploded.

It is certain, that neither the grammatical, nor popular sense of the term requires that construction. According to both, *necessary* often means no more than *needful, requisite, incidental, useful,* or *conducive to.* It is a common mode of expression to say, that it is *necessary* for a government or a person to do this or that thing, when nothing more is intended or understood, than that the interests of the government or person require, or will be promoted, by the doing of this or that thing. The imagination can be at no loss for exemplifications of the use of the word in this sense.

And it is the true one in which it is to be understood as used in the constitution. The whole turn of the clause containing it, indicates, that it was the intent of the convention, by that clause to give a liberal latitude to the exercise of the specified powers. The expressions have peculiar comprehensiveness. They are—"to make *all laws,* necessary & proper for *carrying into execution* the foregoing powers & all *other powers* vested by the constitution in the *government* of the United States, or in any *department* or *officer* thereof." To understand the word as the Secretary of State does, would be to depart from its obvious & popular sense, and to give it a *restrictive* operation; an idea never before entertained. It would be to give it the same force as if the word *absolutely* or *indispensibly* had been prefixed to it.

Such a construction would beget endless uncertainty & embarassment. The cases must be palpable & extreme in which it could be pronounced with certainty, that a measure was absolutely necessary, or one without which the exercise of a given power would be nugatory. There are few measures of any government, which would stand so severe a test. To insist upon it, would be to make the criterion of the exercise of any implied power a *case of extreme necessity,* which is rather a rule to justify the overleaping of the bounds of constitutional authority, than to govern the ordinary exercise of it.

It may be truly said of every government, as well as of that of the United States, that it has only a right, to pass such laws as are necessary & proper to accomplish the objects intrusted to it. For no government has a right to do *merely what it pleases.* Hence by a process of reasoning similar to that of the Secretary of State, it might be proved, that neither of the State governments has a right to incorporate a bank. It might be shewn, that all the public business of the State, could be performed without a bank, and inferring thence that it was unnecessary it might be argued that it could not be done, because it is against the rule which has been just mentioned. A like mode of reasoning would prove, that there was no power to incorporate the Inhabitants of a town, with a view to a more perfect police: For it is certain, that an incorporation may be dispensed with, though it is better to have one. It is to be remembered, that there is no *express* power in any State constitution to erect corporations.

The *degree* in which a measure is necessary, can never be a test of the *legal* right to adopt it. That must ever be a matter of opinion; and can only be a test of expediency. The *relation* between the *measure* and the *end*, between the *nature* of *the mean* employed towards the execution of a power and the object of that power, must be the criterion of constitutionality not the more or less of *necessity* or *utility.*

The practice of the government is against the rule of construction advocated by the Secretary of State. Of this the act concerning light houses, beacons, buoys & public piers, is a decisive example. This doubtless must be referred to the power of regulating trade, and is fairly relative to it. But it cannot be affirmed, that the exercise of that power, in this instance, was strictly necessary; or that the power itself would be *nugatory* without that of regulating establishments of this nature.

This restrictive interpretation of the word *necessary* is also contrary to this sound maxim of construction namely, that the powers contained in a constitution of government, especially those which concern the general administration of the affairs of a country, its finances, trade, defence &c ought to be construed liberally, in advancement of the public good. This rule does not depend on the particular form of a government or on the particular demarkation of the boundaries of its powers, but on the nature and objects of government itself. The means by which national exigencies are to be provided for, national inconveniencies obviated, national prosperity promoted, are of such infinite variety, extent and complexity, that there must, of necessity, be great latitude of discretion in the selection & application of those means. Hence consequently, the necessity & propriety of exercising the authorities intrusted to a government on principles of liberal construction.

The Attorney General admits the *rule*, but takes a distinction between a State, and the fœderal constitution. The latter, he thinks, ought to be construed with greater strictness, because there is more danger of error in defining partial than general powers.

But the reason of the *rule* forbids such a distinction. This reason is—the variety & extent of public exigencies, a far greater proportion of which and of a far more critical kind, are objects of National than of State administration. The greater danger of error, as far as it is supposeable, may be a prudential reason for caution in practice, but it cannot be a rule of restrictive interpretation.

In regard to the clause of the constitution immediately under consideration, it is admitted by the Attorney General, that no *restrictive* effect can be ascribed to it. He defines the word necessary thus. "To be necessary is to be *incidental*, and may be denominated the natural means of executing a power."

But while, on the one hand, the construction of the Secretary of State is deemed inadmissible, it will not be contended on the other, that the clause in question gives any *new* or *independent* power. But it gives an explicit sanction to the doctrine of *implied* powers, and is equivalent to an admission of the proposition, that the government, *as to its specified powers* and *objects*, has plenary & sovereign authority, in some cases paramount to that of the States, in others co-ordinate with it. For such is the plain import of the declaration, that it may pass *all laws* necessary & proper to carry into execution those powers.

It is no valid objection to the doctrine to say, that it is calculated to extend the powers of the general government throughout the entire sphere of State legislation. The same thing has been said, and may be said with regard to every exercise of power by implication or construction. The moment the literal meaning is departed from, there is a chance of error and abuse. And yet an adherence to the letter of its powers would at once arrest the motions of the government. It is not only agreed, on all hands, that the exercise of constructive powers is indispensible, but every act which has been passed is more or less an exemplification of it. One has been already mentioned, that relating to light houses &c. That which declares the power of the President to remove officers at pleasure, acknowlidges the same truth in another, and a signal instance.

The truth is that difficulties on this point are inherent in the nature of the fœderal constitution. They result inevitably from a division of the legislative power. The consequence of this division is, that there will be cases clearly within the power of the National Government; others clearly without its power; and a third class, which will leave room for controversy & difference of opinion, & concerning which a reasonable latitude of judgment must be allowed.

But the doctrine which is contended for is not chargeable with the consequence imputed to it. It does not affirm that the National government is sovereign in all respects, but that it is sovereign to a certain extent: that is, to the extent of the objects of its specified powers.

It leaves therefore a criterion of what is constitutional, and of what is not so. This criterion is the *end* to which the measure relates as a *mean*. If the end be clearly comprehended within any of the specified powers, & if the measure have an obvious relation to that end, and is not forbidden by any particular provision of the constitution—it may safely be deemed to come within the compass of the national authority. There is also this further criterion which may materially assist the decision. Does the proposed measure abridge a preexisting right of any State, or of any individual? If it does not, there is a strong presumption in favour of its constitutionality; & slighter relations to any declared object of the constitution may be permitted to turn the scale.

The general objections which are to be inferred from the reasonings of the Secretary of State and of the Attorney General to the doctrine which has been advanced, have been stated and it is hoped satisfactorily answered. Those of a more particular nature shall now be examined.

The Secretary of State introduces his opinion with an observation, that the proposed incorporation undertakes to create certain capacities properties or attributes which are *against* the laws of *alienage, descents, escheat* and *forfeiture, distribution* and *monopoly,* and to confer a power to make laws paramount to those of the States. And nothing says he, in another place, but a *necessity invincible by other means* can justify such a *prostration* of *laws* which constitute the pillars of our whole system of jurisprudence, and are the foundation laws of the State Governments.

If these are truly the foundation laws of the several states, then have most of them subverted their own foundations. For there is scarcely one of them which has not, since the establishment of its particular constitution, made material alterations in some of those branches of its jurisprudence especially the law of descents. But it is not conceived how any thing can be called the fundamental law of a State Government which is not established in its constitution unalterable by the ordinary legislature. And with regard to the question of necessity it has been shewn, that this can only constitute a question of expediency, not of right.

To erect a corporation is to substitute a *legal* or *artificial* to a *natural* person, and where a number are concerned to give them *individuality*. To that legal or artificial person once created, the common law of every state of itself *annexes* all those incidents and attributes, which are represented as a prostration of the main pillars of their jurisprudence. It is certainly not accurate to say, that the erection of a corporation is *against* those different *heads* of the State laws; because it is rather to create a kind of person or entity, to which *they* are inapplicable, and to which the general rule of those laws assign a different regimen. The laws of alienage cannot apply to an artificial person, because it can have no country. Those of descent cannot apply to it, because it can have no heirs. Those of escheat are foreign from it for the same reason. Those of forfeiture, because it cannot commit a crime. Those of distribution, because, though it may be dissolved, it cannot die. As truly might it be said, that the exercise of the power of prescribing the rule by which foreigners shall be naturalised, is *against* the law of alienage; while it is in fact only to put them in a situation to cease to be the subject of that law. To do a thing which is *against* a law, is to do something which it forbids or which is a violation of it.

But if it were even to be admitted that the erection of a corporation is a direct alteration of the State laws in the enumerated particulars; it would do nothing towards proving, that the measure was unconstitutional. If the government of the United States can do no act, which amounts to an alteration of a State law, all its powers are nugatory. For almost every new law is an alteration, in some way or other of an old *law*, either *common*, or *statute*.

There are laws concerning bankruptcy in some states— some states have laws regulating the values of foreign coins. Congress are empowered to establish uniform laws concerning bankruptcy throughout the United States, and to regulate the values of foreign coins. The exercise of either of these powers by Congress necessarily involves an alteration of the laws of those states.

Again: Every person by the common law of each state may export his property to foreign countries, at pleasure. But Congress, in pursuance of the power of regulating trade, may prohibit the exportation of commodities: in doing which, they would alter the common law of each state in abridgement of individual rights.

It can therefore never be good reasoning to say—this or that act is unconstitutional, because it alters this or that law of a State. It must be shewn, that the act which makes the alteration is unconstitutional on other accounts, not *because* it makes the alteration.

There are two points in the suggestions of the Secretary of State which have been noted that are peculiarly incorrect. One is, that the proposed incorporation is against the laws of monopoly, because it stipulates an exclusive right of banking under the national authority. The other that it gives power to the institution to make laws paramount to those of the states.

But with regard to the first point, the bill neither prohibits any State from erecting as many banks as they please, nor any number of Individuals from associating to carry on the business: & consequently is free from the charge of establishing a monopoly: for monopoly implies a *legal impediment* to the carrying on of the trade by others than those to whom it is granted.

And with regard to the second point, there is still less foundation. The bye-laws of such an institution as a bank can operate only upon its own members; can only concern the disposition of its own property and must essentially resemble the rules of a private mercantile partnership. They are expressly not to be contrary to law; and law must here mean the law of a State as well as of the United States. There never can be a doubt, that a law of the corporation, if contrary to a law of a state, must be overruled as void; unless the law of the State is contrary to that of the United States; and then the question will not be between the law of the State and that of the corporation, but between the law of the State and that of the United States.

Another argument made use of by the Secretary of State, is, the rejection of a proposition by the convention to empower Congress to make corporations, either generally, or for some special purpose.

What was the precise nature or extent of this proposition, or what the reasons for refusing it, is not ascertained by any authentic document, or even by accurate recollection. As far as any such document exists, it specifies only canals. If this was the amount of it, it would at most only prove, that it was thought inexpedient to give a power to incorporate for the purpose of opening canals, for which purpose a special power would have been necessary; except with regard to the Western Territory, there being nothing in any part of the constitution respecting the regulation of canals. It must be confessed however, that very different accounts are given of the import of the proposition and of the motives for rejecting it. Some affirm that it was confined to the opening of canals and obstructions in rivers; others, that it embraced banks; and others, that it extended to the power of incorporating generally. Some again alledge, that it was disagreed to, because it was thought improper to vest in Congress a power of erecting corporations—others, because it was thought unnecessary to *specify* the power, and inexpedient to furnish an additional topic of objection to the constitution. In this state of the matter, no inference whatever can be drawn from it.

But whatever may have been the nature of the proposition or the reasons for rejecting it concludes nothing in respect to the real merits of the question. The Secretary of State will not deny, that whatever may have been the intention of the framers of a constitution, or of a law, that intention is to be sought for in the instrument itself, according to the usual & established rules of construction. Nothing is more common than for laws to *express* and *effect*, more or less than was intended. If then a power to erect a corporation, in any case, be deducible by fair inference from the whole or any part of the numerous provisions of the constitution of the United States, arguments drawn from extrinsic circumstances, regarding the intention of the convention, must be rejected.

Most of the arguments of the Secretary of State which have not been considered in the foregoing remarks, are of a nature rather to apply to the expediency than to the constitutionality of the bill. They will however be noticed in the discussions which will be necessary in reference to the particular heads of the powers of the government which are involved in the question.

Those of the Attorney General will now properly come under review.

His first observation is, that the power of incorporation is not *expressly* given to congress. This shall be conceded, but in *this sense* only, that it is not declared in *express terms* that congress may erect a *corporation*. But this cannot mean, that there are not certain *express* powers, which *necessarily* include it.

For instance, Congress have express power "to exercise exclusive legislation in all cases whatsoever, over such *district* (not exceeding ten miles square) as may by cession of particular states, & the acceptance of Congress become the seat of the government of the United states; and to exercise *like authority* over all places purchased by consent of the legislature of the State in which the same shall be for the erection of forts, arsenals, dock yards & other needful buildings."

Here then is express power to exercise *exclusive legislation in all cases whatsoever over certain places*; that is to do in respect to those places, all that any government whatever may do: For language does not afford a more complete designation of sovereign power, than in those comprehensive terms.

It is in other words a power to pass all laws whatsoever, & consequently to pass laws for erecting corporations, as well as for any other purpose which is the proper object of law in a free government. Surely it can never be believed, that Congress with *exclusive power of legislation in all cases whatsoever*, cannot erect a corporation within the district which shall become the seat of government, for the better regulation of its police. And yet there is an unqualified denial of the power to erect corporations in every case on the part both of the Secretary of State and of the Attorney General. The former indeed speaks of that power in these emphatical terms, that it is *a right remaining exclusively with the states.*

As far then as there is an express power to do any *particular act of legislation*, there is an express one to erect corporations in the cases above described. But accurately speaking, no *particular power* is more than *implied* in a *general one*. Thus the power to lay a duty on a *gallon of rum*, is only a particular *implied* in the general power to lay and collect taxes, duties, imposts and excises. This serves to explain in what sense it may be said, that congress have not an express power to make corporations.

This may not be an improper place to take notice of an argument which was used in debate in the House of Representatives. It was there urged, that if the constitution intended to confer so important a power as that of erecting corporations, it would have been expressly mentioned. But the case which has been noticed is clearly one in which such a power exists, and yet without any specification or express grant of it, further than as every *particular implied* in a general power, can be said to be so granted.

But the argument itself is founded upon an exaggerated and erroneous conception of the nature of the power. It has been shewn, that it is not of so transcendent a kind as the reasoning supposes; and that viewed in a just light it is a mean which ought to have been left to *implication*, rather than an *end* which ought to have been *expressly* granted.

Having observed, that the power of erecting corporations is not expressly granted to Congress, the Attorney General proceeds thus . . . .

"If it can be exercised by them, it must be

1. because the nature of the fœderal government implies it.
2. because it is involved in some of the specified powers of legislation or
3. because it is necessary & proper to carry into execution some of the specified powers."

To be implied in the *nature of the fœderal government,* says he, would beget a doctrine so indefinite, as to grasp every power.

This proposition it ought to be remarked is not precisely, or even substantially, that, which has been relied upon. The proposition relied upon is, that the *specified powers* of Congress are in their nature sovereign—that it is incident to sovereign power to erect corporations; & that therefore Congress have a right within the *sphere* & *in relation to the objects of their power, to erect corporations.*

It shall however be supposed, that the Attorney General would consider the two propositions in the same light, & that the objection made to the one, would be made to the other.

To this objection an answer has been already given. It is this; that the doctrine is stated with this express *qualification,* that the right to erect corporations does *only* extend to *cases* & *objects* within the *sphere* of the *specified powers* of the government. A general legislative authority implies a power to erect corporations *in all cases*—a particular legislative power implies authority to erect corporations, in relation to cases arising under that power only. Hence the affirming, that as an *incident* to sovereign power, congress may erect a corporation in relation to the *collection* of their taxes, is no more than to affirm that they may do whatever else they please; than the saying that they have a power to regulate trade would be to affirm that they have a power to regulate religion: or than the maintaining that they have sovereign power as to taxation, would be to maintain that they have sovereign power as to every thing else.

The Attorney General undertakes, in the next place, to shew, that the power of erecting corporations is not involved in any of the specified powers of legislation confided to the National government.

In order to this he has attempted an enumeration of the particulars which he supposes to be comprehended under the

several heads of the *powers* to lay & collect taxes &c—to borrow money on the credit of the United States—to regulate
commerce with foreign nations—between the states, and with
the Indian Tribes—to dispose of and make all needful rules &
regulations respecting the territory or other property belonging to the United States; the design of which enumeration is
to shew *what is* included under those different heads of
power, & *negatively*, that the power of erecting corporations
is not included.

The truth of this inference or conclusion must depend on
the accuracy of the enumeration. If it can be shewn that the
enumeration is *defective*, the inference is destroyed. To do this
will be attended with no difficulty.

The heads of the power to lay & collect taxes, he states
to be

1. To ascertain the subject of taxation &c
2. to declare the quantum of taxation &c
3. to prescribe the *mode* of *collection*.
4. to ordain the manner of accounting for the taxes &c

The defectiveness of this enumeration consists in the generality of the third division "*to prescribe the mode* of collection"; which is in itself an immense chapter. It will be shewn
hereafter, that, among a vast variety of particulars, it com-
prises the very power in question; namely to *erect corporations.*

The heads of the power to borrow money are stated to be

1. to stipulate the sum to be lent.
2. an interest or no interest to be paid.
3. the time & manner of repaying, unless the loan be
   placed on an irredeemable fund.

This enumeration is liable to a variety of objections. It
omits, in the first place, the *pledging* or *mortgaging* of a fund
for the security of the money lent, an usual and in most cases
an essential ingredient.

The idea of a stipulation of *an interest or no interest* is too
confined. It should rather have been said, to stipulate the
consideration of the loan. Individuals often borrow upon
considerations other than the payment of interest. So may
government; and so they often find it necessary to do. Every
one reCollects the lottery tickets & other douceurs often

given in Great Britain, as collateral inducements to the lending of money to the Government.

There are also frequently collateral conditions, which the enumeration does not contemplate. Every contract which has been made for monies borrowed in Holland includes stipulations that the sum due shall be *free from taxes*, and from sequestration in time of war, and mortgages all the land & property of the United States for the reimbursement.

It is also known, that a lottery is a common expedient for borrowing money, which certainly does not fall under either of the enumerated heads.

The heads of the power to regulate commerce with foreign nations are stated to be

1. to prohibit them or their commodities from our ports.
2. to impose duties on *them* where none existed before, or to increase existing duties on them.
3. to subject *them* to any species of custom house regulation
4. to grant *them* any exemptions or privileges which policy may suggest.

This enumeration is far more exceptionable than either of the former. It omits *every thing* that relates to the *citizens vessels* or *commodities* of the United States. The following palpable omissions occur at once.

1. Of the power to prohibit the exportation of commodities which not only exists at all times, but which in time of war it would be necessary to exercise, particularly with relation to naval and war-like stores.
2. Of the power to prescribe rules concerning the *characteristics* & *priviledges* of an american bottom—how she shall be navigated, as whether by citizens or foreigners, or by a proportion of each.
3. Of the power of regulating the manner of contracting with seamen, the police of ships on their voyages &c of which the act for the government & regulation of seamen in the merchants service is a specimen.

That the three preceding articles are omissions, will not be doubted. There is a long list of items in addition, which admit of little, if any question; of which a few samples shall be given.

1. The granting of bounties to certain kinds of vessels, & certain species of merchandise. Of this nature is the allowance on dried & pickled fish & salted provisions.
2. The prescribing of rules concerning the *inspection* of commodities to be exported. Though the states individually are competent to this regulation, yet there is no reason, in point of authority at least, why a general system might not be adopted by the United States.
3. The regulation of policies of insurance; of salvage upon goods found at sea, and the disposition of such goods.
4. The regulation of pilots.
5. The regulation of bills of exchange drawn by a merchant of *one state* upon a merchant of *another state*. This last rather belongs to the regulation of trade between the states, but is equally omitted in the specification under that head.

The last enumeration relates to the power "to dispose of & make *all needful rules and regulations* respecting the territory *or other property* belonging to the United States."

The heads of this power are said to be

1. to exert an ownership over the territory of the United States, which may be properly called the property of the United States, as in the Western Territory, and to *institute a government therein*: or
2. to exert an ownership over the other property of the United States.

This idea of exerting an ownership over the Territory or other property of the United States, is particularly indefinite and vague. It does not at all satisfy the conception of what must have been intended by a power, to make all needful *rules* and *regulations*; nor would there have been any use for a special clause which authorised nothing more. For the right of exerting an ownership is implied in the very definition of property.

It is admitted that in regard to the western territory some thing more is intended—even the institution of a government; that is the creation of a body politic, or corporation of the highest nature; one, which in its maturity, will be able itself to create other corporations. Why then does not the same clause authorise the erection of a corporation in respect to the regulation or disposal of any other of the property of the United States? This idea will be enlarged upon in another place.

Hence it appears, that the enumerations which have been attempted by the Attorney General are so imperfect, as to authorise no conclusion whatever. They therefore have no tendency to disprove, that each and every of the powers to which they relate, includes that of erecting corporations; which they certainly do, as the subsequent illustrations will more & more evince.

It is presumed to have been satisfactorily shewn in the course of the preceding observations

1. That the power of the government, *as to* the objects intrusted to its management, is in its nature sovereign.

2. That the right of erecting corporations is one, inherent in & inseparable from the idea of sovereign power.

3. That the position, that the government of the United States can exercise no power but such as is delegated to it by its constitution, does not militate against this principle.

4. That the word *necessary* in the general clause can have no *restrictive* operation, derogating from the force of this principle, indeed, that the degree in which a measure is, or is not necessary, cannot be a *test* of *constitutional* right, but of expediency only.

5. That the power to erect corporations is not to be considered, as an *independent* & *substantive* power but as an *incidental* & *auxiliary* one; and was therefore more properly left to implication, than expressly granted.

6. that the principle in question does not extend the power of the government beyond the prescribed limits, because it only affirms a power to *incorporate* for *purposes within the sphere of the specified powers.*

   And lastly that the right to exercise such a power, in certain cases, is unequivocally granted in the most *positive* & *comprehensive* terms.

To all which it only remains to be added that such a power has actually been exercised in two very eminent instances: namely in the erection of two governments, One, northwest of the river Ohio, and the other south west—*the last, independent of any antecedent compact.*

And there results a full & complete demonstration, that the Secretary of State & Attorney General are mistaken, when they deny generally the power of the National government to erect corporations.

It shall now be endeavoured to be shewn that there is a power to erect one of the kind proposed by the bill. This will be done, by tracing a natural & obvious relation between the institution of a bank, and the objects of several of the enumerated powers of the government; and by shewing that, *politically* speaking, it is necessary to the effectual execution of one or more of those powers. In the course of this investigation, various instances will be stated, by way of illustration, of a right to erect corporations under those powers.

Some preliminary observations maybe proper.

The proposed bank is to consist of an association of persons for the purpose of creating a joint capital to be employed, chiefly and essentially, in loans. So far the object is not only lawful, but it is the mere exercise of a right, which the law allows to every individual. The bank of New York which is not incorporated, is an example of such an association. The bill proposes in addition, that the government shall become a joint proprietor in this undertaking, and that it shall permit the bills of the company payable on demand to be receivable in its revenues & stipulates that it shall not grant privileges similar to those which are to be allowed to this company, to any others. All this is incontrovertibly within the compass of the discretion of the government. The only question is, whether it has a right to incorporate this company, in order to enable it the more effectually to accomplish *ends*, which are in themselves lawful.

To establish such a right, it remains to shew the relation of such an institution to one or more of the specified powers of the government.

Accordingly it is affirmed, that it has a relation more or less direct to the power of collecting taxes; to that of borrowing money; to that of regulating trade between the states; and to those of raising, supporting & maintaining fleets & armies. To the two former, the relation may be said to be *immediate*.

And, in the last place, it will be argued, that it is, *clearly*, within the provision which authorises the making of all *need-*

ful rules & *regulations* concerning the *property* of the United States, as the same has been practiced upon by the Government.

A Bank relates to the collection of taxes in two ways; *indirectly*, by increasing the quantity of circulating medium & quickening circulation, which facilitates the means of paying—*directly*, by creating a *convenient species* of *medium* in which they are to be paid.

To designate or appoint the money or *thing* in which taxes are to be paid, is not only a proper, but a necessary *exercise* of the power of collecting them. Accordingly congress in the law concerning the collection of the duties on imports & tonnage, have provided that they shall be payable in gold & silver. But while it was an indispensible part of the work to say in what they should be paid, the choice of the specific thing was mere matter of discretion. The payment might have been required in the commodities themselves. Taxes in kind, however ill judged, are not without precedents, even in the United States. Or it might have been in the paper money of the several states; or in the bills of the bank of North America, New York and Massachusetts, all or either of them: or it might have been in bills issued under the authority of the United States.

No part of this can, it is presumed, be disputed. The appointment, then, of the *money* or *thing*, in which the taxes are to be paid, is an incident to the power of collection. And among the expedients which may be adopted, is that of bills issued under the authority of the United States.

Now the manner of issuing these bills is again matter of discretion. The government might, doubtless, proceed in the following manner. It might provide, that they should be issued under the direction of certain officers, payable on demand; and in order to support their credit & give them a ready circulation, it might, besides giving them a currency in its taxes, set apart out of any monies in its Treasury, a given sum and appropriate it under the direction of those officers as a fund for answering the bills as presented for payment.

The constitutionality of all this would not admit of a question. And yet it would amount to the institution of a bank, with a view to the more convenient collection of taxes. For the simplest and most precise idea of a bank, is, a deposit of coin or other property, as a fund for *circulating* a *credit* upon it, which is to answer the purpose of money. That such an arrangement would be equivalent to the establishment of a bank would become obvious, if the place where the fund to be set apart was kept should be made a receptacle of the monies of all other persons who should incline to deposit them there for safe keeping; and would become still more so, if the Officers charged with the direction of the fund were authorised to make discounts at the usual rate of interest, upon good security. To deny the power of the government to add these ingredients to the plan, would be to refine away all government.

This process serves to exemplify the natural & direct relation which may subsist between the institution of a bank and the collection of taxes. It is true that the species of bank which has been designated, does not include the idea of incorporation. But the argument intended to be founded upon it, is this: that the institution comprehended in the idea of a bank being one immediately relative to the collection of taxes, *in regard to the appointment* of *the money or thing* in which they are to be paid; the sovereign power of providing for the collection of taxes necessarily includes the right of granting a corporate capacity to such an institution, as a requisite to its greater security, utility and more convenient management.

A further process will still more clearly illustrate the point. Suppose, when the species of bank which has been described was about to be instituted, it were to be urged, that in order to secure to it a due degree of confidence the fund ought not only to be set apart & appropriated generally, but ought to be specifically vested in the officers who were to have the direction of it, and in their *successors* in office, to the end that it might acquire the character of *private property* incapable of being resumed without a violation of the sanctions by which the rights of property are protected & occasioning more serious & general alarm, the apprehension of which might operate as a check upon the government—such a proposition might be opposed by arguments against the expediency of it or the solidity of the reason assigned for it, but it is not conceivable what could be urged against its constitutionality.

And yet such a disposition of the thing would amount to the erection of a corporation. For the true definition of a corporation seems to be this. It is a *legal* person, or a person created by act of law, consisting of one or more natural persons authorised to hold property or a franchise in succession in a legal as contradistinguished from a natural capacity.

Let the illustration proceed a step further. Suppose a bank of the nature which has been described with or without incorporation, had been instituted, & that experience had evinced as it probably would, that being wholly under public direction it possessed not the confidence requisite to the credit of its bills— Suppose also that by some of those adverse conjunctures which occasionally attend nations, there had been a very great drain of the specie of the country, so as not only to cause general distress for want of an adequate medium of circulation, but to produce, in consequence of that circumstance, considerable defalcations in the public revenues—suppose also, that there was no bank instituted in any State—in such a posture of things, would it not be most manifest that the incorporation of a bank, like that proposed by the bill, would be a measure immediately relative to the *effectual collection* of the taxes and completely within the province of the sovereign power of providing by all laws necessary & proper for that collection?

If it be said, that such a state of things would render that necessary & therefore constitutional, which is not so now— the answer to this, and a solid one it doubtless is, must still be, that which has been already stated—Circumstances may affect the expediency of the measure, but they can neither add to, nor diminish its constitutionality.

A Bank has a direct relation to the power of borrowing money, because it is an usual and in sudden emergencies an essential instrument in the obtaining of loans to Government.

A nation is threatened with a war. Large sums are wanted, on a sudden, to make the requisite preparations. Taxes are laid for the purpose, but it requires time to obtain the benefit of them. Anticipation is indispensible. If there be a bank, the supply can, at once be had; if there be none loans from Individuals must be sought. The progress of these is often too slow for the exigency: in some situations they are not practicable at all. Frequently when they are, it is of great consequence to be able to anticipate the product of them by advances from a bank.

The essentiality of such an institution as an instrument of loans is exemplified at this very moment. An Indian expedition is to be prosecuted. The only fund out of which the money can arise consistently with the public engagements, is a tax which will only begin to be collected in July next. The preparations, however, are instantly to be made. The money must therefore be borrowed. And of whom could it be borrowed; if there were no public banks?

It happens, that there are institutions of this kind, but if there were none, it would be indispensible to create one.

Let it then be supposed, that the necessity existed, (as but for a casualty would be the case) that proposals were made for obtaining a loan; that a number of individuals came forward and said, we are willing to accommodate the government with this money; with what we have in hand and the credit we can raise upon it we doubt not of being able to furnish the sum required: but in order to this, it is indispensible, that we should be incorporated as a bank. This is essential towards putting it in our power to do what is desired and we are obliged on that account to make it the *consideration* or condition of the loan.

Can it be believed, that a compliance with this proposition would be unconstitutional? Does not this alone evince the contrary? It is a necessary part of a power to borrow to be able to stipulate the consideration or conditions of a loan. It is evident, as has been remarked elsewhere, that this is not confined to the mere stipulation of a sum of money by way of interest—why may it not be deemed to extend, where a government is the contracting party, to the stipulation of a *franchise*? If it may, & it is not perceived why it may not, then the grant of a corporate capacity may be stipulated as a consideration of the loan? There seems to be nothing unfit, or foreign from the nature of the thing in giving individuality or a corporate capacity to a number of persons who are willing to lend a sum of money to the government, the better to enable them to do it, and make them an ordinary instrument of loans in future emergencies of the state.

But the more general view of the subject is still more satis-factory. The legislative power of borrowing money, & of mak-ing all laws necessary & proper for carrying into execution that power, seems obviously competent to the appointment of the *organ* through which the abilities and wills of individuals may be most efficaciously exerted, for the accommodation of the government by loans.

The Attorney General opposes to this reasoning, the fol-lowing observation. "To borrow money presupposes the ac-cumulation of a fund to be lent, and is secondary to the creation of an ability to lend." This is plausible in theory, but it is not true in fact. In a great number of cases, a previous ac-cumulation of a fund equal to the whole sum required, does not exist. And nothing more can be actually presupposed, than that there exist resources, which put into activity to the greatest advantage by the nature of the operation with the government, will be equal to the effect desired to be pro-duced. All the provisions and operations of government must be presumed to contemplate things as they *really* are.

The institution of a bank has also a natural relation to the regulation of trade between the States: in so far as it is con-ducive to the creation of a convenient medium of *exchange* between them, and to the keeping up a full circulation by pre-venting the frequent displacement of the metals in reciprocal remittances. Money is the very hinge on which commerce turns. And this does not mean merely gold & silver, many other things have served the purpose with different degrees of utility. Paper has been extensively employed.

It cannot therefore be admitted with the Attorney General, that the regulation of trade between the States, as it concerns the medium of circulation & exchange ought to be consid-ered as confined to coin. It is even supposeable in argument, that the whole, or the greatest part of the coin of the coun-try, might be carried out of it.

The Secretary of State objects to the relation here insisted upon, by the following mode of reasoning—"To erect a bank, says he, & to regulate commerce, are very different acts. He who erects a bank, creates a subject of commerce, so does he, who makes a bushel of wheat, or digs a dollar out of the mines. Yet neither of these persons regulates commerce thereby. To make a thing which may be bought & sold is not to *prescribe* regulations for *buying* & *selling*: thus making the regulation of commerce to consist in prescribing rules for *buying* & *selling*.

This indeed is a species of regulation of trade; but is one which falls more aptly within the province of the local jurisdictions than within that of the general government, whose care must be presumed to have been intended to be directed to those general political arrangements concerning trade on which its aggregate interests depend, rather than to the details of buying and selling.

Accordingly such only are the regulations to be found in the laws of the United States; whose objects are to give encouragement to the entreprise of our own merchants, and to advance our navigation and manufactures.

And it is in reference to these general relations of commerce, that an establishment which furnishes facilities to circulation and a convenient medium of exchange & alienation, is to be regarded as a regulation of trade.

The Secretary of State further argues, that if this was a regulation of commerce, it would be void, *as extending as much to the internal commerce of every state as to its external.* But what regulation of commerce does not extend to the internal commerce of every state? What are all the duties upon imported articles amounting to prohibitions, but so many bounties upon domestic manufactures affecting the interests of different classes of citizens in different ways? What are all the provisions in the coasting act, which relate to the trade between district and district of the same State? In short what regulation of trade between the States, but must affect the internal trade of each State? What can operate upon the whole but must extend to every part!

The relation of a bank to the execution of the powers, that concern the common defence, has been anticipated. It has been noted, that at this very moment the aid of such an institution is essential to the measures to be pursued for the protection of our frontier.

It now remains to shew, that the incorporation of a bank is within the operation of the provision which authorises. Congress to make all needful rules & regulations concerning the property of the United States. But it is previously necessary to advert to a distinction which has been taken by the Attorney General.

He admits, that the word *property* may signify personal property however acquired. And yet asserts, that it cannot signify money arising from the sources of revenue pointed out in the constitution; because, says he, "the disposal & regulation of money is the final cause for raising it by taxes."

But it would be more accurate to say, that the *object* to which money is intended to be applied is the *final cause* for raising it, than that the disposal and regulation of it is *such*. The support of Government; the support of troops for the common defence; the payment of the public debt, are the true *final causes* for raising money. The disposition & regulation of it when raised, are the steps by which it is applied to the *ends* for which it was raised, not the ends themselves. Hence therefore the money to be raised by taxes as well as any other personal property, must be supposed to come within the meaning as they certainly do within the letter of the authority, to make all needful rules & regulations concerning the property of the United States.

A case will make this plainer: suppose the public debt discharged, and the funds now pledged for it liberated. In some instances it would be found expedient to repeal the taxes, in others, the repeal might injure our own industry, our agriculture and manufactures. In these cases they would of course be retained. Here then would be monies arising from the authorised sources of revenue which would not fall within the rule by which the Attorney General endeavours to except them from other personal property, & from the operation of the clause in question.

The monies being in the coffers of the government, what is to hinder such a disposition to be made of them as is contemplated in the bill or what an incorporation of the parties concerned under the clause which has been cited.

It is admitted that with regard to the Western territory they give a power to erect a corporation—that is to institute a government. And by what rule of construction can it be maintained, that the same words in a constitution of government will not have the same effect when applied to one species of property, as to another, as far as the subject is capable of it? or that a legislative power to make all needful rules & regulations, or to pass all laws necessary & proper concerning the public property which is admitted to authorise an incorporation in one case will not authorise it in another? will justify the institution of a government over the western territory & will not justify the incorporation of a bank, for the more useful management of the money of the nation? If it will do the last, as well as the first, then under this provision alone the bill is constitutional, because it contemplates that the United States shall be joint proprietors of the stock of the bank.

There is an observation of the secretary of state to this effect, which may require notice in this place. Congress, says he, are not to lay taxes *ad libitum for any purpose they please*, but only to pay the debts, or provide for the *welfare* of the Union. Certainly no inference can be drawn from this against the power of applying their money for the institution of a bank. It is true, that they cannot without breach of trust, lay taxes for any other purpose than the general welfare but so neither can any other government. The welfare of the community is the only legitimate end for which money can be raised on the community. Congress can be considered as under only one restriction, which does not apply to other governments—They cannot rightfully apply the money they raise to any purpose *merely* or purely local. But with this exception they have as large a discretion in relation to the *application* of money as any legislature whatever. The constitutional *test* of a right application must always be whether it be for a purpose of *general* or *local* nature. If the former, there can be no want of constitutional power. The quality of the object, as how far it will really promote or not the welfare of the union, must be matter of conscientious discretion. And the arguments for or against a measure in this light, must be arguments concerning expediency or inexpediency, not constitutional right. Whatever relates to the general order of the finances, to the general interests of trade &c being general objects are constitutional ones for *the application* of *money*.

A Bank then whose bills are to circulate in all the revenues of the country, is *evidently* a general object, and for that very reason a constitutional one as far as regards the appropriation of money to it. Whether it will really be a beneficial one, or not, is worthy of careful examination, but is no more a constitutional point, in the particular referred to; than the question whether the western lands shall be sold for twenty or thirty cents ℔ acre.

A hope is entertained, that it has by this time been made to appear, to the satisfaction of the President, that a bank has a natural relation to the power of collecting taxes; to that of borrowing money; to that of regulating trade; to that of providing for the common defence: and that as the bill under consideration contemplates the government in the light of a joint proprietor of the stock of the bank, it brings the case within the provision of the clause of the constitution which immediately respects the property of the United States.

Under a conviction that such a relation subsists, the Secretary of the Treasury, with all deference conceives, that it will result as a necessary consequence from the position, that all the specified powers of the government are sovereign as to the proper objects; that the incorporation of a bank is a constitutional measure, and that the objections taken to the bill, in this respect, are ill founded.

But from an earnest desire to give the utmost possible satisfaction to the mind of the President, on so delicate and important a subject, the Secretary of the Treasury will ask his indulgence while he gives some additional illustrations of cases in which a power of erecting corporations may be exercised, under some of those heads of the specified powers of the Government, which are alledged to include the right of incorporating a bank.

1. It does not appear susceptible of a doubt, that if Congress had thought proper to provide in the collection law, that the bonds to be given for the duties should be given to the collector of each district in the name of the collector of the district A. or B. as the case might require, to enure to him & his successors in office, in trust for the United States, that it would have been consistent with the constitution to make such an arrangement. And yet this it is conceived would amount to an incorporation.

2. It is not an unusual expedient of taxation to farm particular branches of revenue, that is to mortgage or sell the

product of them for certain definite sums, leaving the collection to the parties to whom they are mortgaged or sold. There are even examples of this in the United States. Suppose that there was any particular branch of revenue which it was manifestly expedient to place on this footing, & there were a number of persons willing to engage with the Government, upon condition, that they should be incorporated & the funds vested in them, as well for their greater safety as for the more convenient recovery & management of the taxes. Is it supposeable, that there could be any constitutional obstacle to the measure? It is presumed that there could be none. It is certainly a mode of collection which it would be in the discretion of the Government to adopt; though the circumstances must be very extraordinary, that would induce the Secretary to think it expedient.

3. suppose a new & unexplored branch of trade should present itself with some foreign country. Suppose it was manifest, that, to undertake it with advantage, required an union of the capitals of a number of individuals; & that those individuals would not be disposed to embark without an incorporation, as well to obviate that consequence of a private partnership, which makes every individual liable in his whole estate for the debts of the company to their utmost extent, as for the more convenient management of the business—what reason can there be to doubt, that the national government would have a constitutional right to institute and incorporate such a company? None.

They possess a general authority to regulate trade with foreign countries. This is a mean which has been practiced to that end by all the principal commercial nations; who have trading companies to this day which have subsisted for centuries. Why may not the United States *constitutionally* employ the means *usual* in other countries for attaining the ends entrusted to them?

A power to make all needful rules & regulations concerning territory has been construed to mean a power to erect a government. A power to *regulate* trade is a power to make all needful rules & regulations concerning trade. Why may it not then include that of erecting a trading company as well as in the other case to erect a Government?

It is remarkable, that the State Conventions who have proposed amendments in relation to this point, have most, if not all of them, expressed themselves nearly thus—"Congress shall not grant monopolies, nor *erect any company* with exclusive advantages of commerce;" thus at the same time expressing their sense, that the power to erect trading companies or corporations, was inherent in Congress, & objecting to it no further, than as to the grant of *exclusive* priviledges.

The Secretary entertains all the doubts which prevail concerning the utility of such companies; but he cannot fashion to his own mind a reason to induce a doubt, that there is a constitutional authority in the United States to establish them. If such a reason were demanded, none could be given unless it were this—that congress cannot erect a corporation; which would be no better than to say they cannot do it, because they cannot do it: first presuming an inability, without reason, & then assigning that *inability* as the cause of itself.

Illustrations of this kind might be multiplied without end. They shall however be pursued no further.

There is a sort of evidence on this point, arising from an aggregate view of the constitution, which is of no inconsiderable weight. The very general power of laying & collecting taxes & appropriating their proceeds—that of borrowing money indefinitely—that of coining money & regulating foreign coins—that of making all needful rules and regulations respecting the property of the United States—these powers combined, as well as the reason & nature of the thing speak strongly this language: That it is the manifest design and scope of the constitution to vest in congress all the powers requisite to the effectual administration of the finances of the United States. As far as concerns this object, there appears to be no parsimony of power.

To suppose then, that the government is precluded from the employment of so usual as well as so important an instrument for the administration of its finances as that of a bank, is to suppose, what does not coincide with the general tenor & complexion of the constitution, and what is not agreeable to impressions that any mere spectator would entertain concerning it. Little less than a prohibitory clause can destroy the strong presumptions which result from the general aspect of the government. Nothing but demonstration should exclude the idea, that the power exists.

In all questions of this nature the practice of mankind ought to have great weight against the theories of Individuals.

The fact, for instance, that all the principal commercial nations have made use of trading corporations or companies for the purposes of *external commerce*, is a satisfactory proof, that the Establishment of them is an incident to the regulation of that commerce.

This other fact, that banks are an usual engine in the administration of national finances, & an ordinary & the most effectual instrument of loans & one which in this country has been found essential, pleads strongly against the supposition, that a government clothed with most of the most important prerogatives of sovereignty in relation to the revenues, its debts, its credit, its defence, its trade, its intercourse with foreign nations—is forbidden to make use of that instrument as an appendage to its own authority.

It has been stated as an auxiliary test of constitutional authority, to try, whether it abridges any preexisting right of any state, or any Individual. The proposed incorporation will stand the most severe examination on this point. Each state may still erect as many banks as it pleases; every individual may still carry on the banking business to any extent he pleases.

Another criterion may be this, whether the institution or thing has a more direct relation as to its uses, to the objects of the reserved powers of the State Governments, than to those of the powers delegated by the United States. This rule indeed is less precise than the former, but it may still serve as some guide. Surely a bank has more reference to the objects entrusted to the national government, than to those, left to the care of the State Governments. The common defence is decisive in this comparison.

It is presumed, that nothing of consequence in the observations of the Secretary of State and Attorney General has been left unnoticed.

There are indeed a variety of observations of the Secretary of State designed to shew that the utilities ascribed to a bank in relation to the collection of taxes and to trade, could be obtained without it, to analyse which would prolong the discussion beyond all bounds. It shall be forborne for two reasons—first because the report concerning the Bank may speak for itself in this respect; and secondly, because all those observations are grounded on the erroneous idea, that the *quantum* of necessity or utility is the test of a constitutional exercise of power.

One or two remarks only shall be made: one is that he has taken no notice of a very essential advantage to trade in general which is mentioned in the report, as peculiar to the existence of a bank circulation equal, in the public estimation to Gold & silver. It is this, that it renders it unnecessary to *lock* up the money of the country to accumulate for months successively in order to the periodical payment of interest. The other is this; that his arguments to shew that treasury orders & bills of exchange from the course of trade will prevent any considerable displacement of the metals, are founded on a partial view of the subject. A case will prove this: The sums collected in a state may be small in comparison with the debt due to it. The balance of its trade, direct & circuitous, with the seat of government may be even or nearly so. Here then without bank bills, which in that state answer the purpose of coin, there must be a displacement of the coin, in proportion to the difference between the sum collected in the State and that to be paid in it. With bank bills no such displacement would take place, or, as far as it did, it would be gradual & insensible. In many other ways also, would there be at least a temporary & inconvenient displacement of the coin, even where the course of trade would eventually return it to its proper channels.

The difference of the two situations in point of convenience to the Treasury can only be appreciated by one, who experiences the embarassments of making provision for the payment of the interest on a stock continually changing place in thirteen different places.

One thing which has been omitted just occurs, although it is not very material to the main argument. The Secretary of State affirms, that the bill only contemplates a re-payment, not a loan to the government. But here he is, certainly mistaken.

It is true, the government invests in the stock of the bank a sum equal to that which it receives on loan. But let it be remembered, that it does not, therefore, cease to be a proprietor of the stock; which would be the case, if the money received back were in the nature of a repayment. It remains a proprietor still, & will share in the profit, or loss, of the institution, according as the dividend is more or less than the interest it is to pay on the sum borrowed. Hence that sum is manifestly, and, in the strictest sense, a loan.

Philadelphia February 23d. 1791.

Report on the Subject of Manufactures

The Secretary of the Treasury in obedience to the order of ye House of Representatives, of the 15th day of January 1790, has applied his attention, at as early a period as his other duties would permit, to the subject of Manufactures; and particularly to the means of promoting such as will tend to render the United States, independent on foreign nations, for military and other essential supplies. And he there upon respectfully submits the following Report.

The expediency of encouraging manufactures in the United States, which was not long since deemed very questionable, appears at this time to be pretty generally admitted. The embarrassments, which have obstructed the progress of our external trade, have led to serious reflections on the necessity of enlarging the sphere of our domestic commerce: the restrictive regulations, which in foreign markets abrige the vent of the increasing surplus of our Agricultural produce, serve to beget an earnest desire, that a more extensive demand for that surplus may be created at home: And the complete success, which has rewarded manufacturing enterprise, in some valuable branches, conspiring with the promising symptoms, which attend some less mature essays, in others, justify a hope, that the obstacles to the growth of this species of industry are less formidable than they were apprehended to be; and that it is not difficult to find, in its further extension; a full indemnification for any external disadvantages, which are or may be experienced, as well as an accession of resources, favourable to national independence and safety.

There still are, nevertheless, respectable patrons of opinions, unfriendly to the encouragement of manufactures. The following are, substantially, the arguments, by which these opinions are defended.

"In every country (say those who entertain them) Agriculture is the most beneficial and *productive* object of human industry. This position, generally, if not universally true, applies with peculiar emphasis to the United States, on account of their immense tracts of fertile territory, uninhabited and unimproved. Nothing can afford so advantageous an employment for capital and labour, as the conversion of this extensive wilderness into cultivated farms. Nothing equally with this, can contribute to the population, strength and real riches of the country."

"To endeavor by the extraordinary patronage of Government, to accelerate the growth of manufactures, is in fact, to endeavor, by force and art, to transfer the natural current of industry, from a more, to a less beneficial channel. Whatever has such a tendency must necessarily be unwise. Indeed it can hardly ever be wise in a government, to attempt to give a direction to the industry of its citizens. This under the quick-sighted guidance of private interest, will, if left to itself, infallibly find its own way to the most profitable employment: and 'tis by such employment, that the public prosperity will be most effectually promoted. To leave industry to itself, therefore, is, in almost every case, the soundest as well as the simplest policy."

"This policy is not only recommended to the United States, by considerations which affect all nations, it is, in a manner, dictated to them by the imperious force of a very peculiar situation. The smallness of their population compared with their territory—the constant allurements to emigration from the settled to the unsettled parts of the country—the facility, with which the less independent condition of an artisan can be exchanged for the more independent condition of a farmer, these and similar causes conspire to produce, and for a length of time must continue to occasion, a scarcity of hands for manufacturing occupation, and dearness of labor generally. To these disadvantages for the prosecution of manufactures, a deficiency of pecuniary capital being added, the prospect of a successful competition with the manufactures of Europe must be regarded as little less than desperate. Extensive manufactures can only be the offspring of a redundant, at least of a full population. Till the latter shall characterise the situation of this country, 'tis vain to hope for the former."

"If contrary to the natural course of things, an unseasonable and premature spring can be given to certain fabrics, by heavy duties, prohibitions, bounties, or by other forced expedients; this will only be to sacrifice the interests of the community to those of particular classes. Besides the misdirection of labour, a virtual monopoly will be given to the persons employed on such fabrics; and an enhancement of price, the inevitable consequence of every monopoly, must be defrayed at the expence of the other parts of the society. It is far preferable, that those persons should be engaged in the cultivation of the earth, and that we should procure, in exchange for its productions, the commodities, with which foreigners are able to supply us in greater perfection, and upon better terms."

This mode of reasoning is founded upon facts and principles, which have certainly respectable pretensions. If it had governed the conduct of nations, more generally than it has done, there is room to suppose, that it might have carried them faster to prosperity and greatness, than they have attained, by the pursuit of maxims too widely opposite. Most general theories, however, admit of numerous exceptions, and there are few, if any, of the political kind, which do not blend a considerable portion of error, with the truths they inculcate.

In order to an accurate judgement how far that which has been just stated ought to be deemed liable to a similar imputation, it is necessary to advert carefully to the considerations, which plead in favour of manufactures, and which appear to recommend the special and positive encouragement of them; in certain cases, and under certain reasonable limitations.

It ought readily to be conceded, that the cultivation of the earth—as the primary and most certain source of national supply—as the immediate and chief source of subsistence to man—as the principal source of those materials which constitute the nutriment of other kinds of labor—as including a state most favourable to the freedom and independence of the human mind—one, perhaps, most conducive to the multiplication of the human species—has *intrinsically a strong claim to pre-eminence over every other kind of industry.*

But, that it has a title to any thing like an exclusive predilection, in any country, ought to be admitted with great caution. That it is even more productive than every other branch of Industry requires more evidence, than has yet been given in support of the position. That its real interests, precious and important as without the help of exaggeration, they truly are, will be advanced, rather than injured by the due encouragement of manufactures, may, it is believed, be satisfactorily demonstrated. And it is also believed that the expediency of such encouragement in a general view may be shewn to be recommended by the most cogent and persuasive motives of national policy.

It has been maintained, that Agriculture is, not only, the most productive, but the only productive species of industry. The reality of this suggestion in either aspect, has, however, not been verified by any accurate detail of facts and calculations; and the general arguments, which are adduced to prove it, are rather subtil and paradoxical, than solid or convincing.

Those which maintain its exclusive productiveness are to this effect.

Labour, bestowed upon the cultivation of land produces enough, not only to replace all the necessary expences incurred in the business, and to maintain the persons who are employed in it, but to afford together with the *ordinary profit* on the stock or capital of the Farmer, a nett surplus, or *rent* for the landlord or proprietor of the soil. But the labor of Artificers does nothing more, than replace the Stock which employs them (or which furnishes materials tools and wages) and yield the *ordinary profit* upon that Stock. It yields nothing equivalent to the *rent* of land. Neither does it add any thing to the *total value* of the *whole annual produce* of the land and labour of the country. The additional value given to those parts of the produce of land, which are wrought into manufactures, is counterbalanced by the value of those other parts of that produce, which are consumed by the manufacturers. It can therefore only be by saving, or *parsimony* not by the positive *productiveness* of their labour, that the classes of Artificers can in any degree augment the revenue of the Society.

To this it has been answered—

I   "That inasmuch as it is acknowleged, that manufacturing labour reproduces a value equal to that which is expended or consumed in carrying it on, and continues in existence the original Stock or capital employed—it ought on that account alone, to escape being considered as wholly unproductive: That though it should be admitted, as alleged, that the consumption of the produce of the soil, by the classes of Artificers or Manufacturers, is exactly equal to the value added by their labour to the materials upon which it is exerted; yet it would not thence follow, that it added nothing to the Revenue of the Society, or to the aggregate value of the annual produce of its land and labour. If the consumption for any given period amounted to a *given sum* and the *increased* value of the produce manufactured, in the same period, to a *like sum,* the total amount of the consumption and production during that period, would be equal to the *two sums,* and consequently double the value of the agricultural produce consumed. And though the increment of value produced by the classes of Artificers should at no time exceed the value of the produce of the land consumed by them, yet there would be at every moment, in consequence of their labour, a greater value of goods in the market than would exist independent of it."

II—"That the position, that Artificers can augment the revenue of a Society, only by parsimony, is true, in no other sense, than in one, which is equally applicable to Husbandmen or Cultivators. It may be alike affirmed of all these classes, that the fund acquired by their labor and destined for their support is not, in an ordinary way, more than equal to it. And hence it will follow, that augmentations of the wealth or capital of the community (except in the instances of some extraordinary dexterity or skill) can only proceed, with respect to any of them, from the savings of the more thrifty and parsimonious."

III—"That the annual produce of the land and labour of a country can only be encreased, in two ways—by some improvement in the *productive powers* of the useful labour, which actually exists within it, or by some increase in the quantity of such labour: That with regard to the first, the labour of Artificers being capable of greater subdivision and simplicity of operation, than that of Cultivators, it is susceptible, in a proportionably greater degree, of improvement in its *productive powers,* whether to be derived from an accession of Skill, or from the application of ingenious machinery; in which particular, therefore, the labour employed in the culture of land can pretend to no advantage over that engaged in manufactures: That with regard to an augmentation of the quantity of useful labour, this, excluding adventitious circumstances, must depend essentially upon an increase of *capital,* which again must depend upon the savings made out of the revenues of those, who furnish or manage *that*, which is at any time employed, whether in Agriculture, or in Manufactures, or in any other way."

But while the *exclusive* productiveness of Agricultural labour has been thus denied and refuted, the superiority of its productiveness has been conceded without hesitation. As this concession involves a point of considerable magnitude, in relation to maxims of public administration, the grounds on which it rests are worthy of a distinct and particular examination.

One of the arguments made use of, in support of the idea may be pronounced both quaint and superficial. It amounts to this—That in the productions of the soil, nature cooperates with man; and that the effect of their joint labour must be greater than that of the labour of man alone.

This however, is far from being a necessary inference. It is very conceivable, that the labor of man alone laid out upon a work, requiring great skill and art to bring it to perfection, may be more productive, *in value*, than the labour of nature and man combined, when directed towards more simple operations and objects: And when it is recollected to what an extent the Agency of nature, in the application of the mechanical powers, is made auxiliary to the prosecution of manufactures, the suggestion, which has been noticed, loses even the appearance of plausibility.

It might also be observed, with a contrary view, that the labour employed in Agriculture is in a great measure periodical and occasional, depending on seasons, liable to various and long intermissions; while that occupied in many manufactures is constant and regular, extending through the year, embracing in some instances night as well as day. It is also probable, that there are among the cultivators of land more examples of remissness, than among artificers. The farmer, from the peculiar fertility of his land, or some other favorable circumstance, may frequently obtain a livelihood, even with a considerable degree of carelessness in the mode of cultivation; but the artisan can with difficulty effect the same object, without exerting himself pretty equally with all those, who are engaged in the same pursuit. And if it may likewise be assumed as a fact, that manufactures open a wider field to exertions of ingenuity than agriculture, it would not be a strained conjecture, that the labour employed in the former, being at once more *constant*, more uniform and more ingenious, than that which is employed in the latter, will be found at the same time more productive.

But it is not meant to lay stress on observations of this nature—they ought only to serve as a counterbalance to those of a similar complexion. Circumstances so vague and general, as well as so abstract, can afford little instruction in a matter of this kind.

Another, and that which seems to be the principal argument offered for the superior productiveness of Agricultural labour, turns upon the allegation, that labour employed in manufactures yields nothing equivalent to the rent of land; or to that nett surplus, as it is called, which accrues to the proprietor of the soil.

But this distinction, important as it has been deemed, appears rather *verbal* than *substantial*.

It is easily discernible, that what in the first instance is divided into two parts under the denominations of the *ordinary profit* of the Stock of the farmer and *rent* to the landlord, is in the second instance united under the general appellation of the *ordinary profit* on the Stock of the Undertaker; and that this formal or verbal distribution constitutes the whole difference in the two cases. It seems to have been overlooked, that the land is itself a Stock or capital, advanced or lent by its owner to the occupier or tenant, and that the rent he receives is only the ordinary profit of a certain Stock in land, not managed by the proprietor himself, but by another to whom he lends or lets it, and who on his part advances a second capital to stock & improve the land, upon which he also receives the usual profit. The rent of the landlord and the profit of the farmer are therefore nothing more than the *ordinary profits* of *two* capitals belonging to *two* different persons, and united in the cultivation of a farm: As in the other case, the surplus which arises upon any manufactory, after replacing the expences of carrying it on, answers to the ordinary profits of *one* or *more* capitals engaged in the prosecution of such manufactory. It is said *one* or *more* capitals; because in fact, the same thing which is contemplated, in the case of the farm, sometimes happens in that of a manufactory. There is one, who furnishes a part of the capital, or lends a part of the money, by which it is carried on, and another, who carries it on, with the addition of his own capital. Out of the surplus, which remains, after defraying expences, an interest is paid to the money lender for the portion of the capital furnished by him, which exactly agrees with the rent paid to the landlord; and the residue of that surplus constitutes the profit of the undertaker or manufacturer, and agrees with what is denominated the ordinary profits on the Stock of the farmer. Both together make the ordinary profits of two capitals employed in a manufactory; as in the other case the rent of the landlord and the revenue of the farmer compose the ordinary profits of two Capitals employed in the cultivation of a farm.

The rent therefore accruing to the proprietor of the land, far from being a criterion of *exclusive* productiveness, as has been argued, is no criterion even of superior productiveness. The question must still be, whether the surplus, after defraying expences, of a *given capital*, employed in the *purchase* and *improvement* of a piece of land, is greater or less, than that of a like capital employed in the prosecution of a manufactory: or whether the *whole value produced* from a *given capital* and a *given quantity of labour*, employed in one way, be greater or less, than the *whole value produced* from an *equal capital* and an *equal quantity of labour* employed in the other way: or rather, perhaps whether the business of Agriculture or that of Manufactures will yield the greatest product, according to a *compound ratio* of the quantity of the Capital and the quantity of labour, which are employed in the one or in the other.

The solution of either of these questions is not easy; it involves numerous and complicated details, depending on an accurate knowlege of the objects to be compared. It is not known that the comparison has ever yet been made upon sufficient data properly ascertained and analised. To be able to make it on the present occasion with satisfactory precision would demand more previous enquiry and investigation, than there has been hitherto either leisure or opportunity to accomplish.

Some essays however have been made towards acquiring

the requisite information; which have rather served to throw doubt upon, than to confirm the Hypothesis, under examination: But it ought to be acknowledged, that they have been too little diversified, and are too imperfect, to authorise a definitive conclusion either way; leading rather to probable conjecture than to certain deduction. They render it probable, that there are various branches of manufactures, in which a given Capital will yield a greater *total* product, and a considerably greater *nett* product, than an equal capital invested in the purchase and improvement of lands; and that there are also *some* branches, in which both the *gross* and the *nett* produce will exceed that of Agricultural industry; according to a compound ratio of capital and labour: But it is on this last point, that there appears to be the greatest room for doubt. It is far less difficult to infer generally, that the *nett produce* of Capital engaged in manufacturing enterprises is greater than that of Capital engaged in Agriculture.

In stating these results, the purchase and improvement of lands, under previous cultivation are alone contemplated. The comparison is more in favour of Agriculture, when it is made with reference to the settlement of new and waste lands; but an argument drawn from so temporary a circumstance could have no weight in determining the general question concerning the permanent relative productiveness of the two species of industry. How far it ought to influence the policy of the United States, on the score of particular situation, will be adverted to in another place.

The foregoing suggestions are *not designed to inculcate an opinion that manufacturing industry is more productive than that of Agriculture*. They are intended rather to shew that the reverse of this proposition is not ascertained; that the general arguments which are brought to establish it are not satisfactory; and consequently that a supposition of the superior productiveness of Tillage ought to be no obstacle to listening to any substantial inducements to the encouragement of manufactures, which may be otherwise perceived to exist, through an apprehension, that they may have a tendency to divert labour from a more to a less profitable employment.

It is extremely probable, that on a full and accurate development of the matter, on the ground of fact and calculation, it would be discovered that there is no material difference between the aggregate productiveness of the one, and of the other kind of industry; and that the propriety of the encouragements, which may in any case be proposed to be given to either ought to be determined upon considerations irrelative to any comparison of that nature.

II   But without contending for the superior productiveness of Manufacturing Industry, it may conduce to a better judgment of the policy, which ought to be pursued respecting its encouragement, to contemplate the subject, under some additional aspects, tending not only to confirm the idea, that this kind of industry has been improperly represented as unproductive in itself; but to evince in addition that the establishment and diffusion of manufactures have the effect of rendering the total mass of useful and productive labor in a community, *greater than it would otherwise be.* In prosecuting this discussion, it may be necessary briefly to resume and review some of the topics, which have been already touched.

To affirm, that the labour of the Manufacturer is unproductive, because he consumes as much of the produce of land, as he adds value to the raw materials which he manufactures, is not better founded, than it would be to affirm, that the labour of the farmer, which furnishes materials to the manufacturer, is unproductive, *because he consumes an equal value of manufactured articles.* Each furnishes a certain portion of the produce of his labor to the other, and each destroys a correspondent portion of the produce of the labour of the other. In the mean time, the maintenance of two Citizens, instead of one, is going on; the State has two members instead of one; and they together consume twice the value of what is produced from the land.

If instead of a farmer and artificer, there were a farmer only, he would be under the necessity of devoting a part of his labour to the fabrication of cloathing and other articles, which he would procure of the artificer, in the case of there being such a person; and of course he would be able to devote less labor to the cultivation of his farm; and would draw from it a proportionably less product. The whole quantity of production, in this state of things, in provisions, raw materials and manufactures, would certainly not exceed in value the amount of what would be produced in provisions and raw materials only, if there were an artificer as well as a farmer.

Again—if there were both an artificer and a farmer, the latter would be left at liberty to pursue exclusively the cultivation of his farm. A greater quantity of provisions and raw materials would of course be produced—equal at least—as has been already observed, to the whole amount of the provisions, raw materials and manufactures, which would exist on a contrary supposition. The artificer, at the same time would be going on in the production of manufactured commodities; to an amount sufficient not only to repay the farmer, in those commodities, for the provisions and materials which were procured from him, but to furnish the Artificer himself with a supply of similar commodities for his own use. Thus then, there would be two quantities or values in existence, instead of one; and the revenue and consumption would be double in one case, what it would be in the other.

If in place of both these suppositions, there were supposed to be two farmers, and no artificer, each of whom applied a part of his labour to the culture of land, and another part to the fabrication of Manufactures—in this case, the portion of the labour of both bestowed upon land would produce the same quantity of provisions and raw materials only, as would be produced by the intire sum of the labour of one applied in the same manner, and the portion of the labour of both bestowed upon manufactures, would produce the same quantity of manufactures only, as would be produced by the intire sum of the labour of one applied in the same manner. Hence the produce of the labour of the two farmers would not be greater than the produce of the labour of the farmer and artificer; and hence, it results, that the labour of the artificer is as possitively productive as that of the farmer, and, as positively, augments the revenue of the Society.

The labour of the Artificer replaces to the farmer that portion of his labour, with which he provides the materials of exchange with the Artificer, and which he would otherwise have been compelled to apply to manufactures: and while the Artificer thus enables the farmer to enlarge his stock of Agricultural industry, a portion of which he purchases for his own use, *he also supplies himself with the manufactured articles of which he stands in need.*

He does still more—Besides this equivalent which he gives for the portion of Agricultural labour consumed by him, and this supply of manufactured commodities for his own consumption—he furnishes still a surplus, which compensates for the use of the Capital advanced either by himself or some other person, for carrying on the business. This is the ordinary profit of the Stock employed in the manufactory, and is, in every sense, as effective an addition to the income of the Society, as the rent of land.

The produce of the labour of the Artificer consequently, may be regarded as composed of three parts; one by which the provisions for his subsistence and the materials for his work are purchased of the farmer, one by which he supplies himself with manufactured necessaries, and a third which constitutes the profit on the Stock employed. The two last portions seem to have been overlooked in the system, which represents manufacturing industry as barren and unproductive.

In the course of the preceding illustrations, the products of equal quantities of the labour of the farmer and artificer have been treated as if equal to each other. But this is not to be understood as intending to assert any such precise equality. It is merely a manner of expression adopted for the sake of simplicity and perspicuity. Whether the value of the produce of the labour of the farmer be somewhat more or less, than that of the artificer, is not material to the main scope of the argument, which hitherto has only aimed at shewing, that the one, as well as the other, occasions a positive augmentation of the total produce and revenue of the Society.

It is now proper to proceed a step further, and to enumerate the principal circumstances, from which it may be inferred—That manufacturing establishments not only occasion a positive augmentation of the Produce and Revenue of the Society, but that they contribute essentially to rendering them greater than they could possibly be, without such establishments. These circumstances are—

1. The division of Labour.
2. An extension of the use of Machinery.

3. Additional employment to classes of the community not ordinarily engaged in the business.

4. The promoting of emigration from foreign Countries.

5. The furnishing greater scope for the diversity of talents and dispositions which discriminate men from each other.

6. The affording a more ample and various field for enterprize.

7. The creating in some instances a new, and securing in all, a more certain and steady demand for the surplus produce of the soil.

Each of these circumstances has a considerable influence upon the total mass of industrious effort in a community. Together, they add to it a degree of energy and effect, which are not easily conceived. Some comments upon each of them, in the order in which they have been stated, may serve to explain their importance.

I.   As to the Division of Labour.

It has justly been observed, that there is scarcely any thing of greater moment in the œconomy of a nation, than the proper division of labour. The seperation of occupations causes each to be carried to a much greater perfection, than it could possible acquire, if they were blended. This arises principally from three circumstances.

1st—The greater skill and dexterity naturally resulting from a constant and undivided application to a single object. It is evident, that these properties must increase, in proportion to the separation and simplification of objects and the steadiness of the attention devoted to each; and must be less, in proportion to the complication of objects, and the number among which the attention is distracted.

2nd. The œconomy of time—by avoiding the loss of it, incident to a frequent transition from one operation to another of a different nature. This depends on various circumstances—the transition itself—the orderly disposition of the impliments, machines and materials employed in the operation to be relinquished—the preparatory steps to the commencement of a new one—the interruption of the impulse, which the mind of the workman acquires, from being engaged in a particular operation—the distractions hesitations and reluctances, which attend the passage from one kind of business to another.

3rd. An extension of the use of Machinery. A man occupied on a single object will have it more in his power, and will be more naturally led to exert his imagination in devising methods to facilitate and abrige labour, than if he were perplexed by a variety of independent and dissimilar operations. Besides this, the fabrication of Machines, in numerous instances, becoming itself a distinct trade, the Artist who follows it, has all the advantages which have been enumerated, for improvement in his particular art; and in both ways the invention and application of machinery are extended.

And from these causes united, the mere separation of the occupation of the cultivator, from that of the Artificer, has the effect of augmenting the *productive powers* of labour, and with them, the total mass of the produce or revenue of a Country. In this single view of the subject, therefore, the utility of Artificers or Manufacturers, towards promoting an increase of productive industry, is apparent.

II.   As to an extension of the use of Machinery a point which though partly anticipated requires to be placed in one or two additional lights.

The employment of Machinery forms an item of great importance in the general mass of national industry. 'Tis an artificial force brought in aid of the natural force of man; and, to all the purposes of labour, is an increase of hands; an accession of strength, *unencumbered too by the expence of maintaining the laborer.* May it not therefore be fairly inferred, that those occupations, which give greatest scope to the use of this auxiliary, contribute most to the general Stock of industrious effort, and, in consequence, to the general product of industry?

It shall be taken for granted, and the truth of the position referred to observation, that manufacturing pursuits are susceptible in a greater degree of the application of machinery, than those of Agriculture. If so all the difference is lost to a community, which, instead of manufacturing for itself, procures the fabrics requisite to its supply from other Countries. The substitution of foreign for domestic manufactures is a transfer to foreign nations of the advantages accruing from the employment of Machinery, in the modes in which it is capable of being employed, with most utility and to the greatest extent.

The Cotton Mill invented in England, within the last twenty years, is a signal illustration of the general proposition, which has been just advanced. In consequence of it, all the different processes for spining Cotton are performed by means of Machines, which are put in motion by water, and attended chiefly by women and Children; and by a smaller number of persons, in the whole, than are requisite in the ordinary mode of spinning. And it is an advantage of great moment that the operations of this mill continue with convenience, during the night, as well as through the day. The prodigious affect of such a Machine is easily conceived. To this invention is to be attributed essentially the immense progress, which has been so suddenly made in Great Britain in the various fabrics of Cotton.

III. As to the additional employment of classes of the community, not ordinarily engaged in the particular business.

This is not among the least valuable of the means, by which manufacturing institutions contribute to augment the general stock of industry and production. In places where those institutions prevail, besides the persons regularly engaged in them, they afford occasional and extra employment to industrious individuals and families, who are willing to devote the leisure resulting from the intermissions of their ordinary pursuits to collateral labours, as a resource of multiplying their acquisitions or their enjoyments. The husbandman himself experiences a new source of profit and support from the encreased industry of his wife and daughters; invited and stimulated by the demands of the neighboring manufactories.

Besides this advantage of occasional employment to classes having different occupations, there is another of a nature allied to it and of a similar tendency. This is—the employment of persons who would otherwise be idle (and in many cases a burthen on the community), either from the byass of temper, habit, infirmity of body, or some other cause, indisposing, or disqualifying them for the toils of the Country. It is worthy of particular remark, that, in general, women and Children are rendered more useful and the latter more early useful by manufacturing establishments, than they would otherwise be. Of the number of persons employed in the Cotton Manufactories of Great Britain, it is computed that 4/7 nearly are women and children; of whom the greatest proportion are children and many of them of a very tender age.

And thus it appears to be one of the attributes of manufactures, and one of no small consequence, to give occasion to the exertion of a greater quantity of Industry, even by the *same number* of persons, where they happen to prevail, than would exist, if there were no such establishments.

IV. As to the promoting of emigration from foreign Countries.

Men reluctantly quit one course of occupation and livelihood for another, unless invited to it by very apparent and proximate advantages. Many, who would go from one country to another, if they had a prospect of continuing with more benefit the callings, to which they have been educated, will often not be tempted to change their situation, by the hope of doing better, in some other way. Manufacturers, who listening to the powerful invitations of a better price for their fabrics, or their labour, of greater cheapness of provisions and raw materials, of an exemption from the chief part of the taxes burthens and restraints, which they endure in the old world, of greater personal independence and consequence, under the operation of a more equal government, and of what is far more precious than mere religious toleration—a perfect equality of religious privileges; would probably flock from Europe to the United States to pursue their own trades or professions, if they were once made sensible of the advantages they would enjoy, and were inspired with an assurance of encouragement and employment, will, with difficulty, be induced to transplant themselves, with a view to becoming Cultivators of Land.

If it be true then, that it is the interest of the United States to open every possible avenue to emigration from abroad, it affords a weighty argument for the encouragement of manufactures; which for the reasons just assigned, will have the strongest tendency to multiply the inducements to it.

Here is perceived an important resource, not only for extending the population, and with it the useful and productive labour of the country, but likewise for the prosecution of manufactures, without deducting from the number of hands, which might otherwise be drawn to tillage; and even for the indemnification of Agriculture for such as might happen to be diverted from it. Many, whom Manufacturing views would induce to emigrate, would afterwards yield to the temptations, which the particular situation of this Country holds out to Agricultural pursuits. And while Agriculture would in other respects derive many signal and unmingled advantages, from the growth of manufactures, it is a problem whether it would gain or lose, as to the article of the number of persons employed in carrying it on.

V.   As to the furnishing greater scope for the diversity of talents and dispositions, which discriminate men from each other.

This is a much more powerful mean of augmenting the fund of national Industry than may at first sight appear. It is a just observation, that minds of the strongest and most active powers for their proper objects fall below mediocrity and labour without effect, if confined to uncongenial pursuits. And it is thence to be inferred, that the results of human exertion may be immensely increased by diversifying its objects. When all the different kinds of industry obtain in a community, each individual can find his proper element, and can call into activity the whole vigour of his nature. And the community is benefitted by the services of its respective members, in the manner, in which each can serve it with most effect.

If there be anything in a remark often to be met with— namely that there is, in the genius of the people of this country, a peculiar aptitude for mechanic improvements, it would operate as a forcible reason for giving opportunities to the exercise of that species of talent, by the propagation of manufactures.

VI.   As to the affording a more ample and various field for enterprise.

This also is of greater consequence in the general scale of national exertion, than might perhaps on a superficial view be supposed, and has effects not altogether dissimilar from those of the circumstance last noticed. To cherish and stimulate the activity of the human mind, by multiplying the objects of enterprise, is not among the least considerable of the expedients, by which the wealth of a nation may be promoted. Even things in themselves not positively advantageous, sometimes become so, by their tendency to provoke exertion. Every new scene, which is opened to the busy nature of man to rouse and exert itself, is the addition of a new energy to the general stock of effort.

The spirit of enterprise, useful and prolific as it is, must necessarily be contracted or expanded in proportion to the simplicity or variety of the occupations and productions, which are to be found in a Society. It must be less in a nation of mere cultivators, than in a nation of cultivators and merchants; less in a nation of cultivators and merchants, than in a nation of cultivators, artificers and merchants.

VII.   As to the creating, in some instances, a new, and securing in all a more certain and steady demand, for the surplus produce of the soil.

This is among the most important of the circumstances which have been indicated. It is a principal mean, by which the establishment of manufactures contributes to an augmentation of the produce or revenue of a country, and has an immediate and direct relation to the prosperity of Agriculture.

It is evident, that the exertions of the husbandman will be steady or fluctuating, vigorous or feeble, in proportion to the steadiness or fluctuation, adequateness, or inadequateness of the markets on which he must depend, for the vent of the surplus, which may be produced by his labour; and that such surplus in the ordinary course of things will be greater or less in the same proportion.

For the purpose of this vent, a domestic market is greatly to be preferred to a foreign one; because it is in the nature of things, far more to be relied upon.

It is a primary object of the policy of nations, to be able to supply themselves with subsistence from their own soils; and manufacturing nations, as far as circumstances permit, endeavor to procure, from the same source, the raw materials necessary for their own fabrics. This disposition, urged by the spirit of monopoly, is sometimes even carried to an injudicious extreme. It seems not always to be recollected, that nations, who have neither mines nor manufactures, can only obtain the manufactured articles, of which they stand in need, by an exchange of the products of their soils; and that, if those who can best furnish them with such articles are unwilling to give a due course to this exchange, they must of necessity make every possible effort to manufacture for themselves, the effect of which is that the manufacturing nations abrige the natural advantages of their situation, through an unwillingness to permit the Agricultural countries to enjoy the advantages of theirs, and sacrifice the interests of a mutually beneficial intercourse to the vain project of *selling every thing* and *buying nothing.*

But it is also a consequence of the policy, which has been noted, that the foreign demand for the products of Agricultural Countries, is, in a great degree, rather casual and occasional, than certain or constant. To what extent injurious interruptions of the demand for some of the staple commodities of the United States, may have been experienced, from that cause, must be referred to the judgment of those who are engaged in carrying on the commerce of the country; but it may be safely assumed, that such interruptions are at times very inconveniently felt, and that cases not unfrequently occur, in which markets are so confined and restricted, as to render the demand very unequal to the supply.

Independently likewise of the artificial impediments, which are created by the policy in question, there are natural causes tending to render the external demand for the surplus of Agricultural nations a precarious reliance. The differences of seasons, in the countries, which are the consumers make immense differences in the produce of their own soils, in different years; and consequently in the degrees of their necessity for foreign supply. Plentiful harvests with them, especially if similar ones occur at the same time in the countries, which are the furnishers, occasion of course a glut in the markets of the latter.

Considering how fast and how much the progress of new settlements in the United States must increase the surplus produce of the soil, and weighing seriously the tendency of the system, which prevails among most of the commercial nations of Europe; whatever dependence may be placed on the force of natural circumstances to counteract the effects of an artificial policy; there appear strong reasons to regard the foreign demand for that surplus as too uncertain a reliance, and to desire a substitute for it, in an extensive domestic market.

To secure such a market, there is no other expedient, than to promote manufacturing establishments. Manufacturers who constitute the most numerous class, after the Cultivators of land, are for that reason the principal consumers of the surplus of their labour.

This idea of an extensive domestic market for the surplus produce of the soil is of the first consequence. It is of all things, that which most effectually conduces to a flourishing state of Agriculture. If the effect of manufactories should be to detach a portion of the hands, which would otherwise be engaged in Tillage, it might possibly cause a smaller quantity of lands to be under cultivation but by their tendency to procure a more certain demand for the surplus produce of the soil, they would, at the same time, cause the lands which were in cultivation to be better improved and more productive. And while, by their influence, the condition of each individual farmer would be meliorated, the total mass of Agricultural production would probably be increased. For this must evidently depend as much, if not more, upon the degree of improvement; than upon the number of acres under culture.

It merits particular observation, that the multiplication of manufactories not only furnishes a Market for those articles, which have been accustomed to be produced in abundance, in a country; but it likewise creates a demand for such as were either unknown or produced in inconsiderable quantities. The bowels as well as the surface of the earth are ransacked for articles which were before neglected. Animals, Plants and Minerals acquire an utility and value, which were before unexplored.

The foregoing considerations seem sufficient to establish, as general propositions, That it is the interest of nations to diversify the industrious pursuits of the individuals, who compose them—That the establishment of manufactures is calculated not only to increase the general stock of useful and productive labour; but even to improve the state of Agriculture in particular; certainly to advance the interests of those who are engaged in it. There are other views, that will be hereafter taken of the subject, which, it is conceived, will serve to confirm these inferences.

III Previously to a further discussion of the objections to the encouragement of manufactures which have been stated, it will be of use to see what can be said, in reference to the particular situation of the United States, against the conclusions appearing to result from what has been already offered.

It may be observed, and the idea is of no inconsiderable weight, that however true it might be, that a State, which possessing large tracts of vacant and fertile territory, was at the same time secluded from foreign commerce, would find its interest and the interest of Agriculture, in diverting a part of its population from Tillage to Manufactures; yet it will not follow, that the same is true of a State, which having such vacant and fertile territory, has at the same time ample opportunity of procuring from abroad, on good terms, all the fabrics of which it stands in need, for the supply of its inhabitants. The power of doing this at least secures the great advantage of a division of labour; leaving the farmer free to pursue exclusively the culture of his land, and enabling him to procure with its products the manufactured supplies requisite either to his wants or to his enjoyments. And though it should be true, that in settled countries, the diversification of Industry is conducive to an increase in the productive powers of labour, and to an augmentation of revenue and capital; yet it is scarcely conceivable that there can be any thing of so solid and permanent advantage to an uncultivated and unpeopled country as to convert its wastes into cultivated and inhabited districts. If the Revenue, in the mean time, should be less, the Capital, in the event, must be greater.

To these observations, the following appears to be a satisfactory answer—

1. If the system of perfect liberty to industry and commerce were the prevailing system of nations—the arguments which dissuade a country in the predicament of the United States, from the zealous pursuits of manufactures would doubtless have great force. It will not be affirmed, that they might not be permitted, with few exceptions, to serve as a rule of national conduct. In such a state of things, each country would have the full benefit of its peculiar advantages to compensate

for its deficiencies or disadvantages. If one nation were in condition to supply manufactured articles on better terms than another, that other might find an abundant indemnification in a superior capacity to furnish the produce of the soil. And a free exchange, mutually beneficial, of the commodities which each was able to supply, on the best terms, might be carried on between them, supporting in full vigour the industry of each. And though the circumstances which have been mentioned and others, which will be unfolded hereafter render it probable, that nations merely Agricultural would not enjoy the same degree of opulence, in proportion to their numbers, as those which united manufactures with agriculture; yet the progressive improvement of the lands of the former might, in the end, atone for an inferior degree of opulence in the mean time: and in a case in which opposite considerations are pretty equally balanced, the option ought perhaps always to be, in favour of leaving Industry to its own direction.

But the system which has been mentioned, is far from characterising the general policy of Nations. The prevalent one has been regulated by an opposite spirit.

The consequence of it is, that the United States are to a certain extent in the situation of a country precluded from foreign Commerce. They can indeed, without difficulty obtain from abroad the manufactured supplies, of which they are in want; but they experience numerous and very injurious impediments to the emission and vent of their own commodities. Nor is this the case in reference to a single foreign nation only. The regulations of several countries, with which we have the most extensive intercourse, throw serious obstructions in the way of the principal staples of the United States.

In such a position of things, the United States cannot exchange with Europe on equal terms; and the want of reciprocity would render them the victim of a system, which should induce them to confine their views to Agriculture and refrain from Manufactures. A constant and encreasing necessity, on their part, for the commodities of Europe, and only a partial and occasional demand for their own, in return, could not but expose them to a state of impoverishment, compared with the opulence to which their political and natural advantages authorise them to aspire.

Remarks of this kind are not made in the spirit of complaint. 'Tis for the nations, whose regulations are alluded to, to judge for themselves, whether, by aiming at too much they do not lose more than they gain. 'Tis for the United States to consider by what means they can render themselves least dependent, on the combinations, right or wrong of foreign policy.

It is no small consolation, that already the measures which have embarrassed our Trade, have accelerated internal improvements, which upon the whole have bettered our affairs. To diversify and extend these improvements is the surest and safest method of indemnifying ourselves for any inconveniences, which those or similar measures have a tendency to beget. If Europe will not take from us the products of our soil, upon terms consistent with our interest, the natural remedy is to contract as fast as possible our wants of her.

2. The conversion of their waste into cultivated lands is certainly a point of great moment in the political calculations of the United States. But the degree in which this may possibly be retarded by the encouragement of manufactories does not appear to countervail the powerful inducements to affording that encouragement.

An observation made in another place is of a nature to have great influence upon this question. If it cannot be denied, that the interests even of Agriculture may be advanced more by having such of the lands of a state as are occupied under good cultivation, than by having a greater quantity occupied under a much inferior cultivation, and if Manufactories, for the reasons assigned, must be admitted to have a tendency to promote a more steady and vigorous cultivation of the lands occupied than would happen without them—it will follow, that they are capable of indemnifying a country for a diminution of the progress of new settlements; and may serve to increase both the capital value and the income of its lands, even though they should abrige the number of acres under Tillage.

But it does, by no means, follow, that the progress of new settlements would be retarded by the extension of Manufactures. The desire of being an independent proprietor of land is founded on such strong principles in the human breast, that where the opportunity of becoming so is as great as it is in the United States, the proportion will be small of those, whose situations would otherwise lead to it, who would be diverted from it towards Manufactures. And it is highly probable, as already intimated, that the accessions of foreigners, who originally drawn over by manufacturing views would afterwards abandon them for Agricultural, would be more than equivalent for those of our own Citizens, who might happen to be detached from them.

The remaining objections to a particular encouragement of manufactures in the United States now require to be examined.

One of these turns on the proposition, that Industry, if left to itself, will naturally find its way to the most useful and profitable employment: whence it is inferred, that manufactures without the aid of government will grow up as soon and as fast, as the natural state of things and the interest of the community may require.

Against the solidity of this hypothesis, in the full latitude of the terms, very cogent reasons may be offered. These have relation to—the strong influence of habit and the spirit of imitation—the fear of want of success in untried enterprises—the intrinsic difficulties incident to first essays towards a competition with those who have previously attained to perfection in the business to be attempted—the bounties premiums and other artificial encouragements, with which foreign nations second the exertions of their own Citizens in the branches, in which they are to be rivalled.

Experience teaches, that men are often so much governed by what they are accustomed to see and practice, that the simplest and most obvious improvements, in the most ordinary occupations, are adopted with hesitation, reluctance and by slow gradations. The spontaneous transition to new pursuits, in a community long habituated to different ones, may be expected to be attended with proportionably greater difficulty. When former occupations ceased to yield a profit adequate to the subsistence of their followers, or when there was an absolute deficiency of employment in them, owing to the superabundance of hands, changes would ensue; but these changes would be likely to be more tardy than might consist with the interest either of individuals or of the Society. In many cases they would not happen, while a bare support could be ensured by an adherence to ancient courses; though a resort to a more profitable employment might be practicable. To produce the desireable changes, as early as may be expedient, may therefore require the incitement and patronage of government.

The apprehension of failing in new attempts is perhaps a more serious impediment. There are dispositions apt to be attracted by the mere novelty of an undertaking—but these are not always those best calculated to give it success. To this, it is of importance that the confidence of cautious sagacious capitalists both citizens and foreigners, should be excited. And to inspire this description of persons with confidence, it is essential, that they should be made to see in any project, which is new, and for that reason alone, if, for no other, precarious, the prospect of such a degree of countenance and support from government, as may be capable of overcoming the obstacles, inseperable from first experiments.

The superiority antecedently enjoyed by nations, who have preoccupied and perfected a branch of industry, constitutes a more formidable obstacle, than either of those, which have been mentioned, to the introduction of the same branch into a country, in which it did not before exist. To maintain between the recent establishments of one country and the long matured establishments of another country, a competition upon equal terms, both as to quality and price, is in most cases impracticable. The disparity in the one, or in the other, or in both, must necessarily be so considerable as to forbid a successful rivalship, without the extraordinary aid and protection of government.

But the greatest obstacle of all to the successful prosecution of a new branch of industry in a country, in which it was before unknown, consists, as far as the instances apply, in the bounties premiums and other aids which are granted, in a variety of cases, by the nations, in which the establishments to be imitated are previously introduced. It is well known (and particular examples in the course of this report will be cited) that certain nations grant bounties on the exportation of particular commodities, to enable their own workmen to undersell and supplant all competitors, in the countries to which those commodities are sent. Hence the undertakers of a new manufacture have to contend not only with the natural disadvantages of a new undertaking, but with the gratuities and remunerations which other governments bestow. To be enabled to contend with success, it is evident, that the interference and aid of their own government are indispensible.

Combinations by those engaged in a particular branch of business in one country, to frustrate the first efforts to introduce it into another, by temporary sacrifices, recompensed perhaps by extraordinary indemnifications of the government of such country, are believed to have existed, and are not to be regarded as destitute of probability. The existence or assurance of aid from the government of the country, in which the business is to be introduced, may be essential to fortify adventurers against the dread of such combinations, to defeat their effects, if formed and to prevent their being formed, by demonstrating that they must in the end prove fruitless.

Whatever room there may be for an expectation that the industry of a people, under the direction of private interest, will upon equal terms find out the most beneficial employment for itself, there is none for a reliance, that it will struggle against the force of unequal terms, or will of itself surmount all the adventitious barriers to a successful competition, which may have been erected either by the advantages naturally acquired from practice and previous possession of the ground, or by those which may have sprung from positive regulations and an artificial policy. This general reflection might alone suffice as an answer to the objection under examination; exclusively of the weighty considerations which have been particularly urged.

The objections to the pursuit of manufactures in the United States, which next present themselves to discussion, represent an impracticability of success, arising from three causes—scarcity of hands—dearness of labour—want of capital.

The two first circumstances are to a certain extent real, and, within due limits, ought to be admitted as obstacles to the success of manufacturing enterprize in the United States. But there are various considerations, which lessen their force, and tend to afford an assurance that they are not sufficient to prevent the advantageous prosecution of many very useful and extensive manufactories.

With regard to scarcity of hands, the fact itself must be applied with no small qualification to certain parts of the United States. There are large districts, which may be considered as pretty fully peopled; and which notwithstanding a continual drain for distant settlement, are thickly interspersed with flourishing and increasing towns. If these districts have not already reached the point, at which the complaint of scarcity of hands ceases, they are not remote from it, and are approaching fast towards it: And having perhaps fewer attractions to agriculture, than some other parts of the Union, they exhibit a proportionably stronger tendency towards other kinds of industry. In these districts, may be discerned, no inconsiderable maturity for manufacturing establishments.

But there are circumstances, which have been already noticed with another view, that materially diminish every where the effect of a scarcity of hands. These circumstances are—the great use which can be made of women and children; on which point a very pregnant and instructive fact has been mentioned—the vast extension given by late improvements to the employment of Machines, which substituting the Agency of fire and water, has prodigiously lessened the necessity for manual labor—the employment of persons ordinarily engaged in other occupations, during the seasons, or hours of leisure; which, besides giving occasion to the exertion of a greater quantity of labour by the same number of persons, and thereby encreasing the general stock of labour, as has been elsewhere remarked, may also be taken into the calculation, as a resource for obviating the scarcity of hands—lastly the attraction of foreign emigrants. Whoever inspects, with a careful eye, the composition of our towns will be made sensible to what an extent this resource may be relied upon. This exhibits a large proportion of ingenious and valuable workmen, in different arts and trades, who, by expatriating from Europe, have improved their own condition, and added to the industry and wealth of the United States. It is a natural inference from the experience, we have already had, that as soon as the

United States shall present the countenance of a serious prosecution of Manufactures—as soon as foreign artists shall be made sensible that the state of things here affords a moral certainty of employment and encouragement—competent numbers of European workmen will transplant themselves, effectually to ensure the success of the design. How indeed can it otherwise happen considering the various and powerful inducements, which the situation of this country offers; addressing themselves to so many strong passions and feelings, to so many general and particular interests?

It may be affirmed therefore, in respect to hands for carrying on manufactures, that we shall in a great measure trade upon a foreign Stock; reserving our own, for the cultivation of our lands and the manning of our Ships; as far as character and circumstances shall incline. It is not unworthy of remark, that the objection to the success of manufactures, deduced from the scarcity of hands, is alike applicable to Trade and Navigation; and yet these are perceived to flourish, without any sensible impediment from that cause.

As to the dearness of labour (another of the obstacles alledged) this has relation principally to two circumstances, one that which has been just discussed, or the scarcity of hands, the other, the greatness of profits.

As far as it is a consequence of the scarcity of hands, it is mitigated by all the considerations which have been adduced as lessening that deficiency.

It is certain too, that the disparity in this respect, between some of the most manufacturing parts of Europe and a large proportion of the United States, is not nearly so great as is commonly imagined. It is also much less in regard to Artificers and manufacturers than in regard to country labourers; and while a careful comparison shews, that there is, in this particular, much exaggeration; it is also evident that the effect of the degree of disparity, which does truly exist, is diminished in proportion to the use which can be made of machinery.

To illustrate this last idea—Let it be supposed, that the difference of price, in two Countries, of a given quantity of manual labour requisite to the fabrication of a given article is as 10; and that some *mechanic power* is introduced into both countries, which performing half the necessary labour, leaves only half to be done by hand, it is evident, that the difference in the cost of the fabrication of the article in question, in the two countries, as far as it is connected with the price of labour, will be reduced from 10. to 5, in consequence of the introduction of that *power*.

This circumstance is worthy of the most particular attention. It diminishes immensely one of the objections most strenuously urged, against the success of manufactures in the United States.

To procure all such machines as are known in any part of Europe, can only require a proper provision and due pains. The knowledge of several of the most important of them is already possessed. The preparation of them here, is in most cases, practicable on nearly equal terms. As far as they depend on Water, some superiority of advantages may be claimed, from the uncommon variety and greater cheapness of situations adapted to Mill seats, with which different parts of the United States abound.

So far as the dearness of labour may be a consequence of the greatness of profits in any branch of business, it is no obstacle to its success. The Undertaker can afford to pay the price.

There are grounds to conclude that undertakers of Manufactures in this Country can at this time afford to pay higher wages to the workmen they may employ than are paid to similar workmen in Europe. The prices of foreign fabrics, in the markets of the United States, which will for a long time regulate the prices of the domestic ones, may be considered as compounded of the following ingredients—The first cost of materials, including the Taxes, if any, which are paid upon them where they are made: the expence of grounds, buildings machinery and tools: the wages of the persons employed in the manufactory: the profits on the capital or Stock employed: the commissions of Agents to purchase them where they are made; the expence of transportation to the United States including insurance and other incidental charges; the taxes or duties, if any and fees of office which are paid on their exportation: the taxes or duties and fees of office which are paid on their importation.

As to the first of these items, the cost of materials, the advantage upon the whole, is at present on the side of the United States, and the difference, in their favor, must increase, in proportion as a certain and extensive domestic demand shall induce the proprietors of land to devote more of their attention to the production of those materials. It ought not to escape observation, in a comparison on this point, that some of the principal manufacturing Countries of Europe are much more dependent on foreign supply for the materials of their manufactures, than would be the United States, who are capable of supplying themselves, with a greater abundance, as well as a greater variety of the requisite materials.

As to the second item, the expence of grounds buildings machinery and tools, an equality at least may be assumed; since advantages in some particulars will counterbalance temporary disadvantages in others.

As to the third item, or the article of wages, the comparison certainly turns against the United States, though as before observed not in so great a degree as is commonly supposed.

The fourth item is alike applicable to the foreign and to the domestic manufacture. It is indeed more properly a *result* than a particular, to be compared.

But with respect to all the remaining items, they are alone applicable to the foreign manufacture, and in the strictest sense extraordinaries; constituting a sum of extra charge on the foreign fabric, which cannot be estimated, at less than from 15 to 30 ℀ Cent. on the cost of it at the manufactory.

This sum of extra charge may confidently be regarded as more than a Counterpoise for the real difference in the price of labour; and is a satisfactory proof that manufactures may prosper in defiance of it in the United States. To the general allegation, connected with the circumstances of scarcity of hands and dearness of labour, that extensive manufactures can only grow out of a redundant or full population, it will be sufficient, to answer generally, that the fact has been otherwise— That the situation alleged to be an essential condition of success, has not been that of several nations, at periods when they had already attained to maturity in a variety of manufactures.

The supposed want of Capital for the prosecution of manufactures in the United States is the most indefinite of the objections which are usually opposed to it.

It is very difficult to pronounce any thing precise concerning the real extent of the monied capital of a Country, and still more concerning the proportion which it bears to the objects that invite the employment of Capital. It is not less difficult to pronounce how far the *effect* of any given quantity of money, as capital, or in other words, as a medium for circulating the industry and property of a nation, may be encreased by the very circumstance of the additional motion, which is given to it by new objects of employment. That effect, like the momentum of descending bodies, may not improperly be represented, as in a compound ratio to *mass* and *velocity*. It seems pretty certain, that a given sum of money, in a situation, in which the quick impulses of commercial activity were little felt, would appear inadequate to the circulation of as great a quantity of industry and property, as in one, in which their full influence was experienced.

It is not obvious, why the same objection might not as well be made to external commerce as to manufactures; since it is manifest that our immense tracts of land occupied and unoccupied are capable of giving employment to more capital than is actually bestowed upon them. It is certain, that the United States offer a vast field for the advantageous employment of Capital; but it does not follow, that there will not be found, in one way or another, a sufficient fund for the successful prosecution of any species of industry which is likely to prove truly beneficial.

The following considerations are of a nature to remove all inquietude on the score of want of Capital.

The introduction of Banks, as has been shewn on another occasion has a powerful tendency to extend the active Capital of a Country. Experience of the Utility of these Institutions is multiplying them in the United States. It is probable that they will be established wherever they can exist with advantage; and wherever, they can be supported, if administered with prudence, they will add new energies to all pecuniary operations.

The aid of foreign Capital may safely, and, with considerable latitude be taken into calculation. Its instrumentality has been long experienced in our external commerce; and it has begun to be felt in various other modes. Not only our funds, but our Agriculture and other internal improvements have been animated by it. It has already in a few instances extended even to our manufactures.

It is a well known fact, that there are parts of Europe, which have more Capital, than profitable domestic objects of employment. Hence, among other proofs, the large loans continually furnished to foreign states. And it is equally certain that the capital of other parts may find more profitable employment in the United States, than at home. And notwithstanding there are weighty inducements to prefer the employment of capital at home even at less profit, to an investment of it abroad, though with greater gain, yet these inducements are overruled either by a deficiency of employment or by a very material difference in profit. Both these Causes operate to produce a transfer of foreign capital to the United States. 'Tis certain, that various objects in this country hold out advantages, which are with difficulty to be equalled elsewhere; and under the increasingly favorable impressions, which are entertained of our government, the attractions will become more and More strong. These impressions will prove a rich mine of prosperity to the Country, if they are confirmed and strengthened by the progress of our affairs. And to secure this advantage, little more is now necessary, than to foster industry, and cultivate order and tranquility, at home and abroad.

It is not impossible, that there may be persons disposed to look with a jealous eye on the introduction of foreign Capital, as if it were an instrument to deprive our own citizens of the profits of our own industry: But perhaps there never could be a more unreasonable jealousy. Instead of being viewed as a rival, it ought to be Considered as a most valuable auxiliary; conducing to put in Motion a greater Quantity of productive labour, and a greater portion of useful enterprise than could exist without it. It is at least evident, that in a Country situated like the United States, with an infinite fund of resources yet to be unfolded, every farthing of foreign capital, which is laid out in internal ameliorations, and in industrious establishments of a permanent nature, is a precious acquisition.

And whatever be the objects which originally attract foreign Capital, when once introduced, it may be directed towards any purpose of beneficial exertion, which is desired. And to detain it among us, there can be no expedient so effectual as to enlarge the sphere, within which it may be usefully employed: Though induced merely with views to speculations in the funds, it may afterwards be rendered subservient to the Interests of Agriculture, Commerce & Manufactures.

But the attraction of foreign Capital for the direct purpose of Manufactures ought not to be deemed a chimerial expectation. There are already examples of it, as remarked in another place. And the examples, if the disposition be cultivated can hardly fail to multiply. There are also instances of another kind, which serve to strengthen the expectation. Enterprises for improving the Public Communications, by cutting canals, opening the obstructions in Rivers and erecting bridges, have received very material aid from the same source.

When the Manufacturing Capitalist of Europe shall advert to the many important advantages, which have been intimated, in the Course of this report, he cannot but perceive very powerful inducements to a transfer of himself and his Capital to the United States. Among the reflections, which a most interesting peculiarity of situation is calculated to suggest, it cannot escape his observation, as a circumstance of Moment in the calculation, that the progressive population and improvement of the United States, insure a continually increasing domestic demand for the fabrics which he shall produce, not to be affected by any external casualties or vicissitudes.

But while there are Circumstances sufficiently strong to authorise a considerable degree of reliance on the aid of foreign Capital towards the attainment of the object in view, it is satisfactory to have good grounds of assurance, that there are domestic resources of themselves adequate to it. It happens, that there is a species of Capital actually existing within the United States, which relieves from all inquietude on the score of want of Capital—This is the funded Debt.

The effect of a funded debt, as a species of Capital, has

been Noticed upon a former Occasion; but a more particular elucidation of the point seems to be required by the stress which is here laid upon it. This shall accordingly be attempted.

Public Funds answer the purpose of Capital, from the estimation in which they are usually held by Monied men; and consequently from the Ease and dispatch with which they can be turned into money. This capacity of prompt convertibility into money causes a transfer of stock to be in a great number of Cases equivalent to a payment in coin. And where it does not happen to suit the party who is to receive, to accept a transfer of Stock, the party who is to pay, is never at a loss to find elsewhere a purchaser of his Stock, who will furnish him in lieu of it, with the Coin of which he stands in need. Hence in a sound and settled state of the public funds, a man possessed of a sum in them can embrace any scheme of business, which offers, with as much confidence as if he were possessed of an equal sum in Coin.

This operation of public funds as capital is too obvious to be denied; but it is objected to the Idea of their operating as an *augmentation* of the Capital of the community, that they serve to occasion the *destruction* of some other capital to an equal amount.

The Capital which alone they can be supposed to destroy must consist of—The annual revenue, which is applied to the payment of Interest on the debt, and to the gradual redemption of the principal—The amount of the Coin, which is employed in circulating the funds, or, in other words, in effecting the different alienations which they undergo.

But the following appears to be the true and accurate view of this matter.

1st. As to the point of the Annual Revenue requisite for Payment of interest and redemption of principal.

As a determinate proportion will tend to perspicuity in the reasoning, let it be supposed that the annual revenue to be applied, corresponding with the modification of the 6 per Cent stock of the United States, is in the ratio of eight upon the hundred, that is in the first instance six on Account of interest, and two on account of Principal.

Thus far it is evident, that the Capital destroyed to the capital created, would bear no greater proportion, than 8 to 100. There would be withdrawn from the total mass of other capitals a sum of eight dollars to be paid to the public creditor; while he would be possessed of a sum of One Hundred dollars, ready to be applied to any purpose, to be embarked in any enterprize, which might appear to him eligible. Here then the *Augmentation* of Capital, or the excess of that which is produced, beyond that which is destroyed is equal to Ninety two dollars. To this conclusion, it may be objected, that the sum of Eight dollars is to be withdrawn annually, until the whole hundred is extinguished, and it may be inferred, that in process of time a capital will be destroyed equal to that which is at first created.

But it is nevertheless true, that during the whole of the interval, between the creation of the Capital of 100 dollars, and its reduction to a sum not greater than that of the annual revenue appropriated to its redemption—there will be a greater active capital in existence than if no debt had been Contracted. The sum drawn from other Capitals *in any one year* will not exceed eight dollars; but there will be *at every instant of time* during the whole period, in question a sum corresponding *with so much of the principal*, as remains *unredeemed*, in the hands of some person, or other, employed, or ready to be employed in some profitable undertaking. There will therefore constantly be more capital, in capacity to be employed, than capital taken from employment. The excess for the first year has been stated to be Ninety two dollars; it will diminish yearly, but there always will be an excess, until the principal of the debt is brought to a level with the *redeeming annuity*, that is, in the case which has been assumed by way of example, to *eight dollars*. The reality of this excess becomes palpable, if it be supposed, as often happens, that the citizen of a foreign Country imports into the United States 100 dollars for the purchase of an equal sum of public debt. Here is an absolute augmentation of the mass of Circulating Coin to the extent of 100 dollars. At the end of a year the foreigner is presumed to draw back eight dollars on account of his Principal and Interest, but he still leaves, Ninety two of his original Deposit in circulation, as he in like manner leaves Eighty four at the end of the second year, drawing back then

also the annuity of Eight Dollars: And thus the Matter proceeds; The capital left in circulation diminishing each year,
and coming nearer to the level of the annuity drawnback.
There are however some differences in the ultimate operation
of the part of the debt, which is purchased by foreigners, and
that which remains in the hands of citizens. But the general
effect in each case, though in different degrees, is to add to
the active capital of the Country.

Hitherto the reasoning has proceeded on a concession of
the position, that there is a destruction of some other capital,
to the extent of the annuity appropriated to the payment of
the Interest and the redemption of the principal of the debt
but in this, too much has been conceded. There is at most a
temporary transfer of some other capital, to the amount of
the Annuity, from those who pay to the Creditor who receives; which he again restores to the circulation to resume
the offices of a capital. This he does either immediately by
employing the money in some branch of Industry, or medi-
ately by lending it to some other person, who does so employ
it or by spending it on his own maintenance. In either supposition there is no destruction of capital, there is nothing
more than a suspension of its motion for a time; that is, while
it is passing from the hands of those who pay into the Public
coffers, & thence through the public Creditor into some
other Channel of circulation. When the payments of interest
are periodical and quick and made by instrumentality of
Banks the diversion or suspension of capital may almost be
denominated momentary. Hence the deduction on this Account is far less, than it at first sight appears to be.

There is evidently, as far as regards the annuity no destruction nor transfer of any other Capital, than that portion of the
income of each individual, which goes to make up the Annuity. The land which furnishes the Farmer with the sum which
he is to contribute remains the same; and the like may be observed of other Capitals. Indeed as far as the Tax, which is the
object of contribution (as frequently happens, when it does
not oppress, by its weight) may have been a Motive to *greater
exertion* in any occupation; it may even serve to encrease the
contributory Capital: This idea is not without importance in
the general view of the subject.

It remains to see, what further deduction ought to be made from the capital which is created, by the existence of the Debt; on account of the coin, which is employed in its circulation. This is susceptible of much less precise calculation, than the Article which has been just discussed. It is impossible to say what proportion of coin is necessary to carry on the alienations which any species of property usually undergoes. The quantity indeed varies according to circumstances. But it may still without hesitation be pronounced, from the quickness of the rotation, or rather of the transitions, that the *medium* of circulation always bears but a small proportion to the amount of the *property* circulated. And it is thence satisfactorily deducible, that the coin employed in the Negociations of the funds and which serves to give them activity, as capital, is incomparably less than the sum of the debt negotiated for the purposes of business.

It ought not, however, to be omitted, that the negotiation of the funds becomes itself a distinct business; which employs, and by employing diverts a portion of the circulating coin from other pursuits. But making due allowance for this circumstance there is no reason to conclude, that the effect of the diversion of coin in the whole operation bears any considerable proportion to the amount of the Capital to which it gives activity. The sum of the debt in circulation is continually at the Command, of any useful enterprise—the coin itself which circulates it, is never more than momentarily suspended from its ordinary functions. It experiences an incessant and rapid flux and reflux to and from the Channels of industry to those of speculations in the funds.

There are strong circumstances in confirmation of this Theory. The force of Monied Capital which has been displayed in Great Britain, and the height to which every species of industry has grown up under it, defy a solution from the quantity of coin which that kingdom has ever possessed. Accordingly it has been Coeval with its funding system, the prevailing opinion of the men of business, and of the generality of the most sagacious theorists of that country, that the operation of the public funds as capital has contributed to the effect in question. Among ourselves appearances thus far favour the same Conclusion. Industry in general seems to have been reanimated. There are symptoms indicating an extension of our Commerce. Our navigation has certainly of late had a Considerable spring, and there appears to be in many parts of the Union a command of capital, which till lately, since the revolution at least, was unknown. But it is at the same time to be acknowledged, that other circumstances have concurred, (and in a great degree) in producing the present state of things, and that the appearances are not yet sufficiently decisive, to be intirely relied upon.

In the question under discussion, it is important to distinguish between an *absolute increase of Capital, or an accession of real wealth*, and *an artificial increase of Capital*, as an engine of business, or as an instrument of industry and Commerce. In the first sense, a funded debt has no pretensions to being deemed an increase of Capital; in the last, it has pretensions which are not easy to be controverted. Of a similar nature is bank credit and in an inferior degree, every species of private credit.

But though a funded debt is not in the first instance, an absolute increase of Capital, or an augmentation of real wealth; yet by serving as a New power in the operation of industry, it has within certain bounds a tendency to increase the real wealth of a Community, in like manner as money borrowed by a thrifty farmer, to be laid out in the improvement of his farm may, in the end, add to his Stock of real riches.

There are respectable individuals, who from a just aversion to an accumulation of Public debt, are unwilling to concede to it any kind of utility, who can discern no good to alleviate the ill with which they suppose it pregnant; who cannot be persuaded that it ought in any sense to be viewed as an increase of capital lest it should be inferred, that the more debt the more capital, the greater the burthens the greater the blessings of the community.

But it interests the public Councils to estimate every object as it truly is; to appreciate how far the good in any measure is compensated by the ill; or the ill by the good, Either of them is seldom unmixed.

Neither will it follow, that an accumulation of debt is desireable, because a certain degree of it operates as capital. There may be a plethora in the political, as in the Natural body; There may be a state of things in which any such artificial capital is unnecessary. The debt too may be swelled to such a size, as that the greatest part of it may cease to be useful as a Capital, serving only to pamper the dissipation of idle and dissolute individuals: as that the sums required to pay the Interest upon it may become oppressive, and beyond the means, which a government can employ, consistently with its tranquility, to raise them; as that the resources of taxation, to face the debt, may have been strained too far to admit of extensions adequate to exigencies, which regard the public safety.

Where this critical point is, cannot be pronounced, but it is impossible to believe, that there is not such a point.

And as the vicissitudes of Nations beget a perpetual tendency to the accumulation of debt, there ought to be in every government a perpetual, anxious and unceasing effort to reduce that, which at any time exists, as fast as shall be practicable consistently with integrity and good faith.

Reasonings on a subject comprehending ideas so abstract and complex, so little reducible to precise calculation as those which enter into the question just discussed, are always attended with a danger of runing into fallacies. Due allowance ought therefore to be made for this possibility. But as far as the Nature of the subject admits of it, there appears to be satisfactory ground for a belief, that the public funds operate as a resource of capital to the Citizens of the United States, and, if they are a resource at all, it is an extensive one.

To all the arguments which are brought to evince the impracticability of success in manufacturing establishments in the United States, it might have been a sufficient answer to have referred to the experience of what has been already done. It is certain that several important branches have grown up and flourished with a rapidity which surprises: affording an encouraging assurance of success in future attempts: of these it may not be improper to enumerate the most considerable.

I
of
Skins.
{ Tanned and tawed leather dressed skins, shoes, boots and Slippers, harness and sadlery of all kinds. Portmanteau's and trunks, leather breeches, gloves, muffs and tippets, parchment and Glue.

II of Iron	Barr and Sheet Iron, Steel, Nail-rods & Nails, implements of husbandry, Stoves, pots and other household utensils, the steel and Iron work of carriages and for Shipbuilding, Anchors, scale beams and Weights & Various tools of Artificers, arms of different kinds; though the manufacture of these last has of late diminished for want of demand.
III of Wood	Ships, Cabinet Wares and Turnery, Wool and Cotton cards and other Machinery for manufactures and husbandry, Mathematical instruments, Coopers wares of every kind.
IV of flax & Hemp.	Cables, sail-cloth, Cordage, twine and pack-thread.
V	Bricks and coarse tiles & Potters Wares.
VI	Ardent Spirits, and malt liquors.
VII	Writing and printing Paper, sheathing and wrapping Paper, pasteboards, fillers or press papers, paper hangings.
VIII	Hats of furr and Wool and of mixtures of both, Womens Stuff and Silk shoes.
IX	Refined Sugars.
X	Oils of Animals and seeds; Soap, Spermaceti and Tallow Candles.
XI	Copper and brass wares, particularly utensils for distillers, Sugar refiners and brewers, And—Irons and other Articles for household Use, philosophical apparatus
XII	Tin Wares, for most purposes of Ordinary use.
XIII	Carriages of all kinds
XIV	Snuff, chewing & smoking Tobacco.
XV	Starch and Hairpowder.
XVI	Lampblack and other painters colours,
XVII	Gunpowder

Besides manufactories of these articles which are carried on as regular Trades, and have attained to a considerable degree of maturity, there is a vast scene of household manufacturing, which contributes more largely to the supply of the Community, than could be imagined; without having made it an object of particular enquiry. This observation is the pleasing result of the investigation, to which the subject of the report has led, and is applicable as well to the Southern as to the middle and Northern States; great quantities of coarse cloths, coatings, serges, and flannels, linsey Woolseys, hosiery of Wool, cotton & thread, coarse fustians, jeans and Muslins, checked and striped cotton and linen goods, bed ticks, Coverlets and Counterpanes, Tow linens, coarse shirtings, sheetings, toweling and table linen, and various mixtures of wool and cotton, and of Cotton & flax are made in the household way, and in many instances to an extent not only sufficient for the supply of the families in which they are made, but for sale, and (even in some cases) for exportation. It is computed in a number of districts that 2/3 3/4 and even 4/5 of all the clothing of the Inhabitants are made by themselves. The importance of so great a progress, as appears to have been made in family Manufactures, within a few years, both in a moral and political view, renders the fact highly interesting.

Neither does the above enumeration comprehend all the articles, that are manufactured as regular Trades. Many others occur, which are equally well established, but which not being of equal importance have been omitted. And there are many attempts still in their Infancy, which though attended with very favorable appearances, could not have been properly comprized in an enumeration of manufactories, already established. There are other articles also of great importance, which tho' strictly speaking manufactures are omitted, as being immediately connected with husbandry: such are flour, pot & pearl ash, Pitch, tar, turpentine and the like.

There remains to be noticed an objection to the encouragement of manufactures, of a nature different from those which question the probability of success. This is derived from its supposed tendency to give a monopoly of advantages to particular classes at the expence of the rest of the community, who, it is affirmed, would be able to procure the requisite supplies of manufactured articles on better terms from foreigners, than from our own Citizens, and who it is alledged, are reduced to a necessity of paying an enhanced price for whatever they want, by every measure, which obstructs the free competition of foreign commodities.

It is not an unreasonable supposition, that measures, which serve to abridge the free competition of foreign Articles, have a tendency to occasion an enhancement of prices and it is not to be denied that such is the effect in a number of Cases; but the fact does not uniformly correspond with the theory. A reduction of prices has in several instances immediately succeeded the establishment of a domestic manufacture. Whether it be that foreign Manufacturers endeavour to supplant by underselling our own, or whatever else be the cause, the effect has been such as is stated, and the reverse of what might have been expected.

But though it were true, that the immediate and certain effect of regulations controuling the competition of foreign with domestic fabrics was an increase of price, it is universally true, that the contrary is the ultimate effect with every successful manufacture. When a domestic manufacture has attained to perfection, and has engaged in the prosecution of it a competent number of Persons, it invariably becomes cheaper. Being free from the heavy charges, which attend the importation of foreign commodities, it can be afforded, and accordingly seldom or never fails to be sold Cheaper, in process of time, than was the foreign Article for which it is a substitute. The internal competition, which takes place, soon does away every thing like Monopoly, and by degrees reduces the price of the Article to the *minimum* of a reasonable profit on the Capital employed. This accords with the reason of the thing and with experience.

Whence it follows, that it is the interest of a community with a view to eventual and permanent oeconomy, to encourage the growth of manufactures. In a national view, a temporary enhancement of price must always be well compensated by a permanent reduction of it.

It is a reflection, which may with propriety be indulged here, that this eventual diminution of the prices of manufactured Articles; which is the result of internal manufacturing establishments, has a direct and very important tendency to benefit agriculture. It enables the farmer, to procure with a smaller quantity of his labour, the manufactured produce of which he stands in need, and consequently increases the value of his income and property.

The objections which are commonly made to the expediency of encouraging, and to the probability of succeeding in manufacturing pursuits, in the United states, having now been discussed; the Considerations which have appeared in the Course of the discussion, recommending that species of industry to the patronage of the Government, will be materially strengthened by a few general and some particular topics, which have been naturally reserved for subsequent Notice.

I There seems to be a moral certainty, that the trade of a country which is both manufacturing and Agricultural will be more lucrative and prosperous, than that of a Country, which is, merely Agricultural.

One reason for this is found in that general effort of nations (which has been already mentioned) to procure from their own soils, the articles of prime necessity requisite to their own consumption and use; and which serves to render their demand for a foreign supply of such articles in a great degree occasional and contingent. Hence, while the necessities of nations exclusively devoted to Agriculture, for the fabrics of manufacturing states are constant and regular, the wants of the latter for the products of the former, are liable to very considerable fluctuations and interruptions. The great inequalities resulting from difference of seasons, have been elsewhere remarked: This uniformity of demand on one side, and unsteadiness of it, on the other, must necessarily have a tendency to cause the general course of the exchange of commodities between the parties to turn to the disadvantage of the merely agricultural States. Peculiarity of situation, a climate and soil adapted to the production of peculiar commodities, may, sometimes, contradict the rule; but there is every reason to believe that it will be found in the Main, a just one.

Another circumstance which gives a superiority of commercial advantages to states, that manufacture as well as cultivate, consists in the more numerous attractions, which a more diversified market offers to foreign Customers, and greater scope, which it affords to mercantile enterprise. It is a position of indisputable truth in Commerce, depending too on very obvious reasons, that the greatest resort will ever be to those marts where commodities, while equally abundant, are most various. Each difference of kind holds out an additional inducement. And it is a position not less clear, that the field of enterprise must be enlarged to the Merchants of a Country, in proportion to the variety as well as the abundance of commodities which they find at home for exportation to foreign Markets.

A third circumstance, perhaps not inferior to either of the other two, conferring the superiority which has been stated has relation to the stagnations of demand for certain commodities which at some time or other interfere more or less with the sale of all. The Nation which can bring to Market, but few articles is likely to be more quickly and sensibly affected by such stagnations, than one, which is always possessed of a great variety of commodities. The former frequently finds too great a proportion of its stock of materials, for sale or exchange, lying on hand—or is obliged to make injurious sacrifices to supply its wants of foreign articles, which are *Numerous* and *urgent*, in proportion to the smallness of the number of its own. The latter commonly finds itself indemnified, by the high prices of some articles, for the low prices of others—and the Prompt and advantageous sale of those articles which are in demand enables its merchant the better to wait for a favorable change, in respect to those which are not. There is ground to believe, that a difference of situation, in this particular, has immensely different effects upon the wealth and prosperity of Nations.

From these circumstances collectively, two important inferences are to be drawn, one, that there is always a higher probability of a favorable balance of Trade, in regard to countries in which manufactures founded on the basis of a thriving Agriculture flourish, than in regard to those, which are confined wholly or almost wholly to Agriculture; the other (which is also a consequence of the first) that countries of the former description are likely to possess more pecuniary wealth, or money, than those of the latter.

Facts appear to correspond with this conclusion. The importations of manufactured supplies seem invariably to drain the merely Agricultural people of their wealth. Let the situation of the manufacturing countries of Europe be compared in this particular, with that of Countries which only cultivate, and the disparity will be striking. Other causes, it is true, help to Account for this disparity between some of them; and among these causes, the relative state of Agriculture; but between others of them, the most prominent circumstance of dissimilitude arises from the Comparative state of Manufactures. In corroboration of the same idea, it ought not to escape remark, that the West India Islands, the soils of which are the most fertile, and the Nation, which in the greatest degree supplies the rest of the world, with the precious metals, exchange to a loss with almost every other Country.

As far as experience at home may guide, it will lead to the same conclusion. Previous to the revolution, the quantity of coin, possessed by the colonies, which now compose the United states, appeared, to be inadequate to their circulation; and their debt to Great-Britain was progressive. Since the Revolution, the States, in which manufactures have most increased, have recovered fastest from the injuries of the late War, and abound most in pecuniary resources.

It ought to be admitted, however in this as in the preceding case, that causes irrelative to the state of manufactures account, in a degree, for the Phœnomena remarked. The continual progress of new settlements has a natural tendency to occasion an unfavorable balance of Trade; though it indemnifies for the inconvenience, by that increase of the national capital which flows from the conversion of waste into improved lands: And the different degrees of external commerce, which are carried on by the different States, may make material differences in the comparative state of their wealth. The first circumstance has reference to the deficiency of coin and the increase of debt previous to the revolution; the last to the advantages which the most manufacturing states appear to have enjoyed, over the others, since the termination of the late War.

But the uniform appearance of an abundance of specie, as the concomitant of a flourishing state of manufactures and of the reverse, where they do not prevail, afford a strong presumption of their favourable operation upon the wealth of a Country.

Not only the wealth; but the independence and security of a Country, appear to be materially connected with the prosperity of manufactures. Every nation, with a view to those great objects, ought to endeavour to possess within itself all the essentials of national supply. These comprise the means of *Subsistence habitation clothing* and *defence.*

The possession of these is necessary to the perfection of the body politic, to the safety as well as to the welfare of the society; the want of either, is the want of an important organ of political life and Motion; and in the various crises which await a state, it must severely feel the effects of any such deficiency. The extreme embarrassments of the United States during the late War, from an incapacity of supplying themselves, are still matter of keen recollection: A future war might be expected again to exemplify the mischiefs and dangers of a situation, to which that incapacity is still in too great a degree applicable, unless changed by timely and vigorous exertion. To effect this change as fast as shall be prudent, merits all the attention and all the Zeal of our Public Councils; 'tis the next great work to be accomplished.

The want of a Navy to protect our external commerce, as long as it shall Continue, must render it a peculiarly precarious reliance, for the supply of essential articles, and must serve to strengthen prodigiously the arguments in favour of manufactures.

To these general Considerations are added some of a more particular nature.

Our distance from Europe, the great fountain of manufactured supply, subjects us in the existing state of things, to inconvenience and loss in two Ways.

The bulkiness of those commodities which are the chief productions of the soil, necessarily imposes very heavy charges on their transportation, to distant markets. These charges, in the Cases, in which the nations, to whom our products are sent, maintain a Competition in the supply of their own markets, principally fall upon us, and form material deductions from the primitive value of the articles furnished. The charges on manufactured supplies, brought from Europe are greatly enhanced by the same circumstance of distance. These charges, again, in the cases in which our own industry maintains no competition, in our own markets, also principally fall upon us; and are an additional cause of extraordinary deduction from the primitive value of our own products; these being the materials of exchange for the foreign fabrics, which we consume.

The equality and moderation of individual property and the growing settlements of new districts, occasion in this country an unusual demand for coarse manufactures; The charges of which being greater in proportion to their greater bulk augment the disadvantage, which has been just described.

As in most countries domestic supplies maintain a very considerable competition with such foreign productions of the soil, as are imported for sale; if the extensive establishment of Manufactories in the United states does not create a similar competition in respect to manufactured articles, it appears to be clearly deducible, from the Considerations which have been mentioned, that they must sustain a double loss in their exchanges with foreign Nations; strongly conducive to an unfavorable balance of Trade, and very prejudicial to their Interests.

These disadvantages press with no small weight, on the landed interest of the Country. In seasons of peace, they cause a serious deduction from the intrinsic value of the products of the soil. In the time of a War, which shou'd either involve ourselves, or another nation, possessing a Considerable share of our carrying trade, the charges on the transportation of our commodities, bulky as most of them are, could hardly fail to prove a grievous burthen to the farmer; while obliged to depend in so great degree as he now does, upon foreign markets for the vent of the surplus of his labour.

As far as the prosperity of the Fisheries of the United states is impeded by the want of an adequate market, there arises another special reason for desiring the extension of manufactures. Besides the fish, which in many places, would be likely to make a part of the subsistence of the persons employed; it is known that the oils, bones and skins of marine animals, are of extensive use in various manufactures. Hence the prospect of an additional demand for the produce of the Fisheries.

One more point of view only remains in which to Consider the expediency of encouraging manufactures in the United states.

It is not uncommon to meet with an opinion that though

the promoting of manufactures may be the interest of a part of the Union, it is contrary to that of another part. The Northern & southern regions are sometimes represented as having adverse interests in this respect. Those are called Manufacturing, these Agricultural states; and a species of opposition is imagined to subsist between the Manufacturing and Agricultural interests.

This idea of an opposition between those two interests is the common error of the early periods of every country, but experience gradually dissipates it. Indeed they are perceived so often to succour and to befriend each other, that they come at length to be considered as one: a supposition which has been frequently abused and is not universally true. Particular encouragements of particular manufactures may be of a Nature to sacrifice the interests of landholders to those of manufacturers; But it is nevertheless a maxim well established by experience, and generally acknowledged, where there has been sufficient experience, that the *aggregate* prosperity of manufactures, and the *aggregate* prosperity of Agriculture are intimately connected. In the Course of the discussion which has had place, various weighty considerations have been adduced operating in support of that maxim. Perhaps the superior steadiness of the demand of a domestic market for the surplus produce of the soil, is alone a convincing argument of its truth.

Ideas of a contrariety of interests between the Northern and southern regions of the Union, are in the Main as unfounded as they are mischievous. The diversity of Circumstances on which such contrariety is usually predicated, authorises a directly contrary conclusion. Mutual wants constitute one of the strongest links of political connection, and the extent of these bears a natural proportion to the diversity in the means of mutual supply.

Suggestions of an opposite complexion are ever to be deplored, as unfriendly to the steady pursuit of one great common cause, and to the perfect harmony of all the parts.

In proportion as the mind is accustomed to trace the intimate connexion of interest, which subsists between all the parts of a Society united under the *same* government—the infinite variety of channels which serve to Circulate the pros-

perity of each to and through the rest—in that proportion
will it be little apt to be disturbed by solicitudes and Apprehensions which originate in local discriminations. It is a truth
as important as it is agreeable, and one to which it is not easy
to imagine exceptions, that every thing tending to establish
substantial and *permanent order*, in the affairs of a Country,
to increase the total mass of industry and opulence, is ultimately beneficial to every part of it. On the Credit of this
great truth, an acquiescence may safely be accorded, from
every quarter, to all institutions & arrangements, which
promise a confirmation of public order, and an augmentation
of National Resource.

But there are more particular considerations which serve to
fortify the idea, that the encouragement of manufactures is
the interest of all parts of the Union. If the Northern and
middle states should be the principal scenes of such establishments, they would immediately benefit the more southern, by
creating a demand for productions; some of which they have
in common with the other states, and others of which are either peculiar to them, or more abundant, or of better quality,
than elsewhere. These productions, principally are Timber,
flax, Hemp, Cotton, Wool, raw silk, Indigo, iron, lead, furs,
hides, skins and coals. Of these articles Cotton & Indigo are
peculiar to the southern states; as are hitherto *Lead* & *Coal*.
Flax and Hemp are or may be raised in greater abundance
there, than in the More Northern states; and the Wool of Virginia is said to be of better quality than that of any other
state: a Circumstance rendered the more probable by the reflection that Virginia embraces the same latitudes with the
finest Wool Countries of Europe. The Climate of the south is
also better adapted to the production of silk.

The extensive cultivation of Cotton can perhaps hardly be
expected, but from the previous establishment of domestic
Manufactories of the Article; and the surest encouragement
and vent, for the others, would result from similar establishments in respect to them.

If then, it satifactorily appears, that it is the Interest of the
United states, generally, to encourage manufactures, it merits
particular attention, that there are circumstances, which Render the present a critical moment for entering with Zeal upon

the important business. The effort cannot fail to be materially seconded by a considerable and encreasing influx of money, in consequence of foreign speculations in the funds—and by the disorders, which exist in different parts of Europe.

The first circumstance not only facilitates the execution of manufacturing enterprises; but it indicates them as a necessary mean to turn the thing itself to advantage, and to prevent its being eventually an evil. If useful employment be not found for the Money of foreigners brought to the country to be invested in purchases of the public debt, it will quickly be reexported to defray the expence of an extraordinary consumption of foreign luxuries; and distressing drains of our specie may hereafter be experienced to pay the interest and redeem the principal of the purchased debt.

This useful employment too ought to be of a Nature to produce solid and permanent improvements. If the money merely serves to give a temporary spring to foreign commerce; as it cannot procure new and lasting outlets for the products of the Country; there will be no real or durable advantage gained. As far as it shall find its way in Agricultural ameliorations, in opening canals, and in similar improvements, it will be productive of substantial utility. But there is reason to doubt, whether in such channels it is likely to find sufficient employment, and still more whether many of those who possess it, would be as readily attracted to objects of this nature, as to manufacturing pursuits; which bear greater analogy to those to which they are accustomed, and to the spirit generated by them.

To open the one field, as well as the other, will at least secure a better prospect of useful employment, for whatever accession of money, there has been or may be.

There is at the present juncture a certain fermentation of mind, a certain activity of speculation and enterprise which if properly directed may be made subservient to useful purposes; but which if left entirely to itself, may be attended with pernicious effects.

The disturbed state of Europe, inclining its citizens to emigration, the requisite workmen, will be more easily acquired, than at another time; and the effect of multiplying the opportunities of employment to those who emigrate, may be an increase of the number and extent of valuable acquisitions to the population arts and industry of the Country. To find pleasure in the calamities of other nations, would be criminal; but to benefit ourselves, by opening an asylum to those who suffer, in consequence of them, is as justifiable as it is politic.

A full view having now been taken of the inducements to the promotion of Manufactures in the United states, accompanied with an examination of the principal objections which are commonly urged *in opposition*, it is proper in the next place, to consider the means, by which it may be effected, as introductory to a Specification of the objects which in the present state of things appear the most fit to be encouraged, and of the particular measures which it may be adviseable to adopt, in respect to each.

In order to a better judgment of the Means proper to be resorted to by the United states, it will be of use to Advert to those which have been employed with success in other Countries. The principal of these are.

I   Protecting duties—or duties on those foreign articles which are the rivals of the domestic ones, intended to be encouraged.

Duties of this Nature evidently amount to a virtual bounty on the domestic fabrics since by enhancing the charges on foreign Articles, they enable the National Manufacturers to undersell all their foreign Competitors. The propriety of this species of encouragement need not be dwelt upon; as it is not only a clear result from the numerous topics which have been suggested, but is sanctioned by the laws of the United states in a variety of instances; it has the additional recommendation of being a resource of revenue. Indeed all the duties imposed on imported articles, though with an exclusive view to Revenue, have the effect in Contemplation, and except where they fall on raw materials wear a beneficent aspect towards the manufactures of the Country.

II.   Prohibitions of rival articles or duties equivalent to prohibitions.

This is another and an efficacious mean of encouraging national manufactures, but in general it is only fit to be employed when a manufacture, has made such a progress and is in so many hands as to insure a due competition, and an adequate supply on reasonable terms. Of duties equivalent to prohibitions, there are examples in the Laws of the United States, and there are other Cases to which the principle may be advantageously extended, but they are not numerous.

Considering a monopoly of the domestic market to its own manufacturers as the reigning policy of manufacturing Nations, a similar policy on the part of the United states in every proper instance, is dictated, it might almost be said, by the principles of distributive justice; certainly by the duty of endeavouring to secure to their own Citizens a reciprocity of advantages.

III   Prohibitions of the exportation of the materials of manufactures.

The desire of securing a cheap and plentiful supply for the national workmen, and, where the article is either peculiar to the Country, or of peculiar quality there, the jealousy of enabling foreign workmen to rival those of the nation, with its own Materials, are the leading motives to this species of regulation. It ought not to be affirmed, that it is in no instance proper, but it is certainly one which ought to be adopted with great circumspection and only in very plain Cases. It is seen at once, that its immediate operation, is to abridge the demand and keep down the price of the produce of some other branch of industry, generally speaking, of Agriculture, to the prejudice of those, who carry it on; and though if it be really essential to the prosperity of any very important national Manufacture, it may happen that those who are injured in the first instance, may be eventually indemnified, by the superior steadiness of an extensive domestic market, depending on that prosperity: yet in a matter, in which there is so much room for nice and difficult combinations, in which such opposite considerations combat each other, prudence seems to dictate, that the expedient in question, ought to be indulged with a sparing hand.

IV   Pecuniary bounties

This has been found one of the most efficacious means of encouraging manufactures, and it is in some views, the best. Though it has not yet been practiced upon by the Government of the United states (unless the allowance on the exportation of dried and pickled Fish and salted meat could be

considered as a bounty) and though it is less favored by public opinion than some other modes.

Its advantages, are these—

1 It is a species of encouragement more positive and direct
than any other, and for that very reason, has a more immediate tendency to stimulate and uphold new enterprises, increasing the chances of profit, and diminishing the risks of
loss, in the first attempts.

2. It avoids the inconvenience of a temporary augmentation of price, which is incident to some other modes, or it
produces it to a less degree; either by making no addition to
the charges on the rival foreign article, as in the Case of protecting duties, or by making a smaller addition. The first happens when the fund for the bounty is derived from a different
object (which may or may not increase the price of some
other article, according to the nature of that object) the second, when the fund is derived from the same or a similar object of foreign manufacture. One per cent duty on the foreign
article converted into a bounty on the domestic, will have an
equal effect with a duty of two per Cent, exclusive of such
bounty; and the price of the foreign commodity is liable to be
raised, in the one Case, in the proportion of 1 ℀ Cent; in the
other, in that of two ℀ Cent. Indeed the bounty when
drawn from another source is calculated to promote a reduction of price, because without laying any new charge on
the foreign article, it serves to introduce a competition
with it, and to increase the total quantity of the article in the
Market.

3 Bounties have not like high protecting duties, a tendency
to produce scarcity. An increase of price is not always the immediate, though, where the progress of a domestic Manufacture does not counteract a rise, it is commonly the ultimate
effect of an additional duty. In the interval, between the laying of the duty and a proportional increase of price, it may
discourage importation, by interfering with the profits to be
expected from the sale of the article.

4. Bounties are sometimes not only the best, but the only
proper expedient, for uniting the encouragement of a new
object of agriculture, with that of a new object of manufacture. It is the Interest of the farmer to have the production of

the raw material promoted, by counteracting the interference of the foreign material of the same kind. It is the interest of the manufacturer to have the material abundant and cheap. If prior to the domestic production of the Material, in sufficient quantity, to supply the manufacturer on good terms; a duty be laid upon the importation of it from abroad, with a view to promote the raising of it at home, the Interests both of the Farmer and Manufacturer will be disserved. By either destroying the requisite supply, or raising the price of the article, beyond what can be afforded to be given for it, by the Conductor of an infant manufacture, it is abandoned or fails; and there being no domestic manufactories to create a demand for the raw material, which is raised by the farmer, it is in vain, that the Competition of the like foreign article may have been destroyed.

It cannot escape notice, that a duty upon the importation of an article can no otherwise aid the domestic production of it, than giving the latter greater advantages in the home market. It can have no influence upon the advantageous sale of the article produced, in foreign markets; no tendency, therefore to promote its exportation.

The true way to conciliate these two interests, is to lay a duty on foreign *manufactures* of the material, the growth of which is desired to be encouraged, and to apply the produce of that duty by way of bounty, either upon the production of the material itself or upon its manufacture at home or upon both. In this disposition of the thing, the Manufacturer commences his enterprise under every advantage, which is attainable, as to quantity or price, of the raw material: And the Farmer if the bounty be immediately to him, is enabled by it to enter into a successful competition with the foreign material; if the bounty be to the manufacturer on so much of the domestic material as he consumes, the operation is nearly the same; he has a motive of interest to prefer the domestic Commodity, if of equal quality, even at a higher price than the foreign, so long as the difference of price is any thing short of the bounty which is allowed upon the article.

Except the simple and ordinary kinds of household Manufactures, or those for which there are very commanding local advantages, pecuniary bounties are in most cases indispensable to the introduction of a new branch. A stimulus and a support not less powerful and direct is generally speaking essential to the overcoming of the obstacles which arise from the Competitions of superior skill and maturity elsewhere. Bounties are especially essential, in regard to articles, upon which those foreigners, who have been accustomed to supply a Country, are in the practice of granting them.

The continuance of bounties on manufactures long established must almost always be of questionable policy: Because a presumption would arise in every such Case, that there were natural and inherent impediments to success. But in new undertakings, they are as justifiable, as they are oftentimes necessary.

There is a degree of prejudice against bounties from an appearance of giving away the public money, without an immediate consideration, and from a supposition, that they serve to enrich particular classes, at the expence of the Community.

But neither of these sources of dislike will bear a serious examination. There is no purpose, to which public money can be more beneficially applied, than to the acquisition of a new and useful branch of industry; no Consideration more valuable than a permanent addition to the general stock of productive labour.

As to the second source of objection, it equally lies against other modes of encouragement, which are admitted to be eligible. As often as a duty upon a foreign article makes an addition to its price, it causes an extra expence to the Community, for the benefit of the domestic manufacturer. A bounty does no more: But it is the Interest of the society in each case, to submit to a temporary expence, which is more than compensated, by an increase of industry and Wealth, by an augmentation of resources and independence; & by the circumstance of eventual cheapness, which has been noticed in another place.

It would deserve attention, however, in the employment of this species of encouragement in the United states, as a reason for moderating the degree of it in the instances, in which it might be deemed eligible, that the great distance of this country from Europe imposes very heavy charges on all the fabrics which are brought from thence, amounting from 15 to 30 ℔ Cent on their value, according to their bulk.

A Question has been made concerning the Constitutional right of the Government of the United States to apply this species of encouragement, but there is certainly no good foundation for such a question. The National Legislature has express authority "To lay and Collect taxes, duties, imposts and excises, to pay the debts and provide for the *Common defence* and *general welfare*" with no other qualifications than that "all duties, imposts and excises, shall be *uniform* throughout the United states, that no capitation or other direct tax shall be laid unless in proportion to numbers ascertained by a census or enumeration taken on the principles prescribed in the Constitution, and that "no tax or duty shall be laid on articles exported from any state." These three qualifications excepted, the power to *raise money* is *plenary*, and *indefinite*; and the objects to which it may be *appropriated* are no less comprehensive, than the payment of the public debts and the providing for the common defence and "*general Welfare.*" The terms "*general Welfare*" were doubtless intended to signify more than was expressed or imported in those which Preceded; otherwise numerous exigencies incident to the affairs of a Nation would have been left without a provision. The phrase is as comprehensive as any that could have been used; because it was not fit that the constitutional authority of the Union, to appropriate its revenues shou'd have been restricted within narrower limits than the "General Welfare" and because this necessarily embraces a vast variety of particulars, which are susceptible neither of specification nor of definition.

It is therefore of necessity left to the discretion of the National Legislature, to pronounce, upon the objects, which concern the general Welfare, and for which under that description, an appropriation of money is requisite and proper. And there seems to be no room for a doubt that whatever concerns the general Interests of *learning* of *Agriculture* of *Manufactures* and of *Commerce* are within the sphere of the national Councils *as far as regards an application of Money.*

The only qualification of the generallity of the Phrase in

question, which seems to be admissible, is this—That the object to which an appropriation of money is to be made be *General* and not *local*; its operation extending in fact, or by possibility, throughout the Union, and not being confined to a particular spot.

No objection ought to arise to this construction from a supposition that it would imply a power to do whatever else should appear to Congress conducive to the General Welfare. A power to appropriate money with this latitude which is granted too in *express terms* would not carry a power to do any other thing, not authorised in the constitution, either expressly or by fair implication.

V.   Premiums

These are of a Nature allied to bounties, though distinguishable from them, in some important features.

Bounties are applicable to the whole quantity of an article produced, or manufactured, or exported, and involve a correspondent expence. Premiums serve to reward some particular excellence or superiority, some extraordinary exertion or skill, and are dispensed only in a small number of cases. But their effect is to stimulate general effort. Contrived so as to be both honorary and lucrative, they address themselves to different passions; touching the chords as well of emulation as of Interest. They are accordingly a very economical mean of exciting the enterprise of a Whole Community.

There are various Societies in different countries, whose object is the dispensation of Premiums for the encouragement of *Agriculture Arts manufactures* and *Commerce*; and though they are for the most part voluntary associations, with comparatively slender funds, their utility has been immense. Much has been done by this mean in great Britain: Scotland in particular owes materially to it a prodigious amelioration of Condition. From a similar establishment in the United states, supplied and supported by the Government of the Union, vast benefits might reasonably be expected. Some further ideas on this head, shall accordingly be submitted, in the conclusion of this report.

VI   The Exemption of the Materials of manufactures from duty.

The policy of that Exemption as a general rule, particularly in reference to new Establishments, is obvious. It can hardly ever be adviseable to add the obstructions of fiscal burthens to the difficulties which naturally embarrass a new manufacture; and where it is matured and in condition to become an object of revenue, it is generally speaking better that the fabric, than the Material should be the subject of Taxation. Ideas of proportion between the quantum of the tax and the value of the article, can be more easily adjusted, in the former, than in the latter case. An argument for exemptions of this kind in the United States, is to be derived from the practice, as far as their necessities have permitted, of those nations whom we are to meet as competitors in our own and in foreign Markets.

There are however exceptions to it; of which some examples will be given under the next head.

The Laws of the Union afford instances of the observance of the policy here recommended, but it will probably be found adviseable to extend it to some other Cases. Of a nature, bearing some affinity to that policy is the regulation which exempts from duty the tools and implements, as well as the books, cloths and household furniture of foreign artists, who come to reside in the United states; an advantage already secured to them by the Laws of the Union, and which, it is, in every view, proper to Continue.

VII   Drawbacks of the duties which are imposed on the Materials of Manufactures.

It has already been observed as a general rule that duties on those materials, ought with certain exceptions to be foreborne. Of these exceptions, three cases occur, which may serve as examples—one—where the material is itself, an object of general or extensive consumption, and a fit and productive source of revenue: Another, where a manufacture of a simpler kind the competition of which with a like domestic article is desired to be restrained, partakes of the Nature of a raw material, from being capable, by a further process to be converted into a manufacture of a different kind, the introduction or growth of which is desired to be encouraged; a third where the Material itself is a production of the Country, and in sufficient abundance to furnish cheap and plentiful supply to the national Manufacturer.

Under the first description comes the article of Molasses. It is not only a fair object of revenue; but being a sweet, it is just that the consumers of it should pay a duty as well as the Consumers of sugar.

Cottons and linens in their White state fall under the second description. A duty upon such as are imported is proper to promote the domestic Manufacture of similar articles in the same state. A drawback of that duty is proper to encourage the printing and staining at home of those which are brought from abroad: When the first of these manufactures has attained sufficient maturity in a Country, to furnish a full supply for the second, the utility of the drawback ceases.

The article of Hemp either now does or may be expected soon to exemplify the third Case, in the United states.

Where duties on the materials of manufactures are not laid for the purpose of preventing a competition with some domestic production, the same reasons which recommend, as a general rule, the exemption of those materials from duties, would recommend as a like General rule, the allowance of draw backs, in favor of the manufacturer. Accordingly such drawbacks are familiar in countries which systematically pursue the business of manufactures; which furnishes an argument for the observance of a similar policy in the United states; and the Idea has been adopted by the laws of the Union in the instances of salt and Molasses. It is believed that it will be found advantageous to extend it to some other Articles.

VIII   The encouragement of new inventions and discoveries, at home, and of the introduction into the United States of such as may have been made in other countries; particularly those, which relate to machinery.

This is among the most useful and unexceptionable of the aids, which can be given to manufactures. The usual means of that encouragement are pecuniary rewards, and, for a time, exclusive privileges. The first must be employed, according to the occasion, and the utility of the invention, or discovery: For the last, so far as respects "authors and inventors" provision has been made by Law. But it is desireable in regard to improvements and secrets of extraordinary value, to be able to extend the same benefit to Introducers, as well as Authors and Inventors; a policy which has been practiced with advantage in other countries. Here, however, as in some other cases, there is cause to regret, that the competency of the authority of the National Government to the *good*, which might be done, is not without a question. Many aids might be given to industry; many internal improvements of primary magnitude might be promoted, by an authority operating throughout the Union, which cannot be effected, as well, if at all, by an authority confined within the limits of a single state.

But if the legislature of the Union cannot do all the good, that might be wished, it is at least desirable, that all may be done, which is practicable. Means for promoting the introduction of foreign improvements, though less efficaciously than might be accomplished with more adequate authority, will form a part of the plan intended to be submitted in the close of this report.

It is customary with manufacturing nations to prohibit, under severe penalties, the exportation of implements and machines, which they have either invented or improved. There are already objects for a similar regulation in the United States; and others may be expected to occur from time to time. The adoption of it seems to be dictated by the principle of reciprocity. Greater liberality, in such respects, might better comport with the general spirit of the country; but a selfish and exclusive policy in other quarters will not always permit the free indulgence of a spirit, which would place us upon an unequal footing. As far as prohibitions tend to prevent foreign competitors from deriving the benefit of the improvements made at home, they tend to increase the advantages of those by whom they may have been introduced; and operate as an encouragement to exertion.

IX   Judicious regulations for the inspection of manufactured commodities.

This is not among the least important of the means, by which the prosperity of manufactures may be promoted. It is indeed in many cases one of the most essential. Contributing to prevent frauds upon consumers at home and exporters to foreign countries—to improve the quality & preserve the character of the national manufactures, it cannot fail to aid the expeditious and advantageous Sale of them, and to serve as a guard against successful competition from other quarters.

The reputation of the flour and lumber of some states, and of the Pot ash of others has been established by an attention to this point. And the like good name might be procured for those articles, wheresoever produced, by a judicious and uniform system of Inspection; throughout the ports of the United States. A like system might also be extended with advantage to other commodities.

X   The facilitating of pecuniary remittances from place to place is a point of considerable moment to trade in general, and to manufactures in particular; by rendering more easy the purchase of raw materials and provisions and the payment for manufactured supplies. A general circulation of Bank paper, which is to be expected from the institution lately established will be a most valuable mean to this end. But much good would also accrue from some additional provisions respecting inland bills of exchange. If those drawn in one state payable in another were made negotiable, everywhere, and interest and damages allowed in case of protest, it would greatly promote negotiations between the Citizens of different states, by rendering them more secure; and, with it the convenience and advantage of the Merchants and manufacturers of each.

XI   The facilitating of the transportation of commodities.

Improvements favoring this object intimately concern all the domestic interests of a community; but they may without impropriety be mentioned as having an important relation to manufactures. There is perhaps scarcely any thing, which has been better calculated to assist the manufactures of Great Britain, than the ameliorations of the public roads of that Kingdom, and the great progress which has been of late made in opening canals. Of the former, the United States stand much in need; and for the latter they present uncommon facilities.

The symptoms of attention to the improvement of inland Navigation, which have lately appeared in some quarters, must fill with pleasure every breast warmed with a true Zeal for the prosperity of the Country. These examples, it is to be hoped, will stimulate the exertions of the Government and the Citizens of every state. There can certainly be no object, more worthy of the cares of the local administrations; and it were to be wished, that there was no doubt of the power of the national Government to lend its direct aid, on a comprehensive plan. This is one of those improvements, which could be prosecuted with more efficacy by the whole, than by any part or parts of the Union. There are cases in which the general interest will be in danger to be sacrificed to the collission of some supposed local interests. Jealousies, in matters of this kind, are as apt to exist, as they are apt to be erroneous.

The following remarks are sufficiently judicious and pertinent to deserve a literal quotation. "Good roads, canals, and navigable rivers, by diminishing the expence of carriage, put the *remote parts of a country* more nearly upon a level with those in the neighborhood of the town. They are *upon that account* the greatest of all improvements. They encourage the cultivation of the remote, which must always be the most extensive circle of the country. They are advantageous to the Town by breaking down the monopoly of the country in its neighborhood. They are advantageous *even to that part of the Country.* Though they introduce some rival commodities into the old Market, they open many new markets to its produce. Monopoly besides is a great enemy to good management, which can never be universally established, but in consequence of that free and universal competition, which forces every body to have recourse to it for the sake of self defence. It is not more than Fifty years ago that *some of the countries in the neighborhood of London petitioned the Parliament, against the extension of the turnpike roads, into the remoter counties. Those remoter counties, they pretended, from the cheapness of Labor, would be able to sell their grass and corn cheaper in the London Market, than themselves, and they would thereby reduce their rents and ruin their cultivation.* Their rents however have risen and their cultivation has been improved, since that time."

Specimens of a spirit, similar to that which governed the counties here spoken of present themselves too frequently to the eye of an impartial observer, and render it a wish of patriotism, that the body in this Country, in whose councils a local or partial spirit is least likely to predominate, were at liberty to pursue and promote the general interest, in those instances, in which there might be danger of the interference of such a spirit.

The foregoing are the principal of the means, by which the growth of manufactures is ordinarily promoted. It is, however, not merely necessary, that the measures of government, which have a direct view to manufactures, should be calculated to assist and protect them, but that those which only collaterally affect them, in the general course of the administration, should be gaurded from any peculiar tendency to injure them.

There are certain species of taxes, which are apt to be oppressive to different parts of the community, and among other ill effects have a very unfriendly aspect towards manufactures. All Poll or Capitation taxes are of this nature. They either proceed, according to a fixed rate, which operates unequally, and injuriously to the industrious poor; or they vest a discretion in certain officers, to make estimates and assessments which are necessarily vague, conjectural and liable to abuse. They ought therefore to be abstained from, in all but cases of distressing emergency.

All such taxes (including all taxes on occupations) which proceed according to the amount of capital *supposed* to be employed in a business, or of profits *supposed* to be made in it are unavoidably hurtful to industry. It is in vain, that the evil may be endeavoured to be mitigated by leaving it, in the first instance, in the option of the party to be taxed, to declare the amount of his capital or profits.

Men engaged in any trade of business have commonly weighty reasons to avoid disclosures, which would expose, with any thing like accuracy, the real state of their affairs. They most frequently find it better to risk oppression, than to avail themselves of so inconvenient a refuge. And the consequence is, that they often suffer oppression.

When the disclosure too, if made, is not definitive, but controulable by the discretion, or in other words, by the passions & prejudices of the revenue officers, it is not only an ineffectual protection, but the possibility of its being so is an additional reason for not resorting to it.

Allowing to the public officers the most equitable dispositions; yet where they are to exercise a discretion, without certain data, they cannot fail to be often misled by appearances. The quantity of business, which seems to be going on, is, in a vast number of cases, a very deceitful criterion of the profits which are made; yet it is perhaps the best they can have, and it is the one, on which they will most naturally rely. A business therefore which may rather require aid, from the government, than be in a capacity to be contributory to it, may find itself crushed by the mistaken conjectures of the Assessors of taxes.

Arbitrary taxes, under which denomination are comprised all those, that leave the *quantum* of the tax to be raised on each person, to the *discretion* of certain officers, are as contrary to the genius of liberty as to the maxims of industry. In this light, they have been viewed by the most judicious observers on government; who have bestowed upon them the severest epithets of reprobation; as constituting one of the worst features usually to be met with in the practice of despotic governments.

It is certain at least, that such taxes are particularly inimical to the success of manufacturing industry, and ought carefully to be avoided by a government, which desires to promote it.

The great copiousness of the subject of this Report has insensibly led to a more lengthy preliminary discussion, than was originally contemplated, or intended. It appeared proper to investigate principles, to consider objections, and to endeavour to establish the utility of the thing proposed to be encouraged; previous to a specification of the objects which might occur, as meriting or requiring encouragement, and of the measures, which might be proper, in respect to each. The first purpose having been fulfilled, it remains to pursue the second. In the selection of objects, five circumstances seem intitled to particular attention; the capacity of the Country to furnish the raw material—the degree in which the nature of the manufacture admits of a substitute for manual labour in machinery—the facility of execution—the extensiveness of the uses, to which the article can be applied—its subserviency to other interests, particularly the great one of national defence. There are however objects, to which these circumstances are little applicable, which for some special reasons, may have a claim to encouragement.

A designation of the principal raw material of which each

manufacture is composed will serve to introduce the remarks upon it. As, in the first place—

Iron

The manufactures of this article are entitled to preeminent rank. None are more essential in their kinds, nor so extensive in their uses. They constitute in whole or in part the implements or the materials or both of almost every useful occupation. Their instrumentality is everywhere conspicuous.

It is fortunate for the United States that they have peculiar advantages for deriving the full benefit of this most valuable material, and they have every motive to improve it, with systematic care. It is to be found in various parts of the United States, in great abundance and of almost every quality; and fuel the chief instrument in manufacturing it, is both cheap and plenty. This particularly applies to Charcoal; but there are productive coal mines already in operation, and strong indications, that the material is to be found in abundance, in a variety of other places.

The inquiries to which the subject of this report has led have been answered with proofs that manufactories of Iron, though generally understood to be extensive, are far more so than is commonly supposed. The kinds, in which the greatest progress has been made, have been mentioned in another place, and need not be repeated; but there is little doubt that every other kind, with due cultivation, will rapidly succeed. It is worthy of remark that several of the particular trades, of which it is the basis, are capable of being carried on without the aid of large capitals.

Iron works have very greatly increased in the United States and are prosecuted, with much more advantage than formerly. The average price before the revolution was about Sixty four Dollars ℔. Ton—at present it is about Eighty; a rise which is chiefly to be attributed to the increase of manufactures of the material.

The still further extension and multiplication of such manufactures will have the double effect of promoting the extraction of the Metal itself, and of converting it to a greater number of profitable purposes.

Those manufactures too unite in a greater degree, than almost any others, the several requisities, which have been mentioned, as proper to be consulted in the selection of objects.

The only further encouragement of manufactories of this article, the propriety of which may be considered as unquestionable, seems to be an increase of the duties on foreign rival commodities.

Steel is a branch, which has already made a considerable progress, and it is ascertained that some new enterprizes, on a more extensive scale, have been lately set on foot. The facility of carrying it to an extent, which will supply all internal demands, and furnish a considerable surplus for exportation cannot be doubted. The duty upon the importation of this article, which is at present seventy five cents ℔ Cwt., may it is conceived be safely and advantageously extended to 100 Cents. It is desireable, by decisive arrangements, to second the efforts, which are making in so very valuable a branch.

The United States already in a great measure supply themselves with Nails & Spikes. They are able, and ought certainly, to do it intirely. The first and most laborious operation, in this manufacture is performed by water mills; and of the persons afterwards employed a great proportion are boys, whose early habits of industry are of importance to the community, to the present support of their families, and to their own future comfort. It is not less curious than true, that in certain parts of the country, the making of Nails is an occasional family manufacture.

The expendiency of an additional duty on these articles is indicated by an important fact. About one million 800,000 pounds of them were imported into the United States in the course of a year ending the 30th. of September 1790. A duty of two Cents ℔ lb would, it is presumeable, speedily put an end to so considerable an importation. And it is in every view proper that an end should be put to it.

The manufacture of these articles, like that of some others, suffers from the carelessness and dishonesty of a part of those who carry it on. An inspection in certain cases might tend to correct the evil. It will deserve consideration whether a regulation of this sort cannot be applied, without inconvenience, to the exportation of the articles either to foreign countries, or from one state to another.

The implements of husbandry are made in several States in great abundance. In many places it is done by the common blacksmiths. And there is no doubt that an ample supply for the whole country can with great ease be procured among ourselves.

Various kinds of edged tools for the use of Mechanics are also made; and a considerable quantity of hollow wares; though the business of castings has not yet attained the perfection which might be wished. It is however improving, and as there are respectable capitals in good hands, embarked in the prosecution of those branches of iron manufactories, which are yet in their infancy, they may all be contemplated as objects not difficult to be acquired.

To ensure the end, it seems equally safe and prudent to extend the duty ad valorem upon all manufactures of Iron, or of which iron is the article of chief value, to ten per Cent.

Fire arms and other military weapons may it is conceived, be placed without inconvenience in the class of articles rated at 15 ℔. Cent. There are already manufactories of these articles, which only require the stimulus of a certain demand to render them adequate to the supply of the United States.

It would also be a material aid to manufactures of this nature, as well as a mean of public security, if provision should be made for an annual purchase of military weapons, of home manufacture to a certain determinate extent, in order to the formation of Arsenals; and to replace from time to time such as should be withdrawn for use, so as always to have in store the quantity of each kind, which should be deemed a competent supply.

But it may hereafter deserve legislative consideration, whether manufactories of all the necessary weapons of war ought not to be established, on account of the Government itself. Such establishments are agreeable to the usual practice of Nations and that practice seems founded on sufficient reason.

There appears to be an improvidence, in leaving these essential instruments of national defence to the casual speculations of individual adventure; a resource which can less be relied upon, in this case than in most others; the articles in question not being objects of ordinary and indispensable private consumption or use. As a general rule, manufactories on the immediate account of Government are to be avoided; but this seems to be one of the few exceptions, which that rule admits, depending on very special reasons.

Manufactures of Steel, generally, or of which steel is the article of chief value, may with advantage be placed in the class of goods rated at 7½ per Cent. As manufactures of this kind have not yet made any considerable progress, it is a reason for not rating them as high as those of iron; but as this material is the basis of them, and as their extension is not less practicable, than important, it is desireable to promote it by a somewhat higher duty than the present.

A question arises, how far it might be expedient to permit the importation of iron in pigs and bars free from duty. It would certainly be favourable to manufactures of the article; but the doubt is whether it might not interfere with its production.

Two circumstances, however, abate if they do not remove apprehension, on this score; one is, the considerable increase of price, which has been already remarked, and which renders it probable, that the free admission of foreign iron would not be inconsistent with an adequate profit to the proprietors of Iron Works; the other is, the augmentation of demand, which would be likely to attend the increase of manufactures of the article, in consequence of the additional encouragements proposed to be given. But caution nevertheless in a matter of this kind is most adviseable. The measure suggested ought perhaps rather to be contemplated, subject to the lights of further experience, than immediately adopted.

Copper

The manufactures of which this article is susceptible are also of great extent and utility. Under this description, those of brass, of which it is the principal ingreedient, are intended to be included.

The material is a natural production of the Country. Mines of Copper have actually been wrought, and with profit to the undertakers, though it is not known, that any are now in this condition. And nothing is easier, than the introduction of it, from other countries, on moderate terms, and in great plenty.

Coppersmiths and brass founders, particularly the former, are numerous in the United States; some of whom carry on business to a respectable extent.

To multiply and extend manufactories of the materials in question is worthy of attention and effort. In order to this, it is desireable to facilitate a plentiful supply of the materials. And a proper mean to this end is to place them in the class of free articles. Copper in plates and brass are already in this predicament, but copper in pigs and bars is not—neither is *lapis calaminaris*, which together with *copper* and *charcoal*, constitute the component ingredients of brass. The exemption from duty, by parity of reason, ought to embrace all such of these articles, as are objects of importation. An additional duty, on brass wares, will tend to the general end in view. These now stand at 5 ℔. Cent, while those of tin, pewter and copper are rated at 7½. There appears to be a propriety in every view in placing brass wares upon the same level with them; and it merits consideration whether the duty upon all of them ought not to be raised to 10 ℔. Cent.

Lead

There are numerous proofs, that this material abounds in the United States, and requires little to unfold it to an extent, more than equal to every domestic occasion. A prolific mine of it has long been open in the South Western parts of Virginia, and under a public administration, during the late war, yielded a considerable supply for military use. This is now in the hands of individuals, who not only carry it on with spirit; but have established manufactories of it, at Richmond, in the same State.

The duties, already laid upon the importation of this article, either in its unmanufactured, or manufactured state, ensure it a decisive advantage in the home market—which amounts to considerable encouragement. If the duty on pewter wares should be raised it would afford a further encouragement. Nothing else occurs as proper to be added.

Fossil Coal

This, as an important instrument of manufactures, may without impropriety be mentioned among the subjects of this Report.

A copious supply of it would be of great consequence to the iron branch: As an article of household fuel also it is an interesting production; the utility of which must increase in proportion to the decrease of wood, by the progress of settlement and cultivation. And its importance to navigation, as an immense article of transportation coastwise, is signally exemplified in Great Britain.

It is known, that there are several coal mines in Virginia, now worked; and appearances of their existence are familiar in a number of places.

The expediency of a bounty on all the species of coal of home production, and of premiums, on the opening of new mines, under certain qualifications, appears to be worthy of particular examination. The great importance of the article will amply justify a reasonable expence in this way, if it shall appear to be necessary to and shall be thought it likely to answer the end.

Wood

Several manufactures of this article flourish in the United States. Ships are no where built in greater perfection, and cabinet wares, generally, are made little if at all inferior to those of Europe. Their extent is such as to have admitted of considerable exportation.

An exemption from duty of the several kinds of wood ordinarily used in these manufactures seems to be all, that is requisite, by way of encouragement. It is recommended by the consideration of a similar policy being pursued in other countries, and by the expediency of giving equal advantages to our own workmen in wood. The abundance of Timber proper for ship building in the United States does not appear to be any objection to it. The increasing scarcity and the growing importance of that article, in the European countries, admonish the United States to commence, and systematically to pursue, measures for the preservation of their stock. Whatever may promote the regular establishment of Magazines of Ship Timber is in various views desireable.

Skins

There are scarcely any manufactories of greater importance, than of this article. Their direct and very happy influence upon Agriculture, by promoting the raising of Cattle of different kinds, is a very material recommendation.

It is pleasing too, to observe the extensive progress they have made in their principal branches; which are so far matured as almost to defy foreign competition. Tanneries in particular are not only carried on as a regular business, in numerous instances and in various parts of the Country; but they constitute in some places a valuable item of incidental family manufactures.

Representations however have been made, importing the expediency of further encouragement to the Leather-Branch in two ways—one by increasing the duty on the manufactures of it, which are imported—the other by prohibiting the exportation of bark. In support of the latter it is alleged that the price of bark, chiefly in consequence of large exportations, has risen within a few years from about three Dollars to four dollars and a half per cord.

These suggestions are submitted rather as intimations, which merit consideration, than as matters, the propriety of which is manifest. It is not clear, that an increase of duty is necessary: and in regard to the prohibition desired, there is no evidence of any considerable exportation hitherto; and it is most probable, that whatever augmentation of price may have taken place, is to be attributed to an extension of the home demand from the increase of manufactures, and to a decrease of the supply in consequence of the progress of Settlement; rather than to the quantities which have been exported.

It is mentioned however, as an additional reason for the prohibition, that one species of the bark usually exported is in some sort peculiar to the country, and the material of a very valuable dye, of great use in some other manufactures, in which the United States have begun a competition.

There may also be this argument in favor of an increase of duty. The object is of importance enough to claim decisive encouragement and the progress, which has been made, leaves no room to apprehend any inconvenience on the score of supply from such an increase.

It would be of benefit to this branch, if glue which is now rated at 5 perCent, were made the object of an excluding duty. It is already made in large quantities at various tanneries; and like paper, is an entire œconomy of materials, which if not manufactured would be left to perish. It may be placed with advantage in the class of articles paying 15 perCent.

Grain

Manufactures of the several species of this article have a title to peculiar favor; not only because they are most of them immediately connected with the subsistence of the citizens; but because they enlarge the demand for the most precious products of the soil.

Though flour may with propriety be noticed as a manufacture of Grain, it were useless to do it, but for the purpose of submitting the expediency of a general system of inspection, throughout the ports of the United states; which, if established upon proper principles, would be likely to improve the quality of our flour every where, and to raise its reputation in foreign markets. There are however considerations which stand in the way of such an arrangement.

Ardent spirits and malt liquors are, next to flour, the two principal manufactures of Grain. The first has made a very extensive, the last a considerable progress in the United States. In respect to both, an exclusive possession of the home market ought to be secured to the domestic manufacturers; as fast as circumstances will admit. Nothing is more practicable & nothing more desireable.

The existing laws of the United States have done much towards attaining this valuable object; but some additions to the present duties, on foreign distilled spirits, and foreign malt liquors, and perhaps an abatement of those on home made spirits, would more effectually secure it; and there does not occur any very weighty objection to either.

An augmentation of the duties on imported spirits would

favour, as well the distillation of Spirits from molasses, as that from Grain. And to secure to the nation the benefit of the manufacture, even of foreign materials, is always of great, though perhaps of secondary importance.

A strong impression prevails in the minds of those concerned in distilleries (including too the most candid and enlightened) that greater differences in the rates of duty on foreign and domestic spirits are necessary, completely to secure the successful manufacture of the latter; and there are facts which entitle this impression to attention.

It is known, that the price of molasses for some years past, has been successively rising in the West India Markets, owing partly to a competition, which did not formerly exist, and partly to an extension of demand in this country; and it is evident, that the late disturbances in those Islands, from which we draw our principal supply, must so far interfere with the production of the article, as to occasion a material enhancement of price. The destruction and devastation attendant on the insurrection in Hispaniola, in particular, must not only contribute very much to that effect, but may be expected to give it some duration. These circumstances, and the duty of three cents per Gallon on molasses, may render it difficult for the distillers of that material to maintain with adequate profit a competition, with the rum brought from the West Indies, the quality of which is so considerably superior.

The consumption of Geneva or Gin in this country is extensive. It is not long since distilleries of it have grown up among us, to any importance. They are now becoming of consequence, but being still in their infancy, they require protection.

It is represented, that the price of some of the materials is greater here, than in Holland, from which place large quantities are brought, the price of labour considerably greater, the capitals engaged in the business there much larger, than those which are employed here, the rate of profits, at which the Undertakers can afford to carry it on, much less—the prejudices, in favor of imported Gin, strong. These circumstances are alleged to outweigh the charges, which attend the bringing of the Article, from Europe to the United states and the present difference of duty, so as to obstruct the prosecution of the manufacture, with due advantage.

Experiment could perhaps alone decide with certainty the justness of the suggestions, which are made; but in relation to branches of manufacture so important, it would seem inexpedient to hazard an unfavourable issue, and better to err on the side of too great, than of too small a difference, in the particular in question.

It is therefore submitted, that an addition of two cents per Gallon be made to the duty on imported spirits of the first class of proof, with a proportionable increase on those of higher proof; and that a deduction of one cent per Gallon be made from the duty on spirits distilled within the United states, beginning with the first class of proof, and a proportionable deduction from the duty on those of higher proof.

It is ascertained, that by far the greatest part of the malt liquors consumed in the United States are the produce of domestic breweries. It is desireable, and, in all likelihood, attainable, that the whole consumption should be supplied by ourselves.

The malt liquors, made at home, though inferior to the best are equal to a great part of those, which have been usually imported. The progress already made is an earnest of what may be accomplished. The growing competition is an assurance of improvement. This will be accelerated by measures, tending to invite a greater capital into this channel of employment.

To render the encouragement to domestic breweries decisive, it may be adviseable to substitute to the present rates of duty eight cents per gallon generally; and it will deserve to be considered as a gaurd against evasions, whether there ought not to be a prohibition of their importation, except in casks of considerable capacity. It is to be hoped, that such a duty would banish from the market, foreign malt liquors of inferior quality; and that the best kind only would continue to be imported till it should be supplanted, by the efforts of equal skill or care at home.

Till that period, the importation so qualified would be an useful stimulus to improvement: And in the mean time, the payment of the increased price, for the enjoyment of a luxury, in order to the encouragement of a most useful branch of domestic industry, could not reasonably be deemed a hardship.

As a further aid to the manufactures of grain, though upon a smaller scale, the articles of Starch, hair powder and wafers, may with great propriety be placed among those, which are rated at 15 perCent. No manufactures are more simple, nor more completely within the reach of a full supply, from domestic sources, and it is a policy, as common as it is obvious, to make them the objects either of prohibitory duties, or of express prohibition.

Flax and Hemp

Manufactures of these articles have so much affinity to each other, and they are so often blended, that they may with advantage be considered in conjunction. The importance of the linnin branch to agriculture—its precious effects upon household industry—the ease, with which the materials can be produced at home to any requisite extent—the great advances, which have been already made, in the coarser fabricks of them, especially in the family way, constitute claims, of peculiar force, to the patronage of government.

This patronage may be afforded in various ways; by promoting the growth of the materials; by increasing the impediments to an advantageous competition of rival foreign articles; by direct bounties or premiums upon the home manufacture.

First. As to promoting the growth of the materials.

In respect to hemp, something has been already done by the high duty upon foreign hemp. If the facilities for domestic production were not unusually great, the policy of the duty, on the foreign raw material, would be highly questionable, as interfering with the growth of manufactures of it. But making the proper allowances for those facilities, and with an eye to the future and natural progress, of the country, the measure does not appear, upon the whole, exceptionable. A strong wish naturally suggests itself, that some method could be devised of affording a more direct encouragement to the growth both of flax and hemp; such as would be effectual, and at the same time not attended with too great inconveniences. To this end, bounties and premiums offer themselves to *consideration*; but no modification of them has yet occurred, which would not either hazard too much expence, or operate unequally in reference to the circumstances of different parts of the Union; and which would not be attended with very great difficulties in the execution.

Secondly—

As to encreasing the impediments to an advantageous competition of rival foreign articles.

To this purpose, an augmentation of the duties on importation is the obvious expedient; which, in regard to certain articles, appears to be recommended by sufficient reasons.

The principal of these articles is Sail cloth; one intimately connected with navigation and defence; and of which a flourishing manufactory is established at Boston and very promising ones at several other places.

It is presumed to be both safe and adviseable to place this in the class of articles rated at 10 Per cent. A strong reason for it results from the consideration that a bounty of two pence sterling per ell is allowed, in Great Britain, upon the exportation of the sail cloth manufactured in that Kingdom.

It would likewise appear to be good policy to raise the duty to 7½ perCent on the following articles. Drillings, Osnaburghs, Ticklenburghs, Dowlas, Canvas, Brown Rolls, Bagging, and upon all other linnens the first cost of which at the place of exportation does not exceed 35 cents per yard. A bounty of 12½ ℔ Cent, upon an average on the exportation of such or similar linens from Great-Britain encourages the manufacture of them in that country and increases the obstacles to a successful competition in the countries to which they are sent.

The quantities of tow and other household linnens manufactured in different parts of the United States and the expectations, which are derived from some late experiments, of being able to extend the use of labour-saving machines, in the coarser fabrics of linnen, obviate the danger of inconvenience, from an increase of the duty upon such articles, and authorize a hope of speedy and complete success to the endeavours, which may be used for procuring an internal supply.

Thirdly. As to direct bounties, or premiums upon the manufactured articles.

To afford more effectual encouragement to the manufacture, and at the same time to promote the cheapness of the article for the benefit of navigation, it will be of great use to allow a bounty of two Cents ℈ yard on all Sail Cloth, which is made in the United States from materials of their own growth. This would also assist the Culture of those materials. An encouragement of this kind if adopted ought to be established for a moderate term of years, to invite to new undertakings and to an extension of the old. This is an article of importance enough to warrant the employment of extraordinary means in its favor.

Cotton

There is something in the texture of this material, which adapts it in a peculiar degree to the application of Machines. The signal Utility of the mill for spinning of cotton, not long since invented in England, has been noticed in another place; but there are other machines scarcely inferior in utility which, in the different manufactories of this article are employed either exclusively, or with more than ordinary effect. This very important circumstance recommends the fabricks of cotton, in a more particular manner, to a country in which a defect of hands constitutes the greatest obstacle to success.

The variety and extent of the uses to which the manufactures of this article are applicable is another powerful argument in their favor.

And the faculty of the United States to produce the raw material in abundance, & of a quality, which though alledged to be inferior to some that is produced in other quarters, is nevertheles capable of being used with advantage, in many fabrics, and is probably susceptible of being carried, by a more experienced culture, to much greater perfection—suggests an additional and a very cogent inducement to the vigorous pursuit of the cotton branch, in its several subdivisions.

How much has been already done has been stated in a preceding part of this report.

In addition to this, it may be announced, that a society is forming with a capital which is expected to be extended to at least half a million of dollars; on behalf of which measures are already in train for prosecuting on a large scale, the making and printing of cotton goods.

These circumstances conspire to indicate the expediency of removing any obstructions, which may happen to exist, to the advantageous prosecution of the manufactories in question, and of adding such encouragements, as may appear necessary and proper.

The present duty of three cents ℔ lb. on the foreign raw material, is undoubtedly a very serious impediment to the progress of those manufactories.

The injurious tendency of similar duties either prior to the establishment, or in the infancy of the domestic manufacture of the article, as it regards the manufacture, and their worse than inutility, in relation to the home production of the material itself, have been anticipated particularly in discussing the subject of pecuniary bounties.

Cotton has not the same pretensions, with hemp, to form an exception to the general rule.

Not being, like hemp an universal production of the Country it affords less assurance of an adequate internal supply; but the chief objection arises from the doubts; which are entertained concerning the quality of the national cotton. It is alledged, that the fibre of it is considerably shorter and weaker, than that of some other places; and it has been observed as a general rule, that the nearer the place of growth to the Equator, the better the quality of the cotton. That which comes from Cayenne, Surrinam and Demarara is said to be preferable, even at a material difference of price, to the Cotton of the Islands.

While a hope may reasonably be indulged, that with due care and attention the national cotton may be made to approach nearer than it now does to that of regions, somewhat more favored by climate; and while facts authorize an opinion, that very great use may be made of it, and that it is a resource which gives greater security to the cotton fabrics of this country, than can be enjoyed by any which depends wholly on external supply it will certainly be wise, in every view, to let our infant manufactures have the full benefit of the best materials on the cheapest terms.

It is obvious that the necessity of having such materials is proportioned to the unskilfulness and inexperience of the workmen employed, who if inexpert, will not fail to commit great waste, where the materials they are to work with are of an indifferent kind.

To secure to the national manufactures so essential an advantage, a repeal of the present duty on imported cotton is indispensible.

A substitute for this, far more encouraging to domestic production, will be to grant a bounty on the national cotton, when wrought at a home manufactory; to which a bounty on the exportation of it may be added. Either or both would do much more towards promoting the growth of the article, than the merely nominal encouragement, which it is proposed to abolish. The first would also have a direct influence in encouraging the manufacture.

The bounty which has been mentioned as existing in Great Britain, upon the exportation of coarse linnens not exceeding a certain value, applies also to certain discriptions of cotton goods of similar value.

This furnishes an additional argument for allowing to the national manufacturers the species of encouragement just suggested, and indeed for adding some other aid.

One cent per yard, not less than of a given width, on all goods of cotton, or of cotton and linnen mixed, which are manufactured in the United States; with the addition of one cent ℔ lb weight of the material; if made of national cotton; would amount to an aid of considerable importance, both to the production and to the manufacture of that valuable article. And it is conceived, that the expence would be well justified by the magnitude of the object.

The printing and staining of cotton goods is known to be a distinct business from the fabrication of them. It is one easily accomplished and which, as it adds materially to the value of the article in its white state, and prepares it for a variety of new uses, is of importance to be promoted.

As imported cottons, equally with those which are made at home, may be the objects of this manufacture, it will merit consideration, whether the whole, or a part of the duty, on the white goods, ought not to be allowed to be drawn back in favor of those, who print or stain them. This measure would certainly operate as a powerful encouragement to the business; and though it may in a degree counteract the original fabrication of the articles it would probably more than compensate for this disadvantage, in the rapid growth of a collateral branch, which is of a nature sooner to attain to maturity. When a sufficient progress shall have been made, the drawback may be abrogated; and by that time the domestic supply of the articles to be printed or stained will have been extended.

If the duty of 7½ ₧. Cent on certain kinds of cotton goods were extended to all goods of cotton, or of which it is the principal material, it would probably more than counterbalance the effect of the drawback proposed, in relation to the fabrication of the article. And no material objection occurs to such an extension. The duty then considering all the circumstances which attend goods of this description could not be deemed inconveniently high; and it may be inferred from various causes that the prices of them would still continue moderate.

Manufactories of cotton goods, not long since established at Beverly, in Massachusetts, and at Providence in the state of Rhode Island and conducted with a perseverence corresponding with the patriotic motives which began them, seem to have overcome the first obstacles to success; producing corduroys, velverets, fustians, jeans, and other similar articles of a quality, which will bear a comparison with the like articles brought from Manchester. The one at Providence has the merit of being the first in introducing into the United States the celebrated cotton mill; which not only furnishes materials for that manufactory itself, but for the supply of private families for household manufacture.

Other manufactories of the same material; as regular businesses, have also been begun at different places in the state of Connecticut, but all upon a smaller scale, than those above mentioned. Some essays are also making in the printing and staining of cotton goods. There are several small establishments of this kind already on foot

Wool.

In a country, the climate of which partakes of so considerable a proportion of winter, as that of a great part of the

United States, the woolen branch cannot be regarded, as inferior to any, which relates to the cloathing of the inhabitants.

Household manufactures of this material are carried on, in different parts of the United States, to a very interesting extent; but there is only one branch, which, as a regular business, can be said to have acquired maturity. This is the making of hats.

Hats of wool, and of wool mixed with furr, are made in large quantities, in different States; & nothing seems wanting, but an adequate supply of materials, to render the manufacture commensurate with the demand.

A promising essay, towards the fabrication of cloths, cassimires and other woolen goods, is likewise going on at *Hartford* in Connecticut. Specimens of the different kinds which are made, in the possession of the Secretary, evince that these fabrics have attained a very considerable degree of perfection. Their quality certainly surpasses anything, that could have been looked for, in so short a time, and under so great disadvantages; and conspires with the scantiness of the means, which have been at the command of the directors, to form the eulogium of that public spirit, perseverance and judgment, which have been able to accomplish so much.

To cherish and bring to maturity this precious embryo must engage the most ardent wishes—and proportionable regret, as far as the means of doing it may appear difficult or uncertain.

Measures, which should tend to promote an abundant supply of wool, of good quality, would probably afford the most efficacious aid, that present circumstances permit.

To encourage the raising and improving the breed of sheep, at home, would certainly be the most desireable expedient, for that purpose; but it may not be alone sufficient, especially as it is yet a problem, whether our wool be capable of such a degree of improvement, as to render it fit for the finer fabrics.

Premiums would probably be found the best means of promoting the domestic, and bounties the foreign supply. The first may be within the compass of the institution hereafter to be submitted—The last would require a specific legislative provision. If any bounties are granted they ought of course to be adjusted with an eye to quality, as well as quantity.

A fund for the purpose may be derived from the addition of 2½ per Cent, to the present rate of duty, on Carpets and Carpeting; an increase, to which the nature of the Articles suggests no objection, and which may at the same time furnish a motive the more to the fabrication of them at home; towards which some beginnings have been made.

Silk.

The production of this Article is attended with great facility in most parts of the United States, Some pleasing essays are making in Connecticut, as well towards that, as towards the Manufacture of what is produced. Stockings, Handkerchiefs Ribbons & Buttons are made though as yet but in small quantities.

A Manufactory of Lace upon a scale not very extensive has been long memorable at Ipswich in the State of Massachusetts.

An exemption of the material from the duty, which it now pays on importation, and premiums upon the production, to be dispensed under the direction of the Institution before alluded to, seem to be the only species of encouragement adviseable at so early a stage of the thing.

Glass

The Materials for making Glass are found every where. In the United States there is no deficiency of them. The sands and Stones called Tarso, which include flinty and chrystalline substances generally, and the Salts of various plants, particularly of the Sea Weed Kali or Kelp constitute the essential ingredients. An extraordinary abundance of Fuel is a particular advantage enjoyed by this Country for such manufactures. They, however, require large Capitals and involve much manual labour.

Different manufactories of Glass are now on foot in the United States. The present duty of 12½ per Cent on all imported articles of glass amount to a considerable encouragement to those Manufactories. If any thing in addition is judged eligible, the most proper would appear to be a direct bounty, on Window Glass and black Bottles.

The first recommends itself as an object of general convenience; the last adds to that character, the circumstance of being an important item in breweries. A Complaint is made of great deficiency in this respect.

Gun Powder

No small progress has been of late made in the manufacture of this very important article: It may indeed be considered as already established; but its high importance renders its further extension very desireable.

The encouragements, which it already enjoys, are a duty of 10 per Cent on the foreign rival article, and an exemption of Salt petre one of the principal ingredients of which it is composed, from duty. A like exemption of Sulphur, another chief ingredient, would appear to be equally proper. No quantity of this Article has yet been produced, from internal sources. The use made of it in finishing the bottoms of Ships, is an additional inducement to placing it in the class of free goods. Regulations for the careful inspection of the article would have a favourable tendency.

Paper

Manufactories of paper are among those which are Arrived at the greatest maturity in the United States, and are most adequate to national supply. That of paper hangings is a branch, in which respectable progress has been made.

Nothing material seems wanting to the further success of this valuable branch which is already protected by a competent duty on similar imported Articles.

In the enumeration of the several kinds, made subject to that duty, Sheathing and Cartridge paper have been omitted. These, being the most simple manufactures of the sort, and necessary to military supply, as well as Ship building, recommend themselves equally with those of other descriptions, to encouragement, and appear to be as fully within the compass of domestic exertions.

Printed books

The great number of presses disseminated throughout the Union, seem to afford an assurance, that there is no need of being indebted to foreign Countries for the printing of the Books, which are used in the United States. A duty of ten per Cent instead of five, which is now charged upon the Article, would have a tendency to aid the business internally.

It occurs, as an objection to this, that it may have an unfavourable aspect towards literature, by raising the prices of Books in universal use in private families Schools and other Seminaries of learning. But the difference it is conceived would be without effect.

As to Books which usually fill the Libraries of the wealthier classes and of professional Men, such an Augmentation of prices, as might be occasioned by an additional duty of five per Cent would be too little felt to be an impediment to the acquisition.

And with regard to books which may be specially imported for the use of particular seminaries of learning, and of public libraries, a total exemption from duty would be adviseable, which would go far towards obviating the objection just mentioned. They are now subject to a duty of 5 ₧ Cent.

As to the books in most general family use, the constancy and universality of the demand would insure exertions to furnish them at home and the means are compleatly adequate. It may also be expected ultimately, in this as in other cases, that the extension of the domestic manufacture would conduce to the cheapness of the article.

It ought not to pass unremarked, that to encourage the printing of books is to encourage the manufacture of paper.

Refined Sugars and Chocolate.

Are among the number of extensive and prosperous domestic manufactures.

Drawbacks of the duties upon the materials, of which they are respectively made, in cases of exportation, would have a beneficial influence upon the manufacture, and would conform to a precedent, which has been already furnished, in the instance of molasses, on the exportation of distilled spirits.

Cocoa the raw material now pays a duty of one cent ₧ lb.,

while chocolate which is a prevailing and very simple manufacture, is comprised in the mass of articles rated at no more
than five ₰ Cent.

There would appear to be a propriety in encouraging the
manufacture, by a somewhat higher duty, on its foreign rival,
than is paid on the raw material. Two cents ₰ lb. on imported chocolate would, it is presumed, be without inconvenience.

The foregoing heads comprise the most important of the
several kinds of manufactures, which have occurred as requiring, and, at the same time, as most proper for public encouragement; and such measures for affording it, as have appeared
best calculated to answer the end, have been suggested.

The observations, which have accompanied this delineation
of objects, supercede the necessity of many supplementary
remarks. One or two however may not be altogether superfluous.

Bounties are in various instances proposed as one species of
encouragement.

It is a familiar objection to them, that they are difficult to
be managed and liable to frauds. But neither that difficulty
nor this danger seems sufficiently great to countervail the advantages of which they are productive, when rightly applied.
And it is presumed to have been shewn, that they are in some
cases, particularly in the infancy of new enterprises indispensable.

It will however be necessary to guard, with extraordinary
circumspection, the manner of dispensing them. The requisite
precautions have been thought of; but to enter into the detail
would swell this report, already voluminous, to a size too inconvenient.

If the principle shall not be deemed inadmissible the means
of avoiding an abuse of it will not be likely to present insurmountable obstacles. There are useful guides from practice in
other quarters.

It shall therefore only be remarked here, in relation to this
point, that any bounty, which may be applied to the *manufacture* of an article, cannot with safety extend beyond those
manufactories, at which the making of the article is a *regular
trade.*

It would be impossible to annex adequate precautions to a benefit of that nature, if extended to every private family, in which the manufacture was incidentally carried on, and its being a merely incidental occupation which engages a portion of time that would otherwise be lost, it can be advantageously carried on, without so special an aid.

The possibility of a diminution of the revenue may also present itself, as an objection to the arrangements, which have been submitted.

But there is no truth, which may be more firmly relied upon, than that the interests of the revennue are promoted, by whatever promotes an increase of National industry and wealth.

In proportion to the degree of these, is the capacity of every country to contribute to the public Treasury; and where the capacity to pay is increased, or even is not decreased, the only consequence of measures, which diminish any particular resource is a change of the object. If by encouraging the manufacture of an article at home, the revenue, which has been wont to accrue from its importation, should be lessened, an indemnification can easily be found, either out of the manufacture itself, or from some other object, which may be deemed more convenient.

The measures however, which have been submitted, taken aggregately, will for a long time to come rather augment than decrease the public revenue.

There is little room to hope, that the progress of manufactures, will so equally keep pace with the progress of population, as to prevent, even, a gradual augmentation of the product of the duties on imported articles.

As, nevertheless, an abolition in some instances, and a reduction in others of duties, which have been pledged for the public debt, is proposed, it is essential, that it should be accompanied with a competent substitute. In order to this, it is requisite, that all the additional duties which shall be laid, be appropriated in the first instance, to replace all defalcations, which may proceed from any such abolition or diminution. It is evident, at first glance, that they will not only be adequate to this, but will yield a considerable surplus.

This surplus will serve.

First. To constitute a fund for paying the bounties which shall have been decreed.

Secondly. To constitute a fund for the operations of a Board, to be established, for promoting Arts, Agriculture, Manufactures and Commerce. Of this institution, different intimations have been given, in the course of this report. An outline of a plan for it shall now be submitted.

Let a certain annual sum, be set apart, and placed under the management of Commissioners, not less than three, to consist of certain Officers of the Government and their Successors in Office.

Let these Commissioners be empowered to apply the fund confided to them—to defray the expences of the emigration of Artists, and Manufacturers in particular branches of extraordinary importance—to induce the prosecution and introduction of useful discoveries, inventions and improvements, by proportionate rewards, judiciously held out and applied—to encourage by premiums both honorable and lucrative the exertions of individuals, And of classes, in relation to the several objects, they are charged with promoting—and to afford such other aids to those objects, as may be generally designated by law.

The Commissioners to render to the Legislature an annual account of their transactions and disbursments; and all such sums as shall not have been applied to the purposes of their trust, at the end of every three years, to revert to the Treasury. It may also be enjoined upon them, not to draw out the money, but for the purpose of some specific disbursment.

It may moreover be of use, to authorize them to receive voluntary contributions; making it their duty to apply them to the particular objects for which they may have been made, if any shall have been designated by the donors.

There is reason to believe, that the progress of particular manufactures has been much retarded by the want of skilful workmen. And it often happens that the capitals employed are not equal to the purposes of bringing from abroad workmen of a superior kind. Here, in cases worthy of it, the auxiliary agency of Government would in all probability be useful. There are also valuable workmen, in every branch, who are prevented from emigrating solely by the want of means. Occasional aids to such persons properly administered might be a source of valuable acquisitions to the country.

The propriety of stimulating by rewards, the invention and introduction of useful improvements, is admitted without difficulty. But the success of attempts in this way must evidently depend much on the manner of conducting them. It is probable, that the placing of the dispensation of those rewards under some proper discretionary direction, where they may be accompanied by *collateral expedients*, will serve to give them the surest efficacy. It seems impracticable to apportion, by general rules, specific compensations for discoveries of unknown and disproportionate utility.

The great use which may be made of a fund of this nature to procure and import foreign improvements is particularly obvious. Among these, the article of machines would form a most important item.

The operation and utility of premiums have been adverted to; together with the advantages which have resulted from their dispensation, under the direction of certain public and private societies. Of this some experience has been had in the instance of the Pennsylvania society, for the Promotion of Manufactures and useful Arts; but the funds of that association have been too contracted to produce more than a very small portion of the good to which the principles of it would have led. It may confidently be affirmed that there is scarcely any thing, which has been devised, better calculated to excite a general spirit of improvement than the institutions of this nature. They are truly invaluable.

In countries where there is great private wealth much may be effected by the voluntary contributions of patriotic individuals, but in a community situated like that of the United States, the public purse must supply the deficiency of private resource. In what can it be so useful as in prompting and improving the efforts of industry?

All which is humbly submitted

Alexander Hamilton
Secy of the Treasury

December 5, 1791

"A PROMISE MUST NEVER BE BROKEN"

To Philip A. Hamilton

Philadelphia December 5
1791

I received with great pleasure My Dear Philip the letter which you wrote me last week. Your Mama and myself were very happy to learn that you are pleased with your situation and content to stay as long as shall be thought for your good. We hope and believe that nothing will happen to alter this disposition.

Your Master also informs me that you recited a lesson the first day you began, very much to his satisfaction. I expect every letter from him will give me a fresh proof of your progress. For I know that you can do a great deal, if you please, and I am sure you have too much spirit not to exert yourself, that you may make us every day more and more proud of you.

Your Mama has got an Ovid for you and is looking up your Mairs introduction. If it cannot be found tomorrow another will be procured and the books with the other articles she promised to send you will be forwarded in two or three days.

You remember that I engaged to send for you next Saturday and I will do it, unless you request me to put it off. For a promise must never be broken; and I never will make you one, which I will not fulfil as far as I am able. But it has occurred to me that the Christmas holidays are near at hand, and I suppose your school will then break up for some days and give you an opportunity of coming to stay with us for a longer time than if you should come on Saturday. Will it not be best for you, therefore, to put off your journey till the holidays? But determine as you like best and let me know what will be most pleasing to you.

A good night to my darling son.   Adieu   A Hamilton

"A FACTION DECIDEDLY HOSTILE TO ME"

To Edward Carrington

My Dear Sir   Philadelphia May 26th, 1792

Believing that I possess a share of your personal friendship and confidence and yielding to that which I feel towards you—persuaded also that our political creed is the same on *two essential points*, 1st the necessity of *Union* to the respectability and happiness of this Country and 2 the necessity of an *efficient* general government to maintain that Union—I have concluded to unbosom myself to you on the present state of political parties and views. I ask no reply to what I shall say. I only ask that you will be persuaded, the representations I shall make are agreable to the real and sincere impressions of my mind. You will make the due allowances for the influence of circumstances upon it—you will consult your own observations and you will draw such a conclusion as shall appear to you proper.

When I accepted the Office, I now hold, it was under a full persuasion, that from similarity of thinking, conspiring with personal goodwill, I should have the firm support of Mr. Madison, in the *general course* of my administration. Aware of the intrinsic difficulties of the situation and of the powers of Mr. Madison, I do not believe I should have accepted under a different supposition.

I have mentioned the similarity of thinking between that Gentleman and myself. This was relative not merely to the general principles of National Policy and Government but to the leading points which were likely to constitute questions in the administration of the finances. I mean 1 the expediency of *funding* the debt 2 the inexpediency of *discrimination* between original and present holders 3 The expediency of *assuming* the state Debts.

As to the first point, the evidence of Mr. Madisons sentiments at one period is to be found in the address of Congress of April 26th 1783, which was planned by him in conformity to his own ideas and without any previous suggestions from the Committee and with his hearty cooperation in every part of the business. His conversations upon various occasions since have been expressive of a continuance in the same sentiment, nor indeed, has he yet contradicted it by any part of his official conduct. How far there is reason to apprehend a change in this particular will be stated hereafter.

As to the second part, the same address is an evidence of Mr. Madison's sentiments at the same period. And I had been informed that at a later period he had been in the Legislature of Virginia a strenuous and successful opponent of the principle of discrimination. Add to this that a variety of conversations had taken place between him and myself respecting the public debt down to the commencement of the New Government in none of which had he glanced at the idea of a change of opinion. I wrote him a letter after my appointment in the recess of Congress to obtain his sentiments on the subject of the Finances. In his answer there is not a lisp of his new system.

As to the third point, the question of an assumption of the state Debts by the U States was in discussion when the Convention that framed the present Government was sitting at Philadelphia; and in a long conversation, which I had with Mr. Madison in an afternoon's walk I well remember that we were perfectly agreed in the expediency and propriety of such a measure, though we were both of opinion that it would be more adviseable to make it a measure of administration than an article of constitution; from the impolicy of multiplying obstacles to its reception on collateral details.

Under these circumstances, you will naturally imagine that it must have been matter of surprize to me, when I was apprised, that it was Mr. Madison's intention to oppose my plan on both the last mentioned points.

Before the debate commenced, I had a conversation with him on my report, in the course of which I alluded to the calculation I had made of his sentiments and the grounds of that calculation. He did not deny them, but alledged in his justification that the very considerable alienation of the debt, subsequent to the periods at which he had opposed a discrimination, had essentially changed the state of the question —and that as to the assumption, he had contemplated it to take place as matters stood at the peace.

While the change of opinion avowed on the point of discrimination diminished my respect for the force of Mr. Madison's mind and the soundness of his judgment—and while the idea of reserving and setting afloat a vast mass of already extinguished debt as the condition of a measure the leading objects of which were an accession of strength to the National Government and an assurance of order and vigour in the national finances by doing away the necessity of thirteen complicated and conflicting systems of finance—appeared to me somewhat extraordinary: Yet my previous impressions of the fairness of Mr. Madison's character and my reliance on his good will towards me disposed me to believe that his suggestions were sincere; and even, on the point of an assumption of the debts of the States as they stood at the peace, to lean towards a cooperation in his view; 'till on feeling the ground I found the thing impracticable, and on further reflection I thought it liable to immense difficulties. It was tried and failed with little countenance.

At this time and afterwards repeated intimations were given to me that Mr. Madison, from a spirit of rivalship or some other cause had become personally unfriendly to me; and one Gentleman in particular, whose honor I have no reason to doubt, assured me, that Mr. Madison in a conversation with him had made a pretty direct attempt to insinuate unfavourable impressions of me.

Still I suspended my opinion on the subject. I knew the malevolent officiousness of mankind too well to yield a very ready acquiescence to the suggestions which were made, and resolved to wait 'till time and more experience should afford a solution.

It was not 'till the last session that I became unequivocally convinced of the following truth—*"That Mr. Madison cooperating with Mr. Jefferson is at the head of a faction decidedly hostile to me and my administration, and actuated by views in my judgment subversive of the principles of good government and dangerous to the union, peace and happiness of the Country."*

These are strong expressions; they may pain your friendship for one or both of the Gentlemen whom I have named. I have not lightly resolved to hazard them. They are the result of a *Serious alarm* in my mind for the public welfare, and of a full conviction that what I have alledged is a truth, and a truth, which ought to be told and well attended to, by all the friends of Union and efficient National Government. The suggestion will, I hope, at least awaken attention, free from the byass of former prepossessions.

This conviction in my mind is the result of a long train of circumstances; many of them minute. To attempt to detail them all would fill a volume. I shall therefore confine myself to the mention of a few.

First—As to the point of opposition to me and my administration.

Mr. Jefferson with very little reserve manifests his dislike of the funding system generally; calling in question the expediency of funding a debt at all. Some expressions which he has dropped in my own presence (sometimes without sufficient attention to delicacy) will not permit me to doubt on this point, representations, which I have had from various respectable quarters. I do not mean, that he advocates directly the undoing of what has been done, but he censures the whole on principles, which if they should become general, could not but end in the subversion of the system.

In various conversations with *foreigners* as well as citizens, he has thrown censure on my *principles* of government and on my measures of administration. He has predicted that the people would not long tolerate my proceedings & that I should not long maintain my ground. Some of those, whom he *immediately* and *notoriously* moves, have *even* whispered suspicions of the rectitude of my motives and conduct. In the question concerning the Bank he not only delivered an opinion in writing against its constitutionality & expediency; but he did it *in a stile and manner* which I felt as partaking of asperity and ill humour towards me. As one of the trustees of the sinking fund, I have experienced in almost every leading question opposition from him. When any turn of things in the community has threatened either odium or embarrassment to me, he has not been able to suppress the satisfaction which it gave him.

A part of this is of course information, and might be misrepresentation. But it comes through so many channels and so well accords with what falls under my own observation that I can entertain no doubt.

I find a strong confirmation in the following circumstances. *Freneau* the present Printer of the National Gazette, who was a journeyman with Childs & Swain at New York, was a known anti-federalist. It is reduced to a certainty that he was brought to Philadelphia by Mr. Jefferson to be the conductor of a News Paper. It is notorious that cotemporarily with the commencement of his paper he was a Clerk in the department of state for foreign languages. Hence a clear inference that his paper has been set on foot and is conducted under the patronage & not against the views of Mr. Jefferson. What then is the complexion of this paper? Let any impartial man peruse all the numbers down to the present day; and I never was more mistaken, if he does not pronounce that it is a paper devoted to the subversion of me & the measures in which I have had an Agency; and I am little less mistaken if he do not pronounce that it is a paper of a tendency *generally unfriendly* to the Government of the U States.

It may be said, that a News Paper being open to all the publications, which are offered to it, its complexion may be influenced by other views than those of the Editor. But the fact here is that wherever the Editor appears it is in a correspondent dress. The paragraphs which appear as his own, the publications, not original which are selected for his press, are of the same malignant and unfriendly aspect, so as not to leave a doubt of the temper which directs the publication.

Again *Brown*, who publishes an Evening paper called *The Federal Gazette* was originally a zealous federalist and personally friendly to me. He has been employed by Mr. Jefferson as a Printer to the Government for the publication of the laws; and for some time past 'till lately the complexion of his press was equally bitter and unfriendly to me & to the Government.

Lately, Col Pickering in consequence of certain attacks upon him, got hold of some instances of malconduct of his which have served to hold him in Check and seemed to have varied his tone a little. I dont lay so much stress on this last case as on the former. There, I find an internal evidence which is as conclusive as can be expected in any similar case. Thus far, as to Mr. Jefferson.

With regard to Mr. Madison—the matter stands thus. I have not heard, but in the one instance to which I have alluded, of his having held language unfriendly to me in private conversation. But in his public conduct there has been a more uniform & persevering opposition than I have been able to resolve into a sincere difference of opinion. I cannot persuade myself that Mr. Madison and I, whose politics had formerly so much the *same point of departure*, should now diverge so widely in our opinions of the measures which are proper to be pursued. The opinion I once entertained of the candour and simplicity and fairness of Mr. Madisons character has, I acknowledge, given way to a decided opinion that *it is one of a peculiarly artificial and complicated kind.*

For a considerable part of the last session, Mr. Madison lay in a great measure *perdu.* But it was evident from his votes & a variety of little movements and appearances, that he was the prompter of Mr. Giles & others, who were the open instruments of opposition. Two facts occurred, in the course of the session, which I view as unequivocal demonstrations of his disposition towards me. In one, a direct and decisive blow was aimed. When the department of the Treasury was established Mr. Madison was an unequivocal advocate of the principles which prevailed in it and of the powers and duties which were assigned by it to the head of the department. This appeared both from his private and public discourses; and I will add, that I have personal evidence that Mr. Madison is as well convinced as any man in the U States of the necessity of the arrangement which characterizes that establishment to the orderly conducting of the business of the Finances.

Mr. Madison nevertheless opposed directly a reference to me to report *ways* & *means* for the Western expedition, & combatted *on principle* the propriety of such references.

He well knew, that, if he had prevailed, a certain consequence was, my *resignation*—that I would not be fool enough to make pecuniary sacrifices and endure a life of extreme drudgery without opportunity either to do material good or to acquire reputation; and frequently with a responsibility in reputation for measures in which I had no hand, and in respect to which, the part I had acted, if any, could not be known.

To accomplish this point, an effectual train, as was supposed, was laid. Besides those who ordinarily acted under Mr.

Madison's banners, several, who had generally acted with me from various motives, vanity, self importance, &c. &c. were enlisted.

My overthrow was anticipated as certain and Mr. Madison, *laying aside his wonted caution*, boldly led his troops as he imagined to a certain victory. He was disappointed. Though, *late* I became apprized of the danger. Measures of counteraction were adopted, & when the Question was called, Mr. Madison was confounded to find characters voting against him, whom he had counted upon as certain.

Towards the close of the Session, another, though a more covert, attack was made. It was in the shape of a proposition to insert in the supplementary Act respecting the public Debt something by way of instruction to the Trustees "to make their purchases of the debt at the *lowest* market price." In the course of the discussion of this point, Mr. Madison dealt much in *insidious insinuations* calculated to give an impression that the public money under my particular direction had been unfaithfully applied to put undue advantages in the pockets of speculators, & to support the debt at an *artificial* price for their benefit. The whole manner of this transaction left no doubt in any ones mind that Mr. Madison was actuated by *personal* & political animosity.

As to this last instance, it is but candid to acknowledge, that Mr. Madison had a better right to act the enemy than on any former occasion. I had some short time before, subsequent to his conduct respecting the reference, declared openly my opinion of the views, by which he was actuated towards me, & my determination to consider & treat him as a political enemy.

An intervening proof of Mr. Madisons unfriendly intrigues to my disadvantage is to be found in the following incident which I relate to you upon my honor but from the nature of it, you will perceive in the *strictest confidence*. The president having prepared his speech at the commencement of the ensuing session communicated it to Mr. Madison for his remarks. It contained among other things a *clause* concerning weights & measures, hinting the advantage of an invariable standard, which *preceded*, in the original state of the speech, a clause concerning the Mint. Mr. Madison suggested a transposition of these clauses & the addition of certain words, which I now forget importing an *immediate connection* between the two subjects. You may recollect that Mr. Jefferson proposes that the *unit of weight* & the *unit in the coins* shall be the same, & that my propositions are to preserve the Dollar as the Unit, adhering to its present quantity of Silver, & establishing the same proportion of alloy in the silver as in the gold Coins. The evident design of this manoeuvre was to connect the Presidents opinion in favour of Mr. Jefferson's idea, in contradiction to mine, &, the worst of it is, *without his being aware of the tendency of the thing.* It happened, that the President shewed me the Speech, altered in conformity to Mr. Madisons suggestion, just before it was copied for the purpose of being delivered. I remarked to him the tendency of the alteration. *He declared that he had not been aware of it & had no such intention; & without hesitation agreed to expunge the words which were designed to connect the two subjects.*

This transaction, in my opinion, not only furnishes a proof of Mr. Madisons *intrigues*, in opposition to my measures, but charges him with an *abuse* of the Presidents confidence in him, by endeavouring to make him, without his knowledge, take part with one officer against another, in a case in which they had given different opinions to the Legislature of the Country. *I forbore to awaken the President's mind to this last inference*; but it is among the circumstances which have convinced me that Mr. Madisons true character is the reverse of that *simple, fair, candid one*, which he has assumed.

I have informed you, that Mr. Freneau was brought to Philadelphia, by Mr. Jefferson, to be the Conductor of a News Paper. My information announced Mr. Madison as the mean of negotiation while he was at New York last summer. This and the general coincidence & close intimacy between the two Gentlemen leave no doubt that their views are substantially the same.

Secondly As to the tendency of the views of the two Gentlemen who have been named.

Mr. Jefferson is an avowed enemy to a funded debt. Mr. Madison disavows in public any intention to *undo* what has been done; but in a private conversation with Mr. Charles

Carroll (Senator), this Gentlemans name I mention confidentially though he mentioned the matter to Mr. King & several other Gentlemen as well as myself; & if any chance should bring you together you would easily bring him to repeat it to you, he favoured the sentiment in Mr. Mercers speech that a Legislature had no right to *fund* the debt by mortgaging permanently the public revenues because they had no right to bind posterity. The inference is that what has been unlawfully done may be undone.

The discourse of partizans in the Legislature & the publications in the party news-papers direct their main battery against the *principle* of a funded debt, & represent it in the most odious light as a perfect *Pandoras box.*

If Mr. Barnewell of St. Carolina, who appears to be a man of nice honor, may be credited, Mr. Giles declared in a conversation with him that if there was a question for reversing the funding system on the abstract point of the right of pledging & the futility of preserving public faith, he should be for reversal; merely to demonstrate his sense of the defect of right & the inutility of the thing. If positions equally extravagant were not publicly advanced by some of the party & secretly countenanced by the most guarded & *discreet* of them, one would be led, from the absurdity of the declaration, to suspect misapprehension. But from what is *known* any thing may be *believed.*

Whatever were the original merits of the funding system, after having been so solemly adopted, & after so great a transfer of property under it, what would become of the Government should it be reversed? What of the National Reputation? Upon what system of morality can so atrocious a doctrine be maintained? In me, I confess it excites *indignation* & *horror*!

What are we to think of those maxims of Government by which the power of a Legislature is denied to bind the Nation by a *Contract* in an affair of *property* for twenty four years? For this is precisely the case of the debt. What are to become of all the legal rights of property, of all charters to corporations, nay, of all grants to a man his heirs & assigns for ever, if this doctrine be true? What is the term for which a government is in capacity to *contract*? Questions might be multiplied without end to demonstrate the perniciousness & absurdity of such a doctrine.

In almost all the questions great & small which have arisen, since the first session of Congress, Mr. Jefferson & Mr. Madison have been found among those who were disposed to narrow the Federal authority. The question of a National Bank is one example. The question of bounties to the Fisheries is another. Mr. Madison resisted it on the ground of constitutionality, 'till it was evident, by the intermediate questions taken, that the bill would pass & he then under the wretched subterfuge of a change of a single word "bounty" for "allowance" went over to the Majority & voted for the bill. In the Militia bill & in a variety of minor cases he has leaned to abridging the exercise of foederal authority, & leaving as much as possible to the States & he has lost no opportunity of *sounding the alarm* with great affected solemnity at encroachments meditated on the rights of the States, & of holding up the bugbear of a faction in the Government having designs unfriendly to Liberty.

This kind of conduct has appeared to me the more extraordinary on the part of Mr. Madison as I know for a certainty it was a primary article in his Creed that the real danger in our system was the subversion of the National authority by the preponderancy of the State Governments. All his measures have proceeded on an opposite supposition.

I recur again to the instance of Freneaus paper. In matters of this kind one cannot have direct proof of men's latent views; they must be inferred from circumstances. As the coadjutor of Mr. Jefferson in the establishment of this paper, I include Mr. Madison in the consequences imputable to it.

In respect to our foreign politics the views of these Gentlemen are in my judgment equally unsound & dangerous. *They have a womanish attachment to France and a womanish resentment against Great Britain.* They would draw us into the closest embrace of the former & involve us in all the consequences of her politics, & they would risk the peace of the country in their endeavours to keep us at the greatest possible distance from the latter. This disposition goes to a length particularly in Mr. Jefferson of which, till lately, I had no adequate Idea. Various circumstances prove to me that if these Gentlemen were left to pursue their own course there would be in less than six months *an open War between the U States & Great Britain.*

I trust I have a due sense of the conduct of France towards this Country in the late Revolution, & that I shall always be among the foremost in making her every suitable return; but there is a wide difference between this & implicating ourselves in all her politics; between bearing good will to her, & hating and wranggling with all those whom she hates. The Neutral & the Pacific Policy appear to me to mark the true path to the U States.

Having now delineated to you what I conceive to be the true complexion of the politics of these Gentlemen, I will now attempt a solution of these strange appearances.

Mr. Jefferson, it is known, did not in the first instance cordially acquiesce in the new constitution for the U States; he had many doubts & reserves. He left this Country before we had experienced the imbicillities of the former.

In France he saw government only on the side of its abuses. He drank deeply of the French Philosophy, in Religion, in Science, in politics. He came from France in the moment of a fermentation which he had had a share in exciting, & in the passions and feelings of which he shared both from temperament and situation.

He came here probably with a too partial idea of his own powers, and with the expectation of a greater share in the direction of our councils than he has in reality enjoyed. I am not sure that he had not peculiarly marked out for himself the department of the Finances.

He came electrified *plus* with attachment to France and with the project of knitting together the two Countries in the closest political bands.

Mr. Madison had always entertained an exalted opinion of the talents, knowledge and virtues of Mr. Jefferson. The sentiment was probably reciprocal. A close correspondence subsisted between them during the time of Mr. Jefferson's absence from this country. A close intimacy arose upon his return.

Whether any peculiar opinions of Mr. Jefferson concerning the public debt wrought a change in the sentiments of Mr.

Madison (for it is certain that the former is more radically wrong than the latter) or whether Mr. Madison seduced by the expectation of popularity and possibly by the calculation of advantage to the state of Virginia was led to change his own opinion—certain it is, that a very material *change* took place, & that the two Gentlemen were united in the new ideas. Mr. Jefferson was indiscreetly open in his approbation of Mr. Madison's principles, upon his first coming to the seat of Government. I say indiscreetly, because a Gentleman in the administration in one department ought not to have taken sides against another, in another department.

The course of this business & a variety of circumstances which took place left Mr. Madison a very discontented & chagrined man and begot some degree of ill humour in Mr. Jefferson.

Attempts were made by these Gentlemen in different ways to produce a Commercial Warfare with Great Britain. In this too they were disappointed. And as they had the liveliest wishes on the subject their dissatisfaction has been proportionally great; and as I had not favoured the project, I was comprehended in their displeasure.

These causes and perhaps some others created, much sooner than I was aware of it, a systematic opposition to me on the part of those Gentlemen. My subversion, I am now satisfied, has been long an object with them.

Subsequent events have encreased the Spirit of opposition and the feelings of personal mortification on the part of these Gentlemen.

A mighty stand was made on the affair of the Bank. There was much *commitment* in that case. I prevailed.

On the Mint business I was opposed from the same Quarter, & with still less success. In the affair of ways & means for the Western expedition—on the supplementary arrangements concerning the debt except as to the additional assumption, my views have been equally prevalent in opposition to theirs. This current of success on one side & defeat on the other have rendered the Opposition furious, & have produced a disposition to subvert their Competitors even at the expence of the Government.

Another circumstance has contributed to widening the breach. 'Tis evident beyond a question, from every movement, that Mr Jefferson aims with ardent desire at the Presidential Chair. This too is an important object of the party-politics. It is supposed, from the nature of my former personal & political connexions, that I may favour some other candidate more than Mr. Jefferson when the Question shall occur by the retreat of the present Gentleman. My influence therefore with the Community becomes a thing, on ambitious & personal grounds, to be resisted & destroyed.

You know how much it was a point to establish the Secretary of State as the Officer who was to administer the Government in defect of the President & Vice President. Here I acknowledge, though I took far less part than was supposed, I run counter to Mr. Jefferson's wishes; but if I had had no other reason for it, I had already *experienced opposition* from him which rendered it a measure of *self defence.*

It is possible too (for men easily heat their imaginations when their passions are heated) that they have by degrees persuaded themselves of what they may have at first only sported to influence others—namely that there is some dreadful combination against State Government & republicanism; which according to them, are convertible terms. But there is so much absurdity in this supposition, that the admission of it tends to apologize for their hearts, at the expence of their heads.

Under the influence of all these circumstances, the attachment to the Government of the U States originally weak in Mr Jeffersons mind has given way to something very like dislike; in Mr. Madisons, it is so counteracted by personal feelings, as to be more an affair of the head than of the heart —more the result of a conviction of the necessity of Union than of cordiality to the thing itself. I hope it does not stand worse than this with him.

In such a state of mind, both these Gentlemen are prepared to hazard a great deal to effect a change. Most of the important measures of every Government are connected with the Treasury. To subvert the present head of it they deem it expedient to risk rendering the Government itself odious; perhaps foolishly thinking that they can easily recover the lost affections & confidence of the people, and not appreciating as they ought to do the natural resistance to Government which in every community results from the human passions, the degree to which this is strengthened by the *organised rivality* of State Governments, & the infinite danger that the National Government once rendered odious will be kept so by these powerful & indefatigable enemies.

They forget an old but a very just, though a coarse saying—That it is much easier to raise the Devil than to lay him.

Poor *Knox* has come in for a share of their persecution as a man who generally thinks with me & who has a portion of the Presidents good Will & confidence.

In giving you this picture of political parties, my design is I confess, to awaken your attention, if it has not yet been awakened to the conduct of the Gentlemen in question. If my opinion of them is founded, it is certainly of great moment to the public weal that they should be understood. I rely on the strength of your mind to appreciate men as they merit—when you have a clue to their real views.

A word on another point. I am told that serious apprehensions are disseminated in your state as to the existence of a Monarchical party meditating the destruction of State & Republican Government. If it is possible that so absurd an idea can gain ground it is necessary that it should be combatted. I assure you on my *private faith* and *honor* as a Man that there is not in my judgment a shadow of foundation of it. A very small number of men indeed may entertain theories less republican than Mr Jefferson & Mr. Madison; but I am persuaded there is not a Man among them who would not regard as both *criminal* & *visionary* any attempt to subvert the republican system of the Country. Most of these men rather *fear* that it may not justify itself by its fruits, than feel a predilection for a different form; and their fears are not diminished by the factions & fanatical politics which they find prevailing among a certain set of Gentlemen and threatening to disturb the tranquillity and order of the Government.

As to the destruction of State Governments, the *great* and *real* anxiety is to be able to preserve the National from the too potent and counteracting influence of those Governments. As to my own political Creed, I give it to you with the utmost sincerity. I am *affectionately* attached to the Republican theory. I desire *above all things* to see the *equality* of political rights exclusive of all *hereditary* distinction firmly established by a practical demonstration of its being consistent with the order and happiness of society.

As to State Governments, the prevailing byass of my judgment is that if they can be circumscribed within bounds consistent with the preservation of the National Government they will prove useful and salutary. If the States were all of the size of Connecticut, Maryland or New Jersey, I should decidedly regard the local Governments as both safe & useful. As the thing now is, however, I acknowledge the most serious apprehensions that the Government of the U States will not be able to maintain itself against their influence. I see that influence already penetrating into the National Councils & preverting their direction.

Hence a disposition on my part towards a liberal construction of the powers of the National Government and to erect every fence to guard it from depredations, which is, in my opinion, consistent with constitutional propriety.

As to any combination to prostrate the State Governments I disavow and deny it. From an apprehension lest the Judiciary should not work efficiently or harmoniously I have been desirous of seeing some rational scheme of connection adopted as an amendment to the constitution, otherwise I am for maintaining things as they are, though I doubt much the possibility of it, from a tendency in the nature of things towards the preponderancy of the State Governments.

I said, that I was *affectionately* attached to the Republican theory. This is the real language of my heart which I open to you in the sincerity of friendship; & I add that I have strong hopes of the success of that theory; but in candor I ought also to add that I am far from being without doubts. I consider its success as yet a problem.

It is yet to be determined by experience whether it be consistent with that *stability* and *order* in Government which are essential to public strength & private security and happiness. On the whole, the only enemy which Republicanism has to fear in this Country is in the Spirit of faction and anarchy. If this will not permit the ends of Government to be attained under it—if it engenders disorders in the community, all regular & orderly minds will wish for a change—and the demagogues who have produced the disorder will make it for their own aggrandizement. This is the old Story.

If I were disposed to promote Monarchy & overthrow State Governments, I would mount the hobby horse of popularity—I would cry out usurpation—danger to liberty &c. &c—I would endeavour to prostrate the National Government—raise a ferment—and then "ride in the Whirlwind and direct the Storm." That there are men acting with Jefferson & Madison who have this in view I verily believe. I could lay my finger on some of them. That Madison does *not* mean it I also verily believe, and I rather believe the same of Jefferson; but I read him upon the whole thus—"A man of profound ambition & violent passions."

You must be by this time tired of my epistle. Perhaps I have treated certain characters with too much severity. I have however not meant to do them injustice—and from the bottom of my soul believe I have drawn them truly and that it is of the utmost consequence to the public weal they should be viewed in their true colors. I yield to this impression. I will only add that I make no clandestine attacks on the gentlemen concerned. They are both apprized indirectly from myself of the opinion I entertain of their views. With the truest regard and esteem.

THE NECESSITY OF REELECTION

To George Washington

Sir   Philadelphia July 30th 1792

I received the most sincere pleasure at finding in our last conversation, that there was some relaxation in the disposition you had before discovered to decline a reelection. Since your departure, I have lost no opportunity of sounding the opinions of persons, whose opinions were worth knowing, on these two points—1st the effect of your declining upon the public affairs, and upon your own reputation—2dly. the effect of your continuing, in reference to the declarations you have made of your disinclination to public life—And I can truly say, that I have not found the least difference of sentiment, on either point. The impression is uniform—that your declining would be to be deplored as the greatest evil, that could befall the country at the present juncture, and as critically hazardous to your own reputation—that your continuance will be justified in the mind of every friend to his country by the evident necessity for it. Tis clear, says every one, with whom I have conversed, that the affairs of the national government are not yet firmly established—that its enemies, generally speaking, are as inveterate as ever—that their enmity has been sharpened by its success and by all the resentments which flow from disappointed predictions and mortified vanity—that a general and strenuous effort is making in every state to place the administration of it in the hands of its enemies, as if they were its safest guardians—that the period of the next house of representatives is likely to prove the crisis of its permanent character—that if you continue in office nothing materially mischievous is to be apprehended—if you quit much is to be dreaded—that the same motives which induced you to accept originally ought to decide you to continue till matters have assumed a more determinate aspect—that indeed it would have been better, as it regards your own character, that you had never consented to come forward, than now to leave the business unfinished and in danger of being undone—that in the event of storms arising there would be an imputation either of want of foresight or want of firmness—and, in fine, that on public and personal accounts, on patriotic and prudential considerations, the clear path to be pursued by you will be again to obey the voice of your country; which it is not doubted will be as earnest and as unanimous as ever.

On this last point, I have some suspicion that it will be insinuated to you, and perhaps (God forgive me, if I judge hardly) with design to place before you a motive of declining—that there is danger of a division among the electors and of less unanimity in their suffrages than heretofore. My view of this matter is as follows:

While your first election was depending I had no doubt, that there would be characters among the electors, who if they durst follow their inclinations, would have voted against you; but that in all probability they would be restrained by an apprehension of public resentment—that nevertheless it was possible a few straggling votes might be found in opposition, from some headstrong and fanatical individuals—that a circumstance of this kind would be in fact, and ought to be estimated by you, as of no importance—since their would be sufficient unanimity to witness the general confidence and attachment towards you.

My view of the future accords exactly with what was my view of the past. I believe the same motives will operate to produce the same result. The dread of public indignation will be likely to restrain the indisposed few. If they can calculate at all, they will naturally reflect that they could not give a severer blow to their cause than by giving a proof of hostility to you. But if a solitary vote or two should appear wanting to perfect unanimity, of what moment can it be? Will not the fewness of the exceptions be a confirmation of the devotion of the community to a character, which has so generally united its suffrages, after an administration of four years at the head of a new government, opposed in its first establishment by a large proportion of its citizens and obliged to run counter to many prejudices in devising the arduous arrangements, requisite to public Credit and public Order? Will not those, who may be the authors of any such exceptions, manifest more their own perverseness and malevolence than any diminution of the affection and confidence of the Nation? I am persuaded, that both these questions ought to be answered in the affirmative; and that there is nothing to be looked for, on the score of diversity of sentiment which ought to weigh for a moment.

I trust, Sir, and I pray God that you will determine to make a further sacrifice of your tranquillity and happiness to the public good. I trust that it need not continue above a year or two more—And I think that it will be more eligible to retire from office before the expiration of the term of an election, than to decline a reelection.

The sentiments I have delivered upon this occasion, I can truly say, proceed exclusively from an anxious concern for the public welfare and an affectionate personal attachment. These dispositions must continue to govern in every vicissitude one who has the honor to be very truly and respectfully

Sir   Your most Obedt. & hum serv   A Hamilton

August 3d. Since writing the foregoing I am favoured with your interesting letter of the 29th of July. An answer to the points raised is not difficult & shall as soon as possible be forwarded.

An American No. I

For the Gazette of the United States

Mr. Fenno

It was easy to foresee, when the hint appeared in your Gazette of   that the Editor of the National Gazette received a salary from the General Government, advantage would be taken of its *want* of explicitness and particularity to make the circumstance matter of merit in Mr. Freneau and an argument of his independent disinterestedness. Such a turn of the thing cannot be permitted to succeed. It is now necessary that the whole truth should be told, and that the real state of the affair should be well understood.

Mr. Freneau before he came to this City to conduct the National Gazette was employed by Childs & Swaine Printers of the Dayly Advertiser in the City of New York in capacity of   . A paper more devoted to the views of a certain party of which Mr. Jefferson is the head than any to be found in this City was wanted. Mr. Freneau was thought a fit instrument. His talents for invective and abuse had before been tried as Conductor of the Freemans Journal in this City. A negotiation was opened with him, which ended in the establishment of the National Gazette under his direction. There is good ground to believe that Mr. Madison while in New York in the summer of   was the medium of that Negotiation.

Mr. Freneau came here at once Editor of the National Gazette and Clerk for foreign languages in the department of Mr. Jefferson, Secretary of State; an experiment somewhat new in the history of political manœvres in this Country; a news paper instituted by a public officer, and the Editor of it regularly pensioned with the public money, in the disposal of that officer; an example savouring not a little of that spirit, which in the enumeration of European abuses is the continual theme of declamatory censure with the party whose leader is the author of it; an example which could not have been set by any other head of a department without having long since rung throughout the UStates.

Mr. Freneau is not then, as he would have supposed, the Independent Editor of a News Paper, who though receiving a salary from Government has firmness enough to expose its maladministration. He is the faithful and devoted servant of the head of a party, from whose hand he receives the boon. The whole complexion of his paper is an exact copy of the politics of his employer foreign and domestic, and exhibits a decisive internal evidence of the influence of that patronage under which he acts.

Whether the services rendered by him are an equivalent for the compensation he receives is best known to his employer and himself. There is however some room for doubt. Tis well known that his employer is himself well acquainted with the French language; the only one of which he is the translator; and it may be a question how often his aid is necessary.

It is somewhat singular too that a man acquainted with but one foreign language engaged in a particular trade, which it may be presumed occupies his whole time and attention, the Editor of a News Paper, should be the person selected as the Clerk for foreign languages, in the department of the United States for foreign affairs. Could no person have been found acquainted with more than one foreign language, and who, in so confidential a trust, could have been regularly attached to, in the constant employ of the department and immediately under the eye of the head of it?

But it may be asked—Is it possible that Mr. Jefferson, the head of a principal department of the Government can be the Patron of a Paper, the evident object of which is to decry the Government and its measures? If he disapproves of the Government itself and thinks it deserving of opposition, could he reconcile to his own personal dignity and the principles of probity to hold an office under it and employ the means of official influence in that opposition? If he disapproves of the leading measures, which have been adopted in the course of its administration, could he reconcile it with the principles of delicacy and propriety to continue to hold a place in that administration, and at the same time to be instrumental in vilifying measures which have been adopted by majorities of both branches of the Legislature and *sanctionned by the Chief Magistrate of the Union*?

These questions would certainly be natural. An answer to them might be left to the facts which establish the relation between the Secretary of State and the Editor of the National Gazette, as the text, and to the general tenor of that paper as the Commentary. Let any intelligent man read the paper, from the commencement of it, and let him determine for himself, whether it be not a paper virulently hostile both to the Government and to its measures. Let him then ask himself, whether considering the connection which has subsisted between the Secretary of State and the Editor of that Paper, cœval with its first establishment, it be probable that the complexion of the paper is contrary to the views of that officer.

If he wishes a confirmation of the inference, which he cannot fail to draw, as a probable one, let him be informed in addition—

1   That while the Constitution of the United States was depending before the People of this Country, for their consideration and decision, Mr. Jefferson, being in France, was opposed to it, in some of its most important feautures, and wrote his objections to some of his friends in Virginia. That he, at first, went so far as to discountenance its adoption; though he afterwards recommended it, on the ground of expediency, in certain contingencies.

2   That he is the declared opponent of almost all the important measures which have been devised by the Government; more especially the provision which has been made for the public Debt, the institution of the Bank of the United States, and such other measures as relate to the Public Credit and the Finances of the UStates.

It is proper that these facts should be known. If the People of the UStates believe, that their happiness and their safety are connected with the existence and maintenance of an efficient National or Fœderal Government—if they continue to think that, which they have created and established, worthy of their confidence, if they are willing, that the powers they have granted to it should be exercised with sufficient latitude to attain the ends they had in view in granting them and to do the essential business of the Nation—If they feel an honest pride in seeing the Credit of their country, so lately prostrate, elevated to an equal station with that of any Nation upon earth—if they are conscious that their own importance is increased by the increased respectability of their Country, which from an abject and degraded state, owing to the want of government, has, by the establishment of a wise constitution and by the measures which have been pursued under it, become a theme for the praise and admiration of mankind—if they experience that their own situation is improved and improving—that commerce and navigation have advanced—that manufactures are progressing—that agriculture is thriving— that property is more secure than it was—industry more certain of real not nominal reward, personal liberty perfectly protected—that notwithstanding the unavoidable demands upon them to satisfy the justice retrieve the reputation and answer the exigencies of the Country they are either less burthened than they were or more equal to the burthen which they have to sustain—if these are their opinions and their experience, let them know and understand, that the sentiments of the officer who has been mentioned, both as to the principles and the practice of the Constitution, which was framed by them and has been administered by their representatives, freely chosen, are essentially different from theirs.

If on the contrary—The People of the United States are of opinion that they erred in adopting their present constitution—that it contains pernicious principles and dangerous powers—that is has been administered injudiciously and wickedly—that men whose abilities and patriotism were tried in the worst of times have entered into a league to betray and oppress them—that they are really oppressed and ruined or in imminent danger of being so—If they think the preservation of National Union a matter of no or small consequence—if they are willing to return to the situation, from which they have just escaped, and to strip the government of some of the most necessary powers with which they have cloathed it—if they are desirous that those which are permitted to remain should be frittered away by a narrow timid and feeble exercise of them—If they are disposed to see the National Government transformed into the skeleton of Power—and the separate omnipotence of the state Governments exalted upon its ruins—If they are persuaded that Nations are under no ties of moral obligation that public Credit is useless or something worse—that public debts may be paid or cancelled at pleasure; that when a provision is not likely to be made for them, the discontents to be expected from the omission may honestly be transferred from a Government able to vindicate its rights to the breasts of Individuals who may first be encouraged to become the Substitutes to the Original Creditor, and afterwards defrauded without danger.* If to National Union, national respectability Public Order and public Credit they are willing to substitute National disunion, National insignificance, Public disorder and discredit—then let them unite their acclamations and plaudits in favour of Mr. Jefferson: Let him be the toast of every political club, and the theme of every popular huzza. For to those points, without examining his motives do assuredly tend the political tenets, real or pretended, of that Gentleman.

These strictures are made from a Conviction, that it is important to the People to know the characters intrusted with their public affairs.

As Mr. Jefferson is emulous of being the head of a party, whose politics have constantly aimed at elevating State-power, upon the ruins of National Authority—Let him enjoy all the glory and all the advantage of it. But Let it at the same time be understood by those, who are persuaded that the real and permanent welfare of the Country is to be promoted by other means that such are the views by which he is actuated.

An American

---

*Such was the advice given by Mr. Jefferson, when Minister Plenipotentiary to the Court of France, to Congress, respecting the debt due to France. The precise terms are not recollected but the substance may be depended upon. The poor Hollanders were to be the victims.

August 4, 1792

POLITICAL AND PERSONAL DEFENSE

To George Washington

Sir   Philadelphia Aug 18. 1792

I am happy to be able, at length, to send you, answers to the objections, which were communicated in your letter of the 29th of July.

They have unavoidably been drawn in haste, too much so, to do perfect justice to the subject, and have been copied just as they flowed from my heart and pen, without revision or correction. You will observe, that here and there some severity appears. I have not fortitude enough always to hear with calmness, calumnies, which necessarily include me, as a principal Agent in the measures censured, of the falsehood of which, I have the most unqualified consciousness. I trust that I shall always be able to bear, as I ought, imputations of error of Judgment; but I acknowlege that I cannot be intirely patient under charges, which impeach the integrity of my public motives or conduct. I feel, that I merit them *in no degree*; and expressions of indignation sometimes escape me, in spite of every effort to suppress them. I rely on your goodness for the proper allowances.

With high respect and the most affectionate attachment, I have the honor to be,   Sir   Your most Obedient & humble servant

Alexander Hamilton

Objections and Answers respecting the Administration
of the Government

1   Object. The public Debt is greater than we can possibly pay before other causes of adding to it will occur; and this has been artificially created by adding together the *whole amount* of the Debtor and Creditor sides of the Account.

Answer. The public Debt was produced by the late war. It is not the fault of the present government that it exists; unless it can be proved, that public morality and policy do not require of a Government an honest provision for its debts.

Whether it is greater than can be paid before new causes of adding to it will occur is a problem incapable of being solved, but by experience; and this would be the case if it were not one fourth as much as it is. If the policy of the Country be prudent, cautious and *neutral* towards foreign nations, there is a rational probability, that war may be avoided long enough to wipe off the debt. The Dutch in a situation, not near so favourable for it as that of the UStates have enjoyed intervals of peace, longer than with proper exertions would suffice for the purpose. The Debt of the UStates compared with its present and growing abilities is really a very light one. It is little more than 15.000000 of pounds Sterling, about the annual expenditure of Great Britain.

But whether the public Debt shall be extinguished or not within a moderate period depends on the temper of the people. If they are rendered dissatisfied by misrepretations of the measures of the government, the Government will be deprived of an efficient command of the resources of the community towards extinguishing the Debt. And thus, those who clamour are likely to be the principal causes of protracting the existence of the debt.

As to having been artificially increased, this is denied; perhaps indeed the true reproach of the system, which has been adopted, is that it has artificially diminished the debt as will be explained by and by.

The assertion, that the Debt has been increased, by adding together the whole amount of the Debtor and Creditor sides of the account, not being very easy to be understood is not easy to be answered.

But an answer shall be attempted.

The thirteen States in their *joint* capacity owed a *certain* sum. The same states, in their separate capacities, owed *another sum*. These two sums constituted the *aggregate* of the *public Debt*. The PUBLIC, in a political sense, compounded of the Governments of the Union and of the several states, was the DEBTOR. The individuals who held the various evidences of debt were the CREDITORS. It would be non-sense to say, that the combining of *the two parts* of the public Debt is adding together the Debtor and Creditor sides of the account. So great an absurdity cannot be supposed to be intended by the objection. Another meaning must therefore be sought for.

It may possibly exist in the following misconception. The states individually, when they liquidated the accounts of Individuals for services and supplies towards the common defence during the late war, and gave certificates for the sums due would naturally charge them to the UStates as contributions to the common cause. The UStates in assuming to pay those certificates charge themselves with them. And it may be supposed that here is a double charge for the same thing.

But as the amount of the sum assumed for each state is by the system adopted to be charged to such state, it of course goes in extinguishment of so much of the first charge as is equal to the sum assumed, and leaves the UStates chargeable only once, as ought to be the case.

Or perhaps the meaning of the objection may be found in the following mode of reasoning. Some states, from having disproportionately contributed during the war, would probably on a settlement of accounts be found debtors, independently of the Assumption. The assuming of the debts of such states increases the ballances against them, and as these ballances will ultimately be remitted from the impracticability of enforcing their payment, the sums assumed will be an extra charge upon the U States increasing the mass of the debt.

This objection takes it for granted that the ballances of the Debtor States will not be exacted; which by the way is no part of the system and if it should eventually not prove true, the foundation of the reasoning would fail. For it is evident if the ballances are to be collected (unless there be some undiscovered error in the principle by which the accounts are to be adjusted) that one side of the account will counterpoise the other. And every thing as to the quantum of debt will remain *in statu quo*.

But it shall be taken for granted that the ballances will be remitted; and still the consequence alleged does not result. The reverse of it may even take place. In reasoning upon this point, it must be remembered that impracticability would be alike an obstacle to the collection of ballances without as with the Assumption.

This being the case, whether the ballances to be remitted will be increased or diminished must depend on the relative proportions of outstanding debts. If a former *debtor* State owes to individuals a smaller sum in proportion to its contributive faculty, than a former *Creditor* state, the assumption of the debts of both to be provided for out of a *common fund* raised upon them proportionally must necessarily, on the idea of a remission of ballances, tend to restore equality between them, and lessen the ballance of the debtor state to be remitted.

How the thing may work upon the whole, cannot be pronounced without a knowlege of the situation of the account of each State, but all circumstances that are known render it probable that the ultimate effect will be favourable to justice between the states and that there will be inconsiderable ballances either on one side or on the other.

It was observed that perhaps the true reproach of the system which has been adopted is that it has artificially decreased the Debt. This is explained thus—

In the case of the debt of the UStates interest upon two thirds of the principal only at 6 ⅌ Cent is immediately paid—interest upon the remaining third was deferred for ten years—and only three ⅌ Cent has been allowed upon the arrears of interest, making one third of the whole debt.

In the case of the separate debts of the States interest upon $\frac{4}{9}$ only of the intire sum is immediately paid; interest upon $\frac{2}{9}$ was deferred for 10 years and only three per Cent allowed on $\frac{3}{9}$.

The Market rate of interest at the time of adopting the funding system was 6 ⅌ Cent. Computing according to this rate of interest—the then present value of 100 Dollars of debt upon an average, principal and interest, was about 73 Dollars.

And The present *actual* value, in the Market, of 100 Dollars, as the several kinds of Stock are sold, is no more than 83 Dollars & 61 Cents. This computation is not made on equal sums of the several kinds of Stock according to which the average value of 100 Dollars would be only 78.75 but it is made on the proportions which constitute the Mass of the debt.

At 73 to 100 The diminution on 60 000 000 is 16.200 000 Dollars; at 83.61 to 100 it is 9.834 000 Dollars.

But as the UStates having a right to redeem in certain proportions need never give more than par for the 6 ⅌ Cent, the diminution to them as purchasers at the present market prices is 12.168 000 Dollars.

If it be said that the UStates are engaged to pay the whole sum at the Nominal value, the answer is that they are always at liberty if they have the means to purchase at the market prices and in all those purchases they gain the difference between the nominal sums and the lesser market rates.

If the whole debt had been provided for at 6 ⅌ Cent the market rate of Interest when the funding system passed the market value throughout would undoubtedly have been 100 for 100. The Debt may then rather be said to have been artificially decreased by the Nature of the provision.

The conclusion from the whole, is that assuming it as a principle that the public debts of the different descriptions were honestly to be provided for and paid—it is the reverse of true that there has been an artificial increase of them. To argue on a different principle is to presuppose dishonesty, and make it an objection to doing right.

Objection II This accumulation of debt has taken for ever out of our power those easy sources of revenue which applied &c.

Answer. There having been no accumulation of debt, if what is here pretended to have been the consequence were true, it would only be to be regretted as the unavoidable consequence of an unfortunate state of things. But the supposed consequence does by *no means* exist. The only sources of taxation which have been touched are imported articles and the single internal object of distilled spirits. Lands, houses, the great mass of personal as well as the whole of real property remain essentially free. In short, the chief sources of taxation are free for extraordinary conjunctures; and it is one of the distinguishing merits of the system which has been adopted, that it has rendered this far more the case than it was before. It is only to look into the different states to be convinced of it. In most of them real estate is wholly exempted. In some very small burthens rest upon it for the purpose of the internal Governments. In all the burthens of the people have been lightened. It is a mockery of truth to represent the U States as a community burthened and exhausted by taxes.

Objection 3

Answer. This is a mere painting and exaggeration. With the Exception of a very few articles, the duties on imports are still moderate, lower than in any Country of whose regulations we have knowlege, except perhaps Holland, where having few productions or commodities of their own, their export trade depends on the reexportation of foreign articles.

It is true the Merchants have complained, but so they did of the first impost law for a time and so men always will do at an augmentation of taxes which touch the business they carry on, especially in a country where no or scarcely any *such* taxes before existed. The Collection, it is not doubted will be essentially secure. Evasions have existed in a degree and will continue to exist. Perhaps they may be somewhat increased; to what extent can only be determined by experience, but there are no symptoms to induce an opinion that they will materially increase. As to the idea of a war upon the citizens to collect the impost duties, it can only be regarded as a figure of rhetoric.

The Excise law no doubt is a good topic of declamation. But can it be doubted that it is an excellent and a very fit mean of revenue?

As to the partiality of its operation, it is no more so than any other tax on a consumeable commodity; adjusting itself upon exactly the same principles. The consumer in the main pays the tax—and if some parts of the U States consume more domestic spirits, others consume more foreign—and both are taxed. There is perhaps, upon the whole, no article of more *general* and *equal consumption* than distilled spirits.

As to its *unproductiveness*, unless inforced by *arbitrary* and *vexatious* means, facts testify the contrary. Already, under all the obstacles arising from its novelty and the prejudices against it in some states, it has been considerably productive. And it is not inforced by any arbitrary or vexatious means; at least the precautions in the existing laws for the collection of the tax will not appear in that light but to men who regard all taxes and all the means of enforcing them as arbitrary and vexatious. Here however there is abundant room for fancy to operate. The standard is in the mind, and different minds will have different standards.

The observation relating to the commitment of the authority of the Government, in parts where resistance is most probable and coertion least practicable has more weight than any other part of this objection. It must be confessed that a hazard of this nature has been run but if there were motives sufficiently cogent for it, it was wisely run. It does not follow that a measure is bad because it is attended with a degree of danger.

The general inducements to a provision for the public Debt are—I   To preserve the public faith and integrity by fulfilling as far as was practicable the public engagements. II   To manifest a due respect for property by satisfying the public obligations in the hands of the public Creditors and which were as much their property as their houses or their lands their hats or their coats. III   To revive and establish public Credit; the palladium of public safety. IV   To preserve the Government itself by shewing it worthy of the confidence which was placed in it, to procure to the community the blessings which in innumerable ways attend confidence in the Government and to avoid the evils which in as many ways attend the want of confidence in it.

The particular inducements to an assumption of the state Debts were   I   To consolidate the finances of the country and give an assurance of permanent order in them; avoiding the collisions of thirteen different and independent systems of finance under concurrent and coequal authorities and the scramblings for revenue which would have been incident to so many different systems. II   To secure to the Government of the Union, by avoiding those entanglements, an effectual command of the resources of the Union for present and future exigencies. III   To *equalize the condition* of the *citizens* of the several states in the important article of taxation; rescuing a part of them from being oppressed with burthens, beyond their strength, on account of extraordinary exertions in the war and through the want of certain adventitious resources, which it was the good fortune of others to possess.

A mind naturally attached to order and system and capable of appreciating their immense value, unless misled by particular feelings, is struck at once with the prodigious advantages which in the course of time must attend such a simplification of the financial affairs of the Country as results from placing all the parts of the public debt upon one footing—under one direction—regulated by one provision. The want of this sound policy has been a continual source of disorder and embarrassment in the affairs of the United Netherlands.

The true justice of the case of the public Debt consists in that equalization of the condition of the Citizens of all the states which must arise from a consolidation of the debt and common contributions towards its extinguishment. Little inequalities, as to the past, can bear no comparison with the more lasting inequalities, which, without the assumption, would have characterised the future condition of the people of the UStates; leaving upon those who had done most or suffered most a great additional weight of burthen.

If the foregoing inducements to a provision for the public Debt (including an assumption of the state debts) were sufficiently cogent—then the justification of the Excise law lies within a narrow compass. Some further source of revenue, besides the duties on imports, was indispensable, and none equally productive, would have been so little exceptionable to the Mass of the People.

Other reasons cooperated in the minds of some able men to render an excise at an early period desireable. They thought it well to lay hold of so valuable a resource of revenue before it was generally preoccupied by the State Governments. They supposed it not amiss that the authority of the National Government should be visible in some branch of internal Revenue; lest a total non-exercise of it should beget an impression that it was never to be exercised & next that it ought not to be exercised. It was supposed too that a thing of the kind could not be introduced with a greater prospect of easy success than at a period when the Government enjoyed the advantage of first impressions—when state-factions to resist its authority were not yet matured—when so much aid was to be derived from the popularity and firmness of the actual chief Magistrate.

Facts hitherto do not indicate the measure to have been rash or ill advised. The law is in operation with perfect acquiescence in all the states North of New York, though they contribute most largely. In New York and New Jersey it is in full operation with some very partial complainings fast wearing away. In the greatest part of Pensylvania it is in operation and with increasing good humour towards it. The four Western

Counties continue exceptions. In Delaware it has had some struggle, which by the last accounts was surmounted. In Maryland and Virginia, it is in operation and without material conflict. In South Carolina it is now in pretty full operation, though in the interior parts it has had some serious opposition to overcome. In Georgia no material difficulty has been experienced. North Carolina Kentucke & the four Western Counties of Pensylvania present the only remaining impediments of any consequence to the full execution of the law. The latest advices from NC & Kentuke were more favourable than the former.

It may be added as a well established fact that the effect of the law has been to encourage new enterprises in most of the states in the business of domestic distillation. A proof that it is perceived to operate favourably to the manufacture, and that the measure cannot long remain unpopular any where.

Objection IV Propositions have been made in Congress & projects are on foot still to increase the Mass of the Debt.

Ans. Propositions have been made, and no doubt will be renewed by the States interested to complete the assumption of the State Debts. This would add in the first instance to the mass of the *Debt of the UStates* between three and four Millions of Dollars but it would not increase the mass of the *public Debt* at all. It would only transfer from particular States to the Union debts which already exist and which if the states indebted are honest must be provided for. It happens that Massachusettes and South Carolina would be chiefly benefitted. And there is a moral certainty that Massachusettes will have a ballance in her favour more than equal to her remaining debt and a probability that South Carolina will have a ballance sufficient to cover hers—so that there is not likely to be an eventual increase even of the *debt of the United States* by the further assumption. The immense exertions of Massachusettes during the late war and particularly in the latter periods of it when too many of the States failed in their fœderal Duty are known to every well informed man. It would not be too strong to say, that they were in a great degree the pivot of the revolution. The exertions sufferings sacrifices and losses of South Carolina need not be insisted upon. The other States have comparitively none or inconsiderable Debts. Can that policy be condemned which aims at putting the burthened states upon an equal footing with the rest? Can that policy be very liberal which resists so equitable an arrangement? It has been said that if they had exerted themselves since the peace their situation would have been different. But Massachusettes threw her Citizens into Rebellion by heavier taxes than were paid in any other State and South Carolina has done as much since the peace as could have been expected considering the exhausted state in which the War left her.

The only proposition during the last session or at any antecedent one which would truly have swelled the debt artificially was one which Mr Maddison made in the first session & which was renewed in the last and generally voted for by those who oppose the system that has prevailed. The object of this proposition was *that all the parts* of the State debts which have been *paid* or other*wise absorbed by them* should be assumed for the benefit of the States, and funded by the UStates. This measure if it had succeeded would truly have produced an immense artificial increase of the debt; but it has twice failed & there is no probability that it will ever succeed.

Objection 5.   By borrowing at ⅔ &c.

Answer. First—All the foreign loans which were made by the UStates prior to the present Government taking into the calculation charges & premiums cost them more than 6 ℔ Cent. Since the establishment of the present Government they borrowed first at about 5¼ including charges & since at about 4¼ including charges. And it is questionable in the present state of Europe whether they can obtain any further loans at so low a rate.

The System which is reprobated is the very cause that we have been able to borrow monies on so good terms. If one, that would have inspired less confidence, certainly if the substitutes which have been proposed, from a certain quarter, had obtained, we could not have procured loans even at six per Cent. The Dutch were largely adventurers in our domestic debt before the present Government. They did not embark far till they had made inquiries of influential public characters, as to the light in which the Debt was & would be considered in the hands of alienees—and had received assurances that Assignees would be regarded in the same light as original holders. What would have been the state of our Credit with them, if they had been disappointed, or indeed if our conduct had been in any respect inconsistent with the notions entertained in Europe concerning the maxims of public Credit?

The inference is that our being able to borrow on low terms is a consequence of the system which is the object of censure and that the thing itself, which is made the basis of another system, would not have existed under it.

Secondly. It will not be pretended that we could have borrowed at the proposed low rate of interest in the UStates; and all our exertions to borrow in Europe which have been unremitted, as occasions presented, have not hitherto produced above   of Dollars in space of   ; not even a sufficient sum to change the form of our foreign debt.

Thirdly If it were possible to borrow the whole sum abroad within a short period, to pay off our debt, it is not easy to imagine a more pernicious operation than this would have been. It would first have transferred to foreigners by a violent expedient the whole amount of our debt; and creating a money plethora in the Country a momentary scene of extravagance would have followed & the excess would quickly have flowed back: The evils of which situation need not be enlarged upon. If it be said that the operation might have been gradual, then the end proposed would not have been attained.

Lastly The plan which has been adopted secures in the first instance the *identical advantage*, which in the other plan would have been *eventual* and *contingent*. It puts one third of the whole Debt at an interest of 3 ℔Ct. only—and by deferring the payment of interest on a third of the remainder effectually reduces the interest on that part. It is evident that a *suspension* of interest is in fact a *reduction* of interest. The money which would go towards paying interest in the interval of suspension is an accumulating fund to be applied towards payment of it when it becomes due, proportionably reducing the provision then to be made.

In reality, on the principles of the funding system, the United States reduced the interest on their whole Debt upon *an average* to about 4½ ℔Cent, nearly the lowest rate they have any chance to borrow at, and lower than they could possibly have borrowed at, in an attempt to reduce the interest on the whole Capital by borrowing and paying; probably by one ₽ Cent. A demand for large loans by forcing the market would unavoidably have raised their price upon the borrower. The above average of 4½ ₽ Ct. is found by calculation, computing the then present value of the deferred Stock at the time of passing the funding Act and of course 3 ₽ Cent on the three per Cent Stock.

The funding system, then, secured in the very outset the *precise advantage* which it is alleged would have accrued from leaving the whole debt redeemable at pleasure. But this is not all. It did more. It left the Government still in a condition to enjoy upon ⅚ of the intire debt the advantage of extinguishing it, by loans at a low rate of interest, if they are obtainable. The 3 ₽ Cents which are one third of the whole may always be purchased in the market below par, till the market rate of interest falls to 3 ₽ Ct. The deferred will be purchaseable below par till near the period of the actual payment of interest. And this further advantage will result; in all these purchases the public will enjoy not only the advantage of a reduction of interest on the sums borrowed but the additional advantage of purchasing the debt under par, that is for less than 20/ in the pound.

If it be said that the like advantage might have been enjoyed under another system, the assertion would be without foundation. Unless some equivalent had been given for the reduction of interest in the irredeemable quality annexed to the Debt, nothing was left consistently with the principles of public Credit but to provide for the whole debt at 6 ₽ Cent. This evidently would have kept the whole at par, and no advantage could have been derived by purchases under the nominal value. The reduction of interest by borrowing at a lower rate is all that would have been practicable and this advantage has been secured by the funding system in the very outset and without any second process.

If no provision for the interest had been made, not only public Credit would have been sacrificed; but by means of it the borrowing at a low rate of interest or at any rate would have been impracticable.

There is no reproach which has been thrown upon the funding system so unmerited as that which charges it with being a bad bargain for the public or with a tendency to prolong the extinguishment of the Debt. The bargain has if any thing been too good on the side of the public; and it is impossible for the debt to be in a more convenient form than it is for a rapid extinguishment.

Some Gentlemen seem to forget that the faculties of every Country are limited. They talk as if the Government could extend its revenue *ad libitum* to pay off the debt. Whereas every rational calculation of the abilities of the Country will prove that the power of redemption which has been reserved over the debt is quite equal to those abilities, and that a greater power would be useless. If happily the abilities of the Country should exceed this estimate, there is nothing to hinder the surplus being employed in purchases. As long as the three ℔ Cents & deferred exist those purchases will be under par. If for the Stock bearing an immediate interest of six ℔ Cent more than par is given—the Government can afford it from the saving made in the first instance.

Upon the whole then it is the merit of the funding System to have conciliated these three important points—the restoration of public Credit—a reduction of the rate of interest—and an organisation of the Debt convenient for speedy extinguishment.

Object 6   The irredeemeable quality was given to the debt for the *avowed* purpose of inviting its transfer to foreign countries.

This assertion is a palpable misrepresentation. The *avowed purpose* of that quality of the Debt, as explained in the report of the Secretary of the Treasury, and in the arguments in Congress was to give an *equivalent* for the reduction of Interest, that is for deferring the payment of interest on ⅓ of the principal for three years and for allowing only 3 ℔ Cent on the arrears of Interest.

It was indeed argued, in confirmation of the reality of the equivalent, that foreigners would be willing to give more, where a high rate of Interest was *fixed*, than where it was liable to fluctuate with the market. And this has been verified by the fact—for the 6 ℔ Cents could not have risen for a moment above par, if the rate could have been lowered by redeeming the Debt at pleasure. But the inviting of the transfer to foreigners was never assigned as a motive to the arrangement.

And what is more, that transfer will be probably slower with the portion of irredeemability which is attached to the Debt than without it because a larger capital would be requisite to purchase 100 Dollars in the former than in the latter case. And the Capital of foreigners is limited as well as our own.

It appears to be taken for granted that if the Debt had not been funded in its present shape foreigners would not have purchased it as they now do; than which nothing can be more ill founded or more contrary to experience. Under the old Confederation when there was no provision at all foreigners had purchased five or six millions of the Debt. If any provision had been made, capable of producing confidence, their purchases would have gone on just as they now do; and the only material difference would have been that what they got from us then would have cost them less than what they now get from us does cost them. Whether it is to the disadvantage of the Country that they pay more is submitted.

Even a provision which should not have inspired full confidence would not have prevented foreign purchases. The commodity would have been cheap in proportion to the risks to be run. And full-handed Dutchmen would not have scrupled to amass large sums, for trifling considerations, in the hope, that time & experience would introduce juster notions into the public councils.

Our Debt would still have gone from us & with it our reputation & Credit.

Objection 7

Answer. The same glooming forebodings were heared in England in the early periods of its funding system. But they have never been realized. The money invested by foreigners in the purchase of its Debt being employed in its commerce agriculture and manufactures increased the wealth and Capital of the Nation, more than in proportion to the annual drain for the payment of interest and created the ability to bear it.

The objection seems to forget that the Debt is not transferred for Nothing—that the Capital paid for the Debt is
always an equivalent for the interest to be paid to the purchasers. If that Capital is well employed in a young country,
like this, it must be considerably increased so as to yield a
greater revenue than the interest of the money. The Country
therefore will be a gainer by it and will be able to pay the interest without inconvenience.

But the objectors suppose that all the money which come
in goes out again in an increased consumption of foreign luxuries. This however is taking for granted what never happened in any industrious country & what appearances among
us do not warrant. The expense of living generally speaking is
not sensibly increased. Large investments are every day making in ship building, house building, manufactures & other
improvements public & private.

The transfer too of the whole debt is a very improbable
supposition. A large part of it will continue to be holden by
our own citizens. And the interest of that part which is owned
by foreigners will not be annually exported as is supposed. A
considerable part will be invested in new speculations, in
lands canals roads manufactures commerce. Facts warrant this
supposition. The Agents of the Dutch have actually made
large investments in a variety of such speculations. A young
Country like this is peculiarly attractive. New objects will be
continually opening and the money of foreigners will be made
instrumental to their advancement.

8.th Object

Ans   This is a mere hypothesis in which theorists differ.
There are no decisive facts on which to rest the question.

The supposed tendency of bank paper to banish specie is
from its capacity of serving as a substitute for it in circulation.
But as the quantity circulated is proportioned to the demand for it, in circulation, the presumption is that a greater
quantity of industry is put in motion by it, so as to call for a
proportionably greater quantity of *circulating medium* and
prevent the banishment of the specie.

But however this may be it is agreed among sound theroists
that Banks more than compensate for the loss of the specie in
other ways. SMITH who was witness to their effects in Scot-

land; where too a very adverse fortune attended some of them bears his testimony to their beneficial effects in these strong Terms (Wealth of Nations Vol. I Book II. Ch. II. Page 441. to 444).

9 Objection

The 10 or 12 ℔ Ct &c.

Answer 1 The profits of the Bank have not hitherto exceeded the rate of 8 ℔ Ct. per annum & perhaps never may. It is questionable whether they can legally make more than *10 ℔ Ct.*

2 These profits can in no just sense be said to be taken out of the pockets of the people. They are compounded of two things—1 the interest paid by the Government on that part of the public Debt which is incorporated in the stock of the Bank—2 the interest paid by those *Individuals who borrow* money of the Bank on the *sums they borrow.*

As to the first, it is no *new grant* to the bank. It is the old interest on a part of the old Debt of the Country, subscribed by the proprietors of that Debt towards constituting the Stock of the Bank. It would have been equally payable if the Bank had never existed. It is therefore nothing new taken out of the pockets of the people.

As to the second, it may with equal propriety be said, when one individual borrows money of another, that the interest, which the borrower pays to the lender, is taken out of the *pockets of the people.* The case here is not only parallel but the same. It is a case of one or more individuals borrowing money of a company of individuals associated to lend. None but the actual borrowers pay in either case. The rest of the community have nothing to do with it.

If a man receives a bank bill for the ox or the bushel of wheat which he sells he pays no more interest upon it than upon the same sum in gold or silver; that is he pays none at all.

So that whether the paper banishes specie or not it is the same thing to every individual through whose hands it circulates, as to the point of Interest. Specie no more than Bank paper can be borrowed without paying interest for it, and when either is not borrowed no interest is paid. As far as the Government is a sharer in the profits of the Bank which is in the proportion of ⅕ the contrary of what is supposed happens. *Money is put into the pockets of the People.*

All this is so plain and so palpable that the assertion which is made betrays extreme ignorance or extreme disingenuousness. It is destitute even of colour.

10 Objection

This is a copious subject which has been fully discussed in the report of the Secretary of the Treasury on the subject of Manufactures from Page   to   . It is true that the Capital, that is the *specie*, which is employed in paper speculation, while so employed, is barren and useless, but the paper itself constitutes a *new Capital*, which being saleable and transferrable at any moment, enables the proprietor to undertake any piece of business as well as an equal sum in Coin. And as the amount of the Debt circulated is much greater than the amount of the *specie* which circulates it, the new Capital put in motion by it considerably exceeds the old one which is *suspended*. And there is more capital to carry on the productive labour of the Society. Every thing that has value is Capital— an acre of ground a horse or a cow or a public or a private obligation; which may with different degrees of convenience be applied to industrious enterprise. That which, like public Stock, can at any instant be turned into money is of equal utility with money as Capital.

Let it be examined whether at those places where there is most debt afloat and most money employed in its circulation, there is not at the same time a greater plenty of money for every other purpose. It will be found that there is.

But it is in fact quite immaterial to the Government, as far as regards the propriety of its measures.

The Debt existed. It was to be provided for. In whatever shape the provision was made the object of speculation and the speculation would have existed. Nothing but abolishing the Debt could have obviated it. It is therefore the fault of the Revolution not of the Government that paper speculation exists.

An unsound or precarious provision would have increased this species of speculation in its most odious forms. The defects & casualties of the system would have been as much subjects of speculation as the Debt itself.

The difference is that under a bad system the public Stock would have been too uncertain an article to be a substitute for money & all the money employed in it would have been diverted from useful employment without any thing to compensate for it. Under a good system the Stock becomes more than a substitute for the money employed in negotiating it.

Objection 11   Paper Speculation nourishes in our Citizens &c.

Answer   This proposition within certain limits is true. Jobbing in the funds has some bad effects among those engaged in it. It fosters a spirit of gambling, and diverts a certain number of individuals from other pursuits. But if the proposition be true, that Stock operates as Capital, the effect upon the Citizens at large is different. It promotes among them industry by furnishing a larger field of employment. Though this effect of a funded debt has been called in question in England by some theorists yet most theorists & all practical men allow its existence. And there is no doubt, as already intimated, that if we look into those scenes among ourselves where the largest portions of the Debt are accumulated we shall perceive that a new spring has been given to Industry in various branches.

But be all this as it may, the observation made under the last head applies here. The Debt was the creature of the Revolution. It was to be provided for. Being so, in whatever form, it must have become an object of speculation and jobbing.

Objection 12

The funding of the Debt has furnished effectual means of corrupting &c.

Answer   This is one of those assertions which can only be denied and pronounced to be malignant and false. No facts exist to support it, and being a mere matter of fact, no *argument* can be brought to repel it.

The Assertors beg the question. They assume to themselves and to those who think with them infallibility. Take their words for it, they are the only honest men in the community. But compare the tenor of mens lives and *at least* as large a proportion of virtuous and independent characters will be found among those whom they malign as among themselves.

A member of a majority of the Legislature would say to these Defamers—

"In your vocabulary, Gentlemen, *creditor* and *enemy* appear to be synonimous terms—the *support of public credit* and *corruption* of similar import—an *enlarged* and *liberal* construction of the constitution for the public good and for the maintenance of the due energy of the national authority of the same meaning with usurpation and a conspiracy to overturn the republican government of the Country—every man of a different opinion from your own an ambitious despot or a corrupt knave. You bring every thing to the standard of your narrow and depraved ideas, and you condemn without mercy or even decency whatever does not accord with it. Every man who is either too long or too short for your political couch must be stretched or lopped to suit it. But your pretensions must be rejected. Your insinuations despised. Your Politics originate in immorality, in a disregard of the maxims of good faith and the rights of property, and if they could prevail must end in national disgrace and confusion. Your rules of construction for the authorities vested in the Government of the Union would arrest all its essential movements and bring it back in practice to the same state of imbecillity which rendered the old confederation contemptible. Your principles of liberty are principles of licentiousness incompatible with all government. You sacrifice every thing that is venerable and substantial in society to the vain reveries of a false and new fangled philosophy. As to the motives by which I have been influenced, I leave my general conduct in private and public life to speak for them. Go and learn among my *fellow citizens* whether I have not uniformly maintained the character of an honest man. As to the love of liberty and Country you have given no stronger proofs of being actuated by it than I have done. Cease then to arrogate to yourself and to your party all the patriotism and virtue of the Country. Renounce if you can the intolerant spirit by which you are governed—and begin to reform yourself instead of reprobating others, by beginning to doubt of your own infallibility."

Such is the answer which would naturally be given by a member of the Majority in the Legislature to such an Objector. And it is the only one that could be given; until some evidence of the supposed corruption should be produced.

As far as I know, there is not a member of the Legislature who can properly be called a Stock-jobber or a paper Dealer. There are several of them who were proprietors of public debt in various ways. Some for money lent & property furnished for the use of the public during the War others for sums received in payment of Debts—and it is supposeable enough that some of them had been purchasers of the public Debt, with intention to hold it, as a valuable & convenient property; considering an honorable provision for it as matter of course.

It is a strange perversion of ideas, and as novel as it is extraordinary, that men should be deemed corrupt & criminal for becoming proprietors in the funds of their Country. Yet I believe the number of members of Congress is very small who have ever been considerably proprietors in the funds.

And as to improper speculations on measures depending before Congress, I believe never was any *body* of men freer from them.

There are indeed several members of Congress, who have become proprietors in the Bank of the United States, and a *few* of them to a pretty large amount say 50 or 60 shares; but all operations of this kind were necessarily subsequent to the determination upon the measure. The subscriptions were of course subsequent & purchases still more so. Can there be any thing really blameable in this? Can it be culpable to invest property in an institution which has been established for the most important national purposes? Can that property be supposed to corrupt the holder? It would indeed tend to render him friendly to the preservation of the Bank; but in this there would be no collision between duty & interest and it could give him no improper byass in other questions.

To uphold public credit and to be friendly to the Bank must be presupposed to be *corrupt things* before the being a proprietor in the funds or of bank Stock can be supposed to have a *corrupting influence*. The being a proprietor in either case is a very different thing from being, in a proper sense of the term, a Stock jobber. On this point of the corruption of the Legislature one more observation of great weight remains. Those who oppose a *funded* debt and mean any provision for it contemplate an *annual* one. Now, it is impossible to conceive a more fruitful source of legislative corruption than this. All the members of it who should incline to speculate would have an annual opportunity of speculating upon their influence in the legislature to promote or retard or put off a provision. Every session the question whether the annual provision should be continued would be an occasion of pernicious caballing and corrupt bargaining. In this very view when the subject was in deliberation, it was impossible not to wish it declared upon once for all & out of the way.

Objection the 13   The Corrupt Squadron &c

Here again the objectors beg the question. They take it for granted that their constructions of the constitution are right and that the opposite ones are wrong, and with great good nature and candor ascribe the effect of a difference of opinion to a disposition to get rid of the limitations on the Government.

Those who have advocated the constructions which have obtained have met their opponents on the ground of fair argument and they think have refuted them. How shall it be determined which side is right?

There are some things which the General Government has clearly a right to do—there are others which it has clearly no right to meddle with, and there is a good deal of middle ground, about which honest & well disposed men may differ. The most that can be said is that some of this middle ground may have been occupied by the National Legislature; and this surely is no evidence of a disposition to get rid of the limitations in the constitution; nor can it be viewed in that light by men of candor.

The truth is one description of men is disposed to do the essential business of the Nation by a liberal construction of the powers of the Government; another from disaffection would fritter away those powers—a third from an overweening jealousy would do the same thing—a fourth from party & personal opposition are torturing the constitution into objections to every thing they do not like.

The Bank is one of the measures which is deemed by some the greatest stretch of power; and yet its constitutionality has been established in the most satisfactory manner.

And the most incorrigible theorist among its opponents would in one months experience as head of the Department of the Treasury be compelled to acknowlege that it is an absolutely indispensable engine in the management of the Finances and would quickly become a convert to its perfect constitutionality.

Objection XIV   The ultimate object of all

To this there is no other answer than a flat denial—except this that the project from its absurdity refutes itself.

The idea of introducing a monarchy or aristocracy into this Country, by employing the influence and force of a Government continually changing hands, towards it, is one of those visionary things, that none but madmen could meditate and that no wise men will believe.

If it could be done at all, which is utterly incredible, it would require a long series of time, certainly beyond the life of any individual to effect it. Who then would enter into such plot? For what purpose of interest or ambition?

To hope that the people may be cajoled into giving their sanctions to such institutions is still more chimerical. A people so enlightened and so diversified as the people of this Country can surely never be brought to it, but from convulsions and disorders, in consequence of the acts of popular demagogues.

The truth unquestionably is, that the only path to a subversion of the republican system of the Country is, by flattering the prejudices of the people, and exciting their jealousies and apprehensions, to throw affairs into confusion, and bring on civil commotion. Tired at length of anarchy, or want of government, they may take shelter in the arms of monarchy for repose and security.

Those then, who resist a confirmation of public order, are the true Artificers of monarchy—not that this is the intention of the generality of them. Yet it would not be difficult to lay the finger upon some of their party who may justly be suspected. When a man unprincipled in private life desperate in his fortune, bold in his temper, possessed of considerable talents, having the advantage of military habits—despotic in his ordinary demeanour—known to have scoffed in private at the principles of liberty—when such a man is seen to mount the hobby horse of popularity—to join in the cry of danger to liberty—to take every opportunity of embarrassing the General Government & bringing it under suspicion—to flatter and fall in with all the non sense of the zealots of the day—It may justly be suspected that his object is to throw things into confusion that he may "ride the storm and direct the whirlwind."

It has aptly been observed that *Cato* was the Tory—*Cæsar* the whig of his day. The former frequently resisted—the latter always flattered the follies of the people. Yet the former perished with the Republic the latter destroyed it.

No popular Government was ever without its Catalines & its Cæsars. These are its true enemies.

As far as I am informed the anxiety of those who are calumniated is to keep the Government in the state in which it is, which they fear will be no easy task, from a natural tendency in the state of things to exalt the local on the ruins of the National Government. Some of them appear to wish, in a constitutional way, a change in the judiciary department of the Government, from an apprehension that an orderly and effectual administration of Justice cannot be obtained without a more intimate connection between the state and national Tribunals. But even this is not an object of any set of men as a party. There is a difference of opinion about it on various grounds among those who have generally acted together. As to any other change of consequence, I believe nobody dreams of it.

Tis curious to observe the anticipations of the different parties. One side appears to believe that there is a serious plot to overturn the state Governments and substitute monarchy to the present republican system. The other side firmly believes that there is a serious plot to overturn the General Government & elevate the separate power of the states upon its ruins. Both sides may be equally wrong & their mutual jealousies may be materially causes of the appearances which mutually disturb them, and sharpen them against each other.

Objection the 15   This change was contemplated &c

This is a palpable misrepresentation. No man, that I know of, contemplated the introducing into this country of a monarchy. A very small number (not more than three or four) manifested theoretical opinions favourable in the abstract to a constitution like that of Great Britain, but every one agreed that such a constitution except as to the general distribution of departments and powers was out of the Question in reference to this Country. The Member who was most explicit on this point (a Member from New York) declared in strong terms that the republican theory ought to be adhered to in this Country as long as there was any chance of its success—that the idea of a perfect equality of political rights among the citizens, exclusive of all permanent or hereditary distinctions, was of a nature to engage the good wishes of every good man, whatever might be his theoretic doubts—that it merited his best efforts to give success to it in practice—that hitherto from an incompetent structure of the Government it had not had a fair trial, and that the endeavour ought then to be to secure to it a better chance of success by a government more capable of energy and order.

There is not a man at present in either branch of the Legislature who, that I recollect, had held language in the Convention favourable to Monarchy.

The basis therefore of this suggestion fails.

16   So many of them &c.

This has been answered above. Neither description of character is to be found in the Legislature. In the Senate there are 9 or ten who were members of the Convention; in the house of Representatives not more than six or seven. Of those who are in the lastmentioned house—none can be considered as influential but Mr. Madison and Mr. Gerry. Are they monarchy men?

As to the 17. 18th and 19th heads—They are rather inferences from and comments upon what is before suggested than specific objections. The answer to them must therefore be derived from what is said under other heads.

It is certainly much to be regretted that party discriminations are so far Geographical as they have been; and that ideas of a severance of the Union are creeping in both North and South. In the South it is supposed that more government than is expedient is desired by the North. In the North, it is believed, that the prejudices of the South are incompatible with the necessary degree of Government and with the attainment of the essential ends of National Union. In both quarters there are respectable men who talk of separation, as a thing dictated by the different geniusses and different prejudices of the parts. But happily their number is not considerable—& the prevailing sentiment of the people is in favour of their true interest, UNION. And it is to be hoped that the Efforts of wise men will be able to prevent a scism, which would be injurious in different degrees to different portions of the Union; but would seriously wound the prosperity of all.

As to the sacrifice of Southern to Northern prejudices—if the conflict has been between *prejudices* and *prejudices*, it is certainly to be wished for mutual gratification that there had been mutual concession; but if the conflict has been between *great* and *substantial* national objects on the one hand, and theoretical prejudices on the other, it is difficult to desire that the former should in any instance have yielded.

Objection 20   The Owers of the Debt are in the Southern and the holders of it in the Northern Division.

Answer. If this were literally true, it would be no argument for or against any thing. It would be still politically and morally right for the Debtors to pay their Creditors.

But it is in *no sense* true. The OWERS of the Debt are the people of *every* State, South Middle North. The holders are the Individual Creditors—citizens of the United Netherlands, Great Britain, France & of these States, North, Middle, South. Though some men, who constantly substitute hypothesis to fact, imagination to evidence, assert and reassert that the inhabitants of the South contribute *more* than those of the North; yet there is no pretence that they contribute *all*; and even the assertion of greater contribution is unsupported by documents facts, or, it may be added, probabilities. Though the inhabitants of the South manufacture less than those of the North, which is the great argument, yet it does not follow that they consume more of taxable articles. It is a solid answer to this, that *whites* live better, wear more and better cloaths, and consume more luxuries, than blacks who constitute so considerable a part of the population of the South—that the Inhabitants of Cities and Towns, which abound so much more in the North than in the South, consume more of foreign articles, than the inhabitants of the Country—that it is a general rule that communities consume & contribute in proportion to their active or circulating wealth and that the Northern Regions have more active or circulating wealth than the Southern.

If official documents are consulted, though for obvious reasons they are not decisive, they contradict rather than confirm the hypothesis of greater proportional contribution in the Southern Division.

But to make the allegation in the objection true, it is necessary not merely that the Inhabitants of the South should contribute more, but that they should contribute *all*.

It must be confessed that a much larger proportion of the Debt is *owned* by inhabitants of the States from Pensylvania to New Hampshire inclusively than in the States South of Pensylvania.

But as to the primitive Debt of the United States, that was the case in its original concoction. This arose from two causes. I, from the war having more constantly been carried on in the Northern Quarter, which led to obtaining more men and greater supplies in that quarter, and credit having been, for a considerable time, the main instrument of the Government, a consequent accumulation of debt in that quarter took place. II from the greater ability of the Northern and middle States to furnish men money and other supplies; and from the greater quantity of men money and other supplies which they did furnish. The loan office Debt; the army debt, the debt of the five great departments was *contracted* in a much larger proportion in the Northern and middle, than in the Southern States.

It must be confessed too that by the attractions of a superior monied Capital the disparity has increased, but it was great in the beginning.

As to the assumed debt the proportion in the South was at the first somewhat larger than in the North; and it must be acknowleged that this has since, from the same superiority of monied Capital in the North, ceased to be the case.

But if the Northern people who were originally greater Creditors than the Southern have become still more so, as purchasers, is it any reason that an honorable provision should not be made for their Debt? Or is the Government to blame for having made it? Did the Northern people take their property by violence from the Southern, or did they purchase and pay for it?

It may be answered that they obtained a considerable part of it by speculation, taking advantage of superior opportunities of information.

But admitting this to be true in all the latitude in which it is commonly stated—Is a government to bend the general maxims of policy and to mould its measures according to the accidental course of private speculations? Is it to do this or omit that in cases of great national importance, because one set of Individuals may gain, another lose, from unequal opportunities of information, from unequal degrees of resource, craft confidence or enterprise?

More over—There is much exaggeration in stating the manner of the alienation of the Debt. The principal speculations in state debt, whatever may be pretended certainly began, after the promulgation of the plan for assuming by the Report of the Secy of the Treasury to the House of Representatives. The resources of Individuals in this Country are too limited to have admitted of much progress in purchases before the knowlege of that plan was diffused throughout the Country. After that, purchasers and sellers were upon equal ground. If the purchasers speculated upon the sellers, in many instances, the sellers speculated upon the purchasers. Each made his calculation of chances, and founded upon it an exchange of money for certificates. It has turned out generally that the buyer had the best of the bargain; but the seller got the value of his commodity according to his estimate of it, and probably in a great number of instances more. This shall be explained:

It happened that Mr. Maddison and some other distinguished characters of the South started in opposition to the Assumption. The high opinion entertained of them made it be taken for granted in that quarter, that the opposition would be successful. The securities quickly rose by means of purchases beyond their former prices. It was imagined that they would soon return to their old station by a rejection of the proposition for assuming. And the certificate holders were eager to part with them at their current prices; calculating on a loss to the Purchasers from their future fall. The representation is not conjectural; it is founded in information from respectable and intelligent Southern characters—And may be ascertained by Inquiry.

Hence it happened, that the inhabitants of the Southern states sustained a considerable loss, by the opposition to the assumption, from Southern Gentlemen, and their too great confidence in the efficacy of that opposition.

Further—A great part of the Debt which has been purchased by Northern of Southern Citizens has been at high prices; in numerous instances beyond the true value. In the late delirium of speculation large sums were purchased at 25 ⅌ Cent above par and upwards.

The Southern people upon the whole have not parted with their property for nothing. They parted with it voluntarily—in most cases, upon fair terms, without surprize or deception, in many cases for more than its value. Tis their own fault, if the purchase money has not been beneficial to them—and the presumption is that it has been so in a material degree.

Let then any candid and upright mind, weighing all the circumstances, pronounce whether there be any real hardship in the inhabitants of the South being required to contribute their proportion to a provision for the Debt as it now exists—whether, if at liberty, they could honestly dispute the doing of it, or whether they can even in candor and good faith complain of being obliged to do it.

If they can, it is time to unlearn all the ancient notions of justice and morality, and to adopt a new system of Ethics.

Observation 21   The Antifœderal Champions &c

Answer   All that can be said in answer to this has been already said.

It is much to be wished, that the true state of the case may not have been, that the Antifœderal Champions have been encouraged in their activity, by the countenance which has been given to their principles, by certain fœderalists, who in an envious and ambitious struggle for power influence and preeminence have imbraced as auxiliaries the numerous party originally disaffected to the Government in the hope that these united with the factious and feeble minded fœderalists whom they can detach will give them the prœdominancy. This would be nothing more than the old story of personal and party emulation.

The Antifœderal Champions alluded to may be taught to abate their exultation by being told that the great body of the fœderalists, or rather the great body of the people are of opinion that none of their predictions have been fulfilled—That the beneficial effects of the Government have exceeded expectation and are witnessed by the general prosperity of the Nation.

REPRIMANDING ADAMS

To John Adams

My Dear Sir   Philadelphia Sepr. 9. 1792

I trust you are sufficiently convinced of my respect for and attachment to you to render an apology for the liberty, I am going to take unnecessary. I learnt with pain that you may not probably be here 'till late in the session. I fear that this will give some handle to your enemies to misrepresent—and though I am persuaded you are very indifferent personally to the event of a certain election, yet I hope you are not so as it regards the cause of good Government. The difference in that view is in my conception immense between the success of Mr. Clinton or yourself; and some sacrifices of feeling are to be made. But this is not the only relation, in which I deem your early presence here desireable. Permit me to say it best suits the firmness and elevation of your character to meet all events, whether auspicious or otherwise, on the ground where station & duty, call you. One would not give the ill disposed the triumph of supposing that an anticipation of want of success had kept you from your post.

You observe My Dr Sir, I speak without much *menagement*. You will ascribe it to my confidence and esteem. It is not necessary in any view to multiply words. I forbear it. But allow me to add that it is the universal wish of your friends you should be as soon as possible at Philadelphia.

I have the honor to remain very respectfully   and truly Dr
Sir Yr friend & Obed servant

A Hamilton

RESPONDING TO A PLEA FOR PEACE

To George Washington

Philadelphia September 9
Sir   1792

I have the pleasure of your private letter of the 26th of August.

The feelings and views which are manifested in that letter are such as I expected would exist. And I most sincerely regret the causes of the uneasy sensations you experience. It is my most anxious wish, as far as may depend upon me, to smooth the path of your administration, and to render it prosperous and happy. And if any prospect shall open of healing or terminating the differences which exist, I shall most chearfully embrace it; though I consider myself as the deeply injured party. The recommendation of such a spirit is worthy of the moderation and wisdom which dictated it; and if your endeavours should prove unsuccessful, I do not hesitate to say that in my opinion the period is not remote when the public good will require *substitutes* for the *differing members* of your administration. The continuance of a division there must destroy the energy of Government, which will be little enough with the strictest Union. On my part there will be a most chearful acquiescence in such a result.

I trust, Sir, that the greatest frankness has always marked and will always mark every step of my conduct towards you. In this disposition, I cannot conceal from you that I have had some instrumentality of late in the retaliations which have fallen upon certain public characters and that I find myself placed in a situation not to be able to recede *for the present.*

I considered myself as compelled to this conduct by reasons public as well as personal of the most cogent nature. I know that I have been an object of uniform opposition from Mr. Jefferson, from the first moment of his coming to the City of New York to enter upon his present office. I know, from the most authentic sources, that I have been the frequent subject of the most unkind whispers and insinuating from the same quarter. I have long seen a formed party in the Legislature, under his auspices, bent upon my subversion. I cannot doubt, from the evidence I possess, that the National Gazette was instituted by him for political purposes and that one leading object of it has been to render me and all the measures connected with my department as odious as possible.

Nevertheless I can truly say, that, except explanations to confidential friends, I never directly or indirectly retaliated or countenanced retaliation till very lately. I can even assure you, that I was instrumental in preventing a very severe and systematic attack upon Mr. Jefferson, by an association of two or three individuals, in consequence of the persecution, which he brought upon the Vice President, by his indiscreet and light letter to the Printer, transmitting *Paine's* pamphlet.

As long as I saw no danger to the Government, from the machinations which were going on, I resolved to be a silent sufferer of the injuries which were done me. I determined to avoid giving occasion to any thing which could manifest to the world dissentions among the principal characters of the government; a thing which can never happen without weakening its hands, and in some degree throwing a stigma upon it.

But when I no longer doubted, that there was a formed party deliberately bent upon the subversion of measures, which in its consequences would subvert the Government— when I saw, that the undoing of the funding system in particular (which, whatever may be the original merits of that system, would prostrate the credit and the honor of the Nation, and bring the Government into contempt with that description of Men, who are in every society the only firm supporters of government) was an avowed object of the party; and that all possible pains were taking to produce that effect by rendering it odious to the body of the people—I considered it as a duty, to endeavour to resist the torrent, and as an essential mean to this end, to draw aside the veil from the principal Actors. To this strong impulse, to this decided conviction, I have yielded. And I think events will prove that I have judged rightly.

Nevertheless I pledge my honor to you Sir, that if you shall hereafter form a plan to reunite the members of your administration, upon some steady principle of cooperation, I will faithfully concur in executing it during my continuance in office. And I will not directly or indirectly say or do a thing, that shall endanger a feud.

I have had it very much at heart to make an excursion to Mount Vernon, by way of the Fœderal City in the course of this Month—and have been more than once on the point of asking your permission for it. But I now despair of being able to effect it. I am nevertheless equally obliged by your kind invitation.

The subject mentioned in the Postscript of your letter shall with great pleasure be carefully attended to. With the most faithful and affectionate attachment I have the honor to remain

Sir   Your most Obed & humble servant   A Hamilton

P.S   I had written you two letters on public business, one of which will go with this; but the other will be witheld, in consequence of a slight indisposition of the Attorney General, to be sent by express sometime in the course of tomorrow.

Amicus

For the National Gazette.

A writer in the Gazette of Saturday last, after several observations, with regard to certain charges, which have lately been brought forward against the Secretary of State, proceeds to make or insinuate several charges against another public character.

As to the observations which are designed to exculpate the Secretary of State, I shall do nothing more than refer to the discussions which have taken place and appear to be in a train to be pursued, in the Gazette of the United States.

As to the charges which have been bro't against the other public character alluded to, I shall assert generally, from a long, intimate, and confidential acquaintance with him, added to some other means of information, that the matters charged, as far as they are intelligible, are either grossly misrepresented or palpably untrue.

A part of them, is of a nature to speak itself, without comment, the malignity and turpitude of the accuser, denoting clearly the personal enemy in the garb of the political opponent.

The subject and the situation of the parties naturally impose silence—but this is not the first attempt of the kind that has been made; fruitlessly hitherto, and I doubt not equally fruitlessly in time to come. An opinion on the experience of fifteen years, the greatest part of the time, under circumstances affording the best opportunity for an accurate estimate of character, cannot be shaken by slanderous surmises. The charge of which I shall take more particular notice, is contained in the following passage—"Let him explain the public character, who, if uncontradicted fame is to be regarded, *opposed* the Constitution in the Grand Convention, because it was *too republican*, and advocated the *British monarchy as the perfect standard* to be approached as nearly as the people could be *made to bear*."

This I affirm, to be a gross misrepresentation. To prove it so, it were sufficient to appeal to a single fact, namely, that the gentleman alluded to, was the only member from the state to which he belonged who signed the Constitution, and, it is notorious, against the prevailing weight of the official influence of the state, and against what would probably be the opinion of a large majority of his fellow-citizens, till better information should correct their first impressions—how then can he be believed to have opposed a thing, which he actually agreed to, and that, in so unsupported a situation, and under circumstances of such peculiar responsibility? To this I shall add two more facts; one, that the member in question, never made a single proposition to the Convention, which was not conformable to the republican theory; the other, that the highest-toned of any of the propositions made by him was actually voted for by the representations of several states, including some of the principal ones; and including individuals, who, in the estimation of those who deem themselves the only republicans, are pre-eminent for republican character—more than this I am not at liberty to say. It is a matter generally understood, that the deliberations of the Convention which were carried on in private, were to remain undisturbed. And every prudent man must be convinced of the propriety both of the one and the other. Had the deliberations been open while going on, the clamours of faction would have prevented any satisfactory result. Had they been afterwards disclosed, much food would have been afforded to inflammatory declamation. Propositions made without due reflection, and perhaps abandoned by the proposers themselves, on more mature reflection, would have been handles for a profusion of ill-natured accusation.

Every infallible declaimer taking his own ideas as the perfect standard, would have railed without measure or mercy at every member of the Convention who had gone a single line beyond his standard.

The present is a period fruitful in accusation. Much anonymous slander has and will be vented. No man's reputation can be safe, if charges in this form are to be lightly listened to. There are but two kinds of anonymous charges that can merit attention—where the evidence goes along with the charge—and where reference is made to *specific facts*, the evidence of the truth or falsehood of which, is in the power or possession of the party accused, and he at liberty to make a free use of it. None of the charges brought forward in the present instance, fall within either of these rules.

AMICUS.

Sept. 11.

AN EMBRYO-CÆSAR

To an Unknown Correspondent

Philadelphia Sept. 26.
1792

My Dear Sir

Some days since, I was surprised with the following intelligence, in a letter from Mr. King (whose name I disclose to you in confidence).

"*Burr* is industrious in his Canvass and his object is well understood by our Antis. Mr. Edwards is to make interest for him in Connecticut and Mr. Dallas, who is here, and quite in the circle of the Governor and the party informs us, that Mr. Burr will be supported as Vice President in Pensylvania. Nothing which has heretofore happened so decisively proves the inveteracy of the opposition. Should they succeed much would be to be apprehended"

Though in my situation I deem it most proper to avoid interference in any matter relating to the elections for Members of the Government—Yet I feel reasons of sufficient force to induce a departure from that rule in the present instance.

Mr. Burr's integrity as an Individual is not unimpeached. As a public man he is one of the worst sort—a friend to nothing but as it suits his interest and ambition. Determined to climb to the highest honours of State, and as much higher as circumstances may permit—he cares nothing about the means of effecting his purpose. Tis evident that he aims at putting himself at the head of what he calls the "popular party" as affording the best tools for an ambitious man to work with. Secretly turning Liberty into ridicule, he knows as well as most men how to make use of the name. In a word, if we have an embryo-Cæsar in the United States 'tis Burr.

Draft of a Defense of the Neutrality Proclamation

1. It is a melancholy truth, which every new political occurrence more and more unfolds, that there is a discription of men in this country, irreconcileably adverse to the government of the United States; whose exertions, whatever be the springs of them, whether infatuation or depravity or both, tend to disturb the tranquillity order and prosperity of this now peaceable flourishing and truly happy land. A real and enlightened friend to public felicity cannot observe new confirmations of this fact, without feeling a deep and poignant regret, that human nature should be so refractory and perverse; that amidst a profusion of the bounties and blessings of Providence, political as well as natural, inviting to contentment and gratitude, there should still be found men disposed to cherish and propagate disquietude and alarm; to render suspected and detested the instruments of the felicity, in which they partake; to sacrifice the most substantial advantages, that ever fell to the lot of a people at the shrine of personal envy rivalship and animosity, to the instigations of a turbulent and criminal ambition, or to the treacherous phantoms of an ever craving and never to be satisfied spirit of innovation; a spirit, which seems to suggest to its votaries that the most natural and happy state of Society is a state of continual revolution and change—that the welfare of a nation is in exact ratio to the rapidity of the political vicissitudes, which it undergoes—to the frequency and violence of the tempests with which it is agitated.

2 Yet so the fact unfortunately is—such men certainly are—and it is essential to our dearest interests to the preservation of peace and good order to the dignity and independence of our public councils—to the real and permanent security of liberty and property—that the Citizens of the UStates should open their eyes to the true characters and designs of the men alluded to—should be upon their guard against their insidious and ruinous machinations.

3 At this moment a most dangerous combination exists. Those who for some time past have been busy in undermining

the constitution and government of the UStates, by indirect attacks, by labouring to render its measures odious, by striving to destroy the confidence of the people in its administration—are now meditating a more direct and destructive war against it—and embodying and arranging their forces and systematising their efforts. Secret clubs are formed and private consultations held. Emissaries are dispatched to distant parts of the United States to effect a concert of views and measures, among the members and partisans of the disorganising corps, in the several states. The language in the confidential circles is that the constitution of the United States is too complex a system—that it savours too much of the pernicious doctrine of "ballances and checks" that it requires to be simplified in its structure, to be purged of some monarchical and aristocratic ingredients which are said to have found their way into it and to be stripped of some dangerous prerogatives, with which it is pretended to be invested.

4   The noblest passion of the human soul, which no where burns with so pure and bright a flame, as in the breasts of the people of the UStates, is if possible to be made subservient to this fatal project. That zeal for the liberty of mankind, which produced so universal a sympathy in the cause of France in the first stages of its revolution, and which, it is supposed, has not yet yielded to the just reprobation, which a sober temperate and humane people, friends of religion, social order, and justice, enemies to tumult and massacre, to the wanton and lawless shedding of human blood cannot but bestow upon those extravagancies excesses and outrages, which have sullied and which endanger that cause—that laudable, it is not too much to say that holy zeal is intended by every art of misrepresentation and deception to be made the instrument first of controuling finally of overturning the Government of the Union.

5   The ground which has been so wisely taken by the Executive of the UStates, in regard to the present war of Europe against France, is to be the pretext of this mischievous attempt. The people are if possible to be made to believe, that the Proclamation of neutrality issued by the President of the US was unauthorised illegal and officious—inconsistent with the treaties and plighted faith of the Nation—inconsistent

with a due sense of gratitude to France for the services rendered us in our late contest for independence and liberty—inconsistent with a due regard for the progress and success of republican principles. Already the presses begin to groan with invective against the Chief Magistrate of the Union, for that prudent and necessary measure; a measure calculated to manifest to the World the pacific position of the Government and to caution the citizens of the UStates against practices, which would tend to involve us in a War the most unequal and calamitous, in which it is possible for a Country to be engaged—a war which would not be unlikely to prove pregnant with still greater dangers and disasters, than that by which we established our existence as an Independent Nation.

6 What is the true solution of this extraordinary appearance? Are the professed the real motives of its authors? They are not. The true object is to disparage in the opinion and affections of his fellow citizens that man who at the head of our armies fought so successfully for the Liberty and Independence, which are now our pride and our boast—who during the war supported the hopes, united the hearts and nerved the arm of his countrymen—who at the close of it, unseduced by ambition & the love of power, soothed and appeased the discontents of his suffering companions in arms, and with them left the proud scenes of a victorious field for the modest retreats of private life—who could only have been drawn out of these favourite retreats, to aid in the glorious work of ingrafting that liberty, which his sword had contributed to win, upon a stock of which it stood in need and without which it could not flourish—endure—a firm adequate national Government—who at this moment sacrifices his tranquillity and every favourite pursuit to the peremptory call of his country to aid in giving solidity to a fabric, which he has assisted in rearing—whose whole conduct has been one continued proof of his rectitude moderation disinterestedness and patriotism, who whether the evidence of a uniform course of virtuous public actions be considered, or the motives likely to actuate a man placed precisely in his situation be estimated, it may safely be pronounced, can have no other ambition than that of doing good to his Country & transmitting his fame unimpaired to posterity. For what or for whom

is he to hazard that rich harvest of glory, which he has acquired that unexampled veneration and love of his fellow Citizens, which he so eminently possesses?

7   Yet the men alluded to, while they contend with affected zeal for gratitude towards a foreign Nation, which in assisting us was and ought to have been influenced by considerations relative to its own interest—forgetting what is due to a fellow Citizen, who at every hazard rendered essential services to his Country from the most patriotic motives—insidiously endeavour to despoil him of that precious reward of his services, the confidence and approbation of his fellow Citizens.

8   The present attempt is but the renewal in another form of an attack some time since commenced, and which was only dropped because it was perceived to have excited a general indignation. Domestic arrangements of mere convenience, calculated to reconcile the œconomy of time with the attentions of decorum and civility were then the topics of malevolent declamation. A more serious article of charge is now opened and seems intended to be urged with greater earnestness and vigour. The merits of it shall be examined in one or two succeeding papers, I trust in a manner, that will evince to every candid mind to futility.

9   To be an able and firm supporter of the Government of the Union is in the eyes of the men referred to a crime sufficient to justify the most malignant persecution. Hence the attacks which have been made and repeated with such persevering industry upon more than one public Character in that Government. Hence the effort which is now going on to depreciate in the eyes and estimation of the People the man whom their unanimous suffrages have placed at the head of it.

10   Hence the pains which are taking to inculcate a discrimination between *principles* and *men* and to represent an attachment to the one as a species of war against the other; an endeavour, which has a tendency to stifle or weaken one of the best and most useful feelings of the human heart—a reverence for merit—and to take away one of the strongest incentives to public virtue—the expectation of public esteem.

11   A solicitude for the character who is attacked forms no part of the motives to this comment. He has deserved too

much, and his countrymen are too sensible of it to render any advocation of him necessary. If his virtues and services do not secure his fame and ensure to him the unchangeable attachment of his fellow Citizens, twere in vain to attempt to prop them by anonymous panygeric.

12 The design of the observations which have been made is merely to awaken the public attention to the views of a party engaged in a dangerous conspiracy against the tranquillity and happiness of their country. Aware that their hostile aims against the Government can never succeed til they have subverted the confidence of the people in its present Chief Magistrate, they have at length permitted the suggestions of their enmity to betray them into this hopeless and culpable attempt. If we can destroy his popularity (say they) our work is more than half completed.

13 In proportion as the Citizens of the UStates value the constitution on which their union and happiness depend, in proportion as they tender the blessings of peace and deprecate the calamities of War—ought to be their watchfulness against this success of the artifices which will be employed to endanger that constitution and those blessings. A mortal blow is aimed at both.

14 It imports them infinitely not to be deceived by the protestations which are made—that no harm is meditated against the Constitution—that no design is entertained to involve the peace of the Country. These appearances are necessary to the accomplishment of the plan which has been formed. It is known that the great body of the People are attached to the constitution. It would therefore defeat the intention of destroying it to avow that it exists. It is also known that the People of the UStates are firmly attached to peace. It would consequently frustrate the design of engaging them in the War to tell them that such an object is in contemplation.

15 A more artful course has therefore been adopted. Professions of good will to the Constitution are made without reserve: But every possible art is employed to render the administration and the most zealous and useful friends of the Government odious. The reasoning is obvious. If the people can be persuaded to dislike all the measures of the Government and to dislike all or the greater part of those who have

been most conspicuous in establishing or conducting it—the passage from this to the dislike and change of the constitution will not be long nor difficult. The abstract idea of regard for a constitution on paper will not long resist a thorough detestation of its practice.

16   In like manner, professions of a disposition to preserve the peace of the Country are liberally made. But the means of effecting the end are condemned; and exertions are used to prejudice the community against them. A proclamation of neutrality in the most cautious form is represented as illegal—contrary to our engagements with and our duty towards one of the belligerent powers. The plain inference is that in the opinion of these characters the UStates are under obligations which do not permit them to be neutral. Of course they are in a situation to become a party in the War from duty.

17   Pains are likewise taken to inflame the zeal of the people for the cause of France and to excite their resentments against the powers at War with her. To what end all this—but to beget if possible a temper in the community which may overrule the moderate or pacific views of the Government.

c. May 1793

Pacificus No. I

As attempts are making very dangerous to the peace, and it is to be feared not very friendly to the constitution of the UStates—it becomes the duty of those who wish well to both to endeavour to prevent their success.

The objections which have been raised against the Proclamation of Neutrality lately issued by the President have been urged in a spirit of acrimony and invective, which demonstrates, that more was in view than merely a free discussion of an important public measure; that the discussion covers a design of weakening the confidence of the People in the author of the measure; in order to remove or lessen a powerful obstacle to the success of an opposition to the Government, which however it may change its form, according to circumstances, seems still to be adhered to and pursued with persevering Industry.

This Reflection adds to the motives connected with the measure itself to recommend endeavours by proper explanations to place it in a just light. Such explanations at least cannot but be satisfactory to those who may not have leisure or opportunity for pursuing themselves an investigation of the subject, and who may wish to perceive that the policy of the Government is not inconsistent with its obligations or its honor.

The objections in question fall under three heads—

1   That the Proclamation was without authority
2   That it was contrary to our treaties with France
3   That it was contrary to the gratitude, which is due from this to that country; for the succours rendered us in our own Revolution.
4   That it was out of time & unnecessary.

In order to judge of the solidity of the first of these objections, it is necessary to examine what is the nature and design of a proclamation of neutrality.

The true nature & design of such an act is—to *make known* to the powers at War and to the Citizens of the Country, whose Government does the Act that such country is in the condition of a Nation at Peace with the belligerent parties, and under no obligations of Treaty, to become an *associate in the war* with either of them; that this being its situation its intention is to observe a conduct conformable with it and to perform towards each the duties of neutrality; and as a consequence of this state of things, to give warning to all within its jurisdiction to abstain from acts that shall contravene those duties, under the penalties which the laws of the land (of which the law of Nations is a part) annexes to acts of contravention.

This, and no more, is conceived to be the true import of a Proclamation of Neutrality.

It does not imply, that the Nation which makes the declaration will forbear to perform to any of the warring Powers any stipulations in Treaties which can be performed without rendering it an *associate* or *party* in the War. It therefore does not imply in our case, that the UStates will not make those distinctions, between the present belligerent powers, which are stipulated in the 17th and 22d articles of our Treaty with France; because these distinctions are not incompatible with a state of neutrality; they will in no shape render the UStates an *associate* or *party* in the War. This must be evident, when it is considered, that even to furnish *determinate* succours, of a certain number of Ships or troops, to a Power at War, in consequence of *antecedent treaties having no particular reference to the existing war*, is not inconsistent with neutrality; a position well established by the doctrines of Writers and the practice of Nations.*

But no special aids, succours or favors having relation to war, not positively and precisely stipulated by some Treaty of the above description, can be afforded to either party, without a breach of neutrality.

In stating that the Proclamation of Neutrality does not imply the non performance of any stipulations of Treaties which are not of a nature to make the Nation an associate or party in the war, it is conceded that an execution of the clause of Guarantee contained in the 11th article of our Treaty of Alliance with France would be contrary to the sense and spirit of the Proclamation; because it would engage us with our whole force as an *associate* or *auxiliary* in the War; it would

---

* See Vatel Book III Chap. VI § 101.

be much more than the case of a definite limited succour, previously ascertained.

It follows that the Proclamation is virtually a manifestation of the sense of the Government that the UStates are, *under the circumstances of the case, not bound* to execute the clause of Guarantee.

If this be a just view of the true force and import of the Proclamation, it will remain to see whether the President in issuing it acted within his proper sphere, or stepped beyond the bounds of his constitutional authority and duty.

It will not be disputed that the management of the affairs of this country with foreign nations is confided to the Government of the UStates.

It can as little be disputed, that a Proclamation of Neutrality, where a Nation is at liberty to keep out of a War in which other Nations are engaged and means so to do, is a *usual* and a *proper* measure. *Its main object and effect are to prevent the Nation being immediately responsible for acts done by its citizens, without the privity or connivance of the Government, in contravention of the principles of neutrality.**

An object this of the greatest importance to a Country whose true interest lies in the preservation of peace.

The inquiry then is—what department of the Government of the UStates is the proper one to make a declaration of Neutrality in the cases in which the engagements of the Nation permit and its interests require such a declaration.

A correct and well informed mind will discern at once that it can belong neither to the Legislative nor Judicial Department and of course must belong to the Executive.

The Legislative Department is not the *organ* of intercourse between the UStates and foreign Nations. It is charged neither with *making* nor *interpreting* Treaties. It is therefore not naturally that Organ of the Government which is to pronounce the existing condition of the Nation, with regard to foreign Powers, or to admonish the Citizens of their obligations and duties as founded upon that condition of things. Still less is it charged with enforcing the execution and observance of these obligations and those duties.

* See Vatel Book III Chap VII § 113.

It is equally obvious that the act in question is foreign to the Judiciary Department of the Government. The province of that Department is to decide litigations in particular cases. It is indeed charged with the interpretation of treaties; but it exercises this function only in the litigated cases; that is where contending parties bring before it a specific controversy. It has no concern with pronouncing upon the external political relations of Treaties between Government and Government. This position is too plain to need being insisted upon.

It must then of necessity belong to the Executive Department to exercise the function in Question—when a proper case for the exercise of it occurs.

It appears to be connected with that department in various capacities, as the *organ* of intercourse between the Nation and foreign Nations—as the interpreter of the National Treaties in those cases in which the Judiciary is not competent, that is in the cases between Government and Government—as that Power, which is charged with the Execution of the Laws, of which Treaties form a part—as that Power which is charged with the command and application of the Public Force.

This view of the subject is so natural and obvious—so analogous to general theory and practice—that no doubt can be entertained of its justness, unless such doubt can be deduced from particular provisions of the Constitution of the UStates.

Let us see then if cause for such doubt is to be found in that constitution.

The second Article of the Constitution of the UStates, section 1st, establishes this general Proposition, That "The Executive Power shall be vested in a President of the United States of America."

The same article in a succeeding Section proceeds to designate particular cases of Executive Power. It declares among other things that the President shall be Commander in Cheif of the army and navy of the UStates and of the Militia of the several states when called into the actual service of the UStates, that he shall have power by and with the advice of the senate to make treaties; that it shall be his duty to receive ambassadors and other public Ministers and to take care that the laws be faithfully executed.

It would not consist with the rules of sound construction to consider this enumeration of particular authorities as derogating from the more comprehensive grant contained in the general clause, further than as it may be coupled with express restrictions or qualifications; as in regard to the cooperation of the Senate in the appointment of Officers and the making of treaties; which are qualifications of the general executive powers of appointing officers and making treaties: Because the difficulty of a complete and perfect specification of all the cases of Executive authority would naturally dictate the use of general terms—and would render it improbable that a specification of certain particulars was designd as a substitute for those terms, when antecedently used. The different mode of expression employed in the constitution in regard to the two powers the Legislative and the Executive serves to confirm this inference. In the article which grants the legislative powers of the Governt. the expressions are— *"All Legislative powers herein granted shall be vested in a Congress of the UStates;"* in that which grants the Executive Power the expressions are, as already quoted "The EXECUTIVE POWER shall be vested in a President of the UStates of America."

The enumeration ought rather therefore to be considered as intended by way of greater caution, to specify and regulate the principal articles implied in the definition of Executive Power; leaving the rest to flow from the general grant of that power, interpreted in conformity to other parts of the constitution and to the principles of free government.

The general doctrine then of our constitution is, that the EXECUTIVE POWER of the Nation is vested in the President; subject only to the *exceptions* and *qualifications* which are expressed in the instrument.

Two of these have been already noticed—the participation of the Senate in the appointment of Officers and the making of Treaties. A third remains to be mentioned the right of the Legislature "to declare war and grant letters of marque and reprisal."

With these exceptions the EXECUTIVE POWER of the Union is completely lodged in the President. This mode of construing the Constitution has indeed been recognized by Congress in formal acts, upon full consideration and debate. The power of removal from office is an inportant instance.

And since upon general principles for reasons already given, the issuing of a proclamation of neutrality is merely an Executive Act; since also the general Executive Power of the Union is vested in the President, the conclusion is, that the step, which has been taken by him, is liable to no just exception on the score of authority.

It may be observed that this Inference would be just if the power of declaring war had not been vested in the Legislature, but that this power naturally includes the right of judging whether the Nation is under obligations to make war or not.

The answer to this is, that however true it may be, that the right of the Legislature to declare war includes the right of judging whether the Nation be under obligations to make War or not—it will not follow that the Executive is in any case excluded from a similar right of Judgment, in the execution of its own functions.

If the Legislature have a right to make war on the one hand—it is on the other the duty of the Executive to preserve Peace till war is declared; and in fulfilling that duty, it must necessarily possess a right of judging what is the nature of the obligations which the treaties of the Country impose on the Government; and when in pursuance of this right it has concluded that there is nothing in them inconsistent with a *state* of neutrality, it becomes both its province and its duty to enforce the laws incident to that state of the Nation. The Executive is charged with the execution of all laws, the laws of Nations as well as the Municipal law, which recognises and adopts those laws. It is consequently bound, by faithfully executing the laws of neutrality, when that is the state of the Nation, to avoid giving a cause of war to foreign Powers.

This is the direct and proper end of the proclamation of neutrality. It declares to the UStates their situation with regard to the Powers at war and makes known to the Community that the laws incident to that situation will be enforced. In doing this, it conforms to an established usage of Nations, the operation of which as before remarked is to obviate a responsibility on the part of the whole Society, for secret and unknown violations of the rights of any of the warring parties by its citizens.

Those who object to the proclamation will readily admit that it is the right and duty of the Executive to judge of, or to interpret, those articles of our treaties which give to France particular privileges, in order to the enforcement of those privileges: But the necessary consequence of this is, that the Executive must judge what are the proper bounds of those privileges—what rights are given to other nations by our treaties with them—what rights the law of Nature and Nations gives and our treaties permit, in respect to those Nations with whom we have no treaties; in fine what are the reciprocal rights and obligations of the United States & of all & each of the powers at War.

The right of the Executive to receive ambassadors and other public Ministers may serve to illustrate the relative duties of the Executive and Legislative Departments. This right includes that of judging, in the case of a Revolution of Government in a foreign Country, whether the new rulers are competent organs of the National Will and ought to be recognised or not: And where a treaty antecedently exists between the UStates and such nation that right involves the power of giving operation or not to such treaty. For until the new Government is *acknowleged*, the treaties between the nations, as far at least as regards *public* rights, are of course suspended.

This power of determining virtually in the case supposed upon the operation of national Treaties as a consequence, of the power to receive ambassadors and other public Ministers, is an important instance of the right of the Executive to decide the obligations of the Nation with regard to foreign Nations. To apply it to the case of France, if there had been a Treaty of alliance *offensive* and defensive between the UStates and that Country, the unqualified acknowlegement of the new Government would have put the UStates in a condition to become an associate in the War in which France was engaged—and would have laid the Legislature under an obligation, if required, and there was otherwise no valid excuse, of exercising its power of declaring war.

This serves as an example of the right of the Executive, in certain cases, to determine the condition of the Nation, though it may consequentially affect the proper or improper exercise of the Power of the Legislature to declare war. The Executive indeed cannot control the exercise of that power—further than by the exercise of its general right of objecting to all acts of the Legislature; liable to being overruled by two thirds of both houses of Congress. The Legislature is free to perform its own duties according to its own sense of them—though the Executive in the exercise of its constitutional powers, may establish an antecedent state of things which ought to weigh in the legislative decisions. From the division of the Executive Power there results, in referrence to it, a *concurrent* authority, in the distributed cases.

Hence in the case stated, though treaties can only be made by the President and Senate, their activity may be continued or suspended by the President alone.

No objection has been made to the Presidents having acknowleged the Republic of France, by the Reception of its Minister, without having consulted the Senate; though that body is connected with him in the making of Treaties, and though the consequence of his act of reception is to give operation to the Treaties heretofore made with that Country: But he is censured for having declared the UStates to be in a state of peace & neutrality, with regard to the Powers at War; because the right of *changing* that state & *declaring war* belongs to the Legislature.

It deserves to be remarked, that as the participation of the senate in the making of Treaties and the power of the Legislature to declare war are exceptions out of the general "Executive Power" vested in the President, they are to be construed strictly—and ought to be extended no further than is essential to their execution.

While therefore the Legislature can alone declare war, can alone actually transfer the nation from a state of Peace to a state of War—it belongs to the "Executive Power," to do whatever else the laws of Nations cooperating with the Treaties of the Country enjoin, in the intercourse of the UStates with foreign Powers.

In this distribution of powers the wisdom of our constitution is manifested. It is the province and duty of the Executive to preserve to the Nation the blessings of peace. The

Legislature alone can interrupt those blessings, by placing the Nation in a state of War.

But though it has been thought adviseable to vindicate the authority of the Executive on this broad and comprehensive ground—it was not absolutely necessary to do so. That clause of the constitution which makes it his duty to "take care that the laws be faithfully executed" might alone have been relied upon, and this simple process of argument pursued.

The President is the constitutional EXECUTOR of the laws. Our Treaties and the laws of Nations form a part of the law of the land. He who is to execute the laws must first judge for himself of their meaning. In order to the observance of that conduct, which the laws of nations combined with our treaties prescribed to this country, in reference to the present War in Europe, it was necessary for the President to judge for himself whether there was any thing in our treaties incompatible with an adherence to neutrality. Having judged that there was not, he had a right, and if in his opinion the interests of the Nation required it, it was his duty, as Executor of the laws, to proclaim the neutrality of the Nation, to exhort all persons to observe it, and to warn them of the penalties which would attend its non observance.

The Proclamation has been represented as enacting some new law. This is a view of it entirely erroneous. It only proclaims a *fact* with regard to the *existing state* of the Nation, informs the citizens of what the laws previously established require of them in that state, & warns them that these laws will be put in execution against the Infractors of them.

Gazette of the United States,
June 29, 1793

"CONTEMPTIBLE AS YOU ARE"

To Andrew G. Fraunces

Contemptible as you are, what answer could I give to your last letter?

The enclosed is a copy of what will shortly appear in one of the Gazettes of the city of New-York.   A. Hamilton

Albany, October 1, 1793.

One Andrew G. Fraunces, lately a clerk in the treasury department, has been endeavoring to have it believed, that he is possessed of some facts, of a nature to criminate the official conduct of the Secretary of the Treasury; an idea to which, for obvious reasons, an extensive circulation has been given, by a certain description of persons. The Public may be assured, that the said Fraunces has been regularly and repeatedly called upon, to declare the grounds of his suggestion; that he has repeatedly evaded the enquiry; that he possesses no facts of the nature pretended; and that he is a despicable calumniator.

ADVICE TO A DAUGHTER

To Angelica Hamilton

I was very glad to learn, my dear daughter, that you were going to begin the study of the French language. We hope you will in every respect behave in such a manner as will secure to you the good-will and regard of all those with whom you are. If you happen to displease any of them, be always ready to make a frank apology. But the best way is to act with so much politeness, good manners, and circumspection, as never to have occasion to make any apology. Your mother joins in best love to you. Adieu, my very dear daughter.

c. November 1793

CRISIS WITH BRITAIN

To George Washington

Sir   Philadelphia April 1794

The present is beyond question a great, a difficult & a perilous crisis in the affairs of this country. In such a crisis it is the duty of every man, according to situation, to contribute all in his power towards preventing evil and producing good. This consideration will I trust be a sufficient apology for the liberty I am about to take of submitting without an official call the ideas which occupy my mind concerning the actual posture of our public affairs. It cannot but be of great importance that the chief Magistrate should be informed of the real state of things; and it is not easy for him to have this information but through those principal officers who have most frequent access to him. Hence an obligation on their part to communicate information on occasions like the present.

A course of accurate observation has impressed on my mind a full conviction, that there exist in our councils three considerable parties—one decided for preserving peace by every effort which shall any way consist with the ultimate maintenance of the national honor and rights and disposed to cultivate with all nations a friendly understanding—another decided for war and resolved to bring it about by every expedient which shall not too directly violate the public opinion— a third not absolutely desirous of war but solicitous at all events to excite and keep alive irritation and ill humour between the UStates and Great Britain, not unwilling in the pursuit of this object to expose the peace of the country to imminent hazards.

The views of the first party in respect to the questions between G Britain and us favour the following course of conduct—To take effectual measures of military preparation, creating in earnest force and revenue—to vest the President with important powers respecting navigation and commerce for ulterior contingencies—to endeavour by another effort of negotiation confided to hands able to manage it and friendly to the object, to obtain reparation for the wrongs we suffer and a demarkation of a line of conduct to govern in future—to avoid 'till the issue of that experiment all measures of a nature to occasion a conflict between the motives which might dispose the British Government to do us the justice to which we are intitled and the sense of its own dignity—If that experiment fails then and not till then to resort to reprisals and war.

The views of the second party, in respect to the same questions favour the following courses of conduct—to say and to do every thing which can have a tendency to stir up the passions of the people and beget a disposition favourable to war—to make use of the inflamation which is excited in the community for the purposes of carrying through measures calculated to disgust Great Britain and to render an accommodation impracticable, without humiliation to her, which they do not believe will be submitted to—in fine, to provoke and bring on war by indirect means without declaring it or even avowing the intention; because they know the public mind is not yet prepared for such an extremity and they fear to encounter the direct responsibility of being the authors of a War.

The views of the third party lead them to favour the measures of the second—but without a perfect coincidence in the result. They weakly hope that they may hector and vapour with success—that the pride of Great Britain will yield to her interest—and that they may accomplish the object of perpetuating animosity between the two countries without involving War.

There are some characters, not numerous, who do not belong to either of these classes—but who fluctuate between them as in the conflict between Reason & Passion, the one or the other prevails.

It may seem difficult to admit in the situation of this Country that there are parties of the description of the two last men who can either systematically meditate war or can be willing to risk it otherwise than by the use of means which they deem necessary to insure reparation for the injuries we experience.

But a due attention to the course of the human passions as recorded in history and exemplified by daily occurrences is sufficient to obviate all difficulty on this head.

Wars oftener proceed from angry and perverse passions than from cool calculations of Interest. This position is admitted without difficulty when we are judging of the hostile appearances in the measures of Great Britain towards this country. What reason can there be why it should not be as good a test of similar appearances on our part? As men, it is equally applicable to us—and the symptoms are strong of our being readily enough worked up into a degree of rage and phrenzy, which goes very far towards silencing the voice of reason and interest.

Those who compose the parties whose measures have a War-Aspect are under the influence of some of the strongest passions that can actuate human conduct. They unite from habitual feeling in an implacable hatred to Great Britain and in a warm attachment to France. Their animosity against the former is inflamed by the most violent resentment for recent and unprovoked injuries—in many instances by personal loss and suffering or the loss and suffering of intimate friends and conections. Their sympathy with the latter is increased by the idea of her being engaged in defending the cause of liberty against a combination of despots who meditate nothing less than the destruction of it throughout the world. In hostility with Britain they seek the gratification of revenge upon a detested enemy with that of serving a favourite friend and in this the cause of liberty. They anticipate also, what is in their estimation a great political good, a more complete and permanent alienation from Great Britain and a more close approximation to France. Those even of them who do not wish the extremity of war consider it as a less evil than a thorough and sincere accommodation with Great Britain and are willing to risk the former rather than lose an opportunity so favourable as the present to extend and rivet the springs of ill will against that Nation.

However necessary it is to viel this policy in public—in private there are not much pains taken to disguise it. Some Gentlemen do not scruple to say that pacification is and ought to be out of the question.

What has been heretofore said relates only to persons in public character. If we extend our view from these to the community at large, we shall there also find a considerable diversity of opinion—partizans of patience negotiation and peace, if possible, and partisans of war. There is no doubt much of irritation now afloat—many advocates for measures tending to produce war. But it would be a great mistake to infer from these appearances that the prevailing sentiment of the Country is for war—or that there would be either a willing acquiescence or a zealous cooperation in it if the proceedings of the government should not be such as to render it manifestly beyond question, that war was inevitable but by an absolute sacrifice of the rights and interests of the Nation—that the race of prudence was completely run and that nothing was done to invite hostility or left undone to avoid it.

It is to my mind unequivocal, that the great mass of opinion in the Eastern States and in the State of New York is against War if it can be avoided without absolute dishonor or the ultimate sacrifice of essential rights and interests—and I verily believe that the same sentiment is the radical one throughout the UStates, *some* of the towns perhaps exepted, where even it is much to be doubted whether there would not be a minority for the affirmative of the naked question of war or of measures which should be acknowleged to have a tendency to promote or produce it.

The natural inference from such a state of the public mind is—that if measures are adopted with the disapprobation and dissent of a large and enlightened minority of Congress, which in the event should appear to have been obstacles to a peaceable adjustment of our differences with Great Britain—there would be under the pressure of the evils produced by them a deep and extensive dissatisfaction with the conduct of the Government—a loss of confidence in it—and an impatience under the measures which War would render unavoidable.

Prosperous as is truly the situation of this country, great as would be the evils of War to it, it would hardly seem to admit of a doubt, that no chance for preserving peace ought to be lost or diminished, in compliance either with resentment or the speculative ideas, which are the arguments for a hostile course of conduct.

At no moment were the indications of a plan on the part of Great Britain to go to War with us sufficiently decisive to preclude the hope of averting it by a negotiation conducted with prudent energy and seconded by such military preparations as should be demonstrative of a Resolution eventually to vindicate our rights. The revocation of the instructions of the 6th of November even with the relaxation of some pretensions which Great Britain has in former wars maintained against Neutral Powers is full evidence that if the system was before for War it was then changed. The events which have taken place in Europe are of a nature to render it probable that such a system will not be revived and that by prudent management we may still escape a calamity which we have the strongest motives internal as well as external to shun.

I express myself thus because it is certainly not an idle apprehension that the example of France (whose excesses are with too many an object of apology if not of justification) may be found to have unhinged the orderly principles of the People of this country and that War by putting in motion all the turbulent passions and promoting a further assimilation of our principles with those of France may prove to be the threshold of disorganization and anarchy.

The late successes of France have produced in this country conclusions much too sanguine with regard to the event of the Contest. They no doubt afford a high probability of her being able eventually to defend herself especially under a form of administration of such unexampled vigour as that by which she has of late managed her affairs. But there will be nothing wonderful in a total reverse of fortune during the ensuing campaign. Human nature must be an absolutely different thing in France from what it has hitherto shewn itself to be throughout the globe and in all ages if there do not exist in a large proportion of the French Nation germs of the profoundest discontent ready to burst into vegetation the moment there should appear an efficacious prospect of protection and shade from the progress of the invading armies. And if having possessed themselves of some of the keys of France the principle of the commencing campaign should be different from that of the past—active field operations succeeding to the wasteful and dilatory process of seiges—who can say that Victory may not so far crown the enterprises of the coalesced powers as to open the way to an internal explosion which may prove fatal to the Republic? Tis now evident that another vigorous campaign will be essayed by the Allies. The result is and must be incalculable.

To you, Sir, it is unnecessary to urge the extreme precariousness of the events of War. The inference to be drawn is too manifest to escape your penetration. This Country ought not to set itself afloat upon an ocean so fluctuating so dangerous and so uncertain but in a case of absolute necessity.

That necessity is certainly not yet apparent. The circumstances which have been noticed with regard to the recent change of conduct on the part of G Britain authorise a strong hope that a negotiation conducted with ability and moderation and supported at home by demonstrations of vigour and seriousness would obviate those causes of collision which are the most urgent—might even terminate others which have so long fostered dissatisfaction and enmity. There is room to suppose that the moment is pecularily favourable to such an attempt. On this point there are symptoms of a common sentiment between the advocates and the opposers of an unembarrassed attempt to negotiate—the former desiring it from the confidence they have in its probable success—the latter from the same cause endeavouring either to prevent its going on under right auspices or to clog it with impediments which will frustrate its effect.

All ostensibly agree that one more experiment of negotiation ought to precede actual war; but there is this serious difference in the practice. The sincere friends of peace and accommodation are for leaving things in a state which will enable Great Britain without abandoning self-respect to do us the justice we seek. The others are for placing things upon a footing which would involve the disgrace or disrepute of having receded through intimidation.

This last scheme indubitably ends in War. The folly is too great to be seriously entertained by the discerning part of those who affect to believe the position—that Great Britain fortified by the alliances of the greatest part of Europe will submit to our demands urged with the face of coertion and preceded by acts of reprisal. She cannot do it without renouncing her pride and her dignity, without losing her consequence and weight in the scale of Nations—and consequently it is morally certain that she will not do it. A proper estimate of the operation of the human passions must satisfy us that she would be less disposed to receive the law from us than from any other nation—a people recently become a nation, not long since one of her dependencies, and as yet, if a Hercules—a Hercules in the cradle.

When one nation inflicts injuries upon another, which are causes of war, if this other means to negotiate before it goes to War, the usual and received course is to prepare for War and proceed to negotiation—avoiding reprisals till the issue of the Negotiation. This course is recommended by all enlightened Writers on the laws of Nations as the course of moderation propriety and wisdom and it is that commonly pursued except where there is a disposition to go to war or a commanding superiority of Power.

Preparation for War in such cases contains in it nothing offensive. It is a mere precaution for self defence under circumstances which endanger the breaking out of War. It gives rise to no point of honor which can be a bar to equitable and amicable negotiation. But acts of reprisal speak a contrary effect—they change negotiation into peremptory demand and they brandish a rod over the party on whom the demand is made. He must be humble indeed, if he comply with the demand to avoid the stripe.

Such are the propositions which have lately appeared in the House of Representatives for the sequestration or arrestation of British Debts—for the cutting off of all intercourse with Great Britain till she shall do certain specific things. If such propositions pass they can only be regarded as provocatives to a Declaration of War by Great Britain.

The sequestration of Debts is treated by all writers as one of the highest species of Reprisal. It is moreover contrary to the most approved practice of the present century, to what may be safely pronounced to be the modern rule of the law of Nations—to what is so plainly dictated by original principles of Justice and good faith that nothing but the barbarism of times in which war was the principal business of man could ever have tolerated an opposite practice—to the manifest interest of a people situated like that of the UState; which having a vast fund of materials for improvement in various ways ought to invite into the channels of their industry the Capital of Europe, by giving to it inviolable security—which, giving little facility to extensive revenue from taxation, ought for its own safety in war to cherish its credit by a religious observance of the maxims of credit in all their branches.

The proposition for cutting off all intercourse with G Britain has not yet sufficiently devellopped itself to enable us to pronounce what it truly is. It may be so extensive in its provisions as even to include in fact though not in form sequestration by rendering remittances penal or impracticable. Indeed it can scarcely avoid so far interfering with the payment of debts already contracted as in a great degree to amount to a virtual sequestration. But however this may be—being adopted for the express purpose of retaliating or punishing injuries to continue until those injuries are redressed it is in the spirit of a reprisal—Its principle is avowedly coercion—a principle directly opposite to that of negotiation, which supposes an appeal to the reason and justice of the party. Caustic and stimulant in the highest degree, it cannot fail to have a correspondent effect upon the minds of those against whom it is directed. It cannot fail to be viewed as originating in motives of the most hostile and overbearing kind—to stir up all the feelings of pride and resentment in the nation as well as in the cabinet—and consequently to render negotiation abortive.

It will be wonderful if the immediate effect of either of these measures be not either War or the seizure of our vessels wherever they are found, on the ground of keeping them as hostages for the debts due to the British Merchants and on the additional ground of the measures themselves being either acts of hostility or evidence of a disposition to hostility.

The interpretation will naturally be that our views originally pacific have changed with the change in the affairs of France, and are now bent towards War.

The measures in question, besides the objection to them resulting from their tendency to produce war, are condemned by a comprehensive and enlightened view of their operation in other respects.

They cannot but have a malignant influence upon our public and mercantile credit. They will be regarded abroad as violent and precipitate. It will be said there is no reliance to be placed on the steadiness or solidity of concerns with this people. Every gust that arises in the political sky is the signal for measures tending to destroy their ability to pay or to obstruct the course of payment. Instead of a people pacific, forbearing moderate and of rigid probity we see in them a people turbulent hasty intemperate and loose—sporting with their individual obligations and disturbing the general course of their affairs with levity and inconsiderateness.

Such will indubitably be the comments upon our conduct. The favourable impressions now entertained of the character of our government and Nation will infallibly be reversed.

The cutting off of intercourse with Great Britain to distress her seriously must extend to the prohibition of all her commodities indirectly as well as directly. Else it will have no other operation than to transfer the Trade between the two countries to the hands of foreigners to our disadvantage more than to that of Great Britain.

If it extends to the total prohibition of her commodities, however brought, it deprives us of a supply, for which no substitute can be found elsewhere, a supply necessary to us in peace and more necessary to us if we are to go to War. It gives a sudden and violent blow to our revenue which cannot easily if at all be repaired from other resources. It will give so great an interruption to commerce as may very possibly interfere with the payment of the duties which have heretofore accrued and bring the Treasury to an absolute stoppage of payment—an event which would cut up credit by the roots.

The consequences of so great and so sudden a disturbance of our Trade which must affect our exports as well as our Imports are not to be calculated. An excessive rise in the price of foreign commodities—a proportional decrease of price and demand for our own commodities—the derangement of our revenue and credit—these circumstances united may occasion the most dangerous dissatisfactions & disorders in the community and may drive the governt. to a disgraceful retreat—independent of foreign causes.

To adopt the measure in *terrorem* and postpone its operation will be scarcely a mitigation of the Evil. The expectation of it will as to our imports have the effect of the reality; since we must obtain what we want chiefly upon credit. Our supply and our revenue therefore will suffer nearly as much as if there was an immediate interruption.

The effect, with regard to our peace will be the same. The principle being menace and coertion will equally recommend resistance to the policy as well as the pride of the other party. Tis only to consult our own hearts to be convinced that nations like individuals revolt at the idea of being guided by external compulsion. They will at least only yield to that idea after resistance has been fruitlessly tried in all its forms.

Tis as great an error for a nation to overrate as to underrate itself. Presumption is as great a fault as timidity. Tis our error to overrate ourselves and to underrate Great Britain. We forget how little we can annoy how much we may be annoyed.

Tis enough for us, situated as we are, to be resolved to vindicate our honor and our rights in the last extremity. To precipitate a great conflict of any sort is utterly unsuited to our condition to our strength or to our resources. This is a truth to be well weighed by every wise and dispassionate man as the rule of public action.

There are two ideas of immense consequence to us in the event of War. The disunion of our enemies—the perfect union of our own citizens. Justice and moderation united with firmness are the means to secure both these advantages. Injustice or Intemperance will lose both.

Unanimity among ourselves, which is the most important of the two ideas, can only be secured by its being manifest, if war ensues, that it was inevitable by another course of conduct. This cannot and will not be the case, if measures so intemperate as those which are meditated take place. The inference will be that the war was brought on by the design of some and the rashness of others. This inference will be universal in the Northern States, and to you Sir I need not urge the importance of those states in war.

Want of unanimity will naturally tend to render the operations of War feeble and heavy—to destroy both effort and perseverance. War undertaken under such auspices can scarcely end in any thing better than an inglorious and disadvantageous peace. What worse it may produce is beyond the reach of human foresight.

The foregoing observations are designed to convey to the mind of the President information of the true state of things at the present juncture and to present to his consideration the general reasons which have occurred to me against the course of proceeding which appears to be favoured by a majority of the House of Representatives.

My solicitude for the public interest, according to the view I have of it, and my real respect and regard for him to whom I address myself lead me to subjoin some reflections of a more delicate nature.

The crisis is such a one as involves the highest responsibility on the part of every one who may have to act a part in it. It is one in which every man will be understood to be bound to act according to his judgment without concession to the ideas of others. The President, who has by the constitution a right to object to laws, which he deems contrary to the public interest, will be considered as under an indispensable obligation to exercise that right against any measure, relating to so vast a point as that of the peace of the Country, which shall not accord with his opinion. The consideration of its having been adopted by both Houses of Congress and of respect for their opinion will have no weight in such a case as a reason for forbearing to exercise the right of objection. The consequence is that the not objecting will be deemed conclusive evidence of approbation and will implicate the President in all the consequences of the measure.

In such a position of things it is therefore of the utmost importance to him as well as to the community that he should trace out in his own mind such a plan as he thinks it would be eligible to pursue and should endeavour by proper and constitutional means to give the deliberations of Congress a direction towards that plan.

Else he runs the risk of being reduced to the dilemma either of assenting to measures, which he may not approve, with a full responsibility for consequences—or of objecting to measures which have already received the sanction of the two houses of Congress with the responsibility of having resisted and probably prevented what they meditated. Neither of these alternatives is a desireable one.

It seems adviseable, then, that The President should come

to a conclusion, whether the plan ought to be preparation for war and negotiation unincumbered by measures which forbid the expectation of success—or immediate measures of a coercive tendency to be accompanied with the ceremony of a demand of redress. For I believe there is no middle plan between those two courses.

If the former appears to him to be the true policy of the Country, I submit it as my conviction that it is *urgent* for him to demonstrate that opinion as a preventive of wrong measures and future embarrassment.

The mode of doing it which occurs is this—to nominate a person, who will have the confidence of those who think peace still within our reach, and who may be thought qualified for the mission as envoy extraordinary to Great Britain— to announce this to the one as well as the other House of Congress with an observation that it is done with an intention to make a solemn appeal to the justice and good sense of the British Government to avoid if possible an ulterior rupture and adjust the causes of misunderstanding between the two Countries—and with an earnest recommendation that vigorous and effectual measures may be adopted to be prepared for war should it become inevitable—abstaining for the present from measures which may be contrary to the spirit of an attempt to adjust existing differences by Negotiation.

Knowing as I do Sir that I am among the persons who have been in your contemplation to be employed in the capacity I have mentioned, I should not have taken the present step, had I not been resolved at the same time to advise you with decision to drop me from the consideration and to fix upon another character. I am not unapprised of what has been the byass of your opinion on the subject. I am well aware of all the collateral obstacles which exist and I assure you in the utmost sincerity that I shall be completely and intirely satisfied with the election of another.

I beg leave to add that of the persons whom you would deem free from any constitutional objections—Mr. Jay is the only man in whose qualifications for success there would be thorough confidence and him whom alone it would be adviseable to send. I think the business would have the best chance possible in his hands. And I flatter myself that his mission would issue in a manner that would produce the most important good to the Nation.

Let me add Sir that those whom I call the soberminded men of the Country look up to You with solicitude upon the present occasion. If happily you should be the instrument of still rescuing the Country from the dangers and calamities of War, there is no part of your life, Sir, which will produce to you more real satisfaction or true Glory than that which shall be distinguished by this very important service.

In any event I cannot doubt Sir that you will do justice to the motives which impel me and that you will see in this proceeding another proof of my sincere wishes for your honor & happiness and anxiety for the public weal.

With the truest respect and attachment   I have the Honor to be   Sir   Your most obedient & humble servant

Alexander Hamilton

April, 14, 1794

THE WHISKEY REBELLION

To George Washington

Sir   Treasury Department August 2d. 1794

In compliance with your requisition I have the honor to submit my Opinion as to the course which it will be adviseable for the President to pursue in regard to the armed Opposition recently given in the four Western Counties of Pennsylvania to the execution of the laws of the U. States laying duties upon Spirits distilled within the United States and upon Stills.

The case upon which an Opinion is required is summarily as follows. The four most Western Counties of Pennsylvania since the Commencement of those laws a period of more than three Years, have been in steady and Violent Opposition to them. By formal public meetings of influential individuals, whose resolutions and proceedings had for undisguised objects, to render the laws odious, to discountenance a compliance with them, and to intimidate individuals from accepting and executing Offices under them—by a general Spirit of Opposition (thus fomented) among the Inhabitants—by repeated instances of armed parties going in disguise to the houses of the Officers of the Revenue and inflicting upon them personal violence and outrage—by general combinations to forbear a compliance with the requisitions of the laws by examples of injury to the Property and insult to the persons of individuals who have shewn by their conduct a disposition to comply and by an almost universal noncompliance with the laws—their execution within the Counties in question has been completely frustrated.

Various Alterations have been made in the laws by the Legislature to obviate as far as possible the objections of the Inhabitants of those Counties.

The executive, on its part has been far from deficient in forbearance lenity or a Spirit of Accomodation.

But neither the Legislative nor the Executive accomodations have had any effect in producing compliance with the laws.

The Opposition has continued and matured, till it has at length broke out in Acts which are presumed to amount to Treason.

Armed Collections of men, with the avowed design of Opposing the execution of the laws, have attacked the house of the Inspector of the Revenue, burnt and destroyed his Property and Shed the blood of Persons engaged in its defence—have made Prisoner of the Marshall of the District and did not release him till for the Safety of his life he stipulated to execute no more processes within the disaffected counties—have compelled both him and the Inspector of the Revenue to fly the Country by a circuitous route to avoid personal injury perhaps Assassination—have proposed the Assembling of a Convention of delegates from these Counties and the Neighbouring ones of Virginia probably with a view to systematise measures of more effectual Opposition—have forcibly seized Opened & Spoliated a Mail of the United States.

What in this State of things is proper to be done?

The President has with the advice of the heads of the Departments and the Attorney General, caused to be submitted all the evidence of the foregoing facts to the Consideration of an Associate Judge under the Act intitled "An Act to provide for calling forth the Militia to execute the laws of the Union Suppress Insurrection and repel Invasion."

If the Judge shall pronounce that the case described in the second section of that Act exists—it will follow that a competent force of Militia should be called forth and employed to suppress the insurrection and support the Civil Authority in effectuating Obedience to the laws and the punishment of Offenders.

It appears to me that the very existence of Government demands this course and that a duty of the highest nature urges the Chief Magistrate to pursue it. The Constitution and laws of the United States, contemplate and provide for it.

What force of Militia shall be called out, and from What State or States?

The force ought if attainable to be an imposing one, such if practicable, as will deter from opposition, save the effusion of the blood of Citizens and secure the object to be accomplished.

The quantum must of course be regulated by the resistance to be expected. Tis computed, that the four opposing Counties contain upwards of sixteen thousand males of 16 years and more, that of these about seven thousand may be expected to be armed. Tis possible that the union of the nieghbouring Counties of Virginia may augment this force. Tis not impossible, that it may receive an accession from some adjacent Counties of this state on this side of the Alleghany Mountain.

To be prepared for the worst, I am of opinion, that twelve thousand Militia ought to be ordered to assemble; 9000 foot and 3000 horse. I should not propose so many horse, but for the probability, that this description of Militia, will be more easily procured for the service.

From what State or States shall these come?

The Law contemplates that the Militia of a State, in which an insurrection happens, if willing & sufficient shall first be employed, but gives power to employ the Milita of other States in the case either of refusal or insufficiency.

The Governor of Pennsylvania in an Official conference this

day, gave it explicitly as his opinion to the President, that the Militia of Pennsylvania alone would be found incompetent to the suppression of the insurrection.

This Opinion of the Chief Magistrate of the State is presumed to be a sufficient foundation for calling in, in the first instance, the aid of the Militia of the Neighbouring States.

I would submit then, that Pennsylvania be required to furnish 6000 men of whom 1000 to be horse, New–Jersey 2000 of whom 800 to be horse, Maryland 2000 of whom 600 to be horse, Virginia 2000, of whom 600 to be horse.

Or perhaps it may be as eligible to call upon each State for such a number of Troops, leaving to itself the proportion of horse and foot according to convenience. The Militia called for to rendezvous at Carlisle in Pensylvania & Cumberland Fort in Virginia on the 10th of September next.

The law requires that previous to the using of force a Proclamation shall issue, commanding the Insurgents to disperse and return peaceably to their respective abodes within a limited time. This step must of course be taken.

The application of the force to be called out and other ulterior measures must depend on circumstances as they shall arise.

With the most perfect respect   I have the Honor to be Sir   Your Most Obedient Servant

Alexander Hamilton

Tully No. I

For the American Daily Advertiser.
To the PEOPLE *of the* UNITED STATES.

LETTER I.

It has from the first establishment of your present constitution been predicted, that every occasion of serious embarrassment which should occur in the affairs of the government— every misfortune which it should experience, whether produced from its own faults or mistakes, or from other causes, would be the signal of an attempt to overthrow it, or to lay the foundation of its overthrow, by defeating the exercise of constitutional and necessary authorities. The disturbances which have recently broken out in the western counties of Pennsylvania furnish an occasion of this sort. It remains to see whether the prediction which has been quoted, proceeded from an unfounded jealousy excited by partial differences of opinion, or was a just inference from causes inherent in the structure of our political institutions. Every virtuous man, every good citizen, and especially EVERY TRUE REPUBLICAN must fervently pray, that the issue may confound and not confirm so ill omened a prediction.

Your firm attachment to the government you have established cannot be doubted.

If a proof of this were wanting to animate the confidence of your public agents, it would be sufficient to remark, that as often as any attempt to counteract its measures appear, it is carefully prepared by strong professions of friendship to the government, and disavowals of any intention to injure it. This can only result from a conviction, that the government carries with it YOUR affections; and that an attack upon it to be successful, must veil the stroke under appearances of good will.

It is therefore very important that YOU should clearly discern in the present instance, the shape in which a design of turning the existing insurrection to the prejudice of the government would naturally assume. Thus guarded, you will more readily discover and more easily shun the artful snare which may be laid to entangle your feelings and your judgment, and will be the less apt to be misled from the path by which alone you can give security and permanency to the blessings you enjoy, and can avoid the incalculable mischiefs incident to a subversion of the just and necessary authority of the laws.

The design alluded to, if it shall be entertained, would not appear in an open justification of the principles or conduct of the insurgents, or in a direct dissuasion from the support of the government. These methods would produce general indignation and defeat the object. It is too absurd and shocking a position to be directly maintained, that forcible resistance by a sixtieth part of the community to the representative will of the WHOLE, and its constitutional laws expressed by that will, and acquiesced in by the people at large, is justifiable or even excusable. It is a position too untenable and disgustful to be directly advocated—that the government ought not be supported in exertions to establish the authority of the laws against a resistance so incapable of justification or excuse.

The adversaries of good order in every country have too great a share of cunning, too exact a knowledge of the human heart, to pursue so unpromising a cause. Those among us would take upon the present occasion one far more artful, and consequently far more dangerous.

They would unite with good citizens, and perhaps be among the loudest in condemning the disorderly conduct of the insurgents. They would agree that it is utterly unjustifiable, contrary to the vital principle of republican government, and of the most dangerous tendency—But they would, at the same time, slily add, that excise laws are pernicious things, very hostile to liberty, (or perhaps they might more smoothly lament that the government had been imprudent enough to pass laws so contrary to the genius of a free people) and they would still more cautiously hint that it is enough for those who disapprove of such laws to submit to them—too much to expect their aid in enforcing them upon others. They would be apt to intimate further, that there is reason to believe that the Executive has been to blame, sometimes by too much forbearance, encouraging the hope that laws would not be enforced, at other times in provoking violence by severe and irritating measures; and they would generally remark, with an affectation of moderation and prudence, that the case is to be lamented, but difficult to be remedied; that a trial of force would be delicate and dangerous; that there is no forseeing how or where it would end; that it is perhaps better to temporize, and by mild means to allay the ferment and afterwards to remove the cause by repealing the exceptionable laws. They would probably also propose, by anticipation of and in concert with the views of the insurgents, plans of procrastination. They would say, if force must finally be resorted to let it not be till after Congress have been consulted, who, if they think fit to persist in continuing the laws, can make additional provisions for enforcing their execution. This too, they would argue, will afford an opportunity for the public sense to be better known, which (if ascertained to be in favor of the laws) will give the government a greater assurance of success in measures of coercion.

By these means, artfully calculated to divert YOUR attention from the true question to be decided, to combat by prejudices against a particular system, a just sense of the criminality and danger of violent resistance to the laws; to oppose the suggestion of misconduct on the part of government to the fact of misconduct on the part of the insurgents; to foster the spirit of indolence and procrastination natural to the human mind, as an obstacle to the vigor and exertion which so alarming an attack upon the fundamental principles of public and private security demands; to distract YOUR opinion on the course proper to be pursued, and consequently on the propriety of the measures which may be pursued. They would expect (I say) by these and similar means, equally insidious and pernicious, to abate YOUR just indignation at the daring affront which has been offered to YOUR authority and YOUR zeal for the maintenance and support of the laws to prevent a competent force, if force is finally called forth, from complying with the call—and thus to leave the government of the Union in the prostrate condition of seeing the laws trampled under foot by an unprincipled combination of a small portion of the community, habitually disobedient to laws, and itself destitute of the necessary aid for vindicating their authority.

Virtuous and enlightened citizens of a now happy country! ye could not be the dupes of artifices so detestable, of a scheme so fatal; ye cannot be insensible to the destructive consequences with which it would be pregnant; ye cannot but remember that the government is YOUR OWN work—that those who administer it are but your temporary agents; that YOU are called upon not to support their power, BUT YOUR OWN POWER. And you will not fail to do what your rights, your best interests, your character as a people, your security as members of society conspire to demand of you.

TULLY

Dunlap and Claypoole's American Daily Advertiser,
August 23, 1794

Tully No. III

For the American Daily Advertiser.
To the PEOPLE *of the* UNITED STATES.

LETTER III.

If it were to be asked, What is the most sacred duty and the greatest source of security in a Republic? the answer would be, An inviolable respect for the Constitution and Laws—the first growing out of the last. It is by this, in a great degree, that the rich and powerful are to be restrained from enterprises against the common liberty—operated upon by the influence of a general sentiment, by their interest in the principle, and by the obstacles which the habit it produces erects against innovation and encroachment. It is by this, in a still greater degree, that caballers, intriguers, and demagogues are prevented from climbing on the shoulders of faction to the tempting seats of usurpation and tyranny.

Were it not that it might require too lengthy a discussion, it would not be difficult to demonstrate, that a large and well organized Republic can scarcely lose its liberty from any other cause than that of anarchy, to which a contempt of the laws is the high road.

But, without entering into so wide a field, it is sufficient to present to your view a more simple and a more obvious truth, which is this—that a sacred respect for the constitutional law is the vital principle, the sustaining energy of a free government.

Government is frequently and aptly classed under two descriptions, a government of FORCE and a government of LAWS; the first is the definition of despotism—the last, of liberty. But how can a government of laws exist where the laws are disrespected and disobeyed? Government supposes controul. It is the POWER by which individuals in society are kept from doing injury to each other and are bro't to co-operate to a common end. The instruments by which it must act are either the AUTHORITY of the Laws or FORCE. If the first be destroyed, the last must be substituted; and where this becomes the ordinary instrument of government there is an end to liberty.

Those, therefore, who preach doctrines, or set examples, which undermine or subvert the authority of the laws, lead us from freedom to slavery; they incapacitate us for a GOVERNMENT of LAWS, and consequently prepare the way for one of FORCE, for mankind MUST HAVE GOVERNMENT OF ONE SORT OR ANOTHER.

There are indeed great and urgent cases where the bounds of the constitution are manifestly transgressed, or its constitutional authorities so exercised as to produce unequivocal oppression on the community, and to render resistance justifiable. But such cases can give no colour to the resistance by a comparatively inconsiderable part of a community, of constitutional laws distinguished by no extraordinary features of rigour or oppression, and acquiesced in by the BODY OF THE COMMUNITY.

Such a resistance is treason against society, against liberty, against every thing that ought to be dear to a free, enlightened, and prudent people. To tolerate were to abandon your most precious interests. Not to subdue it, were to tolerate it. Those who openly or covertly dissuade you from exertions adequate to the occasion are your worst enemies. They treat you either as fools or cowards, too weak to perceive your interest and your duty, or too dastardly to pursue them. They therefore merit, and will no doubt meet your contempt.

To the plausible but hollow harangues of such conspirators, ye cannot fail to reply, How long, ye Catilines, will you abuse our patience.

TULLY.

Dunlap and Claypoole's American Daily Advertiser,
August 28, 1794

"WICKED INSURGENTS OF THE WEST"

To Angelica Church

Bedford Pensylvania
October 23. 1794
205 Miles Westward of
Philadelphia

I am thus far my dear Angelica on my way to attack and subdue the wicked insurgents of the West. But you are not to promise yourself that I shall have any trophies to lay at your feet. A large army has cooled the courage of those madmen & the only question seems now to be how to guard best aganst the return of the phrenzy.

You must not take my being here for a proof that I continue a quixot. In popular governments 'tis useful that those who propose measures should partake in whatever dangers they may involve. Twas very important there should be no mistake in the management of the affair—and I *might* contribute to prevent one. I wish to have every thing well settled for Mr. Church & you, that when you come, you may tread on safe ground. Assure him that the insurrection will do us a great deal of good and add to the solidity of every thing in this country. Say the same to Mr Jay to whom I have not time to write & to Mr Pinkney.

God bless You Dear Sister & make you as happy as I wish you. Love to Mr. Church.

A Hamilton

To Angelica Church

Philadelphia, December 8, 1794.

You say I am a politician, and good for nothing. What will you say when you learn that after January next, I shall cease to be a politician at all? So is the fact. I have formally and definitely announced my intention to resign at that period, and have ordered a house to be taken for me at New York.

My dear Eliza has been lately very ill. Thank God, she is now quite recovered, except that she continues somewhat weak. My absence on a certain expedition was the cause. You will see, notwithstanding your disparagement of me, I am still of consequence to her.

Liancourt has arrived, and has delivered your letter. I pay him the attentions due to his misfortunes and his merits. I wish I was a Croesus; I might then afford solid consolations to these children of adversity, and how delightful it would be to do so. *But now*, sympathy, kind words, and *occasionally a dinner, are all I can contribute.*

Don't let Mr. Church be alarmed at my retreat—all is well with the public. Our insurrection is most happily terminated. Government has gained by it reputation and strength, and our finances are in a most flourishing condition. *Having contributed to place those of the Nation on a good footing, I go to take a little care of my own; which need my care not a little.*

Love to Mr. Church. Betsy will add a line or two. Adieu.

Memorandum on the French Revolution

In the early periods of the French Revolution, a warm zeal for its success was in this Country *a sentiment truly universal.* The love of Liberty is here the ruling passion *of the Citizens of the UStates* pervading every class animating every bosom. As long therefore as the Revolution of France bore the marks of being the cause of liberty it united all hearts concentered all opinions. But this unanimity of approbation has been for a considerable time decreasing. The excesses which have constantly multiplied, with greater and greater aggravations have successively though slowly detached reflecting men from their partiality for an object which has appeared less and less to merit their regard. Their reluctance to abandon it has however been proportioned to the ardor and fondness with which they embraced it. They were willing to overlook many faults—to apologise for some enormities—to hope that better justifications existed than were seen—to look forward to more calm and greater moderation, after the first shocks of the political earthquake had subsided. But instead of this, they have been witnesses to one volcano succeeding another, the last still more dreadful than the former, spreading ruin and devastation far and wide—subverting the foundations of right security and property, of order, morality and religion—sparing neither sex nor age, confounding innocence with guilt, involving the old and the young, the sage and the madman, the long tried friend of virtue and his country and the upstart pretender to purity and patriotism—the bold projector of new treasons with the obscure in indiscriminate and profuse destruction. They have found themselves driven to the painful alternative of renouncing an object dear to their wishes or of becoming by the continuance of their affection for it accomplices with Vice Anarchy Depotism and Impiety.

But though an afflicting experience has materially lessened the number of the admirers of the French Revolution among us and has served to chill the ardor of many more, who profess still to retain their attachment to it, from what they suppose to be its ultimate tendency; yet the effect of Experience has been thus far much less than could reasonably have been expected. The predilection for it still continues extensive and ardent. And what is extraordinary it continues to comprehend men who are able to form a just estimate of the information which destroys its title to their favour.

It is not among the least perplexing phœnomina of the present times, that a people like that of the UStates—exemplary for humanity and moderation surpassed by no other in the love of order and a knowlege of the true principles of liberty, distinguished for purity of morals and a just reverence for Religion should so long perservere in partiality for a state of things the most cruel sanguinary and violent that ever stained the annuals of mankind, a state of things which annihilates the foundations of social order and true liberty, confounds all moral distinctions and *substitutes to* the mild & beneficent religion of the Gospel a gloomy persecuting and desolating atheism. To the eye of a wise man, this partiality is the most inauspicious circumstance, that has appeared in the affairs of this country. It leads involuntarily and irresistibly to apprehensions concerning the soundness of our principles and the stability of our welfare. It is natural to fear that the transition may not be difficult from the approbation of bad things to the imitation of them; a fear which can only be mitigated by a careful estimate of the extraneous causes that have served to mislead the public judgment.

But though we may find in these causes a solution of the fact calculated to abate our solicitude for the consequences; yet we can not consider the public happiness as out of the reach of danger so long as our principles continue to be exposed to the debauching influence of admiration for an example which, it will not be too strong to say, presents the caricature of human depravity. And the pride of national character at least can find no alleviation for the wound which must be inflicted by so ill-judged so unfortunate a partiality.

If there be any thing solid in virtue—the time must come when it will have been a disgrace to have advocated the Revolution of France in its late stages.

This is a language to which the ears of the people of this country have not been accustomed. Every thing has hitherto conspired to confirm the pernicious fascination by which they are enchained. There has been a positive and a negative conspiracy against the truth which has served to shut out its enlightening ray. Those who always float with the popular gale perceiving the prepossession of the people have administered to it by all the acts in their power—endeavouring to recommend themselves by an exaggerated zeal for a favourite object. Others through timidity caution or an ill-judged policy unwilling to expose themselves to the odium of resisting the general current of feeling have betrayed by silence that Truth which they were unable not to perceive. Others, whose sentiments have weight in the community have been themselves the sincere dupes of   . Hence the voice of reason has been stifled and the Nation has been left unadmonished to travel on in one of the most degrading delusions that ever disparaged the understandings of an enlightened people.

To recal them from this dangerous error—to engage them to dismiss their prejudices & consult dispassionately their own good sense—to lead them to an appeal from their own enthusiasm to their reason and humanity would be the most important service that could be rendered to the UStates at the present juncture. The error entertained is not on a mere speculative question. The French Revolution is a political convulsion that in a great or less degree shakes the whole civilized world and it is of real consequence to the principles and of course to the happiness of a Nation to estimate it rightly.

1794

RESIGNING FROM OFFICE

To George Washington

Philadelphia February
Sir   3. 1795

My particular acknowlegements are due for your very kind letter of yesterday. As often as I may recall the vexations I have endured, your approbation will be a great and precious consolation.

It was not without a struggle, that I yielded to the very urgent motives, which impelled me to relinquish a station, in which I could hope to be in any degree instrumental in promoting the success of an administration under your direction; a struggle which would have been far greater, had I supposed that the prospect of future usefulness was proportioned to the sacrifices to be made.

Whatsoever may be my destination hereafter, I entreat you to be persuaded (not the less for my having been sparing in professions) that I shall never cease to render a just tribute to those eminent and excellent qualities which have been already productive of so many blessings to your country—that you will always have my fervent wishes for your public and personal felicity, and that it will be my pride to cultivate a continuance of that esteem regard and friendship, of which you do me the honor to assure me. With true respect and affectionate attachment I have the honor to be

Sir   Your obliged & obedt servt

A Hamilton

FEDERALIST LEADER
AND ATTORNEY
1795–1804

To Rufus King

My Dear King   Kingston Feby. 21. 1795
   The unnecessary capricious & abominable assassination of
the National honor by the rejection of the propositions respecting the unsubscribed debt in the House of Representatives haunts me every step I take, and afflicts me more than I
can express. To see the character of the Government and the
country so sported with, exposed to so indelible a blot puts
my heart to the Torture. Am I then more of an American
than those who drew their first breath on American Ground?
Or What is it that thus torments me at a circumstance so
calmly viewed by almost every body else? Am I a fool—a Romantic quixot—Or is there a constitutional defect in the
American Mind? Were it not for yourself and a few others, I
could adopt the reveries of De Paux as substantial truths, and
would say with him that there is something in our climate
which belittles every Animal human or brute.
   I conjure you, my friend, Make a vigorous stand for the
honor of your Country. Rouse all the energies of your mind,
and measure swords in the Senate with the great Slayer of
public faith—the hacknied *Veteran* in the violation of public
engagements. Prevent him if possible from triumphing a second time over the prostrate credit* and injured interests of his
Country. Unmask his false and horrid hypothesis. Display the
immense difference between an able statesman and the *Man
of subtilties.* Root out the distempered and noisome *weed*
which is attempted to be planted in our political garden—to
choak and wither in its infancy the fair plant of public credit.
   I disclose to you without reserve the state of my mind. It is
discontented and gloomy in the extreme. I consider the cause
of good government as having been put to an issue & the verdict against it.
   Introduce I pray you into the Senate, when the bill comes
up the clause which has been rejected freed from embarrassment by the bills of Credit bearing interest on the nominal

*Witness the 40 for 1 scheme a most unskilful measure, to say the best of it.

value. Press its adoption in this the most unexceptionable shape & let the *yeas* & *nays* witness the result.

Among other reasons for this is my wish that the true friends of public credit may be distinguished from its enemies. The question is too great a one not to undergo a thorough examination before the Community. It would pain me not to be able to distinguish. Adieu.

God bless you   A Hamilton

P.S. Do me the favour to revise carefully the course of the bill respecting the unsubscribed Debt & let me know the particulars. I wish to be able to judge more particularly of the under plot I suspect.

"PUBLIC FOOLS"

To Robert Troup

Albany April 13. 1795

I should want feeling & friendship were I not penetrated by the affectionate concern you so repeatedly manifest for my interest.

Without knowing the particulars of the plan to which you refer I ought not to decide finally against it. But I very much believe that it will not comport with my general system which is to avoid large or complicated speculations especially where foreigners are concerned.

Tis not my Dear Friend that I think there is any harm or even indelicacy in the thing—I am now in no situation that restrains me—But 'tis because I think there is at present a great crisis in the affairs of mankind which may in its consequences involve this country in a sense most affecting to every true friend to it—because concerns of the nature alluded to, though very harmless in the *saints*, who may even fatten themselves on the opportunities or if you please spoils of office, as well as profit by every good thing that is going—who may [   ] agents & tools of foreign *Governments* without hazarding their popularity yet those who are not of the *regenerating* tribe may not do the most unexceptionable things without its being thundered in their ears—without being denounced as speculators peculators British Agents &c. &c. Because there must be some *public fools* who sacrifice private to public interest at the certainty of ingratitude and obloquy—because my *vanity* whispers I ought to be one of those fools and ought to keep myself in a situation the best calculated to render service—because I dont want to be rich and if I cannot live *in splendor* in Town, with a moderate fortune moderately acquired, I can at least live *in comfort* in the country and I am content to do so.

The game to be played may be a most important one. It may be for nothing less than true liberty, property, order, religion and of course *heads*. I will try Troupe if possible to guard yours & mine.

You are good enough to offer to stand between me and ostensibility. I thank you with all my soul. You cannot doubt that I should have implicit confidence in you but it has been the rule of my life to do nothing for my own emolument *undercover*—what I would not promulge I would avoid. This may be too great refinement. I know it is pride. But this pride makes it part of my plan to *appear truly what I am.*

God bless you. Always Affectionately Yrs.   A Hamilton

The Defence No. I

IT was to have been foreseen, that the treaty which Mr. Jay was charged to negociate with Great Britain, whenever it should appear, would have to contend with many perverse dispositions and some honest prejudices. That there was no measure in which the government could engage so little likely to be viewed according to its intrinsic merits—so very likely to encountre misconception, jealousy, and unreasonable dislike. For this many reasons may be assigned.

It is only to know the vanity and vindictiveness of human nature, to be convinced, that while this generation lasts, there will always exist among us, men irreconciliable to our present national constitution—embittered in their animosity, in proportion to the success of its operation, and the disappointment of their inauspicious predictions. It is a material inference from this, that such men will watch with Lynx's eyes for opportunities of discrediting the proceedings of the government, and will display a hostile and malignant zeal upon every occasion, where they think there are any prepossessions of the community to favor their enterprizes. A treaty with Great Britain was too fruitful an occasion not to call forth all their activity.

It is only to consult the history of nations to perceive, that every country, at all times, is cursed by the existence of men, who, actuated by an irregular ambition, scruple nothing which they imagine will contribute to their own advancement and importance. In monarchies, supple courtiers; in republics, fawning or turbulent demagogues, worshipping still the idol power wherever placed, whether in the hands of a prince, or of the people, and trafficking in the weaknesses, vices, frailties, or prejudices of the one or the other. It was to have been expected, that such men, counting more on the passions than on the reason of their fellow citizens, and anticipating that the treaty would have to struggle with prejudices, would be disposed to make an alliance with popular discontent, to nourish it, and to press it into the service of their particular views.

It was not to have been doubted, that there would be one or more foreign powers, indisposed to a measure which accommodated our differences with Great Britain, and laid the foundation of future good understanding, merely because it had that effect.

Nations are never content to confine their rivalships and enmities to themselves. It is their usual policy to disseminate them as widely, as they can, regardless how far it may interfere with the tranquility or happiness of the nations which they are able to influence. Whatever pretentions may be made, the world is yet remote from the spectacle of that just and generous policy, whether in the cabinets of republics or of kings, which would dispose one nation, in its intercourses with another; satisfied with a due proportion of privileges and benefits to see that other pursue freely, its true interest, with regard to a third; though at the expence of no engagement, nor in violation of any rule of friendly or fair procedure. It was natural that the contrary spirit should produce efforts of foreign counteraction to the treaty, and it was certain that the partizans of the counteracting power would second its efforts by all the means which they thought calculated to answer the end.

It was known, that the resentment produced by our revolution war with Great-Britain had never been entirely extinguished, and that recent injuries had rekindled the flame with additional violence. It was a natural consequence of this, that many should be disinclined to any amicable arrangement with Great Britain, and that many others should be prepared to acquiesce only in a treaty which should present advantages of so striking and preponderant a kind, as it was not reasonable to expect could be obtained, unless the United States were in a condition to give the law to Great Britain, and as if obtained under the coercion of such a situation could only have been the short lived prelude of a speedy rupture to get rid of them.

Unfortunately too the supposition of that situation has served to foster exaggerated expectations, and the absurd delusion to this moment prevails, notwithstanding the plain evidence to the contrary, which is deducible from the high and haughty ground still maintained by Great Britain, against victorious France.

It was not to be mistaken that an enthusiasm for France and her revolution throughout all its wonderful vicissitudes has continued to possess the minds of the great body of the people of this country, and it was to be inferred, that this sentiment would predispose to a jealousy of any agreement or treaty with her most persevering competitior—a jealousy so excessive as would give the fullest hope to insidious arts to perplex and mislead the public opinion. It was well understood, that a numerous party among us, though disavowing the design, because the avowal would defeat it, have been steadily endeavouring to make the United States a party in the present European war, by advocating all those measures which would widen the breach between us and Great Britain, and by resisting all those which could tend to close it; and it was morally certain, that this party would eagerly improve every circumstance which could serve to render the treaty odious, and to frustrate it, as the most effectual road to their favorite goal.

It was also known beforehand that personal and party rivalships of the most active kind, would assail whatever treaty might be made, to disgrace, if possible, its organ.

There are three persons prominent in the public eye, as the successor of the actual President of the United States in the event of his retreat from the station, Mr. Adams, Mr. Jay, Mr. Jefferson.

No one has forgotten the systematic pains which have been taken to impair the well earned popularity of the first gentleman. Mr. Jay too has been repeatedly the object of attacks with the same view. His friends as well as his enemies anticipated that he could make no treaty which would not furnish weapons against him—and it were to have been ignorant of the indefatigable malice of his adversaries to have doubted that they would be seized with eagerness and wielded with dexterity.

The peculiar circumstances which have attended the two last elections for governor of this state, have been of a nature to give the utmost keenness to party animosity. It was impossible that Mr. Jay should be forgiven for his double, and in the last instance triumphant success; or that any promising opportunity of detaching from him the public confidence should pass unimproved.

Trivial facts frequently throw light upon important designs.

It is remarkable, that in the toasts given on the 4th of July, wherever there appears a direct or indirect censure on the treaty, it is pretty uniformly coupled with compliments to Mr. Jefferson, and to our late governor Mr. Clinton, with an evident design to place those gentlemen in contrast with Mr. Jay, and decrying him to elevate them. No one can be blind to the finger of party spirit, visible in these and similar transactions. It indicates to us clearly, one powerful source of opposition to the treaty.

No man is without his personal enemies. Pre-eminence even in talents and virtue is a cause of envy and hatred of its possessor. Bad men are the natural enemies of virtuous men. Good men sometimes mistake and dislike each other.

Upon such an occasion as the treaty, how could it happen other wise, than that *personal enmity* would be unusually busy, enterprising and malignant?

From the combined operation of these different causes, it would have been a vain expectation that the treaty would be generally contemplated with candor and moderation, or that reason would regulate the first impressions concerning it. It was certain on the contrary, that however unexceptionable its true character might be, it would have to fight its way through a mass of unreasonable opposition; and that time, examination and reflection would be requisite to fix the public opinion on a true basis. It was certain that it would become the instrument of a systematic effort against the national government and its administration; a decided engine of party to advance its own views at the hazard of the public peace and prosperity.

The events which have already taken place, are a full comment of these positions. If the good sense of the people does not speedily discountenance the projects which are on foot, more melancholy proofs may succeed.

Before the treaty was known, attempts were made to prepossess the public mind against it. It was absurdly asserted, that it was not expected by the people, that Mr. Jay was to make any treaty; as if he had been sent, not to accommodate differences by negociation and agreement, but to dictate to Great Britain the terms of an unconditional submission.

Before it was published at large, a sketch, calculated to

produce false impressions, was handed out to the public through a medium noted for hostility, to the administration of the government. Emissaries flew through the country, spreading alarm and discontent: the leaders of clubs were every where active to seize the passions of the citizens and preoccupy their judgments against the treaty.

At Boston it was published one day, and the next a town meeting was convened to condemn it, without ever being read; without any serious discussion, sentence was pronounced against it.

Will any man seriously believe that in so short a time, an instrument of this nature could have been tolerably understood by the greater part of those who were thus induced to a condemnation of it? Can the result be considered as any thing more than a sudden ebullition of popular passion, excited by the artifices of a party, which had adroitly seized a favourable moment to surprize the public opinion? This spirit of precipitation and the intemperance which accompanied it, prevented the body of merchants and the greatest part of the most considerate citizens from attending the meeting, and left those who met, wholly under the guidance of a set of men, who, with two or three exceptions, have been the uniform opposers of the government.

The intelligence of this event had no sooner reached New York, than the leaders of the clubs were seen haranguing in every corner of the city to stir up our citizens into an imitation of the example of the meeting at Boston. An invitation to meet at the City Hall quickly followed, not to consider or discuss the merits of the treaty, but to unite with the meeting at Boston to address the president against its ratification.

This was immediately succeeded by a hand bill, full of invectives against the treaty as absurd as they were inflammatory, and manifestly designed to induce the citizens to surrender their reason to the empire of their passions.

In vain did a respectable meeting of the merchants endeavour, by their advice, to moderate the violence of these views, and to promote a spirit favourable to a fair discussion of the treaty; in vain did a respectable body of citizens of every discription, attend for that purpose. The leaders of the clubs resisted all discussion, and their followers, by their clamours and vociferations, rendered it impracticable, notwithstanding the wish of a manifest majority of the citizens convened upon the occasion.

Can we believe, that the leaders were really sincere, in the objections they made to a decision, or that the great and mixed mass of citizens then assembled had so thoroughly mastered the merits of the treaty, as that they might not have been enlightened by such a discussion.

It cannot be doubted that the real motive to the opposition, was the fear of a discussion; the desire of excluding light; the adherence to a plan of surprize and deception. Nor need we desire any fuller proof of that spirit of party which has stimulated the opposition to the treaty, than is to be found in the circumstances of that opposition.

To every man who is not an enemy to the national government, who is not a prejudiced partizan, who is capable of comprehending the argument, and passionate enough to attend to it with impartiality, I flatter myself I shall be able to demonstrate satisfactorily in the course of some succeeding papers—

1. That the treaty adjusts in a reasonable manner the points in controversy between the United States and Great-Britain, as well those depending on the inexecution of the treaty of peace, as those growing out of the present European war.

2. That it makes no improper concessions to Great-Britain, no sacrifices on the part of the United States.

3. That it secures to the United States equivalents for what they grant.

4. That it lays upon them no restrictions which are incompatible with their honour or their interest.

5. That in the articles which respect war, it conforms to the laws of nations.

6. That it violates no treaty with, nor duty toward any foreign power.

7. That compared with our other commercial treaties, it is upon the whole, entitled to a preference.

8. That it contains concessions of advantages by Great-Britain to the United States, which no other nation has obtained from the same power.

9. That it gives to her no superiority of advantages over other nations with whom we have treaties.

10. That interests of primary importance to our general welfare, are promoted by it.

11. That the too probable result of a refusal to ratify is war, or what would be still worse, a disgraceful passiveness under violations of our rights, unredressed and unadjusted; and consequently, that it is the true interest of the United States, that the treaty should go into effect.

It will be understood, that I speak of the treaty as advised to be ratified by the Senate—for this is the true question before the public.

CAMILLUS.

The Argus, or Greenleaf's New Daily Advertiser,
July 22, 1795

Memorandum on the Design for Seal of the United States

A Globe with Europe and part of Africa on one side—America on the other—the Atlantic Ocean between. The portion occupied by America to be larger than that occupied by Europe. A Colossus to be placed on this Globe, with one foot on Europe, the other extending partly over the Atlantic towards America, having on his head a *quintuple* crown in his right hand an *Iron*-Sceptre projected but broken in the middle—in his left hand a *Pileus* reversed, the staff intwined by a snake with its head downward having the staff in its mouth and folding in its tail (as if in the act of strangling) a label with these words "Rights of Man."

Upon a base, supported by fifteen columns, erected on the Continent of America, to be placed the *Genius* of America, represented by *Pallas*—a female figure with a firm composed countenance, in an attitude of defiance, cloathed in armour with a golden breast plate, a spear in her right hand and an *Ægis* or shield in her left, decorated with the scales of Justice instead of the Medusa's head—her helmet incircled with wreaths of Olive—her spear striking upon the Sceptre of the Colussus and breaking it obliquely over her head a radiated Crown or *Glory*.

EXPLANATION

The Globe is an antient symbol of universal Dominion. This, with the Colossus alluding to the Directory, will denote the project of acquiring it—the position of one leg of the colussus will signify the *attempt* to extend it to America. The Columns will represent the American States. Pallas, as the Genius of America will denote, that though loving Peace (of which the Olive wreath is the emblem) yet guided by *Wisdom*, or an enlightened sense of her own rights and interests, she is determined to exert and does successfully exert her *valour*, in breaking the sceptre of the Tyrant. The *Glory* is the usual type of Providential interposition.

It would improve it if it did not render it too complicated to represent the Ocean in Tempest & Neptune striking with his Trident the projected leg of the Colussus.

But perhaps instead of all this it may suffice to have the figure of Pallas on horse back the harp placed on the Columns these on a small mount—her spear breaking a Sceptre projected by a *Herculean Arm*.

c. May 1796

A DRAFT OF THE FAREWELL ADDRESS

To George Washington

Sir   New York July 30. 1796
I have the pleasure to send you herewith a certain draft which I have endeavoured to make as perfect as my time and engagements would permit. It has been my object to render this act *importantly* and *lastingly* useful, and avoiding all just cause of present exception, to embrace such reflections and sentiments as will wear well, progress in approbation with time, & redound to future reputation. How far I have succeeded you will judge.

I have begun the second part of the task—the digesting the supplementary remarks to the first address which in a fortnight I hope also to send you—yet I confess the more I have considered the matter the less eligible this plan has appeared to me. There seems to me to be a certain awkwardness in the thing—and it seems to imply that there is a doubt whether the assurance without the evidence would be believed. Besides that I think that there are some ideas which will not wear well in the former address, & I do not see how any part can be omitted, if it is to be given as the thing formerly prepared. Nevertheless when you have both before you you can better judge.

If you should incline to take the draft now sent—and after perusing and noting any thing that you wish changed & will send it to me I will with pleasure shape it as you desire. This may also put it in my power to improve the expression & perhaps in some instances condense.

I rejoice that certain clouds have not lately thickened & that there is a prospect of a brighter horison.

With affectionate & respectful attachment I have the honor to be
Sir   Yr. Very Obed Serv   A Hamilton

The period for a new election of a Citizen to administer the Executive Gov of the U States being not very distant and the time actually arrived when your thoughts must be employed in designating the person who is to be cloathed with that important trust for another term, it appears to me proper, and especially as it may conduce to a more distinct expression of the public voice, that I should now apprize you of the resolution I have formed to decline being considered among the number of those out of whom a choice is to be made.

I beg you nevertheless to be assured that the resolution, which I announce, has not been taken without a strict regard to all the considerations attached to the relation which as a dutiful Citizen I bear to my Country; and that in withdrawing the tender of my service, which silence in my situation might imply, I am influenced by no diminution of zeal for its future interest nor by any deficiency of grateful respect for its past kindness, but by a full conviction that such a step is compatible with both.

The acceptance of and continuance hitherto in the office to which your suffrages have twice called me has been a uniform sacrifice of private inclination to the opinion of public duty coinciding with what appeared to be your wishes. I had constantly hoped that it would have been much earlier in my power consistently with motives which I was not at liberty to disregard to return to that retirement from which those motives had reluctantly drawn me.

The strength of my desire to withdraw previous to the last election had even led to the preparation of an address to declare it to you—but deliberate reflection on the very critical and perplexed posture of our affairs with foreign nations and the unanimous advice of men of every way intitled to my confidence obliged me to abandon the idea.

I rejoice that the state of your national Concerns external as well as internal no longer renders the pursuit of my inclination incompatible with the sentiment of duty or propriety, and that whatever partiality any portion of You may still retain for my services, they, under the existing circumstances of our Country, will not disapprove the resolution I have formed.

The impressions under which I first accepted the arduous trust of chief Magistrate of the U States were explained on the proper occasion. In the discharge of this trust I can only say that I have with pure intentions contributed towards the organisation and administration of the Government the best exertions of which a very fallible judgment was capable. Not unconscious at the outset of the inferiority of my qualifications for the station, experience in my own eyes and perhaps still more in those of others has not diminished in me the diffidence of myself—and every day the increasing weight of years admonishes me more and more that the shade of retirement is as necessary to me as it will be welcome to me. Satisfied that if any circumstances have given a peculiar value to my services they were temporary, I have the consolation to believe that while inclination and prudence urge me to recede from the political scene patriotism does not forbid it—May I also have that of perceiving in my retreat that the involuntary errors which I have probably committed have been the causes of no serious or lasting mischief to my Country and thus be spared the anguish of regrets which would disturb the repose of my retreat and embitter the remnant of my life! I may then expect to realize without alloy the purest enjoyment of partaking, in the midst of my fellow citizens of the benign influence of good laws under a free Government; the ultimate object of all my wishes and to which I look as the happy reward I hope of our mutual cares labours and dangers.

In looking forward to the moment which is to terminate the carreer of my public life, my sensations do not permit me to suspend the deep acknowlegements required by that debt of gratitude which I owe to my beloved country for the many honors it has conferred upon me still more for the distinguished and steadfast confidence it has reposed in me and for the opportunities it has thus afforded me of manifesting my inviolable attachment by services faithful and persevering—however the inadequateness of my faculties may have ill seconded my zeal. If benefits have resulted to you my fellow Citizens from these services, let it always be remembered to your praise and as an instructive example in our annals that the constancy of your support amidst appearances sometimes dubious vicissitudes of fortune often discouraging and in situations in which not infrequently want of success has seconded the criticisms of malevolence was the essential prop of the efforts and the guarantee of the measures by which they were atchieved. Profoundly penetrated with this idea, I shall carry it with me to my retirement and to my grave as a lively incitement to unceasing vows (the only returns I can henceforth make) that Heaven may continue to You the choicest tokens of the beneficence merited by national piety and morality—that your union and brotherly affection may be perpetual—that the free constitution, which is the work of your own hands may be sacredly maintained—that its administration in every department may be stamped with wisdom and virtue—that in fine the happiness of the People of these States under the auspices of liberty may be made complete by so careful a preservation & so prudent a use of this blessing as will acquire them the glorious satisfaction of recommending it to the affection the praise—and the adoption of every nation which is yet a stranger to it.

Here perhaps I ought to stop. But a solicitude for your welfare, which cannot end but with my life, and the fear that there may exist projects unfriendly to it against which it may be necessary you should be guarded, urge me in taking leave of you to offer to your solemn consideration and frequent re-view some sentiments the result of mature reflection con-firmed by observation & experience which appear to me essential to the permanency of your felicity as a people. These will be offered with the more freedom as you can only see in them the disinterested advice of a parting friend who can have no personal motive to tincture or byass his counsel.

Interwoven as is the love of Liberty with every fibre of your hearts no recommendation is necessary to fortify your attach-ment to it. Next to this that unity of Government which constitutes you one people claims your vigilant care & guardianship—as a main pillar of your real independence of your peace safety freedom and happiness.

This being the point in your political fortress against which the batteries of internal and external enemies will be most con-stantly and actively however covertly and insidiously levelled, it is of the utmost importance that you should appreciate in its full force the immense value of your political Union to your national and individual happiness—that you should cherish to-wards it an affectionate and immoveable attachment and that you should watch for its preservation with jealous solicitude.

For this you have every motive of sympathy and interest. Children for the most part of a common country, that coun-try claims and ought to concentrate your affections. The name of American must always gratify and exalt the just pride of patriotism more than any denomination which can be de-rived from local discrimination. You have with slight shades of difference the same religion manners habits & political insti-tutions & principles. You have in a common cause fought and triumphed to gether. The independence and liberty you enjoy are the work of joint councils efforts—dangers sufferings & successes. By your Union you atchieved them, by your union you will most effectually maintain them.

The considerations which address themselves to your sensi-bility are greatly strengthened by those which apply to your interest. Here every portion of our Country will find the most urgent and commanding motives for guarding and preserving the Union of the Whole.

The North in free & unfettered intercourse with the South under the equal laws of one Government will in the production of the latter many of them peculiar find vast additional resources of maritime and commercial enterprise and precious materials of their manufacturing industry. The South in the same intercourse will share in the benefits of the Agency of the North will find its agriculture promoted and its commerce extended by means of Navigation which the North more abundantly affords and while it contributes to extend the national navigation will participate in the protection of a maritime strength to which itself is unequally adapted. The East in a like intercourse with the West finds and in the progressive improvement of internal navigation will more & more find, a valuable vent for the commodities which it brings from abroad or manufactures at home. The West derives through this Channel an essential supply of its wants—and what is far more important to it, it must owe the secure and permanent enjoyment of the indispensable outlets for its own productions to the weight influence & maritime resources of the Atlantic States directed by an indissoluble community of interest. The tenure by which it could hold this advantage either from its own separate strength or by an apostate and unnatural connection with any foreign Nation must be intrinsically & necessarily precarious at every moment liable to be disturbed by the fluctuating combinations of those primary European interests which constantly regulate the conduct of every portion of Europe—And where every part finds a particular interest in the Union All the parts of our Country will find in their Union greater independence from the superior abundance & variety of production incident to the diversity of soil & climate, all the parts of it must find in the aggregate assemblage & reaction of their mutual population production greater strength, proportional security from external danger, less frequent interruption of their peace with foreign nations and what is far more valuable an exemption from those broils & wars between the parts if disunited which their own rivalships fomented by foreign intrigue, or the opposite alliances with foreign nations engendered by their mutual jealousies would inevitably produce—a consequent exemption from the necessity of those military establishments upon a large scale which bear in every country so menacing an aspect toward Liberty.

These considerations speak a conclusive language to every virtuous and considerate mind. They place the continuance of our Union among the first objects of patriotic desire. Is there a doubt whether a common government can long embrace so extensive a sphere? Let Time & Experience decide the question. Speculation in such a case ought not to be listened to— And tis rational to hope that the auxiliary agency of the governments of the subdivisions, with a proper organisation of the whole will secure a favourable issue to the Experiment. Tis allowable to believe that the spirit of party the intrigues of foreign nations, the corruption & the ambition of Individuals are likely to prove more formidable adversaries to the unity of our Empire than any inherent difficulties in the scheme. Tis against these that the guards of national opinion national sympathy national prudence & virtue are to be erected. With such obvious motives to Union there will be always cause from the fact itself to distrust the <u>patriotism</u> of those who in any quarter may endeavour to weaken its bands. And by all the love I bear you My fellow Citizens I conjure you as often as it appears to frown upon the attempt.

Besides the more serious causes which have been hinted at, as endangering our Union there is another less dangerous but against which it is necessary to be on our guard. I mean the petulance collisions & disgusts of party differences of Opinion. It is not uncommon to hear the irritations which these excite vent themselves in declarations that the different parts of the Union are ill assorted and cannot remain together—in menaces from the inhabitants of one part to those of another that it will be dissolved by this or that measure. Intimations of the kind are as indiscreet as they are intemperate. Though frequently made with levity and without being in earnest they have a tendency to produce the consequence which they indicate. They teach the minds of men to consider the Union as precarious as an object to which they are not to attach their hopes and fortunes and thus weaken the sentiment in its favour. By rousing the resentment and alarming the pride of those to whom they are addressed they set ingenuity to work to depreciate the value of the object and to discover motives of Indifference to it. This is not wise. Prudence demands that we should habituate ourselves in all our words and actions to reverence the Union as a sacred and inviolable palladium of our happiness—and should discountenance whatever can lead to a suspicion that it can in any event be abandonned.

Tis matter of serious concern that parties in this Country for some time past have been too much characterised by geographical discriminations—Northern and Southern States Atlantic and Western Country. These discriminations of party which are the mere artifice of the spirit of party (always dexterous to avail itself of every source of sympathy of every handle by which the passions can be taken hold of and which has been careful to turn to account the circumstance of territorial vicinity) have furnished an argument against the Union as evidence of a real difference of local interests and views and serve to hazard it by organising large districts of country under the direction of the leaders of different factions whose passions & prejudices rather than the true interests of the Country, will be too apt to regulate the use of their influence. If it be possible to correct <u>this poison</u> in the affairs of our Country it is worthy the best endeavours of moderate & virtuous men to effect it.

One of the expedients which the partisans of Faction employ towards strengthening their influence by local discriminations is to misrepresent the opinions and views of rival districts—The People at large cannot be too much on their guard against the jealousies which grow out of these misrepresentations. They tend to render aliens to each other those who ought to be tied together by fraternal affection. The Western Country have lately had a useful lesson on this subject. They have seen in the negotiation by the Executive & in the unanimous ratification of the Treaty with Spain by the Senate & in the universal satisfaction at that event in all parts of the Country a decisive proof how unfounded have been the suspicions that have been instilled in them of a policy in the Atlantic States & in the different departments of the General Government hostile to their interests in relation to the Mississipian. They have seen two treaties formed which secure to them every thing that they could desire to confirm their prosperity. Will they not henceforth rely for the preservation of these advantages on that union by which they were procured? Will they not reject those counsellors who would render them alien to their brethren & connect them with Aliens?

To the duration and efficacy of your Union a Government extending over the whole is indispensable. No alliances however strict between the parts could be an adequate substitute. These could not fail to be liable to the infractions and interruptions which all alliances in all times have suffered. Sensible of this important truth you have lately established a Constitution of General Government, better calculated than the former for an intimate union and more adequate to the direction of your common concerns. This Government the offspring of your own choice uninfluenced and unawed, completely free in its principles, in the distribution of its powers uniting energy with safety and containing in itself a provision for its own amendment is well entitled to your confidence and support—Respect for its authority, compliance with its laws, acquiescence in its measures, are duties dictated by the fundamental maxims of true Liberty. The basis of our political systems is the right of the people to make and to alter their constitutions of Government. But the constitution for the time, and until changed by an explicit and authentic act of the whole people, is sacredly binding upon all. The very idea of the right and power of the people to establish Government presupposes the duty of every individual to obey the established Government.

All obstructions to the execution of the laws—all <u>combinations</u> and <u>associations</u> under whatever plausible character with the real design to direct counteract countroul influence or awe the regular deliberation or action of the constituted authorities are contrary to this fundamental principle & of the most fatal tendency. They serve to organise Faction to give it an artificial force; and to put in the stead of the delegated will of the whole nation the will of a party. often a small but artful & enterprising minority of the community—and according to the alternate triumphs of different parties to make the public administration reflect the ill concerted schemes and projects of faction rather than the wholesome plans of common councils and deliberations. However combinations or associations of this description may occasionally promote popular ends and purposes they are likely to produce in the course of time and things the most effectual engines by which artful ambitious and unprincipled men will be enabled to subvert the power of the people and usurp the reins of Government.

Towards the preservation of your government and the permanency of your present happy state, it is not only requisite that you steadily discountenance irregular oppositions to its authority but that you should be upon your guard against the spirit of innovation upon its principles however specious the pretexts. One method of assault may be to effect alterations in the forms of the constitution tending to impair the energy of the system and so to undermine what cannot be directly overthrown. In all the changes to which you may be invited remember that time and habit are as necessary to fix the true character of governments as of any other human institutions, that experience is the surest standard by which the real tendency of existing constitutions of government can be tried—that changes upon the credit of mere hypothesis and opinions exposes you to perpetual change from the successive and endless variety of hypothesis and opinion—and remember also that for the efficacious management of your common interests in a country so extensive as ours a Government of as much force and strength as is consistent with the perfect security of liberty is indispensable. Liberty itself will find in such a Government, with powers properly distributed and arranged, its surest guardian—and protector. In my opinion the real danger in our system is that the General Government organised as at present will prove too weak rather than too powerful.

I have already observed the danger to be apprehended from founding our parties on Geographical discriminations. Let me now enlarge the view of this point and caution you in the most solemn manner against the baneful effects of party spirit in general. This spirit unfortunately is inseperable from human nature and has its root in the strongest passions of the human heart.—It exists under different shapes in all governments but in different degrees stifled controuled or repressed in those of the popular form it is always seen in its utmost vigour & rankness and it is their worst enemy. In republics of narrow extent, it is not difficult for those who at any time possess the reins of administration, or even for partial combinations of men, who from birth riches and other sources of distinction have an extraordinary influence by possessing or acquiring the direction of the military force or by sudden efforts of partisans & followers to overturn the established order of things and effect a usurpation. But in republics of large extent the one or the other is scarcely possible. The powers and opportunities of resistance of a numerous and wide extended nation defy the successful efforts of the ordinary military force or of any collections which wealth and patronage may call to their aid—especially if there be no city of overbearing force resources and influence. In such Republics it is perhaps safe to assert that the conflict of popular faction offer the only avenues to tyranny & usurpation. The domination of one faction over another stimulated by that spirit of Revenge which is apt to be gradually engendered and which in different ages and countries have produced the greatest enormities is itself a frightful despotism. But this leads at length to a more formal and permanent despotism. The disorders and miseries which result predispose the minds of men to seek repose & security in the absolute power of a single man. And some leader of a prevailing faction more able or more fortunate than his competitors turns this disposition to the purpose of an ambitious and criminal self aggrandisement.

Without looking forward to such an extremity (which however ought not to be out of sight) the ordinary and continual mischief of the spirit of party make it the interest and the duty of a wise people to discountenance and repress it.

It serves always to distract the Councils & enfeeble the administration of the Government. It agitates the community with ill founded jealousies and false alarms embittering one part of the community against another, & producing occasionaly riot & insurrection. It opens inlets for foreign corruption and influence—which find an easy access through the channels of party passions—and cause the true policy & interest of our own country to be made subservient to the policy and interest of one and another foreign Nation; sometimes enslaving our own Government to the will of a foreign Government.

There is an opinion that parties in free countries are salutary checks upon the administration of the Government & serve to invigorate the spirit of Liberty. This within certain limits is true and in governments of a monarchical character or byass patriotism may look with some favour on the spirit of party. But in those of the popular kind in those purely elective, it is a spirit not to be fostered or encouraged. From the natural tendency of such governments, it is certain there will always be enough of it for every salutary purpose and there being constant danger of excess the effort ought to be by force of public opinion to mitigate & correct it. Tis a fire which cannot be quenched but demands a uniform vigilance to prevent its bursting into a flame—lest it should not only warm but consume.

It is important likewise that the habits of thinking of the people should tend to produce caution in their agents in the several departments of Government, to retain each within its proper sphere and not to permit one to encroach upon another—that every attempt of the kind from whatever quarter should meet with the discountenance of the community, and that in every case in which a precedent of encroachment shall have been given, a corrective be sought in (revocation be effected by) a careful attention to the next choice of public Agents. The spirit of encroachment tends to absorb & consolidate the powers of the several branches and departments into one, and thus to establish under whatever forms a despotism. A just knowlege of the human heart, of that love of power which predominates in it, is alone sufficient to establish this truth. Experiments ancient and modern—some in our own country and under our own eyes serve to confirm it. If in the public opinion the distribution of the constitutional powers be in any instance wrong or inexpedient—let it be corrected by the authority of the people in a legitimate constitutional course—Let there be no change by usurpation, for though this may be the instrument of good in one instance, it is the ordinary and natural instrument of the destruction of free Government—and the influence of the precedent is always infinitely more pernicious than any thing which it may atchieve can be beneficial.

To all those dispositions which promote political happiness, Religion and Morality are essential props. In vain does that man claim the praise of patriotism who labours to subvert or undermine these great pillars of human happiness these firmest foundations of the duties of men and citizens. The mere politician equally with the pious man ought to respect and cherish them. A volume could not trace all their connections with private and public happiness. Let it simply be asked where is the security for property for reputation for life if the sense of moral and religious obligation deserts the oaths which are administered in Courts of Justice? Nor ought we to flatter ourselves that morality can be separated from religion. Concede as much as may be asked to the effect of refined education in minds of a peculiar structure—can we believe—can we in prudence suppose that national morality can be maintained in exclusion of religious principles? Does it not require the aid of a generally received and divinely authoritative Religion?

Tis essentially true that virtue or morality is a main & necessary spring of popular or republican Governments. The rule indeed extends with more or less force to all free Governments. Who that is a prudent & sincere friend to them can look with indifference on the ravages which are making in the foundation of the Fabric? Religion? The uncommon means which of late have been directed to this fatal end seem to make it in a particular of manner the duty of the Retiring Chief of a nation to warn his country against tasting of the poisonous draught.

Cultivate also industry and frugality. They are auxiliaries of good morals and great sources of private and national prosperity. Is there not room for regret that our propensity to expence exceeds the maturity of our Country for expense? Is there not more luxury among us, in various classes, than suits the actual period of our national progress? Whatever may be the apology for luxury in a Country mature in all the arts which are its ministers and the means of national opulence—can it promote the advantage of a young agricultural Country little advanced in manufactures and not much advanced in wealth?

Cherish public Credit as a mean of strength and security. As one method of preserving it, use it as little as possible. Avoid occasions of expence by cultivating peace—remembering always that the preparation against danger by timely and provident disbursements is often a mean of avoiding greater disbursements to repel it. Avoid the accumulation of debt by avoiding occasions of expence and by vigorous exertions in time of peace to discharge the debts which unavoidable wars may have occasionned—not transferring to posterity the burthen which we ought to bear ourselves. Recollect that towards the payment of debts there must be Revenue, that to have revenue there must be taxes, that it is impossible to devise taxes which are not more or less inconvenient and unpleasant—that they are always a choice of difficulties—that the intrinsic embarrassment which never fails to attend a selection of objects ought to be a motive for a candid construction of the conduct of the Government in making it—and that a spirit of acquiescence in those measures for obtaining revenue which the public exigencies dictate is in an especial manner the duty and interest of the citizens of every State.

Cherish good faith and Justice towards, and peace and harmony with all nations. Religion and morality enjoins this conduct And It cannot be, but that true policy equally demands it. It will be worthy of a free enlightened and at no distant period a great nation to give to mankind the magnanimous and too novel example of a people invariably governed by those exalted views. Who can doubt that in a long course of time and events the fruits of such a conduct would richly repay any temporary advantages which might be lost by a steady adherence to the plan? Can it be that Providence has not connected the permanent felicity of a nation with its virtue? The experiment is recommended by every sentiment which ennobles human nature. Alas! is it rendered impossible by its vices?

Toward the execution of such a plan nothing is more essential than that antipathies against particular nations and passionate attachments for others should be avoided—and that instead of them we should cultivate just and amicable feelings towards all. That nation, which indulges towards another a habitual hatred or a habitual fondness is in some degree a slave. It is a slave to its animosity or to its affection—either of which is sufficient to lead it astray from its duty and interest. Antipathy against one nation which never fails to beget a similar sentiment in the other disposes each more readily to offer injury and insult to the other—to lay hold of slight causes of umbrage and to be haughty and intractable when accidental or trifling differences arise. Hence frequent quarrels and bitter and obstinate contests. The nation urged by resentment and rage sometimes impels the Government to War contrary to its own calculations of policy. The Government sometimes participates in this propensity & does through passion what reason would forbid—at other times it makes the animosity of the nations subservient to hostile projects which originate in ambition & other sinister motives. The peace often and sometimes the liberty of Nations has been the victim of this cause.

In like manner a passionate attachment of one nation to another produces multiplied ills. Sympathy for the favourite nations, promoting the illusion of a supposed common interest in cases where it does not exist and communicating to one the enmities of the one betrays into a participation in its quarrels & wars without adequate inducements or justifications. It leads to the concession of privileges to one nation and to the denial of them to others—which is apt doubly to injure the nation making the concession by an unnecessary yielding of what ought to have been retained and by exciting jealousy ill will and retaliation in the party from whom an equal privilege is witheld. And it gives to ambitious corrupted or deluded citizens, who devote themselves to the views of the favourite foreign power, facility in betraying or sacrificing the interests of their own country without odium & even with popularity gilding with the appearance of a virtuous impulse the base yieldings of ambition or corruption.

As avenues to foreign influence in innumerable Ways such attachments are peculiarly alarming to the enlightened independent Patriot. How many opportunities do they afford to intrigue with domestic factions to practice with success the arts of seduction—to mislead public opinion—to influence or awe the public Councils! Such an attachment of a small or weak towards a great & powerful Nation destines the former to revolve round the latter as its satellite.

Against the Mischiefs of Foreign Influence all the Jealousy of a free people ought to be constantly continually exerted. All History & Experience prove that foreign influence is one of the most baneful foes of republican Governt—but that jealousy of it to be useful must be impartial else it becomes an instrument—of the very influence to be avoided instead of a defence against it.

Excessive partiality for one foreign nation & excessive dislike of another, leads to see danger only on one side and serves to viel & second the arts of influence on the other. Real Patriots who resist the intrigues of the favorite become suspected & odious. Its tools & dupes usurp the applause & confidence of the people to betray their interests.

The great rule of conduct for us in regard to foreign Nations ought to be to have as little <u>political</u> connection with them as possible—so far as we have already formed engagements let them be fulfilled—with circumspection indeed but with perfect good faith. Here let us stop.

Europe has a set of primary interests which have none or a very remote relation to us. Hence she must be involved in frequent contests the causes of which will be essentially foreign to us. Hence therefore it must necessarily be unwise on our part to implicate ourselves by an artificial connection in the ordinary vicissitudes of European politics—in the combination, & collisions of her friendships or enmities.

Our detached and distant situation invites us to a different course & enables us to pursue it. If we remain a united people under an efficient Government the period is not distant when we may defy material injury from external annoyance—when we may take such an attitude as will cause the neutrality we shall at any time resolve to observe to be violated with caution—when it will be the interest of belligerent nations under the impossibility of making acquisitions upon us to be very careful how either forced us to throw our weight into the opposite scale—when we may choose peace or war as our interest guided by justice shall dictate.

Why should we forego the advantages of so felicitous a situation? Why quit our own ground to stand upon Foreign ground? Why by interweaving our destiny with any part of Europe should we intangle our prosperity and peace in the nets of European Ambition rivalship interest or Caprice?

Permanent alliance, intimate connection with any part of the foreign world is to be avoided. so far (I mean) as we are now at liberty to do it: for let me never be understood as patronising infidelity to preexisting engagements. These must be observed in their true and genuine sense. But tis not necessary nor will it be prudent to extend them. Tis our true policy as a general principle to avoid permanent or close alliance—Taking care always to keep ourselves by suitable establishments in a respectably defensive posture we may safely trust to occasional alliances for extraordinary emergencies.

Harmony liberal intercourse and commerce with all nations are recommended by justice humanity & interest. But even our commercial policy should hold an equal hand—neither seeking nor granting exclusive favours or preferences—consulting the natural course of things—<u>diffusing</u> and <u>diversifying</u> by gentle means the streams of Commerce but forcing nothing—establishing with powers so disposed in order to give to Trade a stable course, to define the rights of our Merchants and enable the Government to support them—conventional rules of intercourse the best that present circumstances and mutual opinion of interest will permit but temporary—and liable to be abandonned or varied as time experience & future circumstances may dictate—remembering alway that tis folly in one nation to expect disinterested favour in another—that to accept any thing under that character is to part with a portion of its independence—and that it may find itself in the condition of having given equivalents for nominal favours and of being reproached with ingratitude in the bargain. There can be no greater error in national policy than to desire expect or calculate upon real favours. Tis an illusion that experience must cure, that a just pride ought to discard.

In offering to you My Countrymen! these counsels of an old and affectionate friend—counsels suggested by labourious reflection and matured by a various experience—I dare not hope that they will make the strong and lasting impressions I wish—that they will controul the current of the passions or prevent our nation from running the course which has hitherto marked the destiny of all nations. But if they even produce some partial benefits, some occasional good—that they sometimes recur to moderate the violence of party spirit—to warn against the evils of foreign intrigue—to guard against the impositions of pretended patriotism—the having offered them must always afford me a precious consolation.

How far in the execution of my present Office I have been guided by the principles which have been inculcated the public records & the external evidences of my conduct must witness. My conscious assures me that I have at least believed myself to be guided by them.

In reference to the present War of Europe my Proclamation of the 22d of April 1793 is the key to my plan. Sanctioned by your approving voice and that of your representatives in Congress the spirit of that measure has continually governed me uninfluenced and unawed by the attempts of any of the warring powers their agents or partizans to deter or divert from it.

After deliberate consideration and the best lights I could obtain (and from men who did not agree in their views of the origin progress & nature of that war) I was satisfied that our Country, under all the circumstances of the case, had a right and was bound in propriety and interest to take a neutral position—And having taken it, I determined as far as should depend on me to maintain it steadily and firmly.

Though in reviewing the incidents of my administration I am unconscious of intentional error—I am yet too sensible of my own deficiencies not to think it probable that I have committed many errors. I deprecate the evils to which they may tend—and fervently implore the Almighty to avert or mitigate them. I shall carry with me nevertheless the hope that my motives will continue to be viewed by my Country with indulgence & that after forty five years of my life devoted with an upright zeal to the public service the faults of inadequate abilities will be consigned to oblivion as myself must soon be to the mansions of rest.

Neither Ambition nor interest has been the impelling cause of my actions. I never designedly misused any power confided to me. The fortune with which I came into office is not bettered otherwise than by that improvement in the value of property which the natural progress and peculiar prosperity of our country have produced. I retire without cause for a blush—with a pure heart with no alien sentiment to the ardor of those vows for the happiness of his Country which is so natural to a Citizen who sees in it the native soil of himself and his progenitors for four generations.

CRISIS WITH FRANCE

To William Loughton Smith

Dr Sir

Since my last to you I have perused with great satisfaction your little work on our Governments. I like the execution no less than the plan. If my health & leisure should permit, I would make some notes, but you cannot depend on it, as I am not only extremely occupied but in feeble health.

I send you My ideas of the course of Conduct proper in our present situation. It is unpleasant to me to know that I have for some time differed materially from many of my friends on public subjects; and I particularly regret that at the present critical juncture there is in my apprehension much danger that *sensibility* will be an overmatch for *policy*. We seem not to feel & reason as the *Jacobins* did when Great Britain insulted and injured us, though certainly we have at least as much need of a temperate conduct now as we had then. I only say, God Grant, that the public interest may not be sacrificed at the shrine of irritation & mistaken pride. Farewell

Affectly Yrs.   A H
                                               April 10. 1797

It must be acknowleged by all who can comprehend the subject that the present situation of the UStates is in an extreme degree critical, demanding in our public councils a union of the greatest prudence with the greatest firmness. To appreciate rightly the course which ought to be pursued it is an essential preliminary to take an accurate view of the situation.

That the preservation of peace is a leading article in the policy of this country has been peculiarly the tenet of the friends of the Government. It is a tenet supported by conclusive reasons. In addition to the general motives to peace which are common to other nations—it is of the utmost consequence to us that our progress to that degree of maturity which puts humanly speaking our fortunes absolutely in our hands shall not be retarded by a premature war.

But the state of affairs externally and internally suggests the strongest imaginable auxiliary motives to avoid, if possible, at this time a rupture with France. Externally we behold France most formidably successful—extending too her connections and influence, while the affairs of her remaining enemies decline. The late events in Italy have for the present put that Country intirely in the power of France with all its resources. It was evident that the Emperor had made a violent exertion for the relief of Mantua. The issue has been to him a terrible one. He will probably be able to bring forward new and powerful forces but it is likely to be attended with great difficulty and embarrassment—and there is too much reason to suspect that these new forces will be under the disadvantage, of *raw-troops* contending with Veterans led by a General who seems to have chained Victory to his chair. It would seem too that France has awed or seduced Naples into her alliance. And who can say what she may not do as to Venice? Does not every thing seem to promise her the intire command of Italy and its cooperation against the Emperor?

What is the situation of Great Britain? Triumphant at sea but deeply, if not mortally wounded in her vital part, in that which is the vital energy of the Opposition to France—I mean in her pecuniary system. The late measures with regard to the Bank, however vieled, amount to nothing less than a stoppage of payment and an act of bankruptcy in that Institution. The magic which surrounded it, and gave it its principal force exists no longer. Opinion must be injured and with it credit. The consequences are incalculable. An incapacity to afford further subsidies or loans to the Emperor may be inferred with almost moral certainty. Though the great national resources of England and the universal interest in public Credit may arrest and abrige the extent of the evil yet it is scarcely possible that it shall not very much enervate the future efforts against France & it may be expected to fortify extremely the desire of peace in the Nation.

The conduct of the present Emperor of Russia is at best equivocal. Having departed from the engagements of his predecessor towards the Emperor it is in the course of calculation that he may be thrown into the opposite scale. What is the King of Prussia about? Nothing friendly to the Emperor of Germany, if we may reason from his conduct for sometime past—though if we were to reason from his solid interest we ought to conclude that he would not be willing to have France for a contiguous neighbour commanding Holland, and the Emperor of Germany so weakened as to be a counterpoise neither to *France* nor *Russia*. Yet a crooked policy pursuing some immediate interest seems most likely to be his governing motive.

According to appearances then there is great danger that the Emperor and England may be compelled to subscribe to the conditions of France, or to continue the contest on unequal and ruinous terms. It is true in the shifting scenes of Europe the political hemisphere may quickly wear a totally different aspect, but such as it is, it exhibits every evil omen to the enemies of France.

To be involved in a contest with France at this time and under such circumstances would be in the highest degree inauspicious. If the war continues between her and her present enemies the contest can still promise nothing but evil to us without a possibility of Gain. If a sudden peace in Europe takes place and we are left to contend alone the prospect is a most uncomfortable one. France will have large bodies of troops that she will be glad to get rid of and it cannot be doubted that she will be governed by a spirit of *domination* and *Revenge*.

Internally, though our situation in this respect, mends, it is certain that there is a very large party infatuated by a blind devotion to France. Who will guarantee that in a contest so dangerous these men on considerations of ambition fear interest and predilection would not absolutely join France? There is at least enough of danger of this to furnish a strong reason for avoiding if possible rupture.

In the South we have a vast body of blacks. We know how successful the French have been in innoculating this description of men and we ought to consider them as the probable auxiliaries of France. Let us add that we may have to contend on the South & West with Spain & all the Savage tribes they can influence.

The aggregate of these considerations is little less than awful.

In such a state of things large and dispassionate views are indispensible. Neither the suggestion of pride nor timidity ought to guide. There ought to be much cool calculation united with much *calm* fortitude. The Government ought to be all intellect while the people ought to be all feeling.

The result is in my mind that there ought to be 1 a further attempt to negotiate & 2 vigorous preparation for war with an intermediate embargo.

As to a further attempt to negotiate—let a Commission extraordinary consisting of three persons be sent to France, and let *Jefferson* or *Madison* be at the head of this Commission, perhaps as the Ostensible Minister, but obliged to cooperate with his Colleagues & to conform to the Major opinion. Let General *Pinckney* be one of the Commission, and let Mr. King or Mr. Cabot or some other able man of the Northern Region be the third. If thought expedient the Com~. May go to Amsterdam & announce their mission by a Courier asking for passports &c.

Let two leading principles of action be prescribed to these Commissioners. They must not directly or indirectly acknowlege any fault or culpability in the U States—they must not stipulate any succour to France of any kind or in any shape in the present War—they must stipulate nothing inconsistent with any existing treaty with another Power.

What may they do? They may now modify our Treaties with France so as to assimilate the Commercial one with that with Great Britain and so as mutually to *do away*, or liquidate with an eye to future *defensive* wars the guarantee contained in the Treaty of alliance, substituting specific succours in defined cases to the *general guarantee.*

This measure will keep open the door of accommodation and give us the chance of favorable events. It will furnish a bridge to the pride of France to retreat. It will give her the motive of endeavouring to strengthen her party by appearing to yield peace to a leader of that party. It will convince the people completely that the Government is at least as solicitous to avoid War with France as it was to avoid it with Great Britain. It will take from the partisans of France the argument that as much has not been done in her case as in that of Great Britain & thus it will contribute, if the measure fails, to the all important end of uniting Opinion at home.

Let us see the objections to this measure and the answers they admit.

Objection 1. The conduct of France has been so violent & insulting towards us that we cannot without disgrace make a further Overture for negotiation.

Answer. This was the opinion of many with regard to Great Britain when Mr. Jay was sent & in all appearance her conduct was very outrageous. Yet our moderation on that occasion not only averted war but raised the character of the Country abroad. It is true France has gone much further than Great Britain ever did. But on the other hand the state of things, and of opinion, requires greater circumspection in the case of France, than was necessary in that of Great Britain. If we couple this measure with others which will evince that we are in earnest about defending ourselves and repelling aggression, our honor will be saved and our moderation only will be displayed. When also it shall be known that our ministers were prohibited from unworthy concessions, it will be demonstrated that we did nothing more than wave *punctilio* in favour of peace. It is often too wise by some early *condescension* to avoid the danger of future *humiliation*. Our Country is not a military one. Our people are divided. France may present herself to their imaginations as the terrible and invincible conqueror of Europe. Who will answer for their fortitude and exertion under such circumstances? Will it not be prudent to avoid if we can the Experiment by a little condescension now?

But this is not all. The measure will tend to *unite* and *fortify* & this may ensure that very fortitude which in a different state of things might be wanting. It may beget the noble resolution to die in the last ditch.

2 Object: The sending of a man unfriendly to the course of our Government & devoted to France may give an opportunity to play into the hands of France & leave greater odium upon the Government for not acceding to inadmissible terms of accommodation. He may be a medium of Cabal between France and the party rather than the Negotiator of accommodation.

Answer. There is perhaps more weight in this than in any other Objection which can be made. But it seems to admit of a satisfactory answer. First. It goes further in ascribing *Turpitude* to the character in question than perhaps is warrantable. It is far from certain that he would be disposed to make an absolute sacrifice of his country and it is to be remembered that in accepting the appointment with known restrictions he agrees to their reasonableness & engages his reputation upon the issue of success. Considerable securities result from these considerations. But admit the disposition to do what is feared, If he is coupled with men of address a counter game may be played & such a complexion may be given to the thing as may put both him and France intirely in the wrong. All will depend on the characters combined. Pinckney, it may be depended on, is a man of honor & loves his Country. Unite with him a man of *skill* and an effectual counteraction is provided. Such a man can certainly be found in a case where the Government may command any of its citizens.

3 Objection. If the measure succeeds under such a man it will strengthen his hands and through him increase the influence of France from which it is of the utmost importance to emancipate the Country.

Answer. There will be some evil of this sort. But this must be weighed against the good obtained. That will be the preservation of peace in the most dangerous crisis that can well be imagined. Besides the credit of the measure will at least be divided between the Authors & the Agent. The President and the Government will have a large share. And the poison will carry with it its antidote. Moreover it is morally certain that the course of things in France will furnish every day some new cure to a moral and orderly people like the people of this Country. But this objection such as it is lies against the *person* not the *measure*.

4th Objection. The conduct of France has been such as to free us from the shakles of Treaties which present only nominal advantages to us or such as in future will be real to her (alluding chiefly to the mutual guarantee).

Answer. This may be true, but the consequence can only take place in a final Rupture. And this would be to stake perhaps our political existence against a partial incumbrance.

Surely it could not be wise to attempt to disengage ourselves from our connection with France by a War with her at such a juncture. It might happen that in the end we might be obliged to consent to be fettered in a much greater degree, and increase rather than diminish the evil for which the rupture was hazarded. Expediency is so clearly against it that it is unnecessary to examine the morality of such a policy.

Objection 5 The conduct of France leaves no hope that such a measure will be useful or even that the mission will be heared. There will then be pure disgrace without any advantage.

Answer. The course of things in France does not authorise us to expect any very steady plan there. Events within and without will govern—and there may exist when the Minister arrives a good disposition to receive and hear him. The refusal to receive a minister Plenipotentiary may mean only *an ordinary one to reside* & may not extend to an extraordinary one *pro hac vice*. But suppose the worst, it will tend to the most precious of all things *Union* at home. The repetition of effort to avoid war and of Insult from France will have the most happy influence upon the Temper of our Country.

Object 6. The policy of remodifying our Treaty of Alliance is very questionable. It converts a vague into a specific contract, and substitutes precise obligations to such as each party may interpret according to its convenience.

Answer. This is not an essential part of the plan & may be rejected if thought inexpedient.

But considering the Treaty of alliance as the *price*, no less than the instrument of the assistance from France, morality, which is most consistent with good policy, requires it should be paid. The genuine meaning of that alliance, as to the obligation of the U States, seems to be that when France is *really* & *truly* engaged in a *defensive* war & her West India possessions are attacked the U States ought to assist in their defence with their whole force. In future the U States will not have the excuse of *inability*. They are becoming dayly a powerful nation. They must then either evade their obligation, or as often as France is engaged in a defensive war with a maritime power, take part with her with their whole force. Hence they may be exposed to frequent wars. The denial of their duty besides the guilt & disgrace of broken faith may not avoid that consequence, for as it would be a just so it might be the actual cause of War with the ally.

The vagueness of the Obligation as a source of reciprocal Controversy is in itself an evil which it would be important to get rid of.

Specific succours by either party to the other would not necessarily have the effect of involving the Giver in War. It is settled that such succours in consequence of a Treaty antecedent to the War are not a cause of War.

It would therefore seem to be a great point to the UStates to convert its obligation into that of a specific succour to be defined & thus lessen the danger of a quarrel either with France or its enemies and likewise the evils of a general War.

It is bad to be under obligations which it will be a violation of good faith not to perform & which it will certainly compromit the peace of the Country to perform.

In addition to the reasons already given for pacificatory measures are these cogent ones. The plan of the Government and of the Fœderal party has been to avoid becoming a party in the present War. If any measure it has taken is either the cause or pretext of a War with France, the end will be lost. The credit of preserving peace will not exist. The wisdom of the plan pursued will be questionned. The confidence in the Government will be shaken. The adverse party will acquire the Reputation & the influence of superior foresight. The evil avoided will be forgotten. The evil incurred will be felt. The doubt entertained by many of the justifiableness of the Treaty with G B in respect to France may increase with suffering and danger—& the management of Affairs may be thrown into the hands of the opposite party by the Voice of the people & the Government & the Country sacrificed to France.

Hence it is all important to avoid War if we can—if we cannot to strengthen as much as possible the Opinion that it proceeds from the *Unreasonableness* of France.

As to preparation for War they ought in my opinion to consist of these particulars.

I REVENUE, which ought to go as far as not to be really oppressive. A large sum may be raised within this limit. The objects may be hereafter designated.

II   A loan of five Millions of Dollars on the basis of that Revenue. This may be put on a footing which will ensure its gradual, yet timely success.

III   The completion of the three frigates with all possible speed & the purchase of *Twenty* ships the most fit to be armed and equipped as Cutters & Sloops of War. These will serve to guard our Trade against the Pickeroons of France in the West Indies which are chiefly dangerous. They are to be used in the first instance merely as convoys with instructions purely defensive—prohibitted from cruising for prizes or from attacking, or from *capturing except when attacked.*

IV   Instructions to our Minister in Great Britain, if the Negotiation fails, to endeavour to purchase from Great Britain or obtain on a loan Two ships of the line & three frigates. It will be her interest to do this as she has more ships than she can well man & our men employed in them will increase the force to be employed against the common enemy. This may be the most expeditious mode to augment our navy.

V   To grant Commissions to such of our Merchantmen as choose to take them authorising them to arm and defend themselves but not to cruise and not to capture unless attacked.

VI   To lay a general Embargo with authority to The President to grant licenses to sail, if the Vessels go themselves armed or with Convoys either of our own or of any foreign Nation. This will serve our Vessels and our seamen without arresting our Trade. In a short time, it will go on as usual under protection.

VI   To raise upon the *Establishment* some additional Artillery and Two thousand additional Cavalry. These will be useful guards against the Insurrection of the Southern Negroes—and they will be a most precious arm in case of Invasion. Cavalry will be of infinite importance as auxiliary to *new* against *veteran* Troops.

VII   The establishment of a provisional army of Twenty thousand infantry. They may be engaged to serve if a War breaks out with any foreign power, and may receive *certain* emoluments in the mean time—cloaths, full wages when they assemble to exercise, a dollar ℔ Month at other times. This corps must be regularly organised & officered by the United

States. The Officers to take rank with those of the establishment. Its advantage will be to have a body of men at a small expence ready for emergencies. The chance of not being employed will facilitate the obtaining of the men on moderate terms.

There may be a disposition to rely wholly on the Militia on three grounds—the supposed improbability of an Invasion—the belief that Militia are sufficient—the Expence in the first instance.

Those who may think an Invasion improbable ought to remember that it is not long since there was a general Opinion the U States was in no danger of War. They see how difficult it has been and is to avoid one. They ought to suspect that the present opinion that there is no danger of invasion may be as chimerical as that other which experience proves to be false.

If France can transport her troops here what is to hinder an invasion? Will she not be very likely to imagine that numerous partisans will join her standard so as to enable her to effect a Revolution & place us more completely under her influence? What if the corps destined to this service be lost? Will it not be to get rid of an incumbrance rather than to sustain a loss? While the War with Great Britain continues it will be difficult though not impossible to throw any considerable Corps into our Country. But if the War with G Britain should end there is no longer any thing to hinder. It is then an event so much in the compass of possibility that it ought to enter seriously into our calculations by anticipation. The situation of Europe is so extraordinary that the most improbable enterprizes in ordinary times become now probable.

Should an invasion take place, though the Militia & after raised troops may finally rescue us, yet there will be no comparison in the expence and evils with or without such a corps prepared beforehand as the *trunk* of our Military force.

VIII   Fortification of our Principal Ports. This ought seriously to be attended to but it is a source of expence not requited beyond the utility to embrace more than the principal port in each state.

In addition to these measures it may be proper by some religious solemnity to impress seriously the minds of the

People. A philosopher may regard the present course of things in Europe as some great providential dispensation. A Christian can hardly view it in any other light. Both these descriptions of persons must approve a national appeal to Heaven for protection. The politician will consider this as an important mean of influencing Opinion, and will think it a valuable resource in a contest with France to set the Religious Ideas of his Countrymen in active Competition with the Atheistical tenets of their enemies. This is an advantage which we shall be very unskilful, if we do not improve to the utmost. And the impulse cannot be too early given. I am persuaded a day of humiliation and prayer besides being very proper would be extremely useful.

Perhaps attempts to engage the *good offices*, not the *mediation*, of some other foreign powers may be useful. In this light Spain Holland & Prussia present themselves. This however is a very delicate point.

But we have a further object in the Mission—to obtain compensation and redress for the Spoliations on our Trade. This is an object which our Government ought not to lose sight of. Here however it may be expedient to facilitate the matter by allowing as an offset to France some of her gratuities during the late War. It is useful to get rid of obligations as fast and as fully as we can; for we see the compensation hitherto claimed is nothing less than the sacrifice of our Independence.

INTRODUCTION TO AN UNCLE

To William Hamilton

Albany State of New York

My Dear Sir   May the 2d. 1797

Some days since I received with great pleasure your letter of the 10th. of March. The mark, it affords, of your kind attention, and the particular account it gives me of so many relations in Scotland are extremely gratifying to me. You no doubt have understood that my fathers affairs at a very early day went to wreck; so as to have rendered his situation during the greatest part of his life far from eligible. This state of things occasionned a separation between him and me, when I was very young, and threw me upon the bounty of my mothers relations, some of whom were then wealthy, though by vicissitudes to which human affairs are so liable, they have been since much reduced and broken up. Myself at about sixteen came to this Country. Having always had a strong propensity to literary pursuits, by a course of steady and laborious exertion, I was able, by the age of Nineteen to qualify myself for the degree of Batchelor of Arts in the College of New York, and to lay a foundation, by preparatory study, for the future profession of the law.

The American Revolution supervened. My principles led me to take part in it. At nineteen I entered into the American army as Captain of Artillery. Shortly after, I became by his invitation Aide De Camp to General Washington, in which station, I served till the commencement of that Campaign which ended with the seige of York, in Virginia, and the Capture of Cornwallis's Army. This Campaign I made at the head of a corps of light infantry, with which I was present at the seige of York and engaged in some interesting operations.

At the period of the peace with Great Britain, I found myself a member of Congress by appointment of the legislature of this state.

After the peace, I settled in the City of New York in the practice of the law; and was in a very lucrative course of practice, when the derangement of our public affairs, by the feebleness of the general confederation, drew me again reluctantly into public life. I became a member of the Convention which framed the present Constitution of the U States; and having taken part in this measure, I conceived myself to be under an obligation to lend my aid towards putting the machine in some regular motion. Hence I did not hesitate to accept the offer of President Washington to undertake the office of Secretary of the Treasury.

In that office, I met with many intrinsic difficulties, and many artificial ones proceeding from passions, not very worthy, common to human nature, and which act with peculiar force in republics. The object, however, was effected, of establishing public credit and introducing order into the finances.

Public Office in this Country has few attractions. The pecuniary emolument is so inconsiderable as too amount to a sacrifice to any man who can employ his time with advantage in any liberal profession. The opportunity of doing good, from the jealousy of power and the spirit of faction, is too small in any station to warrant a long continuance of private sacrifices. The enterprises of party had so far succeeded as materially to weaken the necessary influence and energy of the Executive Authority, and so far diminish the power of doing good in that department as greatly to take the motives which a virtuous man might have for making sacrifices. The prospect was even bad for gratifying in future the love of Fame, if that passion was to be the spring of action.

The Union of these motives, with the reflections of prudence in relation to a growing family, determined me as soon as my plan had attained a certain maturity to withdraw from Office. This I did by a resignation about two years since; when I resumed the profession of the law in the City of New York under every advantage I could desire.

It is a pleasing reflection to me that since the commencement of my connection with General Washington to the present time, I have possessed a flattering share of his confidence and friendship.

Having given you a brief sketch of my political career, I proceed to some further family details.

In the year 1780 I married the second daughter of General Schuyler, a Gentleman of one of the best families of this Country; of large fortune and no less personal and public consequence. It is impossible to be happier than I am in a wife and I have five Children, four sons and a daughter, the eldest a son somewhat passed fifteen, who all promise well, as far as their years permit and yield me much satisfaction. Though I have been too much in public life to be wealthy, my situation is extremely comfortable and leaves me nothing to wish but a continuance of health. With this blessing, the profits of my profession and other prospects authorise an expectation of such addition to my resources as will render the eve of life, easy and agreeable; so far as may depend on this consideration.

It is now several months since I have heared from my father who continued at the Island of St Vincents. My anxiety at this silence would be greater than it is, were it not for the considerable interruption and precariousness of intercourse, which is produced by the War.

I have strongly pressed the old Gentleman to come to reside with me, which would afford him every enjoyment of which his advanced age is capable. But he has declined it on the ground that the advice of his Physicians leads him to fear that the change of Climate would be fatal to him. The next thing for me is, in proportion to my means to endeavour to increase his comforts where he is.

It will give me the greatest pleasure to receive your son Robert at my house in New York and still more to be of use to him; to which end my recommendation and interest will not be wanting, and, I hope, not unavailing. It is my intention to embrace the Opening which your letter affords me to extend intercourse with my relations in your Country, which will be a new source of satisfaction to me.

The "Reynolds Pamphlet"

*Observations on Certain Documents Contained in No. V
& VI of "The History of the United States for the Year
1796," In Which the Charge of Speculation Against
Alexander Hamilton, Late Secretary of the Treasury, is
Fully Refuted. Written by Himself*

THE spirit of jacobinism, if not entirely a new spirit, has at
least been cloathed with a more gigantic body and armed
with more powerful weapons than it ever before possessed. It
is perhaps not too much to say, that it threatens more extensive and complicated mischiefs to the world than have hitherto flowed from the three great scourges of mankind, WAR,
PESTILENCE and FAMINE. To what point it will ultimately
lead society, it is impossible for human foresight to pronounce; but there is just ground to apprehend that its
progress may be marked with calamities of which the dreadful
incidents of the French revolution afford a very faint image.
Incessantly busied in undermining all the props of public security and private happiness, it seems to threaten the political
and moral world with a complete overthrow.

A principal engine, by which this spirit endeavours to accomplish its purposes is that of calumny. It is essential to its
success that the influence of men of upright principles, disposed and able to resist its enterprises, shall be at all events
destroyed. Not content with traducing their best efforts for
the public good, with misrepresenting their purest motives,
with inferring criminality from actions innocent or laudable,
the most direct falshoods are invented and propagated, with
undaunted effrontery and unrelenting perseverance. Lies often detected and refuted are still revived and repeated, in the
hope that the refutation may have been forgotten or that the
frequency and boldness of accusation may supply the place of
truth and proof. The most profligate men are encouraged,
probably bribed, certainly with patronage if not with money,
to become informers and accusers. And when tales, which
their characters alone ought to discredit, are refuted by evidence and facts which oblige the patrons of them to abandon

their support, they still continue in corroding whispers to wear away the reputations which they could not directly subvert. If, luckily for the conspirators against honest fame, any little foible or folly can be traced out in one, whom they desire to persecute, it becomes at once in their hands a two-edged sword, by which to wound the public character and stab the private felicity of the person. With such men, nothing is sacred. Even the peace of an unoffending and amiable wife is a welcome repast to their insatiate fury against the husband.

In the gratification of this baleful spirit, we not only hear the jacobin news-papers continually ring with odious insinuations and charges against many of our most virtuous citizens; but, not satisfied with this, a measure new in this country has been lately adopted to give greater efficacy to the system of defamation—periodical pamphlets issue from the same presses, full freighted with misrepresentation and falshood, artfully calculated to hold up the opponents of the FACTION to the jealousy and distrust of the present generation and if possible, to transmit their names with dishonor to posterity. Even the great and multiplied services, the tried and rarely equalled virtues of a WASHINGTON, can secure no exemption.

How then can I, with pretensions every way inferior expect to escape? And if truly this be, as every appearance indicates, a conspiracy of vice against virtue, ought I not rather to be flattered, that I have been so long and so peculiarly an object of persecution? Ought I to regret, if there be any thing about me, so formidable to the Faction as to have made me worthy to be distinguished by the plentitude of its rancour and venom?

It is certain that I have had a pretty copious experience of its malignity. For the honor of human nature, it is to be hoped that the examples are not numerous of men so greatly calumniated and persecuted, as I have been, with so little cause.

I dare appeal to my immediate fellow citizens of whatever political party for the truth of the assertion, that no man ever carried into public life a more unblemished pecuniary reputation, than that with which I undertook the office of Secretary of the Treasury; a character marked by an indifference to the acquisition of property rather than an avidity for it.

With such a character, however natural it was to expect criticism and opposition, as to the political principles which I might manifest or be supposed to entertain, as to the wisdom or expediency of the plans, which I might propose, or as to the skill, care or diligence with which the business of my department might be executed, it was not natural to expect nor did I expect that my fidelity or integrity in a pecuniary sense would ever be called in question.

But on this head a mortifying disappointment has been experienced. Without the slightest foundation, I have been repeatedly held up to the suspicions of the world as a man directed in his administration by the most sordid views; who did not scruple to sacrifice the public to his private interest, his duty and honor to the sinister accumulation of wealth.

Merely because I *retained* an opinion once common to me and the most influencial of those who opposed me, *That the public debt ought to be provided for on the basis of the contract upon which it was created*, I have been wickedly accused with wantonly increasing the public burthen many millions, in order to promote a stock-jobbing interest of myself and friends.

Merely because a member of the House of Representatives entertained a different idea from me, as to the legal effect of appropriation laws, and did not understand accounts, I was exposed to the imputation of having committed a deliberate and criminal violation of the laws and to the suspicion of being a defaulter for millions; so as to have been driven to the painful necessity of calling for a formal and solemn inquiry.

The inquiry took place. It was conducted by a committee of fifteen members of the House of Representatives—a majority of them either my decided political enemies or inclined against me, some of them the most active and intelligent of my opponents, without a single man, who being known to be friendly to me, possessed also such knowledge and experience of public affairs as would enable him to counteract injurious intrigues. Mr. Giles of Virginia who had commenced the attack was of the committee.

The officers and books of the treasury were examined. The transactions between the several banks and the treasury were scrutinized. Even my *private accounts* with those institutions were laid open to the committee; and every possible facility given to the inquiry. The result was a complete demonstration that the suspicions which had been entertained were groundless.

Those which had taken the fastest hold were, that the public monies had been made subservient to loans, discounts and accommodations to myself and friends. The committee in reference to this point reported thus: "It appears from the affidavits of the Cashier and several officers of the bank of the United States and several of the directors, the Cashier, and other officers of the bank of New-York, that the Secretary of the Treasury never has either directly or indirectly, for himself or any other person, procured any discount or credit from either of the said banks upon the basis of any public monies which at any time have been deposited therein under his direction: And the committee are satisfied, that no monies of the United States, whether before or after they have passed to the credit of the Treasurer have ever been directly or indirectly used for or applied to any purposes but those of the government, except so far as all monies deposited in a bank are concerned in the general operations thereof."

The report, which I have always understood was unanimous, contains in other respects, with considerable detail the materials of a complete exculpation. My enemies, finding no handle for their malice, abandoned the pursuit.

Yet unwilling to leave any ambiguity upon the point, when I determined to resign my office, I gave early previous notice of it to the House of Representatives, for the declared purpose of affording an opportunity for legislative crimination, if any ground for it had been discovered. Not the least step towards it was taken. From which I have a right to infer the universal conviction of the House, that no cause existed, and to consider the result as a complete vindication.

On another occasion, a worthless man of the name of Fraunces found encouragement to bring forward to the House of Representatives a formal charge against me of unfaithful conduct in office. A Committee of the House was appointed to inquire, consisting in this case also, partly of some of my most intelligent and active enemies. The issue was an unanimous exculpation of me as will appear by the following extract from the Journals of the House of Representatives of the 19th of February 1794.

"The House resumed the consideration of the report of the Committee, to whom was referred the memorial of Andrew G. Fraunces: whereupon,

"_Resolved_, That the reasons assigned by the secretary of the treasury, for refusing payment of the warrants referred to in the memorial, are fully sufficient to justify his conduct; and that in the whole course of this transaction, the secretary and other officers of the treasury, have acted a meritorious part towards the public."

"_Resolved_, That the charge exhibited in the memorial, against the secretary of the treasury, relative to the purchase of the pension of Baron de Glaubeck is wholly illiberal and groundless*."

Was it not to have been expected that these repeated demonstrations of the injustice of the accusations hazarded against me would have abashed the enterprise of my calumniators? However natural such an expectation may seem, it would betray an ignorance of the true character of the Jacobin system. It is a maxim deeply ingrafted in that dark system, that no character, however upright, is a match for constantly reiterated attacks, however false. It is well understood by its disciples, that every calumny makes some proselites and even retains some; since justification seldom circulates as rapidly and as widely as slander. The number of those who from doubt proceed to suspicion and thence to belief of imputed guilt is continually augmenting; and the public mind fatigued at length with resistance to the calumnies which eternally assail it, is apt in the end to sit down with the opinion that a person so often accused cannot be entirely innocent.

Relying upon this weakness of human nature, the Jacobin Scandal-Club though often defeated constantly return to the charge. Old calumnies are served up a-fresh and every pretext is seized to add to the catalogue. The person whom they seek to blacken, by dint of repeated strokes of their brush, becomes a demon in their own eyes, though he might be pure

---

*Would it be believed after all this, that Mr. Jefferson Vice President of the United States would write to this Fraunces friendly letters? Yet such is the fact as will be seen in the Appendix, Nos. XLIV & XLV.

and bright as an angel but for the daubing of those wizard painters.

Of all the vile attempts which have been made to injure my character that which has been lately revived in No. V and VI, of the history of the United States for 1796 is the most vile. This it will be impossible for any *intelligent*, I will not say *candid*, man to doubt, when he shall have accompanied me through the examination.

I owe perhaps to my friends an apology for condescending to give a public explanation. A just pride with reluctance stoops to a formal vindication against so despicable a contrivance and is inclined rather to oppose to it the uniform evidence of an upright character. This would be my conduct on the present occasion, did not the tale seem to derive a sanction from the names of three men of some weight and consequence in the society: a circumstance, which I trust will excuse me for paying attention to a slander that without this prop, would defeat itself by intrinsic circumstances of absurdity and malice.

The charge against me is a connection with one James Reynolds for purposes of improper pecuniary speculation. My real crime is an amorous connection with his wife, for a considerable time with his privity and connivance, if not originally brought on by a combination between the husband and wife with the design to extort money from me.

This confession is not made without a blush. I cannot be the apologist of any vice because the ardour of passion may have made it mine. I can never cease to condemn myself for the pang, which it may inflict in a bosom eminently intitled to all my gratitude, fidelity and love. But that bosom will approve, that even at so great an expence, I should effectually wipe away a more serious stain from a name, which it cherishes with no less elevation than tenderness. The public too will I trust excuse the confession. The necessity of it to my defence against a more heinous charge could alone have extorted from me so painful an indecorum.

Before I proceed to an exhibition of the positive proof which repels the charge, I shall analize the documents from which it is deduced, and I am mistaken if with discerning and candid minds more would be necessary. But I desire to obviate the suspicions of the most suspicious.

The first reflection which occurs on a perusal of the documents is that it is morally impossible I should have been foolish as well as depraved enough to employ so vile an instrument as *Reynolds* for such *insignificant ends*, as are indicated by different parts of the story itself. My enemies to be sure have kindly pourtrayed me as another *Chartres* on the score of moral principle. But they have been ever bountiful in ascribing to me talents. It has suited their purpose to exaggerate such as I may possess, and to attribute to them an influence to which they are not intitled. But the present accusation imputes to me as much folly as wickedness. All the documents shew, and it is otherwise matter of notoriety, that Reynolds was an obscure, unimportant and profligate man. Nothing could be more weak, because nothing could be more unsafe than to make use of such an instrument; to use him too without any intermediate agent more worthy of confidence who might keep me out of sight, to write him numerous letters recording the objects of the improper connection (for this is pretended and that the letters were afterwards burnt at my request) to unbosom myself to him with a prodigality of confidence, by very unnecessarily telling him, as he alleges, of a connection in speculation between myself and Mr. Duer. It is very extraordinary, if the head of the money department of a country, being unprincipled enough to sacrifice his trust and his integrity, could not have contrived objects of profit sufficiently large to have engaged the co-operation of men of far greater importance than Reynolds, and with whom there could have been due safety, and should have been driven to the necessity of unkennelling such a reptile to be the instrument of his cupidity.

But, moreover, the scale of the concern with Reynolds, such as it is presented, is contemptibly narrow for a rapacious speculating secretary of the treasury. *Clingman, Reynolds* and his wife were manifestly in very close confidence with each other. It seems there was a free communication of secrets. Yet in clubbing their different items of information as to the supplies of money which Reynolds received from me, what do they amount to? *Clingman* states, that Mrs. Reynolds told him, that at a certain time her husband had received from me upwards of eleven hundred dollars. A note is produced which shews that at one time fifty dollars were sent to him, and another note is produced, by which and the information of Reynolds himself through Clingman, it appears that at another time 300 dollars were asked and refused. Another sum of 200 dollars is spoken of by *Clingman* as having been furnished to Reynolds at some other time. What a scale of speculation is this for the head of a public treasury, for one who in the very publication that brings forward the charge is represented as having procured to be funded at forty millions a debt which ought to have been discharged at ten or fifteen millions for the criminal purpose of enriching himself and his friends? He must have been a clumsy knave, if he did not secure enough of this excess of twenty five or thirty millions, to have taken away all inducement to risk his character in such bad hands and in so huckstering a way—or to have enabled him, if he did employ such an agent, to do it with more means and to better purpose. It is curious, that this rapacious secretary should at one time have furnished his speculating agent with the paltry sum of fifty dollars, at another, have refused him the inconsiderable sum of 300 dollars, declaring upon his honor that it was not in his power to furnish it. This declaration was true or not; if the last the refusal ill comports with the idea of a speculating connection—if the first, it is very singular that the head of the treasury engaged without scruple in schemes of profit should have been destitute of so small a sum. But if we suppose this officer to be living upon an inadequate salary, without any collateral pursuits of gain, the appearances then are simple and intelligible enough, applying to them the true key.

It appears that *Reynolds* and *Clingman* were detected by the then comptroller of the treasury, in the odious crime of suborning a witness to commit perjury, for the purpose of obtaining letters of administration on the estate of a person who was living in order to receive a small sum of money due to him from the treasury. It is certainly extraordinary that the confidential agent of the head of that department should have been in circumstances to induce a resort to so miserable an expedient. It is odd, if there was a speculating connection, that it was not more profitable both to the secretary and to his agent than are indicated by the circumstances disclosed.

It is also a remarkable and very instructive fact, that notwithstanding the great confidence and intimacy, which subsisted between *Clingman, Reynolds* and his wife, and which continued till after the period of the liberation of the two former from the prosecution against them, neither of them has ever specified the objects of the pretended connection in speculation between Reynolds and me. The pretext that the letters which contained the evidence were destroyed is no answer. They could not have been forgotten and might have been disclosed from memory. The total omission of this could only have proceeded from the consideration that detail might have led to detection. The destruction of letters besides is a fiction, which is refuted not only by the general improbability, that I should put myself upon paper with so despicable a person on a subject which might expose me to infamy, but by the evidence of extreme caution on my part in this particular, resulting from the laconic and disguised form of the notes which are produced. They prove incontestibly that there was an unwillingness to trust Reynolds with my hand writing. The true reason was, that I apprehended he might make use of it to impress upon others the belief of some pecuniary connection with me, and besides implicating my character might render it the engine of a false credit, or turn it to some other sinister use. Hence the disguise; for my conduct in admitting at once and without hesitation that the notes were from me proves that it was never my intention by the expedient of disguising my hand to shelter myself from any serious inquiry.

The accusation against me was never heard of 'till Clingman and Reynolds were under prosecution by the treasury for an infamous crime. It will be seen by the document No. 1 (a) that during the endeavours of *Clingman* to obtain relief, through the interposition of Mr. Mughlenberg, he made to the latter the communication of my pretended criminality. It will be further seen by document No. 2 that Reynolds had while in prison conveyed to the ears of Messrs. Monroe and Venable that he could give intelligence of my being concerned in speculation, and that he also supposed that he was kept in prison by a design on my part to oppress him and drive him away. And by his letter to *Clingman* of the 13 of

December, after he was released from prison, it also appears that he was actuated by a spirit of revenge against me; for he declares that he will have *satisfaction* from me *at all events*, adding, as addressed to *Clingman*, "And *you only I trust.*"

Three important inferences flow from these circumstances—one that the accusation against me was an auxiliary to the efforts of *Clingman* and *Reynolds* to get released from a disgraceful prosecution—another that there was a vindicative spirit against me at least on the part of Reynolds—the third, that he confided in *Clingman* as a coadjutor in the plan of vengeance. These circumstances, according to every estimate of the credit due to accusers, ought to destroy their testimony. To what credit are persons intitled, who in telling a story are governed by the double motive of escaping from disgrace and punishment and of gratifying revenge? As to Mrs. Reynolds, if she was not an accomplice, as it is too probable she was, her situation would naturally subject her to the will of her husband. But enough besides will appear in the sequel to shew that her testimony merits no attention.

The letter which has been just cited deserves a more particular attention. As it was produced by Clingman, there is a chasm of three lines, which lines are manifestly essential to explain the sense. It may be inferred from the context, that these deficient lines would unfold the cause of the resentment which is expressed. 'Twas from them that might have been learnt the true nature of the transaction. The expunging of them is a violent presumption that they would have contradicted the purpose for which the letter was produced. A witness offering such a mutilated piece descredits himself. The mutilation is alone satisfactory proof of contrivance and imposition. The manner of accounting for it is frivolous.

The words of the letter are strong—satisfaction is to be had *at all events, per fas et nefas,* and *Clingman* is the chosen confidential agent of the laudable plan of vengeance. It must be confessed he was not wanting in his part.

Reynolds, as will be seen by No. II (a) alleges that a merchant came to him and offered as a volunteer to be his bail, who he suspected had been instigated to it by me, and after being decoyed to the place the merchant wished to carry him to, he refused being his bail, unless he would deposit a sum of money to some considerable amount which he could not do and was in consequence committed to prison. Clingman (No. IV a) tells the same story in substance though with some difference in form leaving to be implied what Reynolds expresses and naming *Henry Seckel* as the merchant. The deposition of this respectable citizen (No. XXIII) gives the lie to both, and shews that he was in fact the agent of *Clingman*, from motives of good will to him, as his former book-keeper, that he never had any communication with me concerning either of them till after they were both in custody, that when he came as a messenger to me from one of them, I not only declined interposing in their behalf, but informed Mr. Seckel that they had been guilty of a crime and advised him to have nothing to do with them.

This single fact goes far to invalidate the whole story. It shews plainly the disregard of truth and the malice by which the parties were actuated. Other important inferences are to be drawn from the transaction. Had I been conscious that I had any thing to fear from *Reynolds* of the nature which has been pretended, should I have warned Mr. *Seckel* against having any thing to do with them? Should I not rather have encouraged him to have come to their assistance? Should I not have been eager to promote their liberation? But this is not the only instance, in which I acted a contrary part. *Clingman* testifies in No. V. that I would not permit *Fraunces* a clerk in my office to become their bail, but signified to him that if he did it, he must quit the department.

Clingman states in No. IV. (a) that my note in answer to Reynolds' application for a loan towards a subscription to the *Lancaster Turnpike* was in his possession from about the time it was written (June 1792.) This circumstance, apparently trivial, is very explanatory. To what end had *Clingman* the custody of this note all that time if it was not part of a project to lay the foundation for some false accusation?

It appears from No. V. that *Fraunces* had said, or was stated to have said, something to my prejudice. If my memory serves me aright, it was that he had been my agent in some speculations. When *Fraunces* was interrogated concerning it, he absolutely denied that he had said any thing of the kind. The charge which this same *Fraunces* afterwards preferred against me to the House of Representatives, and the fate of it, have been already mentioned. It is illustrative of the nature of the combination which was formed against me.

There are other features in the documents which are relied upon to constitute the charge against me, that are of a nature to corroborate the inference to be drawn from the particulars which have been noticed. But there is no need to be over minute. I am much mistaken if the view which has been taken of the subject is not sufficient, without any thing further, to establish my innocence with every discerning and fair mind.

I proceed in the next place to offer a frank and plain solution of the enigma, by giving a history of the origin and progress of my connection with Mrs. Reynolds, of its discovery, real and pretended by the husband, and of the disagreeable embarrassments to which it exposed me. This history will be supported by the letters of Mr. and Mrs. Reynolds, which leave no room for doubt of the principal facts, and at the same time explain with precision the objects of the little notes from me which have been published, shewing clearly that such of them as have related to money had no reference to any concern in speculation. As the situation which will be disclosed, will fully explain every ambiguous appearance, and meet satisfactorily the written documents, nothing more can be requisite to my justification. For frail indeed will be the tenure by which the most blameless man will hold his reputation, if the assertions of three of the most abandoned characters in the community, two of them stigmatized by the discrediting crime which has been mentioned, are sufficient to blast it. The business of accusation would soon become in such a case, a regular trade, and men's reputations would be bought and sold like any marketable commodity.

Some time in the summer of the year 1791 a woman called at my house in the city of Philadelphia and asked to speak with me in private. I attended her into a room apart from the family. With a seeming air of affliction she informed that she was a daughter of a Mr. Lewis, sister to a Mr. G. Livingston of the State of New-York, and wife to a Mr. Reynolds whose father was in the Commissary Department during the war with Great Britain, that her husband, who for a long time had treated her very cruelly, had lately left her, to live with another woman, and in so destitute a condition, that though desirous of returning to her friends she had not the means—that knowing I was a citizen of New-York, she had taken the liberty to apply to my humanity for assistance.

I replied, that her situation was a very interesting one—that I was disposed to afford her assistance to convey her to her friends, but this at the moment not being convenient to me (which was the fact) I must request the place of her residence, to which I should bring or send a small supply of money. She told me the street and the number of the house where she lodged. In the evening I put a bank-bill in my pocket and went to the house. I inquired for Mrs. Reynolds and was shewn up stairs, at the head of which she met me and conducted me into a bed room. I took the bill out of my pocket and gave it to her. Some conversation ensued from which it was quickly apparent that other than pecuniary consolation would be acceptable.

After this, I had frequent meetings with her, most of them at my own house; Mrs. Hamilton with her children being absent on a visit to her father. In the course of a short time, she mentioned to me that her husband had solicited a reconciliation, and affected to consult me about it. I advised to it, and was soon after informed by her that it had taken place. She told me besides that her husband had been engaged in speculation, and she believed could give information respecting the conduct of some persons in the department which would be useful. I sent for Reynolds who came to me accordingly.

In the course of our interview, he confessed that he had obtained a list of claims from a person in my department which he had made use of in his speculations. I invited him, by the expectation of my friendship and good offices, to disclose the person. After some affectation of scruple, he pretended to yield, and ascribed the infidelity to Mr. Duer from whom he said he had obtained the list in New-York, while he (Duer) was in the department.

As Mr. Duer had resigned his office some time before the seat of government was removed to Philadelphia; this discovery, if it had been true, was not very important—yet it was the interest of my passions to appear to set value upon it, and to continue the expectation of friendship and good offices. Mr.

Reynolds told me he was going to Virginia, and on his return would point out something in which I could serve him. I do not know but he said something about employment in a public office.

On his return he asked employment as a clerk in the treasury department. The knowledge I had acquired of him was decisive against such a request. I parried it by telling him, what was true, that there was no vacancy in my immediate office, and that the appointment of clerks in the other branches of the department was left to the chiefs of the respective branches. Reynolds alleged, as *Clingman* relates No. IV (a) as a topic of complaint against me that I had promised him *employment* and had *disappointed* him. The situation with the wife would naturally incline me to conciliate this man. It is possible I may have used vague expressions which raised expectation; but the more I learned of the person, the more inadmissible his employment in a public office became. Some material reflections will occur here to a discerning mind. Could I have preferred my private gratification to the public interest, should I not have found the employment he desired for a man, whom it was so convenient to me, on my own statement, to lay under obligations. Had I had any such connection with him, as he has since pretended, is it likely that he would have wanted other employment? Or is it likely that wanting it, I should have hazarded his resentment by a persevering refusal? This little circumstance shews at once the delicacy of my conduct, in its public relations, and the impossibility of my having had the connection pretended with Reynolds.

The intercourse with Mrs. Reynolds, in the mean time, continued; and, though various reflections, (in which a further knowledge of Reynolds' character and the suspicion of some concert between the husband and wife bore a part) induced me to wish a cessation of it; yet her conduct, made it extremely difficult to disentangle myself. All the appearances of violent attachment, and of agonizing distress at the idea of a relinquishment, were played off with a most imposing art. This, though it did not make me entirely the dupe of the plot, yet kept me in a state of irresolution. My sensibility, perhaps my vanity, admitted the possibility of a real fondness; and led me to adopt the plan of a gradual discontinuance rather than of a sudden interruption, as least calculated to give pain, if a real partiality existed.

Mrs. Reynolds, on the other hand, employed every effort to keep up my attention and visits. Her pen was freely employed, and her letters were filled with those tender and pathetic effusions which would have been natural to a woman truly fond and neglected.

One day, I received a letter from her, which is in the appendix (No. I. b) intimating a discovery by her husband. It was matter of doubt with me whether there had been really a discovery by accident, or whether the time for the catastrophe of the plot was arrived.

The same day, being the 15th of December 1791, I received from Mr. Reynolds the letter (No. II. b) by which he informs me of the detection of his wife in the act of writing a letter to me, and that he had obtained from her a discovery of her connection with me, suggesting that it was the consequence of an undue advantage taken of her distress.

In answer to this I sent him a note, or message desiring him to call upon me at my office, which I think he did the same day.

He in substance repeated the topics contained in his letter, and concluded as he had done there, that he was resolved to have satisfaction.

I replied that he knew best what evidence he had of the alleged connection between me and his wife, that I neither admitted nor denied it—that if he knew of any injury I had done him, intitling him to satisfaction, it lay with him to name it.

He travelled over the same ground as before, and again concluded with the same vague claim of satisfaction, but without specifying the kind, which would content him. It was easy to understand that he wanted money, and to prevent an explosion, I resolved to gratify him. But willing to manage his delicacy, if he had any, I reminded him that I had at our first interview made him a promise of service, that I was disposed to do it as far as might be proper, and in my power, and requested him to consider in what manner I could do it, and to write to me. He withdrew with a promise of compliance.

Two days after, the 17th of December, he wrote me the letter (No. III. b). The evident drift of this letter is to exaggerate the injury done by me, to make a display of sensibility and to magnify the atonement, which was to be required. It however comes to no conclusion, but proposes a meeting at the *George Tavern*, or at some other place more agreeable to me, which I should name.

On receipt of this letter, I called upon Reynolds, and assuming a decisive tone, told him, that I was tired of his indecision, and insisted upon his declaring to me explicitly what it was he aimed at. He again promised to explain by letter.

On the 19th, I received the promised letter (No. IV. b) the essence of which is that he was willing to take a thousand dollars as the plaister of his wounded honor.

I determined to give it to him, and did so in two payments, as per receipts (No. V and VI) dated the 22d of December and 3d of January. It is a little remarkable, that an avaricious speculating secretary of the treasury should have been so straitened for money as to be obliged to satisfy an engagement of this sort by two different payments!

On the 17th of January, I received the letter No. V. by which Reynolds invites me to *renew my visits to his wife*. He had before requested that I would see her no more. The motive to this step appears in the conclusion of the letter, "*I rely* upon your befriending me, *if there should any thing offer that should be to my advantage*, as you *express a wish to befriend me.*" Is the pre-existence of a speculating connection reconcileable with this mode of expression?

If I recollect rightly, I did not immediately accept the invitation, nor 'till after I had received several very importunate letters from Mrs. Reynolds—See her letters No. VIII, (b) IX, X.

On the 24th of March following, I received a letter from *Reynolds*, No. XI, and on the same day one from his wife, No. XII. These letters will further illustrate the obliging co-operation of the husband with his wife to aliment and keep alive my connection with her.

The letters from Reynolds, No. XIII to XVI, are an additional comment upon the same plan. It was a persevering scheme to spare no pains to levy contributions upon my passions on the one hand, and upon my apprehensions of discovery on the other. It is probably to No. XIV that my note, in these words, was an answer; "To-morrow what is requested will be done. 'Twill hardly be possible *to-day*." The letter presses for the loan which is asked for *to-day*. A scarcity of cash, which was not very uncommon, is believed to have modelled the reply.

The letter No. XVII is a master-piece. The husband there forbids my future visits to his wife, chiefly because I was careful to avoid publicity. It was probably necessary to the project of some deeper treason against me that I should be seen at the house. Hence was it contrived, with all the caution on my part to avoid it, that *Clingman* should occasionally see me.

The interdiction was every way welcome, and was I believe, strictly observed. On the second of June following, I received the letter No. XVIII, from Mrs. Reynolds, which proves that it was not her plan yet to let me off. It was probably the prelude to the letter from Reynolds, No. XIX, soliciting a *loan* of 300 dollars towards a subscription to the Lancaster Turnpike. *Clingman's* statement, No. IV, admits, on the information of Reynolds, that to this letter the following note from me was an answer—"*It is utterly out of my power I assure you 'pon my honour to comply with your request. Your note is returned.*" The letter itself demonstrates, that here was no concern in speculation on my part—that the money is asked as a *favour* and as a *loan*, to be reimbursed simply and without profit *in less than a fortnight*. My answer shews that even the loan was refused.

The letter No. XX, from *Reynolds*, explains the object of my note in these words, "*Inclosed are 50 dollars, they could not be sent sooner,*" proving that this sum also was begged for in a very apologetic stile as a mere loan.

The letters of the 24th and 30th of August, No. XXI and XXII, furnish the key to the affair of the 200 dollars mentioned by *Clingman* in No. IV, shewing that this sum likewise was asked by way of loan, towards furnishing a small boardinghouse which *Reynolds* and his wife were or pretended to be about to set up.

These letters collectively, furnish a complete elucidation of the nature of my transactions with *Reynolds*. They resolve them into an amorous connection with his wife, detected, or pretended to be detected by the husband, imposing on me the necessity of a pecuniary composition with him, and leaving me afterwards under a duress for fear of disclosure, which was the instrument of levying upon me from time to time *forced loans.* They apply directly to this state of things, the notes which *Reynolds* was so careful to preserve, and which had been employed to excite suspicion.

Four, and the principal of these notes have been not only generally, but particularly explained—I shall briefly notice the remaining two.

"My dear Sir, I expected to have heard the day after I had the pleasure of seeing you." This fragment, if truly part of a letter to *Reynolds*, denotes nothing more than a disposition to be civil to a man, whom, as I said before, it was the interest of my passions to conciliate. But I verily believe it was not part of a letter to him, because I do not believe that I ever addressed him in such a stile. It may very well have been part of a letter to some other person, procured by means of which I am ignorant, or it may have been the beginning of an intended letter, torn off, thrown into the chimney in my office, which was a common practice, and there or after it had been swept out picked up by Reynolds or some coadjutor of his. There appears to have been more than one clerk in the department some how connected with him.

The endeavour shewn by the letter No. XVII, to induce me to render my visits to Mrs. Reynolds more public, and the great care with which my little notes were preserved, justify the belief that at a period, before it was attempted, the idea of implicating me in some accusation, with a view to the advantage of the accusers, was entertained. Hence the motive to pick up and preserve any fragment which might favour the idea of friendly or confidential correspondence.

2dly. "The person Mr. Reynolds inquired for on Friday waited for him all the evening at his house from a little after seven. Mr. R. may see him at any time to-day or to-morrow between the hours of two and three."

Mrs. Reynolds more than once communicated to me, that Reynolds would occasionally relapse into discontent to his situation—would treat her very ill—hint at the assassination of me—and more openly threaten, by way of revenge, to inform Mrs. Hamilton—all this naturally gave some uneasiness. I could not be absolutely certain whether it was artifice or reality. In the workings of human inconsistency, it was very possible, that the same man might be corrupt enough to compound for his wife's chastity and yet have sensibility enough to be restless in the situation and to hate the cause of it.

Reflections like these induced me for some time to use palliatives with the ill humours which were announced to me. Reynolds had called upon me in one of these discontented moods real or pretended. I was unwilling to provoke him by the appearance of neglect—and having failed to be at home at the hour he had been permitted to call, I wrote her the above note to obviate an ill impression.

The foregoing narrative and the remarks accompanying it have prepared the way for a perusal of the letters themselves. The more attention is used in this, the more entire will be the satisfaction which they will afford.

It has been seen that an explanation on the subject was had cotemporarily that is in December 1792, with three members of Congress—F. A. Muhlenberg, J. Monroe, and A. Venable. It is proper that the circumstances of this transaction should be accurately understood.

The manner in which Mr. Muhlenberg became engaged in the affair is fully set forth in the document (No. I. a). It is not equally clear how the two other gentlemen came to embark in it. The phraseology, in reference to this point in the close of (No. I.) and beginning of (No. II.) is rather equivocal. The gentlemen, if they please, can explain it.

But on the morning of the 15th of December 1792, the above mentioned gentlemen presented themselves at my office. Mr. Muhlenberg was then speaker. He introduced the subject by observing to me, that they *had discovered a very improper connection* between me and a Mr. Reynolds: extremely hurt by this mode of introduction, I arrested the progress of the discourse by giving way to very strong expressions of indignation. The gentlemen explained, telling me in substance that I had misapprehended them—that they did not intend to take the fact for established—that their meaning was to apprise me that unsought by them, information had been given them of an improper pecuniary connection between Mr. Reynolds and myself; that they had thought it their duty to pursue it and had become possessed of some documents of a suspicious complexion—that they had contemplated the laying the matter before the President, but before they did this, they thought it right to apprise me of the affair and to afford an opportunity of explanation; declaring at the same time that their agency in the matter was influenced solely by a sense of public duty and by no motive of personal ill will. If my memory be correct, the notes from me in a disguised hand were now shewn to me which without a moment's hesitation I acknowledged to be mine.

I replied, that the affair was now put upon a different footing—that I always stood ready to meet fair inquiry with frank communication—that it happened, in the present instance, to be in my power by written documents to remove all doubt as to the real nature of the business, and fully to convince, that nothing of the kind imputed to me did in fact exist. The same evening at my house was by mutual consent appointed for an explanation.

I immediately after saw Mr. Wolcott, and for the first time informed him of the affair and of the interview just had; and delivering into his hands for perusal the documents of which I was possessed, I engaged him to be present at the intended explanation in the evening.

In the evening the proposed meeting took place, and Mr. Wolcott according to my request attended. The information, which had been received to that time, from *Clingman*, *Reynolds* and his wife was communicated to me and the notes were I think again exhibited.

I stated in explanation, the circumstances of my affair with Mrs. Reynolds and the consequences of it and in confirmation produced the documents (No. I. b, to XXII.) One or more of the gentlemen (Mr. Wolcott's certificate No. XXIV, mentions one, Mr. Venable, but I think the same may be said of Mr. Muhlenberg) was struck with so much conviction, before I had gotten through the communication that they delicately urged me to discontinue it as unnecessary. I insisted upon going through the whole and did so. The result was a full and unequivocal acknowlegement on the part of the three gentlemen of perfect satisfaction with the explanation and expressions of regret at the trouble and embarrassment which had been occasioned to me. Mr. Muhlenberg and Mr. Venable, in particular manifested a degree of sensibility on the occasion. Mr. Monroe was more cold but intirely explicit.

One of the gentlemen, I think, expressed a hope that I also was satisfied with their conduct in conducting the inquiry. I answered, that they knew I had been hurt at the opening of the affair—that this excepted, I was satisfied with their conduct and considered myself as having been treated with candor or with fairness and liberality, I do not now pretend to recollect the exact terms. I took the next morning a memorandum of the substance of what was said to me, which will be seen by a copy of it transmitted in a letter to each of the gentlemen No. XXV.

I deny absolutely, as alleged by the editor of the publication in question, that I intreated a suspension of the communication to the President, or that from the beginning to the end of the inquiry, I asked any favour or indulgence whatever, and that I discovered any symptom different from that of a proud consciousness of innocence.

Some days after the explanation I wrote to the three gentlemen the letter No. XXVI already published. That letter evinces the light in which I considered myself as standing in their view.

I received from Mr. Muhlenberg and Mr. Monroe in answer the letters No. XXVII and XXVIII.

Thus the affair remained 'till the pamphlets No. V and VI of the history of the U. States for 1796 appeared; with the exception of some dark whispers which were communicated to me by a friend in Virginia, and to which I replied by a statement of what had passed.

When I saw No. V though it was evidence of a base infidelity somewhere, yet firmly believing that nothing more than a want of due care was chargeable upon either of the three gentlemen who had made the inquiry, I immediately wrote to each of them a letter of which No. XXV is a copy in full confidence that their answer would put the whole business at rest. I ventured to believe, from the appearances on their part at closing our former interview on the subject, that their answers would have been both cordial and explicit.

I acknowledge that I was astonished when I came to read in the pamphlet No. VI the conclusion of the document No.

V, containing the equivocal phrase *"We left him under an impression our suspicions were removed,"* which seemed to imply that this had been a mere piece of management, and that the impression given me had not been reciprocal. The appearance of duplicity incensed me; but resolving to proceed with caution and moderation, I thought the first proper step was to inquire of the gentlemen whether the paper was genuine. A letter was written for this purpose the copy of which I have mislaid.

I afterwards received from Messrs. Muhlenberg and Venable the letters No. XXIX, XXX, and XXXI.

Receiving no answer from Mr. Monroe, and hearing of his arrival at New-York I called upon him. The issue of the interview was that an answer was to be given by him, in conjunction with Mr. Muhlenberg and Mr. Venable on his return to Philadelphia, he thinking that as the agency had been joint it was most proper the answer should be joint, and informing me that Mr. Venable had told him he would wait his return.

I came to Philadelphia accordingly to bring the affair to a close; but on my arrival I found Mr. Venable had left the city for Virginia.

Mr. Monroe reached Philadelphia according to his appointment. And the morning following wrote me the note No. XXXII. While this note was on its way to my lodgings I was on my way to his. I had a conversation with him from which we separated with a repetition of the assurance in the note. In the course of the interviews with Mr. Monroe, the *equivoque* in document No. V, (a) and the paper of January 2d, 1793, under his signature were noticed.

I received the day following the letter No. XXXIII, to which I returned the answer No. XXXIV,—accompanied with the letter No. XXXV. which was succeeded by the letters No. XXXVI—XXXVII—XXXVIII—XXXIX—XL. In due time the sequel of the correspondence will appear.

Though extremely disagreeable to me, for very obvious reasons, I at length determined in order that no cloud whatever might be left on the affair, to publish the documents which had been communicated to Messrs. Monroe, Muhlenberg and Venable, all which will be seen in the appendix from No. I, (b) to No. XXII, inclusively.

The information from *Clingman* of the 2d January 1793, to which the signature of Mr. Monroe is annexed, seems to require an observation or two in addition to what is contained in my letter to him No. XXXIX.

Clingman first suggests that he had been apprized of my vindication through Mr. Wolcott a day or two after it had been communicated. It did not occur to me to inquire of Mr. Wolcott on this point, and he being now absent from Philadelphia, I cannot do it at this moment. Though I can have no doubt of the friendly intention of Mr. Wolcott, if the suggestion of Clingman in this particular be taken as true; yet from the condition of secrecy which was annexed to my communication, there is the strongest reason to conclude it is not true. If not true, there is besides but one of two solutions, either that he obtained the information from one of the three gentlemen who made the inquiry, which would have been a very dishonourable act in the party, or that he conjectured what my defence was from what he before knew it truly could be. For there is the highest probability, that through Reynolds and his wife, and as an accomplice, he was privy to the whole affair. This last method of accounting for his knowledge would be conclusive on the sincerity and genuineness of the defence.

But the turn which *Clingman* gives to the matter must necessarily fall to the ground. It is, that Mrs. Reynolds denied her amorous connection with me, and represented the suggestion of it as a mere contrivance between *her husband* and *myself* to cover me, alleging that there had been a fabrication of letters and receipts to countenance it. The plain answer is, that Mrs. Reynolds' own letters contradict absolutely this artful explanation of hers; if indeed she ever made it, of which *Clingman's* assertion is no evidence whatever. These letters are proved by the affidavit No. XLI, though it will easily be conceived that the proof of them was rendered no easy matter by a lapse of near five years. They shew explicitly the connection with her, the discovery of it by her husband and the pains she took to prolong it when I evidently wished to get rid of it. This cuts up, by the root, the pretence of a contrivance between the husband and myself to fabricate the evidences of it.

The variety of shapes which this woman could assume was endless. In a conversation between her and a gentleman whom I am not at liberty publicly to name, she made a voluntary confession of her belief and even knowledge, that I was innocent of all that had been laid to my charge by *Reynolds* or any other person of her acquaintance, spoke of me in exalted terms of esteem and respect, declared in the most solemn manner her extreme unhappiness lest I should suppose her accessary to the trouble which had been given me on that account, and expressed her fear that the resentment of Mr. Reynolds on *a particular score*, might have urged him to improper lengths of revenge—appearing at the same time extremely agitated and unhappy. With the gentleman who gives this information, I have never been in any relation personal or political that could be supposed to bias him. His name would evince that he is an impartial witness. And though I am not permitted to make a public use of it, I am permitted to refer any gentleman to the perusal of his letter in the hands of William Bingham, Esquire; who is also so obliging as to permit me to deposit with him for similar inspection all the original papers which are contained in the appendix to this narrative. The letter from the gentleman above alluded to has been already shewn to *Mr. Monroe.*

Let me now, in the last place, recur to some comments, in which the hireling editors of the pamphlets No. V and VI has thought fit to indulge himself.

The first of them is that the *soft* language of one of my notes addressed to a man in the habit of threatening me with disgrace, is incompatible with the idea of innocence. The threats alluded to must be those of being able to hang the Secretary of the Treasury. How does it appear that Reynolds was in such a *habit?* No otherwise than by the declaration of *Reynolds* and *Clingman*. If the assertions of these men are to condemn me, there is an end of the question. There is no need, by elaborate deductions from *parts* of their assertions, to endeavour to establish what their assertions collectively affirm in express terms. If they are worthy of credit I am guilty; if they are not, all wire-drawn inferences from parts of their story are mere artifice and nonsense. But no man, not as debauched as themselves, will believe them, independent of the positive disproof of their story in the written documents.

As to the affair of threats (except those in Reynolds letters respecting the connection with his wife, which it will be perceived were very gentle for the occasion) not the least idea of the sort ever reached me 'till after the imprisonment of Reynolds. Mr. Wolcott's certificate shews my conduct in that case—notwithstanding the powerful motives I may be presumed to have had to desire the liberation of Reynolds, on account of my situation with his wife, I cautioned Mr. Wolcott not to facilitate his liberation, till the affair of the threat was satisfactorily cleared up. The solemn denial of it in Reynold's letter No. XLII was considered by Mr. Wolcott as sufficient. This is a further proof, that though in respect to my situation with his wife, I was somewhat in Reynolds's power. I was not disposed to make any improper concession to the apprehension of his resentment.

As the threats intimated in his letters, the nature of the cause will shew that the soft tone of my note was not only compatible with them, but a natural consequence of them.

But it is observed that the dread of the disclosure of an amorous connection was not a sufficient cause for my humility, and that I had nothing to lose as to my reputation for chastity concerning which the world had fixed a previous opinion.

I shall not enter into the question what was the previous opinion entertained of me in this particular—nor how well founded, if it was indeed such as it is represented to have been. It is sufficient to say that there is a wide difference between vague rumours and suspicions and the evidence of a positive fact—no man not indelicately unprincipled, with the state of manners in this country, would be willing to have a conjugal infidelity fixed upon him with positive certainty. He would know that it would justly injure him with a considerable and respectable portion of the society—and especially no man, tender of the happiness of an excellent wife could without extreme pain look forward to the affliction which she might endure from the disclosure, especially a *public disclosure*, of the fact. Those best acquainted with the interior of my domestic life will best appreciate the force of such a consideration upon me.

The truth was, that in both relations and especially the last, I dreaded extremely a disclosure—and was willing to make large sacrifices to avoid it. It is true, that from the acquiescence of Reynolds, I had strong ties upon his secrecy, but how could I rely upon any tie upon so base a character. How could I know, but that from moment to moment he might, at the expence of his own disgrace, become the *mercenary* of a party, with whom to blast my character in *any way* is a favorite object!

Strong inferences are attempted to be drawn from the release of *Clingman* and *Reynolds* with the consent of the Treasury, from the want of communicativeness of Reynolds while in prison—from the subsequent disappearance of Reynolds and his wife, and from their not having been produced by me in order to be confronted at the time of the explanation.

As to the first, it was emphatically the transaction of Mr. Wolcott the then Comptroller of the Treasury, and was bottomed upon a very adequate motive—and one as appears from the document No. I, (a) early contemplated in this light by that officer. It was certainly of more consequence to the public to detect and expel from the bosom of the Treasury Department an unfaithful Clerk to prevent future and extensive mischief, than to disgrace and punish two worthless individuals. Besides that a powerful influence foreign to me was exerted to procure indulgence to them—that of Mr. Muhlenberg and Col. Burr—that of Col. Wadsworth, which though insidiously placed to my account was to the best of my recollection utterly unknown to me at the time, and according to the confession of Mrs. Reynolds herself, was put in motion by her entreaty. Candid men will derive strong evidence of my innocence and delicacy, from the reflection, that under circumstances so peculiar, the culprits were compelled to give a real and substantial equivalent for the relief which they obtained from a department, *over which I presided.*

The backwardness of Reynolds to enter into detail, while in jail, was an argument of nothing but that conscious of his inability to communicate any particulars which could be supported, he found it more convenient to deal in generals, and to keep up appearances by giving promises for the future.

As to the disappearance of the parties after the liberation, how am I answerable for it? Is it not presumable, that the instance discovered at the Treasury was not the only offence of the kind of which they were guilty? After one detection, is it not very probable that Reynolds fled to avoid detection in other cases? But exclusive of this, it is known and might easily be proved, that Reynolds was considerably in debt! What more natural for him than to fly from his creditors after having been once exposed by confinement for such a crime? Moreover, atrocious as his conduct had been towards me, was it not natural for him to fear that my resentment might be excited at the discovery of it, and that it might have been deemed a sufficient reason for retracting the indulgence, which was shewn by withdrawing the prosecution and for recommending it?

One or all of these considerations will explain the disappearance of Reynolds without imputing it to me as a method of getting rid of a dangerous witness.

That disappearance rendered it impracticable, if it had been desired to bring him forward to be confronted. As to *Clingman* it was not pretended that he knew any thing of what was charged upon me, otherwise than by the notes which he produced, and the information of Reynolds and his wife. As to Mrs. Reynolds, she in fact appears by *Clingman's* last story to have remained, and to have been accessible through him, by the gentlemen who had undertaken the inquiry. If they supposed it necessary to the elucidation of the affair, why did not they bring her forward? There can be no doubt of the sufficiency of Clingman's influence, for this purpose, when it is understood that Mrs. Reynolds and he afterwards lived together as man and wife. But to what purpose the confronting? What would it have availed the elucidation of truth, if Reynolds and his wife had impudently made allegations which I denied. Relative character and the written documents must still determine These could decide without it, and they were relied upon. But could it be expected, that I should so debase myself as to think it necessary to my vindication to be confronted with a person such as Reynolds? Could I have borne to suffer my veracity to be exposed to the humiliating competition?

For what?—why, it is said, to tear up the last twig of jealousy—but when I knew that I possessed written documents which were decisive, how could I foresee that any twig of jealousy would remain? When the proofs I did produce to the gentlemen were admitted by them to be completely satisfactory, and by some of them to be more than sufficient, how could I dream of the expediency of producing more—how could I imagine that every twig of jealousy was not plucked up?

If after the recent confessions of the gentlemen themselves, it could be useful to fortify the proof of the full conviction, my explanation had wrought, I might appeal to the total silence concerning this charge, when at a subsequent period, in the year 1793, there was such an active legislative persecution of me. It might not even perhaps be difficult to establish, that it came under the eye of Mr. Giles, and that he discarded it as the plain case of a private amour unconnected with any thing that was the proper subject of a public attack.

Thus has my desire to destroy this slander, completely, led me to a more copious and particular examination of it, than I am sure was necessary. The bare perusal of the letters from Reynolds and his wife is sufficient to convince my greatest enemy that there is nothing worse in the affair than an irregular and indelicate amour. For this, I bow to the just censure which it merits. I have paid pretty severely for the folly and can never recollect it without disgust and self condemnation. It might seem affectation to say more.

To unfold more clearly the malicious intent, by which the present revival of the affair must have been influenced—I shall annex an affidavit of Mr. Webster tending to confirm my declaration of the utter falsehood of the assertion, that a menace of publishing the papers which have been published had arrested the progress of an attempt to hold me up as a candidate for the office of President. Does this editor imagine that he will escape the just odium which awaits him by the miserable subterfuge of saying that he had the information from a respectable citizen of New-York? Till he names the author the inevitable inference must be that he has fabricated the tale.

ALEXANDER HAMILTON.

Philadelphia, July, 1797.

August 25, 1797

AN APPEAL TO WASHINGTON

To George Washington

My Dear Sir　　　　　　　　　New York May 19. 1798

At the present dangerous crisis of public affairs, I make no apology for troubling you with a political letter. Your impressions of our situation, I am persuaded, are not different from mine. There is certainly great probability that we may have to enter into a very serious struggle with France; and it is more and more evident that the powerful faction which has for years opposed the Government is determined to go every length with France. I am sincere in declaring my full conviction, as the result of a long course of observation, that they are ready to *new model* our constitution under the *influence* or *coertion* of France—to form with her a perpetual alliance *offensive* and *defensive*—and to give her a monopoly of our Trade by *peculiar* and *exclusive* privileges. This would be in substance, whatever it might be in name to make this Country a province of France. Neither do I doubt, that her standard displayed in this country would be directly or indirectly seconded by them in pursuance of the project I have mentioned.

It is painful and alarming to remark that the Opposition-Faction assumes so much a Geographical complexion. As yet from the South of Maryland nothing has been heared but accents of disapprobation of our Government and approbation of or apology for France. This is a most portentous symptom & demands every human effort to change it.

In such a state of public affairs it is impossible not to look up to you; and to wish that your influence could in some proper mode be brought into direct action. Among the ideas which have passed through my mind for this purpose—I have asked myself whether it might not be expedient for you to make a circuit through Virginia and North Carolina under some pretence of health &c. This would call forth addresses public dinners &c. which would give you an opportunity of expressing sentiments in Answers Toasts &c. which would throw the weight of your character into the scale of the

Government and revive an enthusiasm for your person that may be turned into the right channel.

I am aware that the step is delicate & ought to be well considered before it is taken. I have even not settled my own opinion as to its propriety—but I have concluded to bring the general idea under your view, confident that your judgment will make a right choice and that you will take no step which is not well calculated. The conjuncture however is extraordinary & now or very soon will demand extraordinary measures.

You ought also to be aware, My Dear Sir, that in the event of an open rupture with France, the public voice will again call you to command the armies of your Country; and though all who are attached to you will from attachment, as well as public considerations, deplore an occasion which should once more tear you from that repose to which you have so good a right—yet it is the opinion of all those with whom I converse that you will be compelled to make the sacrifice. All your past labour may demand to give it efficacy this further, this very great sacrifice.

Adieu My Dear Sir   Respectfully & Affecly Yr very obed servt   A Hamilton

"MY GOOD GENIUS"

To Elizabeth Hamilton

Philadelphia
Nov 1798

I am always very happy My Dear Eliza when I can steal a few moments to sit down and write to you. You are my good genius; of that kind which the ancient Philosophers called a *familiar*, and you know very well that I am glad to be in every way as familiar as possible with you. I have formed a sweet project, of which I will make you my confident when I come to New York, and in which I rely that you will cooperate with me chearfully.

> "You may guess and guess and guess again
> Your guessing will be still in vain."

But you will not be the less pleased when you come to understand and realize the scheme.

Adieu best of wives & best of mothers. Heaven ever bless you & me in you A H

November 19, 1798

THE PROBLEM OF VIRGINIA

To Theodore Sedgwick

New York Feby 2. 1799

What, My Dear Sir, are you going to do with Virginia? This is a very serious business, which will call for all the wisdom and firmness of the Government. The following are the ideas which occur to me on the occasion.

The first thing in all great operations of such a Government as ours is to secure the opinion of the people. To this end, the proceedings of Virginia and Kentucke with the two laws complained of should be referred to a special Committee. That Committee should make a report exhibiting with great luminousness and particularity the reasons which support the constitutionality and expediency of those laws—the tendency of the doctrines advanced by Virginia and Kentucke to destroy the Constitution of the UStates—and, with calm dignity united with pathos, the full evidence which they afford of a regular conspiracy to overturn the government. And the Report should likewise dwell upon the inevitable effect and probably the intention of these proceedings to encourage a hostile foreign power to decline accommodation and proceed in hostility. The Government must not merely defend itself but must attack and arraign its enemies. But in all this, there should be great care to distinguish the people of Virginia from the legislature and even the greater part of those who may have concurred in the legislature from the Chiefs; manifesting indeed a strong confidence in the good sense and patriotism of the people, that they will not be the dupes of an insidious plan to disunite the people of America to break down their constitution & expose them to the enterprises of a foreign power.

This Report should conclude with a declaration that there is no cause for a Repeal of the laws. If however on examination any modifications consistent with the general design of the laws, but instituting better guards, can be devised it may well to propose them as a bridge for those who may incline to retreat over. Concessions of this kind adroitly made have a good rather than a bad effect. On a recent though hasty revision of the Alien law it seems to me deficient in precautions against abuse and for the security of Citizens. This should not be.

No pains or expence should be spared to desseminate this Report. A little pamphlet containing it should find its way into every house in Virginia.

This should be left to work and nothing to court a shock should be adopted.

In the mean time the measures for raising the Military force should proceed with activity. Tis much to be lamented that so much delay has attended the execution of this measure. In times like the present not a moment ought to have been lost to secure the Government so powerful an auxiliary. Whenever the experiment shall be made to subdue a *refractory* & powerful *state* by Militia, the event will shame the advocates of their sufficiency. In the expedition against the Western Insurgents I trembled every moment lest a great part of the Militia should take it into their heads to return home rather than go forward.

When a clever force has been collected let them be drawn towards Virginia for which there is an obvious pretext—& then let measures be taken to act upon the laws & put Virginia to the Test of resistance.

This plan will give time for the fervour of the moment to subside, for reason to resume the reins, and by dividing its enemies will enable the Government to triumph with ease.

As an auxiliary measure, it is very desireable that the Provisional Army Bill should pass & that the Executive should proceed to the appointment of the Officers. The tendency of this needs no comment.

Yrs. affecy

A Hamilton

DISPLAYING STRENGTH "LIKE A HERCULES"

To James McHenry

Private   New York March 18. 1799

Beware, my Dear Sir, of magnifying a riot into an insurrection, by employing in the first instance an inadequate force. Tis better far to err on the other side. Whenever the Government appears in arms it ought to appear like a *Hercules*, and inspire respect by the display of strength. The consideration of expence is of no moment compared with the advantages of energy. Tis true this is always a relative question—but tis always important to make no mistake. I only offer a *principle* and a *caution.*

A large corps of auxiliary cavalry may be had in Jersey New York Delaware Maryland without interfering with farming pursuits.

Will it be inexpedient to put under marching Orders a large force provisionally, as in eventual support of the corps to be employed—to awe the disaffected?

Let all be well considered.

Yrs. truly

A Hamilton

Memorandum on Measures for Strengthening the Government

An Accurate view of the internal situation of the UStates presents many discouraging reflections to the enlightened friends of our Government and country. Notwithstanding the unexampled success of our public measures at home and abroad—notwithstanding the instructive comments afforded by the disastrous & disgusting scenes of the french Revolution, public opinion has not been ameliorated—sentiments dangerous to social happiness have not been diminished—on the contrary there are symptoms which warrant the apprehension that among the most numerous class of citizens errors of a very pernicious tendency have not only preserved but have extended their empire. Though something may have been gained on the side of men of information and property, more has probably been lost on that of persons of different description. An extraordinary exertion of the friends of Government, aided by circumstances of momentary impression, gave in the last election for members of Congress a more favourable countenance to some states than they had before worne. Yet it is the belief of well informed men that no real or desirable change has been wrought in those States. On the other hand it is admitted by close observers that some of the parts of the Union which in time past have been the soundest have of late exhibited signs of a gangrene begun and progressive.

It is likewise apparent that opposition to the government has acquired more system than formerly—is bolder in the avowal of its designs—less solicitous than it was to discriminate between the Constitution and the Administration—more open and more enterprising in its projects.

The late attempt of Virginia & Kentucke to unite the state legislatures in a direct resistance to certain laws of the Union can be considered in no other light than as an attempt to change the Government.

It is stated, in addition, that the opposition-Party in Virginia, the head Quarters of the Faction, have followed up the hostile declarations which are to be found in the resolutions of their General Assembly by an actual preparation of the means of supporting them by force—That they have taken measures to put their militia on a more efficient footing—are preparing considerable arsenals and magazines and (which is an unequivocal proof how much they are in earnest) have gone so far as to lay new taxes on their citizens.

Amidst such serious indications of hostility, the safety and the duty of the supporters of the Government call upon them to adopt vigorous measures of counteraction. It will be wise in them to act upon the hypothesis that the opposers of the Government are resolved, if it shall be practicable to make its existence a question of force. Possessing as they now do all the constitutional powers, it will be an unpardonable mistake on their part if they do not exert them to surround the constitution with new ramparts and to disconcert the schemes of its enemies.

The measures proper to be adopted may be classed under   heads:

1   Establishments which will extend the influence and promote the popularity of the Government.

Under this head three important expedients occur—1 The Extension of the Judiciary system. 2 The improvement of the great communications as well interiorly as coastwise by turnpike roads. 3 The institution of a Society with funds to be employed in premiums for new inventions discoveries and improvements in Agriculture and in the Arts.

The extension of the Judiciary system ought to embrace two objects—one The subdivision of each state into small Districts (suppose Connecticut into four and so in proportion) assigning to each a Judge with a moderate salary—the other the appointment in each Country of Conservators or Justices of the Peace with only Ministerial functions and with no other compensations than fees for the services they shall perform.

This measure is necessary to give efficacy to the laws the execution of which is obstructed by the want of similar organs and by the indisposition of the local Magistrates in some states. The constitution requires that *Judges* shall have fixed salaries—but this does not apply to mere Justices of the peace without Judicial powers. Both those descriptions of persons are essential as well to the energetic execution of the laws as to the purpose of salutary patronage.

The thing would no doubt be a subject of clamour, but it would carry with it its own antidote, and when once established would bring a very powerful support to the Government.

The improvement of the roads would be a measure universally popular. None can be more so. For this purpose a regular plan should be adopted coextensive with the Union to be successively executed—and a fund should be appropriated sufficient for the basis of a loan of a Milion of Dollars. The revenue of the Post office naturally offers itself. The future revenue from tolls would more than reimburse the expence; and public utility would be promoted in every direction.

The institution of a society with the aid of proper funds to encourage Agriculture and the arts, besides being productive of general advantage, will speak powerfully to the feelings and interests of those classes of men to whom the benefits derived from the Government have been heretofore the least manifest.

2   Provisions for augmenting the means and consolidating the strength of the Government.

A Milion of Dollars may without difficulty be added to the Revenue, by increasing the rates of some existing indirect taxes and by the addition of some new items of a similar character. The direct taxes ought neither to be increased nor diminished.

Our naval force ought to be completed to six Ships of the line Twelve frigates and twenty four sloops of War. More at this juncture would be disproportioned to our resources. Less would be inadequate to the end to be accomplished.

Our Military force should for the present be kept upon its actual footing; making provision for a reinlistment of the men for five years in the event of a settlement of differences with France—with this condition that in case of peace between Great Britain France and Spain, the UStates being then also at peace, all the Privates of twelve additional Regiments of Infantry and of the Regiment of Dragoons exceeding Twenty to a Company shall be disbanded. The corps of Artillerists may be left to retain the numbers which it shall happen to have; but without being recruited until the number of privates shall fall below the standard of the Infantry & Dragoons. A power ought to be given to the President to augment the four Old Regiments to their War Establishmt.

The laws respecting volunteer Companies & the *Eventual army* should be rendered permanent and the Executive should proceed without delay to organise the latter. Some modifications of the discretion of the President will however be proper in a permanent law. And it will be a great improvement of the plan if it shall be thought expedient to allow the inlistment, for the purpose of instruction, of a corps of serjeants equal to the number requisite for the Eventual Army.

The Institution of a Military Academy will be an auxiliary of great importance.

Manufactories of every article, the woolen parts of cloathing included, which are essential to the supply of the army ought to be established.

3 Arrangements for confirming and enlarging the legal Powers of the Government.

There are several temporary laws which in this view ought to be rendered permanent, particularly that which authorises the calling out of the Militia to suppress unlawful combinations and Insurrections.

An article ought to be proposed to be added to the constitution for empowering Congress to open canals in all cases in which it may be necessary to conduct them through the territory of two or more states or through the territory of a State and that of the UStates. The power is very desireable for the purpose of improving the prodigious facilities for inland navigation with which nature has favoured this Country. It will also assist commerce and agriculture by rendering the transportation of commodities more cheap and expeditious. It will tend to secure the connection by facilitating the communication between distant portions of the Union. And it will be a useful source of influence to the Government.

Happy would it be if a clause would be added to the constitution, enabling Congress on the application of any considerable portion of a state, containing not less than a hundred thousand persons, to erect it into a separate state on the condition of fixing the quota of contributions which it shall make towards antecedent debts, if any there shall be, reserving to Congress the authority to levy within such state the taxes necessary to the payment of such quota, in case of neglect on the part of the State. The subdivision of the great states is indispensable to the security of the General Government and with it of the Union. Great States will always feel a rivalship with the common head, will often be disposed to machinate against it, and in certain situations will be able to do it with decisive effect. The subdivision of such states ought to be a cardinal point in the Fœderal policy: and small states are doubtless best adapted to the purposes of local regulation and to the preservation of the republican spirit. This suggestion however is merely thrown out for consideration. It is feared that it would be inexpedient

& even dangerous to propose at this time an amendment of the kind.

4 Laws for restraining and punishing incendiary and seditious practices.

It will be useful to declare that all such writings &c which at common law are libels if levelled against any Officer whatsoever of the UStates shall be cognizable in the Courts of UStates.

To preserve confidence in the Officers of the General Government, by preserving their reputations from malicious and unfounded slanders, is essential to enable them to fulfil the ends of their appointment. It is therefore both constitutional and politic to place their reputations under the guardianship of the Courts of the United States. They ought not to be left to the cold and relucant protection of state courts always temporising sometimes disaffected.

But what avail laws which are not executed? Renegade Aliens conduct more than one of the most incendiary presses in the UStates—and yet in open contempt and defiance of the laws they are permitted to continue their destructive labours. Why are they not sent away? Are laws of this kind passed merely to excite odium and remain a dead letter? Vigour in the Executive is at least as necessary as in the legislative branch. If the President requires to be stimulated those who can approach him ought to do it.

c. 1799

To Josiah Ogden Hoffman

Sir

"GREENLEAFS NEW DAYLY ADVERTISER" of this morning contains a publication intitled "Extract of a letter from Philadelphia dated September 20th," which charges me with being at the "bottom" of an "effort recently made to suppress the AURORA" (a news paper of that City) by pecuniary means.

It is well known that I have long been the object of the most malignant calumnies of the faction opposed to our government, through the medium of the papers devoted to their views. Hitherto I have foreborne to resort to the laws for the punishment of the authors or abettors; and were I to consult personal considerations alone I should continue in this course, repaying hatred with contempt. But public motives now compel me to a different conduct. The design of that faction to overturn our government, and with it the great pillars of social security and happiness, in this country, become every day more manifest, and have of late acquired a degree of system, which renders them formidable. One principal Engine for effecting the scheme is by audacious falsehoods to destroy the confidence of the people in all those who are in any degree conspicuous among the supporters of the Government: an Engine which has been employed in time past with too much success, and which unless counteracted in future is likely to be attended with very fatal consequences. To counter act it is therefore a duty to the community.

Among the specimens of this contrivance, that which is the subject of the present letter demands peculiar attention. A bolder calumny; one more absolutely destitute of foundation was never propagated. And its dangerous tendency needs no comment; being calculated to inspire the belief that the Independence and liberty of the press are endangered by the intrigues of ambitious citizens and by foreign gold.

In so flagrant a case the force of the laws must be tried. I therefore request that you will take immediate measures towards the prosecution of the persons who conduct the inclosed paper.

With great consideration   I am Sir   yr Obed ser

November 6, 1799

THE DEATH OF WASHINGTON

To Charles Cotesworth Pinckney

Philadelphia Decr.

Sir   1799

The death of our beloved commander in Chief was known to you before it was to me. I can be at no loss to anticipate what have been your feelings. I need not tell you what are mine. Perhaps no friend of his has more cause to lament, on personal account, than my self. The public misfortune is one which all the friends of our Government will view in the same light. I will not dwell on the subject. My Imagination is gloomy my heart sad.

Inclosed is an order relative to the occasion which speaks its own object.

With the sincerest esteem and most affectionate regard   I remain Sir   Yr very Obed ser

December 22, 1799

"SO HEART-RENDING AN AFFLICTION"

To Martha Washington

New York Jany. 12. 1800

I did not think it proper, Madam, to intrude amidst the first effusions of your grief. But I can no longer restrain my sensibility from conveying to you an imperfect expression of my affectionate sympathy in the sorrows you experience. No one, better than myself, knows the greatness of your loss, or how much your excellent heart is formed to feel it in all its extent. Satisfied that you cannot receive consolation, I will attempt to offer none. Resignation to the will of Heaven, which the practice of your life ensures, can alone alleviate the sufferings of so heart-rending an affliction.

There can be few, who equally with me participate in the loss you deplore. In expressing this sentiment, I may without impropriety allude to the numerous and distinguished marks of confidence and friendship, of which you have yourself been a Witness; but I cannot say in how many ways the continuance of that confidence and friendship was necessary to me in future relations.

Vain, however, are regrets. From a calamity, which is common to a mourning nation, who can expect to be exempt? Perhaps it is even a privilege to have a claim to a larger portion of it than others.

I will only add, Madam, that I shall deem it a real and a great happiness, if any future occurrence shall enable me to give you proof of that respectful and cordial attachment with which I have the honor to be

Your obliged & very obedient servant

AN ELECTORAL STRATAGEM

To John Jay

Dear Sir   New York May 7. 1800
    You have been informed of the loss of our Election in this City. It is also known that we have been unfortunate throughout Long Island & in West Chester. According to the Returns hitherto, it is too probable that we lose our Senators for this District.

The moral certainty therefore is that there will be an Antifœderal Majority in the Ensuing Legislature, and this very high probability is that this will bring *Jefferson* into the Chief Magistracy; unless it be prevented by the measure which I shall now submit to your consideration, namely the immediate calling together of the existing Legislature.

I am aware that there are weighty objections to the measure; but the reasons for it appear to me to outweigh the objections. And in times like these in which we live, it will not do to be overscrupulous. It is easy to sacrifice the substantial interests of society by a strict adherence to ordinary rules.

In observing this, I shall not be supposed to mean that any thing ought to be done which integrity will forbid—but merely that the scruples of delicacy and propriety, as relative to a common course of things, ought to yield to the extraordinary nature of the crisis. They ought not to hinder the taking of a *legal* and *constitutional* step, to prevent an *Atheist* in Religion and a *Fanatic* in politics from getting possession of the helm of the State.

You Sir know in a great degree the Antifœderal party, but I fear that you do not know them as well as I do. Tis a composition indeed of very incongruous materials but all tending to mischief—some of them to the overthrow of the Government by stripping it of its due energies others of them to a Revolution after the manner of Buonaparte. I speak from indubitable facts, not from conjectures & inferences.

In proportion as the true character of this party is understood is the force of the considerations which urge to every effort to disappoint it. And it seems to me that there is a very solemn obligation to employ the means in our power.

The calling of the Legislature will have for object the choosing of Electors by the people in Districts. This (as Pennsylvania will do nothing) will insure a Majority of votes in the U States for Fœderal Candidates.

The measure will not fail to be approved by all the Fœderal Party; while it will no doubt be condemned by the opposite. As to its intrinsic nature it is justified by unequivocal reasons for *public safety.*

The reasonable part of the world will I believe approve it. They will see it as a proceeding out of the common course but warranted by the particular nature of the Crisis and the great cause of social order.

If done the motive ought to be frankly avowed. In your communication to the Legislature they ought to be told that Temporary circumstances had rendered it probable that without their interposition the executive authority of the General Government would be transfered to hands hostile to the system heretofore pursued with so much success and dangerous to the peace happiness and order of the Country—that under this impression from facts convincing to your own mind you had thought it your duty to give the existing Legislature an opportunity of deliberating whether it would not be proper to interpose and endeavour to prevent so great an evil by referring the choice of Electors to the People distributed into Districts.

In weighing this suggestion you will doubtless bear in mind that Popular Governments must certainly be overturned & while they endure prove engines of mischief—if one party will call to its aid all the resources which *Vice* can give and if the other, however pressing the emergency, confines itself within all the ordinary forms of delicacy and decorum.

The legislature can be brought together in three weeks. So that there will be full time for the objects; but none ought to be lost.

Think well my Dear Sir of this proposition. Appreciate the extreme danger of the Crisis; and I am unusually mistaken in my view of the matter, if you do not see it right and expedient to adopt the measure.

Respectfully & Affecty   Yrs.   A Hamilton

WITHDRAWING SUPPORT FROM ADAMS

To Theodore Sedgwick

Dr Sir   New York May 10. 1800

I am very sorry for the information contained in your letter of the 7th. But I am not intimate enough with Dexter to put myself upon Paper to him. If on his return I can catch him at New York I shall have a particular conversation with him.

He is I am persuded much mistaken as to the opinion entertained of Mr Adams by the Fœderal party. Were I to determine from my own observation I should say, *most* of the *most influential men* of that party consider him as a very *unfit* and *incapable* character.

For my individual part my mind is made up. I will never more be responsible for him by my direct support—even though the consequence should be the election of *Jefferson*. If we must have an *enemy* at the head of the Government, let it be one whom we can oppose & for whom we are not responsible, who will not involve our party in the disgrace of his foolish and bad measures. Under *Adams* as under *Jefferson* the government will sink. The party in the hands of whose chief it shall sink will sink with it and the advantage will all be on the side of his adversaries.

Tis a notable expedient for keeping the Fœderal party together to have at the head of it a man who hates and is dispised by those men of it who in time past have been its most efficient supporters.

If the cause is to be sacrificed to a weak and perverse man, I withdraw from the party & act upon my own ground—never certainly against my principles but in pursuance of them in my own way. I am mistaken if others will not do the same.

The only way to prevent a fatal scism in the Fœderal party is to support G Pinckney in good earnest.

If I can be perfectly satisfied that Adams & Pinckney will be upheld in the East with intire good faith, on the ground of conformity I will wherever my influence may extend pursue the same plan. If not I will pursue Mr. Pinkny as my single object.

Adieu Yrs. truly   A H

SUPPORTING PINCKNEY

To Charles Carroll of Carrollton

Dear Sir: New-York, July 1st, 1800.

I yesterday returned from an excursion through three of the four eastern States, and found your letter of the 18th of April. It is very necessary that the true and independent friends of the government should communicate and understand each other at the present very embarrassed and dangerous crisis of public affairs. I am glad, therefore, of the opportunity which your letter affords me of giving you some explanations which may be useful. They are given without reserve, because the times forbid temporising, and I hold no opinions which I have any motives to dissemble. As to the situation of this State, with regard to the election of President, it is perfectly ascertained that on a joint ballot of the two houses of our legislature, the opposers of the government will have a majority of more than twenty; a majority which can by no means be overcome. Consequently all our electors will vote for Mr. Jefferson, and Mr. Burr. I think there is little cause to doubt that the electors in the four eastern States will all be federal.

The only question seems to be as to Rhode Island, where there is some division, and a state of things rather loose. Governor Fenner, as far as he may dare, will promote the interest of Jefferson.

A considerable diversion in favor of the opposition has lately been made in New Jersey. But the best and best informed men there entertain no doubt that all her electors will still be federal, and I believe this opinion may be relied upon.

I go no further south, as I take it for granted your means of calculation with regard to that quarter are, at least, equal to mine.

The result of a comprehensive view of the subject, seems to me to be, that the event is uncertain, but that the probability is, that a universal adherence of the federalists to Pinckney will exclude Jefferson.

On this point there is some danger, though the greatest number of strong minded men in New England are not only satisfied of the expediency of supporting *Pinckney*, as giving the best chance against Jefferson, but even prefer him to *Adams*, yet in the body of that people there is a strong personal attachment to this gentleman, and most of the leaders of the second class are so anxious for his re-election that it will be difficult to convince them that there is as much danger of its failure as there unquestionably is, or to induce them faithfully to co-operate in Mr. Pinckney, notwithstanding their common and strong dread of Jefferson.

It may become advisable, in order to oppose their fears to their *prejudices*, for the middle States to declare that Mr. Adams will not be supported at all, when, seeing his success desperate, they would be driven to adhere to *Pinckney*. In this plan New Jersey, and even Connecticut, may be brought to concur. For both these States have generally lost confidence in Mr. Adams.

But this will be best decided by future events and elucidations. In the mean time it is not advisable that Maryland should be too deeply pledged to the support of Mr. Adams.

That this gentleman ought not to be the object of the federal wish, is, with me, reduced to demonstration. His administration has already very materially disgraced and sunk the government. There are defects in his character which must inevitably continue to do this more and more. And if he is supported by the federal party, his party must in the issue fall with him. Every other calculation will, in my judgment, prove illusory.

Doctor *Franklin*, a sagacious observer of human nature, drew this portrait of Mr. Adams:—"He is always honest, *sometimes* great, but *often mad.*" I subscribe to the justness of this picture, adding as to the first trait of it this qualification—"as far as a man excessively *vain* and *jealous*, and *ignobly* attached to *place* can be."

With great consideration and esteem, I am, dear Sir, &c.

RESPONSE TO AN ACCUSATION

To John Adams

Sir   New York August 1. 1800

It has been repeatedly mentioned to me that you have, on different occasions, asserted the existence of a *British Faction* in this Country, embracing a number of leading or influential characters of the *Fœderal Party* (as usually denominated) and that you have sometimes named me, at other times plainly alluded to me, as one of this description of persons: And I have likewise been assured that of late some of your warm adherents, for electioneering purposes, have employed a corresponding language.

I must, Sir, take it for granted, that you cannot have made such assertions or insinuations without being willing to avow them, and to assign the reasons to a party who may conceive himself injured by them. I therefore trust that you will not deem it improper that I apply directly to yourself, to ascertain from you, in reference to your own declarations, whether the information, I have received, has been correct or not, and if correct what are the grounds upon which you have founded the suggestion.

With respect   I have the honor to be   Sir   Your obedient servt.

Alexander Hamilton

"I AM IN A VERY BELLIGERENT HUMOUR"

To Oliver Wolcott Jr.

Dear Sir   New York Aug 3. 1800
I have two days since written to Mr. Adams a *respectful* letter on the subject I heretofore mentioned to you. Occupations at Court prevented its being sooner done.

But I wait with impatience for the statement of facts which you promised me. It is plain that unless we give our reasons in some form or other—Mr. Adam's personal friends seconded by the Jacobins will completely *run us down in the public opinion.* Your name in company with mine that of T Pickering &c. is in full circulation as one of the *British Faction* of which Mr. Adams has talked so much

I have serious thoughts of giving to the public my opinion respecting Mr. Adams with my reasons in a letter to a friend with my signature. This seems to me the most authentic way of conveying the information & best suited to the plain dealing of my character. There are however reasons against it and a very strong one is that some of the principal causes of my disapprobation proceed from yourself & other members of the Administration who would be understood to be the sources of my information whatever cover I might give the thing.

What say you to this measure? I could predicate it on the fact that I am abused by the friends of Mr. Adams who ascribe my opposition to pique & disappointment & would give it the shape of a *defence of my self.*

You have doubtless seen The Aurora publications of Treasury Documents & the manner in which my name is connected with it. These publications do harm with the ignorant who are the greatest number. I have thoughts of instituting an action of slander to be tried by a struck jury against the Editor. If I do it I should claim you & the Supervisors Collectors & Loan Officers of all the States from Maryland to N York inclusively as Witnesses to demonstrate completely the malice & falsity of the accusation. What think you of this? You see I am in a very belligerent humour.

But I remember that at the outset before the sums payable for interest pensions &c. were ascertained I placed the money in the hands of the paying officers upon estimate & that to avoid disappointment I made the estimates large. Pray look into this & see how far it may give any colour to the calumny.

Let me hear from you soon

Yrs. very truly   A Hamilton

"THE MOST HUMILIATING CRITICISM"

To William Jackson

My dear Jackson.   New-York Aug 26 1800.

Never was there a more ungenerous persecution of any man than of myself.—Not only the worst constructions are put upon my conduct as a public man but it seems my birth is the subject of the most humiliating criticism.

On this point as on most others which concern me, there is much mistake—though I am pained by the consciousness that it is not free from blemish.

I think it proper to confide to your bosom the real history of it, that among my friends you may if you please wipe off some part of the stain which is so industriously impressed.

The truth is that on the question who my parents were, I have better pretensions than most of those who in this Country plume themselves on Ancestry.

My Grandfather by the mothers side of the name of Faucette was a French Huguenot who emigrated to the West Indies in consequence of the revocation of the Edict of Nantz and settled in the Island of Nevis and there acquired a pretty fortune. I have been assured by persons who knew him that he was a man of letters and much of a gentleman. He practiced as a Physician, whether that was his original profession, or one assumed for livelihood after his emigration is not to me ascertained.

My father now dead was certainly of a respectable Scotch Family. His father was, and the son of his Eldest brother now is Laird of Grange. His mother was the sister of an ancient Baronet *Sir Robert Pollock*.

Himself being a younger son of a numerous family was bred to trade. In capacity of merchant he went to St Kitts, where from too generous and too easy a temper he failed in business, and at length fell into indigent circumstances. For some time he was supported by his friends in Scotland, and for several years before his death by me. It was his fault to have had too much pride and two large a portion of indolence—but his character was otherwise without reproach and his manners those of a Gentleman.

So far I may well challenge comparison, but the blemish remains to be unveiled.

A Dane a fortune-hunter of the name of *Lavine* came to Nevis bedizzened with gold, and paid his addresses to my mother then a handsome young woman having a *snug* fortune. In compliance with the wishes of her mother who was captivated by the glitter of the   but against her own inclination she married Lavine. The marriage was unhappy and ended in a separation by divorce. My mother afterwards went to St Kitts, became acquainted with my father and a marriage between them ensued, followed by many years cohabitation and several children.

But unluckily it turned out that the divorce was not absolute but qualified, and thence the second marriage was not lawful. Hence when my mother died the small property which she left went to my half brother Mr Lavine who lived in South Carolina and was for a time partner with Mr Kane. He is now dead.

As to my fathers family Mr McCormick of this city, merchant, can give testimony and will corroborate what I have stated.

Your truly and affectionately.   Alexander Hamilton

Rules for Philip Hamilton

Rules for *Mr Philip Hamilton* from the first of April to the first of October he is to rise not later than Six Oclock—The rest of the year not later than Seven. If Earlier he will deserve commendation. Ten will be his hour of going to bed throughout the year.

From the time he is dressed in the morning till nine o clock (the time for breakfast Excepted) he is to read Law.

At nine he goes to the office & continues there till dinner time—he will be occupied partly in the writing and partly in reading law.

After Dinner he reads law at home till five O clock. From this hour till Seven he disposes of his time as he pleases. From Seven to ten he reads and Studies what ever he pleases.

From twelve on Saturday he is at Liberty to amuse himself.

On Sunday he will attend the morning Church. The rest of the day may be applied to innocent recreations.

He must not Depart from any of these rules without my permission.

1800

"A BASE WICKED AND CRUEL CALUMNY"

To John Adams

Sir   New York October 1. 1800

The time which has elapsed since my letter of the first of August was delivered to you precludes the further expectation of an answer.

From this silence, I will draw no inference; nor will I presume to judge of the fitness of silence on such an occasion, on the part of The Chief Magistrate of a Republic, towards a citizen, who without a stain has discharged so many important public trusts.

But this much I will affirm, that by whomsoever a charge of the kind mentioned in my former letter may, at any time, have been made or insinuated against me, it is a base wicked and cruel calumny; destitute even of a plausible pretext to excuse the folly or mask the depravity which must have dictated it.

With due respect   I have the honor to be   Sir   Your obed Servt

                                                A Hamilton

Letter from *Alexander Hamilton,* Concerning the Public Conduct and Character of John Adams, Esq. President of the United States

Sir,

Some of the warm personal friends of Mr. ADAMS are taking unwearied pains to disparage the motives of those Federalists, who advocate the equal support of Gen. PINCKNEY, at the approaching election of President and Vice-President. They are exhibited under a variety of aspects equally derogatory. Sometimes they are versatile, factious spirits, who cannot be long satisfied with any chief, however meritorious:—Sometimes they are ambitious spirits, who can be contented with no man that will not submit to be governed by them:—Sometimes they are intriguing partisans of Great-Britain, who, devoted to the advancement of her views, are incensed against Mr. ADAMS for the independent impartiality of his conduct.

In addition to a full share of the obloquy vented against this description of persons collectively, peculiar accusations have been devised, to swell the catalogue of my demerits. Among these, the resentment of disappointed ambition, forms a prominent feature. It is pretended, that had the President, upon the demise of General WASHINGTON, appointed me Commander in Chief, he would have been, in my estimation, all that is wise, and good and great.

It is necessary, for the public cause, to repel these slanders; by stating the real views of the persons who are calumniated, and the reasons of their conduct.

In executing this task, with particular reference to myself, I ought to premise, that the ground upon which I stand, is different from that of most of those who are confounded with me as in pursuit of the same plan. While our object is common, our motives are variously dissimilar. A part, well affected to Mr. ADAMS, have no other wish than to take a double chance against Mr. JEFFERSON. Another part, feeling a diminution of confidence in him, still hope that the general tenor of his conduct will be essentially right. Few go as far in their objections as I do. Not denying to Mr. ADAMS patriotism and integrity, and even talents of a certain kind, I should be deficient in candor, were I to conceal the conviction, that he does not possess the talents adapted to the *Administration* of Government, and that there are great and intrinsic defects in his character, which unfit him for the office of Chief Magistrate.

To give a correct idea of the circumstances which have gradually produced this conviction, it may be useful to retrospect to an early period.

I was one of that numerous class who had conceived a high veneration for Mr. ADAMS, on account of the part he acted in the first stages of our revolution. My imagination had exalted him to a high eminence, as a man of patriotic, bold, profound, and comprehensive mind. But in the progress of the war, opinions were ascribed to him, which brought into question, with me, the solidity of his understanding. He was represented to be of the number of those who favored the enlistment of our troops annually, or for short periods, rather than for the term of the war; a blind and infatuated policy, directly contrary to the urgent recommendation of General WASHINGTON, and which had nearly proved the ruin of our cause. He was also said to have advocated the project of appointing yearly a new Commander of the Army; a project which, in any service, is likely to be attended with more evils than benefits; but which, in ours, at the period in question, was chimerical, from the want of persons qualified to succeed, and pernicious, from the peculiar fitness of the officer first appointed, to strengthen, by personal influence, the too feeble cords which bound to the service, an ill-paid, ill-clothed, and undisciplined soldiery.

It is impossible for me to assert, at this distant day, that these suggestions were brought home to Mr. ADAMS in such a manner as to ascertain their genuineness; but I distinctly remember their existence, and my conclusion from them; which was, that, if true, they proved this gentleman to be infected with some visionary notions, and that he was far less able in the practice, than in the theory, of politics. I remember also, that they had the effect of inducing me to qualify the admiration which I had once entertained for him, and to reserve for opportunities of future scrutiny, a definitive opinion of the true standard of his character.

In this disposition I was, when just before the close of the war, I became a member of Congress.

The situation in which I found myself there, was far from being inauspicious to a favorable estimate of Mr. ADAMS.

Upon my first going into Congress, I discovered symptoms of a party already formed, too well disposed to subject the interests of the United States to the management of France. Though I felt, in common with those who had participated in our Revolution, a lively sentiment of good will towards a power, whose co-operation, however it was and ought to have been dictated by its own interest, had been extremely useful to us, and had been afforded in a liberal and handsome manner; yet, tenacious of the real independence of our country, and dreading the preponderance of foreign influence, as the natural disease of popular government, I was struck with disgust at the appearance, in the very cradle of our Republic, of a party actuated by an undue complaisance to foreign power; and I resolved at once to resist this bias in our affairs: a resolution, which has been the chief cause of the persecution I have endured in the subsequent stages of my political life.

Among the fruits of the bias I have mentioned, were the celebrated instructions to our Commissioners, for treating of peace with Great-Britain; which, not only as to final measures, but also as to preliminary and intermediate negociations, placed them in a state of dependence on the French ministry, humiliating to themselves, and unsafe for the interests of the country. This was the more exceptionable, as there was cause to suspect, that in regard to the two cardinal points of the fisheries and the navigation of the Mississippi, the policy of the cabinet of Versailles did not accord with the wishes of the United States.

The Commissioners, of whom Mr. ADAMS was one, had the fortitude to break through the fetters which were laid upon them by those instructions; and there is reason to believe, that by doing it, they both accelerated the peace with Great-Britain, and improved the terms, while they preserved our faith with France.

Yet a serious attempt was made to obtain from Congress a formal censure of their conduct. The attempt failed, and instead of censure, the praise was bestowed which was justly due to the accomplishment of a treaty advantageous to this country, beyond the most sanguine expectation. In this result, my efforts were heartily united.

The principal merit of the negociation with Great-Britain, in some quarters, has been bestowed upon Mr. ADAMS; but it is certainly the right of Mr. JAY, who took a lead in the several steps of the transaction, no less honorable to his talents than to his firmness. The merit, nevertheless, of a full and decisive co-operation, is justly due to Mr. ADAMS.

It will readily be seen, that such a course of things was calculated to impress me with a disposition friendly to Mr. ADAMS. I certainly felt it, and gave him much of my consideration and esteem.

But this did not hinder me from making careful observations upon his several communications, and endeavoring to derive from them an accurate idea of his talents and character. This scrutiny enhanced my esteem in the main for his moral qualifications, but lessened my respect for his intellectual endowments. I then adopted an opinion, which all my subsequent experience has confirmed, that he is a man of an imagination sublimated and eccentric; propitious neither to the regular display of sound judgment, nor to steady perseverance in a systematic plan of conduct; and I began to perceive what has been since too manifest, that to this defect are added the unfortunate foibles of a vanity without bounds, and a jealousy capable of discoloring every object.

Strong evidence of some traits of this character, is to be found in a Journal of Mr. ADAMS, which was sent by the then Secretary of Foreign Affairs to Congress. The reading of this Journal, extremely embarrassed his friends, especially the delegates of Massachusetts; who, more than once, interrupted it, and at last, succeeded in putting a stop to it, on the suggestion that it bore the marks of a private and confidential paper, which, by some mistake, had gotten into its present situation, and never could have been designed as a public document for the inspection of Congress. The good humor of that body yielded to the suggestion.

The particulars of this Journal cannot be expected to have remained in my memory—but I recollect one which may serve as a sample. Being among the guests invited to dine with the Count de Vergennes, Minister for Foreign Affairs, Mr. ADAMS thought fit to give a specimen of American politeness, by conducting Madame de Vergennes to dinner; in the way, she was pleased to make retribution in the current coin of French politeness—by saying to him, *"Monsieur Adams, vous etes le* WASHINGTON *de negociation."** Stating the incident, he makes this comment upon it: "These people have a very pretty knack of paying compliments." He might have added, they have also a very dexterous knack of disguising a sarcasm.

This opinion, however, which I have avowed, did not prevent my entering cordially into the plan of supporting Mr. ADAMS for the office of Vice-President, under the new Constitution. I still thought that he had high claims upon the public gratitude, and possessed a substantial worth of character, which might atone for some great defects. In addition to this, it was well known, that he was a favorite of New-England, and it was obvious that his union with General WASHINGTON would tend to give the government, in its outset, all the strength which it could derive from the character of the two principal magistrates.

But it was deemed an essential point of caution to take care, that accident or an intrigue of the opposers of the Government, should not raise Mr. ADAMS, instead of General WASHINGTON, to the first place. This, every friend of the Government would have considered as a disastrous event; as well because it would have displayed a capricious operation of the system in elevating to the first station, a man intended for the second; as because it was conceived that the incomparably superior weight and transcendant popularity of Gen. WASHINGTON, rendered his presence at the head of the Government, in its first organization, a matter of primary and indispensable importance. It was therefore agreed that a few votes should be diverted from Mr. ADAMS to other persons, so as to insure to General WASHINGTON a plurality.

*Mr. Adams, you are the WASHINGTON of negociation.

Great was my astonishment, and equally great my regret, when, afterwards, I learned from persons of unquestionable veracity, that Mr. ADAMS had complained of unfair treatment, in not having been permitted to take an equal chance with General WASHINGTON, by leaving the votes to an uninfluenced current.

The extreme egotism of the temper, which could blind a man to considerations so obvious as those that had recommended the course pursued, cannot be enforced by my comment. It exceeded all that I had imagined, and shewed, in too strong a light, that the vanity which I have ascribed to him, existed to a degree that rendered it more than a harmless foible.

Mr. ADAMS was elected Vice-President. His public conduct, in that station, was satisfactory to the friends of the Government, though they were now and then alarmed by appearances of some eccentric tendencies.

It is, in particular, a tribute due from me, to acknowledge, that Mr. ADAMS, being in quality of Vice-President, *ex officio*, one of the Trustees of the Sinking Fund, I experienced from him the most complete support; which was the more gratifying to me, as I had to struggle against the systematic opposition of Mr. JEFFERSON, seconded occasionally by Mr. RANDOLPH. Though it would be an ill compliment to Mr. ADAMS, not to presume that the support which he gave me, was the dictate of his sense of the public interest; yet, so cordial and useful a co-operation, at a moment when I was assailed with all the weapons of party rancor, won from me an unfeigned return of the most amicable sentiments.

I lost no opportunity of combating the prejudices industriously propagated against him by his political enemies; and, for a considerable time, went quite as far as candor would permit, to extenuate the failings which more and more alarmed and dissatisfied his friends.

The epoch at length arrived, when the retreat of General WASHINGTON made it necessary to fix upon a successor. By this time, men of principal influence in the Federal Party, whose situation had led them to an intimate acquaintance with Mr. ADAMS's character began to entertain serious doubts about his fitness for the station; yet, his pretensions, in several respects, were so strong, that after mature reflection, they thought it better to indulge their hopes than to listen to their fears. To this conclusion, the desire of preserving harmony in the Federal Party, was a weighty inducement. Accordingly it was determined to support Mr. ADAMS for the Chief Magistracy.

It was evidently of much consequence to endeavor to have an eminent Federalist Vice-President. Mr. THOMAS PINCKNEY, of South Carolina, was selected for this purpose. This gentleman, too little known in the North, had been all his life time distinguished in the South, for the mildness and amiableness of his manners, the rectitude and purity of his morals, and the soundness and correctness of his understanding, accompanied by a habitual discretion and self-command, which has often occasioned a parallel to be drawn between him and the venerated WASHINGTON. In addition to these recommendations, he had been, during a critical period, our Minister at the Court of London, and recently Envoy Extraordinary to the Court of Spain; and in both these trusts, he had acquitted himself to the satisfaction of all parties. With the Court of Spain he had effected a Treaty, which removed all the thorny subjects of contention, that had so long threatened the peace of the two countries, and stipulated for the United States, on their Southern frontier, and on the Mississippi, advantages of real magnitude and importance.

Well-informed men knew that the event of the Election was extremely problematical; and, while the friends of Mr. JEFFERSON predicted his success with sanguine confidence, his opposers feared that he might have at least an equal chance with any Federal Candidate.

To exclude him, was deemed, by the Federalists, a primary object. Those of them who possessed the best means of judging, were of opinion that it was far less important, whether Mr. ADAMS or Mr. PINCKNEY was the successful Candidate, than that Mr. JEFFERSON should not be the person; and on this principle, it was understood among them, that the two first mentioned gentlemen should be equally supported; leaving to casual accessions of votes in favor of the one or the other, to turn the scale between them.

In this plan I united with good faith; in the resolution, to which I scrupulously adhered, of giving to each Candidate an equal support. This was done, wherever my influence extended; as was more particularly manifested in the State of New-York, where all the Electors were my warm personal or political friends, and all gave a concurrent vote for the two Federal Candidates.

It is true that a faithful execution of this plan would have given Mr. PINCKNEY a somewhat better chance than Mr. ADAMS; nor shall it be concealed, that an issue favorable to the former would not have been disagreeable to me; as indeed I declared at the time, in the circles of my confidential friends.* My position was, that if chance should decide in favor of Mr. PINCKNEY, it probably would not be a misfortune; since he, to every essential qualification for the office, added a temper far more discreet and conciliatory than that of Mr. ADAMS.

This disposition, on my part, at that juncture, proves, at least, that my disapprobation of Mr. ADAMS has not originated in the disappointment, to which it has been uncandidly attributed. No private motive could then have entered into it. Not the least collision or misunderstanding had ever happened between that gentleman and myself—on the contrary, as I have already stated, I had reason individually to be pleased with him.

No: The considerations which had reconciled me to the success of Mr. PINCKNEY, were of a nature exclusively public. They resulted from the disgusting egotism, the distempered jealousy, and the ungovernable indiscretion of Mr. ADAMS's temper, joined to some doubts of the correctness of his maxims of Administration. Though in matters of Finance he had acted with the Federal Party; yet he had, more than once, broached theories at variance with his practice. And in conversation, he repeatedly made excursions in the field of foreign politics, which alarmed the friends of the prevailing system.

The plan of giving equal support to the two Federalist Candidates, was not pursued. Personal attachment for Mr.

*I appeal particularly to Lt. Governor VAN RENSSELAER and R. TROUP, Esq.

ADAMS, especially in the New-England States, caused a number of the votes to be withheld from Mr. PINCKNEY, and thrown away. The result was, that Mr. ADAMS was elected President by a majority of two votes, and Mr. JEFFERSON Vice-President.

This issue demonstrated the wisdom of the plan which had been abandoned, and how greatly, in departing from it, the cause had been sacrificed to the man. But for a sort of miracle, the departure would have made Mr. JEFFERSON President. In each of the States of Pennsylvania, Virginia and North-Carolina, Mr. ADAMS had one vote. In the two latter States, the one vote was as much against the stream of popular prejudice, as it was against the opinions of the other Electors. The firmness of the individuals who separated from their colleagues, was so extraordinary, as to have been contrary to all probable calculation. Had only one of them thrown his vote into the other scale, there would have been an equality, and no election. Had two done it, the choice would have fallen upon Mr. JEFFERSON.

No one, sincere in the opinion that this gentleman was an ineligible and dangerous Candidate, can hesitate in pronouncing, that in dropping Mr. PINCKNEY, too much was put at hazard; and that those who promoted the other course, acted with prudence and propriety.

It is a fact, which ought not to be forgotten, that Mr. ADAMS, who had evinced discontent, because he had not been permitted to take an equal chance with General WASHINGTON, was enraged with all those who had thought that Mr. PINCKNEY ought to have had an equal chance with him. But in this there is perfect consistency. The same turn of temper is the solution of the displeasure in both cases.

It is to this circumstance of the equal support of Mr. PINCKNEY, that we are in a great measure to refer the serious scism which has since grown up in the Federal Party.

Mr. ADAMS never could forgive the men who had been engaged in the plan; though it embraced some of his most partial admirers. He has discovered bitter animosity against several of them. Against me, his rage has been so vehement, as to have caused him more than once, to forget the decorum, which, in his situation, ought to have been an inviolable law. It will not

appear an exaggeration to those who have studied his character, to suppose that he is capable of being alienated from a system to which he has been attached, because it is upheld by men
whom he hates. How large a share this may have had in some
recent aberrations, cannot easily be determined.

Occurrences which have either happened or come to light
since the election of Mr. ADAMS to the Presidency, confirming my unfavorable forebodings of his character, have given
new and decisive energy, in my mind, to the sentiment of his
unfitness for the station.

The letter which has just appeared in the public prints,
written by him, while Vice-President, to TENCH COXE, is of
itself conclusive evidence of the justness of this sentiment. It
is impossible to speak of this transaction in terms suited to its
nature, without losing sight that Mr. ADAMS is the President
of the United States.

This letter avows the *suspicion*, that the appointment of Mr.
PINCKNEY to the Court of London, had been procured or
promoted by British Influence. And considering the parade
with which the story of the Duke of Leeds is told, it is fair to
consider that circumstance as the principal, if not the sole,
ground of the odious and degrading suspicion.

Let any man of candor or knowledge of the world, pronounce on this species of evidence.

It happened unfortunately for the PINCKNEYS, that, while
boys, and long before our revolution, they went to school
with a British Duke, who was afterwards Minister of the
British Government for the foreign department. This indiscreet Duke, perhaps for no better reason than the desire of
saying something to a parting American Minister, and the
want of something better to say, divulges to him the dangerous secret, that the two PINCKNEYS had been his class-mates,
and goes the alarming length of making enquiry about their
health. From this, it is sagaciously inferred, that these gentlemen have *"many powerful old friends in England;"* and from
this again, that the Duke of Leeds (of course of the number
of these old friends) had procured by intrigue the appointment of one of his class-mates to the Court of London; or, in
the language of the letter, that much British influence had
been exerted in the appointment.

In the school of jealousy, stimulated by ill-will, logic like this may pass for substantial; but what is it in the school of reason and justice?

Though this contaminating connection of the PINCKNEYS with the Duke of Leeds, in their juvenile years, did not hinder them from fighting for the independence of their native country throughout our revolution; yet the supposition is, that the instant the war was terminated, it transformed them from the soldiers of liberty into the tools of the British Monarchy.

But the hostility of the PINCKNEYS to Mr. ADAMS, evidenced by their "long intrigue" against him, of which he speaks in the letter, is perhaps intended as a still stronger proof of their devotion to Great-Britain—the argument may be thus understood: Mr. ADAMS is the bulwark of his country against foreign influence. The batteries of every foreign power, desirous of acquiring an ascendant in our affairs, are of consequence always open against him—and, the presumption therefore must be, that every citizen who is his enemy, is the confederate of one or another of those foreign powers.

Let us, without contesting this argument of self-love, examine into the facts upon which its applicability must depend.

The evidence of "the long intrigue" seems to be, that the family of the PINCKNEY's contributed to limit the duration of Mr. ADAMS's commission to the Court of London to the term of three years, in order to make way for some of themselves to succeed him. This, it must be confessed, was a long-sighted calculation in a government like ours.

A summary of the transaction, will be the best comment on the inference which has been drawn.

The resolution of Congress by which Mr. ADAMS's commission was limited, was a general one, applying to the Commissions of all Ministers to foreign Courts. When it was proposed and adopted, it is certain that neither of the two PINCKNEY's was a member of Congress; and it is believed that they were both at Charleston, in South Carolina, their usual place of abode, more than eight hundred miles distant from the seat of Government.

But they had, it seems, a *cousin*, Mr. CHARLES PINCKNEY, who was in Congress; and this cousin it was who moved the restrictive resolution. Let us enquire who seconded and who voted for it.

It was seconded by Mr. HOWELL, a member from Rhode Island, *the very person who nominated Mr. Adams as Minister to Great-Britain*, and was voted for by the four Eastern States, with New-York, New-Jersey, Maryland and South Carolina. Mr. GERRY, always a zealous partisan of Mr. ADAMS, was among the supporters of the resolution. To make out this to be a machination of the two PINCKNEYS, many things must be affirmed: First, that their cousin CHARLES is always subservient to their views (which would equally prove that they have long been, and still are, opposers of the Federal Administration:)—Second, that this cunning wight had been able to draw the *four Eastern States* into his plot, as well as New-York, New-Jersey, Maryland, and South-Carolina:—Third, that the PINCKNEYS could foresee, at the distance of three years, the existence of a state of things which would enable them to reap the fruit of their contrivance.

Would not the circumstances better warrant the suspicion that the resolution was a contrivance of the friends of Mr. ADAMS, to facilitate in some way his election, and that Mr. PINCKNEY was their coadjutor, rather than their prompter?

But the truth most probably is, that the measure was a mere precaution to bring under frequent review the propriety of continuing a Minister at a particular Court, and to facilitate the removal of a disagreeable one, without the harshness of formally displacing him. In a policy of this sort, the cautious maxims of New-England would very naturally have taken a lead.

Thus in the very grounds of the suspicion, as far as they appear, we find its refutation. The complete futility of it will now be illustrated by additional circumstances.

It is a fact, that the rigor with which the war was prosecuted by the British armies in our Southern quarter, had produced among the friends of our Revolution there, more animosity against the British Government, than in the other parts of the United States: and it is a matter of notoriety, in the same quarter, that this disposition was conspicuous among the PINCKNEYS, and their connections. It may be added, that they were likewise known to have been attached to the French Revolution, and to have continued so, till long after the appointment of Mr. THOMAS PINCKNEY to the Court of London.

These propensities of the gentlemen, were certainly not such as to make them favorites of Great-Britain, or the appointment of one of them to that Court, an object of particular solicitude.

As far as appeared at the time, the idea of nominating Mr. THOMAS PINCKNEY, originated with the then President himself: but whatever may have been its source, it is certain that it met the approbation of the whole Administration, Mr. JEFFERSON included. This fact alone, will go far to refute the surmise of a British agency in the appointment.

Supposing, that, contrary to all probability, Great-Britain had really taken some unaccountable fancy for Mr. PINCKNEY, upon whom was her influence exerted?

Had the virtuous, circumspect *Washington* been ensnared in her insidious toils? Had she found means for once to soften the stern, inflexible hostility of JEFFERSON? Had RANDOLPH been won by her meretricious caresses? Had KNOX, the uniform friend of Mr. ADAMS, been corrupted by her seducing wiles? Or was it all the dark work of the *alien* Secretary of the Treasury? Was it this arch juggler, who debauched the principles, or transformed the prejudices, of Mr. PINCKNEY; who persuaded the British Government to adopt him as a pliant instrument; who artfully induced the President to propose him as of his own selection; who lulled the zealous vigilance of JEFFERSON and RANDOLF, and surprised the unsuspecting friends of KNOX?

But when the thing had been accomplished, no matter by what means, it was surely to have been expected that the man of its choice would have been treated at the Court of London with distinguished regard, and that his conduct towards that Court would have been marked, if not by some improper compliances, at least by some displays of extraordinary complaisance.

Yet, strange as it may appear, upon Mr. ADAMS's hypothesis, it might be proved, if requisite, that neither the one nor the other took place. It might be proved that, far from Mr. PINCKNEY's having experienced any flattering distinctions, incidents not pleasant to his feelings, had occurred, and that in the discharge of his official functions, he had advanced pretensions in favor of the United States, from which, with the approbation of the then Secretary of State, Mr. JEFFERSON, he was instructed to desist.

What will Mr. ADAMS or his friends reply to all these facts? How will he be excused for indulging and declaring, on grounds so frivolous, a suspicion so derogatory, of a man so meritorious—of a man who has acted in a manner so unexceptionable?

But a more serious question remains: How will Mr. ADAMS answer to the Government and to his Country, for having thus wantonly given the sanction of his opinion to the worst of the aspersions which the enemies of the Administration have impudently thrown upon it? Can we be surprised that such a torrent of slander was poured out against it, when a man, the second in official rank, the second in the favor of the friends of the Government, stooped to become himself one of its calumniators? It is peculiarly unlucky for Mr. ADAMS in this affair, that he is known to have desired, at the time, the appointment which was given to Mr. PINCKNEY. The President declined the measure, thinking that it was compatible neither with the spirit of the constitution nor with the dignity of the Government, to designate the Vice-President to such a station.

This letter, better than volumes, developes the true, the unfortunate character of Mr. ADAMS.

The remaining causes of dissatisfaction with him respect his conduct in the office of President; which, in my opinion, has been a heterogeneous compound of right and wrong, of wisdom and error.

The outset was distinguished by a speech which his friends lamented as temporising. It had the air of a lure for the favor of his opponents at the expense of his sincerity; but being of an equivocal complexion, to which no precise design can be annexed, it is barely mentioned as a circumstance, which, in conjunction with others of a more positive tint, may serve to explain character.

It is in regard to our foreign relations, that the public measures of Mr. ADAMS first attract criticism.

It will be recollected that General PINCKNEY, the brother of THOMAS, and the gentleman now supported together with Mr. ADAMS, had been deputed by President WASHINGTON, as successor to Mr. MONROE, and had been refused to be received by the French Government in his quality of Minister Plenipotentiary.

This, among those of the well-informed, who felt a just sensibility for the honor of their country, excited much disgust and resentment. But the Opposition-Party, ever too ready to justify the French Government at the expense of their own, vindicated or apologized for the ill treatment: and the mass of the community, though displeased with it, did not appear to feel the full force of the indignity.

As a final effort for accommodation, and as a mean, in case of failure, of enlightening and combining public opinion, it was resolved to make another, and a more solemn, experiment, in the form of a commission of three.

This measure (with some objections to the detail) was approved by all parties; by the Antifederalists, because they thought no evil so great as the rupture with France; by the Federalists, because it was their system to avoid war with every power, if it could be done without the sacrifice of essential interests or absolute humiliation.

Even such of them who conceived that the insults of the French Government, and the manifestation of its ill will, had already gone far enough to call for measures of vigor; perceiving that the nation was not generally penetrated with the same conviction, and would not support with zeal measures of that nature, unless their necessity was rendered still more apparent, acquiesced in the expediency of another mission. They hoped that it would serve either to compose the differences which existed, or to make the necessity of resistance to the violence of France, palpable to every good citizen.

The expediency of the step was suggested to Mr. ADAMS, through a Federal channel, a considerable time before he determined to take it. He hesitated whether it could be done after the rejection of General PINCKNEY, without national debasement. The doubt was an honorable one; it was afterwards very properly surrendered to the cogent reasons which pleaded for a further experiment.

The event of this experiment is fresh in our recollection. Our Envoys, like our Minister, were rejected. Tribute was demanded as a preliminary to negociation. To their immortal honor, though France at the time was proudly triumphant, they repelled the disgraceful pretension. Americans will never forget that General PINCKNEY was a member, and an efficient member, of this Commission.

This conduct of the French Government, in which it is difficult to say, whether despotic insolence or unblushing corruption was most prominent, electrified the American people with a becoming indignation. In vain the partisans of France attempted to extenuate. The public voice was distinct and audible. The nation, disdaining so foul an overture, was ready to encounter the worst consequences of resistance.

Without imitating the flatterers of Mr. ADAMS, who, in derogation from the intrinsic force of circumstances, and from the magnanimity of the nation, ascribe to him the whole merits of producing the spirit which appeared in the community, it shall with cheerfulness be acknowledged, that he took upon the occasion a manly and courageous lead—that he did all in his power to rouse the pride of the nation—to inspire it with a just sense of the injuries and outrages which it had experienced, and to dispose it to a firm and magnanimous resistance; and that his efforts contributed materially to the end.

The friends of the Government were not agreed as to ulterior measures. Some were for immediate and unqualified war; others for a more mitigated course; the dissolution of treaties, preparation of force by land and sea, partial hostilities of a defensive tendency; leaving to France the option of seeking accommodation, or proceeding to open war. The latter course prevailed.

Though not as bold and energetic as the other; yet, considering the prosperous state of French affairs, when it was adopted, and how many nations had been appalled and prostrated by the French Power—the conduct pursued bore sufficiently the marks of courage and elevation to raise the national character to an exalted height throughout Europe.

Much is it to be deplored that we should have been precipitated from this proud eminence without necesity, without temptation.

The latter conduct of the President forms a painful contrast to his commencement. Its effects have been directly the reverse. It has sunk the tone of the public mind—it has impaired the confidence of the friends of the Government in the Executive Chief—it has distracted public opinion—it has unnerved the public councils—it has sown the seeds of discord at home, and lowered the reputation of the Government abroad. The circumstances which preceded, aggravate the disagreeableness of the results. They prove that the injudicious things which have been acted, were not the effects of any regular plan, but the fortuitous emanations of momentary impulses.

The session, which ensued the promulgation of the dispatches of our Commissioners, was about to commence. Mr. ADAMS arrived at Philadelphia from his seat at Quincy. The tone of his mind seemed to have been raised, rather than depressed.

It was suggested to him, that it might be expedient to insert in his Speech to Congress, a sentiment of this import: That after the repeatedly rejected advances of this country, its dignity required that it should be left with France in future to make the first overture; that if, desirous of reconciliation, she should evince the disposition by sending a Minister to this Government, he would be received with the respect due to his character, and treated with in the frankness of a sincere desire of accommodation.

The suggestion was received in a manner both indignant and intemperate.

Mr. Adams declared as a sentiment which he had adopted on mature reflection: *That if France should send a Minister tomorrow, he would order him back the day after.*

So imprudent an idea was easily refuted. Little argument was requisite to shew that by a similar system of retaliation, when one Government in a particular instance had refused the Envoy of another, nations might entail upon each other perpetual hostility; mutually barring the avenues of explanation.

In less than forty-eight hours from this extraordinary sally, the mind of Mr. Adams underwent a total revolution—he resolved not only to insert in his speech the sentiment which had been proposed to him, but to go farther, and to declare, that if France would give explicit assurances of receiving a Minister from this country, with due respect, he would send one.

In vain was this extension of the sentiment opposed by all his Ministers, as being equally incompatible with good policy, and with the dignity of the nation—he obstinately persisted, and the pernicious declaration was introduced.

I call it pernicious, because it was the ground-work of the false steps which have succeeded.

The declaration recommended to the President was a prudent one.

The measures of Congress, by their mitigated form, shewed that an eye had been still kept upon pacification. A numerous party were averse from war with France at any rate. In the rest of the community, a strong preference of honorable accommodation to final rupture was discernible, even amidst the effusions of resentment.

The charges which we had exhibited in the face of the world against the French Government, were of a high and disgraceful complexion; they had been urged with much point and emphasis.

To give an opening to France, to make conciliatory propositions, some salve for her pride was necessary. It was also necessary she should be assured that she would not expose herself to an affront by a refusal to receive the agent whom she might employ for that purpose. The declaration proposed fulfilled both objects.

It was likely to have another important advantage. It would be a new proof to the American people of the moderate and pacific temper of their Government; which would tend to preserve their confidence, and to dispose them more and more to meet inevitable extremities with fortitude and without murmurs.

But the supplement to the declaration was a blameable excess. It was more than sufficient for the ends to be answered. It waved the point of honor, which, after two rejections of our Ministers, required that the next Mission between the two countries, should proceed from France. After the mortifying humiliations we had endured, the national dignity demanded that this point should not be departed from without necessity. No such necessity could be pretended to exist: moreover, another mission by us would naturally be regarded as evidence of a disposition on our part to purchase the friendship of revolutionary France, even at the expense of honor; an impression which could hardly fail to injure our interests with other countries: and the measure would involve the further inconvenience of transferring the negociation from this country, where our government could regulate it according to its own view of exigencies, to France, where that advantage would be enjoyed by her Government, and where the power of judging for us must be delegated to Commissioners; who, acting under immense individual responsibility, at a distance too great for consultation, would be apt to act with hesitancy and irresolution, whether the policy of the case required concession or firmness. This was to place it too much in the power of France to manage the progress of the negociation according to events.

It has been said that Paris was wisely preferred as the place of negociation, because it served to avoid the caballings of a French Minister in this country. But there is not enough in this argument to counterbalance the weighty considerations on the other side. The intrigues of GENET and his successors were perplexing to the Government, chiefly because they were too well seconded by the prepossessions of the people. The great alteration in public opinion, had put it completely in the power of our Executive to controul the machinations of any future public Agent of France. It ought also to be remembered, that if France has not known agents, she never will be without secret ones, and that her partisans among our citizens, can much better promote her cause, than any Agents she can send. In fact, her Agents, by their blunders, were in the event rather useful than pernicious to our affairs.

But is it likely that France would have sent a minister to this country? When we find, that from calculations of policy she could brook the ignominy which the publication of the dispatches of our commissioners was calculated to bring upon her; and stifling her resentment, could invite the renewal of negociation; what room can there be to doubt, that the same calculations would have induced her to send a minister to this country when an opening was given for it?

The French minister for foreign relations, through the French Diplomatic Agent at the Hague, had opened a communication with Mr. MURRAY, our Resident there, for the purpose of reviving negociation between the two countries. In this manner, assurances were given that France was disposed to treat, and that a Minister from us would be received and accredited. But they were accompanied with intimations of the characters proper to be employed, and who would be likely to succeed; which was exceptionable, both as it savored of the pretension (justly censured by the President himself) of prescribing to other Governments how they were to manage their own affairs; and as it might, according to circumstances, be construed into a tacit condition of the promise to receive a Minister. Overtures so circuitous and informal, through a person who was not the regular organ of the French government for making them, to a person who was not the regular organ of the American government for receiving them, might be a very fit mode of preparing the way for the like overtures in a more authentic and obligatory shape: But they were a very inadequate basis for the institution of a new Mission.

When the President pledged himself in his speech to send a minister, if satisfactory assurances of a proper reception were given, he must have been understood to mean such as were direct and official, not such as were both informal and destitute of a competent sanction.

Yet upon this loose and vague foundation, Mr. ADAMS precipitately nominated Mr. MURRAY as Envoy to the French Republic, without previous consultation with any of his Ministers. The nomination itself was to each of them, even to the Secretary of State, his Constitutional Counsellor, in similar affairs, the first notice of the project.

Thus was the measure wrong, both as to mode and substance.

A President is not bound to conform to the advice of his Ministers. He is even under no positive injunction to ask or require it. But the Constitution presumes that he will consult them; and the genius of our government and the public good recommend the practice.

As the President nominates his Ministers, and may displace them when he pleases, it must be his own fault if he be not surrounded by men, who for ability and integrity deserve his confidence. And if his ministers are of this character, the consulting of them will always be likely to be useful to himself and to the State. Let it even be supposed that he is a man of talents superior to the collected talents of all his ministers, (which can seldom happen, as the world has seen but few FREDERICKS) he may, nevertheless, often assist his judgment by a comparison and collision of ideas. The greatest genius, hurried away by the rapidity of its own conceptions, will occasionally overlook obstacles which ordinary and more phlegmatic men will discover, and which, when presented to his consideration, will be thought by himself decisive objections to his plans.

When, unhappily, an ordinary man dreams himself to be a FREDERICK, and through vanity refrains from counselling with his constitutional advisers, he is very apt to fall into the hands of miserable intriguers, with whom his self-love is more at ease, and who without difficulty slide into his confidence, and by flattery, govern him.

The ablest men may profit by advice. Inferior men cannot dispense with it; and if they do not get it through legitimate channels, it will find its way to them, through such as are clandestine and impure.

Very different from the practice of Mr. ADAMS was that of the modest and sage WASHINGTON. He consulted much, pondered much, resolved slowly, resolved surely.

And as surely, Mr. ADAMS might have benefited by the advice of his ministers.

The stately system of not consulting Ministers is likely to have a further disadvantage. It will tend to exclude from places of primary trust, the men most fit to occupy them.

Few and feeble are the interested inducements to accept a place in our Administration. Far from being lucrative, there is not one which will not involve pecuniary sacrifice to every *honest* man of preeminent talents. And has not experience shewn, that he must be fortunate indeed, if even the successful execution of his task can secure to him consideration and fame? Of a large harvest of obloquy he is sure.

If excluded from the counsels of the Executive Chief, his office must become truly insignificant. What able and virtuous man will long consent to be so miserable a pageant?

Every thing that tends to banish from the Administration able men, tends to diminish the chances of able counsels. The probable operation of a system of this kind, must be to consign places of the highest trust to incapable honest men, whose inducement will be a livelihood, or to capable dishonest men, who will seek indirect indemnifications for the deficiency of direct and fair inducements.

The precipitate nomination of Mr. MURRAY, brought Mr. ADAMS into an aukward predicament.

He found it necessary to change his plan in its progress, and instead of one, to nominate three Envoys, and to superadd a promise, that, though appointed, they should not leave the United States till further and more perfect assurances were given by the French Government.

This remodification of the measure was a virtual acknowledgment that it had been premature. How unseemly was this fluctuation in the Executive Chief. It argued either instability of views, or want of sufficient consideration beforehand. The one or the other, in an affair of so great moment, is a serious reproach.

Additional and more competent assurances were received; but before the Envoys departed, intelligence arrived of a new Revolution in the French Government; which, in violation of the Constitution, had expelled two of the Directory.

Another Revolution: Another Constitution overthrown: Surely here was reason for a pause, at least till it was ascertained that the new Directory would adhere to the engagement of its predecessors, and would not send back our Envoys with disgrace.

In the then posture of French affairs, which externally as well as internally, were unprosperous, a pause was every way prudent. The recent Revolution was a valid motive for it.

Definitive compacts between nations, called real Treaties, are binding, notwithstanding Revolutions of Governments. But to apply the maxim to Ministerial acts, preparatory only to negociation, is to extend it too far; to apply it to such acts of an unstable revolutionary Government (like that of France at that time) is to abuse it.

Had any policy of the moment demanded it, it would have been not at all surprising to have seen the new Directory disavowing the assurance which had been given, and imputing it as a crime to the Ex-Directors, on the pretence that they had prostrated the dignity of the Republic by courting the renewal of negociation with a government, which had so grossly insulted it.

Yet our Envoys were dispatched without a ratification of the assurance by the new Directory, at the hazard of the interests and the honor of the country.

Again, the dangerous and degrading system of not consulting Ministers, was acted upon.

When the news of the Revolution in the Directory arrived, Mr. Adams was at his seat in Massachusetts. His Ministers addressed to him a joint letter, communicating the intelligence, and submitting to his consideration, whether that event ought not to suspend the projected mission. In a letter which he afterwards wrote from the same place, he directed the preparation of a draft of instructions for the Envoys, and intimated that their departure would be suspended *for some time*.

Shortly after he came to Trenton, where he adjusted with his Ministers the tenor of the instructions to be given; but he observed a profound silence on the question, whether it was expedient that the Mission should proceed. The morning after the instructions were settled, he signified to the Secretary of State that the Envoys were immediately to depart.

He is reported to have assigned as the reason of his silence, that he knew the opinions of his Ministers from their letter; that he had irrevocably adopted an opposite one; and that he deemed it most delicate not to embarrass them by a useless discussion.

But would it not have been more prudent to have kept his judgment in some degree in suspense, till after an interview and discussion with his Ministers? Ought he to have taken it for granted that the grounds of his opinion were so infallible, that there was no possibility of arguments being used which were sufficient to shake them? Ought he not to have recollected the sudden revolution which his judgment had undergone in the beginning of the business, and to have inferred from this, that it might have yielded in another instance to better lights? Was it necessary for him, if he had had a conference with his ministers, to have alarmed their delicacy, by prefacing the discussion with a declaration that he had fixed an unalterable opinion? Did not the intimation respecting a suspension of the departure of the Envoys, imply that this would continue till there was a change of circumstances? Was it not a circumstance to strengthen expectation in the Ministers, when consulted about the instructions, that they would be heard as to the principal point, previous to a definitive resolution?

Giving Mr. ADAMS credit for sincerity, the desolutoriness of his mind is evinced by the very different grounds upon which, at different times, he has defended the propriety of the mission.

Sometimes he has treated with ridicule the idea of its being a measure which would terminate in peace; asserting that France would not accommodate, on terms admissible by the United States, and that the effect to be expected from the mission, was the demonstration of this truth, and the union of public opinion on the necessity of war.

Sometimes, and most frequently, he has vindicated the measure as one conformable with the general and strong wish of the country for peace, and as likely to promote that desirable object.

It is now earnestly to be hoped, that the final issue, of the Mission, in an honorable accommodation, may compensate for the sacrifice of consistency, dignity, harmony and reputation, at which it has been undertaken.

But even in relation to the adjustment of differences with the French Republic, the measure was injudicious. It was probable that it would delay, rather than accelerate, such an adjustment.

The situation of French affairs, at the time of the overtures for renewing the negociation, coincides with the solicitude which was manifested for that object, to render it likely that, at this juncture, France really desired accommodation. If this was so, it is presumeable (as observed in another place) that, had not the declaration about sending a Minister to her intervened, she would have sent one to us, with adequate powers and instructions. Towards a Minister here, our Government might have acted such a part as would have hastened a conclusion; and the Minister, conforming to the impressions of his

Government when he was sent, it is not improbable that a desirable arrangement might sometime since have been effected.

Instead of this, the mode pursued, naturally tended to delay. A lapse of time, by changing the circumstances, is very apt to change the views of Governments. The French Agents, charged with the negociation at Paris, could find little difficulty in protracting it till events (such as the fate of a campaign) should be ascertained, as a guide to rise or fall in their pretensions. And in this way, obstacles might supervene, which would not have existed in the beginning, and which might render accommodation impracticable—or practicable only on terms injurious to our interests.

Thus, on every just calculation, whatever may be the issue, the measure, in reference either to our internal or foreign affairs, even to our concerns with France herself, was alike impolitic.

It is sometimes defended by the argument, that when our Commissioners departed, there were circumstances in the position of Europe which made a general peace during the succeeding winter probable, and that it would have been dangerous for this country, remote as it is from Europe, to have been without agents on the spot authorized to settle its controversy with France, at the same epoch. The country, it is said, might otherwise have been left in the perilous situation of having a subsisting quarrel with France, after she had disembarrassed herself of all her European enemies.

The idea that a general peace was likely to happen during that winter, was, I know, entertained by Mr. ADAMS himself; for, in a casual conversation at Trenton, he expressed it to me, and I supported a different opinion. But waving now a discussion of the point, and admitting that the expectation was entertained on substantial grounds, though it has not been verified by experience, still the argument derived from it is not valid.

The expediency of the measure must be tested by the state of things when it had its inception. At the time the foundation was laid for it by the speech, when even the nomination of Mr. MURRAY took place, the affairs of France and of her enemies, portended a result very inauspicious to her, and very different from that of a general peace, on conditions which

LETTER CONCERNING JOHN ADAMS 959

would leave her the inclination or the power to prosecute hostilities against this country.

But even on the supposition of other prospects, Mr. ADAMS had the option of a substitute far preferable to the expedient which he chose.

He might secretly and confidentially have nominated one or more of our Ministers actually abroad for the purpose of treating with France; with *eventual* instructions predicated upon appearances of an approaching peace.

An expedient of this sort, merely provisionary, could have had none of the bad effects of the other. If the secret was kept, it could have had no inconvenient consequences; if divulged, it would have been deemed here and elsewhere, a prudent precaution only, recommended by the distant situation of the country, to meet future casualties, with which we might otherwise not have been able to keep pace. To the enemies of France, it could have given no ill impression of us; to France, no motive to forbear other conciliatory means, for one and the same reason, namely, because the operation was to be eventual.

There are some collateral incidents connected with this business of the Mission, which it may not be useless to mention, as they will serve still farther to illustrate the extreme propensity of Mr. ADAMS's temper to jealousy.

It happened that I arrived at Trenton a short time before the President—Chief Justice ELSWORTH a short time after him. This was considered as evidence of a combination between the heads of Departments, the Chief Justice and myself, to endeavor to influence or counteract him in the affair of the Mission.

The truth, nevertheless, most certainly is, that I went to Trenton with General WILKINSON, pursuant to a preconcert with him of some weeks standing, to accelerate, by personal conferences with the Secretary of War, the adoption and execution of arrangements which had been planned between that General and myself, for the future disposition of the Western Army; that when I left New-York upon this journey, I had no expectation, whatever, that the President would come to Trenton, and that I did not stay at this place a day longer than was indispensable to the object I have stated. General

WILKINSON, if necessary, might be appealed to, not only as knowing that this was a real and sincere purpose of my journey, but as possessing satisfactory evidence, that in all probability, I had no anticipation of the movement of the President.

As to Chief Justice ELSWORTH, the design of his journey was understood to be to meet his colleague, Governor DAVY, at the seat of the Government, where they would be at the fountain head of information, and would obtain any lights or explanations which they might suppose useful. This was manifestly a very natural and innocent solution of the Chief Justice's visit, and I believe the true one.

Yet these simple occurrences were to the jealous mind of Mr. ADAMS, "confirmations strong," of some mischievous plot against his independence.

The circumstance, which next presents itself to examination, is the dismission of the two Secretaries, PICKERING and M'HENRY. This circumstance, it is known, occasioned much surprise, and a strong sensation to the disadvantage of Mr. ADAMS.

It happened at a peculiar juncture, immediately after the unfavorable turn of the election in New-York, and had much the air of an explosion of combustible materials which had been long prepared, but which had been kept down by prudential calculations respecting the effect of an explosion upon the friends of those Ministers in the State of New-York. Perhaps, when it was supposed that nothing could be lost in this quarter, and that something might be gained elsewhere by an atoning sacrifice of those Ministers, especially Mr. PICKERING, who had been for some time particularly odious to the opposition party, it was determined to proceed to extremities. This, as a mere conjecture, is offered for as much as it may be worth.

One fact, however, is understood to be admitted, namely, that neither of the dismissed Ministers had given any new or recent cause for their dismission.

A primary cause of the state of things which led to this event, is to be traced to the ungovernable temper of Mr. ADAMS. It is a fact that he is often liable to paroxysms of anger, which deprive him of self command, and produce very outrageous behaviour to those who approach him. Most, if not all his Ministers, and several distinguished Members of the two Houses of Congress, have been humiliated by the effects of these gusts of passion.

This violence, and the little consideration for them which was implied in declining to consult them, had occasioned great dryness between the President and his Ministers, except, I believe, the Secretary of the Navy.

The neglect was of course most poignant to Mr. PICKERING, because it had repeatedly operated in matters appertaining to his office. Nor was it in the disposition of this respectable man, justly tenacious of his own dignity and independence, to practise condescentions towards an imperious chief. Hence the breach constantly grew wider and wider, till a separation took place.

The manner of the dismission was abrupt and uncourteous; ill-suited to a man, who, in different stations, had merited so much from his country.

Admitting that when the President and his Minister had gotten into a situation thus unpleasant, a separation was unavoidable; still, as there was no surmise of misconduct, the case required a frank politeness, not an uncouth austerity.

But the remark most interesting in this particular, to the character of the President, is, that it was by his own fault that he was brought into a situation which might oblige him to displace a Minister, whose moral worth has his own suffrage, and whose abilities and services have that of the public.

The dismission of this Minister was preceded by a very curious circumstance. It was, without doubt, announced as a thing shortly to happen in an opposition circle, before any friend of the Government had the slightest suspicion of it. This circumstance, taken in connection with the period at which it happened, naturally provokes the conjecture that there may have been some collateral inducements to the step.

The dismission of the Secretary at War took place about the same time. It was declared in the sequel of a long conversation between the President and him, of a nature to excite alternately pain and laughter; pain, for the weak and excessive indiscretions of a Chief Magistrate of the United States; laughter at the ludicrous topics which constituted charges against this officer.

A prominent charge was, that the Secretary, in a Report to the House of Representatives, had *eulogized General Washington*, and had attempted to eulogize General *Hamilton*, which was adduced as one proof of a combination, in which the Secretary was engaged, to depreciate and injure him, the President.

Wonderful! passing Wonderful! that an Eulogy of the dead patriot and hero, of the admired and beloved WASHINGTON, consecrated in the affections and reverence of his country, should, in any shape, be irksome to the ears of his successor!

Singular, also, that an encomium on the officer, first in rank in the armies of the United States, appointed and continued by Mr. ADAMS, should in his eyes have been a crime in the head of the War Department, and that it should be necessary, in order to avert his displeasure, to obliterate a compliment to that officer from an official Report.

Another principal topic of accusation was, that the Secretary had, with the other Ministers, signed the joint letter, which had been addressed to the President respecting a suspension of the Mission to France. It was ostentatiously asked, how he or they should pretend to know any thing of *diplomatic affairs*; and it was plainly intimated that it was presumption in them to have intermeddled in such affairs.

A variety of things equally frivolous and *outré* passed. By way of episode, it fell to my lot to be distinguished by a torrent of gross personal abuse; and I was accused of having contributed to the loss of the election in New-York, out of ill will to Mr. ADAMS: a notable expedient truly for giving vent to my ill will. Who is so blind as not to see, that if actuated by such a motive, I should have preferred by the success of the election, to have secured the choice of electors for the State of New-York, who would have been likely to co-operate in the views by which I was governed?

To those who have not had opportunities of closely inspecting the weaknesses of Mr. ADAMS's character, the details of this extraordinary interview would appear incredible; but to those who have had these opportunities, they would not even furnish an occasion of surprise. But they would be, to all who knew their truth, irrefragable proofs of his unfitness for the station of Chief Magistrate.

Ill treatment of Mr. M'HENRY cannot fail to awaken the sympathy of every person well acquainted with him. Sensible, judicious, well-informed, of an integrity never questioned, of a temper, which, though firm in the support of principles, has too much moderation and amenity to offend by the manner of doing it—I dare pronounce that he never gave Mr. ADAMS cause to treat him, as he did, with unkindness. If Mr. ADAMS thought that his execution of his office indicated a want of the peculiar qualifications required for it, he might have said so with gentleness, and he would have only exercised a prerogative entrusted to him by the Constitution, to which no blame could have attached; but it was unjustifiable to aggravate the deprivation of office by humiliating censures and bitter reproaches.

The last material occurrence in the administration of Mr. ADAMS, of which I shall take notice, is the pardon of *Fries,* and other principals in the late insurrection in Pennsylvania.

It is a fact that a very refractory spirit has long existed in the Western Counties of that State. Repeatedly have its own laws been opposed with violence, and as often, according to my information, with impunity.

It is also a fact, which every body knows, that the laws of the Union, in the vital article of revenue, have been twice resisted in the same State by combinations so extensive, and under circumstances so violent, as to have called for the employment of military force; once under the former President, and once under the actual President; which together cost the United States nearly a million and a half of dollars

In the first instance it happened, that by the early submission of most of the leaders, upon an invitation of the government, few offenders of any consequence remained subject to prosecution. Of these, either from the humanity of the juries or some deficiency in the evidence, not one was capitally convicted. Two poor wretches only were sentenced to die, one of them little short of an ideot, the other a miserable follower in the hindmost train of rebellion, both beings so insignificant in all respects, that after the lenity shewn to the chiefs, justice would have worn the mien of ferocity, if she had raised her arm against them. The sentiment that their punishment ought to be remitted was universal; and the President, yielding to the special considerations, granted them pardons.

In the last instance, some of the most important of the offenders were capitally convicted—one of them by the verdicts of two successive juries. The general opinion of the friends of the Government demanded an example, as indispensable to its security.

The opinion was well founded. Two insurrections in the same State, the one upon the heels of the other, demonstrated a spirit of insubordination or disaffection which required a strong corrective. It is a disagreeable fact, forming a weighty argument in the question, that a large part of the population of Pennsylvania is of a composition which peculiarly fits it for the intrigues of factious men, who may desire to disturb or overthrow the Government. And it is an equally disagreeable fact, that disaffection to the national Government is in no other State more general, more deeply rooted, or more envenomed.

The late Governor Mifflin himself informed me that in the first case, insurrection had been organized down to the very liberties of Philadelphia, and that had not the Government anticipated it, a general explosion would speedily have ensued.

It ought to be added, that the impunity, so often experienced, had made it an article in the creed of those who were actuated by the insurgent spirit, that neither the General nor the State Government dared to inflict capital punishment.

To destroy this persuasion, to repress this dangerous spirit, it was essential that a salutary rigor should have been exerted, and that those who were under the influence of the one and the other should be taught that they were the dupes of a fatal illusion.

Of this, Mr. ADAMS appeared so sensible, that while the trials were pending, he more than once imprudently threw out, that the accused must found their hopes of escape either in their innocence or in the lenity of the juries; since from him, in case of conviction, they would have nothing to expect. And a very short time before he pardoned them, he declared (b) with no small ostentation, that the mistaken clemency of WASHINGTON on the former occasion, had been the cause of the second insurrection, and that he would take care there should not be a third, by giving the laws their full course against the convicted offenders.

Yet he thought proper, as if distrusting the courts and officers of the United States, to resort through the Attorney-General to the counsel of the culprits, for a statement of their cases; (c) in which was found, besides some objections of form, the novel doctrine, disavowed by every page of our law books, that treason does not consist of resistance by force to a public law; unless it be an act relative to the militia, or other military force.

And upon this, or upon some other ground, not easy to be comprehended, he of a sudden departed from all his former declarations, and against the unanimous advice of his Ministers, with the Attorney General, came to the resolution, which he executed, of pardoning all those who had received sentence of death.

No wonder that the public was thunderstruck at such a result—that the friends of the Government regarded it as a virtual deriliction—it was impossible to commit a greater error. The particular situation of Pennsylvania, the singular posture of human affairs, in which there is so strong a tendency to the disorganization of Government—the turbulent and malignant humors which exist, and are so industriously nourished throughout the United States; every thing loudly demanded that the Executive should have acted with exemplary vigor, and should have given a striking demonstration, that condign punishment would be the lot of the violent opposers of the laws.

The contrary course, which was pursued, is the most inexplicable part of Mr. ADAMS's conduct. It shews him so much at variance with himself, as well as with sound policy, that we are driven to seek a solution for it in some system of concession to his political enemies; a system the most fatal for himself, and for the cause of public order, of any that he could possibly devise. It is by temporisings like these, that men at the head of affairs, lose the respect both of friends and foes— it is by temporisings like these, that in times of fermentation and commotion, Governments are prostrated, which might easily have been upheld by an erect and imposing attitude.

(b) (c) Of these two facts, my evidence is inferior to that which supports the other allegations of this letter; yet it is so strong that I feel myself warranted to state them.

I have now gone through the principal circumstances in Mr. ADAMS's conduct, which have served to produce my disapprobation of him as Chief Magistrate. I pledge my veracity and honor, that I have stated none which are not either derived from my own knowledge, or from sources of information, in the highest degree, worthy of credit.

I freely submit it, Sir, to your judgment, whether the grounds of the opinion I have expressed, are not weighty; and whether they are not sufficient to exculpate those Federalists, who favor the equal support of Mr. PINCKNEY, from all blame, and myself in particular, from the unworthy imputation of being influenced by private resentment.

At the same time, I will admit, though it should detract from the force of my representations, that I have causes of personal dissatisfaction with Mr. ADAMS. It is not my practice to trouble others with my individual concerns; nor should I do it at present, but for the suggestions which have been made. Even with this incentive, I shall do it as little as possible.

The circumstances of my late military situation, have much less to do with my personal discontent than some others. In respect to them, I shall only say, that I owed my appointment to the station and rank I held, to the *express stipulation* of General Washington, when he accepted the command of the Army, afterwards *peremptorily insisted upon* by him, in *opposition* to the *strong wishes* of the President; and that, though second in rank, I was not promoted to the first place, when it became vacant, by the death of the Commander in Chief. As to the former, I should have had no cause to complain, if there had not been an apparent inconsistency in the measures of the President; if he had not nominated me first on the list of Major Generals, and attempted afterwards to place me third in rank. As to the latter, the Chief Command, not being a matter of routine, the not promoting me to it, cannot be deemed a wrong or injury; yet certainly I could not see, in the omission, any proof of good will or confidence—or of a disposition to console me for the persecutions which I had incessantly endured. But I dismiss the subject, leaving to others to judge of my pretensions to the promotion, and of the weight, if any, which they ought to have had with the President.

On other topics, my sensations are far less neutral. If, as I have been assured from respectable authorities, Mr. ADAMS has repeatedly indulged himself in virulent and indecent abuse of me; if he has denominated me a man destitute of every moral principle; if he has stigmatised me as the leader of a British Faction; then certainly I have right to think that I have been most cruelly and wickedly traduced; then have I right to appeal to all those who have been spectators of my public actions; to all who are acquainted with my private character, in its various relations, whether such treatment of me, by Mr. ADAMS, is of a nature to weaken or to strengthen his claim to the approbation of wise and good men; then will I so far yield to the consciousness of what I am, as to declare, that in the cardinal points of public and private rectitude, above all, in pure and disinterested zeal for the interests and service of this country—I shrink not from a comparison with any arrogant pretender to superior and exclusive merit.

Having been repeatedly informed, that Mr. ADAMS had delineated me as the leader of a British Faction, and having understood that his partisans, to counteract the influence of my opinion, were pressing the same charge against me, I wrote him a letter on the subject, dated the first of August last. No reply having been given by him to this letter, I, on the first of the present month, wrote him another; of both which letters I send you copies.

Of the purity of my public conduct in this, as in other particulars, I may defy the severest investigation.

Not only is it impossible for any man to give color to this absurd charge, by a particle of proof, or by any reasonable presumption; but I am able to shew, that my conduct has uniformly given the lie to it.

I never advised any connection* with Great-Britain, other than a commercial one; and in this I never advocated the giving to her any privilege or advantage which was not to be

---

*I mean a lasting connection. From what I recollect of the train of my ideas, it is possible I may at some time have suggested a *temporary* connection for the purpose of co-operating against France in the event of a definitive rupture; but of this I am not certain, as I well remember that the expediency of the measure was always problematical in my mind, and that I have occasionally discouraged it.

imparted to other nations. With regard to her pretensions as a belligerent power in relation to neutrals, my opinions, while in the Administration, to the best of my recollection, coincided with those of Mr. JEFFERSON. When in the year 1793, her depredations on our commerce discovered a hostile spirit, I recommended one definitive effort to terminate differences by negociation, to be followed, if unsuccessful, by a declaration of war. I urged, in the most earnest manner, the friends of the Administration, in both houses of Congress, to prepare by sea and land for the alternative, to the utmost extent of our resources; and to an extent far exceeding what any member of either party was found willing to go. For this alternative, I became so firmly pledged to the friends and enemies of the Administration, and especially to the President of the United States, in writing as well as verbally, that I could not afterwards have retracted without a glaring and disgraceful inconsistency. And being thus pledged, I explicitly gave it as my opinion to Mr. JAY, Envoy to Great-Britain, that *"unless an adjustment of the differences with her could be effected on solid terms, it would be better to do nothing."* When the treaty arrived, it was not without full deliberation and some hesitation, that I resolved to support it. The articles relative to the settlement of differences were upon the whole satisfactory; but there were a few of the others which appeared to me of a different character. The article respecting contraband, though conformable with the general law of nations, was not in all its features such as could have been wished. The XXVth article, which gave asylum in our ports, under certain exceptions, to privateers with their prizes, was in itself an ineligible one, being of a nature to excite the discontent of nations against whom it should operate, and deriving its justification from the example before set of an equivalent stipulation in our Treaty with France. The XIIth article, was in my view inadmissible. The enlightened negociator, not unconscious that some parts of the Treaty were less well arranged than was to be desired, had himself hesitated to sign: but he had resigned his scruples to the conviction that nothing better could be effected, and that aggregately considered, the instrument would be advantageous to the United States. On my part, the result of mature reflection was, that as the subjects of controversy which had threatened the peace of the two nations, and which implicated great interests of this country, were in the essential points well adjusted, and as the other articles would expire in twelve years after the ratification of the Treaty, it would be wise and right to confirm the compact, with the exception of the XIIth article. Nevertheless, when an account was received that the British cruizers had seized provisions going to ports of the French dominions, not in fact blockaded or besieged, I advised the President to ratify the Treaty conditionally only, that is, with express instructions not to exchange ratifications, unless the British Government would disavow a construction of the instrument authorising the practice and would discontinue it.

After the rejection of Mr. PINCKNEY by the Government of France, immediately after the installment of Mr. ADAMS as President, and long before the measure was taken, I urged a member of Congress, then high in the confidence of the President, to propose to him the immediate appointment of three Commissioners, of whom Mr. *Jefferson*, or Mr. *Madison* to be one, to make another attempt to negociate. And when afterwards Commissioners were appointed, I expressly gave it as my opinion, that indemnification for spoliations, should not be a *sine qua non* of accommodation. In fine, I have been disposed to go greater lengths to avoid rupture with France than with Great-Britain; to make greater sacrifices for reconciliation with the former than with the latter.

In making this avowal, I owe it to my own character to say, that the disposition I have confessed, did not proceed from predilection for France (revolutionary France, after her early beginnings, has been always to me an object of horror) nor from the supposition that more was to be feared from France, as an enemy, than from Great-Britain, (I thought that the maritime power of the latter, could do us most mischief) but from the persuasion that the sentiments and prejudices of our country, would render war with France a more unmanageable business, than war with Great Britain.

Let any fair man pronounce, whether the circumstances which have been disclosed, bespeak the partisan of Great-Britain, or the man exclusively devoted to the interests of this country. Let any delicate man decide, whether it must not be shocking to an ingenuous mind, to have to combat a slander so vile, after having sacrificed the interests of his family, and devoted the best part of his life to the service of that country, in counsel and in the field.

It is time to conclude—The statement, which has been made, shews that Mr. ADAMS has committed some positive and serious errors of Administration; that in addition to these, he has certain fixed points of character which tend naturally to the detriment of any cause of which he is the chief, of any Administration of which he is the head; that by his ill humors and jealousies he has already divided and distracted the supporters of the Government; that he has furnished deadly weapons to its enemies by unfounded accusations, and has weakened the force of its friends by decrying some of the most influential of them to the utmost of his power; and let it be added, as the necessary effect of such conduct, that he has made great progress in undermining the ground which was gained for the government by his predecessor, and that there is real cause to apprehend, it might totter, if not fall, under his future auspices. A new government, constructed on free principles, is always weak, and must stand in need of the props of a firm and good administration; till time shall have rendered its authority venerable, and fortified it by habits of obedience.

Yet with this opinion of Mr. ADAMS, I have finally resolved not to advise the withholding from him a single vote. The body of Federalists, for want of sufficient knowledge of facts, are not convinced of the expediency of relinquishing him. It is even apparent, that a large proportion still retain the attachment which was once a common sentiment. Those of them, therefore, who are dissatisfied, as far as my information goes, are, generally speaking, willing to forbear opposition, and to acquiesce in the equal support of Mr. ADAMS with Mr. PINCKNEY, whom they prefer. Have they not a claim to equal deference from those who continue attached to the former? Ought not these, in candor, to admit the possibility that the friends who differ from them, act not only from pure motives, but from cogent reasons? Ought they not, by a co-operation in General PINCKNEY, to give a chance for what will be a *safe* issue, supposing that they are right in their preference, and the best issue, should they happen to be mistaken? Especially, since by doing this, they will increase the probability of excluding a third candidate, of whose unfitness all sincere federalists are convinced. If they do not pursue this course, they will certainly incur an immense responsibility to their friends and to the Government.

To promote this co-operation, to defend my own character, to vindicate those friends, who with myself have been unkindly aspersed, are the inducements for writing this letter. Accordingly, it will be my endeavor to regulate the communication of it in such a manner as will not be likely to deprive Mr. ADAMS of a single vote. Indeed, it is much my wish that its circulation could forever be confined within narrow limits. I am sensible of the inconveniences of giving publicity to a similar developement of the character of the Chief Magistrate of our country; and I lament the necessity of taking a step which will involve that result. Yet to suppress truths, the disclosure of which is so interesting to the public welfare as well as to the vindication of my friends and myself, did not appear to me justifiable.

The restraints, to which I submit, are a proof of my disposition to sacrifice to the prepossessions of those, with whom I have heretofore thought and acted, and from whom in the present question I am compelled to differ. To refrain from a decided opposition to Mr. ADAMS's re-election has been reluctantly sanctioned by my judgment; which has been not a little perplexed between the unqualified conviction of his unfitness for the station contemplated, and a sense of the great importance of cultivating harmony among the supporters of the Government; on whose firm union hereafter will probably depend the preservation of order, tranquillity, liberty, property; the security of every social and domestic blessing.

October 24, 1800

JEFFERSON OVER BURR

To Gouverneur Morris

Dr Sir   New York 26 Decr. 1800

The post of yesterday gave me the pleasure of a letter from you. I thank you for the communication. I trust that a letter which I wrote you the day before the receipt of yours will have duly reached you as it contains some very free & confidential observations ending in two results—1 That The Convention with France ought to be ratified as the least of two evils   2 That *on the same ground Jefferson* ought to be preferred to *Burr*.

I trust the Fœderalists will not finally be so mad as to vote for the *latter*. I speak with an intimate & accurate knowlege of character. His elevation can only promote the purposes of the desperate and proflicate. If there be a man in the world I ought to hate it is Jefferson. With *Burr* I have always been personally well. But the public good must be paramount to every private consideration. My opinion may be freely used with such reserves as you shall think discreet.

Yrs.   very truly   A H

ANXIETY ABOUT THE ELECTION

To John Rutledge Jr.

Confidential

My Dear Sir   New York Jany. 4. 1801

My extreme anxiety about the ensuing election of President by the House of Representatives will excuse to you the liberty I take in addressing you concerning it without being consulted by you. Did you know Mr. *Burr* as well as I do, I should think it unnecessary. With your honest attachment to the Country and correctness of views, it would not then be possible for you to hesitate, *if you now do*, about the course to be taken. You would be clearly of opinion with me that Mr. Jefferson is to be preferred.

As long as the Fœderal party preserve their high ground of integrity and principle, I shall not despair of the public weal. But if they quit it and descend to be the willing instruments of the Elevation of the most unfit and most dangerous man of the Community to the highest station in the Government—I shall no longer see any anchor for the hopes of good men. I shall at once anticipate all the evils that a daring and unprincipled ambition wielding the lever of Jacobinism can bring upon an infatuated Country.

The enclosed paper exhibits a faithful sketch of Mr. Burr's character as I believe it to exist, with better opportunities than almost any other man of forming a true estimate.

The expectation, I know, is, that if Mr. Burr shall owe his elevation to the Fœderal party he will judge it his interest to adhere to that party. But it ought to be recollected, that he will owe it in the first instance to the Antifoederal party; that among these, though perhaps not in the House of Representatives, a numerous class prefers him to Mr. Jefferson as best adapted by the boldness and cunning of his temper to fulfill their mischievous views; and that it will be the interest of his Ambition to preserve and cultivate these friends.

Mr. Burr will doubtless be governed by his interest as he views it. But *stable* power and Wealth being his objects—and there being no prospect that the respectable and sober fœderalists will countenance the projects of an irregular Ambition or prodigal Cupidity, he will not long lean upon them—but selecting from among them men suited to his purpose he will seek with the aid of those and of the most unprincipled of the opposite party to accomplish his ends. At least such ought to be our calculation. From such a man as him, who practices all the maxims of a Catiline, who, while despising, has played the whole game of, democracy, what better is to be looked for. Tis not to a Chapter of Accidents, that we ought to trust the Government peace and happiness of our Country. Tis enough for us to know that Mr. Burr is one of the most unprincipled men in the UStates in order to determine us to decline being responsible for the precarious issues of his calculations of Interest.

Very different ought to be our plan. Under the uncertainty of the Event we ought to seek to obtain from Mr. Jefferson these assurances 1 That the present Fiscal System will be maintained. 2 That the present neutral plan will be adhered to. 3 That the Navy will be preserved and gradually increased. 4 That Fœderalists now in office, not being heads of the great departments, will be retained. As to the heads of Departments & other matters he ought to be free.

You cannot in my opinion render a greater service to your Country than by exerting your influence to counteract the *impolitic* and *impure* idea of raising Mr. Burr to the Chief Magistracy.

Adieu My Dear Sir   Yrs. with sincere esteem & regard

A Hamilton

Confidential

A Burr

1   He is in every sense a profligate; a voluptuary in the extreme, with uncommon habits of expence; in his profession extortionate to a proverb; suspected on strong grounds of having *corruptly* served the views of the Holland Company, in the capacity of a member of our legislature*; and understood to have been guilty of several breaches of probity in his pecuniary transactions. His very friends do not insist upon his integrity.

2   He is without doubt insolvent for a large *deficit*. All his visible property is deeply mortgaged, and he is known to owe other large debts, for which there is no specific security. Of the number of these is a Judgment in favour of Mr. Angerstien for a sum which with interest amounts to about 80,000 Dollars.

3   The fair emoluments of any station, under our government, will not equal his expences in that station; still less will they suffice to extricate him from his embarassments & he must therefore from the necessity of his situation have recourse to unworthy expedients. These may be a *bargain* and *sale* with some foreign power, or combinations with public agents in projects of gain by means of the public monies; perhaps and probably, to enlarge the sphere—a *War*.

---

*He cooperated in obtaining a law to permit Aliens to hold & convey lands.

4   He has no pretensions to the Station from services. He acted in different capacities in the last war finally with the rank of Lt. Col in a Regiment, and gave indications of being a good officer; but without having had the opportunity of performing any distinguished action. At a *critical period* of the War, he resigned his commission, assigning for cause ill-health, and went to reside at *Paramus* in the State of New Jersey. If his health was bad he might without difficulty have obtained a furlough and was not obliged to resign. He was afterwards seen in his usual health. The circumstance excited much jealousy of his motives. In civil life, he has never projected nor aided in producing a single measure of important public utility.

5   He has *constantly* sided with the party hostile to *fœderal* measures before and since the present constitution of the U States. In opposing the adoption of this constitution he was engaged covertly and insidiously; because, as he said at the time "it was too strong and too weak" and he has been uniformly the opposer of the Fœderal Administration.

6   No mortal can tell what his political principles are. He has talked *all round the compass. At times* he has dealt in all the jargon of Jacobinism; at other times he has proclaimed decidedly the total insufficiency of the Fœderal Government and the necessity of changes to one far more energetic. The truth seems to be that he has no plan but that of *getting* power by *any* means and *keeping* it by *all* means. It is probable that if he has any theory 'tis that of a simple *despotism*. He has intimated that he thinks the present French constitution not a bad one.

7   He is of a temper bold enough to think no enterprize too hazardous and sanguine enough to think none too difficult. He has censured the leaders of the Fœderal party as wanting in vigour and enterprise, for not having established a strong Government when they were in possession of the power and influence.

8   Discerning men of all parties agree in ascribing to him an irregular and inordinate ambition. Like *Catiline*, he is indefatigable in courting the *young* and the *profligate*. He knows well the weak sides of human nature, and takes care to play in with the passions of all with whom he has intercourse.

By natural disposition, the haughtiest of men, he is at the same time the most creeping to answer his purposes. Cold and collected by nature and habit, he never loses sight of his object and scruples no means of accomplishing it. He is artful and intriguing to an inconceivable degree. In short all his conduct indicates that he has in view nothing less than the establishment of Supreme Power in his own person. Of this nothing can be a surer index than that having in fact high-toned notions of Government, he has nevertheless constantly opposed the *fœderal* and courted the *popular* party. As he never can effect his wish by the aid of good men, he will court and employ able and daring scoundrels of every party, and by availing himself of their assistance and of all the bad passions of the Society, he will in all likelihood attempt an usurpation.

8   Within the last three weeks at his own Table, he drank these toasts successively   1 The French Republic   2 The Commissioners who negotiated the Convention   3 *Buonaparte*   4 *La Fayette*; and he countenanced and seconded the positions openly advanced by one of his guests that it was the interest of this Country to leave it free to the Belligerent Powers to sell their prizes in our ports and to build and equip ships for their respective uses; a doctrine which evidently aims at turning all the naval resources of the UStates into the channel of France; and which by making these states the most pernicious enemy of G Britain would compel her to go to War with us.

9   Though possessing infinite art cunning and address—he is yet to give proofs of great or solid abilities. It is certain that at the Bar he is more remarkable for ingenuity and dexterity than for sound judgment or good logic. From the character of his understanding and heart it is likely that any innovations which he may effect will be such as to serve the turn of his own power, not such as will issue in establishments favourable to the permanent security and prosperity of the Nation— founded upon the principles of a *strong free* and *regular* Government.

BURR HAS "NO FIXED THEORY"

To James A. Bayard

New-York Jany. 16th. 1801.

I was glad to find my dear sir, by your letter, that you had not yet determined to go with the current of the Fœderal Party in the support of Mr *Burr* & that you were resolved to hold yourself disengaged till the moment of final decision. Your resolution to separate yourself, in this instance, from the Fœderal Party if your conviction shall be strong of the unfitness of Mr Burr, is certainly laudable. So much does it coincide with my ideas, that if the Party Shall by supporting Mr Burr as President adopt him for their official Chief—I shall be obliged to consider myself as an *isolated* man. It will be impossible for me to reconcile with my notions of *honor* or policy, the continuing to be of a Party which according to my apprehension will have degraded itself & the country. I am sure nevertheless that the motives of many will be good, and I shall never cease to esteem the individuals, tho' I shall deplore a step which I fear experience will show to be a very fatal one. Among the letters which I receive assigning the reasons *pro* & *con* for prefering Burr to J. I observe no small exaggeration to the prejudice of the latter & some things taken for granted as to the former which are at least questionable. Perhaps myself the first, at some expence of popularity, to unfold the true character of Jefferson, it is too late for me to become his apologist. Nor can I have any disposition to do it. I admit that his politics are tinctured with fanaticism, that he is too much in earnest in his democracy, that he has been a mischevous enemy to the principle measures of our past administration, that he is crafty & persevering in his objects, that he is not scrupulous about the means of success, nor very mindful of truth, and that he is a contemptible hypocrite. But it is not true as is alleged that he is an enemy to the power of the Executive, or that he is for confounding all the powers in the House of Rs. It is a fact which I have frequently mentioned that while we were in the administration together he was generally for a large construction of the

Executive authority, & not backward to act upon it in cases which coincided with his views. Let it be added, that in his theoretic Ideas he has considered as improper the participations of the Senate in the Executive Authority. I have more than once made the reflection that viewing himself as the reversioner, he was solicitous to come into possession of a Good Estate. Nor is it true that Jefferson is zealot enough to do anything in pursuance of his principles which will contravene his popularity, or his interest. He is as likely as any man I know to temporize—to calculate what will be likely to promote his own reputation and advantage; and the probable result of such a temper is the preservation of systems, though originally opposed, which being once established, could not be overturned without danger to the person who did it. To my mind a true estimate of Mr J.'s character warrants the expectation of a temporizing rather than a violent system. That Jefferson has manifested a culpable predilection for France is certainly true; but I think it a question whether it did not proceed quite as much from her *popularity* among us, as from sentiment, and in proportion as that popularity is diminished his zeal will cool. Add to this that there is no fair reason to suppose him capable of being corrupted, which is a security that he will not go beyond certain limits. It is not at all improbable that under the change of circumstances Jefferson's Gallicism has considerably abated.

As to Burr these things are admitted and indeed cannot be denied, that he is a man of *extreme* & *irregular* ambition—that he is *selfish* to a degree which excludes all social affections & that he is decidedly *profligate*. But it is said, 1st. that he is *artful* & *dexterous* to accomplish his ends—2nd. that he holds no pernicious theories, but is a mere *matter of fact* man—3rd. that his very selfishness* is a guard against mischevous foreign predilections. 4th That his *local situation* has enabled him to appreciate the utility of our Commercial & fiscal systems, and the same quality of selfishness will lead him to support & invigorate them. 5th. that he is now disliked by the Jacobins, that his elevation will be a mortal stab to them, breed an invincible hatred to him, & compel him to lean on the Fed-

---

*It is always very dangerous to look to the *vices* of men for *Good*.

eralists. 6th. That Burr's ambition will be checked by his good sense, by the manifest impossibility of succeeding in any scheme of usurpation, & that if attempted, there is nothing to fear from the attempt. These topics are in my judgment more plausible than solid. As to the 1st point the fact must be admitted, but those qualities are objections rather than recommendations when they are under the direction of bad principles. As to the 2nd point too much is taken for granted. If Burr's conversation is to be credited he is not very far from being a visionary.* It is ascertained in some instances that he has talked perfect *Godwinism*. I have myself heard him speak with applause of the French system as unshackling the mind & leaving it to its natural energies, and I have been present when he has contended against Banking Systems† with earnestness & with the same arguments that Jefferson would use. The truth is that *Burr* is a man of a very subtile imagination, and a mind of this make is rarely free from ingenious whimsies. Yet I admit that he has no fixed theory & that his peculiar notions will easily give way to his interest. But is it a recommendation to have *no theory*? Can that man be a systematic or able statesman who has none? I believe not. *No general principles* will hardly work much better than erroneous ones. As to the 3rd. point—it is certain that Burr generally speaking has been as warm a partisan of France as Jefferson—that he has in some instances shewn himself to be so with passion. But if it was from calculation who will say that his calculations will not continue him so? His selfishness‡ so far from being an obstacle may be a prompter. If corrupt as well as selfish he may be a partisan for gain—if ambitious as well as selfish, he may be a partisan for the sake of aid to his views. No man has trafficked more than he in the floating passions of the multitude. Hatred to G. Britain & attachment to France in the public mind will naturally lead a man of his

*He has quoted to me *Connecticut* as an example of the success of the Democratic theory, and as authority, serious doubts whether it was not a good one.

†Yet he has lately by a trick established a *Bank*, a perfect monster in its principles; but a very convenient instrument of *profit* & *influence*.

‡Unprincipled selfishness is more apt to seek rapid gain in disorderly practices than slow advantages from orderly systems.

selfishness, attached to place and power, to favour France &
oppose G. Britain. The Gallicism of many of our patriots is to
be thus resolved, & in my opinion it is morally certain that
Burr will continue to be influenced by this calculation. As to
the 4th point the instance I have cited with respect to Banks
proves that the argument is not to be relied on. If there was
much in it, why does Chancellor Livingston maintain that we
ought not to cultivate navigation but ought to let foreigners
be our Carriers? France is of this opinion too & Burr for some
reason or other, will be very apt to be of the opinion of
France. As to the 5th point—nothing can be more fallacious.
It is demonstrated by recent facts* that Burr is *solicitous* to
keep upon *Antifœderal ground*, to avoid compromitting himself by any engagements† with the Fœderalists. With or without such engagements he will easily persuade his former
friends that he does stand on that ground, & after their first
resentment they will be glad to rally under him. In the mean
time he will take care not to disoblige them & he will always
court those among them who are best fitted for tools. He will
never choose to lean on good men because he knows that
they will never support his bad projects: but instead of this he
will endeavour to disorganize both parties & to form out of
them a third composed of men fitted by their characters to be
conspirators, & instruments of such projects. That this will be
his future conduct may be inferred from his past plan, & from
the admitted quality of irregular ambition. Let it be remembered that Mr Burr has never appeared solicitous for fame, &
that great Ambition unchecked by principle, or the love of
Glory, is an unruly Tyrant which never can keep long in a
course which good men will approve. As to the last point—
The propostion is against the experience of all times. Ambition without principle never was long under the guidance of
good sense. Besides that, really the force of Mr Burrs understanding is much overrated. He is far more *cunning* than *wise*,
far more *dexterous* than *able*. In my opinion he is inferior in
real ability to Jefferson. There are also facts against the supposition. It is past all doubt that he has blamed me for not

---

*My letter to Mr Morris states some of them.
†He trusts to their *prejudices* and *hopes* for support.

having improved the situation I once was in to change the Government. That when answered that this could not have been done without guilt—he replied—"Les grands ames se soucient peu des petits morceaux"—that when told the thing was never practicable from the genious and situation of the country, he answered, "that depends on the estimate we form of the human passions and of the means of influencing them." Does this prove that Mr Burr would consider a scheme of usurpation as visionary. The truth is with great apparent coldness he is the most sanguine man in the world. He thinks every thing possible to adventure and perseverance. And tho' I believe he will fail, I think it almost certain he will attempt usurpation. And the attempt will involve great mischief.

But there is one point of view which seems to me decisive. If the Antifœderalists who prevailed in the election are left to take their own man, they remain responsible, and the Fœderalists remain *free united* and without *stain*, in a situation to resist with effect pernicious measures. If the Fœderalists substitute Burr, they adopt him and become answerable for him. Whatever may be the theory of the case, abroad and at *home* (for so from the beginning will be taught) Mr Burr will become *in fact* the man of our party. And if he acts ill, we must share in the blame and disgrace. By adopting him we do all we can to reconcile the minds of the Fœderalists to him, and prepare them for the effectual operation of his arts. He will doubtless gain many of them, & the Fœderalists will become a disorganized and contemptible party. Can there be any serious question between the policy of leaving the Antifœderalists to be answerable for the elevation of an exceptionable man, & that of adopting ourselves & becoming answerable for a man who on all hands is acknowledged to be a complete *Cataline* in his practice & principles? 'Tis enough to state the question to indicate the answer, if reason not passion presides in the decision. You may communicate this & my former letter to discreet & confidential friends.

Your's very truly, A H

Proposal for the New York Legislature for Amending the Constitution

Resolved, as the sense of the Legislature, that the following amendments ought to be incorporated into the Constitution of the United States as a necessary safeguard in the choice of a President and Vice President against pernicious dissensions as the most eligible mode of obtaining a full and fair expression of the public will in such election.

1st. That Congress shall from time to time divide each State into Districts equal to the whole number of Senators and Representatives from such state in the Congress of the United States, and shall direct the mode of choosing an Elector of President and Vice President in each of the said Districts, who shall be chosen by Citizens who have the qualifications requisite for Electors of the most numerous branch of the State Legislature, and that the districts shall be formed, as nearly as may be, with an equal proportion of population in each, and of Counties and, if necessary, parts of Counties contiguous to each other, except when there may be any detached portion of territory not sufficient of itself to form a District which then shall be annexed to some other part nearest thereto.

2nd. That in all future elections of President and Vice President the persons voted for shall be particularly designated by declaring which is voted for as President and which as Vice President.

Resolved that the President of the Senate and Speaker of the Assembly transmit a copy of the preceding Resolutions to the Senators and Representatives in Congress from this State with an earnest request that they would use their best exertions for obtaining the adoption of the above amendments or other amendments in substance equivalent so as that the President and Vice President may be separately designated in voting for them and that the electors for both may be chosen in distinct Districts.

January 1802

Remarks on the Repeal of the Judiciary Act

To these remarks General Hamilton rose again to reply—he remarked in substance that he had fostered the hope, that on this occasion, by cautiously avoiding to say any thing on the point of the constitutionality of the proposed repeal, and stating only the opinion of the New-York bar on that of its *inexpediency*, there would have been but one sentiment—He regretted, deeply regretted, that on this point there was a diversity of sentiment; he foresaw the unhappy effects that would hence result; he deplored them, not from any private or contracted view, but turning his eye inward on his heart, and looking to heaven as the witness of his motives, he declared he knew of none that influenced him but the sincerest attachment to the public good. So far as respected the unconstitutionality of the proposed repeal, he had no hesitation in avowing his own opinion. He considered it a most direct, and fatal violation of the most essential, the most *vital* principle of the constitution. The independence of the judges once destroyed, the constitution is gone, it is a dead letter; it is a vapor which the breath of faction in a moment may dissipate, and this boasted union the labor of true patriots, the hope of our country, which in the last 12 years has raised us to the most enviable height of prosperity, dissolves and dies.

He had cherished the idea, he said, that this part of the Constitution was the last that party violence would attack. That although certain extensions of executive authority, certain changes in the finances, or in diplomatic arrangements abroad might take place, yet that the essential rights of the judiciary in which foreigners and citizens, but more especially the mercantile interests of the U. States are so deeply concerned, would have been preserved inviolate. He had looked forward to many evils that he thought likely to flow from the known principles of the leading characters now in authority, but indeed, he had not calculated on such a rapid progression of evil. He had little hope that any thing that could now be *said* or done, would assist in averting the impending blow. He knew full well that the plan now going into effect had long been meditated and resolved on, and hence, his zeal was much abated, yet could any thing he could do have any effect in saving the constitution from the fatal blow that now menaced it, he would labor day and night; he would not give 'sleep to his eyes, nor slumber to his eye-lids,' while he had hope to support his exertions; nay, 'I would give a drop of my heart's blood,' said he, to save this *vital* principle of the constitution. There is no motive which induced me to put my life at hazard through our revolutionary war, that would not now as powerfully operate on me, to put it again in jeopardy, in defence of the independence of the judiciary; for remember what is said this night; if this fatal measure is not by *some means* arrested, if the *laws* are not suffered to controul the passions of individuals, thro the organs of an extended, firm and independent judiciary, the bayonet must. There is no alternative; we must be ruled by municipal law, or by—a military force: and I beg gentlemen to recollect what I now say, without aspiring to the character of a prophet, that if this rash unadvised repeal takes place, mutual confidence will be destroyed—the union will gradually crumble to pieces and in a few, very few years, the present confederation will either be parcelled out into separate territories, with clashing interests, and you will see the hand of brother, raised to shed a brother's blood, or you will see this country become the prey of a usurper, and sink into the calm of a military despotism. On those gentlemen, then, who truly value our republican government, I call, to banish for an instant, the influence of party-spirit, and to lend their aid in extinguishing a rising conflagration, which threatens to involve this devoted country in miseries incalculable. On the point of *expediency*, he observed, that he could, in no one point of view, consider the proposed repeal as defensible. Every gentleman present, who had been concerned in business depending in the circuit court of the United States, knew, without his going into details, the vices of the *old system*. Many of its defects were indeed removed by the present, which, however, was not to be considered as perfect. On this, certain improvements could be advantageously engrafted—which would render it a very eligible and convenient system. But he was surprised, greatly surprised indeed, to hear any gentleman who had any respect to his own character, risk an opinion, that the district courts, with the supreme court of the United States, were fully competent to all the business of the United States. The business of the former he said, from revenue and admiralty causes, and from what arose under the late bankrupt law, furnished full employ for the most industrious judge. Beside, if all suits were originally to be commenced in the district courts, no suitor would rest satisfied with the decision of a single man, but would remove the cause for a final hearing to the supreme court of the United States, in which case parties would be constantly obliged to travel with papers and vouchers from the extremities of the Union to the seat of government, there to retain new counsel, be at heavy expences, and far from their families, which would produce inconveniences that would not long be submitted to.

February 11, 1802

"MINE IS AN ODD DESTINY"

To Gouverneur Morris

My Dr. Sir

Your letter of the 22d is the third favour for which I am indebted to you since you left N York.

Your frankness in giving me your opinion as to the expediency of an application of our bar to Congress obliges me. But you know we are not readily persuaded to think we have been wrong. Were the matter to be done over I should pursue the same course. I did not believe the measure would be useful as a preventative, and for the people an expression of an opinion by letter would be as good as in a memorial. It appeared to me best because it saved our delicacy and because in the abstract I am not over fond of the precedent of the bar addressing Congress. But I did what I thought likely to do more good—*I induced* the Chamber of Commerce to send a memorial.

As to the rest, I should be a very unhappy man, if I left my tranquillity at the mercy of the misinterpretations which friends as well as foes are fond of giving to my conduct.

Mine is an odd destiny. Perhaps no man in the UStates has sacrificed or done more for the present Constitution than myself—and contrary to all my anticipations of its fate, as you know from the very begginning I am still labouring to prop the frail and worthless fabric. Yet I have the murmurs of its friends no less than the curses of its foes for my rewards. What can I do better than withdraw from the Scene? Every day proves to me more and more that this American world was not made for me.

The suggestions with which you close your letter suppose a much sounder state of the public mind than at present exists. Attempts to make a show of a general *popular* dislike of the pending measures of the Government would only serve to manifest the direct reverse. Impressions are indeed making but as yet within a very narrow sphere. The time may ere long arrive when the minds of men will be prepared to make an offer to *recover* the Constitution, but the many cannot now be brought to make a stand for its preservation. We must wait awhile.

I have read your speeches with great pleasure. They are truly worthy of you. Your real friends had many sources of satisfaction on account of them. The conspiracy of Dulness was at work. It chose to misinterpret your moderation in certain transactions of a personal reference. A public energetic display of your talents and principles was requisite to silence the Cavillers. It is now done. You, friend Morris, are by *birth* a native of this Country but by *genius* an exotic. You mistake if you fancy that you are more a favourite than myself or that you are in any sort upon a theatre suited to you.

Adieu   Yrs. ever   A H
Feby 29.

1802

THE DEATH OF PHILIP HAMILTON

To Benjamin Rush

Dear Sir   New York March 29. 1802

I felt all the weight of the obligation which I owed to you and to your amiable family, for the tender concern they manifested in an event, beyond comparison, the most afflicting of my life. But I was obliged to wait for a moment of greater calm, to express my sense of the kindness.

My loss is indeed great. The highest as well as the eldest hope of my family has been taken from me. You estimated him rightly—He was truly a fine youth. But why should I repine? It was the will of heaven; and he is now out of the reach of the seductions and calamities of a world, full of folly, full of vice, full of danger—of least value in proportion as it is best known. I firmly trust also that he has safely reached the haven of eternal repose and felicity.

You will easily imagine that every memorial of the goodness of his heart must be precious to me. You allude to one recorded in a letter to your son. If no special reasons forbid it, I should be very glad to have a copy of that letter.

Mrs. Hamilton, who has drank deeply of the cup of sorrow, joins me in affectionate thanks to Mrs. Rush and yourself. Our wishes for your happiness will be unceasing.

Very sincerely & cordially   Yrs.   A Hamilton

THE CHRISTIAN CONSTITUTIONAL SOCIETY

To James A. Bayard

Dear Sir.   New-York April 1802

Your letter of the 12th inst. has relieved me from some apprehension. Yet it is well that it should be perfectly understood by the truly sound part of the Fœderalists, that there do in fact exist intrigues in good earnest, between several individuals not unimportant, of the Fœderal Party, and the person in question; which are bottomed upon motives & views, by no means auspicious to the real welfare of the country. I am glad to find that it is in contemplation to adopt a plan of conduct. It is very necessary; & to be useful it must be efficient & comprehensive in the means which it embraces, at the same time that it must meditate none which are not really constitutional & patriotic. I will comply with your invitation by submitting some ideas which from time to time have passed through my mind. Nothing is more fallacious than to expect to produce any valuable or permanent results, in political projects, by relying merely on the reason of men. Men are rather reasoning than reasonable animals for the most part governed by the impulse of passion. This is a truth well understood by our adversaries who have practised upon it with no small benefit to their cause. For at the very moment they are eulogizing the reason of men & professing to appeal only to that faculty, they are courting the strongest & most active passion of the human heart—*VANITY!*

It is no less true that the Fœderalists seem not to have attended to the fact sufficiently; and that they erred in relying so much on the rectitude & utility of their measures, as to have neglected the cultivation of popular favour by fair & justifiable expedients. The observation has been repeatedly made by me to individuals with whom I particularly conversed & expedients suggested for gaining good will which were never adopted. Unluckily however for us in the competition for the passions of the people our opponents have great advantages over us; for the plain reason, that the vicious are far more active than the good passions, and that to win the latter to our side we must renounce our principles & our objects, & unite in corrupting public opinion till it becomes fit for nothing but mischief. Yet unless we can contrive to take hold of & carry along with us some strong feelings of the mind we shall in vain calculate upon any substantial or durable results. Whatever plan we may adopt, to be successful must be founded on the truth of this proposition. And perhaps it is not very easy for us to give it full effect; especially not without some deviations from what on other occasions we have maintained to be right. But in determining upon the propriety of the deviations, we must consider whether it be possible for us to succeed without in some degree employing the weapons which have been employed against us, & whether the actual state & future prospect of things, be not such as to justify the reciprocal use of them. I need not tell you that I do not mean to countenance the imitation of things intrinsically unworthy, but only of such as may be denominated irregular, such as in a sound & stable order of things ought not to exist. Neither are you to infer that any revolutionary result is contemplated. In my opinion the present Constitution is the standard to which we are to cling. Under its banners, *bona fide* must we combat our political foes—rejecting all changes but through the channel itself provides for amendments. By these general views of the subject have my reflections been guided. I now offer you the outline of the plan which they have suggested. Let an Association be formed to be denominated, "The Christian Constitutional Society." It's objects to be

1st The support of the Christian Religion.
2nd The support of the Constitution of the United States.

Its Organization.

1st A directing council consisting of a President & 12 Members, of whom 4 & the President to be a quorum.
2nd A sub-directing council in each State consisting of a Vice-President & 12 Members, of whom 4 with the Vice-President to be a quorum & 3rd As many societies in each State, as local circumstances may permit to be formed by the Sub-directing council.

The Meeting at Washington to Nominate the *President* & *Vice-President* together with *4 Members of each* of the councils, who *are to complete* their own numbers respectively.

Its Means.

1st The diffusion of information. For this purpose not only the Newspapers but pamphlets must be largely employed & to do this a fund must be created. 5 dollars annually for 8 years, to be contributed by each member who can really afford it, (taking care not to burden the less able brethren) may afford a competent fund for a competent time. It is essential to be able to disseminate *gratis* useful publications. Whenever it can be done, &

there is a press, clubs should be formed to meet once a week, read the newspapers & prepare essays paragraphs &ct.

2nd   The use of all lawful means in concert to promote the election of *fit men*. A lively correspondence must be kept up between the different Societies.

3rd   The promoting of institutions of a charitable & useful nature in the management of Fœderalists. The populous cities ought particularly to be attended to. Perhaps it will be well to institute in such places 1st Societies for the relief of Emigrants—2nd. Academies each with one professor for instructing the different Classes of Mechanics in the principles of Mechanics & Elements of Chemistry. The cities have been employed by the Jacobins to give an impulse to the country. And it is believed to be an alarming fact, that while the question of Presidential Election was pending in the House of Rs. parties were organized in several of the Cities, in the event of there being no election, to cut off the leading Fœderalists & sieze the Government. An Act of association to be drawn up in concise general terms. It need only designate the "name" "objects" & contain an engagement to promote the objects by all lawful means, and particularly by the diffusion of Information. This act to be signed by every member.

especially confidential

The foregoing to be the principal Engine. In addition let measures be adopted to bring as soon as possible the repeal of the Judiciary law before the Supreme Court. Afterwards, if not before, let as many Legislatures as can be prevailed upon, instruct their Senators to endeavour to procure a repeal of the repealing law. The body of New-England speaking the same language will give a powerful impulse. In Congress our friends to *propose* little, to agree candidly to all good measures, & to resist & expose all bad. This is a general sketch of what has occurred to me. It is at the service of my friends for so much as it may be worth. With true esteem & regard

Dr Sir   Yours   AH

"A MOST VISIONARY THEORY PRESIDES"

To Rufus King

My Dear Sir   New York June 3. 1802

I have been long very delinquent towards you, as a correspondent, and am to thank you that you have not cast me off altogether as an irretrievable reprobate. But you knew how to appreciate the causes and you have made a construction equally just and indulgent.

In your last you ask my opinion about a matter delicate and important both in a public and in a personal view. I shall give it with the frankness to which you have a right, and I may add that the impressions of your other friends, so far as they have fallen under my observation do not differ from my own. While you were in the midst of a negotiation interesting to your country, it was your duty to keep your post. You have now accomplished the object and have the good fortune not very common of having the universal plaudit. This done, it seems to me most adviseable that you return home. There is little probability that your continuance in your present station will be productive of much positive good. Nor are circumstances such as to give reason to apprehend that the substitute for you, whoever he may be, can do much harm. Your stay or return therefore, as it regards our transatlantic concerns, is probably not material: While your presence at home may be useful in ways which it is not necessary to particularise. Besides, it is questionable whether you can continue longer in the service of the present administration consistently with what is due as well to your own character as to the common cause. I am far from thinking that a man is bound to quit a public office, merely because the administration of the Government may have changed hands. But when those who have come into power are undisguised persecutors of the party to which he has been attached and study with ostenstation to heap upon it every indignity and injury—he ought not in my opinion to permit himself to be made an exception or to lend his talents to the support of such characters. If in addition to this, it be true that the principles and plans of the men at the head of affairs tend to the degradation of the Government and to their own disgrace it will hardly be possible to be in any way connected with them without sharing in the disrepute which they may be destined to experience.

I wish I had time to give you a comprehensive & particular map of our political situation. But more than a rude outline is beyond my leisure, devoted as I am more than ever to my professional pursuits.

You have seen the course of the Administration hitherto, especially during the last session of Congress; and I am persuaded you will agree in opinion with me that it could hardly have been more diligent in mischief. What you will ask, has been and is likely to be the effect on the public mind?

Our friends are sanguine that a great change for the better has been wrought and is progressive. I suppose good has been done—that the Fœderalists have been reconciled and cemented—have been awakened and alarmed. Perhaps too there may be some sensible and moderate men of the adverse party who are beginning to doubt. But I as yet discover no satisfactory symptoms of a revolution of opinion in the *mass* "informe in gens cui lumen ademptum." Nor do I look with much expectation to any serious alteration until inconveniences are extensively felt or until time has produced a disposition to coquet it with new lovers. Vibrations of power, you are aware, are of the genius of our Government.

There is however a circumstance which may accelerate the fall of the present party. There is certainly a most serious scism between the chief and his heir apparent; a scism absolutely incurable, because founded in the breasts of both in the rivalship of an insatiable and unprincipled ambition. The effects are already apparent, and are ripening into a more bitter animosity between the partizans of the two men than ever existed between the Fœderalists and Antifœderalists.

Unluckily we are not as neutral to this quarrel as we ought to be. You saw how far our friends in Congress went in polluting themselves with the support of the second personage for the presidency. The Cabal did not terminate there. Several men, of no inconsiderable importance among us, like the enterprising and adventurous character of this man, and hope to soar with him to power. Many more through hatred to the

Chief and through an impatience to recover the reins are linking themselves with the vice-Chief, almost without perceiving it and professing to have no other object than to make use of him; while he knows that he is making use of them. What this may end in, it is difficult to foresee.

Of one thing only I am sure, that in no event will I be directly or indirectly implicated in a responsibility for the elevation or support of either of two men, who in different senses, are in my eyes equally unworthy of the confidence of intelligent or honest men.

Truly, My dear Sir, the prospects of our Country are not brilliant. The mass is far from sound. At headquarters a most visionary theory presides. Depend upon it this is the fact to a great extreme. No army, no navy no *active* commerce—national defence, not by arms but by embargoes, prohibition of trade &c.—as little government as possible within—these are the pernicious dreams which as far and as fast as possible will be attempted to be realized. Mr. Jefferson is distressed at the codfish having latterly emigrated to the Southern Coast lest the people there should be tempted to catch them, and commerce of which we have already too much receive an accession. Be assured this is no pleasantry, but a very sober anecdote.

Among Fœderalists old errors are not cured. They also continue to dream though not quite so preposterously as their opponents. "All will be very well (say they) when the power once more gets back into Fœderal hands. The people convinced by experience of their error will repose a *permanent* confidence in good men." Rescum teneatis—Adieu.

Yrs. ever   A H

P.S. The bearer our acquaintance Wm Bayard continues worthy of high esteem & regard.   A H

To Charles Cotesworth Pinckney

Grange (NY)

Decr. 29. 1802

My Dear Sir

A garden, you know, is a very usual refuge of a disappointed politician. Accordingly, I have purchased a few acres about 9 Miles from Town, have built a house and am cultivating a Garden. The melons in your country are very fine. Will you have the goodness to send me some seed both of the Water & Muss Melons?

My daughter adds another request, which is for three or four of your peroquets. She is very fond of birds. If there be any thing in this quarter the sending of which can give you pleasure, you have only to name them. As Farmers a new source of sympathy has risen between us; and I am pleased with every thing in which our likings and tastes can be approximated.

Amidst the triumphant reign of Democracy, do you retain sufficient interest in public affairs to feel any curiosity about what is going on? In my opinion the follies and vices of the Administration have as yet made no material impression to their disadvantage. On the contrary, I think the malady is rather progressive than upon the decline in our Northern Quarter. The last *lullaby* message, instead of inspiring contempt, attracts praise. Mankind are forever destined to be the dupes of bold & cunning imposture.

But a difficult *knot* has been twisted by the incident of the cession of Louisian and the interruption of the Deposit at New Orleans. You have seen the soft tun given to this in the message. Yet we are told the President in conversation is very stout. The great embarrassment must be how to carry on war without taxes. The pretty scheme of substituting œconomy to taxation will not do here; and a war would be a terrible comment upon the abandonment of the Internal Revenue. Yet how is popularity to be preserved with the Western partisans if their interests are tamely sacrificed? Will the artifice be for the Chief to hold a bold language and the subalters to act a public part? Time must explain.

You know my general theory as to our Western affairs. I have always held that the Unity of our empire and the best interests of our Nation require that we should annex to the UStates all the territory East of the Mississippia, New Orleans included. Of course I infer that in an emergency like the present, Energy is Wisdom.

Adieu My Dear Sir   Ever Yrs   A H

Mrs. H joins me in affectionate Compliments to Mrs. Pinckney.

"A WORLD FULL OF EVIL"

To Elizabeth Hamilton

March 1803

I thank you My Betsy for your letter from Fish Kill. I hope the subsequent part of your journey has proved less fatiguing than the two first days.

I have anticipated with dread your interview with your father. I hope your prudence and fortitude have been a match for your sensibility. Remember that the main object of visit is to console him; that his own burthen is sufficient, and that it would be too much to have it increased by the sorrows of his Children.

Arm yourself with resignation. We live in a world full of evil. In the later period of life misfortunes seem to thicken round us; and our duty and our peace both require that we should accustom ourselves to meet disasters with christian fortitude.

Kiss Kitty for me & give my love to Angelica, & all the friends & connections round you.

Adieu My excellent wife.   A H

Your Children are all well. I write your father by this oppy.

March 17, 1803

Purchase of Louisiana

At length the business of New-Orleans has terminated favourably to this country. Instead of being obliged to rely any longer on the force of treaties, for a place of deposit, the jurisdiction of the territory is now transferred to our hands and in future the navigation of the Mississippi will be ours unmolested. This, it will be allowed is an important acquisition, not, indeed, as territory, but as being essential to the peace and prosperity of our Western country, and as opening a free and valuable market to our commercial states. This purchase has been made during the period of Mr. Jefferson's presidency, and, will, doubtless, give eclat to his administration. Every man, however, possessed of the least candour and reflection will readily acknowledge that the acquisition has been solely owing to a fortuitous concurrence of unforseen and unexpected circumstances, and not to any wise or vigorous measures on the part of the American government.

As soon as we experienced from Spain a direct infraction of an important article of our treaty, in withholding the deposit of New-Orleans, it afforded us justifiable cause of war, and authorised immediate hostilities. Sound policy unquestionably demanded of us to begin with a prompt, bold and vigorous resistance against the injustice: to seize the object at once; and having this *vantage ground*, should we have thought it advisable to terminate hostilities by a purchase, we might then have done it on almost our own terms. This course, however, was not adopted, and we were about to experience the fruits of our folly, when another nation has found it her interest to place the French Government in a situation substantially as favourable to our views and interests as those recommended by the federal party here, excepting indeed that we should probably have obtained the same object on better terms.

On the part of France the short interval of peace had been wasted in repeated and fruitless efforts to subjugate St. Domingo; and those means which were originally destined to the colonization of Louisiana, had been gradually exhausted by the unexpected difficulties of this ill-starred enterprize.

To the deadly climate of St. Domingo, and to the courage and obstinate resistance made by its black inhabitants are we indebted for the obstacles which delayed the colonization of Louisiana, till the auspicious moment, when a rupture between England and France gave a new turn to the projects of the latter, and destroyed at once all her schemes as to this favourite object of her ambition.

It was made known to Bonaparte, that among the first objects of England would be the seizure of New-Orleans, and that preparations were even then in a state of forwardness for that purpose. The First Consul could not doubt, that if an English fleet was sent thither, the place must fall without resistance; it was obvious, therefore, that it would be in every shape preferable that it should be placed in the possession of a neutral power; and when, besides, some millions of money, of which he was extremely in want, were offered him, to part with what he could no longer hold it affords a moral certainty, that it was to an accidental state of circumstances, and not to wise plans, that this cession, at this time, has been owing. We shall venture to add, that neither of the ministers through whose instrumentality it was effected, will ever deny this, or even pretend that previous to the time when a rupture was believed to be inevitable, there was the smallest chance of inducing the First Consul, with his ambitious and aggrandizing views, to commute the territory for any sum of money in their power to offer. The real truth is, Bonaparte found himself absolutely compelled by situation, to relinquish his darling plan of colonising the banks of the Mississippi: and thus have the Government of the United States, by the unforseen operation of events, gained what the feebleness and pusillanimity of its miserable system of measures could never have acquired. Let us then, with all due humility, acknowledge this as another of those signal instances of the kind interpositions of an over-ruling Providence, which we more especially experienced during our revolutionary war, & by which we have more than once, been saved from the consequences of our errors and perverseness.

We are certainly not disposed to lessen the importance of this acquisition to the country, but it is proper that the public should be correctly informed of its real value and extent as well as of the terms on which it has been acquired. We perceive by the newspapers that various & very vague opinions are entertained; and we shall therefore, venture to state our ideas with some precision as to the territory; but until the instrument of cession itself is published, we do not think it prudent to say much as to the conditions on which it has been obtained.

Prior to the treaty of Paris 1763, France claimed the country on both sides of the river under the name of Louisiana, and it was her encroachments on the rear of the British Colonies which gave rise to the war of 1755. By the conclusion of the treaty of 1763, the limits of the colonies of Great Britain and France were clearly and permanently fixed; and it is from that and subsequent treaties that we are to ascertain what territory is really comprehended under the name of Louisiana. France ceded to Great-Britain all the country east and south-east of a line drawn along the middle of the Mississippi from its source to the Iberville, and from thence along that river and the Lakes Maurepas and Pontchartrain to the sea; France retaining the country lying west of the river, besides the town and Island of New-Orleans on the east side. This she soon after ceded to Spain who acquiring also the Floridas by the treaty of 1783, France was entirely shut out from the continent of North America. Spain, at the instance of Bonaparte, ceded to him Louisiana, including the Town and Island (as it is commonly called) of New-Orleans. Bonaparte has now ceded the same tract of country, and this only, to the United States. The whole of East and West-Florida, lying south of Georgia and of the Mississippi Territory, and extending to the Gulf of Mexico, still remains to Spain, who will continue, therefore, to occupy, as formerly, the country along the southern frontier of the United States, and the east bank of the river, from the Iberville to the American line.

Those disposed to magnify its value will say, that this western region is important as keeping off a troublesome neighbour, and leaving us in the quiet possession of the Mississippi. Undoubtedly this has some force, but on the other hand it may be said, that the acquisition of New-Orleans is perfectly adequate to every purpose; for whoever is in possession of that, has the uncontrouled command of the river. Again, it may be said, and this probably is the most favourable point of view in which it can be placed, that although not valuable to the United States for settlement, it is so to Spain, and will become more so, and therefore at some distant period will form an object which we may barter with her for the Floridas, obviously of far greater value to us than all the immense, undefined region west of the river.

It has been usual for the American writers on this subject to include the Floridas in their ideas of Louisiana, as the French formerly did, and the acquisition has derived no inconsiderable portion of its value and importance with the public from this view of it. It may, however, be relied on, that no part of the Floridas, not a foot of land on the east of the Mississippi, excepting New-Orleans, falls within the present cession. As to the unbounded region west of the Mississippi, it is, with the exception of a very few settlements of Spaniards and Frenchmen bordering on the banks of the river, a wilderness through which wander numerous tribes of Indians. And when we consider the present extent of the United States, and that not one sixteenth part of its territory is yet under occupation, the advantage of the acquisition, as it relates to actual settlement, appears too distant and remote to strike the mind of a sober politician with much force. This, therefore, can only rest in speculation for many years, if not centuries to come, and consequently will not perhaps be allowed very great weight in the account by the majority of readers. But it may be added, that should our own citizens, more enterprizing than wise, become desirous of settling this country, and emigrate thither, it must not only be attended with all the injuries of a too widely dispersed population, but by adding to the great weight of the western part of our territory, must hasten the dismemberment of a large portion of our country, or a dissolution of the Government. On the whole, we think it may with candor be said, that whether the possession at this time of any territory west of the river Mississippi will be advantageous, is at best extremely problematical. For ourselves, we are very much inclined to the opinion, that after all, it is the Island of N. Orleans by which the command of a free navigation of the Mississippi is secured, that gives to this interesting cession, its greatest value, and will render it in every view of immense benefit to our country. By this cession we hereafter shall hold within our own grasp, what we have heretofore enjoyed only by the uncertain tenure of a treaty, which might be broken at the pleasure of another, and (governed as we now are) with perfect impunity. Provided therefore we have not purchased it too dear, there is all the reason for exultation which the friends of the administration display, and which all Americans may be allowed to feel.

As to the pecuniary value of the bargain; we know not enough of the particulars to pronounce upon it. It is understood generally, that we are to assume *debts* of France to our own citizens not exceeding four millions of dollars; and that for the remainder, being a very large sum, 6 per cent stock to be created, and payment made in that. But should it contain no conditions or stipulations on our part, no "tangling alliances" of all things to be dreaded, we shall be very much inclined to regard it in a favorable point of view though it should turn out to be what may be called a costly purchase. By the way a question here presents itself of some little moment: Mr. Jefferson in that part of his famous electioneering message, where he took so much pains to present a flattering state of the Treasury in so few words that every man could carry it in his noddle and repeat it at the poll, tells us, that "experience too so far authorizes us to believe, *if no extraordinary event supervenes, and the expences which will be actually incurred shall not be greater than was contemplated* by Congress at their last session, that we shall not be disappointed in the expectations formed" that the debt would soon be paid, &c. &c. But the first and only measure of the administration that has really been of any material service to the country (for they have hitherto gone on the strength of the provisions made by their predecessors) is really *"an extraordinary event,"* and calls for more money than they have got. According to Mr. Gallatin's report, they had about 40.000 to spare for contingencies, and now the first *"extraordinary event"* that *"supervenes"* calls upon them for several millions. What a poor starvling system of administering a government! *But how is the money to be had? Not by taxing luxury and wealth and whiskey, but by increasing the taxes on the necessaries of life.* Let this be remembered.

But we are exceeding our allowable limits. It may be satisfactory to our readers, that we should finish with a concise account of New-Orleans itself.

The Island of New-Orleans is in length about 150 miles; its breadth varies from 10 to 30 miles. Most of it is a marshy swamp, periodically inundated by the river. The town of New-Orleans, situated about 105 miles from the mouth of the river, contains near 1300 houses, and about 8000 inhabitants, chiefly Spanish and French. It is defended from the overflowings of the river, by an embankment, or *leveé*, which extends near 50 miles.

The rights of the present proprietors of real estate in New-Orleans and Louisiana, whether acquired by descent or by purchase, will, of course, remain undisturbed. How they are to be governed is another question; whether as a colony, or to be formed into an integral part of the United States, is a subject which will claim consideration hereafter. The probable consequences of this cession, and the ultimate effect it is likely to produce on the political state of our country, will furnish abundant matter of speculation to the American statesman.

———

If reliance can be placed on the history given of the negociation of *Louisiana* in private letters, from persons of respectability residing at Paris, and who speak with confidence, the merit of it, after making due allowance for the great events which have borne it along with them, is due to our ambassador, Chancellor Livingston, and not to the Envoy Extraordinary. "The cession was voted in the Council of State on the 8th of April, and Mr. Munro did not even arrive till the 12th." Judging from Mr. Munro's former communications to the French Government on this subject, we really cannot but regard it as fortunate, that the thing was concluded before he reached St. Cloud.

New-York Evening Post, July 5, 1803

EXPLAINING A PLAN OF GOVERNMENT

To Timothy Pickering

New York September 16
1803

My Dear Sir

I will make no apology for my delay in answering your inquiry some time since made, because I could offer none which would satisfy myself. I pray you only to believe that it proceeded from any thing rather than want of respect or regard. I shall now comply with your request.

The highest toned propositions, which I made in the Convention, were for a President, Senate and Judges during good behaviour—a house of representatives for three years. Though I would have enlarged the Legislative power of the General Government, yet I never contemplated the abolition of the State Governments; but on the contrary, they were, in some particulars, constituent parts of my plan.

This plan was in my conception comfortable with the strict theory of a Government purely republican; the essential criteria of which are that the principal organs of the Executive and Legislative departments be elected by the people and hold their offices by a *responsible* and temporary or *defeasible* tenure.

A vote was taken on the proposition respecting the Executive. Five states were in favour of it; among those Virginia; and though from the manner of voting, by delegations, individuals were not distinguished, it was morally certain, from the known situation of the Virginia members (six in number, two of them *Mason* and *Randolph* possessing popular doctrines) that *Madison* must have concurred in the vote of Virginia. Thus, if I sinned against Republicanism, Mr. Madison was not less guilty.

I may truly then say, that I never proposed either a President, or Senate for life, and that I neither recommended nor meditated the annihilation of the State Governments.

And I may add, that in the course of the discussions in the Convention, neither the propositions thrown out for debate, nor even those voted in the earlier stages of deliberation were considered as evidences of a definitive opinion, in the proposer or voter. It appeared to me to be in some sort understood, that with a view to free investigation, experimental propositions might be made, which were to be received merely as suggestions for consideration.

Accordingly, it is a fact, that my final opinion was against an Executive during good behaviour, on account of the increased danger to the public tranquility incident to the election of a Magistrate of this degree of permanency. In the plan of a Constitution, which I drew up, while the convention was sitting & which I communicated to Mr. Madison about the close of it, perhaps a day or two after, the Office of President has no greater duration than for three years.

This plan was predicated upon these bases— 1 That the political principles of the people of this country would endure nothing but republican Government. 2 That in the actual situation of the Country, it was in itself right and proper that the republican theory should have a fair and full trial— 3 That to such a trial it was essential that the Government should be so constructed as to give it all the energy and stability reconciliable with the principles of that theory. These were the genuine sentiments of my heart, and upon them I acted.

I sincerely hope, that it may not hereafter be discovered, that through want of sufficient attention to the last idea, the experiment of Republican Government, even in this Country, has not been as complete, as satisfactory and as decisive as could be wished.

Very truly   Dear Sir   Yr friend & servt   A Hamilton

Speech to a Federalist Meeting in Albany

Reasons why it is desirable that Mr. Lansing rather than Col. Burr should succeed.

1. Col Burr has steadily pursued the track of democratic policies. This he has done either from *principle* or from *calculation*. If the former he is not likely now to change his plan, when the fœderalists are prostrate and their enemies predominent. If the latter, he will certainly not at this time relinquish the ladder of his ambition and espouse the cause or views of the weaker party.

2. Though detested by some of the leading Clintonians, he is certainly not personally disagreeable to the great body of them, and it will be no difficult task for a man of talents intrigue and address possessing this chair of Government to rally the great body of them under his standard and thereby to consolidate for personal purposes the mass of Clintonians, his own adherents among the democrats and such fœderalists as from personal good will or interested motives may give him support.

3. The effect of his elevation will be to reunite under a more adroit able and daring chief the now scattered fragments of the democratic party and to reinforce it by a strong detachment from the fœderalists. For though virtuous fœderalists who from miscalculation may support him, would afterwards relinquish his standard a large number from various motives would continue attached to it.

4. A further effect of his elevation by the aid of fœderalists will be to present to the confidence of New England a man already the man of the democratic leaders of that Country, and towards whom the mass of the people have no weak predilection as their countryman, as the Grandson of President Edwards, and the son of President Burr. In vain will certain men resist this predilection when it can be said that he was chosen Governor of this state, in which he was best known principally or in a great degree by the aid of fœderalists.

5. This will give him fair play to disorganize New England if so disposed; a thing not very difficult when the strength of the

democratic party in each of the N E states is considered and the natural tendency of our civil institutions is duly weighed.

6.   The ill opinion of Jefferson and jealousy of the ambition of Virginia is no inconsiderable prop of good principles in that Country. But these causes are leading to an opinion that a dismemberment of the Union is expedient. It would probably suit Mr. Burrs views to promote this result to be the chief of the Northern portion—And placed at the head of the state of New York no man would be more likely to succeed.

7   If he be truly, as the fœderalists have believed, a man of irregular and insatiable ambition; if his plan has been to rise to power on the ladder of Jacobinic principles, it is natural to conclude that he will endeavor to fix himself in power by the same instrument, that he will not lean on a fallen and falling party, generally speaking of a character not to favour usurpation and the ascendancy of a despotic chief. Every day shews more and more the much to be regretted tendency of Governments intirely popular to dissolution and disorder. Is it rational to expect, that a man who had the sagacity to foresee this tendency, and whose temper would permit him to bottom his aggrandisement on popular prejudices and vices would desert this system at a time, when more than ever the state of things invites him to adhere to it?

8   If Lansing is Governor his personal character affords some security against pernicious extremes, and at the same time renders it morally certain, that the democratic party already much divided and weakened will moulder and break asunder more and more. This is certainly a state of things favorable to the future ascendancy of the wise and good. May it not lead to a recasting of parties by which the fœderalists will gain a great accession of force from former opponents? At any rate, is it not wiser in them to promote a course of things by which scism among the democrats will be fostered and increased, than one likely, upon a fair calculation to give them a chief better able than any they have yet had to unite and direct them and in a situation to infuse rottenness in the only part of our Country which still remains sound—the fœderal states of New England.

February 10, 1804

Propositions on the Law of Libel

I. The Liberty of the press consists in the right to publish with impunity Truth with good motives for justifiable ends though reflecting on Govt. Magistracy or Individuals.

II. That the allowance of this right is essential to the preservation of free Governmt. The dissallowance of it fatal.

III. That its abuse is to be guarded against by subjecting the exercise of it to the animadversion and controul of the Tribunals of Justice; but that this controul cannot safely be entrusted to a permanent body of Magistracy and requires the effectual cooperation of Court and Jury.

IV. That to confine the Jury to the mere question of publication and the application of terms; without the right of inquiry into the intent or tendency reserving to the Court the exclusive right of pronouncing upon the construction tendency and intent of the alleged libel, is calculated to render nugatory the function of the Jury; enabling the Court to make a libel of any writing whatsoever the most innocent or commendable.

V. That it is the general rule of criminal law that the intent constitutes the crime and that it is equally a general rule, that the intent, mind or *quo animo* is an inference of fact to be drawn by the Jury.

VI. That if there are exceptions to this rule they are confined to cases on which not only the principal fact but its circumstances can be and are specifically defined by Statute or Judicial Precedents.

VII. That in respect to libel there is no such specific and precise definition of facts and circumstances to be found; that consequently it is difficult if not impossible to pronounce that any writing is per se and exclusive of all circumstances libellous: That its libellous character must depend on intent and tendency the one and the other being matter of fact.

VIII. That the definitions or descriptions of libels to be found in the books predicate them upon some malicious or mischievous intent or tendency; to expose individuals to hatred or contempt or to occasion a disturbance or breach of the peace.

IX. That in determining the character of a libel the Truth or falsehood is in the nature of things a material ingredient though the truth may not always be decisive but being abused may still admit of a malicious and mischievous intent which may constitute a libel.

X. That in the Roman Law one source of the doctrine of libel, the truth in cases interesting to the public may be given in evidence. That the antient Statutes probably declaratory of the common make the falsehood an ingredient of the Crime; that antient precedents in the Court of Justice correspond and that the precedents to this day charge a malicious intent.

XI. That the doctrine of excluding the truth as immaterial originate in a tyrannical and polluted source, the Court of Star Chamber and that though it prevailed a considerable length of time yet there are leading precedents down to the Revolution and ever since in which a contrary practice prevailed.

XII. That this doctrine being against reason and natural justice and contrary to the original principles of the common law enforced by Statutory provisions, precedents which support it deserve to be considered in no better light than as malus usus which ought to be abolished.

XIII. That in the general distribution of powers in our System of Jurisprudence the cognizance of law belongs to the Court, of fact to the Jury; that as often as they are not blended the powers of the Court is absolute and exclusive. That in civil cases it is always so and may rightfully be so exerted. That in criminal cases the law and fact being always blended, the Jury for reasons of a political and peculiar nature, for the security of life and liberty, is entrusted with the power of deciding both law and fact.

XIV. That this distinction results.

1. from the ancient forms of pleading in civil cases none but special pleas being allowed in matter of law, in criminal none but the general issue.

2. from the liability of the Jury to attaint on civil cases and the general power of the Court, as its substitute in granting new trials and from the exemption of the Jury from attaint in criminal cases and the defect of power to controul their verdicts by new trials; the test of every legal power being its

capacity to produce a definitive effect liable neither to punishment nor controul.

XV. That in criminal cases nevertheless the Court are the constitutional advisers of the Jury in matter of law; who may compromit their consciences by lightly or rashly disregarding that advice; but may still more compromit their consciences by following it, if exercising their judgments with discretion and honesty they have a clear conviction that the charge of the Court is wrong.

February 15, 1804

ORIGINS OF A DISPUTE

From Aaron Burr

Sir,   Nyork 18 June 1804

I send for your perusal a letter signed Ch. D. Cooper which, though apparently published some time ago, has but very recently come to my knowledge. Mr Van Ness who does me the favor to deliver this, will point out to you that Clause of the letter to which I particularly request your attention.

You might perceive, Sir, the necessity of a prompt and unqualified acknowledgment or denial of the use of any expressions which could warrant the assertions of Dr Cooper.

I have the honor to be   Your Obt Svt   A. Burr

SIR,

The malignant attack which my character has sustained in an anonymous hand-bill, to which your letter of the 21st inst. directed to the chairman of the Federal electioneering committee of this city is annexed; and in which you contradict certain facts contained in a letter, said to have been written by me to ANDREW BROWN, Esq. of Bern, will be my apology for repelling the unfounded aspersions which have been thus dishonorably obtruded on the public. My letter to Mr. BROWN was committed to the care of JOHAN J. DEITZ, Esq. of Bern;

but to this gentleman, I hope, cannot be imputed the embezzling and breaking open of a letter, a crime which in England has met with the most ignominious punishment.

Admitting the letter published to be an exact transcript of the one intended for Mr. BROWN, and which, it seems, instead of being delivered according to promise, was EMBEZZLED and BROKEN OPEN; I aver, that the assertions therein contained are substantially true, and that I can prove them by the most unquestionable testimony. I assert that Gen. HAMILTON and Judge KENT have declared, in substance, that they looked upon Mr. BURR to be a dangerous man, and one who ought not to be trusted with the reins of government. If, Sir, you attended a meeting of federalists, at the city tavern, where Gen. HAMILTON made a speech on the pending election, I might appeal to you for the truth of so much of this assertion as relates to him. I have, however, other evidence to substantiate the fact. With respect to Judge KENT's declaration, I have only to refer to THEODORUS V. W. GRAHAM, Esq. and Mr. JAMES KANE, of this city, whose veracity, I trust, will not be impeached; but should the fact have escaped their recollection, I am not in want of other evidence, equally respectable, to support it. Mr. VAN RENSSELAER, a few days before he left town for New-York, in a conversation with me, declared in substance what I communicated in the letter to Mr. BROWN, as coming from him; and I am perfectly willing to repose myself on his well-known candour for the truth of this declaration.

I asserted, in the letter which has been so disgracefully EMBEZZLED, and the BREAKING OPEN of which must be ranked with the lowest species of villainy, that many of the reflecting federalists would support Judge LEWIS. Will this be considered a rash assertion, when it is known, that two federal gentlemen, high in office in this city, have declared they would vote for him? Judge PENDLETON, of New-York, made the same declaration in this city, under the impression, however, that no federal candidate was to be offered. OLIVER PHELPS, when in this city, on his way to Canandaigua, stated, that Gen. HAMILTON, and about one hundred federalists in New-York, would not vote for Mr. BURR.

It is true, that Judge TAYLER intimated to me, the conversation Mr. VAN RENSSELAER had with him, to which you allude, but it was subsequent to my having written and dispatched the letter for Mr. BROWN.

I beg leave to remark, sir, that the anxiety you discovered, when his Honor the Chancellor was about to be nominated, induced me to believe, that you entertained a bad opinion of Mr. BURR, especially when taken in connection with General HAMILTON's harangue at the city tavern; and although I have never suggested that you would act on the one side or the other in this election—yet, presuming on the correctness of your mind, and the reputation you sustain of an upright and exemplary character, I could not suppose you would support a man whom I had reason to believe, you held in the lowest estimation.

It is sufficient for me, on this occasion, to substantiate what I have asserted. I have made it an invariable rule of my life, to be circumspect in relating what I may have heard from others; and in this affair, I feel happy to think, that I have been unusually cautious—for really sir, I could detail to you a still more despicable opinion which General HAMILTON has expressed of Mr. BURR.

I cannot conclude, without paying some attention to your friend, Dr. STRINGER; I have to regret that this gentleman, so renowned for the Christian virtues, should have consented to dishonour your name, by connecting your letter with an anonymous production, replete with the vilest falsehood and the foulest calumny.

I am, Sir, with due respect,   Your humble servant,
                                CHARLES D. COOPER.
April 23, 1804.

DECLINING TO AVOW OR DISAVOW

To Aaron Burr

Sir   New York June 20. 1804
    I have maturely reflected on the subject of your letter of the 18th instant; and the more I have reflected the more I have

become convinced, that I could not, without manifest impropriety, make the avowal or disavowal which you seem to think necessary.

The clause pointed out by Mr. Van Ness is in these terms "I could detail to you a *still more despicable opinion*, which General Hamilton has expressed of Mr. Burr." To endeavour to discover the meaning of this declaration, I was obliged to seek in the antecedent part of the letter, for the opinion to which it referred, as having been already disclosed. I found it in these words "General Hamilton and Judge Kent have declared, *in substance*, that they looked upon Mr. Burr to be *a dangerous man*, and one *who ought not to be trusted with the reins of Government*". The language of Doctor Cooper plainly implies, that he considered this opinion of you, which he attributes to me, as a *despicable* one; but he affirms that I have expressed some other *still more despicable*; without however mentioning to whom, when, or where. 'Tis evident, that the phrase "still more dispicable" admits of infinite shades, from very light to very dark. How am I to judge of the degree intended? Or how shall I annex any precise idea to language so indefinite?

Between Gentlemen, *despicable* and *more despicable* are not worth the pains of a distinction. When therefore you do not interrogate me, as to the opinion which is specifically ascribed to me, I must conclude, that you view it as within the limits, to which the animadversions of political opponents, upon each other, may justifiably extend; and consequently as not warranting the idea of it, which Doctor Cooper appears to entertain. If so, what precise inference could you draw as a guide for your future conduct, were I to acknowlege, that I had expressed an opinion of you, *still more despicable*, than the one which is particularised? How could you be sure, that even this opinion had exceeded the bounds which you would yourself deem admissible between political opponents?

But I forbear further comment on the embarrassment to which the requisition you have made naturally leads. The occasion forbids a more ample illustration, though nothing would be more easy than to pursue it.

Repeating, that I cannot reconcile it with propriety to make the acknowlegement, or denial, you desire—I will add, that I deem it inadmissible, on principle, to consent to be interrogated as to the justness of the *inferences*, which may be drawn by *others*, from whatever I may have said of a political opponent in the course of a fifteen years competition. If there were no other objection to it, this is sufficient, that it would tend to expose my sincerity and delicacy to injurious imputations from every person, who may at any time have conceived the import of my expressions differently from what I may then have intended, or may afterwards recollect.

I stand ready to avow or disavow promptly and explicitly any precise or definite opinion, which I may be charged with having declared of any Gentleman. More than this cannot fitly be expected from me; and especially it cannot reasonably be expected, that I shall enter into an explanation upon a basis so vague as that which you have adopted. I trust, on more reflection, you will see the matter in the same light with me. If not, I can only regret the circumstance, and must abide the consequences.

The publication of Doctor Cooper was never seen by me 'till after the receipt of your letter.

I have the honor to be   Sir   Your obed. servt

A Hamilton

NEW REASONS FOR A DEFINITE REPLY

From Aaron Burr

Sir   Nyork 21 June 1804
Your letter of the 20th. inst. has been this day received. Having Considered it attentively I regret to find in it nothing of that sincerity and delicacy which you profess to Value.

Political opposition can never absolve Gentlemen from the necessity of a rigid adherence to the laws of honor and the rules of decorum: I neither claim such priviledge nor indulge it in others.

The Common sense of Mankind affixes to the epithet adopted by Dr Cooper the idea of dishonor: it has been publicly applied to me under the Sanction of your name. The question is not whether he has understood the meaning of the word or has used it according to Syntax and with grammatical accuracy, but whether you have authorised this application either directly or by uttering expressions or opinions derogatory to my honor. The time "when" is in your own knowledge, but no way material to me, as the calumny has now first been disclosed so as to become the Subject of my Notice, and as the effect is present and palpable.

Your letter has furnished me with new reasons for requiring a definite reply.

I have the honor to be   sir   your obt st   A. Burr

"EXPRESSIONS INDECOROUS AND IMPROPER"

To Aaron Burr

Sir   New York June 22d. 1804

Your first letter, in a style too peremptory, made a demand, in my opinion, unprecedented and unwarrantable. My answer, pointing out the embarrassment, gave you an opportunity to take a less exceptionable course. You have not chosen to do it, but by your last letter, received this day, containing expressions indecorous and improper, you have increased the difficulties to explanation, intrinsically incident to the nature of your application.

If by a "definite reply" you mean the direct avowal or disavowal required in your first letter, I have no other answer to give than that which has already been given. If you mean any thing different admitting of greater latitude, it is requisite you should explain.

I have the honor to be   Sir   Your obed servt.

A Hamilton

"THE COURSE I AM ABOUT TO PURSUE"

From Aaron Burr

Sir   Nyork June 22d. 1804

Mr. V Ness has this evening reported to me Verbally that you refuse to answer my last letter, that you consider the course I have taken as intemperate and unnecessary and some other conversation which it is improper that I should notice.

My request to you was in the first instance proposed in a form the most simple in order that you might give to the affair that course to which you might be induced by your temper and your knowledge of facts. I relied with unsuspecting faith that from the frankness of a Soldier and the Candor of a gentleman I might expect an ingenuous declaration; that if, as I had reason to believe, you had used expressions derogatory to my honor, you would have had the Spirit to Maintain or the Magnanimity to retract them, and, that if from your language injurious inferences had been improperly drawn, Sincerity and delicacy would have pointed out to you the propriety of correcting errors which might thus have been widely diffused.

With these impressions, I was greatly disappointed in receiving from you a letter which I could only consider as evasive and which in manner, is not altogether decorus. In one expectation however, I was not wholly deceived, for at the close of your letter I find an intimation, that if I should dislike your refusal to acknowledge or deny the charge, you were ready to meet the consequences. This I deemed a sort of defiance, and I should have been justified if I had chosen to make it the basis of an immediate message: Yet, as you had also said something (though in my opinion unfounded) of the indefiniteness of my request; as I believed that your communication was the offspring, rather of false pride than of reflection, and, as I felt the utmost reluctance to proceed to extremities while any other hope remained, my request was repeated in terms more definite. To this you refuse all reply, reposing, as I am bound to presume on the tender of an alternative insinuated in your letter.

Thus, Sir, you have invited the course I am about to pursue, and now by your silence impose it upon me. If therefore your determinations are final, of which I am not permitted to doubt, Mr. Van Ness is authorised to communicate my further expectations either to yourself or to such friend as you may be pleased to indicate.

I have the honor to be   Your Ob st   A. Burr

Response to a Letter from William P. Van Ness

Whether the observations in this letter are designed merely to justify the result, which is indicated in the close of the letter, or may be intended to give an opening for rendering any thing explicit which may have been deemed vague heretofore can only be judged of by the sequel. At any rate it appears to me necessary not to be misunderstood. Mr. Pendleton is therefore authorised to say that in the course of the present discussion, whether written or verbal, there has been no intention to evade defy or insult, but a sincere disposition to avoid extremities, if it could be done with propriety. With this view G H—— has been ready to enter into a frank and free explanation on any and every object of a specific nature; but not to answer a general and abstract enquiry, embracing a period too long for any accurate recollection, and exposing him to unpleasant criticisms from or unpleasant discussions with any and every person, who may have understood him in an unfavourable sense. This (admitting that he could answer in a manner the most satisfactory to Col Burr) he should deem inadmissible, in principle and precedent, and humiliating in practice. To this therefore he can never submit. Frequent allusion has been made to slanders said to be in circulation. Whether this be openly or in whispers they have a form and shape and might be specified.

If the alternative alluded to in the close of the letter is definitively tendered, it must be accepted, the time place and

manner to be afterwards regulated. I should not think it right
in the midst of a circuit Court to withdraw my services from
those who may have confided important interests to me and
expose them to the embarrassment of seeking other counsel
who may not have time to be sufficiently instructed in their
causes. I shall also want a little time to make some arrangements respecting my own affairs.

June 28, 1804

Statement Regarding Financial Situation

Herewith is a general statement of my pecuniary affairs; in
which there can be no material error. The result is that calculating my property at what it stands me in, I am now worth
about Ten thousand pounds, and that estimating according to
what my lands are now selling for and are likely to fetch, the
surplus beyond my debts may fairly be stated at nearly double
that sum. Yet I am pained to be obliged to entertain doubts
whether, if an accident should happen to me, by which the
sales of my property should come to be forced, it would be
even sufficient to pay my debts.

In a situation like this, it is perhaps due to my reputation to
explain why I have made so considerable an establishment in
the country. This explanation shall be submitted.

To men, who have been so much harassed in the busy
world as myself, it is natural to look forward to a comfortable
retirement, in the sequel of life, as a principal desideratum.
This desire I have felt in the strongest manner; and to prepare
for it has latterly been a favourite object. I thought that I
might not only expect to accomplish the object, but might
reasonably aim at it and pursue the preparatory measures,
from the following considerations.

It has been for some time past pretty well ascertained to my
mind, that the emoluments of my profession would prove
equal to the maintenance of my family and the gradual discharge of my debts, within a period to the end of which my

faculties, for business might be expected to extend, in full energy. I think myself warranted to estimate the annual product of those emoluments at Twelve* Dollars at the least. My expences while the first improvements of my country establishment were going on have been great; but they would this summer and fall reach the point, at which it is my intention they should stop, at least 'till I should be better able than at present to add to them; and after a fair examination founded upon an actual account of my expenditures, I am persuaded that a plan I have contemplated for the next and succeeding years would bring my expences of every kind within the compass of four thousand Dollars yearly, exclusive of the interest of my country establishment. To this limit, I have been resolved to reduce them, even though it should be necessary to lease that establishment for a few years.

In the mean time, my lands now in a course of sale & settlement would accelerate the extinguishment of my debt, and in the end leave me a handsome clear property. It was also allowable for me to take into view, collaterally, the expectations of my wife; which have been of late partly realised. She is now intitled to a property of between two and three thousand pounds (as I compute) by descent from her mother; and her father is understood to possess a large estate. I feel all the delicacy of this allusion; but the occasion I trust will plead my excuse. And that venerable father, I am sure, will pardon. He knows well all the nicety of my past conduct.

Viewing the matter in these different aspects, I trust the opinion of candid men will be, that there has been no impropriety in my conduct; especially when it is taken into the calculation that my Country establishment, though costly, promises, by the progressive rise of property on this Island, and the felicity of its situation to become more and more valuable.

My chief apology is due to those friends, who have from mere kindness, indorsed my paper discounted at the Banks. On mature reflection I have thought it justifiable to secure them in preference to other Creditors, lest perchance there should be *a deficit*. Yet while this may save them from even-

---

*thousand must have been omitted through inadvertence.

tual loss, it will not exempt them from some present inconvenience. As to this I can only throw myself upon their kindness, and entreat the indulgence of the Banks for them. Perhaps this request may be supposed intitled to some regard.

In the event, which would bring this paper to the public eye, one thing at least would be put beyond a doubt. This is, that my public labours have amounted to an absolute sacrifice of the interests of my family—and that in all pecuniary concerns the delicacy, no less than the probity of my conduct in public stations, has been such as to defy even the shadow of a question.

Indeed, I have not enjoyed the ordinary advantages incident to my military services. Being a member of Congress, while the question of the commutation of the half pay of the army in a sum in gross was in debate, delicacy and a desire to be useful to the army, by removing the idea of my having an interest in the question, induced me to write to the Secretary of War and relinquish my claim to half pay; which, or the equivalent, I have accordingly never received. Neither have I ever applied for the lands allowed by the United States to Officers of my rank. Nor did I ever obtain from this state the allowance of lands made to officers of similar rank. It is true that having served through the latter period of the War on the general staff of the UStates and not in the line of this State, I could not claim that allowance as a matter of course. But having before the War resided in this State and having entered the military career at the head of a company of Artillery raised for the particular defence of this State, I had better pretensions to the allowance than others to whom it was actually made—Yet has it not been extended to me.

A H

July 1, 1804

"FLY TO THE BOSOM OF YOUR GOD"

To Elizabeth Hamilton

This letter, my very dear Eliza, will not be delivered to you, unless I shall first have terminated my earthly career; to begin, as I humbly hope from redeeming grace and divine mercy, a happy immortality.

If it had been possible for me to have avoided the interview, my love for you and my precious children would have been alone a decisive motive. But it was not possible, without sacrifices which would have rendered me unworthy of your esteem. I need not tell you of the pangs I feel, from the idea of quitting you and exposing you to the anguish which I know you would feel. Nor could I dwell on the topic lest it should unman me.

The consolations of Religion, my beloved, can alone support you; and these you have a right to enjoy. Fly to the bosom of your God and be comforted. With my last idea; I shall cherish the sweet hope of meeting you in a better world.

Adieu best of wives and best of Women. Embrace all my darling Children for me.

Ever yours   AH

July 4. 1804

Statement Regarding the Duel with Burr

On my expected interview with Col Burr, I think it proper to make some remarks explanatory of my conduct, motives and views.

I am certainly desirous of avoiding this interview, for the most cogent reasons.

1   My religious and moral principles are strongly opposed to the practice of Duelling, and it would even give me pain to be obliged to shed the blood of a fellow creature in a private combat forbidden by the laws.

2   My wife and Children are extremely dear to me, and my life is of the utmost importance to them, in various views.

3   I feel a sense of obligation towards my creditors; who in case of accident to me, by the forced sale of my property, may be in some degree sufferers. I did not think my self at liberty, as a man of probity, lightly to expose them to this hazard.

4   I am conscious of no *ill-will* to Col Burr, distinct from political opposition, which, as I trust, has proceeded from pure and upright motives.

Lastly, I shall hazard much, and can possibly gain nothing by the issue of the interview.

But it was, as I conceive, impossible for me to avoid it. There were *intrinsick* difficulties in the thing, and *artificial* embarrassments, from the manner of proceeding on the part of Col Burr.

Intrinsick—because it is not to be denied, that my animadversions on the political principles character and views of Col Burr have been extremely severe, and on different occasions, I, in common with many others, have made very unfavourable criticisms on particular instances of the private conduct of this Gentleman.

In proportion as these impressions were entertained with sincerity and uttered with motives and for purposes, which might appear to me commendable, would be the difficulty (until they could be removed by evidence of their being erroneous), of explanation or apology. The disavowal required of me by Col Burr, in a general and indefinite form, was out of my power, if it had really been proper for me to submit to be so questionned; but I was sincerely of opinion, that this could not be, and in this opinion, I was confirmed by that of a very moderate and judicious friend whom I consulted. Besides that Col Burr appeared to me to assume, in the first instance, a tone unnecessarily peremptory and menacing, and in the second, positively offensive. Yet I wished, as far as might be practicable, to leave a door open to accommodation. This, I think, will be inferred from the written communications made by me and by my direction, and would be confirmed by the conversations between Mr van Ness and myself, which arose out of the subject.

I am not sure, whether under all the circumstances I did

not go further in the attempt to accommodate, than a punctilious delicacy will justify. If so, I hope the motives I have stated will excuse me.

It is not my design, by what I have said to affix any odium on the conduct of Col Burr, in this case. He doubtless has heared of animadversions of mine which bore very hard upon him; and it is probable that as usual they were accompanied with some falshoods. He may have supposed himself under a necessity of acting as he has done. I hope the grounds of his proceeding have been such as ought to satisfy his own conscience.

I trust, at the same time, that the world will do me the Justice to believe, that I have not censured him on light grounds, or from unworthy inducements. I certainly have had strong reasons for what I may have said, though it is possible that in some particulars, I may have been influenced by misconstruction or misinformation. It is also my ardent wish that I may have been more mistaken than I think I have been, and that he by his future conduct may shew himself worthy of all confidence and esteem, and prove an ornament and blessing to his Country.

As well because it is possible that I may have injured Col Burr, however convinced myself that my opinions and declarations have been well founded, as from my general principles and temper in relation to similar affairs—I have resolved, if our interview is conducted in the usual manner, and it pleases God to give me the opportunity, to *reserve* and *throw away* my first fire, and I *have thoughts* even of *reserving* my second fire—and thus giving a double opportunity to Col Burr to pause and to reflect.

It is not however my intention to enter into any explanations on the ground. Apology, from principle I hope, rather than Pride, is out of the question.

To those, who with me abhorring the practice of Duelling may think that I ought on no account to have added to the number of bad examples—I answer that my *relative* situation, as well in public as private aspects, enforcing all the considerations which constitute what men of the world denominate honor, impressed on me (as I thought) a peculiar necessity not to decline the call. The ability to be in future useful, whether in resisting mischief or effecting good, in those crises of our public affairs, which seem likely to happen, would probably be inseparable from a conformity with public prejudice in this particular.

AH

c. July 10, 1804

"OUR REAL DISEASE; WHICH IS DEMOCRACY"

To Theodore Sedgwick

My Dear Sir   New York July 10. 1804

I have received two letters from you since we last saw each other—that of the latest date being the 24 of May. I have had in hand for some time a long letter to you, explaining my view of the course and tendency of our Politics, and my intentions as to my own future conduct. But my plan embraced so large a range that owing to much avocation, some indifferent health, and a growing distaste for Politics, the letter is still considerably short of being finished. I write this now to satisfy you, that want of regard for you has not been the cause of my silence.

I will here express but one sentiment, which is, that Dismemberment of our Empire will be a clear sacrifice of great positive advantages, without any counterballancing good; administering no relief to our real Disease; which is DEMOCRACY, the poison of which by a subdivision will only be the more concentered in each part, and consequently the more virulent.

King is on his way for Boston where you may chance to see him, and hear from himself his sentiments.

God bless you   A H

AN OBLIGATION OWED

To Elizabeth Hamilton

My beloved Eliza

Mrs. Mitchel is the person in the world to whom as a friend I am under the greatest Obligations. I have not hitherto done my duty to her. But resolved to repair my omission as much as possible, I have encouraged her to come to this Country and intend, if it shall be in my power to render the Evening of her days comfortable. But if it shall please God to put this out of my power and to inable you hereafter to be of service to her, I entreat you to do it and to treat her with the tenderness of a Sister.

This is my second letter.

The Scruples of a Christian have determined me to expose my own life to any extent rather than subject my self to the guilt of taking the life of another. This must increase my hazards & redoubles my pangs for you. But you had rather I should die innocent than live guilty. Heaven can preserve me and I humbly hope will but in the contrary event, I charge you to remember that you are a Christian. God's Will be done. The will of a merciful God must be good.

Once more Adieu My Darling darling Wife

A H

Tuesday Evening 10 oClock

July 10, 1804

APPENDIX:

STATEMENTS ON THE HAMILTON-BURR DUEL

Joint Statement by William P. Van Ness and Nathaniel Pendleton

Col: Burr arrived first on the ground as had been previously agreed. When Genl Hamilton arrived the parties exchanged salutations and the Seconds proceeded to make their arrangments. They measured the distance, ten full paces, and cast lots for the choice of positions as also to determine by whom the word should be given, both of which fell to the Second of Genl Hamilton. They then proceeded to load the pistols in each others presence, after which the parties took their stations. The Gentleman who was to give the word, then explained to the parties the rules which were to govern them in firing which were as follows: The parties being placed at their stations The Second who gives the word shall ask them whether they are ready—being answered in the affirmative, he shall say *"present"* after which the parties shall present & fire when they please. If one fires before the other the opposite second shall say one two, three, fire, and he shall fire or loose his fire. And asked if they were prepared, being answered in the affirmative he gave the word *present* as had been agreed on, and both of the parties took aim, & fired in succession, the Intervening time is not expressed as the seconds do not precisely agree on that point. The pistols were discharged within a few seconds of each other and the fire of Col: Burr took effect; Genl Hamilton almost instantly fell. Col: Burr then advanced toward Genl H——n with a manner and gesture that appeared to Genl Hamilton's friend to be expressive of regret, but without Speaking turned about & withdrew. Being urged from the field by his friend as has been subsequently stated, with a view to prevent his being recognised by the Surgeon and Bargemen who were then approaching. No farther communications took place between the principals and the Barge that carried Col: Burr immediately returned to the City. We conceive it proper to add that the conduct of the parties in that interview was perfectly proper as suited the occasion.

July 17, 1804

Statement by Nathaniel Pendleton

The statement containing the facts that led to the interview between General Hamilton and Col. Burr, published in the Evening Post on Monday, studiously avoided mentioning any particulars of what past at the place of meeting. This was dictated by suitable considerations at the time, and with the intention, that whatever it might be deemed proper to lay before the public, should be made the subject of a future communication. The following is therefore now submitted.

In the interviews that have since taken place between the gentlemen that were present, they have not been able to agree in two important facts that passed there—for which reason nothing was said on those subjects in the paper lately published as to other particulars in which they were agreed.

Mr. P. expressed a confident opinion that General Hamilton did not fire first—and that he did not fire at all *at Col. Burr.* Mr. V. N. seemed equally confident in the opinion that Gen. H. did fire first—and of course that it must have been *at* his antagonist.

General Hamilton's friend thinks it to be a sacred duty he owes to the memory of that exalted man, to his country, and his friends, to publish to the world such facts and circumstances as have produced a decisive conviction in his own mind, that he cannot have been mistaken in the belief he has formed on these points.

1st. Besides the testimonies of Bishop Moore, and the paper containing an express declaration, under General Hamilton's own hand, enclosed to his friend in a packet, not to be delivered but in the event of his death, and which have already been published, General Hamilton informed Mr. P. at least ten days previous to the affair, that he had doubts whether he would not receive and not return Mr. Burr's first fire. Mr. P. remonstrated against this determination, and urged many considerations against it, as dangerous to himself and not necessary in the particular case, when every ground of accommodation, not humiliating, had been proposed and rejected. He said he would not decide lightly, but take time to deliberate fully. It was incidentally mentioned again at their occasional subsequent conversations, and on the evening preceding the time of the appointed interview, he informed Mr. P. he had made up his mind *not to fire at Col. Burr the first time, but to receive his fire, and fire in the air.* Mr. P. again urged him upon this subject, and repeated his former arguments. His final answer was in terms that made an impression on Mr. P's mind which can never be effaced. "My friend, it is the effect of A RELIGIOUS SCRUPLE, and does not admit of reasoning, it is useless to say more on the subject, as my purpose is definitely fixed."

2d. His last words before he was wounded afford a proof that this purpose had not changed. When he received his pistol, after having taken his position, he was asked if he would have the hair spring set? His answer was, *"Not this time."*

3d. After he was wounded, and laid in the boat, the first words he uttered after recovering the power of speech, were, (addressing himself to a gentleman present, who perfectly well remembers it) *"Pendleton knows I did not mean to fire at Col. Burr the first time."*

4th. This determination had been communicated by Mr. P. to that gentleman that morning, before they left the city.

5th. The pistol that had been used by General Hamilton, lying loose over the other apparatus in the case which was open; after having been some time in the boat, one of the boatmen took hold of it to put it into the case. General Hamilton observing this, said *"Take care of that pistol—it is cocked. It may go off and do mischief."* This is also remembered by the gentleman alluded to.

This shews he was not sensible of having fired at all. If he had fired *previous* to receiving the wound, he would have remembered it, and therefore have known that the pistol could not go off; but if *afterwards* it must have been the effect of an involuntary exertion of the muscles produced by a mortal wound, in which case, he could not have been conscious of having fired.

6. Mr. P. having so strong a conviction that if General Hamilton had fired first, it could not have escaped his attention (all his anxiety being alive for the effect of the first fire, and having no reason to believe the friend of Col. Burr was not sincere in the contrary opinion) he determined to go to

the spot where the affair took place, to see if he could not discover some traces of the course of the ball from Gen. Hamilton's pistol.

He took a friend with him the day after General Hamilton died, and after some examination they fortunately found what they were in search of. They ascertained that the ball passed through the limb of a cedar tree, at an elevation of about twelve feet and a half, perpendicularly from the ground, between thirteen and fourteen feet from the mark on which General Hamilton stood, and about four feet wide of the direct line between him and Colonel Burr, on the right side; he having fallen on the left. The part of the limb through which the ball passed was cut off and brought to this city, and is now in Mr. Church's possession.

No inferences are pointed out as resulting from these facts, nor will any comments be made. They are left to the candid judgment and feelings of the public.

July 19, 1804

Statement by William P. Van Ness

The second of G H having considered it proper to subjoin an explanatory note to the statement mutually furnished, it becomes proper for the gentleman who attended Col Burr to state also his impressions with respect to those points on which their exists a variance of opinion. In doing this he pointedly disclaims any idea disrespectful to the memory of G H, or an intention to ascribe any conduct to him that is not in his opinion perfectly honorable & correct.

The parties met as has been above related & took their respective stations as directed: the pistols were then handed to them by the seconds. Gen Hamilton elevated his, as if to try the light, & lowering it said I beg pardon for delaying you but the direction of the light renders it necessary, at the same time feeling his pockets with his left hand, & drawing forth his spectacles put them on. The second then asked if they were prepared which was replied to in the affirmative. The word *present* was then given, on which both parties took aim. The pistol of General Hamilton was first discharged, and Col Burr fired immediately after, only five or six seconds of time intervening. On this point the second of Col Burr has full & perfect reccollection. He noticed particularly the discharge of G H's pistol, & looked to his principal to ascertain whether he was hurt, he then clearly saw Col Bs pistol discharged. At this moment of looking at Col B on the discharge of G H's pistol he perceived a slight motion in his person, which induced the idea of his being struck. On this point he conversed with his principal on their return, who ascribed that circumstance to a small stone under his foot, & observed that the smoke of G Hs pistol obscured him for a moment in the interval of their firing.

When G H fell Col B advanced toward him as stated & was checked by his second who urged the importance of his immediately repairing to the barge, conceiving that G H was mortally wounded, & being desirous to secure his principal from the sight of the surgeon & bargemen who might be called in evidence. Col B complied with his request.

He shortly followed him to the boat, and Col B again expressed a wish to return, saying with an expression of much concern, I must go & speak to him. I again urged the obvious impropriety stating that the G was surrounded by the Surgeon & Bargemen by whom he must not be seen & insisted on immediate departure.

July 21, 1804

Chronology

1755   Born January 11 in the British West Indies, probably on the island of Nevis, the second child of Rachel Faucett Lavien and James Hamilton. (Father was born c. 1718 in Scotland, the fourth son of Alexander Hamilton, Laird of Grange in Ayrshire, and his wife, Elizabeth, and went to the West Indies around 1736 to seek his fortune. Mother was born c. 1729 on Nevis, the daughter of John Faucett, a physician and planter of Huguenot descent, and his wife, Mary. She married Johann Michael Lavien, a wealthy merchant, on St. Croix in the Danish West Indies around 1745, and their son, Peter, was born in 1746. The marriage was unhappy, and in 1750 Rachel left her husband and son. By 1752 she was living out of wedlock with James Hamilton, possibly on St. Kitts. Their first child, James, was born in 1753. Alexander Hamilton apparently believed he had been born in 1757, but the year 1755 is supported by a 1768 probate document.)

1759   Johann Michael Lavien obtains divorce that forbids Rachel from remarrying.

1765   Family moves to St. Croix. Father leaves family and never returns. Mother opens small store in Christiansted selling provisions and plantation supplies.

1768   Mother falls ill with fever and dies on February 19. Peter Lavien, her sole legitimate child, inherits her entire estate. Hamilton becomes clerk in the mercantile firm of Beckman & Cruger, while brother James is apprenticed to a carpenter.

1772   Letter by Hamilton describing hurricane is published in the St. Croix *Royal Danish American Gazette* on October 3. Hugh Knox, minister of the Presbyterian church in Christiansted, collects funds to send Hamilton to the North American mainland for an education. Hamilton sails to Boston and then travels to New York, carrying letters of introduction from Knox. Sponsored by William Livingston and Elias Boudinot, both successful attorneys and acquaintances of Knox, Hamilton begins study of Latin and Greek at Presbyterian academy taught by Francis Barber in Elizabethtown, New Jersey, where Livingston and Boudinot live.

1773   Requests entrance to the College of New Jersey (now Princeton) with permission to advance as quickly as he can work, but his request is denied by the trustees. Enters King's College (now Columbia) in New York City as a special student. Lodges in a room at the college with Robert Troup, who becomes a lifelong friend. Through the Livingston family, meets New York attorney John Jay.

1774 Formally enters King's College. Studies Latin, Greek, anatomy, and mathematics. Forms a writing and debating society with friends. In response to a pamphlet by leading New York Loyalist Samuel Seabury, Hamilton writes *A Full Vindication of the Measures of Congress*, pamphlet published December 15.

1775 After Seabury responds to *A Full Vindication*, Hamilton counters with pamphlet *The Farmer Refuted*, published on February 23. Helps protect Myles Cooper, the Loyalist president of King's College, from a patriotic mob on May 10. Studies gunnery and joins New York provincial militia, attending daily drill sessions. Publishes letters in *Rivington's New-York Gazetteer*, June 15 and June 22, criticizing the Quebec Act of 1774 for establishing "arbitrary power" and the Roman Catholic Church in the province. Sees action for the first time, August 23–24, when he comes under fire from a British warship in New York harbor while helping to remove cannon from the Battery.

1776 New York Provincial Congress orders the organization of an artillery company, and on March 14 Hamilton is appointed its commander with rank of captain. Leaves King's College without obtaining a degree. Spends months equipping and drilling his company, which is assigned to fortifications in New York City. Retreats with his company to Harlem Heights in northern Manhattan on September 15 after the British land at Kips Bay. Company withdraws with Continental army to White Plains in October and is sent to Hackensack, New Jersey, in November. Helps cover withdrawal from New Brunswick on December 1 during American retreat across New Jersey, and participates in Washington's surprise attack on the Hessians at Trenton on December 26.

1777 Fights in battle of Princeton, January 3. Becomes an aide-de-camp to George Washington, with rank of lieutenant colonel in the Continental army, on March 1, a position he holds until 1781. During this period Hamilton keeps close company with Washington at headquarters and in the field, drafts hundreds of letters for him on political, military, and diplomatic subjects, and frequently serves as his emissary. From March 20 to September 1, Hamilton also writes regular military reports to the committee of correspondence of the New York Provincial Convention. Becomes friends with the Marquis de Lafayette when Lafayette joins Washington's staff as a volunteer in August. Serves in the field with Washington during American defeat at Brandywine Creek, Pennsylvania, on September 11. After narrowly escaping from a British cavalry patrol along the Schuylkill River on September 18, sends message warning the Continental Congress to leave Philadelphia (Congress flees to York, Pennsylvania, and the British occupy Philadelphia on September 26). Serves with Washington during unsuccessful American attack at Germantown, Pennsylvania, on October 4. Travels to Albany, New York, in November to obtain reinforcements from the command of General Horatio Gates. Returns to Pennsylvania and spends winter with the army at Valley Forge.

1778   Drafts report for Washington to the Continental Congress on reorganization of the army in January. Continental army leaves Valley Forge on June 19 after British evacuate Philadelphia. Hamilton gathers intelligence and helps coordinate troop movements as Washington pursues British army across New Jersey. Sees action at battle of Monmouth Court House on June 28. Criticizes conduct of General Charles Lee in the battle and testifies on July 4 and July 13 as a prosecution witness at Lee's court-martial for insubordination. Publishes three letters signed "Publius" in the *New-York Journal*, October 19–November 16, attacking Samuel Chase, a Maryland delegate to Congress, for using official information to speculate in the flour market. In December Hamilton's friend and fellow aide John Laurens challenges Charles Lee to a duel over Lee's slurs against Washington. Hamilton acts as Laurens' second in the duel, fought on December 23, in which Laurens wounds Lee.

1779   Spends most of winter and spring at army headquarters in Middlebrook, New Jersey. Helps prepare English version of manual by Friedrich von Steuben, inspector general of the Continental army, on army regulations, drill, and tactics. Writes to John Jay, now the president of Congress, in support of John Laurens' plan to arm slaves in South Carolina. In summer, moves with headquarters to New Windsor and West Point, New York. Engages in heated exchange of correspondence with the Rev. William Gordon, a Massachusetts clergyman whom Hamilton accuses of defaming him by spreading a rumor that he had called for the overthrow of Congress. Spends winter at headquarters in Morristown, New Jersey.

1780   Asks Washington for a field command in January, but request is denied. Begins courtship of Elizabeth Schuyler, born 1757, the daughter of wealthy New York landowner General Philip Schuyler, during her visit to Morristown. Assists Washington in his efforts to obtain sufficient men, supplies, and funds from Congress and the states. Spends summer at headquarters in northeastern New Jersey. Writes long letter to his friend James Duane, a New York delegate to Congress, on September 3, proposing a series of political and financial measures for strengthening the central government, including organizing a national bank and calling a convention to revise the Articles of Confederation. Continues to seek a field command without success. Accompanies Washington on inspection of West Point, September 25, during which the treachery of Benedict Arnold is uncovered. Hamilton is sympathetic toward Major John André, the British officer captured in civilian disguise after meeting with Arnold, and supports André's request to Washington for an honorable execution by firing squad; Washington refuses, and André is hanged. Hamilton and Elizabeth Schuyler marry on December 14 at the Schuyler home in Albany.

1781   Returns to headquarters at New Windsor, New York, in January. Resigns staff position during a dispute with Washington on February 16. Refuses Washington's offer of reconciliation, but remains at headquarters until late April waiting for a replacement to be found. On April 30 writes lengthy letter to Robert Morris, the recently appointed superintendent of finance, detailing plan for restoring public credit. Publishes first of six "Continentalist" essays, advocating a broad interpretation of the powers given to Congress under the Articles of Confederation, in the *New-York Packet* on July 12 (series runs until July 4, 1782). Appointed commander of a New York light infantry battalion, July 31, and joins siege of Yorktown in late September. Leads successful night assault on British redoubt on October 14. Returns to Schuyler home in Albany soon after the British surrender on October 19. Leaves active service in the army while retaining his commission.

1782   First child, Philip, is born January 22. Begins intensive study of the law, making comprehensive and methodical notes (his notes will form the basis for *New York Supreme Court Practice*, a manual published by William Wyche in 1794). Although legal study in New York usually requires a three-year clerkship, Hamilton takes advantage of a temporary suspension of the rule for army veterans and is admitted to practice before the state supreme court in July. Appointed receiver of continental taxes for New York on July 2 by Robert Morris. On July 21,

New York legislature adopts resolutions, probably drafted by Hamilton, calling for a general convention to revise the Articles of Confederation (the first such call made by a public body). Appointed as a delegate to Congress by the state legislature on July 22. Writes detailed letter to Morris in August on economic and political situation in New York State. Serves as receiver through the end of October. Travels to Philadelphia and takes his seat in Congress on November 25. Works with Virginia delegate James Madison on measures for raising funds to pay the army and the public creditors.

1783   Writes to Washington on February 13 suggesting that the growing discontent in the army be used to pressure Congress and the states into adopting new revenue measures. Praises Washington in March when he acts decisively to stop a possible mutiny by officers camped at Newburgh, New York. Takes active role in committees of Congress concerned with military and foreign affairs. Congress ratifies peace treaty with Britain on April 15. Hamilton votes against series of revenue measures proposed to the states by Congress on April 18, believing them to be insufficient. Serves on committee that confers with Pennsylvania executive council during mutiny by unpaid Pennsylvania soldiers in late June. After soldiers surround building where Congress is meeting on June 21, the delegates leave Philadelphia and reconvene in Princeton. Hamilton drafts resolution calling for a convention to revise the Articles of Confederation, but does not submit it to Congress "for want of support." Leaves Congress in late July and returns to Albany in August. Becomes active member of the Society of the Cincinnati, an order formed by Continental army officers that draws criticism for plans to makes its membership hereditary. Settles family in New York City in November, establishing his home and law offices at 57 Wall Street. Attends emotional farewell meeting of Washington and his officers at Fraunces Tavern on December 4.

1784   Publishes two pamphlets under the name "Phocion" in January and April remonstrating against state legislative acts punishing Loyalists. Drafts constitution of the Bank of New York in early March and becomes a member of its board of directors. Appears for the defendant before the mayor's court of New York on June 29 in *Rutgers* v. *Waddington*, lawsuit brought under the 1783 Trespass Act by an elderly widow against a British merchant for damages to her brewery during the British occupation of New York City. Hamilton argues that the Trespass Act, a state law, violates the law of nations and the 1783 peace treaty with Britain and therefore should be held void. In August the court issues a ruling limiting the defendant's liability and accepts one of Hamilton's arguments, holding that the Trespass Act must be interpreted in accordance with the powers given to occupying armies under the law of nations. Second child, Angelica, is born September 25.

1785   Dedicates most of his time to building his law practice; continues to represent British subjects and Loyalists sued under the Trespass Act. Helps organize Society for Promoting the Manumission of Slaves in February. Receives rare letter from his brother James and lends him £50. (Evidence indicates that James died in the West Indies in 1785 or 1786.)

1786   Elected in April to the New York assembly for one-year term beginning in 1787. Appointed by New York legislature on May 5 as delegate to conference on interstate commerce. Third child, Alexander, born May 16. Convention in Annapolis, September 11–14, is attended by only 12 delegates from five states, before adjourning, it unanimously adopts resolution, drafted by Hamilton, proposing that a general convention meet in Philadelphia in May 1787 to consider constitutional changes.

1787   Takes seat in the assembly in January. Unsuccessfully attempts to win approval for measure granting Congress the power to levy a 5 percent tax on imports. Appointed by the legislature on March 6 as a delegate to the Philadelphia convention along with Robert Yates and Robert Lansing Jr., who oppose creating a stronger central government. Takes seat in the convention, May 18. Convention achieves quorum on May 25 and adopts rule giving each state delegation one vote; outnumbered by Yates and Lansing, Hamilton is unable to give voting support to proposals he favors. Delivers lengthy speech on June 18 praising the British system of government and outlining plan for an elected government modeled on it. (Although proceedings of convention are secret, reports of the speech will cause opponents to denounce Hamilton as a monarchist for the rest of his life.) Leaves Philadelphia after June 29 session to tend to his legal practice in New York; will sporadically attend convention during July and August. Publishes unsigned letter in the New York *Daily Advertiser*, July 21, attacking New York governor George Clinton for opposing the convention. Resumes regular attendance in the convention, September 6, and signs the finished Constitution on September 17. Publishes first number of *The Federalist*, essay series advocating ratification of the Constitution, in the New York *Independent Journal* on October 27. (Hamilton eventually writes 51 of the 85 *Federalist* essays, with James Madison contributing 29 and John Jay five; all appear under the name "Publius" and are published several times a week in different New York newspapers over the next five months.) Becomes a trustee of Columbia College (formerly King's College).

1788   Elected by New York legislature as a delegate to Congress, January 22, and takes his seat on February 25; attends sporadically because of his involvement in ratification struggle and the demands of his legal practice. First 36 *Federalist* essays are published in book form on March 22 by John and Archibald McLean in New York. Corresponds regularly with Madison, who has returned to Virginia to attend its ratifying convention. Fourth child, James Alexander, born April 14. Elected as delegate to the New York ratifying convention on April 29. Remaining 49 *Federalist* essays, including eight which had not appeared in newspapers, are published by McLean in second volume on May 28. New York convention opens in Poughkeepsie on June 17 with Antifederalists (opponents of ratification) in the majority. Hamilton takes leading role in the debates, engaging in extended exchanges with prominent Antifederalist Melancton Smith. Federalist position is strengthened when express rider brings news on July 2 that Virginia has become the tenth state to ratify. Debate shifts to possible forms of ratification; Hamilton strongly opposes suggestions by some Antifederalists that New York should conditionally ratify the Constitution. On July 26 convention approves, 30–27, an unconditional ratification that includes recommendations for amendments. Hamilton attends Congress for the last time on October 10.

1789   Hoping to defeat Governor George Clinton, who continues to oppose the new federal government, Hamilton becomes chairman on February 11 of committee of correspondence supporting candidacy of Robert Yates. Writes public letters on behalf of Yates, as well as 16 "H.G." letters attacking Clinton that appear in newspapers from February 20 to April 9. Supports candidacy of John Laurance, a Federalist who is elected to the new House of Representatives on March 4. Clinton wins reelection as governor on April 28. Washington is inaugurated as president on April 30. In response to a request for advice from Washington, Hamilton counsels him to adopt as much formality in presidential etiquette as public sentiment will allow.

Hamilton alienates powerful Livingston family by supporting election of Rufus King to the U.S. Senate from New York over James Duane. Washington signs bill establishing Treasury Department, September 2, and nominates Hamilton as Secretary of the Treasury on September 11; he is confirmed by the Senate on the same day. House of Representatives directs Hamilton on September 21 to submit a plan for the support of the public credit when Congress reconvenes in January 1790. Hamilton works to organize chaotic national finances, collecting information, seeking advice, establishing standard forms and procedures, and commencing regular correspondence with Treasury employees throughout the nation. In October, begins series of conversations with Major George Beckwith, unofficial British minister to the United States, with the aim of improving Anglo-American trade relations.

1790 Submits report on public credit on January 14, asserting that a well-financed national debt will stimulate the economy and strengthen the Union. Report calls for funding the $54 million national debt and for federal assumption of $25 million of state debts incurred during the Revolutionary War; holders of depreciated Continental securities would be allowed to exchange them for new bonds at face value, and import and excise taxes would provide revenue for paying interest on the debt. Plan proves highly controversial and is opposed in the House by Madison, who favors discrimination between the original holders of securities and those who later purchased them at depreciated prices, and who believes the plan for assuming state debts is unfair to Virginia and other states that have already paid much of their war debt. House votes against discrimination, 36–13, on February 22, but defeats assumption measure, 31–29, on April 12, and sends bill for funding the debt to the Senate on June 2. In late June Hamilton, Madison, and Secretary of State Thomas Jefferson agree that in exchange for southern support of assumption, northern members of Congress will vote for locating the national capital in Philadelphia for ten years and then permanently establishing it along the Potomac River in 1800. Bills for national assumption of state debts and the location of the capital pass the House by narrow margins in July after being approved by the Senate. Hamilton resumes meetings with Beckwith in July, reporting regularly to Washington and Jefferson on their conversations. Moves with Elizabeth and their four children to Philadelphia in November. Advises Washington on his second annual message to Congress. Proposes series of excise taxes on spirits in report to the House on December 13 (taxes are approved by Congress, January–February 1791). Submits report to the House on December 14 calling for the chartering of a national bank, which he argues will increase the circulation of currency, encourage investment, and facilitate the financial operations of the national government.

1791   Bill chartering Bank of the United States passes Senate on January 20 and is sent to the House. Hamilton submits report on establishing a national mint to the House on January 28 (mint is established by Congress in April 1792). Madison opposes bank bill, arguing that the Constitution does not give Congress the power to charter a corporation, but it is approved by the House, 39–20, on February 8. Upon receiving the bill, Washington seeks written opinions from Attorney General Edmund Randolph and Jefferson, who agree with Madison that the measure is unconstitutional. Washington submits both opinions to Hamilton on February 16 and asks for a response. Hamilton replies on February 23 with a lengthy treatise arguing that the Constitution gives Congress implied powers and that incorporation of a bank is a "necessary and proper" means of attaining constitutional ends. Washington signs bill on February 25. During the summer, while Elizabeth and the children are at the Schuyler home in Albany, Hamilton is called on by Maria Reynolds, a woman who claims to have been abandoned by her husband and who asks him for financial assistance; they quickly begin an adulterous affair. Helps establish the Society for Useful Manufactures, corporation sponsoring an experimental industrial site in Paterson, New Jersey, that soon sells $600,000 worth of stock. After a year of preparation, Hamilton submits a report on manufactures to the House on December 5. The report advocates making manufacturing a major part of the American economy and proposes to encourage industrial development by government subsidies and protective tariffs, citing the "general welfare" clause of the Constitution to justify public spending in support of manufacturing. Plan is opposed on constitutional and economic grounds and is not acted upon by Congress. Hamilton begins series of conversations with George Hammond, the newly arrived British minister to the United States, hoping to make progress toward negotiating an Anglo-American commercial treaty. Begins making blackmail payments to James Reynolds, Maria's husband.

1792 *National Gazette*, newspaper founded in 1791 by Philip Freneau with support from Madison and Jefferson, begins printing attacks on Hamilton in March as his policies face increasing opposition in Congress. Hamilton helps contain financial panic caused by bankruptcy in early March of William Duer, governor of the Society for Useful Manufactures and a major speculator in bank stocks and government securities. Ends affair with Maria Reynolds. Launches extensive newspaper campaign, publishing 20 essays under nine different pseudonyms between July 25 and December 22, in which he defends his policies and accuses Jefferson of hiring Freneau as a State Department translator in order to sponsor his partisan editorship of the *National Gazette*. Urges Washington to serve for a second term. At the President's request, sends Washington a lengthy defense of his principles and programs on August 18. Fifth child, John Church, is born on August 22. Controversy over Hamilton's programs contributes to emergence of two political alliances, with Madison, Jefferson, and their supporters calling themselves Republicans, and Hamilton and his supporters calling themselves Federalists. Representatives Frederick Muhlenberg and Abraham Venable and Senator James Monroe question Hamilton on December 15 about his payments to James Reynolds, who has accused Hamilton of having used him to illicitly speculate in Treasury funds; in a meeting at his home, Hamilton confesses to his adulterous affair and to the blackmail he has been paying out of his own funds. Muhlenberg, Venable, and Monroe pledge to keep the matter secret.

1793 On January 23 Representative William Branch Giles of Virginia submits five resolutions to the House questioning Hamilton's management of foreign loans. Although Republicans expect that he will be unable to respond before adjournment of Congress on March 3, Hamilton submits several lengthy and detailed reports by February 19. Giles then introduces nine resolutions, drafted by Jefferson, condemning Hamilton's conduct; all nine are defeated on March 1. After learning of France's declaration of war on Great Britain, Washington issues proclamation of neutrality on April 22 while deciding to maintain the 1778 treaty of alliance with France. Hamilton informs Washington on June 21 that he intends to resign at the close of the next congressional session in June 1794. When neutrality proclamation is criticized by Republicans on constitutional grounds, Hamilton publishes seven "Pacificus" essays in the *Gazette of the United States*, June 29–July 27, defending presidential power to declare neutrality and interpret treaties. Continues newspaper campaign with nine "No Jacobin" essays, July 31–August 28, criticizing French envoy Edmond Genet for failing to respect the neutrality proclamation. At the urging of Jefferson, Madison responds to "Pacificus" with five "Helvidius" essays, published in the *National Gazette* between August 24 and September 18, arguing that Congress has the constitutional power to declare neutrality and interpret treaties. In early September Hamilton and Elizabeth contract yellow fever during epidemic in Philadelphia; they send their children to the Schuyler home in Albany and join them there after their recovery. Hamilton returns to Philadelphia on October 23. Seeking official exoneration, Hamilton submits request to the House on December 16 for a formal inquiry into his conduct as Secretary of the Treasury. Jefferson resigns as Secretary of State on December 31.

1794   Hamilton publishes two "Americanus" essays criticizing France and its American supporters in *Dunlap and Claypoole's American Daily Advertiser* on January 31 and February 7. Meets sporadically with the House select committee appointed on February 24 to investigate him. News in March of the British capture of more than 250 American merchant ships trading with the French West Indies causes crisis in Anglo-American relations. Hamilton urges Washington to send John Jay to Britain as a special envoy and, after Jay is appointed on April 16, helps draft his instructions. House committee issues report favorable to Hamilton on May 22. Citing the continuing threat of war with Britain, Hamilton informs Washington on May 27 that he will postpone his resignation. Resistance to excise tax on whiskey leads to violence against federal officials in western Pennsylvania during summer. Hamilton calls for use of force to restore order and publishes four "Tully" essays, August 23–September 2, denouncing the insurgents. Helps organize military expedition against the "Whiskey Rebellion" and accompanies Washington when the President leaves Philadelphia on September 30 to take command of an army of 12,000 militia. Remains in western Pennsylvania to interview witnesses and prisoners after the insurrection collapses and Washington returns to the capital in October. Returns to Philadelphia in late November and informs Washington on December 1 that he will resign in two months.

1795   Submits extensive report on the further support of public credit to the House on January 19, reviewing his fiscal program and proposing new measures for paying the national debt (most of his proposals become law on March 3). Resigns on January 31 and is succeeded by Oliver Wolcott Jr., who has served as the Comptroller of the Treasury since 1791. Departs for New York on February 17. Family spends March through June at Schuyler home in Albany before returning to New York City, where Hamilton resumes successful law practice (will also appear frequently before state courts in Albany). On June 24 the Senate ratifies Anglo-American treaty negotiated by Jay; its terms provide for British evacuation of frontier outposts in the Northwest Territory but contain few British concessions regarding American maritime rights or terms of Anglo-American commerce. Treaty is published on July 1 and is widely attacked. Hamilton sends Washington a lengthy memorandum urging him to sign the treaty despite its shortcomings (President signs treaty on August 18). Attempts to defend treaty at public meeting in New York City on July 18 but is shouted down by hostile crowd and possibly struck by thrown stones. Quarrels with New York Republicans James Nicholson and Maturin Livingston while leaving meeting and challenges them to duels; disputes are resolved peacefully. Writing as "Camillus," begins "The Defence," series of newspaper essays in support of the Jay Treaty, on July 22. (Series runs until January 9, 1796, with Hamilton writing 28 and Rufus King ten of its 38 essays.) Continues to advise Washington on foreign and domestic matters and outlines the President's annual message to Congress. On November 20, publishes lengthy response in the *Daily Advertiser* to charges that Washington has habitually overdrawn his presidential salary.

1796   Appears for the government before the U.S. Supreme Court in *Hylton* v. *United States*, defending the constitutionality of a federal tax on carriages by arguing that it is not a "direct tax" and thus does not have to be apportioned by population. Court upholds the tax on March 8, ruling for the first time on the constitutionality of an act of Congress and accepting Hamilton's broad construction of congressional taxing power. After suffering major financial losses, the Society for Useful Manufactures collapses. Hamilton works closely with Washington during the spring and summer on successive drafts of the President's farewell address, which is published on September 19. Continues to advise Washington and drafts his annual message to Congress in November. Writes private letters urging Federalists to support John Adams and Thomas Pinckney equally in the presidential election. Campaigns extensively for James Watson, the unsuccessful Federalist candidate for Congress from New York City. Adams is elected president with 71 electoral votes, and Jefferson, the Republican candidate, is elected vice-president with 68 electoral votes.

1797   Writing as "Americus" in the *Gazette of the United States*, January 27–March 27, Hamilton publishes "The Warning," series of six essays denouncing French seizures of American ships trading with Britain. Adams retains Secretary of State Timothy Pickering, Secretary of War James McHenry, and Secretary of the Treasury Oliver Wolcott Jr. from the Washington administration; the three cabinet secretaries continually seek advice from Hamilton, who corresponds with them on a regular basis. James Callender, a Philadelphia journalist, publishes pamphlets in June and July accusing Hamilton of having used James Reynolds to speculate in public funds and having falsely confessed to having had an affair with Maria Reynolds when he was questioned by Monroe, Muhlenberg, and Venable in 1792. Hamilton asks the three men to deny publicly Callender's charges, affirm their belief in the explanation he gave them in 1792, and offer assurances that they are not the source of documents quoted by Callender. Angry conversation between Hamilton and Monroe regarding Reynolds scandal on July 11 almost results in a duel. Sixth child, William Stephen, born August 4. Hamilton publishes pamphlet *Observations on Certain Documents . . . in which the Charge of the Speculation against Alexander Hamilton, late Secretary of the Treasury, is Fully Refuted* on August 25, in which he makes a detailed confession regarding his adulterous affair with Maria Reynolds. Remains engaged with his busy law practice throughout the scandal.

1798   Elected a counselor to the New York Society for Promoting the Manumission of Slaves on January 16. Continues correspondence with McHenry, Pickering, and Wolcott as Franco-American relations worsen; Hamilton opposes declaration of war while calling for expanding the army and navy. Writing as "Titus Manlius," publishes "The Stand," series of seven newspaper essays decrying French aggression in Europe, continued French depredation of American shipping, and attempts by the French Directory to extort bribes from American envoys John Marshall, Elbridge Gerry, and Charles Cotesworth Pinckney in the "XYZ Affair." John Jay, now governor of New York, asks Hamilton to accept appointment to vacant seat in the U.S. Senate, but Hamilton declines on April 24, declaring his unwillingness to sacrifice family interests yet again. Adams administration begins an undeclared naval war against France during the summer, and Adams commissions Washington as commander in chief of an expanded army on July 4. Washington insists upon having Hamilton serve as inspector general of the army, and he is appointed to the position on July 25 with rank of major general. Hamilton begins working on army administration, seeking references on extensive lists of potential officers and revising standing regulations regarding recruitment, tactics, and discipline. Supervises fortification of New York City for both the state and federal governments. After prolonged dispute regarding his rank relative to Henry Knox and Charles Cotesworth Pinckney, Adams reluctantly appoints Hamilton as second in command of the army on October 15. Hamilton struggles to maintain his law practice while awaiting compensation for his military service. Contemplates using army to seize Florida and Louisiana from Spain (a French ally).

1799 Alarmed by the Kentucky and Virginia Resolutions declaring the federal Alien and Sedition Acts unconstitutional, writes letter to Federalist senator Theodore Sedgwick proposing sending federal troops to Virginia to suppress resistance to national authority. Continues reorganization of the army, appointing officers, designing and procuring uniforms, and collecting information regarding fortifications and weapons. Father dies on island of St. Vincent in the West Indies sometime during the year. During a heated conference with Adams at Trenton, New Jersey, in early October, Hamilton objects to the President's decision to send a new diplomatic mission to France. Asks New York state authorities to bring libel prosecution against David Frothingham, printer of *The Argus, or Greenleaf's New Daily Advertiser of New York*, for publishing allegation that Hamilton had used British secret service money in attempt to suppress the *Aurora*, an anti-administration newspaper. (Frothingham is convicted in November 1799 and jailed for four months.) Seventh child, Eliza, born November 20. Hamilton drafts plan for a national military academy. Washington dies on December 14.

1800 Adams refuses to promote Hamilton to commander in chief of the army, leaving the post unfilled. Hamilton continues to attend to both army administration and his law practice. Joins with Aaron Burr and Brockholst Livingston in April to successfully defend Levi Weeks in a sensational murder case in

New York City. Hamilton is chosen to succeed Washington as president general of the Society of the Cincinnati. After Republicans win New York state elections and secure control of the new state legislature, which will choose presidential electors in the fall, Hamilton writes John Jay on May 7, proposing that he call the existing legislature into session and have the method of choosing electors changed to popular voting by district; Jay refuses. In May Adams demands the resignation of McHenry and dismisses Pickering, accusing them of being subservient to Hamilton, and orders demobilization of the "Additional Army" created in 1798. Hamilton takes military inspection trip through Connecticut, Rhode Island, Massachusetts, and New Hampshire, June 7–30, during which he meets with leading Federalists and urges them to support Charles Cotesworth Pinckney for the presidency over Adams. Military service ends on June 15 with demobilization of the "Additional Army." Begins constructing country house in upper Manhattan about nine miles north of New York City and names it "The Grange," after the ancestral Hamilton family home in Scotland and his uncle's estate in St. Croix. Writes letters in support of Pinckney and collects material for a pamphlet, which he plans to circulate privately among Federalists, describing Adams as unfit for the presidency. After Republican newspapers obtain copies of Hamilton's pamphlet attack on Adams, it is published on October 24, dividing the Federalists and seriously damaging Hamilton's political influence and reputation. Voting in electoral college results in tie between Republican candidates Thomas Jefferson and Aaron Burr, forcing the presidential election into the Federalist controlled House of Representatives. Hamilton writes series of letters urging Federalists to support Jefferson over Burr.

1801   House begins voting on February 11 and remains deadlocked until February 17, when Jefferson is elected president and Burr vice-president on the 36th ballot. Hamilton writes pamphlet and makes campaign speeches in support of Stephen Van Rensselaer, the Federalist candidate for governor. Burr campaigns for George Clinton, who wins the election in late April. In the fall Hamilton helps found the *New-York Evening Post*, which publishes its first number on November 16. Eldest son, Philip, age 19, is mortally wounded in duel fought on November 23 with George Eacker, a Republican attorney who had criticized Hamilton's policies in a Fourth of July oration, and dies on November 24 with Hamilton at his bedside. Writing as "Lucius

Crassus," Hamilton begins "The Examination," series attacking the Jefferson administration in the *New-York Evening Post* on December 17 (last of 18 articles appears on April 18, 1802).

1802 Drafts resolution calling for a constitutional amendment providing for separate balloting by electors for president and vice-president and requiring that electors be chosen by popular vote in districts established by Congress. Resolution is adopted by New York state legislature and presented to the House of Representatives in February. (Provision for separate balloting becomes part of the Twelfth Amendment, ratified on September 25, 1804.) In February Hamilton secures adoption by the New York City bar and chamber of commerce of memorials protesting Republican effort to repeal the Judiciary Act of 1801 that enlarged and reorganized the federal court system (repeal measure becomes law on March 8). Advocates changes in Federalist political methods to better attract popular support, but his proposals are largely ignored by other Federalist leaders. Campaigns in April for Federalist candidates for the state senate and the House of Representatives. Eighth child is born on June 2 and named Philip. Family moves into "The Grange" in late summer.

1803 Hamilton helps found Merchants' Bank in New York City in April. Campaigns for Federalist candidates for the state legislature. Publishes unsigned article in the *New-York Evening Post* on July 5 supporting the Louisiana Purchase. Continues to dedicate most of his time to his legal practice.

1804 Appears before the New York supreme court in February as counsel for Harry Croswell, who had been convicted in 1803 of libeling President Jefferson in his newspaper *The Wasp*. Hamilton argues that in the interest of protecting freedom of the press, defendants in libel cases should be allowed to offer the truth of their statements as a defense. Although the court refuses to grant Croswell a new trial, the state legislature begins revision of the libel law to allow truth to be admitted as a defense (new law is passed on April 6, 1805). Rival Republican factions nominate Burr and Morgan Lewis, chief justice of the state supreme court, to run for governor after George Clinton declines to seek reelection. Alarmed by support for Burr among Federalists, Hamilton denounces him in writing and in person during the campaign. Burr carries New York City in voting at the end of April but loses election statewide. On June 18 Burr writes to Hamilton demanding an explanation for a letter printed in the *Albany Register* in which Hamilton was reported to have declared Burr to be "a dangerous man" and to have expressed "a still more despicable opinion" of him. After nine days of negotiation, Burr challenges Hamilton on June 27 and Hamilton accepts. In duel fought at Weehawken, New Jersey, on the morning of July 11, Hamilton is struck by pistol ball that perforates his liver before lodging in his spine. Brought back across the river to the house of a friend in Greenwich Village, he sees his wife and children and receives communion from an Episcopal bishop while suffering intense pain. Dies at 2 P.M. on July 12. After a large public funeral procession on July 14, Hamilton is buried in the yard of Trinity Church in lower Manhattan.

Note on the Texts

This volume prints the texts of 172 letters, essays, pamphlets, reports, speeches, resolutions, and memoranda written or delivered by Alexander Hamilton between 1769 and 1804, as well as the text of a memorandum written in 1789 by British envoy George Beckwith recording a conversation with Hamilton and the texts of three letters written to Hamilton in 1804 by Aaron Burr during the correspondence that led to their duel. (In addition, the texts of three statements written by William P. Van Ness and Nathaniel Pendleton, the seconds in the Hamilton-Burr duel, are printed in an appendix in this volume.) With one exception, the texts printed here—including the documents written by Beckwith, Burr, Van Ness, and Pendleton—are taken from *The Papers of Alexander Hamilton* (27 volumes; New York: Columbia University Press, 1961–87), edited by Harold C. Syrett, with associate editors Jacob E. Cooke (vols. 1–15), Patricia Syrett (vols. 16–27), Cara-Louise Miller (vol. 16), Dorothy Twohig (vol. 16), Barbara A. Chernow (vols. 17–26), Brigid Allen (vols. 18–21), Joseph G. Henrich (vols. 22–24), Irene R. Diamant (vols. 25–26), Richard J. Morris (vol. 26), and Sara Solberg (vol. 26). Because *The Papers of Alexander Hamilton* does not include documents relating to Hamilton's law practice, the text of "Propositions on the Law of Libel" is taken from Volume I of *The Law Practice of Alexander Hamilton: Documents and Commentary*, edited by Julius Goebel Jr. (New York: Columbia University Press, 1964), pages 840–42.

Although the majority of these documents existed only in manuscript at the time of Hamilton's death, some of them were printed during his lifetime. Hamilton wrote prolifically for the press, publishing numerous pamphlets and newspaper essays both under his own name and under a variety of pseudonyms. His contributions to *The Federalist* were published contemporaneously in book form; speeches he made in the New York ratifying convention and at political meetings were recorded in shorthand and then published in book form or in newspapers; and some of the reports he submitted to Congress while serving as Secretary of the Treasury were printed as pamphlets.

Three major editions of Hamilton's writings have been published: *The Works of Alexander Hamilton*, edited by his son John Church Hamilton (7 volumes, 1850–51); *The Works of Alexander Hamilton*, edited by Henry Cabot Lodge (9 volumes, 1885–86); and *The Papers of Alexander Hamilton*, edited by Harold C. Syrett (27 volumes, 1961–87). In his edition, John Church Hamilton freely altered his father's spelling, punctuation, capitalization, and paragraphing, and sometimes omitted words or passages from the documents he printed. Henry Cabot Lodge also made frequent alterations in Hamilton's spelling, punctuation, and capitalization in preparing his edition.

In 1955 work began on *The Papers of Alexander Hamilton*, a new edition sponsored by Columbia University and published by Columbia University Press. The editors of *The Papers of Alexander Hamilton* collected copies of more than 19,000 documents relating to Hamilton's life from libraries, archives, manuscript dealers, and private collections. Documents were transcribed and printed without alteration in their spelling and paragraphing, and with minimal alterations in their capitalization and punctuation, mostly in the substitution of periods for dashes used to end sentences and the omission of dashes in instances where a dash appears following a period. Wherever possible, the editors of *The Papers of Alexander Hamilton* used an autograph manuscript as the source of their text. In cases where no autograph manuscript, manuscript copy, or contemporary printed version of a document was available, the editors of *The Papers of Alexander Hamilton* took their text from a later printed version, such as the John Church Hamilton or Henry Cabot Lodge editions. For the texts of the first 43 of Hamilton's 51 contributions to *The Federalist*, the editors of *The Papers of Alexander Hamilton* used the newspaper versions published between October 27, 1787, and April 2, 1788, incorporating into these texts some of the variants (largely corrections of errors) that appeared in the first book edition, published in New York by John and Archibald McLean in two volumes on March 22 and May 28, 1788. The texts of Hamilton's final eight *Federalist* essays, which did not appear in newspapers prior to book publication, are taken from the McLean first edition.

This volume prints texts as they appeared in the Syrett and Goebel editions, but with a few alterations in editorial procedure. The bracketed conjectural readings of the editors of *The Papers of Alexander Hamilton*, in cases where original manuscripts or printed texts were damaged or difficult to read, are accepted without brackets in this volume when those readings seem to be the only possible ones; but when they do not, or when the editor made no conjecture, the missing word or words are indicated by a bracketed two-em space, i.e., [   ]. In cases where *The Papers of Alexander Hamilton* supplied in brackets letters or words that were omitted from the source text by an obvious slip of the pen or printer's error, this volume removes the

brackets and accepts the editorial emendation. Bracketed editorial in-
sertions used in *The Papers of Alexander Hamilton* to expand con-
tractions, identify speakers, clarify meaning, or supply place names
have been deleted in this volume. *The Papers of Alexander Hamilton*
used brackets to indicate which portions of a document were in
Hamilton's handwriting, as opposed to that of a government clerk,
as well as to indicate which portions of the text of a document were
taken from an incomplete manuscript source, as opposed to a later
printed source; in both cases, this volume omits the brackets. In
cases where *The Papers of Alexander Hamilton* printed a document
from a complete manuscript source and used brackets to insert material that was added in a later printed version of the document, this
volume deletes the inserted material and prints the manuscript version of the document. (The material added to "American No. I,"
which was most likely added by Hamilton, is presented in the notes
in this volume.)

In *The Papers of Alexander Hamilton*, Hamilton's letter to Philip
Schuyler of February 18, 1781, is presented in a text in which material deleted by Hamilton while drafting the letter is printed with lines
through the deleted material and with material substituted or added
by Hamilton printed in interlined form. This volume omits the canceled material and prints the interlined material on the line. The
draft of the Farewell Address enclosed by Hamilton in his letter to
George Washington of July 30, 1796, is presented by *The Papers of
Alexander Hamilton* in a similar manner, with the difference that in
this instance the interlined material also includes words or passages
offered by Hamilton as alternatives to uncanceled words and passages in the draft. This volume omits the canceled material and
prints interlined material containing added or substituted wording
on the line. Three of Hamilton's errors in the draft of the Farewell
Address are treated as slips of the pen and corrected in this volume,
even though they were not corrected in *The Papers of Alexander
Hamilton*: at 860.18, "successessive" becomes "successive"; at 865.13,
"and a and" becomes "and"; and at 868.38, "it vows for" becomes
"it."

In the texts of "A Full Vindication of the Measures of the Congress" and "The Continentalist No. I" presented in *The Papers of
Alexander Hamilton*, errata that were printed in newspapers contemporaneously with the initial printing of Hamilton's essays are
printed as footnotes. In this volume, these corrections have been accepted and incorporated into the text printed here: at 15.16, "falibility"
becomes "fallibility"; at 16.24, "nutral" becomes "neutral"; at 18.6,
"hideous" replaces "tedious"; at 21.8, "engredient" becomes "ingre-

dient"; at 21.17, "denied" replaces "desired"; at 23.28, "commerce; I know" replaces "commerce; know"; at 26.11, "would" replaces "could"; at 30.7–8, "is, not because" replaces "is, because"; at 31.38, "you, how and" replaces "you, and"; at 37.36, "arguments" replaces "argument"; at 39.38, "heineous" becomes "heinous"; at 41.1 "can" replaces "can't"; at 42.6, "devised" replaces "desired"; at 42.14, "advices" becomes "advice"; at 42.39, "best" replaces "left"; at 98.17, "coloneal" becomes "colonial"; at 99.39, "security" replaces "felicity"; at 100.3, "vigour" replaces "rigour"; at 100.11, "commonwealths" replaces "commonwealth"; at 100.27, "In a comparison" replaces "In comparison"; at 100.39–40, "our particular constitutions" replaces "our constitutions."

This volume presents the texts of the two editions chosen as sources here but does not attempt to reproduce features of their typographic design. Some headings have been changed, and addresses and endorsements at the end of letters have been omitted, as have the date lines uniformly supplied by *The Papers of Alexander Hamilton* at the beginning of documents. The texts are printed without alteration except for the changes previously discussed and for the correction of typographical errors. Spelling, punctuation, and capitalization are often expressive features, and they are not altered, even when inconsistent or irregular. The following is a list of typographical errors corrected, cited by page and line number: 19.40, flourshes; 30.22, bitterst; 34.2, imprisioned; 50.35, amy; 76.27, impossibily; 105.24–25, dismembrement; 135.26, compliance.; 135.27, power?; 171.25, judicous; 181.32, Massachusettes; 183.17, exit; 185.4, acquiese; 188.19, individuals; 205.38, reamin; 213.1–2, diference; 302.24, *imports,*; 344.24, that; 474.19, *government.**; 541.37, confederation."; 758.9, agrigulcure; 778.14, two; 793.28, il-natured; 794.33, ridicule he,; 844.30, weaknessess; 853.39, remmant; 858.5, characteristed; 865.7, hostiles; 885.9, his; 922.21, thing; 939.37 ADAM'S; 950.19, Speech of; 994.17, Decomocracy; 1007.25, Court.

Notes

In the notes below, the reference numbers denote page and line of this volume (the line count includes headings). No note is made for material included in standard desk-reference books such as Webster's *Collegiate*, *Biographical*, and *Geographical* dictionaries. Footnotes in the text are Hamilton's own. For further biographical background, references to other studies, and more detailed notes, see Broadus Mitchell, *Alexander Hamilton* (2 vols., New York: The Macmillan Company, 1957–62); *The Papers of Alexander Hamilton*, edited by Harold C. Syrett (27 vols., New York: Columbia University Press, 1961–87); and *The Law Practice of Alexander Hamilton: Documents and Commentary*, edited by Julius Goebel Jr. and Joseph H. Smith (5 vols., New York: Columbia University Press, 1964–81).

THE WEST INDIES, THE REVOLUTION, AND THE CONFEDERATION, 1769–1786

3.2   *Edward Stevens*] Hamilton's friend Edward Stevens (d. 1834) was the son of Thomas Stevens, a St. Croix merchant who may have taken Hamilton into his home after the death of Hamilton's mother in 1768. Hamilton sent this letter to New York City, where Stevens attended King's College (now Columbia University). Stevens later studied medicine in Edinburgh and treated Hamilton and his wife during the 1793 yellow fever epidemic in Philadelphia.

4.2   *Nicholas Cruger*] Nicholas Cruger (1743–1801) took control of the Beekman and Cruger trading company in 1769 when David Beekman left the firm. While Cruger was in New York City between October 1771 and March 1772, Hamilton managed much of the firm's business.

4.16   ps.] Pieces of eight (Spanish coins).

5.21   Sti] Stiver (a Dutch coin).

6.2   *To The Royal Danish American Gazette*] Hamilton sent this letter to his father, who was living on St. Kitts at the time. Its publication was arranged by Hugh Knox, the Presbyterian minister on St. Croix who helped sponsor Hamilton's education in North America; see Chronology, 1772.

9.11   Our General] Ulrich Wilhelm Roepstorff, the Danish governor general of St. Croix.

10.1   *A Full Vindication*] Hamilton was responding to a pamphlet dated November 16, 1774, and titled *Free Thoughts on the Proceedings of the*

Continental Congress, Held at Philadelphia, Sept 5, 1774: Wherein Their Errors are exhibited, their Reasonings Confuted, and the fatal Tendency of their Non-Importation, Non-Exportation, and Non-Consumption Measures, are laid open to the plainest Understandings; and the Only Means pointed out for Preserving and Securing Our present Happy Constitution: In a Letter to the Farmers and other inhabitants of North America in General, and to those of the Province of New-York in Particular. By a Farmer. Hear me, for I Will speak! Most likely, the author was Samuel Seabury, an Anglican rector in Westchester County. The "Farmer" responded to Hamilton's *A Full Vindication* with the pamphlet *A View of the Controversy Between Great-Britain and her Colonies . . .* dated December 24, 1774. Hamilton responded in turn with *The Farmer Refuted: or A more impartial and comprehensive View of the Dispute between Great-Britain and the Colonies . . .* published on February 23, 1775.

10.14   measures . . . congress] The First Continental Congress met in Philadelphia from September 5 to October 26, 1774, and adopted an agreement for the colonies to cease importing goods from Britain, Ireland, and the West Indies after December 1, 1774, to cease consuming British goods after March 1, 1775, and, if necessary, to halt exports to Britain, Ireland, and the West Indies after September 10, 1775.

13.2   invasion of our rights] The First Continental Congress convened in response to the "Intolerable Acts" passed by Parliament in the spring of 1774, which closed Boston harbor, abrogated the royal charter of Massachusetts, allowed royal officials accused of capital crimes in Massachusetts to be tried outside the colony, and permitted the quartering of troops in occupied dwellings throughout the 13 colonies.

14.23–24   popery . . . Canada] The Quebec Act, signed by George III on June 22, 1774, established a civil government for Quebec without an elected assembly, gave the Roman Catholic Church the power to collect tithes, and extended the borders of the province to the Mississippi and Ohio rivers.

14.26   the revolution] The 1688 "Glorious Revolution" in England.

14.38   The Premier] Lord North (1732–92), prime minister of Britain from 1770 to 1782.

15.31   *vi & armis*] By force of arms.

27.16   Georgia] Georgia did not send delegates to the First Continental Congress.

35.39–40   not *classical*] In his pamphlet *Free Thoughts* the "Farmer" had written: "We are ordered *to kill them sparingly:* a queer phrase; however, let is pass. If it is not *classical*, it is *congressional;* and that's enough."

36.1   Mr. Johnson's dictionary] Samuel Johnson, *A Dictionary of the English Language* (first edition, 1755).

38.28   weathers]   Castrated rams.

43.33–34   Capt Sears . . . Mr. Rivington's types]   Isaac Sears (1730–86), a leader of the New York Sons of Liberty, recruited men from Connecticut to attack the press of James Rivington, the Loyalist editor and printer of *Rivington's New-York Gazetteer*.

46.12   your constitution]   New York adopted its first state constitution on April 20, 1777.

47.35   family]   An 18th-century term for a military commander's staff.

48.4   St. John's]   Town in southern Quebec used by the British as a base for operations on Lake Champlain.

51.15   a certain faction]   In the winter of 1777–78 Major General Thomas Conway (1735–1800?) allegedly plotted with some delegates to Congress to have Major General Horatio Gates replace George Washington as commander in chief of the Continental army. The movement to oust Washington eventually collapsed, and Conway resigned from the army in April 1778.

52.28   *primum mobile*]   Prime mover.

53.6   Lord Stirling]   William Alexander (1726–83), a major general in the Continental army, had unsuccessfully claimed the earldom of Stirling while living in England from 1756 to 1762 and continued to use the title Lord Stirling after he returned to America.

54.19–20   hug himself . . . win laurels]   During the first (September 19, 1777) and second (October 7, 1777) battles of Bemis Heights (Saratoga), Horatio Gates had remained distant from the fighting while his subordinate, Major General Benedict Arnold, led American troops on the battlefield.

56.2   *John Jay*]   Jay (1745–1829) served as president of the Continental Congress from December 1778 to September 1779.

56.4   Col Laurens]   Lieutenant Colonel John Laurens (1755–82), the son of Henry Laurens, a prominent South Carolina planter and political leader, had become a close friend of Hamilton's after joining Washington's staff in 1777. He was killed in a skirmish in South Carolina in August 1782.

56.13   recommended by Congress]   On March 29, 1779, Congress recommended that Georgia and South Carolina recruit 3,000 slaves to serve in separate battalions under white officers. Slaveowners would receive up to $1,000 for each slave who enlisted, and at the end of the war, the slaves would be freed and paid $50 for their service. The proposal was rejected by the government of South Carolina in May 1779.

56.36–37   want of cultivation . . . probably as good]   Hamilton first wrote "spontaniety," crossed it out and wrote "want of knowledge," and then crossed out "knowledge" and wrote "cultivation." He also changed "perhaps" to "probably."

59.5–6   application to the Assembly]   See note 56.13.

60.7   the Indian command]   Washington was organizing a punitive expedition against the Iroquois of central New York, who had allied themselves with the British.

60.15–16   *soi-disante . . . épouse*]   "Supposedly the kinswoman of Madame, your wife." Laurens was studying law in London when the Revolutionary War began. He married Martha Manning in October 1776, then returned to America in January 1777.

60.17   perhaps [   ].]   The end of the sentence was crossed out in the manuscript of the letter, probably by John Church Hamilton while preparing his edition of his father's papers, *The Works of Alexander Hamilton* (7 volumes, 1850–51). Penciled at the top of the letter, presumably by John Church Hamilton, are the words: "I must not publish the whole of this."

61.13   length of my nose . . . I [   ].]   The end of the sentence was crossed out. Hamilton was possibly using "nose" as a double entendre for "penis," as in the novel *The Life and Opinions of Tristram Shandy* (1759–67) by Laurence Sterne.

61.25   Fleury]   François Louis Teisseydre, Marquis de Fleury, sought a position as secretary to the French diplomatic mission to the United States.

61.30   *To William Gordon*]   Gordon (1728–1807) was a Congregational clergyman in Massachusetts. In a letter of August 10, 1779, Hamilton had asked Gordon to identify the source of a rumor that Hamilton had declared in a public coffee house in Philadelphia that "it was high time for the people to rise, join Genl. Washington, and turn Congress out of Doors."

65.20–21   Governor Martin . . . the fleet]   Josiah Martin (1737–86), the royal governor of North Carolina, was driven from the colony in 1775. He sailed from New York City on December 26, 1779, as part of the British invasion fleet bound for South Carolina.

65.27   a certain commission]   Laurens had urged Congress to appoint Hamilton as a secretary to Benjamin Franklin, who was serving as the American minister to France. In a letter of December 18, 1779, Laurens, the favored candidate, told Hamilton that he felt compelled to accept the post if Congress could agree on no other candidate, and identified the other men under consideration as Massachusetts delegate James Lovell, Colonel Walter Stewart, and Gouverneur Morris.

66.17   leave to go to the Southward]   Hamilton was seeking a field command.

67.14–15   Meade . . . his widow]   Lieutenant Colonel Richard Kidder Meade was an aide-de-camp to Washington. In 1780 he married Mary Fitzhugh Grymes Randolph, a widow.

67.21   Portia] Portia (or Porcia) was the daughter of Cato the Younger and the wife of Brutus, the leader of the conspirators who assassinated Julius Caesar.

70.2   *James Duane*] James Duane (1733–97) was a delegate to Congress from New York, 1774–79 and 1781–83. He later served as the mayor of New York City, 1784–89, and as the U.S. district judge for New York, 1789–94.

71.5   appointing a dictator] On December 27, 1776, Congress granted Washington extraordinary powers for a six-month period, including the authority to raise troops, appoint officers, requisition supplies, and arrest persons suspected of disloyalty.

71.9–10   The confederation] The Articles of Confederation were proposed to the states by Congress on November 15, 1777, but their ratification was not completed until March 1, 1781.

73.7   United provinces] The Netherlands

87.22   Liberty Pole] A tavern in Englewood, New Jersey.

87.30   the Marquis] The Marquis de Lafayette (1757–1834).

88.19–21   the poet . . . or fair."] Alexander Pope (1688–1744), "Of the Characters of Women, an Epistle to a Lady" (1735).

88.22–23   "*a fair . . . nature.*"] John Milton (1608–74), *Paradise Lost* (1667), Book X, 891–92.

89.20   about Fleury] The Marquis de Fleury may have been interested in Elizabeth's younger sister, Margarita Schuyler.

90.4   amiable woman] Margaret (Peggy) Shippen Arnold (1760–1804), Benedict Arnold's wife.

91.19   André's request to be shot] After being condemned as a spy, André asked to be executed with honor by a firing squad, rather than be hanged. Washington denied his request, and André was hanged on October 2, 1780.

92.30   *To Margarita Schuyler*] Hamilton wrote this message as a postscript in a letter from Elizabeth Hamilton to her younger sister.

93.32   Mr. Tilghman] Lieutenant Colonel Tench Tilghman (1744–86), an aide-de-camp to Washington.

94.21   ¹ that] The text printed here is taken from Hamilton's draft. The superscript numerals probably indicate the order in which Hamilton planned to arrange the sentences in the final version of the letter.

94.37–39   Mr. Humphrey's . . . Mr. Harrison] Lieutenant Colonel David Humphreys (1752–1818) and Lieutenant Colonel Robert Hanson Harrison were aides-de-camp to Washington.

98.1   *The Continentalist No. I*] Hamilton wrote six "Continentalist" essays; they were published on July 12, July 19, August 9, August 30, 1781, and April 18, July 4, 1782.

98.2   MR. LOUDON] Samuel Loudon was the editor of *The New-York Packet*.

102.31   two of them] Georgia and South Carolina.

102.33   General without an army] Major General Nathanael Greene (1742–86) led a numerically weak army in a successful campaign against the British in the Carolinas in 1781.

105.4–5   war with the Dutch] Britain declared war on the Netherlands on December 20, 1780.

105.30   Empress Queen] Maria Theresa of Austria died on November 29, 1780.

110.35–36   Superintendant of their Finances] On February 20, 1781, Robert Morris (1735–1806) of Pennsylvania was named Superintendent of Finance. He served until November 1, 1784.

119.5–6   our little stranger] Hamilton's first child, Philip, was born on January 22, 1782.

120.7   *Remarks . . . Raising Funds*] These remarks, and those on page 121, were recorded as part of the notes James Madison kept on debates in the Continental Congress.

120.8   the subject] On January 25, 1783, Congress began debating how to fund the national debt.

121.2   Mr. Elseworth] Connecticut delegate Oliver Ellsworth (1745–1807).

121.8–11   pervading & uniting . . . power of Congress] Madison wrote in his notes that Hamilton's "remark was imprudent & injurious to the cause wch. it was meant to serve. This influence was the very source of jealousy which rendered the States averse to a revenue under the collection as well as appropriation of Congress. All the members of Congress who concurred in any degree with the States in this jealousy smiled at the disclosure." Virginia delegates Theodorick Bland and Arthur Lee remarked in conversation with Madison that Hamilton "had let out the secret."

121.21   temper . . . of the army] On January 6, 1783, a delegation of officers from the Continental army encampment at Newburgh, New York, presented a memorial to Congress protesting its failure to pay them and asking that officers receive several years' full pay in lieu of the lifetime pensions at half pay granted them in 1780. The memorial warned that further inaction "may have fatal consequences."

123.11   General Knox]   Major General Henry Knox (1750–1806) signed the Newburgh petition.

123.22   steps of so inflammatory]   On March 10, 1783, an anonymous address written by Major John Armstrong (1758–1843) was circulated among the officers at Newburgh, denouncing Congress for its failure to pay them and inciting the army to rebellion if its demands were not met. In response, Washington called a general meeting of officers on March 15. At the meeting Washington strongly condemned the address and successfully called upon the officers to express their obedience to Congress.

123.32   provisional articles]   On March 12, 1783, Congress received the provisional peace treaty signed in Paris on November 30, 1782.

124.6   Lord Shelburne]   Sir William Petty, second Earl of Shelburne (1737–1805), was prime minister of Great Britain from July 1782 to February 1783.

127.1   A Letter from Phocion]   In April 1784 Hamilton published a second Letter from Phocion in response to the pamphlet Mentor's Reply to Phocion's Letter; With Some Observations on Trade (the identity of "Mentor" is not known).

127.14–16   violate . . . treaty]   After Congress ratified the Treaty of Paris on April 15, 1783, the New York legislature passed several laws punishing Loyalists, despite the prohibition in the sixth article of the treaty against further prosecutions and confiscations. The New York courts also continued to enforce earlier laws that authorized the confiscation of Tory property and the staying of debts owed to Loyalists.

128.39   Coke upon Magna Carta]   Sir Edward Coke (1552–1634), The Second Part of the Institutes of the Laws of England, posthumously published in 1642.

132.26–27   imperium in imperio]   Government within a government.

133.15   the fisheries]   The treaty recognized American fishing rights off Canada.

135.39   Vatel . . . Grotius]   Emmerich de Vatel (1714–67), The Law of Nations (1758); Hugo Grotius (1583–1645), On the Law of War and Peace (1625).

FRAMING AND RATIFYING THE CONSTITUTION, 1787–1789

149.1   Plan of Government]   Hamilton included this plan as part of his lengthy speech to the Federal Convention on June 18, 1787. In mid-September 1787, around the time of the close of the Convention, Hamilton presented James Madison with a more detailed draft of a proposed constitution; some of the changes and additions included in the later draft are noted below.

149.4   *Assembly . . . senate*]   Hamilton specified in his later draft that initially the Assembly would have 100 members and the Senate 40, both apportioned among the states according to population. Bills for raising revenue, for support of the navy and army, and for appropriating money to pay the salaries of government officials would originate in the Assembly, but could be altered and amended by the Senate.

149.6   pass all *laws whatsoever*]   In his later draft Hamilton included prohibitions against the passing of bills of attainder and ex post facto laws, the granting of titles of nobility, and the establishment of religious denominations and of religious tests for office.

149.8   *by the People*]   Hamilton specified in his later draft that members of the Assembly were to be chosen by "the free male citizens and inhabitants" of the states over the age of 21.

149.11–12   *Electors . . . People*]   In his later draft Hamilton specified that the senatorial electors were to be chosen by males who would hold an estate in land for life or for at least 14 years.

149.17   *governor*]   In the later draft, "President of the United States."

149.19   by the people]   Hamilton specified in his later draft that the presidential electors would be chosen by citizens "having an estate of inheritance or for three lives in land" or a personal estate of at least $1,000.

149.24–25   Commander in Chief]   Hamilton added in his later draft that the President would not take actual command in the field without the consent of the Senate and the Assembly.

150.7   twelve Judges]   In his later draft Hamilton wrote that the "Supreme Court" should consist of "not less than six nor more than twelve judges" and be headed by a "Chief Justice."

150.9–10   original jurisdiction . . . appellative jurisdiction]   Hamilton added in his later draft that the Supreme Court would have original jurisdiction in all cases "in which the United States shall be a party, in all controversies between the United States and a particular state or between two or more states" and appellate jurisdiction in all cases "in which the fundamental rights of this constitution are involved." All crimes (except impeachment) would be tried by a 12-man jury in the state where the crime occurred. The later draft also included an article on the trial of territorial claims.

150.20–21   impeachments . . . judges]   Hamilton's later draft added that a majority of judges present could convict.

151.1–2   *Speech . . . Plan of Government*]   This speech, delivered on June 18, 1787, and lasting between five and six hours, constituted Hamilton's principal contribution to the convention debates. In addition to the versions of the speech recorded by James Madison and Robert Yates that are presented here, John Lansing Jr. and Rufus King also recorded shorter versions in their notes. Yates' version of the speech was first published in 1821, Madison's in 1840, King's in 1894, and Lansing's in 1939.

151.14   both plans] The Virginia Plan, presented to the Convention by Edmund Randolph on May 29, 1787, and the New Jersey Plan, presented by William Paterson on June 15. While the Virginia Plan proposed creating a supreme national government with distinct executive, legislative, and judicial branches, the New Jersey Plan proposed retaining the existing Congress while granting it additional powers.

151.33   (Mr. R.)] Virginia governor Edmund Randolph (1753–1813).

153.9–10   Masss. . . . necessity] A series of protests by farmers in western Massachusetts against tax collections and farm foreclosures led in September 1786 to the outbreak of "Shays' Rebellion," named after one of its leaders, the Revolutionary War veteran Daniel Shays (1747?–1825). The uprising was suppressed by Massachusetts militia in February 1787.

156.17   Mr. Neckar] Jacques Necker (1732–1804), French director-general of finance, 1777–81.

156.34–35   Senate (of Maryland)] Under the 1776 state constitution, the Maryland senate was elected indirectly by an electoral college chosen by the voters.

156.37–38   a paper emission] The Maryland senate rejected bills issuing paper money passed by the house of delegates in December 1785 and December 1786.

158.14   Report . . . the whole] The Convention met as a committee of the whole from May 30 to June 13, 1787, to debate the Virginia Plan and then prepared a report in the form of 19 resolutions.

158.31   sketch of a plan] See pp. 149–50 in this volume.

166.9   my arrival here] Hamilton left Philadelphia on June 29 and returned to New York City to attend to private business.

167.27   *Conjectures . . . Constitution*] Hamilton did not publish this memorandum, and is not known to have circulated it.

171.1   *The Federalist No. 1*] The *Federalist* eventually included 85 essays, 51 of which were written by Hamilton, 29 by James Madison, and five by John Jay. (Hamilton and Madison subsequently made conflicting claims regarding the authorship of some of the essays, all of which appeared under the name "Publius"; modern scholarship accepts the accuracy of Madison's attributions.) Each *Federalist* essay appeared in several New York newspapers over the course of several days; this volume gives the newspaper and date of first publication at the end of each essay, except for *The Federalist No. 78–No. 85*, which first appeared in book form. Hamilton corrected and revised *The Federalist* for its first book edition, published in two volumes by John and

Archibald McLean on March 22 and May 28, 1788. Some significant differences between the newspaper and McLean versions of the essays are noted below.

176.1   *The Federalist No. 6*]   This essay draws upon notes Hamilton made for his June 18, 1787, speech to the Federal Convention.

178.17   SHAYS]   See note 153.9–10.

178.39   Dutchess of Marlborough]   Sarah (nee Jennings) Churchill, Duchess of Marlborough (1660–1744), held influence over Queen Anne until her dismissal from the royal household in 1711.

180.30–181.12   and sometimes even . . . beneficial fruits.]   This passage was added in the McLean edition and did not appear in the newspaper text.

180.33   last war . . . and Spain]   Fought from 1739 until 1748, it was known in Britain at first as the War of Jenkins' Ear, after an alleged Spanish atrocity, and then after 1744 as the War of the Austrian Secession.

181.30   North-Carolina]   In 1784 settlers in four counties in western North Carolina organized the state of "Franklin." Both Congress and North Carolina refused to recognize the new state, and in 1788 North Carolina reestablished jurisdiction over the region, which eventually became the state of Tennessee.

181.31   menancing . . . in Pennsylvania]   In 1787 settlers in the Wyoming Valley of Pennsylvania who held land titles from Connecticut agitated for the creation of a new state. (Royal charters granted to Connecticut colonists in 1662 and to William Penn in 1681 resulted in conflicting claims to jurisdiction over the Wyoming region; in 1782 a commission appointed by Congress awarded jurisdiction to Pennsylvania.)

182.9   Vide Principes . . . Mably]   Gabriel Bonnot de Mably, *Des Principes des Négociations* (1757).

185.7–8   controversy . . . Vermont]   Settlers in Vermont declared their independence from both Great Britain and New York in 1777. Vermont was admitted to the United States in 1791 after the resolution of its dispute with New York.

188.22–24   Connecticut . . . Rhode-Island]   In May 1786 the Rhode Island legislature issued £100,000 in paper money and made it legal tender for all debts, but refused to permit non-resident debtors to use the money. The Connecticut assembly debated retaliatory measures against Rhode Island creditors in 1787 and sent a remonstrance to Congress declaring Rhode Island's policies to be a violation of the Articles of Confederation.

191.37   the only rational precaution]   In the newspaper text, "the only natural precaution."

199.39   Spirit of Laws]   Baron Montesquieu (1689–1755), *The Spirit of the Laws* (1748).

208.21   Recherches . . . Americains]   Published in 1770 by Cornelius Pauw (1739–99)

219.19–21   valuable territories . . . surrendered?]   The British continued to occupy several frontier posts in the Northwest Territory ceded to the United States by the 1783 peace treaty, claiming that the United States had not fulfilled its treaty obligations to secure the payment of debts owed to British creditors and to compensate Loyalists for seized property.

230.24   levity or rashness]   In the newspaper text, "liberty or rashness."

240.6–7   Kings County . . . Montgomery]   Kings County is at the western end of Long Island and is now coterminous with the borough of Brooklyn. In 1787 Montgomery was the largest county in the state and extended over a wide area in central and western New York.

243.27   Mr. Jenkinson]   Charles Jenkinson (1727–1808), later first Earl of Liverpool.

244.39   Encyclopedie]   Denis Diderot, *Encyclopédie, ou Dictionnaire Raisonné des Sciences, des Arts and des Métiers* (1751–76).

247.6–7   a single veto]   In the newspaper text, "a single vote."

249.16   Earl of Chesterfield]   The fourth Earl of Chesterfield served as British minister to the Netherlands, 1728–32.

249.23   limited monarch . . . single day]   Gustavus III staged a coup d'etat against the Swedish *Riksdag* (parliament) on August 19, 1772.

267.32–33   Pennsylvania at this instant]   On October 31, 1787, the Pennsylvania assembly resolved to raise a permanent force of enlisted troops in response to the threat of renewed disorder in the Wyoming Valley (see note 181.31).

284.1   *The Federalist No. 29*]   This essay appeared as *Federalist No. 35* in the newspapers.

285.11   POSSE COMITATUS]   Power of the county.

289.23   duty and sympathy.]   This was followed in the newspaper text by an additional paragraph: "I have now gone through the examination of such of the powers proposed to be vested in the United States, which may be considered as having an immediate relation to the energy of the government; and have endeavoured to answer the principal objections which have been made to them. I have passed over in silence those minor authorities which are either too inconsiderable to have been thought worthy of the hostilities of the opponents of the Constitution, or of too manifest propriety to admit of controversy. The mass of judiciary power however might have claimed an inves-

tigation under this head, had it not been for the consideration that its organization and its extent may be more advantageously considered in connection. This has determined me to refer it to the branch of our enquiries, upon
which we shall next enter."

290.1   *The Federalist No. 30*]   *The Federalist No. 30* and *No. 31* in the
McLean edition appeared as *The Federalist No. 29* and *No. 30* in the newspapers.

301.1   *The Federalist No. 32*]   *The Federalist No. 32* and *No. 33* in the
McLean edition appeared together as *The Federalist No. 31* in the newspapers.

305.3–5   The residue . . . following clauses;]   This phrase did not appear
in the newspaper text.

310.1   *The Federalist No. 34*]   *The Federalist No. 34, No. 35,* and *No. 36* in
the McLean edition appeared as *The Federalist No. 32, No. 33,* and *No. 34* in
the newspapers.

328.23–329.5   I have now . . . example to mankind!]   This paragraph did
not appear in the newspaper text. It concluded the first volume of the
McLean edition, published on March 22, 1788.

330.1   *The Federalist No. 59*]   The *Federalist* essays numbered from 37 to
77 in the McLean edition were numbered from 36 to 76 in the newspapers.
The remaining eight essays in the series first appeared in the second volume
of the McLean edition, published on May 28, 1788, and were numbered from
78 to 85.

330.15   a gentleman]   Noah Webster (1758–1843), writing as "A Citizen of
America," in the pamphlet *An Examination Into the Leading Principles of the
Federal Constitution*, published on October 17, 1787.

348.37   that it would tend]   In the newspaper text, "that it could tend."

358.39   Cato]   Seven Antifederalist articles by "Cato" appeared in New
York newspapers between September 27, 1787, and January 3, 1788. Their authorship is uncertain, although they often have been attributed to New York
governor George Clinton.

362.36   Federal Farmer]   *Observations leading to a Fair Examination of
the System of Government, Proposed by the Late Convention; and to Several
Essential and Necessary Alterations in it. In a Number of Letters from the
Federal Farmer to the Republican*, an Antifederalist pamphlet published in
New York in early November 1787. The authorship of the "Federal Farmer"
letters is uncertain, although they often have been attributed to Richard
Henry Lee of Virginia.

364.29   president, will seldom]   In the newspaper text, "president, will
never."

365.6–7 "For forms . . . is best."] Cf. Alexander Pope, *An Essay on Man* (1733–34), Epistle III, lines 303–4: "For forms of government let fools contest; / Whate'er is best administer'd is best."

367.4 Governors of Virginia] In the newspaper text, "Governors of Maryland."

367.12 disuse of that power] In March 1708, Queen Anne became the last English monarch to exercise the royal veto.

368.30 A writer . . . Tamony] The letter from "Tamony" appeared in the *Virginia Independent Chronicle* on January 9, 1788, and was reprinted in the Philadelphia *Independent Gazetteer* on February 1, 1788.

368.34 Blackstone] Sir William Blackstone (1723–80), *Commentaries on the Laws of England* (1765).

380.36 the celebrated Junius] The author of a series of letters criticizing George III, Lord Chief Justice Mansfield, and the ministry of the Duke of Grafton that were published in the London *Public Advertiser* between 1769 and 1772.

380.39 De Lome] Jean Louis Delolme (1740–1806), author of *Constitution de l'Angleterre* (1771).

387.11 Mr. Fox's India bill] In 1783 the House of Commons passed a bill for the reorganization of the East India Company that had been proposed by Charles James Fox. The bill was criticized in pamphlets and satirical prints as an attempt by Fox to secure a permanent majority in the House of Commons by controlling the patronage of the Company, and it was defeated in the House of Lords after George III declared himself a personal enemy to anyone who supported it.

399.37 Mr. Abraham Yates] Abraham Yates Jr. of Albany (1724–96) served in the New York provincial congress, 1775–77, the New York state senate, 1778–90, and the Continental Congress, 1787–88.

418.12 a Mr. V Der Kemp] Francis Adrian van der Kemp (1752–1829), a Dutch Mennonite minister who came to America as a political refugee in 1788.

420.1 *The Federalist No. 78*] *Federalist* essays 78–85 first appeared in the second volume of the McLean edition of *The Federalist* and were reprinted in the *Independent Journal* and the *New-York Packet* between June 14 and August 16, 1788.

425.38–39 Protest of the minority . . . Martin's speech] "The Address and Reasons of Dissent of the Minority" was published by 21 members of the Pennsylvania convention in the *Pennsylvania Packet* on December 18, 1787, six days after the convention voted 46–23 in favor of ratification. Luther Martin (1744–1826), a Maryland delegate to the Federal Convention, gave a lengthy address to his state legislature on November 29, 1787, in which he attacked the Constitution and revealed some of the proceedings of the Convention. An expanded version of his speech was published in 12 installments, December 28, 1787–February 8, 1788, and as a pamphlet, *The Genuine Information*, in April 1788.

432.36   *lex loci*]   The law of the place.

433.12   Maximilian]   Maximilian I, Holy Roman Emperor from 1493 to 1519, created the Imperial Chamber in 1495.

454.21–455.4   But that there . . . a criminal nature.]   This passage was deleted in the second book edition of *The Federalist*, printed by George Hopkins in 1802.

459.40   minority of Pennsylvania]   On December 12, 1787, the Pennsylvania ratifying convention rejected by a 46–23 vote 15 proposed amendments to the Constitution, including one that guaranteed trial by jury in federal civil cases.

462.24   proposition of Massachusetts]   The Massachusetts convention voted 187–168 on February 6, 1788, to ratify the Constitution while recommending the subsequent adoption of nine amendments, including the one cited by Hamilton.

473.4   Montgomery county]   See note 240.6–7.

474.38   Rutherford's Institutes]   Thomas Rutherforth (1712–71), *Institutes of Natural Law: Being the Substance of a Course of Lectures on Grogius de Jure Belli et Pacis* (1754–56).

481.39   "An Address . . . New-York."]   Written by John Jay and published on April 15, 1788.

484.36   Hume's . . . sciences]   David Hume (1711–76), "Of the Rise and Progress of the Arts and Sciences" (1742).

487.1–2   *Speech . . . on Representation*]   The New York ratifying convention opened in Poughkeepsie on June 17, 1788, with Antifederalists outnumbering Federalists among the delegates 46 to 19. At the time, eight states had ratified the Constitution, leaving only one more ratification necessary to put the Constitution into effect. The texts of Hamilton's speeches in the convention are taken from *Debates and Proceedings of the Convention of the State of New-York*, transcribed and edited by Francis Childs (1788).

487.4   the committee]   The convention had resolved itself into a committee of the whole and begun a clause-by-clause debate of the Constitution.

487.14   the gentlemen contend]   Delegates John Williams (1752–1806) and Melancton Smith (1744–98), who had spoken before Hamilton.

489.27   an honorable gentleman]   John Williams.

492.15   the Federal Farmer]   See note 362.36.

496.1–2   *Speech . . . and Corruption*]   This was the third of four speeches that Hamilton made on June 21, 1788.

496.4   hon. member from Ulster]   Governor George Clinton, who had called for a more "comprehensive" representation in Congress.

496.7–8   gentlemen from Albany and Dutchess]   John Lansing Jr. (1754–1829) and Melancton Smith, both of whom had advocated a larger representation in Congress.

501.1   honorable member]   George Clinton.

504.2   the gentleman]   Melancton Smith.

506.3   idea of exclusive revenues]   John Williams had offered a resolution on June 26 calling for limitations on federal taxing power, including a requirement that Congress first requisition funds from the states before imposing its own taxes.

506.32–33   honorable member from New-York]   Chancellor Robert R. Livingston (1746–1813).

507.20   a celebrated writer]   Montesquieu.

510.18   one gentleman]   Melancton Smith.

511.34–512.1   the watch . . . Major Cochran]   Hamilton was assisting Alexander Cochrane, a captain in the Royal Navy, in his attempts to recover a watch belonging to his late brother. The watch was eventually sent by George Washington to Hamilton, who arranged for General Daniel Morgan to receive 50 guineas for it.

514.7   defect in the constitution]   As originally specified in the Constitution, presidential electors in each state voted for two candidates, one of whom could not be from their home state; when the votes from all of the states were tallied, the man who received the most votes became president and the runner-up vice-president.

514.19–20   Rutlege . . . Clinton]   John Rutledge (1739–1800) of South Carolina and New York governor George Clinton.

514.32   exclusive of New York]   In 1789 a dispute between Federalists and Antifederalists in the New York legislature prevented the election of presidential electors in the state.

515.17   *To George Washington*]   Upon assuming office, Washington asked for advice on presidential etiquette from James Madison, John Adams, John Jay, and Robert R. Livingston, as well as Hamilton.

516.3   a levee day once a week]   Washington adopted the practice of holding a formal levee every Tuesday afternoon and a small public dinner on Thursday evenings, while generally refusing private invitations.

SECRETARY OF THE TREASURY, 1789–1795

521.31   Neckar]   Jacques Necker, who had served as director-general of fi-
nance from 1777 to 1781, was returned to his former position in August 1788.
Dismissed and then reappointed by Louis XVI under pressure in July 1789,
Necker served until his resignation in September 1790.

523.1   *Memorandum by George Beckwith*]   George Beckwith (1753–1823), a
British army officer, served as the unofficial British minister to the United
States from 1787 until the arrival in 1791 of George Hammond, the first offi-
cial minister. In the text of the memorandum printed in this volume,
Beckwith's comments appear in a smaller font than Hamilton's.

523.3   Seventh]   In his correspondence, Beckwith used the code name
"Seven" for Hamilton.

523.34   Lord Lansdowne]   The second Earl of Shelburne (see note 124.6)
was made Marquis of Lansdowne in 1784.

523.37   Navigation and regulating Acts]   Parliament passed a series of acts
between 1783 and 1789 restricting American trade with Britain, Ireland, and
the West Indies.

525.11   (see second)]   Beckwith used "Second" as a code name for Philip
Schuyler, Hamilton's father-in-law, who served as a U.S. senator from New
York, 1789–91.

525.12–13   Revenue Bill . . . discriminating clauses]   Earlier in 1789 James
Madison introduced revenue legislation in the House imposing higher
tonnage duties on British shipping in retaliation for British restrictions on
American commerce. The discriminatory clauses were removed by the Senate
and the final law imposed a uniform duty on all foreign shipping.

526.25   *Western Forts, And the Negroes*]   Regarding the dispute over the
frontier posts, see note 219.19–21. More than 10,000 escaped slaves left the
United States during the British evacuation at the end of the Revolutionary
War. The British government responded to American demands for their return, or for the payment of compensation, by asserting that the slaves had become free when they entered British lines and therefore had left legally and
voluntarily.

526.26   Lord Dorchester]   Sir Guy Carleton (1724–1808), after 1786
Baron Dorchester, was the British commander in chief in America, 1782–83.
He served as governor of Quebec, 1786–91, and received Beckwith's reports
before forwarding them to the ministry in London.

527.6   the gentleman, to be Employed]   On October 13, 1789, Washington appointed Hamilton's friend and ally Gouverneur Morris as a special
emissary to Great Britain.

530.7   your queries]   In his letter Lee had asked Hamilton for information concerning the funding of the national debt for his "private informa-

tion," while acknowledging that his request might be improper. The two men had been friends since the Revolutionary War.

547.8   schedule A.]   The schedules that accompanied Hamilton's report are not printed in this volume.

575.10   report No. 1]   Hamilton submitted his first report to the House on the "further provision . . . necessary for establishing public credit" on December 13, 1790, the same day he presented his report on a bank.

613.1–2   *Opinion . . . National Bank*]   See Chronology, 1791.

617.34–36   arguments . . . certain State-banks]   In the opinion he submitted to President Washington, Thomas Jefferson argued that a national bank was not necessary because "existing banks will without a doubt, enter into arrangements for lending their agency: & the more favorable, as there will be a competition among them for it."

621.7   power . . . to remove officers]   Congress gave the president the power to remove executive officers at pleasure in legislation establishing the State, War, and Treasury departments passed in the summer of 1789 after first debating whether the consent of the Senate was constitutionally required for removals.

626.22–23   an argument . . . debate in the House]   By James Madison on February 2, 1791.

647.1   *Report . . . Manufactures*]   Hamilton was assisted in writing this report by Tench Coxe (1755–1824), the Assistant Secretary of the Treasury from 1790 to 1792. Coxe drafted a preliminary and much shorter version of the report, supplied information on manufacturing, and commented on Hamilton's later drafts.

706.19   objects for a similar regulation]   Pennsylvania had adopted an "Act to encourage and protect the Manufactures of this State" in March 1788.

708.8–9   The following . . . quotation]   The passage is from *An Inquiry into the Nature and Causes of the Wealth of Nations* (1776) by Adam Smith (1723–90).

719.19   insurrection in Hispaniola]   On August 22, 1791, a slave revolt began in Haiti that eventually resulted in the establishment of an independent republic in 1804.

723.37–38   a society is forming]   The Society for Useful Manufactures. See Chronology, 1791.

735.2   *To Philip A. Hamilton*]   Philip (1782–1801), Hamilton's eldest child, was attending an Episcopal boarding school in Trenton, New Jersey.

735.19   Mairs introduction]   John Mair, *An Introduction to Latin Syntax . . .* (1775).

736.2 *To Edward Carrington*] Carrington (1748–1810) had served in the Continental army with Hamilton and had been a Virginia delegate to the Continental Congress, 1785–86. In 1791 he was appointed supervisor of the revenue for Virginia.

740.2 *Freneau . . .* National Gazette] Supported by Jefferson and Madison, Philip Freneau (1752–1832) began publishing the *National Gazette* in Philadelphia on October 31, 1791.

740.32 Col Pickering] Timothy Pickering (1745–1829) was appointed Postmaster General in August 1791. Early in 1792 he became involved in a public dispute with Andrew Brown (1744?–97), publisher of the *Federal Gazette and Philadelphia Daily Advertiser*, over the postal rates for newspapers. After Brown questioned his truthfulness, Pickering responded by reprinting a public notice from 1786 in which Brown admitted to having falsely accused another man of fraud.

741.15 Mr. Giles] William Branch Giles (1762–1830) of Virginia served in the House of Representatives, 1790–98, where he became a leading member of the Republican opposition.

741.28–30 Mr. Madison . . . such references] The legislation establishing the Treasury Department, passed in 1789 with Madison's support, authorized its secretary, unlike the secretaries of State and War, to communicate directly with Congress. In March 1792 Madison and other Republicans in the House opposed a motion directing Hamilton to report on ways to finance army reinforcements for the Northwest frontier, arguing that the request improperly shifted a legislative responsibility onto the executive.

742.34–35 The president . . . speech] Washington's third annual message to Congress, October 25, 1791.

743.40–744.2 Charles Carroll . . . Mr. King] Charles Carroll of Carrollton (1737–1832) was a Federalist senator from Maryland, 1789–92. Rufus King (1755–1827) was a Federalist senator from New York, 1789–96, and one of Hamilton's particular friends; he later served as U.S. minister to Great Britain, 1796–1803.

744.5 Mr. Mercers speech] John Francis Mercer (1759–1821) was a Republican representative from Maryland, 1792–94. He made these remarks in a speech of March 30, 1792.

744.14 Mr. Barnewell] Robert Barnwell (1761–1814) was a Federalist representative from South Carolina, 1791–93.

745.7 bounties to the Fisheries] The bill for aiding the cod fishery was debated and passed by the House in February 1792.

745.13   the Militia bill]   The bill, which authorized the president to call forth state militias in case of an insurrection against federal authority, became law on May 2, 1792.

749.8   Poor *Knox*]   Henry Knox (1750–1806) served as Secretary of War in the Washington administration from 1789 to 1794.

751.7–8   "ride in . . . the Storm."]   Joseph Addison (1672–1719), *The Campaign* (1705), line 291, later used by Alexander Pope in *The Dunciad* (1728), Book III, line 264.

754.5   your interesting letter . . . An answer]   See pp. 760–88 in this volume.

755.1   *An American No. I*]   Hamilton published two additional "American" letters on August 11 and 18, 1792.

755.4–5   the hint appeared in your Gazette of]   The text printed here is taken from Hamilton's manuscript; in the printed version that appeared in the *Gazette of the United States* on August 4, 1792, this appeared as "the hint appeared in your Gazette of 25th July." The "hint" was a short piece by Hamilton, writing as "T.L.," in which he questioned whether Philip Freneau was paid his government salary for translations or for publications designed to "vilify" the administration.

755.15–16   in capacity of]   In the printed version: "in capacity of editor or superintendant."

755.19–21   His talents for . . . this City.]   This sentence did not appear in the printed version. Freneau edited the *Freeman's Journal: or the North-American Intelligencer* from June 1781 through the fall of 1782.

755.23–25   There is good . . . that Negotiation.]   This sentence did not appear in the printed version.

760.5–6   the objections . . . 29th of July]   The objections included by Washington in his letter were copied almost verbatim from a letter Jefferson had written to the President on May 23, 1792. Washington did not identify Jefferson as their source, but told Hamilton that "sensible & moderate men" in Virginia were alarmed by Hamilton's policies, and that "Others, less friendly perhaps to the Government, and more disposed to arraign the conduct of its Officers" had enumerated the objections he listed.

764.38   Objection 3]   As stated in Washington's letter, the third objection protested that the new government already had been forced to raise impost taxes and impose an excise tax on distilled spirits, which would encourage tax evasion and thereby force the government to collect taxes by "arbitrary & vexatious means."

769.21   Objection 5]   Washington wrote: "They say that by borrowing at 2/3 of the interest, we might have paid off the principal in 2/3 of the time;

but that from this we are precluded by its being made irredeemable but in small portions, & long terms."

771.7–8   time of . . . funding Act]   The act funding the debt was passed in August 1790.

773.32   Objection 7]   Washington wrote: "They predict that this transfer of the principal, when compleated, will occasion an exportation of 3 Millions of dollars annually for the interest; a drain of Coin, of which as there has been no example, no calculation can be made of its consequences."

774.28   8.th Object]   Washington wrote: "That the banishment of our Coin will be compleated by the creation of 10 millions of paper money, in the form of Bank-bills now issuing into circulation."

775.5   9 Objection]   Washington wrote: "They think the 10 or 12 pr Ct. annual profit, paid to the lenders of this paper medium, are taken out of the pockets of the people, who would have had without interest the coin it is banishing."

776.6   10 Objection]   Washington wrote: "That all the Capitol employed in paper speculation is barren & useless, producing, like that on a gaming table, no accession to itself, and is withdrawn from Commerce and Agriculture where it would have produced addition to the common mass."

777.7   Objection 11]   Washington wrote: "That it nourishes in our citizens vice & idleness instead of industry & morality."

777.26–27   must have become . . . jobbing.]   Following this passage in his draft of the letter, Hamilton wrote and then crossed out: "Land-jobbing has at least as many bad sides as stock-jobbing and yet it has been a great cause of accelerating."

777.28   Objection 12]   Washington wrote: "That it has furnished effectual means of corrupting such a portion of the legislature, as turns the balance between the honest Voters which ever way it is directed."

780.11   Objection the 13]   Washington wrote: "That this corrupt squadron, deciding the voice of the legislature, have manifested their dispositions to get rid of the limitations imposed by the Constitution on the general legislature; limitations, on the faith of which, the States acceded to that instrument."

781.7   Objection XIV]   Washington wrote: "That the ultimate object of all this is to prepare the way for a change, from the present republican form of Government, to that of a monarchy; of which the British Constitution is to be the model."

782.6   "ride the storm . . . whirlwind."]   Cf. note 751.7–8.

782.36   Objection the 15]   Washington wrote: "That this was contemplated in the Convention, they say is no secret, because its partisans have made none of it—to effect it then was impracticable; but they are still eager after their object, and are predisposing every thing for its ultimate attainment."

783.4–5   The Member . . . from New York)]   Hamilton is referring to his own speech of June 18, 1787, at the Federal Convention; see pp. 151–66 in this volume.

783.21   16]   Washington wrote: "So many of them have got into the legislature, that, aided by the corrupt squadron of paper dealers, who are at their devotion, they make a majority of both houses."

783.27   Mr. Gerry]   Elbridge Gerry (1744–1814) attended the Federal Convention as a delegate from Massachusetts but refused to sign or support the Constitution. He served in the House of Representatives from 1789 to 1793.

783.29   17. 18th and 19th heads]   In Washington's letter, these paragraphs were concerned with the alliance in Congress between "republicans" and "antifederalists"; the danger posed by a corrupted legislature; and the possibility of a division of the Union along sectional lines.

787.6   a considerable loss]   At this point in the draft, Hamilton wrote and then crossed out: "by Mr. Maddison's."

787.29   Objection 21]   Washington had repeated Jefferson's assertion that the actions of the "Monarchial federalists" had "disarmed" the "republican federalists" who supported the Constitution, while fulfilling the predictions made by the "antifederal champions" who had opposed it.

788.16–17   you may not probably be here]   Vice-President Adams had left Philadelphia and returned to his home in Quincy, Massachusetts.

788.22–23   Mr. Clinton or yourself]   Governor George Clinton of New York was supported by many Republicans for vice-president in the 1792 presidential election. (Adams eventually received 77 votes in the electoral college, Clinton 50, Jefferson 4, and Aaron Burr 1.)

789.8–9   letter of the 26th of August]   In his letter Washington alluded to the bitter feud between Hamilton and Jefferson and expressed his hope that "liberal allowances" would be made "for the political opinions of one another," adding that without such "mutual forbearances and temporising yieldings *on all sides*," he did not see how the Union could survive. The President had made a similar plea for reconciliation in a letter to Jefferson of August 23, 1792.

789.30–31   the retaliations . . . certain public characters]   Hamilton refers to his ongoing newspaper campaign against Jefferson; see Chronology, 1792.

790.17–19   the persecution . . . *Paine's* pamphlet]   In 1791 Jefferson had sent a copy of Thomas Paine's *Rights of Man* to Samuel Harrison Smith, a

Philadelphia printer, along with a brief note decrying "the political heresies which have sprung up among us"; without Jefferson's permission, Smith included the note in the pamphlet's preface. Jefferson's remark regarding "political heresies" was widely understood to be a criticism of *Discourses on Davila* (1790–91), a series of essays by John Adams attacking the French Revolution.

791.15   The subject . . . Postscript]   Washington had asked Hamilton to note down ideas for inclusion in his address to Congress at the opening of the upcoming session.

794.14   Mr. Edwards . . . and Mr. Dallas]   Pierpont Edwards (1750–1826), Aaron Burr's uncle, and Alexander Dallas (1759–1817) of Pennsylvania.

795.1–2   *Draft . . . Neutrality Proclamation*]   After learning in early April 1793 of France's declaration of war on Great Britain, President Washington consulted with his cabinet and then issued a proclamation of neutrality on April 22, 1793.

796.6   Secret clubs are formed]   Many "Democratic Societies" were organized in the spring of 1793 by supporters of the French Republic.

801.1   *Pacificus No. I*]   Seven "Pacificus" essays appeared in the *Gazette of the United States* on June 29, July 3, 6, 10, 13–17, 17, and 27, 1793.

801.25   three heads]   The text printed here is taken from Hamilton's manuscript; in the printed version, this appeared as "four heads."

802.39   Vatel]   See note 135.39.

810.2   *To Andrew G. Fraunces*]   Andrew Fraunces, the son of Washington's steward, Samuel Fraunces, had been dismissed from a clerkship in the Treasury Department in March 1793. Denied payment of two warrants issued by the Board of Treasury, he countered by publishing a pamphlet accusing Hamilton of allowing personal considerations to guide his administrative decisions, and then submitted his pamphlet to Congress to request payment on his warrants. Hamilton's letter and enclosure were printed in two New York newspapers on October 11, 1793.

810.20   *To Angelica Hamilton*]   The Hamilton children, including Hamilton's oldest daughter, nine-year-old Angelica, had been sent to the Albany home of their grandfather, Philip Schuyler, during the yellow fever epidemic in Philadelphia.

811.4–5   a great . . . crisis]   See Chronology, 1794.

815.4–5   revocation . . . 6th of November]   On November 6, 1793, the British ministry had issued instructions ordering commanders of warships and privateers to detain ships bringing goods to or from any French colony. These instructions were revoked on January 8, 1794, in favor of directives aimed more specifically at trade between French colonies and European nations.

817.25–27   propositions . . . British Debts] In March 1794 the House
had debated proposals to sequester British debts in the United States and pay
them into the U.S. Treasury as compensation for damages caused by British
seizure of American ships.

817.27–28   the cutting off . . . Great Britain] In April 1794 the House
had debated a resolution to cut off all trade with Great Britain until restitution was made for damages sustained at sea, and until the British relinquished
frontier posts ceded to the United States under the 1783 peace treaty.

825.3   Associate Judge] An associate justice of the U.S. Supreme Court.

827.1   *Tully No. I*] Hamilton published four "Tully" essays; the other
three appeared on August 26, 28, and September 2, 1794.

832.8   *To Angelica Church*] Angelica Church, Hamilton's sister-in-law,
lived in England.

832.29   Mr Pinkney] Thomas Pinckney (1750–1828) was the American
minister to Great Britain, 1792–96.

833.14   Liancourt has arrived] The Duc de La Rochefoucauld-Liancourt
fled France for Britain in August 1792; he arrived in America in November 1794.

836.21–22   your very kind letter] In a formal farewell letter, Washington
had written that "in every relation, which you have borne to me, I have
found that my confidence in your talents, exertions and integrity, has been
well placed," assuring Hamilton of the "sincere esteem, regard and friendship
of . . . Your affectionate Go: Washington."

FEDERALIST LEADER AND ATTORNEY, 1795–1804

841.5–6   propositions . . . unsubscribed debt] In his "Report on a Plan
for the Further Support of Public Credit," received by the House on January
16, 1795, Hamilton included a provision for payment of the unsubscribed
debt. The provision was rejected by the House, with some Federalist representatives joining Republicans in voting against it.

841.16   De Paux] See note 208.21.

841.37   the 40 for 1 scheme] In 1780 the Continental Congress had proposed retiring existing Continental paper money, which it valued at 40-to-1
against specie.

842.14   *To Robert Troup*] On March 31, 1795, Hamilton's old friend
Robert Troup (1757–1823) had asked Hamilton to join him in a land speculation scheme organized by a former British officer, Charles Williamson.

843.17–18   offer to stand . . . ostensibility] To enable Hamilton to keep
his name unassociated with the speculation, Troup had offered to act as
Hamilton's trustee.

844.1   *The Defence No. I*]   Writing as "Camillus," Hamilton published 28 essays in defense of the Jay Treaty between July 22, 1795, and January 9, 1796. Rufus King wrote another ten essays in the series.

846.33–34   peculiar circumstances . . . elections for governor]   In the 1792 election the votes of three counties were discounted because of technicalities, giving the election to George Clinton over John Jay; in the 1795 election, Jay was nominated while still serving as a special envoy in Britain, but went on to win.

847.40–848.1   a sketch, . . . false impressions]   On June 29, 1795, the *Aurora*, a Republican newspaper in Philadelphia, published a rough outline of the treaty.

848.35–38   respectable meeting . . . the treaty]   New York Republicans organized a mass rally on July 18, 1795, to protest the Jay Treaty. Meeting the night before, Hamilton and a handful of merchants drafted a hasty public appeal for citizens to attend the rally and demand a fair discussion. See Chronology, 1795.

850.23   a *Pileus*]   In the margin, Hamilton wrote "Cap of Liberty."

851.22   *To George Washington*]   On May 15, 1796, Washington sent Hamilton a draft of a farewell address, based largely on a draft prepared by James Madison in 1792 in anticipation of Washington's retirement after one term. The President asked Hamilton either to revise the old draft or to prepare a new one. Hamilton did both, first outlining a new version of the 1792 address, and then preparing a new draft of his own, which he included with his July 30 letter. Although the opening and closing of the new draft followed the 1792 version, the middle section was entirely Hamilton's work. He later sent Washington a revised version of the draft he had received on May 15, but the President rejected it in favor of Hamilton's new draft, which he revised and then published on September 19, 1796.

858.30   the Treaty with Spain]   The treaty was signed October 27, 1795.

869.2   *To William Loughton Smith*]   William Loughton Smith (1758–1812) was a Federalist representative from South Carolina, 1789–96.

869.5   work on our Governments]   *Comparative View of the Constitutions of the Several States with each other, and with that of the United States* (1796).

870.10   the Emperor]   Francis (1768–1835), Holy Roman Emperor, 1792–1806, and Emperor of Austria, 1804–35.

870.16   a General]   Napoléon Bonaparte.

872.16–17   General *Pinckney* . . . or Mr. Cabot]   Charles Cotesworth Pinckney (1745–1825) of South Carolina and George Cabot (1752–1823), a Federalist senator from Massachusetts, 1791–96.

872.28   the Commercial one]   The 1778 treaty of amity and commerce between France and the United States, signed at the same time as the treaty of alliance.

877.4   the three frigates]   Construction of the frigates *United States, Constitution*, and *Constellation* had been authorized by Congress in 1794.

879.28   *To William Hamilton*]   William Hamilton, Alexander Hamilton's uncle, was Laird of the Grange in Ayrshire, Scotland.

882.15–17   your son Robert . . . use to him]   Robert Hamilton sought a commission in the U.S. Navy. With some assistance from Hamilton, he was made a lieutenant and sent to serve on the *Constitution*.

883.1   *The "Reynolds Pamphlet"*]   Hamilton wrote this pamphlet to defend himself against accusations made by journalist James Thomson Callender in a series of pamphlets published in book form as *The History of the United States for 1796; Including a Variety of Interesting Particulars Relative to the Federal Government Previous to That Period* (1797). See Chronology, 1791, 1792, 1797.

883.2–6   *Observations . . . Himself*]   The actual title of the pamphlet.

885.28   a formal and solemn inquiry]   See Chronology, 1793, 1794.

886.34–35   a worthless man . . . Fraunces]   See note 810.2.

887.40   Appendix, Nos. XLIV & XLV]   The appendix is not printed in this volume. In the letters, written on June 27 and 28, 1797, Jefferson declined to lend Fraunces money or provide him with letters of reference.

888.4–5   No. V and VI, . . . for 1796]   These two installments in James Thomson Callender's series of pamphlets appeared in late June and early July 1797.

889.6   another *Chartres*]   Louis Philippe d'Orleans, duc de Chartres, deserted to the Austrians in 1793 and spent three years in exile in Europe before arriving in Philadelphia in October 1796.

889.23   Mr. Duer]   William Duer (1747–1799) served as Assistant Secretary of the Treasury under Hamilton, 1789–90. He was financially ruined in 1792 by the collapse of his speculative schemes in bank stocks and government securities.

890.31   comptroller of the treasury]   Oliver Wolcott Jr. (1760–1833).

891.31   document No. 1 (a)]   The document is a statement by Frederick Muhlenberg, dated December 13, 1792.

891.35   document No. 2]   The document is a statement by James Monroe and Abraham Venable, dated December 13, 1792.

892.33   *per fas et nefas*]   Through right and wrong.

893.3   (No. IV a)]   Jacob Clingman's statement is dated December 13, 1792.

893.6   (No. XXIII)]   The deposition is dated July 19, 1797.

893.25   in No. V]   Hamilton is referring to document No. IV (a) in the appendix.

893.35   No. V.]   Hamilton is referring to a document in Callender's *History.*

897.9   a letter from her,]   Maria Reynolds wrote: "I have not tim to tell you the cause of my present troubles only that Mr. has rote to you this morning and I know not wether you have got the letter or not and he has swore that If you do not answer It or If he dose not se or hear from you to day he will write Mrs. Hamilton he has just Gone oute and I am a Lone I think you had better come here one moment that you May know the Cause then you will better know how to act Oh my God I feel more for you than myself and I wish I had never been born to give you so mutch unhappiness do not rite him no not a Line but come here soon do not send or leave any thing in his power."

898.21   the letter No. V]   Hamilton is referring to document No. VII in the appendix.

899.7   No. XVII is a master-piece.]   James Reynolds wrote: "I must now for ever forbid you of visiting Mrs. R any more I was in hopes that it would in time ware off, but I find there is no hopes. So I am determed to put a finell end to it. if its in my power. for I find by your Seeing her onely Renews the Friendship, and likewise when you Call you are feareful any person Should See you am I a person of Such a bad Carector. that you would not wish to be seen in Coming in my house in the front way. all any Person Can say of me is that I am poore and I dont know if that is any Crime. So I must meet my fate. I have my Reasons for it for I cannot be Reconsiled to it. for there is know person Can tell the pain it give me except they were plased in my sutivation I am shure the world would despise me if they Onely knew what I have bin Reconsiled to, I am in hopes in a short time to make you amends for your favour Rendered me I am Sir your humble Servant."

901.19   A. Venable]   Abraham Venable (1758–1811) was a representative from Virginia, 1791–99.

902.32   Mr. Wolcott's certificate No. XXIV]   The certificate is dated July 12, 1797.

903.14   I deny absolutely . . . the editor]   In his pamphlet, Callender had stated that when the incriminating documents were first presented to Hamilton, and he was told that they were to be given to Washington, "he entreated, in the most anxious tone of deprecation, that this measure might be suspended. . . . They gave their consent to it, on his express promise of a guarded behaviour in future, and because he attached to the suppression of these papers, a mysterious degree of solicitude."

905.33   affidavit No. XLI] The affidavit, dated July 21, 1797, was sworn by Mary Williams, a boarding house keeper who recognized the handwriting on the letters to Hamilton shown to her as Maria Reynolds'.

907.10–11   Reynold's letter No. XLII] The letter to Wolcott was dated December 5, 1792.

908.24   Col. Wadsworth] Jeremiah Wadsworth (1743–1804) served as a representative from Connecticut, 1789–95.

910.27   affidavit of Mr. Webster] The affidavit was sworn by Noah Webster on July 13, 1797.

912.30–31   a sweet project] Hamilton is possibly referring to his plan to build a country home in upper Manhattan.

913.7   *To Theodore Sedgwick*] Theodore Sedgwick (1746–1813) was a Federalist senator from Massachusetts, 1796–99, and served in the House, 1789–96 and 1799–1801.

913.15   proceedings of Virginia and Kentucke] The Kentucky and Virginia Resolutions of 1798, which denounced the Alien and Sedition Acts as unconstitutional and asserted the right of states to determine the constitutionality of congressional legislation.

915.4–5   riot . . . insurrection] On March 7, 1799, a party of armed men led by John Fries (1750–1818) forced the release of 18 men arrested in eastern Pennsylvania for resisting the 1798 federal property tax. Fries was later arrested, convicted of treason, and sentenced to hang, but was pardoned by President Adams on May 23, 1800.

915.21–22   *Memorandum . . . the Government*] Hamilton showed this document to Jonathan Dayton (1760–1824), a Federalist representative (1791–99) and senator (1799–1805) from New Jersey, and possibly to other Federalists in Congress.

916.7–8   more favourable countenance to some states] The number of Federalists elected to Congress had increased in Virginia, North and South Carolina, and Georgia.

920.28   *To Josiah Ogden Hoffman*] Josiah Ogden Hoffman (1766–1837) was attorney general of New York State from 1798 to 1801.

921.27   foreign gold] The letter alleged that Hamilton had used British secret service money in his attempt to suppress the *Aurora*.

921.29   take immediate measures] Hamilton was asking Hoffman to press charges against David Frothingham, the printer of *Greenleaf's New Daily Advertiser*. Found guilty of libel on November 16, 1799, Frothingham was sentenced to pay a $500 fine and spend four months in prison.

922.5   death of our beloved commander] George Washington died from a throat infection at Mount Vernon on December 14, 1799.

922.13 an order relative to the occasion] Hamilton enclosed the general orders he issued to the army on December 21, 1799, quoting President Adams's official recognition of Washington's death, and detailing a military ceremony to mark the occasion.

925.12 Think well . . . proposition] Jay rejected Hamilton's proposal and noted at the bottom of the letter: "Proposing a measure for party purposes wh. I think it wd. not become me to adopt." The New York legislature chose a slate of Republican electors.

925.21 Dexter] In a letter of May 7, 1800, Sedgwick had informed Hamilton that Federalist senator Samuel Dexter of Massachusetts wanted to support John Adams for president, rather than attempt to elect Charles Cotesworth Pinckney of South Carolina in his place.

926.24–25 an excursion . . . eastern States] See Chronology, 1800.

928.12–13 Doctor *Franklin* . . . Mr. Adams] In a letter to Robert R. Livingston on July 22, 1783, Benjamin Franklin wrote that Adams "means well for his Country, is always an honest Man, often a wise one, but sometimes, and in some things, absolutely out of his senses."

929.15 the statement of facts] On July 1, 1800, Hamilton had asked Wolcott, the Secretary of the Treasury since 1795, for confidential details about Adams's administration. Hamilton eventually used this information in writing his pamphlet attacking Adams; see pp. 934–71 in this volume.

929.20 T Pickering] Timothy Pickering had served as Secretary of State from August 1795 until May 12, 1800, when he was dismissed by Adams.

930.1 The Aurora publications] In June and July 1800 the Philadelphia *Aurora* printed an exposé of the Treasury in which Hamilton was accused of making improper payments to Treasury officials in order to provide them with funds for Federalist electioneering.

930.19 *To William Jackson*] William Jackson (1759–1828) was an old friend of Hamilton's from the Revolutionary War. Hamilton ultimately sent this letter to James McHenry rather than Jackson.

930.23–24 my birth . . . criticism] Hamilton was born out-of-wedlock. See Chronology, 1755.

932.4 *Rules for Philip Hamilton*] Philip Hamilton graduated from Columbia College in 1800.

934.1–3 *Letter . . . Character of John Adams*] Hamilton originally intended this pamphlet be circulated privately; see Chronology, 1800.

936.25 instructions to our Commissioners] In June 1781 Congress instructed John Adams, John Jay, Benjamin Franklin, and Henry Laurens to conduct peace negotiations with the "knowledge and concurrence" of the French ministry.

937.32   Secretary of Foreign Affairs] Robert R. Livingston.

938.36–37   a few votes . . . Mr. ADAMS] See pp. 513–15 in this volume.

941.38   Lt. Governor VAN RENSSELAER and R. TROUP] Stephen Van Rensselaer was married to Hamilton's sister-in-law, Margarita. Robert Troup was a longtime friend from Hamilton's time as a student at King's College.

943.11   The letter . . . public prints] The letter, written by Adams to Tench Coxe in May 1792, was partially published by the Philadelphia *Aurora* in the summer of 1799 and printed in full by the *Aurora* on August 28, 1800.

943.25   the PINCKNEYS] Thomas Pinckney and Charles Cotesworth Pinckney were brothers.

947.32   a speech] Adams's inaugural address in 1797, which referred to the French in friendly terms.

948.4   Mr. MONROE] James Monroe (1758–1831) was the American minister to France, 1794–96.

948.17   commission of three] On May 31, 1797, Adams appointed John Marshall, Elbridge Gerry, and Charles Cotesworth Pinckney as special envoys to France.

949.1   event of this experiment] The commissioners were approached by three French diplomatic agents, later referred to in dispatches as X, Y, and Z, who solicited a $240,000 bribe.

950.19   Speech to Congress] Adams's second annual message to Congress, delivered on December 8, 1798.

952.22   The intrigues of GENET] French minister Edmond Genet arrived in the United States in April 1793. Genet soon angered the administration by arming and commissioning privateers in American ports in defiance of Washington's proclamation of neutrality, and then by threatening to make a direct appeal to the American public against the neutrality policy. In August 1793 the administration asked for his recall.

953.3   Mr. MURRAY] William Vans Murray (1760–1803).

955.11   three Envoys] Murray, Chief Justice Oliver Ellsworth, and North Carolina governor William R. Davie.

959.25   I arrived at Trenton] In October 1799.

960.16   dismission of the two Secretaries] In May 1800; see Chronology.

961.7   the Secretary of the Navy] Benjamin Stoddart, who was appointed by Adams in 1798 and served until 1801.

963.15   the pardon of *Fries*] See note 915.4–5.

966.21–23   owed my appointment . . . WASHINGTON] See Chronology, 1798.

967.24–25   both which letters I send you copies] The letters were printed in an appendix to the pamphlet; for their texts, see pp. 928–29, 932–33 in this volume.

968.33   The XIIth article] The article severely restricted the ability of American ships to trade with the West Indies.

972.8–9   Convention with France] On September 30, 1800, the peace negotiators sent to France by Adams signed a treaty ending the undeclared "Quasi-War" with France and suspending the 1778 treaty of alliance.

972.10   *Jefferson* ought to be preferred to *Burr*] By the time Hamilton wrote this letter it was generally known that the official counting of the electoral vote on February 11, 1801, would reveal a tie between Republican presidential candidate Thomas Jefferson and Republican vice-presidential candidate Aaron Burr, leaving the election to be decided in the House.

972.21   *To John Rutledge Jr.*] John Rutledge Jr. (1766–1819) was a Federalist representative from South Carolina, 1797–1803.

975.7   reside at *Paramus*] Burr's future wife, Theodosia Prevost, lived in Paramus, New Jersey.

977.2   *To James A. Bayard*] Bayard (1767–1815) was a Federalist representative from Delaware, 1797–1803. Since Delaware had only one seat in the House, Bayard carried an entire state with his single vote, giving him a potentially pivotal role in resolving the election of 1800. In February 1801 Bayard voted for Burr on 35 ballots, then cast a blank vote on the 36th and final ballot.

979.11   perfect *Godwinism*] English political philosopher William Godwin (1756–1836), author of *Enquiry concerning Political Justice and its influence on general virtue and happiness* (1793), believed that society should be ruled by innate reason rather than codified laws.

979.37   by a trick established a *Bank*] Wanting to found a bank that was favorable to the Republican cause, Burr accomplished his purposes in 1799 by inserting a clause into the charter of the Manhattan Company, an enterprise intended to improve New York City's water supply.

980.38   letter to Mr Morris] In a January 13, 1801, letter to Gouverneur Morris, Hamilton described how Burr was using the Federalists to gain the presidency, welcoming their overtures but stating that he could not overtly help them without losing Republican support and thus the contest as a whole.

981.1–2   the situation . . . change the Government] In a private conversation, Burr had allegedly criticized Hamilton for not taking advantage of his position as inspector general of the army to overturn the government. In the margin next to this passage, Hamilton wrote "very very confidential."

981.3–4 "Les grands . . . petit morceaux"] "Great souls care little for petty crumbs."

981.34 my former letter] Hamilton had written a letter highly critical of Burr to Bayard on December 27, 1800.

982.1–2 *Proposal for . . . the Constitution*] The resolution was adopted by the New York legislature and proposed to the House by New York representative Benjamin Walker on February 25, 1802, beginning the process that resulted in the ratification of the Twelfth Amendment in 1804.

983.1–2 *Remarks on . . . Judiciary Act*] The text of Hamilton's remarks is taken from the New York *Commercial Advertiser*, February 26, 1802. The Judiciary Act of 1801, signed by Adams on February 13, relieved Supreme Court justices from circuit duty and created 16 new circuit court and five new district court judgeships. When the Republicans in Congress moved on January 6, 1802, to repeal the act and abolish the new judgeships, Federalists protested that removing judges already in office would violate the constitutional independence of the judiciary. The repeal measure became law on March 8, 1802.

984.5 'sleep . . . eye-lids,'] Cf. Psalm 132:4, Proverbs 6:4.

986.10 The suggestions . . . your letter] In his letter of February 22, 1802, Morris had suggested establishing committees of correspondence to express public discontent with the repeal of the 1801 Judiciary Act.

986.20 your speeches] Morris spoke against the repeal of the 1801 Judiciary Act in the Senate on January 8 and 14, 1802.

987.6–7 an event . . . most afflicting of my life] On November 23, 1801, Hamilton's 19-year-old son Philip was mortally wounded in a duel with George Eacker, a Republican lawyer who had criticized Hamilton's policies in a Fourth of July oration.

988.2 person in question] In a letter of April 12, 1802, Bayard had assured Hamilton that Burr's appearance at a recent Federalist celebration of George Washington's birthday did not herald a planned collaboration between Burr and the Federalists.

991.15 your post] American minister to Great Britain; see note 743.40–744.2.

992.21 "informe in gens cui lumen ademptum."] Virgil, *Aeneid*, Book 3, line 659: "shapeless, huge, blind."

993.31 Wm Bayard] William Bayard (1761–1826) was a New York City merchant. Hamilton died in his home after his 1804 duel with Burr.

994.3 Grange] Between 1800 and 1802, Hamilton built a country home in upper Manhattan and named it the "Grange."

994.23   last *lullaby* message] Jefferson's second annual message to Congress, December 15, 1802.

994.27–28   cession of Louisian . . . Deposit at New Orleans] Spain ceded Louisiana to France in 1801, but still administered the province in 1802. The Spanish-American treaty signed in 1795 gave Americans the right to store goods at New Orleans for later shipment, but on October 16, 1802, the Spanish intendant of the port rescinded this right.

995.13   your journey] Elizabeth Hamilton was traveling to Albany to console her father after the death of her mother on March 7, 1803.

995.26   Kitty . . . Angelica] Elizabeth's sister-in-law Catherine Van Rensselaer Schuyler and her sister Angelica Schuyler Church.

996.5   territory is now transferred to our hands] The purchase of the Louisiana territory from France

996.33   short interval of peace] France and Britain signed a preliminary peace treaty on October 1, 1801; war between the two nations resumed on May 18, 1803.

998.11   war of 1755] The French and Indian War, also known as the Seven Years' War.

1000.3   uncertain tenure of a treaty] The Spanish-American treaty of 1795.

1000.20–21   famous electioneering message] Jefferson's second annual message to Congress, December 15, 1802.

1000.34   Mr. Gallatin's report] Secretary of the Treasury Albert Gallatin submitted a report on the state of finances to Congress on December 20, 1802.

1001.26   Chancellor Livingston] Robert R. Livingston of New York.

1001.29–30   Mr. Munro's . . . French Government] James Monroe had served as American minister to France from 1794 until 1796, when he was re-called by the Washington administration.

1002.5–6   your inquiry] On April 5, 1803, Pickering asked Hamilton to describe his proposed plan of government at the 1787 Federal Convention after relating a recent Republican claim that Hamilton had advocated electing the national executive and senators for life as a step toward establishing a monarchy. See pp. 149–66 in this volume.

1003.13   no greater duration than for three years] In his September 1787 draft of a constitution, Hamilton retained his earlier proposal that the president should be elected and then hold office during good behavior.

1004.1   *Speech to a Federalist Meeting in Albany*] The text of this speech is taken from Hamilton's manuscript.

1004.2   Mr. Lansing] John Lansing Jr. was the initial nominee for governor of the Clinton faction of the New York Republicans. He soon withdrew and was replaced as a candidate by Morgan Lewis, the chief justice of the state supreme court.

1004.31–32   President Edwards . . . President Burr] Theologian Jonathan Edwards was president of the College of New Jersey (now Princeton University) from 1757 to 1758; the elder Aaron Burr was president of the college from 1748 to 1757.

1006.1   *Propositions on the Law of Libel*] Hamilton read these propositions at the close of his argument in *People* v. *Croswell*; see Chronology, 1804.

1007.13–14   Court of Star Chamber] An English court used during the reign of Charles I to suppress religious and political dissent. It was abolished by Parliament in 1641.

1007.15–16   the Revolution] The English Revolution of 1688.

1008.14   letter signed Ch. D. Cooper] The enclosed letter from Federalist Charles D. Cooper to Philip Schuyler was printed in the *Albany Register* on April 24, 1804.

1008.16   Mr Van Ness] William P. Van Ness, a New York lawyer and political supporter of Burr who acted as Burr's second in the duel.

1009.10   Judge KENT] James Kent (1763–1847), a Federalist, served as a judge on the New York supreme court from 1798 to 1823.

1009.13   meeting of federalists, at the city tavern] See pp. 1004–05 in this volume.

1010.4   the Chancellor] John Lansing Jr.

1015.8–9   *Response to a Letter from William P. Van Ness*] Van Ness refused to accept this document, which Hamilton wrote in response to a June 27 letter from Van Ness to Nathaniel Pendleton, the lawyer who served as Hamilton's second. The letter from Van Ness largely repeated the contents of Burr's June 22 letter to Hamilton.

1015.33   the alternative alluded . . . the letter] Van Ness's June 27 letter concluded by suggesting the need for a "personal interview" (duel) between Burr and Hamilton.

1016.9   *Statement Regarding Financial Situation*] Hamilton included this document in a packet of papers to be opened in the event of his death.

1019.22   *Statement Regarding the Duel with Burr*] This statement was also included in the packet of papers Hamilton left to be opened in the event of his death.

1020.31   moderate and judicious friend] Hamilton consulted with Rufus King about the propriety of Burr's demand for an explanation.

1022.20–21   Dismemberment of our Empire]   Some New England Federalists were considering plans to secede from the Union.

1023.4   Mrs. Mitchel]   Ann Mitchell, Hamilton's cousin, supported him during his youth in the West Indies. This letter was included among the packet of papers to be opened in the event of Hamilton's death.

APPENDIX

1027.1–2   *Joint Statement . . . Pendleton*]   This statement first appeared in the New York *Morning Chronicle* on July 17, 1804. The subsequent individual statements by Pendleton and Van Ness also appeared in New York newspapers.

1027.21   took aim]   On July 18, 1804, Van Ness and Pendleton published a correction stating that "presented" should have been used in place of "take aim" in their joint statement.

1027.31   the Surgeon and Bargemen]   Dr. David Hosack, Hamilton's attending physician, and the men who rowed Hamilton across the Hudson River to Weehawken, New Jersey.

1028.26–27   testimonies of Bishop Moore . . . express declaration]   In his account of Hamilton's deathbed conversation, Bishop Benjamin Moore noted that Hamilton had said that he met Burr "with a fixed resolution to do him no harm." For Hamilton's "express declaration," see pp. 1019–22 in this volume.

1029.14   hair spring set]   The pistol could be set so that a light pressure on the trigger would fire it.

1030.14   Mr. Church's]   John Barker Church, the husband of Elizabeth's sister, Angelica.

Index

Library of Congress Cataloging-in-Publication Data

Hamilton, Alexander, 1757–1804.
  [Selections. 2001]
  Writings/Alexander Hamilton.
    p. cm.— (The Library of America ; 129)
  Includes bibliographical references and index.
  ISBN 1–931082–04–9 (alk. paper)
    1. Hamilton, Alexander, 1757–1804—Archives. 2. Hamilton, Alexander,
1757–1804—Correspondence. 3. United States—Politics and
government—1775–1783—Sources. 4. United States—Politics and
government—1783–1809—Sources. 5. Hamilton, Alexander, 1757–1804—
Political and social views. I. Title. II. Series.

E302.H22   2001
973.4'092—dc21

                                        2001023043

THE LIBRARY OF AMERICA SERIES

The Library of America fosters appreciation and pride in America's literary heritage by publishing, and keeping permanently in print, authoritative editions of its best and most significant writing. An independent nonprofit organization, it was founded in 1979 with seed money from the National Endowment for the Humanities and the Ford Foundation.

This book is set in 10 point Linotron Galliard,
a face designed for photocomposition by Matthew Carter
and based on the sixteenth-century face Granjon. The paper is
acid-free Ecusta Nyalite and meets the requirements for permanence
of the American National Standards Institute. The binding
material is Brillianta, a woven rayon cloth made by
Van Heek-Scholco Textielfabrieken, Holland.
The composition is by The Clarinda
Company. Printing and binding by
R.R.Donnelley & Sons Company.
Designed by Bruce Campbell.

DATE			